An Equal Place

An Equal Place

Lawyers in the Struggle for Los Angeles

SCOTT L. CUMMINGS

OXFORD
UNIVERSITY PRESS

Oxford University Press is a department of the University of Oxford. It furthers the University's objective of excellence in research, scholarship, and education by publishing worldwide. Oxford is a registered trade mark of Oxford University Press in the UK and certain other countries.

Published in the United States of America by Oxford University Press
198 Madison Avenue, New York, NY 10016, United States of America.

© Oxford University Press 2021

All rights reserved. No part of this publication may be reproduced, stored in a retrieval system, or transmitted, in any form or by any means, without the prior permission in writing of Oxford University Press, or as expressly permitted by law, by license, or under terms agreed with the appropriate reproduction rights organization. Inquiries concerning reproduction outside the scope of the above should be sent to the Rights Department, Oxford University Press, at the address above.

You must not circulate this work in any other form
and you must impose this same condition on any acquirer.

Library of Congress Control Number: 2018029428
ISBN 978-0-19-021592-7

1 3 5 7 9 8 6 4 2

Printed by Sheridan Books, Inc., United States of America

To Ingrid—
For building a place with me.

CONTENTS

Preface ix
Abbreviations xvii

1. *From Riots to Recession: The Challenge to Low-Wage Work in Los Angeles* 1

2. *Garment Workers: Fighting to End Sweatshops* 32

3. *Day Laborers: Organizing the Corner* 91

4. *Retail Workers: Negotiating Community Benefits* 164

5. *Grocery Workers: Blocking the Big-Box Invasion* 264

6. *Truck Drivers: Challenging Misclassification* 311

7. *An Equal Place? Empirical Appraisal and Theoretical Implications* 446

Notes 509
Index 625

PREFACE

For nearly two decades, I have had the enormous privilege of teaching law to students passionately committed to social justice at a proudly public university in one of the most diverse and dynamic cities in the world. This book is a product of that privilege. It is, first and foremost, the product of inspiration I have drawn from incredible students over the years, who have always taught me more than I could ever teach them about what it takes to ensure that our society gives more to those with less. With their enormous talents, they could choose to do anything. The fact that they choose to stand with people with less privilege—to struggle as equals alongside them—always moves and motivates me.

I wanted to write about lawyers dedicated to the ideal of equality to capture what that struggle looks like, how it plays out over the arc of time, and why it matters so profoundly for our future. When I was a law student, stories about social justice lawyers were my sustenance. Learning about the work of old giants like Gary Bellow, Ruth Bader Ginsburg, Cruz Reynoso, Thurgood Marshall, and Marian Wright Edelman, and new visionaries like Luke Cole and Jennifer Gordon got me through. For this book, I wanted to write accounts of contemporary lawyers that would resonate with the current generation—my own students who would go (and literally have gone) out to carry on the movements I describe. In this regard, the book is dedicated to all the public interest students I have known who have worked to make our city, state, and nation more equal places. They are the coauthors of this book's ongoing stories.

That I have been able to author this book is also a product of my own unique institutional place. The UCLA School of Law has been my irreplaceable home since 2002. Every day, when I take the glorious walk, rain or shine (mostly shine), across the iconic quad, anchored by four landmark Romanesque Revival buildings built nearly a century ago, I feel humbled to live in a state that has made (and continues to make, albeit to a lesser degree) such an enormous investment in its people and that has been particularly committed to ensuring access to education for so many for whom being on campus is the fulfillment of their family's struggle to achieve the American Dream. Passing by the students each day is to profoundly appreciate the strength in our nation's incredible diversity.

My law school, nestled on the eastern perimeter of campus where I end my daily walk, has itself been a beacon of egalitarian values. As an upstart founded in 1949, it was one of the first law schools in the country to hire women and faculty of color; to grant full tenure to clinical faculty; to foster sociolegal scholarship on law as an instrument of social justice; to create a specialization in critical race studies; and to establish a specialization in public interest law—now called the Epstein Program in Public Interest Law and Policy (or Public Interest Law Program, for short)—which is the community that has nurtured and supported me since I was a junior faculty member. I could not have written this book anywhere else.

The genesis of the book was a 2004 seminar I taught called "Problem Solving in the Public Interest"—a required second-year course for students in our Public Interest Law Program, in which I served as faculty director for six years and continue to play an active role. The seminar was designed to expose students to different "modes of advocacy," emphasizing the theme that social change happens when lawyers work in coordination with other actors—organizers, community residents, researchers, communications specialists, and political officials—and that struggle is ongoing and adaptive. In this particular class, I decided to illustrate these themes by focusing on case studies of local advocacy. The initial choices were not systematic. I was originally drawn to a campaign I had observed as a newly minted community economic development lawyer a few years earlier: the movement to win the nation's first community benefits agreement in downtown Los Angeles, in connection with the project now known as L.A. Live. For the course, I assigned background materials on redevelopment in Los Angeles, current news articles, and materials from the campaign; we took a field trip to the area; and I invited in key advocates, including Jerilyn López Mendoza from Environmental Defense. The class was a tremendous success and a profound learning experience for the students and me. Two years later, I taught the seminar around paired case studies: the legal resistance to sweatshops in the garment industry and the fight to stop Wal-Mart's planned opening of a Supercenter, which housed a cut-rate grocery staffed by nonunionized workers and thus posed an existential threat to Los Angeles's unionized grocery sector.

As that course ended, I had two important insights. First, the stories were interconnected, and the individual campaigns aspired to broader movement-building and city transformation. There were overlapping organizations and actors; and it was clear that there was a larger goal—reforming the burgeoning low-wage economy—that animated the campaigns. Second, I realized that I needed to disseminate the stories beyond the confines of my classroom. The lessons they taught spoke more broadly to students and practicing lawyers interested in understanding the impact they could make and responded directly to ongoing scholarly debates about the role of lawyers in social movements. The seeds of the book project were thus planted.

My first insight led me to more systematically study the role of lawyers in the place immediately around me: my own City of Los Angeles. When I arrived in Los Angeles in the summer of 1998, on the cusp of a Skadden Fellowship in Public Counsel Law Center's Community Development Project, it was clear to me the city was in the midst of a tectonic change. There was a feeling of motion. Important coalitions were taking shape: the L.A. Living Wage Coalition, anchored by the still nascent Los Angeles Alliance for a New Economy, which was formed to create synergies between community organizing and the labor movement; and the Metropolitan Alliance, anchored by Action for Grassroots Empowerment and Neighborhood Development—known as AGENDA—which had grown out of the 1992 uprising to tackle the root causes of disinvestment and disenfranchisement in South Los Angeles. These coalitions were developing alongside the birth of the Los Angeles worker center movement. Richard Riordan, a business-friendly Republican, was mayor, but the gathering strength of progressive activism pointed toward impending political change at the city level. Confronting these grassroots developments were brewing challenges, including gentrification fueled by city-subsidized redevelopment and the proliferation of low-wage work. Therefore, when I decided to write this book, I was motivated by wanting to better understand the changes around me and how they impacted the communities with which I had worked. As I began to develop the case studies, I also realized that—in addition to providing accounts of legal mobilization—they traced the broader rise of progressive activism in Los Angeles and the resurgence of the labor movement in local politics. As this project began to unfold, Los Angeles became both an object of study and an ideal of diversity, inclusion, and solidarity to be realized.

My second insight—that the stories needed to be widely shared—was strengthened by conversations with students and young attorneys, which fueled my broader reaction against the critical views of social change lawyers that I had been taught in law school. Many students came into the UCLA Public Interest Law Program with a serious skepticism about their ability to make a difference as lawyers. They questioned their role and their purpose. What value could they add to the crucial grassroots mobilization and policy work happening on the ground? This was, of course, an important question with a complex set of answers—many, if not most, of which could not be discovered by reference to case studies in a book. But I sensed a larger progressive legal malaise, coming out of the disappointments of the Civil Rights era and codified by academic work that cast doubt on the political efficacy of lawyers who, in Stuart Scheingold's famous phrase, pursued the "myth of rights."

This book became my effort to assert a counter-narrative to this critical vision of lawyers, rooted in the rigor of the sociolegal tradition that I had been taught. In this regard, I was inspired—as I always am—by my dear friend and role model, Rick

Abel, who encouraged this project when he generously shared with me materials from a Law and Social Change course he taught on the living wage and community benefits movements in Los Angeles, which contained original empirical research conducted by his students. When I finally decided to pursue this book, I wanted it to aspire to the sweep and richness of Rick's monumental account of legal resistance to apartheid in South Africa. Although nothing could live up to that standard, it has been my guiding star.

Other mentors have been essential to me. Gary Blasi, a founder of our Public Interest Law Program (like Rick) and legendary public interest lawyer in Los Angeles, helped me conceptualize the scope of the project, while Joe Doherty, former director of our Empirical Research Group, provided crucial assistance with the methodological design. Cathy Mayorkas, the founding director of the Public Interest Law Program, who left an indelible imprint, was also generous with her contacts and always encouraging in her words. I could not have written the book without the crucial support of my other UCLA colleagues. Noah Zatz's endless enthusiasm and advice about substance and structure was a continuous lifeline, while Kathy Stone helped me to see the importance of the stories to labor law and think through their implications. Sameer Ashar, now our vice dean of Experiential Learning, has been a stalwart friend, commenting on every piece of this project. I am also grateful to Stuart Banner, David Binder, Devon Carbado, Jennifer Chacón, Sharon Dolovich, Laura Gómez, Cheryl Harris, Sean Hecht, Jasleen Kohli, Máximo Langer, Rachel Moran, Hiroshi Motomura, Steve Yeazell, and Jonathan Zasloff for all of their help along the way.

As it always does, my own institution rallied around me. I am indebted to former dean Rachel Moran, for encouragement and assistance at critical stages, and to our current dean, Jennifer Mnookin, for giving me the space I needed to get this project over the finish line. Nor could I have done it all without the generous and enduring support of the UCLA Institute for Research on Labor and Employment (IRLE) and its leaders, particularly Chris Tilly and Abel Valenzuela, the latter of whom was also generous in sharing his data on day labor with me. The current Empirical Research Group team of Ben Nyblade and Henry Kim assembled data about the Los Angeles low-wage economy. Henry, in particular, put in a huge amount of time piecing together industry data with skill and precision. No list of thank-yous could ever be complete without recognition of the sustained support of the staff of our school's "crown jewel": the library. A special thanks to the library director, Kevin Gerson, for his steadfast friendship and empathy; to Linda Karr O'Connor, director of the Research Assistant Program, for always finding me research assistants who are the perfect fit; and to Elyse Meyers, assistant director of that program, for going well above and beyond the call of duty to help problem-solve, edit, and otherwise push forward this colossus. And last, but certainly not least, I am eternally grateful to my incredible faculty assistants, Jamie Libonate and Trinh Bui.

I have also been lucky to have had the most talented and enthusiastic research assistants one could ever hope for. They have spanned a decade of work and are literally the reason that this book exists. Doug Smith did me a tremendous service by producing the maps on day labor ordinances, organizing and digitizing materials, and updating the chapters on garment workers and Wal-Mart. Danae McElroy produced a magnificent overview of the anti-sweatshop campaign that formed the backbone of that chapter. Alejandra Cruz, Stephanie Lamb, and Jessica Rutter tracked down materials and created a research database for the day labor chapter. Alyssa Titche spent more than a year wrestling the industry data to the ground and helped figure out the daunting "crosswalks" between the 1990 and 2010 census information. Bob Kim helped put together historical background on the L.A. economy for the first chapter, while also digitizing archival materials. Lindsay Cutler and Michael Fenne assembled documents for, edited, and cite checked the ports chapter. Brenna Wylder provided invaluable help at the end, synthesizing a trove of materials and providing an essential update to the community benefits chapter, while Yani Jacobs did a magnificent job with final updates to the day labor chapter. Michelle Alig, Vidaur Durazo, Dana Ontiveros, John Trang, and Julia Vázquez also provided critical research support along the journey.

Outside of UCLA, I have been lucky to have colleagues in interdisciplinary fields—the legal profession, social movements, labor law, and local government law—who have been critical interlocutors. Catherine Fisk was an early supporter, inviting me to conferences that helped develop what are now the chapters on garment workers and port truckers. Deborah Rhode and David Wilkins have been incredible mentors and models of how to research the role of lawyers in society. Tony Alfieri taught me an enormous amount about grounded scholarship. There have been so many other essential contributors to whom I am grateful: Mark Aaronson, Muneer Ahmad, Catherine Albiston, Michelle Wilde Anderson, Fran Ansley, Wendy Bach, Elizabeth Bartholet, Steve Boutcher, Lynette Chua, Paul Diller, Veena Dubal, Rashmi Dyal-Chand, Ann Eisenberg, Peter Enrich, Laurel Fletcher, Sheila Foster, Jody Freeman, Brian Glick, Thalia Gonzalez, Jennifer Gordon, Robert Gottlieb, Bruce Green, Lani Guinier, Angela Harris, Kevin Johnson, Michael Klarman, Nelson Lichtenstein, Michael McCann, Kathleen Morris, Frank Munger, Doug NeJaime, John Nockleby, Russell Pearce, Nancy Polikoff, Dean Hill Rivkin, Leonard Rubinowitz, Ben Sachs, Austin Sarat, Chris Schmidt, Rich Schragger, Jeff Selbin, Bill Simon, Louise Trubek, Dave Trubek, Deborah Weissman, Lucie White, and Kim Yuracko. Finally, I must thank my mentors and friends from practice, who have taught me what it means to use law for justice: Dan Grunfeld, Gilda Haas, Madeline Janis, Victor Narro, Tom Saenz, and Julie Su.

Part of the challenge of doing contemporary history is knowing when (and how) to stop—because all the campaigns I document live on in some form. Susan Carle helped me to see the end and get over the final hurdles. Part of doing this involved splitting off a more theoretical project on *Lawyers and Social Movements*, which will be published as a separate book, though its central thrust—contesting the fundamental critiques of social movement lawyers—animates this project.

This book is built upon the foundation of five case studies, which I originally produced as journal articles and a book chapter. These appeared as: *Preemptive Strike: Law in the Campaign for Clean Trucks*, 4 UC IRVINE LAW REVIEW 939 (2014); *Litigation at Work: Defending Day Labor in Los Angeles*, 58 UCLA LAW REVIEW 1617 (2011); *Hemmed In: Legal Mobilization in the Los Angeles Anti-Sweatshop Movement*, 30 BERKELEY JOURNAL OF EMPLOYMENT AND LABOR LAW 1 (2009); *Law in the Labor Movement's Challenge to Wal-Mart: A Case Study of the Inglewood Site Fight*, 95 CALIFORNIA LAW REVIEW 1927 (2007); and *Mobilization Lawyering: Community Economic Development in the Figueroa Corridor*, in CAUSE LAWYERS AND SOCIAL MOVEMENTS 302 (Austin Sarat & Stuart Scheingold eds., 2006). In addition, I conducted an analysis of some local labor initiatives documented in this book in *Mobilizing Local Government Law for Low-Wage Workers* (with Steven A. Boutcher), 2009 UNIVERSITY OF CHICAGO LEGAL FORUM 187 (2009). I am grateful to the publishers of these works for granting me permission to adapt them for this book. And, most of all, I am grateful to David McBride and Holly Mitchell at Oxford University Press for helping me see that the whole was greater than the parts and patiently waiting for the whole to come together.

I benefited from feedback from many people in different workshops, including multiple Law and Society Association meetings; the Conference on Race, Class, Gender, and Ethnicity at the University of North Carolina School of Law in 2005; the Minnesota Law Review conference in 2007; the University of Chicago Legal Forum Symposium on Civil Rights Law and the Low-Wage Worker in 2008; the Loyola Law Review Symposium on Access to Justice in 2009; the Northwestern Law School Employment Law Colloquium in 2009; the 2009 AALS Mid-Year Meeting Workshop on Work Law; the Northeastern School of Law's Law, Policy and Society's 2010 Speaker Series; the UCLA IRLE Colloquium in 2010; the University of San Francisco Symposium on Lawyering for Equality in 2010; the Labor Law Group meeting at Lake Arrowhead in 2010; the 2011 UCLA Law Review Symposium; the 2011 Loyola Law School Sixth Annual Labor and Employment Law Colloquium; the Harvard Law School program on the legal profession in 2012; the Access to Justice Speaker Series at Occidental College in 2012; the UC Irvine Law Review Conference, Re-imagining Labor Law, in 2013; the UCLA Low-Wage Workers and Worker Organizing Conference in 2013; the International Legal Ethics Conference VI in London in 2014; the Harvard Law School Faculty Workshop in 2014; the ClassCrits VIII conference at the University of Tennessee, the Northeastern Law School conference on The Puzzle of the Urban Core, and the UCLA IRLE workshop on Southern California Port Truckers, all in 2015; the 2016 AALS Annual Meeting panel on Local Laboratories of Workplace Regulation; and the 2018 symposia on Reimagining Localism at Fordham Law School, Just Transitions at the University of South Carolina, and Legal Ethics and Professionalism at the University of Georgia.

As this long list suggests, this book is, perhaps more than anything, about the value of perseverance: my own, but more importantly, that of the people the book depicts. The stories it tells about lawyers and activists attempting to make our city work better for those who make it work are alternatively inspirational and dispiriting. One of the most essential themes, in the end, is that social justice is never achieved, it is only struggled for. And in uplifting the stories of that struggle, I hope that this book will help it persevere.

My family is also an essential part of the story I tell—not visible on the page but animating its spirit. My wife and incredible life partner, Ingrid Eagly, to whom I dedicate this book, has given me so much love and support throughout our amazing journey together that I could never fully express how important she is to me. I have the most enormous gratitude for her and the most profound admiration for who she is and what she does. She is my shining star. My parents, Ron Cummings and Wilma Nash, taught me not just to care about people, but to use my time to make a difference in the world immediately around me. My father was my first and greatest teacher: of writing and of social justice. His stories inspired my love of words and his stands for justice inspired me to become a lawyer of conscience. My mother still gets up every morning and drives an hour to work to help ensure that students with disabilities get the education they deserve. She is my model of persistence and care. I am grateful to Jennifer Vanica and Dennis Brown, also my parents, who helped to raise me and my children, and who have been essential role models for how to live lives dedicated to helping others. My relationship with my brothers, Eric and Josh, has sustained me through the years. This book, I hope, warrants all of your investment in me. Finally, this book would not be possible without my amazing daughters, Caroline and Audrey, who anchor me in what matters, fill me with joy, and inspire me to always be better.

I began writing this book in earnest a decade ago, in a moment of abounding hope symbolized by the election of President Barack Obama, born to a white mother from Kansas and a Kenyan immigrant father. As a boy, Obama spent four years in Indonesia, returning to Hawaii to live with his grandparents, who raised him through high school. He started college in Los Angeles at Occidental, a progressive liberal arts bastion, and then transferred to Columbia. He spent two years after college organizing on Chicago's South Side, providing job training and leadership development, while supporting low-income tenants. He graduated from Harvard Law School, becoming the first black president of the prestigious *Harvard Law Review*. As a third-year Harvard law student with a sterling pedigree, Obama could have literally taken any job he wanted. He could have become immediately and fantastically wealthy. Instead, he chose to be a civil rights lawyer, litigating discrimination cases at Davis, Miner, Barnhill & Galland, a small civil rights and economic development firm in Chicago.

I recount this story for two reasons. One is to highlight how much choices matter in shaping careers in the public interest. Obama's choices took him on a path now well known, but at the time a distant and seemingly impossible dream. One need not reach such heights to appreciate the courage and vision required to choose to pursue justice—to turn away from Wall Street to organize on the South Side, to turn away from Big Law for Civil Rights—when everything is open. That is what he did. That is what the lawyers in this book did. And that is what my students and others like them do throughout their careers.

The second reason for this story is to mark the distance between the hopefulness of where I started and where we now stand. I began writing this book in my own hope that the story of economic justice advocacy in Los Angeles, with all of its potential and problems, perhaps could serve as a guide to realize a more progressive future for our country. The book was meant to be a work of history, a sociology of social change, but also a vision of future reform. That I write now at a very different moment, one marred by the resurgence and amplification of racial resentment and xenophobia, challenges that vision and raises serious questions about whether Los Angeles and other progressive cities are exemplars for our nation or islands drifting away from large swaths of America. I still believe that there is hope for reconciliation and that economic justice can spread and rise. In times of darkness, bringing to light stories of resistance feels more important than ever. For if there is to be a future of inclusion and equality—one that looks more like the future imagined by the courageous lawyers, activists, and ordinary people of my city—it must be fought for from the ground up.

—Los Angeles, California

ABBREVIATIONS

A.B.	Assembly Bill
ACJC	Alameda Corridor Jobs Coalition
ACLU	American Civil Liberties Union
ACORN	Association of Community Organizations for Reform Now
ACTWU	Amalgamated Clothing and Textile Workers Union
AEG	Anschutz Entertainment Group
AFL-CIO	American Federation of Labor and Congress of Industrial Organizations
AGENDA	Action for Grassroots Empowerment and Neighborhood Development Alternatives
AMI	area median income
APALC	Asian Pacific American Legal Center
AQMD	Air Quality Management District
ARSAC	Alliance for a Regional Solution to Airport Congestion
ATA	American Trucking Associations
ATLF	Asociación de Trabajadores de Lake Forest
BCG	Boston Consulting Group
BID	business improvement district
BNSF	Burlington Northern and Santa Fe
BRU	Bus Rider's Union
CAAP	Clean Air Action Plan
Cal/OSHA	California Division of Occupational Safety and Health
CARB	California Air Resources Board
CARECEN	Central American Resource Center

CBA	community benefits agreement
CBD	central business district
CBE	Communities for a Better Environment
CBI	Coalition for a Better Inglewood
CCC	Community Coalition for Change
CD Tech	Community Development Technologies Center
CDC	Community Development Corporation
CED	community economic development
CEQA	California Environmental Quality Act
CERA	California Environmental Rights Alliance
China Shipping	China Shipping Holding Company
CHIRLA	Coalition for Humane Immigrant Rights of Los Angeles
CIO	Congress of Industrial Organizations
CIR	community impact report
CLEAN	Community Labor Environmental Action Network
CLUE	Clergy and Laity United for Economic Justice
COSCO	China Ocean Shipping Company
CRA	Community Redevelopment Agency
CUP	conditional use permit
CWA	Communications Workers of America
DLC	Downtown Labor Center
DLSE	Division of Labor Standards Enforcement
DOL	Department of Labor
EBASE	East Bay Alliance for a Sustainable Economy
EIR	environmental impact report
EIS	environmental impact statement
EIS/EIR	environmental impact statement/environmental impact report
Environmental Defense	Environmental Defense–Environmental Justice Project
EPA	Environmental Protection Agency
ERA	Equal Rights Advocates
FAA	Federal Aviation Administration
FAAAA	Federal Aviation Administration Authorization Act
FCCEJ	Figueroa Corridor Coalition for Economic Justice

FLSA	Fair Labor Standards Act
GE	General Electric
GWC	Garment Worker Center
HDV	heavy duty vehicle
HERE	Hotel Employees and Restaurant Employees
HS	high school
ICC	Interstate Commerce Commission
ICTF	Intermodal Container Transfer Facility
IDEPSCA	Instituto de Educación Popular del Sur de California (Institute of Popular Education of Southern California)
ILA	International Longshoremen's Association
ILGWU	International Ladies' Garment Workers' Union
ILWU	International Longshore and Warehouse Union
INS	Immigration and Naturalization Service
IPO	initial public offering
IRCA	Immigration Reform and Control Act of 1986
JfJ	Justice for Janitors
KIWA	Koreatown Immigrant Workers Alliance
LA CAN	Los Angeles Community Action Network
LAANE	Los Angeles Alliance for a New Economy
LAFCO	Los Angeles County Local Area Formation Commission
LAFLA	Legal Aid Foundation of Los Angeles
LAWA	Los Angeles World Airports
LAX	Los Angeles International Airport
LBACA	Long Beach Alliance for Children with Asthma
LCCR	Lawyers' Committee for Civil Rights
LEED	Leadership in Energy and Environmental Design
LGBT	lesbian, gay, bisexual, and transgender
LMC	licensed motor carrier
LNG	liquid natural gas
LPA	Labor Peace Agreement
MALDEF	Mexican American Legal Defense and Educational Fund
MATES	Multiple Air Toxics Exposure Study
MFA	Multi-Fiber Arrangement

MOCA	Museum of Contemporary Art
MTA	Metropolitan Transportation Authority
NAACP	National Association for the Advancement of Colored People
NAFTA	North American Free Trade Agreement
NDLON	National Day Laborer Organizing Network
NELP	National Employment Law Project
NEPA	National Environmental Policy Act
NILC	National Immigration Law Center
NLG	National Lawyers Guild
NLRA	National Labor Relations Act
NLRB	National Labor Relations Board
NOx	nitrogen oxide
NRDC	Natural Resources Defense Council
OC	Orange County
Pac 9	Pacific 9 Transportation
PMA	Pacific Maritime Association
PMSA	Pacific Merchant Shipping Association
RFP	request for proposal
RICO	Racketeer Influenced and Corrupt Organizations Act
RLA	Rebuild Los Angeles
S.B.	Senate Bill
SAJE	Strategic Actions for a Just Economy
SCAQMD	South Coast Air Quality Management District
SCLC	Southern Christian Leadership Conference
SEIU	Service Employees International Union
SLAPP	Strategic Litigation Against Public Participation
SMO	social movement organization
SRO	single room occupancy
TELACU	The East Los Angeles Community Union
TEU	twenty-foot equivalent unit
TIDC	Tourism Industry Development Council
TIF	tax increment financing
TMA	Transport Maritime Association
TRO	temporary restraining order

TWIC	Transportation Workers Identification Credential
UC	University of California
UCLA	University of California, Los Angeles
UFCW	United Food and Commercial Workers Union
ULAX	Unionize LAX
ULP	unfair labor practice
UNIDAD	United Neighbors in Defense Against Displacement
UNITE	Union of Needletrades, Industrial and Textile Employees
UP	Union Pacific
USC	University of Southern California
WRTU	Waterfront Rail Truckers Union
WTO	World Trade Organization
YWCA	Young Women's Christian Association

1

From Riots to Recession

The Challenge to Low-Wage Work in Los Angeles

Overview

This book is about the role of lawyers in the movement to challenge economic inequality in one of America's most unequal cities: Los Angeles. Covering a transformative period of city history—from the 1992 riots to the 2008 recession—the book examines how law has been used, and what it has achieved, in the struggle to improve conditions for workers in the low-wage economy. It is, at bottom, about the quest by social movement lawyers, in alliance with activists and workers, to build a more *equal place*: one defined by shared prosperity in which workers gain greater economic security by asserting a larger voice in city policymaking. In this quest, the idea of an equal place has a twofold meaning. It expresses an approach to social movement advocacy in which lawyers and activists work on terms of equality in leading campaigns, while also prescribing the substantive movement goal of greater equality in a city riven by economic and racial division.

The backdrop is the dramatic growth of low-wage work powered by global outsourcing, declining unionism, increasing labor contingency, and surging immigration. The narrative focus is on five pivotal campaigns in which lawyers allied with the city's dynamic labor, immigrant rights, and environmental movements mobilize law to reform key sectors of the regional economy. These campaigns, analyzed through in-depth studies, reveal how law has shaped low-wage work in Los Angeles—and at times provided a potent weapon to contest it.[1] Throughout, lawyers are not conventional client agents, but rather essential producers of community-based knowledge and power.

Using the L.A. movement to challenge low-wage work as a foundational case, this book aims to rethink the relationship between lawyers and social movements in American politics, while contributing to scholarship on the potential of local government to reshape labor law. In doing so, it spotlights the crucial role of lawyers in defining the city as a space for redefining work. Challenging critical accounts of lawyers in social movements, the book's central claim is that by advancing an innovative model of legal mobilization, the L.A. campaigns have achieved meaningful regulatory reform, while strengthening the position of workers in the field of local politics. Through multidimensional advocacy to promote worker organizing, lawyers and activists have succeeded in converting policy change into greater interest group power—forging a new model of progressive city-building for the twenty-first century.

This introductory chapter provides an overview of the book's main goals and contributions. It begins by placing local legal mobilization in theoretical perspective and situating the L.A. campaigns in relation to the city's broader postwar economic and political transformation. It concludes with a demographic overview of the industries targeted by the L.A. campaigns and a roadmap of the chapters that follow.

Lawyers and Social Movements in Los Angeles

This book is motivated by an impulse to deepen scholarship on lawyers and social movements by closely attending to the richness and complexity of contemporary practice. More than a half century after the March on Washington, the field's foundational stories and theoretical insights still flow from the fount of the Civil Rights movement—with the National Association for the Advancement of Colored People (NAACP) Legal Defense and Educational Fund's drive to win *Brown v. Board of Education* remaining a touchstone of American analysis.[2] Yet *Brown* in particular, and the larger canon of mid-century progressive law reform efforts in general, while still crucially important as historical markers of legal struggle with much to teach,[3] no longer speak in the same powerful register to the current generation of lawyers and activists—many of whom have internalized the criticisms of *Brown*-era impact litigation and are deploying law in creative ways to advance social movements.[4]

The stories from Los Angeles begin where canonical accounts of lawyers and social movements end: asking what can be learned from a new generation of lawyers—coming of age after the Civil Rights period—who respond to its legacy by rejecting the centrality of courts and reclaiming the centrality of economic rights.[5] These lawyers view law as an important, though not decisive, part of comprehensive strategies to change the legal framework of low-wage work in order to redistribute economic benefits and build worker power. Toward this end, they mobilize law in connection with movement campaigns: advocating across institutional spaces, coordinating legal and extralegal tactics, planning for backlash, and building alliances. Why and how movement lawyers adopt this approach—and what it can accomplish—are defining questions.

The book offers a unique perspective on these questions by turning toward the local policy arena as a site of mobilizing law. There, it seeks to widen the scope of analysis beyond litigation to investigate lawyers' contributions to legislative advocacy, economic development built through transactional law, community legal education, and legally oriented media strategies. The approach is to explore how these strategies are deployed at the grassroots level in pursuit of economic rights in the context of local labor markets segmented by race and immigration status—tracing the labor movement's struggle to redefine its relationship to civil rights and for broader relevance in the face of rapidly expanding inequality. In this struggle, activism is channeled to the city level, where workers seek to strengthen local law to augment a weak federal labor system. Toward this end, local government law is repurposed to enhance the quality of work, construct new spaces for unionization, and ultimately build a more equitable vision of the city economy. On the leading edge of this movement, Los Angeles presents a test case for local labor policymaking that pushes the limits of federalism: raising fundamental questions about the scope of local power, the suitability of local solutions, and the scalability of local victories.

Encountering Los Angeles at the crossroads of change, the book unfolds around an original history of high-profile campaigns to reform legal rules—and thereby enhance labor conditions—in vital industries.[6] Each campaign emerged from the profound realignment of Los Angeles's economy beginning in the 1980s, marked by the growth of service employment, labor flexibility, and immigration.[7] Within each industry, law shaped the structure of low-wage work through employer practices (e.g., contracting out and wage theft) and governmental policies (e.g., deregulation and underenforcement). In response, the campaigns have sought to build alternative legal frameworks to reconstruct a foundation for greater economic equality and mobilize workers. Taken together, the campaigns have enacted new legal formats for worker protection and organizing—and pointed to a new localist regime for workplace regulation.

Over the past two decades, the L.A. campaigns have become iconic social movement stories, drawing attention and informing strategy across the United States. They are:

- the struggle to end sweatshop production in the garment industry by assigning legal responsibility for labor abuse to manufacturers and retailers;
- the coordinated litigation and organizing campaign to challenge anti-solicitation ordinances preventing day laborers from seeking work on street corners;
- the grassroots effort to force private developers in gentrifying neighborhoods around downtown and the airport to enter community benefits agreements to enhance conditions for retail workers;
- the fight to stop Wal-Mart from opening big-box stores in the L.A. area, threatening the city's unionized grocery sector; and
- the movement to redesign the trucking industry at the Port of Los Angeles to eliminate independent contracting and promote unionization among drivers.

In analyzing the L.A. campaigns, this book places social movement actors—lawyers and nonlawyers alike—at the forefront of lawmaking processes designed to change local economic rules. From this perspective, law does not belong solely to lawyers or operate only within courts. To the contrary, law is a pragmatic tool of social movement organizations, activists, and lawyers, who often collaborate—and sometimes compete—in efforts to author a new legal framework for regulating work. Significantly, while movement actors operate in an institutional environment that promotes exchange and coordination, they are not directed by one organization. Rather, their joint activity is episodic and instrumental, characterized by the formation of shifting coalitions to advance different goals. Thus, how coalitions form, who controls them, and how lawyers relate to their leaders is a key story line—one that is generally underexamined in the law and social movement literature.[8] Although there is not a single vanguard group, there are critical organizational leaders—such as the Los Angeles Alliance for a New Economy (LAANE) and the UCLA Downtown Labor Center—that set the agenda and shape strategy. Within this environment, organized labor has significant power, which sometimes creates disagreement and division, but also gives coalitions the political strength to move policy.

The relationship between lawyers and social movement organizations is a central lens through which the stories unfold.[9] Movement organizations are networked with and seek advice from a cadre of lawyers who practice both in nonprofit public interest organizations and for-profit firms. In contrast to the paradigmatic top-down civil rights model, these lawyers are valued as partners because of their strategic knowledge as well as their expertise in performing discrete functions in relation to larger campaign projects. Litigation is an important component of these projects, although courts are typically used to promote movement-building or to protect policy gains.[10] Lawyers are crucial throughout the phases of campaign mobilization: helping to identify problems; finding legal hooks to solve them; devising legal theories to advance policy; and mobilizing legal doctrine to persuade allies, policymakers, and judges. In these struggles, lawyers seek to coordinate law and politics—and ultimately challenge the division between the two.

Theoretical Framework: Local Legal Mobilization

This book explores the role of lawyers challenging low-wage work in Los Angeles through the lens of *local legal mobilization*. It focuses on the deployment of integrated political and legal strategies, coordinated with social movements, which leverage local government processes toward the end of producing new forms of labor regulation in the city. In doing so, this book contributes to scholarly research at the intersection of three fields: (1) lawyers and social movements, (2) labor law and labor studies, and (3) local government law and urban planning.

Lawyers

The question of whether lawyers help or hurt social movements has been deeply contested since the Civil Rights era. As progressive social movements declined in the 1970s, scholars developed a powerful critical account of the role that lawyers had played, asserting that lawyer control and overinvestment in legal tactics had worked against grassroots activism.[11] This account coalesced around two foundational critiques. The first centered on lawyer *accountability*, claiming that lawyers advancing rights on behalf of marginalized constituencies risked letting their own ideological commitments undercut the interests of those they served.[12] The second centered on legal *efficacy*, claiming that court-centered legal strategies were ineffective at best, unable to change social practice on the ground, and detrimental at worst, causing social movement demobilization and backlash while legitimizing the status quo.[13] Despite significant changes in politics and the profession, these foundational critiques of progressive lawyering have persisted, fostering skepticism about what lawyers can do "for and to" social movements.[14]

This book reconsiders these critiques in relation to contemporary legal practice. It does so by adopting *comparative institutional analysis*.[15] This theoretical framework builds upon foundational legal and social scientific approaches to lawyering and legal mobilization,[16] while integrating interdisciplinary insights on the form and impact of activism outside of law.[17] In this framework, legal and political mobilization are viewed in context as strategies that complement and conflict, shaping each other over time. The key focus of comparative institutional analysis is on situating legal mobilization in relation to available nonlegal alternatives—thereby illuminating how lawyers and activists make choices in the real world of opportunity and constraint. This lens highlights why specific groups make distinctive tactical decisions while also facilitating evaluation of outcomes by presenting the full range of options at the time lawyers and activists confront them.

Comparative institutional analysis functions by placing lawyers and nonlawyers within the broader field of social movement action in which community grievances are ultimately translated into legal and political mobilization.[18] Figure 1.1 maps the actors, institutions, and outcomes in the framework. As it shows, there are different organizations through which lawyers and activists pursue strategies of social change: legal groups that mobilize within the legal field, interest groups that mobilize within institutional politics, and social movement organizations (SMOs) that mobilize outside of institutional politics. In reality, these groups overlap. There may be one group advancing multiple strategies or a coalition of groups coordinating efforts. All organizations operate in a wider environment in which they seek to represent the interests of a broader constituency, mobilizing available opportunities and resources that are shaped by other actors (elites, the public, government officials, funders, opponents, and other movements).

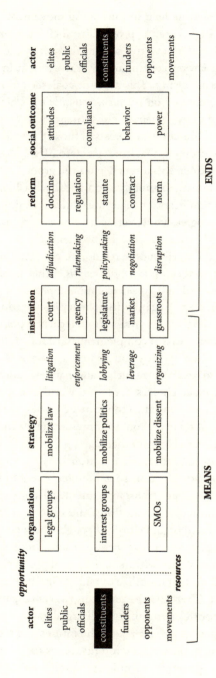

Figure 1.1 Comparative institutional framework.

The theoretical framework is divided into two hemispheres. On the *means* side, inquiry centers on how political opportunities, organizational resources, and individual choices shape the development of social change groups, the strategies and tactics they deploy, and the role that law comes to play within movements.[19] On the *ends* side, the focus is on how mobilization is translated into concrete change, both at the level of specific reforms achieved through legal and political action (policy change) and at the level of social outcomes (changes in attitudes, behavior, policy implementation, and political power).[20] Ultimately, mobilization seeks to change law on the books and law in action[21]—building political power to transform the attitudes and behaviors of the very actors who affect the environment in the first instance. Mobilization produces outcomes through different institutional venues— courts, agencies, legislatures, private markets, and the street—where organizations bring demands on behalf of constituents. A critical feature of the comparative institutional framework is that it illuminates how these organizational demands occur in tandem, influencing each other in ways that shape results—which are then challenged in additional rounds of "contentious politics."[22]

By presenting a richer conception of SMOs and their relationship to formal lawmaking, this framework draws on neglected aspects of social science to reveal how legal and nonlegal actors within movements face parallel challenges to advancing movement claims: struggles over leadership, conflicts of interest, dependency on external funding, debates over incrementalism versus radical change, and the constant threat of reversal and backlash.[23] Within the comparative institutional framework, evaluative analysis is oriented *prospectively*, through the lens of movement decision-making processes.[24] This orientation reveals the range of alternatives available at the point of movement planning and execution, and permits a fuller appraisal of decisional trade-offs. In this perspective, it is the *campaign*—a series of interconnected operations intended to achieve a specific object—and not the lawyers or the case, that is the relevant unit of analysis. The focus is on how lawyers and legal strategy come to fit into the broader process of issue framing, power mapping, and strategic development in the campaigns themselves—in which accountability and efficacy can then be assessed on their own terms.

With respect to accountability, the book explores factors shaping the development and execution of movement lawyering approaches focused on building local coalitions to strengthen city regulation and enhance worker power. In these approaches, law is given an *equal place* with politics: Lawyers and activists coordinate to design comprehensive strategies in which legal and political mobilization are interconnected tools. The book seeks to capture why this coordination happens and what it looks like through two important shifts in emphasis. The first shift is geographic. In contrast to the civil rights model of invoking federal power to protect minority interests at the local level, this book examines the movement to *build local power to resist, and potentially transform, federal authority*. It thus analyzes how networks of local lawyers and activists develop over time to engage in repeated advocacy efforts in a defined place where connections to affected communities are immediate and sustained. This leads to the second shift in emphasis, which is strategic. By tracing the development of *integrated legal and political strategies* to challenge low-wage work, the book illuminates how lawyers navigate their relationships with other movement activists and community members, particularly around issues of racial difference and class privilege; how they mobilize law throughout campaigns to persuade policymakers and private actors to support movement claims; and how they ultimately embed law in local policies that themselves become the subject of ongoing legal dispute. In so doing, the book investigates the ways in which lawyers in the L.A. campaigns exercise accountable leadership—deploying professional expertise while promoting community empowerment—and asks what their efforts teach about the nature of representation in contemporary reform efforts.

With respect to efficacy, the book seeks to evaluate the campaigns' impact by examining how they have contributed to making Los Angeles itself a more *equal place*. It does so by exploring the degree to which Los Angeles as a city has redressed inequality, both in terms of the local regulatory regime governing work and the lived experience of the L.A. working class. Movement impact is measured by assessing the extent to which the campaigns have succeeded in changing local law in a proworker direction and exploring how legal reforms have affected the conditions of workers in industries targeted by campaigns. Outcome evaluation also focuses on whether legal mobilization has enabled low-wage workers to achieve more power in city governance—a more equal place at the political bargaining table. This analysis traces the development of movement organizations, the rise of movement leaders in local politics, and the degree to which those leaders can exert influence over city elections and policy development.

Labor

Engaging the debate about the role of law as a tool to contest local economic inequality has important implications for contemporary research on the labor movement and labor law. Over the past quarter-century, labor scholars have argued over the appropriate regulatory framework for collective rights, and the appropriate strategies for collective action, against the backdrop of labor law's "ossification" and the changing nature of the workplace.[25] As statutory revisions and judicial interpretations have limited the utility of the federal labor law system of collective bargaining for promoting employee interests,[26] and corporate practices have placed a growing number of workers beyond the "reach and grasp" of employment and labor law altogether,[27] scholars and practitioners have searched for alternative structures of protection and mobilization. A fundamental question has been the degree to which the traditional regulatory framework and organizational structures (i.e., unions) are worth salvaging or whether the future of workers' rights lies in "reimagining" labor law in relation to different legal regimes, forms of mobilization, and scales of intervention.[28]

Underlying this question are several important trends. One is the changing demographics of low-wage work, particularly the growth of immigrant workers (some undocumented),[29] which has occurred alongside ongoing racial division in the low-wage marketplace. Working-class whites have become deeply disaffected from the labor movement's historical political home, the Democratic Party, and black workers are often left out of the conversation about the problem of low-wage work and how to address it.[30] In addition, the development of new forms of organization designed to channel the "hydraulic pressure" of worker organizing into substantive workplace gains[31]—like worker centers and community–labor groups[32]—has continued to run up against the limited power of nonunionized workers to challenge industry employment practices and respond to the rise of independent contracting and other forms of risk-shifting in the new "gig" economy.[33] Finally, the hostility of the Republican Party to the enforcement and expansion of labor rights has resulted in federal gridlock on issues as basic as an increased minimum wage and has succeeded in producing an entrenched majority against labor rights on the Supreme Court.[34] For organized labor, this has spurred efforts to identify and build on opportunities for state and local labor reforms—like the $15 minimum wage—which have resulted in important successes, but continue to beg critical questions about how to bridge gaping red-blue state divides and translate local energy into a broader national resurgence of the American labor movement.

This book situates the L.A. campaigns at the intersection of these trends and illuminates central dynamics of "labor activism in local politics."[35] First, it reveals how low-wage worker organizing *outside* of the federal labor law regime interacts with (and may be leveraged to reinforce) unionization, while also demonstrating the limits of this approach in industries defined by informality and contracting. Second, it shows how *legal analysis* is an inescapable element of organizing strategy—necessary to understand whether labor unions go through or around federal collective bargaining law; how local government law, particularly in the areas of land use planning and contracting, can be used to advance labor objectives; and how federal preemption may operate to limit the scope of local efforts. Third, the book traces the evolving relationship between worker organizing and labor's *political strategy*, in which organizing success is translated into policy reform and greater influence by the labor movement in local politics. This feeds into the final dynamic: the unstable *alliance* between labor and other progressive movements, particularly immigrant rights and environmental justice, which are key partners in many campaigns, but which also have to navigate labor's growing political influence in ways that create challenges to sustained collaboration in pursuit of a more equal place.

Localism

By locating labor activism in the context of a broader project of city reform, this book reframes Los Angeles's low-wage worker campaigns as not simply about reconstituting labor law outside of the federal sphere, but also about reimagining the city as a space for economic redistribution. In this sense, Los Angeles is not merely a setting for movement activity, but a tool and a target of struggle. Viewing Los Angeles from this perspective speaks to current debates within local government law on the potential and trade-offs of the "progressive city."[36] Contrary to scholarly accounts emphasizing how law constructs urban inequality,[37] the case studies explore the ways local government law is being used to build alternative regulatory frameworks to promote "shared prosperity."[38] From a theoretical standpoint, this analysis raises questions about how far cities can and should go in pursuing redistributive policies that extract economic benefits from immobile local employers.[39] In terms of policy and legal doctrine, the pursuit of local redistribution tests the boundaries of city lawmaking and the validity of adapting municipal law to advance labor rights, highlighting the clash between municipal authority and federal preemption.

Local analysis also focuses attention on inequality across jurisdictional lines. Los Angeles County is comprised of eighty-eight separately incorporated cities, of which the City of Los Angeles is by far the largest, with roughly 40% of the county's population (4 million people in 2017).[40] The greater L.A. area is even larger, covering a five-county region with a population of close to twenty million. As the campaigns reveal, a significant part of what advocates do is pursue worker rights in one jurisdiction, only to see another lower standards in ways that threaten an inter-jurisdictional race to the bottom. How advocates think about reform in *the city* in relation to the broader movement for *regional* equity is thus a critical theme.

Los Angeles has always existed between the space of myth and reality. Its allure as a magical place of reinvention where dreams come true has fit uneasily with stories of graft, oppression, and violence. Hollywood has peddled both images: *La La Land* and *Crash*; *Pretty Woman* and *Boyz in the Hood*; *L.A. Story* and *L.A. Confidential*—the idyllic and the noir. Urbanists have similarly characterized Los Angeles in schizophrenic terms: presented simultaneously as a bellwether of national urban trends and dysfunctional anomaly,[41] a site of innovation and unstinting deprivation,[42] a place enriched by radical diversity and inescapably divided by race and class.[43] This book probes the power of both visions and suggests how each is necessary to sustain the other—and how the very tension between myth and reality generates the energy to demand that the city can and should be better. It is in this sense that place matters in the campaigns for economic justice: revealing Los Angeles as a citadel of intransigent inequality, where hope springs eternal.

The Arc of L.A. History: Foundations of Inequality and Activism

This book analyzes a transformative time in L.A. history, shaped by complex forces flowing from the cauldron of economic restructuring, immigration, racial conflict, and political realignment. It covers a pivotal period in the city's evolution: from the 1992 civil unrest through the 2008 recession. During this less than two-decade span, the city confronted the consequences of tectonic demographic, economic, and political shifts—the roots of which had been growing for some time. Compared to the postwar period, Los Angeles in the early 1990s was a city with more racial diversity, more immigrants, and more income inequality.[44] The changing demography and economy spawned new demands for representation and redress, dramatically shifting local politics, which moved from a business friendly, tough-on-crime conservatism to a pro-labor, more inclusive progressivism. The struggle to reclaim the dignity of work, led by low-income communities of color, was a product of this shift and contributed to its velocity.

On April 29, 1992, in Simi Valley northwest of Los Angeles, the jury foreman in the prosecution of five police officers charged with the brutal videotaped beating of a handcuffed black man, Rodney King, uttered words that would ignite the city: "Not guilty. Not guilty. Not guilty. Not guilty . . . ."[45] Protests erupted immediately, exposing long-seething anger in the black community over police abuse in South Los Angeles.[46] In 1965, protesters in Watts had chanted "burn baby burn" after highway patrolmen arrested a woman on suspicion of drunk driving and then proceeded to arrest her mother and brother in the ensuing scuffle.[47] This was followed by a continuous scourge of unchecked police brutality, which regularly broke into public view: the 1978 killing of a black woman triggered by an unpaid utility bill; the 1989 killing of a black Muslim man after a traffic stop; and untold killings of purported gang members in the name of Operation Hammer instituted by reviled police chief Daryl Gates.[48] After the 1992 riots ended, the city took stock of its toll: 60 dead, 2,383 injured, roughly 10,000 arrested, 623 fires, and $1 billion in total damage.[49] In the aftermath, city and community leaders looked backward and forward: analyzing the causes of the unrest and taking tentative steps toward reconciliation and rebuilding.

Looking back with the perspicuity of hindsight, it was clear that, through the 1992 unrest, South L.A. residents were uncorking years of frustration over joblessness, inadequate schools, and discriminatory housing practices that segregated African Americans in less desirable neighborhoods close to freeways and other environmental hazards.[50] As the Civil Rights movement revealed the intransigence of segregation, efforts to address some of these problems seemed to only make things worse. School integration provoked acrimonious boycotts from white parents, who kept ten thousand children home on the first day of the L.A. busing plan in 1978 and increasingly abandoned the school system altogether,[51] draining resources from central city schools and the city's economic infrastructure.[52]

Frustration in the black community was also a product of shifting economic fortunes. World War II had brought African Americans to Los Angeles from the South in search of opportunity, which many found in military-related industries.[53] After World War II, the city experienced tremendous economic growth. Wartime production of military airplanes and other manufacturing items was retooled for postwar civilian production, galvanizing a manufacturing boom, particularly in the aerospace, electronics, and automotive industries, which were all heavily unionized. In addition, light manufacturing industries—like garment production—and some service industries—notably construction, janitorial services, and trucking—were important growth sectors with high union density in the postwar period.[54] Despite persistent inequalities based on race and immigration status, a diverse middle class emerged in Los Angeles, bolstered by the heavy manufacturing sector (which employed one in five county residents in 1970[55]), as well as the unionized service industries.

The foundation of middle-class Los Angeles crumbled as quickly as it had been built. The manufacturing base that powered Los Angeles's mid-century growth began to decline in the 1970s and 1980s.[56] Trade liberalism and workplace restructuring produced Los Angeles's own version of deindustrialization, shifting the economic balance toward low-wage service industries.[57] Between 1978 and 1982, the city lost nearly one hundred thousand manufacturing jobs, primarily in the automobile industry.[58] As Edward Soja describes, one consequence was the westward migration of African Americans from South Los Angeles to places like Inglewood, which were closer to the airport and the still-strong aerospace industry.[59] However, recession in the early 1990s decimated aerospace as well, causing the loss of three hundred thousand more manufacturing jobs.[60] Between 1990 and 1994, the largely unionized durable goods manufacturing sector declined by one-third.[61] A critical pillar of middle-class Los Angeles was irreversibly degenerating.

In its place, the economically bipolar service sector rose to dominate the L.A. economy, distributing enormous wealth at the high end and economic insecurity at the low end. As an emerging global city, Los Angeles developed a dense economic network of finance, real estate, and professional service industries like law and accounting that reshaped the market, creating a new class of professionals connected to the central city who relied on cheap labor, often accessed through the informal economy, to provide the food, child care, maintenance, and other services that facilitated their lives.[62] Low-end service sector jobs—in growth industries like retail sales and hospitality—lacked the high wages, labor protections, and job security that had undergirded the postwar middle class. Abuse was rampant in the burgeoning informal economy, while even in the formal economy, there were increasing rates of labor violations.[63]

In addition, corporate strategies to restructure work undermined union density and degraded labor standards. Companies in previously unionized industries (such as janitorial services and garment production) launched subcontracting practices— outsourcing work to small independently owned companies—that broke the unions, drove down wages, and promoted exploitation while shielding those with economic power from legal responsibility.[64] Although Los Angeles still remained the manufacturing capital of the United States in the 1990s, the bulk of those jobs were in light manufacturing—like garment and furniture production—which were not unionized and paid low wages.[65] The labor movement's decline in Los Angeles was part of a national corporate strategy to undermine unions' economic standing and political clout. Labor protections atrophied. As a prominent symbol of labor's weakened state, the federal minimum wage declined by nearly 40% in real terms from the late 1960s to the late 1980s.[66] Added to this was a shrinking safety net, culminating in the 1996 federal welfare reform law, forcing more people to rely on precarious work.

It was in this context that income inequality surged in Los Angeles—built on the backs of the new working poor.[67] The Gini coefficient (a prominent metric of inequality measured on a scale of 0, the lowest, to 1, the highest) grew from .544 in 1980 to .575 in 1990 for adults in Los Angeles County.[68] Inequality was driven by astonishing income increases at the high end, much from investment, and the spread of poverty at the bottom. In 1993, nearly one-quarter of Los Angeles County residents (more than two million people) lived in poverty,[69] which was concentrated in neighborhoods with the highest percentage of residents of color: East Los Angeles (90% Latino) and South Los Angeles (half black and half Latino).[70] Inequality was also a function of the shrinking middle class. In 1990, the average salary for all workers in Los Angeles County was $24,258—$22,298 for blacks and $15,857 for Latinos (declining from 1980). Over the next decade, middle-income workers saw a more than 10% decline in average earnings, while the earnings ratio of the top quintile of workers compared to the middle quintile grew by nearly 17%.[71] By the end of the 1990s, over 40% of Los Angeles County residents lived below the needs-based poverty threshold (200% of the federal poverty level) and roughly two-thirds of them lived in a household with at least one full-time worker.[72] More than one million individual workers in Los Angeles County earned less than the needs-based income threshold, nearly 80% of whom worked full-time.[73] These working poor Angelenos were disproportionately Latino and foreign-born.[74]

Beginning in the 1980s, with job growth exploding in the low-wage market, immigration to the region expanded as employers took advantage of workers forced to accept degraded conditions in newly restructured workplaces.[75] As immigration increased, particularly from Mexico and other Latin American countries, the demography and residential patterns of Los Angeles shifted. Attracted by the promise of prosperity, immigration to the L.A. metropolitan area grew sharply, from roughly half a million in 1984, to a peak of 1.8 million in 1991.[76] In 1994, one-fifth of immigrants to Los Angeles came from Mexico, with significant proportions also coming from Russia, the Philippines, China, and El Salvador.[77] A large number of entrants were undocumented immigrants—with estimates of Los Angeles County's undocumented population ranging from 533,000 to 1.5 million in 1992.[78] As a result of migration, the overall demographic composition of Los Angeles shifted toward a higher proportion of Latino and foreign-born residents. In 1965, when Watts burned, the population of greater Los Angeles was 80% white, and African Americans were by far the largest minority group.[79] In the 1980s, "the county added 1.4 million residents. Nearly 1.3 million of them—92.9%—were Latino. Outnumbered 8-1 by Anglos in 1960, Latinos were nearly on par by 1990," with 37% of the county population Latino compared to 41% white (Asian and African Americans were 11% each).[80] By the start of the new millennium, the City of Los Angeles was 47% Latino, 30% white, 10% Asian American, and 11% African American.[81] Reflecting this overall trend, between 1970 and 1990, the composition of the workforce changed dramatically, from 75% white to less than 50%; while African Americans held constant at 10%, "the Latino and Asian workforce grew by more than 300 percent and 463 percent, respectively."[82] The foreign-born population in the region rose from 1 million in 1970 to nearly 4 million in 1990 (with 54% of Latinos foreign-born) and close to 5.5 million by 2010,[83] as the overall population increased from 11 to 17 million over the same forty-year span.[84]

Growth reshuffled residential patterns and realigned local politics. Both changes created friction. In South Los Angeles, the demographic shift was dramatic as new immigrants moved into traditionally African American neighborhoods.[85] In 1970, South Los Angeles was overwhelmingly African American; during the course of that decade, 100,000 Latinos settled there.[86] By 1990, Latinos comprised nearly half of South L.A. residents, fueling economic competition and sometimes violence.[87] Following the models of Chinatown and Little Tokyo, established nearly a century earlier, Asian American immigrants during this period concentrated in ethnic communities.[88] The growth of Koreatown, in mid-city Los Angeles between Hancock Park and downtown, was one of the most prominent. Beginning in the late 1960s, as white flight drained the central city, Korean immigrants (newly authorized to enter by the 1965 Immigration and Nationality Act) began buying housing and opening businesses around a stretch of Wilshire Boulevard formerly known as the "Miracle Mile." During the 1970s, the Korean population in the city increased from 5,700 to 33,100, half of whom lived in Koreatown.[89] Yet even then, Korean immigrants were a minority in Koreatown, which had nearly three times as many black and over five times as many Latino residents.[90] The result of residential intermixing and change was dynamic—and also combustible. During the 1992 riots, conflict between communities of color broke into painful view. Although their businesses were concentrated in Koreatown, Korean Americans also owned a significant number of stores in South Los Angeles's predominantly black neighborhoods, some purchased at low prices during white flight. Resentment at these owners draining money from the black community was inflamed by the 1991 shooting of a fifteen-year-old black customer, Latasha Harlins, by a Korean convenience store owner.[91] During the civil unrest, many Korean American-owned stores in South Los Angeles were burned—a prominent symbol of the interracial conflict that erupted.[92]

The 1992 riots constituted a pivot point in L.A. politics. The Civil Rights era saw the rise of black political power in the city, culminating in the election of Tom Bradley as mayor in 1974. Yet as the city's composition changed, so did its politics. The most immediate consequence of the riots was backlash. After five terms as mayor, Bradley declined to seek reelection in 1993, opening the door for Republican lawyer and businessman Richard Riordan to claim a resounding victory built on promises to promote economic development and crack down on crime (his campaign slogan was "Tough Enough to Lead L.A."). Yet the Riordan interregnum served as a bridge between the Bradley era and the rise of Latino political influence. As prominent L.A. urbanist Mike Davis argues, during this period, Latinos were not just "reinventing" the city economy, they were also shaking up its political structure.[93] In 1992, at the time of civil unrest, the fifteen-seat Los Angeles City Council had two Latino members (Mike Hernandez and Richard Alatorre) and three African American members (Mark Ridley-Thomas, Rita Walters, and Nate Holden). By 2003, there were four Latino members (Ed Reyes, Tony Cardenas, Alex Padilla, and Antonio Villaraigosa), alongside two African Americans (Bernard Parks and Jan Perry). Although the City Council was never as pro-business as Mayor Riordan, by 2003, it had shifted more forcefully toward organized labor: symbolized by the election of Antonio Villaraigosa (who had been an organizer for United Teachers Los Angeles) to the fourteenth district, and Martin Ludlow (a former organizer for the Service Employees International Union (SEIU)) to the tenth.

The election of Villaraigosa and Ludlow, along with the broader ascendance of pro-worker politics, was the product of labor's own reinvention. As Ruth Milkman documents, organized labor in Los Angeles had followed an atypical path that made it well-positioned to respond to the growth of service industries and immigrant workers.[94] Unionism during Los Angeles's postwar period occurred primarily in "older, occupationally based, nonfactory unions" affiliated with the American Federation of Labor (AFL),[95] which used a sectoral strategy of taking wages out of competition by pressuring and negotiating with employers industry-wide, rather than mobilizing workers on the shop floor—the strategy adopted by Congress of Industrial Organizations (CIO) unions.[96] Through the 1950s, AFL unions achieved notable success organizing janitors, truck drivers, garment workers, and construction workers,[97] and by 1955, 37% of L.A. workers were unionized—the vast majority in AFL unions.[98] As elsewhere, deindustrialization and neoliberal restructuring hit the L.A. labor movement hard. By 1986, union density had dropped sharply to 22% and was concentrated in heavy manufacturing.[99] In former labor strongholds like construction, janitorial services, and trucking, "deunionization and employment restructuring" was "followed by an exodus of native-born workers, [and] an immigrant influx."[100] By the mid-1980s, organized labor had gone into steep decline, hemorrhaging members and resources.[101]

Nevertheless, in the seeds of decline were sown labor's rebirth, which it achieved by building closer ties with Los Angeles's burgeoning community groups and committing to organize new immigrants in the precise service industries where AFL unions had historic strength. Early precursors of community–labor alliance grew out of deindustrialization and plant closings in the 1980s. When General Electric (GE) announced its intent to close a flat-iron plant in Ontario, California, in 1980, the plant's United Electrical Workers union reached out to the Los Angeles Coalition Against Plant Shutdowns, an umbrella organization that brought together community groups and religious leaders.[102] Although the alliance did not prevent the closure, it did succeed in generating publicity, putting forward a plant closing bill in the state legislature, developing a worker buyout proposal, and helping other GE workers win job security language in national union contracts.[103]

The L.A. model of community–labor mobilization was also a product of deliberate union strategy—innovation born of desperate times and guided by organizers who had cut their teeth as architects of earlier efforts by the United Farm Workers to mobilize low-wage immigrants against contract-based corporate farmers.[104] Perhaps no other campaign heralded the renaissance of the L.A. labor movement more than Justice for Janitors (JfJ), led by SEIU Local 399, which put Los Angeles on the map by showing that unions could win collective bargaining agreements in the new environment of subcontracting and immigrant work.[105] In this environment, Los Angeles's historic weakness in industrial unionism became its "comparative advantage,"[106] allowing AFL unions to build on prior nonfactory organizing traditions. Janitorial service epitomized the transformation of the L.A. economy. Composed of a largely unionized, African American workforce in the 1970s (Rodney King's father was a janitor), janitorial service was a low-wage, nonunionized industry a decade later—transformed by building owners that contracted out service to low-wage outfits that hired mostly Latino immigrants, many undocumented.[107] The JfJ campaign in the late 1980s was built on nontraditional tactics—reclaiming and updating the AFL approach of taking wages out of competition across an entire industry. Instead of targeting the subcontractors, which had little power, the SEIU pressured building owners by protesting in the streets, alongside community organizations and religious leaders, and using savvy public relations—capitalizing on popular outrage after a televised police attack on peaceful marchers in Century City galvanized official support.[108] The end result was a union contract in 1990 covering thousands of janitors in downtown Los Angeles.[109]

The JfJ campaign had powerful ripple effects, not the least of which was to reshape the labor movement's approach to local politics. Throughout the tenure of Mayor Bradley, organized labor continued to exercise significant local political influence through the vaunted Los Angeles County Federation of Labor (County Fed), whose close relations with city officials permitted union members, particularly in the building trades, to benefit from city-sponsored redevelopment projects in the 1980s.[110] However, the 1992 riots and the end of Bradley's reign left the County Fed at a crossroads—with the critical issue of how to deal with Los Angeles's growing population of immigrant workers unresolved. At the national level, the AFL-CIO had endorsed the 1986 Immigration Reform and Control Act (IRCA), which imposed sanctions on employers for hiring undocumented immigrants—signaling that the union movement did not envision a future partnership with immigrant workers. Although the County Fed did not explicitly co-sign the national labor movement's support for IRCA, there was significant local disagreement over whether to embrace organizing immigrant workers, who many viewed as unorganizable.[111] This debate reached a crescendo after JfJ, leading to the narrow 1996 election of a new leader of the County Fed, Miguel Contreras, who had built his reputation organizing Latino immigrant workers for the Hotel Employees and Restaurant Employees (HERE) Local 11 union.

Contreras's election cemented the County Fed's movement toward closer collaboration with the immigrant community, punctuated two years earlier by the County Fed's agreement to co-sponsor a 100,000-person march against anti-immigrant state Proposition 187—demonstrating a "new and powerful political alliance between Labor and the Latino community."[112] Contreras led a shift away from the County Fed's Bradley-era insider politics, rebuilding labor's power through a sophisticated get-out-the-vote operation predicated on an innovative strategy of mobilizing occasional voters, securing the elections of Villaraigosa and Ludlow to the City Council in 2003—and paving the way for Villaraigosa's successful bid for mayor in 2005.[113] The County Fed was also instrumental in engineering the national AFL-CIO's 2000 decision to reverse its previous stance on immigration policy and support a pathway to citizenship for undocumented workers.[114]

In addition to fostering political realignment, JfJ also underscored the power of community partnerships, helping galvanize a new brand of community–labor activism in Los Angeles that sought to connect labor's resurgence with efforts to promote cross-racial collaboration in the wake of the riots.[115] This new activism reshaped progressive political and legal advocacy while challenging the underlying structure of low-wage work.[116] At the grassroots level, the new activism built on Los Angeles's base of community organizations, some dating back to the 1960s and others emerging out of 1980s restructuring.[117] The Watts Labor Community Action Committee was established just before the Watts riots to address the lack of economic opportunity in South Los Angeles.[118] It became the model for other community development corporations that followed: CHARO Community Development Corporation (1967), the East Los Angeles Community Union, or TELACU (1968), and Little Tokyo Service Center (1979). Esperanza Community Housing Corporation, located in an immigrant-dense neighborhood adjacent to the University of Southern California (USC) just south of downtown, was started in

1985 by a nun from the local Catholic parish, Sister Diane Donoghue, who worked to stop resident displacement by a proposed garment sweatshop.[119] Esperanza grew rapidly to support the neighborhood's immigrant community, mostly from Mexico and Central America, providing English language and other classes, and beginning in 1994, building much-needed affordable housing.[120]

As Martha Matsuoka shows, these community development groups were initially place-based, but soon engaged in new forms of regional organizing that responded to the same forces of economic restructuring and demographic change that reshaped the labor movement.[121] By adopting cross-sectoral, multiracial approaches, these groups sought to address the widening chasm of inequality that cut across neighborhood lines. One effort that reflected the potential of sectoral initiatives was the 1998 Alameda Corridor Jobs Coalition (ACJC) campaign to win local hiring and other community benefits in connection with the billion-dollar expansion of the Alameda Corridor rail line linking the ports to downtown Los Angeles—at the time the largest public works project in the United States.[122] ACJC also demonstrated the importance of legal partnerships in sectoral initiatives as the final agreement codifying the coalition's gains was negotiated and drafted by lawyers from the Los Angeles Legal Aid Foundation and San Francisco's Employment Law Center.

The new wave of aggressive, coalition-led organizing to promote equitable development ran counter to the city-sponsored effort to subsidize industry in the aftermath of the 1992 civil unrest. The city's official program, dubbed Rebuild LA (RLA), was launched by Mayor Bradley and Governor Pete Wilson, who persuaded Peter Ueberroth, who had organized the 1984 L.A. Olympics, to lead the effort. Ueberroth's approach was to "use his considerable skills to influence the heads of corporations to donate money, people, and equipment to RLA and persuade large businesses, especially chain retail outlets, to open branches in South Central and other inner-city areas. He also hoped to coordinate large amounts of government funds."[123] When this failed, new RLA leadership focused on "bottom-up" development, mapping existing economic assets in South Los Angeles and working to support their expansion based on "competitive advantage."[124] Mirroring the federal movement to provide business incentives through "Empowerment Zones," RLA sought to channel resources and information, through conferences and networking opportunities, to strengthen extant industries in the inner city: garment, furniture, food, and toy manufacturing[125]—the very light manufacturing industries contributing to the rise of low-wage work. In parallel, the Riordan administration pushed initiatives to cut business regulation and promote city-subsidized retail redevelopment in the downtown area, which further added to the glut of low-wage jobs.[126]

In 1992, students from the UCLA Department of Urban Planning's nascent Community Scholars program conducted a research project, led by Professor Gilda Haas, which critiqued the city-sponsored expansion of tourism-related industries and offered a plan for growth that focused on equity for workers.[127] Their report, titled "Accidental Tourism," was the template for what would become LAANE (founded in 1994 as the Tourism Industry Development Council), which won its first victory—the nation's second living wage law in 1997—by convincing the City Council to override a veto by Mayor Riordan. The seminal Bus Rider's Union (BRU) campaign was also launched in 1992, organized by the Labor/Community Strategy Center,[128] whose founder, Eric Mann, had been involved in the General Motors plant closing movement a decade earlier. The BRU—a multiracial coalition of low-income, largely immigrant workers—targeted the linked problems of transit racism and pollution, provoked by the Metropolitan Transportation Authority (MTA) decision to raise bus fares and reduce routes to poor neighborhoods. Teaming up with the L.A. branch of the NAACP, the BRU filed a civil rights lawsuit that resulted in a 1996 consent decree in which the MTA promised affordable and accessible service for Los Angeles's working poor.[129] Two years later, protests at USC over outsourcing janitorial and food service workers launched a grassroots movement that coalesced around another new group, Strategic Actions for a Just Economy (SAJE), started by Haas, which spearheaded an alliance between labor and community members concerned over gentrification and displacement.[130]

Into this welter of activity entered a small but influential number of worker centers: grassroots groups experimenting with new ways of organizing and protecting worker rights outside of traditional unionism.[131] As they evolved, worker centers focused on immigrants, emphasizing policy advocacy and legal redress for labor abuse.[132] One of the earliest worker centers in Los Angeles was Korean Immigrant Workers Advocates (KIWA, which later changed its name to the Koreatown Immigrant Workers Alliance). Founded in 1992, just before the Rodney King verdict, KIWA gained notoriety by helping Latino and Asian American workers receive compensation from stores shut down by the unrest. Its major campaign was an effort started in 1997 to organize Latino and Asian American workers fighting wage theft by Korean-owned restaurants and groceries.[133] The campaign, in partnership with local unions and civil rights organizations, combined boycotts with legal action—taking a stand for cross-racial workers' rights over ethnic solidarity, winning back pay and living wage agreements from employers, and bringing public attention to the problem of labor abuse in Koreatown.[134]

In 2002, the UCLA Labor Center, established nearly forty years earlier to promote research and policy development on workers' issues, opened its flagship downtown office overlooking MacArthur Park in a bustling community of Latino immigrants. The Downtown Labor Center (DLC) aimed to build bridges between worker centers, organized labor, and immigrant communities in the surrounding neighborhood and beyond. It was there that the National Day Laborer Organizing Network (NDLON) and the Community Labor Environmental Action Network (CLEAN) Car Wash Campaign were officially launched as the DLC became a key meeting place and strategic headquarters for the worker center movement, strengthening ties to organized labor while also helping establish networks of movement lawyers, like the Coalition of Immigrant Workers Advocates.[135] Crucially, the DLC also sought to build bridges to African American workers concerned about being marginalized by organized labor's growing focus on Latinos. This effort to promote multiracial solidarity, albeit not without friction, was reinforced by partnerships between the County Fed and groups like Action for Grassroots Empowerment and Neighborhood Alternatives, which advocated for better jobs for black workers in South Los Angeles and teamed up with the County Fed to mobilize black voters in support of progressive political leaders.[136] From the ashes of the L.A. riots, a new foundation for progressive activism in Los Angeles was thus built—one that weaved together multiple strands of mobilization into a coordinated challenge to inequality.

Industries Targeted by the L.A. Campaigns

This book's account of the L.A. campaigns follows the arc of low-wage worker mobilization over a roughly two-decade span through the 2008 Great Recession, when the collapse of the housing market produced global economic crisis and steep local decline. Up to that point, the L.A. economy continued to grow—and to shift toward the service sector.[137] The campaigns took aim at the last bastion of manufacturing (the garment industry), as well as critical service industries with existing or historical union strength (grocery and trucking), large-scale organizing potential (retail and hospitality), and rampant worker abuse (day labor). Each industry had geographic ties to the region, making them sticky—not amenable to outsourcing—and thus prime sites for collective action and, in some cases, possible unionization.

The following tables provide an overview of the industries targeted by the campaigns (each industry is the subject of one chapter, with the exception of chapter 4 on the community benefits movement, which focuses on retail and hospitality workers). Tables 1.1 through 1.3 compare county-level demographic and earnings data from the 1990 and 2010 censuses for all target industries except day labor, for which no census data are available (the tables use the term "Hispanic" following the census category). Table 1.4 shows education level, citizenship, and nativity status for workers in all target industries except day labor as of 2010.[138] Day labor demographics are presented in Table 1.5 based on the best available source, which is the 2004 National Day Labor Survey. Figure 1.2 shows the trajectory of private sector unionization in Los Angeles County compared to state and national trends.

Table 1.1 presents the gender and racial composition of the target industry workforces as of 1990. As it shows, white workers formed the largest percentage of the total countywide workforce (45%), followed by Hispanic (35%), Asian American (10%), and black (10%) workers. The total workforce in the target industries constituted just less than 10% of the countywide workforce with retail and hospitality the largest sectors (70% of the target industry workforce). Garment

Table 1.1 **Demographic overview of target industries, 1990.**

	Total	Male	Female	Hispanic	White	Black	Native American	Asian	Other
Garment Workers	56,545	15,981	40,564	47,240	1,131	509	7	7,586	72
Retail Workers	131,455	56,213	75,242	39,437	61,241	12,906	467	17,136	268
Hospitality Workers	157,849	98,036	59,813	91,042	41,698	6,890	453	17,366	400
Grocery Workers	42,380	21,697	20,683	16,378	16,049	3,914	91	6,810	63
Truckers	30,514	29,215	1,299	14,425	10,671	3,953	248	1,123	94
Target Industry Workforce	418,743	221,142	197,601	208,522	130,790	28,172	1,266	50,021	897
Los Angeles Countywide Workforce	4,538,364	2,571,269	1,967,095	1,572,010	2,029,860	437,134	16,779	473,874	8,707

Source: U.S. Dep't of Commerce, Bureau of the Census, Census of Population and Housing, 1990 [United States]: EEO Supplemental Tabulations File, Part I. Ann Arbor, MI: Inter-university Consortium for Political and Social Research [distributor], 2006-01-12.

workers were disproportionately female (72%) and Hispanic (84%), while truckers were more racially mixed (47% Hispanic and 35% white) but almost entirely male (96%). Black workers had the highest representation in the retail (10%), grocery (9%), and trucking (13%) industries, although this was consistent with black worker representation in the countywide workforce. Overall, Hispanic workers were overrepresented in the target industries by 15% relative to their share of the countywide workforce.

Table 1.2 shows total figures for the same industries as of 2010 and the percentage change from 1990. Overall, the countywide workforce declined slightly, reflecting the impact of the recession; however, the percentage of Hispanic and Asian American workers grew significantly (approximately 24% and 41% respectively). The total workforce in the target industries also declined slightly (−.54%), while Hispanic workers were the only identified group to show growth (nearly 20%). The garment sector suffered significant job loss with employment falling by more than 40%, while the grocery sector also contracted significantly (−14%). In contrast, the hospitality and trucking sectors both grew by roughly one-sixth. By 2010, the number of Hispanic workers had increased significantly in all industries except garment, reflecting that industry's overall job loss, while the number of white and black workers declined across the board. The Asian American workforce grew modestly in hospitality (23%) and significantly in trucking (79%), although the number of Asian American truckers remained small. Hispanic workers continued to be significantly overrepresented in the target industries (constituting 60% of the workforce) relative to their share of the countywide workforce (totaling only 43%), while white workers were the most underrepresented (21% of the target industry workforce compared to 33% countywide).

Table 1.3 shows earnings in the target industries from 1990 to 2010 (in constant 1990 dollars). Overall, it confirms that workers in target industries were disproportionately concentrated in the lowest earnings category, with roughly 70% making less than $15,000 per year relative to approximately 40% of the countywide workforce in 1990 and 2010. The table also shows relative stability in earnings across all industries during this twenty-year span. The notable changes are that the proportion of retail workers in the lowest earnings category decreased by 10 percentage points over the time period, while the share of grocery workers in that category increased by about 15 points.

As Table 1.4 shows, as of 2010, target industry workers were disproportionately less educated and foreign-born. Retail workers were the closest to countywide figures, while garment workers were the most dissimilar, with over 75% not graduating high school and over 97% foreign-born (80% were noncitizens).

Table 1.5 presents data for day laborers collected in 2004, the only date for which data are available. As it suggests, day labor was the most homogenous industry by race and gender: Nearly all workers were foreign-born Hispanic men. They were disproportionately undocumented and, given their marginal status in the informal

Table 1.2 **Demographic overview of target industries, 2010.**

	Total	Male	Female	Hispanic	White	Black	Native American	Asian	Other
Garment Workers	32,515	13,100	19,420	27,970	330	0	0	4,165	50
	−42.5%	−18.0%	−52.1%	−40.8%	−70.8%	−100.0%	−100.0%	−45.1%	−30.6%
Retail Workers	129,569	55,369	74,180	59,144	38,958	11,909	148	16,399	3,031
	−1.4%	−1.5%	−1.4%	50.0%	−36.4%	−7.7%	−68.3%	−4.3%	1031.0%
Hospitality Workers	181,935	102,245	79,695	116,010	35,235	5,815	244	21,375	3256
	15.3%	4.3%	33.2%	27.4%	−15.5%	−15.6%	−46.1%	23.1%	714.0%
Grocery Workers	36,420	17,280	19,140	20,100	7,605	2,455	30	5,740	490
	−14.1%	−20.4%	−7.5%	22.7%	−52.6%	−37.3%	−67.0%	−15.7%	677.8%
Truckers	36,030	35,125	905	26,230	5,535	2,345	35	2,015	115
	18.1%	20.2%	−30.3%	81.8%	−48.1%	−40.7%	−85.9%	79.4%	22.3%
Target Industry Workforce	416,469	223,119	193,340	249,454	87,663	22,524	457	49,694	6,942
	−0.54%	0.89%	−2.16%	19.63%	−32.97%	−20.05%	−63.90%	−0.65%	673.91%
Los Angeles Countywide Workforce	4,530,880	2,506,420	2,024,460	1,945,215	1,493,815	340,320	8,605	669,585	73,345
	−0.16%	−2.52%	2.92%	23.74%	−26.41%	−22.15%	−48.72%	41.30%	742.37%

Source: U.S. Census Bureau, The EEO Tabulation: 2006–2010.

Table 1.3 Earnings distribution in target industries (by percentage), 1990 and 2010.

	1990							2010						
	Under $15k	$15k–$25k	$25k–$35k	$35k–$50k	$50k–$75k	Over $75k		Under $15k	$15k–$25k	$25k–$35k	$35k–$50k	$50k–$75k	Over $75k
Garment Workers	84.66	11.29	2.27	1.04	0.45	0.29		83.13	10.71	3.43	1.83	0.41	0.49
Retail Workers	71.21	15.62	6.99	3.34	1.67	1.16		61.46	16.77	8.20	6.51	3.95	3.11
Hospitality Workers	75.49	17.89	4.38	1.50	0.48	0.26		73.54	18.77	4.84	1.81	0.67	0.37
Grocery Workers	68.51	16.71	9.07	3.94	1.40	0.37		84.15	10.18	3.09	2.08	0.20	0.30
Truckers	42.36	23.49	16.68	12.85	3.19	1.43		41.32	29.77	16.02	9.26	2.58	1.04
Target Industry Workforce	70.51	16.97	6.89	3.68	1.26	0.69		70.91	15.80	6.33	3.91	1.78	1.26
Los Angeles Countywide Workforce	43.00	20.28	14.52	11.79	5.32	4.09		40.85	21.17	13.04	11.77	7.70	5.46

Source: For 1990, U.S. Dep't of Commerce, Bureau of the Census, Census of Population and Housing, 1990 [United States]: EEO Supplemental Tabulations File, Part I. Ann Arbor, MI: Inter-university Consortium for Political and Social Research [distributor], 2006-01-12. For 2010, Steven Ruggles et al, IPUMS USA: Version 8.0 [dataset]. Minneapolis, MN: IPUMS, 2018. Figures are in 1990 dollars.

Table 1.4 Education, citizenship, and nativity in target industries (by percentage), 2010.

	Education					Citizenship and Nativity		
	Not HS Grad	HS Grad	Some College	College Grad	Postgrad Degree	US Citizens	Noncitizens	Foreign-Born
Garment Workers	76.03	18.42	4.31	0.94	0.29	19.87	80.13	97.32
Retail Workers	19.44	30.68	37.90	10.82	1.16	75.87	24.13	41.30
Hospitality Workers	37.89	27.03	24.48	9.60	1.00	51.98	48.02	62.37
Grocery Workers	29.02	36.06	27.45	6.42	1.05	60.14	39.86	68.50
Truckers	39.49	36.80	19.95	3.29	0.47	67.48	32.52	50.96
Target Industry Workforce	36.19	28.63	25.85	8.38	0.95	57.36	42.64	59.63
Los Angeles Countywide Workforce	18.61	20.49	28.97	20.98	10.95	18.61	20.49	28.97

Source: U.S. Census Bureau, The EEO Tabulation: 2006–2010.

Table 1.5 **Demographic overview and earnings of day laborers, 2004.**

	Los Angeles	United States
Estimated Total	19,500	120,000
Gender		
Male	98.9%	97.4%
Female	1.1%	2.5%
Ethnicity		
Hispanic	98.3%	96.6%
White	1.7%	.9%
Black	—	2.1%
Native American	—	—
Asian	—	—
Other	—	.2%
Citizenship Status		
U.S. Born	2.2%	4.5%
Naturalized U.S. Citizens or Legal Permanent Residents	9.4%	5.7%
Noncitizens, Temporary Resident	4.4%	5.1%
Noncitizens, Undocumented	78.3%	76.8%
Unknown	5.6%	7.9%
Work and Earnings		
Months Worked per Year as Day Laborer	3.41	2.62
Hours of Work per Week as Day Laborer	9.25	8.33
Earnings per Month as Day Laborer	$597.53	$678.93

Source: National Day Labor Survey, 2004.

economy, earnings were strikingly low, at less than $7,200 per year for day laborers in Los Angeles County.

Finally, to give context on the environment for labor organizing, Figure 1.2 compares private sector union density in Los Angeles County to state and national figures over time. While there is a steady decline in national union density from 1990 to 2010 (from nearly 12% to just over 7%), until the 2008 recession, Los Angeles County stayed consistently around 10%, albeit with significant fluctuation. In 2010, density by industry varied significantly. In the garment industry, it was less than 1%, compared to unionization rates of just over 40% for grocery workers, 16% for retail workers, 3% for hospitality workers, and 16% for truckers.[139]

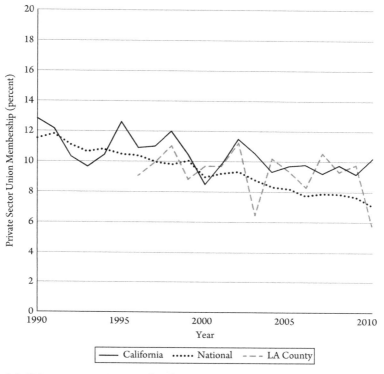

Figure 1.2 Private sector union membership, 1990 to 2010. *Source*: Sarah Flood et al., Integrated Public Use Microdata Series, Current Population Survey: Version 6.0 [dataset]. Minneapolis, MN: IPUMS, 2018.

Design

The campaigns recounted in this book grew out of the emerging community–labor challenge to inequality after the 1992 unrest and fundamentally contributed to its rise. As the demographic data suggests, the campaigns targeted industries that, in general, were disproportionately comprised of Latino immigrant workers and thus the theme of immigrant worker organizing features prominently. However, low-wage work cut across race and the campaigns themselves aspired to be self-consciously cross-racial, attending to the varied racial composition of different industries. In doing so, the campaigns fused different types of organizing approaches (inside and outside of unionism) and social movements (labor, immigrant rights, environmental justice, and others), while also creating a central role for lawyers and law. The chapters that follow pull back the curtain on the campaigns to reveal the often hidden, but crucially important, ways in which lawyers made contributions to the struggle for Los Angeles.

Chapter 2 begins with an iconic campaign that woke the city (and nation) to the severe exploitation of immigrant workers—and created a new model for change. Launched in 1995 with the discovery of more than seventy enslaved Thai workers in a suburban apartment complex surrounded by barbed wire fence, the campaign—led by the Asian Pacific American Legal Center—pioneered the integration of strategic litigation and worker organizing, marking the emergence of a movement to contest garment sweatshops. The sweatshop regime was built on a legal foundation of subcontracting: insulating retailers and manufacturers, which sold and created clothes, from the contractors actually producing them. At its most ambitious, the campaign sought to make legal responsibility follow economic power, rupturing the legal fiction that protected retailers and manufacturers from labor abuses such as those uncovered in the Thai worker case. The chapter shows how lawyers built a powerful alliance with labor and grassroots organizers, won important legal victories in court, and achieved passage of a landmark state law creating manufacturer liability for contract labor violations. It then traces the campaign through the fierce fight against retailer Forever 21, which showed the power of industry countermobilization and ultimately marked the end of the litigation campaign. This outcome underscored a central lesson of the new economy: Individual enforcement and litigation strategies, even when paired with innovative organizing and media campaigns, confronted formidable barriers in challenging abuse enabled by extensive contracting and—crucially—the threat of global outsourcing. Nonetheless, in fusing law and organizing to mount this challenge, the anti-sweatshop campaign marked a new beginning in the movement against low-wage work—one in which lawyers and activists would apply the tools honed in the manufacturing context to target Los Angeles's immobile service industries.

Chapter 3 examines a pivotal battle in this new movement: the two-decade-long legal campaign led by the Mexican American Legal Defense and Educational Fund (MALDEF) to contest anti-solicitation ordinances—local laws prohibiting the public solicitation of work by day laborers. The relationship between day laborers and those who use their labor is defined through contracting, with day laborers negotiating for daily rates and often experiencing labor abuse. Although part of the underground economy, during the 1990s, day laborers became some of the most visible immigrant workers, standing on the corners in affluent communities to find jobs. They also became the target of legal backlash, with nearly forty anti-solicitation ordinances passed by cities in the greater L.A. area by 2000. Chapter 3 charts the course of the legal campaign to challenge these ordinances, beginning with the alliance between MALDEF and NDLON, which together created a litigation model built around organizing worker committees to be plaintiffs in federal First Amendment lawsuits. This model created legal standing while protecting workers from intrusive discovery. After a series of legal battles, joined by the American Civil Liberties Union, the campaign won a monumental Ninth Circuit Court of Appeals en banc ruling striking down the Redondo Beach anti-solicitation ordinance as an overbroad regulation of commercial speech. The ruling had the effect of invalidating similar ordinances and thus preserving significant parts of the region's sidewalks for day laborers to seek work. It therefore showed the power of litigation to create the conditions for collective action by sweeping aside barriers to its realization. It also underscored litigation's limits: Although the campaign succeeded in protecting the "corner" as a place for contracting work, it could not prevent the labor abuse that followed—or stop the creation of the next generation of anti-solicitation ordinances tailored to circumvent the Ninth Circuit's ruling.

Chapter 4 analyzes a campaign that emerged at the intersection of Los Angeles's living wage movement and efforts to challenge gentrification. Led by LAANE and SAJE, the campaign sought to leverage community benefits from publicly subsidized development, particularly in gentrifying neighborhoods where displacement of low-income residents was occurring. These developments produced significant numbers of retail and hospitality jobs (along with jobs in ancillary industries like janitorial services and security); a primary goal of the campaign was to ensure these jobs would go to local residents and pay a living wage. The benefits strategy was advanced through interlocking coalitions that negotiated with developers to create contracts—known as community benefits agreements (CBAs)—that traded developer promises to provide specific benefits (living wage guarantees, job training programs, local hiring, and affordable housing) for coalition promises to support the projects. The first campaign, targeting the development of a sports and entertainment complex in downtown Los Angeles, won a multimillion-dollar package of benefits, including an agreement by the developer to ensure that retailers ultimately occupying the complex as tenants would pay workers at the living wage rate. This filled a gap in the L.A. living wage ordinance, which excluded tenants in publicly subsidized commercial projects. It also laid the foundation for two other major CBAs: a half-billion-dollar agreement with Los Angeles International Airport (LAX) in relation to airport expansion, and a CBA with the developer of a transformative mixed-used downtown development known as the Grand Avenue Project. Both of these were significant for different reasons: The LAX agreement showed the power of a nascent labor-environmental—or "blue-green"—alliance to negotiate a monumental benefits package with a public entity, whereas the Grand Avenue CBA revealed how organized labor's growing power permitted it to achieve community benefits through insider political strategies while community groups focused on affordable housing continued to pursue CBAs through outsider challenges. Overall, the CBA campaign was important for its innovative use of private contracting mechanisms to promote labor standards and unionization—through living wage, card check neutrality, and local hiring provisions—which were ultimately embedded in local policy.

Chapter 5 analyzes the campaign to challenge the retail giant Wal-Mart, whose announced plan in 2002 to bring forty Supercenters into California threatened to undercut wages in the unionized grocery sector. It focuses on LAANE's confrontation with Wal-Mart in the separately incorporated City of Inglewood, a historically working-class African American community in South Los Angeles. The chapter offers a close account of the labor-backed campaign to stop the development of the Inglewood Supercenter through legislative and legal challenges—a technique known as a "site fight" because of its focus on blocking Wal-Mart at a specific location. It concentrates on how labor and community groups enlisted legal advocacy to mobilize community opposition to Wal-Mart's Inglewood initiative and later to craft a set of policy responses to limit Wal-Mart's ability to enter the Los Angeles market. It then traces the story to Wal-Mart's effort to circumvent the laws passed after the Inglewood site fight by opening a small-format grocery store in the historic Chinatown neighborhood in downtown Los Angeles.

The final case study in chapter 6 examines the campaign to raise work and environmental standards at the ports of Los Angeles and Long Beach—known as the Campaign for Clean Trucks. This blue-green campaign, led by LAANE and the Teamsters union (on the labor side) and the Natural Resources Defense Council (on the environmental side), emerged as a fight over air quality, but developed as a struggle over the conditions of short-haul truck drivers, whose misclassification as independent contractors contributed to poorly maintained trucks viewed as a key cause of air pollution, while precluding labor organizing. The campaign rested on an innovative legal foundation: the port, as a publicly owned and operated entity, had the power to define the terms of entry for trucking companies through concession agreements. The campaign therefore hinged on how those agreements treated truck drivers and what types of environmental standards they set. In 2006, labor unions, environmental activists, and community residents formed the Coalition for Clean and Safe Ports, which passed a Clean Truck Program two years later through the L.A. Board of Harbor Commissioners. The program conditioned port concession agreements on two requirements: first, that trucking companies convert their fleets to low-emissions vehicles, and, second, that they convert all their drivers to employees. Under this new program, the environmental movement advanced a long-standing goal—"greening" the port—while the Teamsters could pursue driver unionization. It was a win-win designed to take maintenance out of the low-paid drivers' hands, making companies internalize the costs, thus creating a sustainable foundation for clean trucking over time. Lawyers working with the coalition crafted the program to minimize the legal risk that it would be preempted by federal law, all the while planning for a federal preemption challenge by the American Trucking Associations. That lawsuit came quickly, resulting in a Ninth Circuit ruling invalidating the program's requirement of employee drivers. As a result, the labor-environmental alliance's joint policy victory was torn asunder through litigation—with port truck drivers forced to carry the economic burdens of heightened environmental compliance without the economic benefits of enhanced labor standards. The ports campaign thus presents a cautionary tale—demonstrating law's potential to build coalition-led reform but also to split it apart.

It further highlights the power of movement resilience: tracing how organized labor responded to legal setback through an innovative new strategy to maneuver around preemption and reassert its challenge to driver misclassification.

Chapter 7 considers the larger meaning of the five campaigns by exploring how they have contributed to making Los Angeles a more equal place. It evaluates equality as a process and an outcome of local legal mobilization, assessing how new forms of movement lawyering have challenged low-wage work in the city. From an empirical perspective, the chapter synthesizes findings across campaigns, offering an overall appraisal of legal mobilization's role in redefining local economic policy, rebuilding labor movement power in local politics, and reshaping Los Angeles as a progressive city. From a theoretical perspective, the chapter reflects on what the case studies teach about the place of lawyers in progressive social movements in contemporary American politics and considers the potential of building more robust systems of labor regulation for vulnerable workers by transforming local government law.

2

Garment Workers

Fighting to End Sweatshops

Overview

Launched in 1995 with the discovery of garment workers imprisoned in a suburban apartment complex surrounded by barbed wire fence, the movement to end sweatshops—led by the Asian Pacific American Legal Center (APALC)—pioneered the integration of strategic litigation and worker organizing to challenge inequality in Los Angeles. This chapter recounts the decade-long campaign to bring accountability to the country's largest garment production sector, constructed on an elaborate system of subcontracting that insulated powerful industry retailers and manufacturers from legal liability for employment violations committed by garment contractors. The campaign, which began in the mid-1990s, developed on the cusp of a new wave of low-wage worker organizing—and marked a pivotal juncture in its evolution. While dramatizing the extremes of immigrant labor abuse in the United States, the anti-sweatshop movement also revealed its pervasiveness and nexus to the mainstream economy. The campaign burst onto the international stage in early August 1995 when more than seventy undocumented Thai workers were found in slave-like conditions in a garment subcontracting company in a suburb of Los Angeles,[1] where they labored eighty hours a week for less than $2 a day,[2] producing clothing for brand-name manufacturers and major retailers, including Mervyn's.[3] The Thai worker story was an iconic moment in the emergent anti-sweatshop movement, drawing intense media attention to the workers' struggle to recover stolen wages and reconstruct their lives.

The campaign also illustrated the divergent fortunes of union-driven and extraunion legal mobilization. As the Thai worker case made its way through the litigation process, it underscored the critical role of legal action in defending workers' rights—providing a counter-narrative to the tale of organized labor's declining power to protect garment workers. The case occurred at a crucial point along the arc of labor activism in the L.A. garment sector—just as the Union of Needletrades,

Industrial and Textile Employees (UNITE) was planning a major campaign to unionize the designer clothing manufacturer Guess, Inc.—and offered a study in contrasts. While the Guess campaign, which included a wage-and-hour class action to pressure the company, failed in its bid to organize workers at Guess and its contractors, the civil lawsuit filed in the Thai worker case resulted in a favorable legal ruling—stating that the manufacturers contracting with the sweatshop could be liable as "joint employers"[4]—and a multimillion dollar settlement for the workers.

Finally, the anti-sweatshop campaign, as it developed in the wake of the Thai worker case, pioneered the strategic integration of targeted litigation with grassroots worker organizing in a way that challenged conventional wisdom about the demobilizing impact of legal action and directed significant attention to new legal strategies to organize workers outside of the traditional labor law regime. The legal campaign, directed by APALC, was used to spur further legal and political mobilization, contributing to the creation of new anti-sweatshop organizations and the passage of a statewide joint employer law covering the garment industry. APALC lawyers thus broke with traditional conceptions of professional role, orchestrating a political campaign that not only rattled a global industry, but also provided a template for law and organizing that was widely emulated by groups around the country. They did so against enormous odds, challenging major companies in a low-wage manufacturing sector increasingly vulnerable to the forces of global outsourcing. Their campaign thus tested new-wave law and organizing techniques in an industry closely identified with the old economy, underscoring both the promise and perils of this approach.

Law in the Construction of Garment Sweatshops

The structure of the garment industry is commonly represented by a pyramid with garment retailers at the apex, manufacturers in the middle, and contractors at the base.[5] The pyramid, like the one shown in Figure 2.1, is meant to depict market relationships in the industry: a small group of powerful giant retailers like Wal-Mart and Target operate on a national scale and control access to consumers;[6] retailers purchase garments from a diverse cohort of manufacturers, which design "brands" and thus are the creative force in the industry;[7] the manufacturers, in turn, externalize production through the use of contractors, typically operating as small shops with short-term orders from multiple manufacturers, which they meet by hiring workers to cut and sew—and sometimes placing orders with their own subcontractors.[8]

Within this pyramid system, power flows downward. Retailers have substantial bargaining power to determine the wholesale price to the manufacturer, which, in turn controls the price paid to contract shops. Because contractors compete for bids and face the threat of foreign competition, they are under intense pressure to cut costs, which they must achieve by reducing wages.[9] Pressure on contractors to

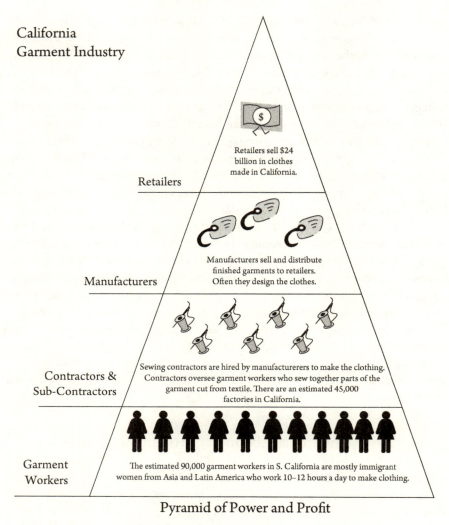

Figure 2.1 Pyramid of Power and Profit. *Source*: Sweatshop Watch (2005).

reduce labor costs often translates into illegal labor abuse committed against the workforce. In the worst cases, contract shops become sweatshops,[10] characterized by "extreme exploitation, including the absence of a living wage or benefits," "poor working conditions, such as health and safety hazards," and "arbitrary discipline."[11] How could a production system built upon systematic labor violations exist in the heavily regulated modern U.S. economy? This section describes the legal rules that enabled sweatshop employment to flourish in the garment industry in the 1980s and 1990s.

Union Organizing

Garment sweatshops have a long history in the United States.[12] Their initial demise is largely a story about the successful unionization of the garment industry during the first half of the twentieth century. This effort was led by the International Ladies' Garment Workers' Union (ILGWU), which used a model of "triangular" negotiation between the union, manufacturers, and contractors to effectively take wages out of competition. To achieve this goal, the union negotiated jointly with the garment contractors and manufacturer associations, agreeing with both on a wage scale to be paid by the contractors to the garment workers, which was predicated on adequate manufacturer payments to contractors.[13] This triangular system was permitted by National Labor Relations Act (NLRA) § 8(e), which specifically exempted union actions against manufacturers forming part of an "integrated process of production in the apparel and clothing industry" from the prohibition on secondary boycotts (i.e., actions against companies doing business with the targets of union organizing, in this case, garment contractors).[14] Section 8(e) thus legally permitted the ILGWU to strike manufacturers that failed to source jobs to union contractors, even though the ILGWU had no unionized workers directly employed by the manufacturers.[15] This arrangement institutionalized a system of "joint employership" in the garment industry that empowered the union to deal directly with manufacturers, which set the ultimate price for labor. Under this system, the ILGWU represented nearly 450,000 workers—over 70% of the garment industry—at its peak in the mid-1950s.[16]

The success of this model of garment unionization at the mid-point of the twentieth century rested on four pillars: the power of unions to effectively bargain with manufacturers, the physical concentration of production in New York, the constriction of the immigrant labor market in the interwar and immediate postwar period, and the relative power of manufacturers to set prices vis-à-vis retailers. These pillars began to crumble in the 1970s.

As a legal matter, unionization was hindered by the deficiencies of the NLRA election process, which permitted employer intimidation and failed to provide union organizers meaningful protection from employer retaliation.[17] In addition, manufacturers deliberately undercut garment union power by moving domestic production out of New York, where garment sector unionism was strong. Starting in the 1970s, Los Angeles emerged as the nonunion production alternative to New York because of its weaker tradition of unionism.[18] By 1992, Los Angeles's garment work force was nearly double what it had been two decades before,[19] while New York had lost a third of its garment workforce during the same period.[20] The expansion of the garment industry in Los Angeles occurred on an entirely nonunion basis, with union density standing at only 1% by the mid-1990s[21]—down from 15% two decades before.[22]

International Trade

The shift in production from New York to Los Angeles was part of a broader global movement of garment production that reinforced the decline of garment unionism. The outsourcing of garment production from its hub in the Northeast began in the 1950s and 1960s, with apparel assembly sourced first to the American South, then to East Asia.[23] The impact of this first wave of foreign outsourcing was limited by a series of voluntary bilateral agreements negotiated under the General Agreement on Tariffs and Trade that restricted the importation of specified foreign-made garment products.[24] In 1974, however, these agreements were replaced by the Multi-Fiber Arrangement (MFA),[25] which continued import quotas for twenty years but allowed the quotas to grow in a way that facilitated more outsourcing to developing countries where labor costs were low.[26] As a result, foreign outsourcing grew in the 1980s, producing an increase in garment imports and a decrease in domestic garment sector employment.[27] Asian countries, particularly China, emerged during this period as major apparel exporters, followed by countries in Latin America and the Caribbean that benefited from special tariff reductions on apparel assembly.[28]

The outsourcing trend accelerated in the 1990s, propelled by the passage of the North American Free Trade Agreement (NAFTA) in 1994 and the advent of the World Trade Organization (WTO) in 1995. NAFTA generated a significant shift in production to Mexican maquiladoras and led to an explosion in apparel and textile imports from Mexico.[29] With the creation of the WTO, the MFA was formally replaced by the Agreement on Textiles and Clothing, which provided for the gradual phaseout of all garment quotas by 2005[30]—further accelerating the outsourcing trend.[31]

California remained the one bright spot in the domestic garment industry. While garment production in the rest of the country fell, California—particularly Los Angeles—saw an increase in employment between 1978 and 1997.[32] The peak year of garment employment in Los Angeles County was 1996, with approximately ninety-eight thousand "cut-and-sew" apparel workers industry-wide.[33] This growth in garment employment reflected the drive to move production from New York to union-free shops in Los Angeles. It also underscored the interplay between the international legal regime and domestic production. The continuation of import quotas throughout the 1990s trapped some garment production in the United States. An important focus of the production that remained was on the high fashion market, characterized by cutting-edge design and quickly changing styles, which called for tighter quality control and quick-turnaround production. Los Angeles, with its high concentration of fashion designers, became a garment production magnet.[34] By the mid-1990s, the L.A. garment industry had grown to be the nation's biggest and was the largest manufacturing industry in the city,[35] powered by the production of women's outerwear.[36]

Immigration

As global companies sought a competitive edge by moving production to take advantage of low-paid foreign workers living *outside* the United States, domestic contractors responded in kind by focusing on hiring foreign workers already *inside* American borders: immigrants willing (or forced) to accept the low pay and benefits policies that contractors had come to demand as the industry standard.

While the halcyon days of garment union organizing coincided with racially restrictive controls on immigration,[37] the era of deunionization occurred during the liberalization of immigration law, which (paradoxically) resulted in an expansion of undocumented entry. The passage of the 1965 Immigration and Nationality Act amendments eliminated the discriminatory national origin quota system, which had blocked Asian immigration, and imposed new limits on Latin American immigrants.[38] While this spurred the entry of Asians, it capped legal Mexican immigration at levels that proved too low to meet demand, resulting in a dramatic increase in undocumented entry.[39] After the passage of the 1986 Immigration Reform and Control Act, which increased border security and imposed sanctions on employers that hired undocumented workers,[40] undocumented immigration not only grew,[41] but also changed in ways that exposed immigrants to greater economic and legal insecurity. Because it was harder to cross the border, immigrants began to stay longer and moved out of seasonal agricultural work into the urban low-wage sector.[42] Although Asian immigrants were less prominent in the undocumented flow, they too became bound up in the system of labor abuse as disproportionate victims of human trafficking.[43]

By 1990, Los Angeles had emerged as the immigration capital of the United States, surpassing New York as the region with the largest foreign-born population (4 million).[44] The growth in the L.A. foreign-born population was fueled by the rapid rise of immigrants from Latin America, with the majority coming from Mexico,[45] though the Asian population (mostly Filipino, Chinese, and Korean) also grew rapidly in the 1980s.[46] Significantly, Los Angeles was also the center of undocumented immigration, with one estimate of 1.5 million undocumented residents in 1992, the largest contingent being from Mexico.[47] Los Angeles's pool of immigrant labor made it a magnet for manufacturers seeking labor flexibility and the garment industry readily incorporated immigrants as the mainstay of its workforce. In 1990, 85% of the garment sector workforce was immigrant (and over 70% women), with half from Mexico and roughly one-seventh from Asia.[48] Although the proportion of undocumented garment workers was not known with precision,[49] a 1980 study finding that over 80% of Latino and Latina garment workers were undocumented was suggestive of the magnitude of the industry's reliance on undocumented labor.[50] These workers, in particular, were more prone to tolerate sweatshop conditions for fear of employers exposing their lack of legal status if they complained of abuse.

Corporate Organization

Organized labor's lack of success in the L.A. garment industry was partly a product of the relative weakness of unionism there, but it also reflected organizational changes in the garment industry itself that disrupted the stable relationship between manufacturers and contractors allowing unions to thrive in mid-century New York.

At the bottom of the industry pyramid, the system of garment contracting changed in ways that challenged union organizing. Whereas the old New York model was to source production to a small group of large contractors, the L.A. model was to source production to a large number of small-scale, high-turnover firms, any one of which could be shut down by the withdrawal of manufacturer contracts.[51] These small firms engaged in fierce competition to outbid each other,[52] driving down prices in order to attract business from manufacturers.[53] While the L.A. garment industry still constituted an integrated production system under the NLRA, manufacturers were able to effectively thwart unionization by shifting production among small contracting shops—undercutting collaborative wage setting and rendering union efforts to organize any one shop extremely difficult.

Manufacturers moved toward this more aggressive contracting posture in part because of changes at the pinnacle of the industry pyramid that threatened their economic position. As the number of contractors grew, the number of retailers diminished, concentrating power in the hands of a small cohort of giant department stores and discount chains like Wal-Mart.[54] The new market dominance of these retail giants conferred greater power to set prices, which allowed the retailers to drive a harder bargain with manufacturers, particularly those outside the high-end sector especially vulnerable to outsourcing.[55] In addition, many retailers began to produce their own brand labels, which competed directly with traditional manufacturers in price and quality. As a result, retailers increasingly dictated the industry's cost structure by setting prices through bulk purchasing and offshoring their own private-label production.[56] Manufacturers, their profits diminished, looked to make up the difference by forcing lower prices on their network of contractors.

Labor Enforcement

For manufacturers, extracting cost savings at the contractor level meant setting the price of jobs at low margins that created incentives for contractors to "sweat out" profits by paying below the minimum wage, eliminating employee benefits, and reducing investments in employee safety.[57] It also meant that manufacturers sought to insulate themselves from the legal consequences of contractor abuse. Contracting was therefore done not just to implement an *economic division of labor*, but also to enforce a *legal division of accountability*. Whereas manufacturers in the postwar era had entered into triangular agreements with contractors and unions under the old joint employership system as a way of sharing legal responsibility for labor compliance, manufacturers in the modern era entered individual contracts in order to disclaim legal liability. The shift from a regime of collective bargaining agreements to individual contracts attempted to draw a clear legal line between manufacturers and contractors, and changed the focus of labor dispute resolution from the systemwide enforcement of collective bargaining rights administered by unions to the individual-level enforcement of minimum statutory employment protections.

This system depended on two actors—the government and the worker—to enforce state and federal statutory employment rights (such as minimum wage and overtime rules) against contractors that violated them. At the state level, the California Division of Labor Standards Enforcement (DLSE) was empowered to bring civil actions under state law to recover unpaid wages and impose civil penalties (it also administered an individual wage claim process),[58] while enforcement of the federal Fair Labor Standards Act (FLSA) was entrusted to the Department of Labor's Wage and Hour Division, which possessed similar powers to bring lawsuits to collect back wages and seek liquidated damages.[59] Each agency attempted to focus attention on labor abuse in the garment industry in the 1990s.[60] Although there were some important initiatives,[61] governmental enforcement efforts were generally impeded by insufficient funding,[62] as well as political disagreements over how to allocate resources between monitoring and enforcement.[63]

As a result, the onus of labor enforcement was placed on workers, whose pursuit of individual claims against employers was hindered by multiple obstacles, including the fear of reprisal; limits on class actions; barriers to accessing legal assistance, particularly in cases for low damages insufficient to attract private lawyers dependent on attorney's fees;[64] and the difficulty of recovering against contractors, which often refused to pay and even went out of business to avoid labor lawsuits.[65] In the face of lax public and private enforcement efforts, labor violations by contractors reached systemic proportions. In 1994, the federal government reported that there were forty-five hundred sweatshops in Los Angeles,[66] while a state study found that half of California's garment shops were in violation of minimum wage laws and two-thirds broke overtime laws.[67] A 1998 Department of Labor survey repeated similar conclusions, finding that nearly two-thirds of garment firms in Los Angeles were violating wage-and-hour regulations, underpaying workers by over $70 million per year.[68] As these figures underscored, the shift in the garment industry from joint production to individual contract subverted the system of labor compliance—normalizing the sweatshop and rendering exceptional the garment firm that complied with labor law.

Law in the Resistance to Garment Sweatshops

The anti-sweatshop movement in Los Angeles took shape around the goal of reconstituting the fractured system of garment regulation. At its most ambitious, the objective was to make legal responsibility follow economic power by rupturing the legal fiction that protected profitable manufacturers and retailers from the labor abuses committed by their contractors. Beginning in the mid-1990s, at the height of the L.A. garment industry's employment strength and on the cusp of the decline caused by the phaseout of foreign production quotas, a coalition of activists and lawyers pursued this goal—sometimes in coordination and at other times in isolation. This anti-sweatshop movement developed along four interrelated paths: union organizing, impact litigation, policy advocacy, and grassroots organizing.

A Fledgling Coalition

The story of anti-sweatshop activism unfolded in dramatic fashion, with lawyers and activists seizing upon prominent cases of abuse to achieve policy change. Yet it began, more tentatively, with the development of relationships among advocates and the formation of an anti-sweatshop coalition. In the 1980s, though the problem of garment sweatshops was familiar to individual advocates who saw abuse through the eyes of clients and community members, it was still largely hidden from public view. The low political profile of garment sweatshops meant limited opportunities for collaboration among advocates. Moreover, despite the small size of the advocacy community, there were no formal mechanisms of inter-organizational exchange and coordination. This situation began to change in the early 1990s as high-profile stories of garment industry abuse emerged, highlighting the extent of the sweatshop problem—both in Los Angeles and San Francisco—and creating openings for collaboration around legislative and grassroots initiatives. These openings allowed advocates from multiple disciplines to come together in different types of alliances to chart new strategies for shifting accountability for sweatshop violations to manufacturers and retailers.

Organized labor emerged at the forefront of the drive to resuscitate joint employer status between manufacturers and contractors—though this time in the form of statewide legislation, rather than through collective bargaining. The political opportunity to press for a state joint employer bill first came in 1990, when reports of sweatshop raids revealing widespread wage-and-hour violations committed by judgment-proof garment contractors prompted state policymakers to take up the matter.[69] The joint employer legislative campaign was led by the ILGWU, which joined with a range of California organizations to form the Coalition to Eliminate Sweatshop Conditions as a vehicle to lobby for the bill.[70] For the first time, the coalition formally brought together major anti-sweatshop players, which included the ILGWU, immigrant rights organizations, worker centers, and women's rights groups. The coalition, in conjunction with the California Labor Federation, succeeded in gaining passage of joint liability bills by the California state legislature in 1990, 1991, and 1994,[71] only to see them vetoed by Republican Governors George Deukmejian and Pete Wilson.[72]

At the grassroots level, groups also came together in campaign-specific alliances. In 1992, the Asian Immigrant Women Advocates, based in Oakland's Chinatown, mounted a campaign against the dress designer Jessica McClintock after a dozen Asian immigrant women complained of being denied $15,000 in wages by one of McClintock's defunct contractors.[73] The campaign took out prominent advertisements in *The New York Times* and picketed McClintock boutiques, drawing public attention to the discrepancy between the designer's profit and the workers' penury, while also enlisting the San Francisco-based Asian Law Caucus and American Civil Liberties Union (ACLU) to fight McClintock's legal challenges to the boycotts.[74] In Los Angeles, the Korean Immigrant Workers Advocates (KIWA) coordinated boycotts, prompting a lawsuit by McClintock to prevent picketing in front of her Beverly Hills store. APALC represented KIWA and student protesters in the lawsuit.

As the anti-sweatshop coalition developed, there were a number of nonlawyers who made key contributions. Katie Quan, a former ILGWU organizer (and later co-director of the UC Berkeley Labor Center), and Roy Hong, founder of KIWA, were both important leaders who helped to articulate the coalition's campaign agenda.[75] In addition, UNITE's regional director, Steve Nutter, made crucial connections between the coalition and organized labor and promoted a statewide legislative approach.[76] The coalition also drew heavily from the ranks of legal organizations, which brought together the experience of senior attorneys with the energy of brand new lawyers. Lora Jo Foo, a former garment worker and labor organizer in San Francisco, moved to the Asian Law Caucus in 1992 after seven years at a labor-side law firm. She focused on litigating immigrant labor cases in sweatshop industries, particularly in San Francisco's Chinatown. Foo was joined in the early anti-sweatshop network by another senior lawyer from San Francisco, Rose Fua, who worked at Equal Rights Advocates (ERA), an impact litigation group focusing on women's rights. An infusion of younger lawyers occurred through legal fellowship programs, which provided a key stimulus to the incipient movement. In 1994, the Asian Law Caucus and ERA were both awarded fellows to work on garment issues: Leti Volpp, a Columbia graduate, won the prestigious Skadden Fellowship to build a garment worker project at ERA (and later moved to the ACLU Immigrants' Rights Project), while Laura Ho, from Yale, received the National Association of Public Interest Law fellowship to work with Foo at the Asian Law Caucus. That same year, Julie Su also received the Skadden Fellowship to provide legal assistance to low-wage Asian American workers, with a special focus on the garment industry, at APALC in Los Angeles.[77]

The Rise of Law: The Thai Worker Case

Su's arrival at APALC in 1994 was something of a homecoming. The daughter of Chinese immigrants, Su had grown up in Cerritos, southeast of downtown Los

Angeles, where her parents owned a laundromat. She was acutely aware of the impact of discrimination against immigrants and the grinding toll of low-wage work. When she got to APALC, the group was not focused on legal advocacy for low-wage workers, but concentrated instead on a range of identity-based civil rights issues, including language access and voting rights for Asian Americans, as well as domestic violence and hate crimes.[78] Although the organization's lawyers had represented individual employees in wage-and-hour cases, they had not attempted to invest resources in combating labor abuse in targeted industries with large concentrations of immigrant workers.[79] Su's fellowship project was meant to change this through an industry-focused approach to immigrant labor violations, but her initial proposal was quite broad, reflecting her inexperience and limited understanding of the structure of the garment industry.[80] She was drawn to litigation, but was interested in structural reform, not simply individual representation: "I felt like if we could attack a structure, we might not just help individual workers, but prevent the abuse before it happened."[81] She recognized the limits of legal action and from the beginning sought to use litigation as a vehicle not just to achieve joint liability, but ultimately to organize workers.[82] Thus, in the first year of her fellowship, she sought to learn from experienced lawyers like Foo and Fua, but also to help support direct organizing efforts, conducting some limited background research to assist in planning the impending union campaign against Guess.[83] She met actively with other groups as APALC's representative in the Coalition to Eliminate Sweatshop Conditions.[84]

When seventy-two Thai workers (sixty-seven women and five men) were discovered on August 2, 1995 after state and federal labor agents raided a factory in El Monte, Su—still a first-year lawyer—could no longer proceed to study the industry at a comfortable pace. Instead, she was forced to take a crash course that placed her at the center of the case that came to define anti-sweatshop activism. The Thai workers found in El Monte were smuggled there by an organized crime ring that took their passports and withheld their earnings as payment for transporting the workers to the United States.[85] They were held by force, imprisoned behind a barbed wire fence, cowed by threats that if they tried to escape, their families would be murdered and they would be reported to the Immigration and Naturalization Service (INS).[86]

They lived in squalid conditions, their lives confined to a claustrophobic sewing room by day and a one-room sleeping area by night. In 1995, a worker who escaped through an air conditioning duct contacted the INS and the DLSE about abuses occurring at the El Monte factory.[87] As the INS sought to gather enough information to get a federal warrant, state labor department agents, supported by their federal labor department counterparts and the L.A. and El Monte police, executed a warrant and conducted the raid.[88]

Once discovered, the Thai workers were not immediately freed. Instead, the INS put the workers into detention at a federal penitentiary.[89] Su, part of a group of Asian American activists, demanded the workers' release, arguing that their detention

Figure 2.2 El Monte compound. *Source*: Bob Carey, *Los Angeles Times* (August 12, 1995).

Figure 2.3 Thai workers outside El Monte compound. *Source*: Rick Meyer, *Los Angeles Times* (August 3, 1995).

sent the wrong message by discouraging other abused workers from reporting violations.[90] When calls for immediate release went unheeded, the group set up an office in the INS building and resorted to "aggression and street tactics."[91] Twenty-one workers were released on $500 bail each after one week;[92] the rest were released two days later.[93] On top of managing the Thai workers' mounting legal issues, Su spent the next several weeks providing logistical support to help the workers transition to their new lives—searching for housing, recruiting volunteers to teach English, and making doctor appointments—while taking the workers to L.A. attractions like Griffith Park and Disneyland.[94] This was done to help the workers reintegrate after the twin horrors of enslavement by their El Monte employers and incarceration by the U.S. government. In addition, the workers received significant community support from the Thai Community Development Corporation, which helped to find new jobs and homes.[95]

The legal process related to the Thai worker case proceeded on multiple tracks. The operators of the El Monte shop—ten Thai nationals, including a sixty-six-year-old grandmother known as "Auntie," who ran the shop, and her five sons[96]—were indicted on federal charges of kidnapping, which carried a potential life sentence, as well as lesser charges of conspiracy, indentured servitude, and harboring and concealing illegal immigrants.[97] Eight pled guilty to the lesser charges in exchange for the government dropping the kidnapping count and were given sentences of up to seven years; two remained fugitives thought to be in Thailand.[98]

The released Thai workers faced the immediate problem of their undocumented immigration status. Their dilemma was resolved in the short term when a federal immigration agent came up with the idea of granting the workers S visas under a newly enacted program providing temporary status for noncitizens providing law enforcement "critical reliable information" concerning "a criminal organization or enterprise."[99] Under the S visa program, the Thai workers were allowed to remain in the United States in exchange for being willing to testify as material witnesses in the criminal case against the sweatshop operators.[100] Although the law provided that S visa holders could adjust to permanent resident status after three years if they "substantially contributed to the success of an authorized criminal investigation,"[101] the Thai workers were not granted permanent residency until 2002.[102] The lengthy negotiations between the workers' lawyers and INS officials centered on the use of the S visa law, originally passed to help prosecute drug trafficking and terrorism cases, to provide permanent status to victims of human trafficking.[103] It was only after a series of meetings between Su and federal officials—including a meeting with Attorney General Janet Reno—that the INS was ultimately persuaded to give the workers permanent residency.[104]

Recovery of the estimated $5 million the workers were owed in back wages was pursued by public officials and private lawyers. On the public side, the California DLSE took a leading role investigating the El Monte sweatshop, called SK Fashions, and the manufacturers with which it did business.[105] The DLSE first imposed fines on several manufacturers dealing with SK Fashions for failing to follow a state licensing law.[106] The DLSE then moved to distribute back pay awards from assets it had seized from the El Monte shop operators and some of its manufacturers during the initial raid.[107] In March of 1996, the state paid the workers $1 million from the seized assets of SK Fashions and money received from five manufacturers that paid into a fund as part of a settlement with the state, which had threatened prosecution under a state law holding manufacturers liable for the labor violations of unlicensed contractors.[108]

On the private side, just over a month after the El Monte raid, a coalition of legal organizations led by APALC filed a federal civil lawsuit on behalf of sixty-four Thai workers against the sweatshop operators,[109] both individually and as SK Fashions, seeking hundreds of millions of dollars in damages for involuntary servitude, fraud, misrepresentation, assault, false imprisonment, and violations of the Racketeer Influenced and Corrupt Organizations Act (RICO).[110] In an amended complaint filed in October 1995, the plaintiffs added ten "manufacturer" defendants, including Mervyn's, which allegedly used the shop to produce its private-label items, and Tomato, LF Sportswear, Ms. Tops, Topson Downs of California, F-40, New Boys, Bigin, Italian Club, and B.U.M. International.[111] The amended complaint incorporated a range of employment claims against these manufacturer defendants, asserting that they failed to pay minimum wage and engaged in illegal industrial homework under federal law. It also alleged that the manufacturers violated state laws prohibiting contracting with unlicensed entities, negligent hiring, and unfair business practices.[112] Later amended complaints added defendants Montgomery Ward and Hub Distributing.

The federal lawsuit, *Bureerong v. Uvawas*, announced by Su and the workers on September 5, 1995, forged new connections between APALC and the labor and civil rights legal community, while drawing upon relationships formed through the earlier process of anti-sweatshop coalition building. Su, along with the director of APALC, Stewart Kwoh, realized at the outset that they were going to need co-counsel given the magnitude of the case.[113] Through UNITE's regional director Steve Nutter, Su was connected to Della Bahan—a labor lawyer at the Pasadena law firm of Rothner, Segall, Bahan & Greenstone—and the two formed the lead counsel team in the case.[114] Bahan brought in Dan Stormer from the civil rights law firm of Hadsell & Stormer. The firm had a reputation as a litigation powerhouse and Stormer was considered to be extremely strong in settlement negotiations.[115] Because there was great interest from nonprofit legal groups in supporting the anti-sweatshop cause, Su, Bahan, and Stormer convened an early discussion about how large the legal team should be, ultimately deciding to bring in all the organizations that wanted to partner.[116] In the end, the team included attorneys from nonprofit public interest law organizations allied with the anti-sweatshop cause: Lora Jo Foo and Laura Ho from the Asian Law Caucus; Lucas Guttentag and Leti Volpp from

Figure 2.4 Julie Su and Thai workers announcing lawsuit. *Source*: Dan Groshong, AFP, Getty Images (September 5, 1995).

the ACLU Immigrants' Rights Project; and Mark Rosenbaum, Daniel Tokaji, and David Schwartz from the ACLU of Southern California.[117]

In terms of division of labor, Bahan was responsible for case management and APALC maintained primary contact with the client group, though Su, as a young attorney, was careful not to be pigeonholed as client liaison and worked to ensure that the nonprofit lawyers generally were involved in discovery, brief writing, and arguing motions.[118] Since the younger attorneys at APALC, the Asian Law Caucus, and the ACLU were eager to be part of the case and gain experience working with some of the state's top public interest attorneys, they put in a substantial amount of hours on discovery and legal research.[119] Although they deferred to the judgment of the more experienced litigators—particularly Bahan, Stormer, and Rosenbaum—on issues of strategy, they played important roles by helping to draft the complaint, taking depositions, and arguing some early motions.[120] For instance, Su and Tokaji worked closely together to help file the initial complaint, draft the opposition to the companies' motions to dismiss, and handle the massive discovery.[121] Although decisions were generally by consensus, some tensions arose. In particular, there was a feeling among some of the younger attorneys that the senior lawyers were skeptical about their capabilities and their choice to invest time in client empowerment activities. Su bristled at "the attorneys *on our side* who say, 'If you want to do all that political and educational stuff, organize meetings with the workers and visit them in their homes at night, go ahead and do that. But leave the 'real' lawyering—the hard-core strategizing, brief writing and arguing—to the real lawyers.'"[122] Yet for Su, client education and empowerment were integral to the broader anti-sweatshop strategy, providing the glue to hold the workers together during the litigation process and build a foundation for future activism. In addition, while tensions arose in the case, which was strategically complex and litigated under difficult circumstances, deep friendships were also forged. Bahan—"a woman in a sea of men"—was a role model for Su, teaching her "everything from where to look for the applicable rule for a specific judge to strategizing in an enormously complex and unprecedented case."[123] Su recalled being "in awe of her," and counted her friendship with Bahan as one of the important legacies of the case.[124] In addition, Su pointed to the opportunity to work with "some of the premier attorneys in the country working for social and economic justice" as a "gift" that not only allowed her to hone her litigation skills, but also brought her into contact with a group of highly respected lawyers who would remain professional mentors and friends.[125]

The key to the case was surviving the defendants' motion to dismiss. The defendants' motion struck at the heart of the workers' claims, which sought to extend liability for the El Monte abuses to the manufacturers that had contracted with SK Fashions. At one level, the focus on manufacturer liability recognized the economic realities of the case: with the individual sweatshop operators incarcerated and their business assets already seized, the claims against the manufacturers held the only possibility of recovery. Yet the focus on the manufacturers was also an effort to address the broader economic structure of the garment industry by sending a message to the manufacturers that they would be held to account for their contractors' labor abuses. As a legal matter, this argument was framed in terms of applying FLSA's "joint employer" test—which had long been used to target labor violations in subcontractor relationships[126]—to the garment industry.[127]

The strategy paid off. On March 21, 1996, District Court Judge Audrey Collins, a former legal aid lawyer and one of the few African American women appointed by President Bill Clinton, denied key parts of the defendants' motion to dismiss. In particular, she denied the defendants' effort to dismiss the joint employer liability claim, citing the "economic realities" of the contractors' relationship to the manufacturers.[128] Despite the fact that Judge Collins found the defendant manufacturers were "clearly removed from the actual garment manufacturing process that transpired in the El Monte facility" and that there was "no 'traditional' employment relationship," she pointed to allegations that the manufacturers contracted out to avoid liability and set unfairly low prices in concluding that the plaintiffs had sufficiently stated a claim of manufacturer "control" over the sweatshop employees.[129]

The victory on the motion to dismiss was followed by a series of legal maneuvers that ultimately resulted in settlement. On the heels of the ruling, the plaintiffs' lawyers amended their case to include back pay claims for a group of Latino garment workers employed in the downtown L.A. "front store" owned by the El Monte factory operators.[130] The amendment was filed, in part, to bolster the Thai worker case: by demonstrating that the downtown store had too few workers and sewing machines to produce the quantity of garments in the time frame demanded by the manufacturers, the amendment argued that the manufacturers' quality control agents "either knew or should have known" that the garments were being produced elsewhere by exploited labor.[131] Because it was brought on behalf of Latino workers who were not enslaved—but denied wages in the normal course of employment— the claim was also designed to highlight the endemic problem of labor abuse outside the extreme situation of El Monte, while fostering cross-racial collaboration between Asians and Latinos in the garment industry.

This amendment was followed by another amended complaint in the Thai worker case that incorporated multiple claims against manufacturer Hub Distributing, Inc., including a novel state law theory arguing that Hub had negligently sold goods tainted by sweatshop labor for profit. This theory was modeled on the "hot goods" provision of FLSA, which prohibited the sale of goods made in violation of labor law across state lines but contained no individual right of action. Hub moved to dismiss. On March 3, 1997, Judge Collins issued an order denying critical parts of Hub's motion.[132] Although she did dismiss the sale of tainted goods claim, she granted plaintiffs' leave to amend the complaint to include a properly pleaded negligence per se claim based on FLSA's hot goods provision.[133] This was significant because under the negligence per se theory, plaintiffs could show a defendant's negligent conduct based purely on the technical violation of a law designed to protect the public interest—here the hot goods law—rather than having to undertake the more difficult task of proving a defendant's lack of due care.

Settlement negotiations took place in the context of intensive media coverage that generated an enormous wellspring of public sympathy for the Thai workers.[134] Rather than face a possible trial, with the negative exposure that it would have involved, the main defendants moved to jointly settle the case before summary judgment. On the plaintiffs' side, though Su wanted to gain a definitive court judgment on the joint liability issue, the workers were eager to put the case behind them— and the lawyers had already won favorable rulings on the motions to dismiss. In late October 1997, five of the manufacturer defendants—Mervyn's, Montgomery Ward, B.U.M. International, and LF Sportswear, and (in a separate undisclosed agreement) Hub—settled for more than $2 million while admitting no wrongdoing.[135] This was in addition to previous settlements with other manufacturers totaling $300,000,[136] and on top of the $1 million already given to the workers as part of the DLSE's back pay award. Although the workers could not regain the time lost in bondage and most still labored in the L.A. garment industry, the settlement punctuated a dramatic turnaround. Two years after the El Monte raids, they had recovered over three-fifths of their back wages.

The October settlement with the main defendants also raised the issue of payment for the lawyers. Su was concerned about the collection of attorney's fees

Figure 2.5 Julie Su and Thai workers signing settlement agreement. *Source*: M. Jamie Watson (October 1997).

because she did not want to play into "the rumors and deep distrust coming from some segments" of the Asian American community, evident in media stories in Thai news outlets suggesting that APALC simply wanted to use the case to make money.[137] As a result, the lawyers agreed after the October settlement (for which the lawyers received fees) that APALC would proceed pro bono against the remaining defendants and that Stormer and Bahan, whose firms relied on fees to function, would withdraw. Stormer and Bahan were replaced by Ekwan Rhow, a law school classmate of Su, who worked at the L.A. law firm of Bird Marella, which agreed to take the case on a pro bono basis. Bird Marella handled depositions, preparation for summary judgment, and settlement negotiations with the remaining defendants.[138] The case finally drew to a close in 1999, when the plaintiffs won a final $1.2 million settlement from Tomato, Inc., the El Monte sweatshop's largest customer.[139] In total, when one added the settlements from the APALC litigation to those from the earlier DLSE actions, the workers' ultimate recovery stood at over $4.5 million—$10,000 to $80,000 per worker based on the length of employment.[140]

The Decline of Union Organizing: The Guess Campaign

As a matter of principle, the Thai worker litigation shared much in common with the garment union's organizing drive against the L.A.-based designer jeans manufacturer Guess, which developed along a parallel path during the same five-year period at the end of the 1990s. Both sought to impose legal responsibility on targeted manufacturers as a way to improve labor conditions and empower garment workers. Yet, as a matter of strategy and outcome, the two campaigns were strikingly different. While the Thai worker case represented the use of law to enforce legal minimum standards in response to unanticipated events, the Guess campaign involved the strategic deployment of legal and organizing resources to take wages out of competition in the Guess production sector through collective bargaining. And while the Thai worker case resulted in compelling victory, the Guess union campaign ended in acrimonious defeat.

As a matter of chronology, the genesis of the union drive occurred just before the Thai worker case exploded into public view. At the moment of the El Monte raid, the ILGWU was in the midst of planning its own campaign to jumpstart the union's flagging fortunes in the L.A. garment industry. By 1992, the ILGWU had barely two thousand members in Los Angeles (down from four to five thousand in the mid-1970s),[141] with virtually all of them outside the garment industry.[142] Accordingly, in 1994 the ILGWU's L.A. organizing staff, with the reluctant blessing of the more powerful union leaders in New York, developed a plan to target Los Angeles's largest and most successful garment manufacturer, Guess.[143] This offered a number of strategic advantages from an organizing perspective. Guess had built a visible brand name producing designer jeans and was the most profitable apparel manufacturer in Southern California.[144] Its production system was large (thirty-five hundred workers employed mostly through seventy contractors) and geographically concentrated in downtown Los Angeles,[145] making sectoral organizing possible. Also, Guess had emphasized in its advertising that its products were "Made in the USA," rendering the firm susceptible to a media campaign sullying that claim.[146] Moreover, the union believed that there were economic factors keeping high-end denim production in the United States, including the need for quality fabric, skilled production workers, and quick turnaround.

The ILGWU organizers decided that targeting Guess offered a second-best solution to labor's problems in the L.A. garment industry. They understood that shop-by-shop organizing was doomed to fail since manufacturers could easily move work from one contractor to another,[147] and that the optimal solution would be to take wages out of competition in the entire regional garment industry.[148] However, although the union local had a good reputation for organizing immigrants, it faced resource constraints and internal problems, including a shortage of Spanish-speaking representatives,[149] and lacked critical national-level support for an industry-wide campaign.[150] Thus, the Guess campaign was conceived as a transitional strategy, giving the union a prominent beachhead in the industry,[151] while allowing it to claim progress in a broader campaign to revitalize the labor movement.[152]

The specific strategy was two-pronged. On the ground, union leaders planned to organize five hundred to one thousand workers to conduct shop-level "unfair labor practice" (ULP) strikes over specific illegal practices by employers.[153] The advantage of ULP strikes from a legal perspective was that workers who undertook them could not be permanently replaced by employers, as they could in strikes over general economic concerns.[154] ULP strikers would thus be freed to walk picket lines without the fear of losing their jobs. This "ground war" was to be combined with a corporate campaign—an "air war"—designed to publicize the sweatshop conditions of Guess workers in order to damage its image and reduce sales.[155] The objective was to obtain a collective bargaining agreement that would cover Guess and its contractors, raising wages while obtaining a commitment from Guess not to outsource production work.[156]

The environment for the air war seemed auspicious. In 1992, the company had been the target of a Clinton administration probe finding that several Guess contractors had committed substantial labor violations.[157] In the face of a threatened government lawsuit, Guess became the first garment manufacturer in the country to participate in the Department of Labor's industry compliance program, signing an agreement to monitor contractors, pay back wages, and refrain from doing business with offending shops.[158] Thus, Guess had already been publicly shamed and was under intense scrutiny.

Yet internal changes at the union challenged the organizing plan. In 1995, the ILGWU merged with its counterpart, the Amalgamated Clothing and Textile Workers Union (ACTWU), to become UNITE.[159] In the aftermath of the merger, UNITE's New York-based national leaders, reflecting their skepticism about the wisdom of any type of garment industry organizing, halved the number of organizers working on the ULP strikes to fifteen and instructed the local union to focus instead on the corporate campaign, which it viewed as more likely to succeed.[160]

The emphasis on the corporate campaign, while diminishing the role of organizing, simultaneously elevated the role of law as a key component of the air war.[161] The affirmative use of a lawsuit to draw attention to labor abuse was a common tactic in corporate campaigns.[162] As a union conducted research on corporate operations, labor violations were often uncovered, giving rise to the potential for a lawsuit that focused negative media attention on the company.[163] With advanced planning, the filing of the lawsuit could be timed for maximum public relations effect.

UNITE followed this playbook in the first phase of the Guess campaign, deftly orchestrating its legal and media strategy to seize the offensive against the company. At the outset, UNITE received an unintended gift from the Department of Labor, which named Guess as one of only thirty-one companies nationwide on its 1995 Fair Labor Fashions Trendsetter List.[164] This gave UNITE a chance to draw a sharp distinction between image and reality, of which it took full advantage in July 1996, when state labor regulators—acting upon a complaint filed by UNITE on the basis of its Guess research[165]—raided eight illegal home-sewing operations they claimed had produced garments for Guess contractors.[166] Guess lawyer Daniel Petrocelli from the L.A. firm of Mitchell Silberberg & Knupp (who would later gain fame for winning the civil wrongful death suit against O.J. Simpson) disputed the connection to Guess; however, the allegations raised concerns about Guess's labor practices just as the company was preparing for an initial public offering (IPO) to raise $200 million in capital.[167]

The IPO was a key pressure point for UNITE, offering both media attention and the chance to inflict real economic damage on Guess by shaking investor confidence in the company and reducing the IPO price—thereby reducing total capital raised.[168] The IPO, initially scheduled for August 1, 1996, was delayed after the revelations of home-sewing operations—combined with UNITE picketing at Guess's investor meeting at New York's Waldorf-Astoria hotel—rattled investors' nerves.[169] In the interim period, UNITE organized demonstrations at Guess IPO functions, Guess retail outlets, and the L.A. office of Merrill Lynch, one of the banking firms underwriting the IPO.[170]

When Guess regrouped to launch its IPO on August 7, UNITE counterpunched the same day by filing a class action lawsuit in California Superior Court on behalf of two thousand workers claiming labor abuse.[171] The lawsuit named the company and sixteen contractors (fifteen cut-and-sew shops and one laundry[172]) as defendants and included federal and state wage-and-hour claims, as well as state unfair business practices and negligent hiring claims.[173] In addition, the complaint alleged that Guess was liable for its contractors' violations under a third-party beneficiary theory, arguing that the company owed obligations to the workers based on its compliance agreement with the Department of Labor.[174] A key argument was that Guess had detailed information from its contractors about how long it took to produce individual garments (based on the monitoring it undertook in accordance with the compliance agreement), and that it therefore must have known that its contract prices were insufficient to provide for legal wage payments to the workers. Along these lines, the complaint asserted that "Guess engaged and continues to engage in a pattern and practice of contracting at unfairly low prices by utilizing garment contractors who are chronic violators of labor laws."[175] The factual allegations in the complaint drew, in part, on information uncovered in the state labor raids on the home-sewing sites.[176] Petrocelli again disputed Guess's relation to the offending contractors and called the lawsuit "a case that is by and for the benefit of UNITE."[177] While Guess had hoped that its IPO would be priced at between $21 and $23 a share, it had to settle for only $18—reducing the amount of capital raised from an expected $200 million to $125 million.[178] Although market conditions and investor discomfort with Guess's debt burden were cited as key factors influencing the IPO price, the bad publicity generated by the lawsuit also played a role.[179]

The class action suit occupied a central place in the Guess campaign strategy—and highlighted the complexities of using litigation to advance union organizing. The suit sought to use law to both remedy specific employment grievances by workers and bring attention to the broader issue of sweatshop abuse by challenging Guess's reputation as a "good guy" garment manufacturer.[180] In this sense, it was analogous to the lawsuit in the Thai worker case, which was similarly brought to achieve the twin goals of recovering unpaid wages and raising public awareness. But the Guess campaign presented distinct circumstances that made the lawsuit a more problematic tool. Specifically, the endgame was not just to win the lawsuit, but to win the "air war," with victory ultimately measured by Guess's recognition of UNITE as the workers' union. While it was one thing to use a lawsuit to generate publicity, it was another to translate publicity to concrete gains at the bargaining table.

Determining how best to coordinate the class action and organizing drive also raised issues of legal ethics since lawyers for the class ultimately had to look out for the class's interest in recovering damages, which was not coextensive with UNITE's interest in winning a union contract—for which Guess might demand that workers give up damages as part of a final bargain. Although the workers were told about the relationship between the lawsuit and the organizing drive and consented to the representation in light of the potential for conflict, the appearance of competing loyalties haunted the campaign. Moreover, the reliance on law by UNITE made the organizing campaign susceptible to the countervailing use of law by Guess. And while the plaintiffs in the class action could rely on the strength of legal protections for victims of wage-and-hour violations, it proved more difficult for the union to contest Guess's actions under the NLRA, reflecting the unequal legal playing field on which union battles played out.

Della Bahan, co-lead counsel in the Thai worker case, was charged with navigating this difficult legal terrain. Bahan, who represented the class and UNITE in subsequent legal battles with Guess, came in with a distinguished and diverse public interest background. After graduating from UC Berkeley's Boalt Hall School of Law in 1979, she moved to Los Angeles where she was a fellow at the Center for Law in the Public Interest and represented Central American asylum seekers at El Rescate. From there, Bahan practiced labor law, first at Reich, Adell & Crost and then as a partner at Rothner, Segall, Bahan & Greenstone, where she was at the time of the Guess campaign.[181] Bahan had long represented the ILGWU and after the UNITE merger continued to be the union's main outside counsel.[182] Bahan was given "a couple of months head's up" by David Young, the organizing director at UNITE, about the Guess campaign and participated in formulating legal strategy.[183] Young was the main client contact at UNITE, which paid for Bahan's time as class counsel and in connection with the other Guess litigation that ensued.[184] Bahan was assisted by David Prouty, a lawyer who had joined UNITE from ACTWU, where he had focused on union campaigns in Southern textile mills.[185] While Prouty represented some workers in their ULP actions in front of the National Labor Relations Board (NLRB), his primary role was to supervise litigation as UNITE's in-house counsel.[186]

That task turned out to be a monumental one, as Guess bounced back from its early setbacks to launch a legal counteroffensive that stretched union resources to the limit. The Guess corporate leadership was adamantly opposed to unionization and the company invested significantly in opposing the UNITE effort.[187] To thwart UNITE's legal strategy, Guess's lawyers responded on two fronts: playing vigorous defense against the UNITE lawsuits while simultaneously going on the legal offensive with affirmative litigation of their own.

First, the Guess lawyers attempted to negate the union's litigation efforts, which included the class action and ULP complaints to the NLRB. A key defensive strategy in the class action was to undermine the strength of the class by soliciting workers to "opt out." Specifically, Guess lawyers attempted to persuade workers to opt out of the class in the course of conducting fact-finding interviews at their worksites. Through this process, the lawyers succeeded in obtaining opt-out declarations from more than four hundred workers before the plaintiffs' lawyers learned of the practice and filed a motion to stop it.[188] An L.A. Superior Court Commissioner initially ordered Guess to halt the solicitation, but refused to invalidate the opt-outs already received.[189] The Superior Court appointed a referee to investigate the workers' claims of coercion and ordered them to testify about the company's opt-out solicitation practices in a trailer set up in the Guess parking lot.[190] The process placed tremendous strain on Bahan, who enlisted the help of Dan Stormer and Bob Newman, a well-known litigator from the Western Center on Law and Poverty (who also had his own practice on the side). With their assistance, Bahan was able to invalidate the opt-outs altogether—though by this time Guess had succeeded in diverting the focus of the case away from labor abuse and significantly delaying the litigation process.

Meanwhile, Guess pursued a parallel strategy of attacking Bahan as class counsel. Exploiting the potential conflict in Bahan's dual role as class counsel and counsel for UNITE, Guess won a protective court order prohibiting Bahan from sharing any discovery from the class action with the union. When Bahan disclosed to the NLRB that one contractor had admitted in a deposition for the class action that he threatened workers with closing down his shop in retaliation for their union organizing, Guess moved to amend the protective order to prevent her from sharing this information. The court amended the order and Bahan was required to pay Petrocelli's attorney's fees as a discovery sanction.[191] Placed in the middle of a conflict over her proper role, Bahan withdrew from the class action after the opt-out dispute had been resolved, handing the case over to Michael Rubin at the San Francisco-based labor law firm Altshuler Berzon, who brought in the Santa Monica litigation boutique Strumwasser & Woocher to help litigate the case along with Newman.[192] Going forward, Rubin and Fred Woocher played the role of legal strategists, while Strumwasser associates Sean Hecht and Kevin Reed were responsible for coordinating discovery and preparing the class certification petition.

With respect to the ULP complaints filed by UNITE and the workers with the NLRB, Guess followed the common employer playbook of delaying remedial action. The goal of seeking delay was to take away organizing momentum during the critical early stages of the campaign. A common employer practice in union campaigns was to fire workers in response to organizing, contest the ULP charges, and then reinstate workers after the organizing campaign had been defeated (or lost steam) in order to comply with NLRA rules.[193] This was the path Guess took to counter UNITE's ULP-focused ground war. After UNITE launched its campaign in August 1996, Guess fired twenty workers engaged in union organizing activity. Because this was illegal retaliation under the NLRA, UNITE immediately brought a complaint to the NLRB regional board challenging the firings, while also charging Guess with illegal surveillance and threatening to move production abroad in the event of union success.[194] Guess agreed to settle the complaint by reinstating the workers in January 1997, though it denied wrongdoing, stating instead that the firings were a "seasonal adjustment to employment."[195]

Guess quickly invoked the ultimate sanction, announcing its intention to move a significant portion of its production to Mexico and South America.[196] In an article that ran in *The Wall Street Journal* on January 14, 1997, Chief Executive Officer Maurice Marciano stated that the union campaign was a "factor" in the move, which had been initiated five months earlier and was set to reduce the volume of Guess apparel produced in Los Angeles from 75% to 35%.[197] Bahan, on behalf of UNITE, promptly filed another ULP complaint challenging the threatened move as illegal retaliation.[198] The NLRB stayed its approval of the January ULP settlement and scheduled a hearing on UNITE's charges.[199] After nearly two hundred workers demonstrated *against* UNITE in May 1997, UNITE filed another complaint alleging that Guess had illegally organized the protest, though the company denied any involvement.[200] UNITE filed other ULP charges, although Guess's strategy of contesting each one (and filing ULP charges of its own against UNITE) allowed it to defer the ultimate NLRB reckoning of the ULP complaints—including the key one concerning the decision to offshore production.

As it sought to limit the scope of UNITE's affirmative litigation, Guess deployed a second strategy focused on battering the union with a series of new lawsuits to force it into a defensive legal position. The Guess lawyers designed these suits to drain union litigation resources, while also chilling UNITE's boycott activity. The company was particularly concerned about boycotts at its flagship Rodeo Drive store in Beverly Hills, which UNITE launched on August 20, 1996. The next day, Guess moved in state court for a temporary restraining order and an order to show cause why a preliminary injunction should not be issued to limit UNITE activities at all of Guess's Southern California stores.[201] The preliminary injunction was issued on September 12, imposing restrictions on the number, noise level, and location of the picketers.[202] Guess then filed several motions to hold UNITE in contempt of the injunction based on union activities at Guess's Rodeo Drive and Orange County South Coast Plaza stores. The trial court found UNITE in contempt of the injunction and ordered the union to pay fines and $50,000 in opposing counsel's legal fees. UNITE's appeal failed.[203] UNITE filed a related lawsuit on state constitutional grounds seeking to enjoin six L.A.-area malls from restricting its access to protest Guess stores. The trial court in that case refused to issue an injunction and the California Court of Appeal, in a devastating published decision, held that the malls' rules limiting boycotts to identified persons in designated areas at specific times, restricting the size and content of posters, and requiring the union to purchase liability insurance and post a damage deposit were reasonable time, place, and manner restrictions that did not violate UNITE's free speech rights.[204]

Guess brought two additional state court lawsuits that added to UNITE's legal strain. In the first, filed after the launch of the campaign in 1996, Guess charged UNITE and the women's group Common Threads with libel and defamation in connection with their use of the Guess logo on protest signs and their participation in a poetry reading at the Santa Monica bookstore Midnight Special, at which activists criticized Guess labor practices.[205] Guess dropped part of the suit in March 1997, citing "many reasons, including but not limited to the cost and expenses of litigation."[206] The remainder of the suit settled shortly thereafter. In early 1998, Guess filed another action alleging that the union had stolen the company's trade secrets by illegally obtaining its confidential list of specialty stores that carried the Guess brand and contacting the stores to persuade them to stop purchasing Guess items.[207] Guess won a temporary restraining order prohibiting UNITE from using the list and the case quickly settled.

In the face of these legal skirmishes—and under mounting pressure after Guess's offshoring announcement—UNITE soldiered on with its air war, but the cumulative effect of the lawsuits began to take its toll on the campaign, with UNITE incurring substantial legal fees.[208] The union did succeed in mounting some high-profile public actions, the largest of which brought out nearly a thousand people—including Guess workers, clergy, college students, and community activists—in a march on the L.A. garment district in October of 1997.[209] The union also orchestrated a protest in front of the Santa Monica branch of retailer Robinsons-May, in which Rage Against the Machine guitarist Tom Morello was arrested,[210] and planned a Guess boycott during the holiday shopping season.[211]

Yet the media campaign collapsed under the weight of mounting legal setbacks. The campaign's fatal blow came in April 1998, when the NLRB, while acknowledging that Guess had engaged in a series of ULPs,[212] rejected UNITE's most serious charge—that Guess's decision to move production to Mexico was retaliatory—finding instead that the decision had been made before the union drive started.[213] With the campaign reeling from the now legally sanctioned move, Guess finally agreed to reinstate thirteen workers fired for union organizing and pay $113,000 in back wages to the twenty employees fired in the immediate wake of the campaign.[214] Guess also agreed to eliminate company-sponsored employee committees that the union claimed were behind the anti-UNITE employee demonstrations.[215] Yet, at this point, these gestures were largely symbolic. Although UNITE would continue with the campaign, even intensifying the ULP litigation,[216] Guess had won a decisive victory. UNITE put a brave face on the ruling, vowing to carry the fight overseas by enlisting foreign unions to put pressure on Guess distributors and retailers in other countries,[217] but by the end of 1998 the campaign was in retreat. While there was no public statement of surrender, the union withdrew funds from further garment organizing.[218]

The one outstanding matter was the class action lawsuit, which would end as a bittersweet victory for the workers who endured nearly three years of litigation. Despite the dissolution of the organizing drive, class counsel still had obligations to obtain the best financial outcome for the class members, many of whom had been disillusioned by the delay and the failure of the union drive. The case dragged on for over a year after the NLRB issued its ruling on Guess's offshoring decision. The turning point came when lawyers at Strumwasser & Woocher successfully moved the court to order Guess to turn over documents related to its industry compliance program (showing whether Guess knew of its contractors' labor violations), which the company had withheld on the ground of attorney-client privilege.[219] Shortly thereafter, in July 1999, UNITE and Guess settled the suit for nearly $1 million, with Guess admitting no wrongdoing.[220] UNITE's lawyers stated that while two thousand workers would be eligible to receive back pay awards under the settlement, only 15% were expected to come forward since many class members had long since left the industry.[221] Although some workers felt that they had waited too long for too little, the relative success of the wage-and-hour class action was a fitting epilogue to the story of UNITE's failed organizing campaign. While the class action settlement dramatized the limits of using law to spur union organizing, it also reinforced the power of law as a tool to enforce employment law compliance on recalcitrant manufacturers. Indeed, the legal outcome of the Guess class action was based on a joint employer theory that held Guess legally liable for the abuse of its contractors—precisely the same outcome as in the Thai worker case, which announced its final settlement that same month. The end of both cases thus marked a pivotal point in the anti-sweatshop movement: away from traditional labor organizing toward an alternative model focused on using employment law to promote industry-wide legal reform and grassroots worker mobilization.

The Integration of Law and Grassroots Organizing

Although Guess's decision to shift production outside of the United States technically only impacted the union campaign, it was an ominous portent of the broader challenges confronting anti-sweatshop activists at the turn of the millennium. By 1999, the full force of NAFTA and declining apparel quotas was being felt in the garment industry:[222] employment in Los Angeles's garment manufacturing sector was ten thousand jobs lower than at its peak three years earlier and the trajectory was downward.[223] And there was evidence that piece rates were declining as a result, with the brunt of the industry's downturn falling hardest on the most vulnerable workers, particularly undocumented immigrants.[224] From this vantage point, Guess's move symbolized a larger trend.

Nonetheless, the political momentum from the Thai worker case was significant. In the immediate aftermath of El Monte, state and federal labor officials increased resources for monitoring garment production and enforcing labor rights.[225] Secretary of Labor Robert Reich, in particular, became actively involved in the sweatshop issue. Under his leadership, the Department of Labor began more aggressively using FLSA's hot goods provision (which could only be enforced by the government) against garment manufacturers and retailers accused of selling apparel made under illegal conditions across state lines, threatening to sue unless they entered into compliance agreements.[226] Reich also issued a No Sweat Garment Enforcement Report, which listed contractors that had violated labor laws, along with the manufacturers for which they worked. In August 1996, President Clinton convened industry stakeholders—including retailer, manufacturer, union, and human rights groups—to form an Apparel Industry Partnership to develop a code of conduct and to monitor industry labor standards.[227] Manufacturers and retailers started implementing their own labor monitoring programs and working with anti-sweatshop groups, though critics argued that these voluntary schemes were too lenient.[228] While the failure of UNITE's organizing drive dampened the garment reform mood, the heavily publicized victory in the Thai worker case still presented an opportunity for further action.

Impact Litigation Phase I: Momentum

APALC moved quickly to capitalize on the Thai worker success. In 1997, Su was joined by Harvard Law School-trained Skadden Fellow Muneer Ahmad, Yale Law School graduate and Echoing Green Fellow Betty Hung, and Michigan Law School graduate Christina Chung. As the Thai worker case was coming to a close, the APALC lawyers decided to focus their efforts on a litigation campaign targeting the garment industry. The campaign presented trade-offs for the organization. It meant concentrating on fewer high-impact cases rather than handling a larger number of individual actions—though this was mitigated by the fact that the impact cases privileged group representation.[229] Through this high-impact strategy, APALC would seek to extend the joint employer theory developed in the Thai worker case more broadly within the industry—setting precedent that would force other manufacturers and retailers to take seriously their responsibility to ensure labor standards were met.[230] Toward this end, cases would be coordinated with a media campaign: the filing of each suit would be timed with a press conference and media contacts would be used to pressure defendants to agree to worker demands.

In addition, the garment industry focus meant elevating the theme of workers' rights in an organization historically known for its dedication to Asian American legal issues more broadly. The garment industry was targeted, in part, because a significant portion of its workforce was Asian. Yet it was primarily the lawyers' commitment to attacking the exploitation of low-wage workers that animated their garment strategy.[231] In the specific context of the garment industry in Los Angeles, there was a strong possibility that APALC would be on the side of representing the largely Latina workforce against the predominantly Asian-immigrant-owned contract shops. While the lawyers realized that their garment litigation would create tensions with some segments of the Asian American community, they viewed it as their responsibility as members of a progressive legal organization to side with workers.[232] As an internal matter, the lawyers tried to choose garment cases based not just on their public impact, but also on their potential to promote cross-racial alliances among workers in the industry in order to build worker solidarity.[233] However, where cases did not present this opportunity, APALC pursued them nonetheless in the name of workers' rights.[234]

Deploying this model, APALC won a string of quick successes in the immediate wake of the Thai worker case. In November 1999, APALC filed a lawsuit in federal court on behalf of an Asian garment worker employed by a Walnut, California contractor that produced clothing for the L.A. manufacturers City Girl, Inc., BCBG Max Azria, and Hobby Horse, Inc.[235] The worker suffered "regular headaches, sleeplessness and high blood pressure" as a result of the poor conditions in her factory.[236] City Girl filed a defamation suit against the worker, APALC as an organization, and APALC lawyer Ahmad for his role speaking at a press conference and to the media.[237] However, after APALC publicized the effort to intimidate the worker, the defendants settled in May 2000 in an agreement that paid the worker $20,000 in damages and $10,000 to APALC for attorney's fees.[238] Also in November 1999, APALC filed a suit on behalf of three garment workers—Garciela Ceja, Samuel Guerra, and their daughter—who alleged that they were denied minimum wage and overtime, and fired for reporting labor violations at their shop. The shop contracted with and was monitored by two manufacturers, John Paul Richards Inc. and Francine Browner Inc. (a division of the same company that owned BCBG), which settled the case in September 2000 for $134,000, admitting no liability and calling it a "business decision."[239]

In December 1999, APALC's Su and Ahmad teamed up with Julia Figueira-McDonough—a Skadden Fellow and UCLA School of Law alumna who was working at the Legal Aid Foundation of Los Angeles (LAFLA)—to sue another garment manufacturer, J.H. Design Group. This case was designed to reinforce the emerging student anti-sweatshop movement, which had gained steam the year before with the formation of United Students Against Sweatshops (a more aggressive alternative to the industry-sponsored Fair Labor Association that focused on gaining commitments from university administrators to develop and enforce codes of conduct for university contractors).[240] APALC filed the complaint in federal court on behalf of eight Latino garment workers who worked for a manufacturer that sold jackets to universities, including UCLA, USC, Indiana, Michigan, Wisconsin, and Florida. The case, like its predecessors, alleged federal and state violations of minimum wage and overtime laws, and claimed that two workers were fired in retaliation for raising the violations with government regulators, while another was fired for raising complaints directly with the employer.[241] Correcting the problem that had led to partial dismissal in the Thai worker case, plaintiffs in this matter alleged that by transporting illegally produced garments across state lines, the defendant committed negligence per se, incorporating FLSA's hot goods provision as the predicate violation.[242] In addition, the plaintiffs asserted—as they had in the Thai worker case—that the manufacturer engaged in an "unlawful, unfair or fraudulent business act or practice" under California Business and Professions Code § 17200 by using illegally underpaid labor.[243] Because damages were unavailable under § 17200, the plaintiffs sued for injunctive relief and restitution on this claim.[244] J.H. Design settled the case in March 2000 for $172,000.[245]

In November 2000, APALC and LAFLA filed a similar federal lawsuit against XOXO Clothing Company and its contractor on behalf of twelve garment workers who alleged that they were not paid wages for work performed over a six-week period.[246] The suit was well-publicized and featured a press conference and a statement of support for XOXO workers by actress Sarah Jessica Parker, who starred in the popular television show *Sex in the City*.[247] XOXO settled a mere two weeks after the suit was filed for $62,000—a figure that included liquidated damages and was therefore roughly five times the amount of unpaid wages.[248]

Legislation: Assembly Bill 633

The anti-sweatshop lawyers did not rely on litigation alone to change industry practice. Rather, they viewed litigation pragmatically as one part of a politically multifaceted campaign that included efforts "above" in the legislative arena and "below" at the grassroots level. This pragmatism reflected both a generational divide and the influence of legal training. The lawyers involved had come of age during the era of public interest law's reappraisal—attending elite law schools where critical dialogue about public interest law was robust—and had assimilated a skeptical view of the power of law to change society. This is not to suggest that their approach was entirely informed by academic debates. For her part, Su's feelings about the limits of law were "totally gut," formed in response to her disaffection with law school,[249] where she was part of a group of students who conducted a sit-in outside the dean's office in protest of Harvard's failure to appoint faculty of color.[250] Her views were also forged through exposure to role models outside the law, like organizers at KIWA, with whom she worked during her early days at APALC on the boycott against Jessica McClintock.[251] Su cited that campaign, which focused on McClintock's "ethical responsibility" to its workers, as "a powerful early education in both the importance of legal strategies and their limits."[252] Through these experiences, Su became committed not just to law as such, but rather to law as a spur to broader organizing and advocacy.

Su and her colleagues' interest in law as a tool of broader mobilization was evident well before the impact litigation campaign started, when just before the El Monte raid, APALC and many of the other groups that had previously assembled as the Coalition to Eliminate Sweatshop Conditions decided to formally launch Sweatshop Watch.[253] Although the group was formed to broadly handle anti-sweatshop advocacy,[254] it also became a vehicle to support the Thai workers, since Su and other advocates believed that it was not useful to create an additional coalition just for that purpose.[255] The founding organizations of Sweatshop Watch were APALC, UNITE, the Asian Law Caucus, the Coalition for Humane Immigrant Rights of Los Angeles (CHIRLA), KIWA, Asian Immigrant Women Advocates, and ERA.[256] From its inception, Sweatshop Watch was designed to be the media advocacy and public policy arm of the anti-sweatshop movement. The group was led by Director Nikki Fortunato Bas, herself a former garment worker, who collaborated with board members like Su and Lora Jo Foo of the Asian Law Caucus. The group's early efforts included mounting a Retailer Accountability Campaign that used protests and letter-writing to generate public pressure on retailers accused of selling goods produced by workers in the El Monte sweatshop.[257]

Sweatshop Watch's major test came in 1999 when it spearheaded the effort to pass a statewide law to extend liability for wage-and-hour violations to garment manufacturers and retailers. Sweatshop Watch was joined in this effort by a larger group of advocacy organizations doing garment worker cases, including legal services groups LAFLA and Bet Tzedek, which had joined with APALC to form their own coalition for garment workers.[258] Thus, at the moment APALC was launching its impact litigation campaign in court to establish joint liability under federal law, Sweatshop Watch pursued a parallel campaign at the state legislative level to codify joint liability under California law. The two efforts were meant to complement each other. As Su stated: "We used the constant threat of litigation to bring manufacturers to the table. . . . The reason they were there was that they didn't want to be sued any more."[259]

Sweatshop Watch's 1999 legislative campaign built upon a longer history of advocating for garment manufacturer liability. Garment worker advocates in California first pressed for manufacturer joint liability in the late 1970s.[260] The apparel industry blocked the attempt and a softer piece of legislation, the Garment Registration Act, was passed in 1980.[261] That legislation simply required manufacturers and contractors to register with the state and pass examinations in order to receive operating licenses.[262] The Act only held manufacturers liable for labor violations when they used unregistered shops.[263] However, because registration was easy to obtain and labor enforcement of contractor shops was lax, the law did little to deter abuse. As the 1998 Department of Labor survey of the garment industry revealed, it was nearly two-thirds of *registered* shops that were found violating wage-and-hour laws.[264] Moreover, registration did not solve the problem of how to recover back wages when contractors went out of business.[265]

Although the Coalition to Eliminate Sweatshop Conditions had tried and failed to pass a joint liability law as late as 1994,[266] the post-El Monte climate provided a unique opportunity that Sweatshop Watch and APALC seized. With a democratic governor, Gray Davis, finally in Sacramento and publicity from the El Monte and Guess campaigns heightening consumer awareness about sweatshops, apparel industry representatives, recognizing that some change was inevitable, were pressured into participating in a dialogue of reform—or else risk passage of a much more pro-worker bill than they wanted to accept.[267]

California State Assemblyman Darrell Steinberg (a Democrat from Sacramento) sponsored legislation, referred to as Assembly Bill (A.B.) 633, and worked with Tom Hayden (a Democrat from Los Angeles) in the state senate to advance the bill through the legislature.[268] On the anti-sweatshop side, the Asian Law Caucus's Foo and APALC's Su were the key lawyers, drafting the main provisions of A.B. 633 and its amendments.[269] Su also helped to promote garment worker participation in the process of developing the bill, at one point coordinating a legislative visit by some of the Thai workers, who testified in front of a state assembly committee.[270] In the draft bill, workers were given a private right of action to sue manufacturers and retailers in court to hold them strictly liable for any wage-and-hour or health and safety violations committed by their contractors.[271] This met with stiff resistance from the garment industry, whose lawyer, Stanley Levy, a partner at Manatt, Phelps & Phillips, argued instead for tightening registration requirements and increasing labor enforcement.[272]

The private right of action became a crucial sticking point. It was fiercely opposed by industry leaders who believed that it would expose manufacturers and retailers

Figure 2.6 El Monte worker Rojana Cheunchujit speaking at A.B. 633 hearing. *Source*: Asian Americans Advancing Justice Archive (1999).

to class actions and unlimited liability.[273] Even while conceding some form of joint liability, the industry tried to channel enforcement through the state DLSE, which they knew from experience was too under-funded to adequately police abuse.[274] Industry representatives proposed that a civil action only be allowed if the DLSE's labor commissioner did not resolve claims through the administrative enforcement process in a timely fashion, and then only if workers waived their right to bring class actions and recover attorney's fees.[275]

Sweatshop Watch rejected this proposal, knowing that it would make it economically infeasible for private attorneys to take on joint liability cases.[276] Garment advocates and industry representatives remained at an impasse on the private right of action issue until the senate scheduled the bill for debate. Fearing that Governor Davis would veto a bill that threatened increased litigation, Sweatshop Watch and other garment advocates made a difficult decision: Bowing to the "political realities," they agreed to the removal of the private right of action provision altogether.[277] With that impediment gone, the bill was passed by the legislature and signed into law on September 28, 1999, taking effect on January 1, 2000.

Although industry had achieved a significant goal by individualizing the case processing of A.B. 633 claims through the DLSE—thereby minimizing liability exposure—the final bill nonetheless represented a major step forward in garment regulation. For the first time, it established as a matter of state law that "a person engaged in garment manufacturing . . . shall guarantee payment of the applicable minimum wage and overtime compensation, as required by law, that are due" from its contractors.[278] Although workers were allowed to enforce this wage guarantee "solely by filing a claim with the Labor Commissioner,"[279] A.B. 633 set up an expedited administrative process within the DLSE designed to resolve claims within 120 days of being filed.[280] Either party could appeal the labor commissioner's decision to state court.[281] In terms of remedies, in addition to imposing guarantor status on manufacturers, A.B. 633 also provided for the recovery of liquidated damages against contractors in an amount equal to unpaid wages and overtime.[282] To incentivize claims, A.B. 633 provided for attorney's fees for workers who prevailed at the DLSE hearing,[283] although guarantors were jointly and severally liable for the fees only if they were found to have acted in bad faith.[284]

Once the bill was passed, the focus of Sweatshop Watch quickly turned to implementation.[285] A key battle shaped up over A.B. 633's implementing regulations. While A.B. 633 was touted as establishing joint liability for manufacturers and retailers, the language of the bill, which imposed the wage guarantee on "a person engaged in garment manufacturing," was not so clear. The law defined persons engaged in "garment manufacturing" as those "sewing, cutting, making, processing, repairing, finishing, assembling, or otherwise preparing any garment . . . for sale or resale . . . or any persons contracting to have those operations performed."[286] The dispute centered on whether this definition covered retailers, which were not explicitly included or excluded from the bill. When the DLSE finally issued its proposed regulations in 2001, it did not clarify the matter, instead providing a circular definition of "manufacturers" as "persons who are engaged in 'garment manufacturing', within the meaning of the law, but who are not contractors."[287] During the public comment period, comments were submitted from Sweatshop Watch and its allies.[288] After public hearings on the proposed regulations ended, the advocacy groups continued to meet with California labor officials to discuss their concerns with industry efforts to narrow the meaning of "manufacturer" under the law.[289]

These concerns focused on the written and public comments of Paul Gill, an industry consultant, who proposed revising the definition of manufacturer to create a "safe harbor" for retailers by providing that "any individual or company that purchases finished goods of wearing apparel from a registered manufacturer or purchases services incidental to the manufacturing process from a registered manufacturer shall not be required to register with the Labor Commissioner and shall not be presumed to be engaged in garment manufacturing."[290] The garment advocates rejected this definition as creating "loopholes" and supported the labor commissioner's "less detailed definition of 'manufacturer' " as a "better approach to ensuring that A.B. 633's wage guarantee will not be defeated by changes in industry business practices."[291] The labor commissioner ultimately agreed with the advocates' position and left the definition of manufacturer as it was, clarifying that "these regulations neither automatically exempt nor automatically include retailers."[292] When the regulations became final in October 2002, Sweatshop Watch claimed victory in beating back industry's attempt to exclude retailers.[293] As they stood, the regulations could be read to allow workers to recover against those retailers that engaged in "garment manufacturing" either by directly producing their own brand labels or contracting with a manufacturer to do so.[294] With the battle over the regulations concluded, advocates turned their attention to monitoring implementation of the bill[295]—and to educating workers so that they would be empowered to enforce the new guarantee.

Legal Consciousness: The Garment Worker Center

The vehicle designed for worker empowerment was the Garment Worker Center (GWC), which was created in the wake of A.B. 633 by garment workers and representatives of Sweatshop Watch, APALC, CHIRLA, and KIWA[296]—four organizations that became part of the GWC's steering committee.[297] The GWC built on models from the burgeoning national worker center movement, while charting a distinctive path.[298] Whereas most worker centers were place-based, focused on a particular city or neighborhood rather than an employment sector,[299] the GWC was specifically created as the L.A. anti-sweatshop movement's organizing arm to target labor abuse in the garment industry[300]—one of the first "multiracial, multilingual garment workers' center[s] in the country."[301]

The GWC was created at the intersection of UNITE's failed Guess organizing drive and Sweatshop Watch's successful A.B. 633 campaign. In the early 1990s, UNITE had established a Garment Workers Justice Center to respond to workers' claims of labor abuse, but shut it down in the wake of the Guess defeat,[302] raising a concern among advocates about how to provide continued institutional support to organize garment workers.[303] This concern was heightened with the enactment of A.B. 633, which advocates knew could only be effectively enforced through coordinated outreach to workers and assistance in bringing claims.

The twin concerns about legal enforcement and organizing were reflected in GWC's original mission: to support workers in recovering unpaid wages while also promoting collective worker efforts to reform the garment industry.[304] The task of melding these two goals fell to Kimi Lee, the GWC's founding director.[305] Lee brought to the job unique experience combining law and organizing, along with a deep personal connection to garment labor abuse. In the early 1970s, her parents had fled the military crackdown on ethnic Chinese in Burma, where her mother was a garment worker—a job she continued to hold after moving to San Francisco.[306] In college, Lee was active on the Jessica McClintock campaign and in 1998 became a field organizer at the ACLU of Southern California, where she conducted community outreach on civil rights legal issues.[307]

Lee was hired at the GWC in 2000 with funding from the progressive Los Angeles Liberty Hill Foundation and began working from a desk in APALC's office. In January of 2001, the GWC—with $100,000 from Liberty Hill and other small foundations—opened its own office in the downtown garment district to maximize worker accessibility, though it formally remained a project of Sweatshop Watch.[308] The GWC reached out to workers by distributing multilingual flyers and setting up a toll-free hotline in English, Spanish, Thai, and Mandarin, which workers could call to get information on their rights.[309] It also organized workshops and distributed booklets on labor laws that explained what garment workers could do to pursue their claims.[310] The GWC, which had a staff of three Asian Americans including Lee and Taiwanese American organizer Joann Lo, took steps to reach out to the Spanish-speaking community (Lo spoke fluent Spanish), while seeking to build bridges between Asian and Latina garment workers.[311]

In its early phase, the GWC patterned its activities after other worker centers, like the well-known Workplace Project on Long Island, which used the draw of legal service provision to bring workers into the center's organizing activities.[312] At the beginning, there was a workers' committee that advised GWC staff, but the development of worker membership and a formal Worker Board did not occur until later.[313] Although it conducted educational workshops and provided social service referrals,[314] the GWC's primary focus was to help workers resolve wage-and-hour violations through the A.B. 633 process.[315] To implement this system, GWC staff, with assistance from between fifteen and twenty volunteers, used a three-tiered process.[316] First, volunteers would assist workers in researching the manufacturers that had contracts with the workers' shops in order to identify potential guarantors. Second, cases would be handed off to GWC staff to help the workers with their wage claims in the DLSE. Frequently, cases settled before claims were even filed, after contractors received demand letters from the GWC. When that did not occur, staff would help workers file their claims with the labor commissioner and prepare for the initial meet-and-confer conference. In the third phase, cases that proceeded beyond meet-and-confer were typically referred to lawyers at APALC, LAFLA, or Bet Tzedek. During its first year of existence, the GWC helped about a dozen workers through the wage claim process.[317]

As was evident from the fact that Lee started off in an APALC office, relations between the GWC and APALC were close. Yet, aside from the GWC's practice of referring wage claims to APALC at the hearing stage, there was no formal plan to coordinate strategy between the groups. That changed quickly, as workers who made clothes for L.A.-based Forever 21, a popular retailer of young women's clothing, began coming to the GWC in April 2001 complaining of labor abuse.[318] By June, nineteen Latino and Latina workers had come to the GWC,[319] claiming that they had labored in unsafe factories for up to twelve hours a day and were owed several hundred thousands of dollars in unpaid wages and overtime.[320] Some alleged that they had been fired for protesting their treatment.[321] The GWC "helped the nineteen workers strategize how they could work as a group to support each other in their cases," which led to the workers' decision to target the individual factories as well as Forever 21.[322] After meeting with the workers as a group to formulate a collective strategy to recover from Forever 21,[323] GWC staff attempted to contact the company's president, Do Won Chang, to resolve the workers' claims. When he refused a meeting and his assistant rejected demands to improve factory conditions, GWC staff and APALC lawyers began laying the groundwork for a coordinated legal and organizing campaign against the company.[324]

Impact Litigation Phase II: Retrenchment

When APALC filed suit against Forever 21 on September 6, 2001,[325] it began its most ambitious and sophisticated campaign to date. For the first time, the campaign put the role of retailers in workplace abuse front and center. Forever 21 was targeted as a high-profile retailer based in Los Angeles that produced its own label and therefore was responsible for contracting the production of its garments, 95% of which was done in the city.[326] Because Forever 21 was focused on young women's clothing, with a short fashion cycle, it was believed that the company would be reluctant to outsource to foreign contractors that would create delay.[327] Thus, the Forever 21 campaign struck at the pinnacle of the garment industry's pyramid structure. As a tactical matter, the lawsuit was specifically designed to be part of a larger national campaign against the retailer that was coordinated at the grassroots level by the GWC, with media assistance by Sweatshop Watch. In this way, it was a test of the new multidisciplinary organizational structure that had been put into place in order to wage anti-sweatshop campaigns. It was also a chance for the GWC, a new organization, to make its name as a worker organizing group.

From APALC's perspective, the Forever 21 case was, in addition, part of the broader litigation effort to advance its goal of extending joint liability into the retail sphere. Building on the momentum of the Forever 21 suit's public launch, APALC moved three months later, on December 18, 2001, to sue Bebe,[328] another popular vendor of its own brand-name young women's clothes based south of San Francisco. The history of both cases was closely intertwined, with each lawsuit winding its way through nearly three years of complex legal proceedings while advocates attempted to coordinate public pressure through boycott actions. They were premised, however, on two different legal theories.

Because of the absence of a strong control relationship between Forever 21 and its contractors, the legal strategy in that case—crafted by APALC's Christina Chung—focused on establishing liability under state law, rather than pressing for FLSA joint employer status. Chung and Su—assisted by Bird Marella, the L.A. firm that had provided pro bono support in the Thai worker case—therefore initially brought the case in state court on behalf of nineteen workers against the contract shops for which they worked, the manufacturing entities that contracted with the shops (the "manufacturer defendants"), and Forever 21 and its owners (who contracted with the manufacturer defendants).[329] The original state court complaint alleged no federal claims against the manufacturers or contractors, instead asserting violations of California wage-and-hour law. The initial state claims against Forever 21 alleged unfair competition under California Business and Professions Code § 17200 for using subminimum wage labor, violations of record keeping requirements, negligence per se for selling hot goods and allowing industrial homework, and negligent supervision of contractors.[330]

In contrast, the suit against Bebe (brought by APALC's Su, Chung, and Figueira-McDonough, who had just joined APALC from LAFLA) was built around federal law claims.[331] The case was brought in federal court on behalf of seven Chinese garment workers claiming labor violations against Bebe and its contractor Apex Clothing Corporation.[332] The complaint looked similar to those filed in the previous City Girl and XOXO cases, combining FLSA wage-and-hour claims with state law claims for negligence per se; negligent hiring, supervision, and entrustment; and unfair business practices.[333] Although the state claims were significant, the focus of the case was on establishing joint employer status under FLSA, which APALC lawyers believed they could do given Bebe's level of operational control over Apex. Specifically, the workers claimed that Bebe controlled all aspects of production and that Apex effectively operated as a department of Bebe, existing merely to supply the labor.

With the key legal issue thus defined, the Bebe suit proceeded in straightforward fashion. In September 2002, the plaintiffs moved for partial summary judgment on the issue of joint employer status, arguing that "Bebe quality control personnel conducted daily, on-site inspections to ensure compliance with Bebe's detailed quality standards and then inspected garments before shipping them."[334] Yet, in sharp contrast to the favorable joint employer ruling APALC had received in the Thai worker case, District Court Judge Gary Feess, a Clinton appointee and former U.S. Attorney, issued a legal rebuke to the Bebe plaintiffs, holding that they could not pursue claims against the retailer as a joint employer.[335] In particular, the court found that the plaintiffs had not shown control under the "economic realities" test, emphasizing that "Apex contracted with companies other than Bebe Stores; Bebe Stores contracted with garment sewers other than Apex; Apex owned and operated its own production facility; Apex had sole control over and responsibility for hiring and firing its employees; and Apex controlled the working conditions of its employees."[336] As for the fact that one of Bebe's quality control managers "maintained an office at Apex to deal with quality control problems as they arose," the court said that plaintiffs did not show that the manager exerted day-to-day control over Apex employees—that job, the court found, was left to Apex supervisors.[337] Thus, whereas the court in the Thai worker case held out the possibility of joint liability based on structural market dynamics,[338] the Bebe court limited its inquiry to a formalistic analysis of the contractual relationships at stake. The analysis suggested that a retailer or manufacturer could only be a joint employer when its representatives were primarily responsible for the day-to-day management of the contractor's employees—a standard that would be almost impossible to meet because of the contractual separation between the parties. APALC contemplated an appeal of the district court's ruling, but Su believed that "the tide had turned," with the courts becoming resistant to the notion of expanding corporate liability.[339]

After the district court's ruling in late 2002,[340] APALC pressed ahead while the GWC and Sweatshop Watch organized a grassroots campaign to pressure Bebe to settle. Supporters sent postcards with anti-sweatshop messages to Bebe President Manny Mashouf, and protested outside Bebe stores, distributing flyers to customers with the campaign's slogan, "to be . . . or not to be . . . a sweatshop."[341] In February 2003, the GWC, Sweatshop Watch, and United Students Against Sweatshops organized a three hundred–person march outside a Santa Monica Bebe store calling on Bebe and other manufacturers to stop using sweatshops.[342] Yet the district court ruling prefigured the outcome, which came on March 3, 2004 in the form of a confidential settlement agreement with Bebe.[343] APALC continued to pursue its claims against Apex and was awarded a default judgment against the company for $1.4 million, which it was unable to collect.[344]

Although the Forever 21 case produced no negative legal precedent, it raised a different set of challenges to APALC's litigation strategy. At one level, Forever 21 highlighted the lengths that retailers were willing to go to resist legal responsibility for contractor labor abuse. The case thus involved much more aggressive legal maneuvering than Bebe or any other case that had preceded it. This was apparent at the very outset when Forever 21, realizing that the workers' case rested on the strength of their state law claims, immediately sought to remove the case to federal court. APALC, not wanting to get bogged down in removal proceedings, agreed to amend its complaint to create federal jurisdiction by asserting FLSA claims, but only against the contractors and manufacturers (no federal claims were asserted against Forever 21).[345] After some additional wrangling over the propriety of federal jurisdiction, APALC refiled its complaint in federal court on November 5, 2001.[346] Less than two weeks later, the GWC announced a boycott of Forever 21 stores, which drew garment workers and community members to picket stores every Saturday through the end of the year.[347] The GWC's Joann Lo was the key organizer who worked on the campaign.

In December 2001, Forever 21 moved to dismiss all but the unfair business practices claim. APALC then settled with the other defendants that had appeared: manufacturers One Clothing and Sany Fashion.[348] At that point, APALC filed its own motion to dismiss the action—without prejudice—against Forever 21 for lack of federal jurisdiction, since the only remaining claims in the lawsuit involved the pendant state law violations against Forever 21.[349] APALC's goal was to get out of federal court and refile its claims against the retailer in state court. Forever 21 opposed the motion and filed an additional motion for partial summary judgment. At a hearing on all the motions, District Court Judge Manuel Real—a cantankerous Lyndon Johnson appointee—dismissed *all* of plaintiffs' claims, including the unfair business practices claim that Forever 21 had not tried to dismiss.[350] The dismissal was *with prejudice* and, as such, blocked APALC from refiling in state court.

In the wake of the district court's dismissal of the claims against Forever 21, the case split along two tracks. On the heels of its legal victory, Forever 21 sought to quell ongoing boycotts, filing two suits against individuals and groups involved in the demonstrations. One suit charged the GWC, Sweatshop Watch, and the GWC's Lee and Lo with libel and other torts.[351] The other alleged defamation, interference with prospective business advantage, unfair business practices, and nuisance against the nineteen plaintiffs, CHIRLA, and Victor Narro,[352] who was about to move from CHIRLA, where he directed the Workers' Rights Project, to become Sweatshop Watch's co-executive director. The ACLU of Southern California, assisted pro bono by the law firm Loeb & Loeb in conjunction with lawyers from the National Lawyers Guild, took the cases and moved to strike the complaints by filing motions under the state Strategic Litigation Against Public Participation (SLAPP) statute, which allowed a court to dismiss causes of action "arising from any act of that person in furtherance of the person's right of petition or free speech."[353] Under public pressure, Forever 21 dropped the claims against the workers, but continued on against the organizations and advocates.[354]

By targeting the organizing and public relations arms of the campaign, Forever 21's lawsuits attempted to neutralize the use of the boycott to bring public pressure to bear on the company to settle. Forever 21 thus struck at the heart of the

Figure 2.7 Garment Worker Center protests against Forever 21. *Source*: Garment Worker Center (2001).

advocates' attempt to integrate law and organizing. The suits also led to a showdown between Forever 21 and the advocacy groups, which responded by ratcheting up their organizing efforts. After the suits were filed, the workers organized a press conference condemning Forever 21 for retaliation,[355] which was followed by a series of actions, including a campaign to put up billboards reading "Forever 21, Sweatshop Made" around Los Angeles in August 2002.[356] The workers also organized a national speaking tour in the fall of 2002.[357] In the meantime, workers continued reaching out to universities and community organizations, while staging demonstrations at local Forever 21 stores.[358]

These public actions proceeded in tandem with the two SLAPP motions to strike the Forever 21 complaints. In both cases, the advocates suffered early setbacks. The trial court in the GWC case continued the GWC's motion to strike and permitted Forever 21 to conduct limited discovery,[359] while the court in the CHIRLA case denied CHIRLA's motion to strike, finding that Forever 21 had a "probability" of prevailing on its claims based on videotaped footage of Narro handing out allegedly defamatory flyers at a demonstration.[360] However, both of these rulings were reversed on appeal. In April 2004, the California Court of Appeal issued a writ of mandate to stay discovery in the GWC case,[361] and reversed the dismissal of CHIRLA's motion to strike on the ground that the statements contained in Narro's flyer, which recounted the workers' claims against Forever 21, were not false.[362]

By this point, however, the campaign had already dragged on for nearly two and a half years and the coalition the advocates had worked so hard to create began to show signs of strain.[363] GWC staff and workers were reportedly bored and frustrated by the ongoing picketing,[364] and the deteriorating relationships between the organizers and attorneys led to "conflict resolution meetings" and a feeling among the attorneys that they could not "discuss litigation and organizing strategies with the organizers because of the different legal issues highlighted by [the federal employment and state SLAPP] cases."[365]

Nonetheless, after extensive discussions between APALC's Chung, the GWC's Lo, and the workers involved, the plaintiffs decided to move forward on the second track of the legal case: appealing the district court's dismissal on the ground that its supplemental jurisdiction over the state claims ceased once the federal claims were dismissed,[366] and therefore the state claims should have been dismissed *without prejudice* to a subsequent state court case on the same grounds. Chung was the primary author of the legal brief to the Ninth Circuit Court of Appeals making this case and, with Su, argued the appeal. In March 2004, the Ninth Circuit agreed with the plaintiffs and reversed the district court, stating that the state claims presented novel issues of California law and that it was "inappropriate for the district court to have retained the supplemental state claims against the Forever 21 defendants after the federal claims were dismissed."[367] This decision cleared the way for APALC to bring the state law claims against Forever 21 in state superior court,[368] which it did in May 2004.[369]

With this victory coming within a month of the favorable state appellate court decisions in the SLAPP suits, the campaign received a considerable boost that rejuvenated public demonstrations and placed pressure on Forever 21 to settle, which was heightened by the prospect of ugly boycotts during the holiday shopping season.[370] On December 14, 2004, the plaintiffs reached a confidential settlement agreement with Forever 21. Their press release provided few details: "[The parties] have reached an agreement to resolve all litigation between them. In addition, the parties have agreed to take steps to promote greater worker protection in the local garment industry.... Under the parties' agreement, the national boycott of Forever 21 and related protests at the Company's retail stores, initiated by the GWC in 2001, have ended."[371]

The resolution of the Forever 21 case, in conjunction with the Bebe settlement earlier in the year, constituted a turning point in the anti-sweatshop movement in Los Angeles. On the one hand, the outcome of both cases allowed advocates to claim success. For APALC, the cases reaffirmed the power of law to hold retailers to account, with each case deploying different joint liability theories to ultimately win settlements for workers. For the GWC, in turn, the Forever 21 campaign helped to establish the organization as a major player in the industry, providing media attention that allowed it to recruit new worker members and build worker leadership.[372]

Yet the cases also revealed difficulties and divisions that would become magnified as the movement progressed. As the Bebe ruling demonstrated, litigation was risky: Even in a case with strong facts showing an intricate relationship between Bebe and its contractors, the court found an absence of control in language that seemed to immunize retailers and manufacturers from liability so long as their representatives were not on the shop floor supervising garment workers. In addition, as the bruising litigation against Forever 21 underscored, retailers and manufacturers were becoming more sophisticated and aggressive when contesting joint liability in the courts. Particularly as outrage from the Thai worker case subsided, retailers and manufacturers were under less public pressure to bend quickly to garment litigation demands and were willing to fight to keep large-scale impact cases out of court—preferring instead to confine garment labor disputes to the A.B. 633 process, which provided administrative enforcement of individual claims. In addition, the garment industry was dramatically contracting—it was nearly one-third smaller in 2004 than it was in 2000—and the impending phaseout of apparel quotas under the MFA raised concerns about the industry's continued relevance. APALC never formally ended its impact litigation campaign and remained ready and willing to litigate more garment cases. However, against the backdrop of these structural changes, Forever 21 turned out to be the last garment case that the organization filed.

Moreover, the Forever 21 case laid bare tensions underlying the ambitious effort to combine law and organizing as a strategy to attack sweatshop abuse. At one level, the case—which saw APALC take the side of Latino and Latina workers against successful Korean American business owners—strained ties with this segment of the group's Asian American constituency.[373] At the grassroots level, the length and complexity of the case frustrated some GWC organizers, who began to view impact suits as too top-down to complement the group's worker empowerment goals. For instance, the GWC's Lee viewed the confidential settlement as a "downside" to the case, since it could not be used to publicly advance worker organizing goals.[374]

The cessation of APALC's impact litigation drive to establish joint liability in court refocused attention on the pursuit of garment workers' rights in alternative venues. Two strategies emerged, reflecting the new political terrain that antisweatshop activism encountered in the decade after the El Monte raid. First, the move away from courts as a forum for pursuing systemic reform magnified the importance of the A.B. 633 administrative process as a route for enforcing individual rights. Second, in the absence of unionization—and in the aftermath of Forever 21—advocates sought to develop different methods for linking individual case representation to the goal of promoting collective worker organizing.

Individual Rights: The Limits of Enforcement

The enactment of A.B. 633 posed a classic problem of legal reform: how to translate law on the books to change on the ground.[375] In what came as no surprise to those who had followed the DLSE's history of inadequate enforcement efforts, a report produced by UCLA School of Law Professor Gary Blasi revealed significant problems with the early phase of A.B. 633 implementation.[376] To begin with, workers were not using the process in significant numbers. Looking at claims in the Southern California DLSE office during the first fifteen months of A.B. 633's operation, the report found that only 382 workers had filed claims, a number that "likely represent[ed] well under one percent of those who ha[d] potential claims."[377] The report attributed the low number of filings to administrative difficulties in initiating the claims process and the lack of information about A.B. 633 provided in languages that community members could understand. More distressing than the lack of claimants was the lack of success of those who did file claims in recovering against the statutorily defined "guarantors." The wage guarantee was touted as the critical advance in the law, permitting workers to recover against economically viable manufacturers and retailers. Yet the report revealed that the DLSE had been able to identify guarantors for only 30 of the 189 contractors named in the claims.[378] More disturbing still were the figures on financial recovery. Although the report showed that the labor commissioner had awarded workers over $320,000 in back pay, *nothing had been recovered from the guarantors.*[379]

The report's conclusions pointed advocates in two directions—increasing the number of claims filed and augmenting enforcement of the wage guarantee. The GWC was on the frontlines of A.B. 633 enforcement and invested heavily in reaching out to workers and helping guide them through the administrative process. Yet without meaningful enforcement of joint liability, the law was an empty letter—simply an additional layer of bureaucracy to navigate for those with individual wage claims. And particularly after advocates had succeeded in thwarting the industry's attempt to draft A.B. 633's implementing regulations so as to exclude retailers from the wage guarantee, attention was focused on how the labor commissioner and the courts would deal with retailer liability.

The opportunity to test A.B. 633's treatment of retailers arose in a case that came out of the GWC in 2002. Four Latina garment workers claimed that their contractor, D.T. Sewing, forced them to work seventy-hour weeks at less than $4 per hour for several years.[380] The contractor produced garments sold by young women's fashion retailer Wet Seal. The workers, represented by Cassandra Stubbs, a Skadden Fellow at Bet Tzedek, sought recovery against Wet Seal. The contractor and manufacturer had shut down. At a hearing, the workers won a favorable ruling from the Labor Commission, which found that the presence of Wet Seal monitors at the contract shop "established a direct working relationship between the Wet Seal and D.T. Sewing."[381] Wet Seal, which the labor commissioner held liable for $90,000 of the $240,000 owed in back wages to the workers, responded by invoking its right to appeal the decision to the state superior court.[382] While trial was pending, the GWC organized several actions against the company to pressure it to settle, which it did in January 2004. In addition to paying the $90,000 ordered by the labor commissioner, Wet Seal agreed to give $40,000 to Bet Tzedek to support its anti-sweatshop activities,[383] hire an independent monitor to oversee production, and provide quarterly monitoring reports upon request.[384]

Yet while the Wet Seal case brought notoriety and favorable precedent on retailer liability, its very uniqueness begged the question of how much A.B. 633 had actually improved industry conditions for garment workers more broadly. Drawing upon data collected for nearly three years after the period covered in the Blasi report, the Garment Workers Collaborative sought to provide an answer to that question with a comprehensive evaluation of A.B. 633 in 2005 that was drafted primarily by Christina Chung.[385] The verdict was not good. The report found that "poor implementation of A.B. 633 by the DLSE and flagrant disregard of the law by many apparel companies effectively strip A.B. 633 of its power."[386] On the positive side of the ledger, the number of claimants had risen fourfold since the law's passage,[387] and the DLSE seemed to be doing a better job of identifying guarantors, finding them in about half of the cases studied.[388] In addition, there were significant improvements in the average worker recovery—up from $417 to $1,365.[389]

However, the good news stopped there. Workers were recovering, on average, less than one-third of the total amount of unpaid wages owed to them and were typically not recovering any liquidated damages or penalties provided by A.B. 633.[390] Contractors were settling claims for about 30% of what the workers were owed, while guarantors settled infrequently and when they did, paid an average of only 16% of what the workers claimed in back wages.[391] Only 15% of guarantors paid anything to workers and, even when workers received a labor commissioner order directing guarantors to pay, a full 60% of guarantors still paid nothing.[392] Thus, it appeared that most guarantors were opting out of the process, forcing workers to come after them in court, while contractors were offering workers low-ball settlements in the knowledge that workers would be reluctant to incur the costs and risks of fully litigating their claims.[393]

The report attributed the problems to poor enforcement by the DLSE, which regularly failed to subpoena records and did not adequately enforce the law requiring contractors to keep written records of guarantors.[394] Furthermore, although the DLSE had the legislative authority to pursue collections, it seldom used it,[395] leaving workers to options like referring collections to the California Franchise Tax Board,[396] which had a weak reputation for collecting judgments.[397] In this environment, where contractors and guarantors could successfully settle claims for amounts far below what they were worth—or get out of paying altogether—there was "no incentive to ensure that workers [were] paid their wages in the first place."[398] Although the report made the appropriate recommendations, calling on the DLSE to step up its enforcement efforts, the echoes of similar calls long since unheeded left little room for optimism that change would come soon.

Away from Law

With the MFA set to expire on January 1, 2005—eliminating textile and apparel quotas that had restricted imports from developing countries—advocates braced for the impact on Los Angeles's garment industry and began thinking of possible responses. In the run up to the expiration, experts predicted that eighty-one thousand apparel positions would be eliminated in California,[399] and that about half of the garment workers in Los Angeles would lose their jobs.[400] Garment advocates convened a meeting in mid-November 2004, called "The Future of California's Garment Industry: Strengthening Opportunities for Immigrant Workers," at which they discussed different models for holding retailers accountable, the potential of international campaigns, options for job retraining and transitional support for ex-garment workers, and the possibilities for worker-ownership and other types of development initiatives.[401] In their final report, the convening groups seemed resigned to losing a significant part of the garment industry that they had fought so hard to protect. Although the report called for promoting "sweatshop-free, locally produced apparel that boasts high quality and quick turnaround," its recommendations suggested that advocates were also thinking about transitions, emphasizing the general need to improve the quality of work, increase job training, legalize immigrants, improve the social safety net, support responsible trade policy, and expand economic opportunities.[402]

The worst predictions about the demise of the garment industry in a post-MFA world did not materialize in the short term. American garment imports from China did increase sharply immediately after the MFA quota phaseout,[403] but a number of factors combined to staunch the outward flow of garment jobs, including the continuation of some tariffs, and the reintroduction of limits on Chinese imports based on China's WTO accession agreement providing for safeguards against market disruption.[404] By 2006, the Los Angeles County Economic Development Corporation, using industry-wide data, reported that roughly sixty thousand apparel manufacturing jobs still remained in Los Angeles.[405]

Yet there was no question that the industry had fundamentally changed. And as they stepped back to survey the damage, both advocates and industry leaders held law at least partly to blame for the industry's declining fortunes—albeit for different reasons. While advocates cited the inadequacy of legal enforcement as a cause of poor working conditions, industry leaders argued that intensive government regulation had demonstrated a "hostile attitude" that prompted producers to leave.[406]

The disenchantment with law in the anti-sweatshop movement was apparent at the grassroots level, where the GWC began disinvesting in legal activities after the Forever 21 campaign. The GWC's decision to deemphasize direct staff involvement in legal processes stemmed from an internal evaluation of how best to promote its organizational mission. Although the GWC had from its inception focused on helping workers file wage claims, the volume of individual claims began to clash with its goal of fostering worker collective action. The ministerial nature of the wage claims was time consuming and GWC organizers found themselves asking: "What's our purpose? How's this tied to organizing? How much of our resources do we want going to this?"[407] Particularly after the Forever 21 campaign stretched the GWC's resources to the limit, the organization decided to restructure its legal clinic by emphasizing more of a "self-help" approach to wage claim filings.[408] Under this model, the GWC trained about a dozen workers to serve as "peer counselors" to new workers who approached the GWC for assistance.[409] The peer counselors helped workers through the full range of the A.B. 633 process: collecting documentation on unpaid wages, making a demand on the employer, filing the claim, and conducting settlement negotiations.[410] If negotiations failed to yield a settlement, workers were expected to represent themselves at the labor commissioner hearing aided by a peer counselor; as a quid pro quo for this peer assistance, workers were required to become members of the GWC.[411]

The self-help model was designed to build worker capacity by giving individual workers the tools to pursue their own claims, while also helping to create a new cadre of peer counselors with the knowledge to help other workers navigate the A.B. 633 process. By requiring membership in exchange for services, the GWC sought to expose workers to the larger anti-sweatshop movement, provide opportunities to engage in collective action, and cultivate new leaders with a stake in the GWC to guide future organizing drives. Under this model, legal enforcement through the A.B. 633 process became a means to the end of promoting worker empowerment.

The move toward self-help reflected a broader shift in the GWC away from legal engagement. For the GWC, the lesson from the Forever 21 campaign was that lawyer-driven social reform could overwhelm the objective of promoting worker leadership and development.[412] Instead of having its involvement in law reform campaigns drive the deployment of worker organizing, the GWC decided to make worker organizing the centerpiece of all its activities. This meant freeing itself from other organizational ties that would place restrictions on its ability to foster worker participation. Toward this end, the GWC decided to withdraw from funding arrangements that did not centrally involve worker organizing, reverting back to its initial funding structure of relying on smaller foundation grants.[413] As a result, the group shrank in numbers, from eight staff members in 2005 to just two in 2007, producing a greater reliance on volunteers and members.[414] It also ceased its involvement with the Los Angeles Workers Advocates Coalition—created to focus on legal strategy—which the GWC came to view as outside the scope of its immediate mission. Additionally, the GWC cut back on policy work because of resource constraints.[415] In 2006, in a move that had been contemplated from the organization's inception, the GWC formally separated from Sweatshop Watch, where it had been a project, and established itself as an independent nonprofit organization.

The GWC's activities changed as well. Although it still helped workers file wage claims, and referred some workers to legal groups for assistance, the GWC relied even more heavily on upfront education to help workers file claims on their own. In turn, the GWC began concentrating its efforts on popular education workshops to promote worker political consciousness and leadership development, while launching an initiative to form worker committees inside factories to improve health and safety conditions.[416] The goal of this new strategy was to create "systemic changes" through organizing in the garment industry while endowing the workers with a stronger sense of "ownership" in the GWC.[417]

On the cusp of the Great Recession, while the GWC reverted to its core mission of organizing, APALC and Sweatshop Watch tentatively charted new directions that pointed to the local and international spheres—moving from adversarial strategies to impose legal reform to more collaborative efforts to develop incentives to promote voluntary labor compliance. At the local level, APALC and Sweatshop Watch jointly focused on taking advantage of Los Angeles's location as the epicenter of high-end fashion to move garment producers onto the "high-road," where the efficient production of high-quality, market-competitive items complemented respect for workers' rights. Their focus was on niche industries, such as premium denim production, which remained in Los Angeles because of quick turnaround times and specialized finishing processes that required close monitoring.[418] Instead of imposing accountability through regulation—a goal that receded in the face of political resistance, market outsourcing, and ineffective enforcement—the new advocacy strategy emphasized identifying producers that had strong local ties, fostering best practices, and cultivating relationships between industry, worker, and governmental stakeholders to promote high-road employment standards with industry leaders and seek out collaborative models for industry development.

As the legal organization responsible for the impact litigation campaign, APALC's move toward collaborating with industry leaders challenged its litigation identity and tested its credibility with the industry it had strenuously fought. It also underscored the political pragmatism that animated its work from the inception of the anti-sweatshop struggle. While the group did not eschew litigation—and emphasized that the threat of litigation was still necessary to respond to abusive garment companies[419]—it adopted a more conciliatory approach, not out of an ideological commitment to a collaborative methodology, but from practical recognition of the barriers to other strategies. In particular, Su viewed collaboration around policy reform as a way "to try to get the city to invest in the industry and make a difference in remaining jobs."[420] With the industry at a crossroads, she believed that "the policy approach may be one of the strongest weapons currently for creating better working conditions in Los Angeles' garment industry, particularly in light of the strong global forces."[421]

To advance this strategy, APALC and students in the UCLA School of Law Community Economic Development Clinic produced a report in 2006 proposing a mix of supply-side and demand-side incentives to promote high-road local garment production. On the supply side, it proposed production incentives for high-road manufacturers, such as tax breaks and below-market loans, as well as assistance in procuring start-up capital through investment funds and business development programs. Another proposal involved assisting producers through the formation of a garment industry advocacy group that would work in the interests of both workers and manufacturers to provide technical and training assistance to local manufacturers and contractors seeking to adopt high-road production. On the demand side, the report offered proposals to incentivize local sweat-free production by marketing to customers who valued sweat-free clothing and had the disposable income to be able to purchase such items.

For Sweatshop Watch, as a policy advocacy organization, the move toward collaborative strategies to voluntarily enhance labor standards was more consonant with its core mission and perhaps for that reason it took the lead role in advancing the high-road strategy. One of its key initiatives was the "Made in L.A." project that sought to attract and retain socially responsible companies in Los Angeles, while encouraging them to adhere to a sweat-free standard by providing economic incentives for voluntary compliance.[422] In 2006, Sweatshop Watch reported it would "develop proposals for how the City can stimulate local production and promote model working conditions within Los Angeles's garment industry."[423] Toward this end, Sweatshop Watch leaders met with local city officials to develop ideas about appropriate types of incentives and to consider the designation of locally made sweat-free garments as "Made in L.A." as a marketing tool to appeal to consumers who desired clothing produced under ethical conditions.[424] The ultimate goal was to make Los Angeles "the capital of sweat-free fashion."[425]

Sweatshop Watch also, more tentatively, began looking outside the United States to build the transnational reach of the anti-sweatshop movement—effectively meeting the industry on its own global terms. These efforts also reflected the movement's overall pivot away from litigation, which had been more central a decade earlier. In 1999, Sweatshop Watch was involved in one of a trio of lawsuits that sought to internationalize the legal struggle against sweatshops by targeting producers in Saipan, the capital of the U.S. Commonwealth of the Northern Mariana Islands, which as part of the United States could export goods duty free while being exempt from labor laws. Sweatshop Watch (along with Global Exchange, UNITE, and the Asian Law Caucus) was a party in the first case, which was filed in state court against U.S. retailers, including Abercrombie and Fitch, Calvin Klein, J. Crew, J.C. Penny, Levis, Liz Claiborne, May, Nordstrom, Polo, Sears, The Gap, and Tommy Hilfiger. The suit alleged that the retailers violated California's unfair business practices law by, among other things, advertising that their garments were sweat-free and shipping hot goods. In addition, there were two federal class action lawsuits filed on behalf of Chinese female workers, one against the same retailers alleging violations of RICO and the Alien Tort Statute,[426] and the other against Saipan contractors for violations of federal and Commonwealth employment laws.[427] The cases were litigated by Michael Rubin, the labor lawyer from Altshuler Berzon who helped to litigate the Guess class action, and lawyers from Milberg Weiss Hynes & Lerach. All of the defendants ultimately settled in 2003 for a total of $20 million and agreed to a code of conduct for Saipan workers and independent factory monitoring.[428]

Although interest in litigation targeting foreign sweatshops remained, by the mid-2000s, Sweatshop Watch was pursuing a less litigious transnational path focused on network building. In 2005, it organized a convening of anti-sweatshop groups from Canada, China, Guatemala, and Mexico to strategize about how to address sweatshops in the post-MFA era. Sweatshop Watch staff also went to China to meet with labor rights groups about sweatshop conditions there. In Mexico, Sweatshop Watch staff sought to build ties with independent labor organizations and supported a campaign by the Coalition for Justice in the Maquiladoras on behalf of Mexican workers fired for organizing a plant that produced jeans for Levis—writing letters to Levis headquarters protesting the factory's actions.

These efforts were in their embryonic state when the garment industry—in Los Angeles and around the world—was rocked by the 2008 recession. The economic crisis accelerated downsizing trends already underway, contributing to the contraction of an industry that had been the mainstay of L.A. manufacturing. Between 1996, the peak of L.A. garment employment, and 2009, the L.A. garment workforce declined by over 50%—a downward trajectory that would continue.[429] While garment production remained Los Angeles's biggest post-recession manufacturing sector, the local economy had shifted profoundly toward service work. While this shift created opportunities for low-wage worker organizing in service industries—a project that would build on the model anti-sweatshop advocates pioneered and to which they would continue to contribute—it signaled the end of the concentrated campaign to reform the L.A. garment industry. Although the fight was carried forward and important enforcement efforts continued, resources dried up and advocates moved on. Once the hub of an innovative effort to merge law, policy, and organizing to end garment worker abuse, Sweatshop Watch closed in 2009, drawing a symbolic curtain on the campaign for corporate accountability in an industry slashed by globalization, abandoned by unions, and unredeemed by law.

Analysis

Although the anti-sweatshop movement did not achieve its most ambitious goal of extending joint employment in the L.A. garment industry, it produced important positive outcomes, both at the individual and systemic levels, in the face of significant structural challenges, which included an uneven legal playing field, strong industry countermobilization, and internal dissent.

Consequences

Individual

On an individual scale, the campaign brought about two types of changes: restoring wages and dignity for injured garment workers and creating new leadership in the field of low-wage worker advocacy.

From a financial perspective, APALC's litigation campaign, combined with the GWC's program of assisting workers in the A.B. 633 wage claims process, accounted for monetary recoveries that totaled more than $6 million. This included the roughly $3.5 million APALC won in the Thai worker case, along with smaller settlements in City Girl, John Paul Richards, J.H. Design, and XOXO. It also included the approximately $2.5 million the GWC helped workers recover through 2005 in the A.B. 633 process.[430] In addition, the Thai workers recovered $1 million from the DLSE's back pay award. Although the confidential settlements in the Forever 21 and Bebe cases did not reveal whether there were monetary payments, if there were, they would raise this total. Also, if the $1-million recovery for workers in the Guess class action is added, the total monetary recovery from 1995 to 2005 exceeds $8 million.

There were non-monetary outcomes that benefited workers as well. By the recession, the GWC had provided educational and leadership training to thousands of garment workers and claimed over one hundred active members. Similarly, according to Su, one of the movement's "biggest successes was just how workers involved in cases developed in terms of their consciousness, leadership, and engagement."[431] There is no systematic evidence of the impact of movement experiences on the workers' legal consciousness or sense of individual empowerment. However, there were opportunities for worker participation in movement activities that advanced empowerment goals. Some of the Thai workers, for instance, spoke publicly about sweatshop conditions, testified on A.B. 633, and met with leaders at the AFL-CIO about the relationship between law and organizing. This engagement, according to Su, "helped them to feel greater control over the circumstances of their lives."[432] And partly because of this participation, individual workers received significant public attention for their roles in the anti-sweatshop movement, which complemented other efforts to promote empowerment. In this regard, the Forever 21 workers were the subject of a powerful documentary, *Made in L.A.*, which aired in 2007. The Thai workers, for their part, were the subject of intense media coverage and received substantial civic support in making the transition from the El Monte compound to life in the community. The press highlighted individual success stories, such as one Thai worker starting her own restaurant.[433] And there was celebration of collective achievements. Perhaps most prominently, in 2008, the Thai workers became U.S. citizens with one proudly proclaiming, "I am an American and this is my home now!"[434]

From a professional standpoint, the anti-sweatshop campaign also enhanced the careers of many involved in ways that strengthened the legal capacity of immigrant worker labor enforcement. APALC's Julie Su won several prestigious awards, including the Reebok International Human Rights Award in 1996 and the MacArthur Fellowship, commonly known as the "genius grant," in 2001.[435] In 2011, after a decade and a half of leadership at APALC—and in a move hailed by workers' rights advocates around the state—Su was appointed by Governor Jerry Brown to be the California labor commissioner, running the very agency she had worked tirelessly to reform and directing agency resources to garment industry enforcement. APALC also attracted an impressive group of young lawyers who went on to continue their leadership roles in the low-wage worker field. Christina Chung was a key member of APALC's anti-sweatshop litigation team, the intellectual architect of the Forever 21 case, and the only lawyer besides Su who worked on all of the garment litigation. She went on to work at the Employment Law Center-Legal Aid Society in San Francisco, where she continued her workers' rights advocacy. Muneer Ahmad became a professor at American University's Washington College of Law and in 2009 was appointed to the Yale Law School faculty, where he has focused on immigrant rights. Betty Hung became the directing attorney of the Employment Project at LAFLA, worked at the Inner City Law Center, and then joined the UCLA Labor Center. Julia Figueira-McDonough became a city attorney focusing on labor enforcement in low-wage industries and then went to work with Julie Su at the DLSE, as did Yungsuhn Park, a 2005 Skadden Fellow from the Boalt

Hall School of Law. Judy Marblestone, a 2003 Equal Justice Works Fellow from the UCLA School of Law (and co-author of the 2002 A.B. 633 report with Gary Blasi), became a lawyer at the New York union-side labor law firm Gladstein, Reif & Meginniss.

Systemic

From a system-wide perspective, there were a number of changes wrought by the anti-sweatshop campaign at the levels of industry practice, governmental policy, and organizational action.

At the industry level, although retailers and manufacturers ultimately resisted the imposition of a strong form of joint liability, there was evidence that at least some nonetheless changed their way of doing business with contractors. Instead of turning a blind eye to contractor labor abuse, there were visible industry efforts to implement monitoring systems and work with anti-sweatshop groups on reform. Some companies hired private monitoring firms to police their contract shops, while a handful of conscientious retailers sat down with activists to develop responses to labor abuse.[436] Observers debated whether these efforts were sincere or simply window-dressing to insulate retailers and manufacturers from charges of insensitivity and protect their images.[437] However, particularly after the El Monte raid, heightened public awareness of garment labor abuse constrained the ability of industry actors to conduct "business as usual."[438] As a result of anti-sweatshop activism, retailers were, for the first time, pressured to disclose where their clothes were made and ensure that they were produced under appropriate conditions.[439] Giant retailers like Wal-Mart incorporated codes of conduct into their contracts with suppliers stating that the suppliers were bound to comply with labor laws.[440] And in the period after the Thai worker case, advocates believed that they had the "green light" to sue noncompliant companies, which may have deterred some of the most egregious abuse.[441] In addition, the public outrage over garment sweatshops fed into the growing consumer appetite for "sweat-free" production alternatives. This created a market space for companies promoting sweat-free policies, like American Apparel, the once high-flying retailer and manufacturer that boasted of its pro-labor (and anti-union) policies (and flamed out after a CEO scandal), as well as the short-lived SweatX, launched by Ben & Jerry's founder Ben Cohen and unionized by UNITE.[442]

There were also identifiable changes in government enforcement practices and labor policies. Although labor enforcement resources ebbed and flowed—and were never at a level that was satisfactory to advocates—the public backlash against sweatshops after El Monte forced some reforms. In the short term, the federal Department of Labor under Secretary Reich stepped up enforcement efforts, particularly through the use of hot goods prosecutions, and in 1996 claimed that it had recovered $7.3 million in back wages for twenty-five thousand workers during the three years prior.[443] The federal Trendsetter List and President Clinton's Apparel Industry Partnership also promoted monitoring programs that proponents argued reduced the incidence of labor abuse in monitored shops.[444] Similarly, the California DLSE reported increased enforcement activity in the period after El Monte, while California Governor Arnold Schwarzenegger announced a 2005 budget that provided $6.5 million in funding to add new enforcement and audit positions to state agencies, including the DLSE, in an effort to launch a coordinated Economic and Employment Enforcement Coalition.[445] However, while the Schwarzenegger initiative conducted nearly 950 "sweeps" during its first year and assessed $3 million in penalties for violations of workers' compensation and other rules, critics noted that it had issued less than twenty wage-and-hour citations and completed no wage audits.[446]

Moreover, anti-sweatshop advocates could point to new laws on the books as an important result of their efforts. The most visible achievement was A.B. 633 but there were other laws passed as a result of movement activism. In 2004, the Los Angeles City Council enacted a local anti-sweatshop ordinance requiring city garment contractors to pledge compliance with employment and labor laws and pay workers a "procurement living wage," while providing for penalties and contract termination in the event of noncompliance.[447] Following passage of the sweat-free ordinance, Sweatshop Watch fought for its enforcement, achieving a victory when the Los Angeles City Council agreed to hire the Worker Rights Consortium—a labor rights organization that grew out of United Students Against Sweatshops to monitor conditions in factories that produced university logo apparel[448]—to monitor contractors' compliance with the law.[449] In the wake of the L.A. procurement ordinance, Sweatshop Watch worked to establish a national consortium of sweat-free cities and states. The goal was to have consortium members agree to coordinate their monitoring programs and contract only with certified vendors in order to leverage the purchasing power of government agencies to sustain factories that paid living wages. At home, Sweatshop Watch made preliminary efforts to work with L.A.-based companies to gain sweat-free certification and procure government contracts.

The anti-sweatshop movement produced other important policy reforms. In 2004, the state legislature passed Senate Bill (S.B.) 179 (co-sponsored by the GWC) permitting garment (and other low-wage) employees to recover damages and attorney's fees from a manufacturer that "knows or should know" that its agreement with a contractor "does not include funds sufficient to allow the contractor to comply with all applicable local, state, and federal laws or regulations governing the labor or services to be provided."[450] S.B. 179 was designed to reduce the barriers to manufacturer liability by making it easier to show manufacturer control. At the federal level, outrage over El Monte was cited as one of the motivating factors that spurred passage of the Trafficking Victims Protection Act of

2000, which made trafficking a federal crime and provided a pathway to legal residence for trafficking victims.[451] Advocates also pressed for changes to A.B. 633 after reports of its inadequacies. Lobbying by Sweatshop Watch in 2005 and 2006 led to a change in the administration of the Garment Special Account—the fund garment workers could tap to collect awards by the labor commissioner that went unpaid by contractors and guarantors.[452] As a result, the legislature more than doubled the annual appropriation for the fund and developed a "streamlined" process to release funds if demand for monies exceeded that amount.[453]

Finally, the anti-sweatshop movement in Los Angeles generated an infrastructure of organizations and a network of alliances that fueled continued low-wage worker activism. Sweatshop Watch and the GWC were created as separate entities and, though some collaborations dissipated, others like the Garment Workers Collaborative persisted. In addition, some of the relationships forged during the height of the campaign spawned new alliances, such as the Coalition of Immigrant Worker Advocates—which included CHIRLA, the GWC, the Institute of Popular Education of Southern California (or IDEPSCA, its Spanish acronym), KIWA, La Raza Centro Legal, LAFLA, the Maintenance Cooperation Trust Fund, NDLON, and Sweatshop Watch—and the Multi-Ethnic Immigrant Workers Organizing Network—which included CHIRLA, the GWC, IDEPSCA, KIWA, and the Pilipino Workers Center of Southern California. Sweatshop Watch also helped to found the Worker Rights Consortium and Sweatshop Watch's first director, Nikki Bas, was on its advisory board. Even the failed Guess campaign was credited with forging alliances between labor activists, students, and religious groups.[454] Victor Narro left Sweatshop Watch in 2003 to join the UCLA Downtown Labor Center, directing a project bringing together unions and immigrant workers to improve conditions in low-wage industries.[455] In 2007, the Wage Justice Center was formed by two USC Law School graduates, who used seed funding from the Echoing Green foundation to create an organization dedicated to enforcing judgments for unpaid wages in the garment industry and other low-wage sectors.[456]

Challenges

While the movement's accomplishments were real and far-reaching, garment retailers and manufacturers remained generally insulated from legal liability for labor abuse, while advocates struggled to achieve a minimal level of enforcement of the individual labor claims of garment workers left in the shrinking L.A. industry.[457] In one sense, these outcomes reinforced familiar critiques of legal mobilization efforts: Judicial decrees do not change facts on the ground, state bureaucracies do not enforce the law, and socially powerful actors undo even minor gains achieved by marginalized groups. But while the attempt to combine law and organizing in the anti-sweatshop movement was limited by these factors, a more nuanced account suggests that setbacks could be attributed not to the nature of legal mobilization itself, but to its particular application in the L.A. garment production context.

The Limits of Law: Scale and Contingency

In campaigns for social reform, where law is deployed matters.[458] In the garment context, advocates were sophisticated about playing at all levels where they felt there were advantages to be gained. This was apparent throughout the impact litigation campaign: APALC sought to leverage the benefits of federal court when its lawyers believed it had strong claims of manufacturer "control" and state court when it viewed retailer liability as more likely under state law theories of unfair business practices and negligence per se. Advocates also took advantage of the relatively labor-friendly Clinton administration to press for greater Department of Labor involvement and lobbied for more state enforcement resources from the DLSE. With respect to legislative reform, advocacy similarly occurred at different tiers. A.B. 633 leveraged the power of the California labor enforcement system under the DLSE to establish a statewide wage guarantee, while the L.A. anti-sweatshop procurement ordinance used the hook of the city's contracting power to establish sweat-free standards.

Anti-sweatshop advocacy was also notable for the places it avoided or could not reach. Lawyers did not, for instance, seek to litigate federal cases up the ladder to the Supreme Court, which was viewed as a venue unlikely to provide a favorable ruling on issues related to immigrant labor. In the Bebe case, APALC even declined to appeal to the Ninth Circuit, fearing that the political climate might produce an appellate court decision upholding—and thus adding further weight to—the damaging district court ruling on joint liability. This skepticism was motivated in part by the 2002 Supreme Court decision in *Hoffman Plastic Compounds, Inc. v. NLRB*, which held that undocumented workers fired illegally for participating in union organizing were not protected by federal labor laws guaranteeing back pay in such situations.[459] This anti-immigrant message made lawyers loath to litigate other immigrant worker claims to higher levels of the federal court system.[460] The ruling also affected litigation efforts on the ground, as lawyers reported that employer defendants sought to intimidate immigrant workers by requesting information about their legal status in discovery.[461] The Coalition of Immigrant Worker Advocates was able to mitigate the damage to ongoing litigation efforts by successfully advocating for the passage of a state law, S.B. 1818,[462] clarifying that all California labor laws apply to workers irrespective of immigration status.[463] But the threat of exposing undocumented workers remained.

Ultimately, garment advocates could not affect the global rules of the game that profoundly influenced the macro-level distribution of garment production. Thus, the impact of NAFTA and the phaseout of MFA quotas fundamentally altered the economic terrain on which anti-sweatshop activism played out. Particularly as 2005 approached, there was a recognition of inevitable industry decline and the enormous difficulty of organizing in the face of the offshoring threat. In that sense, the harbinger of Guess had come to fruition. It is, however, too simplistic to suggest that anti-sweatshop activism was defeated by globalization, both because free trade did not eliminate garment production from Los Angeles and because the movement suffered other blows unrelated to market dynamics. But it did seem clear that the inability to influence the scope and content of trade pacts at the level of global governance limited the options for legal and political intervention at the national level. While advocates gained leverage at the outset of the campaign from the fact that part of the industry was effectively trapped inside the United States by trade rules, once that leverage was lost advocates saw their power limited by the newly expanded threat of manufacturers to ship production elsewhere. From this perspective, it was not the weakness of law that failed the anti-sweatshop movement, but rather the relative power of law as it operated at the global level to overshadow countervailing efforts at the local level. The reform of international trade rules had economic impacts that overpowered legal and organizing efforts to improve conditions at the local and state level. Unable to play at all levels of the system, advocates were badly handicapped in their struggle—underscoring the lesson that legal change in one arena competes with, and may be diminished by, change in another.

This is not to suggest that local law was completely subservient to global governance. In the garment context there were other barriers to the movement that were not related to the location of legal reform efforts. One important impediment turned out to be the courts themselves. Impact litigation is inherently uncertain, both because lawyers cannot control which judge they draw in any given case and, once the judge is assigned, what the ruling on the merits will be. In the Thai worker case, the lawyers struck gold: they were assigned Judge Collins, a legal-aid-lawyer-turned-federal-judge, who was willing to listen to arguments of structural injustice and publish an opinion that extended the concept of joint employment to redress violations against undocumented immigrant workers. This was in sharp contrast with the Bebe case, in which APALC drew another Clinton appointee, Judge Feess, who—in a case that was weaker in sympathy value but arguably stronger on the facts showing Bebe's control—granted the employer's motion to dismiss based on a narrow reading of FLSA's "economic realities" test that found no control despite Bebe's on-site monitor. The contrast with Collins was stronger still when the Forever 21 plaintiffs drew Judge Real, a notoriously difficult and idiosyncratic appointee of President Lyndon Johnson, who threw out the entire state law case with prejudice on what the Ninth Circuit later agreed were the flimsiest of grounds. The assignment of different judges in Bebe and Forever 21 might not have changed the outcome of the overall campaign but might have strengthened APALC's hand in continuing to use litigation to pursue the worst offenders. Instead, the legal outcome in these cases contributed to the cessation of garment impact litigation efforts.

The Opposition to Law: Industry Resistance and Internal Dissent

The retailers and manufacturers, for their part, left nothing to chance. Although they, too, had to face the uncertainty of judicial assignments when sued, the outcomes in the cases may have owed as much to legal maneuvering as to judicial ideology. Particularly in Forever 21, the defendants combined hardball tactics in the plaintiffs' lawsuit—aggressive removal and the pugnacious pursuit of dismissal with prejudice—with their own SLAPP suits against activists involved in the retail boycott. The case therefore had much in common with the litigation strategy deployed by Guess to thwart UNITE's organizing drive. In both cases, though the companies ultimately settled, they could claim victory in the larger battle: Forever 21 by winning a confidential settlement that appeared to resist major changes to company practices and Guess by staving off unionization.

Outside of the judicial arena, companies learned how to adapt to the stricter regulatory environment after El Monte. While companies complained about the negative business impact of lawsuits, they also took steps to insulate themselves from their reach. In negotiations over A.B. 633, industry leaders were able to excise a private right of action, channeling workers into an administrative process where class actions were not allowed—and where contractors and guarantors could effectively undercut enforcement efforts by stonewalling investigations, providing low-ball settlement offers, and failing to pay out even when so ordered by the labor commissioner. Although some companies responded conscientiously by instituting legitimate contractor monitoring to prevent abuse, others tried to game the system by sourcing production to a larger number of contractors in order to attenuate the appearance of legal control.[464] In addition, companies like Bebe used monitoring not as a way to promote labor compliance but rather to shield themselves from joint liability. One facet of the Bebe case involved the question of whether the company's use of a private monitoring company gave rise to legal control. In response to the Department of Labor's "No Sweat Initiative," Bebe had contracted with the private monitoring firm Apparel Resources to visit its contract shops, check time cards and payroll records, and interview workers.[465] The court held that the use of the monitor did not demonstrate Bebe's "control" over its contractor (Apex), and suggested that if it did, the federal policy promoting monitoring would be defeated since no company would opt to monitor for fear of joint liability.[466] Thus, as a matter of law, by contracting out monitoring services, manufacturers could avoid liability.

The unified industry effort to resist legal enforcement of employment law stood in contrast to the cracks that developed on the garment advocates' side, where grassroots opposition to the primacy of legal tactics eventually resulted in estrangement between the coalition's organizing base—the GWC—and its legal and policy wings. This division likely had much to do with personalities and power, but it also spoke to the difficult marriage of law and organizing in pursuit of progressive political causes built on the active participation of—and control by—those on the bottom. Without minimizing the real economic divisions between retailers, manufacturers, and contractors, it was perhaps easier for them to coalesce around the clear goal of profit-maximization than it was for garment advocates to stay aligned around the more contested concept of worker empowerment, which encompassed elements of worker participation and structural reform.

The APALC lawyers, for their part, were focused on linking law to organizing and engaged in a model of empowerment-oriented lawyering that was a thoughtful effort to navigate the tensions between legal action and democratic accountability. The tensions that emerged, therefore, did not stem from the typical top-down lawyering that drew criticism during the Civil Rights period. To the contrary, the tensions stemmed from the structural challenges of integrating law and organizing, as well as from the specific dynamics of the anti-sweatshop effort in Los Angeles. In particular, the Forever 21 campaign, with its protracted legal wrangling and unsatisfying outcome, sharpened the distinction between the reality of what was provided through law and the image of what was possible through worker struggle—even if this image was a romantic one. And in the fallout from the campaign, as a more radical notion of democratic accountability came to hold sway within the ranks of the GWC, the ideal of social change desired by its staff and members appeared beyond the reach of what law could afford. This is not to suggest that organizing emerged as a more effective tool of reform in the garment industry. There is no evidence that the model of worker organizing employed by the GWC increased worker solidarity or promoted industry reform beyond what was accomplished through coordinated legal and organizing efforts. Rather, what the GWC's movement away from APALC highlighted was the challenge inherent in forging lasting bonds between organizations that shared complementary social change philosophies but had divergent organizational priorities and tactical preferences.

Coda

In the end, the campaign challenging garment sweatshops in Los Angeles was unraveled not by internecine disagreements over strategy, but by macroeconomic forces that made the apparel industry less appealing as a site of sustained workplace struggle. In the wake of the recession, industry observers noted that the more things seemed to change, the more they stayed the same. The diminished L.A. garment industry—by 2016, barely a third of what it was at the time of the El Monte case—had come to concentrate on high-end "fast fashion," which required close proximity between production and design. However, despite all of the attention and resources devoted over the prior two decades to enforcing legal liability in the fragmented industry, there continued to be overwhelming evidence of systematic labor abuse. Multiple reports revealed damning facts.[467] A 2010 survey of low-wage workers found that more than half of garment workers were paid less than the minimum wage and over 90% reported overtime violations.[468] From 2007 to 2012, federal labor officials discovered workplace violations in 93% of fifteen hundred garment industry investigations, amounting to $11 million in back wages owed to eleven thousand workers.[469] In 2014, the Department of Labor reported that 1,549 garment workers were owed more than $3 million in unpaid wages.[470] Around the same time, the garment industry was found to have the most violations of any industry surveyed by the Occupational Safety and Health Administration.[471] Even Forever 21, the company at the center of APALC's litigation campaign, seemed not to have learned its lesson. The Department of Labor investigated the company in 2012 for producing clothing in "sweatshop-like conditions," while a class action filed against the company that same year alleged workers were locked in after clocking out to be searched for stolen goods.[472] When asked about its contractors' labor practices, Forever 21 CEO Do Won Chang had this to say: "Regarding that problem, those are actually not my employees. Those are people who work at a company that sells products to us."[473]

And yet, looking back from this vantage point, it was hard to ignore how much had, in fact, been accomplished. The struggle against sweatshops in Los Angeles was an effort that challenged a complex, global economic system with a sophisticated approach that sought to fuse law and organizing into a potent weapon to change an industry built on labor exploitation. It was, of course, an ambitious undertaking and one that perhaps could only have been advanced by a band of young, idealistic lawyers and activists undaunted by power and untainted by experience. In the face of mighty adversaries, the advocates managed to leverage public outrage and legal might to shine the spotlight of attention on an industry operating in the shadows. They managed to defy the odds, win significant cases, pass major laws, and garner the support of powerful allies. And for a moment, they were able to knock the industry back on its heels.

That they did not deliver the final blow is not an indictment of their efforts, but rather an acknowledgment of the magnitude of their task. The anti-sweatshop campaign met resistance by well-resourced and coordinated adversaries and was undercut by the forces of macro-level global change. Precisely for this reason, garment advocates shifted their strategy away from litigation and toward efforts to collaborate with those manufacturers who remained to craft a solution that both promoted the bottom line and respected workers' rights. Yet the movement's efforts to integrate law and organizing endured in the form of organizational alliances and individual leaders whose experience shaped advocacy in other low-wage sectors where the threat of global outsourcing could not be invoked to chill worker organizing. In this sense, the story of garment advocacy in Los Angeles was not merely the final act in the drama of deindustrialization—but a bridge to a new model of low-wage worker organizing in the service sector.

3

Day Laborers

Organizing the Corner

Overview

Day laborers are predominantly immigrant men who seek daily employment on street corners, often next to home improvement stores and other venues trafficked by contractors and do-it-yourselfers. The relationship between day laborers and those who use their labor is defined through contracting, with day laborers negotiating rates for daily work (called a *jornal* in Spanish, giving rise to the Spanish-language name for day laborers: *jornaleros*). The informality of such transactions often results in labor abuse. The combination of a strong construction market and rising undocumented immigration powered the growth of day labor through the 1990s. Although part of the underground economy, day laborers were some of the most visible immigrant workers, standing on the corners in affluent communities to find jobs. As a result, they became the target of legal backlash, with more than forty cities in the greater L.A. area passing anti-solicitation ordinances making it a crime for day laborers to solicit work from the street corner. This chapter examines the coordinated legal and organizing campaign to challenge these ordinances led by the Mexican American Legal Defense and Educational Fund (MALDEF) and National Day Laborer Organizing Network (NDLON), culminating in the seminal 2011 appellate court decision—*Comite de Jornaleros v. Redondo Beach*—striking down the most expansive anti-solicitation ordinances on First Amendment grounds.

Local Regulation: Controlling Immigration via Land Use Law

Economics: All in a Day's Work

Part of the informal economy, day laborers have long been a particularly disadvantaged class of workers. Research from the early 2000s found that day laborers in

Southern California were "primarily undereducated [with] limited English proficiency, which severely hinder[ed] them socially and economically."[1] Most were relatively recent immigrants, with a majority living in the United States five years or less, and three-quarters in the country ten years or less.[2] Day laborers were predominantly young men, almost all of whom came from Mexico (77.5%) and Central America (20.1%).[3] Nationwide, three-quarters of day laborers were reported to be undocumented immigrants.[4]

The same research found that the work environment of day laborers was unregulated and, as a result, frequently exploitative. Although day laborers solicited work in groups at day labor sites,[5] they performed work in relative isolation in unsteady jobs. Day laborers were concentrated in industries that required skill—construction, painting, gardening, plumbing, and carpentry[6]—but market informality produced low pay. Although day laborers earned an average hourly rate above the minimum wage, their average annual income was at the poverty threshold because of the volatile nature of their work schedules.[7] As repeat players in the market, day laborers had incentives to be compliant, particularly when there was a surfeit of workers and the assertion of employment rights would mean that employers looked elsewhere for more quiescent labor. The undocumented immigration status of some day laborers also made them loath to complain about mistreatment, despite evidence of systematic abuse—particularly the nonpayment or underpayment of wages.[8] Moreover, even though day laborers were generally covered by employment laws, enforcement by public agencies was inconsistent because of nonstandard work arrangements and lack of awareness by enforcement officials of the scope of employment abuse and the application of employment protections.[9]

Politics: Regulating Day Labor as a Public Nuisance

Beginning in the 1980s, growing numbers of day laborers fueled local complaints that their presence constituted a threat to community safety and injured local businesses.[10] These complaints characterized day laborers as a public nuisance,[11] citing a range of negative externalities produced by their solicitation. These externalities clustered around three perceived threats: (1) to public safety (based on claims that day laborers created traffic congestion and accidents); (2) to public welfare (based on claims that they littered, urinated in public, bothered women, and generally intimidated residents); and (3) to private economic interests (based on claims that they undercut legitimate businesses and scared away customers).

The construction of the day labor "crisis" as a nuisance problem reflected the complicated politics of the underlying immigration debate. The nuisance framing elided a central concern of day labor opponents: the perceived intrusion of outsiders into community space defined as racially and economically incompatible with their presence. The outsider status of day laborers was reinforced by the perception that they were undocumented immigrants without any legal right to be present in the community, where they came to take jobs from law-abiding citizens.[12]

Framing day labor as a nuisance problem rather than an immigration problem had pragmatic political benefits for city officials. Local opposition to day labor was not monolithic, particularly within the business community, where some (especially in the construction and home improvement trades) welcomed day laborers as a low-cost workforce. Defining day labor as a nuisance left open the possibility that day laborers could be regulated out of public view (meeting resident concerns), but still be available to fill local demand for cheap services (meeting business needs). Moreover, the nuisance frame underscored the central legal reality that local governments were limited in their capacity to remove day laborers based on their immigration status—a task reserved to the federal government. Thus, even if communities were indeed motivated by a desire to rid themselves of "illegal immigrants," they did not have the legal power to do so (nor would it have been a completely effective strategy since not all day laborers lacked legal status).

Against this backdrop, the nuisance frame not only expressed local opposition to day labor, but also provided a legal hook to regulate it. The argument made by local jurisdictions was that, to the extent that the congregation of immigrant men on the corner imposed negative community externalities, localities could exercise their land use authority to mitigate them.[13] By enacting anti-solicitation ordinances restricting day laborers' access to public space, municipalities claimed to regulate conduct—rather than status—thus avoiding controversy over the local enforcement of immigration law. In so doing, local officials focused debate over the legality of day labor solicitation on the question of whether the conduct at issue (the act of seeking work in public) was constitutionally protected speech. This, in turn, shifted the emphasis of day labor advocacy from enforcing economic rights to protecting civil liberties—though the two were inextricably linked. Indeed, ensuring day laborers' civil right to seek work became a legal precondition to protecting their economic right to be treated fairly while engaged in the act of working.

Advocacy: Litigation When Nothing Else Works

The movement lawyers who took up the challenge of protecting day laborers' right to seek work adopted a classic test-case strategy. They mounted legal challenges to ordinances in jurisdictions with strong enforcement efforts, ultimately seeking to win a favorable ruling on the merits by the federal Ninth Circuit Court of Appeals, covering the western part of the United States, where immigrants were most concentrated. In doing so, the lawyers proceeded in an environment that was relatively conducive to a litigation strategy—though one that nonetheless presented serious risks.

Several positive factors pointed in favor of an impact litigation approach. Beginning in the mid-1990s, there was strong legal capacity, with resources and expertise devoted to the anti-solicitation campaign by MALDEF. Because anti-solicitation ordinances purported to limit conduct deemed a public nuisance, they gave rise to a credible First Amendment argument that was potentially more legally and politically appealing to conservative courts than a claim of discrimination based on race or national origin. Further, a successful case would result in an injunction blocking enforcement of the ordinance, resulting in resumption of the voluntary job-seeking activity of day laborers rather than requiring ongoing bureaucratic enforcement. In addition, the creation of NDLON brought grassroots organizing resources that strengthened monitoring and enforcement; it also created strong ties with workers that enhanced their understanding of their rights and their participation in the litigation process.

On the other side of the ledger, there was weak political capacity to thwart the spread of anti-solicitation ordinances. Despite the existence of NDLON, day laborers were a classically underrepresented political constituency. They were small in number, often not residents of the communities in which they sought work (and therefore not voters), and politically marginalized by race, class, and immigrant status. Their vulnerability contrasted sharply with the power of day labor opponents—neighborhood groups, business interests, and anti-immigrant organizations—whose combined political might rendered resistance through conventional political channels implausible, leaving day laborers few alternate avenues of redress. The fractured geography of the greater L.A. area—with 183 separately incorporated cities, plus unincorporated areas, inside 5 county-level administrative units (Los Angeles County surrounded by Ventura to the north, San Bernardino and Riverside to the east, and Orange to the south)—reinforced the political deficits of day laborers. This fragmented jurisdictional context, where localities varied dramatically by political ideology and receptivity to immigrants, made it much harder for day labor advocates to consider politically contesting—much less actually stopping—the spread of ordinances. This was particularly true in jurisdictions in which the presence of pro-day labor actors, such as unions or immigrant rights groups, was weak.

The absence of a viable political strategy strengthened the case for legal intervention as a means of advancing the day laborers' policy objective: the eradication of anti-solicitation ordinances. Yet litigation was not without risks. In particular, there were a number of contingencies that could be estimated but not known with any degree of certainty. Although the right to communicate one's availability for work in a public forum rested on solid free speech foundations, there was precedent upholding other anti-solicitation laws as valid time, place, and manner restrictions. Accordingly, the litigation strategy rested, in part, on how well day labor lawyers could marshal First Amendment arguments in their favor and distinguish adverse cases. Perhaps more crucially, the extent to which those arguments would prove successful hinged on who was selected to hear them in the lottery of judicial assignments—and what political predilections the jurists brought to the cases. Finally, changes in the broader political culture could affect the way that legal cases were framed and adjudicated. How judges would view anti-solicitation ordinances—as an unfair sanction against hardworking immigrants taking jobs native-born workers did not want or as an acceptable device to protect communities against illegal immigrants stealing opportunities from American workers—would depend profoundly on the economic and political moment at which the question was ultimately called.

Local Resistance: The Campaign to Defend Day Labor

The campaign to challenge anti-solicitation ordinances across the greater L.A. area sought to leverage scarce legal and organizing resources to maximal geographic effect—selecting strategic cases to abrogate the most egregious ordinances, deter copycats, and develop the legal and factual foundation for a positive resolution with precedential value. The overarching strategy emphasized protecting the sidewalks as a venue for solicitation and promoting access to private property with a nexus to the day labor market (such as home improvement stores). To advance this strategy, lawyers—from 1991 through 2011—litigated eight lawsuits to enjoin ordinances in jurisdictions across the greater L.A. area. Why did the lawyers choose to assert legal challenges where they did? And how did the legal challenges differ in their conception, execution, and outcome?

Litigation Before Organizing: The State Court–Civil Rights Approach

The Origins of Anti-Solicitation

The initial flashpoints of anti-day labor hostility occurred in more politically conservative jurisdictions in Orange County (OC) and the South Bay area of Los Angeles County. The earliest efforts to restrict day labor focused on heightened enforcement of traffic laws to prevent solicitation at day labor sites. In 1985, the City of Orange, in the heart of OC, passed one of the first local ordinances to limit solicitation in response to complaints by local merchants that day laborers were "killing business" by "scaring off customers, blocking driveways and creating a nuisance."[14] The Orange ordinance sought to prevent solicitation by empowering citizens to arrest "trespassers" on private property and creating a no-stopping zone around the corner that served as an informal day labor site.[15] Facing the threat of a lawsuit from the National Immigration Law Center (NILC) in Los Angeles, Orange officials decided not to enforce the trespass provision; nonetheless, the city succeeded in cutting the number of day laborers at the site by over half by citing prospective employers for traffic violations.[16] Following this traffic enforcement model, neighboring Santa

Ana—also responding to business complaints "that many of the [day laborers] loiter, block traffic and drive away customers"—mounted a five-day crackdown in April 1986, although instead of citing employers, Santa Ana police issued tickets directly to day laborers for impeding traffic.[17]

Beginning in 1986, local efforts to restrict day labor shifted to the more systematic creation and enforcement of anti-solicitation ordinances. This was driven by two legal changes. The first was the enactment of the Immigration Reform and Control Act of 1986 (IRCA),[18] which imposed sanctions on employers who hired undocumented workers. In the wake of IRCA's passage, formal employers began firing immigrant workers suspected of being undocumented, which swelled the ranks of workers pursuing jobs through the informal market.[19] Nonetheless, some day labor sites reported a significant drop in day labor activity out of worker fear of Immigration and Naturalization Service (INS) enforcement.[20] The prospect of enhanced enforcement produced two alternate responses by local governments. Some sought to preserve day labor hiring—acknowledging its benefits to employers—but to confine it to formal day labor centers. Others moved more aggressively to eliminate day labor altogether, building upon the anti-immigrant sentiment to pass broad prohibitions designed to sweep day labor off the streets.

The second legal development altering the day labor landscape was the Ninth Circuit's 1986 ruling in *Association of Community Organizations for Reform Now (ACORN) v. City of Phoenix*.[21] That decision gave legal ammunition to local officials seeking to ban day labor by upholding a Phoenix ordinance that prohibited ACORN's solicitation of monetary contributions from drivers of cars stopped at traffic lights (so-called "tagging").[22] Although the court acknowledged that ACORN members were exercising their free speech rights in a public forum, it nonetheless held that the ordinance—as a content-neutral time, place, and manner restriction—advanced the city's interest in promoting traffic safety while allowing for alternative means of communicating ACORN's message (such as distributing pamphlets to drivers).[23] Cities interested in prohibiting the solicitation of work on the border of street and sidewalk now had legal precedent they could marshal in support of their goal.

The first city to test the anti-solicitation approach was Redondo Beach in the South Bay. Business complaints that day laborers were driving away customers led Redondo Beach in 1986 to follow a path similar to Orange, enacting an ordinance that banned cars from stopping near the intersection of the day labor site.[24] When the Legal Aid Foundation of Los Angeles (LAFLA) filed suit challenging the ban,[25] the city responded not by backing down, but rather by dramatically extending the geographic reach of the ordinance. In 1987, Redondo Beach— following the Phoenix ordinance nearly to the letter—became the first city in the greater L.A. area to make it illegal for "any person to stand on a street or highway and solicit, or attempt to solicit, employment, business, or contributions from an occupant of any motor vehicle."[26] "Street or highway" was explicitly defined to include "sidewalks." Redondo Beach's law was amended to also apply to motorists, making it illegal for them "to stop, park or stand a motor vehicle on a street or highway from which any occupant attempts to hire or hires for employment another person or persons." The anti-solicitation ordinance was born.

The Redondo Beach ordinance provided a template that emboldened other cities to pursue similar repressive tactics—which, in turn, began to generate more organized resistance.[27] In 1988, the City of Glendale (in northeast Los Angeles County) proposed to ban day labor solicitation to address what local government officials called an "ongoing problem" at an intersection near a Dunn-Edward's paint store and a 7-Eleven.[28] Business owners in that area echoed concerns that day laborers scared off customers by "making comments and leaving trash," while city officials argued that day laborers were prone to "disrupt businesses, create traffic congestion, cause litter problems and bother women."[29]

The controversy generated by Glendale's proposal galvanized a coalition of legal and grassroots organizations, which would form the foundation of day labor advocacy for the next twenty years. On the heels of the proposal, the ACLU threatened to sue the city for turning the act of "looking for an honest day's work [into] a crime,"[30] while a number of grassroots organizations began to mobilize in the streets. Included among them were three relatively new immigrant rights groups: El Rescate, founded in 1981 to provide legal and social services to Salvadoran refugees fleeing the country's civil war; the Central American Resource Center (CARECEN), created in 1983 to assist Central American refugees more broadly; and CHIRLA, started after the passage of IRCA to facilitate legalization for eligible immigrants.[31] These organizations were joined by LAFLA and lawyers from the National Lawyers Guild (NLG), which together had formed the Los Angeles Labor Defense Network to protect the rights of workers in the informal economy. The Network, led by CHIRLA, created an Adopt-a-Corner program in 1989 that sent student-led groups to day labor corners to conduct know-your-rights trainings.[32] In addition, faith-based leaders from local churches—such as Our Lady Queen of Angels pastor Luis Olivares, who had opened his downtown church as a sanctuary for undocumented immigrants, and clergy from Dolores Mission in Boyle Heights—joined to support the day labor cause.

In response to the proposed ordinance, these groups launched protests in Glendale, which prompted meetings between city officials and coalition representatives from CARECEN, El Rescate, the Salvation Army, and the Glendale-based Catholic Youth Organization.[33] Opposition from the coalition succeeded in persuading Glendale City Council members to defer their vote on an anti-solicitation ordinance,[34] creating space for the negotiation of an alternative plan between the city and the Catholic Youth Organization, which agreed to set up a formal day labor hiring center.[35] Under this plan, day laborers could assemble on the organization's property from 6 a.m. to 9 a.m. each day to meet contractors, and would be permitted after that time period to solicit work on the sidewalk in front of the organization's property.[36] This plan placated day labor opponents and led to a one-year moratorium on consideration of the ordinance.[37] It also underscored the political alignment in favor of day labor, with local contractors supporting the plan as a way to maintain access to a cheap labor pool.[38]

The following year, as police sweeps of day labor corners drew praise from many business owners,[39] the Los Angeles City Council proposed its own ordinance banning solicitation on the streets and sidewalks.[40] This triggered a protest led by CHIRLA, which was shedding its social service image to develop more aggressive advocacy strategies that included the Day Labor Outreach Project, established in 1989 by Nancy Cervantes to inform day laborers of their rights.[41] Cervantes was a recent USC School of Law graduate, who had been one of the founders of CARECEN and a student organizer in the Glendale campaign. After the protest, L.A. city officials convened stakeholders to work out a compromise to protect the rights of day laborers while respecting the concerns of business owners and community residents over unregulated hiring sites. Out of these discussions, the city agreed to fund a six-month pilot project to launch six city-run day labor hiring centers opened to all workers irrespective of immigration status.[42] To spearhead this program—one of the first of its kind in the country—the city hired Cervantes, who helped open a day labor center in the South Bay's Harbor City in 1989, and another in North Hollywood the following year.[43]

Some cities in OC followed the hiring center approach, although the general direction of local policymaking was toward greater restriction of day labor activity.[44] In 1988, Costa Mesa created the nation's first day labor hiring center, which hosted nearly nine hundred workers in its first month; however, by requiring workers to present legal documents as a condition of entry, the site invited controversy and provoked threats by the ACLU to sue.[45] Costa Mesa coupled its hiring center with an ordinance (taking effect in 1989), which imposed a citywide ban on soliciting employment from a car.[46] Despite stepped-up enforcement, resulting mostly in the arrest of day laborers,[47] the market remained active in Costa Mesa, fueled by a booming economy and employers (particularly in the construction and car wash industry) who reported relying on undocumented workers for jobs that legal residents would not take.[48] The city then amended its ordinance to further prohibit day laborers from being in certain high-activity zones with the "intent" to solicit work.[49] The ACLU sued to enjoin the amendment in state court on behalf of a Costa Mesa resident (neither a day laborer nor an employer) on the ground that it was unconstitutionally vague.[50] The court agreed, striking down the amended portion of the law in 1990.[51] In 1992, the hiring center was opened to all workers (both documented and undocumented) after the state took it over for financial reasons.[52] The broader anti-solicitation ordinance, however, remained on the books.

Further south, Dana Point pursued a slightly different path. In August 1989, the city enacted an anti-solicitation ordinance,[53] but opted not to mount a vigorous enforcement effort. Instead, it attempted to facilitate hiring off the streets by setting up a telephone job bank to link day laborers and employers.[54] The City of Orange, in contrast, followed the Costa Mesa playbook more closely, expanding its ordinance in 1989 to prohibit solicitation on the streets and in private parking lots after its program of arresting hundreds of day laborers on misdemeanor charges and then turning them over to the INS failed to stem hiring activity.[55] Orange deferred enforcement, however, until after the opening of a city-sponsored day labor center, which was limited to documented workers.[56] Elsewhere, Laguna Beach and Brea both sanctioned day labor centers,[57] while other OC cities—Placentia, San Juan Capistrano, and Stanton—were considering the enactment of a uniform ordinance barring public solicitation.[58]

By the beginning of the 1990s, cities had thus developed three tactics to deal with day laborers. One approach was to enact anti-solicitation ordinances—citywide, in certain zones, or on private parking lots. A second was to increase police enforcement—either of existing traffic laws or newly minted anti-solicitation ordinances. And a third was to sanction day labor hiring in geographically bounded centers. These tactics often formed an interlocking framework. Cities like Costa Mesa and Orange sanctioned day labor centers, enacted ordinances to ban solicitation in other city locations, and increased police enforcement to secure the boundaries of this spatial division. In response, day labor advocates began to develop their own model for protecting day labor that sought to disentangle these city tactics: resisting ordinances and enhanced police enforcement, while promoting inclusive hiring centers.[59]

The First Test Case: Agoura Hills

The first opportunity for executing the day labor advocacy strategy came in the City of Agoura Hills, a suburban enclave in northwest Los Angeles County.[60] When about one hundred men started to solicit work outside of a shopping mall in 1989, the city responded to local merchant complaints by setting up a hiring center on a vacant lot, where jobs were distributed via a lottery system.[61] The center, which was donated by its owner and subsidized by the city's Chamber of Commerce, led to a doubling of day laborers, most of whom traveled from Los Angeles and the San Fernando Valley.[62] Although the center was initially deemed successful, it quickly came to be viewed as a "serious public nuisance," with allegations that the workers were "catcalling" women, urinating and defecating in public, and engaging in a "mad dash" to prospective employers, causing "many near-accidents."[63] The city also claimed that day laborers continued to congregate at the old informal hiring site, prompting the city to put up no-stopping signs at that intersection.

On March 27, 1991, responding to local pressure, the City Council passed an ordinance prohibiting any person from standing "on a public sidewalk, street or highway, or in a vehicle parking area located adjacent thereto," to solicit work from an occupant of a motor vehicle.[64] Upon the recommendation of the local community services department,[65] the city also instituted a phone bank system modeled on the Dana Point program. The hiring center was closed,[66] which—once the ordinance took effect in June—left day laborers with no public space in which to seek work. The ordinance was quickly denounced by a coalition that included CHIRLA and the ACLU, which spearheaded a protest of the law and drafted a letter to the City Council demanding its repeal.[67] The city countered by ratcheting up enforcement, conducting a police sweep that resulted in the arrest of sixteen day laborers.[68]

In response, the ACLU filed suit challenging the Agoura Hills ordinance on behalf of the workers.[69] It did so in concert with a team of lawyers from L.A. immigrant rights legal organizations: the Immigrant Rights Project of Public Counsel, the Immigrants' Rights Office of LAFLA, NILC, MALDEF, and CARECEN. This team included notable immigration lawyers (Public Counsel's Niels Frenzen, LAFLA's Michael Ortiz, NILC's Linton Joaquin, and MALDEF's Vibiana Andrade), along with veterans of the day labor movement, including Cervantes, who had joined Public Counsel after establishing the Harbor City and North Hollywood day labor centers.

To lay the groundwork for its attack, the legal team set up a "sting operation to demonstrate how [the city was] grabbing anyone who was a male Latino."[70] The sting was coordinated by Robin Toma, an ACLU staff attorney who had joined the group on a fellowship in 1988 after graduating from the UCLA School of Law. Toma organized UCLA students to stand as day laborers on the corner and coordinated with the local NBC news station, which secretly filmed the students being arrested and sheriffs telling prospective employers, "Don't you know you are not allowed to hire Mexicans?"[71] Cervantes also helped set up the sting and, despite the criticism of more senior colleagues who urged her to "just litigate,"[72] sought to advance a vision of lawyering in which the lawsuit was complemented by efforts to build an organizing base. Toward that end, she collaborated with CHIRLA and CARECEN, although those groups "didn't have formal organizing then, [but rather] were more militant and activist driven."[73] After the sting, Cervantes was the main liaison to the plaintiff group, which was composed partly of Kanjobal Indians from Guatemala, who were "really brave" in the face of what Cervantes recalled as "super angry anti-immigrant sentiment" that was "uglier than anything I had dealt with."[74]

The legal strategy had two prongs. First, in terms of venue, the team opted to file suit in state court, where Toma thought the day laborers had a better chance to get a "fair shot" in light of the "problematic" federal *ACORN* precedent.[75] Second, on the merits, the complaint was framed broadly, with twenty causes of action, which included a facial First Amendment challenge, but emphasized discriminatory application of the anti-solicitation law.[76] The legal team drew on the ACLU's previous suit against Costa Mesa, which rested on First Amendment grounds but, as Toma put it, "fashioned a whole other thing" since there was a "stronger case of discriminatory intent."[77] The complaint was framed as a "civil rights and taxpayer action" on behalf of "thirteen Latino and Latino-appearing individuals who have been arrested, criminally prosecuted, or discriminated against."[78] The complaint sought to enjoin the ordinance and also asserted a claim for monetary relief against the city and fast food restaurant Jack-in-the-Box for racially discriminatory practices in denying day laborers service.[79]

Neither prong of the legal strategy proved successful. The trial court denied the motion for a preliminary injunction in December 1991,[80] under circumstances suggesting that the decision to file in state court was a tactical miscalculation. According to Toma, after filing the petition, the ACLU "had [the] misfortune of realizing that [it] had earlier filed litigation against all superior court judges for granting continuances in criminal cases that violated defendants' right to a speedy trial."[81] As a result, many judges had to recuse themselves; one of the few who did not was assigned to the Agoura Hills case. The judge "was not very sympathetic," which Toma believed may have been due to the adversarial posture the ACLU had taken against the entire bench.[82] Nor did the lawyers get what they viewed as serious consideration on appeal. As one sign of this, when Toma stood up to argue the appeal, he was asked by one of the appellate judges if the plaintiff "was arguing on his own behalf."[83] The judge had mistaken him for one of the Latino day laborer plaintiffs.[84] The venue decision also did not avoid the appellate court's consideration of the *ACORN* precedent, which it cited liberally in holding that the Agoura Hills ordinance was a constitutionally permissible time, place, and manner restriction.[85]

Neither did the complaint's emphasis on discrimination succeed in gaining legal traction. Indeed, after the lower court dismissed the plaintiffs' equal protection arguments, the lawyers shifted course on appeal by resting their constitutional challenge on First Amendment grounds[86]—and dropping an explicit discrimination claim.[87] The appellate court nonetheless considered and rejected the discrimination claim for good measure, summarily concluding that the plaintiffs had "not shown a practice or pattern of unconstitutional enforcement," and suggesting that if individual day laborers had been treated unconstitutionally, they could "assert such conduct as a defense to any prosecution and conceivably could have a cause of action against that deputy."[88] The court also rejected the plaintiffs' facial First Amendment challenge in terms that Toma thought sounded like they had been "lifted... straight out of [the city's] brief"[89]—holding that the ordinance was content-neutral, served a legitimate interest in safety, and provided ample alternative venues of communication.[90] Although the plaintiffs did manage to settle for $7,500 against Jack-in-the-Box,[91] the first frontal challenge to an anti-solicitation ordinance in the greater L.A. area had failed. As an immediate consequence, the number of day laborers in Agoura Hills went from "250... down to 10 because of repression."[92] The case also cast a negative light on the approach of filing suit in state court, which some advocates began to criticize as inhospitable to day laborers' rights.[93]

Litigation Coordinated with Organizing:
The Federal Court–Civil Liberties Approach

Roots: The Legal-Organizing Alliance

By the time of the Agoura Hills appellate decision in 1994, the terrain of day labor advocacy had begun to change. The momentum in favor of anti-solicitation ordinances was building, with a total of seventeen bans in the L.A. region by 1994—including one ordinance enacted by Laguna Beach that prohibited hiring outside its city-sanctioned day labor center.[94] Yet the infrastructure of day labor advocacy was also growing stronger, resulting in an incipient alliance between law and organizing groups that would shape the future of the day labor movement.

On the law side, the arrival of Thomas Saenz as a staff attorney at MALDEF in the fall of 1993 marked a significant milestone. Saenz, whose family was of Mexican descent, grew up in Alhambra on the east side of Los Angeles, heading off to Yale for college and law school, where he displayed the oratorical skills that would make him a formidable litigator, winning the school's Potter Stewart Prize for moot court. After law school, Saenz clerked for liberal icon Stephen Reinhardt on the Ninth Circuit—a clerkship reserved for only the most academically elite and politically progressive law school graduates.

Saenz then joined MALDEF, where "one of [his] first assignments was the Agoura Hills case pending on appeal."[95] His marginal work on that case did not influence the appellate outcome, but did mark the start of his sustained day labor advocacy. Once the appellate court's ruling came down, Saenz and his colleague Vibiana Andrade filed a petition for rehearing to depublish the opinion.[96] The petition failed, but served to introduce Saenz to the key legal arguments over anti-solicitation—and pointed toward future strategies to avoid repeating the Agoura Hills loss.

At the time, however, the loss dealt the day labor movement a heavy blow. Across the greater L.A. area, it raised the stakes for advocates who saw other cities enact ordinances that followed the letter of the law upheld in the Agoura Hills case. Moreover, with bad precedent on the books, legal organizations were reluctant "to come back and try again to challenge these ordinances."[97] In terms of legal groups dedicated to fighting anti-solicitation, "MALDEF was on its own."[98]

Yet new nonlegal allies emerged. Saenz's arrival at MALDEF coincided with the development of a day labor organizing infrastructure that brought new advocates into the field. Among them was Victor Narro, who joined MALDEF as a community liaison in 1992 immediately after graduating from the University of Richmond Law School. Two key institutional developments further strengthened day labor organizing. The first was the 1991 creation of the Instituto de Educación del Sur de California (IDEPSCA), a grassroots, volunteer-based organization that used Paulo Freire's philosophy of nonhierarchical learning to promote leadership among Latino immigrants in Pasadena.[99] IDEPSCA initiated leadership development workshops for day laborers that led to the creation of the Association of Day Laborers of Pasadena, which "served as a mediator between day laborers, the city of Pasadena, police, and residents."[100] IDEPSCA's day labor work influenced the second crucial institutional development: the expansion of CHIRLA's day labor advocacy under the leadership of Cervantes, who had left Public Counsel in 1993 to direct CHIRLA's Workers' Rights Project, which focused on stemming employment abuse of day laborers, household workers, and street vendors through popular education, organizing, and rights enforcement.[101]

Breakthrough: Los Angeles County

The first test for this new constellation of advocates came before the Agoura Hills case had reached its end. The flashpoint was a corner adjacent to the HomeBase store in Ladera Heights, a historically middle-class African American community in an unincorporated area of South Los Angeles under Los Angeles County's jurisdiction.[102] Residents, organized as the Ladera Heights Civic Association, pressed Yvonne Brathwaite Burke, the area's county supervisor, to take action against roughly one hundred day laborers assembled at the site.[103] The laborers were accused of "loitering, obstructing traffic, whistling at women, drinking, and even engaging in theft."[104] While the Agoura Hills case was on appeal, Burke proposed an ordinance barring solicitation in public areas and private parking lots and imposing fines of up to $1,000 and jail time for violators.[105]

The advocates' initial response was to organize workers at the site and reach out to local residents and officials. CHIRLA's Cervantes was on the ground first, joined by activists from the Southern Christian Leadership Conference (SCLC) and the Multicultural Collaborative, lawyers from the ACLU (including Toma), and MALDEF's Narro, who was assigned to "connect MALDEF to meetings and events in the community" and "work closely with CHIRLA" to mobilize support for the day laborers.[106] The coalition members worked on multiple levels. They organized meetings with Burke in which they sought to "bust myths" about day laborers as undocumented workers, and brought in respected residents (including SCLC Director Joe Hicks, Southwestern Law Professor Isabelle Gunning, and community leader Genethia Hayes) to emphasize that day labor opponents "did not speak for me or my neighborhood."[107] Advocates also testified against the ordinance in front of the Los Angeles County Board of Supervisors.[108] Coalition members met with the managers of HomeBase to find a solution that would allow the workers to stay in the parking lot,[109] and reached out to the local sheriff's office to encourage the creation of a day labor center.[110] This grassroots effort was fruitful. Captain Jack Scully, who commanded the area's sheriff station, became, in Cervantes's terms, a "missionary for the cause" of setting up a day labor center, and District Attorney Gil Garcetti agreed not to prosecute anyone under the ordinance.[111] Even the

HomeBase manager showed signs of support, calling the workers at the day labor site "pretty well-behaved."[112]

Despite these efforts, the residents opposing day labor were intransigent and Burke continued to advance their cause. In Narro's view, the Agoura Hills trial court decision denying a preliminary injunction had strengthened the residents' resolve because they "thought the law was on their side."[113] Day labor advocates responded with efforts to pressure Burke to withdraw the proposed ordinance. In January 1994, they organized a protest march,[114] which was followed by an op-ed in the *Los Angeles Times* (written by Cervantes, along with Public Counsel's Frenzen and the SCLC's Hicks) calling the ordinance "overkill" and suggesting that instead of criminalizing immigrants seeking employment, Burke should seize the opportunity to create visionary change and "mediat[e] Latino-black friction."[115] Though the op-ed brought significant attention to the issue, advocates believed it poisoned the well with Burke.[116] Nonetheless, the coalition again reached out to Burke in a letter signed by MALDEF President Antonia Hernández proposing worker–resident mediation organized by CHIRLA. Burke agreed.[117]

In the mediation sessions, Cervantes recalled that day laborers attempted to "extend the olive branch"[118] and "humanize the issue" by telling their personal stories.[119] However, the sessions quickly deteriorated. The Ladera Heights Civic Association president countered the Cervantes op-ed with one of her own, asserting that the county had an obligation "to seek protection for its residents" through an ordinance.[120] This adversarial posture carried through to the mediation sessions, where, as Cervantes recalled, only the "most hateful residents" turned out.[121] As she recounted, Burke sent the "squeakiest wheels" to the mediation—those who were "making her field staff's lives miserable."[122] Sensing that the residents were "not at the table in good faith," the workers became disillusioned and the mediators grew frustrated.[123] After only two sessions, the residents told Burke that "it wasn't working."[124] Burke moved forward with the ordinance to ban solicitation, stating that "[a] residential area cannot accommodate that type of activity."[125] From the advocates' point of view, what began as a promising organizing campaign had turned into a "horrible disaster."[126]

The final hearing on the ordinance was held on March 25, 1994. It was marked by anti-immigrant hostility, including testimony in support of the ordinance by the author of Proposition 187, the voter initiative prohibiting undocumented immigrants from accessing social services in California that would pass in November of that year.[127] At the hearing's conclusion, the Board of Supervisors voted three to one to outlaw solicitation in Los Angeles County's unincorporated areas.[128] The ordinance, to take effect on July 1, 1994, was virtually identical to the one in Agoura Hills, prohibiting someone "standing in any portion of the public right-of-way," including sidewalks, from solicitating another person "traveling in a vehicle along a public right-of-way."[129]

After the ordinance passed, Saenz gathered with colleagues from Public Counsel and the ACLU to discuss legal strategy. Saenz was eager to file a lawsuit that would chart a different legal course than the one followed in Agoura Hills.[130] However, an immediate challenge did not materialize. The day laborers still needed time to form an association to be ready to pursue a lawsuit. In addition, after Proposition 187 passed, Saenz became devoted to litigating that case.[131] As a consequence, the county ordinance remained on the books for four years before MALDEF was able to challenge that law.

The interregnum, however, proved fruitful for day labor organizing, as new leadership emerged. When Cervantes left CHIRLA in 1996 to become the field director for Los Angeles City Councilwoman Jackie Goldberg, Narro was tapped to replace her as director of the Workers' Rights Project. At CHIRLA, Narro joined Pablo Alvarado, who in 1990 had emigrated from El Salvador with a university degree in sociology.[132] Alvarado initially worked as a day laborer, primarily as a painter and gardener,[133] and volunteered as an organizer at IDEPSCA, where he collaborated with CHIRLA's Adopt-a-Corner program.[134] In 1995, he was hired by CHIRLA as the lead organizer in Ladera Heights to "make sure day laborers would participate in the negotiations."[135] Toward that end, Alvarado organized the Day Labor Union (Sindicato de Trabajadores por Día), gaining "needed legitimacy" through intensive engagement with the workers, which included the formation of a soccer team.[136]

Together with the Sindicato, Narro and Alvarado pursued what Narro called a "human relations approach to continue the dialogue with the community stakeholders" in Ladera Heights after the ordinance was passed.[137] This approach built upon the efforts initiated by Cervantes, who launched the Ladera Heights Task Force—which included Captain Scully and other deputy sheriffs, residents, and members of the business community[138]—prior to the ordinance's enactment. As part of the Task Force, the sheriffs observed the operation of the hiring site and held a number of meetings with the workers.[139] As a result, the sheriffs agreed not to ticket any day laborers under the ordinance, thereby achieving an important outcome around the county. As Narro stated, although there was still "law on the books..., it wasn't being enforced."[140]

Yet Saenz remained committed to "righting the wrong of Agoura Hills" by negating the legal validity of the county ordinance,[141] which covered 10% of the county's population—and offered an appealing test case. When the Proposition 187 litigation concluded, Saenz turned his attention back to the county ordinance, which MALDEF formally challenged in June 1998 on behalf of CHIRLA and the Sindicato. The complaint sought an injunction against the ordinance, damages caused by enforcement, and a declaration of the ordinance's unconstitutionality.[142] Saenz asked CHIRLA to be a named plaintiff because of its growing day labor organizing work; CHIRLA, in turn, believed that it was important to "contribute to the lawsuit and mobilize workers," while also recognizing that serving as plaintiff might provide "legitimacy to the organization" and help it "raise money to keep going."[143]

MALDEF's strategy was to challenge the ordinance squarely on First Amendment grounds, offering two alternative theories in its complaint. As a primary matter, MALDEF argued that the ordinance was content-discriminatory (and therefore presumptively unconstitutional) because it only targeted solicitation speech (and not other sorts of speech) in public right-of-ways.[144] Alternatively, MALDEF suggested that even if the ordinance was content-neutral, it was nonetheless not a reasonable time, place, and manner restriction because the county lacked a substantial interest in its enforcement and did not leave open adequate alternative channels of speech.[145] The case was assigned to District Court Judge George King, a President Clinton appointee and former U.S. Attorney, who split the case into a two-step joint motion for summary judgment: first considering the issue of content neutrality and then deciding the ultimate question of whether the ordinance passed constitutional muster.[146]

From MALDEF's point of view, the court got the issues half right—though the half decided in the day laborers' favor was what ultimately counted the most. On the issue of content neutrality, the court in its October 1999 ruling held that although the ordinance did regulate a particular type of speech, it was nonetheless content-neutral because it was enacted to deal with undesirable "secondary effects" of day labor solicitation—traffic disruption, harassment, littering, and public defecation and urination.[147]

In September 2000, the court turned to the question of whether the ordinance was a reasonable time, place, and manner restriction. Here, the court broke with the Agoura Hills analysis and issued a stinging rebuke to the county, holding that the ordinance neither was narrowly tailored nor provided adequate alternative means of communication.[148] In addressing the force of the Agoura Hills precedent, the court noted that it was not bound by the state court decision, which it did not find "persuasive" in any event.[149] The court explicitly distinguished *ACORN* as a case that dealt only with "ACORN's face-to-face method of soliciting motorists while they were still in the flow of traffic and only temporarily stopped at a light."[150] In contrast, the county ordinance reached "even a solicitor who stands on the sidewalk, away from the curb, and unobtrusively attempts to make known to the occupants of vehicles his availability for work."[151] The court further held that there was "not a reasonable fit between the Ordinance, which reaches even the individual solicitor, and the quality-of-life concerns identified by the County."[152] It similarly rejected the notion that day laborers had adequate alternative means of communicating their desire to work, stating that the county had not shown that any of the proposed alternatives (door-to-door canvassing, telephone solicitation, solicitation of parked vehicles, and solicitation on private property) were either available or reasonable.[153] Despite losing their lead argument, the MALDEF lawyers nonetheless won a sweeping victory—one that marked the first major legal setback to anti-solicitation proponents.[154]

In the process, the day labor movement was itself born. In Cervantes's view, the long battle in Ladera Heights forged new "alliances and true friendships" among advocates that pointed the way toward the future.[155] In addition, innovative law and organizing strategies were developed. The implacable public opposition of residents reinforced the necessity of legal action as a last resort—but also illuminated the importance of sustained grassroots action. While the "lawsuit was essential,"[156] the "human relations" model of building ties with the local law enforcement and business community paid crucial dividends.[157] By the time the court struck down the county ordinance, CHIRLA's outreach had secured a nonenforcement policy that had already effectively nullified it. The organizing complemented the litigation, like "carrot and stick," showing cities that there was a high road toward cooperative solutions on day labor, but that movement lawyers could prevail on the legal merits if necessary.[158]

Leveraging Success: The City-by-City Approach

Strategic Foundation: The Mobilization Template
The county case, *CHIRLA v. Burke*,[159] became the template for a succession of lawsuits filed to break the tide of anti-solicitation around the greater L.A. area, in which nearly forty ordinances had been enacted by 2000.[160] The campaign was orchestrated as a collaborative legal and organizing effort. On the law side, MALDEF took the lead. Buoyed by its success in Ladera Heights and supported by a grant from the Rosenberg Foundation, MALDEF began developing a litigation campaign to strike down ordinances across the region, with the ultimate goal of winning a positive precedent in the Ninth Circuit Court of Appeals.[161] As an initial matter, a list of ordinances was compiled and Saenz sent letters to each city requesting compliance with the *Burke* decision. From the outset, this campaign was envisioned as integrating a crucial role for community organizing and was crafted in close alliance with day labor organizers, particularly CHIRLA's Alvarado.

One of the first moves was to revisit the Agoura Hills ordinance, this time threatening to file a lawsuit in federal court on the basis of the *Burke* precedent.[162] MALDEF drafted the complaint, while organizers coordinated a protest to pressure Sheriff Lee Baca not to enforce the ordinance in Agoura Hills (which was within the Sheriff Department's jurisdiction). After reviewing a letter from MALDEF (which laid out the First Amendment case against the ordinance), Baca agreed to take no enforcement action.[163] In turn, MALDEF dropped its complaint.[164] The positive resolution in Agoura Hills followed the Ladera Heights model by combining a credible legal threat with a "human relations" approach to engaging key decisionmakers. While underscoring the strategic importance of MALDEF's legal advocacy, it also signaled the growing power of activists on the organizing side, who were on the cusp of creating their own institution.

The groundwork for an independent day labor organizing group was built by CHIRLA's Narro and Alvarado in the late 1990s. In 1996, CHIRLA took over management of the day labor centers in Harbor City and North Hollywood, drawing on the organizing lessons learned in Ladera Heights to introduce leadership committees, workers' rights courses, and other community education programs.[165] Often these programs occurred "under the table"—for instance, in the evenings at the CHIRLA office—since the city made clear that the centers were not to be used for "organizing projects."[166] CHIRLA's goal was to transform the culture of the centers, which had been poorly run in a "top down" manner with security guards setting a tone of repression in response to internal problems, such as worker drinking and drug use.[167] CHIRLA also sought to make the centers operate more efficiently as hiring halls by bringing employers to the centers and creating a lottery system to organize the distribution of work.[168] CHIRLA and IDEPSCA shared responsibility for running the city-sponsored centers, with CHIRLA taking on a new center in Cypress Park, while IDEPSCA agreed to manage centers in downtown, Hollywood, and West Los Angeles.[169]

By this point, Alvarado had become the driving force behind day labor organizing in Los Angeles. His vision was to build upon core day labor sites to promote new leadership and establish a countywide network.[170] In 1997, Alvarado organized the first Intercorner Day Labor Conference in CHIRLA's parking lot, which built toward the creation of a formal Los Angeles County Day Labor Association, whose leaders were elected in 1998.[171] The Association was financially sponsored by IDEPSCA, but was largely run by Alvarado and other staff at CHIRLA.[172] The Association's goal was to take over the day labor centers and coordinate street corner organizing; however, due to resource constraints, that vision was never realized and the Association dissolved in 2000.[173] Out of its ashes, however, arose a national organization: NDLON. Founded in 2001 as a coalition of fifteen day labor organizations from around the country,[174] NDLON's goal was "not just to affect members, but to affect the entire day labor industry."[175] Alvarado was elected the leader of NDLON, which promulgated a "unified agenda"—a central pillar of which was defeating the proliferation of anti-solicitation ordinances.[176] A crucial feature of this strategy was the promotion of "constructive approaches" to day labor through the creation of formal day labor hiring centers.[177] Yet Alvarado was aware that funding would be an ongoing constraint on the expansion of formal centers and thus emphasized the importance of sustaining the legal fight to block anti-solicitation ordinances: "Unless you fund centers everywhere, you need to protect the corners."[178]

The strategy that developed drew upon the experience and input of advocates working in the day labor field since its early phase. It was also the product of "a special relationship between two people"[179]—Alvarado and Saenz—initially forged during the Ladera Heights campaign and reinforced when both participated in the

Rockefeller Foundation's Next Generation Leadership Program in 2000. Their connection was crucial to developing the sophisticated law and organizing campaign that ensued.

The campaign model was elegantly simple. Since all the ordinances at the time were virtually "carbon copies" of the complete ban pioneered by Redondo Beach,[180] targets were selected by MALDEF and NDLON staff based on evidence of strong enforcement efforts.[181] Advocates also assessed whether cities had viable hiring centers.[182] At enforcement hotspots, NDLON helped to organize corners and develop committees of local workers, while MALDEF drafted a complaint on behalf of the committees and NDLON. This structure was designed to ensure legal standing while protecting the interests of the workers. While Saenz viewed NDLON as having organizational standing in its own right, the committee was added as a plaintiff because of the direct harm the ordinance imposed on the workers. The committee—rather than the workers individually—was named because of "concerns about transience" and to protect workers from intrusive discovery about their immigration status, which Saenz viewed as legally irrelevant, both because IRCA exempted day laborers (as casual workers or independent contractors),[183] and because "their status doesn't affect their First Amendment right to seek employment."[184] When defendants sought to discover the immigration status of the workers, MALDEF moved for a protective order to prevent those inquiries. Even if the protective order motion was unsuccessful, the committee structure prevented individual workers from being singled out for questioning.

The complaint itself was grounded on the succinct First Amendment theory crafted by Saenz in the Los Angeles County case, presenting a powerful free speech argument uncluttered by other claims.[185] To mark the filing of the lawsuit, NDLON and MALDEF would stage a public event, marching from the day labor site to city hall.[186] This was done both to advance the legal strategy—generating publicity in order to exert pressure on city officials to negotiate—and the organizing strategy—giving day laborers ownership over the struggle and a platform to make normative arguments casting their right to seek work in moral terms. As Saenz recounted, the mobilization template was designed to promote mutually reinforcing law and organizing objectives: "Working together we could accomplish the legal policy goal and NDLON could organize groups around California."[187]

An Easy Win: Rancho Cucamonga–Upland

This strategy was first deployed to challenge joint ordinances in the cities of Rancho Cucamonga and Upland, which abutted one another in San Bernardino County. Both cities passed ordinances in 2001 to enforce anti-solicitation at one street corner, located at the cities' boundary.[188] The police mounted an enforcement campaign that involved weekly raids of the site.[189] Alvarado attempted to organize the workers on his own, since NDLON had no staff at this time, but "wasn't making progress."[190] He therefore gave the workers an ultimatum: "This is the last time I'll come here. We can fight back. We have the lawyers and have them ready."[191] The workers agreed to sue and MALDEF drafted a complaint,[192] which was served on the Rancho Cucamonga mayor by five hundred workers who "knocked on [his] door and said, 'We are taking you to court.... You are not going to intimidate us.'"[193] Once the suit was filed, the cities came to the table to start "discussing solutions almost right away."[194] In January 2003, the cities agreed to amend their ordinances so as to only prohibit solicitation "on a street or highway" and to explicitly "not prohibit solicitation by persons off the street or highway, or on a sidewalk."[195] In addition, the cities entered a settlement agreement in which they pledged to train police officers in appropriate enforcement measures and to establish a day laborer task force to "jointly address issues faced by each side."[196] The following year, Rancho Cucamonga officials worked with the nonprofit arm of a local church to open a day labor center in the city.[197]

The victory in these cases appeared to reflect a broader tapering in the push toward anti-solicitation. A number of cities—Cypress, Lawndale, and Lake Forest—announced that they were going to stop enforcing their ordinances in light of the *Burke* decision.[198] Huntington Beach and Costa Mesa were also considering revisions to their ordinances to clarify that solicitation was not banned on the sidewalks.[199] The strategy of using *Burke* as a deterrent to protect public space for solicitation was meeting with some success. Yet day labor advocates were still worried about cities enacting cosmetic changes that complied with *Burke*, but that did not alter the ordinances' ultimate impact. This concern grew as cities sought to craft ordinances to more carefully hew to the public safety justification that supported the tagging restriction in *ACORN*.[200] In this vein, Huntington Beach's ordinance was amended to explicitly permit sidewalk solicitation, while the proposed Costa Mesa ordinance barred solicitation that diverted the attention of drivers.[201] Advocates objected that such laws still threatened the right of day laborers to seek work by preventing the crucial curbside interaction with prospective employers. As Alvarado put it, "If you think employers are going to exit their vehicles, park in permitted areas and talk to people on sidewalks, it's not going to happen."[202] As this new generation of ordinances sought to draw a finer line between street and sidewalk, advocates were forced to determine whether they genuinely preserved day laborers' right to seek work or were just a clever repackaging of the flat ban in more legally legitimate terms.

Transition: Glendale Redux
A new front in the campaign opened in Glendale, where the fragile peace achieved by activists in the 1980s was broken after the demise of the nonprofit-run center they had helped to create. Despite a truce between the city and day labor advocates, local merchants and residents continued to complain that day laborers presented a public nuisance: "drinking alcohol, harassing women, breaking bottles, urinating in public."[203] Business owners near the Home Depot store where day laborers gathered

were particularly vociferous in their complaints.[204] However, Glendale city officials in the early 1990s were cautious about enacting an ordinance as they watched the lawsuit in Agoura Hills unfold. By 1994, the city attorney's office had prepared a draft ordinance to ban solicitation, but withheld it from City Council pending resolution of the Agoura Hills appeal,[205] arguing that it was "important that the city have the Agoura Hills law to lean on in case civil rights groups decide to legally challenge any similar law Glendale might enact."[206]

After the Agoura Hills ordinance was upheld, Glendale moved forward with its ordinance in earnest. However, in doing so, the city sought to forge a more humane path, which combined a public solicitation ban with the creation of a viable city-sponsored hiring center to provide day laborers with real opportunities for employment, job training, and education.[207] Glendale's goal (following the City of Los Angeles model) was to create the hiring center as part of a "fair and balanced approach" that would respond to the concerns of residents and businesses "without infringing on the workers' rights."[208] The Glendale ordinance, which went into effect in September 1996, made day labor solicitation a misdemeanor.[209] The city contributed $75,000 to help construct a day labor center to be run by a private charity,[210] which opened the following year.[211] At the outset, Glendale's plan was greeted with cautious optimism by day laborers, who welcomed the chance to use a center that would "make it . . . easier to get work," and by advocates, who believed the hiring center model had "tremendous value."[212]

Yet, by 2004, this optimism faded in the wake of police enforcement of the ban and worker frustration with the center. Because Glendale's ordinance prohibited solicitation in any portion of the public right-of-way, including sidewalks, workers were effectively forced to use the hiring center. To ensure that workers did so, police began issuing citations for "quality-of-life" offenses such as "trespassing, littering and public urination" based on complaints from residents and Home Depot managers.[213] Glendale officials denied enforcing the ordinance per se, which they were careful not to do in light of the *Burke* decision.[214] However, advocates complained that this was a distinction without a difference. They were also frustrated with the hiring center: "just a tarp over an area where workers could go" that was not seen as effectively allowing workers to signal their availability.[215] Moreover, the center instituted some unpopular policies, such as a $25 monthly user fee, which workers had to pay retroactively when returning from extended absences.[216]

This frustration motivated workers to contact MALDEF, which by this time had built its day labor litigation capacity to its high-water mark. In 2001, Saenz had hired Belinda Escobosa Helzer as a staff attorney for immigrant rights—a position that soon became almost exclusively focused on day labor.[217] Helzer, who grew up in OC, graduated from Southwestern Law School and then clerked on the New Mexico Supreme Court before starting at MALDEF. One of her first assignments was finalizing the settlement in the Rancho Cucamonga case.[218] From there, she began working with Saenz, who by then had become MALDEF's vice president, to identify ordinances and monitor enforcement efforts.[219] When Helzer and Saenz identified strong enforcement activity at specific day labor sites, they asked city officials to voluntarily cease enforcement or repeal their ordinances in light of *Burke*.[220] As Helzer recalled, it was "through that process that [MALDEF] identified Glendale as a problem."[221] Helzer's investigation of Glendale revealed selective enforcement of traffic laws: "Police would sit outside of Home Depot monitoring the workers. If they jay-walked, they got a ticket. If business people did the same thing, they didn't get a ticket."[222]

With this evidence of selective enforcement in hand, MALDEF and NDLON launched their campaign. The organizing component was led by NDLON's Veronica Federosky. An immigrant from Argentina, Federosky began working in 1998 as an organizer for IDEPSCA, where she helped to open the downtown L.A. day labor site.[223] She joined NDLON in 2003 and, after working on the final stages of the Rancho Cucamonga campaign, Federosky entered the Glendale fight.[224] Her initial organizing challenge was winning worker confidence: Because "other organizers [from the center] had been there and promised things that hadn't come true and there had been so many abuses by the police, it was difficult for the workers to trust."[225] Federosky sought to build rapport through education sessions focused on the workers' legal right to seek employment and earn a minimum wage.[226] She also coordinated leadership training programs, established a worker committee, and organized a task force of city officials, police, Home Depot management, and day laborers.[227]

Helzer accompanied Federosky to the Glendale corner to discuss the workers' rights and to consider the possibility of legal action.[228] MALDEF lawyers also met several times with Glendale officials to try to work out a compromise.[229] Although City Attorney Scott Howard gave MALDEF a written agreement that the city would not enforce the ordinance,[230] the persistent issuance of quality-of-life citations against day laborers led MALDEF to file suit in May 2004 on behalf of NDLON and the worker committee organized by Federosky.[231] Helzer was the main lawyer on the case (with Saenz supervising), taking the lead in writing the complaint and subsequent motion for a preliminary injunction.[232]

The initial complaint—filed by Saenz and a group of day laborers—asserted a facial challenge to the Glendale ordinance, following the *Burke* template: first claiming that the ordinance was content-discriminatory and, in the alterative, that it was not a valid time, place, or manner restriction.[233] Glendale responded with a curveball. In June, the city amended its ordinance to delete the explicit prohibition of solicitation on sidewalks in an attempt to blunt the plaintiffs' argument that the ordinance was not narrowly tailored to address safety concerns.[234] MALDEF then filed an amended complaint arguing that the new ordinance—insofar as it did not explicitly *permit* sidewalk solicitation—was "similar" to the previous one and thus still unconstitutional on its face.[235] In MALDEF's motion for a preliminary injunction, Helzer

Figure 3.1 Tom Saenz and day laborers marching to Glendale City Hall. *Source*: MALDEF (March 20, 2004).

argued both that the ordinance was content-discriminatory and an invalid time, place, and manner restriction.[236] As to the latter, she asserted that the ordinance was overbroad since it barred speech that was not connected to safety: "Instead, the ordinance regulates *all* solicitation speech (and even attempted solicitation) regardless of whether the speaker approaches a vehicle, whether vehicles stop, impede or block traffic."[237] Moreover, Helzer argued that no viable alternatives to solicit work existed. The ordinance's lack of clarity about the legality of sidewalk solicitation combined with continued police enforcement of quality-of-life infractions to deter workers from solicitation in public—while the hiring center proved an inadequate substitute.[238]

In ruling on the preliminary injunction motion, District Court Judge S. James Otero, a nominee of President George W. Bush, rejected MALDEF's content neutrality argument under the secondary effects doctrine.[239] However, Judge Otero agreed that the ordinance was not narrowly tailored. Since it was "unclear where the curb ends and where the sidewalk begins," the ordinance's vagueness was "likely to chill permissible speech."[240] The court also agreed that the plaintiffs had not been afforded adequate alternatives since the ordinance did nothing to assure the continued availability of the hiring center, which was contingent on "the funding and management decisions of a private organization."[241] The court issued a preliminary injunction in January 2005 and the plaintiffs quickly moved for summary judgment to impose a permanent injunction,[242] which the court—echoing its earlier holding—granted in May.[243]

It was a resounding victory, but one that marked a transition point in the movement. Glendale appealed the permanent injunction in fall 2005.[244] By this time, the legal team was in the midst of a profound change. Part of the change was a consequence of routine personnel issues, with Helzer and her MALDEF colleague, Shaheena Simons (a Yale Law School graduate who had joined MALDEF on a Fried Frank public interest fellowship in 2003), both taking family leave in 2005, before resolution of the Glendale summary judgment motion.[245] These departures were followed by other major losses that occurred against the backdrop of the 2004 resignation of MALDEF's long-time president, Antonia Hernández, and her replacement by Ann Marie Tallman, a senior finance executive from Fannie Mae. In August 2005, Saenz announced that he was leaving to become general counsel for L.A. Mayor Antonio Villaraigosa. Soon thereafter, MALDEF's regional counsel, Hector Villagra—another Judge Reinhardt clerk and Fried Frank fellow who had spent his career at MALDEF—announced his departure. In September, just before Glendale filed its appeal, Saenz, Villagra, Helzer, and Simons withdrew as counsel of record for the plaintiffs; in their place, Araceli Perez, a junior MALDEF attorney, assumed counsel's role.[246] Yet MALDEF was not to be in charge of the appeal. Instead, NDLON retained a team from the Lawyers' Committee for Civil Rights (LCCR) in San Francisco led by two lawyers: Legal Director Robert Rubin and Staff Attorney Philip Hwang.

These transitions strained relations between the advocates and day laborers. Yet Federosky worked to make sure that the changes were communicated to the worker committee and that its leaders continued to make crucial decisions about the progress of the case.[247] When Glendale filed its appeal, the plaintiffs were therefore cognizant of the risks of proceeding to the Ninth Circuit. They had lost their main lawyers, while the factual and legal posture of the case was not ideal given that Glendale's ordinance excised sidewalks and the city had a functioning hiring center. Serious settlement talks ensued (building on those begun in district court), led by LCCR attorneys, who along with Glendale counsel moved to delay oral argument to finalize a deal. In early 2008, the two sides reached a settlement in which Glendale agreed to adopt a revised ordinance that narrowly targeted traffic interference,[248] prohibiting solicitation on "any street, roadway, curb, or highway that is within, or immediately adjacent to, any industrial or commercial zone" from any vehicle either traveling in the street, or "stopped in or blocking a lane of traffic."[249] It explicitly did not prohibit solicitation "directed at the occupant of a vehicle that is stopped at the side of the roadway and out of the lanes of traffic."[250] This resolution constituted a victory—the Glendale sidewalks had been preserved for day labor solicitation that did not threaten traffic—but one that left open the crucial question: Who would lead the legal campaign against anti-solicitation ordinances into its culminating phase?

The Height of Intransigence: Redondo Beach

The question was quickly posed in Redondo Beach, where a lawsuit filed before the departure of Saenz and his colleagues from MALDEF would ultimately proceed without them. Redondo Beach's 1987 ordinance was the first in Southern California to ban anyone from standing on the street or sidewalk to solicit employment.[251] Yet, for over fifteen years, the city had a lax approach to enforcement and thus was not one of the initial targets of the legal campaign.

This changed in October 2004, when Redondo Beach launched a month-long enforcement crackdown that resulted in sixty-three worker arrests.[252] Precipitated by "complaints from a couple of businesses in two strip malls" near the day labor site,[253] the crackdown included a sting operation in which local police went undercover posing as employers and arrested day laborers who entered their vehicles.[254] The workers called NDLON,[255] whose organizers had earlier left business cards with workers on the corner during a visit to evaluate enforcement activity.[256]

Day labor advocates responded swiftly, moving forward along interrelated tracks. First, NDLON's Federosky launched an effort to organize the corner, following the well-honed model: establishing "a committee, creating rules for the corner, [conducting] leadership training, identifying leaders, and talking to workers about their responsibilities at the corner."[257] Unlike in Glendale, however, Federosky believed that the prospects for collaboration with local officials were dim. As she stated: "In Redondo Beach, the politics were more racist from the city and the police, so it was a different dynamic. We were basically alone."[258] In this context, NDLON organized protests in support of the workers.

Advocates also confronted the immediate challenge of supporting the defense of day laborers facing criminal charges as a result of the sting operation. This job fell to a newcomer, Chris Newman, who had arrived at NDLON to launch its in-house legal department. As a law student at the University of Denver, Newman had helped to start

Figure 3.2 Day laborers waiting for work in Redondo Beach. *Source*: Robert Harbison, *The Christian Science Monitor* Archive (January 10, 2004).

Figure 3.3 Day labor protests in Redondo Beach. *Source*: Brian Vander Brug, *Los Angeles Times* via Getty Images (November 18, 2004).

a day labor center "as an outlet to get away from law school."[259] Through this work, he met Alvarado and Saenz, and then had a "light bulb" moment at an NDLON conference in San Francisco: He would make defending the rights of day laborers his life's work.[260] Upon graduation, he won a Ford Foundation New Voices fellowship, which funded him to provide employment law services to day laborers through NDLON.[261] However, the Redondo Beach case—which "came out of the blue"—quickly changed the fellowship plan, shifting Newman's focus to contesting solicitation bans.[262]

When the Redondo Beach crackdown occurred, Newman was awaiting his bar results; thus, his role was limited to acting as a liaison between the workers and lawyers. One important part of this role was reaching out to the local public defenders who had been assigned to represent day laborers in their criminal cases.[263] Newman recalled that some of the defenders viewed the misdemeanor cases as a "hassle" and thus he took it upon himself to "get them enthused about representing the day laborers" as a part of the broader campaign.[264] Newman also took the lead in meeting with the workers about legal strategy. "Almost every other day," Newman would meet workers on the corner, typically with Federosky, but sometimes also with Alvarado and Narro (who was acting as a legal observer).[265] Because Newman "was not involved in drafting" legal briefs, he was able to "mak[e] sure that the workers had ownership over their own claims and underst[ood] . . . all aspects of the case."[266]

As Federosky recalled, the workers viewed the lawsuit as the only viable course of action: "They didn't see any other way out of it. They were so scared."[267] For the lawyers, Redondo Beach presented an appealing case to pursue on the merits. Unlike in Glendale—where a challenge had been filed six months earlier and was still pending[268]—the Redondo Beach ordinance was a complete ban, the city had no organized day labor center, and enforcement was substantial. MALDEF lawyers (Saenz, Helzer, and Simons) filed for an injunction on behalf of two clients: the worker committee (Comite de Jornaleros de Redondo Beach) and NDLON. MALDEF's Simons drafted the federal complaint,[269] which was served on the city after a march in November 2004. MALDEF faced off against Redondo Beach's City Attorney Michael Webb, who Newman saw as "a bit of an ideologue" who "liked the attention" brought by the suit.[270] From Saenz's perspective, the plaintiffs drew a "good judge":[271] Consuelo Marshall, a President Carter appointee and path-breaking liberal jurist, who was the first woman hired by the L.A. city attorney's office and the first African American woman judge appointed in the Central District of California.

The case "moved fast."[272] Judge Marshall granted the plaintiffs' motion for a temporary restraining order within three weeks of the initial filing.[273] Less than two weeks later, the court issued a preliminary injunction, finding that there were "serious questions" about whether the ordinance was content-based; the order also expressed skepticism about the degree of narrow tailoring (stating that Redondo Beach "could simply enforce traffic laws" to protect public safety and that activities such as vandalism and littering had "nothing to do with speech pertaining to solicitation") and the adequacy of alternate channels of communication (noting that the ordinance prohibited workers from soliciting work from drivers who had pulled over and parked their cars).[274] The city appealed the preliminary injunction decision to the Ninth Circuit, which affirmed in an unpublished opinion in May 2005.[275]

From there, however, the dynamic changed. As part of its discovery request, the city sought to acquire information about the legal status of the workers involved in the lawsuit. The plaintiffs, in turn, moved for a protective order arguing that the "discovery is intended to intimidate and harass Plaintiffs' members."[276] The magistrate judge initially refused to issue a protective order, but Judge Marshall reversed that decision, ruling that the plaintiffs' immigration status was irrelevant to the organizational plaintiffs' standing to bring the case and thus not subject to discovery.[277] The plaintiffs moved for summary judgment.

By this stage, MALDEF's litigation team had largely disbanded. Helzer had taken leave and Simons had moved to MALDEF's Washington, D.C. office. Saenz formally withdrew in August 2005 and Perez substituted in as lead counsel, finishing the motion for summary judgment before herself withdrawing in November 2005.[278] LCCR's Rubin and Hwang entered in MALDEF's place to complete the summary judgment briefing (although MALDEF Litigation Director Cynthia Valenzuela continued to review the briefs, along with Saenz).[279] The city filed a cross-motion, arguing that it was entitled to a dismissal because the plaintiffs did not have standing to sue and, even if they did, the ordinance was nonetheless valid. Rubin argued the motion for summary judgment. In her 2006 ruling, Judge Marshall issued a sweeping and carefully documented decision in the plaintiffs' favor, permanently enjoining the ordinance on the ground that it was not narrowly tailored to promote traffic safety, crime prevention, or aesthetics, and did not allow day laborers alternative channels of solicitation.[280]

Yet the victory was bittersweet. Saenz, the architect of the litigation campaign, was gone and the legal department he had built was decimated. Moreover, Redondo Beach showed no sign of conceding the fight. The city promptly appealed the permanent injunction to the Ninth Circuit. Briefing was scheduled for mid-2007, and LCCR set to work on the appeal. On the ground, Federosky continued monitoring the Redondo Beach site to ensure that the police abided by the injunction,[281] which remained in effect pending the appeal.[282] The day laborers returned, but with a sense of caution described by Federosky: "At least for now," they thought, "it is safe."[283]

The Next Generation: Lake Forest, Costa Mesa, and Baldwin Park

BEHIND THE ORANGE CURTAIN It was not safe for day laborers in other parts of the region, where anti-solicitation ordinances had spread "like wildfire."[284] By the time Saenz left MALDEF in 2005, forty-two jurisdictions in the greater L.A. area had enacted anti-solicitation ordinances, although lawyers had succeeded in enjoining two (Los Angeles County and Glendale) and forcing day labor–friendly amendments in two others (Rancho Cucamonga and Upland).[285] In terms of enforcement activity, there were still a number of OC hotspots, where the intensity of anti-immigrant sentiment grew after September 11, 2001. Even places with histories of supporting day labor witnessed escalating hostility. In Laguna Beach, one of the region's first city-sanctioned day labor centers came under vigorous attack by activists from the so-called Minutemen—a vigilante group opposed to immigration, launched in 2004—and the California Coalition for Immigration Reform.[286] After one anti-immigrant activist determined that the center was actually on state-owned land, she sued to eliminate it; the center was saved only after the city agreed to repurchase it from the state.[287]

The City of Lake Forest, just east of Laguna Beach, was another hotspot with a history of tension. Lake Forest had enacted an anti-solicitation ordinance in 1993 that followed the Redondo Beach model by prohibiting any person from soliciting, or attempting to solicit, work in any public right-of-way, including the sidewalk.[288] In the late 1990s, CHIRLA had received complaints of sheriff harassment that resulted in a departmental review and a promise by OC Sheriff Mike Corona to halt enforcement.[289] Conditions improved temporarily, but by the mid-2000s, problems returned when the city—responding to business and Minutemen complaints— voted to allow local shopping mall merchants to pay for a private security guard to file trespass complaints against day laborers.[290] On the basis of these complaints, sheriffs could arrest the day laborers. In so doing, the city could achieve the anti-solicitation ordinance's objective—removing day laborers—without its direct enforcement.

As the next wave of day labor conflicts shifted south, so too did the advocacy resources to address them. Although MALDEF was no longer involved in the litigation fight over day labor, its former lawyers were—albeit under the auspices of a different public interest organization, the ACLU. The campaign that Saenz had initiated was carried on in OC by two of his MALDEF protégés. Villagra left MALDEF in September 2005 to start the ACLU's OC office, recruiting Helzer to follow. They were joined that same year by Nora Preciado, a Berkeley Law School graduate who had won an Equal Justice Works fellowship to address language access issues in health care.[291] Together, in early 2006, they considered the possibility of suing Lake Forest.

From a policy point of view, the new ACLU lawyers were intent on counteracting the spread of anti-immigrant sentiment in OC and viewed the defense of day laborers as a key substantive and symbolic battle.[292] As they reviewed OC cities with ordinances, they found a variety of approaches. Some had complete bans, like Lake Forest, while others, such as Orange, were considering amendments that attempted to draw a tighter connection between anti-solicitation and public safety. The ACLU supported the Laguna Beach hiring center approach and wanted to push cities in that direction, rather than toward more punitive measures. As Preciado put it, "We didn't want Lake Forest setting up a terrible precedent right down the street from [the Laguna Beach] workers' center."[293] Thus, after evaluating the ordinances and enforcement activity in the area, Villagra and his ACLU colleagues determined that "Lake Forest was clearly the type of ordinance we wanted to take aim at initially."[294]

The ACLU was also drawn to Lake Forest by NDLON, which in 2005, had sent in organizers, led by Federosky, to support a day labor march protesting Minutemen harassment and city enforcement. NDLON organized the corners, which had between fifty and eighty workers.[295] However, NDLON's efforts were challenged by its lack of OC-based resources and the fact that there were several corners in Lake Forest—with some tension among them.[296] Because of the city's general political conservatism, Federosky also found it "more difficult to build relations with other community members ... [and to] look for solutions so we don't have to litigate."[297] Federosky attempted to reach out to several churches from different denominations, but "they didn't want anything to do with day laborers."[298] Because of these constraints, NDLON could not implement its full organizing model in Lake Forest, but Villagra still "felt that it was important to do something there" to take a stand against day labor repression.[299] NDLON organizers contacted Villagra and Helzer—whom they knew from MALDEF—and enlisted them to investigate. Preciado, who was bilingual, was the main point of contact with the workers and spent one day a week for several months going out to the sites with NDLON organizers to take "worker declarations of what was happening regarding enforcement."[300]

What they found was a new pattern, one that combined private security enforcement with what Villagra called a model of "nonenforcement enforcement" by the sheriffs,[301] who would not issue citations (in keeping with Sheriff Corona's earlier promise), but instead would try "shooing the workers away" by telling them it was illegal to do work, for which they could be fined and deported.[302] Armed with this information, the lawyers—after months of community-building by NDLON—approached the worker committee, called the Asociación de Trabajadores de Lake Forest (ATLF), to discuss filing suit. Preciado found the workers to be "really fed up with the daily harassment" and therefore "very enthusiastic," although they were worried about retaliation "because of immigration status" and "being the targets of violence."[303] After discussing concerns about confidentiality and the process of seeking a protective order, the workers "collectively decided it was worth risk."[304]

The ACLU filed its complaint (in conjunction with a press conference and protest march) on March 1, 2007, seeking to enjoin the Lake Forest ordinance and to require the city to pay restitution to the workers for fines incurred.[305] The complaint named the city as a defendant, along with several individual city officials (including the mayor, city council members, and the police chief). The case was filed on behalf of ATLF, NDLON, and a student organizing group, Colectivo Tonantzin, which had organized counter-Minutemen demonstrations and volunteered to monitor the enforcement of Lake Forest's ordinance. The case was assigned to District Court Judge David Carter—a Vietnam veteran, former OC district attorney, and superior court judge—who was appointed to the federal bench by President Clinton. From the outset, Carter was aggressive in pushing both sides to settle, and the city quickly agreed to halt enforcement.[306] Shortly thereafter, the city repealed its ordinance.[307]

Despite the swift repeal, however, workers continued to complain that sheriffs engaged in the same enforcement activity. For proof, the ACLU recruited students to pose as employers. Villagra recalled that the students picked up three workers and were immediately pulled over by sheriffs, who claimed hiring day laborers was illegal and warned that the workers could "sue you, rob you, and molest your children."[308] With this evidence of ongoing enforcement, the ACLU filed an amended complaint in April 2007 dropping the facial challenge to the ordinance and instead arguing that the city continued to target the expressive activities of day laborers.[309] The complaint also added a new individual defendant: Sheriff Mike Corona, whose deputies were responsible for enforcement.[310] The city moved to dismiss on the ground that the repeal had mooted the plaintiffs' challenge.[311] The court rejected the defendants' motion, stating that the plaintiffs' allegations that defendants had overseen and managed law enforcement operations in the city was "ample basis upon which to reasonably infer that the Individual Defendants incurred liability in their supervisory capacities."[312]

During this whirlwind of activity, Preciado sought to keep the workers informed of the proceedings and to gather their input about next steps. In these discussions, she recalled that the workers were inclined to "defer to [our assessment of] the best legal tactics so long as they knew the consequences."[313] The key issues revolved around worker confidentiality and which parties to sue. In terms of confidentiality, Preciado made it clear that there were risks but also assured the workers that if "at any point names had to be disclosed, if it meant we had to drop the case, we would."[314] After the court rejected the defendants' motion to dismiss, there was also discussion of whether to add new defendants: Securtec, the private security company hired to patrol the shopping center, and individual sheriffs accused of misconduct. Preciado worried that, in both cases, naming those defendants could "make life miserable for the workers in the short term."[315] However, adding them as defendants also presented the chance to recover monetary damages, which might increase pressure on all defendants to settle. With the workers' consent, plaintiffs further amended their complaint in December 2007 to add the new parties.[316]

The defendants then adopted an aggressive discovery strategy, embroiling the parties in a series of high-stakes disputes. In order to substantiate their claims of ongoing misconduct, plaintiffs submitted fifty-four "Doe" declarations by day laborers, collected by Preciado, which detailed the persistence of enforcement activities. In turn, the defendants moved for information regarding the identity of the Doe declarants, as well as information about NDLON members.[317] The ACLU filed for a protective order, but the magistrate judge rejected its request to bar defendants from acquiring identifying information about the Doe declarants, although he did prevent the disclosure of immigration status.[318] In addition, defendants moved to depose Preciado about communications she had with workers while collecting the declarations. Although the court rejected this motion on the ground of attorney-client privilege,[319] it appeared that part of the defendants' strategy was to discredit the plaintiffs, by casting them as illegal immigrants, and their counsel, by casting her as unethical.

This strategy continued as the case moved toward trial in summer 2008[320]— even after the parties narrowed their disagreements. In June, the ACLU settled its claims against Securtec and all of the city defendants (who agreed not to enforce the ordinance).[321] A compromise, however, could not be reached with the county defendants: the OC sheriff, the Lake Forest police chief (employed by the sheriff), and two individual sheriff deputies. As the August trial date drew near, the county defendants proposed a jury instruction titled "Undocumented Aliens—Right to Work in the United States," which suggested that they planned to introduce evidence about plaintiffs' legal status and discuss immigration law provisions related to undocumented immigrants.[322] The defendants then moved to dismiss the plaintiffs' claims on the grounds that all three (ATLF, NDLON, and Colectivo) lacked standing.[323] The defendants argued that because ATLF did not have identifiable members, it was not possible to show that the members would have standing in their own right, while NDLON and Colectivo had not suffered any organizational harm.[324] Judge Carter, in a blow to the plaintiffs, granted the motion dismissing

Figure 3.4 Hector Villagra and Belinda Escobosa Helzer at the Orange County ACLU.
Source: Paul Rodriguez, *Orange County Register*/SCNG (November 14, 2008).

NDLON and Colectivo; ATLF was allowed to remain in the case based on evidence of actual day laborer membership.[325]

As Villagra recalled, the ACLU lawyers quickly held "an attorney-client meeting on the sidewalk" to discuss "what a bottom-line settlement might look like."[326] Immediately thereafter—and on the eve of trial—a settlement was reached, in which the county defendants agreed not to "interfere with the right of, or take any action for the purposes of discouraging, day laborers to stand, individually or in groups, on any public sidewalk in the city of Lake Forest, as long as no law is violated."[327]

Plaintiffs could again declare victory, but at some cost. They had received a negative decision on the important issue of organizational standing and defendants would not agree in the settlement to give plaintiffs any attorney's fees, which the court later refused to award. Not wanting to abide these negative rulings, the plaintiffs appealed them to the Ninth Circuit, which offered a split decision, holding that the ACLU was entitled to attorney's fees, but continuing to deny that NDLON had standing.[328] In the end, the Lake Forest case could be counted as a success. The plaintiffs had won a hard-fought battle in the heart of OC to repeal Lake Forest's ordinance and secure a strong agreement of nonenforcement. In addition, the ACLU had prevailed in a new type of case that went beyond a facial challenge to require intensive documentation of enforcement practice. Villagra acknowledged that it was a learning experience, which the lawyers would not necessarily repeat: "We had done a lot on the fly in Lake Forest and compressed a lot into a short time."[329]

The next time, in Orange, the lawyers proceeded more deliberately. There, after a legal review prompted by the threat of litigation, the city enacted a panoply of new laws in 2007: requiring identification to access the day labor center, establishing an anti-solicitation "buffer zone" around the center, banning solicitation next to streets without parking lanes, and requiring private owners to get a permit to allow day laborers on their property.[330] As the day labor population precipitously declined,[331] the ACLU spent "a year going out and making sure the workers knew who we were and keeping tabs on the police department."[332] However, instead of suing, lawyers decided to take a wait-and-see approach, educating the workers about where they *could* legally solicit—next to streets with public parking—rather than suing over where they could not.[333]

The ACLU, however, could not afford to wait in Costa Mesa—another OC city with a long history of day labor tensions. After the city agreed to open its hiring center to all workers in the early 1990s, there was a period of fragile détente between the city and day laborers.[334] By the mid-2000s, that was broken as day labor opponents succeeded in pressuring the city to close the center, which opponents called "the illegal alien day-labor center,"[335] despite evidence that nearly all of the laborers were documented.[336] In 2005, the city amended its anti-solicitation ordinance (in response to a threatened lawsuit by MALDEF) to ban the "active solicitation" of employment "from any person in a motor vehicle traveling along a street."[337] Active solicitation was defined as "solicitation accompanied by action intended to attract the attention of a person in a vehicle traveling in the street such as waving arms, making hand signals, shouting to someone in a traveling vehicle, jumping up and down, waving signs pointed so as to be readable by persons in traveling vehicles, quickly approaching nearer to vehicles which are not lawfully parked, and entering the roadway portion of a street."[338] The aim of the ordinance, as stated in its preamble, was to ban solicitation activity that posed public safety risks (by distracting drivers).[339] Costa Mesa Mayor Allan Mansoor also suggested another goal: "The real question I have is . . . do you want a bunch of unknown people loitering in front of your home or soliciting near your home or in front of your business, especially when many of them are here illegally? I think the answer is no."[340]

Heightened enforcement activity followed,[341] culminating in 2009 with what Villagra described as "a sting operation where officers posed as contractors, picked up a van full of workers and drove them straight to" immigration authorities.[342] NDLON's Federosky came in to organize, but the distance and lack of resources meant that "the follow up with workers wasn't as often" as organizers believed necessary.[343] As a result, she "called in Colectivo and asked if they could go to the corner."[344] In February 2010, the ACLU's Helzer (on behalf of a worker committee and Colectivo) sued to enjoin the ordinance's enforcement on the ground that its vague proscription against "active" solicitation "suppresses and unduly chills protected speech."[345] The city agreed to place enforcement on hold pending the resolution of the case, which was itself stayed pending the outcome of the Redondo Beach appeal.[346]

MALDEF'S RETURN In Costa Mesa, Helzer was joined by MALDEF's Saenz, who had returned to the organization in 2009 when he was named president and general counsel. His return marked the culmination of organizational changes that started soon after he had left. The tenure of Tallman came to an abrupt end in 2006, and she was replaced on an interim basis by John Trasviña, a former Justice Department lawyer who had worked early in his career for MALDEF in Washington, D.C. Trasviña's arrival coincided with that of staff attorney Kristina Campbell, who came from the farmworker program at Phoenix's Community Legal Services.

Campbell immediately became involved in the day labor issue in Baldwin Park, an eastern L.A. suburb, where a site adjacent to Home Depot provoked nuisance claims. The city passed an anti-solicitation ordinance on June 8, 2007,[347] after a city attorney review prompted by "two letters from MALDEF questioning the validity of" a proposed ban.[348] Like other cities in the post-*Burke* period, Baldwin Park focused its ordinance on public safety concerns, making it unlawful for "any person to solicit while lying, sitting, standing or walking in any place which is a street or parking area."[349] The ordinance also banned solicitation on the sidewalk "if such use results in there being less than three (3) feet of free and clear passageway in, along, and through such pedestrian area."[350]

NDLON assumed the familiar role as vanguard, with Marco Amador organizing a few dozen workers on the corner in the lead-up to the ordinance's enactment. In coordination with Amador, Campbell visited the workers to discuss the "goals, risks and benefits" of a lawsuit.[351] She recalled that the workers were "aware of the risks" and "very pragmatic," asking: "Will you be the lawyer? Who will be the judge? Will we get arrested? How long will it take?"[352] Campbell also plotted legal strategy with NDLON's Newman and new attorney Marissa Nuncio.

Within MALDEF, Campbell was primarily responsible for handling the case, joined by Litigation Director Cynthia Valenzuela and a new Fried Frank fellow, Gladys Limón. Together, they attended City Council meetings and tried to negotiate a resolution with the city attorney. Yet, in Campbell's view, those efforts did not produce any "serious discussions" due to the "gung ho" position taken by Baldwin Park Mayor Manny Lozano,[353] who suggested at a hearing on the ordinance that he did not want MALDEF coming to Baldwin Park and telling city officials what to do.[354] Campbell did not see the tension in Baldwin Park as fundamentally a racial one: The city was 80% Latino as were all five city council members. Instead, it was about "Latino versus Latino class bias . . . about third-, fourth-, and fifth-generation Chicanos and Latinos not wanting new arrivals to have a place in their city."[355]

In June 2007, Campbell sued the city on behalf of the Jornaleros Unidos de Baldwin Park and NDLON (which had not yet experienced the standing setback

Figure 3.5 Tom Saenz speaking and day laborers protesting in Costa Mesa. *Source*: AP Photo/ Nick Ut (Feb. 2, 2010); Ken Steinhardt, *Orange County Register*/SCNG (2010).

in Lake Forest).[356] NDLON and MALDEF organized a well-publicized rally to announce the lawsuit—replete with workers carrying signs that read (in Spanish) "Reward Hard Work, Do Not Criminalize It" and "Work Yes, Ordinance No!"[357] The complaint followed the familiar model laid down by MALDEF—first arguing content discrimination, then contesting the ordinance's validity as a time, place, and manner restriction. The one wrinkle this time was triggered by a 2006 Ninth Circuit decision, *ACLU v. City of Las Vegas*,[358] in which the court struck down an ordinance barring solicitation from a redevelopment area as content-based because it prohibited one type of speech (solicitation) while permitting others (nonsolicitation).[359] MALDEF sought to apply the *Las Vegas* ruling to negate the Baldwin Park ordinance on content-discrimination grounds.

It worked. The district court, in a July 2007 order by Judge Edward Rafeedie (a President Reagan appointee), found the ordinance to be content-based and issued a preliminary injunction.[360] Immediately thereafter, the city's outside counsel called Campbell "and said if they repealed are you willing to dismiss?"[361] The lawyers wrote up a stipulation binding Baldwin Park to repeal the ordinance, with each party agreeing to bear its own legal costs.[362] MALDEF's Campbell told the clients that "the city would voluntarily rescind the ordinance; they would get no damages; but we couldn't guarantee that the city wouldn't reintroduce an ordinance in the future. That was satisfactory to them."[363]

The stipulation was signed less than ten days after the preliminary injunction was issued. However, the dismissal took until October 2007 to finalize.[364] The delay occurred as the mayor began "making noises about coming back with a constitutional ordinance."[365] At one point, a new ordinance was noticed for a City Council meeting, but Campbell and Newman were able to organize to quash it—encouraging California congresswoman Hilda Solis, who represented the district encompassing Baldwin Park, to speak to Mayor Lozano.[366] After she did, the mayor "took the ordinance off the agenda" and promised to create an organized day labor center.[367] The workers negotiated directly with Home Depot management to create a formal center,[368] out of which "a self-sustaining worker committee" was born in Baldwin Park.[369]

Organizing for Policy Impact: The AFL-CIO Partnership and Home Improvement Stores Ordinance

In the midst of these litigation battles, NDLON turned its organizing efforts to the policy arena, with campaigns to influence interconnected legislation at the local and federal levels. Since the late 1990s, day labor advocates had been working to advance an ordinance to require home improvement stores in Los Angeles to provide access to day labor hiring. The campaign was built around the basic fact that Home Depot was a magnet for day labor activity—and hence a flashpoint of hostility. The idea of enacting an ordinance was conceived as a way to both counteract city efforts to disperse day laborers and to create viable, self-financing centers for organizing. It was linked to the expansion of Home Depot in the L.A. market,[370] which advocates viewed as an opportunity to shift part of the cost of day labor centers to the company.

Narro, while at CHIRLA in the late 1990s, began advocating that Home Depot be required to establish a day labor hiring center as a condition of new store approval by the city. Narro first advanced this idea in Cypress Park, where Home Depot proposed to open a store in the early 2000s. Narro contacted the L.A. city council member representing the area, Mike Hernandez, who agreed to facilitate a deal. With Hernandez's support, Narro negotiated a license agreement with Home Depot under which the store allowed CHIRLA to operate a day labor center in a city-funded trailer on the store's parking lot.[371] In exchange, Hernandez agreed to facilitate city land use approval. Day labor advocates hoped to convert that victory into formal policy requiring home improvement stores to establish day labor centers. This approach avoided the contentious question of whether day laborers had a First Amendment right to solicit and instead emphasized the "win-win" scenario of mitigating the externalities of day labor by organizing workers at a single location—Home Depot—which (the argument was) would benefit from increased patronage by customers buying products and hiring day laborers at the same time. As Narro put it, "We didn't [go to] Home Depot saying, 'hey, we've got the First Amendment right to be here . . . .' [Instead, we said,] 'let's work on a mitigation plan that benefits you guys and benefits us.'"[372]

Against this backdrop,[373] the Los Angeles City Council began to move toward passage of an ordinance to require similar day labor centers in connection with all large-scale home improvement stores. In 2005, the Planning Commission recommended approval of a draft ordinance changing the conditional use permit for home improvement stores to require that they set aside areas for day laborers.[374]

However, this effort ran into the buzzsaw of national immigration reform. In 2005, the U.S. House of Representatives proposed a comprehensive immigration overhaul, known as the Sensenbrenner bill, named after its sponsor, Republican Jim Sensenbrenner from Wisconsin.[375] One of its provisions required all day labor centers to implement a system of employer verification, and another—in direct response to the pending L.A. legislation—preempted any city ordinance tying home improvement store approval to the creation of day labor centers.[376] Home Depot lobbied for this latter provision, which was inserted by Representative Chris Cannon from Utah.[377]

NDLON leaders went to Washington, D.C. to lobby against the bill, retaining Fred Feinstein, former general counsel to the National Labor Relations Board, to help NDLON make its case to Congress. Alvarado, Newman, and Feinstein met with House Speaker Nancy Pelosi's staff, but the initial reception was chilly. As Alvarado put it, "No one was going to help day laborers and we had to step in to fight."[378] Yet NDLON and its immigrant rights allies did not have the power to remove the anti-day labor provisions by themselves and were thus advised to seek reinforcement. As Alvarado recalled sympathetic lawmakers' blunt political assessment: "If you don't have [organized] labor with you, we can't help."[379] As a result, Alvarado reached out to union leaders in an effort to generate the necessary support.[380]

He succeeded in persuading a delegation from the AFL-CIO to meet with NDLON in Los Angeles. There, Alvarado and other NDLON staff took delegates to the Agoura Hills day labor site, where they witnessed a discussion among the day laborers over whether they should collectively agree to raise the minimum hourly wage at the corner from $12 to $15. As Alvarado recalled, when "eighty-five out of one hundred day laborers raised their hands" to increase the minimum wage, AFL-CIO officials recognized the historical parallel to "how the unions began."[381] In Alvarado's view, making this connection between day laborers and the formal union movement was key to solidifying AFL-CIO support.[382]

From there, the two sides began discussions about a formal affiliation, which was understood to be in both of their best interests. As Alvarado put it, "They needed us and we needed them."[383] The AFL-CIO was motivated by a desire to build support among immigrant workers—made more urgent in 2005 when several unions associated with aggressive organizing in communities of color broke away to form Change to Win.[384] For Alvarado, the motivation was "protection" since he believed that NDLON did not have the power to "protect day labor rights without having [union] support."[385] In August 2006, the AFL-CIO passed a historic policy, called the National Partnership Agreement Between the AFL-CIO and NDLON, permitting NDLON members to become affiliates of the AFL-CIO.[386] Under this agreement, the partners vowed to pursue comprehensive pro-immigrant reform at the federal level, while coordinating efforts to enforce immigrant rights at the local level.[387] It therefore promised greater resources for NDLON's ongoing battle to stem the tide of anti-solicitation back home.[388]

At the federal level, the AFL-CIO partnership immediately lent crucial muscle to NDLON's effort to prevent anti-day labor provisions from being included in the Senate's version of the immigration reform bill,[389] which was introduced in May 2007 as part of a "grand bargain" that included enhanced border security and a pathway to citizenship for undocumented immigrants. During consideration of the bill, Senator Johnny Isakson, a Republican from Georgia, where Home Depot was headquartered,[390] introduced an amendment that would have (like its House counterpart) prevented cities from requiring home improvement stores to establish day labor centers as a condition of opening.[391] Although NDLON leaders were able to secure commitments from all Democratic Senators (except Diane Feinstein of California) to vote against the amendment, they nonetheless worried that a lengthy floor debate over day labor would be politically damaging.[392] To put pressure on Home Depot to withdraw the amendment, NDLON threatened to organize large protests at its Atlanta headquarters. When it did, "Home Depot got scared . . . and negotiations began."[393] However, when it became clear that there were not enough votes to end debate on the overall bill, the grand bargain collapsed and the bill died without the amendment being considered.

Figure 3.6 NDLON's Pablo Alvarado and AFL-CIO President John Sweeney announcing day labor partnership. *Source*: Tim Boyle/Getty Images (August 9, 2006).

With the specter of federal preemption lifted, the path was cleared for Los Angeles to reconsider its Home Improvement Stores Ordinance. Indeed, the ugly federal preemption fight was viewed by some day labor advocates as adding momentum to the local effort to pass the ordinance, which became a symbolic test of the city's power to use land use laws to influence labor standards.[394] It was in this context that the Los Angeles City Council—led by Bernard Parks, who had a large Home Depot store in his district[395]—enacted the Home Improvement Stores Ordinance in August 2008,[396] after four years of advocacy.[397] The ordinance gave the city discretion to require large-scale (a hundred thousand or more square feet) home improvement stores to establish an accessible day labor center in order to obtain a conditional use permit.[398] A year later, in the midst of recession, although no Home Depots had yet created day labor centers, there were thirteen proposed stores pending.[399]

Litigation Above (and Beyond) Organizing: The Uncertain Appeal of Law

Reckoning in Redondo Beach

The momentum gained by day labor advocates through 2008 in the litigation and policymaking realms was challenged by a changing economic, political, and legal terrain. The recession devastated the day labor market, particularly as construction came to a halt. While some day laborers returned to their countries of origin, many stayed and tried to scrape by.[400] In this environment, organizing proceeded apace, with a major workshop at the Downtown Labor Center in 2008 to discuss policy options to strengthen the enforcement of wage and hour laws for day laborers.

The political environment changed too, as immigrants again were scapegoated for economic insecurity and the emerging Tea Party movement made anti-immigration policy a key tenet. Localities around the country took repressive steps to criminalize immigrants' status and activity, symbolized by the 2010 passage of Arizona's Senate Bill (S.B.) 1070, which included provisions subjecting undocumented immigrants to state criminal penalties (a provision later invalidated by the Supreme Court) and authorizing state law enforcement officers to demand documentation from anyone suspected of lacking legal authorization (a provision left standing).[401] In addition, the law banned day laborers and prospective employers from impeding traffic[402]—a provision directly traceable to anti-solicitation ordinances pioneered in the greater L.A. area. A team of legal rights groups, featuring the ACLU and MALDEF, came together to challenge the various provisions of S.B. 1070 in a case that would make

Figure 3.7 Victor Narro (bottom row, third from left) and day laborers convening workshop on wage theft at the UCLA Downtown Labor Center. *Source*: UCLA Downtown Labor Center (2008).

its way to the U.S. Supreme Court. However, for MALDEF and the day labor legal team, there was still unfinished business at home.

In that regard, the legal strategy carefully built by Saenz and his colleagues suffered a major setback in the Redondo Beach appeal.[403] Whereas Glendale had appealed to gain leverage in settlement, Redondo Beach took its resistance one step further by rejecting any notion of compromise.[404] Instead, Redondo Beach sought to set precedent upholding the legality of anti-solicitation ordinances by reclaiming the Ninth Circuit's 1986 *ACORN* decision—in which the court upheld Phoenix's ordinance prohibiting the practice of tagging, defined as soliciting funds from passing motorists—as doctrinal support.

To do so, the Redondo Beach city attorney had to invalidate the careful district court record that had been compiled by Saenz—but did not have to contend with Saenz directly. When Saenz left for the mayor's office, LCCR's Robert Rubin and Philip Hwang took the reins of the appeal—joined by pro bono lawyers from the law firm Morrison & Foerster, and supported by MALDEF's Kristina Campbell and Cynthia Valenzuela.[405] In the appellate process, Hwang was lead attorney, following much of the strategy and substance laid out by MALDEF while "updating the cases and arguments, and adding examples."[406] Briefing was completed in 2007 and Hwang argued the 2008 appeal as the lawyer most "involved in briefing at that point."[407]

After the argument but before its decision, the Ninth Circuit issued an en banc opinion in *Berger v. City of Seattle*,[408] which struck down rules that set locations for street performances, permitted only passive solicitation of money, and prohibited performers from communicating with visitors waiting in line at the Seattle Center.[409] The panel handling the Redondo Beach appeal asked for supplemental briefing on the impact of *Berger*, which Hwang viewed as an "optimistic" sign since the logic of *Berger* argued against the Redondo Beach ordinance's legality.[410]

This optimism proved to be misplaced. On June 9, 2010, the panel—consisting of Ninth Circuit Judges Kim Wardlaw, a Clinton appointee, and Sandra Ikuta, a George W. Bush appointee, alongside Alaska-based District Court Judge Ralph Beistline, another Bush appointee (sitting by designation)—reversed the lower court injunction in a split decision, with Wardlaw issuing a scathing dissent. The majority agreed with the district court that the ordinance was content-neutral, distinguishing the *Berger* case on the ground that the ordinance there had discriminatorily outlawed a particular type of speech—"requests for donations, such as 'I'd like you to give me some money if you enjoyed my performance' "—rather than prohibiting the general, content-neutral "act of solicitation" as Redondo Beach had done.[411]

The circuit court, however, then departed significantly from the lower court on the issues of narrow tailoring and alternative means of communication. Relying heavily on *ACORN*, the majority found that day labor solicitation raised the same "risks of traffic disruption and injury" as the tagging activity in that case.[412] It thus concluded that the ordinance "targets only in-person demands directed at occupants of vehicles, and thus specifically addresses traffic flow and safety, the evils Redondo Beach sought to combat."[413] On the issue of alternatives, the court held that ample means for solicitation still existed since employers "can park legally and respond to solicitations made by individuals on foot without either party to the transaction violating the ordinance."[414] Wardlaw's dissent vigorously disputed the application of ACORN and the majority's conclusions as to the reasonableness of the restrictions. Yet the damage had been done. The decade-long path to a definitive ruling on the merits by the Ninth Circuit striking down anti-solicitation ordinances had resulted in just the opposite.

The panel decision, however, did not ultimately end the case. By the time the Ninth Circuit panel's ruling was issued in June 2010, Saenz had returned to MALDEF and he, along with Valenzuela, Campbell, and Limón, worked with LCCR lawyers to draft a petition for rehearing en banc, arguing that review was "necessary to maintain the uniformity of this Court's precedent, and to preserve the quintessential nature of sidewalks as public fora."[415] Rehearings en banc, conducted by an eleven-judge panel, were reserved for cases presenting the most important legal issues and could only be granted by an affirmative vote of the majority of active, nonrecused Ninth Circuit judges. It was, as the lawyers knew, a long shot—but it was the only shot left. To make it count, on June 30, the day labor legal team submitted a petition for rehearing that put forward their premier arguments: distinguishing ACORN as inapplicable to sidewalk speech restrictions, applying Berger's content-discrimination analysis, and emphasizing the overbroad nature of the Redondo Beach ordinance.[416]

In a rare and significant move, on October 15, the Ninth Circuit agreed rehear the case en banc, which meant it would be reargued and decided by an eleven-judge panel, whose decision would supersede the June 2010 three-judge panel ruling. No further briefing was required because the en banc panel reviewed the briefs previously submitted to the three-judge panel. It was a remarkable decision—a lifeline in a case on life support. Yet the day labor legal team's euphoria was quickly tempered by the announcement of the eleven en banc judges: Alex Kozinski, Sidney Thomas, Susan Graber, Ronald Gould, Marsha Berzon, Jay Bybee, Consuelo Callahan, Carlos Bea, Milan Smith Jr., Sandra Ikuta, and Randy Smith. From an ideological perspective—in the mythically liberal Ninth Circuit[417]—the panel could not have been much worse. Seven of the judges were appointed by Republican presidents, all but one of whom, Judge Kozinski (a Reagan appointee), by President George W. Bush (this included Judge Ikuta, who had already ruled against the plaintiffs in the underlying panel decision).[418] In addition, although Judges Graber and Gould were Clinton appointees, they were considered conservative.[419] This draw underscored the roulette nature of judicial assignment and the peculiarity of the en banc process in the very large Ninth Circuit, in which a majority of judges could vote to approve a rehearing en banc (suggesting support for reversing the panel), but those actually selected by lottery to sit on the panel (a subset of the total court) could be ideologically disinclined to reverse. Oral arguments were set for March 21, 2011, in San Francisco. Saenz and his colleagues prepared furiously, trying to remain optimistic in the face of such a disappointing luck of the draw.

If Saenz himself was concerned, his performance at oral argument did not betray any doubt.[420] As lawyer for the appellees, Saenz followed Redondo Beach City Attorney Michael Webb, whose workmanlike argument stressed that the city "after several years of extreme difficulty dealing with traffic issues caused by persons soliciting employment from the highway or roadway . . . copied, word-for-word, an ordinance that had been approved by this court some eight months before" in *ACORN*. Webb was immediately challenged on the issue of overbreadth—whether the statute was narrowly drafted to address the city's purported traffic concerns. Judge Berzon directly called this question: "One of my overall reactions to this case is: Why didn't you write the ordinance to cover what you wanted it to cover rather than all manner of other things?" Webb responded that the city was only trying to do what the Ninth Circuit had instructed in *ACORN*, but the panel appeared unmoved.

Sensing an opening, when Saenz took the podium, he immediately homed in on the ordinance's scope: "This action relates to a Redondo Beach ordinance adopted some twenty-four years ago. As this case went along, Redondo Beach added a contention that despite the plain language of this ordinance, its only effort was to bar that solicitation that resulted in a car stopping in traffic. Now that concern . . . could have been easily addressed through existing laws against jaywalking, against obstructing traffic, against illegally stopping." Judge Kozinski, considered a free speech stalwart, interrupted.

Kozinski: But they say that's not adequate. That's what they say.
Saenz: Yes, but they've put nothing in the record to indicate why it is not adequate. And as you know, your honor, one of the tests they have to satisfy to render this ordinance constitutional is that it's narrowly tailored to serve a significant government interest. The first test that's been articulated by the Supreme Court for determining—
Kozinski: But narrowly tailored doesn't mean it has to be *the* narrowest way of doing it or there isn't a better way of achieving the same ends.
Saenz: That's correct. You have to be able to demonstrate—*prove*, because it is the burden of the city—that its aims could not be achieved less effectively absent the regulation. Well, they've *asserted* that, but I don't think there is anything in the record or anything in logic to explain why, if your concern is about—
Kozinski: They say: "We've tried it the other way, it didn't work."
Saenz: [Pause] Well, I have to say, your honor, twenty-four years later there are still day laborers on the streets of Redondo Beach so it appears that this ordinance doesn't work either.

Staring down Kozinski, who throughout the argument would remain the ordinance's strongest defender, Saenz had set the tone. Drawing on the skills that made him a decorated oralist in law school and seizing the moment that he had carefully built over the preceding decade, Saenz proceeded to spar with a lively panel, parrying questions from all quarters with clarity and steady confidence. Although he asserted that "*ACORN* is a decision that is no longer good law and the court should say that," he nonetheless parsed the numerous factual distinctions between the tagging targeted by the Phoenix ordinance and day labor solicitation. Unpersuaded, Kozinski pressed Saenz to explain the difference between the solicitation of funds from motorists, at issue in *ACORN*, and the solicitation of work by day laborers, both of which Kozinski argued involved a financial transaction. When Saenz pointed out that tagging tended to be a more protracted transaction, Kozinski stated, "I bet you if we had a race, I could pull out a dollar faster than you could load a couple of people in your car." Without missing a beat, Saenz responded, "I'd take that bet, your honor."

To distinguish *ACORN*, Judge Smith focused on the "(b) portion" of the Redondo Beach ordinance, which prohibited *drivers* from trying to hire day laborers. When Saenz agreed that, unlike the Phoenix ordinance, Redondo Beach's law prohibited *both* parties in a willing commercial exchange, Kozinski pounced again, suggesting that Saenz's acknowledgment that "this is a marketplace" cut against his position because the burden of overturning government regulation of *commercial* transactions was much higher. Keeping his wits in the face of another one of Kozinski's repeated interruptions, Saenz replied flatly, "The City of Redondo Beach has never attempted to defend this as a regulation of commercial speech." Kozinski persisted, contending in regard to alternative channels of communication that the day laborers, unlike organizers of a parade or protest, could assemble "in a stadium, in a basketball court, . . . in an outdoor theater." Saenz was nonplussed: "With a parade, a demonstration, *and* day labor, it is a matter of reaching your intended audience."

Pressing his advantage, Saenz sought to undercut the argument that the ordinance should be construed narrowly in relation to the city's limited enforcement of solicitation that interfered with traffic. He emphasized the danger that the ordinance's plain language would chill day labor speech that the city conceded was legal—like signaling from the sidewalk for a driver to pull over to a safe location outside the flow of traffic. Highlighting the contradiction at the heart of the city's position, Saenz pointed out, "If the day laborer is doing what the city concedes is permissible under this ordinance, under this ordinance [he] will still be violating it." When Kozinski, in a last-ditch effort, stated that he had personally never seen a day laborer signal for a driver to pull over to a safe position, Saenz—who had dedicated his entire professional career to standing with day laborers—only had to reply: "I have seen it your honor, seen them say, 'Pull over into a parking lot.' It does occur." Kozinski, for once, was silent. Although there were additional skirmishes over standing, the argument was effectively over—with the general consensus on the day labor side that it could not have gone better. There was nothing left to do but wait.

Although only six months, the wait must have seemed like an eternity for everyone involved in the day labor movement, whose monumental struggle—from the early failure in Agoura Hills, to the first victory in Los Angeles County, through the pitched battles in Orange County—had culminated to this point. But when the decision was handed down, on September 16, 2011, it must have all seemed worthwhile. It was a stunning victory for the day laborers. In a majority opinion authored by conservative Milan Smith, a Brigham Young University graduate and George W. Bush appointee who had been a Republican senator from Oregon, the court held that Redondo Beach's ordinance, although content-neutral, was not narrowly tailored and thus violated the First Amendment.[421] Completely buying into Saenz's framing of the case, the majority rejected the city's invitation to read the statute so as to only prohibit solicitation by day laborers who "cause motorists to stop in traffic lanes in response to the solicitation," stating that the "plain language of the Ordinance ... is not reasonably susceptible to the City's narrowing construction."[422] The court criticized the "illogic" of the city's position on appeal, in which it argued that "the Ordinance would not apply to a person standing on the sidewalk holding a sign that says 'Looking for work.' In the district court, the City asserted that the ordinance *would* apply to a person standing on the sidewalk holding a sign that says, 'I'm available to be hired today, Please stop and talk to me.' The proposed distinguishing feature—*please stop and talk to me*—is wholly absent from the face of the Ordinance, and we cannot rewrite the Ordinance to supply the missing concept."[423]

Moving on to narrow tailoring, the court adopted the plaintiffs' argument that the ordinance was significantly overinclusive as to speech, its language applying to "children selling lemonade on the sidewalk in front of their home, as well as Girl Scouts selling cookies on the sidewalk outside of their school," while also prohibiting "sidewalk food vendors from advertising their wares to passing motorists" and even "school children shouting 'carwash' at passing vehicles."[424] The court further asserted that the ordinance was also "geographically overinclusive" since it applied to all city streets even though there was only evidence that solicitation-related traffic was a problem at a few sites.[425] Because the city had less restrictive means available to address traffic concerns—such as enforcing laws against jaywalking, parking at red curbs, and standing in the street—the court concluded that the ordinance failed to pass the First Amendment test.[426] In the end, aside from assuming "for the purposes of our decision that the Ordinance is content-neutral,"[427] the court gave the plaintiffs nearly everything they could have wanted. It overruled *ACORN* "to the extent that it is inconsistent with our en banc decision in this case" and effectively overturned the earlier Lake Forest decision on standing by adopting the three-judge panel's conclusion that the Redondo Beach ordinance had injured NDLON—frustrating its mission and causing it to divert resources to litigation—thus conferring organizational standing.[428] Judge Smith himself, along with Judges

Thomas and Graber, would have gone even further to hold—as they argued in a special concurrence—that the Redondo Beach ordinance was "content based on its face" because "it prohibits certain subject matters—any solicitation related to 'employment, business, or contributions'—and allows other solicitation (such as political solicitation) to continue unabated."[429]

In what came as no surprise to those who watched oral argument, Judge Kozinksi, joined by Judge Bea, offered a "deep dissent," which began by stating, "This is folly," and went on to offer a stridently toned defense of the Redondo Beach ordinance that—while making a plausible case for upholding the law—undercut its own power by its flippant tone.[430] As if hoping to win the argument by hyperbole, Kozinski opened by stating that the "majority is demonstrably, egregiously, recklessly wrong. If I could dissent twice, I would."[431] Referring to day laborers as "a bunch of scraggly men smoking and spitting while waiting for jobs," Kozinski cast about for arguments, going so far as to deny that speech was even at issue in the case, instead claiming that what the ordinance did was "to regulate a very narrow and finely drawn class of conduct: standing around on sidewalks and street corners in order to interact with passing motorists."[432] At his most cogent, Kozinski questioned the majority's decision to read the ordinance in its broadest terms, suggesting that the narrower construction of solicitation as "requiring a face-to-face conversation with a vehicle occupant for the purpose of consummating a transaction on the spot," was "at least plausible."[433] As Kozinski concluded, "For us to now find Redondo Beach's ordinance 'not reasonably susceptible' to an interpretation the city adopted by slavishly copying language we ourselves approved is so strange I have trouble wrapping my head around it."[434] Going all in, Kozinski further suggested curing the ordinance's constitutional defect by preserving "part (b)" and queried why day laborers lacked alternative channels of communication since no one prohibited them "from advertising in the newspaper or on Craigslist—as many do."[435] Yet, for all of his rhetorical flare and superheated claims, Kozinski was tilting at windmills. The Redondo Beach anti-solicitation ordinance—enacted nearly twenty-five years earlier as the region's pioneering symbol of anti-day labor animus—was no more.

Aftermath

MALDEF's victory in *Comite de Jornaleros v. Redondo Beach* was a peak moment in a day labor movement marked by persistence in the face of implacable hostility by (mostly) white communities against the brown men who assembled each morning to earn a living. It was a career-defining win for Saenz and his team: the type of success that rarely comes for any lawyer, much less one on the side of the most marginalized members of society—but made all the more sweet by that very fact. The litigation itself was in many ways the culmination of a conventional test-case strategy in which MALDEF, the ACLU, and LCCR had built favorable precedent over time, waiting for the moment to call the ultimate legal question, and hoping when the question did get called, there would be receptive judges to answer it. In that regard, the legal team likely breathed a collective sigh of relief when the U.S. Supreme Court, on February 21, 2012, denied certiorari, letting stand the Ninth Circuit en banc panel decision. Yet in winning that decision, the day labor lawyers had also redefined the test-case strategy, melding it with a grassroots effort to build day labor power, and in the process helping to spark a movement with the capacity to carry forward the struggle after the thrill of the legal win subsided.

For their part, the MALDEF lawyers wasted little time celebrating. Instead, less than a month after the Supreme Court refused the *Redondo Beach* appeal, Saenz sent letters to a dozen cities with ordinances like the one the Ninth Circuit had struck down, demanding that the cities repeal their laws or face litigation. *The New York Times* editorial board weighed in on the day laborers' behalf, noting—in a piece titled "They Want to Work"—that MALDEF had recently demanded that the cities "erase these unconstitutional blots from their books and spare themselves the effort and expense of litigation that they would certainly lose. They should listen."[436] The editorial board went on:

> Officials who strike harsh poses on immigration often focus their anger and law-enforcement firepower on day laborers, who are among the most visible and vulnerable of the recent immigrant population. It doesn't matter to them that these laborers are violating no laws and personify hallowed conservative ideals of hard work and self-sufficiency. But, in criminalizing the act of looking for work, these hard-liners are not only being cruel and counterproductive. They are putting themselves on the wrong side of the most fundamental law of the land.[437]

In the end, many cities opted not to be on the wrong side. Sixteen repealed anti-solicitation ordinances after the *Redondo Beach* ruling, including the day labor movement's bitter nemesis, Costa Mesa, which rescinded its traffic interference ban in 2013.[438] However, it was clear that day labor advocates would not be taking an easy victory lap and calling the battle over. There were already signs that local resistance to day labor would continue, albeit in different legal or extralegal forms. Some cities that repealed ordinances continued targeting day laborers by enforcing existing traffic laws against them or through sheer harassment. Others, like Tustin and Cypress, amended their ordinances to more directly prohibit solicitation that interfered with traffic—precisely the type of narrow tailoring that that the *Redondo Beach* court suggested could pass constitutional muster. There were other legal tensions in the day laborers' First Amendment argument, revealed during the *Redondo Beach* case, which potentially opened the door to stricter regulation. Most notably, as Judge Kozinski raised hypothetically during oral argument, if day laborers were engaged in commercial speech—an issue not argued by the city on appeal—the government would have more latitude to impose restrictions.

The issues of commercial speech and narrow tailoring were front and center in the Arizona S.B. 1070 case, as immigrant rights groups, including MALDEF, challenged that law's provisions prohibiting day laborers from soliciting work from a stopped car that impeded traffic (motorists were also subject to the ban). Two years after *Redondo Beach*, the Ninth Circuit again was asked to rule on the constitutionality of an anti-solicitation law—and to answer questions left open by the earlier precedent. From the day labor movement's standpoint, the outcome was positive, although the legal route the court used to get there raised concerns. Directly answering Kozinski's *Redondo Beach* hypothetical, the Ninth Circuit determined that the solicitation provision of S.B. 1070 did, in fact, only restrict "commercial speech."[439] However, addressing the content question it had avoided in *Redondo Beach*, the court held that the Arizona provisions were content-based because they "target one type of speech—day labor solicitation that impedes traffic—but say nothing about other types of roadside solicitation and nonsolicitation speech."[440] From there, the court went on to rule that, although the Arizona law—because it only banned solicitation blocking traffic—was less restrictive than Redondo Beach's, it still failed under the narrow tailoring prong of the First Amendment test, since Arizona had other laws at its disposal to "address legitimate traffic safety concerns without burdening speech."[441] Accordingly, the Ninth Circuit upheld the district court's injunction against S.B. 1070's solicitation provisions. In doing so, it reaffirmed the fundamental right of day laborers to seek work in public places—albeit on grounds that suggested the fluidity of the doctrine and the potential fault lines of future legal battles.

Analysis

At the outset of the L.A. day labor movement, conditions were relatively favorable for an impact litigation campaign to challenge anti-solicitation ordinances given the legal and organizing capacity to support the campaign, and the nature of the right asserted, which was grounded upon credible First Amendment precedent protecting the freedom of day laborers to voluntarily seek work in public space. There were also challenges (strong countermovement opposition and jurisdictional fragmentation) as well as risks (some adverse precedent combined with the unpredictability of judicial assignments). How did advocates succeed and what did they achieve? This part appraises the litigation campaign by examining how changing personnel and tactics interacted with evolving policy and politics to shape the urban geography of anti-solicitation in the greater L.A. area.

Building a Legal Field

Leadership

The trajectory of day labor advocacy can be understood, in part, through the stories of individual lawyers and activists who assumed leadership positions, built new organizational structures, and invested time and resources to develop and implement strategies. This leadership was institutionally embedded, occurring within an evolving field in which each success created new opportunities for advocates to take on important roles. However, success ultimately depended on individuals seizing those opportunities to advance the day labor cause. It is useful, therefore, to trace the contributions of the intellectual architects and organizational entrepreneurs who made choices—often in the face of political and professional risk—to defend day labor.

On the legal side, Nancy Cervantes blazed an important early path. A law student organizer in the initial Glendale campaign, she founded CHIRLA's Day Labor Outreach Project, then launched the L.A. day labor pilot program, after which she helped litigate the Agoura Hills case as an attorney at Public Counsel. Cervantes later became director of the Workers' Rights Project at CHIRLA, where she led an expansion of the group's day labor organizing. At each step, she left behind institutional building blocks that were used by advocates who followed.

One of these was Thomas Saenz, the chief architect of the federal litigation strategy, which he pushed at a time when "MALDEF was on its own" due to the reluctance of other legal groups after Agoura Hills to wade into anti-solicitation litigation. Saenz's approach built upon the claims advanced in Agoura Hills but honed and repackaged them in a way he believed would present the most compelling case. His contribution, however, went beyond the development of litigation strategy to also include institution-building efforts that extended outside of MALDEF and endured after his 2005 departure—while paving the way for his 2009 return. Saenz raised money from the Rosenberg Foundation to establish a day labor project at MALDEF, created an internal database of ordinances, made key hires including Belinda Escobosa Helzer, Shaheena Simons, and Araceli Perez,[442] and built partnerships with outside organizations, like LCCR, to facilitate skilled stewardship of the Glendale and Redondo Beach cases in his absence. Finally, his personal capacity to relate to day laborers and value the contributions of organizers helped build relationships that were crucial to creating long-term alliances. This quality was noted by Victor Narro, who observed a "different dynamic" between lawyers and organizers after Saenz left for the L.A. mayor's office. While Saenz "really believed in the concept of transparency and working things out, others were paternalistic, creating a lot of tension."[443] NDLON's Veronica Federosky echoed this sentiment, placing Saenz in the category of lawyers who would "make the effort to earn the workers' trust, instead of just going and reporting" on the litigation.[444] He imbued this spirit in his protégés, particularly Helzer, who left MALDEF to carry on the day labor struggle in OC. As she put it, a key part of her lawyering involved working with NDLON to build trust with the workers, showing them "that we are here to help you and are not going to expose you, report you, or trick you."[445]

On the organizing front, Pablo Alvarado's rise as NDLON's leader was a crucial movement development. A highly educated former day laborer, he had the unique combination of legitimacy, intellectual vision, and charisma that allowed him to bring together day laborers from around the country to build an independent movement base. A key strength was his ability to operate effectively at different institutional levels. As Chris Newman recounted, Alvarado was a committed practitioner of popular education, who was able to build grassroots leadership (evident in his success forming day labor committees), thereby "empower[ing] day laborers to be protagonists in their own stories."[446] At the same time, he was a full partner in strategic agenda-setting with lawyers and unions (as his successful alliances with MALDEF and the AFL-CIO highlight), while having the organizational wherewithal to shift day labor organizing from a small program housed at CHIRLA to a separately funded organizational structure, NDLON, which by 2010 had fourteen staff members, including two development staff and three attorneys.

The establishment of NDLON created space for other leaders to emerge. Newman, in particular, benefited from Alvarado's trailblazing, which not only served as professional inspiration, but also gave him the organizational opportunity to pursue his calling as an NDLON attorney. Newman used that opportunity to expand NDLON's in-house legal capacity. In 2010, he was serving as the group's national legal director—responsible for developing strategic partnerships and connecting member organizations with legal services—joined by Jessica Karp, a staff attorney working on anti-solicitation, and Nadia Marin, former director of the Workplace Project on Long Island, who focused on employment rights.

As Newman's career path underscored, the exercise of leadership paid career dividends. This was true of other actors in the movement, particularly Alvarado, who gained widespread attention when featured in a *Time* magazine profile of the "25 Most Influential Hispanics in America" as "the new Cesar Chavez."[447] However, the exercise of leadership also exacted professional costs. Although Saenz assumed the presidency of MALDEF, he was passed over (after initially being selected) for the position of assistant attorney general for civil rights in the Obama Department of Justice because of the controversial nature of his immigrant rights advocacy.

Networks

The individual choices and trajectories of the advocates were woven into a broader tapestry in which advocates shifted organizational affiliations but continued to engage in day labor networks as a way to promote continuity, extend expertise, and maintain solidarity. The networks operated at two levels.

First, there were formal networks established to create opportunities for advocates to make contacts and share resources. The original coalition that challenged Glendale's proposed ordinance in 1988 grew out of the Los Angeles Labor Defense Network, which had been created to support low-wage workers across different industries. CHIRLA and then NDLON were both coalitions founded upon organizational networks in order to facilitate exchange among member groups.

Second, there were informal, albeit powerful, personal and professional networks among advocates, which stimulated innovative collaborations and sustained commitment over time. Perhaps the most important collaboration was between MALDEF and NDLON, giving rise to the mobilization template used throughout the campaign. This collaboration was forged by Saenz and Alvarado and deepened by other actors who played significant roles. Narro, who began with Saenz at MALDEF, helped to incubate NDLON as part of CHIRLA's Workers' Rights Project and continued to support its work at the UCLA Downtown Labor Center, which became NDLON's host site. Network participation also served to vouch for commitment to the day labor cause, resulting in new career opportunities and sustained professional relationships. For instance, when Villagra left MALDEF to open the ACLU office in OC, his first hire was Helzer, who had been his MALDEF colleague. Simons, who succeeded Helzer at MALDEF, emphasized the enduring personal bonds forged through the day labor network: "There was a deep respect that we all had for each other. I look back at that work as a very special time and a time of growth as a lawyer, as a person, and in terms of my understanding of the world."[448]

Integrated Advocacy

Litigation on the Edge of Occam's Razor

How much did the lawyering itself affect the outcome of the day labor cases? Did the choice of venue, the nature of the claims, or the quality of the advocacy affect outcomes on the merits? Although there are no definitive answers to these questions because single variables cannot be isolated, it is possible to highlight some of the key aspects of the legal strategy and the trade-offs they involved.

Central to the MALDEF litigation strategy was Saenz's "Occam's Razor" approach:[449] Focus on free speech, not identity-based discrimination, and present a single, powerful argument, rather than cluttering the complaint with multiple causes of action. With this strategy in place, the key issue was limiting the Ninth Circuit's *ACORN* decision on tagging to its facts.

The benefits of this strategy were apparent. Free speech was a political value that cut across identity groups, and the "right to work" unfettered by government regulation could be presented as a core principle that resonated with both redistributive and libertarian politics. The First Amendment frame cast day laborers in their most favorable light: active, diligent, and contributing to the economic good by taking jobs no one else wanted. As Villagra suggested, this frame presented day laborers as agents, while "soften[ing] the [case's] edges to gain broader appeal."[450] A discrimination frame, in contrast, would label day laborers as victims and suggest that they needed special solicitude. Though that may have been true, the lawyers decided that it made for a less compelling and possibly less winnable legal argument: Without evidence of intent, a race or national origin discrimination claim was unlikely to prevail.

Yet this approach also risked imposing movement costs. As a "surrogate" for a race or national origin claim,[451] the free speech argument potentially elided what was ultimately at stake in the anti-solicitation ordinances by obscuring the real motivation of its proponents: to eliminate immigrant workers from the street. Failing to name that reality in litigation risked undermining its power to mobilize public opinion and advance the broader goal of the immigrant rights movement: promoting a more inclusive immigration policy.[452] If the ordinances were only about speech, and not about membership, then that objective would not be explicitly named.

Ultimately, the legal team made a calculation that the discrimination argument would have less legal traction and be more likely to generate political backlash. The lawyers made a choice to maximize the chance for success on the legal merits to advance the immediate movement goal (eliminating ordinances) rather than to make stronger claims that may have supported the immigrant rights movement's most ambitious agenda. As Table 3.1 shows, the campaign's federal court–civil liberties approach produced a series of court wins (cutting across judicial ideology) and positive settlements.

The favorable outcomes all occurred in federal court; the unfavorable outcomes were in state superior court (in the Agoura Hills case) and federal appellate court (in the *Redondo Beach* panel decision, which was superseded by the en banc court's ruling). Of the positive outcomes prior to the 2011 *Redondo Beach* en banc decision, two resulted in ordinances being repealed (Lake Forest and Baldwin Park), two resulted in settlements that required cities to amend their ordinances to permit solicitation on the sidewalk (Rancho Cucamonga–Upland and Glendale), and one (Los Angeles County) resulted in the ordinance being permanently enjoined (though it remained on the books). The *Redondo Beach* en banc decision permanently enjoined the Redondo Beach ordinance—and effectively nullified all similar citywide bans. In the wake of that decision, Costa Mesa formally repealed its ordinance, as did fifteen other jurisdictions. Of the post-Agoura Hills lawsuits, all involved facial First Amendment challenges, except Lake Forest, which involved an applied challenge to ongoing enforcement practices after the ordinance's formal repeal. The initial six lawsuits challenged first-generation ordinances—the complete citywide solicitation ban, applying to streets and sidewalks, pioneered by Redondo Beach—while the last two challenged second-generation ordinances—those that attempted to move beyond the complete ban model to more narrowly target solicitation that interfered with traffic (Baldwin Park's ordinance banned solicitation "while lying, sitting, standing or walking in any place which is a street or parking area," while Costa Mesa's prohibited "active" solicitation designed to distract drivers). The free speech challenges to first-generation ordinances emphasized overbreadth, while the challenges to second-generation ordinances claimed vagueness (Glendale's ordinance was also struck down in part on vagueness grounds).

Table 3.1 Outcome of day labor cases in greater L.A. area.

Jurisdiction	Agoura Hills	Los Angeles County	Rancho Cucamonga–Upland	Glendale	Redondo Beach	Lake Forest	Baldwin Park	Costa Mesa
Year Filed	1991	1998	2002	2004	2004	2007	2007	2010
Result	Law upheld	Permanent injunction	Settled + law amended	Settled + law amended	Permanent injunction	Law repealed + settled	Preliminary injunction + law repealed	Law repealed

In terms of organizational leadership, the first four federal court cases (Los Angeles County, Rancho Cucamonga–Upland, Glendale, and Redondo Beach), involved MALDEF and Saenz at the district court level; the Redondo Beach appeal was handled by LCCR, although the en banc appeal was again handled by MALDEF upon Saenz's return. The Lake Forest and Costa Mesa cases were brought by the ACLU in OC, and the Baldwin Park case was brought by MALDEF before Saenz's return.

Lawyering Outside the Box

Although the day labor movement lawyers opted for an impact litigation strategy, they did so as part of a broader integrated approach, in which they targeted different advocacy domains (courts, legislatures, media), at different levels (federal, state, and local), with different tactics (litigation, popular education/organizing, and lobbying).[453] Their goals were both defensive (to resist anti-solicitation ordinances) and offensive (to promote organized day labor hiring centers while creating a more positive public narrative about day labor). The lawyers engaged in a range of tactics "outside the box" of conventional lawyering—all with an eye toward advancing their goals through the most effective channels available.

There were repeated examples of this integrated approach throughout the campaign. In Agoura Hills, lawyers organized students to pose as day laborers and coordinated with local news media to film their arrest. In Ladera Heights, lawyers engaged Supervisor Burke through private meetings and mediation sessions, organized outreach to HomeBase management and law enforcement officials, and conducted a media strategy that included a sharply worded op-ed criticizing the proposed ordinance. After the county case, *CHIRLA v. Burke*, lawyers pursued a model that combined litigation with mass demonstration and street-level organizing. In Redondo Beach, NDLON's Newman coordinated with the public defender's office to make sure the lawyers understood how individual prosecutions related to the broader advocacy strategy; he also worked behind the scenes to organize amicus briefs to the Ninth Circuit and to place a *Los Angeles Times* editorial urging the court to strike down the ordinance.[454] Individual lawyers performed other tasks, which included testifying at a City Council hearing on the proposed ordinance in Baldwin Park and educating day laborers about where they could legally solicit in Orange. In addition, Victor Narro played a key role in drafting the L.A. Home Improvement Stores Ordinance and pressing for its enactment.

These activities matched the lawyers' attitudes about lawyering, which were generally framed in multidimensional terms. Helzer, for instance, stated that she approached cases as problems, always asking, "What is the best solution?"[455] The answer could be litigation, but also policy advocacy or organizing, depending on the situation. "You try to use all the tools in your toolbox" in "a collaborative effort.... It can't be from the top down."[456] Preciado echoed this point, asserting that "you have to have advocacy, organizing [and other strategies] as part of one package to be effective."[457] Newman, a self-described "Freire guy" inspired by the Workplace Project, believed in advocacy that was "keyed into different ways that lawyers could help."[458] Villagra had a related perspective on how he framed legal arguments, stating that "we move from mode to mode," adapting underlying legal theories depending on a pragmatic assessment of what is likely to be most effective in a given context.[459]

In general, the day labor lawyers were candid and self-conscious about the limits of litigation, while nonetheless acknowledging its importance in creating space for day laborers to find work. Saenz acknowledged that "litigation is not a stand-alone" because it is "too slow moving and episodic," and that a "sustained effort" to organize workers was an essential part of advancing their rights.[460] Narro put the point more directly: "Lawyers should never litigate without organizing."[461]

From Cervantes's perspective, litigation had been "equally important" as organizing in the day labor movement: While organizing gave the workers a "voice," litigation was "another feather in the quill," necessary to "send a message" to cities that day labor rights would be defended in multiple venues.[462] Similarly, Newman saw the value of litigation in terms of its potential to change public attitudes: "It will be a Pyrrhic legal victory if we only win legal doctrine but don't shift morality and public opinion. The legal argument becomes a vehicle by which you mobilize public relations."[463] Yet he was careful to distinguish between the positive use of litigation in the day labor campaign and the typical civil rights model: "Impact litigators are like surgeons. They identify the problem, sedate the patient, operate, wake the patient up and say, 'You are free to go home.' But the people involved in litigation don't want to be sedated in the process."[464] LCCR's Hwang also viewed day labor litigation as "a model of how public interest litigation should happen" in that the lawyers were not "dictating" to clients, who "took it upon themselves to discuss issues and take ownership and make decisions."[465] He noted, however, that even in the context of day labor litigation, there were serious challenges, including the difficulty of translating complex litigation into something understandable for clients: "There would be twists and turns, and there is something unnerving about it . . . . In the moment, you don't know where the case is going to end up."[466]

Others stressed the value added to litigation by organizing. For instance, Helzer saw organizing as essential to the "intense relationship building that needs to be done" with day laborers in order to help them understand unfamiliar court processes and what they could do to protect their own livelihood.[467] Simons noted that her direct involvement in organizing enriched her personally: "Considering that day laborers are such a vulnerable target of anti-immigrant feelings, I think that they are very brave and very organized and very opinionated. As a young lawyer, that was something that I appreciated and that I learned from."[468]

While most lawyers believed that litigation was useful, some had a less sanguine view. MALDEF's Kristina Campbell, for example, viewed litigation as "kind of a bandaid that addresses an immediate harm—the inability to seek work—but doesn't really address the larger goal of integrating day laborers into society and getting rid of stigma based on race, class, and immigration status. Personally, I feel like we won all those cases and it's great—it puts food on the table. But it is micro as opposed to macro. Nothing has changed. Has anything changed at Home Depot? No."[469] However, while Campbell believed that "as an impact litigation strategy, the impact has been small," she did not know "if there is a better solution."[470] Newman, in contrast, emphasized the positive consequences of the Baldwin Park litigation (which Campbell handled): "Jornaleros in Baldwin Park not only beat back an unconstitutional ordinance in court and in the court of public opinion; in the process, they made political alliances with the City Council and with Congresswoman Solis, and they eventually gained power to open an organized hiring site with established minimum wages right there within the Home Depot parking lot."[471]

While the lawyers expressed a deep respect for and sensitivity to the organizing efforts, the organizers, in turn, tended to support litigation as an essential means to advance the movement's goals. For NDLON's Alvarado, "litigation is a tool that we can use to build power."[472] Federosky saw organizing as essential to give workers "ownership of the struggle," but also believed that litigation was necessary—even if as a last resort: "I think litigation is a very important tool for workers to be able to defend their lives. They can organize, mobilize, and write letters, but if you have really racist politicians and a racist environment, you have to have lawyers. It is sad, but I think that sometimes the work the lawyers did was essential."[473]

Standing Conflicts

The post-Agoura Hills cases generally involved a dual-plaintiff structure with NDLON (or CHIRLA in Los Angeles County) asserting organizational standing and a committee of affected workers claiming direct harm. This structure was designed to facilitate coordination between the legal and organizing wings of the campaign. NDLON was formally involved in strategic decision-making in the case and was able to serve as a conduit to the worker committees that its organizers helped to establish—providing crucial information to the workers and giving them confidence that the lawsuit was, in fact, advancing their interests. NDLON's presence also addressed concerns about the transience of workers, who cycled in and out of hiring sites. For those workers who assumed leadership roles, the committee structure was designed to shield their identity during discovery in order to protect them from retaliation.

Although this arrangement formalized an integrated law and organizing approach to attacking ordinances, it did raise the potential for divergence between NDLON's interests—which may have emphasized longer-term movement goals—and that of the workers—who may have been more concerned with the immediate protection of their right to work. However, from the lawyers' perspective, such concerns were mitigated in practice by a commitment to transparency and the strength of

NDLON's relationship with the workers, which was seen as promoting a general alignment of interests.

In terms of transparency, Saenz emphasized that it was important up front "to be as clear and informative as you can about how the process works."[474] In initial conversations with the client groups, the lawyers were explicit about the trade-offs and risks of having two organizational plaintiffs. According to Campbell, "We definitely had conversations about how [the workers] were a separate client group from NDLON and that NDLON couldn't make decisions for them."[475] Their retainers included language informing both client groups about the potential for conflicts and gaining their consent to the joint representation.

Because NDLON worked to build trust and rapport with the workers, the lawyers tended to view the interests of NDLON and the committees as "totally aligned,"[476] so that the dual-plaintiff structure "seemed very natural."[477] Because the lawyers represented the worker committee only after it had been organized by NDLON, the workers already "knew and trusted" NDLON as an ally and "believed that NDLON was joining the lawsuit . . . because its goals were same as theirs: to get the ordinance repealed."[478] The lawyers worked to reinforce this trust by making a fundamental compact with the workers: They would protect worker identity, even if it meant ultimately dismissing the case. As Villagra affirmed, "We made that promise and they trusted us."[479]

The later OC cases, particularly Lake Forest, challenged this representational model on legal and practical grounds.[480] As a legal matter, the lawyers in Lake Forest were unable to completely protect workers' identity, as the court ruled that basic demographic information (though not immigration status) must be revealed in discovery. The Lake Forest case also resulted in a setback to the dual-plaintiff structure when the court denied NDLON organizational standing. Because NDLON had legal staff, however, it was able to maintain its collaboration going forward (in the Costa Mesa case) by changing its involvement from plaintiff to co-counsel. Moreover, the *Redondo Beach* en banc panel effectively reversed the Lake Forest court on the standing point, holding that "[b]ecause there is a causal connection between Redondo Beach's ordinance and NDLON's injury, and NDLON's injury would be redressable by a favorable decision, we conclude that NDLON has standing to bring this appeal."[481]

As a practical matter, the connections among client groups also produced legal complications and generated some friction in the Lake Forest case. During discovery, ATLF elected NDLON's Federosky as its representative to be deposed, to which the city objected based on the fact that she was not part of the worker committee. The court resolved the matter by requiring other worker representatives to be deposed in addition to Federosky. But the episode highlighted the fuzzy boundary between ATLF and NDLON as plaintiff organizations. The politics of the Lake Forest case were also more complex with the addition of Colectivo as a plaintiff based on the group's active support of day labor and proximity to the campaign.

As a more radical group comprised of mostly college-aged activists committed to more confrontational mobilization, Colectivo did not always see eye to eye with NDLON organizers, whom, according to Villagra, Colectivo members viewed "as not progressive enough."[482]

The Politics of Time

Because the legal campaign occurred over a nearly twenty-year period, its effectiveness was influenced not only by the particularities of individual lawyers and strategies, but also by changes in the political and legal environment.

During the campaign, immigration politics shifted significantly. In the 1990s, when day labor advocacy started to grow, day labor organizing was happening in relative obscurity and the booming economy created an essential role for immigrant workers. The following decade, immigration politics were transformed. The surge in undocumented immigration provoked an increasingly virulent response from the Minutemen movement, while 9/11 inflamed xenophobia. In this context, day laborers became, in Newman's terms, a "visible symbol (to some) of a broken system."[483] Animus against day laborers was underscored in the employer verification and home improvement store provisions in the Sensenbrenner bill, which reshaped the policy discussion around how to deal with day labor conflicts.[484] The landscape changed even further in 2008, with the economic collapse weakening the argument for the presence of immigrant workers to take "jobs that American workers don't want," and the rise of the Tea Party movement shifting Republicans further to the right on immigration issues.[485]

In this context, day labor advocates found themselves in an increasingly defensive position. Helzer noted that the "main challenge of the work is just the distraction by the ... anti-immigrant community. The most hate mail I have gotten is when I do day labor cases.... [Opponents believe] that the folks we represent are less than human."[486] From Newman's perspective, as the immigration "debate has coarsened, ... day laborers have been more exposed to abuses of all kinds. There is a slide toward dehumanization," forcing advocates to focus on defending day laborers' basic civil rights.[487] Newman also believed that the vilification of immigrants influenced the negative legal outcome in the *Redondo Beach* three-judge panel decision in 2010. Whereas in 2004, when the case was filed, day laborers had not yet come to symbolize the "quintessential illegal population,"[488] by 2010, the tenor of the debate had soured dramatically, leading Newman to believe that "we'd have won [*Redondo Beach*] 3-0 if it was heard in 2004."[489]

The fact that day laborers ultimately did win the *Redondo Beach* en banc appeal in 2011 highlights a final puzzle about the case. In a hostile political climate, in front of an eleven-judge panel with only two bona fide liberals (Judges Berzon and Thomas), how did the day laborers mobilize conservatives, led by Judge Milan Smith, to win a 9-2 victory? And what explains the fact that Judge Kozinksi, famous for his defense of free speech, ended up writing a blistering dissent, while Judge Ikuta, who ruled against the day laborers on the three-judge panel, switched to side in their favor in the identical case en banc? One can only speculate. But perhaps in a legal context in which the First Amendment had been "weaponized" by the conservative movement to weaken campaign finance regulation, limit gun control, opt out of lesbian, gay, bisexual, and transgender (LGBT) rights enforcement, and undermine unionism,[490] the conservative judges in the *Redondo Beach* case were playing a longer game—one in which strengthening the scaffolding of free speech jurisprudence in a case sympathetic to liberals would ultimately help advance the conservative agenda. This reading of the case might explain why Judge Ikuta switched sides, perhaps convinced to co-sign her conservative colleagues' broader First Amendment arguments; and why Judge Kozinski, a defender of commercial speech but never a movement conservative, refused to play along.

As the Redondo Beach fight underscored, the relationship between legal rules and immigration politics was constantly shifting throughout the campaign—with each responding to the other over time in an ongoing cycle in which the only long-term certainty was the ephemerality of short-term success. In meeting the anti-solicitation challenge, day labor lawyers continuously sought to mobilize doctrinal developments in their favor, changing course when needed and trying to anticipate their opponents' response. Failure in Agoura Hills on discrimination grounds motivated lawyers to hone their free speech attack against citywide solicitation bans. When that succeeded in *Burke*, some cities passed ordinances to more specifically target traffic safety concerns they associated with day labor. This happened in Baldwin Park and Costa Mesa, and although neither case turned out negatively for day laborers, both revealed the advocacy challenge of responding to cities' efforts to create more narrowly tailored safety-oriented restrictions. Indeed, in *Redondo Beach*, the city attempted to defend its ordinance by arguing that its broad formal scope was limited in practice to banning solicitation that impacted traffic safety. Day labor lawyers were disappointed that the Ninth Circuit three-judge panel ruled against them despite the intervening *Berger* authority, which they believed directly supported their argument that restrictions on solicitation that did not have a safety impact were overbroad.[491] The en banc panel reversed on this point, but left open the possibility that traffic interference bans, if well crafted, could qualify as reasonable time, place, and manner restrictions on day labor speech. That some cities have revised their ordinances in an effort to meet this qualification underlines the point that in movements for social change, there is no such thing as a decisive victory, only new phases of contention.

The Urban Geography of Anti-Solicitation

In order to assess the impact of the day labor litigation campaign, it is helpful to step back to look at the trend line of anti-solicitation ordinances in the 5-county greater L.A. area (Los Angeles County, Ventura, San Bernardino, Riverside, and OC) covering 188 jurisdictional units (183 cities and 5 counties). Beginning with Redondo Beach in 1987, these jurisdictions enacted forty-four anti-solicitation ordinances; thus, roughly one-quarter (24%) of jurisdictions in the area had at some point passed such laws. Figure 3.8 charts the growth of these ordinances over time. In order to illustrate the trajectory of initial ordinance enactment, it shows the total number of all ordinances passed in their original form (it does not account for ordinances that were later amended or repealed).

The rate of increase of ordinances slowed in the pre-recession decade (1999–2008) to 29% (from 34 to 44) when compared to the preceding decade (1990–1999), when ordinances grew by 750% (from 4 to 34). There are many variables that might explain this decrease, including the fact that the most anti-day labor jurisdictions enacted ordinances in the early wave, leaving fewer opportunities for enactment over the next decade. It is notable, however, that the slowdown also coincided with the 2000 *Burke* decision and MALDEF's strategy of warning cities not to pass ordinances and suing those that nonetheless did.

In terms of the types of ordinances passed, there were four basic categories (a complete list of ordinances in their original form by local jurisdiction is provided in Table 3.2 at the end of the chapter). The first, and most common, was the *complete*

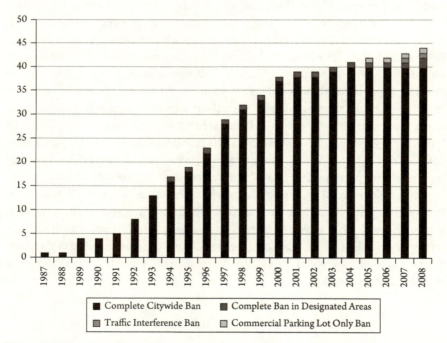

Figure 3.8 Number of anti-solicitation ordinances in greater L.A. area by year. *Source*: Compiled by author.

citywide ban, which prohibited all solicitation from public right-of-ways, including sidewalks. A second type, the *complete ban in designated areas*, applied the complete ban concept to a specific area in the city where day labor activity occurred. The third type was the *traffic interference ban*, which applied to sidewalks but targeted activity linked with traffic safety concerns. The fourth type was the *commercial parking lot only ban*, which prohibited solicitation in commercial parking lots without owner permission but did not restrict public solicitation in other areas. As Figure 3.8 shows, complete citywide bans were by far the most common over time (forty total).[492] There were two ordinances originally passed as complete bans in designated areas, one traffic interference ban, and one commercial parking lot only ban.

What Figure 3.8 does not show is how ordinances themselves changed over time *in response to the litigation campaign*, which resulted in some ordinances being enjoined, repealed, or amended. It is therefore useful to map the geographic impact of the litigation campaign by comparing the status quo in the absence of litigation with the geography of anti-solicitation after the *Redondo Beach* litigation.

Figure 3.9 maps the greater L.A. area as it would look if all the ordinances enacted since 1987 remained on the books *in their original form*. It therefore shows what the geographic reach of anti-solicitation ordinances would have been if the litigation campaign had not occurred.

Figure 3.10 by contrast, shows the geography of anti-solicitation ordinances prior to the *Redondo Beach* en banc decision, reflecting changes resulting from the litigation campaign *up to that point*. It thus eliminates those ordinances that were either enjoined or repealed as the direct result of the litigation campaign, and also shows where ordinances were amended as a result of litigation (or the threat thereof) to be less restrictive.

As this comparison reveals, even the litigation campaign pre-*Redondo Beach* had protected a significant area for unrestricted or sidewalk-based solicitation. In all, ten jurisdictions reduced or eliminated restrictions on solicitation as a result of the campaign. Three jurisdictions went from complete citywide bans to no bans. The Los Angeles County ordinance was enjoined in 2000 as a result of MALDEF's lawsuit; Lake Forest repealed its ordinance in 2007 in response to the ACLU's suit; and Dana Point repealed its ordinance in 2007 after a legal review prompted by contact from MALDEF. One jurisdiction, Baldwin Park (2007), repealed its traffic interference ban as part of its settlement with MALDEF. Six jurisdictions changed their ordinances from complete citywide bans to traffic interference bans: Costa Mesa (2005) and Orange (2007) after a legal review prompted by the threat of litigation by MALDEF; Rancho Cucamonga (2003), Upland (2003), and Glendale (2008) as a result of settlements with MALDEF and LCCR; and Huntington Beach (2001) after a legal review prompted by the *Burke* decision.

Figure 3.11 shows the situation after the Ninth Circuit en banc panel struck down Redondo Beach's ordinance—and thus effectively invalidated those ordinances in other cities that had copied the Redondo Beach model. At the time of the *Redondo*

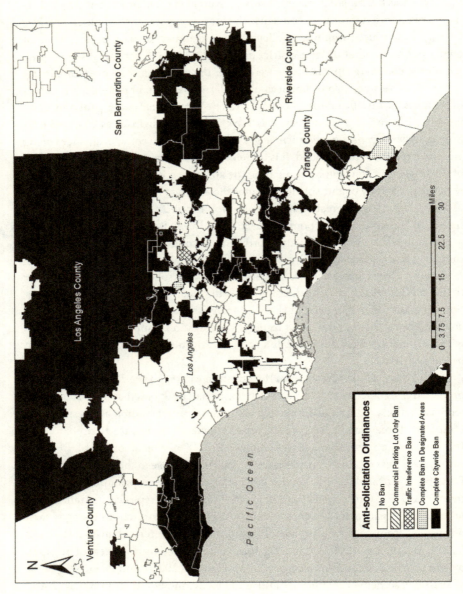

Figure 3.9 Anti-solicitation ordinances in the greater L.A. area prelitigation. *Source*: Compiled by author.

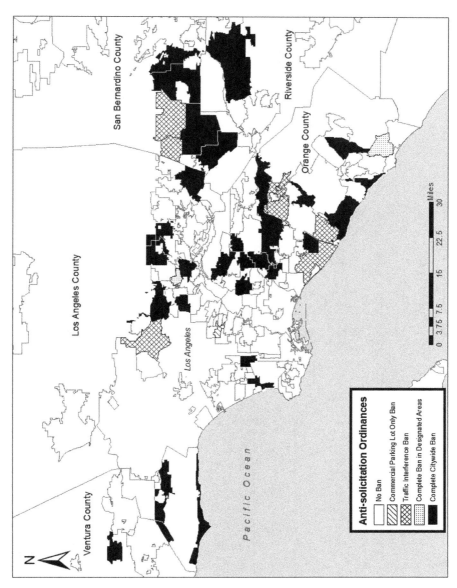

Figure 3.10 Anti-solicitation ordinances in the greater L.A. area prior to *Redondo Beach* en banc decision. *Source:* Compiled by author.

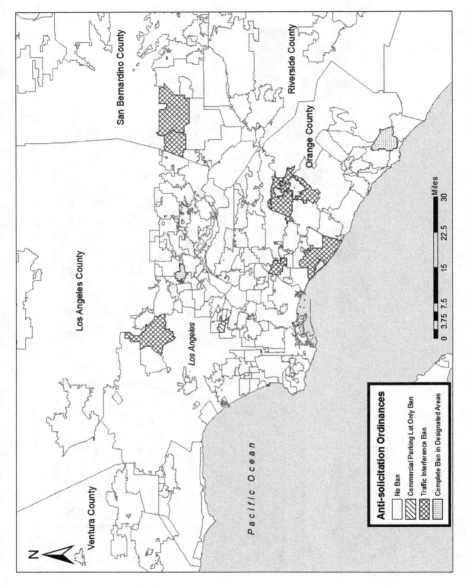

Figure 3.11 Anti-solicitation ordinances in the greater L.A. area after *Redondo Beach* en banc decision. *Source:* Compiled by author.

Beach en banc appeal, thirty-one of the remaining forty L.A.-area ordinances (78%) were still crafted as complete citywide bans.[493] After the en banc ruling, these thirty-one complete citywide bans were no longer valid, opening up wide regional space for day labor solicitation, and leaving a patchwork of less intrusive ordinances, including seven traffic interference bans (Cypress, Glendale, Huntington Beach, Orange, Rancho Cucamonga, Tustin, and Upland), two bans in designated areas (San Juan Capistrano and Temple City), and one commercial parking lot only ban (Huntington Park).[494]

In addition, the maps may understate the impact of the litigation campaign in three ways. First, the threat of litigation, particularly after the success in *Burke*, may have caused some cities to withdraw proposed ordinances—thus preventing their enactment in the first instance. Second, there were some cities with ordinances in which advocates persuaded local officials to *refrain* from robust enforcement, such as Agoura Hills. In these locations, the ordinances were on the books but did not prevent solicitation in practice. Third, litigation (or its threat) may have also contributed to cities opting for less repressive responses to day labor activity, such as the creation of day labor centers. Although there are not systematic data on the relationship between litigation and the development of day labor centers in the greater L.A. area, evidence from a national survey of day labor centers suggests that center growth corresponded to the period of greatest success in the litigation campaign, with approximately 60% of centers opening between 2000 and 2005.[495]

While litigation made a positive impact on the work lives of day laborers, the campaign itself revealed a number of limits. Although litigation created space for organizing and protected the baseline right to seek work in public, it was not able to raise minimum work standards. In this sense, opponents of day laborers succeeded in shifting the terrain of struggle away from promoting more robust economic rights toward simply protecting the basic civil right to find a job. In addition, there was no guarantee that minimum standards would be enforced going forward given lax oversight of those who employed day laborers. Cities, too, still had ways of circumventing the Ninth Circuit's ruling, both by harassing workers through traffic citations and threats of immigration enforcement, and by crafting "smarter" ordinances that homed in on the safety concerns that the Ninth Circuit found were not narrowly targeted by Redondo Beach. Although litigation helped to create the essential conditions for day labor organizing, it could not ensure better economic outcomes on its own.

Yet that fact—the result of deep structural problems in the American immigration and labor systems—could hardly be blamed on the day labor lawyers or their legal mobilization against anti-solicitation ordinances. In the final analysis, it was clear that day laborers as a whole were better off than they would have been without the Southern California litigation campaign, which spanned nearly two decades and attacked ordinances covering hundreds of squares miles. It was certainly true that, despite litigation success, day laborers continued to face harassment and marginalization. But their right to seek work—the powerful magnet that drew most of them to the greater L.A. area in the first instance—had been validated by one of the most powerful courts in the land and ultimately preserved on sidewalks around the region. Given day laborers' lack of political power and alternative avenues of influence, this was an enormous accomplishment. Moreover, day laborers had been activated. They marched in protest, despite legal risks. They weighed in on legal and political strategy. They built a movement. That litigation could not ultimately deliver the highest movement goals—enhancing the quality of day labor work and bringing day laborers out of the political shadows—did nothing to denigrate litigation as a social change tool or the vision of the lawyers who wielded it. To the contrary, the limits of litigation served to spotlight the inherent political vulnerability of day laborers and the profound unfairness of a system that benefited from immigrant labor but denied immigrants basic dignity and legal recognition. In that sense, the end of anti-solicitation was merely the beginning of the next phase in the long struggle for immigrant rights.

Table 3.2 Anti-solicitation ordinances (original form) in the greater L.A. area, 1987–2011.

Jurisdiction	County	First Passed	Change Due to Litigation Campaign	Complete Citywide Ban	Traffic Interference Ban	Complete Ban in Designated Areas	Applies to Workers	Applies to Employers	Ban in Commercial Parking Lots	Exception for Day Labor Center
Redondo Beach	LA	1987	Complete citywide ban challenged in 2004; ordinance permanently enjoined by Ninth Circuit en banc panel in 2011	x			x	x		
Costa Mesa	OC	1989	Complete citywide ban replaced in 2005 with traffic interference ban, which was repealed in 2013 after the Redondo Beach en banc decision	x			x	x	x	

(continued)

Table 3.2 Continued

Jurisdiction	County	First Passed	Change Due to Litigation Campaign	Complete Citywide Ban	Traffic Interference Ban	Complete Ban in Designated Areas	Applies to Workers	Applies to Employers	Ban in Commercial Parking Lots	Exception for Day Labor Center
Dana Point	OC	1989	Complete citywide ban repealed in 2007	x			x	x		
Orange	OC	1989	Original ordinance, a complete citywide ban, was amended to focus on traffic interference after legal review in 2007	x			x	x		x
Agoura Hills	LA	1991	Complete citywide ban repealed in 2012	x			x	x	x	
Gardena	LA	1992	Complete citywide ban repealed in 2012	x			x	x		
La Mirada	LA	1992	Complete citywide ban repealed in 2012	x			x	x		

Malibu	LA	1992		x	x	x
Anaheim	OC	1993		x	x	
Laguna Beach	OC	1993		x	x	x
Lake Forest	OC	1993	Complete citywide ban repealed after lawsuit filed in 2007; city agreed to nonenforcement in 2008 settlement	x	x	
Rancho Cucamonga	SB	1993	Complete citywide ban amended by settlement in 2003 to focus on traffic interference	x		
Upland	SB	1993	Complete citywide ban amended by settlement in 2003 to focus on traffic interference	x		

(*continued*)

Table 3.2 Continued

Jurisdiction	County	First Passed	Change Due to Litigation Campaign	Complete Citywide Ban	Traffic Interference Ban	Complete Ban in Designated Areas	Applies to Workers	Applies to Employers	Ban in Commercial Parking Lots	Exception for Day Labor Center
Fontana	SB	1994		x			x	x		
Los Angeles County	LA	1994	Complete countywide ban permanently enjoined in 2000	x			x	x	x	
Temple City	LA	1994				x	x	x	x	
Tustin	OC	1994	Complete citywide ban replaced by traffic interference ban in 2012	x			x	x	x	
Calabasas	LA	1995	Complete citywide ban repealed in 2012	x			x	x	x	
Fountain Valley	OC	1995	Complete citywide ban repealed in 2012	x			x	x		

Alhambra	LA	1996	Complete citywide ban repealed in 2012	x	x	x
Glendale	LA	1996	Complete citywide ban changed to traffic interference ban as part of 2008 settlement	x	x	x
Moorpark	V	1996	Complete citywide ban repealed in 2012	x	x	x
Newport Beach	OC	1996	Complete citywide ban repealed in 2012	x	x	
Chino	SB	1997		x	x	x
Duarte	LA	1997	Compete citywide ban repealed in 2014	x	x	x
Mission Viejo	OC	1997		x	x	x
Monrovia	LA	1997	Complete citywide ban repealed in 2012	x	x	x

(continued)

Table 3.2 Continued

Jurisdiction	County	First Passed	Change Due to Litigation Campaign	Complete Citywide Ban	Traffic Interference Ban	Complete Ban in Designated Areas	Applies to Workers	Applies to Employers	Ban in Commercial Parking Lots	Exception for Day Labor Center
Pomona	LA	1997		x			x	x	x	x
Riverside	R	1997		x			x	x		x
Buena Park	OC	1998		x			x	x	x	
Cypress	OC	1998	Complete citywide ban changed to traffic interference ban in 2012	x			x	x	x	
El Monte	LA	1998		x			x	x	x	x
La Habra	OC	1999	Complete citywide ban repealed in 2012	x			x	x		
Whittier	LA	1999	Complete citywide ban repealed in 2012	x			x	x	x	
Azusa	LA	2000	Complete citywide ban repealed in 2012	x			x	x	x	

Huntington Beach	OC	2000	Complete citywide ban amended to focus on traffic interference after legal review in 2001		x	x	x
Ontario	SB	2000	Complete citywide ban repealed in 2012		x	x	x
Westlake Village	LA	2000	Complete citywide ban repealed in 2012		x	x	x
Norwalk	LA	2001			x		
Pasadena	LA	2003				x	
Rialto	SB	2004			x	x	x
Huntington Park	LA	2005					x
Baldwin Park	LA	2007	Traffic interference ordinance repealed after lawsuit filed in 2007	x			
San Juan Capistrano	OC	2008		x	x		

4

Retail Workers

Negotiating Community Benefits

Overview

Whereas the campaigns on behalf of garment workers and day laborers grew out of the immigrant rights movement—merging the quest for civil rights and economic justice—the community benefits campaign to bring affordable housing and good jobs to local workers, primarily in the multifaceted retail industry, was from the outset more firmly anchored in the labor movement. And while garment and day labor mobilization responded to structural market changes in those industries, the pursuit of community benefits challenged city-subsidized redevelopment, resulting in the creation of low-wage jobs and fueling gentrification that displaced existing neighborhood residents. In this sense, it was the campaign that galvanized Los Angeles's community–labor alliance, built on an emergent partnership between community-based groups seeking to promote "equitable development" in the face of gentrification,[1] and the labor movement's new vehicle for community engagement, LAANE. As it took shape at the turn of the millennium, the campaign sought to change city redevelopment practices through grassroots legal and political interventions aimed at increasing community participation in the planning process and forcing local developers and governmental officials to commit to projects responsive to the needs of low-income residents.

From the outset, the campaign for community benefits depended on interest convergence among distinct social movement constituencies. The labor movement generally, and LAANE in particular, sought to challenge the city-sponsored proliferation of low-wage jobs, especially in the retail and hospitality industries, thereby demonstrating to working-class communities that organized labor could provide meaningful benefits beyond union membership—while nonetheless leveraging equitable development to support potential unionization. Because labor groups brought political heft, they were essential partners in persuading city officials to support community benefits demands and bringing private developers to the negotiating table. Community groups, for their part, focused more intently on keeping neighborhoods intact in the face of city-catalyzed private investment, which caused housing costs to spike and undermined local businesses. Their effort, led by groups like SAJE and Esperanza Community Housing Corporation, asserted that low-income people had a "right to the city"—mobilizing communities to resist the development of a gilded Los Angeles. This community–labor partnership was joined by environmental justice advocates, who brought a critical legal weapon—the environmental lawsuit—while seeing in the equitable development movement a way to hold the city accountable for unequal environmental impacts in low-income communities of color.

The legal instrument codifying this interest convergence was the community benefits agreement, or CBA—a contract in which a developer agreed to provide specific levels of living wage jobs, affordable housing, environmental remediation, and other benefits in exchange for community support for project approvals and public subsidies. Because CBAs offered a proactive approach to redress negative development externalities through contractual compromise, they rested on a distinctive model of community organizing—leveraging the power of broad-based coalitions to extract benefits through negotiation, thereby avoiding litigation (though wielding its threat). As such, CBAs enlisted a particular role for lawyers, who identified strategic points of legal leverage in the development process, advised coalitions on legal options, negotiated benefits with developers, and ultimately drafted—and helped to enforce—CBAs.

This chapter traces the evolution and outcomes of Los Angeles's community benefits campaign: from the nation's first CBA with the developer of a transformational downtown sports and entertainment complex anchored around the Staples Center, through a $500 million CBA centered on environmental mitigation in connection with the expansion of the L.A. International Airport (LAX), to the Grand Avenue CBA, which focused on affordable housing production in a proposed upscale development on downtown's Bunker Hill. Following this arc, the chapter shows how CBAs operated as part of a broader strategy to promote accountability in the award of redevelopment subsidies, using the redevelopment process as leverage to extend living wage requirements and facilitate unionization. As such, CBAs conferred significant benefits on low-income communities by providing a mechanism for capturing value from projects that had historically been exclusively appropriated by private developers. However, as the CBA became an institutionalized feature of the city's redevelopment process, the campaign confronted challenges of scope and implementation, while experiencing divergence within the community–labor alliance, whose members had different views about the value of development growth—the essential predicate for CBAs that, as the Great Recession revealed, also made them vulnerable to economic collapse.

Fighting Displacement in the Figueroa Corridor: The Staples CBA

The Legal Origins of Gentrification

The nation's first community benefits campaign grew out of efforts to redevelop the Figueroa Corridor, a working-class neighborhood cutting southward from downtown Los Angeles along a 2.5-mile stretch of Figueroa Street (a main north–south arterial parallel to the 110 Harbor Freeway) toward USC.[2] In 2000, there were just over 200,000 people living in the Figueroa Corridor, 70% of whom were Latino. The median income was approximately $20,000 (about one-third of Los Angeles's area median), and 86% of area residents were renters. Strategically located between the Los Angeles Convention Center downtown and the Los Angeles Memorial Coliseum, a ninety thousand-seat stadium just south of USC (site of the 1984 Olympic games), the Figueroa Corridor became a flashpoint for equitable development activism as city officials sought to remake the neighborhood into Los Angeles's sports and entertainment hub. The key mechanism for implementing this plan was state redevelopment law, which empowered local redevelopment agencies to designate "blighted" communities as project areas, assemble private property through eminent domain, and subsidize private development by issuing debt backed by future property tax increases (known as "tax increment").

Official redevelopment in Los Angeles was initiated in 1948, when the city's Community Redevelopment Agency (CRA) was established.[3] From its inception, the CRA followed the model of "downtown development" that characterized other urban renewal projects during this era designed to eliminate central city "blight": the clearance of low-income residential "slums" in the name of "reviving downtown areas as centers for the rapidly expanding white-collar professions"—leading critics to call urban renewal the "federal bulldozer" and, because it often led to the displacement of African American communities, "Negro Removal."[4] When urban renewal was abandoned in the early 1970s, after mounting criticisms of its top-down format and racially biased implementation,[5] the CRA in Los Angeles did what other local redevelopment agencies in major cities were forced to do: It began to rely more heavily on local tax increment financing (TIF) as a way to pay for redevelopment projects. Under the TIF program, the CRA would freeze the amount of property taxes from a project area flowing to the city's general fund and other taxing agencies (like the school district), allowing the CRA to capture increased property taxes generated by higher-value redevelopment and thereby repay debt used to finance projects in the first instance.[6]

Situated at the intersection of five redevelopment project areas, the Figueroa Corridor was shaped by the Los Angeles CRA.[7] The southern part of the Figueroa Corridor was in the Hoover Redevelopment Project area established in the 1960s to allow USC to expand its campus borders and eliminate surrounding community blight as an inducement to remain at its South Los Angeles location.[8] With the help of the CRA, USC became the largest landowner in the Figueroa Corridor, expanding its northern border into the surrounding community while acquiring a real estate portfolio of over one hundred properties, many devoted to student housing.[9] One of the most controversial sites was a property near the northeast border of campus, where in the 1990s the CRA helped USC to purchase a parking lot at the corner of Figueroa Street and Jefferson Boulevard on which it proposed to build a $70 million, 4.75-acre sports arena to house its basketball and volleyball teams,[10] having scrapped an earlier plan to build a commercial center projected to create twenty-seven hundred jobs for local residents and generate $1.6 million per year in tax increment.[11] Community residents unsuccessfully mobilized against the arena, called the Galen Center (which opened in 2006), arguing that it "must generate—on site or off—substantive, measurable economic benefits consistent with the CRA's mission of redevelopment: building communities with jobs and housing."[12] In 1999, the CRA also helped to finance USC's $25 million acquisition of University Village, a shopping center just north of campus that included a movie theater and drug store.[13]

Other development activities added to pressure in the area. In 1998, 150 property owners and merchants, most of whom were located within a few blocks of Figueroa Street, formed a business improvement district (BID) called the Figueroa Corridor Partnership.[14] The 40-block BID taxed its occupants in order to privately finance patrols of "community ambassadors" who served as tour guides and surrogate police officers, while performing routine services like trash collection.[15] The city-owned Coliseum, located in the Hoover project area just south of the USC campus in Exposition Park, was another key site in the city's plan to promote the Figueroa Corridor as a sports and entertainment zone. The home of USC football, the Coliseum was on the short list of stadium sites for a National Football League (NFL) franchise, which the city was working to attract by developing a subsidy package that included a promised city-funded Coliseum renovation.[16]

To the north, development pressures on the Figueroa Corridor emanated from the redevelopment of downtown Los Angeles, much of which was within the Central Business District redevelopment project area.[17] The southwest corner of the Central Business District (just above the interchange of the 110 Harbor Freeway and the 10 Santa Monica Freeway) was home to the Los Angeles Convention Center, originally built in 1969 with high expectations, but which proved to be a major disappointment for city leaders, requiring a $20 million city operating subsidy because it was unable to attract enough business.[18] In 1993, the CRA financed the property acquisition and resident and business relocation for a significant expansion of the convention center's exhibit space, meeting rooms, special events space, and restaurants.[19]

The catalyst for the Figueroa Corridor's transformation was the 1997 announcement of a plan by Los Angeles real estate developer Ed Roski Jr. and Denver billionaire Phillip Anschutz of Qwest Communications[20]—who together owned the Los Angeles Kings professional hockey team and part of the Los Angeles Lakers professional basketball franchise—to build the twenty thousand-seat Staples Center, which would become home of the Kings and Lakers and a venue for concerts and other entertainment events. Roski and Anschutz had originally purchased land around Chinatown for an arena deal but moved the arena project in response to the city's strong interest in developing the area south of downtown. The $375 million project that resulted, located immediately north of the Los Angeles Convention Center, was developed by the L.A. Arena Land Company (a Roski-Anschutz partnership that subsequently became a wholly owned subsidiary of the Anschutz Entertainment Group, AEG) in a complex public–private deal that involved billionaire Rupert Murdoch's Fox Group purchasing a 40% interest in the arena. The deal was completed with a $71.1 million city financial assistance package,[21] which included a $58.5 million loan from the city to the developer (to be repaid through the dedication of revenues from parking fees and a tax imposed on ticket sales) and a $12.6 million grant from the CRA,[22] which went to fund environmental approvals and assist in the acquisition of 20 acres of property north and east of the arena to be used for interim parking.[23] The Staples Center project, which was completed in 1999, reconfigured the terrain of downtown development, rising as a monument to the new vision of downtown Los Angeles as a dynamic destination for affluent (and, from the plan drawings, mostly white) Angelenos and tourists. It also disrupted the fabric of the existing low-income community. The Staples Center project resulted in the relocation of approximately 130 families and individuals from their downtown residences to government-subsidized housing complexes.[24] Approximately $6.5 million of the city's general fund was allocated for this purpose, $1.3 million of which went directly to displaced residents to assist with rents, with the remaining amount used to defray administrative costs and help finance a nearby child care center.[25] Relocated residents were given packages ranging from $2,000 to $27,000, with the average package being $9,300. While these packages were intended to last for four years, many residents found that the bulk of their money was exhausted by move-in costs.[26] In addition, approximately thirty-five businesses were displaced by the construction of the arena and adjoining parking lots.[27]

The Community–Labor Alliance

Although community organizing—which began after the Staples Center development—grew directly out of residents' response to the disruption, it was built upon a foundation of community–labor cooperation that had evolved during the prior years. On the labor side, collaboration was part of a deliberate strategy by national labor leaders, who promoted grassroots coalitions through programs like Union Cities and organizations like Good Jobs First, which was created to build networks of local activists who would advance equitable development.[28] There were also local efforts to strengthen Los Angeles's dynamic community–labor partnerships, forged by unions like the SEIU, following on the heels of its Justice for Janitors and home health care worker campaigns.[29] The SEIU organizing model linked together union organizers, workers, community activists, students, and religious leaders in Los Angeles, and expanded union membership among immigrant workers, many of whom lived in the Figueroa Corridor.[30]

Most importantly, Los Angeles had LAANE, formed to integrate research, organizing, and advocacy toward the goal of creating worker-friendly local policy and building union density. Created by the HERE union in 1994, the Tourism Industry Development Council (which would change its name to LAANE)— led by Madeline Janis-Aparicio—brought together grassroots organizations, faith-based groups, environmental organizations, labor leaders, and worker representatives in its successful 1997 campaign to pass the Los Angeles Living Wage Ordinance.[31] That ordinance responded to the privatization of city services by Mayor Richard Riordan, a pro-business Republican who took office in 1993. It did so by requiring city contractors, concessionaires, and recipients of significant city financial assistance for economic development to pay employees at the living wage rate[32]—effectively reducing the incentive to outsource city jobs to save money (and undercut the public employees' union). In this regard, the Living Wage Ordinance worked in tandem with the Worker Retention Ordinance, passed in 1995, which required companies that took over terminated city contracts to retain the service workers of the terminated contractors for ninety days (reducing the city's

Figure 4.1 Madeline Janis-Aparicio, founder of LAANE. *Source*: Annie Wells, *Los Angeles Times* via Getty Images (August 21, 2000).

incentive to change to low-wage or nonunion contractors).[33] While the Living Wage Ordinance was a significant advance for low-wage workers, lifting up wages in city concessions (like restaurants at LAX) and requiring publicly subsidized developers to pay their construction workers a living wage, it did not reach the retail and hospitality workers whose jobs were created *after* developments were built: by the restaurants, theaters, hotels, and other companies that occupied development space as tenants. Accordingly, by the late 1990s, LAANE was searching for ways to extend the living wage to those permanent retail and hospitality workers, while also laying the groundwork for their possible unionization.

This search led, in the short term, to a focus on "subsidy accountability"—the idea that projects subsidized with taxpayer funds, through agencies like the CRA, should prioritize projects that would produce quality jobs and other community benefits. By the late 1990s, supported by a grant from the Ford Foundation, LAANE undertook to build out its subsidy expertise and map the ways in which the city provided financial assistance to L.A. developers. In a July 1998 interview in the *Los Angeles Times*, Janis-Aparicio called for community benefits in relation to the proposed expansion of Universal Studios in North Hollywood.[34] The following month, LAANE engaged in a comprehensive mapping of all the mechanisms by which city government provided financial support to developers—loans, tax breaks, and electricity discounts, among others—focusing on the agencies within the administration of Mayor Riordan, particularly the CRA and L.A. Business Team, which were spearheading L.A. redevelopment.[35] On August 27, 1998, the self-styled Subsidy Accountability Project held a meeting to assess the city's claims of redevelopment-induced employment, in which it analyzed overall city expenditures, raising the crucial question: "Are these creating living wage jobs?"[36] In 1999, the group proposed a plan to develop "a cradle to grave process for subsidy accountability."[37] An important step forward in this work was the publication in March 1999 of LAANE's report, *Who Benefits from Redevelopment in Los Angeles?*, which concluded that CRA projects had produced a disproportionate number of low-wage jobs.[38] The LAANE report responded to a 1998 UCLA study, called *Assessment of Fifty Years of Redevelopment in Los Angeles*, commissioned by the CRA, which concluded that seventeen redevelopment projects had produced a favorable overall public benefit. These competing reports caused the city's Community and Economic Development Committee to request more information from the CRA on subsidy accountability, which prompted a CRA promise to place greater emphasis on industrial development, adopt a living wage policy for commercial redevelopment, and support quality jobs.[39]

As LAANE's subsidy accountability work was taking shape at the policy level to promote labor interests, it began to intersect with bottom-up community organizing sparked by economic dislocation and gentrification. The key community-based group in the Figueroa Corridor was SAJE, an economic justice and popular education center established in 1996 to build "economic power for working class people in Los Angeles."[40] SAJE was responsible for uniting the first community–labor network in the Figueroa Corridor, which grew out of a labor dispute at USC that began in 1995 when about 350 food and service workers, represented by HERE Local 11, demanded a guarantee from USC that it would not subcontract out their jobs.[41] In 1998, SAJE organized USC employees, students, local clergy, community activists, and neighborhood residents as the Coalition for a Responsible USC,[42] initiating a series of protests, which included a rolling hunger strike, in support of the union's demands.[43] The Los Angeles City Council amended its Worker Retention Ordinance in 1999 to make clear it applied to recipients of city economic development funds,[44] like USC, thus preventing USC from firing workers within ninety days of contracting out their work. As a result, the dispute was settled, with USC retaining the right to subcontract, but agreeing to a consultation process with the union in order to avoid doing so.[45]

The USC campaign reinforced community–labor relationships, highlighting the common economic concerns of union and nonunion community residents and forging a sense of shared purpose among local block clubs, churches, and other community organizations that had not previously worked together. The coalition members continued to meet regularly in 1999, focusing attention on local development issues, including concerns regarding plans for a light rail line into downtown and USC's continued expansion.[46] The USC campaign also led to changes in the coalition itself. As news stories began to circulate in 1999 about plans to further redevelop the area around the Staples Center, the coalition expanded its mission to focus on gentrification in the Figueroa Corridor, formally restructuring as the Figueroa Corridor Coalition for Economic Justice (FCCEJ),[47] with SAJE serving as the organizational host,[48] and Sandra McNeill as the lead organizer.

The announcement in May 2000 by the owners of the Staples Center of plans to develop a Los Angeles Sports and Entertainment District adjacent to the arena set FCCEJ into motion on what would become the nation's first community benefits campaign.[49] Plans for the proposed 4-million-square-foot, $1 billion project—which came to be known as "L.A. Live"—included a forty-five-story twelve hundred-room convention center hotel (with one hundred condominium units) to be located directly north of the Staples Center, a second smaller three-hundred-room high-end hotel, two apartment towers consisting of eight hundred units, a seventy-four hundred–seat live theater, restaurants, nightclubs, an office tower, a 40,000-square-foot open-air plaza, and a 250,000-square-foot convention center expansion.[50] When the project was announced, FCCEJ initiated a community planning process and SAJE began organizing neighborhood tenants in buildings in the area of the proposed Sports and Entertainment District,[51] many of whom were still upset about the dislocation caused by the Staples Center development and being left out of the planning process.[52]

This organizing occurred against the backdrop of exploding labor protests during the spring and summer of 2000. In April, fifteen hundred janitors staged a two-week

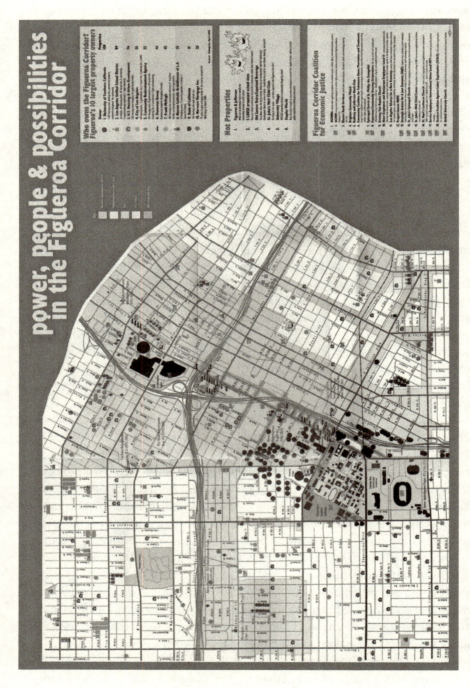

Figure 4.2 FCEEJ map of the Figueroa Corridor. *Source:* Strategic Actions for a Just Economy (2000).

strike in Santa Monica to protest wages in the Santa Monica hotel industry—supported by Democratic presidential candidate Al Gore, alongside activists from HERE Local 11 and Clergy and Laity United for Economic Justice (CLUE), who demanded the janitors be paid a living wage.[53] In July, hotel workers clashed with police in a protest led by HERE Local 11 over conditions at the nonunion New Otani Hotel in the Little Tokyo area of downtown Los Angeles.[54] As labor unrest spotlighted conditions in the hotel industry, FCCEJ focused on the community impacts of the Staples Center. In July, a working group developed—headed by Esperanza, Coalition LA, CARECEN, LAANE, CHIRLA, and SAJE—to conduct a survey of neighborhood residents and discuss potential responses to a post-Lakers game riot around Staples.[55] As August approached, FCCEJ ramped up planning to address disruption anticipated in relation to the Democratic National Convention, which was slated to be held at the Staples Center beginning on August 14.

The convention itself, though mostly peaceful, was marked by ugly moments, with armored police using rubber bullets and pepper spray in clashes with protesters in cordoned-off streets. After the convention ended, FCCEJ intensified its community organizing efforts, convening meetings at the First United Methodist Church for community members upset about convention violence, as well as the ongoing nuisance of reckless drivers, unruly fans, vandalism, and increased parking tickets that were the routine byproducts of Staples Center events.[56] On September 5, 2000, FCCEJ leaders—including SAJE's Sandra McNeill and Gilda Haas; Angelica Salas of CHIRLA; James Elmendorf of Coalition LA; and Erika Zucker, who was LAANE's general counsel—met with Councilman Mike Hernandez, whose district was just across the 110 Freeway west of the Staples Center, to outline the coalition's concerns about the impact of Staples on the neighborhood and the negative consequences of expansion. Two days later, members of the leadership group, joined by Jerilyn López Mendoza of Environmental Defense and Paulina Gonzalez of HERE Local 11, met to start developing potential demands, which included green space and support for union organizing.[57] Demonstrating the coalition's growing focus on subsidies as leverage, a September 20 memorandum from Misty Sanford at Environmental Defense summarized research on Ed Roski's public subsidies, political contributions, and other projects.[58] On October 11, FCCEJ's "Staples Accountable Development Working Groups" met to hone strategy in advance of officially launching a campaign. The groups were set up around discrete issue areas: The community organizing group, led by SAJE's Sandra McNeill and Enrique Velasquez, took on the task of mobilizing residents; the research group was established to respond to the impending Sports and Entertainment District environmental impact review; and a group dedicated to "leveraging public policy" was created to pressure Councilman Hernandez and develop plans for meeting with L.A. Arena Land Company President Tim Leiweke.[59]

By the time that FCCEJ held its first annual assembly meeting in late 2000, the focus of the coalition's efforts had already begun to crystallize around one goal: forcing the Staples Center developers to address community needs in their plans for the Sports and Entertainment District. As this campaign continued to take shape, FCCEJ recruited resident leaders and expanded to its full size of twenty-nine organizations and approximately three hundred residents.[60] Reflecting the broad range of community concerns at stake, there were several categories of member groups:

- *Economic justice*: SAJE, LAANE, and Coalition LA
- *Environmental*: Environmental Defense–Environmental Justice Project
- *Community organizing*: ACORN, Action for Grassroots Empowerment and Neighborhood Development Alternatives (AGENDA), and the Community Coalition
- *Community services*: Blazers Youth Services
- *Religious*: All People's Christian Center, Episcopal Church of St. Phillip the Evangelist, Faithful Service Baptist Church, First United Methodist Church, St. Agnes Catholic Church, St. John's Episcopal Church, St. John's Well Child Center, St. Mark's Lutheran Church, and United University Church
- *Housing and community development*: Esperanza Community Housing Corporation and Concerned Citizens of South Central Los Angeles
- *Health advocacy*: Clinica Oscar Romero and Coalition for Community Health
- *Immigrant rights*: El Rescate, CHIRLA, and CARECEN
- *Neighborhood-based*: Budlong and Jefferson Block Club, and Neighbors for an Improved Community
- *Student-led*: Student Coalition Against Labor Exploitation
- *Unions*: HERE Local 11 and SEIU Local 1877

The Nation's First CBA

FCCEJ's relationship with local unions proved to be one of its critical points of leverage with the developer, L.A. Arena Land Company, and shaped its decision to negotiate with the developer rather than try to block the development altogether. The FCCEJ campaign occurred against the backdrop of labor negotiations between the developer and five unions—HERE Local 11, SEIU Local 1877, Operating Engineers Local 501, Teamsters Local 911, and the International Alliance of Local Stage Employees Local 33—which were attempting to secure union contracts on the project. In contrast to the separate negotiations each union conducted during the original Staples Center development, the unions entered negotiations on the Sports and Entertainment District project committed to a united front, agreeing under the leadership of the Los Angeles County Federation of Labor that "no one would sign an agreement until everyone had an agreement to sign."[61] Eager to demonstrate that labor and community groups could join together to achieve broad gains for working people, the five unions and the County Fed, whose leaders had strong connections to LAANE and other coalition members, agreed to support FCCEJ in its own negotiations for community benefits. As a sign of union support, a labor representative, David Koff of HERE Local 11, was present at all of the meetings between the developer and FCCEJ. Meanwhile, as the unions worked to advance the goals of FCCEJ, LAANE was making efforts to help support the unions.

The developer, realizing that organized labor's influence with local government officials could jeopardize city approval of the deal in the event of labor strife, was eager to reach an accord with the unions that would move the project forward. As the developer's lawyer later recounted, from the developer side, the "fulcrum that brought the parties together" was the calculation that the hotel part of the project would not be approved without the support of organized labor.[62] Not concerned with FCCEJ as such, the developer was nevertheless forced to recognize the coalition's concerns in order to garner the support of unions that had come out behind FCCEJ's efforts. Although union leverage brought FCCEJ to the table with the developer, it also constrained FCCEJ's options in responding to the proposed project. Because the union partners were committed to seeing through a project that would create jobs for their members, there were strong pressures on FCCEJ to negotiate a deal. In this process, FCCEJ could wield the threat of delay, but any expression of outright opposition to the project would have risked union support and weakened its bargaining position.

It was in this context that FCCEJ began zeroing in on the goal of negotiating a legally binding CBA.[63] The CBA model, which had never been tried before, grew out of different strands of activism—and represented an appealing tool to merge community–labor interests around the Staples expansion. Its formal legal structure mirrored the types of agreements entered in the Community Reinvestment Act context, where community organizations committed to supporting bank applications for mergers or branch relocations in front of federal regulators in exchange for bank promises to increase loan activity and banking services in poor neighborhoods. SAJE's Executive Director Gilda Haas, who had been an organizer for the Center for Community Change, had extensive experience negotiating such agreements and brought expertise on this approach to the CBA process.[64] The concept of the CBA—leveraging the need for city development approval to exact developer concessions—also built on organizing pioneered by the HERE and SEIU unions to win living wage jobs for low-wage workers and promote unionization. The unions did this by linking development approval to so-called card-check neutrality agreements—in which developers agreed to refrain from interfering with union organizing (to stay "neutral") and to accept a union if a majority of workers signed union authorization forms (called "cards").[65]

These union agreements formed the essential template for LAANE's initial efforts to promote subsidy accountability by pressuring the CRA to require developers to target benefits to low-income communities affected by CRA-sponsored projects. The first major victory was in 1998, when LAANE and a number of unions worked with local officials, led by Councilwoman Jackie Goldberg, to incorporate a community benefits package into the CRA's agreement with TrizecHahn, the developer of a large entertainment and retail project in Hollywood—built around the centerpiece Kodak Theatre, designed as the new home of the Academy Awards.[66] This Hollywood and Highland project (so called because of the two streets forming the project borders) was erected in the Hollywood redevelopment zone and received significant CRA financing: roughly $100 million for the construction of the theater and parking, and to defray costs associated with land acquisition, tenant relations, and permitting. The financing was secured through the issuance of public bonds to be paid back through tax increment.[67] The Hollywood and Highland project was initially approved by the CRA and City Council in May 1998, following a full year of negotiations between LAANE, the County Fed, and political officials, led by Councilwoman Goldberg, in whose district the project sat. Goldberg's Deputy for Economic Development, Roxana Tynan, was in charge of pushing the deal forward and coordinating stakeholders, which also included the Los Angeles County MTA—persuaded by Goldberg to locate a stop of the new underground Metro Red Line at the project site. A central focus of the negotiations was on extending the city's Living Wage Ordinance to project tenants, incorporating card-check neutrality provisions in leases, and securing a project labor agreement between the developer and the construction unions. In exchange for public financing, TrizecHahn ultimately agreed to use reasonable efforts in all general contracts to ensure that 30% of new hires be from the project area, pay all workers employed by construction contractors and subcontractors a living wage, and "encourage tenants and prospective tenants" to also pay a living wage.[68] In addition to the local hiring plan, TrizecHahn agreed to contribute $100,000 toward a job training program administrated by the CRA.[69] Unlike many earlier developer agreements in which community benefits were promised in principle but never codified, the TrizecHahn commitments were incorporated in the CRA's February 10, 1999 Development and Disposition Agreement, setting forth the terms and conditions of CRA financial assistance. The template for community benefits was thus set.

The Hollywood and Highland agreement was quickly followed with a similar deal nearby in connection with the CRA-sponsored rehabilitation of the historic Cinerama Dome theater on Sunset Boulevard in Hollywood. It was a nearly $100 million project financed with a $32 million contribution from the CRA in the form of parking revenue bonds.[70] Preliminary discussions for the project had begun in 1996 between Jackie Goldberg and Pacific Theaters, which owned the aging site (including adjacent commercial tenant space) and was interested in refurbishing and running the Cinerama Dome under its art-house ArcLight brand. Tynan (Goldberg's deputy) again spearheaded discussions, which were hung up early over demands by organized labor to require ArcLight to pay workers at the reopened theater a living wage. The issue was resolved when the CRA agreed to purchase land from Pacific for an adjacent parking lot at a price over what Pacific was asking (though still below fair market value), effectively subsidizing Pacific to pay employees a living wage. Under the final Owner Participation Agreement between the CRA and the developer (Dome Entertainment Center), the developer agreed to "encourage tenants and prospective tenants of the [project] to pay their employees the Living Wage by, among other things, (i) including in tenant packages references to the Living Wage and the Developer's support thereof, and (ii) implementing the Living Wage Incentive Plan."[71] Under the Incentive Plan, the developer was required to put forth a positive statement about paying a living wage in marketing to tenants; agree to meet and confer with a coalition led by LAANE on potential tenants; and agree "to cause the movie theater operator in the Project to either (i) provide health benefits to each employee of such theater . . .; or (ii) in lieu of providing health benefits . . . pay such employees . . . $1.25 in additional hourly wages."[72]

On top of these LAANE-led projects, there were other important CBA precedents. In 1998, the public transit authority overseeing the Alameda Corridor transportation project—a twenty-mile railway linking the ports of Los Angeles and Long Beach to downtown Los Angeles—bowed to community organizing pressure in requiring the project's general contractor to provide $5 million for job training and to set aside construction jobs for low-income project area residents.[73] The following year, AGENDA successfully petitioned the Los Angeles City Council to require the DreamWorks animation company to enter a development agreement to fund a job training and placement program for low-income workers in exchange for public subsidies approved for the new DreamWorks Playa Vista studio.[74] Such development agreements—like those in the Hollywood and Highland, and Cinerama Dome projects—were required when the city subsidized or transferred public land to a developer. But, up to this point, they had rarely been used to incorporate specific community benefits.

Although representing an important advance for those historically excluded from redevelopment negotiations, the tactic of embedding community benefits within agreements between developers and the city did not include a mechanism for direct enforcement by community organizations. Instead, this tactic relied on government officials to hold developers to their obligations, which—after subsidies were awarded and projects were built—officials often had little incentive to do. It was in response to this problem that Madeline Janis-Aparicio and her colleagues at LAANE started to explore the idea of negotiating a separate contract with a developer *enforceable directly by the community*—what would become the CBA. The first testing ground was in North Hollywood, in connection with organizing commenced by the LAANE-led Valley Jobs Coalition in 2000 around NoHo Commons, a proposed mixed-use project (to be subsidized by the CRA) next to the planned North Hollywood subway station. That organizing eventually resulted in a CBA in late 2001, after events had thrust the Staples Sports and Entertainment District CBA to the fore.

The Staples CBA campaign therefore unfolded against the backdrop of LAANE's wider effort to promote subsidy accountability toward the goal of extending the living wage and requiring a "written contract in every deal that also incorporates public benefits."[75] In early 2000, the Living Wage Coalition, launched after the Living Wage Ordinance was passed and staffed by LAANE's Erika Zucker, was meeting to "[d]evelop a comprehensive policy for subsidy accountability which sets the stage for a citywide campaign to reform the process of awarding subsidies."[76] In a March 15, 2000 memo, LAANE's co-director of research, Jessica Goodheart, presented the central objectives of the subsidy accountability campaign, calling for a "high degree of monitoring and oversight of *highly subsidized large developments*," as well as passage of a CRA living wage policy in Spring 2000.[77] In May, Goodheart and Zucker met with Councilwoman Jackie Goldberg and labor representatives to discuss pushing a "subsidy accountability" policy agenda at city hall. One goal was to link the Living Wage Ordinance to a contractor responsibility policy—effectively barring contractors that did not pay a living wage or already have a union from bidding on city projects—thereby putting pressure on contractors to permit union organizing. In addition, Goodheart and Zucker promoted to Goldberg a policy that would codify the pioneering Hollywood and Highland development agreement by imposing community benefits on all subsidy recipients.[78] Seeking to extend the Living Wage Ordinance to every job on city-financed projects,[79] LAANE published a policy brief in June outlining city development subsidies by type and department, and conducting a power analysis that identified subsidy accountability allies, which included unions, as well as civil rights, environmental, and housing equity groups.[80] In July, LAANE presented research on subsidies to allies across the state.[81] By September, LAANE was developing a plan for a California-wide collaborative, anchored by LAANE, AGENDA, and the Community Coalition in Los Angeles; the East Bay Alliance for a Sustainable Economy (EBASE) and Working Partnerships in the Bay Area; and the Center on Policy Initiatives and Environmental Health Coalition in San Diego.[82] Toward the end of 2000, this alliance added new partners, including Oakland's PolicyLink, and began moving assertively toward developing a statewide economic impact law, modeled on environmental review, which would create a framework for project-by-project community benefits.[83]

In was in the midst of this furious advocacy that the Staples Sports and Entertainment District emerged as the centerpiece of subsidy accountability. Ramping up the Staples campaign, FCCEJ achieved its first major public relations victory in October 2000, when Tim Leiweke, the president of L.A. Arena Land Company, failed to show up to a crowded meeting of community members arranged by Councilwoman Rita Walters.[84] Angry residents and activists shouted at an empty seat with Leiweke's name placard on it.[85] The public fallout led the developer to assign Ted Tanner, senior vice president of the Staples Center, to mend relations with FCCEJ and strike a deal.[86] At a follow-up meeting on November 15, 2000, "residents' anger and frustration was obvious and explicit; Staples people saw that residents aren't patient anymore."[87] A "Big Brains" meeting convened in December 2000 revealed the degree to which the community fight against gentrification had merged with labor's pursuit of subsidy accountability. The meeting was attended by Anthony Thigpenn (AGENDA); Madeline Janis-Aparicio (LAANE); Gilda Haas, Cecilia Brennan, Sandra McNeill, and Enrique Velasquez (SAJE); James Elmendorf (Coalition LA); and Jerilyn López Mendoza (Environmental Defense). The discussion focused on linking the Staples "project to issue of destruction of affordable housing," advancing a solution that built on "Dreamworks and TrizecHahn," promoting high-end jobs, and "lock[ing] components into their Specific Plan" while figuring out "how to deal with gentrification."[88] These big picture ideas were assigned to various FCCEJ committees, which were asked to develop more concrete policy details and report back to the full coalition.

How much affordable housing to demand, and how to fund it, were central questions. In early January 2001, the FCCEJ Ad Hoc Housing Committee developed a plan for setting aside a specific amount of sales tax increment associated with the Staples project for housing, an idea supported by Councilman Hernandez. Committee members were also mulling over the appropriate proportion of affordable housing in the district ("20%? 50%? 100%?"), inclusionary zoning, and a housing trust fund financed from sales tax increment or by the Staples Foundation. Members were instructed that "[a]fter the demands are developed, they should be taken to the Ad Hoc Committee, to [City Council members] Pacheco, Padilla and Wachs, and perhaps to Cindy Miscikowski, and possibly even to Mike Feuer."[89] A week later, on January 10, a working group including Elmendorf, López Mendoza, and Haas discussed how to incorporate community benefits in the Staples Center Specific Plan—a land use document that set out precise zoning requirements in the community—on top of including benefits in the CRA development agreement.[90] That same day, a "Big Brains II" meeting was convened to review the overall framework of a Staples community benefits package, which had coalesced around living wage jobs, first-source hiring, developer and tenant compliance with the Living Wage and Worker Retention Ordinances, card-check neutrality, parks, and open space.

Despite enormous progress, tensions flared among labor and housing advocates concerned about a potential financial trade-off between increased wages and more housing on the project. Describing a community meeting held in February 2001, LAANE's Goodheart told Janis-Aparicio, "The bottom line is that I came out of that meeting thinking that we need to be much more involved in trying to make sure the community–union links really happen with this project."[91] After noting that Coalition LA was seeking $5 to $10 million for housing and open space, Goodheart noted that one coalition member "pulled me out of the meeting at one point saying that she was really, really concerned at the scope of the demands," while another "from ACORN, who happened into the hallway during our conversation also said he was concerned at the scope of the demands, and said he had unsuccessfully tried to talk to Gilda [Haas] about this." For her part, Haas "seemed to feel that the unions needed to be educated more about the need for housing, and that the power that the housing advocates had built up needed to be respected."[92] Expressing concern, Goodheart concluded, "I also feel that this is a very delicate situation, and the most important thing is to work something out that allows us to win something from Staples, and work well together with SAJE in the future. Madeline, I think you're the best situated to do this because of your relationship both with Gilda and Maria Elena [Durazo from HERE Local 11]."[93]

As FCCEJ entered its crucial negotiation phase in 2001, its leaders faced a twin challenge: holding the coalition together from the inside while identifying key sources of leverage on the outside. Intensive coalition research homed in on critical pieces of leverage, all of which were structured by law in important ways. One piece related to electoral term limits. In 1993, Los Angeles voters passed local propositions restricting the mayor and city council members to two four-year terms. That meant that Mayor Riordan, a staunch supporter of the project who had pushed the Planning Commission for fast-track permitting approvals, was set to be termed out of office as of July 1, 2001, with a very tight runoff race underway between Democrats James Hahn and Antonio Villaraigosa, a strong pro-labor candidate.[94] In addition, the City Council—whose members also supported the Sports and Entertainment District—was about to be transformed, with six of its fifteen members—including Councilwoman Rita Walters, whose district encompassed the project—termed out. As a result, the developer was pressing to secure all city land use entitlements before July 1, 2001, which meant ensuring that FCCEJ was on board and would not delay key approvals.

In addition to the leverage gained from term limits, FCCEJ benefited from public participation rights embedded in the legal process for approving development. Local government law set the legal framework for how cities structured the process of granting development entitlements, such as land use and building approvals, while also governing redevelopment. In Los Angeles, developers had to go through the Planning Commission to obtain discretionary land use approvals, with a process for appeal to the City Council generally available. The structure of the entitlements process permitted well-organized opposition groups with strong political connections to delay or even prevent key approvals. With labor unions as coalition members, FCCEJ could make a credible threat of disrupting the land use entitlements process for the Sports and Entertainment District deal, which would increase costs and uncertainty for the developer.[95] Moreover, the deal was from the beginning based on the assumption of public financing, which could only be approved by the CRA and City Council after public hearings, providing another political opportunity for FCCEJ and its union supporters to disrupt the deal.

FCCEJ used the threat of disruption implicit in its participation rights to bring the developer to the negotiating table, where the goal was to hammer out a CBA. From the developer's point of view, the CBA was an "induced agreement," in that the developer would have preferred not to enter into it, but recognized that "there were externalities that the coalition wanted the developer to internalize."[96] In exchange, the developer wanted the certainty of coalition support, which it sought to lock in contractually through pledges by coalition members and their allies not to disrupt project approvals. Although the developer insisted on the certainty of coalition support, it sought flexibility in meeting the coalition's community benefits demands. Accordingly, there was significant push and pull between the developer and coalition representatives on the community benefits package.

It was at this point that lawyers meaningfully contributed to moving negotiations toward final agreement. Julian Gross was the coalition attorney responsible for drafting the CBA. Gross had started out as a Skadden Fellow at the Employment Law Center in San Francisco, where he worked on developing a local hiring policy for the redevelopment agency in East Palo Alto and was involved in the Alameda Corridor Jobs Coalition project in Los Angeles.[97] At the Employment Law Center, Gross had helped win community benefits in connection with an East Palo Alto redevelopment project that was incorporated into the development agreement (though not signed by community groups).[98] In 1999, Gross set up his own solo practice and began working with LAANE on the NoHo Commons CBA campaign.[99] When the Sports and Entertainment District deal was announced, Gross was retained by LAANE to represent the group and provided legal support to the negotiation team throughout the process.[100] Although LAANE was Gross's client, he dealt directly with Janis-Aparicio, Haas, and McNeill. As he recalled, "I went out of my way not to have conversations with other coalition members in order to not make them my client as well," expecting that other member groups would "look at the CBA and have their boards sign off and maybe have their own lawyers look at it."[101]

The negotiation team itself was selected by FCCEJ members on the basis of expertise and negotiating skill. The key members were SAJE's Haas and LAANE's Janis-Aparicio. Although not an attorney, Haas—who held a master's degree in urban planning from UCLA—had started the community economic development unit at LAFLA.[102] Janis-Aparicio was an attorney who, after graduating from the UCLA School of Law, had done slum housing litigation and worked as an associate at the Los Angeles powerhouse firm of Latham & Watkins (which was representing the developer against FCCEJ in the CBA negotiations). Other members of the negotiation team included Adrianne Shropshire from AGENDA, James Elmendorf of Coalition LA, and Jerilyn López Mendoza of Environmental Defense. The FCCEJ team was joined by HERE Local 11's David Koff, who was the crossover participant involved in both the coalition negotiations and organized labor's negotiations for a project labor agreement. The stringent criteria for selection to the negotiating team excluded Figueroa Corridor residents. To address this omission, FCCEJ put together a team of neighborhood leaders—including Esperanza's Sister Diane Donoghue—who attended all of the meetings with the developer, provided

Figure 4.3 Gilda Haas, founder of SAJE (in front of SAJE House). *Source*: The Durfee Foundation (2001).

feedback on developer proposals, and conveyed information on the process back to the community.[103] As Haas recalled, "When we caucused, we would check with them."[104]

To facilitate negotiation, the FCCEJ team presented a weekly briefing paper containing core coalition demands to the developer, which would review and respond at the following meeting. Haas stated that the coalition's demands represented a "floating bottom line" that assigned different weights to housing and jobs depending on the developer's position.[105] As the coalition's lawyer, Gross sought "to minimize the amount my skills [were] needed . . . [letting] the organizers and my clients do most of the negotiating."[106] Although he would fine-tune details of technical issues, such as the duration of local hiring benefits, Gross preferred having the FCCEJ negotiation team talking directly to the developer in order to avoid "the dynamic of seeing how obnoxious lawyers can be in drafting documents."[107] Nonetheless, there were clashes with the developer's lawyer, Bill Delvac, chair of the real estate department at Latham & Watkins, who began working on the Staples Center development in 1996. Although a supporter of affordable housing and committed to expanding the pie, Delvac was viewed by coalition members as a fierce negotiator, often "sneaking in" provisions during contract negotiations that attempted to "shift the framework" of the deal toward his client.[108] Haas came to calling these stealth provisions "Delvacs,"[109] which were sent to Gross to neutralize. From Delvac's vantage point, his proposals were designed to protect his client's interests in preserving

Figure 4.4 Sister Diane Donoghue, founder of Esperanza (at Via Esperanza). *Source*: Carlos Chavez, *Los Angeles Times* via Getty Images (October 3, 2006).

"flexibility" in the implementation of community benefits. In an effort to keep the discussion flowing, when he received a coalition demand, Delvac insisted that his client would "never say no until we've thought about it three times."[110]

As Gross recalled, throughout this process, Haas gave the "best feedback" in ensuring the contract terms were clear. Gross generally did not offer his view of the substantive value of contract provisions, sharing only after Haas would ask him, "What do you think?"[111] As the negotiations advanced, Gross did most of the contract drafting and revision remotely, coming down to Los Angeles only once during the negotiating period. In what became the basic division of labor, Haas and Janis-Aparicio would engage in the substantive negotiations to develop proposals, while McNeill would review those proposals with Gross, whose main task was "trying to put their substantive decisions into language that was legally binding."[112]

Another lawyer on the negotiating team who played a critical—but quite different—role was Jerilyn López Mendoza, a UCLA law graduate with law firm experience, who was an attorney in the Environmental Justice Project at Environmental Defense. López Mendoza's work focused on protecting low-income communities of color against environmental hazards, which she saw as intimately related to FCCEJ's effort to reform a redevelopment system that involved "people with power making decisions that affect people without power."[113] She was attracted to CBAs as "a way of taking a traditional legal concept, a contract, and using it to transfer power. A CBA says to developers: If you want to make this easy for yourself, give us something back."[114] From her perspective, CBAs advanced "the idea of putting the power of decision making and community building in the hands of the people living in the community... giving them a voice" leading to "better results": "developments that are more in tune with community needs."[115] Despite her enthusiasm, López Mendoza was also sensitive about her role as a newcomer to community–labor advocacy, recalling that, because the Staples campaign was "an introduction to the social justice community for me, I didn't want to push too hard and dominate the agenda."[116]

Although she had a humble view of her role, López Mendoza's skill set as an environmental lawyer experienced with the state process for environmental review ended up having a critical impact on the campaign's trajectory. In California, the process for gaining environmental clearance for development projects centered on the California Environmental Quality Act (CEQA), which required that a public agency, such as the city planning commission, evaluate the environmental impact of projects before issuing discretionary development approvals or providing public subsidies.[117] If the project was determined to have a significant environmental impact, an environmental impact report (EIR) had to be prepared and circulated for public comment.[118] The final approval of a project could be challenged in court on the grounds that it did not meet the substantive and procedural requirements of CEQA, forcing the agency to repeat the environmental review process.[119]

Knowing that a defective EIR could significantly delay the project, the FCCEJ environmental team, coordinated by López Mendoza, carefully reviewed the developer's Draft EIR when it was issued in January 2001.[120] FCCEJ's comprehensive forty-six-page response to the Draft EIR, authored by López Mendoza, was submitted to the Planning Commission in late February, highlighting a number of inadequacies, including the developer's failure to include an analysis of the energy impact of the project, which—coming on the heels of Southern California's 2000 energy crisis—was a significant omission. In FCCEJ's response, López Mendoza hammered the draft for this problem:

> Although an EIR should include the energy environmental impacts of a project, the [Draft EIR] for the Project fails to include such an analysis. This omission seems particularly puzzling in light of the ongoing energy crisis facing the state and the region.... In light of the size of the Project and the energy crisis, we believe a full energy analysis should be completed in compliance with requirements set forth in CEQA, and that an energy analysis, complete with required mitigation measures, should be included in the final EIR.[121]

With the prospect of a CEQA lawsuit that could derail the project until well after the July 1, 2001 political transition suddenly a realistic possibility, the developer responded by intensifying the pace of negotiations, which proceeded at breakneck speed. To push the process along, while the negotiating team passed contract drafts back and forth, FCCEJ organizers staged public events to keep up the external pressure. Haas recalled one FCCEJ press conference, at which a community resident told reporters that the developer "wouldn't do this if we were Beverly Hills." Confronted with this claim as he stepped off of a flight returning from the Republican National Convention, Mayor Riordan responded angrily, denouncing the claim as "damn lies,"[122] and provoking a firestorm of negative press. With the publicity increasing and the deadline looming, both parties redoubled their efforts to achieve resolution. It came on May 30, 2001, with the announcement of a final CBA—the first time that a community coalition in a major U.S. city had won a set of contractual concessions directly from any developer, much less a developer with the wealth, status, and power of AEG. The CBA was subsequently attached to the city's development agreement, making it enforceable by the city as well.[123]

There were two related parts to the agreement. Under the first, called the Cooperation Agreement, FCCEJ agreed both to release its right to oppose the development project (which included bringing lawsuits, taking administrative actions, and expressing public opposition) and to provide affirmative support for the project (which included issuing a press release and testifying in support of administrative approvals).[124] There was a split over the final terms of the agreement, with AGENDA and the Community Coalition refusing to sign on as FCCEJ members, citing the waiver of their right to oppose the project as incompatible with their organizational missions.[125] This created a problem for the developer, which wanted to make sure that a few close FCCEJ allies could not opt out of the agreement and protest the project, while the developer bore the full contractual obligations. This "friends of friends" issue, as Delvac put it,[126] was dealt with by contractually designating FCCEJ members that did not sign the agreement as "interested organizations," which—although technically not bound to the agreement—could nevertheless relieve the developer of its community benefits obligations by bringing a suit against the project.[127] In exchange for FCCEJ's cooperation, the developer agreed to the second part of the CBA, called the Community Benefits Program, which was also incorporated as part of the development agreement between the city and the developer. The Community Benefits Program constituted a finely wrought compromise around housing, labor, and other community goals, including these key provisions:

- *Parks and Recreation*: The developer shall provide between $50,000 and $75,000 to fund "an assessment of the need for parks, open space, and recreational facilities" in the project area and subsequently "fund or cause to be privately funded at least one million dollars ($1,000,000) for the creation or improvement of one or more park and recreation facilities."
- *Parking Permit Area*: The developer shall "support" FCCEJ's efforts to have the city establish a residential parking permit district, providing funding of $25,000 per year for five years to the city to develop and implement the program.

- *Living Wage Program*: The developer "shall make all reasonable efforts to maximize the number of living wage jobs" in the project and agree to a 70% Living Wage Goal for the anticipated fifty-five hundred jobs. In the event of failure to achieve "80% of the goal for two consecutive years," the developer "shall meet and confer with the Coalition . . . to determine mutually agreeable steps which can and will be taken to meet the Living Wage Goal." Failure to meet the goal at the "five- and ten-year points" shall not constitute a breach provided the developer comply with obligations to provide an annual report "on the percentage of jobs in the Project that are living wage jobs," and to provide advance notice of prospective tenants to the coalition, giving the coalition an opportunity to meet with prospective tenants to discuss the living wage goal. In addition, "[a]ll Tenants will be offered the opportunity to participate in a Living Wage Incentive Program," providing "various benefits of substantial economic value . . . at no cost to the Developer, to assist the Project in meeting the Living Wage Goal."
- *Local Hiring and Job Training*: The developer shall provide $100,000 in seed funding to establish a First Source Referral System, a nonprofit organization designed to recruit and train targeted job applicants—giving first priority to applicants displaced by the Staples Center or living within a one-half mile radius of the project—and refer them to project employers. The employers, in turn, shall provide notice of job openings to the First Source Referral System and agree to hire only targeted job applicants for a designated period of time after notice of the jobs is provided. An employer who fills 50% of available jobs within a six-month period with targeted job applicants shall be deemed in compliance with the first-source hiring policy.
- *Service Worker Retention and Responsible Contracting*: The developer, its contractors, and tenants in the hotel and theater components of the project shall follow the city's Worker Retention Ordinance requiring the reasonable retention of existing workers in new projects. In addition, the developer shall not retain a contractor failing to meet the city's contractor responsibility policy and shall not lease to tenants without first obtaining "a written account" of the tenant's record of labor compliance.
- *Affordable Housing*: The developer "shall develop or cause to be developed affordable housing equal to 20% of the units constructed" within the project (100–160 affordable units in total). The units shall be targeted as follows: 30% to families earning 50% or less of area median income (AMI); 35% to families earning from 51% to 60% of AMI; and 35% to families earning from 61% to 80% of AMI. Units may be built within the project area or off-site, provided that off-site housing is located "in redevelopment areas within a three-mile radius" of the Staples Center. Residents displaced by the Staples Center shall be given priority in housing selection, and the developer agrees to "meet and confer" with the coalition and city agencies to "seek and obtain permanent affordable housing for families relocated in connection with the development." The developer also must work

cooperatively with community organizations to provide additional affordable housing by contributing up to $650,000 in three-year, interest-free loans to non-profit housing developers building projects in the area (including "pre-qualified" developers such as Esperanza and 1010 Hope Development Corporation).[128]

The Implementation Challenge

Despite the timeliness of the CBA, the project itself did not receive the sought-after approval before the July 1, 2001 political transition because newly elected city council members asked for a delay so that they could review the deal.[129] Whether the city would provide subsidy—and how much—was a sticking point. To decide, after the CBA was inked, the city spent $150,000 on a consultant to advise on funding options,[130] while L.A. Arena Land Company Vice President Ted Tanner insisted that the hotel could not be built without a taxpayer subsidy.[131] Where that money would come from, however, was unclear. Although the developer contended that the project would help the city by generating tax revenue,[132] some officials argued that using tax dollars to supplement a potentially profitable project would benefit already affluent developers.[133] A major legal roadblock was the CRA's authority to use tax increment to subsidize the Sports and Entertainment District. Although the CRA was the natural choice for providing a subsidy (because the CRA could draw upon dedicated redevelopment funds that would not come out of the city's general revenues), it turned out that the CRA was not permitted to offer its typical subsidy because the Central Business District redevelopment zone, in which the Staples project sat, had already reached its legal subsidy cap in 2000.[134] To get around this problem, the city created a new project area, labeled the City Center Redevelopment project, in 2002. The 879-acre project area was expected to generate $2.4 billion in tax revenue over 30 years to finance the construction of twelve thousand nine hundred housing units and 6.7 million square feet of commercial and industrial space, with $150 million to be set aside to help the homeless.[135] A portion of the City Center Redevelopment project area overlapped with 760 acres of the Central Business District, including 43 acres of property allocated to the L.A. Sports and Entertainment District, which the CRA intended to fund.[136] Los Angeles County filed suit to block the City Center area from collecting tax increment, arguing that it would deprive the county of $1 billion in tax revenue (that would otherwise have to be shared with the county in the absence of redevelopment).[137] In 2003, a state superior court agreed, holding that the transfer of Central Business District project area funds to the City Center project was an illegal effort to circumvent the subsidy cap. During this legal wrangling, the Sports and Entertainment District lied fallow.

After it became clear that CRA funds would not be available, the city made a number of other attempts to move the project forward. In mid-July 2004, the developer agreed not to seek city funding paid through general tax revenue and to instead accept the bulk of city assistance in the form of a bed tax waiver.[138] Although this did not placate all critics,[139] it did break the logjam. As a result of these negotiations, it was not until February 2005 that the city finally approved a $177-million financial assistance package for the hotel, consisting of up to $140 million in foregone revenue from hotel bed taxes, $22 million in city loans, $10 million in public improvements, and $5 million in waived building fees.[140] Although construction was not set for completion until 2008, by the time the deal was finalized, the developer had already made good on some of its CBA promises: contributing $1 million to fund Hope and Peace Park and a free family recreational facility in the neighborhood (although the latter was not completed for several years and both required additional public subsidies of nearly $6 million).[141] The developer also assisted in the establishment of Los Angeles's first Poor People's Preferential Parking District, which reserved evening parking for local residents and paid for the first five years of resident permits.[142] The developer further provided $650,000 in low-interest loans to community-based affordable housing developers,[143] which by 2008 had already opened some affordable units.

Implementation of the CBA, however, was not without difficulty.[144] A critical issue involved the CBA's affordable housing provision, under which the developer was required to "develop or cause to be developed affordable housing equal to 20% of the units constructed" within the project, on-site or within a three-mile radius, and targeted to low-income families. This language left a number of enforcement issues unresolved, such as the timing of affordable housing production and how the CBA would apply to developers that purchased discrete parcels within the project from AEG. The timing issue had been initially addressed in the city's development agreement, which conditioned approval of more than 250 market-rate units in the project on the construction of a minimum of 40 affordable units.[145] However, when AEG began to sell parcels off, it asked the city to revise the development agreement to reflect the fact that AEG itself would no longer own the land—and that successor developers were not parties to the CBA. In 2005, the city agreed that going forward new purchasers of development rights in the Sports and Entertainment District could discharge the CBA's affordable housing obligations by providing a $40,000 payment for each required affordable unit to the Figueroa Corridor Community Land Trust—an entity that FCCEJ had established to build affordable housing in the neighborhood—or to another community-based developer in the Figueroa Corridor. Although the city promised the new arrangement would generate several million dollars in contributions to the Land Trust, the coalition objected that $40,000 was inadequate to cover construction costs for a unit of affordable housing.[146] The city also agreed to give developers "half-credits" for already-built affordable units if the developers were willing to provide some additional "gap financing" outside of what was already required by the CBA.[147] Although the coalition objected to this as well, its members believed they had limited leverage to prevent the changes in light of ambiguity in the CBA's affordable housing language,[148] which only stated that the developer directly develop "or cause to be developed" the specified percentage of affordable units.

In its revised development agreement, the city walked back from its strong support for affordable housing in one final respect. In September 2005, Williams and Dame (operating through a subsidiary, Figueroa South Land LLC), one of the developers purchasing project land from AEG, asked the city to be relieved of its affordable housing obligations in light of a preexisting agreement to contribute $8 million toward the YWCA's development of an affordable housing project in downtown (but not within the CBA project area), consisting of two hundred dormitory units for at-risk youth. The coalition once again objected. Putting up a valiant fight, LAFLA attorney Ben Beach drafted a memo contending that the CBA was enforceable against subsequent purchasers and arguing at a city hearing that the revision violated the CBA's affordable housing provisions, which targeted families.[149] However, after a flurry of negotiations, the city and coalition agreed to a plan under which Williams and Dame was given credit for 130 units of affordable housing in exchange for a $400,000 contribution to the Land Trust (split between AEG and Williams and Dame). The plan also included a commitment by Williams and Dame to contribute another $10,000 per unit if it decided to seek credit for the remaining seventy YWCA dormitory units (potentially an additional $700,000 to the Land Trust).[150] With those legal skirmishes settled, only construction remained undone.

Phase One of the L.A. Live project, the seventy-one-hundred–seat Nokia Theater designed to host events such as the American Music Awards and the Emmys, officially opened in 2007. The final construction phases—which included restaurants and entertainment venues (including the GRAMMY Museum, ESPN Zone, the Farm of Beverly Hills, Lawry's, and Starbucks), as well as movie theaters, hotels, and residences—were completed by 2010. Regarding developer compliance with the CBA, a 2006 status update from the coalition stated that a job training program was established in August 2003 and that the developer had provided $62,000 (out of a promised total of $100,000) in seed funding to support the program.[151] By 2009, AEG claimed that all of the jobs in the Nokia Theater met the CBA's living wage requirements and half of the jobs were held by local residents in compliance with the local hiring requirement.[152] A subsequent analysis of CBA implementation concluded that AEG officially reported first meeting the 70% living wage goal for the project in 2013, although that was, in part, because many employers in the project were independently covered by the city's Living Wage Ordinance or (in the case of hotel employees) union contracts.[153] The same analysis found that project developers made affordable housing contributions "with a total nominal value of $13,185,000. This figure, which exclude[d] the $650,000 in interest-free loans [required by the CBA], represent[ed] roughly 10% of the total development cost of 366 units in five projects" (including the 200 YWCA dormitory units deemed "unsuitable for families").[154] In the end, because of the YWCA credits, the "CBA

Figure 4.5 L.A. Live in progress. *Source*: Scott Cummings (2008).

did not produce as many units suitable for families as coalition members sought" (although contributions to the Land Trust may have increased affordable housing production elsewhere), and the achievement of income-targeting goals occurred primarily as the result of the fact that most housing projects were developed with federal tax credits that required lower income restrictions.[155] Moreover, the CBA's 20% inclusionary housing requirement was only marginally higher than the 15% requirement already mandated for new private housing developments under state redevelopment law.

Although the Staples CBA may not have achieved the highest goals FCCEJ had set, it was nonetheless transformative, sparking interest in the CBA as an equitable development tool and setting a model for others to follow in Los Angeles and around the country.[156] In retrospect, while specific provisions might have been drafted more tightly or coalition leverage exerted to larger effect, FCCEJ leaders had to learn an enormous amount on the fly about the redevelopment process and high-stakes negotiation with a powerful developer adversary. From that perspective—and given the baseline of what had been normative for L.A. redevelopment before, with communities receiving nothing beyond legally required minimums—winning a multimillion dollar affordable housing investment, hundreds of living wage jobs, and additional developer-funded community amenities was an accomplishment that could not be sold short. Perhaps most importantly, FCCEJ had asserted standing for community groups to be at the table when development projects were conceived and negotiated—again, a far cry from historic practices, evident in the Staples Center case, in which the first time communities heard about projects was when they were announced by cities and developers as done deals.

In this sense, the Staples CBA campaign reconfigured L.A. redevelopment going forward. Following up on the Staples success, the labor side of the coalition immediately pursued CBAs in Los Angeles's San Fernando Valley, where two publicly subsidized CRA projects became opportunities to test the Staples model. The two CBAs were negotiated in tandem and finalized within a week of each other by the Valley Jobs Coalition (represented by Julian Gross). The coalition, launched in 1999, was led by LAANE, and included CHIRLA, CLUE, HERE Local 11, Pacoima Beautiful, San Fernando Neighborhood Legal Services, United Food and Commercial Workers (UFCW) Local 770, the Van Nuys Worksource Center, and other Valley-based groups. Because the CRA was extending its reach into the Valley, spurred by the new Red Line subway connection running from downtown Los Angeles, LAANE saw another opportunity to advocate that the CRA direct public investment to promote living wage jobs.[157]

The first campaign targeted NoHo Commons, a mixed-use CRA project near the new Metro stop in North Hollywood, set to open in 2000 as the terminus point for the Red Line.[158] To advance the city's goal of promoting transit-oriented development, the NoHo Commons project was slated to receive $43.9 million in public subsidies and loans.[159] The developer, SL NO HO LLC, proposed building 810 housing units as well as 220,000 square feet of office space, a community health center, child care center, and 228,000 square feet of shops and resturants.[160] The project's scale meant that it had to undergo environmental review—making it ripe for CBA organizing. The campaign started in 2000 but was overtaken by the advent of the Staples CBA process, which consumed LAANE resources. As a result, the NoHo Commons CBA was not finalized until November 1, 2001.

The agreement emphasized job quality for local workers and laid the groundwork for a unionization drive at the grocery store at the heart of the project. Toward this end, the CBA included a commitment by the developer to "make all reasonable efforts to maximize the number of living wage jobs in the Development" toward a 75% overall goal, with specific steps constituting reasonable efforts and a $10,000 penalty imposed for failure to make them.[161] In line with the Living Wage Ordinance, the agreement counted as "living wage jobs" those covered by union contract and thus served as a platform for potential union organizing of permanent workers in the retail jobs produced by the project.[162] The central focus of union organizing was the proposed grocery store. In exchange for coalition support, the developer signed a labor neutrality agreement with UFCW Local 770, agreeing that "any retailer who leases space in the development . . . must, as part of the written lease agreement, agree to enter into an agreement with UFCW 770 to ensure an orderly environment for its employees to exercise rights" under federal labor law. The CBA also provided for on-site space for a child care center (with at least fifty spaces reserved for very low- to moderate-income families), a first-source hiring system for employers in the development, a job training program tailored to the needs of employers, seed money for a job training program for day laborers, and developer and contractor compliance with city worker retention and contractor responsibility policies.[163] With the CBA in place, the project won unanimous approval from the Los Angeles City Council.[164]

Around the same time, the Valley Jobs Coalition—this time led by LAANE (represented by Lizette Hernandez), the Sun Valley Neighborhood Improvement Association, Pacoima Beautiful, and UFCW Local 770[165]—homed in on another CRA project: a thirty-three-acre dump site in the Valley, which the developer, SunQuest Development LLC, planned to convert into an industrial and retail complex. Using its now battle-tested approach, the coalition executed the SunQuest CBA on October 25, 2001. It was signed by the individual members of the Valley Jobs Coalition and the developer,[166] which agreed to a 70% living wage goal for jobs in the project, promising a "one-time payment of liquidated damages in the amount of $50,000" in the event of noncompliance at the opening of the site.[167] Because of the site's industrial usage, a significant focus of the CBA was on mitigating environmental impacts—such as limiting commercial trucks accessing the site from using residential streets and from idling for more than ten minutes.[168] In addition, the CBA mandated a process for community input into the development's design, which had to meet strict environmental standards, particularly around landscaping, truck routing, and avoidance of "heat islands."[169] The CBA further required the developer to contribute $150,000 toward a neighborhood improvement fund, provide money for arts programs in local schools, build a new youth center, and establish a first-source hiring policy that covered all employers at the development.[170] The CBA was not incorporated into the CRA's development agreement with SunQuest; instead, the city negotiated a "Community Benefits Plan" in connection with the city's subsequent sale to SunQuest of an adjacent landfill to expand the project's footprint.[171]

With the Valley wins creating additional CBA facts on the ground, LAANE pivoted toward thinking of community benefits in systemic terms—not just as the fruits of ad hoc development campaigns but as a baseline for accountable development codified in city policy.[172] Nevertheless, there were additional CBA site fights in the pipeline. LAANE and AGENDA spearheaded a 2002 CBA with

Capital Vision Equities, developer of Marlton Square in the Crenshaw neighborhood, which included a 70% living wage goal and local hiring.[173] And another project in redevelopment-rich Hollywood, at a Metro stop on the famous corner of Hollywood Boulevard and Vine Street, would result in a LAANE-led CBA two years later.[174]

On top of building expertise among advocates who would lead the next phase of the community benefits campaign in Los Angeles, the Staples CBA also helped to mobilize regulatory reform in support of community benefits policy at the city level.[175] In 2002, coalition members (building on LAANE's earlier statewide subsidy accountability effort) pushed the CRA to codify its Staples success by adopting a Community Impact Report (CIR) policy, which would have required developers within redevelopment project areas to take into account the impact of projects on affordable housing and jobs along the lines of the environmental review system.[176] To promote this policy, LAANE's Goodheart led a research project to create "A Model Community Impact Report," released in August 2002, which applied impact criteria to evaluate a proposed CRA redevelopment project in the South Los Angeles Adams La Brea neighborhood.[177] It was a sophisticated effort, illuminating what rigorous analysis could reveal about the impact of proposed redevelopment projects like Adams La Brea, which the report concluded would mostly create jobs below the living wage line and result in the loss of forty-five unionized grocery positions.[178] Nonetheless, a proposed CIR at the CRA was tabled after strong developer opposition, as was a less onerous requirement for project developers to provide an initial assessment of job and housing impacts and track job and housing outcomes over time. Instead, in May 2005, the CRA mandated that a two-page "community context" report be attached to each project proposal at CRA board meetings highlighting the impact of proposed projects for evaluation.[179]

The CRA eventually did put into place new community benefits policies, spearheaded by LAANE's Madeline Janis-Aparicio, whose success with the Staples CBA resulted in her 2002 appointment to the CRA board by Mayor James Hahn after a strong push from County Fed chief, Miguel Contreras.[180] With Janis-Aparicio's leadership, in 2003, the CRA attached living wage requirements to CRA contractors and recipients of CRA funding over $100,000, adopted a contractor responsibility program requiring CRA contractors and financial assistance recipients to attest to their compliance with labor and other laws (including the Living Wage Ordinance), and passed a worker retention policy. The agency subsequently enacted a labor peace policy requiring hotels developed on city-owned land to agree to card-check neutrality with unions.[181] As this suggested, on the back of the CBA movement, organized labor had achieved influence over L.A. redevelopment in ways that permitted labor leaders to use newly acquired levers of institutional power to promote unionization in the job-rich retail and hospitality industries by attaching community benefits to future projects.

Demanding Environmental Justice from the City: The LAX CBA

When a Public Asset Harms the Public

The next major opportunity to test the CBA model came not with a private developer, but with the City of Los Angeles, which owned one of the region's most important economic assets: the Los Angeles International Airport (LAX). On the cusp of the new millennium, LAX handled roughly 800,000 flights per year, serving 70 million passengers and hauling more than 2 million tons of cargo—making it the third busiest airport in the world.[182] An enormously important and complex economic enterprise, the airport produced forty thousand jobs and constituted an essential stimulus for the region's broader economy.

Yet, at the turn of the millennium, LAX was also an enterprise in need of major renovation. Situated on thirty-five hundred acres near the Pacific Ocean south of Marina del Rey, the airport's vast infrastructure had not received a comprehensive overhaul for a half-century and had not been significantly updated since the 1984 Olympic Games. As a result of growing demand, its facilities were dilapidated and its runway space overtaxed. Airline industry officials and local business leaders worried that LAX could not meet projected increases in passenger and cargo demand over the next decade, causing it to lose market share to other airports. LAX modernization was therefore an urgent priority for Mayor Riordan when he took office in 1993.

Because of LAX's status as a public entity, operated by the city Airport Department—known as Los Angeles World Airports (LAWA)—modernization was a political process: one that required delicate coordination between LAWA and the Federal Aviation Administration (FAA), which had fiscal and regulatory authority over U.S. airports. Any modernization plan would have to come from and ultimately be approved by LAWA, governed by a seven-member Board of Airport Commissioners (appointed by the mayor).[183] Under the city administrative code, LAWA approval would then have to be ratified by the Los Angeles City Council and, from there, by the FAA. In particular, all LAWA expenditures were subject to review by the FAA, which had the statutory authority to deny expenditures "for any purpose other than the capital or operating costs of: (1) the airport; (2) the local airport system; or (3) any other local facility that is owned or operated by the person or entity that owns or operates the airport that is directly and substantially related to the air transportation of passengers or property."[184] Under this rule, any expenditure of airport funds in the process of modernization had to be certified by the FAA as aviation-related.[185] In addition, because of the joint local and federal regulatory oversight of the airport, modernization—which promised to have massive environmental impacts—would have to comply with both the federal National Environmental Protection Act (NEPA), which required an Environmental Impact

Statement (EIS) approved by the lead federal agency (the FAA), and state CEQA law, which required an EIR approved by the lead local agency (LAWA). Accordingly, as in the Staples Sports and Entertainment District project, LAX modernization would require a legally structured environmental review process in which community groups contesting the plan could exert significant influence.

Although the environmental impacts of LAX extended regionwide, the communities with the most at stake were those in the airport's immediate vicinity, which had long suffered disproportionate harm. Noise from plane takeoffs and landings was deafening, rattling homes and other buildings nearby. Toxic air emissions—coming from airplanes, loading equipment, passenger and rental cars, and cargo trucks—were linked to chronic respiratory disease that disproportionately affected local communities, particularly communities of color.[186] LAX thus presented a classic environmental justice problem. LAX's neighboring communities—the separately incorporated City of El Segundo, the Westchester neighborhood of the City of Los Angeles, the separate City of Inglewood, and the community of Lennox in unincorporated Los Angeles County—were demographically distinct but similarly impacted by airport operations.[187] In 2000, El Segundo, to the south of LAX below Imperial Highway, was the whitest (over 80%) and wealthiest (median household income more than $60,000) city adjacent to the airport. Westchester, immediately north of LAX, was 50% white with a median household income around $60,000, although 35% earned less than $40,000 per year. Inglewood, east of the 405 Freeway, had a median household income of $34,000 and was roughly split between black and Latino residents, while Lennox, just south of Inglewood, was 90% Latino with a median household income of less than $30,000. According to U.S. Census data, nearly 20% of Inglewood residents lived below the poverty line; the figure was over 30% in Lennox. Residents of Lennox, in LAX's direct eastward flight path, bore the brunt of airport externalities. Lenox school coaches reported a high incidence of asthma among student athletes, while some classrooms in the district went windowless in order to mitigate noise.[188]

Mayor Riordan ignited these communities' long-simmering discontent when, in October 1994, he launched a three-phase process for designing and approving LAX expansion, called the LAX Master Plan. In Phase One—the research phase—airport planners evaluated more than forty different airfield configurations to address projected increases in passenger and cargo demand. Phase Two, focused on concept development, began in February 1996, and culminated in LAWA unveiling four "alternatives," all of which included plans for additional runways.[189] To lay the groundwork for environmental review, environmental scoping began for the four alternatives in June 1997.[190] Feedback at four public meetings resulted in the elimination of alternatives that added multiple runways—though all the proposals that remained included the addition of one new runway.

Industry representatives and political officials were publicly pressing for airport expansion to accommodate up to 100 million passengers a year and 4 million square feet of cargo space (the latter in response to increased consumer demand from Asia).[191] LAX modernization was projected to create 375,000 jobs and support businesses that needed quick access to foreign markets—at a cost of $8 to $10 billion.[192] The proposed expansion generated fierce opposition from local communities and advocates of regional airport growth. In March 1998, state Senator Tom Hayden, who had opposed Riordan in the prior mayoral election, led representatives from surrounding communities in a protest in front of city hall, proclaiming: "Everything seems so far to be about greed and about glory and not about neighborhood quality."[193] Undaunted, Riordan forged ahead, removing the president of the Airport Commission in May 1998 for failing to generate community support despite significant spending on public relations.[194] Opponents of LAX expansion argued for Palmdale as an alternative site, with Los Angeles County Supervisor Mike Antonovich (representing the Palmdale area) calling for a nonbinding countywide vote on expanding the Palmdale airport.[195] City Councilwoman Ruth Galanter, whose district included communities surrounding LAX, also pushed for alternative sites.

Bowing to this pressure, in June 1999, Riordan introduced a "No Additional Runway Alternative" for LAX modernization, keeping the existing four-runway format, but adding terminal capacity and roadways to accommodate projected passenger and cargo increases. An EIS/EIR for the LAX Master Plan was drafted in 2000 and a Draft EIS/EIR was released in January 2001 with a 180-day public comment period ending on July 25.[196] The fourteen-volume Draft EIS/EIR presented four alternatives. The LAWA staff preference was "Alternative C—the No Additional Runway Alternative," which called for "lengthening and reconfiguring runways, construction of a new terminal, creation of a ring road circulating the airport and extension of the Metro Rail Green Line to the airport."[197]

However, Alternative C did not placate opponents because it still promised growth from 61 million to 90 million annual passengers,[198] while expanding the airport's cargo capacity to 3.1 million tons.[199] Leading the resistance was El Segundo Mayor Mike Gordon, who on the heels of the Draft EIS/EIR's release, launched the Coalition for a Truly Regional Airport Plan comprised of "about 100 cities, counties, civic agencies and school districts, from Manhattan Beach to Riverside and beyond."[200] In Gordon's view, "We had to demonstrate that there was an alternative.... We talked about the economic opportunities for other areas... and came up with a regional plan that was [rooted in] better public policy."[201] Buttressing the opponents' position was a study from the Southern California Association of Governments finding that the economic benefit of a regional airport growth plan was the same as LAX expansion.[202] Nonetheless, pressure for change mounted, as air traffic controllers and pilots urged safety improvements at LAX, which had the worst record of near misses of any airport in the country.[203]

Debate over the LAX Master Plan unfolded against the backdrop of the campaign to elect the new mayor of Los Angeles, pitting frontrunner, City Attorney

James Hahn, against a field that included Steve Soboroff, a former Riordan adviser and LAX expansionist, and Antonio Villaraigosa, who opposed the LAX Master Plan in favor of regional airport growth. During the campaign, Hahn received large donations from the airline industry and construction unions, which were eager for jobs resulting from the projected $12 billion in LAX construction contracts. Because of strenuous objections from homeowner groups, in the lead-up to the April 2001 primary, only Hahn and Soboroff were on record supporting expansion, although both agreed that it should be more limited than the Riordan plan. Ratcheting up the pressure on candidates, Val Velasco, an attorney from Playa del Rey, started the Alliance for a Regional Solution to Airport Congestion (ARSAC) with the goal of mobilizing 10,000 residents to vote for anti-airport expansion candidates in a mayoral election in which experts predicted a candidate would only need 100,000 votes to get into the runoff. ARSAC, composed of mostly Playa del Rey residents with some from Westchester, sought "responsible regionalization."[204] Recognizing the need for homeowner support, Hahn attempted to modulate his position, signing a campaign pledge put forth by the Coalition for a Truly Regional Airport Plan to oppose the Riordan LAX expansion proposal, stating that the airport "should be constrained to operate safely within the capacity of its existing facilities."[205] Elected in the summer of 2001, Hahn thus took office caught between his support for LAX expansion and his commitment to limit its impact.

Seeking to buy more time, one of Hahn's first moves was to extend the comment period on the Draft EIS/EIR by another sixty days: to September 24, 2001. The terrorist attacks on September 11 upended the process, providing Hahn with a potential way out of his dilemma. Although the city had already spent $90 million on LAX Master Plan development, Hahn asked LAWA to come up with another alternative now focused on security—further extending the comment period to November 9, 2001. Adding to the complexity, on September 21, 2001, the Inglewood Unified School District submitted its response to the Draft EIS/EIR, objecting that all alternatives "disproportionately impact[ed] minorities," unfairly burdened minority schools, and produced increased noise and pollution; Inglewood's comments further claimed that the Draft EIS/EIR's analysis of noise was "inadequate," as was the analysis of emissions modeling and traffic impact.[206] Lennox filed comments the same day with a nearly identical analysis (prepared by the same firm, Orbach & Hoff LLP).[207]

In July 2002, after spending another $10 million on plan development, Hahn released LAX Master Plan Alternative D, called the "Enhanced Safety and Security Alternative," which included bigger gates (to accommodate larger aircraft, particularly the 555-seat Airbus A380); greater separation between the two main runways (to avoid near misses); and shops, restaurants, hotels, and even theaters in the central terminal. However, the primary focus was on security: building an underground site for detecting explosives, moving private vehicle passenger unloading outside of the main terminal to a new check-in facility at Manchester Square (a mile and a half from the airport), demolishing central terminal parking structures, consolidating the rental car facility, and building a transit center connecting to the Green Line. Claiming that the "airport doesn't work," Hahn's plan vowed to cap passengers at 78 million per year (down from Riordan's 90 million), in part by demolishing Terminals 1, 2, and 3 (eliminating eleven gates) and scrapping plans for a new terminal.[208] While resident groups supported these modifications, industry officials complained that Alternative D added too little new capacity. Hahn proposed to pay for half of the $9.6 billion project by increasing airline rents and fees, with the other half coming from a $1.50 fee on tickets, supplemented by federal funds and public bonds backed by airport concession revenue.[209] The airlines were not convinced. In an August 2002 letter to the Airport Commission, industry officials wondered "how a plan of this size could be financed. . . . If the city's policy is indeed to constrain the capacity at LAX, it is difficult to believe that the airport could not be improved in a more cost-effective manner and still achieve the benefits of the new alternative."[210] Airline support mattered because the industry had lobbying power with the FAA, whose approval was necessary for any modernization to occur.

On July 9, 2003, LAWA released a Supplement to the Draft EIS/EIR, incorporating an environmental review of Alternative D. Although the draft claimed that modernization would reduce noise, traffic, and air pollution in surrounding neighborhoods, it found that the economic impact of modernization—a $64 billion boost to the regional economy by 2015—was the same as if no LAX expansion occurred based on projections of airport growth in other locations around the region.[211] In late July, Hahn asked for the comment period to be extended from 45 to 120 days and a new round of public hearings commenced.[212]

Alternative D, however, seemed only to succeed in coalescing the opposition. The county remained steadfastly opposed to concentrating the benefits of airport growth in the City of Los Angeles. On August 19, 2003, the County Board of Supervisors, advocating for a regional plan, voted 4-0 to warn Hahn that Alternative D would likely increase passenger traffic beyond the limits Hahn had set.[213] To make matters worse, newly elected City Councilwoman Cindy Miscikowski, whose district included LAX, presented her own plan to enhance airport safety and realign runways at a cost of only $2 billion—challenging Mayor Hahn to explain his price tag and asserting that, until he did, she could not support a plan based on "smoke and mirrors."[214] In a sign of her seriousness, Miscikowski sent an open letter to the City Council urging it to delay Hahn's effort to fast-track his proposal, forcing Hahn to back down.[215] Other problems hounded the Hahn plan. The mayor still needed to acquire 38 houses and 179 apartments to assemble the Manchester Square passenger check-in site—with rapidly rising real estate values making the project increasingly expensive.[216] In addition, Hahn confronted new controversy when Ted Stein, Hahn's handpicked president of the Board of Airport Commissioners, was investigated by the city's Ethics Commission for holding Hahn fundraisers soliciting money from companies seeking LAX contracts.[217] When asked about attending fundraisers, the

County Fed's Miguel Contreras, who had been reappointed by Hahn to the Airport Commission after serving under Riordan, said: "I've never been invited to one of those and I'm not sure we should go."[218] It was the end of 2003 and, after an investment of more than $100 million in planning, Hahn's Alternative D—and the entire project of LAX modernization—appeared deeply imperiled.

In April 2004, LAWA released the Final EIR for the LAX Master Plan, identifying Alternative D as the staff-recommended alternative.[219] But in the face of intractable opposition to Hahn's plan, Councilwoman Miscikowski kept pushing her less-expensive, scaled-back alternative, which embraced widely accepted components of Alternative D—called "green light" projects. These included moving the runways further apart, consolidating the rental car facility, adding gates at the Tom Bradley International Terminal, and making a Green Line connection—all at a cost of roughly $3 billion. Miscikowski's plan deferred the most controversial (and at $8 billion, more expensive) elements (called "yellow light" projects), especially the Manchester Square off-site passenger check-in.[220] While the Chamber of Commerce offered its lukewarm support for Hahn's version, El Segundo Mayor Gordon and ARSAC's Val Velasco spearheaded the resistance: gathering signatures against Alternative D to present at a May 2004 public hearing.[221] At the hearing, Miscikowski promoted what she called her "Consensus Plan" and argued that it was superior to Hahn's because it was less expensive and gave more oversight to the City Council.[222] Realizing he could not secure the City Council's approval without Miscikowski's support, Hahn endorsed the Consensus Plan in June,[223] submitting it to the Airport and Planning Commissions, which each gave their approval on June 14, 2004.[224] An Addendum to the Final EIR was released by LAWA in September including the Consensus Plan. The stage was set for the final City Council approval, which was scheduled for later in the year, and for FAA approval of the EIS.

The Labor Roots of LAX Organizing

The LAX CBA campaign would ultimately seek to intervene in the modernization process set forth by Mayor Hahn, fusing together different constituencies and using their power to disrupt essential city approvals as leverage. The genesis of the LAX CBA campaign occurred as the Staples CBA process was winding down, reuniting some of FCCEJ's key actors—in particular, Environmental Defense and LAANE—while building a more environmentally oriented coalition with LAX community organizational partners. Although LAX presented an opportunity for potential community benefits, there were important differences between the LAX and Staples contexts. Whereas the Staples CBA campaign had taken aim at downtown gentrification, fueled by city-subsidized private development, the LAX campaign confronted a different target—the city—and a different regulatory framework. Moreover, while the Staples campaign had focused on jobs and housing, using the environmental review process as leverage, the LAX campaign—built on an emergent labor–environmental alliance—placed environmental justice concerns at the core of its CBA demands. In this sense, the LAX campaign extended the CBA model into new terrain.

Although environmental issues would be at the center of the LAX campaign, the idea to pursue a CBA in connection with airport modernization emerged from different streams of activism. Environmentalists, long concerned about the public health impacts of airport pollution, found common cause with local communities around the goal of addressing disproportionate environmental harm. These communities, led by homeowner groups and school districts, had their own histories of sustained conflict with LAX and mobilized in opposition to Riordan's original expansion plan and kept up pressure on Hahn. What would bring these groups together with organized labor was the opportunity that labor leaders saw in LAX modernization for deepening preexisting efforts to expand living wage jobs and increase union density in sectors of the service economy tied to local government—which was the driving force behind labor's ongoing support for the CBA model.

For a labor movement seeking to leverage local government to enhance the quality of work, LAX was a job-dense target. In the mid-1990s, the airport had a significant unionized workforce (though still less than half of all workers), mostly in skilled jobs (like mechanics), alongside thousands of nonunionized employees. Some of these nonunionized employees worked for airport restaurants and retail stores, which were public concessions, while others were in jobs contracted out by airlines, such as security, baggage handling, and janitorial services. When labor leaders won passage of the Worker Retention Ordinance in 1995 and the Living Wage Ordinance in 1997, they did so with an eye on unionizing LAX workers as a crucial next step.

Immediately after the Living Wage Ordinance's passage, the Los Angeles Living Wage Coalition sought to promote education and organizing among workers covered by the new law. In a letter to Councilwoman Jackie Goldberg, Madeline Janis-Aparicio noted that the coalition had an agreement with the "Office of Contract Compliance . . . to do a limited, joint worker outreach and education program over the next year."[225] LAX was a key focus of the Living Wage Coalition given that approximately ten thousand LAX workers were set to receive raises under the ordinance.[226] However, the airlines were not inclined to cooperate, threatening to resist application of the ordinance to pre-board screeners, baggage handlers, security workers, janitors, and maintenance workers employed by airlines and their subcontractors. A threshold legal question was whether the airlines counted as city contractors under the terms of the Living Wage Ordinance—a question that the major carriers put to the L.A. city attorney to answer. The city attorney raised additional legal barriers, expressing concern that the ordinance's application to airline employees might be preempted by the federal Airline Deregulation Act. In response, the Living Wage Coalition's lawyer wrote an extensive analysis to City Attorney Frederick Merkin explaining why the ordinance was not preempted.[227] It was into this murky political and legal context that LAANE, still operating as the Tourism Industry Development Council (TIDC), stepped.

Complicated as the legal terrain was, the labor movement sensed tremendous opportunity at LAX. In a bid to capitalize on that opportunity, in 1998, leaders from the TIDC, SEIU, HERE, and AFL-CIO drafted the LAX Organizing Project Proposal, which stated as its goal using the Living Wage and Worker Retention Ordinances "as some of the primary political leverage to help organize the LAX workforce."[228] From the perspective of project leaders, the ordinances could work in tandem to help unionization efforts. Section 10.37.11 of the Living Wage Ordinance allowed employers to "supersede" living wage requirements by entering into a collective bargaining agreement, which could provide lower wages and ensure labor peace. The Worker Retention Ordinance required the retention of contract workers for ninety days after the termination of a city contract—reducing the potential for union busting by switching contract firms. The LAX Organizing Project's goal was to apply the Living Wage Ordinance to airport contractors and subcontractors, seek unionization under the provision permitting collective bargaining agreements, and then protect against union-busting contract terminations with the Worker Retention Ordinance.

The first step in advancing this goal was to apply the ordinances to the airlines as city contractors, which would then permit application to airline subcontractors (who were the major employers). The legal ambiguity in the Living Wage Ordinance arose from the ordinance's original language, which applied living wage requirements to city contractors and subcontractors; a "contractor" was defined as any business that had a "service contract" with the city.[229] "Service contract," in turn, included "a lease or license under which services are rendered for the City" but only when "the services to be rendered probably would otherwise be rendered by City employees."[230] (The Worker Retention Ordinance had a similar definition.) The legal question was whether airlines were in the business of rendering services to the city that would otherwise have been rendered by city employees. It was essential for the unions to be able to convince the city that the airlines qualified as contractors in the first instance; from there, airline contract firms (like those providing security) would count as city subcontractors also subject to the Living Wage and Worker Retention Ordinances (and the airlines could be forced to include compliance with the ordinances as provisions in their subcontracts with service providers). Facing the obligation to pay living wage, and simultaneously confronting pressure from workers to unionize, the subcontractors could then be persuaded by the unions to enter into an orderly process for unionization—under a card-check neutrality framework—which would result in less overall cost and disruption for the firms. With this plan worked out, the LAX Organizing Project was launched around complementary strategies—political, communications, and infrastructure—and governed by a committee of representatives from each of the partner groups. The

SEIU and HERE agreed to devote staff and other resources, while TIDC agreed to contribute half of Janis-Aparicio's time and one full-time worker organizer.[231]

The unions and TIDC met on March 9, 1998, to discuss campaign strategy, which focused on the immediate aim of applying the Living Wage Ordinance to the project's first target, United Airlines, in connection with its impending lease renewal at LAX. The goal, in effect, was to pressure United to accept the status of city contractor, subject to the ordinance, in exchange for lease approval. The campaign's "legal steps" included requesting labor lawyer Richard McCracken at Davis, Cowell & Bowe to help finalize relevant legal documents, including a labor peace and card-check neutrality agreement, by later in the month.[232] The following week, campaign leaders sent a memo to County Fed Director Miguel Contreras outlining the LAX Organizing Project.[233] The memo stated that, although there were already 15,000 unionized workers at the airport, there were "over 20,000 non-union, low wage workers at LAX, including 2,500 pre-board screeners, baggage handlers, skycaps, and wheel chair attendants, as well as nearly 1,000 non-union workers employed in gift shops and restaurants.... The majority are African American and Latino, with many Philippino [sic] workers as well. Most of these workers live in LA's poorest communities; including Compton, Carson, Inglewood, Lennox and South Los Angeles." The memo went on to note, "As the airlines mount a legal fight to block implementation of the [Living Wage] Ordinance, public outrage has continued to grow and workers have been emboldened to take stronger action.... Additionally, with LAX on the verge of beginning a $12 billion expansion for the year 2015, the labor movement in Los Angeles is confronted with a serious challenge of how to ensure that the growth and prosperity of LAX benefits all workers with real opportunities to obtain union jobs at living wages." The memo outlined two proposals designed to enhance union organizing:

> The first proposal is to have the Airport Commission adopt a Labor Peace Agreement (LPA) to cover all service workers hired after the expansion....
> Secondly, we would like to see some airlines meet the requirements of the Living Wage Ordinance (LWO) by adopting a card check-neutrality procedure ... [that] would enable the airline sub-contractors to work out appropriate wages and working conditions through a collective bargaining agreement (or agreements). This process already has the support of [LAWA Executive Director] John Driscoll.... The major theoretical and legal underpinning of this proposal is that a Labor Peace Agreement will prevent future disruptions at the airport, which provides a crucial city service.... As the airline leases come up for renewal (as is the case with United Airlines at the end of this month) the airlines will have to either apply the Living Wage Ordinance to their sub-contracted workers or engage in costly litigation and a very public fight with the Living Wage Coalition to avoid payment of living wages. We believe that the alternative,

a collective bargaining agreement, is a reasonable alternative that would help boost wages while providing workers with union representation while minimizing the costs to the airlines of a protracted fight. We believe that this proposal may be favored by the Mayor who has not supported the LWO but has indicated that he believes it is immoral for LAX workers to earn so little.[234]

On March 18, 1998, project leaders met to plan the campaign's official launch, discussing potential allies (identifying Kent Wong, Miguel Contreras, Jackie Goldberg, and Ruth Galanter) and strategizing about routes for the inaugural protest and the content of the initial press release.[235] Contreras drafted an op-ed for *La Opinion* focusing on the travails of a worker for Argenbright Security, which contracted with United for security screening and other services at the United terminal (and had eight hundred workers at LAX in total). Contreras wrote: "If the City applies the Living Wage Ordinance to the United Airlines lease—as it has applied the law to dozens of airport contracts ranging from parking to janitorial services to baggage cart and car rental concessions—800 to 1,000 workers like Juan Sanchez will soon begin receiving a living wage."[236] On Wednesday, March 25, the Living Wage Coalition put out a press release announcing a Friday march of five hundred protesters against United Airlines to "Inaugurate Public Campaign to Force Living Wage." The following week, Janis-Aparicio wrote a letter to Harold Meyerson, editor of the *L.A. Weekly*, thanking the paper for its coverage of the airlines' failure to comply with the Living Wage Ordinance. She emphasized that the "airlines . . . have refused to require their contractors to pay a living wage, claiming that the Ordinance doesn't cover them. And the City Attorney's office has come up with a baffling legal argument (that a contract is not a service contract unless it is primarily for the purpose of providing services—language that is not in the Ordinance) which seems to support the argument being made by the airlines."[237]

As organizing heated up, the unions requested more resources and the pace of meetings intensified.[238] At a strategy retreat held on April 24 and 25, 1998 at HERE Local 814 in Santa Monica, representatives from the HERE, SEIU, AFL-CIO, and TIDC, as well as Anthony Thigpenn of AGENDA, outlined goals and targets, and discussed a strategy for union organizing under a card-check process, which did not require an NLRA-sanctioned election (in which unions were disadvantaged by employer influence campaigns). Participants also discussed the strategy around labor peace and the Living Wage Ordinance, reviewed the United campaign, and focused on messaging by asking: "What is the glue that holds our campaign together?"[239] By May 1, key campaign committees were formed with Janis-Aparicio and Jon Barton from SEIU Local 1877 serving on the policy committee and representatives from the SEIU and HERE staffing the strategy committee. The AFL-CIO's Leticia Salcedo was appointed director of the LAX Organizing Project. Other staff included Roxane Auer, Jennifer Skurnik, and Tom Walsh from HERE; Ernesto Medrano of the AFL-CIO; and Eddie Iny from the SEIU. Participants at the retreat identified the need for legal support for drafting legislative outputs and union organizing, as well as the need for a legal opinion on how best to navigate the NLRA. Participants also brainstormed key themes around passenger safety ("Our safety is worth more than minimum wage"), how to pay for higher wages ("extra nickel or dollar per flight?"), how to educate the public ("people don't know that jobs aren't union"), and discussed different public messages. These included: "Expansion has to benefit the City not only wealthy employers/business," "Real Welfare Reform," and "This is real 'RLA'—Rebuilding of Los Angeles, therefore real answers to '92 uprising." Finally, participants floated different potential campaign names, including JAWS (Justice for Airport Workers), RELAX (Real Empowerment at LAX), and ULAX (Unionize LAX).[240] These were ultimately rejected in favor of "Respect at LAX," which would become the campaign's signature tagline—reflecting its core demand.

To facilitate the legal work, the Respect at LAX campaign retained Margo Feinberg of Schwartz, Steinsapir, Dohrmann & Sommers in Berkeley. In a letter outlining the scope of work, Feinberg referenced her experience as lead counsel to the Living Wage Coalition, and noted that Erika Zucker, then an associate in the firm's Los Angeles office, also had experience drafting labor regulations. Feinberg then summarized her view of the case:

> Your current plan involves several legal and legislative components. The first is to ensure that the Living Wage Ordinance is applicable to all of the service jobs at the airport, including the jobs that fall under the airline leases. Although it has been the Coalition's position that those jobs were covered, the City Attorney has indicated a narrower reading of the ordinance, indicating that jobs such as security screeners would not be covered since they are not jobs that would otherwise be performed by City employees. However, even if the City Attorney agreed with us, it appears that the Airlines themselves are rumbling about challenging the application of the Ordinance to these positions. Thus, it would be best if a simple amendment was drafted to cover these workers. We would then need to secure the passage of this amendment from the City Council.[241]

Feinberg also noted she would provide legal support for a labor peace agreement and advice on the participation of unions in the LAX environmental review process, which would be necessary for Master Plan expansion as well as for significant projects outside of the Master Plan. Feinberg proposed that her law firm would draft the Living Wage Ordinance amendment, interact with the city attorney and the City Council to get it passed, and "be prepared to respond to arguments raised by the Airlines in this regard, including potential [Airline Deregulation Act] preemption arguments."[242] Following up on Feinberg's letter, Salcedo and Janis-Aparicio asked the AFL-CIO to pay for her services, stressing, "WE ARE

IN 100% AGREEMENT THAT MARGO FEINBERG (AND HER FIRM) ARE ESSENTIAL TO WINNING THIS CAMPAIGN" [because Feinberg has] the political knowledge to not only write and argue these ordinances/resolutions but also knows how and has experience moving the decision makers . . . and understands the relevant law."[243]

After a systematic review, the director of the city's Bureau of Contract Administration determined that, although the Living Wage Ordinance did not apply to "commercial air transportation services," it did apply to airlines' "custodial, building maintenance and security services provided under the lease" with LAX.[244] The coalition pressed board members at United to adhere to this determination as well as to cover screeners, wheelchair attendants, baggage handlers, and other contract employees.[245] But United held fast in its opposition. Campaign leaders, with Feinberg's guidance, thus turned to amending the ordinance to make clear that it applied to all workers subcontracted under airline leases.

The Respect at LAX committees met to chart strategy. Salcedo laid out a calendar that targeted the planned September 1998 full City Council vote on the United lease. Before that deadline, Respect at LAX staff were tasked with submitting evidence of United labor violations to both the Airport Commission and the City Council, and organizing actions to promote the Living Wage Ordinance amendment. To add to the pressure, leaders assembled information on Argenbright employees under contract with United, which showed paltry wages, ranging from $5.75 per hour for baggage handlers to $7.00 per hour for security officers, and revealed that Argenbright workers, many on welfare, received no sick days, confronted disrespect at work, and experienced high turnover. Respect at LAX leaders also developed a plan to enlist other unions, including flight attendants, to join the campaign against United. All of this information was produced in advance of a meeting with Jackie Goldberg about the proposed labor peace agreement and amended Living Wage Ordinance, which would (like the original) include an "opt-out" for companies with unions to promote collective bargaining.[246]

To advance the lease strategy beyond United, in June 1998, Janis-Aparicio asked LAWA Executive Director John Driscoll for a schedule of when airline lease renewals would come before the Airport Commission.[247] This included leases for Continental, American, Air France, Korean, Southwest, and many others. In addition, campaign leaders aimed to win a labor peace agreement between LAWA and all airlines by mid-1999. That left roughly a year to organize, during which time the campaign hoped to win card-check agreements with one or two airlines through lease renewals and achieve amendment of the Living Wage Ordinance so that airline leases were "clearly covered" as the "strongest leverage." With respect to United, the strategy was to "hold up lease until United agrees to card check or at least until [Living Wage Ordinance] applied to lease."[248] Alongside this local advocacy, the AFL-CIO engaged in a national strategy to gain the support of "all major unions representing workers out of LAX."[249]

Operating under a tight timeline, Respect at LAX leaders met furiously in June and July 1998, as the amendment was being prepared. Campaign staff focused on organizing workers, reaching out to community members and national union partners, developing a *Los Angeles Times* profile of the campaign with reporter Jim Newton, and lobbying the Airport Commission. On the legal front, in late July, Feinberg sent another letter to the city attorney explaining why specific airline contract employees were covered by the Living Wage Ordinance.[250] For her part, Janis-Aparicio was busy sending her own letters, explaining the goals of the campaign to allies on July 30,[251] and the next day pivoting to write an outraged letter to Councilwoman Goldberg expressing frustration at the city contract bureau's "disrespectful behavior towards our staff and volunteers" and "lack of cooperation in developing" a training for workers at LAX about their rights under the Living Wage and Worker Retention Ordinances.[252]

The Respect at LAX Coalition held a meeting on August 19, 1998, to discuss community outreach and political strategy. Coalition leaders argued that "the airlines have to see the Living Wage Ordinance amendment as a viable threat i.e., it will pass. . . . If we can make this happen then the airlines are pressured to concede the collective bargaining because of their fear of local government setting a national precedent on how companies should run their business."[253] Following up, the SEIU's Eddie Iny wrote to Contreras, who had been appointed by Mayor Riordan to the Airport Commission in July 1998, noting that "inadequate compensation and poor working conditions experienced by [LAX] workers are serious detriments to ensuring safety and security of passengers and airlines employees."[254] In response, Contreras asked John Driscoll for information on the LAX Master Plan, the status of the project labor agreement review, and the proposed expansion of the United cargo terminal.[255]

With a communication plan finalized, which included distribution of "Respect @ LAX: Good Jobs for a Better LA" passenger leaflets, the campaign sought to exert maximum pressure on the airlines. After meeting with a lobbyist for the Air Transport Association and its lawyer on October 22, 1998, the SEIU's Jon Barton reported that "[t]hey are very concerned about the ordinance and the amendment. While they do not see themselves actively lobbying, when it passes they will attack it in court. Their concern is both federal preemption but also that the FAA and its policies create cohesion in the industry while separate differing local ordinances would create chaos."[256] The machinists union president reached out to airlines with whom it had contracts to get them to support application of the Living Wage Ordinance to contractors: "You may not be aware that an alternative to local regulation is contemplated by the Ordinance. Specifically, the requirements of the Ordinance may be 'superseded' by the terms of a collective bargaining agreement. This means that there is a simple resolution to the concerns expressed about local regulation of the airline industry—that is, for the airlines to encourage their contractors to honor their employees' desire for union representation."[257] The flight attendants union sent similar letters to airlines, while the Inglewood City Council, home to a significant number of LAX workers, drafted a resolution in support of the campaign.

Succumbing to this pressure, on January 14, 1999, the CEO of United announced that the company had "decided to abide by the Living Wage Ordinance."[258] This cleared the way for United's lease renewal. On May 18, 1999, the Board of Airport Commissioners agreed to approve United's revised lease with inclusion of language promising subcontractor compliance with the Living Wage and Worker Retention Ordinances.[259] Specifically, Section 30(f) of the lease provided, "Lessee agrees to include, in every subcontract or sublease covering the Premises . . . a provision pursuant to which Subcontractor (A) agrees to comply with the Living Wage Ordinance and the Service Worker Retention Ordinance with respect to the Premises; (B) agrees not to retaliate against any employee lawfully asserting noncompliance . . .; and (C) acknowledges and agrees that the City, as the intended third-party beneficiary" could enforce the ordinances. However, United's decision did not end the struggle because the lease only applied to the main United terminal, while other airlines facing lease renewals—including American, Northwest, and Southwest—continued to resist application of the living wage.[260]

Moreover, the United lease did not resolve the SEIU's unionization drive against Argenbright, which had workers under contract with other airlines and persisted in its opposition to the union. In March 1999, five hundred Argenbright workers signed petitions requesting a card-check neutrality election. Argenbright refused to recognize the union, telling SEIU Local 1877 President Mike Garcia that if Garcia had the required number of cards to go ahead and "file a petition for election with the NLRB. Continuing to harass our managers, employees, customers and other interested parties does not enhance your position with our employees; it will not result in Argenbright submitting to a 'card check' process, which takes away our employees' right to a secret ballot election."[261] Given United's large contact with Argenbright, which gave United significant leverage, the unions pressed Jim Goodwin, United's CEO, to take a stand in support of the Argenbright workers.[262] Mike Garcia also urged the managing director of United to "have Argenbright Security Inc. to sign the anti-retaliation pledge" for union organizing.[263]

United remained in need of union support for its Century Cargo Facilities Lease, which the Board of Airport Commissioners was slated to review in mid-1999 (and for which United was seeking $41.5 million in tax-exempt public bond financing).[264] Because the lease agreement contemplated an expansion, it raised a question about whether it was subject to CEQA environmental review. To increase the pressure on United, the SEIU funded two legal challenges: one by the City of El Segundo (represented by Shute, Mihaly & Weinberger); and the second by Inglewood City Councilman Jerome Horton, SEIU Local 1877, and Lennox resident Favian Gonzalez (represented by Altshuler Berzon). Both suits questioned LAWA's decision not to complete an EIR. As a result of these challenges, the Board of Airport

Commissioners delayed its vote on the United cargo facility.[265] In October, lawyers for Altshuler Berzon raised objections to LAWA's claim that the project would not have a significant environmental impact, arguing to the contrary that it would "significantly *worsen traffic congestion* on Century Boulevard, *increase air cargo flights*," and cause public exposure to "the *toxic constituents* of increased diesel emissions."[266] Not wanting a protracted legal fight, United and LAWA entered into settlement discussions, which centered on community demands for noise abatement, an agreement by LAX to redirect truck traffic away from residential communities, and a fix to pollution caused by truck idling.[267] The legal challenges were resolved when LAWA agreed to take steps toward these goals and United agreed to use its weight to encourage Argenbright to accept unionization.

The success with United propelled the Respect at LAX campaign toward more ambitious goals. A memo on March 12, 2000 laid out four major objectives: "unionize 2500 workers subcontracted to airlines (SEIU); unionize 1000 non-union concession workers, both food and retail (HERE); achieve a labor peace ordinance at LAX; help raise wages and improve contracts of participating unions" through a "card check neutrality approach."[268] The memo noted successes thus far, which included card-check agreements at W. H. Smith news and gift outlets, the duty free shops, and Host Marriott food concessionaires, as well as an "election with Argenbright (not yet recognized)," affecting nine hundred United, Delta, and Northwest Airlines workers.[269] A year later, on March 1, 2001, SEIU 1877 entered a collective bargaining agreement with Argenbright.[270]

The September 11 attacks, while reorienting the LAX Master Plan process, also brought it into closer connection with the Respect at LAX campaign. On October 4, 2001, Mayor Hahn convened the Los Angeles Economic Impact Task Force, which was chaired by the Chamber of Commerce's George Kieffer—a law firm partner at Manatt, Phelps & Phillips—and included leaders from key businesses, including United Airlines, as well as the president of the Los Angeles Urban League, and LAANE's Janis-Aparicio. The Task Force's goal was to "assess the impact on the Los Angeles economy of the events of 9-11."[271] A key area of focus was the airport, prompting HERE's Tom Walsh to send a letter to the Chief Operating Officer of LAWA recommending that the Task Force take action to "save the jobs" and stressing that any new jobs "should be quality jobs (living wages and benefits)."[272] In March 2002, Respect at LAX leaders recommended that the Task Force's airport committee "be a place for regular updates . . . on all aspects of LAWA developments that may impact workers @ LAX."[273] Soon thereafter, committee members began discussing LAX contractor responsibility as a mechanism for ensuring that new concessionaires were selected based on their record of respect for workers' rights.

By 2002, the Respect at LAX campaign had achieved significant success applying the Living Wage Ordinance to airlines and their subcontractors, led by the United living wage agreement and union contract at Argenbright Security. Yet organizing airport concession workers—food and retail workers at chains not contractually bound to the airlines—remained a challenge. Leaders came to view the campaign's approach of mobilizing around specific concession renewals to ensure that selected firms were unionized as too reactive and resource intensive. To address this, the Respect at LAX campaign continued to seek an airport-wide labor peace policy. However, following nearly three years of delay due to industry resistance to labor peace, campaign leaders also searched for a different path forward. After a February 2002 meeting with Mayor Hahn's chief of staff, Janis-Aparicio directed Nancy Cohen, a researcher at LAANE, to investigate if there was a way that LAX modernization could be leveraged to promote the Respect at LAX goal of labor peace.[274] It was at this point that the campaign for LAX unionization and the drive for environmental justice and community accountability in relation to the LAX Master Plan began to merge.

Defining the Community and Negotiating Benefits

Development of the LAX CBA coalition took shape against the backdrop of the LAX environmental review process, which brought together environmental activism around airport pollution, community resistance to airport expansion, and labor organizing around airport jobs. On the environmental side, support for a CBA built after consideration of more familiar responses to the modernization plan failed to produce a clear path forward. In mid-2000, in the throes of the Staples CBA campaign, Environmental Defense lawyer Jerilyn López Mendoza began monitoring the status of Mayor Riordan's drafting process for the LAX EIS/EIR.[275] Anticipating an environmental justice fight over community impact, López Mendoza initially considered advancing a legal challenge during the 2001 Draft EIS/EIR comment period under Title VI of the Civil Rights Act of 1964, which prohibited race and national origin discrimination in programs receiving federal funds.[276] Adopting a common environmental justice approach, the plan was to argue under recent district court precedent that the increase in airport traffic coming from largely white Orange County (the source of one-third of LAX passengers) would have a disparate impact on LAX's neighboring low-income African American and Latino communities.[277] However, on April 24, 2001, the U.S. Supreme Court held in *Alexander v. Sandoval* that there was no private right of action for disparate impact suits under Title VI,[278] gutting that potential strategy and forcing Environmental Defense to look elsewhere for legal leverage.[279] López Mendoza contemplated a CEQA lawsuit after the release of the Draft EIS/EIR in 2001 and the Supplemental Draft in 2002. However, because a successful CEQA challenge could only overturn an EIR, forcing it to be done over, and because the city could ultimately issue a negative declaration stating that it evaluated environmental impacts but determined the benefits of a project outweighed costs, López Mendoza was reluctant to file suit—which could only stall airport expansion, not fix it.[280] In the wake of September 11, with the Hahn administration emphasizing "safety and security," López Mendoza grew even more pessimistic that a lawsuit could thwart the forward march of modernization.[281]

Just as López Mendoza was confronting this crossroads, in mid-2002, LAANE researcher Nancy Cohen and community organizer Maria Loya reached out to discuss the airport expansion project.[282] For LAANE, it was also a pivotal moment. On the heels of its successful Staples and Valley CBA campaigns, LAANE was pursuing a citywide community benefits policy, while also seeking to extend the Living Wage Ordinance and promote union organizing through the Respect at LAX campaign. LAX modernization offered an opportunity to deepen both efforts. Having previously worked with López Mendoza on the Staples CBA, forging strong personal and organizational ties, LAANE organizers believed that the time was ripe to launch a new, more ambitious effort to mobilize a broad labor–environmental coalition against the city's largest public works project. Although CBA coalitions had never before targeted public developers, Cohen and Loya were confident that the conditions were ripe to pursue an LAX CBA.[283] While advancing goals of good jobs and reduced pollution at LAX, a CBA would also provide the first genuine opportunity for community residents to have meaningful participation in the modernization process.[284]

During the first half of 2003, LAANE and Environmental Defense sought to build out the fledgling LAX Coalition while solidifying political support. An essential predicate for the campaign was ensuring that key political decision-makers ultimately would line up in favor of a CBA at the end of the day. This meant securing commitments from labor unions—eager for jobs produced by modernization—to back a community-based CBA coalition, which could threaten (or at least delay) modernization and also redirect resources from labor toward community and environmental goals. Janis-Aparicio led discussions with unions, encouraging their involvement by arguing that most of the LAX workforce lived in the impacted communities of Lennox and Inglewood, and therefore supporting the community fight would reinforce efforts to unionize community members. She also brokered union support by demonstrating how an LAX CBA, if it incorporated long-sought-after provisions like contractor responsibility and labor peace, could buttress the Respect at LAX campaign to unionize security guards and concession workers. Once Mayor Hahn understood that organized labor expected a CBA in exchange for union support for the LAX Master Plan, he directed LAWA Deputy Executive Director Jim Ritchie and other staff to get a CBA deal done.[285] According to *Los Angeles Times* reporter Jennifer Oldham, the CBA became an "insurance policy" for Hahn, in case he could not generate support for the project on his own.[286] Airport Commissioner Miguel Contreras and City Councilman Tony Cardenas were strong supporters of the CBA concept before the campaign launched, and organized labor brought a half-dozen other council members on board.[287]

With these pieces in place, Janis-Aparicio reached out to union partners, such as SEIU Local 34, where she presented the case for a "CBA at LAX," focusing on the historic "opportunity to advance economic justice and environmental justice for LAX communities."[288] Her presentation reviewed successful CBAs at Staples and SunQuest, and set forth the ultimate goal: passing an LAX Master Plan "with [a] community benefits agreement that provides environmental mitigation, quality jobs and other benefits for the most affected communities."[289] According to the timeline she presented, coalition advocacy would commence in September 2003 toward the goal of finalizing a CBA before a planned City Council vote on the LAX Master Plan slated for September 2004. Negotiations between the coalition and LAWA were set to begin in February 2004.[290]

Coalition building gained momentum during the first half of 2003. LAANE's William Smart—who joined the group as director of training and outreach after four years as senior pastor at Phillips Temple CME Church—was tasked with strengthening support in the communities most impacted by expansion: Lennox and Inglewood.[291] As Smart later recalled, "We looked at organizations that had previously fought against airport expansion and were traditional partners. We did our research on who had previously responded negatively on the EIR."[292]

Simultaneously seeking to build environmental strength, López Mendoza reached out to environmental groups given that environmental remediation would be a core coalition demand—and environmental litigation remained a key lever.[293] Although some groups, like the Natural Resources Defense Council (NRDC), were initially reluctant to give up the right to sue,[294] López Mendoza persisted in making the case in favor of a CBA, ultimately convincing NRDC and other environmental partners that negotiation was a superior strategy in the modernization context. On June 23 and September 11, 2003, coalition leaders held meetings for participating group representatives, political officials, and community members to discuss CBAs, focusing on Staples as a case study.[295] Members of LAANE asked the attendees for suggestions on what to include in a future CBA.[296] "There were around 30 people at the first meeting from nonprofits, churches, communities in affected areas, and politicians," recalled Shabaka Heru of the member group Community Coalition for Change.[297] By fall 2003, members of the growing coalition committed to pursue a CBA as the strategy with the greatest potential for community members to impact the shape of LAX modernization—which many believed was going to happen no matter what.[298] Maria Verduzco-Smith, director of the Lennox Coordinating Council (the main political voice of the unincorporated Lennox community), believed that although the community had a "good neighbor policy" on paper with LAX, the policy's vagueness made it difficult to enforce, and thus CBA negotiations would improve Lennox's position.[299]

While coalition leaders sought broad participation, outreach efforts failed to gain support of key constituents, who chafed at LAANE's leadership and believed their interests were better advanced independently. Although the coalition represented what Smart called a "cross-section" of the community,[300] it did not include leaders from El Segundo, Inglewood, and Westchester—all of whom believed that they could exert more influence over the process by separately negotiating with LAX and, potentially, suing. However, the coalition did include the Inglewood and Lennox School Districts, whose representatives did not trust their cities' political officials to win a deal that addressed their specific needs. Although the coalition reached out to ARSAC, its leaders also declined to participate. ARSAC board member Edgar Saenz, who served as a special assistant to Congresswoman Maxine Waters, criticized the coalition as artificial, calling LAANE a "political scam" that operated as a front for unions, which Hahn had sought to appease by his appointment of Contreras to the Airport Commission.[301] Saenz further claimed that Waters (whose district included the airport, as well as Inglewood, Westchester, and Lennox) and newly elected City Councilman Bernard Parks from South Los Angeles had been deliberately excluded from negotiations. As Saenz's critique underscored, while the coalition ultimately included, in López Mendoza's terms, "people with the same interests, same philosophies,"[302] dissenting voices continued to mobilize against modernization outside of the CBA process.

By the September 2003 meeting, the official LAX Coalition for Economic, Environmental, and Educational Justice had achieved its full strength of twenty-five organizations.[303] These included the Inglewood Unified and Lennox School Districts; community and faith-based groups, AGENDA, CLUE, Community Coalition, Community Coalition for Change, Inglewood Coalition for Drug and Violence Prevention, Inglewood Democratic Club, Inglewood Ministerial Alliance, Lennox Coordinating Council, LAANE, Los Angeles Council of Churches, L.A. Metropolitan Churches, and the Nation of Islam; environmental organizations, the California Environmental Rights Alliance, Coalition for Clean Air, Communities for a Better Environment, Community Action to Fight Asthma, Environmental Defense, NRDC, and Physicians for Social Responsibility; and the HERE Local 11, SEIU Local 1877 and 347, and Teamsters Local 911 unions. The coalition set up a governance structure under which community members transmitted their concerns to their organizational representatives in the coalition, which met once a month; the full coalition, in turn, elected a steering committee to address day-to-day issues and set overall strategy. One of the coalition's first acts, spearheaded by López Mendoza, was to submit comments on the Supplement to the Draft EIS/EIR for the LAX Master Plan before the November 2003 deadline.[304]

From there, the LAX Coalition set to work on its CBA strategy. On January 8, 2004, the coalition convened at the Washington Mutual Bank in Inglewood.[305] Led by LAANE's Smart, coalition leaders constituted a steering committee to "direct the course of the coalition," "make recommendations to coalition members," and "[d]evelop a political strategy that will be implemented to ensure that the Community Benefits Agreement is passed by the various legislative bodies." Smart also proposed a "negotiations committee," estimating that it would work about "10 hours a week once the process starts." Smart made an open call for participation on the negotiations committee but warned everyone to "make sure you have the time commitment." Three other committees were established— environmental/community, jobs/small business, and education —and volunteers were solicited.[306]

Negotiations between the LAX Coalition and airport officials ran from February through December 2004. Each side brought different strengths, but both entered with a will to strike a deal. From Smart's perspective, although the "community brought leverage to the situation [and] . . . understood their self-interests,"[307] the unions held the most power. In his view, community participation was "icing on the cake," providing legitimacy and input.[308] The coalition's major leverage was the threat of mass disruption by a large cross-section of important groups, which could be mobilized in relation to different parts of the Master Plan process. For example, LAWA held biweekly meetings with the City Council, which coalition members could attend to express discontent. In general, LAWA was keen to avoid negative press and coalition leaders were able to trade on this by promising not to publicize meetings in exchange for a commitment on LAWA's part to bargain in good faith.[309] Although the coalition's ultimate threat was the possibility of filing a lawsuit on the Final EIS/EIR, litigation was something that the coalition ultimately wanted to avoid. According to López Mendoza, who was already skeptical of what litigation could accomplish, the coalition knew "that a lawsuit under CEQA was a possibility, but that would be our last resort. . . . When we were negotiating with LAWA, community support for the project was our carrot, but CEQA was the stick."[310]

Moreover, the fact that ARSAC, as well as city and county opponents of expansion, appeared destined to file their own CEQA lawsuits made the coalition's litigation threat seem less consequential. In López Mendoza's view, ARSAC and the city and county opponents—all of which rejected overtures from the coalition to join negotiations—were highly unlikely to compromise with the airport. The county was generally disgruntled about lacking a voice in the expansion process, while ARSAC and other homeowner groups were "trying to delay the project," hoping delay would permit regional airports to take up more slack to "alleviate some of the stress on LAX." As López Mendoza saw it, Inglewood and El Segundo wanted more money for mitigation, while Culver City was using opposition to LAX to gain leverage in its dispute over an unrelated project in Playa Vista, which Culver City wanted the city to stop.[311]

On the city side, in addition to wanting to advance the mayor's goal of getting a deal, LAWA staff articulated their own interests in the negotiation. For his part, LAWA Deputy Executive Director Jim Ritchie expressed support for the adjacent communities' plight. As Ritchie recalled, after joining LAWA in 1999, he heard constant complaints from community groups to the east about nighttime air traffic noise. He initially rejected the complaints as implausible since there was an FAA ban on easterly takeoffs between midnight and 6 a.m.; however, when he went out one night to investigate, Ritchie learned that foreign airport cargo planes had won clearance to take off in the middle of the night over Carson, Lennox, and Westchester—waking residents. He thus came to firmly believe that community residents would be better off if they could "get a good night's rest."[312] Ritchie also understood that the CBA was crucial for the airport to get necessary political support for its modernization project, bringing all the stakeholders together in one place.[313] "When you have a big project that you have to seek outreach support for from various stakeholders, you need to go out and track them down.... The CBA is a one-stop shop."[314]

In explaining why LAX came to the table with the coalition, City Attorney Claudia Culling, who represented the airport in the negotiations, said, "Our attitude was that they had something to offer us and we had something to offer them.... It was also the right thing to do.... The CBA is not required under CEQA, or any law for that matter, but we still went out and did it because it was what the community wanted."[315] Overall, Culling believed that the driving force for an agreement was the mayor's need for coalition support in front of City Council: "The threat of litigation did not give the coalition any leverage.... What kept me in that room was the thought of the coalition not supporting the plan."[316] In Culling's view, the absence of the surrounding cities—Inglewood, El Segundo, and Culver City—at the negotiation table did not affect LAWA's motivation to deal with the coalition since LAWA understood that, no matter what, it was going to be sued by opponents of airport expansion. Culling believed the city opponents were motivated by "greed" and the desire to have LAWA "subsidize their city budgets."[317] Ritchie viewed the homeowner groups as "professional obstructionists."[318]

The negotiation plan, set forth by the coalition in February 2004, aimed to "[e]nsure that every negotiation includes representatives of interested organizations, experts, [and] community members, . . . in order to take advantage of expertise and to efficiently allocate resources of each organization."[319] At the outset, Smart established a code of conduct that prohibited yelling and name-calling—having witnessed prior labor negotiations in which disrespect undermined the project.[320] The protocols developed by Smart also included a commitment to negotiate by issue area, to not revisit issues that had already been finalized, and to only reach formal agreement after an issue had been vetted and approved by the full coalition.[321] Meetings were scheduled to take place every Thursday for three hours.

The coalition's negotiating team was selected by the steering committee. William Smart was the lead negotiator, responsible for organizing meetings and communicating with coalition partners and allies; he was joined in all negotiations by LAANE's Nancy Cohen.[322] The rest of the team was divided by issue area.[323] The Environmental/Community team, focused on environmental mitigation and community-based environmental justice issues, was comprised of Dr. Joe Lyou of the California Environmental Rights Alliance, Jerilyn López Mendoza of Environmental Defense, and Maria Verduzco-Smith of the Lennox Coordinating Council. The Jobs/Small Business team—focused on labor standards, job training, worker health, and the extension of city ordinances to LAX—was led by Susan Minato and Beatriz Silva of HERE Local 11, Danny Tabor of the Inglewood Coalition for Drug and Violence Prevention, and Marqueece Harris-Dawson of the Community Coalition. The school districts held their own negotiations, with Bruce McDaniel negotiating for Lennox and attorney Sima Salek for Inglewood. On the airport's side was LAWA Deputy Executive Director Jim Ritchie, who was chief negotiator; LAWA Chief Operating Officer Samson Mengitsu; consultant Bob Gilbert; and City Attorney Claudia Culling, whose job was to draft the ultimate agreement.[324] On this, Culling worked intensively with Julian Gross, who represented the coalition remotely from San Francisco.

At the first formal meeting, on March 3, 2004, the coalition negotiating team showed up with twenty community representatives. Things got off to a rocky start when Nancy Cohen read a prepared statement and presented 140 demands contained in an Excel spreadsheet, generated from earlier EIR comments and community input. Although the spreadsheet was presented as a "representative document" to show that the coalition was prepared and meant business,[325] airport negotiators were put off since they were expecting a more informal exchange.[326] Smart also believed that some of the airport officials balked at the whole enterprise—unhappy at being directed to negotiate by Hahn.[327] From López Mendoza's perspective, LAWA was initially "baffled" that the coalition was treating the meetings as a real negotiation, not just an opportunity to give community feedback.[328] To complicate matters further, the coalition's initial focus on environmental

Figure 4.6 Danny Tabor, left, speaking on behalf of the LAX Coalition. *Source*: Los Angeles Alliance for a New Economy (2004).

justice issues, in Smart's view, caused the discussions to become "bogged down" in technical details and provoked strong disagreement over basic demands.[329] For example, Bob Gilbert, LAWA's Chief Operating Officer, thought that the coalition's request for gate electrification was "ludicrous."[330]

The coalition quickly corrected course. Some of the coalition's changes were small but significant. For example, instead of presenting positions verbally, which led to miscommunication, the coalition decided to send proposals in writing before every meeting.[331] Although some airport officials were frustrated by the level of generality, the proposals succeeded in focusing discussion during the meetings. Other changes flowed from the developing relations between the negotiating parties. At the third meeting, a Smart sidebar with Ritchie caused Smart to realize that Ritchie was an ally who wanted to help the coalition "get things done."[332] Having established a rapport with Ritchie, Smart decided to hold meetings without the lawyers in attendance, instead giving the lawyers agreed-upon terms after meetings to adapt into legalese. Smart also opened a back channel with Gilbert in order to get a preview of any airport objections before meetings.[333]

With these adjustments in place, the original list of 140 demands was whittled down, eventually to 70, mostly in order to meet the FAA requirement of being aviation-related. FAA approval, in fact, hovered over the negotiations, frequently invoked by LAWA as a bargaining chip. "They would say, 'We want to help you guys, but we are at the mercy of the FAA,'" according to López Mendoza, who pointed to LAWA's resistance to a toxic emissions inventory as one example of how LAWA played the FAA card.[334] FAA approval was also an ongoing constraint in negotiations over job training and local hiring, which LAWA officials fretted were not aviation-related enough.

When LAWA negotiators realized they were in a real negotiation and needed to take the coalition seriously, López Mendoza remembered them resorting to "typical negotiating tactics," like circulating drafts at the last minute and canceling meetings, prompting coalition leaders to cancel a session of their own in response "because we were so annoyed."[335] During negotiations, Smart recalled that Ritchie played the "good cop" to Gilbert's "bad cop."[336] Ritchie believed his role was to bring the coalition down to earth, taking coalition proposals to the LAWA executive and finance boards to determine what LAWA could "realistically offer."[337] As these negotiation rhythms were settling into place, on March 25, 2004, the coalition circulated a draft CBA committing airport officials to "acknowledge the neighborhood context and promote compatibility between LAX and surrounding neighborhoods," while also supporting the goals of promoting economic benefits, controlling noise, and implementing a plan to "reduce air pollution."[338]

It was against this backdrop that the parties sought to make headway on the critical environmental justice issues. From Gilbert's perspective, the environmental justice sessions primarily focused on educating the coalition about what LAWA could and could not do.[339] He found this frustrating but felt that educating the coalition before saying no helped to keep negotiations going. In response to coalition demands, Gilbert—as "bad cop"—frequently found himself having to say "that's not practical because that is not the way things are done in the industry,"[340] while "good cop" Ritchie took a softer approach, responding to controversial coalition requests with: "let us think about this."[341] Other frictions arose. For example, LAANE's Nancy Cohen remembered particular tension around gate electrification, which LAWA wanted to hedge by requiring electrification only if "operationally feasible"—language that concerned the coalition because it introduced wiggle room that threatened enforcement.[342] Confronting this threat, the coalition would go back to environmental partners and legal experts to sharpen terms; this took a long time because the coalition was "pushing the envelope" with the nature of its requests, which provoked resistance from LAWA.[343]

The Lennox Coordinating Committee's Verduzco-Smith recalled that the key environmental justice issue, from the community perspective, was suspension of the airport's so-called avigation easement, under which homeowners in the airport flight path were required to give up their right to sue LAWA for noise if they took any airport money for mitigation. Verduzco-Smith called the easement a "deal breaker," although Smart objected to using that term during the negotiations.[344] To get around this sticking point, City Attorney Culling stated that the airport team ultimately agreed to suspend the easement out of "good will" to please the coalition.[345] In another snag, López Mendoza was surprised that LAWA resisted compliance with Leadership in Energy and Environmental Design (LEED) building standards because of cost, given that LEED certification would bring positive attention to the airport. From López Mendoza's perspective, this impasse was emblematic of an overall pattern of LAWA objecting to mitigation measures on the grounds that they were too expensive or that the airport was not solely responsible for the pollution.[346]

The education negotiations proceeded on a separate track. Culling said she did not understand why the school districts were in the coalition at all since LAWA made it clear it did not want to negotiate with them, given that there had been a prior settlement in 1980 that gave money to the districts for noise mitigation—and the FAA was resistant to providing more.[347] However, during the course of negotiations, Ritchie became convinced that the soundproofing authorized in that earlier settlement had deteriorated and LAWA should do more, while also addressing additional traffic impacts.[348] Because the school districts effectively sought a modification of the prior settlement, they had to negotiate separately from the coalition and each other. Bruce McDaniel, Superintendent of Lennox Unified, negotiated for that district, employing what he called the "giggle test": If he made a request and LAWA did not giggle, he would keep asking for it. While he was pleased to get "more than expected," the giggle test failed to win some of the district's key requests, including relocation of one elementary school and a community health clinic.[349]

The relation between the coalition's lawyer, Julian Gross, and the city attorney, Claudia Culling, was less of a laughing matter. Gross, paid by the California

Partnership for Working Families (an accountable development coalition launched by LAANE and other community–labor groups in 2006),[350] had already negotiated six CBAs and was seen as a national expert. While he sought to use that expertise to advance the coalition's claims, Culling viewed her role as reining in LAWA staff, who she thought were "prepared to give away the farm."[351] Culling found it difficult to work with Gross because he was in San Francisco and she was frustrated to receive revised proposals from Gross that did not track changes.[352] For his part, Gross was frustrated at Culling's slow response time, which was partly dictated by having to run everything past FAA officials. Drafting dynamics were also stressful. As Gross recalled, when he got proposals from LAWA and the coalition, he would make changes designed to ensure enforceability. However, when he sent the drafts back, both sides would often become angry because they thought he had changed the substance. By the end, everyone was so frustrated that both sides told Gross to only make changes that were absolutely necessary. Because of this, Gross thought that the final CBA contained a tension between enforcement language and lawyer "spin."[353]

External challenges to the LAX Master Plan also loomed large.[354] In May 2004, Mike Gordon (who had just resigned as El Segundo's mayor to run for the state assembly) said he could not support Hahn's Alternative D because of the increase in traffic and noise.[355] Gordon and Val Velasco, head of ARSAC, collected twenty thousand signatures in opposition to the plan,[356] signaling their intent to sue if LAWA pursued modernization.[357] As talks progressed through these challenges, with a scheduled May public hearing on the Final EIR (released in April) and a mid-June Airport Commission approval vote approaching, negotiations kicked into high gear. On May 10, 2004, coalition leadership circulated a proposal to be approved by coalition membership. The proposal expressed a commitment to promoting "community accountability" and securing a CBA "enforceable as a contract between LAWA and the Coalition."[358] The proposal's substantive goals included noise and traffic mitigation, $1 million annually for five years to support job training, a first-source hiring program, extending the Living Wage Ordinance throughout the airport, mitigation of noise and pollution in Lennox and Inglewood schools, mitigation of pollution through a mobile health clinic and school-based clinics, air pollution measures including complete gate and hangar electrification within five years, a LAWA incentive program to replace or retrofit diesel trucks, LEED building certification, and small business participation in the Master Plan.[359]

Meanwhile, the coalition developed a media program for the campaign "designed to convey a simple, compelling message through media actions, media stories and editorials . . . crafted to achieve maximum appeal."[360] The plan included the use of "[d]ynamic, articulate spokespeople, both English- and Spanish-speaking" to help frame the problem around the fact that "[r]esidents have not been included in the process" of LAX development, "resulting in negative impacts on our health, our schools and our neighborhoods." The proposed solution was to be presented as a "groundbreaking Community Benefits Agreement" that "protects the rights of residents to have a real say in the region's most important economic development plan." The media program included a release strategy, with a press conference scheduled for June 14, and coordination with the mayor's office.

A crucial May 20 meeting between the coalition and LAWA was set—just days before the planned LAWA and City Council hearing on the LAX Master Plan's Final EIR. In advance, the coalition circulated proposals, eliciting LAWA counterproposals in late April and early May—focused on establishing environmental standards for ground service equipment, converting on-site truck and bus fleets to alternative fuel, mitigating diesel delivery truck emissions, and reducing construction traffic. On May 7, the coalition asked for clarification on a number of factual questions relating to LAWA's counterproposal for gate electrification,[361] focusing on the meaning of "operational feasibility" as a key concern. The coalition also presented its own responses to LAWA's counterproposal on how to monitor compliance with ultra-low diesel fuel standards for construction-related vehicles, stating, "We tried to give you flexibility in the technology mix in the original proposal.... Your counter on the expert [monitor] completely transformed the role of that expert and undermined any possibility for independence. We are countering with specific requirements, as we think this will get us to reduction in construction emissions in the most straightforward way."[362] Jerilyn López Mendoza, Maria Loya, and Nancy Cohen met on May 19 at La Feria Restaurant in Inglewood to discuss negotiation strategy for the next day's meeting, as well as political strategy for June 14,[363] when the Airport Commission was slated to vote on expansion.

At the LAWA administration building's board briefing room on May 20, 2004, the coalition met with LAWA representatives for the eleventh time.[364] One of the coalition's demands was that LAWA conduct credible research on the airport's environmental impact. As an example of the kind of research the coalition did *not* want to see, its negotiators shared a memo critiquing an earlier LAX Air Quality and Source Apportionment Study for failing to use "independent experts" as principal investigators and to include "meaningful involvement" by coalition members. To build a record of solid environmental impact data going forward, the coalition proposed that the CBA include a commitment by LAWA to produce a rigorous air toxic emissions inventory and health exposure assessment study to protect community health.[365]

On Monday, June 14, at a three-and-a-half-hour meeting, the Airport Commission, by resolution No. 22500, approved Miscikowski's Consensus Plan, deferring roughly $8 billion in yellow light projects for further study.[366] Two days later, airport officials indicated that they would support the CBA; however, industry representatives expressed skepticism. As Doug Wills, the Air Transport Association's Vice President of Communications, put it, "Community support is important, but this proposal strikes me as a little off-center."[367] On June 17, 2004, the *Los Angeles Times* reported that the LAX Coalition was negotiating a "precedent-setting deal" for hundreds of millions of dollars in community improvements in connection with modernization.[368] The article stressed the need for FAA approval of community demands, which included $190 million to build and upgrade Lennox schools, a mobile health clinic, low-emission ground service vehicles, local hiring, and an airport-sponsored study of jet fuel emission. The article quoted López Mendoza stating, "This community has been so heavily burdened, it deserves improvement."[369]

Moving toward the final Master Plan approval date in December, LAWA circulated a draft CBA on August 3, 2004, which included much of what the coalition had fought for, though many details—particularly relating to cost—remained unsettled. The draft included unspecified funding for airport noise mitigation, a night curfew for eastern takeoffs, training for airport jobs (with priority going to neighborhood residents), first-source hiring, application of the Living Wage and Worker Retention Ordinances to LAWA contractors and lessees, an "independent study" of air pollutants from jet engine exhaust and other emission sources, a health impacts study, and money for community-based research projects. The draft also provided that grounded aircraft must plug into electricity, mandated electrification of cargo operation areas, required "all construction-related diesel equipment be outfitted with the best available emission control devices," and directed airport contractors and concessionaires to use only alternative-fuel trucks.[370] LAWA denied a request for all airport shuttles to use clean fuel on feasibility grounds and rejected the demand for a community health clinic as not sufficiently aviation-related to pass the FAA. Instead, LAWA committed to an airport-funded health study.[371]

As CBA negotiations and LAX Master Plan review both hurtled forward on the same timeline, the political stars began to align in favor of approval. On September 27, the Air Transport Association endorsed the Consensus Plan.[372] Then, at a news conference following the plan's first public hearing on October 19, the Los Angeles Chamber of Commerce and County Fed directors announced their support. On this business–labor alliance, Chamber President George Kieffer said, "This is our first joint project, but it won't be the last."[373] That same day, the Los Angeles City Council voted to advance the Consensus Plan on a 12-3 vote, with Bernard Parks, Antonio Villaraigosa, and Jack Weiss—all challenging Hahn for mayor—voting no.[374] On November 8, the Airport Commission agreed to a deal with El Segundo to protect the city in the event of expansion, but Mike Gordon was unmoved: "Rest assured, they haven't heard the last from us." Striking a similar note of defiance, County Supervisors Don Knabe and Yvonne Brathwaite Burke made an official board motion stating that the county would sue if City Council gave final approval to the LAX Master Plan.[375]

However, at this stage, approval of modernization and the CBA appeared to be a done deal. A draft of the CBA circulated on November 24, 2004 filled in financial details, with LAWA committing $8.5 million for aircraft noise mitigation and $3 million per year for job training.[376] The draft also provided more detail on community-based research, which LAWA agreed to support by spending "no less than $300,000" to fund studies in relation to future environmental review. That same day, the coalition issued a press release celebrating the deal.[377]

On Monday, December 6, 2004, the CBA went to the Board of Airport Commissioners, which approved it 4-0, noting it would be "tied to City Council and FAA approval of the LAX Master Plan Program."[378] In total, the CBA required LAWA to provide $499.5 million in community benefits.[379] Almost half of the money—$229.5 million—was designated for the Lennox ($111 million) and Inglewood ($118.5 million) school districts for noise-proofing, air conditioning/filtration, and the relocation of Oak Street Elementary in Inglewood (directly in the LAX flight path).[380] These funds were to be distributed at a rate of $4.275 million per year to the cities, with a similar amount going to Los Angeles County.[381] The costs of the CBA were to be paid for through a combination of bonds, airport reserves, passenger charges, and higher land fees and terminal rents. Just before the Airport Commission vote, López Mendoza expressed the coalition's collective excitement: "This agreement is really revolutionary. There are so many of us with such different perspectives, but we've managed to stay together through a long and difficult process."[382]

On December 7, the City Council voted to send the Master Plan for final approval—the same day that the County Board of Supervisors voted to approve Knabe's motion to sue (LAX was in Knabe's district). The City Council vote overrode the Los Angeles County Airport Land Use Commission, which had found that the Master Plan violated county land use law.[383] This cleared the way for final City Council approval of the CBA, which happened a week later.[384]

The LAX CBA—the first ever with a public entity—was extraordinary in its scope and detail, achieving much of what the coalition had struggled for over the previous year. Under the final cooperation agreement, signed by coalition members,[385] the coalition agreed not to "file, prosecute, bring, or advance any suit, claim, or legal action of any kind against LAWA or the FAA based upon any Released Claim," which included any claim "challenging the sufficiency or legal validity of the LAX Master Plan Program and/or associated environmental documents."[386] Because the developer in the LAX deal was the city itself, and the city could not legitimately require coalition groups to provide it with political support, there were no affirmative support obligations as in the Staples Sports and Entertainment District and other private CBAs. The actual terms of the CBA were included as Attachment A to the Cooperation Agreement, in which LAWA agreed to:

- provide $4.275 million per year each to Inglewood and Los Angeles County for noise mitigation with a commitment to accelerate programs for Inglewood (to be completed by 2008) and places of worship (Section III);
- "suspend its requirement that express, full avigation easements . . . be executed by homeowners receiving LAWA provided or funded noise insulation benefits" (Section III);

Figure 4.7 Jerilyn López Mendoza announcing LAX CBA with Mayor James Hahn.
Source: Jerilyn López Mendoza (2004).

- ensure "end-of-block" soundproofing, under which soundproofing money would be allocated to all residents of a block if any house received funding (thereby removing the previous inequity of allocating funding based on an arbitrarily drawn federal map) (Section III);
- provide a total of $15 million over five years to fund job training for airport and aviation-related jobs with first priority given to low-income individuals in the airport project area and then to low-income individuals citywide, people with special needs, and existing airport workers (Section IV);
- create work experience jobs that paid applicable wages and seek out other funds in the event the FAA prohibited job training expenditures (Section IV);

- establish a First Source Hiring Program, included as a material term in all airport contracts as of July 1, 2005, with first priority for the program given to low-income individuals in the project area and then to low-income individuals citywide (Section V);
- implement the First Source Hiring Program in the event the FAA prohibited its application to certain jobs or contribute an additional $200,000 to job training in the event of a complete FAA prohibition (Section V);
- apply the Living Wage Ordinance, Worker Retention Ordinance, and Contractor Responsibility Ordinance to all airport contractors, lessees, and licensees (Section VI);
- fund an independent expert to conduct a study of air pollution from jet engine and other airport sources, a health study of upper respiratory and hearing loss impacts, and community-based research to assess environmental impacts of future LAX Master Plan projects, provided that, in the event the studies were prohibited by the FAA, LAWA would set aside up to $2.8 million for an air quality fund (Sections VII, VIII, IX);
- guarantee electrification of all new passenger gates and cargo areas and, after five years, 100% of all passenger gates and cargo areas, ensuring that aircraft use electricity at passenger gates and cargo areas unless such use was determined to be "operationally infeasible," defined as causing a significant and unreasonable risk of injury, death, or property damage, or other interference or delay (with cost taken into consideration as a feasibility factor) (Section X.A-B);
- conduct an assessment of electrification of passenger loading areas, cargo areas, and hangars to determine whether it would be operationally infeasible and electrify cargo loading areas within five years unless operationally infeasible (Section X.A-C);
- set aside $1.7 million to the air quality fund if the FAA prohibited electrification (Section X.D);
- ensure (through independent monitoring) that all diesel equipment used for construction related to the LAX Master Plan "be outfitted with the best available emission control devices" and construction equipment use only ultra-low sulfur diesel fuel (Section X.F);
- contribute $500,000 to create an incentive program for reduction of diesel emissions and conduct an inventory of ground service equipment on site in order to establish emission rate requirements leading to the use of less polluting equipment (Section X.H);
- fund an independent study of on-road heavy-duty vehicle traffic related to LAX operations toward the goal of ensuring that, within five years, 50% of on-road vehicles operated by airport contractors run on alternative or low-emission fuel (Section X.J);
- incorporate, to the extent "practical and feasible," LEED building standards into the design of the LAX Master Plan program (Section XI);

- designate routes for construction equipment related to LAX Master Plan construction that avoided local communities (Section XII);
- increase participation in planning, construction, operation, and maintenance of LAX by businesses in the project area and by minority- and women-owned business enterprises (Section XIII); and
- establish regular implementation meetings with coalition representatives and provide annual implementation reports, while also reporting back to the coalition on all studies and allowing the coalition to monitor the implementation of various programs (Section XVI).

The CBA, approved in December 2004, was signed by LAWA Executive Director Kim Day on February 15, 2005.[387] The unprecedented agreement was hailed by city officials and coalition representatives alike as symbolizing a new era of community–airport relations characterized by collaboration not conflict.[388] Sweeping as it was, the CBA necessarily left some issues unresolved. There was no money for installing air filtration in homes (only schools), no guarantee of local hiring (only a promise to train and consider residents for jobs), and no living wage goal (as in the Staples CBA). As a result, there were some community members who complained that the LAX CBA did not go far enough and that it unduly benefited coalition members—a

Figure 4.8 LAX Coalition members celebrating CBA. *Source*: Los Angeles Alliance for a New Economy (2004).

point that made López Mendoza bristle: "I really resent those people that call us 'sellouts'... no member of the coalition is getting any funds from this, every single dime is going to mitigation."[389] Yet measured from where the coalition started—excluded from a modernization process barrelling forward without community input—the LAX CBA could be viewed as a striking success. Incorporating more than half of the items on the coalition's original wish list,[390] the CBA gave community residents, in the words of Maria Verduzco-Smith, "more than they ever thought they were going to get."[391] It was the high-water mark of community benefits advocacy in Los Angeles.

Litigation and Enforcement

Even as LAX CBA negotiations were culminating in agreement, city and airport officials were planning for litigation with those who had dissented from the coalition's work. On November 30, 2004, two Los Angeles County supervisors representing the South Bay promised to file suit against the modernization plan on the grounds that county complaints about increases in noise and pollution had gone unheeded.[392] Then, on December 22, 2004—after the CBA had been approved—Inglewood Mayor Roosevelt Dorn threated to sue, claiming that his city did not get its fair share of community benefits and sharply criticizing Hahn: "The agreement you entered with the school districts is atrocious."[393]

True to the opponents' word, in January 2005, four separate CEQA actions were filed against LAWA, the City of Los Angeles, Mayor Hahn, the City Council, and the Board of Airport Commissioners. All sought to enjoin the LAX Master Plan EIR, claiming that it failed to address environmental concerns regarding the plan's anticipated passenger and cargo increase.[394] None of the suits challenged the legitimacy of the CBA, which was not within the ambit of CEQA review.[395] Rather, the challengers' goal was to leverage the power of CEQA, with its relatively low evidentiary threshold for challenging an EIR, to bargain for a better mitigation deal with the city.[396]

Seeking to meet this threshold, the individual suits adopted a similar template. On January 3, 2005, the City of El Segundo filed a CEQA challenge, objecting to what it claimed was the LAX Master Plan's illegal segmenting of environmental review and arguing that, although the "EIR assumes a maximum throughput of 78.9 million annual passengers and 3.1 million annual tons of cargo, the Project provides no assurances that those capacity levels will not be exceeded."[397] Three days later, Los Angeles County and Culver City joined a suit alleging that the LAX Master Plan "fails to disclose or analyze the project's independent and cumulative noise, air, and surface traffic impacts."[398] The same day, ARSAC (represented by Jan Chatten-Brown) challenged approval of the "massive redevelopment and expansion of LAX," which "will result in tremendous adverse environmental impacts on the already severely impacted communities surrounding LAX."[399] On January 7, a group of homeowners, called the Federation of Hillside and Canyon Associations, sued to enjoin the plan, claiming it violated CEQA by "failing to consider a reasonable range of alternatives."[400] Thrown into this combustible mix the following week, the FAA published its Final EIS, with the comment period running through February 22, 2005.[401] At the end of this period, all of the suits were consolidated in the Riverside County Superior Court. In an effort to quell community discontent, the Airport Commission voted to approve $7 million for Inglewood and $1 million of county soundproofing projects, but this did not resolve the conflict.[402]

The CEQA lawsuits played out in the context of another political transition, which would affect settlement negotiations. In May 2005, Antonio Villaraigosa, a staunch opponent of Hahn's LAX Master Plan Alternative D, won a runoff election to succeed Hahn as mayor, while Bill Rosendahl, another Alternative D opponent, won the council seat of Cindy Miscikowski, who was termed out. The new Villaraigosa administration confronted the delicate problem of holding firm to its opposition to Hahn's proposal while embracing the benefits of modernization, which continued to gather political momentum under the green light project framework outlined in Miscikowski's Consensus Plan. On May 20, the FAA approved the LAX Master Plan EIS,[403] thereby authorizing $2.9 billion in green light projects (and provoking a furious denunciation from Representative Maxine Waters).[404] Villaraigosa's first steps as mayor signaled his intent to undercut Hahn's deal, which was most evident in Villaraigosa's appointment of ARSAC's Val Velasco to the Board of Airport Commissioners.[405]

With a more sympathetic administration in place, the CEQA litigants pressed for a settlement. They gained additional leverage in August 2005 by challenging the runway separation project, which required a separate EIR, arguing that the project would increase cancer risk and noise in nearby communities, especially El Segundo.[406] Pushing back, Councilman Tony Cardenas asked City Attorney Rocky Delgadillo to investigate whether Val Velasco had a conflict of interest in voting on Airport Commission matters that were subject to lawsuits in which she was president of the lead plaintiff, ARSAC.[407] Eager to settle the environmental lawsuits and launch the green light projects, Villaraigosa reappointed Lydia Kennard as executive director of LAWA (she had resigned under Hahn in 2003 and was not supportive of Hahn's plan).[408] Villaraigosa claimed he reached out to Kennard before he was sworn in: "I said to her, 'I need you. This airport is an engine for Southern California's economy. I need your leadership, your communication skills. I need your ability to build consensus.'"[409]

Kennard delivered. On December 19, 2005, the Airport Commission gave its initial approval to a settlement of the CEQA lawsuits, which was given final city authorization on January 18, 2006. Under the settlement terms, LAWA agreed to discontinue operations at 10 narrow-body gates and reduce capacity from 183 to 153 gates overall.[410] The settlement also established a community-based planning framework to address yellow light projects—consigning them to a vague future process controlled by project opponents and thus effectively ensuring their demise. Further, the settlement provided $266 million over ten years to fund accelerated noise mitigation, job training, and traffic mitigation for the city plaintiffs, as well as $60 million for additional air quality and environmental justice programs. Bowing to the county and ARSAC, LAWA also agreed to engage the FAA and other counties on a regional solution to air transportation demand. While the environmental litigants claimed victory, the coalition viewed the settlement as a deadweight cost, diverting LAWA staff time to achieve benefits that coalition leaders believed were already contained in the CBA.[411]

Nonetheless, the resolution of the environmental lawsuits opened space for LAWA to focus on CBA implementation.[412] The CBA itself established a framework of co-governance: providing for regular implementation meetings between LAWA and the coalition—to occur once a month in the first year and every other month thereafter—while requiring annual progress reports.[413] It also contained a financial contingency plan in the event that the FAA held any of the CBA programs not to be aviation-related, providing that "LAWA shall maintain accounting set-aside for funds required by this agreement" to be expended on job training and air quality.[414] Anticipating enforcement challenges, after the CBA was signed, LAANE developed an implementation strategy toward the goal of maintaining "community involvement and support during the implementation phase" through ongoing coalition and steering committee meetings; LAANE also sought to keep up ongoing enforcement pressure through meetings with political officials and advocacy to gain FAA approval.[415] To promote implementation, LAANE hired a three-quarter-time community organizer, a half-time researcher, and a one-third-time policy advocate to mobilize resources and allies toward "winnable" goals that "match[ed]" the coalition's core demands. The coalition encountered immediate resistance to the CBA's job-targeting provisions when LAWA sought to reallocate job training dollars to support workers in "other low-income census tracts" in the city. The coalition objected that the move "fundamentally shifts the focus of the intent of the CBA, which is to serve low-income residents within the Project Impact Area."[416] This early skirmish reinforced the importance of close oversight and focused implementation efforts, led by Danny Tabor and Flor Barajas-Tena, on holding LAWA to account for achieving specific CBA goals around noise mitigation, air quality, and jobs.[417]

Tending to the most pressing CBA requirements, LAWA made substantial early progress on noise mitigation. In a status report on February 28, 2006, LAWA stated that it had approved a $7 million grant to Inglewood for soundproofing.[418] LAWA also indicated that it had launched a study of nighttime departures and begun planning for air quality and health impact studies, while it was consulting with the FAA on funding for job training and local hiring—which remained uncertain. To move FAA approval forward, on March 6, 2006, LAWA Deputy Executive Director Jim Ritchie wrote a letter to FAA Manager Mark McClardy, asking for an advisory opinion to permit the use of airport revenues to fund the First Source Hiring Program.[419] On March 23, 2006, Ritchie requested another advisory opinion "regarding the application of existing laws and regulations to the use of LAWA revenues for the job training program."[420] McClardy's reply, on May 16, 2006, was disappointing: "If job training and referral efforts were expanded, as LAWA is proposing to do, LAWA would be funding an economic development program with airport revenue. This would be contrary to 49 USC 47107(1)(2), which prohibits use of airport revenues for general economic development... unrelated to the airport.... We do not doubt that the proposed programs are well intentioned. Nevertheless, it is our opinion that they do not comply with the Policy."[421]

However, LAWA kept up the pressure, fortified by settlement of the CEQA suits, which also called for targeted job training for Inglewood residents.[422] In September 2006, LAWA sent the FAA a revised First Source Hiring Program limited to "outreach and recruitment for LAWA jobs."[423] The FAA approved this modified program, cautioning that "LAWA revenue may be used only for screening for job classifications used by LAWA for hiring its own employees, and not for job classifications used by airport tenants but not LAWA."[424] In a similar concession, the FAA changed its position and agreed in December to support a modified version of the $3.3 million per year job training program—also limited to training for airport jobs, not the jobs of airport contractors.[425] With FAA authorization in place, LAWA began rolling out the First Source Hiring Program: pre-screening job applicants, connecting them with potential employers (through a web-based interface called SkillsMatch), and reimbursing businesses for training expenses.

LAWA's efforts to implement the CBA occurred in tandem with initiation of the enormously complex green light projects. Construction to move the airport's southern runway further away from its northern counterpart commenced in July 2006, reducing runway capacity by one-fourth during the busy summer months.[426] At the same time, in order to alleviate vehicle traffic, a flyaway bus started running from Union Station to LAX, prompting LAWA Executive Director Kennard to question the need to extend the Green Line: "There are a lot of other, better things we can do with our money in terms of getting people to the airport."[427] After residents offered mixed reactions to traffic reduction plans at a public hearing in August 2006,[428] LAWA began requiring hotel shuttles to reduce trips and use clean fuel vehicles.[429] In a sign of its commitment to advancing the CBA, in early 2008, the Board of Airport Commissioners approved $2.2 million to fund the first stage of the CBA-mandated study of air pollution impacts in Westchester, El Segundo, Inglewood, and Lennox.[430]

As the recession took hold, LAWA could boast of substantial progress toward CBA implementation. According to its 2008 Annual Progress Report,[431] the airport had spent a total of $22.5 million on noise mitigation in Los Angeles County, El Segundo, and Inglewood and almost completed $130 million in accelerated soundproofing for surrounding neighborhoods. The much-hated avigation easement was rescinded (although the nighttime departures study was stalled). With respect to jobs, despite the FAA's refusal to permit job training funding for airport contractor jobs, LAWA had succeeded in partnering with other institutions, including Loyola Marymount University and the Los Angeles Community Colleges, to obtain funding for on-the-job training for 259 workers (with 275 more in the pipeline), while the modified First Source Hiring Program had referred 2,015 applicants resulting in 423 hires with 56 program partner companies. All LAWA contracts contained provisions for contractor compliance with the Living Wage, Worker Retention, and Contractor Responsibility Ordinances. While the air quality study was in progress, LAWA reported completing the first phase of its feasibility assessment for gate, hangar, and cargo area electrification; assigning an independent monitor to review the emissions of diesel construction equipment; and incorporating green building design to the extent feasible and practical.

As this suggested, it was relatively easier to meet clearly defined CBA goals that did not excessively impinge on airport operations and over which LAWA could exert top-down control. Thus, soundproofing houses was completed in short order, while programs over which LAWA did not have complete authority (like local hiring) or that raised issues of "operational feasibility" (like electrification) had less definite results. This continued to be true in the period after the recession, which saw dramatic expansion of the Bradley International Terminal (adding nine gates and one million square feet incorporating green design concepts), while revealing uneven compliance with CBA goals. For example, by 2016, LAWA reported that it had completed noise abatement—soundproofing over seventy-three hundred units[432]—but that the FAA had rejected its proposed ban on nighttime departures, leaving the easterly communities in the LAX flightpath subject to ongoing sleep disruption.[433] The FAA also rejected funding for the community health study, sending LAWA back to the drawing board to raise outside funds (even as the air quality study was being finalized). There was similar evidence of mixed results in other areas. While all passenger gates had been electrified, feasibility issues undermined progress in the hangars and cargo areas; although shuttles ran on alternative fuel, emission reductions for other ground service vehicles remained a work-in-progress; and while more than five hundred people completed job training and roughly sixty-seven thousand had been referred to employers through the First Source program, the number of actual local hires was tiny.[434]

Over a decade after the landmark LAX CBA had been reached, the community, environmental, and labor members of the coalition responsible for its achievement could each point to benefits for its constituents: significant noise mitigation and school relocation for the hardest hit LAX communities; genuine progress on electrification, serious study of air pollution, and real programs for phasing out diesel vehicles; and the incorporation of living wage standards into airport contracts alongside job training and placement services for local residents. As with any complex agreement that hinged on bureaucratic enforcement, the long slog of oversight and implementation, punctuated by periodic backsliding, produced inevitable frustration over what remained undone. And yet, overall, the lawyers and activists who built the LAX alliance, and guided it toward the largest CBA in history, could justly claim transformative impact: a half-a-billion dollars in benefits paid by one of Los Angeles's most powerful city agencies to strengthen the very low-income communities of color it had historically marginalized and ignored.

Contesting Gilded Los Angeles: The Grand Avenue CBA

Whose Bunker Hill?

In the trilogy of major Los Angeles CBAs, it was fitting that the final act played out on the site of redevelopment's original sin: Bunker Hill. High atop downtown Los Angeles on a plateau deliberately cut off from Skid Row a mile away, Bunker Hill was home to gleaming skyscrapers that housed the city's corporate, financial, and legal elite. It was not always so. The Los Angeles CRA's first project in Los Angeles was the conversion of Bunker Hill from a working-class residential community dotted with Victorian homes (occupied by a significant Latino immigrant population) to high-rise office space.[435] Redevelopment commenced in 1949 as an urban renewal project approved by the federal government, which then provided the bulk of the funds for property acquisition, relocation, and site preparation.[436] The area was converted by the CRA into the Bunker Hill Urban Renewal Project in 1968, sparking a building boom that transformed the landscape: producing more than eight million square feet of office space and over half-a-million square feet of retail space by the 1990s. However, the imposing corporate skyscrapers—opening only for the daily influx of cars carrying commuters who would flee to their suburban homes as soon as work was over—highlighted the absence of street life and cultural vibrancy. It was, as urbanist Mike Davis described, a coldly efficient space, notable primarily for its desolate indifference to pedestrians and offering a stark contrast with the bustling downtowns of New York, San Francisco, and other global cities.[437]

In an effort to challenge the image of Los Angeles as a city without a center, politicians teamed up with civic leaders to reimagine downtown generally, and Bunker Hill in particular, after the 1992 civil unrest. Leading the revitalization push was billionaire and self-appointed cultural emissary, Eli Broad, who had made a fortune in real estate and insurance and used his wealth to become a force in L.A. art and philanthropy circles in the 1980s and 1990s. It was Broad's initiative and money that helped build the Museum of Contemporary Art (MOCA) as the first cultural addition to Bunker Hill since the late 1960s opening of the Los Angeles Music Center, anchored by the Dorothy Chandler Pavilion (home to opera and dance), on the hill's far north end. In partnership with Mayor Riordan, Broad also helped to spearhead fundraising for the 1996 completion of Frank Gehry's architectural masterpiece, the $275-million Walt Disney Concert Hall, just south of Dorothy Chandler and catty-corner from MOCA on Grand Avenue. By the turn of the millennium, this area—only four blocks from the city hall—was emerging as the cultural and civic center that L.A. boosters had long desired. From the perspective of city leaders, to create a sense of real place, all that was lacking was a residential and retail core to link together the pieces of a burgeoning arts district. It was in this context that what would come to be called the Grand Avenue Project started to take shape, pressed forward by Broad and supported by the CRA in what would be, unbeknownst at the time, its last major attempt at downtown development.

The public announcement of the project came in August 2002, when Eli Broad and developer Jim Thomas, co-chairs of the Grand Avenue Committee, unveiled a proposal for a $1.2 billion residential, retail, and hotel complex, the centerpiece of which was to be built on Grand Avenue, directly east of the Disney Concert Hall between First and Second Streets.[438] As Bunker Hill redevelopment accelerated—with Cardinal Roger Mahony of the Los Angeles Catholic Archdiocese dedicating the stunning new Cathedral of Our Lady of the Angels just north of the Music Center—Broad laid out his vision: "I'm concerned that this city will never really be a city. And for L.A. to be a great city, it has to have a vital center." But just what it meant to have a vital city center was a point of contention—and questions were raised about whether Bunker Hill needed a version of L.A. Live. As a reporter for the *Los Angeles Times* put it: "In a broader sense, the new Grand Avenue is an extension of the retail-entertainment development already being planned for the area around Staples Center."[439] Urbanist Joel Kotkin was more pointed in critique of the Grand Avenue vision: "What's needed are policies that would stimulate [downtown's] existing dynamism. For example, public funds should be spent on improving street lighting, historic restoration, policing and vagrant control."[440]

Advocates of the Broad plan were all in favor of public funding—they just wanted to make sure it went to support the creation of what was being styled as the Champs-Élysées of Los Angeles. In what would be a significant bone of contention, Grand Avenue boosters urged the CRA to contribute $250 to $300 million for infrastructure development in support of the proposed project. However, public outcry over subsidizing a Broad-led luxury development caused Grand Avenue supporters to drop the request in the early stages of the plan. In late 2003, with an eye on securing the necessary approvals, city and county officials created the L.A. Grand Avenue Authority, a unique joint powers entity governed by the CRA and the county—an arrangement necessitated by the fact that of the four parcels (used as parking lots) proposed for the site, two were owned by the city and the other two by the county. As the Grand Avenue Authority reviewed proposed plans (including one put forth in collaboration with real estate mogul Donald Trump),[441] Broad sounded an optimistic note: "We're hopeful we'll be able to create a street where people will stay after work and one that will be a draw for the entire region." Frank Gehry, a leading contender to design the new project, shrugged off the attention: "For me, it's not important if I do a building—I've got Disney Hall. I'm more interested in the urban planning. . . . To create another elitists' enclave is not [the goal]. . . . We've already got Beverly Hills."[442]

In June 2004, the Grand Avenue Authority heard pitches from the two developers selected as finalists for the project: Forest City Enterprises from Cleveland and Related Companies from New York. The Forest City plan envisioned a trolley from Staples to Grand Avenue, while Stephen Ross, chairman of Related, said that he wanted the project to be "complementary to the cultural center that's there and complementary to the Staples Center," adding that he had talked to Cirque du Soleil and Clear Channel about restaurants and comedy clubs.[443] On Monday, August 9, the joint powers authority, chaired by County Supervisor Gloria Molina, selected Related—fresh off completion of the Time Warner Center in New York City—to have exclusive negotiating rights for the Grand Avenue Project. Brady Westwater, head of the downtown neighborhood council, was incredulous that Related was chosen: "They build malls. Why are we handing over the center of our city?"[444]

That concern was shared by others uneasy about the rapid gentrification of downtown. From 1998 to 2005, downtown's population increased from 18,653 to 24,604, and was expected to double over the next decade with newcomers taking residence in the expanding stock of lofts and condominiums. The $1.8 billion Grand Avenue Project—centered around a boutique hotel and luxury condos—would only add to the gentrification trend.[445] Political officials, however, were eager for downtown development and the Grand Avenue Authority voted unanimously to approve the project's Master Plan (also called the implementation plan) on May 23, 2005, in order to bring "night life and a sense of community to a downtown that for decades was known for closing down when the sun set."[446] The envisioned "community" would be located in a mixed-use development covering 3.6 million square feet. The original project design revolved around five skyscrapers: one fifty-story building with the boutique hotel and condominiums and four other towers of thirty stories with expensive condos, affordable housing, 400,000 square feet of retail shops, a movie theater, and a high-end supermarket.[447] The Los Angeles County Economic Development Corporation estimated "that the Grand Avenue Project would create 5,000 full-time jobs and generate approximately $565 million in annual business revenue to the city and county."[448] The implementation plan also included renovation of an underused sixteen-acre park running from the Music Center to the city hall, and streetscape improvements along Grand Avenue from Fifth Street to Cesar Chavez Avenue. It drew the support of former Mayors Riordan and Hahn, and then-Mayor Antonio Villaraigosa.[449]

Backers of the Grand Avenue Project touted a key feature: It would not depend on any public subsidies. In August 2005, Broad bragged that Grand Avenue would be built "without using one dollar of general fund money from the city or the county."[450] However, the complicated financing scheme offered by the city and county made Broad's assertion depend on an assumption of ever-increasing real estate values.

Under the proposed deal, Related would lease the project parcels (owned by the county and CRA) for 99 years, providing an upfront $50 million down payment. However, the down payment would not go back into the public coffers, but rather would be used to fund traffic improvements, renovated streetscapes, and the park.[451] As the *Los Angeles Times* put it, "In effect, the county and city would be allowing the developer to use a valuable public asset—the land—and would use the rent from the land to make the developer's lease more valuable."[452] The county was also considering moving some county offices into the new Grand Avenue buildings— offering another potential financial advantage to Related.

In the most significant potential financial risk to the public fisc, the Grand Avenue deal hinged on Related's payment of so-called incentive rents. On top of the $50 million down payment, the city and county were promising to spend roughly $20 million for upfront streetscape improvements and other upgrades. Because of their commitment not to use general funds to finance the deal, the government agencies were committed to taking out debt or using property tax increment to finance the infrastructure projects. Under the plan, their $70 million upfront investment would then be repaid by Related out of future condo sales and retail rents under a formula setting aside 5% of condo sale prices and 2% of retail rents after four years—but only if property values were to rise.[453] Despite assurance that no public money would be used, the county analyst opined that the county could be at risk if the "project goes over budget or if the downtown real estate market cools," since the government would still be required to fund infrastructure costs.[454] As the report concluded, because the public entities were locked into financial support, "[i]f the costs are understated and in fact become higher, then the need for public assistance and/or the possibility the project would not get built both loom larger."[455] Within this financing framework, the project was nonetheless set to unfold in three phases: with Phase One focused on developing the park and parcel just east of Disney Hall, Phase Two on the parcel to the south of Disney Concert Hall, and Phase Three on the parking lot on Second Street between Hill and Olive Streets. Scoping for the Grand Avenue Project EIR commenced in September 2005.

As AEG broke ground on L.A. Live in the fall of 2005, two visions of downtown development were emerging: with L.A. Live a tourist destination likened to Universal City Walk and the Grand Avenue Project responding to the perceived lack of housing and retail services, like grocery stores and other shopping.[456] Yet both were united in an upscale vision that left little room for low-income communities of color. The Grand Avenue Project contained some gestures toward income diversity. As part of the deal, Related promised to set aside 20% of the project's twenty-one hundred to twenty-six hundred units as low-to-moderate income housing to be reimbursed by the CRA at a rate of $100,000 to $200,000 per unit.[457] However, this promise merely reflected preexisting inclusionary housing obligations under CRA policy, adopted by the joint powers authority, requiring 20% of housing units developed with CRA financial assistance to be set aside for affordable housing.[458] From this point of view, it appeared that Related was only being asked to do the minimum. Moreover, the plan itself contained no environmental, local hiring, or living wage criteria—although CRA policy put in place under the leadership of Madeline Janis (formerly Janis-Aparicio) required tenants in publicly financed projects to pay living wage.[459] Despite the city's professed sensitivity to community concerns, by early 2006, as the Grand Avenue Project was about to enter the crucial environmental review phase, community groups rallying against downtown gentrification and its impact on the poor began turning their attention to preventing a redux of the fateful Bunker Hill redevelopment a half-century earlier.

Community Without Labor

Community mobilization against the Grand Avenue Project reunited the founding partners of the CBA movement—LAANE and SAJE—but that partnership ultimately split onto different tracks as the Grand Avenue CBA campaign developed. This was, in part, a result of the different political landscape in which Grand Avenue mobilization occurred: Organized labor was eager for jobs the development would produce and, with a labor-friendly city administration and LAANE's Madeline Janis on the CRA board, could achieve its goals through the political process. On the other side, community advocates, particularly those focused on housing and homelessness, were still outside of the political establishment and forced to attack a project that, from their perspective, would have negative impacts on low-income residents of downtown.

Organizing for affordable housing stability in gentrifying downtown had its roots in litigation against the CRA over the L.A. Live project at Staples Center in the early 2000s. This litigation challenged the CRA's effort to circumvent the $750 million cap on tax increment from the Central Business District project area to finance L.A. Live by creating a new project area (called the City Center) that included a carve-out of roughly a thousand acres from the Central Business District. (The City Center area, like the Central Business District, ran close to, but did not encompass, the proposed Grand Avenue Project.) The CRA's move precipitated two lawsuits, one by the county, filed in June 2002, arguing that the City Center plan would illegally take tax increment that should otherwise go to the county (which was entitled to a share of Central Business District area tax increment above the cap).[460] It was this lawsuit that had delayed implementation of the Staples CBA.

The second lawsuit, *Wiggins v. CRA*, was brought a month later by LAFLA's Barbara Schultz and Cristian Abasto (along with co-counsel from the Public Interest Law Project) on behalf of the Wiggins family, two day laborers who lived in a downtown Single Room Occupancy (SRO) unit with their infant daughter, and the Los Angeles Coalition to End Hunger and Homelessness, an organizational plaintiff whose members claimed injury caused by the CRA's redrawing of the redevelopment lines.[461] The *Wiggins* suit challenged the City Center project area on the grounds that it constituted "an unlawful attempt to sidestep . . . limitations on the use of tax increments," specifically objecting to the fact that the plan did not adequately account for relocating displaced residents and replacing lost affordable housing, while also failing to provide for job training and permanent employment opportunities for downtown residents.[462] After a February 2003 trial consolidating the *Wiggins* and county cases, the superior court invalidated the City Center plan as contravening the tax increment cap. The California Court of Appeal agreed that the CRA's effort to take tax increment from the thousand acres carved out of the Central Business District violated the cap, but held that the CRA could legally collect tax increment from property in the rest of the City Center project area.[463] On the basis of the appellate court decision, the *Wiggins* and county cases were remanded to the superior court to revise its original order.

On June 15, 2006, the *Wiggins* case settled on terms that reshaped the terrain of affordable housing advocacy in downtown Los Angeles.[464] Under the settlement agreement, the CRA committed to a policy of "no net loss" within the City Center project area (as well as in an adjacent redevelopment zone, the Central Industrial area, covering Skid Row). To advance this policy, the city agreed to maintain an inventory of all housing units developed or rehabbed with CRA funds as well as units subject to demolition or conversion. The goal was to keep the overall inventory of affordable units stable.[465] To implement this part of the settlement, the CRA adopted "Development Guidelines and Controls for Residential Hotels in the City Center and Central Industrial Project Areas," which restricted the redevelopment of SROs (to preserve housing of last resort) and provided one-for-one replacement of SROs when demolition or conversion occurred. The *Wiggins* settlement also established a first-source hiring system, in relation to CRA-funded SRO projects, on which local low-income residents were to make up not less than 30% of the workforce of each permanent employer with ten or more employees.[466] In addition, the CRA promised to establish a $2.5 million job training and development fund for local low-income residents.

Although the *Wiggins* no net loss framework did not technically apply to the land on which the Grand Avenue Project was to be built, it had two important effects that influenced Grand Avenue CBA organizing. One was that the no net loss framework established in the *Wiggins* settlement committed the CRA to a principle of affordable housing preservation in downtown that could be invoked in negotiations around Grand Avenue. In addition, efforts to implement *Wiggins* spawned the Share the Wealth Coalition—a joint organizing effort spearheaded by the L.A. Coalition to End Hunger and Homelessness (the *Wiggins* plaintiff) and FCCEJ (led by SAJE)—which advocated for the rights of SRO tenants while promoting broader inclusionary policies to prevent the loss of affordable housing as a result of downtown development.[467] The coalition also included the Los Angeles Community Action Network (LA CAN), founded in 1999 to address the criminalization of homelessness in Skid Row, and the Downtown Women's Center, a service provider for homeless women that in 2004 had challenged the EIR for a mixed-use development project built adjacent to its office on the gentrifying western border of Skid Row.[468]

Community concerns about gentrification were exacerbated in April 2006, when architect Frank Gehry was selected to design Phase One of the Grand Avenue Project.[469] Gehry's rendering envisioned a 47-story translucent glass tower at the south end of the Grand Avenue parcel immediately across from Disney Concert Hall (along Second Street) and a 24-story L-shaped building at the north end (along First Street). The taller tower, standing at more than six hundred feet, was to have three rooftop pools, 250 luxury condos, a 275-room hotel, spa, and Equinox gym. The second tower, at 250 feet, was to include 100 affordable housing units and 150 condos, as well as a 50,000-square-foot supermarket.[470] Release of the architectural models was followed by a flurry of criticism. The *Los Angeles Times* architecture critic proclaimed that the "public expects more" and objected to the new development "approach that asks developers to build quasi-public space, ringed with retail, in exchange for land, streamlined approval or help with the bottom line."[471] Some condemned the Gehry plan for being less public-oriented than the original design since it contemplated a space filled almost entirely with luxury properties and high-end retail,[472] while others worried that the plan could backfire if the real estate market softened and the wealthy stayed away.[473] The *Los Angeles Times* editorial board denounced the City Council's new proposal to give $66 million in tax breaks to build a hotel with rooms that started at $400 per night.[474]

It was in the context of this controversy that the Grand Avenue Coalition for Community Benefits, building on the backbone of Share the Wealth, was launched in the summer of 2006[475]—at the precise moment that the Grand Avenue Project was entering its period of environmental review. The city issued the Grand Avenue Draft EIR on June 14, 2006, commencing a six-week comment period. Seizing the opportunity to intervene in environmental review that now formed part of the well-worn CBA negotiating strategy, Share the Wealth leaders met with labor counterparts to consider mounting a CBA campaign in relation to the Grand Avenue Project. In July 2006, they held a meeting to discuss a CBA coalition, attended on the labor side by representatives from LAANE, HERE Local 11, and the SEIU. Community-based participants included representatives from SAJE and LA CAN, along with members of two other groups: Concerned Citizens for South Central Los Angeles, a community development organization created in the 1980s to address housing and jobs in historically African American neighborhoods of South Los Angeles (which had been a member of FCCEJ in the Staples CBA campaign); and the Community Development Technologies Center (CD Tech), an organization located in downtown (and aligned with Los Angeles Trade Tech Community College) that focused on community education and leadership training around development issues.

Given the short time frame for input into the Grand Avenue approval process, there was intense pressure on the partner groups to reconcile competing interests and coalesce around common goals. SAJE, led by Gilda Haas, had focused its work primarily in the Figueroa Corridor area of southern downtown, but viewed Grand Avenue as presenting the same gentrification threat as L.A. Live—and brought to the coalition all of the insights and experience from that campaign. As Haas later described, SAJE challenged Grand Avenue because it epitomized downtown development that did not "primarily reflect the needs or interests of the majority of people who live in Los Angeles." Rather, "the majority of those moving into the 'new' downtown are white and wealthy, while most of the thousands of current residents being displaced are black, Latino, and poor."[476] LA CAN viewed its mission as building a resident-led organization in downtown's historic core that would advocate for the rights of low-income renters and homeless people. Becky Dennison was the group's representative in the Grand Avenue Coalition. Trained as a mechanical engineer, Dennison was "looking for a career change" and was "drawn to Skid Row ... given the overwhelming need,"[477] when she started at LA CAN in 2001. Quickly thrown into *Wiggins* and the growing anti-displacement work around redevelopment, Dennison became "really active monitoring" downtown CRA projects. It was in this role that she learned about the Grand Avenue proposal and was "a little taken off guard that [the CRA] was going to present this gigantic mega project with ... just the minimum affordable housing and not much else."[478] LA CAN's special focus, therefore, was on expanding and deepening the affordable housing component of the Grand Avenue Project. CD Tech saw its role as uplifting community voices in the development process, while Concerned Citizens was motivated, in part, by a broader critique of City Councilwoman Jan Perry—whose district included downtown and large parts of South Los Angeles—for Perry's record of "overinvesting in downtown and underinvesting in South Central."[479] For this reason, Concerned Citizens was on board with the coalition's "small but mighty" challenge to the Grand Avenue Project, which was in Perry's council district and had her support.[480]

While LAANE made it clear that it was disqualified from participating in the coalition (because that would have required CRA Commissioner Janis to recuse herself from any decisions related to the project), the unions could not find enough common ground with the community groups to move forward in alliance. Although supportive of the community groups' affordable housing demands, the unions were more focused on leveraging existing CRA policy to extend opportunities for union organizing: applying the CRA's living wage policy to project tenants, winning a project labor agreement with the building and trade unions for construction jobs, and securing a labor peace agreement for the hotel. The unions prioritized these goals over local hiring since local hiring agreements for unionized project jobs meant that workers hired through the local hiring process would effectively jump over existing union members (who were often less diverse) in the hiring queue.

Because Share the Wealth members were committed to housing and local hiring—and issues around substance and strategy could not be resolved—they ultimately decided not to form a community–labor coalition with the unions. From Dennison's point of view, the community groups "were just not aligned with the goals of what [the labor groups] were trying to accomplish," and thought labor was "taking a very insider's approach . . . hoping actually to avoid a CBA and just kind of use their influence to improve the project."[481] Dennison believed that, "especially on the housing side, . . . the CRA minimums were just nowhere near enough."[482] Particularly as community benefits principles had become "institutionalized" as standard CRA policy, Dennison felt like "we should fight for things that aren't standard."[483] As a result, the coalition split not "in any sort of negative way, . . . [rather] there was a group of folks working on an inside strategy and there was a group of folks working on an outside strategy."[484] Janis's perspective was different. Rather than a community–labor split, she viewed Grand Avenue as an example of an effective insider-outsider strategy. While the coalition advocated externally, she and CRA CEO Cecilia Estolano—a progressive leader who cared about development equity—were able to push for a community benefits program from inside the CRA, mobilizing support of the redevelopment board and Mayor Villaraigosa. The end result was a tripartite division of labor: the Grand Avenue Coalition—comprised of SAJE, LA CAN, Concerned Citizens, and CD Tech—pursued a benefits program focused on affordable housing and local hiring; the unions pressed for living wage, a project labor agreement, and labor peace; and Janis and Estolano worked inside the CRA to mesh these demands into a viable benefits program that could be supported by the unions and Related.[485]

Given the preexisting template for Grand Avenue development, with a 20% affordable housing set aside already promised, the coalition's "big asks" were for deeper affordability levels—units for extremely low-income households earning less than 30% of AMI—and affordable housing integrated on-site that included supportive services for formerly homeless residents.[486] The coalition also backed job training and local hiring, focused on project area residents, for construction and permanent jobs. Because of the small number of coalition groups and the need for efficiency, group leaders took the lead in formulating strategy and developing demands, engaging in "report back meetings" to their memberships but not erecting a formal governance structure.[487] For legal support, the coalition retained LAFLA's Ben Beach, who had started as an Equal Justice Works fellow after graduating from the New York University School of Law in 2002 and continued as a staff attorney in LAFLA's Community Economic Development Unit, where he focused on community benefits advocacy. In the Grand Avenue campaign, Beach was asked to help the coalition "navigate the landscape" given the complicated joint powers structure, approval framework, and financing.[488] With this legal and organizing team in place, the Grand Avenue campaign for community benefits commenced.

Benefits without Agreement

The coalition's focus quickly turned to figuring out its points of leverage in order to bring Related to the table and strike a deal within a compressed time frame. From Dennison's perspective, the Grand Avenue Project was presented by the joint powers authority as a "get on board or else" project; as a result, the coalition's initial efforts were "really just about disruption" in order to demonstrate the community's power to stop the sense of inevitability and put pressure on the Grand Avenue Authority and Related to negotiate.[489]

As Beach recalled, although the coalition's "leverage was principally organizing,"[490] its members did seek to mobilize around the Draft EIR,[491] the comment period for which was set to expire in late July 2006. With Beach's assistance, the coalition attacked the draft's assertion that placing jobs and housing in the same area would result in reduced traffic impacts, pointing out that—based on the low wages of service workers to be employed in the project—those workers would not make enough to afford even the most "affordable" unit in the project.[492] The coalition used this argument to support its housing demands, contending that if the project was, in fact, to enable people to live where they work, more units at lower affordability levels were needed as a traffic mitigation measure.[493] Although these comments garnered some attention from the CRA and developer, in Dennison's view, the coalition's environmental critiques of the project were primarily an attempt to "slow it down" since they were ultimately not that strong.[494]

The coalition therefore pivoted toward trying to exert political pressure. Councilwoman Jan Perry, who sat on the joint powers authority, was a key target. As Dennison recalled, because Perry had a reputation for ruling development decisions in her district "with a pretty closed fist" and was "really close with Related," coalition leaders viewed her support as their best bet for making headway. Dennison also viewed Perry as "vulnerable" because she "leaned progressive on housing issues . . . [and] did care about South Central," which allowed the coalition to "get people up in her ear" to ask: "What are you doing?"[495] The coalition deployed Concerned Citizens' director, Noreen McClendon—who had Perry's ear—to make the case for the coalition, which also staged a large protest action at the Central Avenue Jazz festival during the last week of July, which made Perry's "head explode."[496] In response, Perry agreed to help broker a discussion with Related, which was also getting pressure from the CRA's Estolano, who alongside Commissioner Janis, was "super-invested" in the coalition's "collective platform" and willing to push for community benefits negotiations.[497] As Dennison recalled, Estolano "was supportive of enforcing the *Wiggins* Agreement . . . and she knew us and she knew that we were credible. So once we were . . . able to push Jan [Perry] far enough . . . Cecilia Estolano convened the negotiation table with Related."[498] Janis recounted that her work with Estolano involved bringing the unions and Related together around supporting a community benefits program that included deeper housing subsidies and local hiring. This required brokering a deal in which the unions would commit to support community benefits in exchange for project labor and labor peace agreements—and then getting Related on board with the entire package.[499]

Charged with managing this process on Related's side was CEO Bill Witte, a former San Francisco deputy mayor for housing, who was well regarded by business and civic leaders (Eli Broad lauded Witte for being "very credible and want[ing] everyone's input"), and seen as supportive of affordable housing.[500] However, the coalition was not placated by Witte's values and congenial style. To the contrary, advocates denounced the project's Draft EIR, which unveiled Grand Avenue as the L.A. version of Related's swanky Time Warner Center in New York City: home to expensive restaurants, luxury condos, a five-star hotel, and a Whole Foods grocery.[501] Making matters worse, construction cost projections continued to rise. In September 2006, Related announced that there would be a 40% cost increase in Phase One because of the Gehry design.[502] With the project budget ballooning to over $2 billion, Related backtracked from its earlier promise not to seek public subsidies as Witte insisted that the project would be "completely unfeasible" without a twenty-year rebate of the city's 15% hotel bed tax and a temporary rebate of the 10% parking tax.[503]

The Final EIR for the Grand Avenue Project, released in November 2006, analyzed the original Gehry-designed plan alongside five alternatives, including a "No Project" alternative, and other options with density reductions and different designs to mitigate the impact on historical resources. For example, the County Office Building Option included a county building of up to 681,000 square feet, plus 2,060 market-rate housing units and 412 affordable units. The Additional Residential Development Option envisioned 2,660 market-rate units and 532 affordable units. The Final EIR concluded that under any plan there would be significant impacts on traffic, historical resources, and air quality, although it ultimately supported mitigation measures as adequate to address them.[504]

In late November 2006, the Grand Avenue Authority held a public hearing to consider the plan. Witte kept up the pressure for public funds, asking for tax rebates worth $40 million for the 275-room hotel, provoking an incredulous response from CD Tech Director Benjamin Torres: "This project is larger in size, subsidy and government involvement than any other project in Los Angeles, and yet it is smaller in terms of community benefits."[505] In this regard, Related was only promising a modest hundred units of affordable housing in Phase One and the affordability level for those units was set for low-to-moderate income households—no housing was set aside for those who were extremely poor earning less than 30% of AMI. In the face of this paltry community investment, Concerned Citizens' McClendon condemned Grand Avenue as "a project in downtown Los Angeles for the wealthy."[506] These objections, however, fell on deaf ears at the Grand Avenue Authority, the spokesman for which insisted: "If there's no development, there are no benefits." Based on that logic, the authority approved the Gehry-designed plan, sending it to the County Board of Supervisors, City Council, and CRA for their review.

As the plan raced toward final governmental approval, the CRA's Estolano facilitated a flurry of meetings between coalition leaders—SAJE's Haas, LA CAN's Dennison, CD Tech's Torres, and Concerned Citizens' McClendon—and Related's Witte. Over the course of a half-dozen sessions, there was back and forth over the coalition's key housing terms, resulting in significant gains. The coalition used the "threat of public embarrassment" to persuade Related to abandon its plan to create separate entrances for low-income tenants in its residential units—a practice employed by notorious slum lords downtown with whom Related did not want to be associated. However, the coalition ended up trading on-site supportive housing—which the developer viewed as a "nonstarter"[507]—for a $750,000 to $1.5 million revolving loan fund over ten years for supportive housing development within five miles of the project.[508] At first, Related strongly resisted lower affordability levels because, as Dennison put it, of the "stigma that extremely low-income people would be problematic tenants. . . . [Developers] just don't want those folks."[509] But Witte came "around fairly quickly."[510] Indeed, the coalition succeeded in pushing down the income thresholds for affordable housing—which Related agreed to locate on-site. For the entire project, Related committed to making all rental units affordable to households earning 60% of AMI or less, and to set aside half of the affordable for-sale units for low-income households (up to 80% of AMI) and the other half for very low-income households (up to 50% of AMI).[511] For Phase One rental units, Related agreed to lease 35% of the units to extremely low-income tenants (35% of AMI) and the remainder to very low-income tenants.[512] This commitment was "contingent upon the ability of the CRA or other governmental source to provide gap financing at $100,000 per rental unit and $200,000 per for-sale unit."[513]

Because the coalition, in Beach's terms, had "no contractual or other legal power to force the city or the developer to do anything," it agreed—instead of pressing for a full-blown CBA—to include community benefits in a "term sheet" to be incorporated into the CRA's development agreement with Related.[514] As Dennison remembered, the coalition leaders felt the term sheet was the best they could achieve "given that we had gone out of the mainstream . . . and that we had maximized the leverage that we had."[515] Because pressing forward would have cost the CRA's support, the coalition decided to give up "direct accountability" through a contract between the coalition and Related in exchange for a deal enforceable by the city. The coalition's decision to forgo a CBA was also influenced by the fact that the CRA's Estolano strongly believed that the CRA itself could enforce benefits through its development agreement. And since Dennison and other community leaders thought the coalition "already had a lot of legal standing with the CRA, we felt it was maybe better to hold them accountable than the developer directly—[although] there was a lot of debate."[516]

The deal also included substantial developer concessions around local hiring and job training. Using the CRA's Local Hiring Requirements for City Center Redevelopment Projects as a model, in the final benefits program, Related agreed to a 30% local hiring and 10% "at-risk" hiring (of workers with barriers to employment such as limited English proficiency, a criminal record, or lack of a high school degree) goal for the projected twenty-nine thousand construction jobs. The developer agreed to similar goals for the projected fifty-nine hundred permanent jobs in the project.[517] Further, the developer contributed $500,000 to establish a job training program, while the CRA agreed to earmark future project incentive rents "to fund specialized construction and permanent job training programs"—committing $500,000 for Phase One "plus up to $850,000 on a dollar-for-dollar matching basis for any other funding source."[518]

As part of the overall Grand Avenue deal, the unions won their priorities as well. The summary of community benefits attached to the development agreement indicated that the developer was working to execute a project labor agreement for all construction jobs, a neutrality agreement with HERE Local 11 for the hotel, and a collective bargaining agreement with the SEIU for maintenance and security workers. All construction jobs were to comply with the CRA's Prevailing Wage Policy, requiring developers to pay workers at a high construction wage set by the federal government, while all permanent jobs—including those provided by project tenants like restaurants, grocery stores, and retail outlets—were to pay living wage.[519]

With respect to implementation, the CRA agreed to "establish a workforce development, parks, and open space community advisory committee that will meet quarterly, receive quarterly reports on the GA project from the CRA, and design the uses of the job preparation program funds."[520] Related also agreed to provide an estimated $3 million to support public art, make good faith efforts to contract with minority- and women-owned businesses, comply with the CRA service contractor retention policy, and strive toward LEED certification.

With this community benefits program in place, on February 1, 2007, the CRA voted to approve the Grand Avenue Project, agreeing to contribute $24.4 million in payments for streetscape enhancement and affordable housing, in addition to funds already committed to renovate what came to be known as Grand Park.[521] To support park renovation, a number of foundations—including Broad's and the California Community Foundation, led by the Grand Ave Committee Vice President (and former MALDEF President) Antonia Hernández—also contributed donations. However, with a final city and county vote scheduled in mid-February, the project was not yet totally in the clear. Most significantly, the public cost projections continued to grow, with the city's legislative analyst stating that tax rebates could cost $66 million over twenty years.[522] With respect to the need for a public subsidy, influential *Los Angeles Times* columnist Steve Lopez wrote: "Call me a cynic, but I'm not buying it."[523] Nevertheless, proponents found aspects of the project to tout, such as its plan for mixed-income housing. Writing in the *Los Angeles Times*, a fellow from the New America Foundation argued that "what makes this project extraordinary is the range of income earners it promises to attract: those buying seven-figure penthouse condominiums living alongside people who will be asked to shell out only $454 to $649 a month for a one-bedroom apartment. . . ."[524] Weighing in favor of the deal was the *Los Angeles Times* editorial board, which noted the "formidable tower of political consensus" in support, including housing advocates in the Grand Avenue Coalition, and concluded that "the project makes a great deal of sense, and the county Board of Supervisors and City Council should give the Grand Avenue project a green light this week when they take up the matter."[525]

The green light flashed on February 12, 2007, when the City Council and the County Board of Supervisors gave final approval to all three phases of the development, as well as the tax rebates. Councilwoman Jan Perry praised the deal as good for the city.[526] But not everyone was pleased. Critics complained that the deal included a double subsidy: with the city and county leasing land to Related, a profit-making business, while also giving the developer future breaks on hotel and bed taxes. The tax breaks drew particular ire from competing downtown hotels that did not receive such benefits, especially the venerable Westin Bonaventure, whose lawyer threatened to sue. County Supervisor Mike Antonovich also criticized the 30% local hiring provision, calling it "Jim Crow of the 21st century" because other workers in the county did not have access to jobs covered by the agreement. He also joined those condemning the tax rebates: "If the project were a good investment, it would attract more private capital and no subsidy would be required."[527]

These criticisms, however, did nothing to stall final execution of the coalition's community benefits program or sully what it accomplished. After a half-year of intense mobilization, a term sheet containing the community benefits was signed on February 13, 2007.[528] The signatories included the CRA, Related, and coalition members LA CAN, SAJE, Concerned Citizens, and CD Tech.[529] Although the Grand Avenue Coalition had no private enforcement power, the benefits program was included as an attachment to the CRA's development agreement, along with an extensive description of the local hiring responsibilities of construction employers working on the project. In evaluating the deal, LA CAN's Becky Dennison measured its success in relative terms, stressing how much the coalition ultimately gained given the developer's initial response to the idea of providing community benefits, which was: "Absolutely not!"[530] Despite having some "hard feelings" about organized labor through the process, Dennison ultimately viewed the Grand Avenue negotiations as a "learning experience" in which the coalition achieved modest equity enhancements to the project under adverse conditions.[531] As Concerned Citizens' Noreen McClendon put it: "We're basically proud that we got the benefits that we did, but getting any benefits out of anybody in L.A. for very low-income people is still an uphill battle."[532]

Economic Collapse and Uncertain Future

With the major hurdles cleared for the Grand Avenue Project, the city moved forward with more mundane tasks while managing ongoing conflicts. In September 2007, the planning committee voted to approve tract maps for Grand Avenue as the Westin Bonaventure's lawyer tried to block the project, arguing that it created too many housing units, while also accusing Councilwoman Perry of a conflict since she lived less than two blocks from the proposed site.[533] The full City Council dismissed the Bonaventure's objection.[534]

As the collapse of the U.S. subprime market triggered a global financial crisis in late 2007, a much more serious problem emerged: The real estate capital on which the entire project hinged began to dry up. After a big early investment, the California Public Employees' Retirement System withdrew its money from Grand Avenue; in March 2008, a fund controlled by the royal family of Dubai stepped in with $100 million to keep the project afloat.[535] The Dubai money was designed to permit Related to secure construction loans needed to tear down the parking structure across from the Disney Concert Hall, making way for Phase One: a forty-eight–story tower with rooftop pools, condos, a Mandarin Hotel, and Equinox gym, alongside a nineteen-story building containing more condos and a hundred units of affordable housing. However, a week later, Related announced that the project would be delayed until 2012 because of its inability to secure construction loans,[536] prompting Supervisor Antonovich to call on the Grand Avenue Authority to put the project out for new bids.[537] Although not willing to go that far, the authority did deny Related's request for an indefinite extension, giving it until August 15, 2008 to commence construction.[538] In this midst of this uncertainty, a *Los Angeles Times* op-ed by Rich Alossi argued that the development rights for the project—with costs now projected at $3 billion—should be sold to different developers to "allow the free market to take over."[539] However, with no real alternatives in sight, the Grand Avenue Authority moved off its hard-line position in July, granting Related an extension but threatening penalties of $250,000 per month (for two years) if the project did not commence by February 2009—and total renegotiation if the project did not commence by February 2011.[540] Yet when February 2009 came, with no construction loans in sight, the Grand Avenue Authority was openly considering deferring the penalty, which County Supervisor Antonovich condemned as "very much a backroom deal."[541] In August 2010, Related's Bill Witte announced that the project could be delayed for two more years because "[t]here is no chance of financing a significant project in the near term."[542] With opponents continuing to question the need for tax breaks, Related scaled back its vision for an L.A. Champs-Élysées and scrapped plans for luxury condos and the Mandarin Hotel.[543]

Because Grand Park was publicly funded, with the initial $50 million coming from Related's down payment on the project lease, its development proceeded in the face of recession. A public meeting was held at the Dorothy Chandler Pavilion on April 22, 2008, to discuss the design for Grand Park. The following year, the County Board of Supervisors approved the funding and development agreement for the park and ground was broken in July 2010.[544] By June of 2012, the new twelve-acre Grand Park was nearly complete—but the rest of the project lied fallow.[545]

In addition to a sluggish economy, in 2011, the Grand Avenue Project confronted a new financial threat. That summer, the California legislature passed a bill eliminating community redevelopment agencies statewide. It was a complicated law motivated by the state's desire to pull out of its own financial crisis by allocating more local property taxes to school districts while stemming what many believed was city abuse of the redevelopment process. The upshot was that the Los Angeles CRA, dissolved in early 2012, was no longer available to drive forward the Grand Avenue Project—or to play the essential brokering role between developers, labor unions, and community organizations that had come to define its mission in the post-Staples era. While Madeline Janis called the dissolution bill "short-sighted,"[546] and urged that local government continue to "play a role in creating good jobs, affordable housing and a healthy environment in distressed communities across the state,"[547] the city took the legal steps necessary under state law to establish a successor agency to wind down operations and sell off CRA assets. Although a successor agency could honor "enforceable obligations" to complete projects already in progress—and thus the Los Angeles CRA could complete the park and infrastructure development undertaken with its $50 million investment—the CRA did not owe any enforceable obligations to the coalition and, given scarce funds, there were reports that more than $5 million would be cut from planned CRA affordable housing support at Grand Avenue.[548] However, the coalition was able to use Related's promise in the community benefits term sheet to implement the revolving loan fund (managed by the city housing agency) and to hold Related to its commitment to build extremely low-income housing.

It would be seven more years until a less grand version of the Grand Avenue Project would finally break ground: with Phase One scaled back to include a twenty-story, 309-room Equinox hotel alongside a three-story tower with restaurants, shops, and four hundred total residential units, eighty of which designated as affordable housing.[549] As the Grand Avenue Project crept forward, community groups advocated for benefits in relation to other downtown projects—revealing the degree to which CBAs had become an institutionalized part of the development process in Los Angeles, yet how difficult it was to assemble and sustain community–labor partnerships in the face of divergent interests.

As public subsidies evaporated and the CRA was no longer there to exert pressure on developers, coalitions had to find other leverage. In 2011, United Neighbors in Defense Against Displacement (UNIDAD, a successor to FCCEJ that included SAJE, Esperanza, and CD Tech) did just that, striking a CBA deal with developer Geoffrey Palmer in connection with a $250-millon apartment and retail complex, called the Lorenzo, on property that had been owned by Orthopedic Hospital

Figure 4.9 Rendering of Grand Avenue Project. *Source*: Related Companies (October 2018).

next to a planned Expo Line light rail station between the L.A. Convention Center and USC. The agreement was notable because the coalition was able to leverage the property's special zoning designation restricting its use to medical purposes. This allowed the coalition to credibly threaten to block rezoning, which would have reduced community access to health services, and thus pressure Palmer to accept a CBA requiring him to lease seventy-five hundred square feet to a medical clinic rent-free for twenty years, while also committing to local hiring, a living wage goal, and a 5% set aside for affordable housing.[550]

Although the UNIDAD coalition did not include labor, it did have the support of environmentalists as lawyers from NRDC and Chatten-Brown & Carstens (along with Public Counsel, LAFLA, and the Community Benefits Law Center) represented the coalition in the 2011 CBA campaign. This was not the case a year later when Staples owner AEG advanced plans to build a $1.1 billion NFL stadium in downtown by the convention center—to be called Farmers Field. Seeking to preempt an environmental challenge that could stall the project and give leverage to community opponents, AEG had lobbied for passage of a 2011 state law, A.B. 292, which specifically exempted the proposed stadium from normal CEQA review: instead requiring any challenges to the Final EIR to be filed within 30 days in the California Court of Appeal, which was required to issue a final ruling within 175 days. With this bill in place, AEG pressed for stadium approval in the spring of 2012, when the city issued the project's Draft EIR. The coalition that rose to challenge AEG was a faint reflection of the robust community–labor alliance that had sustained the CBA movement over the previous decade. With the building and trades unions staunchly on board for the job benefits, NRDC also broke ranks with the Play Fair at Farmers Field Coalition—led by LA CAN, Physicians for Social Responsibility-LA, and Comunidad Presente (and represented by LAFLA)—instead deciding to support the stadium as an environmentally sensitive infill project. A number of community-based organizations were also unwilling to join the stadium fight because they were already receiving benefits from AEG under the Staples CBA.

That left AEG to deal solely with coalition groups, which filed comments objecting to the April Draft EIR and retained civil rights lawyer Dan Stormer (from the Thai worker sweatshop litigation) to challenge the constitutionality of A.B. 292 in August 2012.[551] When the city approved the stadium's Final EIR the following month, the coalition entered negotiations with AEG to resolve the lawsuit, which resulted in a November settlement agreement that included a $15 million housing trust fund, $1.9 million for air quality and bus rider improvements, and $300,000 for a housing organizer and advocates to provide health education to tenants.[552] In addition, AEG agreed that all on-site jobs would pay the living wage and that 40% of employees would be local hires; AEG also agreed to permit access to street vendors. Against the backdrop of AEG's power and the coalition's limited support, it was a significant victory, but one that depended on AEG convincing the NFL to approve moving a professional football team back to Los Angeles—which it ultimately could not do. With that, after dominating development in Los Angeles for a decade, the CBA movement in Los Angeles saw its last major organizing drive end in a hollow victory.

Analysis

The CBA movement in Los Angeles redefined redevelopment in some of the city's poorest neighborhoods: asserting standing for disenfranchised community groups to participate in and set the terms of development deals—facilitated by public agencies—to transform the local economy. In each case, mobilization depended on a set of underlying conditions that created opportunities but also presented challenges. The conditions grew out of a shift in the basic paradigm of postwar urban development met by a new infrastructure of social movements whose interests converged around interrelated job quality, housing, and environmental goals.

Redevelopment was launched at mid-century in cities like Los Angeles to address "white flight" and capital disinvestment by giving local government a leading role in subsidizing business and housing projects designed to entice the private sector back to the "blighted" central core.[553] First-wave community development organizations entered partnerships with local governments to become developers of last resort: building housing and business projects toward the ever-elusive goal of urban revitalization.

However, by the turn of the millennium, the context had changed profoundly. As cities made "comebacks"[554]—fueled by aggressive urban planning, dissatisfaction with suburban sprawl, and changing demographics—private developers saw opportunity in places they had long shunned. Private investors began to flood disinvested neighborhoods with capital, seeing the potential for massive upside returns. As a result, government agencies accustomed to spending public dollars to lure reluctant businesses to the central city, were now in the role of giving away those funds to aid private developers already eager to come. This development, rather than improving life for existing community members, became the vanguard of gentrification and displacement, while putting local government in the role of subsidizing projects that often resulted in low-wage service sector jobs. It was in this new context that community groups began mobilizing *against* development: if not to stop it, at least to reshape its features and to extract community benefits through negotiated agreements with developers. The CBA movement emerged at this crucial moment. As the Los Angeles experience demonstrates, its success required defining points of leverage in processes of local government approval and building power to influence those processes through coalitions capable of affecting outcomes. For these reasons, CBAs depended on interest convergence among disparate community-based and social movement groups that could bring different assets to campaigns, including the power to disrupt and the clout to negotiate. Community organizations, fighting gentrification under the banner of "better neighborhoods, same neighbors" sought housing stability and local job creation; the labor movement sought a mechanism for building union density through publicly subsidized development; and environmentalists sought to mitigate overall pollution and fight environmental inequality in low-income communities of color.

The CBA movement was thus created with built-in tensions: challenging capitalist development practices, yet dependent upon them for benefits; reliant on public law for leverage, yet codifying benefits in private contract; and requiring solidarity to link together disparate movements, yet constantly managing inter-movement dissent over tactics and goals. Distilling lessons from the seminal CBA campaigns—Staples, LAX, and Grand Avenue—this part examines how the CBA movement shaped conceptions of lawyers' professional role, evaluates the CBA as a tool of urban reform, and considers how institutionalization of the CBA in redevelopment impacted local politics and community–labor relations.

Lawyering for Coalitions

The Los Angeles CBA campaigns were built on the foundation of multi-organizational coalitions, which reflected the diverse interests involved and goals to be achieved. The Staples campaign firmly established a community–labor alliance in pursuit of living wage jobs and affordable housing; LAX cemented a partnership among community, labor, and environmental groups to redress airport environmental impacts in adjacent low-income communities while simultaneously promoting unionized jobs and directing those jobs to community residents; and Grand Avenue assembled an affordable housing coalition to fight gentrification that loosely coordinated with labor groups through an inside-outside strategy to influence the CRA and hold the developer to community demands. In each case, coalitions confronted government and market elites to negotiate benefits and ultimately change the rules of the game for local development practice. CBA coalitions thus undertook local campaigns to mobilize low-income communities, alongside labor and environmental partners, to achieve organizing "wins"—which included variable combinations of enhanced quality jobs, affordable housing, and environmental improvements.

For lawyers representing CBA coalitions (or member groups within them), the critical challenge was navigating complex organizational relationships in order to define common goals and then deploying different lawyering skills to advance those goals—from researching the approval process for public subsidies, to commenting on EIRs, to drafting binding contracts. In each of the CBA campaigns, lawyers were essential to defining leverage and negotiating defensible deals, and often contributed to broader discussions of strategy. Yet their roles were very much shaped by their own professional self-conceptions and the work assigned to them by their clients. CBA lawyers generally entered client relationships with respect for community power and were asked to use specific skill sets to advance coalition-defined ends, engaging in adversarial rights-claiming when necessary, but also backing off from rights to build alliances, broker deals, and craft policy.

In the Staples campaign, the main lawyers were Julian Gross, a public interest lawyer who had just launched a solo law practice in San Francisco focused on supporting community groups in redevelopment, and Jerilyn López Mendoza, an environmental justice lawyer from Environmental Defense. LAANE's Madeline Janis-Aparicio, also a lawyer, brought legal expertise to bear in campaign development and CBA negotiation, but did not act in a traditional representational role. While Gross was retained by LAANE to help negotiate and draft a CBA, López Mendoza came in to help gain leverage through the environmental review process. Each brought to their tasks a complex view of social change, with legal and political advocacy seen as complementary strategies—the utility of each dependent on the particular context of struggle. Instead of top-down legal strategists, they viewed themselves as team members who attempted to cede as much control as possible to the organizers, providing technical expertise only to the limited extent necessary to advance the organizing goal. They were, in short, quite mindful of community concerns about lawyer overreach and careful to respect the governance structures established by coalition members—although they also understood the value of the legal expertise they brought to the campaign.

Gross, a white male lawyer working with a CBA coalition led by women and people of color, articulated his role in narrow terms, stating his goal was "to provide the straight technical side within the standard lawyer–client relationship. My metric is: Am I helping my clients win as much as they can? . . . My other goal is: Am I adding value by transferring whatever experience and opinions I have to clients in a way that is useful and doesn't advance my agenda?"[555] Within this framework, Gross saw himself as providing a skill that was "absolutely needed":[556]

> My job was helping get [CBA] documents written up in a way that is both legally enforceable and covers everything that needs to be covered while giving the client the legal ability to force the developer to do the things [the client] wants. Also, the lawyer's job is to make the documents comprehensible by nonlawyers. . . . It is a common misperception that there is a tension between legal functionality and being comprehensible. The best contract is clear and also comprehensible to the general public.[557]

Although guided by these principles, Gross sometimes found it difficult to reconcile client deference and contract enforceability in practice. For example, in the LAX campaign, despite Gross's commitment to avoid advancing his own agenda, he became subject to criticism for changing terms that he believed enhanced enforcement but both sides objected to for altering substance.

In contrast, López Mendoza—a Chicana from a low-income neighborhood in East Los Angeles—articulated her role in terms of enhancing community power and participation in the planning process. In this sense, she viewed herself a "translator": "taking government laws, environmental laws, redevelopment laws and translating them for community members, translating them into other languages so that the community can understand and taking residents' comments and ideas in terms of job development and housing and translating that back in terms of processes that have been set up. My biggest role sometimes is to get out of the way."[558]

Feeling the need to get out of the way was also a function of client power. Although the strength of coalition leadership may have raised concerns about direct accountability to community members, it insulated the leadership itself from domination by outside lawyers. As Gross recalled in working with FCCEJ on the Staples CBA, although he was careful not to cross professional lines "by throwing policy ideas in a draft without clearing it," he was not worried about "unduly influencing people like SAJE's [Gilda] Hass and [LAANE's] Madeline [Janis-Aparicio]."[559] As this suggests, because CBA coalitions like FCCEJ were empowered political actors, CBA lawyering focused on achieving specific results defined by the coalitions themselves rather than promoting goals envisioned by the lawyers. The CBA movement thus relied on the potency of legal advocacy to create conditions of possibility for successful community mobilization. This was evident in the Staples campaign, where FCCEJ's success in bringing the developer to the negotiating table was predicated on the threat that it could, in fact, successfully litigate an environmental suit over the project's energy impact.

Although the multigroup coalition structure offered advantages from the perspective of client empowerment, it also complicated the lawyer–client relationship.[560] This was apparent in the Staples campaign, where there was a loosely coordinated team of lawyers with different tasks—Gross focused on CBA drafting, Janis-Aparicio on negotiation, and López Mendoza on the environmental response—and a fluid specification of roles with no systematic effort to delineate the client. The lawyers themselves brought vastly different expertise to the project: Gross was trained as an employment attorney; Janis-Aparicio had experience in labor, immigration, and housing; and López Mendoza was an environmental lawyer. And there were times in which the lawyers were both outside and inside the coalition—providing legal advice to the group in their role as attorneys while hashing out policy issues and building group consensus in their role as coalition members. This created the potential for misunderstanding about whom the lawyers represented and when they were acting in their representational capacities.

In Staples, Gross made it clear that he represented LAANE and was careful not to independently talk to other groups in ways that could have created the perception of representation. López Mendoza sought to position herself more as a coalition team member, not a coalition lawyer, who represented Environmental Defense's organizational interests in advocating for an environmentally sustainable Sports and Entertainment District. Other lawyers also came in to play discrete roles. For example, LAFLA's Ben Beach helped resolve the threat to the CBA's affordable housing requirements—when AEG began selling off parcels to developers not technically parties to the contract—by ensuring those developers would pay into a housing land trust.

While the complex nature of coalition representation created the potential for conflicts of interest among member groups, the coalition attempted to deal with them internally: with leaders sorting out disagreements and then conveying instructions to Gross (and later Beach) regarding how to proceed. Nonetheless, the challenge of acting in the coalition's "interests" when those interests were contested was a serious challenge for lawyers learning-by-doing in the groundbreaking Staples CBA. Similar conflicts over competing interests persisted through subsequent CBA campaigns, particularly around the trade-off between jobs and housing benefits. These conflicts were sometimes addressed by assigning separate counsel to negotiate different benefits. For instance, in NoHo Commons, Gross represented the Valley Jobs Coalition in pursuit of a CBA while UFCW counsel simultaneously negotiated with the developer for labor peace in relation to the proposed grocery store.

The CBA movement benefited from, but also shaped the careers of, the lawyers involved—whose work came to be defined by CBA advocacy. Gross emerged as a national expert, co-authoring a foundational legal handbook with Janis-Aparicio and Greg LeRoy of Good Jobs First,[561] and going on to establish the Community Benefits Law Center in 2006, supported by the union-backed Partnership for Working Families, to assist CBA campaigns nationwide (the Center hired Beach in

2008 and he became its director when Gross left in 2010). López Mendoza took her experience from the Staples CBA to play a leading role in the LAX campaign, where she was instrumental building out the environmental justice wing of the coalition, defining the coalition's environmental goals, negotiating the crucial environmental provisions of the CBA, and then participating in the lengthy implementation process. Her leadership role was shaped by the particular environmental focus of the LAX CBA, which sought to address the massive environmental impacts of airport expansion. The scope of environmental concerns at LAX meant that environmental review was more complex and contentious, which gave the coalition more leverage but also required more environmental expertise. Conflicts over how to deal with environmental impacts on neighboring communities also meant that the coalition ultimately did not encompass all constituencies as the cities of El Segundo and Culver City, along with the county, several homeowner groups, and ARSAC, retained their own lawyers and filed their own CEQA lawsuits.

In the Grand Avenue campaign, environmental issues were not salient and thus environmental review as not a key focus of legal advocacy. LAFLA's Beach, having just completed a fellowship promoting equitable development, joined the Share the Wealth Coalition to help implement the no net loss policy established by Beach's LAFLA colleagues in the *Wiggins* lawsuit against the CRA. From there, he was asked to represent the Grand Avenue Coalition, helping them "understand and navigate" the approval process through the unique joint powers authority and identifying any ways to challenge the "bizarre" incentive financing put forward by the CRA.[562] In a political context without labor or environmental coalition partners, where "a few groups sort of grabbed the reins and seized the opportunity in a very short window," Beach helped the lead organizers prepare for and debrief from negotiations in which he did not play a direct role. He also helped to ensure that the negotiated term sheet of community benefits was included in the development agreement to enable city enforcement in a deal in which the coalition members had "no contractual or other legal power to force the city or the developer to do anything—they were reliant on the city completely to enforce the terms that they helped negotiate."[563]

By the time that the UNIDAD coalition won a CBA in the Lorenzo campaign (2011) and the Play Fair at Farmers Field Coalition negotiated a settlement that included community benefits in its legal challenge to the stadium project (2012), legal support for CBA coalitions was being handled primarily by legal services organizations, LAFLA and Public Counsel, suggesting the degree to which CBA advocacy had moved from being a niche field to the mainstream of community development practice. In both of these final campaigns, LAFLA and Public Counsel played lead representational roles: in the UNIDAD campaign supported by environmental lawyers from NRDC and Jan Chatten-Brown's firm (given the complex zoning issues involved) and the Community Benefits Law Center (where Beach had become director); and in Farmers Field supported by civil rights boutique

Hadsell & Stormer in litigating and settling the constitutional challenge to the state law truncating environmental review for the stadium.

Overall, the nature of lawyering for CBA coalitions was driven by the stakeholders involved (housing, labor, environmental) and the structure of the coalition's leverage. While some lawyers, like Gross and Beach, became CBA generalists able to identify leverage in complex regulatory schemes and navigate approval processes, more specialized substantive expertise was typically required to maximize leverage and negotiate contractual terms in distinct legal contexts. This meant that, for any given CBA campaign, there were multiple lawyers with complementary skill sets representing disparate coalition interests toward the goal of achieving a unified final agreement.

Leveraging Public Law in the Service of Private Contract

One of the key roles that lawyers played in the CBA movement was developing a new legal tool: the CBA itself. On its face, the CBA was a standard contract with a clear quid pro quo. It required the coalition to give up its legal right to protest a development project (a cooperation agreement) in exchange for the developer's promise to provide specified benefits. As the Los Angeles campaigns showed, the innovative aspect of the CBA was that it placed the coalition in a direct contractual relationship with the developer, thus permitting the coalition to directly enforce the developer's obligation to provide benefits. This distinguished the CBA from other community benefits arrangements, in which benefits were incorporated into the city's development agreement (as in the 1998 Hollywood and Highland community benefits program or the 2007 Grand Avenue term sheet) and thus were only enforceable by the city itself. Yet, precisely because it was a contract covering a single project, the strength of the CBA tool depended on how well a coalition could convert bargaining power into enforceable provisions—drawing attention to how coalitions translated legal and political leverage into contractual terms and how those terms were ultimately enforced.

As Figure 4.10 shows, the basic strategy of CBA coalitions was to leverage public law approval processes to build power that could be used to create the conditions for effective private law bargaining. The background rules that proved most critical in the Los Angeles CBA campaigns were rights to participate in political decision-making, particularly those embedded in the land use and environmental review process, as well as the process for conferring public subsidies. These rights were a function of the relationship between the city and the developer, with the city providing permits and subsidies that required public approval in exchange for future tax revenues and other economic benefits provided by the project. The participation rights created an opportunity for legal intervention by CBA coalitions. Because the exercise of participation rights was backed by the

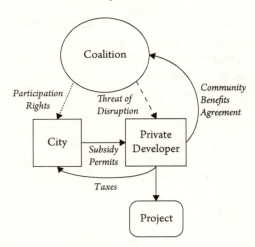

Figure 4.10 Structure of community benefits agreement. *Source:* Scott Cummings (2006).

threat of disruption, participation in project approval processes took on a confrontational tone, with a CBA coalition positioned to derail, or at least stall, a deal supported by the city and developer. In this sense, CBA coalitions used "legal leveraging"—the use of law "as a weapon to 'push' otherwise uncooperative foes into making concessions."[564]

Leverage varied by legal and political context, although it was always structured around approval of land use permits (which often included requests for changes in zoning) and financing—the two central powers local government wielded over large-scale development projects. Land use approvals ran through the Planning Commission and subsidies in redevelopment zones were given by the CRA; both ultimately required City Council approval and thus provided an opportunity for coalitions to exert political power to pressure political officials to support community benefits. It is in this regard that labor partners played key roles in the CBA campaigns around Staples and LAX, forcing officials to take seriously coalition demands or risk losing crucial support from labor unions. In the Staples and LAX campaigns, it was labor's threat to withhold their support for the projects without a CBA deal that pressured city officials—and in the Staples case, the developer—to negotiate. Without labor's participation in the Grand Avenue campaign, the coalition had to look for other pressure points: the coalition's power of protest and its members' relations with City Councilwoman Jan Perry, who had significant influence over the project. In addition, the Grand Avenue Coalition benefited from the participation of the CRA, whose leaders advocated for equity in redevelopment deals by tying CRA financial support to community benefits, such as living wage jobs, local hiring, and job training.

As this suggests, a coalition's ability to deploy leveraging tactics was partly a function of the nature of the coalition and its targets. Coalitions of community, labor, and environmental advocates could maximize leverage through multiple mechanisms: political contacts, threatened lawsuits, and public shaming. Coalitions without the same breadth had less leverage, as the Grand Avenue CBA demonstrated. On the other side, the ultimate impact of leverage depended on the intended target. Private developers attuned to their bottom line tended to be more resistant to CBA negotiations, while public entities, like LAX, were more susceptible to political pressure and more concerned about political accountability.

Because redevelopment projects invariably had environmental consequences, they were also subject to environmental review under state (and sometimes federal) law—which also implicated local agencies, like the CRA, required to lead environmental review for projects they sponsored. Indeed, the CEQA process for environmental review was part of each CBA mobilization to varying degrees. In all cases, coalitions exercised their right to comment on the developers' EIR, holding out the potential threat of a lawsuit to prevent an inadequate EIR from being approved. In the Sports and Entertainment District EIR, FCCEJ objected to the lack of analysis of the project's impact on the electricity grid, threatening substantial costs and the risk of lost political support, which ultimately forced the developer to negotiate.

In the LAX campaign, the lengthy environmental review process was the centerpiece of political and legal contention, providing a springboard for coalition bargaining. From the coalition's standpoint, while environmental review was a potent tool to prod negotiation, it was not a way to ultimately resolve community claims since it could only force the city to redo a faulty review—there was no mechanism for stopping a project or requiring specific mitigation measures. Therefore, as López Mendoza recalled, the LAX Coalition "took the position that we could accomplish more through contract law and private agreement then we could under CEQA. Under CEQA, all LAWA has to do is show that the mitigation measures are not feasible and we would lose out, but by using contract law we are able to get some accountability."[565] In a sign of its potency as a bargaining chip, other actors mobilized around environmental review (toward distinctive ends) throughout the campaigns: ARSAC, homeowners, and local governments filed separate suits under CEQA to challenge the LAX modernization plan; labor lawyers representing El Segundo and Inglewood sued LAWA over the lack of environmental review of the United cargo facility in relation to the drive to unionize the Argenbright Security firm; and the state's attempt to circumvent CEQA in the Farmers Field stadium case provoked a constitutional challenge that ultimately resulted in a community benefits settlement.

Ultimately, leverage mattered to the extent it permitted the negotiation of effective contract terms, which varied by CBA and by provision. Weak coalition leverage translated into weaker substantive terms and mechanisms of coalition enforcement. For example, at Grand Avenue, where the coalition lacked power to block or significantly delay the deal, there was no CBA at all, only a term sheet included in the development agreement. Stronger leverage, provided by the EIR challenge and union support in the Staples campaign, yielded robust terms and direct coalition enforcement rights. Independent of the degree of leverage, across the campaigns, there were contractual terms on which it was relatively easy to gain consensus because they cost the developer little. In the Staples CBA, for instance, the developer's agreement to "support" the coalition's request for a preferential parking district was a low-stakes concession because the developer could comply with minimal out-of-pocket expenses, while generating community goodwill. Revolving loan funds, as in Staples and Grand Avenue, were also relatively easier for developers since they were entitled to recoup loan funds and only lost interest rate points.

Other CBA provisions demanded more from developers and resulted in greater pushback. With respect to affordable housing, the critical sticking points were consistently around the depth of affordability levels and the location of housing (on the development site or elsewhere). In the Staples CBA, units were targeted at the lowest end of affordability, to those earning 50% of AMI, and could be built off site. The Grand Avenue Coalition succeeded in requiring the developer to set aside 35% of Phase One residential units on-site (without separate entrances, which the developer had proposed) for extremely low-income tenants (35% of AMI), although these units were subsidized by the CRA—and the overall number of affordable units was only marginally above what the developer was already required to provide by law.

From the outset, organized labor sought to use CBAs to extend the Living Wage Ordinance to project tenants. This demand generated stiff resistance by developers, who argued that they were in no legal position to force tenants to increase wages and that, even if they could, increased labor costs would mean less left over for rents—which would affect the developers' bottom line. As a result, the living wage provisions of CBAs were often aspirational. The Staples CBA living wage provisions required that the developer use best efforts, imposed flexible benchmarks, and created mechanisms for dispute resolution. Ultimately, failure to comply with the 70% living wage goal did not breach the agreement. Instead, the CBA provided that even if the living wage goal was not met, compliance was presumed so long as the developer made annual living wage reports (detailing the problems of meeting the living wage goal), notified the coalition before selecting project tenants, met with the coalition and prospective tenants to discuss living wage requirements, and "within commercially reasonable limits" took into account "as a substantial factor" the impact of tenant selection on the living wage goal. The strongest living wage language was in the Grand Avenue development agreement, which obligated project tenants to pay living wage—a provision the CRA could demand in exchange for the substantial subsidy it was providing.

There was wiggle room language in other CBA provisions. For example, in the LAX CBA, the coalition agreed that passenger gate, cargo area, and hangar electrification would occur unless "operationally infeasible." The Staples CBA's first-source hiring policy provided that businesses that did not meet the goal of hiring 50% of their workers from a pool of local applicants nevertheless were in compliance with the policy so long as they kept records, provided timely notice of job openings, and held positions for targeted applicants open for designated periods. With respect to parks and open space, AEG was able to negotiate an agreement to "fund or cause to be privately funded" $1 million for park space, which meant that it could use its philanthropic connections—which it did—to raise money for park construction without having to be out of pocket for the costs. Another example of flexibility could be seen in the Staples CBA's affordable housing provision, which required the developer to "develop or cause to be developed" 20% of the total project units as affordable housing. Here again, the developer could use its access to philanthropic sources to reduce its out-of-pocket development costs. In addition, to the extent that nonprofit housing organizations built affordable units in the area with the assistance of interest-free loans provided by the developer, the developer's obligation to build units directly was reduced, although not below 15% of the total units in the project. Thus, in some cases, the strong bargaining power of the developer allowed it to negotiate a relatively soft set of obligations in exchange for a complete waiver of opposition rights by the coalition.

In the FCCEJ context, the demand for waiver caused AGENDA and the Community Coalition to split off, refusing to relinquish their power to disrupt in exchange for the benefits provided in the settlement agreement. Rights-stripping CBAs may be the necessary byproduct of a mobilization strategy premised on the threat of disruption, but the constraining effect runs counter to the ideological goals of many of the grassroots organizations involved. However, coalition member opt-out can undercut the rationale for developer commitment, which is to minimize risk of disruption by placing as many groups under a cooperation agreement as possible. The worst-case scenario for a developer is to give benefits to some groups while letting their allies continue to attack the project. In the Staples context, this was dealt with by designating AGENDA and the Community Coalition as Interested Organizations, effectively bound by the cooperation agreement insofar as any protests by them would relieve the developer of all benefits obligations.

As this suggests, precisely because the CBAs were contracts, they created contractual problems. One key challenge—as the discussion of "operational infeasibility" and living wage goals already highlighted—was defining terms with sufficient specificity so that they could be adequately enforced. Overall, it was relatively easier to enforce provisions with clear mandates and discrete benchmarks: like building Hope and Peace Park in the Figueroa Corridor, soundproofing homes around LAX, or creating a job training program in Grand Avenue. In contrast, provisions with open-ended terms, aspirational language, or unclear benchmarks—like living wage goals or provisions in the LAX agreement requiring independent monitoring of polluting vehicles without prescribing steps to eliminate them—created ongoing enforcement challenges since failure to comply did not breach the agreements.

Another significant challenge was embedding benefits within the developers' chain of contract and ensuring successor liability for CBAs—a problem highlighted when AEG sold off parcels in the Sports and Entertainment District. Although coalitions sought to meet these challenges with implementation strategies and provisions for ongoing community monitoring (as in the LAX CBA), these were limited by the nature of the compliance information developers were required to provide and the brute fact that, over time, community groups with inadequate resources often had to devote attention to other issues. Finally, some CBA provisions were simply easier to enforce than others. For example, affordable housing provisions requiring developers to either build a specified number of units or pay into an affordable housing fund were straightforward to implement because the developers' obligations were clearly defined. In contrast, local hiring and living wage provisions were more difficult to enforce, since they continued throughout the project, posing challenges of ongoing monitoring.

Despite these difficulties, the major benefit of the CBA approach was that it produced a public–private oversight and enforcement scheme. It allowed both the community—through the CBA—and the city—through a development agreement that incorporated the CBA's terms—to watch over developer compliance and intervene to promote accountability. And even though many of the provisions did not provide hard enforcement mechanisms, the goals and standards incorporated in the CBA served as political resources that could be used to pressure developer compliance by generating negative publicity when they were not met.[566] In this sense, the CBA was an important though limited tool of urban reform in Los Angeles, permitting coalitions to press for better jobs and housing, but ultimately constrained by being reactive and one-off—able to gain more than communities were entitled to under the baseline redevelopment regime but not fundamentally disrupting it.

The Institutionalization of CBAs and the Politics of Local Dissent

The CBA movement in Los Angeles emerged as an outsider challenge to business-as-usual in redevelopment—demanding community voice and greater equity. Over time, CBAs became an institutionalized feature of redevelopment in the city, which meant that developers understood that the new business-as-usual meant allocating benefits in order to get deals done. This institutionalization was a testament to the community–labor coalition's achievement in challenging redevelopment practice: creating a new paradigm that demanded developers meet public obligations in exchange for the privilege of public support. However, institutionalization was never complete and the evolution of CBAs as a powerful but imperfect device created a set of political trade-offs. Although some features of CBAs were codified in CRA policy, that policy tended to reflect labor goals, and the city never went so far as to adopt a systematic community benefits law, leaving benefits to be negotiated on a case-by-case basis—and leaving CBA advocates vulnerable to backsliding when the CRA dissolved.

At the project level, the Los Angeles CBAs operated like development regulations in that they forced developers to undertake action they would not otherwise have taken without the threat of community disruption. This is particularly true of the CBAs against private developers: Staples's AEG and Grand Avenue's Related. The outcomes in these cases were redistributive because they extracted greater resources for the community through bargaining than would otherwise have been required under law. The CBA represented a net gain for the developers to the extent that they calculated the costs of providing community benefits as less than the costs of delay, litigation, and the negative publicity associated with a contested approval process. But, in the absence of community challenge, the baseline position was that the developers could undertake the projects without conferring benefits at all. Coordinated community participation therefore constrained the developers' range of action, leveraging the background development rules in such a way that induced agreement.

Some scholars have questioned CBA outcomes on legal and equity grounds.[567] One legal issue that has been raised is whether a city's involvement in brokering a deal that directs benefits to a community coalition in exchange for developer land use approval is an unconstitutional exaction under Supreme Court rules requiring a close and proportional relationship between development conditions and project impact.[568] The Los Angeles CBAs avoided this legal problem because they operated through private contract rather than requiring the city to condition discretionary permit approval on the provision of community benefits. Community groups only exercised their rights to mobilize through preexisting approval processes to raise land use and equity concerns. They did not change the approval rules in any way that explicitly tied public approval to developer obligations. To the extent that community benefits were incorporated in city development agreements, those agreements codified a privately bargained-for deal rather than reflecting publicly imposed conditions. Unless government actors take charge of land use approval processes and become parties to the CBA,[569] constitutional restrictions on exactions are not applicable. Moreover, the practical reality was that developers wanted to see the deals go through and thus had no incentive to retroactively challenge projects based on promises made in CBAs.

From an equity perspective, scholars have raised concerns about sweetheart deals between developers and community groups, in which developers hand-pick pliable community organizations that purport to represent the broader community's interests and essentially pay them off in order to gain the veneer of community support to facilitate project approval. More insidiously, some have suggested that community groups might use their power to hold up projects to extort illegitimate benefits from developers, expropriating what should be public resources for private gain.[570] However, although some New York City CBAs, particularly around the Atlantic Yards basketball arena in Brooklyn, have come under scrutiny for lack of authentic community support, there is no evidence that any of the L.A. agreements were driven by organizational self-interest or were orchestrated by developers.

A final question is how to evaluate what the L.A. CBAs achieved. Against the historical backdrop of community exclusion from prior redevelopment decisions, winning any benefits appears to be an improvement over the status quo. How much of an improvement is difficult to assess. As one perspective on this issue, it is possible to add up the costs of the developer's obligations under the Staples CBA in order to assess the monetary value of the benefits won (Table 4.1).

As this tally shows, from an economic perspective, the developer of L.A. Live (and its successors) made substantial financial commitments to the community. Judging whether those commitments were "enough" requires having a baseline against which to measure. When measured in absolute terms, against the alternative of no agreement, the Staples CBA constitutes a clear success. It provided the most direct support to affordable housing because of the minimal financial outlay for local hiring and training, and the fact that the living wage requirements did not impose direct costs on the developer (although they could have if tenants sought to trade higher wages for reduced rents). However, to the extent that the CRA reimbursed affordable housing expenditures (as it was required to do in the Grand Avenue Project), the developer's direct costs would be reduced. Moreover, in the context of a $1 billion Staples project with a $177 million subsidy, the CBA obligations were less than 1% of overall project cost and less than 5% of the public subsidy.

One can also consider the impact of CBAs on redevelopment over time. After the Staples agreement set CBA precedent, developers could be expected to use the prospect of having to pay out under a CBA to ask for more public subsidy—transferring the cost to taxpayers for providing targeted benefits. This raises questions of fairness and democratic legitimacy insofar as public funds may be allocated based on how much coalitions bargain for through private negotiations rather than based on a publicly accountable decision-making process to determine how best to invest resources toward the goal of promoting affordable housing and living wage jobs citywide. There are additional concerns about neighborhood effects. Once built, redevelopment projects, even with CBAs, often ignite further gentrification. This has certainly been the case in downtown Los Angeles and commentators also have suggested it has happened around the NoHo Commons project, which attracted an influx of developers to North Hollywood.[571] For these reasons, some CBA advocates later questioned the impact of their work. For example, as LA CAN's Becky Dennison reflected, with CBAs "you get jobs, you get housing . . . but the

Table 4.1 Key provisions of the Staples community benefits agreement and cost.

Developer Obligation	Conditions	Cost to Developer
Assessment of need for parks and recreational facilities	None	$50,000–$75,000
"Fund or cause to be privately funded" one or more park and recreational facility	Developer could enlist other funding sources, i.e., philanthropic foundations	$1,000,000
"Support" residential parking permit district, providing seed funding for five years	None	$125,000
"Shall make all reasonable efforts to maximize the number of living wage jobs"	Construction jobs already under union contract and tenants not required to pay	$0
Shall provide seed funding to establish local hiring and training system with first priority to displaced residents	No employer duty to hire specific workers	$100,000
20% affordable housing set aside (100–160 units) in project or off-site (in lieu fee of $40,000 per unit) plus $650,000 revolving loan fund	20% inclusionary requirement already set by CRA, though affordability levels targeted to lower-income residents	$7,000,000 (estimate based on in lieu fee)
Total		$8,300,000 (maximum)

effects of gentrification is just devastating ... [raising] questions about the tool and the approach."[572]

The longer-term objectives of CBA advocacy sought to address some of the short-term trade-offs. In the aftermath of Staples, there were serious efforts to build upon the success of individual CBAs to deepen organizational connections, expand community resources, and develop higher-level coordination (through groups like the California Partnership for Working Families) in order to exert sustained political influence over development decisions. FCCEJ and other equitable development coalitions around the state of California focused on the goal of passing community benefits laws, as well as other reforms, such as no net loss policies guaranteeing that redevelopment did not result in the loss of affordable housing. These efforts resulted in some success, as illustrated by CRA policy changes adopting living wage and local hiring requirements. Although developer resistance thwarted a citywide community benefits policy, overall, one of the positive outcomes of CBA advocacy was translating discrete contractual victories into significant legal reform, demonstrating how struggles at the grassroots level can form the template for policy change.

Nonetheless, due to the local nature of redevelopment, CBA advocacy remained largely decentralized: a fluid network that shared information and strategies, rather than a scaled-up national effort (although the Partnership for Working families played an important national coordinating role). In this sense, despite some policy advances, the very fact that CBAs remained necessary in contesting redevelopment practices could be seen as a disappointing outcome. Developers preferred ad hoc fights over systemic rules, believing they could ultimately out-resource and outlast even the scrappiest of community coalitions. From a regulatory perspective, the CBA could therefore be understood as a second-best solution, reflecting the relative political weakness of accountable development actors to create systemic redevelopment change through conventional political channels. Even at their most effective, CBA coalitions depended on a political constellation in which community and labor partners could exert pressure through political agencies to extract benefits from developers. Within that constellation, the Los Angeles CRA emerged as a guiding star, legally empowered to promote equitable redevelopment and run by leaders politically aligned with the CBA movement's goals. The demise of the CRA therefore weakened the opportunity structure that had supported community benefits advocacy, causing CBAs to decline as a result—and underscoring how reliant CBA mobilization was on insider political support.

The institutionalization of community benefits advocacy, while firmly entrenching CBAs in the development process, also revealed how difficult it was to sustain coalitions in support of their intersecting aims. CBAs were initially predicated on interest convergence between community groups fighting gentrification and labor groups mobilizing around subsidy accountability as a lever to promote living wage jobs and unionization in city-sponsored developments. Labor's ascendance in local politics was enabled by CBAs but also caused labor to be less dedicated to the CBA project over time. In the beginning, CBAs deepened unionization efforts by creating a framework for living wage jobs and labor peace, dovetailing with labor organizing efforts, such as Respect at LAX. From this perspective, the LAX CBA was the highpoint: achieved at the nexus of labor's strong desire to unionize airport workers and the environmental movement's equally strong commitment to mitigate harm from a public asset and forge environmental justice links with surrounding communities. The LAX CBA was also sui generis both because it involved a public agency (with labor representation on the Airport Commission) with the will and resources to strike a deal, and because it did not present the difficult jobs–housing trade-off that ran through the private CBA negotiations. This trade-off was exacerbated by labor's achievement of greater political power and integration into the leadership structure of the CRA, where it could attach union-enhancing conditions, like living wage and labor peace, on redevelopment projects from an advantaged insider position. In this way, labor's pursuit of better jobs invited development that clashed with community groups' quest for affordable housing and resistance to displacement. Although labor leaders remained supportive of community–labor CBA goals, and while labor-friendly officials inside the CRA played an instrumental role helping to win the Grand Avenue community benefits program, it is notable that, after LAX, there were no formal community–labor coalitions advancing CBAs in Los Angeles.

Perhaps the most enduring legacy of the CBA movement was to highlight the contingent nature of redevelopment itself, which depended on a well-functioning economy to provide the opportunity for community negotiations and the resources for community benefits. When that economy broke down, however, as it did after the Great Recession, there was no public works system in place to pick up the slack. There were simply no benefits. The Los Angeles CBA movement thus ends in paradox: constituting a triumph of community–labor mobilization and a stark reminder of the limits of a political system that has privatized core social benefits and forced communities to fight for them through private channels on a case-by-case basis.

5

Grocery Workers

Blocking the Big-Box Invasion

Overview

On a map, the City of Inglewood, California looks like a craggy piece wedged into a jigsaw puzzle. It is one of the eighty-eight separately incorporated cities that give shape to the vast county of Los Angeles,[1] which stretches north-to-south from Lancaster to Long Beach and east-to-west from San Dimas to Santa Monica.[2] In 2000, Inglewood was one of the region's larger cities, with more than one hundred thousand residents—its status as a historically African American community challenged by the arrival of Latino immigrants in the 1980s and 1990s.[3] Located inside a freeway-bound rectangle in the southwestern part of Los Angeles, separated by major arterials from LAX to the west and upscale cities like Beverly Hills and West Hollywood to the north, it was home to the Hollywood Park horseracing track and the "Fabulous" Forum, which had served as an arena for professional basketball and hockey teams through the 1990s, but in 2000 was purchased by the Faithful Central Bible Church. The 1999 closure of the Forum as a regular sports venue, when the Los Angeles Lakers decamped for the new Staples Center, deprived the city of about $1 million in annual tax revenue. However, despite this economic blow, the city retained its working-class character, with a 1999 median income of just under $35,000 per year.[4] As of 2000, Inglewood had only one major supermarket, Vons, within its nearly ten-square-mile city limits.[5] In this sense, Inglewood was not unique among urban communities, in which ready access to grocery stores and other retail businesses was a well-documented problem.[6]

Yet it was precisely because Inglewood's profile mirrored that of many other urban communities that Wal-Mart found it an appealing target for its first Southern California "Supercenter."[7] From an economic standpoint, Inglewood presented a favorable opportunity as an inner city in fiscal need of Wal-Mart's tax revenue boost—and one that housed working-class residents who could potentially benefit from Wal-Mart's "always low prices."[8] From a political perspective, Inglewood was also an attractive locale for urban retail development. It already possessed a large vacant lot adjacent to Hollywood Park that could easily accommodate the Supercenter footprint. And, most critically, Inglewood was *not* part of the City of Los Angeles, which meant that it operated according to its own rules, outside the control of Los Angeles's labor-friendly City Council. Additionally, the fact that Inglewood had a strong African American political base was an important factor because Wal-Mart's urban development strategy emphasized building ties with African American organizations by providing financial contributions.[9] In short, Wal-Mart officials—eager to expand into the lucrative urban market after years of concentrating on rural development—viewed Inglewood as the ideal test case in a larger strategy announced in 2002 to bring forty Supercenters into California.[10]

This chapter explores the labor-backed campaign to stop the development of the Inglewood Supercenter through legislative and legal challenges—a technique known as the "site fight" because of its focus on blocking Wal-Mart at a specific location.[11] It analyzes how labor, environmental, and community groups coalesced to challenge the proposed Supercenter: filing a lawsuit to mobilize opposition to Wal-Mart's Inglewood initiative and redrafting municipal law to limit Wal-Mart's ability to enter the Los Angeles market. It then traces the conflict to Wal-Mart's effort to circumvent the laws passed after the Inglewood site fight by opening a small-format grocery story in the historic Chinatown neighborhood in downtown Los Angeles. In evaluating the campaign, the chapter suggests that the outcome in Inglewood was, in part, a product of Wal-Mart's hubris and political miscalculation. The company's drive for an Inglewood Supercenter failed despite evidence of public support,[12] in large measure because of a politically ill-conceived attempt to gain voter approval of its proposed Supercenter through a city initiative that would have completely circumvented the local planning process. Yet Wal-Mart's Inglewood defeat was not merely self-inflicted. Its miscalculation of the local response to the initiative was politically consequential precisely because there was a sophisticated team of activists and lawyers who used Wal-Mart's disregard of public input to successfully mobilize community opposition to the Supercenter. In that sense, the presence of a political-legal support structure, with experience mounting development-oriented campaigns from the community benefits movement, was essential to Wal-Mart's defeat.

Levers of Labor Reform: Contesting Wal-Mart at the Local Level

The Inglewood site fight occurred within a landscape of larger struggle, in which organized labor and its allies sought to push back against the expansionist impulse of Wal-Mart in order to resist the company's effort to undercut the unionized grocery sector. It was in this broader context that the campaign against Wal-Mart—a global symbol of labor flexibility—evolved as part of an alternative labor strategy to leverage political reforms in local economies, with Los Angeles emerging as a key site of innovation.[13]

Organizing Against Bentonville: The Limits of Traditional Unionism

As one of the world's largest companies[14]—and fiercest union opponents—Wal-Mart was a compelling symbol of labor's organizing dilemma at the turn of the millennium. Wal-Mart's sheer scale was staggering: Its $300 billion in annual sales constituted over 2% of the United States gross national product in the early 2000s, which ranked it as one of the most dominant businesses in economic history.[15] It was this market dominance that made Wal-Mart at once an appealing target for unionization and a mighty adversary.

Wal-Mart's economic power was built upon a retail template that combined low prices with high-volume sales. Wal-Mart founder Sam Walton started his first five-and-dime store in Bentonville, Arkansas in 1950, and built it into a retail giant by undercutting competitor prices, making up for the lower profit margin per unit by selling far more than other retailers.[16] Wal-Mart's corporate operations were characterized by strong centralized managerial control, which allowed it to achieve two different types of cost savings.[17] First, Wal-Mart's command-and-control structure reduced transaction costs by increasing uniformity, predictability, and speed.[18] Perhaps most famously, Wal-Mart was known for its ability to regulate the thermostats of all its retail stores from its headquarters in Bentonville.[19] And Wal-Mart's system of monitoring product movement was one of the most sophisticated in the world, capable of tracking products at any point in the chain from supplier to consumer. This system permitted the company to move quickly to replenish hot-selling items or reduce orders for unpopular goods at any of its retail locations.[20] Second, Wal-Mart's central control over its vast network of retail outlets gave it a strong bargaining position in the market for goods and services, allowing it to reduce the cost of supplies and labor. It used its purchasing power to drive a hard bargain with both domestic and foreign suppliers, who were forced to take the prices that Wal-Mart offered for their goods—or risk losing an enormous customer.[21] Similarly, on the labor front, Wal-Mart achieved low prices by enforcing a uniform low-wage, low-benefits standard and protecting against any sign of union activity.

From organized labor's perspective, Wal-Mart's retail structure extracted cost savings from workers and suppliers, and distributed them to consumers in the form of lower prices and to investors in the form of higher profits. While this structure might have increased overall social welfare—indeed, the central debate over Wal-Mart was the degree to which lower prices compensated for lower wages[22]—organized labor contended that pitting prices against wages presented a false choice.

Contrary to Wal-Mart's claims, labor leaders argued that low prices could coexist with high wages, pointing to Ford Motor Company as the historical prototype and Costco as the modern exemplar of this combination.[23] For labor, the issue was therefore how to improve Wal-Mart's meager and (because of its size) industry-setting labor standards: average annual earnings of just over $17,000 for all hourly workers (below the federal poverty line for a family of four) and health insurance plans that covered less than half of Wal-Mart's employees.[24] Increasing wages and benefits would impose its own trade-offs, requiring some combination of lower profits or lower compensation for higher-level corporate employees, assuming prices were held steady.[25] From labor's perspective, the struggle against Wal-Mart centered on redistributing corporate resources away from managers and investors, and toward workers.

The historical approach to the issue of corporate distribution was unionization, spurred by the ideology of industrial democracy and embodied in the NLRA.[26] Indeed, United States Steel and General Motors—two other archetypes of American capitalism[27]—set the standard for the manufacturing industry by pairing large-scale economic enterprise with traditional unionism.[28] Though the structure of Wal-Mart's retail operations differed in significant ways from the Taylorist production of General Motors assembly plants,[29] there were many echoes of mid-century industrial organization in Wal-Mart's retail design. Like its industrial predecessors, Wal-Mart was characterized by a large-scale, single-employer workforce of over 1.3 million domestic employees,[30] who were engaged in relatively routine job functions and subject to a high degree of central managerial control. Though individual Wal-Mart stores did not contain the massive aggregation of workers associated with industrial shop-floor organizing, Wal-Mart stores were nonetheless large physical workspaces, each home to an average of 325 workers.[31] In contrast to trends toward outsourcing, franchising, and other forms of flexible corporate design,[32] Wal-Mart remained the standard-bearer for unitary commercial organization with a massive workforce of similarly situated employees.

Given the structure of Wal-Mart as a large-scale physical target, many within the labor movement questioned why the UFCW, the major union representing retail and grocery workers, had failed to win a single contract with the retailer. Close observers of Wal-Mart and the UFCW offered explanations for this failure rooted in: (1) the system of federal labor law enforcement; (2) Wal-Mart's flexible organizational structure; (3) Wal-Mart's institutional culture; (4) Wal-Mart's anti-union policies; and (5) the UFCW's organizing model.

Law

The first explanation was not specific to Wal-Mart, but rather pointed more generally to changes in labor law that made union organizing under the NLRA collective bargaining framework difficult. Though the basic legislative structure of labor law had remained intact since the New Deal, administrative and judicial decisions undermined private sector union organizing under the NLRB supervised election process by permitting uncertainty and delay, curtailing employee free speech, and failing to provide sufficient legal protection against employer anti-union retaliation.[33] Unions therefore increasingly opted to circumvent NLRB-supervised union elections in favor of privately negotiated card check neutrality agreements.[34] Wal-Mart, of course, was virulently opposed to card check agreements and was cited for its sophisticated deployment of labor law to thwart incipient organizing attempts.[35] In addition, specific labor organizing rules restricted collective action in support of Wal-Mart workers. For instance, labor law prohibited "secondary activity," which meant that employees of one company could not legally boycott another company subject to a union organizing drive.[36] This prohibition reinforced the difficulty of organizing retail outlets like Wal-Mart, precluding sympathy strikes by transportation unions, like the Teamsters, which could exert significant pressure on Wal-Mart by halting the shipments of goods.[37]

Organization

Another impediment to union organizing stemmed from Wal-Mart's "flexible" labor practices. Wal-Mart relied on part-time employment—a policy that it claimed helped families that needed additional income but also wanted to retain flexibility to care for their children and attend to household tasks.[38] The company kept its part-time workforce at about 20% of the total and even contemplated increasing the proportion to 40% in an effort to cut costs.[39] Part-time workers tended to have less attachment to the company and experienced greater vulnerability—a combination that undercut incentives to organize. Wal-Mart did, in fact, maintain a functioning internal labor market: most of its higher-level managers were recruited from the ranks of hourly employees.[40] However, critics charged that company officials kept the criteria for advancement deliberately vague and used broad discretion to promote workers into training programs, resulting in the systematic under-representation of women in management positions.[41] In fact, female workers, though they comprised nearly 80% of hourly department heads at Wal-Mart in 2001, accounted for only 40% of those in the coveted management trainee program, which operated as the gatekeeper to higher ranking jobs.[42] As a result, women workers at Wal-Mart were disproportionately represented in low-paying, high-turnover jobs perceived as providing limited upward mobility. The precariousness of their work experience constrained opportunities for union activism.

Culture

Observers also pointed to the Wal-Mart "culture" as an additional barrier to unionization. Wal-Mart had its roots in "right-to-work" states in the Deep South,[43] where it promoted an organizational culture that strongly disdained collective worker action. Employees were referred to as "associates," a term that evoked responsibility to the common Wal-Mart enterprise, portrayed in terms of familial obligation and small-town communitarianism.[44] In an effort to promote a team mentality, employees were "coached to achieve their potential,"[45] while the company promoted an "open-door" policy to encourage dissatisfied employees to air concerns with supervisors instead of channeling grievances into labor organizing.[46] A strain of anti-unionism was a core component of Wal-Mart's culture, promulgated through employee literature and meetings that emphasized the dangers of unions, which Wal-Mart portrayed as "victimizing" workers by charging dues and depriving employees of their individual voices in the service of self-interested union goals.[47] The anti-union tenor of Wal-Mart's culture was nurtured in its early period of small-town and rural development, where it tapped themes of community and service to promote the "Wal-Mart Way" as it fanned outward from Arkansas into adjacent Southern and Midwestern states.[48]

Policy

Because of its geographic concentration, Wal-Mart was not a key target of organized labor through the 1980s. This changed in the following decade, as Wal-Mart began to aggressively promote Supercenter development farther from its Bentonville hub in order to wrest market share from the heavily unionized urban grocery industry.[49] As Wal-Mart clashed with labor activists in these new markets, it implemented anti-union policies to thwart organizing drives in their early stages. As a formal matter, Wal-Mart had a clear and well-defined response to signs of union activity. The home office told store managers that defending against unions was a "full-time commitment" and gave them explicit directions on how to deal with potential union threats.[50] Managers were charged with identifying and screening out potentially troublesome employees at the application stage and were required to contact a "Union Hotline" at the first sign of union activity. A call to this hotline dispatched a team from the home office to run a targeted store's anti-union campaign,[51] consisting of mandatory employee meetings with anti-union presentations and propaganda videos.[52] Wal-Mart also imposed a strict anti-solicitation policy to prohibit the distribution of union materials within stores.[53]

Moreover, critics charged Wal-Mart with a tacit policy of intimidating Wal-Mart workers, primarily by firing union activists.[54] Though such terminations were illegal, the traditional labor law remedy of reinstatement with back pay usually represented a hollow victory since it was typically awarded well after a union election had been held (and lost). From 1998 to 2003, the NLRB issued nearly one hundred complaints against Wal-Mart for unfair labor practices, including employee terminations, surveillance, interrogations, and unlawful promises or benefits to dissuade organizing.[55] As a result of Wal-Mart's anti-union policies, only five Wal-Mart stores in the United States had ever held union elections. In the one instance where

U.S. workers voted in favor of the union—in the meat-cutting division at a store in Jacksonville, Texas—Wal-Mart promptly negated the victory by eliminating all of its meat-cutting departments nationwide.[56] In 2005, Wal-Mart closed an entire store in Quebec, Canada after workers voted for union representation.[57] By the mid-2000s, there were no Wal-Mart stores in North America under union contract, despite a nearly decade-long organizing effort by the UFCW.[58]

Labor

While Wal-Mart's anti-union policies erected high barriers to organized labor, part of the failure of the UFCW to make organizing gains was also attributed to its own miscues. With Wal-Mart's focus on preventing unionization clear and resolute, commentators charged the UFCW with failing to respond in kind. In 2004, it devoted only 2% of its national budget to Wal-Mart and was criticized for the absence of a national strategy that tapped into support for Wal-Mart workers.[59] The UFCW abandoned its store-by-store organizing approach in the United States, focusing instead on domestic public relations and policy campaigns.[60] However, even critics acknowledged that systematically organizing Wal-Mart would take more resources than the UFCW could itself devote.[61] There were signs that greater coordination among unions to challenge Wal-Mart was possible, particularly after the 2005 formation of the Change to Win federation. Nonetheless, labor activists expressed skepticism that they could win a traditional organizing campaign against Wal-Mart, even with a large infusion of union resources and a high-level of inter-union coordination, given the company's vast wealth and sophisticated anti-union machinery.[62]

Points of Entry: Localism as an Alternative Labor Strategy

In the face of the challenges to traditional unionism, labor leaders in the Wal-Mart context followed the broader arc of movement activism: turning away from the traditional paradigm of federally supervised union organizing and toward an alternative model emphasizing local coalition building and policy reform designed to increase union density in targeted industries. This turn to localism responded to three central features of the turn-of-the-century field of labor activism. First, it targeted non-exportable industries tied to local economies—because they offered inherently immobile services, had fiscal ties to local governments, or gained economic benefits through association with larger regional economies[63]—that offered key opportunities for union organizing. Second, localism took strategic advantage of the spatial configuration of political power, de-emphasizing advocacy within the more conservative federal government and instead building political alliances with progressive big-city officials who possessed the political will to advance regulation on behalf of their low-wage worker constituents. Third, labor's local strategy presented new opportunities for coalition building and provided distinct legal levers for advancing union organizing goals—embedded in the municipal planning process—which were unavailable at the federal level.

This strategic turn toward the local policy arena also reflected a recognition that litigation against Wal-Mart could only achieve so much. Although litigation was used as an important technique to ensure compliance with minimum workplace standards (evident, for example, in the garment worker class action against Guess during the anti-sweatshop campaign), it had limits from the perspective of organized labor, which sought to mobilize the collective power of workers to raise standards above the legally mandated floor.[64] Nonetheless, strategic lawsuits were used to challenge Wal-Mart's pricing structure and labor practices. In a widely cited policy, the Wal-Mart home office provided detailed budgets to its store managers that set precise targets for revenues and labor costs;[65] because the labor cost projections were so low, critics charged that store managers were effectively forced to violate labor laws in order to satisfy home office standards. Accordingly, prominent lawsuits alleged that Wal-Mart failed to provide state-mandated meal breaks,[66] forced employees to work off the clock,[67] violated child labor laws by requiring minors to work too many hours,[68] and contracted with janitorial services that employed undocumented immigrant workers denied minimum wage and overtime.[69] To the extent that such litigation sought to enforce legal baselines that were systematically flouted, Wal-Mart was forced to reevaluate its pricing and wage policies to ensure ongoing legal compliance. In addition, advocates coordinated impact cases with media strategies to publicize wrongdoing in a way that raised the visibility of labor abuse and increased public pressure for reform. Labor unions generally supported these lawsuits, publicizing them as examples of Wal-Mart's systematic mistreatment of workers.[70]

The most prominent lawsuit against Wal-Mart was *Dukes v. Wal-Mart*, a gender discrimination suit brought by the Berkeley-based Impact Fund in 2004.[71] This lawsuit was certified in 2004 as the largest class action ever, with the Ninth Circuit in 2007 allowing a class of over 1.5 million women seeking back pay, punitive damages, and injunctive relief for unequal pay and promotion.[72] *Dukes* was a traditional employment discrimination suit alleging Title VII violations. Yet to the extent that Wal-Mart deployed gender discrimination as a cost-saving measure, a victory in the class action suit would have had a large-scale effect in raising wages across the board. As the lawsuit progressed, some commentators praised the class action as a vehicle for expressing the collective voice of aggrieved Wal-Mart workers in an environment in which more robust union action was impossible,[73] while others focused on the links between *Dukes* and direct action, highlighting how a union-backed campaign to educate Wal-Mart workers on their rights was partly responsible for empowering female employees to come forward to assert discrimination claims.[74] Some went further, expressing optimism that the *Dukes* suit represented a highly visible rebuke to Wal-Mart's aura of impregnability that could be used to promote greater solidarity and activism among workers.[75] However, that optimism was dashed when the Supreme Court overturned the Ninth Circuit and rejected class certification.

Against the backdrop of litigation constraint and the limits of the federal labor law system, community–labor coalitions sought to reshape local government policy in order to enhance labor standards,[76] exploiting the rising power of progressive city unions to promote labor-friendly urban policy agendas. This strategy was enabled by the fact that labor-enhancing local reforms could be embedded in city ordinances governing contracting and land use regulation—and carried forward by community–labor groups with the resources and sophistication to run effective campaigns.

LAANE had pioneered this strategy, first with the L.A. Living Wage Ordinance, and then with the Staples CBA in 2001. Indeed, at the precise moment LAANE was leading the LAX CBA campaign, it became involved in the Inglewood Wal-Mart struggle. There was a natural connection between the two. The LAX CBA campaign was anchored in Inglewood, which bore the brunt of airport pollution, and therefore LAANE already had personnel on the ground and contacts with important community organizations and political officials. In addition to these community ties, the LAX campaign had also built the foundation for a labor-environmental alliance that would be critical to contesting large-format Wal-Mart stores, which increased traffic and shuttered local businesses, producing blight. Moreover, as in the CBA context, LAANE's challenge to big-box stores spotlighted the problem of local governments approving business development that produced low-wage jobs and thus focused advocacy on containing big-box retailing through local planning mechanisms. One tactic was the site fight, which sought to stop specific development proposals by blocking local land use approval and challenging the environmental soundness of big-box stores. Because the site fight was reactive and resource-intensive,[77] LAANE also sought to persuade local governments to pass ordinances restricting overall big-box development as a way of protecting against the displacement of local businesses and the destruction of housing and green space. These ordinances were intended to influence Wal-Mart either by keeping its Supercenters out of urban areas altogether, and thus protecting higher-wage grocery jobs, or by conditioning Wal-Mart's land use approvals on mitigation measures that would include enhanced wage and benefits standards.

The Inglewood Site Fight

Inglewood emerged in 2003 as labor's signature battle against Wal-Mart, led by activists allied with the UFCW and LAANE, who forged a community–labor coalition to defeat Wal-Mart's bid to open the first Supercenter in metropolitan Los Angeles.[78]

"The No. 1 Enemy": The UFCW's Struggle Against the Supercenter "Invasion"

The struggle over the Inglewood Supercenter was framed by the larger threat that Wal-Mart posed to the unionized grocery sector in California.[79] In 2003, there were about 250,000 unionized grocery workers in California and national figures indicated that they earned about one and a half times as much as their Wal-Mart counterparts.[80] Labor leaders at the UFCW were therefore alarmed at the possible entrance of Wal-Mart Supercenters into the California market, which brought with it the potential to drive unionized grocers out of business and force those that remained to make wage and benefits cuts to stay competitive.[81] Well before Wal-Mart formally announced its plans in 2002 to open forty California Supercenters,[82] the UFCW was therefore actively working to block Wal-Mart from entering the state. In 1998, union and supermarket industry leaders jointly lobbied for a preemptive statewide ban on big-box retail stores that devoted more than fifteen thousand square feet to the sale of non-taxable items like food and drugs.[83] The bill passed the Democratic California legislature but then-Governor Gray Davis vetoed it as "anti-competitive and anti-consumer" after being lobbied by powerful Wal-Mart suppliers.[84]

Defeated at the state, the UFCW took its opposition to Wal-Mart to the local government level, where it attempted to build support for policies barring Supercenter development. This local strategy was part of a broader national campaign by the UFCW (and allied unions like the SEIU) to protect union jobs and reform Wal-Mart's labor practices by redesigning municipal zoning laws to either preclude Supercenter development or condition it on enhanced labor standards.[85] In Los Angeles, the UFCW Local 770's initial strategy focused on enacting a citywide big-box ban—an effort which brought together organizational and legal partners that would play key roles in the subsequent Inglewood campaign. LAANE, in particular, was the central community partner of the UFCW—cementing an alliance established through prior citywide labor campaigns. John Grant, in-house counsel for UFCW Local 770 and coordinator of the union's Wal-Mart strategy, had previously been on the steering committee of the Los Angeles Living Wage Campaign,[86] led by LAANE.[87] In that campaign, Grant coordinated Local 770's efforts with LAANE to negotiate the Living Wage Ordinance with Los Angeles city council members and the Los Angeles city attorney.[88] Subsequently, the UFCW joined LAANE on the CBA campaign (it was part of the coalition targeting SunQuest Industrial Park), which the UFCW supported as a way to promote the inclusion of unionized groceries in publicly subsidized retail developments.[89]

The Los Angeles Living Wage Campaign was also the foundation for the relationship between LAANE and the UFCW's Berkeley-based lawyer, Margo Feinberg, who had spent nearly two decades at the Los Angeles labor-side law firm Schwartz, Steinsapir, Dohrmann & Sommers, which represented the UFCW, as well as other public and private sector unions.[90] Feinberg was instrumental in drafting the Living Wage Ordinance in Los Angeles and other California cities, worked on the Respect at LAX campaign, and developed an expertise in crafting local ordinances to promote labor standards.[91] Feinberg represented the UFCW and LAANE in their initial effort to draft a big-box ban in Los Angeles, which was championed in the late 1990s by legendary progressive City Councilwoman Jackie Goldberg, who represented Hollywood and other neighborhoods in central and northeast Los Angeles.[92] However, the concept of a complete ban was stalled by the opposition of then-Mayor Richard Riordan; skepticism from Assistant City Attorney Cecilia Estolano, who voiced concerns about the legality of a ban that used land use laws to restrict economic competition;[93] and the resistance of key members of the City Council and Planning Commission, who were able to weaken the ban in committee by turning it into a set of aesthetic guidelines.[94]

The UFCW and LAANE took advantage of the 2001 election of Democrat James Hahn as mayor, alongside a new crop of pro-labor council members,[95] to reintroduce a Los Angeles big-box ban in 2002.[96] This time, the groups collaborated with Council members Eric Garcetti—who had replaced the term-limited Goldberg—and Ed Reyes—chair of the powerful Planning and Land Use Management Committee—to advance the bill.[97] However, Wal-Mart lobbied hard against the all-out ban,[98] as did the more union-friendly membership discounter Costco,[99] which chafed against the idea of being lumped in with Wal-Mart given Costco's record of providing higher wages and benefits than its main rival, the membership-based Wal-Mart Sam's Club.[100] In addition, the city attorney's office continued to express reservations about a ban's legal validity.[101]

In 2003, Los Angeles City Councilmembers Garcetti and Reyes brokered a compromise that backed away from a complete ban and proposed instead only to bar big-box stores slated for designated economically blighted zones,[102] where the city already exercised significant power to regulate private development for public purposes. The new proposal banned big-box stores from being built within one mile of city-defined "Economic Assistance Areas" and carved out an exception for membership clubs selling primarily bulk merchandise (i.e., Costco). It followed on the release of a city-commissioned report from consulting firm Rodino Associates, which found that the entrance of Wal-Mart Supercenters into Los Angeles would have a negative impact on small businesses, increase demands on public services, and drive down grocery sector wages.[103] The city attorney's office signed off on this more limited ban,[104] and at the end of 2003 the City Council's Economic Development Committee voted to direct the city attorney to draft an ordinance for its review[105]—a task undertaken in conjunction with Margo Feinberg (who had just helped to draft the recently passed Supercenter ban in Alameda County[106]) working with the UFCW and LAANE.[107] It was widely anticipated that the City Council would vote on the ordinance in early 2004.[108]

However, the timing proved to be unfavorable and the city tabled the geographically limited ban. This was partly due to the newly erupted fissure between the UFCW and major groceries—which had been allies in lobbying for the big-box ban[109]—produced by the deepening Southern California grocery strike. In what observers noted as an ironic twist,[110] at the very moment that the UFCW was working on a ban to ensure that the threat Wal-Mart posed to unionized groceries never materialized, the major grocery chains (Albertsons, Kroger, and Safeway) invoked the specter of Wal-Mart's "invasion" to call for health care cuts during contract negotiations with the union.[111] The proposed cuts, covering 70,000 workers at over 850 Southern and Central California stores, included a cap on employer health care contributions for existing workers and reduced health care benefits for new workers, effectively creating a two-tiered benefits system.[112] The UFCW's response to the proposal was to call a strike of Safeway stores in October 2003, prompting Albertsons and Kroger, which were bargaining jointly with Safeway, to lock out their union employees[113]—thereby precipitating the biggest supermarket strike in Southern California history.[114] Though the UFCW put together a large war chest and mounted a vigorous boycott that lasted over five months and cost the grocery chains $1.5 billion in sales,[115] the settlement of the strike in March 2004 was viewed as a stinging defeat for the UFCW, which ultimately agreed to a two-tier labor system under which new hires would receive lower pensions, health benefits, and wages.[116] While the four-and-a-half-month strike temporarily interrupted labor's pursuit of a big-box ordinance in Los Angeles, its unfavorable resolution lent a heightened sense of urgency to the already heated campaign against the proposed Supercenter in Inglewood.

Inglewood: The Reluctant Test Case

What became a high-profile fight between organized labor and Wal-Mart began as a quiet land deal done well before the grocery strike commenced. In 2002, as part of its plan to bring Supercenters to Southern California, Wal-Mart (through its development proxy, Rothbart Development Corporation) purchased an option to buy the largest undeveloped plot of land in Inglewood: a sixty-acre parcel next to Hollywood Park.[117] The Inglewood site offered Wal-Mart a number of advantages. Inglewood's status as a separately incorporated city within Los Angeles County meant that Wal-Mart could enter the metropolitan market while effectively circumventing the need to gain development approval from Los Angeles's labor-friendly local government. In addition, the fact that Inglewood possessed an already assembled sixty-acre site was a crucial advantage given that the absence of sufficiently large parcels had been a significant impediment to Wal-Mart's urban development plans.[118] Moreover, the identity of Inglewood as a historically African American working-class city was an important feature, which played into Wal-Mart's broader strategy of exploiting tensions between black leaders and organized labor—with its disreputable history of racial discrimination—in order to swing community members in favor of proposed stores.[119] Wal-Mart had already deployed this strategy in Los Angeles, cultivating relationships with local African American leaders in its successful effort to open a traditional Wal-Mart store, without a grocery, in the black community of Baldwin Hills in 2003.[120]

Inglewood was not the first Supercenter skirmish in California. In Palmdale, a mid-sized city sixty miles north of downtown Los Angeles, voters approved a measure in 2000 (over UFCW opposition) to rezone property for a proposed Wal-Mart Supercenter,[121] which later opened as the first Supercenter in Los Angeles County.[122] In 2002, Wal-Mart overturned a city ordinance banning big-box retail development in Calexico, a small border town east of San Diego, though at the time Wal-Mart (which already had a conventional store in the city) had not yet officially announced plans to roll out a Supercenter.[123] Wal-Mart also gained approval for Supercenters in California's vast Inland Empire east of Los Angeles.[124] As these developments highlighted, Wal-Mart's early strategy targeted fast-growing outerlying suburban cities, where retail density was low.[125] This strategy also took advantage of organized labor's relative weakness outside of metropolitan hubs. Although, in 2002, the UFCW raised union dues to create a $3-million war chest to fight Wal-Mart,[126] the union was nonetheless forced to select its battles carefully given the magnitude of Wal-Mart's resources and the vast number of cities it could target.[127] As a result, the UFCW generally opted to forgo challenges to small-market suburban Supercenters, saving resources instead for fights in major urban cities with large numbers of unionized workers and politically powerful labor boards.

It was against this backdrop that Inglewood emerged as a pivotal battle in the UFCW's Wal-Mart campaign—a test of organized labor's ability to block Wal-Mart's entrance into the crucial Los Angeles market. Inglewood also represented one of the first coordinated efforts by a community–labor coalition to thwart an already proposed Wal-Mart Supercenter through the process of local development approval, thus offering a proving ground for the effectiveness of the site fight technique.

The Inglewood campaign began modestly, with the UFCW driving early strategy and LAANE, at that point still a relatively small organization, reluctant to invest major resources. Wal-Mart's plan to develop the Inglewood site became known in March 2002,[128] when LAANE researcher Tracy Gray-Barkan, who was monitoring publicly sponsored development projects in Los Angeles in order to target sites for potential CBAs, learned about the land deal through local government contacts.[129] Once Wal-Mart's intentions were clear, the UFCW and LAANE worked to head off Wal-Mart's development bid, organizing a coalition of community leaders and representatives from the Faithful Central Bible Church, who met regularly for several months with Inglewood City Councilwoman Judy Dunlap to devise a strategy.[130] The UFCW also reached out to Inglewood's Mayor Roosevelt Dorn (who under city law also cast one of five votes on the City Council) and City Councilwoman

Lorraine Johnson, who had been recently appointed to fill a vacant council seat.[131] Both indicated their opposition to Wal-Mart.[132]

While a number of options were discussed, including the possibility of pressing for a CBA, the coalition members ultimately agreed on pushing for an ordinance banning big-box development in Inglewood.[133] The UFCW's John Grant coordinated community testimony in favor of a ban in front of Inglewood's City Council, while Margo Feinberg helped to draft the ordinance,[134] which in its final form barred retail stores larger than one hundred fifty-five thousand square feet that sold more than twenty thousand non-taxable items, such as food.[135] In October 2002, the Inglewood City Council—on a 4-1 vote (with Dunlap, the UFCW ally, opposing on procedural grounds)—passed the ordinance as an emergency measure.[136] Wal-Mart immediately condemned the ordinance and moved to initiate a citywide referendum to repeal it, collecting the required signatures to place the repeal measure on the ballot.[137] In addition, Wal-Mart threatened to sue the city for procedural irregularities associated with the enactment of the ordinance since it was passed on an emergency basis without being drafted by the city attorney.[138] Facing an expensive lawsuit and potentially embarrassing referendum, the City Council reversed course and repealed the ordinance on its own accord in December.[139] Mayor Dorn, Councilwoman Dunlap, and Councilwoman Johnson supported the repeal.[140]

In response to this loss, the UFCW sought to tip the balance of power on the City Council against Wal-Mart by backing Ralph Franklin to run against the incumbent Johnson in the 2003 council election.[141] Grant coordinated the UFCW's get-out-the-vote drive for Franklin,[142] who eventually won the seat in September after the final election was delayed by a series of legal challenges by Johnson.[143] Franklin's overwhelming victory, coupled with that of anti-Wal-Mart Councilman Eloy Morales Jr., gave Wal-Mart foes the upper hand on the City Council and placed Wal-Mart on notice that the council was unlikely to approve a Supercenter project and was poised to revisit a big-box ban. LAANE, for its part, increased its organizing activity in Inglewood after the ordinance's repeal, building support among unionized grocery workers, clergy, community activists, and small business leaders to counter Wal-Mart's quest for development approval.[144]

Wal-Mart's next move, however, came as a surprise. In August of 2003, Wal-Mart, through a front group called the Citizens Committee to Welcome Wal-Mart to Inglewood, began to collect signatures to place an initiative on the local ballot for voter approval of a large-scale commercial development on the Wal-Mart-owned site (called "The Home Stretch at Hollywood Park") that would include a Supercenter and a Sam's Club.[145] The seventy-one page initiative—known as Measure 04-A—sought to amend the city's general land use plan and zoning ordinances to create a commercial zone for the project site (previously zoned for combined commercial/recreational and commercial/residential uses). The initiative also requested voter approval of a specific plan amendment spelling out in precise detail "the uses, development standards, criteria, design, signage and landscaping requirements,

Figure 5.1 Proposed Wal-Mart Supercenter site in Inglewood. *Source*: David McNew/Getty Images (2004).

subdivision requirements, review procedures, exactions, mitigations and other requirements appropriate to the Home Stretch Specific Plan Zone."[146] If passed, the initiative would mandate the project's exact physical site plan and leasable space, its sewage and energy requirements, its transportation plan, its signage, and even its landscape design—all without having to go through the typical city land use approval and environmental review process.[147] Further, Measure 04-A included provisions that would nullify any "Competing Initiative" passed with fewer votes than Measure 04-A,[148] and stated that once approved by a majority vote, it would take a two-thirds supermajority to repeal.[149]

This use of the initiative process to gain approval of a comprehensive development plan constituted a new strategy for Wal-Mart, which had until that point generally focused its ballot campaigns on mobilizing voters to strike down previously approved big-box bans or to authorize limited zoning changes.[150] By October 2003, Wal-Mart collected more than enough signatures to qualify the initiative for the April 2004 ballot.[151] What had begun as a typical skirmish over Supercenter land use approval had grown into a high-profile ballot fight over Wal-Mart's novel attempt to gain comprehensive development approval through Measure 04-A.

The Coalition for a Better Inglewood: Organizing Against Measure 04-A

The Inglewood campaign moved forward on interrelated organizing and legal tracks. LAANE, led by Tracy Gray-Barkan and Reverend William Smart, spearheaded the organizing effort to defeat Measure 04-A, expanding its role in Inglewood dramatically in the fall of 2003 when the UFCW was forced to pull out of Inglewood to devote its resources to full-time work on the grocery strike.[152] LAANE, which had already invested significantly in the Inglewood campaign, knew the election would be a difficult fight, given the public's general support of Wal-Mart. However, based on its previous electoral experiences, LAANE believed it was on the right side of the ballot in that a "no" vote on Measure 04-A would be easier to win given voters' penchant for preserving the status quo.[153] LAANE's major role in the campaign involved forming and supporting the Coalition for a Better Inglewood (CBI),[154] comprised of Inglewood residents and government officials, local UFCW workers, and representatives from a number of organizations, including the progressive faith-based group CLUE,[155] the grassroots economic justice group ACORN,[156] and LAANE itself.[157] Built on the organizational foundation laid by the UFCW and LAANE in early advocacy on the Inglewood big-box ban, CBI was expanded to include new members and infused with new energy as groups coalesced around the clear threat of the Wal-Mart initiative.

In Wal-Mart, CBI faced an opponent with a savvy, experienced public relations team that had cultivated key community supporters. Wal-Mart touted the job-creation and sales tax-generating potential of the proposed store—projecting $3 to $5 million in annual sales tax revenue[158]—and won endorsements from important local politicians like Mayor Dorn, who argued that Measure 04-A was good for Inglewood because it would create two thousand construction and one thousand permanent jobs.[159] As in Baldwin Hills, Wal-Mart's public relations offensive targeted black leaders. The company gave $300,000 to the NAACP in 2001 and another $150,000 in 2003, which critics charged contributed to the civil rights organization's "deafening" silence during the campaign.[160] Moreover, Wal-Mart orchestrated a political operation in favor of Measure 04-A, spending $1 million on outreach and mobilization efforts to influence the roughly ten thousand Inglewood voters who would go to the polls.[161]

To counteract Wal-Mart's efforts, CBI pursued a two-prong strategy for winning the election that emphasized public relations and voter turnout. On the public relations side, CBI worked with Los Angeles-based Democratic political consulting firm SG&A to respond to Wal-Mart's attempt to cultivate a pro-community image.[162] Initially, CBI organizers worked to chip away at Wal-Mart's positive reputation by circulating fact sheets to community members highlighting Wal-Mart's record of labor abuse.[163] This effort to negate Wal-Mart's message of community benefits was adapted for different demographic groups.[164] The campaign to highlight the costs Wal-Mart imposed on communities was reinforced by the late-2003 Rodino report, which found that Wal-Mart Supercenters would injure low-income communities in Los Angeles by shuttering existing businesses and driving down wages and benefits.[165] In response, Wal-Mart funded its own report by the Los Angeles Economic Development Corporation, released in late January 2004, arguing that Supercenter entry into the L.A. city market would generate $668 million in annual consumer savings, while warning that unionization would result in lost jobs and higher prices, thereby eroding the purported benefits.[166] Bob Rodino reviewed the report for the coalition, concluding that the "words sound good but the reality on the ground is quite different." Specifically, he took issue with the cost calculation, suggesting that instead of lower prices, the entry of Wal-Mart would produce "major store closures and the consequent loss of jobs, retail sales taxes, consumer choice and convenience," while producing the "on-going suppression of workers' wages around the region."[167] In a follow-up email, Rodino explained that the "base fallacy of the Wal-Mart report regarding consumer savings-spending and consequent job creation is the spending referred to is not net new spending. It is replacement spending."[168]

While the coalition sought to use these points in its public relations strategy, as the election approached, CBI's internal polling data revealed that the message about Wal-Mart's community costs was not gaining sufficient traction and the initiative was favored by two-thirds of voters.[169] Part of CBI's problem was a lack of sufficient funds: LAANE, for example, was able to spend just $20,000 on its grassroots campaign.[170] The timing of the grocery strike resolution in March 2004 proved fortuitous from a financial perspective, raising the stakes of Inglewood for organized labor, which recognized that a loss there would further erode its already badly damaged credibility as a viable force for grocery worker unionism. The Los Angeles County Fed gave $125,000 to support the final phase of the Inglewood campaign,[171]

Figure 5.2 March against Measure 04-A (Rev. William Smart, right). *Source:* Wally Skalij/ *Los Angeles Times* via Getty Images (March 29, 2004).

and in conjunction with the UFCW and other unions, provided crucial logistical and organizational resources.[172]

However, organized labor's important infusion of funds did nothing to change the faltering appeal of CBI's arguments about Wal-Mart's cost to the community. About one month before the election, CBI leaders therefore concluded that the coalition needed to change the content of its message to emphasize what polling indicated was the most powerful argument against Measure 04-A: that the initiative circumvented the standard legal process in a way that smacked of an illegitimate power grab by Wal-Mart.[173] In the final stretch of the campaign, CBI organized its media and community education efforts around that theme, using phone banks, community presentations, and press conferences to urge voters to reject Measure 04-A on the grounds that it allowed Wal-Mart to circumvent its legal obligations. CBI benefited from the outreach efforts of experienced community partners in communicating its message. LA Metro, a grassroots organizing affiliate of the Industrial Areas Foundation, helped to convene a town hall meeting,[174] while CLUE organized clergy to add moral weight and appeal to African American and Latino churchgoers.[175]

In addition, although CBI could not afford to pay for advertising, it was able to gain media attention through radio talk shows and well-placed opinion pieces in major newspapers like the *Los Angeles Times*.[176] The "Vote No on Measure 04-A" message was also given greater media visibility by the appearance of well-known

Figure 5.3 Altagracia Perez, Rector of Holy Faith Episcopal Church, at Inglewood rally.
Source: LAANE (2004).

Figure 5.4 Jesse Jackson (right) and Maxine Waters (left) meeting with coalition.
Source: LAANE (2004).

political figures, such as the Reverend Jesse Jackson and South Los Angeles Congresswoman Maxine Waters,[177] and was communicated through a direct mail effort organized by the County Fed in conjunction with SG&A.[178]

Finally, CBI and its union allies mounted a vigorous get-out-the-vote campaign in the final weeks before the election, which was coordinated by the County Fed and involved CBI member groups LAANE, ACORN, and LA Metro, as well as the UFCW, HERE, and SEIU unions.[179] This effort included intensive door-to-door vote canvassing, precinct walking, and community meetings.[180] Though under-resourced compared to Wal-Mart, CBI was able to marshal its limited funds and leverage its substantial community connections to orchestrate a highly visible and multifaceted electoral campaign that effectively targeted Inglewood's small pool of likely voters.

The Legal Strategy

CBI's organizing strategy was coordinated with a legal strategy designed to give the coalition an opportunity to defeat the Wal-Mart initiative in court, while also reinforcing grassroots efforts to beat Wal-Mart at the ballot box. CBI therefore viewed the legal strategy as part of a comprehensive effort to use all available tools to gain a "win"—measured by thwarting the Supercenter. The use of legal tactics as part of a "comprehensive campaign" model was consistent with LAANE's general approach—honed in the CBA context—which combined organizing, policy advocacy, research, communications, fundraising, and legal advocacy to build political power.[181]

In Inglewood, the legal prong of the campaign—focused on derailing Measure 04-A in court—underscored the centrality of land use and election law in organized labor's anti-Wal-Mart movement in California. The opportunity to challenge Wal-Mart at the local level turned on the power of cities to control land use planning for the public welfare,[182] which gave municipalities broad discretion over the process of granting development entitlements and codifying general land use plans.[183] As in the CBA context, developers like Wal-Mart were generally required to go through a local planning commission to obtain key discretionary land use approvals, such as zoning variances and conditional use permits, which the city council had to approve.[184] The structure of the entitlements process permitted well-organized opposition groups with strong political connections to delay or even deny key approvals based on legitimate land use concerns,[185] such as limiting sprawl or preventing incompatible uses. Accordingly, politically influential labor groups could lobby governmental officials to deny land use approvals for Wal-Mart Supercenters, which frequently needed zoning changes or amendments to a city's general land use plan to accommodate their massive sites.[186] In addition, the site fight—like the CBA model—derived leverage from the process of environmental clearance for development projects, which required public agencies, like the planning commission, to conduct an environmental review under CEQA.

Finally, the framework of the voter-sponsored initiative and referendum process was an important site of legal contestation over Wal-Mart. California provided a constitutionally guaranteed right to place initiatives (proposing new laws) and referenda (accepting or rejecting previously enacted laws) on state and local ballots,[187] specifically authorizing them to propose or change land use laws.[188] Electoral battles between labor groups and Wal-Mart generally involved three scenarios:[189] (1) Wal-Mart called a referendum to gain voter approval of land use changes already passed by the city to permit Supercenter development (thereby cutting off union efforts to run anti-Wal-Mart candidates who could reverse the approval);[190] (2) Wal-Mart called a referendum to repeal big-box bans enacted by city legislatures;[191] or (3) organized labor called a referendum to reject city approvals of land use changes already passed to permit Supercenter development.[192] While it was no doubt crucial for Wal-Mart opponents to understand the election law framework in each of these instances, because of legal protections favoring citizen access to the ballot, the key fight was over turning out voters rather than challenging the legal validity of the referendum process itself.

Inglewood Measure 04-A was critically different from these typical referenda cases because it was an initiative put on the ballot by Wal-Mart to gain affirmative and absolute land use approval of its Supercenter plans *before* city review. The UFCW and LAANE believed that this distinction made the initiative legally vulnerable and began to assemble a legal team to consider a lawsuit soon after Wal-Mart announced that it would gather signatures to place Measure 04-A on the ballot in the fall of 2003.

UFCW Local 770 and LAANE jointly retained Margo Feinberg to coordinate legal strategy.[193] Feinberg, an expert in neither land use nor election law, contacted Jan Chatten-Brown, an environmental lawyer who she had known for many years through their work on progressive causes (and who would work for ARSAC on the legal challenge to LAX expansion).[194] Chatten-Brown was also not an election law expert (and had never challenged an initiative before), but her environmental law and land use background was deemed critical to stopping an initiative that purported to circumvent conventional environmental and land use processes. Her firm, Chatten-Brown & Associates, was a small public interest law office in Westwood near UCLA, which she had built around representing citizen groups and environmental organizations.[195] The firm had developed a reputation as a sophisticated environmental boutique with a commitment to progressive public interest causes. In addition to its fee-generating work for established environmental organizations,[196] the firm also undertook reduced-fee and pro bono representation for client groups with insufficient resources.[197] In the Measure 04-A challenge, Chatten-Brown and her associate, fellow UCLA School of Law alumnus Doug Carstens, formally represented both LAANE and CBI, although client communications were generally with LAANE representatives Tracy Gray-Barkan and Lizette Hernandez, and LAANE paid for the legal work on a reduced-fee basis.[198]

After preliminary discussions with the city over whether Measure 04-A was eligible for the ballot based on procedural concerns about the city's election report, Chatten-Brown's firm focused on analyzing the legality of the initiative from a constitutional and statutory perspective.[199] Meanwhile, the UFCW and LAANE assembled a larger team of lawyers to consult on the case. Feinberg coordinated this team, which included practicing and academic lawyers identified for their capacity to contribute relevant expertise and bring legitimacy to the cause.[200] One member of this team was David Pettit, a partner at Caldwell Leslie Proctor & Pettit, a small commercial litigation firm in Santa Monica. Another UCLA School of Law graduate, Pettit started out as a legal aid lawyer,[201] and had worked for over a decade at Caldwell Leslie as a land use specialist.[202] Pettit had supported LAANE's Living Wage Campaign in Santa Monica and became involved with LAANE in its work on CBAs.[203] Pettit joined the Inglewood team as pro bono counsel to LAANE, motivated by a commitment to workers' rights and concern about the negative impact of Wal-Mart on low-income communities.[204] Madeline Janis was also on the team, where she was joined by famed constitutional law scholar and then-USC Law Professor Erwin Chemerinsky, and Sean Hecht, recently hired as the executive director of UCLA's Environmental Law Center after several years in the environmental division at the California attorney general's office (before which he worked for the boutique law firm that litigated UNITE's class action against Guess in the anti-sweatshop campaign). A crucial purpose of the legal team, which conferred regularly via conference calls, was to provide additional support for Chatten-Brown by evaluating the strength of possible legal challenges and providing feedback on draft arguments.[205]

A key question raised at the outset was whether to file a pre-election challenge to block the initiative or to wait until after the election to sue in the event that Measure 04-A passed.[206] Although Chatten-Brown was confident about the potential for winning a post-election challenge, she and other members on the legal team were less sanguine about the prospects of prevailing on pre-election review,[207] given the strong judicial bias against preempting the electoral process absent a clear showing of an initiative's invalidity.[208]

Nonetheless, the legal team ultimately decided to pursue a pre-election challenge for two reasons. First, the lawyers and LAANE staff agreed that they should take advantage of the outside chance to succeed on the merits to shut the initiative down.[209] At that stage, LAANE's Gray-Barkan was concerned about the coalition's ability to win the election outright and thus viewed litigation as perhaps its best chance of ultimately gaining victory in Inglewood.[210] Second, Gray-Barkan believed that even if the lawsuit proved unsuccessful, it could serve beneficial purposes. An early filing would put Wal-Mart on notice that, even if it won the election, it would face a strong legal challenge that would at the very least tie up the plan in court for some time.[211] Moreover, she viewed the lawsuit as a way of generating additional media visibility and grassroots momentum for its voter mobilization efforts.[212] Toward this end, Margo Feinberg was able to persuade California Attorney General Bill Lockyer to issue a letter raising legal concerns about the initiative just before filing the lawsuit.[213] Thus, even if the lawsuit did not prevent the election from going forward, LAANE and the broader coalition leadership believed that the publicity it created would amplify its central argument: that Wal-Mart was attempting to place itself "above the law."

Chatten-Brown's firm filed suit on behalf of CBI and LAANE on December 17, 2003 in Los Angeles Superior Court.[214] The lawsuit was styled as a writ of mandate that sought to either prevent the city from submitting the initiative to the electorate or require the county clerk to remove it from the ballot.[215] The petition's complaint centered on the fact that the initiative allowed Wal-Mart to circumvent typical land use approvals and avoid CEQA review. It contained six causes of actions, four of which alleged constitutional violations. The first constitutional claim was that the initiative, by requiring a two-thirds vote to amend, contravened the California Constitution, which required a simple majority vote for all initiatives and referenda.[216] The second was that, by mandating land use changes to the City of Inglewood (which typically required administrative approvals from the city itself), the initiative violated a provision of the California Constitution limiting the use of initiatives to legislative matters.[217] The two other constitutional causes of action faulted the initiative for granting Wal-Mart, as a private corporation, specific development rights and for mandating land use changes (such as the closure of specific streets and the elimination of easements) in conflict with state law requirements for such modifications.[218] The petition also included a claim regarding technical violations of the state law governing subdivisions and alleged that the city clerk had not properly validated the signatures collected in favor of Measure 04-A.[219]

The court's decision came in late February 2004. In a brief four-page ruling, the court expressed "doubts as to the validity of some provisions of the Initiative," but nonetheless held that the petitioners had not made a "clear/compelling showing of invalidity" that would warrant interfering with "the people's constitutional right of initiative."[220] The court's resolution of the petition, though legally disappointing, did not come as a surprise to the legal team or LAANE, which generally credited the lawsuit with providing an important stimulus to the grassroots campaign, attracting widespread national media attention that helped with the final organizing push.[221]

Once it was clear that Measure 04-A would appear on the ballot, the previously assembled legal team focused on preparing for a post-election lawsuit to invalidate Measure 04-A if it passed. Specifically, the lawyers worked to prepare the full legal briefing for both a temporary restraining order to immediately halt implementation of the land use changes called for by the initiative and for a substantive challenge on the merits.[222] Chatten-Brown's firm again took the role of lead counsel in drafting the post-election filing, with David Pettit, Margo Feinberg, and Sean Hecht involved in strategy discussions and substantive reviews of the pleadings.[223] In addition, Feinberg coordinated an effort to put together lawyers who would file amicus briefs with the court on behalf of organizations opposing the initiative from different legal perspectives. Some of the team members themselves were slated to file amicus briefs: Chemerinsky was to file a constitutional law brief, while Hecht and Pettit were to coordinate a land use brief.[224] Feinberg was also in discussion with lawyers associated with the NRDC, labor unions, and historical preservation groups to draft additional briefs.[225] Feinberg was responsible for identifying the lawyers to draft the briefs and putting together the organizations that would sign on as amici.[226] In the weeks leading up to the election, the legal team spent a great deal of energy planning for litigation that its members did not know for sure would ultimately be necessary.[227] Yet the lawyers and organizers did not want to leave anything to chance. On the eve of the election, with LAANE worried about the outcome of the vote,[228] the pieces of an immediate post-election legal challenge were in place.[229]

Figure 5.5 Official announcement of Measure 04-A's defeat (Tracy Gray-Barkan, right). Source: Lawrence K. Ho/*Los Angeles Times* via Getty Images (April 6, 2004).

In the end, a post-election lawsuit was rendered moot by the Inglewood voters, who sent Measure 04-A to defeat by a decisive margin (7,049 voting against and 4,575 voting in favor) in the April 6, 2004 special election for the initiative.[230] At No on Measure 04-A campaign headquarters at La Feria restaurant in Inglewood, official announcement of the final vote tally ignited jubilant celebration. The outcome represented a resounding victory for community–labor action, garnering the anti-Wal-Mart movement national and international media attention.[231] County Fed chief Miguel Contreras, surrounded by community leaders who invested heavily in the anti-Wal-Mart fight, delivered a euphoric speech as celebration lasted well into the night.

It was Wal-Mart's first ballot-box defeat and constituted an embarrassing setback in the company's Southern California expansion plans,[232] particularly in light of the fact that Wal-Mart had spent more than $1 million to secure the initiative's passage.[233] While CBI's victory did not alter Wal-Mart's interest in the sixty-acre parcel of land in Inglewood or its strong desire to develop it into a Supercenter, the defeat of Measure 04-A complicated Wal-Mart's long-term development plan. With the Inglewood City Council lining up against a Supercenter development,[234] it would require a pro-Wal-Mart change in personnel on the council for the possibility of city approval to re-emerge.

Figure 5.6 Miguel Contreras (center) proclaims Measure 04-A's defeat. *Source*: Lawrence K. Ho/*Los Angeles Times* via Getty Images (April 6, 2004).

Figure 5.7 Celebrating Measure 04-A's defeat (Madeline Janis, second from left). *Source*: LAANE (2004).

From Ballot-Box Victory to Local Policy Reform

The Inglewood victory also had repercussions for the ongoing effort to restrict Wal-Mart's ability to enter the L.A. city limits, re-igniting stalled legislative efforts to mitigate the negative impacts of big-box development. After Inglewood, the UFCW and LAANE went back to Los Angeles City Councilman Eric Garcetti, who had championed the Los Angeles big-box ban, about reintroducing legislation. At this point, however, the concept of the ordinance had shifted from a complete ban toward a softer approach in which retailers would be required to conduct a cost-benefit analysis on a case-by-case basis to show that a proposed big-box store would not have adverse economic impacts on the community.[235]

The cost-benefit analysis approach offered distinct political and legal advantages. As the CBI campaign showed, Wal-Mart opponents focused on the economic costs of Wal-Mart as a way to counteract the purported economic benefits of low prices and to gain political traction for legislative efforts to force Wal-Mart to raise wages and health benefits. In this vein, a number of labor-sponsored studies detailed how Wal-Mart's low-wage, low-benefit policies produced "hidden" public costs, measured in terms of the fiscal demands Wal-Mart workers made on taxpayer-financed safety net programs.[236] The 2003 Rodino study, though publicly commissioned, arrived at similar conclusions, finding that the benefits of increased jobs and tax revenue provided by Supercenters would be outweighed by the costs to workers, the broader business community, and taxpayers.[237] In addition, labor groups had also started to document the use of public subsidies to finance Wal-Mart's growth.[238] As these efforts underscored, organized labor saw a political payoff in using the rigor of economic analysis to justify Wal-Mart regulation.

From a legal standpoint, there was still lingering concern that a court might view any type of big-box ban as an impermissible use of zoning law to interfere with private business for economic reasons (protecting labor standards in the grocery industry) unrelated to typical land use concerns (such as preventing blight or reducing traffic).[239] Moreover, even if the city made sure to base a ban on legitimate land use grounds, there was the very real possibility that Wal-Mart would nonetheless sue, tying up the ordinance in costly litigation, or challenge the ordinance through a referendum. Indeed, Wal-Mart had sued Alameda County and the City of Turlock over their big-box bans,[240] and Wal-Mart had already won ballot-box challenges in Contra Costa and Calexico.[241]

LAANE, for its part, had come to oppose an outright ban in Los Angeles, which it argued invited risky litigation and ballot fights.[242] In addition, it was believed that a citywide ban would eliminate the possibility of tying entry of Wal-Mart Supercenters to payment of the living wage. As an alternative, LAANE advocated for adapting the stalled Garcetti-Reyes ordinance to require retailers to submit an "economic impact analysis" demonstrating the absence of adverse economic impacts prior to big-box approval.[243] This idea was roughly modeled on the process for environmental review that had proven to be a potent vehicle for pressing community demands in CBA negotiations. It also mirrored the community impact report that LAANE had promoted to the Los Angeles CRA in the wake of the Staples CBA. While politically infeasible as a general development requirement, the impact report idea gained support in connection with discussions about big-box regulation,[244] and after the Inglewood fight came to represent a way out of the political and legal impasse created by the big-box ban. Only a week after Measure 04-A went down to defeat, Margo Feinberg and Roxana Tynan—who had joined LAANE in 2001 as the project director of accountable development after spearheading the Hollywood and Highland project for Councilwoman Jackie Goldberg—met with Cecilia Estolano of the Los Angeles city attorney's office to review "the new approach to regulating Supercenters."[245] After a thorough legal evaluation by Feinberg, the UFCW signed onto the idea of pursuing an economic impact analysis and a revised ordinance was introduced to the Los Angeles City Planning Commission in May 2004.[246] Flowing out of LAANE's CBA work—and coming in the midst of the LAX CBA campaign—it was clear that the economic impact analysis concept was another effort to deepen and extend the labor movement's living wage and unionization goals. Toward this end, Feinberg took the lead in coordinating with the city attorney's office to draft the new ordinance,[247] which also received key input from UFCW Local 770's John Grant and LAANE's Madeline Janis and Roxana Tynan. Given that LAANE had developed central definitions and concepts in earlier drafts, the major effort involved incorporating a framework for evaluating the economic impact of big-box stores.[248] In addition to drafting, Feinberg testified and prepared other community members to testify at Planning Commission and City Council hearings in order to build a strong public record for the ordinance. In June 2004, she proposed that it would be helpful if Tynan's upcoming remarks at one public hearing "connected the Ordinance to the City's general plan and zoning elements" focusing on the protection of neighborhoods from economic and environmental harm.[249] Taking Feinberg's feedback to heart, Tynan's remarks emphasized "general plan specific goals," while hammering the point that "superstores do have major impacts on community" and that "communities need to decide—case by case."

Feinberg also was involved in briefing the City Council on the goals of the ordinance and coordinating with Councilman Garcetti's representatives on executing changes.[250] LAANE staff, led by Tynan, and UFCW counsel John Grant managed the process of educating council members and coordinating community input.[251] The coalition's talking points emphasized that the ordinance was a "reasonable proposal," "NOT an outright ban." In addition, they stressed the need to protect public investment, noting that the economic impact report would only apply in economic revitalization areas, where "the City has invested large amounts of public money. We don't want to see our public investments undermined by superstores." The coalition also argued that the ordinance was "NOT just targeted at Super Walmarts" and was not simply "a backdoor way to force Walmart to pay a living wage."[252] Highlighting the importance of protecting neighborhoods, Grant mobilized new constituencies in support of the ordinance such as affordable housing groups, like the Southern California Association of Nonprofit Housing, and legal aid lawyers. As a result of this outreach, Beth Steckler, the policy director at the housing group Livable Places, drafted a letter of support to the president of the Planning Commission.[253]

In advance of a critical Planning Commission hearing, Tynan penned a lengthy analysis that responded to a commission staff report proposing significant amendments to the draft ordinance.[254] Referencing the Rodino report's finding that the city had already invested $43,640,000 subsidizing business and retail development in "incentive zones," Tynan stated that "this investment could be seriously jeopardized if the potential negative impacts of big box retailers and superstores are realized."[255] In response to the city's proposal to delete a provision of the ordinance requiring the CRA to address twelve impact factors in conducting its economic review, Tynan objected that "those twelve factors provide critical guidance in clarifying the Council's intent in this matter, and that deleting them significantly undermines the Ordinance."[256] She further argued that Superstores threatened the "reduction of consumer choice due to their tendency to cannibalize competing retail businesses," while forcing store closures that would reduce "sales tax and property tax revenues."[257] Wal-Mart's lawyers from Mayer Brown Rowe & Maw fired back that "it is necessary not only to amend the ordinance as suggested by staff, but also to remove a number of provisions that are either intended to allow the ordinance to be used to regulate economic competition or are inconsistent with current law." Wal-Mart's proposed revisions included extending the ordinance to all retail stores over 100,000 square feet "regardless of merchandise mix," applying the ordinance citywide, eliminating "discriminatory exemptions for wholesale clubs" [like Costco], and "eliminat[ing] any requirement that the economic impact analysis discuss the number of nearby supermarkets, the 'quality' of jobs to be displaced, the cost or quality of goods to be sold, or any other matter not directly related to appropriate land use, as opposed to economic competition, impacts."[258] The coalition punched back, mobilizing other mayors to endorse the ordinance by recounting the costs of Supercenter entry in their cities.[259] As August arrived, there were furious last-minute negotiations and multiple rounds of wordsmithing. As it became clear that the ordinance had the overwhelming support of the City Council,[260] Wal-Mart reversed its early hostility and signaled acquiescence.[261] After roughly three months of negotiations and revisions, in August 2004, Los Angeles passed the nation's first "Superstores Ordinance" requiring an economic impact analysis.[262]

The ordinance applied to any "Superstore"—defined as "a Major Development Project that sells from the premises goods and merchandise, primarily for personal or household use, and whose total Sales Floor Area exceeds 100,000 square feet and which devote more than 10% of sales floor area to the sale of Non-Taxable Merchandise"[263]—slated to be located in an Economic Assistance Area.[264] Such areas included federal and state enterprise zones and city redevelopment project areas covering much of Los Angeles's low-income communities.[265] Because these areas were created through the provision of public subsidies, city officials believed that they could be a legal lever to force Wal-Mart to pay its workers at the living wage rate. The law made the development of a Superstore in such an area contingent on the receipt of a conditional use permit (CUP)—land use approval given by the city on a case-by-case basis to potentially objectionable uses.[266] In order to receive a CUP, a Superstore developer had to submit an "economic impact analysis" to the city's community development department (or CRA if the project was within a redevelopment zone) specifying whether the store would "have an adverse impact or economic benefit on grocery or retail shopping centers," "result in the physical displacement of any businesses," "require the demolition of housing," destroy park space, displace jobs, impact city revenue, and create other "materially adverse or positive economic impacts or blight."[267] The analysis had to specify measures available to "mitigate any materially adverse economic impacts."[268] On the basis of this report and any information submitted in response, the community development department was required to make a recommendation to the Planning Commission as to whether the proposed store would result in a "materially adverse economic impact" and, if so, whether any mitigation measures were available.[269] In order to give final approval to the project, the Planning Commission then had to conclude that no irremediable adverse impacts existed—a determination appealable to the full Los Angeles City Council.[270]

The ordinance aimed to set a high bar for Superstore admission into Los Angeles by requiring the city to create a public record, based on empirical evidence, that the economic benefits of a store would in fact outweigh the costs. It was imagined that, in practice, the economic impact analysis process would conjure a cottage industry of consultants who would produce reports on both sides of the Wal-Mart divide, touting the benefits or condemning the costs depending on the perspective of the commissioning group.[271] The ordinance therefore did not eliminate politics from the siting decision, but rather channeled it into an impact analysis process that placed labor activists on a stronger footing than if they were left solely with the pre-existing land use entitlement and environmental review standards. In particular, the economic impact analysis requirement provided a politically legitimate way for city council members to oppose Wal-Mart because of concerns about its labor practices and negative community effects. Moreover, the structure of the ordinance, which compelled the production of information about the economic impact of Superstores, was designed to be less vulnerable to legal attack than a flat ban on big-box stores.

Of course, passage of the Los Angeles Superstores Ordinance did not affect the status of developments in Inglewood, which remained an active big-box site after the 2004 ballot initiative. In fact, in early 2005, Wal-Mart formally purchased the sixty-acre site it had previously held on option,[272] and it was widely expected that the company would renew its Supercenter proposal that year.[273] In response, community leaders, including California State Assemblyman Jerome Horton and Councilman Ralph Franklin, initially urged Wal-Mart to accept a CBA in exchange for permission to build—a proposal that Wal-Mart rebuffed.[274] Subsequently, the

UFCW and LAANE went back to Inglewood with a strategy of adapting the Los Angeles Superstores Ordinance to Inglewood in order to provide an additional layer of protection from big-box development.[275] Inglewood City Councilman Franklin sponsored the Inglewood ordinance, but while he had the support of the Inglewood City Council, the city attorney opposed the effort. As a result, Franklin circumvented the city attorney, instead directing the city's planning division to send to the full council a proposal that tracked the Los Angeles ordinance.[276] Feinberg, on behalf of the UFCW and LAANE, helped to draft the Inglewood ordinance, which when it passed in July 2006, mirrored its Los Angeles counterpart by requiring big-box developers to pay for an economic impact analysis before building permits could be approved.[277]

The Inglewood Effect: Echoes of Wal-Mart Activism

The adoption of Superstores Ordinances in Los Angeles and Inglewood capped nearly five years of lobbying, organizing, and legal advocacy by the UFCW and LAANE, and legally codified their effort to limit Wal-Mart's entry into metropolitan Los Angeles. When measured against the benchmark of stopping Wal-Mart from penetrating the Los Angeles market, the campaign was by all accounts a striking success. At the end of the 2000s, Wal-Mart had not opened a Supercenter in Los Angeles or Inglewood, and the cities' ordinances held the distinction of having avoided legal challenge from the retailer.

The aftermath of the Inglewood fight, however, underscored the elusiveness of Wal-Mart and the complexities of coordinating labor movement activism on a city-by-city basis. Wal-Mart, for its part, took two lessons from its experiences in Inglewood and Los Angeles. First, as a policy matter, Wal-Mart decided to place less emphasis on targeting Supercenter development in major cities where powerful labor boards raised the costs of entry.[278] Accordingly, Wal-Mart made no effort to come into Los Angeles through the economic impact analysis process set up by the Superstores Ordinance and refocused development away from other union strongholds like Chicago, whose City Council passed a living wage ordinance applicable to big-box stores (vetoed by the mayor in 2006),[279] and New York.[280] As an alternative, Wal-Mart pursued a two-tiered strategy, focusing on the international market,[281] while continuing to vigorously press development plans in small domestic cities where it could use its superior resources to wear down local resistance.[282] In Inglewood, for instance, Wal-Mart did not immediately concede the Supercenter fight, instead attempting—unsuccessfully—to mobilize support for pro-Wal-Mart city council candidates to overturn the existing ordinance.[283]

Second, as a tactical matter, Wal-Mart avoided proposing any new initiatives preempting local planning, which backfired in Inglewood.[284] Instead, it followed the approach pursued successfully before Inglewood, working behind the scenes to secure city approval for Supercenter developments, while referendizing or litigating big-box bans.[285] Its success in this regard was mixed. Wal-Mart did achieve a significant post-Inglewood victory in Rosemead, a small city ten miles east of Los Angeles, where Wal-Mart lobbied the City Council to approve a Supercenter project in 2004. After that approval, a UFCW-led community-labor coalition—bereft of local political support—was forced to litigate its opposition. When the coalition invalidated Wal-Mart's EIR in court,[286] Rosemead simply revised the EIR to address the impact of the store's twenty-four-hour operations and proceeded to confer ultimate environmental approval. Subsequently, the coalition drafted a referendum to repeal the city's development agreement with Wal-Mart, which opponents believed contained zoning changes necessary for Wal-Mart to open. However, the anti-Wal-Mart coalition's legal counsel was poorly advised, as the development agreement contained no such zoning changes. When the city simply rescinded the development agreement in the face of the coalition's challenge, it had the perverse effect of permitting Wal-Mart to accelerate construction of the Supercenter,[287] which opened in September 2006.[288]

Wal-Mart had less success challenging anti-big-box ordinances. This was due, in part, to the fact that some jurisdictions followed the Los Angeles model and adopted ordinances that provided for economic impact analyses rather than imposing bans—thus rendering them less susceptible to legal challenge or ballot referenda.[289] For example, in March 2006—after Alameda County repealed its original ban in the face of a Wal-Mart lawsuit—it enacted the first-ever county-wide big-box ordinance requiring an economic impact analysis.[290] Wal-Mart suffered a major legal setback in its effort to litigate against big-box bans when it lost a challenge to the ban in Turlock, which the California Court of Appeal upheld in 2006 as a constitutional exercise of the city's police powers that did not require further environmental review under CEQA.[291]

The post-Inglewood approach of labor movement opponents of big-box stores was the mirror image of Wal-Mart's. While Wal-Mart retreated from the biggest cities, labor chose those sites to expand restrictive big-box ordinances, taking advantage of the Turlock court's legal validation of big-box bans to advance them in San Diego,[292] Santa Ana,[293] and Long Beach.[294] The Santa Ana ban passed, while the San Diego ban was vetoed and the Long Beach ban repealed after a threatened Wal-Mart referendum. In one unique case, smart growth groups in the tiny Bay Area suburb of Hercules persuaded the city to exercise eminent domain to take land owned by Wal-Mart.[295] Other community groups pursued CEQA litigation to thwart proposed Supercenters,[296] taking advantage of a 2004 California Court of Appeal decision affirming that the environmental review process could consider economic blight induced by big-box competition in addition to traditional environmental impacts.[297] Additional fights in cities like Ventura in Southern California,[298] and Marina in Northern California,[299] contributed to the slowing pace of Wal-Mart's California expansion.[300] Five years after the company announced its plans to bring forty Supercenters to California, it had opened only half that amount.[301]

Wal-Mart Comes to Chinatown

Despite labor's success in keeping Supercenters out of Los Angeles, other threats loomed, and Wal-Mart was not yet done with the city. Girding against the potential acquisition of existing grocery stores by nonunionized competitors, LAANE helped to pass the 2005 Grocery Worker Retention Ordinance, which required new owners of supermarkets to retain the existing workforce for at least ninety days (thereby giving unionized workers the chance to vote to retain their union).[302] Then, in an effort to gain leverage over future grocery store development, in 2006, LAANE helped to launch the Alliance for Healthy & Responsible Grocery Stores, assembling familiar partners—including AGENDA, CLUE, IDEPSCA, KIWA, the County Fed, SEIU, and UFCW—and environmental groups such as the Coalition for Clean Air. Noting the dearth of grocery stores in low-income communities of color, the Alliance sought to use the fact that "virtually every new supermarket must apply for a ... CUP" to advocate for a Grocery Reinvestment Act creating new CUP rules "requiring compliance with anti-redlining and food and job quality criteria," while also "urging major grocery chains to sign Community Benefits Agreements."[303] A key target of this proposal was British food giant, TESCO, the world's third-largest grocery chain, which in 2007 announced its plan to open 100 "Fresh & Easy" markets in Southern California—threatening to bring its low-cost, small-format (10,000 square feet) food stores to "communities chronically ignored by major grocery chains."[304] The markets, though boasting wages of $10 per hour, were nonunion and featured "self-checkout" scanners reducing the number of overall jobs. In response, the Alliance—citing broken promises by the major grocery chains to build thirty-three stores in South Los Angeles after the 1992 civil unrest[305]—urged TESCO to agree to a CBA for its flagship Hollywood market.[306] In the heat of the 2008 presidential race, the bid for a CBA drew support from Democratic candidates John Edwards and Barack Obama.[307] When TESCO refused to negotiate, the Alliance staged rallies at investor meetings and even delivered letters to Prince Andrew, Duke of York, who came to Los Angeles in February 2008 to christen TESCO's Compton store.[308] When TESCO did not budge, the Alliance convened a Blue Ribbon Commission that produced a report in the summer of 2008 advocating for higher job standards in Los Angeles's grocery industry.[309] Yet in the depths of the Great Recession, nearly all development screeched to a halt and the Alliance abandoned its TESCO campaign.

The Alliance did not abandon its effort to promote a version of the Grocery Reinvestment Act. After a CRA-commissioned 2008 study by Rodino Associates documented the public cost to the city of low job standards in the grocery industry and the impact of food deserts, the City Council Planning and Land Use Management Committee initiated hearings in 2009 to consider modifying the CUP process in connection with grocery store development to require evaluation of a proposed store's job and health impacts[310]—effectively extending a version of the Superstores Ordinance into the land use review process for all grocery stores. However, resistance by the grocery lobby combined with the defection of public health advocates—who feared that the proposed law would deter grocery development in communities that had suffered from no access to healthy food—led to the proposal's defeat in 2013.

The Grocery Reinvestment Act's demise coincided with the surprise reemergence of Wal-Mart—this time in Los Angeles's historic Chinatown northeast of rapidly gentrifying downtown. The February 24, 2012 announcement that Wal-Mart had secretly submitted applications for a TESCO-like small-format "neighborhood" market (thirty-three thousand square feet) in Chinatown—and that some permits had already been approved—caught LAANE and its allies off guard, forcing them to make a hard pivot toward beating back the renewed Wal-Mart threat. With Wal-Mart's lease secured in a senior housing and office building across the street from the upscale Orsini Apartment Homes on West Cesar Chavez Avenue,[311] the stage was set for another site fight—though this time labor groups started from the disadvantaged position of having to respond to what appeared to many to be a fait accompli.

Given how much organized labor had staked on keeping Wal-Mart out—and how little time there was for influencing the development process—the struggle over Chinatown escalated with ferocious intensity. On March 16, 2012, Councilman Ed Reyes, who represented the area of the proposed Wal-Mart market, introduced a motion to consider an Interim Control Ordinance to ban large chain stores from opening retail outlets in Chinatown.[312] However, minutes before the full City Council voted to unanimously consider the ban on March 23—which would have tolled all approval processes—an official from the Department of Building

Figure 5.8 Protests against Chinatown Wal-Mart. *Source*: Joe Klamar/AFP/Getty Images (June 30, 2012).

and Safety stated that Wal-Mart had secured the necessary building permits the day before.[313] LAANE and the Asian Pacific American Labor Alliance (APALA) appealed the permits, suing the Department of Building and Safety for failing to properly notify the public of Wal-Mart's application, and thousands marched to protest the Chinatown store.[314] Yet even as Reyes's proposed ban made its way through the policy process, Wal-Mart pressed ahead with construction, successfully defeating a motion by APALA for a temporary restraining order to halt it.[315] When the Chinatown ban failed to muster sufficient City Council votes to pass and a court again refused to block construction,[316] LAANE and APALA were forced back to pursuing their administrative appeal of Wal-Mart building permits for a project already well underway.

Despite large-scale protests and ongoing legal skirmishes, Wal-Mart raced ahead, officially opening its Chinatown Neighborhood Market in September 2013.[317] Although LAANE vowed to carry on the unfinished business of the permit appeal, the point was effectively moot. Revealing a tenacity powered by vast resources, a decade after its loss in Inglewood, Wal-Mart had squeezed its way into the L.A. grocery market. Yet it would—ironically—be a short-lived victory, undone not by labor's resistance, but by the merciless logic of cutthroat competition that Wal-Mart itself had pioneered. In January 2016, with Amazon's online business model decimating its brick-and-mortar adversaries, Wal-Mart announced it was shuttering over 269 stores worldwide—among them its lone and long-sought-after Los Angeles store.[318]

Figure 5.9 L.A. Chinatown Wal-Mart. *Source*: Sterling Davis (2013).

Analysis

This part evaluates how law shaped the development and outcome of the community–labor challenge to Wal-Mart in Los Angeles. It first analyzes the design and implementation of the big-box law reform campaign as a coordinated political-legal effort targeting local government. It then assesses the lawyers' roles in the Inglewood site fight, focusing attention on how the deployment of multifaceted legal tactics and the coordination of legal experts from different practice sites contributed to the campaign's success—while simultaneously raising complex issues of client and community accountability.

Multi-Level Legal Advocacy

The Location of Legal Reform: Bottom-Up

The anti-Wal-Mart campaign reinforced the importance of municipal government as a site of labor struggle and policy reform. The campaign pursued law reform from the "bottom up": deploying legal and organizing techniques to stop the Inglewood Wal-Mart development in a one-off site fight and then, building on the momentum from that victory, to craft citywide policy in the form of the Superstores Ordinance. The city provided the tools of local struggle—in the form of leverage gained through the land use review process—and was itself the ultimate target of policy reform.

The local nature of the campaign resulted, in part, from Wal-Mart's own municipal strategy of identifying struggling cities in need of revenue, where organized labor was weak, and then dangling the prospect of increased taxes and jobs in exchange for permission to operate. Wal-Mart started on the periphery, targeting outlying, more conservative, cities in the complex jurisdictional tapestry of the greater L.A. area. Playing cities off of each other in the scramble for tax revenues, Wal-Mart could encircle the urban core with Supercenters arrayed like advanced sentinels and then systemically assail the big city as the last bastion of labor power. It was precisely this strategy that led Wal-Mart to focus on Inglewood as a vulnerable—and geographically well-positioned—site for entry: an opening wedge that could pierce labor's defenses by creating a Supercenter in the heart of Los Angeles, but not technically in the city proper.

Labor's local response was therefore driven by the need to meet Wal-Mart on its own terms. It also reflected the distinct political opportunity structure facing anti-Wal-Mart labor activists, who could not rely on the conservative federal government as a source of legal protection against the degradation of labor standards that Wal-Mart represented.[319] The Inglewood site fight, from that perspective, was bottom-up in a reactive sense: the product of a larger set of political constraints that forced labor into the defensive posture of protecting progressive islands of relative labor strength, like Los Angeles, from perpetual assault.

Yet it would be inaccurate to suggest that the site fight was only defensive. To the contrary, it represented labor's determination to turn weakness into strength—part of a broader effort to reimagine the city as a site of opportunity. This effort included the UFCW's city-level organizing to protect the unionized grocery sector and LAANE's drive to promote a citywide economic impact policy as a critical tool of the CBA movement, which was occurring simultaneously and in coordinated fashion. Moreover, the local orientation of the site fight presented distinct advantages to organized labor and its allies. The site fight activated labor's traditional research and organizing strengths, and enabled partnerships with community organizations that deepened the community–labor ties that labor leaders believed were essential to the union movement's ultimate resurgence. Together, community and labor coalition partners advanced a local policy strategy built on the CBA model. In this model, the coalition used political capital gained from site-specific victories to craft a local policy codifying community values and then mobilized the new policy to support sustained community organizing. The bottom-up nature of the Inglewood site fight thus represented a deliberate approach to local law reform that asserted policy change should follow the creation of facts on the ground and that policy constructed by affected communities was the only way to effectively respond to their concerns. In this spirit, the Superstores Ordinance that resulted from the Inglewood mobilization succeeded in erecting a structure for regulating big-box stores that could be monitored and enforced by community and labor activists close to the action.

The Nature of Legal Reform: Soft Law

In addition to its bottom-up structure, the Superstores Ordinance was an example of "soft" law that instead of imposing strict regulatory standards on Wal-Mart or barring it outright, set up a framework for assessing economic impacts as a starting point for discussions about how to maximize the benefits of big-box retail while minimizing its costs.[320] As such, the ordinance required that Wal-Mart opponents gather evidence demonstrating the costs of big-box retail in particular communities and offer proposals to mitigate such costs. This meant that community groups would have to monitor proposed developments and provide rigorous empirical documentation of potential impacts. The impact analysis process was unlikely to completely block a big-box project because the ordinance permitted project approval so long as any adverse material impacts were mitigated. Nevertheless, the process required bargaining between Wal-Mart and labor and community stakeholders over the terms of entry.

When enacted, labor imagined that this bargaining might lead to a CBA, like the ones LAANE entered into with publicly subsidized private developers,[321] which would include contractual provisions mandating specific mitigation efforts by Wal-Mart—such as requiring Wal-Mart to pay a living wage and provide a baseline threshold of health benefits in order to gain city approval. This highlights the important role that the CBA tool had come to play in labor's overall strategy, which was reflected in its pursuit of a CBA with TESCO and its promotion of a Grocery Reinvestment Act that would have further expanded the framework for CBA negotiation.

The emphasis on stakeholder negotiation and the reliance on community participation to press for higher labor standards at Wal-Mart raised questions about the ultimate political effectiveness of information-forcing soft laws like the Superstores Ordinance. LAANE justified its support of the ordinance on the grounds that it would avoid unnecessary litigation over its terms—and this held true. Yet the political goal of enhancing labor rights could also have been advanced through either a complete ban, which survived legal challenge in the Turlock case, or a law tying big-box approval directly to living wage requirements, as was tried in Chicago. LAANE's position was that the economic impact approach was superior to these other alternatives, which were politically riskier since they were more likely to invite costly challenges and did not necessarily provide better outcomes for workers given that the Superstores Ordinance would either deter Wal-Mart entry (and thus operate like a complete ban) or result in bargained-for labor improvements (and thus operate like a living wage requirement). Moreover, it was not self-evident that workers in every case were necessarily better off without Wal-Mart and thus the Superstores Ordinance allowed for the possibility of a win-win situation with Wal-Mart permitted to provide low-cost goods and increase jobs in a specific community, but on terms that were acceptable to a wide range of labor and community actors. However, as in the CBA campaign, the risk of a bargaining approach was that a company like Wal-Mart could use its superior power to negotiate a relatively lenient set of obligations in exchange for community support.

Even though that risk was real, one major advantage of the Superstores Ordinance was that it provided a politically legitimate mechanism for imposing stricter standards on Wal-Mart, which distinguished it from the ad hoc CBA approach that relied on leveraging legal mechanisms—like environmental review—that were not designed to facilitate bargaining over economic issues. In this sense, the ordinance provided a stronger legal framework within which to advocate revisions to Wal-Mart economic policies. As a formalistic matter, the economic impact analysis process envisioned under the ordinance ultimately turned on the city's evaluation of competing impact reports—with Wal-Mart consultants touting the community benefits of a Supercenter and labor consultants criticizing the harms. How these reports would be interpreted by city decision-makers and what mitigation requirements were ultimately imposed on Wal-Mart would be a function of political wrangling putting labor's political strength to the test. From a regulatory perspective, the effectiveness of the economic impact analysis process in placing constraints on Supercenter development was contingent on organized labor's ability to sustain political power and mobilize on a case-by-case basis. That the ordinance required ongoing mobilization in order to be an effective check on Wal-Mart's development plans was consistent with labor's larger goal of promoting laws that promised to reinforce organizing.[322]

The Application of Legal Reform: Strategies of Diffusion

By focusing on enacting Superstores Ordinances in Inglewood and Los Angeles, labor activists were able to calibrate strategy based on local political dynamics and adapt policies to local conditions. This approach fed into a broader effort, which involved constructing a set of local policies that forced Wal-Mart to seek public approval for its economic impacts and diffusing those policies on a city-by-city basis in order to establish wide geographic areas where big-box development was accountable to community and labor stakeholders. A key issue raised by this bottom-up approach was labor's capacity to replicate and extend victories without a central means of coordination and given the distinct political dynamics presented by different cities. In addition, as the conflict over TESCO and the Chinatown Wal-Mart revealed, successful policy diffusion often invited a corporate response that circumvented its main thrust and therefore required advanced thinking to limit corporate opportunities for getting around hard-won policy gains.

After Inglewood, a range of formal and informal mechanisms developed to draw attention to big-box mobilizations and foster greater coordination.[323] Lawyers active in the Inglewood campaign developed expertise that positioned them as valuable resources for national groups. Margo Feinberg, in particular, served as a key node of information exchange, giving free advice to community–labor groups around the country who called about drafting big-box ordinances.[324] In addition, labor groups played a critical role in devising ordinances and deliberately exporting them to new locations. LAANE became a key actor in promoting and coordinating anti-Wal-Mart campaigns, producing a resource guide that distilled the collective experiences of community–labor groups around the country and outlined legal and organizing responses to Wal-Mart development.[325] After launching in 2006, the Partnership for Working Families, a statewide network that grew out of the CBA movement, began supporting big-box activism in fifteen cities and sought to double the number of cities with active Wal-Mart campaigns.[326] The goal of these efforts was to enact local policies while changing political discourse to highlight the power of local governments to promote labor standards.

Unions themselves were active participants in the strategic diffusion of Wal-Mart reforms. The UFCW-backed Wakeupwalmart.com and SEIU-sponsored Walmartwatch.com were web-based platforms that provided information about ongoing site fights and legislative proposals, while offering communities step-by-step guides to resist Wal-Mart developments. At the state level, labor groups launched efforts to pass "fair share" laws to force Wal-Mart to increase health care benefits for employees or pay into a state health care fund, though these stalled after Wal-Mart successfully challenged the Maryland Fair Share Health Care Fund Act on the ground that it was preempted by federal employee benefits law.[327] Yet the Maryland case only served to underscore the high-stakes political and legal activism that surrounded Wal-Mart in the post-Inglewood period. While labor and community groups were not able to stop Wal-Mart Supercenter development, they did succeed in placing some limits on its pace, scope, and density.

Tactical Pragmatism

In contrast to the conventional focus on litigation as the movement lawyer's main weapon, the Inglewood case revealed how the tools lawyers used to support political mobilization varied in relation to the type of challenge asserted. Specifically, while the Inglewood lawyers deployed traditional tactics (litigation and legal advising) in an attempt to defeat the Wal-Mart initiative and spur ongoing mobilization, they also incorporated nontraditional techniques (organizing, lobbying, and publicity) as part of a broader advocacy repertoire to advance labor policy goals.[328]

Traditional Advocacy in the Service of Mobilization

In the Inglewood campaign, litigation was deployed as one type of political resource used to advance strategic ends. A legal challenge was undertaken in the context of a broader political strategy in which activists viewed the lawsuit as complementing their get-out-the-vote drive. Although coalition leaders believed the lawsuit had an outside chance of stopping Measure 04-A, they were more realistically focused on using the suit to have a public relations and organizing impact, rather than winning a definitive adjudication of rights. From this perspective, the lawsuit sought to undermine the ordinance's legal legitimacy in the public eye in order to persuade Inglewood voters to oppose Measure 04-A at the ballot box. In this sense, the use of litigation in the Inglewood campaign was politically pragmatic—not viewed as an end in itself, but rather as a way to enhance and supplement movement activity.[329]

In addition, the role of lawyers in helping the UFCW and LAANE to understand and intervene in the local land use planning process was critical to labor's push for big-box reform—and highlighted another way in which lawyering facilitated community mobilization. In organizing against big-box development, community-labor coalitions made political demands on local governments to either block Wal-Mart or condition its development on the promise of benefits for low-income communities. As in the CBA context, these coalitions took advantage of the legal rights to participate in local political decision-making, particularly those embedded in the land use and environmental review process, which permitted public input into Supercenter approval. In this process, lawyers advised coalition leaders to help identify and navigate routes of legal participation, through which coalitions could exercise their rights to advocate against land use and environmental clearance. The leverage afforded by these participation rights was the threat of disruption, which could be actualized by pressuring decision-makers to deny public approval or suing to block developments on the basis of faulty public procedures.

In Inglewood, legal knowledge of the land use process was key to the coalition's campaign against Wal-Mart. First, LAANE's experience working with David Pettit and other lawyers to negotiate CBAs equipped it with a deep understanding of how crucial land use approvals could be as leverage points in negotiations over development conditions. Accordingly, at the outset of the Inglewood campaign, the coalition focused on amending land use laws to ban big-box development as a way of derailing the proposed Supercenter development. Second, when Wal-Mart placed Measure 04-A on the ballot, Jan Chatten-Brown advised coalition members that the initiative constituted a circumvention of their public participation rights. The legal and organizing efforts that followed emphasized the deprivation of public input as both a legal violation and a political power grab. Finally, with Margo Feinberg's assistance, the coalition revised the land use approval process in the Superstores Ordinance to make a Superstore CUP contingent on a favorable economic impact finding. Thus, the community–labor coalition was able to use knowledge of the land use legal system to strengthen community participation rights in the context of Wal-Mart development.

Legal expertise on land use issues continued to be critical to labor's Wal-Mart agenda going forward, as was evident in subsequent efforts to block Supercenter land use approvals and amend local land use laws to limit big-box development in other cities. In Los Angeles, the Grocery Reinvestment Act sought to amend the CUP process to mitigate food deserts and promote job quality in connection with all grocery store sitings, while LAANE's fight against the Chinatown Wal-Mart occurred entirely within the administrative system for conferring and appealing land use and building permits.

The Inglewood campaign and the enactment of big-box ordinances bolstered the Los Angeles labor movement in important ways. In particular, the absence of a Supercenter framed subsequent negotiations over union contracts in the grocery sector, which benefited from the protection against Wal-Mart that the Superstores Ordinances afforded.[330] The UFCW used its success against Wal-Mart to reverse the two-tier wage and benefit system imposed after the 2004 strike. Upon signing a deal with regional chain Stater Bros. to eliminate two-tier benefits,[331] the UFCW struck against Albertsons,[332] which led to a 2007 master agreement with Albertsons, Vons, and Ralphs that raised wages and benefits for most workers and rescinded the detested two-tier system.[333] It was in support of this effort that LAANE launched the Alliance for Healthy & Responsible Grocery Stores, which sponsored a review of the grocery industry calling for the provision of health care benefits for grocery workers, the elimination of the two-tier wage and benefits system, the use of city incentives for groceries with good labor records, and the creation of city policy to prevent grocery stores from redlining low-income communities.[334]

Nontraditional Advocacy in the Service of Legal Reform

To the extent that the Wal-Mart campaign centered on reforming city policy to demand higher standards from the company, it invoked an alternative set of advocacy skills focused on drafting ordinances, coordinating public relations, and mobilizing grassroots support. Margo Feinberg, in particular, was heavily involved in drafting the economic impact ordinance, both in Los Angeles and Inglewood, and contributed to the lobbying efforts to secure its passage. In addition, she performed a number of other campaign tasks, such as negotiating with city council members over the ordinances' terms, coordinating the Inglewood legal team in preparation for its challenge to Measure 04-A, and supporting the Inglewood public relations effort by enlisting legal opinions from high-profile lawyers like the California attorney general. The UFCW's John Grant also made important contributions outside of traditional advocacy, including preparing community members to testify at government hearings and orchestrating the union's get-out-the-vote drive. Madeline Janis, LAANE's director, helped to plan and implement other aspects of the comprehensive campaign, including designing grassroots strategy, fundraising for the legal and organizing efforts, and providing input on the structure of the Superstores Ordinances.

Networked Expertise

The Inglewood case was also notable for its use of a networked team of multiple lawyers to advance its anti-big-box strategy. Although Jan Chatten-Brown was counsel of record in the litigation against Measure 04-A, the campaign was also supported by the ordinance drafting of Margo Feinberg, the policy expertise of John Grant and Madeline Janis, and the land use and environmental legal support of David Pettit and Sean Hecht. This arrangement was notable for connecting lawyers across distinctive practice sites and ideological commitments.

Practice Sites

One distinctive feature of the Inglewood site fight legal team was that many of its key members came from private law firms and law schools, rather than the nonprofit legal sector. This configuration reflected the professional distribution of relevant legal expertise. Labor lawyers were concentrated in private firms serving as outside counsel on a fee-for-service basis to local unions. Thus, to the degree that labor law expertise in the grocery sector was needed, Feinberg's law firm was one of only a handful of viable options. In addition, because land use planning and election law were not topics strongly associated with nonprofit legal groups, LAANE ventured outside of the nonprofit community to find lawyers with the right skills to litigate the ballot initiative. Although nonprofit environmental law groups might have been able to contribute the relevant legal expertise, the politically sensitive nature of the case (using land use law to challenge Wal-Mart on economic impact grounds) and the need to invest a relatively large amount of legal resources within a small time frame cut against their involvement. Further, because the campaign targeted a major corporation, it was outside the ambit of big-firm pro bono, which generally avoided legal challenges to corporate clients.[335] Accordingly, LAANE settled on a fee-for-service arrangement with a small public interest firm, Chatten-Brown & Associates, willing to take on the case for less than market rate because of the firm's political mission and personal ties to the activists involved in the campaign. LAANE did receive pro bono counsel from Pettit, but his role as a partner in a boutique litigation firm with a progressive political orientation gave him greater flexibility in dictating the nature of his pro bono representation. The other members of the legal team, Sean Hecht and Erwin Chemerinsky, were enlisted both because of their relative expertise and because it was thought that they would lend academic legitimacy to the site fight.

Professional Interdisciplinarity and Interlocking Motivation

The second noteworthy feature of the legal team was its interdisciplinary character. Although Inglewood was, at bottom, a labor rights campaign, its focus on leveraging labor reform through local land use planning, coupled with the unique nature of Wal-Mart's invocation of the initiative process, meant that land use and environmental lawyers were enlisted in the service of labor movement objectives. Thus, labor's local strategy drove the UFCW and LAANE to cast their search for legal assistance broadly, blurring the lines between traditional labor law on the one hand, and land use and environmental law on the other—and bringing together lawyers from labor and environmental movements often at odds over perceived trade-offs between promoting job-producing development and preserving the environment. Like the LAX CBA campaign, the Inglewood site fight thus provided a chance to develop a concrete, if still tentative, labor-environmental alliance.

The interdisciplinary nature of the legal team was also reflected in the different motivations that brought each lawyer to the campaign. Although all of the lawyers involved contributed to the ultimate union-defined goal of blocking Wal-Mart to advance labor standards, the lawyers each approached the engagement with unique notions of the "cause."[336] Feinberg and Grant, as labor lawyers, pursued the Wal-Mart case from the standpoint of promoting labor movement goals. However, the other lawyers viewed their involvement through different lenses. For Chatten-Brown, though her firm was on retainer, financial gain was not the prime motivator, given that she was charging LAANE and CBI a reduced rate. Instead, she accepted the Inglewood case as a way of challenging what she viewed as an instance of bad land use planning on behalf of a company that she held in low regard from an environmental perspective.[337] For Pettit, also a land use attorney, the cause was framed in terms of promoting community participation though the framework of land use planning.[338]

Similarly, for Sean Hecht, the UCLA environmental law professor on the legal team, the incentive to get involved was partly personal and partly political. On the one hand, he viewed Inglewood as a compelling case at the intersection of three fields of personal interest: constitutional, land use, and election law.[339] In addition, as a practicing lawyer who had recently moved into an academic setting, he was motivated by the opportunity of reconnecting with the "real world" of practice, particularly in the context of what he viewed as a potential "test case" for land use and environmental law in California.[340] He also got involved based on his policy preferences. As an environmental lawyer, Hecht felt passionately about the integrity of responsible land use planning as a feature of good governance and believed that it was wrong for Wal-Mart to subvert CEQA through initiative, thus carving a huge loophole through the legal framework of environmental review.[341] In this sense, he wanted to help keep Wal-Mart out of Inglewood as a way to promote sound environmental policy.

While the motivations of the lawyers in the Inglewood case coalesced around the goal of supporting the site fight, their distinct conceptions of the cause underlined the challenge of sustaining interdisciplinary coalitions over time—especially in the face of Wal-Mart's deliberate efforts to pull them apart. Indeed, around the country, as Wal-Mart invested in strategies to placate workers to reduce the appeal of unionization,[342] the company was also working to wedge off different factions of the anti-Wal-Mart coalition. Its grant-making to African American civil rights organizations was well known, but Wal-Mart also sought to direct its public relations campaign toward mollifying other critics.[343] For instance, in 2006, Wal-Mart announced an initiative to build environmentally friendly "green" stores,[344] while also providing grants and technical support to small businesses threatened by the Supercenter format.[345] These efforts to cleave off anti-big-box coalition members sought to exploit the different motivations of environmentalists and community groups opposing Wal-Mart in the hope that they would abandon the fight in the face of evidence that the company was making strides toward environmental sustainability and smart growth.

Multi-Tier Accountability

The multiplicity of roles played by lawyers on the anti-Wal-Mart legal team combined with the fluid nature of the activist coalition to raise unique issues of accountability—both the lawyers' accountability to the clients and the clients' accountability to the broader community.

Lawyer–Client

In the Inglewood context, the nature of the client group and the approach of the lawyers diminished traditional concerns about the disempowering impact of legal expertise on client mobilization. On the client end, LAANE, in particular, was a relatively powerful community organization, drawing political clout and resources from its labor affiliation, and governed by politically savvy and influential leaders. LAANE's executive director, Madeline Janis, was an attorney with significant litigation and policy experience, and a CRA commissioner with strong connections to local political officials. As in CBA negotiations, the strength and coherence of LAANE's leadership structure tended to insulate it from undue influence from outside counsel; moreover, LAANE operated as a sophisticated consumer of legal services, selecting lawyers based on how well they advanced LAANE's objectives. In making this selection, LAANE representatives sought out the best technical lawyers for the specific legal tasks, which meant that they evaluated outside counsel based on conventional metrics of legal expertise and capacity—they did not look for lawyers to undertake organizing functions, which they viewed as appropriately kept within LAANE's purview. In this way, the existence of a strong community organization reduced the risk of lawyer domination.

For their part, the lawyers who worked on the campaign approached their engagement with LAANE and CBI from a perspective that mitigated concerns about client autonomy. For one, they were generally private sector lawyers retained by the clients to achieve a well-specified result. Their role conception, informed by their position in the market, emphasized the importance of client-centeredness in representation. The Chatten-Brown & Associates lawyers were specifically brought into the case because of their legal expertise in challenging the ballot initiative, rather than because of their ideological allegiance to the labor movement. From this perspective, the lawyers looked like conventional outside counsel retained to assist an organizational client with a discrete objective (the mirror image, indeed, of the relationship between Wal-Mart and its outside law firm). In addition, the cross-cutting nature of the representation—in which environmental and land use lawyers were enlisted to advance a labor organizing campaign—operated to dampen concerns about lawyers placing cause above client interests.[346]

David Pettit, the small firm lawyer retained by LAANE to be part of the legal team, explicitly adopted what he termed the "David Binder method" of client representation,[347] referring to his UCLA School of Law professor and one of the founders of clinical legal education—famous for his seminal text in client counseling that advocated a "client-centered" approach emphasizing the need to protect client autonomy in all aspects of representation.[348] Thus, Pettit approached his ongoing relationship with LAANE from a very deferential counseling perspective. In any given campaign, he talked to LAANE members and leaders about their short- and long-term objectives—paying close attention to whether LAANE was trying to develop a relationship with city officials in which less adversarial tactics would be appropriate or if the case was a one-shot deal where litigation would be more effective.[349] Feinberg approached her role as coalition lawyer from a similar perspective. Particularly when it came to drafting the Superstores Ordinances, she listened to what coalition members emphasized as their policy interests and then produced multiple drafts based on their input, leaving it to the members to provide feedback for additional changes and to accept the version they believed best served their ultimate purposes.[350]

The conventional nature of the lawyer–client relationship nonetheless raised its own accountability questions. Even within the confines of the lawyer–client relationship as constructed by the parties, the potential for conflicts was ripe.[351] First, there were complexities involved in representing both a multi-organizational coalition (CBI) and the lead organizing group (LAANE) within the same case. Group representation raises difficult questions about who speaks for the group,[352] but here those questions were exacerbated to the degree that CBI itself was an amalgam of several groups that operated with a range of organizational formality and endowed with very different resources. On the one hand, CBI was composed of representatives from LAANE and the UFCW, who brought critical financial and organizational resources; on the other, CBI contained more loosely constituted resident and faith-based groups that lent credibility and authenticity, but did not have the same decision-making clout. This combination created inherent questions of governance and authority to make decisions on behalf of the entire coalition—made more difficult by the fact that LAANE was also named as a separate party to the litigation and was paying for the legal representation.[353] Thus, during the course of the lawsuit, the Chatten-Brown & Associates lawyers coordinated primarily with LAANE representatives—Madeline Janis at the beginning and then Lizette Hernandez and Tracy Gray-Barkan—as the spokespersons for the broader group.[354] This arrangement proceeded by necessity, with LAANE serving as the nodal point and thus well-situated to assimilate the views of coalition members and present a unified position to the lawyers. However, the lack of formal specification of any type of governance structure within the coalition format complicated the lines of client communication.

This complexity was apparent in the ways that the other members of the legal team perceived the "clients" to whom they owed allegiance. Pettit viewed himself as LAANE's lawyer and dealt with Janis as the ultimate decision-maker.[355] John Grant viewed his role less as legal counsel than as an officer of the UFCW accountable to its membership (and leaders), making decisions based on how campaign actions would impact the broader labor movement. Feinberg was on retainer with the UFCW and communicated with its president, Rick Icaza, and John Grant; she was also on retainer with LAANE, where she dealt primarily with Janis. When conflicts arose, she let the organizations work them out and then pursued the commonly agreed upon strategy.[356] Hecht was working in his personal capacity in an advisory role; thus, he did not have a letter of engagement with any specific client.[357]

Client–Community

The multiple and intersecting strands of lawyer–client relationships mapped onto broader divisions between clients and the "community," highlighting challenges to lawyers' efforts to be accountable to the community at large, rather than a particular interest group within it. Indeed, Wal-Mart labor campaigns generally exposed rifts between class- and race-based conceptions of community—rifts that Wal-Mart deliberately exploited as a way to weaken labor opposition to its Supercenter plans. Thus, in Inglewood, Wal-Mart was able to drive a wedge between the labor-backed CBI and traditional African American groups like the Urban League and NAACP by playing upon historical antagonisms. This strategy, replicated in other communities across the country,[358] made it more difficult for lawyers to claim they were representing working-class communities of color in their fight against Wal-Mart, rather than choosing sides in an intra-community dispute over labor versus racial solidarity.

In Inglewood, there were also divisions between residents based on their identification as consumers to be benefited by Wal-Mart or workers to be harmed. And there were a number of potential conflicts among different community constituencies that would be implicated by any Wal-Mart decision to enter the Los Angeles market, thus triggering intense negotiations over what community benefits Wal-Mart would have to provide to gain city approval. As in the CBA context, organized labor's interests were not completely aligned with those of small business owners, environmentalists, and neighborhood organizations. Different types of splits were plausible. On the one hand, community and environmental groups could be more inclined to want to prevent big-box development at all cost, while labor endorsed entry conditioned on Wal-Mart commitments to provide living wage jobs to local residents. On the other hand, labor might seek to resist a Supercenter's degradation of labor standards while other groups welcomed Wal-Mart's promise of local jobs or environmentally conscious design. Moreover, even if all groups were generally supportive of approving Supercenter development with conditions, it was not clear ex ante how Wal-Mart could allocate its resources to mitigate community impacts in a way that would be satisfactory to all stakeholders. There was an upper limit on the amount of money Wal-Mart would commit before a project became cost prohibitive. Should those resources go to enhancing wages, supporting local businesses, providing affordable housing for workers, or building green stores to mitigate energy consumption?

Finally, the interests of labor were not monolithic and even among the core groups of the L.A. labor alliance, there were differences in approach and emphasis. The UFCW, given its mandate, focused on electoral and policy strategies to limit Wal-Mart's threat to union density in the grocery industry, while LAANE used grassroots organizing and coalition building to address wider community concerns about health, housing, and the environment. However, the two groups were intentional about sustaining collaboration over time, and the UFCW understood that community support was essential to its long-term interest in grocery worker unionization—illustrated by the union's decision to send two members to join

LAANE to help coordinate community organizing and training during the Alliance for Healthy & Responsible Grocery Stores campaign.

While the UFCW–LAANE alliance achieved a major victory in Inglewood, even its supporters acknowledged that the site fight's reliance on reactive, case-by-case labor organizing and legal advocacy consumed a great deal of time and resources. Particularly in the greater L.A. area, where the large number of separate jurisdictions gave Wal-Mart many potential targets, the site fight strategy could be easily stretched too thin—or circumvented altogether, as Wal-Mart's stealth Chinatown store revealed. Labor's focus on city ordinances as a shield against Supercenter development responded to the limitations of the site fight, but enacting ordinances on a city-by-city basis was also resource-intensive and politically challenging. Moreover, it was not clear whether labor's effort to promote local policy reform would, in the long term, augment its organizing power or if labor leaders were falling into the same trap of privileging legal reform over sustained collective action that critics claimed caused the decline of the movement in the past century.

Despite these lingering concerns, labor's victory in Inglewood produced important benefits—both symbolic and real—for the labor movement. As a symbol of labor's ability to battle Wal-Mart on its own terms, Inglewood provided a counter-narrative to the dominant story of labor's decline and did some damage (however small) to Wal-Mart's aura of impregnability. The publicity from the site fight galvanized attention from labor and community activists across the country, feeding into new campaigns and raising the visibility of groups like LAANE, which assumed a prominent national role in disseminating organizing models and supporting anti-big-box drives. The Inglewood fight also highlighted the potential of activist city government in which labor and community stakeholders played important parts in shaping local development decisions. But the win in Inglewood was not merely symbolic. It did, in fact, block Wal-Mart's entrance into Los Angeles and strengthen the UFCW's hand in its subsequent round of negotiations against the big grocery store chains. The Inglewood story therefore mattered not just as an allegory of labor smiting the mighty Wal-Mart foe, but as a real-world tale of how local advocacy could recalibrate the legal playing field in ways that enhanced worker power.

6

Truck Drivers

Challenging Misclassification

Overview

This chapter examines the monumental campaign to raise labor and environmental standards in the trucking industry at the Los Angeles and Long Beach ports. Building on the blue-green coalition launched in the CBA and big-box contexts—and incorporating central lessons from a decade of community–labor organizing in Los Angeles—the clean trucks campaign emerged as a fight over air quality but ultimately advanced as a local policy struggle over working conditions for roughly sixteen thousand short-haul, or "drayage," port truck drivers. For these drivers, the central problem was their classification—and misclassification—as independent contractors, which forced them to bear all the costs of operation and precluded them from union organizing. Solving that problem—restoring drivers to the baseline of being organizable as employees—was a central goal of the labor movement, which it pursued by pressing the ports, as public entities, to enact new rules to transform the port trucking industry.

The opportunity to challenge driver misclassification came from outside of the labor field, in a seminal environmental lawsuit against expansion of the Port of Los Angeles, which presented a moment of labor-environmental interest convergence and provided the justification for the campaign's legal strategy: Because independent truck drivers could not afford to acquire and maintain clean fuel trucks, the port had a market-based interest in making trucking companies internalize their labor costs to promote sustainable emission reductions and stop environmental litigation. The blue-green coalition that emerged thus wove environmental compliance into a tapestry of labor reform: leveraging the power of environmental litigation to create space for policy negotiation, linking clean trucks to employee conversion, and nesting employee conversion in a local ordinance predicated on the power of the port to define the terms of entry for trucking companies through concession agreements. The campaign—led by LAANE, the Teamsters union, and

NRDC—leveraged this power to win passage of the landmark 2008 Clean Truck Program, which committed trucking companies seeking to enter the Port of Los Angeles to a double conversion: of dirty to clean fuel trucks (thus reducing pollution) and of independent contractor to employee drivers (thus enabling unionization). However, the program's labor centerpiece—employee conversion—was invalidated by an industry preemption lawsuit that ultimately went to the U.S. Supreme Court. As a result, the policy gains from a blue-green campaign built on mutual interest were split apart and reallocated, resulting in environmental victory but labor setback. Why the coalition won the local policy battle but lost in court—and how the labor movement responded to this legal setback through an innovative strategy to maneuver around preemption—are the central questions this chapter explores.

Law in the Development of the Ports

The Port of Los Angeles sits in the San Pedro Bay, directly adjacent to the Port of Long Beach to the east. The bay itself is tucked under the Palos Verdes Peninsula, which juts out prominently south of Santa Monica. The ports are located in distinct municipalities, subjecting them to different rules and political pressures—and

Figure 6.1 Aerial view of the Ports of Los Angeles and Long Beach. *Source*: Scott Cummings (2018).

making them competitors for cargo business. However, as a functional matter, they form an integrated unit: sharing the same land mass, benefiting from the same infrastructure, and connecting to a unified transportation system of roads and rail.[1] Individually, the Ports of Los Angeles and Long Beach are the first and second largest, respectively, in the United States; together they form one of the largest port complexes in the world.[2]

The geography of the ports, both physical and man-made, has long been a central feature in the struggle over their impact and control. As law contributed to the growth of the port complex, it also distributed the costs and benefits of that growth unequally—enabling some communities to escape the worst impacts, while appropriating others in the project of expanding global trade. This project resulted in transportation and land use decisions that contributed to segregation and environmental degradation in surrounding communities, while also creating winners and losers among workers.

Local Power: Annexation and Autonomy

The history of the ports' legal development can be broken into three phases. In the first, from the mid-1880s through the 1920s, law was used to appropriate the San Pedro harbor—created by and beholden to outside capital—to the project of city building.[3] As U.S. annexation of California and the Gold Rush brought settlers streaming west,[4] the need for transportation infrastructure grew, increasing the economic value of the harbor, which new entrepreneurs struggled to control. Delaware transplant Phineas Banning gained an early advantage by establishing a staging business,[5] and then a railroad line running from Los Angeles to land he purchased north of the harbor, which he named Wilmington.[6] To integrate Los Angeles into the emerging national marketplace, Banning's rail line was sold to the powerful Southern Pacific[7]—part of a political compromise that connected Los Angeles to the transcontinental railroad, which was completed in 1876.[8] After the sale, the City of Los Angeles lacked legal control over the harbor asset, which lay sixteen miles to the south of downtown, within San Pedro and Wilmington,[9] and was still owned by the Southern Pacific.[10]

Recognizing that the harbor was key to municipal development—and eager to capture market share in the face of neighboring Long Beach's ambition to establish a rival port[11]—Los Angeles's business elites pressured the city to annex the port, which it did by first acquiring the unincorporated "shoestring district" from downtown to the harbor,[12] and then consolidating the non-charter cities of San Pedro and Wilmington (promising $10 million in harbor improvements) in 1909.[13] With the support of the local chamber of commerce, the Port of Los Angeles was established as an autonomous, self-financing (through shipping fees on cargo and entry) city agency with broad powers to build the infrastructure necessary to attract growing maritime trade and thereby facilitate Los Angeles's growth as an export-led manufacturing economy.[14] As the city's population grew tenfold between 1900 and 1930, and the discovery of oil and the beginning of Los Angeles's industrialization caused port commerce to shift toward exports, the Port of Los Angeles grew exponentially—becoming the largest on the West Coast.[15] The Port of Long Beach followed closely behind. Awash in "black gold" after the 1921 Signal Hill oil strike, Long Beach used its oil resources to finance massive infrastructure improvements and created its own harbor department in 1921.[16] Rebuffing overtures from Los Angeles to create a unified port district,[17] the Port of Long Beach quadrupled its trade volume by 1930,[18] thus establishing itself as a serious competitor to Los Angeles—causing both ports to ratchet up investment in an inter-jurisdictional competition to capture the shipping market.

Federal Power: Industrialization in the Shadow of Regulation

The second phase of the ports' development, from the Depression to the 1970s, was marked by the rise of the regulatory state and a working compromise among business elites, labor, and local communities to share the profits of industrial growth. The New Deal set the template for postwar expansion. Wartime industrial investment fueled a postwar manufacturing boom, particularly in Southern California, where manufacturing of aircraft and ships was retooled for the peacetime economy. Import tariffs reduced foreign competition and encouraged export-driven industrialization, in which the ports became key distribution centers. Federal regulation of transportation permitted the ports to negotiate favorable terms with shippers and carriers, which they could then reinvest in infrastructure development. Transportation regulation, coupled with newly minted federal labor laws, also gave unions power to negotiate a favorable share of growth for port workers. Those workers, particularly truck drivers, benefited from the postwar regime, while local communities—though increasingly under stress from oil production—had not yet incurred the blight of rapid port expansion. It was a fragile stability that rested on federally regulated industrial prosperity.

Port transportation was tightly controlled by an interlocking regulatory system governing the rates and routes of carriers: the ocean steamship companies,[19] railroad lines,[20] and trucking firms that moved cargo.[21] The key feature of this system was that it produced stable transportation patterns, controlled by federal agencies, that prevented shippers from negotiating single through rates and using the threat of moving cargo through other ports to negotiate lower prices for port services.[22] This allowed the Ports of Los Angeles and Long Beach to use their dominant market position to set relatively higher prices for cargo fees and port access,[23] which they could reinvest in expanding infrastructure that helped further promote regional industrialization.

Federal regulation also shaped labor relations for port workers. For these workers, the Depression exacerbated what had long been the painful reality of substandard and often inhumane working conditions.[24] Harbor railroads had been built using low-paid and sometimes forced labor, while maritime workers on ships and their longshore counterparts, who loaded and unloaded cargo on the docks, labored in dangerous settings and often for little pay.[25] The labor militancy of the 1930s—culminating in the 1935 passage of the NLRA, which established employee collective bargaining rights—began to challenge these conditions. Through a series of dramatic strikes, by the end of the 1930s, the International Longshore and Warehouse Union (ILWU) emerged as a powerful force at the ports.[26] During the same period, the Teamsters union organized a successful boycott of Southern California port trucking firms to unionize the regional trucking industry.[27] Building on the foundation of this agreement, the Teamsters became one of the most successful unions in the state (and also the nation), achieving dramatic union growth that helped increase trucker wages and benefits through the 1960s.[28]

This alignment, which lasted from World War II to the 1970s, marked a transitional moment. As the growth engine of trade shifted from city building to globalization, and the federal regulatory regime governing transportation and labor relations crumbled, the ports and some workers—specifically truckers—lost influence. Globalization, deregulation, and new transport technologies shifted power to global shipping firms, which were increasingly able to dictate financial terms to the ports and carriers. As the ports grew to meet demand for expanded facilities to accommodate rapidly increasing global trade, the ports' relationship with workers and local communities was once again recast—with new tensions emerging.

Global Power: The Logistics Revolution, Free Trade, and Deregulation

The third phase of port development, beginning in the 1970s, was powered by the expanding volume of global trade and its changing composition: from a balanced export-import flow to an import-dominated stream.[29] This transformation profoundly altered the role of the ports: from building the local economy to facilitating the global one.

The result was a growth ratchet. Rapidly expanding global trade and deregulation weakened port negotiating strength, as shippers of goods could drive a harder bargain by threatening to direct cargo to different West Coast ports. To maintain their advantage, the ports had to outcompete rivals—and each other—at the level of infrastructure and service. This required massive new investments, typically publicly financed, in port facilities and transportation networks. As port infrastructure was developed, it became more attractive for shippers; as more goods flowed through the ports, the transportation infrastructure had to be expanded to accommodate the increased volume; as infrastructure was built out, the harbor attracted even more shipping in an iterative cycle. Competition between Los Angeles and

Long Beach contributed to this growth pressure, which was no longer consistent with the interests of labor unions and surrounding communities.

This shift was the product of interlocking technological and legal change. The key technological change was the rise of containerization: the creation of shipping containers in standardized sizes (twenty-foot equivalent units, or TEUs) that could be locked in place and stacked on ships.[30] This allowed goods to be packed in containers at the point of origin and then shipped unaltered via an interconnected transport system to the destination. By enabling low-cost transportation over significant distances, containerization permitted shippers to outsource production to countries with lower labor standards, while also incentivizing ocean carriers to build larger post-Panamex ships (so named because they could not fit through the Panama Canal),[31] reducing per-trip costs and thus increasing revenues.[32] Containerization also facilitated "intermodalism" since containers could be easily transferred from one form (or modality) of transportation—steamships, trains, and trucks—to another.[33] Achieving the efficiencies of containerization, however, required the ports to make substantial upfront capital investments to create the necessary port facilities to accommodate megaships and enable intermodal exchange.

Containerization promoted, and was also a product of, rapidly expanding global trade routed through the ports. Despite the global recession in the mid-1970s, port traffic continued to grow geometrically, increasingly as a result of manufactured imports from the emerging markets of the Pacific Rim.[34] Still critical to regional

Figure 6.2 Post-Panamax container ship at Port of Los Angeles. *Source*: Scott Cummings (2013).

economic activity, with one estimate suggesting that more than two hundred thousand jobs depended on maritime trade,[35] the ports became increasingly geared toward accepting imports,[36] and routing them to delivery points deep within the national economy—and oftentimes beyond to Europe. This transformation of the ports into central links in the global supply chain was authorized and promoted by interrelated legal change.

Trade liberalization through multilateral agreements, particularly the General Agreement on Tariffs and Trade, and bilateral agreements with trading partners, significantly reduced the costs of imports to the United States and thus helped fuel the growth of export-driven economies, particularly those of China and the so-called East Asian Tigers.[37] Whereas in 1970, the United States still had a $3-billion trade surplus, by 1976, it had a deficit, with exported manufactured goods running increasingly behind imports beginning in 1983.[38] As Asia came to dominate the import market, the strategically positioned San Pedro ports reinvented themselves, becoming the gateway of this new trading regime.[39]

Intermodalism was also enabled by legal deregulation, which dismantled the federal rate and route control that had generated transportation industry stability and shared prosperity in the prior period. This had two important effects. First, deregulation of ocean steamshipping, rail, and trucking allowed individual transportation firms to set rates and routes, which permitted price competition and thus facilitated the entry of new low-cost firms into the transportation industry—particularly in the trucking sector because of the lower capital investments required.[40] Second, deregulation allowed transportation firms to set single door-to-door intermodal rates without incurring antitrust liability.[41] As a result, shippers (i.e., manufacturers and retailers that owned cargo) were able to negotiate through rates to provide door-to-door service on one bill of lading.[42] Because standardized rates were no longer required, ocean carriers could bargain directly with individual rail and trucking carriers for the best prices to reduce overall shipping costs.[43] Because ocean carriers dealt in such high container volume, they could exert downward price pressure on rail and trucking companies, which were forced to compete among themselves (and authorized to do so by deregulation) in order to be part of intermodal contacts. In addition, the ability to set door-to-door rates gave shippers greater power vis-à-vis the ports. By threatening to run their intermodal routes through other ports, shippers could negotiate more favorable port access fees and demand improvements to facilitate intermodal connections.

To maintain their dominance over container traffic, the Los Angeles and Long Beach ports were forced to respond to these changes by building the infrastructure needed for efficient intermodal transport. To achieve this, the San Pedro ports coordinated their first major joint project, in concert with the Southern Pacific Railroad (later Union Pacific, or UP): construction of a $50-million Intermodal Container Transfer Facility (ICTF), completed in 1986 to allow mass movement of containers from ships to off-dock rail lines.[44] Although the ICTF was designed to alleviate truck impacts at the ports by routing traffic to a massive facility with ample parking and faster loading service,[45] in its attempt to reduce port congestion, the ICTF introduced a new source of gridlock into the community: increasing drayage truck traffic on the freeways and surface streets coming to and from the ports. In addition, enhanced links to rail transport began to overtax the rail system itself. In response, Los Angeles and Long Beach created a joint powers authority in 1985 authorizing development of the Alameda Corridor project, a twenty-mile high-speed, elevated line from both ports connecting to the transcontinental railroad.[46] The Alameda Corridor rail, running through Wilmington (then north through Carson, Compton, Lynwood, Watts, South Gate, Huntington Park, and Vernon), was completed in 2002 with $2.4 billion in federal, state, and local financing.[47] The Alameda Corridor was one of several large-scale megaprojects coordinated between both ports to deal with massive projected increases in port traffic.[48] In the mid-1980s, both ports adopted the "2020 Plan" to upgrade and integrate maritime trade and land transport systems to deal with an anticipated 250% increase in tonnage.[49]

Although Long Beach eventually withdrew from the plan, both ports nonetheless completed nearly $4 billion in joint investments by 2000, with Long Beach focusing on land acquisition and redevelopment, and Los Angeles on dredging and the creation of new terminals and rail lines.[50] These investments correlated with growth. From 1990 to 2000, total TEUs increased by 130% in the Los Angeles port and by 188% in Long Beach.[51] By 2005, the Los Angeles–Long Beach port complex was the fifth largest in the world, with a combined fourteen million TEUs of traffic.[52] While the ports coordinated on megaprojects, they continued to compete on price and service to attract more tenants and cargo.[53] As Figure 6.3 shows, during the 1990s, both ports saw containerized cargo increase at roughly the same rate, with one port surging ahead and then the other. In 1995, Long Beach surpassed Los Angeles as the nation's biggest port,[54] only to see Los Angeles eke back ahead in 2000, handling 4.9 million TEUs to Long Beach's 4.6 million.[55]

Increasing global trade reduced the power of city governments to mobilize port growth for local benefit. Particularly as shippers could divert cargo to different ports, they gained more bargaining power to drive down rates and demand port amenities that permitted larger volume. The ports were forced to continuously invest in new infrastructure to maintain their advantage. This investment no longer fostered local industrial development as it had in the postwar period. To the contrary, Los Angeles and Long Beach found themselves increasingly under fiscal strain because of deindustrialization, which was now itself intrinsically linked to the ports. The political autonomy the ports had acquired to build the regional economy became an increasing liability, as port revenues were used to benefit the ports' global shipping clientele by continuously upgrading the intermodal system.[56]

As the dividends of export-led growth thus disappeared—and with it the job and tax benefits of local industrialization—the cities of Los Angeles and Long

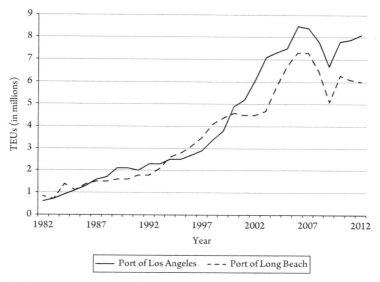

Figure 6.3 Ports of Los Angeles and Long Beach annual container trade in TEUs. *Source*: Ports of Los Angeles and Long Beach (2014).

Beach responded by reasserting greater legal control over the ports in an effort to claim greater local fiscal return. In the late 1980s and early 1990s, Los Angeles and Long Beach—suffering from manufacturer outsourcing and the end of Cold War–driven defense production—sought a share of port resources to infill dwindling city taxes.[57] When this practice was challenged in court, the cities changed course by using port funds to build tax-revenue-generating harbor projects, like the Long Beach Aquarium, under an expanded definition of public benefit.[58] With the ports no longer fueling local industrialization, city governments looked to them to play a new regional role: creating logistics industry jobs and spurring retail growth foundational to the ascendant service-based economy. While this strategy sought to address local fiscal needs, it exacerbated the impact of port expansion on local communities as infrastructure megaprojects like the ICTF and Alameda Corridor rail line resulted in increased congestion and pollution. By linking municipal finances to port growth, cities committed themselves to a development program with increasingly serious local consequences.

Local Impact: Community, Labor, and the Environment

The ports' widening local impact was a function of their expanding role as crucial nodes in the global supply chain, where cargo transportation facilities—for steamships, rail, trucks, and support services—clustered.[59] It was the increasing scale of these facilities and the organization of the trucking industry that connected them together that created negative externalities for surrounding communities and the drivers that serviced the ports.

Harm was concentrated in the communities over which Los Angeles initially exerted dominion to claim access to the port—San Pedro and Wilmington—which suffered economically as the ports, and their global clientele, thrived. At the turn of the millennium, San Pedro, on the Port of Los Angeles's western edge, was a key point of access to the port, which drayage trucks traversed from the Harbor Freeway (Interstate 110) either in order to cross into Terminal Island or to travel down to facilities along the main channel.[60] On-dock rail lines also ran along San Pedro's eastern edge as they snaked their way to the Alameda Corridor exchange. The neighborhood's northeastern border abutted the ConocoPhillips oil refinery in Wilmington, creating a cluster of environmental hazards in that corner. San Pedro's demographic profile reflected its disadvantage. In 2000, its residents were two-fifths Latino and one-quarter immigrant with a median age of thirty-four; roughly one-quarter of residents were college educated with a median household income of $57,000.[61]

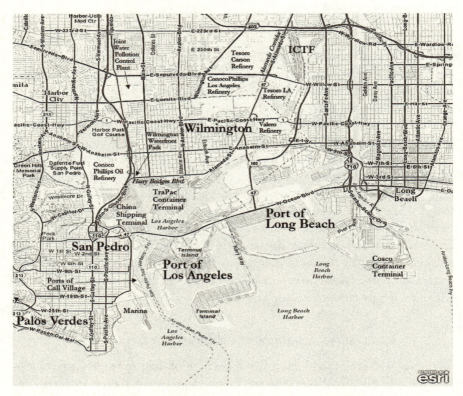

Figure 6.4 Map of ports and surrounding communities. *Source*: Created by Scott Cummings via ESRI (2014).

Wilmington, just north of the port, was even more impacted by environmental hazards: sandwiched between the Harbor and Long Beach Freeways, and bordered by the ConocoPhillips Los Angeles refinery to the north (in addition to the ConocoPhillips oil refinery to the west and Tesoro Los Angeles to the east). The strip of land on its southern border was part of the port's functioning inner channel, lined with terminals (including the massive TraPac container terminal) and crossed by streets and rail lines, separated from the residential part of the city by Harry Bridges Boulevard (named after the founder of the ILWU). Trucks accessed this part of the port from the freeways on both sides, as well as the surface streets, which were often traveled by trucks connecting between the docks and the ICTF. In this way, Wilmington, even more so than San Pedro, existed as an adjunct to the port transportation system. As a result, the community itself was more disadvantaged, with a higher level of segregation and lower socioeconomic indicators than San Pedro. As of 2000, nearly 90% of Wilmington residents were Latino and almost half were immigrants; the community had a median household size of four and a median income of $40,000; and only 5% of residents had a college degree.[62]

As with land use, the labor impacts of port development also varied.[63] Although containerization had initially threatened longshore jobs by reducing the need for loading, ILWU strikes in the 1970s demonstrated the longshoremen's power to disrupt shipping traffic, forcing the Los Angeles and Long Beach ports to invest in labor peace to prevent the diversion of cargo to other West Coast ports. As a result, by the early 2000s, the longshoremen, employed directly by terminal operators, had become the ports' "labor aristocracy"[64]—leveraging their power to choke distribution along the global supply chain to gain job security and negotiate the most lucrative contract in the union's seventy-year history.[65]

Drayage truck drivers, in contrast, had sunk to the bottom of the labor hierarchy.[66] Although also in a position to choke supply, their status as independent contractors—a consequence of deregulation—meant that they could not legally organize and therefore lacked the ability to coordinate labor action that would allow them to leverage collective gains. Prior to deregulation, strong transportation and labor regulation permitted the Teamsters to organize trucking firm employees, which they did with great success.[67] The 1980 Motor Carrier Act deregulated the trucking industry, making it easier for new companies to enter the market, expanding routes, and reducing industry authority to set general rates, which permitted discriminatory pricing. Deregulation introduced fierce competition and increased the number of firms, particularly in the drayage sector.[68] Drayage trucking companies systematically moved to a system of contracting out,[69] under which firms assigned work to nominally "independent" owner-operators,[70] who purchased or rented their own trucks and were paid by the load or trip, rather than by the hour.[71] This insulated companies from driver liability and also significantly reduced labor costs by eliminating the need to pay employment taxes and benefits (such as health care and retirement). It also shifted downside industry risks, particularly the cost of bottlenecks and delays associated with port clearance and cargo identification, to the drivers—who became responsible for truck maintenance, fuel, tolls, taxes, and other expenses. As such, trucking firms became "non-asset-based companies," shedding fixed expenses to increase their share value.[72] In addition, and most crucially, the move to independent contractors undermined unionization, since independent contractors were banned from union organizing under antitrust law.[73]

As a result, the conditions of port truck drivers deteriorated sharply.[74] Dale Belman and Kristen Monaco reported that drivers' wages fell by 21% from 1973 to 1995, and that one-third of that decrease was attributable to deregulation.[75] In Los Angeles and Long Beach, the independent-contractor form came to predominate in the drayage trucking sector, with nearly 90% of truck drivers so designated.[76] For these drivers, the average annual salary, after expenses, was $28,000.[77] In part because of delays, they worked on average fifty-six hours per week, thereby earning an effective wage rate of less than $10 per hour.[78]

The drayage labor force also came to be defined by workers of color. By 2000, in Los Angeles and Long Beach, port truck drivers were almost entirely Latino and nearly half were immigrants.[79] Edna Bonacich and Jake Wilson described the shift from white drivers at mid-century to predominantly nonwhite drivers beginning in the mid-1980s as a product of deregulation and immigration. Entrepreneurialism was long part of the truck driver ethos and, in the immediate wake of deregulation, some white drivers eagerly became owner-operators. Yet the industry rapidly shifted. The increase in immigration during the 1980s, spurred by Central American civil wars, brought more immigrant job seekers into the industry in part because "you didn't need a green card or an I-9 form."[80] Firms became smaller, more immigrants entered, and wages declined.[81] Bonacich and Wilson reported that by 1985 the Teamsters had "lost the harbor."[82] They called a strike, but the "Central Americans did not want the union because of the green card issue," and the strike failed.[83] Tensions between truck drivers and longshoremen flared as drivers felt disrespected by the largely white longshoremen, whose hourly pay structure made them in no hurry to reduce the transport delays that plagued drivers.[84] Observers identified the drayage sector as the most problematic element of port logistics, characterized by delay, poor safety, and pollution.[85] The "handoff" from ocean steamships to trucks was viewed as inefficient.[86] To pick up their cargo, truck drivers had to idle in long queues to enter the port, access the terminal, obtain their chassis, and load their containers.[87] Yet it was a system that benefited trucking companies (which externalized the cost of labor and pollution) and shippers (which were able to pay trucking firms less for their services).[88] Accordingly, those with economic power in the system had no incentive to change the arrangement.[89]

At the start of the new millennium, there were roughly sixteen thousand drayage trucks servicing the Los Angeles and Long Beach ports each day.[90] Because drivers could not generally afford to upgrade, this fleet was aging—the ports were the place

Figure 6.5 Trucks waiting to enter the Port of Los Angeles. *Source*: Barbara Maynard, Teamsters (2016).

where "old trucks went to die"[91]—and ran on diesel fuel, a known carcinogen.[92] Truck emissions, combined with those from ocean carriers and dock transport equipment, caused significant air pollution, which threatened driver and broader community health. A 2007 NRDC report showed that the black carbon inside truck cabs increased "health risks by up to 2,600 excess cancers per million drivers."[93] Overall, the California Air Resources Board (CARB) found that diesel particulate matter emissions from port-related activities constituted roughly one-fifth of all such emissions in the Los Angeles basin.[94] Communities near the ports had cancer risk levels that "exceeded 500 in a million"; further from the port, the risk was less but still significant.[95] From the perspective of community and labor groups, law had contributed to these harmful effects—by disempowering local communities and truck drivers relative to the port. Their response would be to try to reshape law to fix the problems it had produced.

The Port as a Unit of Legal Analysis

Restructuring the Ports of Los Angeles and Long Beach meant leveraging their powers as local government entities to change rules of operations to remedy environmental and economic harm. However, because the ports were also legally bound to the national and global marketplace, any local change had to be compatible with higher order legal regimes that touched upon port operations. With respect to port trucking, this meant navigating around the Federal Aviation Administration Authorization Act (FAAAA),[96] enacted in 1995 to prevent states and localities from passing trucking standards that would circumvent the deregulatory provisions of the 1980 Motor Carrier Act. Designed to be identical with the preemption provision contained in federal airline legislation,[97] the FAAAA provided that a state or locality "may not enact or enforce a law, regulation, or other provision having the force or effect of law related to a price, route, or service of any motor carrier . . . with respect to the transportation of property."[98] Ports seeking to enact any policy change affecting trucking had to avoid the preemptive effect of the FAAAA.[99]

In this regard, federal law had been held to only preempt local action "tantamount to regulation,"[100] not "market participation" by a local entity in its proprietary capacity.[101] Thus, even when federal law had preemptive effect, local action was not generally preempted if it flowed from local government directly participating in the marketplace as a proprietor through the purchase of goods and services.[102] Yet in the early 2000s, on the cusp of the clean trucks campaign, the precedent interpreting market participation in the labor, environmental, and transportation contexts was thin. In 2004, the U.S. Supreme Court held that the Clean Air Act preempted an effort by the South Coast Air Quality Management District (SCAQMD) to set fleet emission standards.[103] However, it invited the parties to consider the market participant exception and, on remand, the district court held that the rules "as applied to state and local government actors, fall within the market participant doctrine and are therefore outside the scope of" the act.[104] In the only reported case on the issue, the Ninth Circuit applied the market participant exception to the FAAAA, upholding a Santa Ana law requiring vehicles be towed by city-approved trucks as an exercise of the city's proprietary power.[105] Therefore, while market participation offered a potential route for local action on port trucking, there was little doctrinal guidance on how to navigate that route in practice. It was into this uncertain space that the Campaign for Clean Trucks cautiously stepped.

Resisting the Ports: Activism in Separate Spheres
The Hundred Years' War: Community Mobilization Against Port Expansion

Although the legal road to clean trucks ultimately ran through the doctrine of preemption, the activism that generated the challenge to port trucking emerged from the specific grievances of local residents affected by port expansion. Activism against port growth—and particularly against its environmental and community impacts—took root in the areas most affected by it: San Pedro, Wilmington, and adjacent neighborhoods through which the port transportation system cut.

Wilmington, occupying nine square miles at the ports' northern border, had long been the region's industrial workhorse. Perched on the massive Wilmington oil field, by the 1980s the community of forty thousand residents was home to dozens of oil refineries and over one hundred working oil wells, as well as numerous waste disposals, auto-wrecking plants, and junk yards.[106] It also contained rail-switching yards and was well traveled by trucks coming to and from the ports. According to the *Los Angeles Times*, Wilmington served as a "regional dumping ground with 13 closed waste dumps—one of the largest concentrations in the City of Los Angeles—and six toxic-waste storage or treatment plants. It also [was] the proposed site of one of the largest hazardous-waste treatment facilities in the state."[107]

Most of the community's ire focused on the Port of Los Angeles, which owned substantial property (including 20% of decaying East Wilmington) and dominated land use decisions, often in disregard of community concerns.[108] Faced with this disregard, in the 1980s, community members began to take matters into their own hands. Residents—then about two-thirds Latino, primarily blue collar, and roughly one-half homeowners—drew upon existing institutions and a sense of cultural pride to begin challenging what many viewed as the community's subservience to the port's industrial needs.[109] As one activist put it, "We are subsidizing the existence of the harbor with our city streets and the air we breathe."[110]

The impact of transportation was a constant concern as truck drivers increasingly used Wilmington streets to access the port and dumped empty containers on vacant lots around the community.[111] In 1987, longtime activist Gertrude Schwab reported to the Los Angeles Harbor Commission that two trucks per minute passed through the intersection at Avalon Boulevard and Anaheim Street—Wilmington's main crossroads.[112] The commission promised to create a dedicated truck route that would bypass residential streets, but the timeline was over a decade long,[113] and the port's immediate decision to approve the notoriously hazardous Wilmington Liquid Bulk Terminals' concrete plant fueled further resentment about increased trucking.[114] Residents also voiced discontent about ongoing environmental degradation, particularly in light of the 2020 Plan, which the ports' own environmental impact review noted would worsen air quality and further restrict commercial fishing and public recreation.[115] As one leader of the Wilmington Home Owners put it, "The conclusion seems to be if it is economically beneficial for the ports, to hell with local communities."[116]

While Wilmington's zoning made it the "backland" for the port's industrial uses, San Pedro emerged as the port's recreational and commercial hub—a fact that Wilmington residents often highlighted with internecine frustration to emphasize their differential treatment.[117] With greater recreational use mandated by state law in 1976, the port adopted a strategy of bifurcation, with San Pedro the recreational choice given its geographic benefits and higher proportion of residentially and commercially zoned land, which precluded Wilmington-style industrial expansion.[118] Against this backdrop, the port and city sought to exploit San Pedro's advantages. The port itself owned several properties on the tidal lands and in the late 1980s pursued aggressive development, investing over $3 million to upgrade Ports O' Call Village, the 1960s-era shopping center on the main channel, while also moving forward with plans to develop a $100-million marina (with over one thousand slips) and recreational complex on Cabrillo Beach,[119] as well as a $60-million facility for cruise ships that included commercial development and a hotel.[120] The recession, however, made sure the good times did not last and the promise of port-led redevelopment turned into another disappointment.

Beset with difficulties, San Pedro and Wilmington began serious efforts to secede from the City of Los Angeles in the late 1990s[121]—a threat made more credible by simultaneous effort by Hollywood and the San Fernando Valley.[122] In a play to tamp down secessionist fever, and quell what activists called the "Hundred Years' War," Mayor Richard Riordan and other city officials made gestures to promote greater community involvement in port planning.[123] The secessionists were not placated. Despite conciliatory efforts by the newly elected mayor—South Los Angeles native and scion of a powerful Democratic family, James Hahn[124]—the secessionists proceeded to advance their bid by making the economic case for independence to the Los Angeles County Local Area Formation Commission (LAFCO), whose approval was required before the issue could be put to city voters.[125] Despite an aggressive case by secession supporters, LAFCO ultimately concluded that an independent harbor city would not be economically viable,[126] particularly in light of a California State Lands Commission recommendation to keep the port with the City of Los Angeles in the event of secession.[127]

It was fitting that the secession movement's decline occurred against the backdrop of yet another dispute between the Los Angeles port and Wilmington residents that tested the genuineness of the port's new community partnership. In 2001, as part of its drive to add twenty-five acres to the TraPac container terminal in the West Basin by expanding it north across Harry Bridges Boulevard to C Street, the port proposed building a twenty-foot-high concrete wall to separate the community from the new terminal boundary.[128] The plan, which had been previously proposed early in the 1990s, brought a firestorm of controversy, as residents once again complained that the port's talk of community collaboration did not match its actions, which would further undermine the goal of harbor access.[129] As one community activist put it bluntly, "We don't need the Berlin Wall."[130]

At a community meeting in April 2001, when the details of the port's plan to expand Harry Bridges Boulevard to accommodate six lanes of truck traffic was revealed, residents exploded.[131] At that meeting was Jesse Marquez, a former aerospace electrician born and raised in Wilmington. As a high school track athlete whose lungs burned when he ran, Marquez was radicalized by a chemical plant fire that injured his family members.[132] At the moment the expansion plan was unveiled, Marquez recalled shouting, "Hell no, over my dead body. If anybody wants it, tell them that [at] my house this Saturday we'll form a committee. We're going to fight this project."[133] A working group of about fifteen residents met to establish the Wilmington Coalition to stop the wall.[134] In the weeks that followed, the meetings grew to fifty residents and the following year the group secured funding from the Liberty Hill Foundation to set up an independent organization that in 2003 changed its name to the Coalition for a Safe Environment—which ultimately succeeded in preventing the wall's construction.[135]

Other port-related projects caused similar disruption—and produced similar community responses. The Alameda Corridor rail line cut through East Wilmington, eliminating many of the gritty neighborhood's only businesses,[136] while intermodal truck and rail traffic disrupted community life in adjacent cities like Carson and

Figure 6.6 Jesse Marquez at community meeting. *Source*: Lawrence K. Ho/*Los Angeles Times* via Getty Images (2009).

around the downtown rail yards.[137] Commerce, home of the UP East L.A. and the Burlington Northern and Santa Fe (BNSF) Hobart yards servicing the ports and bisected by the 710 Freeway, experienced drayage truck increases as port traffic grew in the 1990s.[138] A series of town hall meetings brought out residents concerned with the safety and environmental impact of the trucks.[139] City neglect prompted a handful of families to begin meeting as an ad hoc group. An informal survey confirmed the extent of community concern with the impact of the rail yards and trucking on safety, health, and property.[140] With the leadership of Angelo Logan, an aerospace mechanic, Commerce families formed East Yard Communities for Environmental Justice in 2000.[141] Galvanized by the Alameda Corridor project and plans for a massive expansion of the 710 Freeway to accommodate more port trucks, East Yard Communities became focused on strategies to address the trucks' noxious byproduct: diesel exhaust.[142] Resident research into truck pollution revealed that, while infrastructure design disproportionately impacted their community, the underlying cause of pollution stemmed from the nature of the port trucking industry itself.[143] This point was brought home at a community forum in 2005 to address diesel exhaust, at which resident truck drivers spoke. Logan recalled the event:

> They . . . really laid out their situation in terms of the way in which they were being exploited and their hands being tied in terms of . . . not being able to get into trucks that were safer, that were cleaner and that [allowed]

Figure 6.7 Angelo Logan (right) at the Port of Los Angeles. *Source*: Bob Chamberlin/ *Los Angeles Times* via Getty Images (2009).

them to be good environmental health stewards. And immediately thereafter . . . [we] realized that there was a real issue in terms of the trucking industry and the way that the trucking industry was exploiting the drivers themselves.[144]

Labor's Municipal Strategy: Contracting Around the Independent-Contractor Problem

During this time, leaders within organized labor were also focused on ports, but from a distinct perspective. For the Teamsters, trucking deregulation decimated the ranks of what had been one of the strongest unions in the United States.[145] Whereas 46% of the country's approximately one million truck drivers were unionized in 1978, only 23% of the roughly two million truck drivers were in unions by 1996.[146] An even lower percentage of the nearly four million drivers nationwide were in unions by the early 2000s.[147]

In the wake of deregulation, truck drivers tried to organize independent associations. Central American drivers, who comprised the vast majority at the Los Angeles and Long Beach ports, established their own associations in the 1980s as vehicles for community support and labor struggle. One of these, the Waterfront Rail Truckers Union (WRTU), formed in 1986, spearheaded a series of strikes to address delays and other disputes,[148] one of which involved WRTU members withholding containers until they received payment from a bankrupt trucking company.[149] Members were radical and militant. In the late 1980s, they began challenging their classification as independent contractors by roughly two dozen port trucking companies, including H&M Terminals Transport, Inc.,[150] which drivers challenged through tax filings and picketing.[151] Although the WRTU receded in importance, independent organizing continued into the 1990s,[152] with other groups such as the Latin American Truckers' Association protesting the impact of fuel costs.[153] Some of these independent groups reached out to unions, which were unwilling to invest the resources to support an organizing campaign.[154]

The situation changed in the mid-1990s, when truck drivers initiated a large-scale union organizing drive—led not by the Teamsters, but by the Communications Workers of America (CWA).[155] The drivers' connection to the CWA was partly driven by personal contacts with CWA organizers, but was also a function of the lack of interest shown by the Teamsters.[156] CWA Local 9400 began holding meetings for workers in 1995 and 1996, quickly attracting thousands.[157] To demonstrate its growing strength, in May 1996, CWA organized picketing in front of terminal gates, which was enjoined when the Pacific Maritime Association (PMA) filed suit in Long Beach Superior Court.[158] The truck drivers organized convoys from the ports to highlight their plight and labor leaders persuaded the Los Angeles City Council to pass a resolution in support of unionization.[159]

However, there remained the thorny problem of the drivers' predominantly independent-contractor status, which precluded them from organizing. To get around this problem, CWA launched a dual campaign. One part was a traditional unionization effort directed at the handful of companies that still used employees; the second involved an ambitious plan, to be financed by entrepreneur Donald Allen, to create a new trucking company, the Transport Maritime Association (TMA), which would hire truck drivers as employees and then contract them out to existing companies at higher rates.[160] In May 1996, roughly four thousand drivers declined to accept contracts from their existing companies and instead signed up to be TMA employees with the promise of pay at $25 per hour.[161] Despite a diversion of some cargo, the trucking companies held fast and refused to contract with TMA.[162] When one of the lead organizers suffered a heart attack and it turned out that Allen lacked the resources to bring TMA to scale, the campaign died, with some faulting the CWA for not investigating Allen's finances and for lacking sophisticated knowledge of the port trucking industry.[163] Although the campaign failed to advance truck driver unionization,[164] it did reveal a deep desire among the workers for change, their willingness to take action, and the economic vulnerability of the port to a trucking strike.

The CWA campaign also refocused efforts to address the independent-contractor problem. Labor leaders identified two approaches. One was to find a way to directly organize truck drivers as independent contractors without running afoul of antitrust law. Without amending federal law, which seemed politically impossible, the value of this approach was uncertain, since any state effort to permit independent-contractor organizing could be preempted. The Teamsters did put some effort into this strategy, pursuing a legislative campaign to permit direct organizing of independent contractors; but the union's effort to pass a state law exempting independent contractors from antitrust law failed when Governor Arnold Schwarzenegger vetoed it in 2005.[165]

Instead, the Teamsters pursued a second approach, in which truck drivers would be legally converted into employees and then organized under the NLRA. The CWA campaign attempted to do this by creating the labor-leasing firm, TMA, which was to hire drivers as employees, who would then be unionized—passing the increased costs on to trucking firms in the form of higher contract rates.[166] In the wake of that failed campaign, truck drivers adopted another strategy that echoed earlier WRTU efforts: litigation challenging the drivers' misclassification. In 1996, lawyer Fred Kumetz brought suit on behalf of thirty drivers who claimed that they had been misclassified as independent contractors by forty transportation companies.[167] The suit sought class action certification to represent a larger class of 6,500 harbor truck drivers claiming $250 million in damages—primarily to recover payments made for insurance coverage (which included workers' compensation).[168] Kumetz, a plaintiff's lawyer not associated with organized labor, was approached by drivers after TMA collapsed.[169] In filing the suit, Kumetz argued that "the drivers, nearly all

Latino immigrants, frequently are coerced by 'fly-by-night' companies into signing exploitative contracts without understanding the contents and are duped into paying for workers' compensation and liability insurance without understanding the law."[170] The plaintiffs alleged that having to pay for insurance (and other ownership costs) reduced their earnings to below the poverty level.[171]

The contracts at issue in the case gave truck drivers the choice of obtaining their own insurance or getting it through the trucking firms' less expensive group policies, the cost of which would be deducted from the drivers' compensation.[172] The companies charged the drivers more than the cost of premiums paid and also made the drivers responsible for a $1,000 deductible payment that was not specified in their contracts.[173] In 1999, the case—*Albillo v. Intermodal Container Services*—was certified as a class action.[174] After the trial court ruled against the drivers, the California Court of Appeal, in a 2003 published decision, held that the firms did violate the Labor Code by electing to be covered by workers' compensation while "requiring [drivers] to bear the cost of obtaining workers' compensation insurance."[175] Yet even this success, while compensating workers for wrongful payments, did not achieve the large-scale goal of employee conversion; in fact, it produced the opposite effect by making firms less likely to elect workers' compensation coverage in the first instance.

As the Teamsters watched the CWA campaign and *Albillo* lawsuit unfold, they began devising plans for their own initiative. In 2000, the Teamsters union, through its Port Division, announced a nationwide port truck driver campaign, run by Assistant Director Ron Carver.[176] Coming on the heels of the trial court setback in *Albillo*, lead Teamsters organizer Ed Berk was undaunted: "I don't think they're going to throw in the towel on this one court case."[177] However, the Teamsters had absorbed the lessons of that case, and the CWA campaign before it, concluding that the way to win was not through piecemeal organizing or lawsuits, but through broad change that could convert large numbers of independent contractors back into employees. As Teamsters attorney Mike Manley reflected, the union's view was that "you really can't [address the industry] through a campaign of [federal labor board] elections and slugging it out in representation cases. The industry is too vast . . . you'd be doing it forever."[178] In Los Angeles, there were some unionized firms, like Horizon, and others that still hired truck drivers as employees, like Toll, but without addressing the independent-contractor problem, the industry would remain a low-wage one. The key was to "transform the market."[179]

Port truck driver unionization remained one of the major prizes of Teamsters organizing in the new millennium. In raw numbers, the scale of port trucking nationwide was modest, with approximately forty thousand port drivers operating as independent contractors out of an overall trucking industry of almost four million.[180] However, port trucking was an area of historic strength, and there were practical and strategic reasons to pursue unionization in that sector. As a practical matter, there was a potential legal hook for organizing. The legal status of ports (like Los Angeles and Long Beach) as proprietary departments under the umbrella of local government meant that ports could potentially influence the nature of trucking through their contracting power. Discussions of how to make this happen were underway in 2004 when Mike Manley was hired in the Teamsters' office of general counsel, headed by Pat Szymanski.[181] Manley, from Kansas, worked as an organizer at the East Lawrence Improvement Association before deciding to become a lawyer.[182] In 1980, he enrolled in Kansas Law School, and then went to a Kansas City law firm, Blake & Uhlig, where he eventually became partner.[183] The firm was general counsel to the International Brotherhood of Boilermakers, and Manley remembered that when he was hired by the Teamsters, there was "great interest in the fact that I had done a lot of work for the boilermakers and shipyards—which I guess shows how deep the department was in the [ports] campaign at that point."[184] When Manley started at the Teamsters, and was assigned to the Port Division to help organize port drivers, he remembered incredulously asking Szymanski: "What are you doing? ... They are independent contractors."[185]

As Manley quickly learned, the plan was to change that status by focusing on the ports' role as market participants. In conversations with Ron Carver, the question was: "Is there a way to kind of leverage the port to declare [drivers] to be employees?"[186] Figuring out an affirmative answer to that question was not only important on its own terms but had broader strategic implications. The ports were key links in the larger supply chain that led from manufacturing exporters to regional warehouses, and ultimately to large retail chains, such as Wal-Mart. Some labor leaders believed that if unions could gain a stronger foothold at the ports, it would contribute to a longer-term campaign to organize retail giants.[187] This was something that the Teamsters had argued for, but "didn't get necessarily a lot of traction ... in terms of resources" from union leadership at the AFL-CIO.[188]

That changed with the formation of Change to Win in September 2005.[189] Change to Win—established, in Manley's terms, with "little structure, [but a] big focus on organizing"[190]—set up the Strategic Organizing Center, which was built around different industry sectors, with the goal of identifying "how the pool of existing resources at Change to Win could expand the pace [of] organizing."[191] The center was "like a startup" that put "together experienced organizers and campaigners [to take] a fresh look at industries that were basically nonunion."[192] By bringing together organizers and researchers from different unions, the goal was to innovate according to "best practices."[193] It divided up the economy into different industry sectors: transportation, retail, home construction, and food processing.[194]

John Canham-Clyne and Nick Weiner both volunteered to work on transportation.[195] Canham-Clyne was a former freelance writer who covered the Iran-Contra affair for *In These Times* and wrote a book on single-payer health care.[196] He left journalism in 1996 to work as the research director for Congress Watch at Public Citizen, and from there was recruited to the HERE union to direct campaign research for their hospital-organizing campaigns, first in Las Vegas and then in New

Haven.[197] After Change to Win was formed, Canham-Clyne was recruited to its core staff.[198] There, he was joined by Nick Weiner, who also came from HERE, where he first worked with locals in Baltimore and Washington, D.C., and then joined the national hotel organizing effort at the UNITE HERE office in Washington, D.C.[199]

Together Canham-Clyne and Weiner set out to research the trucking industry, becoming the bridge between Change to Win and the existing Teamsters leadership. Through their research, Canham-Clyne and Weiner identified the ports as a potential target of opportunity. As one of the few publicly owned pieces of freight infrastructure, ports offered "potential hooks" for organizing. Many were in labor-friendly political jurisdictions and drayage was a relatively sticky industry because of the massive infrastructure investment at the ports.[200] On the basis of this research, Change to Win launched a national ports campaign, directed by Canham-Clyne, to build upon the Teamsters' existing organizing efforts and "move [that] work forward faster."[201] The larger goal, in line with that articulated by the Teamsters, was to "organize the supply chain."[202] The ports were the first link in this chain because they were a "chokepoint" that could be used to leverage other wins.[203]

With Change to Win staff and resources in place, a working group was formed and serious planning commenced in 2006.[204] Within the Teamsters, Manley, Carver, and Chuck Mack (West Coast Vice President of the Teamsters and head of the Port Division) met repeatedly with Canham-Clyne and Weiner to develop an organizing theory and strategy, which focused on "strengthening the local political control over the ports."[205] The plan was to target ports in "blue" states or localities with friendly political climates: Los Angeles–Long Beach, Seattle–Tacoma, Oakland, New York–New Jersey, and Miami. From Manley's perspective, if the campaign could get these ports to "adopt a model that made drivers employees," "more than 50% of what was coming into the country would be through facilities where port drivers are employees. And then you'd go to second tier targets . . . [which] are harder nuts to crack."[206] During these meetings, organizers like Weiner drew on their past experiences dealing with local governments and airports to develop a strategy predicated upon a concession model: contractually linking the entry of trucking firms onto port property to the conversion of truck drivers from independent contractors to employees. As Weiner recalled, "once we started looking into port trucking, we kind of came up with [the concession] theory. And then we vetted the theory and that took a few months."[207]

In 2006, there was a meeting of the "legal tribes" in Washington, D.C., where prominent labor lawyers gathered to discuss new organizing strategies.[208] This meeting included the Teamsters' Manley, as well as Szymanski, who had left the Teamsters to become general counsel to Change to Win; Brad Raymond, the new general counsel of the Teamsters; Judy Scott, general counsel to the SEIU; and longtime outside union counsel, Stephen Berzon of Altshuler Berzon, and Richard McCracken of Davis, Cowell & Bowe.[209] One of the issues discussed was the legal feasibility of using the port's status as a city entity to convert truck drivers into

Figure 6.8 Nick Weiner speaking at port driver press conference. *Source*: Asia Morris, *Long Beach Post* (2015).

employees.[210] It was a familiar idea to those present, discussed in various forms for some time. But at that point, with Change to Win backing, the time had finally come to advance the strategy. The question was: "Is this doable?"[211]

The concession model held appeal for a number of reasons. For one, it had been tested in other forms and had proven an effective tool for organizing. In particular, union lawyers had done work on airport organizing—as in the Respect at LAX campaign—in which the airport authorities, as public agencies, had used concession agreements to require food and beverage vendors to remain neutral in union organizing campaigns.[212] Thus, from a mechanical point of view, union lawyers were familiar with the technical aspects of city contracting and how it related to labor issues. Perhaps most crucially, the concession model was viewed as legally defensible against federal preemption. The union lawyers involved had experience with city contracting models to create living wage laws and job training programs, and believed that the same concept could be adapted to the ports under a market participant theory.[213] For this analysis to work, there had to be a justification for the market participation itself. That justification turned out to lie less in trucking's labor relations than in its environmental impact.

The Turning Point: China Shipping and the Clean Air Action Plan

That labor and environmental legal analyses would harmonize around the market participant exception to preemption was not clear on the cusp of the clean trucks campaign. Unlike the labor movement, mainstream environmental organizations could wield legal power through federal and state regulatory regimes, and had not yet clearly defined their relation to locally based initiatives. Judicial recognition of a market participant exception to the Clean Air Act did not occur until 2005.[214] It was at that point, at least in theory, that the legal interests of the labor and environmental movements in asserting the market participant exception were in unison. But there still needed to be a cause upon which to act jointly. That cause would be port pollution.

Environmental attention increasingly focused on the defining problem of the Los Angeles basin: smog. Regulation was shaped by the different tools available to federal and state agencies to deal with key pollution sources. Ships, which used dirty "bunker" fuel high in sulfur content,[215] were known to be significant polluters, but the ports' power to regulate them was ambiguous when ships were in international waters.[216] There was a strong argument that ports could, however, impose rules on ships once docked under an exception to the Clean Air Act permitting local in-use regulations for nonroad sources of emissions.[217] The policy discussion centered on what such on-dock rules should look like. To reduce nitrogen oxide released from port ships burning diesel fuel while idling,[218] the SCAQMD issued a proposed rule requiring ships to plug into dockside electric power[219]—an operation known in the industry as "cold ironing"—which became an important goal of environmental advocacy. Regulators also searched for ways to address diesel truck pollution. While CARB had been granted authority by the federal Environmental Protection Agency (EPA) to set vehicle emission standards, the in-use exception to the Clean Air Act also allowed the ports to regulate the "use, operation, or movement" of trucks,[220] which opened the possibility of imposing restrictions on truck idling.

When it came to air pollution, it was clear that the ports could no longer expect to conduct business as usual, particularly as the environmental and health impacts of diesel fuel vehicles received increasing attention.[221] In 1999, a front-page *Los Angeles Times* story reported on the danger of diesel-fuel-burning vehicles, whose higher fuel content and intense heat-burning engines produced greater concentrations of carbon, sulfur, and nitrogen oxide.[222] "At the Ports of Long Beach and Los Angeles—massive operations that are filled with trucks, ships, trains and cranes—workers breathe some of the most severe doses of diesel exhaust found anyplace in California."[223] A seminal 2000 SCAQMD study on the relation between air pollution and cancer, entitled the Multiple Air Toxics Exposure Study (MATES II), concluded that about 70% of the carcinogenic risk in the Los Angeles basin was "attributed to diesel particulate emissions."[224] The study made specific reference to the negative impact of diesel emissions coming from the ports and connected transportation networks.[225] The communities at greatest risk, unsurprisingly, were adjacent to the ports.[226] A map published with the study (Figure 6.9) highlighted the increased cancer risk in harbor communities and galvanized residents who began to mobilize around environmental justice—distributing the map at official meetings and public actions.[227] At a 2001 conference on air pollution at USC, Coalition for a Safe Environment Director Jesse Marquez challenged assembled scientists to link their findings on air pollution to the unregulated growth of the ports and their impact on local low-income communities.[228] New partnerships between community activists and the scientific community began to develop. The stage for environmental action against the ports was set—though that action initially would play out in court.

It was fitting that in the pivotal environmental fight against the ports, the focal point would be containers arriving from China, which by the mid-1990s was the Los Angeles region's second largest trading partner, accounting for $18 billion of cargo.[229] Long Beach sought to retain the China Ocean Shipping Company (COSCO), a state-run carrier handling a quarter of Chinese trade with the United States,[230] by building a new terminal on the site of a naval station.[231] But that plan

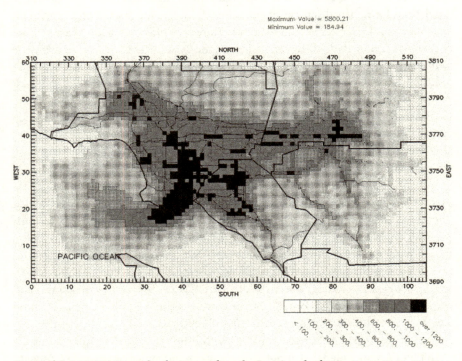

Figure 6.9 MATES II graph of cancer risk in the Los Angeles basin. *Source*: South Coast Air Quality Management District, Multiple Air Toxics Exposure Study Final Report (MATES II) (2000).

was derailed by the combined opposition of environmentalists concerned about contamination from dredging and protecting a habitat for black-crowned night herons,[232] preservationists seeking to block the demolition of historic naval station buildings (represented by environmental lawyer Jan Chatten-Brown before her work on the Inglewood Wal-Mart case),[233] and Republican lawmakers, who viewed COSCO as a security risk.[234]

Meanwhile, the Port of Los Angeles pursued its own China partner. Residents had made inquiries to the Harbor Commission about plans for the West Basin site of the former Todd Shipyard and Chevron area just north of the Vincent Thomas Bridge in San Pedro. Their answer came on March 28, 2001, when the Harbor Commission approved a lease with China Shipping Holding Company (China Shipping).[235] Under the terms of the $650-million lease,[236] China Shipping would occupy a 174-acre terminal built by the port, which would support entry of up to 300 vessels—approximately 1.5 million containers—a year.[237] The terminal—to be located at berths 100 and 102—would be designed to accept 9,100 TEU container vessels, which were larger than any at the time.[238]

Community resistance was swift. San Pedro Peninsula Homeowners United, led by activist Noel Park, and the San Pedro and Peninsula Homeowners Coalition challenged the proposed terminal, which was to include two new wharves and ten massive cranes (up to sixteen stories high) 500 feet from resident homes, along with a backland area with new roads to accommodate traffic.[239] On May 8, 2001, at a tense meeting in which residents were given only five minutes to speak, the Los Angeles City Council rejected resident demands that it conduct an EIR prior to approving the project.[240] Instead, the council approved the project by a unanimous vote.[241] Residents thus turned to court, contacting NRDC to pursue legal action.

On June 14, 2001, NRDC—representing the resident groups San Pedro and Peninsula Homeowners Coalition and San Pedro Peninsula Homeowners United, as well as the Coalition for Clean Air and NRDC's own members—filed suit against the city, port, and harbor commissioners.[242] Petitioners—represented by Gail Ruderman Feuer and Julie Masters of NRDC, along with Jan Chatten-Brown and another private environmental lawyer, Roger Beers—argued that, in approving the project, the city had failed to comply with CEQA,[243] which required an environmental review of significant developments that identified environmental issues and how they would be mitigated, and provided a period for public comment.[244] Petitioners thus sought a writ of mandate directing the city to conduct a new project-specific EIR.[245] "It's time for the port to consider the needs of local communities before it approves a massive expansion in their backyard," claimed NRDC's Masters.[246] The suit emphasized the environmental impact of the incoming ships themselves, as well as increased tugboat activity (over five hundred trips per year) and truck traffic (an estimated one million new trips).[247]

The technical legal issue focused on the port's effort to exempt the China Shipping project from CEQA review by arguing that its approval was encompassed within two EIR processes that predated the lease agreement. The first was a 1997 EIR conducted by the Los Angeles Harbor Department that approved the development of a multifaceted West Basin Transportation Project to "optimize container transport capabilities," which included plans to deepen and widen the basin, create a new on-dock railway linked to the Alameda Corridor, and build a new wharf at berths 98 through 100 to accommodate the largest container vessels.[248] The second was a 2000 EIS/EIR conducted by the U.S. Army Corp of Engineers to evaluate the impacts of a harbor dredging operation that proposed using dredged material to create a landfill between berths 97 through 109 as a potential site for container storage or docking in order to "accommodate the most modern vessels."[249] In preparing for the lease agreement, the Harbor Commission told China Shipping that the "elements contained in the lease have been adequately assessed in the [1997] West Basin Transportation Improvements Program EIR ... and have been adequately assessed in the [2000] Port of Los Angeles Channel Deepening EIS/EIR. ... As such, the Director of Environmental Management has determined that the proposed activity is exempt."[250] The city attorney's office approved a permit authorizing the construction of the China Shipping terminal from landfill taken from the harbor dredging project.[251] Under the final twenty-five-year lease agreement, China Shipping was granted the right to use berths 100 and 102 to construct terminal, wharf, and backland space, to be built in three phases: phase one included construction of the container terminal and first wharf at berth 100 by November 2002; phase two involved the extension of the first wharf and the completion of the second (at berth 102) by March 2005; and phase three involved construction of backland space to support the terminal.[252] Apparently concerned that the scale of the new project might not be encompassed in the prior EIRs, the city also entered into a "side letter agreement," approved by the City Council, which stated that the port and city "will use their best efforts to minimize negative environmental impacts" with respect to emissions from container ships, tugboats, trucks, and rail lines accessing the new terminal.[253]

Petitioners argued that the lease committed the port to all three phases of the development, and that the 1997 and 2000 EIRs did not even address the potential impacts of phase one—much less all three.[254] In particular, the 1997 EIR emphasized near-dock rail access, not container terminal construction, and did not contemplate the much larger scope of environmental impacts—including bigger wharves, larger operation space, more ships, and more trucks—while the 2000 review emphasized dredging.[255] The defendants—represented by lawyers from the city attorney's office and outside counsel Morrison & Foerster and McCutchen, Doyle, Brown & Enersen—denied these allegations.[256]

In 2002, after the suit was filed, activists held a protest in the Knoll Hill neighborhood of San Pedro, just next to the proposed China Shipping project.[257] In a convergence of political interests, harbor secessionists had seized on the project to rally support for their cause, inviting African American leaders angry at newly elected

Mayor James Hahn (a San Pedro resident) for breaking his promise to endorse African American Bernard Parks for a second term as police chief.[258] Hahn's sister, Janice, also a San Pedro resident, represented the Fifteenth District (which linked Watts to the harbor communities of San Pedro and Wilmington) and supported residents pushing for a new environmental review of the China Shipping project.[259] In an effort to tamp down community controversy, Mayor Hahn appointed a Port Community Advisory Committee, which a week prior to the protest had recommended that the U.S. Army Corp of Engineers conduct a new environmental review of the China Shipping site.[260] But that recommendation was rejected by the Harbor Commission and Hahn remained in political hot water.[261]

The state trial court in the NRDC suit provided no relief.[262] On May 30, 2002, the court rejected the environmentalists' challenge, holding that the first phase of the China Shipping project was within the scope of the 1997 EIR and therefore did not have to be redone; because the city and port had apparently conceded that an EIR would have to be done on subsequent project phases for berth expansion, the trial court held those challenges to be moot.[263]

On appeal, the petitioners asserted that the trial court lacked substantial evidence to support a CEQA exemption.[264] In doing so, their brief placed front and center the issue of air pollution caused by diesel-powered vehicles:

> [T]he transportation of . . . containers to and from the site would generate a tremendous increase in the use of diesel trucks, diesel tugboats, and off-road diesel equipment, polluting the air and water and burdening the local streets and freeways. Of particular concern to Appellants who live nearby, and to members of the Appellant environmental groups, is the tremendous quantity of diesel exhaust—a known carcinogen—that would be pumped into the surrounding community.[265]

The attorney general of California weighed in with an amicus brief on behalf of petitioners, arguing that by committing itself to construct all three phases of the development but only purporting to approve phase one, the defendants had improperly segmented the project in direct violation of CEQA, reducing it "to a process whose result will be largely to generate paper, to produce an EIR that describes a journey whose destination is already predetermined and contractually committed to before the public has any chance to see either the road map or the full price tag."[266] As part of its appeal, petitioners asked the appellate court to stay the terminal's construction,[267] which the court declined to do, although it did expedite hearing the case, setting argument for October 18, 2002.[268]

In the meantime, NRDC's Feuer went to federal court arguing that the Army Corps had failed in its 2000 environmental review to adequately evaluate the China Shipping project, again asking for an injunction against further development.[269] District Court Judge Margaret Morrow agreed, issuing a temporary restraining order (TRO) on July 24, "as work crews were pouring 100 feet of new concrete in a rush to complete the China Shipping Holding Co. terminal," which was over halfway done.[270] Fifty residents attended the court hearing, including community activist Jesse Marquez, who was astonished by the court decision: "This kind of thing has never happened before."[271] But the community's enthusiasm was short-lived. Three days later, Judge Morrow refused to convert the TRO into a preliminary injunction, holding that the petitioners had not proved sufficient harm in letting the project proceed, while the port asserted that delay would cost it $1.2 million per day and undermine its reputation in the competitive shipping world.[272]

The state court took a different view. After hearing the case on October 18, the appellate panel decided to issue a stay, blocking construction of the key phase one element: the 1,200-foot wharf at berth 100, which had already been nearly completed.[273] Reversing the decision below, the appellate court curtly dismissed the port's contention that the China Shipping project was encompassed under the previous EIR as "supported neither factually nor legally."[274] Specifically, the court held that because the China Shipping project did not arise until after the completion of either EIR, it could not "be considered part of the overall 'project' addressed in those documents."[275] In a stunning blow to the port, the appellate court not only ordered a new EIR addressing all phases of the project, it also directed "the trial court to issue an injunction consistent with the stay we have issued precluding further construction or operation of the Project pending completion of the environmental review process."[276] The *Los Angeles Times* reported that the injunction barred "the pouring of 200 additional feet of concrete needed to complete the wharf," which was nearly 90% finished.[277]

Court victory did not end the terminal fight. Under the rules of CEQA, it simply required the city and port to go back and conduct an appropriate review.[278] However, since time was of the essence and the port did not want to lose China Shipping's business, the coalition had important leverage, which it used to negotiate an unprecedented—and game-changing—settlement.

On March 5, 2003, in order to circumvent a lengthy battle over the project, the port and environmentalists entered into a $60-million settlement agreement, financed entirely through port revenue.[279] The agreement, approved by Superior Court Judge Dzintra Janavs, permitted the port to finish phase one of the project within weeks while it awaited completion of the EIR, which it was still required to do (the coalition reserved the right to challenge any inadequacy in the EIR).[280] In exchange, the port—in an unprecedented concession to environmental improvements— agreed to specific mitigation measures, which included requiring container handling equipment to use alternative fuel,[281] installing "low profile" cranes,[282] building facilities for "shoreside electrical power for ship hoteling," retrofitting China Shipping vessels to use electrical power while docked,[283] creating a traffic mitigation plan,[284] and setting aside $50 million over five years for community-specific mitigation.[285] This community mitigation fund included $10 million for the Gateway

Cities program to provide "incentives to replace, repower or retrofit existing diesel-powered on-road trucks," $20 million for air quality mitigation, and $20 million for aesthetic improvements to the community, including parks and landscaping.[286] In NRDC lawyer Gail Feuer's words, "Today is Day 1 in the greening of the Port of Los Angeles."[287]

Yet the greening project was nearly over as soon as it began. In a startling setback, it was quickly revealed that the port had not consulted China Shipping about the settlement terms, particularly the requirement that all docked ships turn off their diesel engines and plug into electrical outlets.[288] As it turned out, China Shipping leased its ships and would not commit to the retrofitting needed to convert them to electrical power, which it estimated would cost $300,000 per ship (well beyond the $5 million the port committed in settlement for retrofitting).[289] With the deal in jeopardy, city and port officials engaged in damage control. Port Executive Director Larry Kelly flew to Shanghai to meet with China Shipping representatives, while city officials indirectly blamed NRDC for the failure to notify China Shipping of the settlement terms—arguing that a confidentiality requirement imposed by the plaintiffs prevented city officials from revealing the terms of the settlement until after it was executed.[290] NRDC's Feuer responded in disbelief: "It never actually dawned on us that they weren't talking to China Shipping."[291] If the city had asked for permission to run the settlement by China Shipping—whose buy-in was obviously critical to effectuating the deal—Feuer was sure the plaintiffs would have provided permission to do so.[292]

Figure 6.10 Noel Park (left) and Gail Ruderman Feuer (right) on future site of China Shipping terminal. *Source*: Bob Chamberlin/*Los Angeles Times* via Getty Images (March 6, 2003).

A year after the landmark settlement, the completed terminal sat vacant as city officials worked to salvage the lease. As negotiations unfolded, NRDC agreed to a revised proposal under which China Shipping would commit to plug in 70% of docked ships rather than the 100% proposed in the original agreement, while only making two cranes low profile; however, NRDC held fast to its demand that the port include language in the EIR recognizing the project's "aesthetic impacts" on the surrounding communities.[293] At this the port balked, claiming it did not want to "prejudge" the outcome of the environmental review.[294] After a flurry of meetings, an amended settlement was hammered out, with the port agreeing to make clear that the original $20-million community fund was "being created in part to allow for the mitigation of the aesthetic impacts of the China Shipping terminal off of port lands," while the environmentalists agreed to language that the port was "not prejudging whether these impacts are adverse or significant."[295] This resolution cleared the way for China Shipping to take occupancy, which it did in May 2004[296]—marking the creation of what was hailed as the world's first green terminal, with cold ironing (i.e., dockside electrical plug-in) capability "expected to eliminate more than three tons of nitrogen oxides (NOx) and 350 pounds of diesel particulate matter for each ship that plugs in."[297] Councilwoman Janice Hahn summed up what activists hoped would be the foundation for future change: "The China Shipping Settlement sets a precedent of how we do things at the Port today and into the future."[298]

Hahn's claim turned out to be prescient, as the China Shipping victory reinforced other efforts to stem port-related diesel emissions. At the local level, resident and environmental groups, in newfound alliance, began pressing Mayor James Hahn for stronger city regulation. The ground had already been laid by Mayor Hahn, who as a candidate promised harbor residents that he would commit to a "no net increase" policy capping port emissions at 2001 levels.[299] In the face of an expected quadrupling of container traffic at Los Angeles and Long Beach by 2025,[300] particulate matter from port sources was predicted to increase from one thousand to more than twenty-seven hundred tons per year.[301] In a letter to San Pedro activist Noel Park, Hahn also committed to "review all past, present and future environmental documents in an open public process to ensure that all laws—particularly those related to environmental projects—have been obeyed, all city procedures followed, and all adverse impacts upon the communities mitigated."[302] As secession fever raged and the China Shipping fight was at its height, Mayor Hahn, in his first "state of the harbor address," promised to promote green policies, such as a conversion of port machines to low-emission technology and the creation of a no net increase plan.[303] Some of the items in the speech, such as cold ironing, found their way into the China Shipping agreement. How Hahn planned to implement no net increase remained unclear.

Hahn's plan was pushed forward by mounting evidence of port pollution and regulatory responses to it. In an environmental report card issued in early 2004, NRDC and the Coalition for Clean Air issued Los Angeles a C– and Long Beach a C for their environmental practices.[304] In its press release announcing the report card, NRDC stated that the two ports released as much diesel exhaust as sixteen thousand idling trucks per day.[305] In a subsequent report, NRDC systematically reviewed the negative health impacts of port emissions and made a number of recommendations to mitigate them.[306] Among those recommendations were replacing extremely old trucks, retrofitting others, and mandating the use of cleaner burning fuels.[307] In addition, following the China Shipping model, the report recommended moving ships to shoreside electrical power[308]—a proposal advanced by CARB in April. The NRDC report also identified the need for stricter rules on truck idling,[309] noting that a 2002 bill sponsored by Democratic state Assemblyman Alan Lowenthal from Long Beach—which banned idling for more than thirty minutes outside the port—had been largely circumvented by moving the trucking queue inside port property.[310] In July 2004, CARB approved a rule prohibiting diesel vehicles of ten thousand pounds or more from idling more than five minutes anywhere.[311]

These reports catalyzed ongoing efforts to address port air pollution—including a proposed state no net increase bill by Assemblyman Lowenthal and a battle to stop the expansion of Long Beach's Pier J—both of which brought advocacy around Mayor Hahn's local no net increase initiative to a head. On July 7, 2004, residents were outraged by the release of a Plan to Achieve No Net Increase of Air Emissions at the Port of Los Angeles, authored by the port with the aid of the Houston-based Starcrest Consulting Group.[312] What upset residents most was the plan's claim that the port could achieve Hahn's promise of no net increase without any major new programs by assuming a sharp reduction in air pollution based on the China Shipping truck retrofitting program.[313] Residents objected that the program would only replace four hundred of the more than six thousand trucks that were more than twenty years old—and noted even that would not be completed until 2008.[314]

Embarrassed by the blowback, Mayor James Hahn and Councilwoman Janice Hahn instructed Port of Los Angeles Director Larry Keller to establish a task force to develop a credible strategy.[315] In the wake of the conflict, Keller resigned.[316] Mayor Hahn then appointed a twenty-eight-member No Net Increase Task Force, which began meeting in October 2004 and included Noel Park (also on the Port Community Advisory Committee) and Gail Feuer, along with representatives from industry, labor unions, and other community and environmental groups. Despite this, critics continued to blast the mayor for failing to keep his promise to remediate projects completed prior to 2001.[317]

The task force considered a range of initiatives to deal with port emissions, which included an ambitious (and, at $35 million, expensive) replacement program to convert one thousand old diesel trucks to 2004 clean models.[318] Industry groups participated but were wary, with one terminal operator suggesting that a plan mandating cold ironing would not "survive a constitutional challenge."[319] Although the task force was supposed to present a plan to Hahn by December 31, 2004, election-year politics appeared to intervene, with the group's draft proposal delayed until just before the hotly contested primary between Hahn and challenger Antonio Villaraigosa in March 2005.[320] Released on March 3, the draft contained proposals—without attending to cost or feasibility—for cleaner fuel, subsidized new truck conversion, and cold ironing.[321] Despite progress, the plan was perhaps most notable for what it did not include: support from neighboring Long Beach, which rejected an invitation to participate and instead produced its own green port plan in January 2005 without input from air quality regulators.[322] Opining on the Los Angeles plan, Port of Long Beach Planning Director Robert Kanter complained that "[t]here are some radical ideas, pie-in-the-sky ideas, that I don't think are likely to take place in the near term."[323]

The Los Angeles task force forged ahead in the face of this criticism, producing a final emission reduction plan projected to prevent 2,200 premature deaths over 20 years at a cost of $11 billion.[324] Yet industry resistance to aspects of the plan prevented consensus; as a result, the task force did not vote to endorse the plan,[325] but rather simply turned over its recommendations to Mayor Hahn—who had lost the election—one week before the end of his term.[326] The six-hundred-page report was impressive in its detailed scientific analysis of emissions and in the scope of its policy proposals,[327] which included sixty-eight separate control measures for different emission source categories (ocean-going vessels, harbor craft, cargo-handling equipment, rail, and heavy-duty vehicles).[328] The plan's basic structure was to offer analysis and recommendations proposed by air regulators and environmentalists, while interlineating industry objections throughout.

In addition to fighting over specific regulations, industry and environmental representatives clashed over the port's legal authority to implement proposals—a harbinger of fights to come. Section 5 of the report provided a detailed legal analysis that focused primarily on the issue of federal preemption, particularly with respect to the Clean Air Act.[329] That analysis was drafted through rancorous negotiations between SCAQMD and NRDC (led Gail Feuer) on one side, and lawyers for the rail lines and Pacific Merchant Shipping Association (PMSA)—the industry trade group representing shippers and terminal operators—on the other. The result was a carefully worded analysis that offered a sweeping review of preemption doctrine and a proposal-by-proposal legal analysis, which was impressive in its comprehensiveness, while exposing the deep differences between environmental and industry lawyers on the issue of local authority.

While the SCAQMD and NRDC asserted that the port's implementation of no net increase measures "could be characterized as proprietary conduct that is exempt from federal preemption under the market participant exemption,"[330] rail and PMSA lawyers were much more skeptical, arguing that the Port of Los Angeles "may not adopt a sweeping set of control measures through its contracts and leases in order to implement broad social policy regarding air quality under the guise of the market participant exception."[331] The legal gauntlet was thus thrown down. On July 30, 2005—his last day in office—Hahn endorsed the No Net Increase Task

Force report and recommended "that the Villaraigosa administration adopt the report's finding to make sure that the Port of Los Angeles is the nation's leader in clean air standards."[332] Although many task force members had hailed the plan as a step in the right direction, some community representatives were disappointed with Hahn's failure to keep his no net increase promise, instead tossing the "hot potato" to the next mayor.[333]

For his part, the new mayor seemed determined not to drop it. To the contrary, Villaraigosa—the former Democratic Speaker of the California Assembly, who had campaigned on a platform of green growth and swept into the mayor's office with a coalition of labor, environmental, and other progressive constituencies—appeared committed to aggressive action to meet the seemingly intractable problem of reconciling port expansion with environmental and community health. For Villaraigosa, filling vacancies on the Harbor Commission at the Port of Los Angeles was high on his priority list upon taking office. Against the backdrop of China Shipping and the sense that port expansion was threatened by ongoing environmental clashes, the mayor was committed to appointing board members with environmental experience and community credibility.[334]

To do so, Villaraigosa convened an advisory group of seventy-five diverse stakeholders and asked them to create a pipeline of applicants for commission positions who were "not the usual suspects," but rather people "who think outside the box, who are creative, who come from all over the city."[335] One of those people was Jerilyn López Mendoza, head of the Environmental Justice Project at the Environmental Defense Fund.[336] In addition to environmental expertise, especially around the environmental review process, Mendoza had a deep familiarity with labor issues and the complexity of Los Angeles's proprietary departments, having just finished negotiating the seminal half-billion dollar LAX CBA.[337] Mendoza was contacted by two members of the Villaraigosa transition team, Paula Daniels, former member of the California Coastal Commission, and Cecilia Estolano, then of counsel at Gibson, Dunn & Crutcher.[338] With their encouragement, Mendoza filled out an application and was soon contacted by a screening firm that, she recalled, "asked me . . . pointed questions, like what was my theory of social change and how did I define my work in terms of environmental justice?"[339] At the final interview, Mendoza recalled that she and the mayor engaged in a lengthy "exchange of monologues, where he would sort of explain things to me from his perspective and then I would sort of explain my perspective based on his perspective."[340] In this conversation, Mendoza said the mayor laid out his position:

> [The Port of Los Angeles is] always going to be a working port . . . . It really is just one of our most important economic assets. It's never going to be Marina del Rey. It's never going to be a tourist location . . . . My vision for the port is I want to see the cleanest, greenest port in the world . . . . Do you think that's possible?[341]

Mendoza's answer was yes, "if you have the political will."[342] Her selection as commissioner indicated that the will was indeed there—a view underscored by the appointment of David Freeman, who was former energy secretary to President Carter, general manager of the Tennessee Valley Power Authority, energy czar to Governor Gray Davis, and head of the Los Angeles Department of Water and Power.[343] Freeman, a close adviser to Villaraigosa, was considered someone able to get things done.[344] Freeman and Mendoza were appointed in July 2005 and confirmed in September, along with Kaylynn Kim, a private attorney; Doug Krause, general counsel of East West Bank; and Joe Radisich, president of the Southern California District Council of the ILWU.[345]

The new board immediately signaled a different approach, holding its first scheduled meeting in an overflowing community center in Wilmington,[346] rather than its traditional spot in the San Pedro Harbor Administration Building.[347] There, Freeman, as board president, criticized the Hahn no net increase plan's 2001 emissions baseline, telling the crowd, "[s]urely, you can't settle on that."[348] He asked port staff to evaluate the Hahn task force plan, moving with a greater sense of urgency by requesting a review of which proposals could be accelerated and expanded.[349]

CARB kept on the pressure, releasing a study finding that the port increased cancer risk up to fifteen miles away,[350] while also linking cargo transportation near the port to a host of health problems, which it estimated cost over $6 billion to treat.[351] CARB's study found that twenty-four hundred people died annually as a result of port-related air pollution, many of them in surrounding neighborhoods.[352] In April 2006, as part of a Governor Schwarzenegger-sponsored initiative to meet federal clean air deadlines, CARB approved a plan to reduce goods movement emissions to 2001 levels through a variety of proposals—including cleaner ship fuel, cold ironing, and replacing old diesel trucks.[353] Yet the lack of funding or mandatory requirements caused Harbor Commission President David Freeman to scoff: "Are they ordering people to do things? No? Then what the hell good are they?"[354] For his part, Freeman sought to be more useful. He understood that tackling the green growth problem "was the reason the mayor named me and [Mendoza] and people like that to get the job done. . . . I mean, obviously the exact details of how we were going to go about it were not preordained, but . . . I was put on there because of my environmental credentials and the fact that the mayor knew me as a person that wasn't just a bullshit artist but kind of made things happen that we talked about."[355]

As Mendoza recalled, the board viewed its mission as executing the mayor's goal of making the Port of Los Angeles "the cleanest, greenest port in the world."[356] In discussing how to do that, she said, the commissioners quickly "realized two things: one was everything we did had to be in close coordination with Long Beach. [Without coordination,] the customers and other people who work and live at the port would just move over to Long Beach where they didn't have to deal with it. . . . The second thing we realized was that we weren't going to get anything done unless we adjust all sources of pollution . . . even though we knew that trucks were of primary concern. . . ."[357]

The commission moved assertively on both fronts. To promote inter-port cooperation, the first order of business was hiring a port director to replace Keller who could reach across the bay to Long Beach counterparts. That process was managed within the mayor's office by a small group of advisers that included David Libatique, who became part of Villaraigosa's transition team and then was assigned to the L.A. Business Team as port liaison, under the supervision of Deputy Mayor Bud Ovram.[358] With a master's degree in public policy from Harvard, Libatique joined Villaraigosa's transition team in 2005 after working as a deputy to City Councilman Martin Ludlow.[359] Libatique helped vet the port director candidates, ultimately presenting three to the mayor.[360] The goal was to find a new director who would "focus on dealing with the environmental impacts but create a path forward for the port to continue to be an economic engine for . . . the city."[361] In January 2006, the mayor selected Geraldine Knatz, formerly managing director of the Port of Long Beach, who held a doctorate in biological science and was viewed as a strong supporter of "greening and growing."[362] With twenty-three years of experience at Long Beach, Knatz was also seen as a bridge builder who could promote the coordination agenda.[363]

With Knatz in place, the commission reached out to Long Beach to advance a joint plan that would comprehensively address the port complex's multiple sources of pollution—recognizing that when it came to pollution, there was no "dividing line in the air."[364] Although the mayor made his Harbor Commission and port director selections with "green growth" in mind, Libatique recalled that "there wasn't that much advanced planning about how everything was going to roll out."[365] Instead, the mayor entrusted his new team to develop a plan, which it quickly set to do. Shortly after Knatz was hired, she and Freeman met with their Long Beach counterparts to set a framework for discussions that would lead to a comprehensive policy—to be called the Clean Air Action Plan (CAAP).[366] With the process and goals agreed upon, both ports' Harbor Commissions began holding joint monthly meetings to discuss the details. Mayor Villaraigosa reached out to union leaders to gain their support, arguing that enhanced environmental standards at the port were good for the health of union members.[367] Commissioners and port staff also met with industry leaders to get them on board. According to Freeman, the message to industry representatives was clear: The ports could promise expansion only if shippers and other industry players agreed to clean up the system. In Freeman's terms, the board said "you come to us with an expansion proposal and we'll approve it . . . [if you] clean up what you're doing."[368]

It was ultimately the ports' power to reject or delay expansion that provided the leverage needed to get industry buy-in. And although shippers and carriers had other ports they could use, those ports were generally not as attractive because of preexisting infrastructure investments in Los Angeles and Long Beach, as well as access to the lucrative regional market.[369] It was in this context that the Los Angeles and Long Beach Harbor Commissions developed the outlines of CAAP, a draft of which was circulated in July 2006.[370] The main approach was to regulate emission sources tied to the ports—by, for example, requiring docked ships to burn cleaner fuel or adopt cold ironing.[371] Other parts of the plan referenced ambitious goals for overall emission reductions, but the outlines were still tentative.[372]

By the time the final plan was released in November 2006, a focus on trucks had crystallized.[373] While the draft plan was vague on truck regulation, the final plan emphasized replacing diesel trucks that accessed the ports and offered a clearer road map to effectuate that goal.[374] Although explicitly presented as a "living document," the CAAP Technical Report, through Control Measure HDV1, provided a clear emission control framework for heavy-duty vehicles (HDVs), which formed the foundation for what would ultimately become the Clean Truck Program. The report's central contribution was to recognize that port drayage trucks, on average over ten years old, were a significant source of air pollution and to call for the rapid greening of the entire drayage truck fleet serving the ports within a five-year period.[375] In order to cut diesel emissions by nearly half, the report focused on replacing and retrofitting what it estimated to be the 16,800 trucks that accounted for roughly 80% of all port calls.[376] The goal was to achieve "clean" standards by replacing or upgrading all "frequent caller" trucks (those that made more than seven calls per week) to meet EPA 2007 emission standards. For "semi-frequent caller" trucks (3.5 to 7 calls per week), the goal was to replace or upgrade trucks that were model year 1992 or older, while retrofitting newer trucks with certified emission reduction technologies.[377] To do this, the report proposed that ports would provide "significant incentives to owner/operators to encourage accelerated turnover/retrofits, and on the terminal side to maximize the use of 'clean' trucks through lease requirements and/or other mechanisms."[378]

The financial impacts of various incentive programs were modeled, with the main proposal to replace roughly half the trucks and retrofit the other half estimated to cost approximately $1.8 billion.[379] The report acknowledged that even with ports contributing $300 million and the SCAQMD another $36 million,[380] "additional funding on a massive scale will be needed."[381] Only a tentative implementation framework was provided, with several options put on the table to move the ambitious plan forward, ranging from those imposing costs directly on drivers to those shifting all costs to the public.[382] Each option was evaluated in light of emission goals but also taking into account "wages/quality of life" for truck drivers.[383] The commissioners included a specific timeline for action because, as Mendoza recalled, "we didn't want it to be just a clean air plan that implied it was going to be put on a shelf somewhere."[384] Thus, they asked port staff to develop "further program details" and an "implementation plan" for review and approval "by end of 1st quarter 2007."[385]

On November 20, 2006, after a raucous, four-hour joint session of the Harbor Commissions,[386] at which numerous residents and officials (including the Los Angeles mayor) testified, both ports approved CAAP by a unanimous vote.[387] As if to further underline the importance of the trucking piece, the presidents of both ports read a statement into the record that directed their "respective staffs to work expeditiously to bring forward a plan" to tackle the "dirty truck problem."[388] The "skeletal outline" of this plan included "a 5-year, focused effort to replace or retrofit the entire fleet of over 16,000 trucks that regularly serve our Ports with trucks that at least meet the 2007 control standards and that are driven by people who at least earn the prevailing wage."[389] The directive made clear that the ports were to restrict noncompliant trucks from entry and that the fees necessary to fund the program "would be imposed on 'shippers', and not on the drivers."[390] Furthermore, the ports were instructed to "invite private enterprise trucking companies to hire the drivers on terms that offer the proper incentives and conditions to achieve the Clean Air Action Plan goals while resulting in adequately paid drivers."[391] The goal of CAAP was to reduce diesel truck emissions by 80%.[392]

Although the vote was hailed as a serious step toward addressing the ports' "diesel death zone," large questions remained about CAAP's implementation and funding—despite new pledges from the ports of $200 million and the SCAQMD of $48 million, as well as the passage of state Proposition 1B, which authorized $20 billion in bond funding for transportation projects, $1 billion of which was targeted to support air cleanup.[393] CAAP's focus on trucks previewed—and was pushed forward by—the emergence of an environmental-labor alliance that saw clean trucks as a way to achieve emission reductions, while advancing the Teamsters' long-standing goal of unionizing port truck drivers. Evidence of this alliance was on display at the final joint port meeting on CAAP, where truck drivers testified and parked outside in solidarity, while NRDC lawyer Melissa Lin Perrella made the sustainability argument that would define the clean trucks campaign: "The problem is that if you give a poor truck driver a clean truck, he needs to be able to afford maintaining it."[394] Reducing pollution over the long term would require raising the labor standards of the truck drivers. The Campaign for Clean Trucks was thus born.

Reforming the Ports: The Campaign for Clean Trucks

The Alliance: Forming the Coalition

Personnel

The move toward clean trucks was a product of political opportunity and interest convergence. Opportunity came from the ports' need to develop a sustainable emission control framework that took all stakeholder concerns into account. By highlighting the need to clean up sixteen thousand dirty diesel trucks, CAAP made a link between environmentalism and driver work standards—which organized labor was eager to strengthen. The environmental movement's interest in cleaning up trucks thereby converged with the labor movement's interest in transforming drivers' employment status. For organized labor, environmentalists brought legal leverage and community activists brought grassroots credibility. For environmental and community leaders, labor brought political heft and the ability to move local power.

There were both top-down and bottom-up processes at play in the campaign. The top-down process was driven by Change to Win, which was in the midst of formulating its ports strategy, focused on the concession model, at the very moment the CAAP process was moving toward its approval. The intersection between Change to Win's ports campaign and CAAP occurred by design, but the precise timing was somewhat fortuitous. The Blue-Green Alliance, a formal collaboration between labor and environmental groups, was founded in 2006 as way to overcome historic antagonisms to develop policies that created good jobs and a healthy environment. Carl Pope, director of the Sierra Club, announced an initial agreement between the Sierra Club and the United Steel Workers union in June 2006.[395] He then began meeting with other labor leaders to build out the alliance.

In July, Pope met with top officials at Change to Win to discuss potential collaborations. At that time, although Change to Win had begun to move forward with its five-port concession strategy, the ports team did not have a strong grasp of the local situation in Los Angeles. The Sierra Club, in contrast, had just completed a video about the China Shipping case—called "Terminal Impact"[396]—and, through the local chapter, was deeply engaged in ongoing efforts to stem port pollution. In discussing Change to Win's ports campaign, Pope, who was closely connected to Los Angeles Sierra Club activists, mentioned the CAAP process. Change to Win's Nick Weiner, who was at the July meeting, remembered that Pope's mention of Los Angeles, although "just happenstance," allowed the port team to key in on Los Angeles as an auspicious site and to "connect the dots" between the concession model and environmental compliance.[397] As Weiner recalled, "we discovered that, oh right, these are old polluting trucks and they contribute to the pollution in L.A. in particular. [The Pope meeting] kind of just happened . . . around the same time so that we were able to then further develop [the concession] theory."[398]

From there, Weiner and his colleagues were assigned to "figure out L.A."[399]— a task they undertook with speed and intensity. Weiner and John Canham-Clyne immediately reached out to Maria Elena Durazo, head of the Los Angeles County Fed, and Madeline Janis, director of LAANE,[400] which had by now honed its mission around "championing the role that local government [could] play in nudging either individual industries or the broader regional economy."[401] With LAANE's support, the campaign "took off," toward the goal of passing a concession policy at the Ports of Los Angeles and Long Beach.[402] Although Change to Win launched its campaign nationwide, there was particular optimism about Los Angeles because "the politicians and politics lined up . . . [and] our ability to build a coalition lined up" because the "infrastructure was already there."[403]

The first order of business was to mobilize that infrastructure in support of the campaign. Change to Win chose LAANE, known for its sophisticated campaign research and policy work, to house staff and be the focal point of the coalition building process. As Canham-Clyne recalled, "We did want to make sure that LAANE was involved . . . because they had demonstrated experience in bringing together community organizations and the labor movement in ways that actually functioned."[404] Change to Win thus made an initial funding grant to LAANE in order to support campaign hiring and administrative assistance.[405] Hiring was overseen by Change to Win's Weiner and Canham-Clyne, who sought to bring in personnel with skills necessary to move the port agenda. A key member of this new team was Jon Zerolnick, who joined LAANE in 2006.[406] A Yale undergraduate who pursued graduate labor studies at the University of Massachusetts, Zerolnick was a researcher with deep experience in corporate campaigns.[407] During graduate school, he interned with HERE Local 11 in Los Angeles. When HERE offered to hire him full-time, Zerolnick dropped out of graduate school and went to Las Vegas to work on campaigns to organize culinary workers and employees at the Venetian hotel.[408] From there, Zerolnick went to Denver to join the AFL-CIO on a multi-union organizing campaign at the Denver International Airport and then moved to Los Angeles in 2002 to staff the research department of the United Farm Workers union.[409] When the Change to Win split occurred, he consulted with unions for a while until he received a call from Canham-Clyne in 2006, inviting him to become part of the ports team at LAANE, to which Zerolnick was already attracted because of "the overlap of policy and . . . coalition building and organizing."[410]

Zerolnick was soon joined by Patricia Castellanos, who was technically hired first after an interview with Canham-Clyne but took some time off and thus started just after Zerolnick.[411] Castellanos brought a number of key experiences and skills as an organizer with the proven "ability to build coalitions."[412] She had roots in the South Bay after working there on a number of electoral campaigns in the early 1990s, including the fight against the anti-immigrant initiative, Proposition 187.[413] She then spent nearly a decade at AGENDA, the South Los Angeles-based community organizing group and progressive think tank, where she worked on policy and education campaigns with environmental justice groups around the country.[414]

Castellanos also brought connections to the mayor's office. She had campaigned for Villaraigosa in 2005 and joined his staff once he was elected, working on goods movement policy under Larry Frank in the Neighborhood Services office, where she was "trying to build relationships for the mayor in that area."[415] Like Zerolnick, Castellanos was affirmatively recruited. She had "heard rumblings" about the ports campaign when Canham-Clyne called to ask if she was interested.[416] Roxana Tynan from LAANE also reached out to encourage Castellanos, who joined the staff in

Figure 6.11 Patricia Castellanos at the Los Angeles Harbor Commission. *Source*: Peter Dreier (2013).

August 2006 and spent the first few months applying for foundation grants to staff the project at "a high level."[417] She succeeded in securing an initial grant from Hewlett Packard and gradually increased funding to support two organizers and three researchers at the height of the campaign.[418] Although they were both housed at LAANE, which was the campaign's "glue," Castellanos and Zerolnick worked with Weiner and Canham-Clyne in an "integrated" relationship in which they considered themselves "all staff together."[419]

From the outset, the campaign's mission was to advance the concession concept designed by Weiner and Canham-Clyne. In its basic form, the concept was to use the port's legal authority as a market actor to require drayage trucking companies to effectuate a double conversion: of their fleet to clean trucks and of their drivers to employees. The market-based rationale, which formed the legal foundation upon which the plan rested, was that the double conversion was necessary to provide sustainable emission reductions which were, in turn, necessary to ensure stable port growth. Employee conversion was key to making the trucking companies internalize the long-term costs of clean fleet acquisition and maintenance—and thus stop the ongoing environmental litigation around port expansion. A short-term subsidy could incentivize the drivers to buy clean trucks. But to have those trucks maintained over time required that they be owned by the entities best able to bear that cost: the trucking companies themselves. When Weiner and Canham-Clyne reached out to LAANE, they had already fully "hatched this idea" in D.C.[420] Thus, at the point of initial coalition building, Zerolnick and Castellanos understood that the plan, though still incomplete, would adopt the "essence" of what had been developed by Change to Win, in conversation with LAANE and key environmental groups, and that it involved the "port creating a direct contractual relationship with trucking companies."[421]

Weiner and Canham-Clyne advanced the concession model against the backdrop of careful legal analysis, which had been conducted by the Teamsters' Mike Manley and Andrew Kahn of the Teamsters' outside law firm, Davis, Cowell & Bowe in San Francisco. The Teamsters retained Kahn because they needed California counsel and because Kahn and Richard McCracken, another partner at Davis, Cowell & Bowe, had been involved in the early conversations about port organizing—and were among the nation's leading labor lawyers on strategic campaign work. The legal question to Manley and Kahn was: "politically if we could pull this off, would it withstand challenge?"[422] Their analysis looked at the possibility of a lawsuit based on federal preemption and also researched potential actions by the Federal Maritime Commission under the Shipping Act.[423] On preemption, their conclusion was that "we should be okay. A port would have authority, as a market participant and as a matter of its proprietary rights, to restrict who could come onto its property."[424] The lawyers were sure that the American Trucking Associations (ATA) would sue the ports if the Clean Truck Program passed, but they believed that the ports would ultimately prevail. With Manley and Kahn's analysis of the program as a valid exercise of port authority, the campaign was given legal clearance. As Weiner recalled, "the attorneys thought we had a pretty good case in the Ninth Circuit" and the "likelihood was remote" that the Supreme Court would ultimately take the case.[425]

Partnerships

The campaign's critical first steps involved bringing together a diverse range of partner groups with the expertise to shape policy and the power to move political decision-makers. Key among those groups were unions, environmental and environmental justice organizations, public health advocates, and faith-based groups. For LAANE, the initial goal was to convince partner organizations that addressing environmental and community impacts meant transforming the port trucking industry in a way that achieved employee conversion.[426]

Because the campaign was built upon the political power of organized labor, solidifying local union alliances was a crucial starting point. Getting buy-in from the "blue" side of the blue-green coalition was important, given historical tension between unions and environmentalists, particularly around the port where unions like the ILWU and those affiliated with the Building and Trades Council viewed environmental roadblocks to port expansion as inconsistent with their members' economic interests. As the campaign got underway, LAANE met with local union leaders from ILWU Local 13 and Teamsters Local 848, both of which had been active on port trucking issues.[427] Dave Arian from ILWU Local 13 and Miguel Lopez from Teamsters Local 848 were key leaders, who would come to play important roles in the CAAP implementation process. Yet there were tensions between the ILWU and Teamsters from the outset. The Teamsters had nothing to lose in the campaign and everything to gain. With no port drivers under union contract, the Teamsters saw fixing the independent-contractor problem as a solution to one of the union's most intractable organizing dilemmas. For the ILWU, in contrast, the campaign posed serious risks to its already strong position at the ports since any reduction of port activity meant a potential threat to its membership. Consistent with these divergent positions, the Teamsters locals (848 in Long Beach and 63 in East Los Angeles) signed on to the campaign—with Miguel Lopez eventually joining the campaign's steering committee—while the ILWU declined.

To gain traction with the ports, the coalition had to send a "strong message . . . that you can't expand unless you are going to clean up your pollution."[428] The environmentalists brought the "legal muscle" to make good on this threat and thus were crucial allies in the overall plan.[429] Castellanos was the point person for outreach and took the first steps toward building and deepening relations with environmental partners. Some of this groundwork had already been laid through LAANE's participation in the LAX CBA campaign, in which LAANE worked with environmental advocates—particularly Jerilyn López Mendoza of Environmental Defense—in crafting a half-billion-dollar community benefits package focused on environmental remediation and local hiring. As a result of that campaign, Castellanos recalled that "there was some foundation for our relationship with our environmental partners already established . . . [that we were able to] then use as a building block and go deeper."[430]

Doing so meant linking into preexisting port advocacy networks and capitalizing on areas of interest convergence. NRDC, which played a crucial role shaping port development since the China Shipping case, was an essential partner—already sharing some common political and legal ground with organized labor. Earlier blue-green collaborations built trust: NRDC was involved in the LAX community benefits campaign and had worked with the Teamsters on previous litigation to ban Mexican trucks from entering the United States.[431] There were also overlapping legal interests at stake. As the clean trucks campaign was taking shape, NRDC was simultaneously advancing a theory of market participation that supported labor's vision for the port concession model. In the case of *Engine Manufacturers Association v. SCAQMD*, NRDC argued that the SCAQMD was permitted to develop its own emission rules governing commercial fleet vehicles despite Clean Air Act preemption—"seriously pushing the courts" to recognize "local jurisdiction through the market participant exception."[432] In 2005, a district court recognized the exception under the Clean Air

Act and that decision was affirmed by the Ninth Circuit two years later[433]—at the height of the clean trucks campaign.

It was against this backdrop that Castellanos initially reached out to Adrian Martinez, a staff attorney at NRDC, who had a strong background in environmental justice issues.[434] Martinez studied environmental science in college and received a full-tuition public interest law scholarship to attend the University of Colorado Law School, where he went to pursue environmental law.[435] A second-year internship at NRDC turned into a postgraduate fellowship. When Gail Feuer left to become a superior court judge, Martinez took over her position in NRDC's clean air unit. Soon thereafter, he switched over to environmental justice, which was his passion.[436] With experience on port trucking gained from his participation on Hahn's No Net Increase Taskforce, Martinez became the primary NRDC staff member in the ports coalition, charged with thinking about "how legally they could create a more accountable system."[437]

Martinez teamed up with David Pettit, who had joined NRDC in 2007 coming off his work for LAANE in the Inglewood Wal-Mart campaign. Pettit "came into [the job] thinking, in environmental justice terms, that an alliance of labor and environment, should it happen, would be extremely powerful."[438] Pettit's first meeting as an NRDC attorney was about CAAP. From there, he was "able to figure out fairly

Figure 6.12 Adrian Martinez. *Source*: Environmental Entrepreneurs (2006).

quickly that the interests all pointed in the same direction"—toward "shifting the costs and the economic burden of cleaning the trucks from the drivers to . . . the trucking companies."[439]

Melissa Lin Perrella was another NRDC lawyer involved in the ports campaign. An ethnic studies and social welfare major in college interested in the intersection of "public health, civil rights, and low-income issues," Perrella had gone to Georgetown Law School to pursue a public interest career, initially taking a job as an associate with a big law firm, Orrick, Herrington & Sutcliffe.[440] She was there for five years before applying to work on environmental justice at NRDC, where she started in 2004.[441]

For the NRDC lawyers, joining the coalition was a chance to build "effective power" to protect the community from harmful pollution.[442] The alliance with organized labor helped them better understand how "the economics of the port drayage system . . . impact the environmental conditions."[443] Although NRDC lawyers felt "strongly that the economics of the system need[ed] to be changed" they "didn't take a position on whether or not drivers should be unionized."[444] Martinez became a member of the campaign steering committee, where his role was to put the legal issues "on the table" so that coalition members could understand the "legal constraints" before evaluating the policy issues.[445] In participating in the coalition, NRDC lawyers represented NRDC's own members, not the coalition, although Martinez would address legal issues for the coalition that would "pop up."[446] In developing policy, NRDC lawyers would analyze issues from two perspectives: "[T]rying to do what's best for the environment [and] broader coalition, but [also] mindful of—if this ends up in the courtroom, how is this policy going to play out before a judge?"[447] Generally, other coalition groups did not have separate legal counsel and would rely on NRDC to help them understand the legal stakes.[448]

To expand the coalition, LAANE also built relations with other environmental and environmental justice groups that had begun moving toward similar strategies to reduce port emissions. The idea of using port concessions to reshape trucking was also percolating up from below. Convergence between labor and environmentalists occurred through the portal of CAAP, which provided the "perfect opening" for the concession plan.[449] Thus, the creation of the Clean Truck Program occurred as strains of activism that had been running in parallel began to intersect. What remained, in Weiner's terms, was for the details to be "worked through."[450] To do that, Weiner and Canham-Clyne "had a bunch of meetings with people and got to know them, and build trust with them,"[451] in order to "deepen the community's understanding of the economics by bringing the drivers into the conversation."[452]

Connections to environmental partners were built through different networks and sought to be attentive to the tensions between mainstream environmentalism and the environmental justice movement. Environmental activism around the port itself had multiple sources. Tom Politeo, a computer programmer and software developer who was born and raised in San Pedro, was involved in early environmental advocacy in the harbor area.[453] Like Jesse Marquez, founder of the Coalition for a Safe Environment in Wilmington, Politeo ran high school track and became sensitive to the impact of air quality on his athletic activity; also like Marquez, he was moved to activism after explosions in the 1970s revealed the dangers of chemical and oil storage around the ports.[454] In the face of projected port growth, Politeo and other San Pedro residents, including homeowner activist Noel Park, began regularly attending Harbor Commission meetings in the 1980s. After the MATES II study was released in 2000, residents discussed strategies to reduce air pollution.

Through their own analysis, the San Pedro activists independently arrived at a concession model as a way to force trucking companies to have "consideration for the community where they are working."[455] In early 2000, Park presented the concession model to the Harbor Commission based on what the city, led by Councilwoman Cindy Miscikowski, had done at LAX to force concessionaires to meet codes of conduct.[456] Politeo, a Sierra Club member along with Park, argued that truck drivers "should be paid by the clock and not by the can."[457] Thus, the concept of a concession model to address port trucking pollution was born of "multiple inventors."[458] As Politeo recalled:

> [T]hese trucks were starting to queue up in fairly long lines. The trucks would sit there in idle. All the time they're idling, they're inching forward, and they're polluting. . . . The trucking companies and the shippers who control the terminals don't see any of the costs associated with the truckers waiting in long lines. They don't pay for the extra fuel because the truckers pay for that. They don't pay them for sitting around for three hours because it's the truckers' time. We looked at this, and said, "This is an environment in which the people who have the decision-making power don't feel the effect of whether the decisions are smart or not."[459]

In 2001, Politeo, Park, and a handful of other members of the Los Angeles-Orange County chapter of the Sierra Club formed the Harbor Vision Task Force as a formal standing committee within the Sierra Club focused on the environmental impact of goods movement and how to grow the port "green."[460] The task force held its first meetings at the Long Beach Yacht Club (where one member happened to dock his yacht) and then moved to the San Pedro Public Library. The group was small but active, with a decidedly pro-labor bent. There were "a couple of longshoremen" and two former Teamsters: Sharon Cotrell from Long Beach and Dr. John Miller, who had put himself through college in Tennessee by working on a truck-loading dock.[461] In 2002, Cotrell arranged a meeting with Gary Smith, head of the Teamsters local who was working on Long Beach port issues; the groups collaborated to help gain passage of Lowenthal's anti-idling bill, which had little effect, but cemented a working partnership. According to Politeo, the Sierra Club did not get involved in the China Shipping suit, because it "didn't have the resources to make that happen," and as a matter of triage decided "NRDC is doing that."[462] Organizationally, the Sierra Club did not support Hahn's no net increase initiative, which Politeo believed was insufficient, although Park was active on that task force.[463]

After Villaraigosa's election, his administration brought together stakeholders under the auspices of Green LA (funded by the Liberty Hill Foundation),[464] which formed a Port Working Group with Politeo, Andrea Hricko from USC's Keck School of Medicine, Candice Kim from the Coalition for Clean Air, and other environmental representatives.[465] Politeo suggested reaching out to labor, a move that resulted in a series of "brainstorming" meetings in Wilmington attended by Miguel Lopez from the Teamsters local, and representatives from the ILWU and International Brotherhood of Electrical Workers.[466]

Environmental justice and public health advocates became connected through these networks. Angelo Logan of East Yard Communities for Environmental Justice was a member of the Port Working Group, as was Jesse Marquez.[467] Colleen Callahan, manager of air quality policy for the American Lung Association of California, also became involved.[468] Callahan had been an urban and environmental policy major at Occidental College, where she studied under prominent progressive faculty Peter Dreier and Robert Gottlieb.[469] After a stint at the Center for Food and Justice, in 2006, she joined the American Lung Association, where her charge was getting it "more involve[d] in the environmental health advocacy work locally."[470] As a member of the Green LA Port Working Group, Callahan linked up with other environmental activists and then with LAANE staff.[471] Elina Green, who was project manager at the Long Beach Alliance for Children with Asthma (LBACA), recalled meeting Teamsters leader Miguel Lopez and LAANE's Patricia Castellanos through advocacy on environmental mitigation in relation to a proposed intermodal rail yard for BNSF in West Long Beach called the Southern California International Gateway.[472] Community groups, including LBACA, contested the EIR in that project beginning in 2006, and through that process forged crucial alliances with organized labor. From Green's point of view, the rail yard fight "was actually how the Teamsters sort of started to see the community side of things and they recognized that, well, if they supported us in our ask for that rail yard, then there would be potential for support in their campaign and we started to see the issues from each other's side."[473] For Green, the power of the coalition derived from this assemblage of "crazy-strange bedfellows."[474]

The connection between environmental and community groups, LAANE, and Change to Win occurred through these formal networks and outside of them. Politeo of the Sierra Club recalled being contacted by Weiner in 2006 asking for support in developing a concession plan. "I remember my thought was 'Holy shit! They want to do our work for us.' I'm delighted. I sent a slightly less effusive message back, saying that 'Yes, we're interested in these things and even more.'"[475] Politeo began meeting with Change to Win and LAANE staff. The opportunity, as he saw it, was to leverage the staff and political power that was lacking before. "So, here we've got Change to Win, the Teamsters, and LAANE, all interested in this. Okay, I'm not going to skip on this."[476] Politeo recalled that his meetings with LAANE, Change to Win, and the Teamsters flowed seamlessly out of the Port Working Group. "[I]t's almost as if Nick Weiner walked into the room and said at one of our other meetings, 'I'm taking over. It's my show now.' Over some short period of time, those who acceded to that remained, and the rest left."[477] In short order, the ILWU "sort of disappeared."[478] And other groups began to join, including CLUE, which organized clergy in Long Beach, making arguments for reform that sounded in terms of justice and morality.[479] In addition, the coalition added immigrant rights groups, CHIRLA and Hermandad Mexicana,[480] as well as the San Pedro-based Harbor-Watts Economic Development Corporation, a community-based group created in 1997 that focused on neighborhood capacity building and economic revitalization.

In assembling this coalition, LAANE staff did the bulk of the outreach work. Because of her prior environmental justice organizing and South Bay campaign experience, Castellanos was particularly sensitive to being inclusive: "I did not want to be caught in the scenario where we were just working with the NRDCs and [Coalition for Clean Airs] of the world and not giving equal footing to like the East Yard Communities for Environmental Justice."[481] During July and August 2006, she and Zerolnick conducted a first round of meetings with a number of groups, including East Yard Communities, the Coalition for a Safe Environment, and LBACA, in which they asked the groups to "download" what they knew about trucks and provide input on the potential campaign.[482] In Castellanos's terms, "we didn't come into this campaign thinking there is nothing happening out there.... And so it was an opportunity for us to learn."[483] LAANE had already been in contact with some of the groups in connection with the CAAP process; others they met with for the first time.[484] It was during the second round of meetings that LAANE staff sought to enlist groups to join the campaign. At these meetings, Zerolnick focused on presenting the main conceptual analysis, emphasizing that "the employment status of the drivers had to be addressed" and the ports had to have a direct relationship with the trucking companies in order to create "accountability in the system."[485] According to Zerolnick, the frame was less "Are you with us?" and more "Here's our analysis. Does this make sense?"[486]

The general approach to coalition building was to emphasize the opportunity to create a "potential solution" that would be in the "mutual interest" of labor, community, and environmental groups—creating a platform for long-term benefits and progressive policy change.[487] At outreach meetings, some groups wanted to discuss policy details, while others focused on the working relationship with organized labor.[488] There was "some trepidation" among the environmental justice groups about working with a "humongous labor union."[489] Castellanos shared those concerns and promised to "figure it out together."[490] Although the meetings produced active engagement, Castellanos did not "remember much resistance."[491]

Organizations went through different processes to consider whether to join the coalition. LAANE's Castellanos and Zerolnick reached out to the American Lung

Association's Callahan to ask if her group would join the emerging coalition.[492] Callahan recalled having to raise the issue up to "some pretty high channels" within the national association to get approval to join since there "were some concerns about whether it was necessary to support the concessionary model or whether just pushing for the most current EPA standards . . . was sufficient."[493] LBACA, itself a coalition of local residents and health organizations, had to get approval from the entire membership.[494] East Yard Communities' Logan was one coalition member who was excited about the partnership but wanted details about how it was going to function. He recalled working on CAAP when he was contacted by LAANE after "we had been trying to reach out to labor without success."[495] Although enthusiastic about the partnership, "our group's questions were: How's this all going to work out? What are the power dynamics? What is the decision-making structure? . . . [W]e wanted . . . a governance structure that was really democratic."[496]

The mission statement for what would become the Coalition for Clean and Safe Ports sought to meet this democratic demand, while emphasizing the main goals of the campaign:

> Our objective is to improve the condition of the trucking industry and of truck drivers operating at the San Pedro Bay Ports and along associated goods movement corridors. We are guided by the need to reduce associated health impacts on workers and local communities by resolving shortcomings associated with current port trucking practices. In doing so, we will address port trucking's many challenges that face industry, community, government, labor and the environment.
>
> To accomplish our objective, we will foster an appropriate role for trucking as part of goods movement planning and solutions. We will ensure trucks run cleanly, quietly, safely and efficiently with a stable, employee workforce that pays livable wages and offers drivers all the rights and benefits of an employee. We will make sure improvements adopted in the San Pedro Bay area help create systemic solutions that improve conditions overall and don't simply transfer problems to other areas, such as adjacent communities, our inland ports or other stops along the goods movement chain.
>
> We will act on a timely basis as part of a democratic, broad-based coalition to promote public awareness of trucking problems and solutions and we will seek to influence policymakers to put decisive solutions into effect as rapidly as possible.[497]

Policy

The intense period of initial organizing saw the first instance of organizational coordination among members of the fledging coalition: the filing of written comments on the first public draft of CAAP. Released in July 2006, CAAP required its own EIR and thus both NRDC and LAANE filed comments.[498] Although the CAAP draft identified clean trucks as an issue, it did not make the connection to employment status, providing the coalition with an opening. Zerolnick remembered the CAAP provisions on trucking to read like:

> "We're not really sure how to do it. We'll come back to this." So we submitted public comment and said, "Well, actually we have some ideas for how to do this . . . . [A]nd the basic structural problems are independent-contractor status and the lack of a relationship between the port and this sector of the industry."[499]

Zerolnick drafted a comment letter and circulated it to all coalition partners, who made editorial suggestions.[500] He also worked closely with the Teamsters' Manley and lawyers at NRDC, particularly Adrian Martinez, as he fine-tuned the proposal.[501] The input was focused on sharpening the link between industry accountability, employee status, and emission reduction. In Martinez's terms, the focus was on remedying "the Wild, Wild West situation where there really weren't effective standards and there was no accountability."[502]

The final letter seamlessly integrated these arguments, referencing the research that Change to Win had done as a basis to propose a Clean Truck Program built on the concession approach.[503] The letter, sent to the directors of both ports, was submitted on behalf of LAANE and its "coalition partners."[504] The comments were conceptual, focusing on the "real market forces operating on the Port truckers," as well as "the significant and persistent structural problems in the industry."[505] The bulk of the comments were devoted to detailing the economics of the drayage market and its dysfunctions, while explicating how the concession model would transform the industry. The letter emphasized the twofold problem of independent-contractor drivers and lack of port control over trucking companies.[506] It then proposed a "long-term solution" under which the ports would "jointly enter into a direct contractual relationship with responsible motor carriers to provide drayage services at both Ports, utilizing the same model employed by airports to provide food and other services to air travelers."[507] The comments contemplated a request for proposal process awarding port entry only to trucking companies that met:

> clear standards concerning capitalization requirements, revenues paid to the Ports, environmental standards for trucking equipment operating at the Ports, other environmental mitigation measures and benchmarks, employee status for drivers, employment preferences for the current workforce of owner-operators, and labor peace requirements to ensure that revenue streams to the Ports are uninterrupted.[508]

The letter emphasized that the benefits of this proposal would be clean trucks maintained over the long term, achieving emission reductions while also promoting security and greater accountability.[509] The letter was short on specific policy proposals, but long on analysis and prescription, powerfully laying out the essence of what would become the Clean Truck Program. Although the details were still unclear, the key move was linking clean trucks to employment status through a direct contract between the ports and the trucking companies.[510] CAAP thus provided the critical opportunity to unite disparate labor, environmental, and community interests around a coherent policy program to attack diesel truck emissions and driver misclassification.

The last step was to officially convene the Coalition for Clean and Safe Ports. The launch was timed to happen right before the joint ports' CAAP review meeting on November 20, 2006. In order to maximize publicity, the coalition staged a major press conference,[511] while organizing a "massive community driver turnout," which helped shape the electric environment leading to CAAP approval.[512] Although the coalition grew over the two-year fight for the Clean Truck Program,[513] its initial composition reflected wide support that underscored the success of LAANE's outreach.[514] In the end, the Coalition for Clean and Safe Ports was broad and deep. As Martinez recalled: "We had community, we had faith-based groups, we had the environmental justice community, we had the environmental community, we had economic development groups. . . . We had lawyers, we had scientists involved, we had economic experts, we had people on the ground."[515]

In keeping with its commitment to inclusivity and democracy, while also acknowledging the need for clear and efficient decision-making, the coalition structured a tripartite governance system. Policy decisions were ultimately to be decided by a supermajority vote of the coalition members.[516] To facilitate operations, members agreed to create a steering committee composed of a smaller group of representatives from key organizational partners: three labor, two environmental, two community, two immigration, and one to two research/academic partners.[517] This committee—which "played to the coalition's strengths" by giving voice to the diverse groups involved[518]—was charged with agenda-setting, providing strategic recommendations, and making day-to-day and urgent decisions.[519] The steering committee was created in recognition of the fact that the groups were part of a "live campaign" that required some quick decisions, but also was designed to vet policy and strategy ideas in order to make recommendations for full coalition approval.[520] As necessary, the coalition agreed to set up working subcommittees to deal with various policy issues and give recommendations to the full coalition. These subcommittees were established to develop coalition policy with respect to specific community, environmental, and labor issues. LAANE staffed the subcommittees but did not formally sit on them. Thus structured, the coalition was ready to take action.

The Affirmative Phase: Mobilizing Local Law
The Outside Game: Developing the Program, Exerting Pressure

With the coalition in place, LAANE's effort shifted to rolling out the campaign to pass the Clean Truck Program. The basic approach was twofold. First, the coalition would meet during an intense period to hammer out the details of the program—converting the model taken from Change to Win into a workable policy. Second, the coalition would engage decision-makers and stakeholders to build support for the program. These elements—a clear policy draft and outside pressure—would then be used to move the policy through internal city and port channels.

At the outset of the campaign, both the Los Angeles and Long Beach ports were still aligned in the process, reflecting the ongoing energy around implementing CAAP. In early 2007, the ports established a stakeholder group comprised of representatives from the ports, air agencies, industry, environmental and labor groups, and academia.[521] Several coalition members participated, including Angelo Logan from East Yard Communities, Melissa Lin Perrella from NRDC, Jesse Marquez from Coalition for a Safe Environment, Elina Green from LBACA, Candice Kim from the Coalition for Clean Air, Miguel Lopez from the Teamsters, and Patricia Castellanos from LAANE.[522] The stakeholder group was created to provide input into the ports' larger process of CAAP implementation, which included the development of a detailed Clean Truck Program.[523]

To inform that process—and ultimately shape what the final program would look like—the coalition moved quickly to build out the policy. Following on the heels of CAAP approval, which established the general framework for port truck regulation, "things really kicked into high gear."[524] In late 2006, the coalition set to work on filling in program details in order to shape the final rules. At the outset, the coalition had its basic "yardstick": that any Clean Truck Program had to be "accountable, sustainable, and comprehensive," which meant that it would rest upon fleet *and* employee conversion—thus avoiding a short-term solution converting the fleet to clean trucks through a one-time public subsidy that left the trucking companies without responsibility for long-term maintenance.[525] The question for the coalition members was "what are the standards going to be?"[526]

To answer this question, the coalition engaged in external and internal discussions. Externally, LAANE and Change to Win organizers met with port staff and key elected officials to present the general framework provided by Change to Win. From there, Zerolnick—working closely with the Teamsters' Manley and NRDC's Martinez—began to draft the policy. This was an iterative process that connected to the coalition's internal discussions. Within the coalition, members broke into subcommittees charged with developing standards around labor, environmental, and community issues.[527] To advance this process, the coalition initiated monthly standing meetings, with individual subcommittees engaged in intensive policy discussions that continued during the interim periods.[528] Community partners responded to specific requests for evaluating provisions and came up with some of their own. For example, residents working with coalition member East Yard Communities proposed to make trucking companies park trucks off neighborhood streets and adhere to specified truck routes that would minimize community disruption.[529] Once vetted at the subcommittee level, provisions were passed onto the steering committee for incorporation into the working draft and then presented to the entire coalition for general approval. Although full coalition approval was technically by supermajority vote, Zerolnick recalled that decisions were all made by consensus.[530] As the draft details evolved, LAANE and Change to Win organizers would meet again with city and port officials, getting their feedback and buy-in.[531]

What emerged from this process was a document that the coalition called a request for proposal (RFP) designed as a vehicle for implementing the concession model. The RFP was essentially a scoring system to rate trucking firms as potential concessionaires.[532] Scores were based on responses to application questions designed to ensure that trucking companies met criteria necessary to effectuate the Clean Truck Program.[533] The RFP model was chosen because the coalition assumed that for ease of administration the ports would limit entry to a handful of trucking concessionaires and the RFP provided a standard system to allow the ports to rank applicants.[534] The RFP document was primarily drafted by Zerolnick, shaped by extensive discussions among coalition members, and contained items the coalition viewed as "a bottom line"—phasing out old trucks and employee conversion—and others that were on a "wish list."[535]

The RFP's main purpose was to ensure "that the most responsible entities operate at the Port."[536] Toward that end, the RFP designated responsible business, security, environmental, labor, community, and efficiency standards, though the overall plan hinged on converting old dirty trucks to new clean ones, while also converting the drivers to employees. The standards were to be implemented through the ports' contract power. "Successful applicants will enter into a contract with the Port mandating a turnover of the entire truck fleet over five years."[537] Applicants were also required to "use only employee drivers (as opposed to independent contractors) to provide drayage services."[538] The RFP was structured so as to assign a baseline score to applicants meeting minimum criteria, while then giving extra points to applicants that could demonstrate good business practices and community relations—which were the "wish list" items.[539] The minimum standards were framed to advance core elements of the Clean Truck Program. Applicants were asked, "Does the Applicant utilize only employee drivers to perform drayage services?" and were informed that they "must comply with the requirements of the Clear Bay Clean Air Action Plan (CAAP) regarding the reduction of pollution from diesel trucks."[540] Applicants also had to "provide an assurance of labor peace"[541]—an agreement that they would not disrupt unionization efforts in exchange for a commitment on the part of employees not to strike. The time frame for employee conversion was not specified, though applicants were told that they had five years to convert their entire fleets to EPA 2007 standards (by purchasing new trucks or through retrofit) with a minimum of one-fifth of the fleet converted each year.[542] Applicants were also asked "to make arrangements to provide off-street parking" for out-of-service trucks and to "work with the Port . . . to develop a plan to minimize the impact of HDVs on port-adjacent communities."[543] Concession fees were to be set at an initial level of $5,000 per truck in addition to a 10% monthly revenue fee.[544] In April 2007, the RFP was submitted to both Harbor Commissions, which said that they would take it "under advisement."[545] Although it was not meant to be public, the RFP was leaked to the press.

On April 12, 2007, the ports jointly issued their own Proposed Clean Trucks Program, which gave the coalition most of what it wanted—adopting the concession model as its cornerstone—though in a different format.[546] In what NRDC's Perrella called "a huge, huge step forward in our quest for clean air,"[547] the ports agreed to use their "tariff authority"—their power to pass port rules, called "tariffs"—to "only allow concessionaries operating 'clean' trucks to enter port terminals without having to pay a new Truck Impact Fee at the gate."[548] For the purposes of the program, a clean truck had to meet the so-called "CAAP standard," which meant EPA 2007-compliant new trucks, retrofitted trucks for those of model year 1994 and newer, and trucks replaced through the Gateway Cities program created under the China Shipping settlement.[549] Older trucks would be progressively banned (with a 2012 target date) though could continue to enter if their companies—referred to as licensed motor carriers, or LMCs—paid a truck impact fee of $34 to $54 per container.[550] Proceeds from that fee and a $26 cargo fee, along with other sources of public funding, would be used to subsidize truck replacement and retrofit. Concessionaires would also have to commit to "require employee drivers (after a transition period),"[551] with the goal of achieving full employee conversion by January 1, 2012.[552] Following the coalition model, the ports proposed to confer concessions after an RFP process in which "applicants w[ould] be evaluated for financial strength and asset control."[553] The ports' proposed plan did not go as far as the coalition's in limiting entry to those companies that met best business practice standards. Nonetheless, from the coalition's perspective, "it really did contain most of what we wanted."[554] Industry representatives viewed it through the opposite lens and immediately asserted the threat of litigation. As Curtis Whalen, executive director of the ATA, put it: "We are looking at it now from our lawyers' point of view to see what we might do. I think we might challenge that. . . . By definition, these containers represent interstate commerce. It would impact interstate commerce in a dramatic way. Can a port authority do that?"[555]

The coalition believed that the answer was "yes" and seized the opportunity to push forward. In response to the ports' proposal, Zerolnick (again with input from lawyers Manley and Martinez) drafted another comment letter—this time submitted under the formal auspices of the Coalition for Clean and Safe Ports.[556] Unlike the first letter, which was conceptual, this one was "more concrete," addressing specific policy details.[557] The letter, while commending the ports for their "leadership" and "hard work," sought to offer areas for the plan's improvement.[558] Although it addressed a variety of technical details, the letter emphasized the employee component, which was not explicated in detail in the ports' draft. Specifically, the letter argued that—unlike the conversion to clean trucks—there should be no transition period for the conversion to employee drivers.[559] To do otherwise, the letter suggested, would create potential unfairness for companies that complied earlier and would impose insurmountable administrative problems.[560]

It was the spring of 2007 and negotiations over the terms of the Clean Truck Program had begun in earnest. As the negotiations developed, they would focus on three crucial elements of the program: (1) the nature and timing of the ban on dirty trucks and the related phase-in of clean trucks; (2) the amount and structure of fees imposed on truck cargo, and the related amount of financial incentives allocated to fund clean truck conversion; and (3) the structure and content of the concession agreement, with particular emphasis on the extent and timing of employee conversion.

To advance the coalition's positions on these issues, members sought to "debate it out in public," organizing around a series of port commission meetings to demonstrate that the coalition was "a force to be reckoned with."[561] The Los Angeles and Long Beach Harbor Commissions held regular public meetings to discuss policy development, at which coalition members, community residents, and truck drivers turned out to press the argument that "we need to fix the trucking system."[562] As NRDC's David Pettit described with wry humor, the coalition would turn these normally staid events into dramatic affairs by bringing hundreds of people "with torches and pitchforks."[563] There were also special meetings devoted specifically to the Clean Truck Program, which were in Zerolnick's memory "even longer and even more contentious."[564] In one, held in June 2007, three hundred drivers turned out to support the program. Edgar Sanchez, a driver from Long Beach, credited coalition support with motivating him to speak out:

> Before we didn't have the courage or the confidence to tell people how we feel out of fear we'd be fired or labeled as troublemakers. . . . Not anymore. We see the smoke pouring out of our trucks and we breathe it all day, every day. . . . But we also work long hours at minimum rates. We can be fired at any moment, like slaves without a voice.[565]

A few months later, on October 12, the ports held a Joint Public Workshop on the Clean Truck Program—a six-hour meeting at which the ports took "tons of testimony" from various stakeholders,[566] including LAANE's Castellanos and NRDC's Perrella, as well as numerous truck drivers and community residents.[567] As the Joint Public Workshop underscored, a primary function of the coalition was to turn out members at meetings to testify in favor of the proposed program. These meetings were also a focal point for circulating and responding to draft policies. Drafts would emanate from the ports and Zerolnick would work primarily with NRDC lawyers to craft a response; that response would be circulated among coalition members for comments and then once finalized sent back to the ports for review. Meetings were opportunities for exchange and amplification. During this back-and-forth, coalition members would shape program language and clarify objectives. For instance, a LBACA community resident working with the coalition developed the idea to put placards on trucks indicating a number to call to report any emission and safety issues[568]—an idea that was eventually incorporated into the working plan.

During this period, coalition pressure was applied in open spaces and behind closed doors. The coalition staged a number of public actions, including a caravan of one hundred big rigs down the 110 Freeway to the Port of Long Beach.[569] Coalition members also met privately with harbor commissioners, mayor's office staff, and council staff in both cities—though the approach increasingly diverged between Los Angeles and Long Beach. In Los Angeles, the coalition had allies in key elected politicians and harbor commissioners, and thus the outreach was designed to give them the materials and arguments necessary to hold the line against industry lobbying. The big push, according to the Coalition for Clean Air's Candice Kim, was convincing "people to understand that the employee provision was an environmental provision."[570] This was true at the commission level and in the mayor's office, where there were some divisions among the mayor's staff about whether the program should just advance the green elements or should also include the blue focus on employee drivers. As a result, Nick Weiner remembered having to "fend off repeated attempts by . . . forces within the mayor's office who wanted to jettison the labor components of the Clean Truck Program."[571] In Los Angeles, the coalition also had a powerful champion in Councilwoman Janice Hahn, with whom members met regularly to work out strategy and policy details.[572] In Castellanos's view, Hahn "genuinely was supportive of workers and workers' issues. I think this was in her district and she cared about it."[573]

In Long Beach, the approach was different given the skepticism of recently elected Mayor Bob Foster about the employee provision of the program. Foster, a Democrat who had headed Southern California Edison, won the Long Beach mayor's race in a run-off election in June 2006. He took office that next month, just as CAAP was moving toward approval and the battle for clean trucks was taking shape. Los Angeles Harbor Commissioner Jerilyn López Mendoza recalled having lunch with Foster early in his term to discuss the prospects for port coordination around CAAP. After the lunch, she called LAANE organizer William Smart to ask: "Have you guys talked to Bob Foster yet? . . . I don't think he's on board with an employee mandate. . . . I think you all have some work to do."[574] Coalition members were deployed to increase the pressure on Foster—since unilateral action by Los Angeles could undermine the entire project by diverting cargo to Long Beach.

Elina Green of LBACA mobilized the group's community-based membership to share the challenges they experienced caring for children with asthma and how the Clean Truck Program would promote better public health.[575] As LBACA members worked to "pull any strings" they had with Long Beach officials, they also faced local reprisal: Green recalled one meeting with Mayor Foster and a small group of coalition members in which the mayor was "literally yelling at us the entire meeting."[576]

Coalition members played different roles in exerting outside pressure over the course of the two-year campaign. In private meetings and public hearings, LAANE and Change to Win made the case for industry restructuring, while NRDC emphasized the environmental benefits (and held out the implicit litigation threat). LAANE's Castellanos, Change to Win's Weiner and Canham-Clyne, and NRDC's Martinez, Perrella, and Pettit met regularly with port staff, both mayor's offices, and both city councils, though the emphasis was on the Long Beach City Council because of Janice Hahn's support in Los Angeles.[577] The goal of these meetings was to make the case for sustainability, while also demonstrating the power of the blue-green coalition. In this regard, Castellanos recalled the coalition's first meeting with the Los Angeles mayor's office and port staff: When NRDC showed up with the Teamsters, Port Director Geraldine Knatz was "a little confused" and there was a lot of "brow raising."[578] To complement these efforts, environmental justice organizers mobilized their base,[579] while coalition members engaged in meeting turn out efforts and attended periodic public rallies.

Although all groups played important roles, some acknowledged that LAANE was in charge. While each coalition member spent considerable time and resources advancing the campaign, in the end, as Callahan put it, LAANE "had staff dedicated to this campaign" and was "really in the driver's seat."[580] Some members, like LBACA's Elina Green, expressed concerns about being tokenized but generally praised LAANE's ability to "really listen" to coalition members and bring everyone on board.[581] With the coalition thus united, members worked to hold city officials accountable as they attempted to move the program through internal political channels.

The Inside Game: Mobilizing Legal Expertise, Moving Policy

In Los Angeles, as the campaign heated up, internal policy development proceeded along parallel, though deeply interconnected, paths. It started at the very top, with an effort to obtain a commitment by the Los Angeles mayor and port officials to support clean truck and employee conversion. In November 2006, James Hoffa, president of the Teamsters, met with Los Angeles Mayor Antonio Villaraigosa to seek his support for the Clean Truck Program.[582] The mayor agreed to the concept, which was then tracked for policy development at the port, where the mayor's new appointments to the Harbor Commission and port directorship—made to advance CAAP—would play key roles in the approval of the Clean Truck Program.[583]

Inside the Los Angeles mayor's office, staff understood that a clean truck policy was a priority and worked to advance it. Staff knew about the LAANE campaign and Weiner met directly with some members of the mayor's office to present Change to Win's analysis of the drayage truck market and how the Clean Truck Program would affect it.[584] On the basis of this analysis and their own review, staff concluded that the drayage sector was, in David Libatique's terms, "a perfectly competitive market with . . . a strong negative externality."[585] As the outside pressure of the coalition—and industry opponents—scaled up, the mayor's staff faced multiple challenges. One was "to maintain the integrity of the internal policymaking process . . . by keeping outside influence outside."[586] Libatique and other staffers provided a "buffer" against the coalition.[587]

A key challenge was advancing the program in the face of increasingly intense industry opposition—and, partly as a consequence, some opposition within the mayor's office itself and at the port. To effectively engage that opposition—and to assess whether it was worth spending political capital to do so—the mayor's and port's staffs needed to be comfortable with the legal foundation for the program. In early 2007, the coalition's legal analysis was presented to the mayor's staff members, who wanted assurance that it had been done.[588] Once it became apparent the program was really moving forward, port lawyers began "leading the charge" to make sure they had their "ducks in line" on the legal issues.[589] As a result, there were several meetings between port general counsel, City Attorney Thomas Russell; other lawyers from the city attorney's office assigned to the port, particularly Joy Crose; the Teamsters' Mike Manley; and lawyers from NRDC. These meetings focused on solidifying the legal argument for the concession approach. Manley circulated versions of the memos he had drafted for the Teamsters to the city attorneys, came out to meet with them, and responded to questions and concerns.[590] In these discussions—also attended by LAANE and Change to Win organizers—Manley viewed his role as "trying to convince [port lawyers] not to recommend to the port commission to reject" the program.[591] Manley's analysis when he talked to port counsel was "that the ATA is going to sue you," but "if you're sued you can win."[592] He argued for the program as a "unified whole":

> We had these allies and the thing about labor and environmental groups is we always accuse each other of ditching . . . for our own interests. . . . And so I was careful not to come across as if I were saying, "Well, this 2007 truck stuff doesn't matter as long as they're employees. . . ."[593]

Labor and environmentalists converged around legal theory as well as political strategy. NRDC was present at these meetings as the legal "hammer," but also to help make the case for local authority.[594] As Adrian Martinez recalled, NRDC and other environmental groups were independently "pushing using this market participant exception and at the same time, labor had been eyeing it as a potential approach to resolve several issues. And so it kind of came together where we were both saying" the same thing.⁵⁹⁵ NRDC counsel David Pettit, like the labor lawyers, understood the legal risk of the concession plan and believed that there was "a unified view of how strong the arguments were."⁵⁹⁶

Ultimately, it was port counsel who had the last word on the legal analysis. Much of this work fell to City Attorney Joy Crose, who was lead counsel to the Port of Los Angeles on the Clean Truck Program. Her role was to conduct a "legal review of the program" and prepare all "program implementing documents, including contracts, tariffs, ordinances and resolutions."⁵⁹⁷ To do this, Crose worked with her counterpart in Long Beach, and also engaged outside counsel, Steven Rosenthal, chair of litigation in the Washington, D.C. office of Kaye Scholer. After interviewing a number of law firms toward the end of 2006, the city attorney's office hired Rosenthal and his team to advise the port. Rosenthal had deep expertise on "the commerce clause, federal preemption, and federal statutes relating to the regulation of commerce," gained in representing airports and ports over the course of his thirty-year career.⁵⁹⁸ Together with the city attorneys, Rosenthal advised the port on the legal issues related to enacting the Clean Truck Program. Reflecting on his general approach to city policy, Rosenthal noted that when it came to reviewing "new, complex programs, you [could] identify risks" and suggest "this is why we think this approach is a better idea" but always in a context in which the client understood that "there is no certainty."⁵⁹⁹

The policymakers and their staff were not seeking certainty, just credible assessment. Weiner felt that the campaign's legal groundwork helped to get the port attorneys to "buy into our analysis," which was basically: "yeah, there's a risk. But it's good policy. . . . [W]e've got a good legal case."⁶⁰⁰ NRDC's Martinez described the value of the legal analysis in similar terms. He believed that the legal analysis empowered the city and port to take a stronger position on the bottom-line policy details: If the ATA was going to sue on whatever policy passed, he argued, it freed the port to develop the most effective policy on its own terms and then to "go to court with the best program we have."⁶⁰¹

The initial legal analysis also provided a ready response to the industry's legal pushback that would occur during policy formulation. Martinez recalled that industry groups had "a lot of legal power, so whenever the port or somebody would propose something, they'd give this very long, threatening legal letter that said you can't do this, you can't do this, you can't do this, you can't do this and here's the legal reasons why."⁶⁰² But the coalition had "lawyers on the other side . . . firing back comment letters: oh, but look at this case, look at this case, and making these similar sophisticated arguments on why you can do it. And I think that was the big difference."⁶⁰³ For the mayor's office staff tasked with advancing the program, the coalition's legal analysis was critical as a predicate to moving forward. According to David Libatique: "the legal analysis that was provided by the attorneys basically told us if . . . we're going to have an effect on port trade . . . we would have to act as a market participant and the way we would do that would be through a concession-based model."[604] The mayor's general counsel, Tom Saenz—who had joined Villaraigosa in 2005 in the midst of leadership turmoil at MALDEF that pulled him away from his work on the day labor anti-solicitation campaign—also reviewed the program and provided a legal opinion to his client.

The context of mayoral decision-making was also shaped by politics. Mayor Villaraigosa's first major policy initiative—a controversial attempt to take over the Los Angeles Unified School District board—was held unconstitutional by a superior court judge in late 2006, handing the mayor a stinging defeat.[605] The mayor needed a policy win and a strong pro-environment position at the port promised to deliver political dividends, while also solving a critical regional problem. While Villaraigosa supported employee conversion, and was cautiously optimistic about the overall program's success, he understood its legal and political vulnerabilities—and could not risk a signature policy going down in the courts twice in a row. Accordingly, he sought to ensure the legal severability of program provisions, so that if employee conversion were invalidated, the entire program would not fail, even though truck drivers could be left bearing the cost.

The urgency of solving the trucks problem was underscored as both ports faced community resistance to several massive expansion projects, which were unveiled to the public in mid-2007. These included replacing the Gerald Desmond Bridge to permit entry of larger container vessels; expanding and upgrading facilities in several terminals, including TraPac, China Shipping, and APL; creating new rail and road access; and building a new terminal for crude oil.[606] In the face of resistance, Los Angeles Harbor Commission President David Freeman vowed: "We're going to grow and we're going to clean up this place or my head will be served up on a silver platter in Los Angeles Mayor Antonio Villaraigosa's office."[607] Some coalition members seemed ready to sharpen their knives. The Sierra Club's Tom Politeo warned that the ports' growth rate would outpace mitigation efforts, while LBACA's Green put it more bluntly: "They say growing green means expanding terminals and putting more trucks on the road. What's cleaner about that? It's not logical."[608] Both ports, for their part, seemed to recognize the fight ahead, with the Port of Long Beach director of planning stating that he expected that "every one of the environmental impact documents for these projects will be challenged and end up in court."[609]

The ports simultaneously had to calibrate their response to increasing industry resistance to the Clean Truck Program, which focused on concerns about cost. After the ports released their joint proposal in April 2007, Castellanos said "the real fight began. Once that was public ... industry came out strong and ... the ports, the mayors, the electeds reacted to that."[610] A report by the Los Angeles Economic Development Corporation in May warned that the cargo fee proposed to fund clean trucks might divert cargo to other ports.[611] In June, agricultural exporters complained that the program could make U.S. agriculture "uncompetitive."[612]

The ports' response was to conduct their own economic analysis of the proposed program, which was contracted to outside consultants at Economics & Politics, Inc. Completed in September 2007, the report (called the Husing Report after its main author, economist John Husing), rested on extensive interviews with industry actors, as well as a statistical analysis of a variety of economic data.[613] The report compared the cost of converting the estimated 16,800 trucks regularly serving the ports to clean trucks through the existing structure of independent-contractor drivers to the cost of a plan based on employee conversion. It concluded that the proposal to convert to employee-operated clean trucks would cost LMCs nearly $150,000 per truck, which would include the cost of retrofitting or replacing the trucks and the cost of compensating the drivers—for a total cost of nearly $2.5 billion for converting the entire fleet.[614] This cost was calculated after factoring in port subsidies for fleet conversion, which were to be funded through truck fees and other public sources (including SCAQMD and Proposition 1B funds).[615] The report focused on two driver-related costs. First, the report analyzed the impact of the federal government's new security program, which required anyone accessing foreign entry points, including ports, to obtain a Transportation Workers Identification Credential—a biometric ID card known as a TWIC card.[616] The federal regulations barred undocumented immigrants from obtaining a TWIC card and Husing estimated that this would reduce the supply of port truck drivers by up to 22%, causing LMCs to raise their prices by up to 25% to cover the costs of luring new drivers.[617] The second type of driver-related costs were the payroll and benefit increases associated with the conversion of drivers to employees.[618] Combining these driver costs with the cost of clean truck conversion, the report estimated that LMCs would raise their prices by an average of 80% to offset the cost of implementing the Clean Truck Program.[619]

Worried that the ports would primarily focus on costs, Jon Zerolnick and others at LAANE set out to "quantify the benefits of passing the program."[620] Zerolnick thus took the lead in authoring *The Road to Shared Prosperity*—released a month before the Husing Report—which projected "direct and indirect financial benefits of over $4.2 billion" as a result of increased employee income and taxes, as well as health care savings resulting from better community health and reduced taxpayer subsidies for driver health care.[621] When it was released, the Husing Report also made a nod toward the benefit side by acknowledging an SCAQMD estimate of a "cumulative economic benefit of $4.7 to $5.9 billion due to reductions in premature deaths, lost work time and medical problems."[622] However, its overall conclusions about employee conversion were negative. The Husing Report suggested that shippers "will resist the LMC price increases due to their size" and "would delay such an increase as long as possible and explore other options."[623] Husing predicted that one-third of small LMCs would go out of business.[624] The report did not engage the issue of long-term sustainability emphasized by the coalition.

Predictably, industry reaction focused on the Husing Report's cost analysis, which strengthened opposition to employee conversion. The PMSA and National Industrial Transportation League—jointly representing Wal-Mart, Exxon, General Motors, and other major importers—formally asked the Federal Maritime Commission to intervene to stop the Clean Truck Program.[625] Some trucking company owners threatened dire consequences. One family-run business owner said in response to the Husing Report: "Do the math. They want just a handful of companies to do business with.... I am not interested in having 500 truck drivers as employees. If I have to remodel my business, I will probably walk away. I won't want to go through it."[626] Industry groups pressed their position and ratcheted up the litigation threat. In a letter sent to both Harbor Commissions and mayors, a coalition of business groups urged that the ban on dirty trucks be scrapped in favor of emission standards, and warned that the proposal was "anti-competitive," was outside the ports' "legal authority under state law," and thus "will result in litigation."[627] Against this backdrop, staff members in the Los Angeles mayor's office and port were legitimately concerned and the key question that recurred was why employee conversion was essential to a program that purported to advance environmental goals. In response, coalition members expressed frustration that the ports were mishandling CAAP implementation and had lost valuable momentum. As NRDC's David Pettit put it: "The ports of Los Angeles and Long Beach get a failing grade for slipping behind in the implementation of their landmark Clean Air Action Plan."[628] It was fall 2007 and the program was at a crossroads.

The "turning point" was born out of tragedy,[629] when Los Angeles mayor's office staffer David Libatique was hit and seriously injured by a port drayage truck while leaving a meeting at the TraPac container terminal. Although he would recover to full strength and eventually return, his temporary absence left a personnel gap at the Los Angeles mayor's office. That gap was filled by Sean Arian, who was preternaturally well-suited for the task ahead. Arian was the product of "multiple generations of longshoremen in San Pedro" (he was the son of ILWU leader Dave Arian)—someone who as a boy suffered asthma and thus understood the Clean Truck Program in "very personal" terms.[630] He also had a unique combination of skills. A Columbia Law School-trained lawyer, Arian had spurned the practice of law for the high-powered world of management consulting at McKinsey & Company, which he joined after a Fulbright fellowship in Latin America (where he focused on access to justice) and a federal court clerkship.[631] As a McKinsey analyst, Arian worked for Mayor Villaraigosa setting up a Project Management Unit to audit and track the mayor's accomplishments. In early 2007, Arian left McKinsey and became director of economic development on the L.A. Business Team. Once Libatique was injured, the port portfolio was given to Arian.

Arian entered a situation in which the foundation for a Clean Truck Program had been laid, but significant industry roadblocks remained. Arian took measure of the political context. He was told that the coalition had "done all the legal work," and understood that the coalition had also set forth the "big picture" in a way that made clear "what the community thinks" and what the "political upside and downside were."[632] This gave the mayor "political space" to advance a policy that would be "truly ground breaking."[633] But the case for the link between the environmental benefits of the program and employee conversion had not been persuasively made and industry arguments against it were gaining traction after the Husing Report. Arian sought to more forcefully make the case that port pollution was a "systemic problem" of "market failure," and thus not amenable to environmental regulation by itself.[634] Although the Clean Truck Program was fundamentally about environmental remediation, to get there, Arian argued it was crucial to attack "the root cause of the problem as opposed to just trying to attack one of the externalities."[635]

Two decisions changed the program's course—at least in Los Angeles. First, Arian and others within the Los Angeles mayor's office recognized that for the program to succeed, staff at the port had to buy in. To achieve this, Arian—working closely with Castellanos and Weiner[636]—was able to convince the mayor to "put somebody high ranking" in charge of developing the program at the Los Angeles port.[637]

That person turned out to be John Holmes, who held what was arguably the second most important job in the port: overseeing day-to-day operations as the port's deputy executive director. Holmes had spent nearly thirty years in the Coast Guard, the last three of which directing operations in Southern California—making him a "known quantity" at the port.[638] In Holmes's view, he was charged with designing the Clean Truck Program because figuring out how to get clean trucks in and out of the terminals was ultimately an "operational issue."[639] When he was assigned to the program by Knatz in late 2007, the "two things" he knew were that the program was "going to have a rolling ban ... to culminate in five years in having all the trucks ... be EPA 2007 or newer" and there was going to be employee conversion.[640] As Holmes recalled: "My role was to basically figure it all out."[641]

On the campaign side, it was Weiner's role to facilitate this process. Weiner's goal was to help Holmes credibly advance employee conversion as an integral part of the environmental program and not just a union project.[642] In Weiner's analysis, because port staff were on the front line of dealing with industry opposition, they were under the most pressure to respond to industry claims that "the sky is going to fall."[643] That front line pressure was a constant challenge for the campaign, since port staff would report industry concerns up the ladder, ultimately landing back at the mayor's office, where the mayor's staff would get "nervous and weak-kneed" and the coalition would have to "prop up our supporters" and "beat back all these claims."[644] As a result, the coalition believed it was crucial to have "someone at the staff level at the port ... able to push back and move this agenda."[645] Weiner knew that Holmes was politically astute and appreciated the stakes: that he technically worked for the mayor, while having to deal with industry as the port's primary constituency.[646]

Arian introduced Holmes to Weiner. As Weiner recalled, his pitch to Holmes was: "the mayor really wants this, so I could help you understand why this makes sense and talk it through."[647] Weiner recalled that Holmes' initial posture was "skeptical"—asking "what does this have to do with the Clean Truck Program?"[648] To answer that question, Weiner initiated a series of "one-on-one discussions" with Holmes about the concession model and, specifically, the employee provision. From Weiner's vantage point, these discussions were fruitful as Holmes eventually became comfortable with the idea that "the employee requirement is really so that the companies will be responsible . . . to maintain the trucks and not these drivers."[649] From there, Holmes began to work on the program details. Given concerns about cost, a key issue was determining the appropriate level of financial incentives, which trucking companies had advocated for as necessary to make the conversion "happen as soon as possible."[650] For the incentive piece, Holmes brought in the port's director of finance. But they were working off the basis of the Husing Report, which did not provide a strong framework for advancing the entire clean truck package.

This led to the second crucial decision. After Holmes was on board, Arian received the mayor's permission to bring in another consulting firm to reevaluate the economics of the Clean Truck Program. After reviewing the Husing Report, Arian believed that there was an insufficient "fact base" to convince stakeholders of the need for industry transformation and thus argued for what amounted to a more sophisticated cut at the economics done by "one of the top consulting firms."[651] Using his connections, Arian was able to bring in Boston Consulting Group (BCG) (his former firm's chief rival), which agreed to send in its "A Team" on a pro bono basis to analyze the economic impact of converting to clean trucks. To justify this, Arian dissected the Husing Report in a way that conveyed to port staff that Husing's "analysis didn't go far enough to give us the information we need to evaluate our options."[652] From Weiner's perspective, Arian was able to "basically rip apart" the analysis of John Husing—setting the stage for the entry of BCG.[653] Arian viewed BCG as "potentially a huge risk" because its consultants' reputational capital was based on telling clients "what they think the right answer is" and their analysis would become part of the public record; however, Arian firmly believed that the city "needed to have a really strong fact base by a mutual third party respected organization."[654] Arian recalled that port counsel, Tom Russell, was the "very first person who hopped on board" with the BCG plan since for the market participant theory to work as a legal rationale for the program, there needed to be a strong evidentiary record of why the program made business sense.[655] Holmes's view at this stage was that to get where the Los Angeles port wanted to be "required a sea change in the drayage trucking industry."[656] To do that, he saw the basic choice as regulating or incentivizing the industry—which was not going to go green "just to do the right thing."[657] Industry's basic question was: "Are you going to pay me to do it or make me do it?"[658] The answer was: some combination of both.

Toward that end, Holmes worked intensively with BCG analysts to promote trucking participation in program development and "get the numbers right."[659] BCG modeled industry responses to different program scenarios, in which the main elements were the amount of the cargo fee, the timing of the dirty truck ban, the development of security structures, the nature of driver status (independent contractor or employee), and the amount of incentives (which varied by whether new trucks would run on diesel or alternative fuel). The port wanted to encourage companies to buy liquid natural gas (LNG) trucks, which were an average of $50,000 more expensive than diesel trucks. One issue Holmes grappled with was how much the incentive had to be to persuade companies to buy LNG trucks. In addition, Holmes was focused on working out the details of the concession arrangement and its impact on the community. In his view, the employee mandate was closely associated with the off-street parking provision, since employees would "slip seat"—transfer their trucks to different drivers from one shift to the next—which meant that there needed to be a place to park the trucks during the transfer period.[660] Holmes was sensitive to complaints about traffic and saw off-street parking as an effort to respond to community concerns.[661]

Once the economic models were run, Holmes visited "the twenty-five biggest trucking companies in the country" to validate the results.[662] In these meetings—with major carriers like Schneider, Swift, and Knight, as well as shippers like Wal-Mart—Holmes would say: "We're thinking of doing the program this way. What are we missing?" Through that process, Holmes and the consultants gained "a whole bunch of knowledge" about industry structure and equipment costs that were then factored back into the modeling analysis.[663] Holmes recalled that his meetings with industry were not all adversarial. To the contrary, many representatives of major trucking companies expressed support for minimum standards in an industry they viewed as built on "caveman economics," in which fly-by-night carriers forced a "race to the bottom."[664] Yet although these firms supported many of the environmental elements of the program "and gave good feedback," they uniformly did not agree with employee conversion.[665] Holmes also understood that even those companies that supported the general approach were likely to join an industry lawsuit against the program if it passed, simply because industry rejected port regulation on principle.[666]

As Holmes and BCG carried out their analysis, the commissioners were also working to iron out the policy details. Commissioner Mendoza recalled that her starting point was at odds with Freeman's, who thought that the Los Angeles port should simply "mandate the purchase of 500 LNG trucks" and thus become the direct owner of a portion of the port trucking fleet.[667] However, as the program developed around employee conversion within the mayor's office, Freeman embraced the concept and fought for it like a "momma bear."[668] Together, Mendoza and Freeman took the lead in moving the entire program forward. Mendoza described her approach to dealing with the city attorneys assigned to the program:

We didn't ask them, we would tell them, "This is what we're going to do. You guys have to figure out how to make it work." And although we got a lot of pushback and a lot of "you know, we've never done that before," or "we have outside consultants who have done the analysis and they think that we don't have a really good chance," our response was, "Okay, do we know for certain that this would not be successful in court? No. Well, if we don't try, we won't know."[669]

In Freeman's view, "Holmes was the best staff person there in getting religion and helping to make it happen."[670] Policy issues brought up by port staff were hammered out, either in an ad hoc committee on environmental review staffed by Mendoza and Freeman, or in a closed session of the entire board. In the face of concerns that "truck companies would boycott" the port:[671]

David Freeman and John Holmes would get on a plane and go fly to Wal-Mart in Bentonville, Arkansas, or they'd fly to the different trucking companies that were in Texas and Virginia and places like that, and they would sit down and talk to the business owners and say, "Look, we know this is uncomfortable, we know this is different, we know this is the first time you've been asked to do something like that but at the same time if we clean up, it will allow us to expand in a way that the community will not rise up and riot the way they have in the past. If you want to grow, if you want the port to grow, if you want your goods to get in and out faster, we also have to be as green as possible so that we can grow."[672]

The information gained in these trips allowed Freeman to respond to staff concerns about costs. And Mendoza used her lawyering skills to respond to issues raised about the legality of employee conversion, asking skeptics: "Well, why aren't we a market participant? . . . Why can't we make that argument? What do we have to do to make that argument compelling?"[673] Despite Mendoza's forceful advocacy, Freeman knew that "our furthest reach under the law was to require the truckers to have employees."[674]

The End Game: Passing the Clean Truck Program

As BCG worked on its analysis, the Los Angeles and Long Beach ports initiated a sequential approach to program enactment. Based on a political calculus that it was best to lock in elements of the program in stages—ranging from least to most controversial—the ports began moving forward specific elements of the Clean Truck Program: from clean truck conversion, to industry incentives, to employee conversion. This order tracked the key elements of the program debated from the outset and set an agenda for phased implementation: first, the progressive ban on dirty trucks; second, the Clean Truck Fee and incentives; and third (and most controversially), the concession plan with employee conversion. In the first two steps, the Ports of Los Angeles and Long Beach moved in synch, but in the third, they diverged. Throughout the process, industry pressure mounted to split off the environmental standards from employee conversion—and to sever the environmentalists from organized labor in the coalition.

The first step was, in relative terms, the easiest. On November 1, 2007—as the BCG team was just getting under way—the Port of Los Angeles Board of Harbor Commissioners unanimously approved a progressive dirty truck ban.[675] Following a strong staff recommendation,[676] the board approved Order 6935 to phase in the ban over five years.[677] The legal structure of the ban, drafted by City Attorney Crose, highlighted the legal authority of the port, while the operational structure bore the imprint of Holmes's expertise. Legally, the order amended port Tariff No. 4, which was originally adopted in 1989 to govern the rates and terms of terminal operations.[678] As amended, Tariff No. 4 imposed a prohibition on the terminal operators—not the trucking companies or the truck drivers. Specifically, the ban stated that "no Terminal Operator shall permit access to any Terminal in the Port of Los Angeles" to nonconforming trucks.[679] In the order's findings section, the justification for the ban was made in market participant terms, presenting the port as a proprietary entity with business interests in pollution reduction.

> Independently, the failure of the Port to adequately address air pollution impacts, including diesel truck emissions, would threaten future Port growth both because of legal constraints under the California Environmental Quality Act (CEQA) and the National Environmental Policy Act and the opposition of surrounding residents and communities to further expansion without an actual improvement in environmental conditions surrounding the ports.[680]

The findings focused on trucks as "a critical element in the efficient operations of the Port," and concluded: "Reasonable environmental measures are simply good business practices."[681]

On the operations side, the order established a new system for efficiently identifying clean trucks—requiring all trucks to install a radio frequency identification device by August 1, 2008. The device would contain a unique identification number that could be electronically read by terminal operators, which could cross-reference the number against records showing the vehicle model year and compliance with clean truck standards.[682] The Long Beach Board of Harbor Commissioners unanimously approved an identical dirty truck ban five days later,[683] prompting Long Beach Mayor Foster at a joint news conference with Los Angeles Mayor Villaraigosa to tout the two cities' effort "to lead the world in pushing for cleaner air and healthier environment with our shared goal of having the cleanest ports in the world."[684]

With the dirty truck ban legally and logistically in place, the battle immediately turned to the issues of new truck financing and employee conversion. Upon passage of the Los Angeles ban, Port Director Knatz struck a stern negotiating posture, acknowledging the need for short-term program funding, but making clear "we can't subsidize it forever."[685] With respect to employee conversion, trucking companies again emphasized the litigation threat. Cecilia Ibarra, assistant operations manager for Total Distribution Service of Wilmington was explicit—and articulated industry's particular hostility toward the employee provision. "We want clean air as much as anyone, but the board's actions may drive us into litigation. A concession program is a step toward unionization. I can already hear the ka-chink, ka-chink, ka-chink in union coffers."[686] Despite this effort to isolate employee conversion from the program's environmental elements, coalition members continued to assert a unified front. LBACA's Green made the strong case: "I don't understand why the board decided to vote on just the clean-truck portion of the clean air plan.... It's hard not to think that they were pandering to the environmental community by throwing us a bone, as though we would be happy with just a progressive ban."[687] In an official statement released after the Long Beach ban was adopted, the coalition kept up the pressure to move forward: "Without reform, the Los Angeles and Long Beach ports remain unprepared to meet ever-increasing trade demands, and they will be unequipped to compete in today's rapidly changing economy."[688]

On the financing side, the issue from the outset had been at what price to set the Clean Truck Fee (a charge on containers carried by drayage trucks to be imposed on shippers) in order to create a fund for clean truck conversion. Long Beach made the first move, approving a cargo fee of $35 per loaded twenty-foot container on December 17, 2007.[689] The Clean Truck Fee would be "assessed on containerized merchandise entering or leaving the Ports by Drayage Truck," to be paid by the "Beneficial Cargo Owner," and collected by the terminal operator.[690] The fee was expected to raise $1.6 billion for a Clean Truck Fund,[691] to be used by the port "exclusively for replacement and retrofit of Drayage Trucks serving the Ports of Los Angeles and Long Beach."[692] Still marching in lockstep, the Los Angeles Harbor Commissioners approved an identical fee four days later.[693]

Finally, the stage was set for the showdown over employee conversion. Both sides in the debate pushed hard. In Long Beach, Mayor Foster worked to isolate organized labor. As Weiner recalled, Foster "kept ... wanting to meet with the environmental folks in our coalition without the labor folks ... [asking:] 'Why can't we just do this? Why do you need this employee thing?' "[694] Commissioner Freeman perceived Foster as set against employee conversion: "He just did not believe that we had the right to force these [trucking companies] to have employees."[695] And Foster was worried that "the Teamsters will take over" and undermine future environmental programs.[696]

Figure 6.13 Coalition for Clean and Safe Ports rally. *Source*: Barbara Maynard, Teamsters (2007).

The coalition kept up the pressure with a series of public demonstrations—against the backdrop of ongoing private negotiations. On the day that Long Beach approved its Clean Truck Fee, the coalition organized a rally of 150 truck drivers at the port entrance to stress the need for employee conversion. "We all support cleaner air, but none of us wants a loan or a grant to buy a new truck," said driver Miguel Pineda. "If these plans become law, I won't be able to put food on the family table."[697] He added that "a lot of truckers have stopped spending money on repairs because they aren't sure they will still have jobs next year."[698] A month later, the *Los Angeles Times* ran a front-page story on "unsafe trucks" coming out of the ports, focusing on the plight of low-income independent contractors who could not afford to replace tires on their big rigs and frequented "llanteros" who would use hot blades to carve new grooves into seriously worn tires; the story highlighted other drivers engaged in desperate measures like "lashing bumpers to chassis with bungee cords and smearing mud over cracked parts to hide the problems from [California Highway Patrol] officers."[699]

In the face of pending expansion plans—the *Los Angeles Times* noted that fifteen port projects had been held up since the China Shipping case in 2001—the coalition also pressed to underscore the legal stakes.[700] NRDC's Adrian Martinez and the Teamsters' assistant director of ports, Ron Carver, sent a letter to the ports stating: "Unless we are assured that your plans include reasonable proposals for mitigating the environmental harm of your existing facility, let alone your proposed expansion, we cannot see how we could let the process continue without a challenge."[701] The message was clear—and industry reacted strenuously, with the vice president of the TraPac terminal calling it a "shakedown."[702] Martinez observed that "things are getting nasty out there," while Mayor Villaraigosa tried to give a positive spin: "In the interests of green growth, historic adversaries have become part of a very delicate coalition. It's as though everyone is coming to this party holding hands but reluctant to get on the dance floor. But they will, eventually. They have to."[703]

Before that could happen, the coalition sought to underscore that the legal consequences of inaction would be further logjam. Markers were laid down at both ports. In Los Angeles, the proposed TraPac terminal expansion was the legal flashpoint. On December 6, 2007, the Los Angeles Harbor Commission, in a statement of overriding considerations,[704] unanimously approved the EIR for a $1.5-billion upgrade projected to create six thousand jobs and bring in $200 million annually in taxes.[705] Four individuals and sixteen groups—including the Coalition for Clean and Safe Ports, NRDC, the Coalition for Clean Air, the American Lung Association, Sierra Club, and LAANE—appealed the approval to the Los Angeles City Council on the ground that it did not adequately address the air pollution impact.[706] One of the individual appellants was Kathleen Woodfield, president of the San Pedro and Peninsula Homeowners Coalition, which had been lead plaintiff in the China Shipping litigation.[707] As she recalled, the appellants were not represented by legal counsel: "NRDC was clear that they were not representing us."[708] Yet NRDC did flex its legal muscle, indicating its intent to file a CEQA lawsuit if the council appeal was unsuccessful.[709] In response, Councilwoman Hahn blocked the EIR from getting out of a key council committee and began negotiating with environmental and neighborhood groups.[710]

Two months later, in Long Beach, NRDC and the Coalition for a Safe Environment filed an intent-to-sue letter with the port, asserting an innovative legal theory: The port was an entity subject to oversight as a hazardous waste site under the federal Resource Conservation and Recovery Act.[711] NRDC's Pettit claimed: "We want the court to take over the whole thing at once in order to enforce a new priority of public health over profit.... We think that will require court appointment of a port czar to force the port to use currently available technology to fix the problem."[712] The letter requested that the port stop expansion projects until it could prove they would not "at any time increase the level of hazardous diesel particulates emanating from the port."[713]

If the NRDC letter was meant to put pressure on the Port of Long Beach as the clock ticked down toward a resolution on employee conversion, it did not have that effect. To the contrary, on February 16, 2008, the Port of Long Beach officially broke ranks with its L.A. counterpart, announcing approval of the final element of its Clean Truck Program—a concession plan—without employee conversion.[714] "Their announcement caught us all by surprise," said LAANE's Castellanos.[715] In Long Beach's concession plan, trucks would be granted a "right of access to port property" in exchange for LMCs entering into contracts that ensured compliance with existing laws (including the preexisting elements of the Clean Truck Program), as well as "local truck route and parking restrictions."[716] The ordinance also modified the Clean Truck Fee for cargo moved on trucks not purchased with port subsidies, waiving the fee for containers transported on alternative fuel trucks and halving it for clean diesel trucks.[717]

Released on the cusp of a three-day weekend, the plan was slated for vote the following Tuesday, February 19, by the Long Beach Harbor Commission. Despite the short turnaround, the coalition mobilized to attend the six-hour hearing, with public comments given by several residents, drivers, and coalition members—including Zerolnick, Martinez, Politeo, Kim, Logan, Green, and Callahan.[718] Nonetheless, board approval was unanimous,[719] and port officials touted their program as a "victory for clean air"[720]—one that cleaved apart the environmental and labor elements of the Clean Truck Program.[721] Mayor Foster's chief of staff, responding to the mayor's break with Los Angeles, said: "It doesn't scare us that there is a difference of opinion.... What scares us is not acting to clean the air as quickly as possible. If their board is not ready to go yet, fine.... Ours is."[722] NRDC, unsurprisingly, disagreed in its letter to the board: "Perhaps the most glaring flaw in the port's program is the lack of its key partner and neighbor, the Port of Los Angeles. If Los Angeles decides to go in a different direction in its clean-trucks program, the result would be chaos at the ports."[723]

All eyes therefore turned back to Los Angeles. Industry opponents of employee conversion sought to cast it as a union ploy. NRDC's Martinez perceived that opponents were "freaked out" by the unified front maintained by NRDC and the Teamsters and recalled a lot of "fearmongering."[724] The *Los Angeles Times*, in reporting on the ongoing battle, emphasized the unionization angle: "Critics of the employee provision of the clean truck program . . . are concerned that it could be used by the Teamsters as a springboard to launch unionization efforts at ports nationwide."[725] A month later, an editorial began: "Pollution, death and economic stagnation. These catastrophes are being brought to you by the Natural Resources Defense Council and the International Brotherhood of Teamsters."[726] It argued that the clean trucks deal was being jeopardized over a "dispute that has nothing to do with pollution and everything to do with an unholy alliance between environmentalists and organized labor."[727] Noting that Long Beach had already passed its plan without employee conversion and that Los Angeles seemed on the verge of doing the opposite, the editorial board suggested that the Clean Truck Program of both ports would be tied up for years in litigation—in Long Beach by NRDC and in Los Angeles by the ATA.[728]

Coalition members fought back. In response to the *Los Angeles Times*, Coalition for Clean Air Director Martin Schlageter stated that he was "baffled at your editorial placing the blame for delay on advocates of clean air," noting that it was an NRDC lawsuit that produced CAAP in the first instance and that the Long Beach plan suffered from the "glaring weakness" of failing to influence driver working conditions, which was a concern "for environmentalists and labor advocates alike."[729] Coalition members also sought to make fun of the argument that there must be "something wrong" in a collaboration between labor and environmentalists, with Pettit and his colleagues donning T-shirts with "The Unholy Alliance" printed on them.[730] In retrospect, Pettit thought "we, NRDC—did a poor job of messaging what [the program] had to do with clean air. And I think we came off poorly ... in all the media attention."[731] Yet in a sign that political support was holding firm, the Los Angeles City Council formally adopted the Board of Harbor Commissioners' progressive truck ban and Clean Truck Fee at the end of February.[732]

By March 2008, on the brink of the Los Angeles port's final decision on employee conversion, the political back-and-forth reached a fever pitch. The coalition took out five full-page color advertisements in the *Long Beach Press-Telegram* denouncing Mayor Foster, while Los Angeles City Councilwoman Hahn was privately urging him to reconsider.[733] For their part, the Teamsters were seeking to use their political clout to block state funding for Long Beach to complete renovation of the Gerald Desmond Bridge.[734] LAANE sent Foster a public records request seeking all his communications with industry representatives.[735] Yet Foster remained defiant: "So the end result is, if this happens to be the only office I ever hold and the only term I ever serve, I'm comfortable with that."[736] Industry groups also struck a strident tone in advance of the Los Angeles decision. Curtis Whalen, executive director of the ATA, stated that Villaraigosa's "biggest problem is he has good intentions, but they are not legal."[737]

It was at the height of this debate, on March 7, 2008, that BCG released its long-awaited report—which had been delayed in the wake of the Long Beach decision. At its heart was an analysis of the economics of employee conversion—the sole remaining piece of the Los Angeles Clean Truck Program. In clinical terms, far removed from the supercharged rhetoric of campaign adversaries, the report evaluated different options, which included requiring LMCs to make what it called an "employee commitment."[738] The report's key move—and what made it different than the Husing Report—was that it compared short-term (one to five year) and long-term (more than five year) outcomes in relation to stated environmental, port operations, and safety and security goals.[739] The report's bottom line was that the employee model provided "the best path to long term sustainability" although it posed some "near term risks."[740] Specifically, the report concluded that the employee model would "maximize the likelihood of creating a market in which the reciprocal obligations between the Port (granting a commission) and LMCs (providing drayage services) create a sustainable reliable supply of truckers attracted to stable and relatively well paying jobs in an operationally efficient and orderly drayage market."[741] It went on to recommend that a "100% employee driver requirement, phased in over five years" was the best option: "transparent, aligning incentives and easiest to administer."[742] Financing support for clean truck conversion was set at

80% for new diesel trucks and up to 80% for LNG trucks, with $5,000 given to scrap pre-1989 trucks.[743]

The report was not all rosy. It predicted that under the "employee commitment" scenario, there would be more cargo diversion—approximately 3%—than under the other options, but that this cost would likely be outweighed by overall benefits.[744] The "key risk" was that shippers would divert cargo over and above this 3% threshold based on factors other than increased price,[745] such as fear of "future disruption or instability."[746] This risk would be exacerbated, the report stated, if the Port of Los Angeles and the Port of Long Beach adopted different programs[747]—which, of course, had already happened, though the report seemed to hold out hope that there was still a possibility that Long Beach might reverse course. In reporting on the plan, the *Los Angeles Times* highlighted the cargo risk, beginning its article by emphasizing "that 'substantial diversions' of the Los Angeles port's business probably would shift to the neighboring port of Long Beach or to other harbors."[748]

Despite these market concerns, the BCG report ultimately did the work it was designed to do. At the staff level, the cost analysis permitted Holmes and other port managers to solidify the employee provision and calculate the precise level of financing. On March 12, 2008, a staff report authored by Holmes and Deputy Director of Finance Molly Campbell recommended approval of the concession and incentive plans analyzed in the BCG report.[749] At the board level, Arian recalled that the report was the "key study" that persuaded skeptical commissioners to move toward approval.[750]

On the day the Los Angeles board was set to meet on the concession plan, the *Los Angeles Times* took one last opportunity to hammer home the litigation threat. In an editorial titled "Harbor No Illusions: L.A.'s Plan to Clean Up Port Pollution Is Sure to Wind Up in Court," the editorial board argued that "[i]n the real world of lawsuits and endless court proceedings, [the truck plan] would stall progress on cleaning the air indefinitely."[751] Yet at this stage in the game, the early legal work on the port's authority to pass the program seemed to fortify city staff. As Libatique recalled, staff did not shy away from the concession model: Because of "the amount of work and time we put into the legal underpinnings of the program . . . I think there was a level of confidence here that we had a strong legal case."[752] If litigation came—which it would—the city was prepared to defend its program then, rather than back off it now. The program that the board did adopt on March 20, 2008 contained the signature element of what the coalition had spent almost two years working toward: the concession plan.[753] Resisting industry pressure, the board in Order 6956 (again drafted by Crose) further amended Tariff No. 4 to "require parties who access Port land and terminals for purposes of providing drayage services to the Port of Los Angeles to have a Concession Agreement" with the port.[754] Following the same format used in the earlier order banning dirty trucks, the amendment placed enforcement responsibility on the terminal operators, stating that "no Terminal Operator shall permit access into any Terminal in the Port of Los Angeles to any Drayage Truck unless such Drayage Truck is registered under a Concession."[755] Terminal operators that violated the order were subject to criminal sanction under the tariff's general penalties provision, which made any violation of the tariff a misdemeanor punishable by a fine of up to $500 and imprisonment of up to six months.[756]

The order set forth the legal justification for the concession plan. Expressing concern about the "environmental, operational, and safety and security objectives of the Port" (language adapted from the BCG report), the findings emphasized the goal of encouraging "evolution of the Port drayage market towards an asset-based market in which Licensed Motor Carriers that hold the motor carrier concessions also own the truck assets used to perform under the concession."[757] After noting that the port "currently has no business relationship with the thousands of trucks, drivers or licensed motor carriers" hauling cargo, the order stated that a drayage company "must enter into" an agreement, which would last for a term of five years, "in order to access" the port.[758] Although the order itself did not explicitly discuss employee conversion, a separate transmittal by staff (circulated to the full board) proposed a "non-exhaustive list of the main Concession requirements," which included that LMCs "[t]ransition to 100% employee drivers for Port of Los Angeles drayage in five years, according to a schedule specified by the port."[759] The list also included the concessionaire's commitment to create an "off street parking plan"; to affix "placards on all Concession controlled trucks referring to a 1-800 phone number to report concerns regarding truck emissions, safety and operations"; and to pay a concession fee of "$2500 plus an annual fee of $100 per truck."[760]

In what appeared as a recognition of the legal vulnerability of at least some elements of the concession plan, a severability provision was also added. It stated:

> If any provision of Port of Los Angeles Tariff No. 4 shall be determined by court or agency of competent jurisdiction to be unenforceable, unlawful or subject to an order of temporary or permanent injunction from enforcement, such determination shall only apply to the specific provision and the remainder of the provisions ... shall continue in full force and effect.[761]

The purpose of the provision was to reduce legal and political risk to the overall Clean Truck Program. Legally, the severability provision would permit a court to excise some provisions, while keeping intact the broader plan. Commissioner Freeman recalled "the meeting in the mayor's office where we decided, well, we want a severability clause ... so that if we lose that one, it doesn't contaminate the rest of the case. And we all went ahead with that."[762] Politically, severability maximized the possibility of sustaining some aspects of the Clean Truck Program in the face of legal challenge—allowing the mayor to declare victory while also addressing important policy concerns. Perhaps most crucially, if the employee provision was ultimately struck down, progress could still be made toward greening the port and organized labor would be no worse off than if the effort had not been made at all.

In connection with the board order, a separate resolution drafted by Crose and approved by the board laid out the market participation rationale for the concession plan, while also adding in the core financial incentives. The resolution noted that the objective of the plan was to "create and sustain an efficient, reliable supply of drayage services to the port," which "as land owner of the Harbor District land and assets has the right and the obligation to manage and control the access to its land by tenants and invitees to ensure that operations thereon maintain safety and security of Port operations on a sustainable basis."[763] The resolution went on to stress that the "air quality, port security, and safety goals" of the plan were "more likely to be achieved and sustained over the long term" through concessions. It also pointed to the "[s]erious and long-standing problems" produced by "inadequate maintenance" and "unsafe, negligent or reckless driving of trucks" at the port, and asserted that the concession model was the "most efficient," "greenest," "safest," "most community friendly," "most responsive and flexible," and "easiest model to administer."[764] In addition, the resolution—following the staff report and BCG analysis—authorized a truck funding program, to "provide funding of up to 80% of the value" of clean trucks (in the form of either a lease-to-own agreement or upfront grant to purchase or retrofit) "in order to make the transition... more affordable."[765] Other incentives included a Truck Procurement Assistance Program to "provide volume discounted pricing" to concessionaires and a Scrap Truck Buyback Program providing $5,000 to owners of pre-1989 trucks who turned them in.[766] With that, the centerpiece of the Clean Truck Program was approved. The following day, the ATA's Whalen called it a "scheme to unionize port drivers" and vowed that: "We're going to go after Los Angeles with everything we've got so their plan goes to hell in a handbasket. We will win and we will win handily."[767]

Yet a few steps still remained. The Los Angeles port wanted resolution of the dispute over the TraPac expansion—which had served as the coalition's final "bargaining chip."[768] As homeowner activist Kathleen Woodfield recalled, the port "wanted to move forward with the TraPac project. For as long as it was appealed it was in limbo."[769] To address this dispute, Woodfield, Martinez, and other coalition members met with Councilwoman Hahn, Mayor Villaraigosa, Port of Los Angeles Director Knatz, and Commissioner Freeman to hammer out a deal to approve the EIR.[770] Working closely with Councilwoman Hahn—whose support coalition members thought was "strong and pretty much unequivocal"[771]—the coalition negotiated a settlement in early April.[772] Under its terms—negotiated primarily by NRDC's Martinez and port General Counsel Tom Russell[773]—the port agreed to create a mitigation trust fund with an immediate $12-million contribution toward community improvements and an air filtration system for local schools.[774] The agreement also provided—as a means of avoiding future litigation—that more funds would be contributed for mitigation in conjunction with future expansion projects at the port:[775] $1.50 for each additional cruise ship passenger and $2 for each additional container.[776] The funds were to go to a nonprofit group, the Harbor Community Benefit Foundation, created for the purposes of disbursing the money.[777] The agreement also committed the port to continue working to support the Clean Truck Program.[778] It was the first EIR approved at the port since China Shipping and Commissioner Freeman touted the agreement as a model for pending expansion plans. "The entire environmental community is giving its blessing to Mayor Villaraigosa's green growth program . . . . We will work together on all future [projects] and not resort to litigation."[779] The NRDC's Pettit, though pleased with the outcome, did not go quite that far, emphasizing that: "The agreement does not give up our right to sue on any project other than TraPac."[780]

The accord did, however, clear the way for the concession agreement itself to be approved. The agreement, circulated in early May, spelled out the mechanics of "driver hiring" in detail, setting forth a phased implementation in which a concessionaire "shall be granted a transition period . . . by which to transition its Concession drivers to 100% Employee Concession drivers by no later than December 31, 2013."[781] Under the transition plan, 20% of drivers had to be converted by the end of 2009, 66% by the end of 2010, 85% by the end of 2011, and 100% by the end of 2013.[782] The agreement also required concessionaires to "submit for approval . . . an off-street parking plan," "post placards" on their trucks, agree to regular maintenance, attest to financial capability, and pay the concession fees.[783] The agreement further specified enforcement procedures, identifying (though not defining) minor and major defaults, and listing sanctions, which included revoking the concession agreement itself.[784] The final loose ends were quickly tied. The board approved the concession agreement on May 15, 2008.[785] Then, at a meeting on June 17, the City Council approved the final concession plan.[786] With the mayor's signature, the Clean Truck Program was city law.[787]

In the end, after nearly two years of struggle, the coalition had won a program in Los Angeles that included the twin goals of fleet and employee conversion. Both were achieved through a legal structure that linked the port's contractual and police powers. Trucking companies were required to sign concession agreements to enter the port and terminal operators were required to bar entry to any trucking companies that did not comply with port rules—or incur criminal sanctions. The program was to be financed primarily through the imposition of cargo fees, which would shift the costs of clean truck acquisition to shippers, while providing incentives for trucking companies to upgrade their fleets. Looking at the final program as a whole, there were some details with which the coalition could quibble. At the outset, the coalition had set its sights on full conversion to alternative fuel trucks, a higher fee, and immediate employee conversion.[788] What it got was partial alternative fuel conversion, a lower fee with significant exceptions, and a five-year phase-in for employee conversion. However, these were minor sacrifices to achieve the ultimate program, which closely tracked the outlines proposed in the coalition's RFP a year earlier.

The Defensive Phase: Responding to Federal Law

The ink was barely dry on the Clean Truck Program when legal challenges to it commenced. From the outset, this had been anticipated by the coalition as part of the overall process of enacting and defending the law. As LAANE's Jon Zerolnick described, from the beginning, it "was always a part of the timeline" that the "ATA sues here."[789] Teamsters counsel Mike Manley's early legal opinions had predicted lawsuits on preemption and maritime law grounds—precisely what ended up occurring. The campaign, premised on enacting local law, now turned to defending that law against efforts to negate it on federal grounds.

The Injunctive Phase

As it had long threatened, the ATA was first to the federal courthouse.[790] On July 28, 2008, the ATA filed a complaint in federal district court in Los Angeles for declaratory judgment and injunctive relief.[791] The lawsuit took aim at the concession plans of both the Los Angeles and Long Beach ports, arguing that they were preempted by the FAAAA's prohibition against municipalities enacting "a law, regulation, or other provision having the force and effect of law related to a price, route, or service of any motor carrier."[792] The complaint further alleged that both plans violated the commerce clause by imposing "invasive regulatory requirements on virtually all aspects of the business of a federal motor carrier."[793] Although challenging both ports, the complaint used the fact that Long Beach had broken ranks on employee conversion to buttress its commerce clause argument: "The Port of Los Angeles *prohibits* motor carriers' use of more than 10,000 independent owner-operators of trucks on *their side* of the city line that bisects the San Pedro Bay port complex, while the Port of Long Beach *permits* such subcontracting on *its side* of the line—a text-book case . . . for federal preemption to prevent [the] patchwork of service-determining laws, rules, and regulations from disrupting the motor carriage of property in interstate commerce."[794]

The ATA complaint also sought to distinguish the environmental provisions of the Clean Truck Programs from what it called "extraneous, burdensome regulations regarding wages, benefits, truck ownership, preferences for certain types of trucks, and frequency of service to ports, which have no material environmental impact."[795] Making clear that it did "*not* challenge the Ports' truck engine-retirement programs"[796]—that is, the progressive ban on dirty trucks—the ATA set its sights specifically on the operational provisions of the concession plans. As the ATA's CEO put it, "the litigation is not aimed and should not interfere with the ports' clean air efforts. We are challenging only the intrusive and unnecessary regulatory structure being created under the concession plans."[797]

That the ATA was especially concerned about employee conversion was revealed in its prayer for relief, in which it first sought to enjoin both plans in their entirety

(Count I) and then *separately* sought to enjoin just that portion of the Los Angeles plan that precluded "independent owner-operators" from port entry (Count II).[798] The ATA was thus giving the court a choice: Even if it did not think the concession plans as a whole were preempted, the court could decide to simply enjoin the employee provision. Overall, the ATA's complaint deftly carved lines: distinguishing Long Beach from Los Angeles, and within Los Angeles isolating employee conversion from the other concession provisions. Two days later, the ATA moved for a preliminary injunction to bar implementation of the concession plans.[799] Speaking later about the injunction, the ATA's Whalen sounded what would be the industry group's talking points: "Let's be clear: We are not against clean trucks . . . . We are objecting to concession plans that are going to squeeze out a lot of existing motor carriers and thousands of independent owner-operators."[800] From the coalition's point of view, this argument rang hollow. As NRDC's Martinez recalled, the ATA was "trying to just throw monkey wrenches after monkey wrenches" to stop the plans, while all the time insisting it was "supportive of clean air."[801]

Confronted with a new effort to split the environmental and labor elements of the program and facing the prospect of the cities' legal interests diverging from their own, the coalition—not formally party to the suit—had to decide how to respond. Playing to its legal strength and emphasizing the connection between the environmental and labor pieces of the Los Angeles program, the coalition turned again to its environmental partners. On July 31, 2008, the NRDC, Sierra Club, and Coalition for Clean Air moved to intervene in the case, arguing that its members had "significantly protectable interests" that would not be adequately represented by the defendant ports, which "as public proprietary entities . . . must balance resource constraints and the interests of various constituencies—some of which (such as those of Plaintiff) are at odds with the proposed intervenors' interest—and have often taken positions on port-related policy and regulatory matters contrary to" the intervenors.[802] The court agreed and the intervenors proceeded to make their case in support of the concession plans.

In their brief opposing the ATA's preliminary injunction motion, NRDC's Pettit, Perrella, and Martinez laid out the environmental case for market participation, devoting the first part of their brief to explicating why the plans were "necessary to protect public health."[803] In addition to reviewing the evidence of air pollution and public health impacts, the intervenors' brief stressed how all elements of the concession plans, including employee conversion (not mentioned by name) were "intertwined and . . . all necessary to achieve the Ports' clean air goals."[804] NRDC's Perrella recalled that although it was "very clear that we were in favor of L.A.'s program," NRDC intervened to protect both the Los Angeles and Long Beach plans since "the heart of [the] ATA's argument really attacked the fundamentals of both programs. And so we felt like it was important to protect" them.[805] In the litigation, NRDC represented its own interests, which meant that the organization's lawyers "work[ed] together to figure out the best approach."[806] In also representing the Sierra Club and Coalition for Clean Air, NRDC's retainer identified one person within each organization who served as the representative for client relations purposes, keeping NRDC out of the other client organizations' internal deliberations.[807]

Throughout the litigation, NRDC worked with counsel for the Port of Los Angeles, with whom it had a much closer relationship than with counsel for Long Beach—based on the Los Angeles city attorneys' supportive posture during the policy phase.[808] NRDC lawyers had a "joint defense agreement" with the Port of Los Angeles lawyers,[809] with whom they would discuss "who would take what approach to what issue,"[810] and exchange drafts of legal briefs.[811] Although the city defendants were definitely in the lead, NRDC did not "shy away from . . . being parties in the case."[812] Toward that end, NRDC sought to make arguments that built upon its comparative advantage as environmental experts. In this vein, NRDC pressed the argument that the ports needed to implement the concession plans to avoid potential environmental liability. As the "troublemakers" that initiated port litigation in the first instance, NRDC could make that case "more forcefully" than the city defendants, particularly since the ports were not going to concede that they had ongoing environmental legal risk.[813] In addition, NRDC was well positioned to make the strong case for showing how the employee driver provision "benefits the environment."[814] Particularly to the extent that the ATA was seeking to paint the Los Angeles plan as a sop to unions, having NRDC make the labor argument was a way to keep the entire plan within an environmental frame. During the lawsuit, Teamsters lawyer Mike Manley recalled that the plan was for him to "recede as much as possible to the background," although he believed that the ATA representatives were "going to paint it as a Teamster case anyway—which they did."[815] Manley participated "indirectly" by providing his analyses of the market participant doctrine to NRDC lawyers, whom he told: "here's the argument, here's why it supports us."[816]

Asserting a unified front in the preliminary injunction phase, both ports filed a joint opposition that strongly asserted local authority for their respective concession plans—though with a different emphasis than the environmental intervenors' brief. On the Los Angeles side, outside counsel Steven Rosenthal was the defendants' lead attorney, supported by his colleagues at Kaye Scholer, who worked closely with City Attorneys Tom Russell, Joy Crose, and Simon Kahn. Long Beach was similarly represented by its city attorneys and outside counsel from two law firms.[817]

In their opposition, the ports argued that the programs fell squarely within the market participant exception to federal preemption as the product of "a proprietary action of the Ports in their capacity as commercial enterprises and landlords."[818] Here, the ports emphasized the market dimensions of the concession plans:

> The CTP is a product of the Ports' recognition that in order to grow and to continue to compete successfully in that market, they need to address

major environmental and security issues. The concession programs reflect the Ports' efforts to secure trucking services—services critical to their commercial operation—in a way that will further those objectives.[819]

In making this argument, the ports relied heavily on the *Engine Manufacturers* case, litigated by NRDC, applying the market participant exception to the Clean Air Act in upholding SCAQMD rules setting emission standards for vehicles acquired by the state.[820] Based on that case, the ports emphasized that they were acting as a market participant in the "efficient procurement" of trucking services and that the plans' "narrow scope" defeated an inference that their "primary goal was to encourage a general policy rather than address a specific proprietary problem."[821] As an additional ground of opposition, the ports argued that the concessions fell within a statutory exception to FAAAA preemption, which stated that the act "shall not restrict the safety regulatory authority of a State with respect to motor vehicles."[822] Specifically, the ports claimed that the plans were designed to enhance port security and eliminate unsafe trucks[823]—drawing on arguments that were laid out in the findings sections of the Clean Truck Program legislation. To buttress this argument, the ports submitted an affidavit from John Holmes averring that the Los Angeles program was, in addition to addressing environmental harms, "designed to address other problems that result from the truck activities at the Ports—safety and security."[824]

Weighing these arguments was District Court Judge Christina Snyder, who had been appointed in 1997 by President Clinton after serving as a partner in a Los Angeles law firm.[825] In the early part of her career, Judge Snyder was a founder of Public Counsel Law Center, one of Los Angeles's largest legal aid organizations, serving on its board and as its president.[826] Her first opinion was an early victory for the ports. In an order dated September 9, 2008, she denied the ATA's motion for a preliminary injunction.[827] Yet the scope of the order highlighted the challenges that the ports would face ahead. To begin, the court held that the concession plans likely regulated the "price, route, or service" of trucking companies and thus fell within the scope of FAAAA preemption.[828] The issue was therefore whether an exception to preemption would save the plans. Of the ports' arguments for an exception, Judge Snyder only agreed that "the defendants have shown that there is a significant probability that the concession agreements fall under the safety exception to the FAAAA, and that they may therefore be saved from preemption."[829]

Although acknowledging that there "does not appear to be any case law addressing the question of whether security concerns analogous to the concerns identified by the Ports fall within the safety exception," Judge Snyder ruled that it was likely they did even though the concessions were not passed for the "exclusive purpose of promoting safety."[830] Alarmingly for the ports, the court ruled against application of the market participant exception on the grounds that the programs were not about "efficient procurement" but rather were "akin to a licensing scheme," and they were not sufficiently narrow in scope to qualify as meeting a "specific proprietary problem."[831] Because it lost the motion, the ATA appealed.[832] As both ports separately filed answers to the ATA's complaint, the case now moved—for the first time—to the Ninth Circuit.

As it did, the coalition continued its organizing and media work outside of court to make the case for employee conversion. Part of this strategy involved criticizing Long Beach's program. Speaking for a coalition of civil rights and consumer groups, NAACP President Julian Bond compared Long Beach drivers, who were being forced to take on debt to finance low-emission trucks, to sharecroppers in the Deep South, warning of a wave of "foreclosures on wheels."[833] Under the Long Beach plan, the Mercedes-Benz/Daimler Truck Finance Company was administering a lease-to-own program in which drivers were given loans to purchase new clean trucks worth over $100,000.[834] However, as the coalition stated in a report delivered to Daimler headquarters, even with port incentives many drivers would not be able to meet the payments and would thus be subject to Daimler's aggressive collections department.[835] While the coalition urged Long Beach to adopt the Los Angeles employee conversion approach, some workers were confused, with one quoted as stating: "A lot of truckers have no idea what's going on with all these different plans and protests, so they are just going with the flow."[836] Yet the protests continued, with sixty truck drivers—some chanting "Clean trucks, yes! Bankruptcy, no!"—gathering to condemn the opening of Long Beach's Clean Trucks Center, charged with administering the financial incentive component of the Long Beach program.[837]

Concerns that trucking companies would boycott the Los Angeles program when it officially began on October 1, 2008 were allayed when two large national firms—Swift and Knight—agreed to participate in exchange for financial incentives.[838] This was followed by an announcement that 120 carriers—many members of the ATA—had applied to service the port under program criteria.[839] With the Great Recession taking its economic toll, some viewed both ports' Clean Truck Programs as coming at the most inauspicious economic time as container traffic had dropped sharply from the previous year.[840] However, the recession also made clean truck conversion more attractive for many trucking companies.[841] As diesel prices soared in 2008 and hundreds of companies failed, converting to cleaner technology with port subsidies made economic sense.[842] When the Los Angeles and Long Beach programs were formally initiated on October 1, both mayors hailed them as a success: With 95% of trucks entering the ports meeting program standards, only two thousand had to be turned away.[843] Coalition member Martin Schlageter praised the programs' arrival: "Powerful institutional forces representing billions of dollars had for years urged that the ports not do anything. But the mayors and the ports stood firm."[844]

It was against this backdrop that the ATA's appeal of Judge Snyder's September 2008 denial of injunctive relief took place. On appeal, the industry group contested the lower court's interpretation of the preliminary injunction standard and its ruling that the FAAAA's "safety exception" likely protected the concession plans from federal preemption.[845] The ports countered these arguments and also reasserted their own claims for local authority under the market participant exception.[846] As they had in the court below, the environmental intervenors reiterated the public health benefits of the plans, defended the lower court's application of the safety exception, and then made the case for market participation.[847] The appeal attracted wider attention: the U.S. government (Department of Transportation, Federal Motor Carrier Safety Administration, and Department of Justice) filed an amicus brief in support of the ATA,[848] as did the National Industrial Transportation League[849] and National Association of Waterfront Employers,[850] all arguing against the lower court's application of the safety exception. The California attorney general came in on the side of the ports.[851]

The stage was thus set for a ruling by a three-judge panel of the Ninth Circuit. Although they differed in ideological orientation—Robert Beezer and Ferdinand Fernandez were conservatives appointed by Ronald Reagan, while Richard Paez was a liberal former legal aid lawyer appointed by Clinton—they spoke with a unanimous voice. In an order issued on March 20, 2009, the panel reversed the district court's denial of injunctive relief.[852] The court's key move was to distinguish among the various provisions of the concession plans, holding that "the district court legally erred in not examining the specific provisions of the Concession agreements, and it is likely that many of those provisions are preempted."[853] The panel's analysis rejected the ports' claims with devastating thoroughness.

Although it agreed with the district court on the preliminary injunction standard and its application to the market participant argument,[854] the panel disagreed on the safety exception. Noting that "the mere fact that one part of a regulation or group of regulations might come within an exception to preemption does not mean that all other parts of that regulation or group are also excepted,"[855] the court proceeded to highlight the non-safety rationales for the plans, including "an extensive attempt to reshape and control the economics of the drayage industry" and to "ameliorate . . . adverse economic effects."[856]

The court then turned to analyzing the plans' individual provisions. Homing in on the employee provision in the Los Angeles plan, the court used the very findings the port had included in the ordinance to support market participant status to undercut the safety exception argument, asserting that "the record demonstrates that the Ports' primary concern was increasing efficiency and regulating the drayage market."[857] On that basis, the court held that "as we see it, the independent contractor phase-out provision is one highly likely to be shown to be preempted."[858] The court expressed similar skepticism about provisions in both plans that required job posting, hiring preferences for experienced drivers, and financial disclosure, as well as Los Angeles's off-street parking ban and Long Beach's driver health insurance requirement.[859] Moving through the preliminary injunction test, the court went on to suggest that a company faced with a concession plan would suffer irreparable harm by being put to a "Hobson's choice." If it refused to sign, its port drayage business likely would "evaporate" with the result for a small carrier probably "fatal," while if it did sign, a company would "incur large costs," which would "disrupt and change the whole nature of its business."[860] Noting that the public interest in deregulation further supported issuing a preliminary injunction, the court stopped just short of complete reversal, stating that in light of the severability provision, "we are not prepared to hold that every provision must be preempted."[861] Accordingly, the appellate court remanded the case back to the district court for "further consideration of the specific terms of each agreement and for the issuance of an appropriate preliminary injunction."[862]

Smelling blood, the ATA renewed its motion for preliminary injunction against both ports' plans on the ground of FAAAA preemption.[863] It was at this stage that the Los Angeles and Long Beach ports once again parted ways, each filing separate oppositions. In its brief, the Los Angeles port decided to play defense, conceding the provisions the Ninth Circuit had explicitly addressed (employee conversion, off-street parking, job posting and driver hiring requirements, and financial capability), while arguing against preemption on safety grounds for those that remained.[864] There was a tension in this position given that it conceded the severability of a plan that the port had long argued constituted an indivisible scheme to redress port pollution. Yet the terms of the Ninth Circuit opinion seemed to require this tactical position to salvage any part of the plan. Long Beach was more aggressive, arguing that none of its plan's provisions, including those singled out by the Ninth Circuit, were preempted either because they simply duplicated already existing law or were related to port safety.[865] The ATA responded that duplicative provisions should be removed from the plans and because the preempted provisions were *not* severable, the plans "should be enjoined in their entirety."[866] The *Los Angeles Times* editors, anticipating the district court decision, weighed in against the Los Angeles program, asking Mayor Villaraigosa "and his union backers" to just "[l]et it go."[867]

On April 28, 2009, the district court ruled for the second time on the ATA's motion for preliminary injunction, issuing a split decision.[868] Taking a provision-by-provision approach, the court preliminarily enjoined key elements of the ports' plans—including Los Angeles's employee conversion provision, as well as both ports' provisions on hiring preferences, financial capability, and parking and route restrictions[869]—while letting stand other provisions the court held to be related to port safety.[870] Rejecting the ATA's claim that the plans should rise or fall as unified agreements, the court held that the preempted provisions were severable and that the safety provisions could be effectively implemented on their own.[871] NRDC released a statement criticizing the ruling: "Without the employee program, port cleanup goals could be severely delayed because most independent owner-operators cannot afford to maintain and repair their trucks."[872]

The ATA once again took appeal, disputing the district court's decision not to preempt the provisions deemed safety related.[873] By the time the Ninth Circuit decided the case, however, Long Beach was no longer part of it. With the appeal pending, the Port of Long Beach decided to strike a deal with the ATA, in which the port would permit truck access under a new "Registration and Agreement" to supersede the concession plan.[874] The new agreement stripped away provisions deemed unrelated to clean truck conversion—including those dealing with parking, truck routes, and financial capability.[875] Under the final agreement, concessionaires would certify truck compliance with basic registration, identification, safety, and security standards, while also certifying compliance with the environmental provisions of the Clean Truck Program.[876] On the basis of that settlement, the court dismissed the Long Beach defendants on October 20, 2009.[877] While Port of Long Beach Director Richard Steinke affirmed his port's commitment to going green, Port of Los Angeles Director Geraldine Knatz asked, "Who will pay for the next fleet of clean trucks when today's new trucks will need to be replaced?"[878]

Left to fend for itself, the Port of Los Angeles confronted an invigorated adversary. In court, the ATA sought to compel the disclosure of internal port documents reflecting staff deliberations over the concession agreement, to which the ATA claimed to be entitled in order to rebut port assertions that the agreement was motivated by safety concerns.[879] Although the ATA would ultimately lose this argument on privilege grounds,[880] it suggested the extent to which the ATA was willing to go to win. Out of court, ATA allies sought to take a page from the coalition's book, organizing drivers in opposition to the Los Angeles program. In November 2009, the National Port Drivers Association, claiming to represent independent-contractor drivers, staged a protest in which four hundred truck drivers drove up the 710 Freeway to Los Angeles City Hall, criticizing the fact that clean truck funding had not been given to independent-contractor drivers.[881] Around the same time, the Long Beach port began a marketing campaign to promote its program to community residents, featuring the president of ILWU Local 13, George Lujan, stating that his "union supports the Port of Long Beach Clean Trucks Program."[882]

On appeal, the Port of Los Angeles lost a little more ground in front of a different three-judge panel of the Ninth Circuit.[883] On February 24, 2010, the panel agreed with the district court's decision to enjoin the provisions it did but also decided to enjoin one more—the placard provision, which the court found to be specifically outlawed by a separate section of the FAAAA to which the safety exception did not apply.[884] The overall picture for Los Angeles looked grim. With Long Beach out of the case and the core features of its concession plan subject to a preliminary injunction, the Port of Los Angeles appeared to face long odds heading into trial,[885] which was set for April 2010.

The dramatic turnaround—from the district court's initial support of the concession plan prior to its official launch date in the fall of 2008 to its preliminary injunction in the spring of 2009—affected rollout of the Clean Truck Program. Although scheduled to begin on October 1, 2008, it was widely assumed that the port would not strictly enforce the concession plan until April 2009 as it worked out technical issues and permitted trucking companies to purchase new trucks and begin the phase-in of employee conversion.[886] Despite the ATA lawsuit filed in July 2008, program implementation proceeded apace. As Jon Zerolnick recalled, at first, "nothing changed."[887] Trucking companies drew upon port and state funding to begin converting their fleets, while some, like Southern Counties Express and Swift, took initial steps to convert their drivers to employees.[888] By early 2009, the coalition was supporting Teamsters organizing at companies that had hired employee drivers.[889] The preliminary injunction ruling in April 2009 changed everything. With the threat of port sanction lifted, companies promptly moved back to independent-contractor drivers.

As trucking companies restored independent contractors, they also shifted to drivers the costs associated with purchasing clean trucks. The ban on old, dirty trucks—the second phase of which was set to go into effect on January 1, 2010—forced drivers to purchase or lease expensive new low-emission vehicles. Although the port offered subsidies, some drivers could not take advantage of them to buy their own trucks because they could not qualify for loans to pay off the balance—or simply could not afford to pay off the loans, even with port incentives.[890] As one driver ominously predicted: "The first of the year will probably be the end of my family."[891]

Even for those who could acquire their own trucks, the total burden of the loan payments, higher maintenance and insurance costs, and higher registration fees placed burdens on drivers who struggled before the program was implemented—and who faced even more intense challenges as the recession reduced work opportunities. In this context, trucking companies were cutting contract rates, putting drivers in even more economic peril. The *Los Angeles Times* profiled one driver who sold his old truck and joined a company that still hired employee drivers: "We're like slaves. We've lost our freedom."[892] Those drivers who stayed independent owners appeared to have no more autonomy. Trucking companies that had directly purchased clean trucks made drivers lease them back, deducting insurance and maintenance costs from their pay.[893] The *Los Angeles Times* reported that these new trucks cost 50% more to operate on top of lease payments of $1,000 per month.[894] "Things were bad enough when we owned our trucks, but I would say the situation is desperate now," one driver concluded.[895] Another, with twenty years of trucking experience, reported that his take-home pay was seven dollars an hour—less than the minimum wage. His assessment was harsh: "This program has been a great deception to us . . . . We no longer have hope to be in the middle class. We are all poor now."[896]

The Merits Phase

Punctuating the private litigation was a lawsuit filed by the Federal Maritime Commission, which had been pressured by the ATA to seek an injunction against both ports' Clean Truck Programs pursuant to section 6(h) of the Shipping Act of 1984.[897] That section authorized the commission to bring a civil action if a port rule was "likely, by a reduction in competition, to produce an unreasonable reduction in transportation service or an unreasonable increase in transportation cost."[898] However, when President Obama took office in 2009, he appointed new members to the commission, which promptly moved to dismiss the case in the summer of 2009. The dismissal, at the moment the ATA was taking its appeal from Judge Snyder's second preliminary injunction ruling, raised the stakes of the ATA lawsuit, which was now the only legal barrier to the Los Angeles port's Clean Truck Program. As the case moved toward trial, following the 2010 Ninth Circuit ruling that preliminarily enjoined the employee driver provision, each side focused on strengthening its arguments. Seeking to shore up the economic case in favor of the vulnerable employee provision, LAANE issued a report on the cusp of trial demonstrating that "the combined costs for clean truck leases and vehicle maintenance are out of reach for individual port drivers" thus undermining the "heart of the environmental policy."[899] Timed to correspond with the parties' final briefings, the stage was set for trial.

The trial briefs laid out the now-familiar pattern of disagreement. The ATA argued FAAAA preemption of the Los Angeles concession plan; contended that although it did not have to show each provision was unrelated to safety, it could; and then argued against market participation and in favor of finding that the plan unduly burdened interstate commerce.[900] Narrowing its focus for trial, the ATA only challenged five key provisions of the Los Angeles concession plan related to: (1) employee conversion, (2) off-street parking, (3) maintenance, (4) placards, and (5) financial capability.[901] Reprising a backup argument first made at the preliminary injunction hearing, which had gained increasing court attention throughout the case, the ATA sought to apply the Supreme Court's decision in *Castle v. Hayes Freight Lines*, which held that states were prohibited under the Motor Carrier Act from interfering with a carrier's right to operate in interstate commerce.[902] Although the district court had earlier rejected this argument on the ground that the Motor Carrier Act was passed forty years before the FAAAA—the safety exception of which permitted states to suspend carrier service—the Ninth Circuit had cryptically stated that "this issue is not finally resolved and may be reconsidered in further proceedings for a permanent injunction."[903] The ATA used this opening to argue that *Castle* stood for the proposition that only the federal government could determine a carrier's safety fitness and thus the port could not enforce the safety provisions of its concession agreement by barring truck access.[904]

For its part, the Port of Los Angeles took a slightly different approach than in the preliminary injunction phase. First, the port contended that the concession plan's individual provisions did not have the "force and effect of law related to a price, route, or service" and therefore were not preempted by FAAAA section 14501(c) at all. The port then argued that—assuming preemption did apply—the provisions fell within the market participant exception and also were permitted under the FAAAA's safety exception.[905] This order reflected the port's sense that the safety exception was a relatively weaker argument, but one that it "was kind of stuck with" after the district court upheld several provisions on that basis.[906] Sending a similar message, the port devoted only a page to the ATA's commerce clause argument and relegated the *Castle* claim to a footnote.[907] Not feeling as constrained by the lower court ruling, the NRDC's position at trial emphasized the validity of the concession plan under the market participant exception.[908]

The trial lasted seven days. The ATA's chief counsel, Robert Digges, appeared on behalf of the plaintiffs, alongside outside counsel Christopher McNatt Jr. from Scopelitis, Garvin, Light, Hanson & Feary. On the Los Angeles side, City Attorneys Tom Russell and Simon Kahn appeared with outside counsel from Kaye Scholer (Steven Rosenthal and his team). NRDC lawyers Melissa Lin Perrella and David Pettit appeared on behalf of the environmental intervenors. At trial, port counsel and NRDC each made opening statements, emphasizing distinct themes that foreshadowed counsels' division of labor throughout the remaining litigation. Port counsel Rosenthal sought to lay out the case that the Clean Truck Program was adopted to "address specific proprietary concerns at the port."[909] He suggested that the evidence would show the need for the port as an "enormous commercial enterprise" to address environmental and community impacts that had "brought significant expansion and improvement at the port to a screeching halt."[910] He also stressed the port's need to respond to security risks in laying out the case for application of the safety exception.[911] For the environmental intervenors, NRDC's Perrella focused on "[w]hether the remediation of port-generated air pollution by the Clean Truck Program and specifically by the concession agreement is protected under the market participant doctrine."[912] As she made clear, the intervenors' case would stress the public health impacts of port pollution and tie them directly to the independent-contractor status of the drivers.[913]

During trial, Rosenthal and his team presented evidence to show how the Clean Truck Program responded to proprietary concerns. Rosenthal questioned key port decision-makers: Executive Director Geraldine Knatz, who discussed program details;[914] Commissioner David Freeman, who emphasized that the program was designed to facilitate port expansion;[915] and Deputy Executive Director of Operations John Holmes, who discussed how the program was intended "to provide a level of accountability, but also to insure the program was sustainable and that it met the environmental and security goals of the port."[916] Rosenthal's colleagues elicited testimony from witnesses highlighting how the program responded to local port traffic problems and transportation security concerns.[917] Perrella took the lead in questioning Dr. Elaine Chang, who outlined the case for port-induced air pollution and the need for the Clean Truck Program to address it,[918] and Long Beach resident Bernice Banares, who testified about her own asthma and safety concerns raised by port trucks.[919] According to Perrella, NRDC's role was to "get into the record what the public health and environmental problem is and then to draw out facts related to how the port sought to address those problems and how addressing those problems was really intertwined with its pursuing its commercial interests."[920]

With the evidence thus tendered, the parties waited for Judge Snyder to rule, which she did on August 26, 2010, in a decision that gave a surprisingly sweeping victory to the port. In the court's detailed Findings of Fact and Conclusions of Law, Judge Snyder ruled that none of the provisions challenged by the ATA were preempted—contradicting the Ninth Circuit's assessment during the preliminary injunction phase. The trial court's decision—with an eye on the ATA's inevitable appeal—set forth alternative grounds for different provisions. With respect to the maintenance, placard, and financial capability provisions, the court ruled that there was insufficient evidence that they would affect truck prices, routes, or services and were thus not preempted under section 14501(c);[921] alternatively, the court concluded that even if those provisions were preempted, the maintenance and placard provisions fell within the safety exception (though the financial capability provision, enacted to ensure "the Port will not lose its investment in truck grants," did not).[922] With respect to the employee driver and off-street parking provisions, the court held both covered by the FAAAA and neither within the safety exception.[923]

However, here the court moved to a different rationale: market participation. Rejecting the ATA's narrow definition of proprietary action, the court stated that "where restrictions are placed on services essential to the functioning of a government-run commercial enterprise, the market participant exception applies to non-procurement decisions."[924] The court then ruled that the entire concession agreement was "essentially proprietary"[925]—and thus not preempted—because it was passed "in response to litigation and the threat to [the Port of Los Angeles's] continued economic viability by community groups . . . as a 'business necessity,' in order to eliminate obstacles to its growth."[926] Wanting to cover all its bases, the court also found each individual provision to fall within the market participant exception. Focusing on employee conversion, the court agreed with the port that it was "designed to transfer the financial burden of administration and record-keeping onto the trucking companies," which was "clearly an economically motivated action, and one that a private company with substantial market power—such as the oligopoly power of the Port—would take when possible in pursuit of maximizing profit."[927] Finally rejecting the ATA's *Castle* and dormant commerce clause claims,[928] the court resoundingly validated the port's Clean Truck Program and the legal strategy that produced it—at least for the moment.

That moment passed quickly. In September 2010, the ATA appealed—and back up the ladder the case went. The ATA requested that the court stay the implementation of the Clean Truck Program pending the appeal.[929] Judge Snyder agreed to temporarily enjoin the employee provision, which she held was likely to produce irreparable harm to plaintiffs that was not outweighed by other equities, while permitting implementation of the rest of the concession plan.[930] On appeal, the issues dividing the parties were fully crystalized and their briefs reflected well-worn arguments for and against preemption.[931] However, to underscore the stakes, a number of new amici weighed in on the side of the ATA's appeal: the Intermodal Association of North America, asserting the negative impact of the concession plan on the intermodal industry;[932] the National Right to Work Legal Defense Foundation, which argued that the concessions forced independent-contractor drivers to sacrifice their right to work as such;[933] the Owner Operator Independent Drivers Association, which argued that the concession plan was not responsive to the issues facing non-short-haul drivers;[934] and the Center for Constitutional Jurisprudence, which argued that market participant status could only be exercised through procurement.[935]

The judges assigned to the appellate panel hearing the case were Betty Fletcher, an iconic liberal appointed by President Carter as only the second woman judge in the Ninth Circuit; Randy Smith, a strong conservative from Idaho appointed by President George W. Bush; and Rudi Brewster, a senior district court judge from San Diego who had been appointed by President Reagan. In a two-to-one decision, with Smith in dissent, the panel upheld the bulk of the concession plan—but dealt the decisive blow to employee conversion.[936] Taking an expansive view of market participation, the court held that "when an independent State entity manages access to its facilities, and imposes conditions similar to those that would be imposed by a private landlord in the State's position, the State may claim the market participant doctrine."[937] Here, because the "Port has a financial interest in ensuring that drayage services are provided in a manner that is safe, reliable, and consistent with the Port's overall goals for facilities management," the court concluded that "the Port acted in its proprietary capacity as a market participant when it decided to enter into concession agreements."[938] However, the court stopped short "of holding that every provision in the concession agreement" was therefore valid, instead opting to "examine whether the provisions at issue further the State's interests as a facilities manager, or whether the provisions seek to affect conduct unrelated to those interests."[939]

Turning to the specific provisions at issue, the court upheld four on diverse grounds: it concluded that the financial capability provision did not affect rates, routes, or services and thus was not preempted; it found the maintenance provision to fall within the safety exception; and it upheld the off-street parking and placard provisions as proprietary acts of the port as a market participant.[940] Yet the court could find nothing to save employee conversion, which it concluded sought "to impact third party behavior unrelated to the performance of the concessionaire's obligations to the Port."[941] Recognizing the port's interest in providing higher wages to attract drivers lost to the TWIC program, the court nonetheless concluded that the port could not achieve market stability "by unilaterally inserting itself into the contractual relationship between motor carriers and drivers."[942] Further recognizing the port's interest in protecting its investment in clean trucks, the court concluded that the concession agreements swept too broadly by binding all LMCs, "not merely those who drive Port-subsidized trucks."[943] Finally, acknowledging the port's interest in "streamlined administration" over a smaller number of LMCs, the court found it "insufficient to outweigh the Port's avowed desire to impact wages not subsidized by the State."[944] With this, employee conversion—the lynchpin of a monumental campaign and innovative local policy—was held to be "tantamount to regulation" and thus preempted.[945]

It was September 2011, five years after the Campaign for Clean Trucks had begun, and the piece that had held the labor-environmental alliance together was gone. LAANE's Patricia Castellanos, responding to the decision, stated that it would "have devastating consequences for working families and port communities plagued by dirty air and dead-end jobs."[946] The port's (and coalition's) early calculation that it could win at the Ninth Circuit level—made with full knowledge of the uncertainty—turned out to be wrong as to employee conversion. The editorial board of the *Los Angeles Times*, on the eve of the Ninth Circuit decision, had expressed hope that the court would "end the city's misguided attempt to team up with the Teamsters."[947] And, indeed, the port decided not to appeal the ruling—though not for the reasons suggested by the *Times*. On the negative side of the ledger, the Ninth Circuit ruling sent an undeniable signal: unable to persuade one of the circuit's most liberal judges, Betty Fletcher, it seemed fruitless—even reckless—to press the case for employee conversion in front of the conservative majority on the Supreme Court. On the positive side, it also was possible for the port and coalition to count the Ninth Circuit ruling as a win and walk away. As NRDC's Pettit saw it, the Ninth Circuit ruling endorsed the idea that a port "can have a concession plan and can put conditions on trucks . . . even [those] in interstate commerce."[948] With the basic foundation of the concession concept thus left "intact,"[949] NRDC lawyers "viewed what we got from the Ninth Circuit as a victory."[950] As it turned out, so did the ATA.

The Supreme Court Phase

Refusing to settle for the victory over employee drivers, the ATA again set its sights on gutting the concession plan, this time by appealing to the Supreme Court.[951] NRDC saw the appeal as a statement by the ATA that "state and local government should not be able to place . . . really any requirements on motor carriers, so it was: 'If we can show that you can't even do this placard provision, then that means that you can't do anything.' "[952] In pressing this case, the ATA retained new counsel for the appeal: Supreme Court specialist Roy Englert, an assistant solicitor general under President Reagan who had started his own appellate firm in 2001 and boasted a nearly perfect record in front of the Court. NRDC's Perrella noticed the difference, recalling that the ATA's Supreme Court counsel was "phenomenal," framing the briefs in a way "that was just really compelling."[953]

In its petition for certiorari, the ATA asked the Court to resolve what it characterized as three significant circuit splits: one over the application of the market participant exception to preemption, a second over the scope of FAAAA preemption, and a third over the vitality of *Castle*.[954] In response, the port sought to minimize the legal stakes, arguing that the Ninth Circuit's decision was in fact congruent with those of other circuits on market participation and thus no circuit split existed. Furthermore, the port suggested that the other issues presented were not substantial enough to warrant Court review: specifically, the Ninth Circuit's single ruling that the FAAAA did not preempt the financial capability provision and its narrow application of the safety exception to the maintenance provision were too minor to justify granting cert.[955] For their part, the environmental intervenors stressed that the Ninth Circuit's decision on market participation was based on the trial court's extensive factual findings on the port's health and community impacts, which the ATA did not challenge on appeal.[956] They also continued to emphasize the business benefits of the port going green, which NRDC lawyers believed that they, as representatives of an environmental organization, were better positioned to do.[957] In March 2012, the Supreme Court invited the U.S. solicitor general to express its views on the matter, which it did, coming in on the side of the ATA.[958] In the U.S. brief, Solicitor General Donald Verrilli argued for an expansive concept of preemption, rejecting the idea that a port should be able to establish special rules, claiming instead that the port was "akin to a public managed transportation infrastructure" and thus should not be able to impose restrictions that were inconsistent with other ports.[959] However, the solicitor general also threw a line to the port by recommending that the Court not grant certiorari based on the limited significance of the Los Angeles case.[960]

If supporters of the Clean Truck Program were surprised when the Ninth Circuit struck down the employee driver provision, they were shocked when the Supreme Court agreed to consider the ATA's market participant and *Castle* claims: setting up review of the concession plan's placard and off-street parking provisions.[961] NRDC's Perrella described her response:

> Surprised? . . . It completely devastated us . . . . I don't think I've had that really horrible feeling in my stomach . . . the way I did when I found out the Supreme Court had decided to take the case . . . . [H]ere we go again with a wacky environmental case in the Ninth Circuit before a bunch of conservative judges . . . probably not the best forum for us.[962]

The Court's decision to take the case signaled an interest in perhaps curtailing the market participant doctrine at the core of the Ninth Circuit's decision. Accordingly, the port adjusted its market participant argument in its merits brief. Parrying the ATA's claim that the port did not participate directly in the drayage market, the port emphasized its right as a property owner to enter into agreements affecting access to its land. In summarizing its core position, the port asserted that "absent a statement of clear congressional intent to the contrary, the courts should presume that proprietary state conduct dealing with the management of state-owned property is within the market-participant doctrine."[963] Because the port as property owner had a clear "commercial motivation" in the contested provisions—promoting truck safety and improving community relations—they fell within the scope of the market participant doctrine.[964] NRDC shaped its merits brief in response to the city's draft, emphasizing the commercial benefits of the port's "green growth" strategy.[965] In making the market participant argument, NRDC drew upon its now-deep well of experience and also exchanged views with port counsel and the Teamsters' Mike Manley.[966] In preparing for oral argument, Perrella helped organize two moot courts, one at the University of California, Irvine School of Law, and another at Public Citizen in Washington, D.C., where she persuaded former Solicitor General Seth Waxman to be on the panel.[967]

At oral argument, it was immediately clear that the port's position would be greeted with skepticism. Almost as soon as port counsel Rosenthal began his opening statement, Justice Scalia pounced: "What exception do you appeal to? There are a number of exceptions there."[968] Barely letting him finish a sentence, Scalia insisted that Rosenthal was asking for "an exception for private contract operations as opposed to public matters," adding that "[t]here are exceptions to the preemption [sic] and that is not one of them."[969] For Perrella, this was "difficult" because their argument hinged on the Court recognizing, as a first step, that there was in fact a market participant exception to the FAAAA and she "felt like at least a few of the justices couldn't even get past step one."[970] Contending with Justice Antonin Scalia and Chief Justice John Roberts over enforcement, Rosenthal focused on whether the provisions carried the "force and effect of law" under the FAAAA.[971] This took the conversation away from market participation, meandering through an analysis of *Castle* and then back to questions of concession enforcement[972]—in this way, previewing the grounds for the Court's ultimate resolution.

If the supporters of the Clean Truck Program were bracing for a sweeping curtailment of the market participant exception, what they got on June 13, 2013—in a unanimous decision by Justice Elena Kagan—was a narrow, technical reading of FAAAA section 14501(c)(1)'s operative language, preempting a state "law, regulation, or other provision having the force and effect of law related to a price, route, or service of any motor carrier."[973] Stating that the parties agreed that the provisions at issue related to a motor carrier's price, route, or service, Kagan's decision focused on the "force and effect of law" language.[974] It concluded that the placard and off-street parking provisions, though contained in a contract, were "part and parcel of a governmental program wielding coercive power over private parties, backed by the threat of criminal punishment."[975] Specifically, because the objectives of the agreement were accomplished "by amending the Port's tariff" to impose legal liability on terminal operators—and a violation subjected terminal operators to criminal sanction—the agreement did not stand alone as a contract, but rather was part

Figure 6.14 NRDC lawyers Melissa Lin Perrella, David Pettit, and Morgan Wyenn (from left to right) at the Supreme Court. *Source*: NRDC (2013).

of a comprehensive regulatory scheme backed by "the hammer of criminal law."[976] Although the Court acknowledged that the "line between regulatory and proprietary conduct has soft edges," this case was "nowhere near" that line since "the threat of criminal sanctions" showed the government acting "*qua* government, performing its prototypical regulatory role."[977] What mattered was not the port's intent to "turn a profit," but rather the means used, which in this case involved enforcement of the placard and off-street parking provisions through "a coercive mechanism, available to no private party"—thus bringing them within the FAAAA's preemptive scope.[978] With this characterization of the concession provisions and reading of the statute, the Court sidestepped deep analysis of the scope of market participation.

The court then punted on the ATA's *Castle* claim. Because the port had not yet begun to enforce the financial capability and maintenance provisions, the Court concluded that it was not clear whether enforcement would be for past violations of the concession agreement—which would possibly be barred by *Castle*—or for ongoing violations—which the Court noted that even the ATA agreed would be permissible.[979] Because "the kind of enforcement ATA fears, and believes inconsistent with *Castle*, might never come to pass at all," the Court—threading a very fine needle—decided simply not to decide.[980]

In the end, although the port lost, it did manage to limit the doctrinal damage. The Court, in a footnote, stated that the port had occasionally framed the question as whether "a freestanding 'market-participant exception' limits § 14501(c)(1)'s express terms."[981] However, mirroring the shift to the "force and effect of law" discussion in oral argument, the opinion's text did not mention the market participant doctrine by name, though it asserted that "contract-based participation in a market" was not preempted by the FAAAA[982]—implying that what the port had done with its concession agreement was regulatory and not "contract-based." In that sense, the port—along with the environmental and labor groups that had urged it on—dodged a doctrinal bullet.

Yet that was cold comfort to the city staff and coalition personnel who had struggled so mightily to win passage of the Los Angeles Clean Truck Program. Reflecting on the litigation loss, the port's John Holmes—one of the key architects of the concession plan—saw a contradiction at the heart of the legal outcome. Although the port remained legally liable for environmental compliance, he read the Court's analysis as depriving the port of full legal power to achieve it. The result, in his view, was that the port had "accountability without authority."[983]

For the coalition, the Court's opinion officially laid to rest the boldest aspirations of the Clean Truck Program. Built upon interconnected labor, community, and environmental claims for redress, what remained of the program—clean truck conversion and port financing to achieve it—spoke most directly to the environmental goals. Although community residents would benefit from clean trucks, their other demands—off-street parking and placards to enable reporting of bad drivers—had been legally excised from the concession plan. And one of organized labor's preeminent goals—changing truck drivers from independent contractors to employees—once tantalizingly close, was again a distant dream. Litigation, which had been such a powerful tool in bringing together the coalition, had been used by its adversary to tear its accomplishment apart.

The Aftermath: Maneuvering Around Preemption

The ATA litigation reinforced the outlines of the difficult legal box that the labor movement was in. Although federal labor law did not generally serve the movement's strategic interests—at least when it came to port trucking—federal transportation law was held to preempt local efforts to change the balance of power. The environmental movement, on the other hand, was able to wield strong federal and state law to carve out space for local action. In this regard, the ATA's own strategic behavior helped the environmental cause by foregoing a challenge to the dirty truck ban in order to focus its arguments on the concession plan and, specifically, employee conversion. This was both a tactical and economic choice. Supporting the ports' green initiative demonstrated industry social responsibility and sharpened the union critique. And facing the reality of increasing fuel costs and the promise of a local subsidy, it made economic sense to convert the port fleet.[984] From the industry's point of view, employee conversion was a dead-weight loss to be fought tooth and nail.

As a result of the litigation, environmentalists could claim short-term victory in reducing emissions, but at the cost of long-term uncertainty about maintenance and the effect on truck drivers, who continued as independent contractors—only now with the added burden of having to acquire and maintain expensive new clean trucks.[985] In the face of federal preemption, the coalition pursued two strategies to maneuver around it. One centered on amending the FAAAA to explicitly permit the Clean Truck Program—with employee conversion. The other sought to promote conversion and unionization through a company-by-company approach that combined misclassification litigation and direct driver organizing. Both, again, focused on changing the drivers' independent-contractor status to enable labor action.

A Legislative Window—Closed

By the time the Supreme Court finally resolved the ultimate fate of the concession plan, the coalition had long since turned to "Plan B."[986] After the Ninth Circuit's first preliminary injunction ruling in March 2009—in which it opined that the employee conversion provision was "one highly likely to be shown to be preempted"[987]—the coalition made a strategic decision not to wait idly by for the court process to wend its way toward resolution. As the district court issued its preliminary injunction against key elements of the concession plan a month later, the coalition had already set in motion a legislative campaign to moot the litigation. As Change to Win's Nick Weiner put it after the district court ruling: "We need to talk to our friends in Congress and see what our options are.... We've come this far, and we are not going to give up because there are crummy laws."[988]

The campaign's first move was to the federal government, where it mobilized to amend the FAAAA preemption rule to explicitly permit the Clean Truck Program—employee conversion and all. Jon Zerolnick remembered the coalition's calculation in mid-2009 this way: "So we thought, okay, we're pretty sure that we're going to win the court case. But maybe we're not. Maybe we're wrong. We don't think so. But, you know, if the F-quad-A . . . does preempt what we're doing, well, then let's just clarify the F-quad-A."[989] The legislative campaign started with promise. In mid-2009, President Barack Obama had recently taken office and the Democrats controlled both houses of Congress—with a filibuster-proof majority in the Senate. The political stars were thus aligned and, while the focus was on health care reform, the coalition sought to capitalize on the opportunity.

A key early step was drafting language to modify the FAAAA to carve out an exception for the Los Angeles program. To advance that piece, the Los Angeles city attorneys, with input from NRDC and Teamsters counsel, generated an early draft,[990] which modified section 14501(c) of the FAAAA to make clear that preemption did not limit local authority to "condition entry to Port Facilities for the purpose of . . . improving the environmental, safety, security or congestion conditions of Port facilities or in nearby areas."[991] With that tentative language in hand, the port and coalition sought to secure sponsors in both houses and to persuade the relevant committees—the Committee on Transportation and Infrastructure in the House, and the Committee on Commerce, Science, and Transportation in the Senate—to take up the bill.

In a display of its seriousness, in May 2009, the Port of Los Angeles paid $150,000 to hire former House Majority Leader Richard Gephardt's high-powered political consulting firm, the Gephardt Group, to lobby Congress on behalf of the amendment.[992] To support this effort, the coalition, spearheaded by LAANE, reached out to Southern California Congress members to educate them about the lawsuit and the proposed legislative fix, and to gain their support and potential cosponsorship.[993] To make the coalition's case, LAANE put together a comprehensive briefing book titled, *Clearing the Roadblocks: A Map to Green and Grow a Key American Industry to Create 85,000 Middle-Class Jobs at Our Nation's Ports*, which included an analysis of the "positive impacts" of the Los Angeles port's Clean Truck Program, an overview of the ATA litigation, key reports from the campaign (including the BCG report), press clippings, statements of support from prominent elected officials, and a list of organizational partners.[994] The coalition also assembled a two-page background paper, proclaiming that the "trucking industry, under the leadership of the American Trucking Association . . . is attacking" the Clean Truck Program.[995] This effort bore fruit. On November 4, 2009, twenty-four members of the California congressional delegation wrote to James Oberstar (D-Minnesota), chair of the House Committee on Transportation and Infrastructure, to urge him to "consider making changes to the FAAAA so that California ports can successfully implement and enforce needed truck management programs."[996]

Supporters of the amendment also made their case in the media. On the first anniversary of the Los Angeles Clean Truck Program, Mayor Villaraigosa touted its accomplishments and urged "lawmakers in Washington to update federal law and allow a first-of-its-kind emissions reduction initiative like the Clean Truck Program to flourish."[997] New York City Mayor Michael Bloomberg threw his weight behind the campaign: "Today, I'm calling on Congress to support legislation that will empower ports to implement the L.A. Clean Truck Program, an innovative initiative that will create good, green jobs and improve the quality of the air that New Yorkers breathe."[998] In what came as no surprise, the nation's biggest trade associations were not persuaded: "We strongly oppose the efforts of the port to support changing long-standing federal law ... to include a provision within the Clean Truck Plan that has nothing to do with reducing truck emissions."[999]

For such a small change to an esoteric law, supporters assembled a powerful coalition to make its case on Capitol Hill. It included familiar players from the Los Angeles campaign—including Change to Win, CLUE, East Yard Communities for Environmental Justice, LBACA, LAANE, and NRDC—as well as other powerful supporters (the national Blue-Green Alliance, Steel Workers union, UNITE HERE, and Sierra Club) and community partners from around the country. Thus united, the coalition coordinated congressional visits in late 2009 and early 2010. Change to Win's Weiner helped bring in truck drivers from Los Angeles and coordinated a lobbying day on which Mayor Villaraigosa, consultant Gephardt, and Teamsters President Hoffa met with key lawmakers.[1000] Jonathan Klein, director of CLUE, recalled making the faith case for the amendment, arguing "how unfair" the current law was "in the struggle for working people."[1001] After delays negotiating support due to ILWU resistance, the coalition eventually won crucial backers, including House Speaker Nancy Pelosi and Secretary of Labor Hilda Solis, and—in a key advance—persuaded Democratic Congressman Jerrold Nadler from New York to sponsor the House version of the bill. According to Weiner, Nadler was a "good progressive guy," who had worked on port issues in New York and New Jersey and had strong ties to the Teamsters.[1002]

As this push was underway, the politics began to unravel. The first thread came loose in January 2010, when Republican Scott Brown, in a surprise victory, won the Massachusetts Senate seat vacated by the passing of liberal stalwart Ted Kennedy. Deprived of its filibuster-proof majority in the Senate, the amendment's supporters nonetheless fought on. Their strategy was to attach the amendment to a must-pass transportation reauthorization bill that could be carried in both houses on a Democratic majority.[1003] The enactment of Obama's health care reform law in March 2010 fueled Tea Party resentment and drew predictions of a Republican House majority after the November midterm elections.

With Nadler's support in place, there was a vigorous campaign to pass the amendment before the midterms. In a letter dated April 22, 2010, the coalition—now with over one hundred organizations representing labor, environmental, and community groups from port cities around the country—again urged Oberstar's transportation committee to take up the amendment to "ensure trucks are adequately maintained," "eliminate bad actors," and "prevent fraud."[1004] The coalition concluded: "We can have both high trade volume and clean, safe communities, but only if ports are able to implement programs that give them the tools to address and solve the pollution problem in the ports, including enforcing compliance by bad actors."[1005] The House Committee on Transportation and Infrastructure agreed to move forward, and on May 5, 2010, held a hearing on port trucking conditions,[1006] at which NRDC's Perrella spoke on the status of the litigation.[1007] The draft amendment then was circulated to lawyers in the Department of Transportation. With their "wordsmithing," the draft went back to Nadler and the coalition, which signed off.[1008] With a final "big push," the coalition gained commitments from key cosponsors—Democratic members of the California delegation, plus progressive allies from Maryland, Virginia, Wisconsin, Florida, New Jersey, New York, and Massachusetts—and the bill was ready.

On July 29, 2010, Nadler introduced the Clean Ports Act in the House as H.R. 5967.[1009] The bill—in language that echoed the coalition's early draft—proposed to revise FAAAA section 14501(c)(2)(A) to declare that federal preemption of local laws related to "a price, route, or service of any motor carrier" would *not* apply to local authority:

> to adopt requirements for motor carriers and commercial motor vehicles providing services at port facilities that are reasonably related to the reduction of environmental pollution, traffic congestion, the improvement of highway safety, or the efficient utilization of port facilities . . . .[1010]

The campaign effort now turned to getting sufficient votes to pass—which meant more congressional lobbying—in a harrowingly narrow time frame. To do this, the coalition circulated the results of a survey of driver conditions one year after the ATA litigation, which emphasized that "[m]any port drivers, in order to compensate for new clean truck expenses, are working significantly longer hours, earning less, and feel considerably less optimistic about the future."[1011] Noting that "trucking companies have seized greater control over drivers' work and the trucks they operate through drastic changes in methods of compensation,[1012] the coalition feverishly lobbied to gain support for an omnibus transportation bill. But with Republican electoral chances looking good as the midterm elections drew nearer, House Democrats were reluctant to make a strong push for a labor-backed bill, which was therefore delayed until after November. As Weiner recalled: "And that's when it all fell apart."[1013]

Although launched with great hope, the bill died an untimely death—undone by the catastrophic midterm election loss in November 2010 that negated the Democrats' majority in the House. Deprived of the ability to pass legislation along party lines in either chamber of Congress, Democrats could not persuade any member of the newly energized and more conservative Republican caucus to cross the aisle in support of a union legislative priority. Although the coalition went through the motions, the legislative point was effectively moot. On February 9, 2011, with fifty-nine cosponsors, Nadler's House bill was reintroduced as H.R. 572, with the operative language virtually unchanged.[1014] In a one-page overview, the coalition reiterated its argument that the ATA appeal was "preventing key portions of LA's Clean Truck Program from being enforced, threatening job-creating expansion and infrastructure projects from moving forward."[1015] By late 2011, the coalition had secured a Senate sponsor, newly elected New York Senator Kirsten Gillibrand, who introduced an identical bill, S. 2011, on December 16.[1016] The Senate bill was referred to the Committee on Commerce, Science, and Transportation, where it died stillborn.

In a last-ditch legislative effort, the coalition turned to the California state legislature in the wake of the federal midterm congressional election. On February 18, 2011, with the cosponsorship of staunch labor ally and Assembly Speaker John Perez (representing parts of East and South Los Angeles), and Labor and Employment Committee Chair Sandre Swanson (from Oakland), the coalition helped to introduce the Truck Driver Employment and Public Safety Act, labeled as A.B. 950. The bill sought to amend the California Labor Code "for purposes of all of the provisions of state law that govern employment," to declare that "a drayage truck operator is an employee of the entity or person who arranges for or engages the services of the operator."[1017] As drafted, the bill would have effectuated by state legislative mandate what the coalition had failed to achieve through the port concession plan. However, industry pushback was swift and decisive. Although the bill was read into the Labor and Employment Committee record, and subsequently received a full hearing in May 2011,[1018] it was ordered to the inactive file in June after Perez met with representatives of the California Trucking Association.[1019] In arguing against the bill, the California Trucking Association pointed to the 2008 investigation of drayage trucking companies by state Attorney General Jerry Brown— who found five small companies misclassifying truck drivers at the Los Angeles and Long Beach ports—as evidence that misclassification was not a significant problem.[1020] The irony of this claim could not have been lost on coalition advocates, who knew that the five prosecuted companies represented a lower bound, not an upper limit on violators as the industry suggested. Indeed, as the campaign moved into its final phase, advocates had already begun to challenge driver misclassification as a systemic problem—intent to prove the industry wrong and salvage the effort to reform port trucking.

Law and Organizing—A Renewed Challenge

After the Clean Truck Program was enjoined, the coalition's second backup strategy was to promote misclassification litigation in an effort to move contractor-based companies to an employee model,[1021] while simultaneously organizing unions in employee-based companies that already existed.

Misclassification Litigation
Advocates had long believed that many drayage truck drivers were illegally labeled independent contractors by companies that nonetheless exercised employer-like control. Challenges to misclassification had its roots in the early 1990s campaign

by WRTU and the *Albillo v. Intermodal Container Services* class action at the end of that decade.[1022] Although these efforts did not yield widespread reform, by the late 2000s, the context had changed in ways that refocused attention on the potential to make the misclassification case. The difference was twofold. First, particularly after the congressional midterm elections undercut the effort to amend the FAAAA, the coalition was prepared to invest significant resources to promote a systematic enforcement campaign[1023]—something that had been lacking in previous enforcement efforts. And second, there were political allies in influential positions within relevant federal and state agencies that could contribute additional enforcement resources.

The path was not easy. In an industry of hundreds of small companies, misclassification litigation was necessarily a piecemeal approach. Moreover, the legal argument for misclassification was not straightforward. The test for whether a worker was a statutory employee hinged on the degree of employer control: a murky legal test that looked at the "economic realities" of the working relationship, such as whether the worker was engaged in a distinct business, supplied the materials, provided a special skill, worked without supervision, set the work schedule, and was paid by the job.[1024] Failing to properly classify an employee as such was not an independent legal violation, but rather a predicate to showing an employer violation of other laws—for example, illegally deducting business expenses (like lease payments) from driver paychecks, or failing to pay minimum wage, keep appropriate records, or provide workers compensation and unemployment insurance. For private lawyers, bringing misclassification suits depended on the extent to which the legal violation would generate sufficient legal fees. Cases for back pay involving small numbers of low-paid workers did not always provide fees large enough to entice private lawyers to make the investment. Moreover, even successful cases could not force companies to hire employees—and often had the effect of simply making companies more stringent about following the independent-contractor rules.

It was against this backdrop that the coalition simultaneously pursued public and private enforcement options. The public option avoided the private attorney's fees problem by shifting the cost of litigation to government agencies responsible for enforcing employment law: the Department of Labor (DOL) at the federal level and DLSE at the state level. Both agencies were empowered to investigate and bring enforcement actions against violators of employment laws—and had the resources and staff to conduct large-scale operations. The key was persuading decision-makers to exercise their power.

In 2009, the Obama DOL launched a misclassification initiative to investigate the problem in various industries. At the state level, in February 2008, during the height of the Campaign for Clean Trucks, California Attorney General Jerry Brown appointed a task force to investigate port trucking misclassification, which "uncovered numerous state labor law violations committed by several trucking companies operating at the ports."[1025] As a result, Brown filed lawsuits,[1026] which alleged that port trucking firms had illegally avoided paying employment taxes and workers' compensation benefits, and also gained an unfair business advantage over companies that followed the law.[1027] Although Brown won judgments against small companies,[1028] all went out of business.[1029] Another suit against Pac Anchor Transportation elicited a strong response,[1030] with the company criticizing the attorney general for seeking "political gain" by currying favor with the Teamsters to win their support in his planned 2010 run for governor.[1031]

When Brown was elected governor of California in November 2010, he appointed Julie Su, at that point director of the litigation department at APALC, to head the DLSE.[1032] Su was an inspired choice, whose background battling garment sweatshops generated hope that the DLSE would begin living up its mandate of protecting worker rights. Her groundbreaking advocacy in the Thai worker case, in which she had pressed for garment manufacturer and retailer liability for contract worker abuse under the "economic realities" test,[1033] gave her keen insights into the challenges of proving employee status and how the abuse of contracting relationships harmed low-wage workers. She thus came to the job in early 2011 as someone with deep knowledge and directly relevant experience litigating employment cases in industries defined by contracting.

Coalition members reached out to Su to make the case that the DLSE should devote resources to target misclassification in port trucking. In doing so, they were equipped with multiple pieces of evidence. In December 2010, Rebecca Smith at the National Employment Law Project (NELP)—along with Professor David Bensman of the Rutgers School of Management and Labor Relations, and Paul Marvy of Change to Win—released *The Big Rig*, a carefully documented report on finding that "the typical port truck driver is misclassified as an independent contractor" since drivers were subject to "strict behavioral controls," while being "financially dependent" and "tightly tied" to particular trucking companies.[1034] News reports also highlighted the plight of truck drivers, with one article in the Spanish-language daily, *La Opinión*, quoting a driver lamenting: "We are at the mercy of God."[1035] Other research linked misclassification to the concept of "wage theft," with UCLA researchers finding that nearly one-third of L.A. workers in a typical week were deprived of the minimum wage.[1036] Making the link between wage theft and the government budget, the Obama administration in 2010 estimated that stopping misclassification could generate $7 billion in tax revenue.[1037]

To help develop the case for proactive enforcement—thus advancing what was now "Plan C" since the federal legislative strategy had collapsed—LAANE hired Sanjukta Paul as legal coordinator in early 2011.[1038] Paul had worked at civil rights litigation boutique Hadsell & Stormer and then opened her own solo civil rights and employment firm. On the verge of taking a hiatus from practice, she heard from a colleague that LAANE was looking for a lawyer on a short-term contract to help address misclassification in port trucking.[1039] Attracted to being "part of a larger movement," Paul took the job, which involved advancing the coalition's top-down effort to promote agency enforcement while also developing a bottom-up strategy to link individual enforcement to driver organizing.[1040] She quickly set about "getting up to speed on the legal issues," which involved drafting memos to Change to Win's Weiner to "inform the top-down enforcement approach against the industry."[1041] Toward that end, Paul developed legal theories to strengthen the case for agency enforcement and looked into available damages.[1042]

Paul shared her memos with state regulators, while coalition members, led by LAANE's Castellanos, met with the DLSE's Su in mid-2011. The Teamsters' Mike Manley and Port Division Director Chuck Mack also joined in some of the meetings. As Manley recalled, the thrust of these discussions was: "Here's the evidence. Here's what we found. This is a misclassification . . . . You're losing a whole lot of money by not going after these people."[1043] Manley described the overall goal of the agency meetings as "trying to move them to really do something other than just sit with us . . . and say, 'Oh, my gosh, it's awful.'"[1044] This same approach was taken at the federal DOL, where Weiner coordinated meetings in 2011 to urge Secretary Hilda Solis and top enforcement officials to undertake parallel federal action. Manley attended some of these sessions, as did NELP's Smith, who discussed *The Big Rig* findings.[1045] Both the DLSE and DOL made commitments to ramp up investigations. The wheels of government bureaucracy, however, moved slowly—and industry resistance was strong.

To reinforce the significance of the misclassification drive—and turn up the political pressure—Teamsters President James Hoffa visited the Los Angeles port in December 2011, just after the Ninth Circuit had issued its final ruling in the ATA case invalidating employee conversion. There to meet with striking workers at Toll Group, Inc., his general message to port drivers was that the Teamsters were still in the fight despite the unexpected setback: "We didn't think we were going to lose . . . . We have to go a different way now."[1046] Industry representatives pushed back hard. Robert Millman, a lawyer from Littler Mendleson representing trucking companies, was dismissive of the misclassification campaign: "The short story is nothing (like this) has worked . . . . This is nothing new. The question is: Are they going to be able to come up with some new game plan?"[1047]

Part of the new game plan focused on leases between companies that had converted fleets under the Clean Truck Program and drivers with whom the companies contracted.[1048] The lease arrangements between a company and driver often precluded the driver from working for other firms, thus suggesting a degree of control tantamount to an employer-employee relationship.[1049] Companies deducted loan payments from driver paychecks—a practice that was illegal under state law if the drivers were, in fact, employees. In a legal research memo to the campaign, Paul suggested that the "documentary evidence" of these deductions in paychecks could provide the "monetary hammer" for private lawsuits seeking damages.[1050] Paul also suggested that a new state law sponsored by the Teamsters, the California Willful Misclassification Law (S.B. 459)[1051]—passed in October 2011—provided additional legal leverage. An outgrowth of the legislative effort that had stalled around the more robust A.B. 950 (which would have declared all port drivers employees), S.B. 459 made willful misclassification an independent state law violation, subjecting employers to substantial financial penalties.[1052] In her memo to the coalition, Paul concluded that "the Willful Misclassification Law represents a bold and important advance in the fight against employers' misuse of the 'independent contractor' form to deny employees their basic legal rights."[1053] The industry response to this legal effort was sharp, as companies leasing clean trucks to drivers complained that they were being penalized for simply following the clean truck rule. "It doesn't seem fair. We are following a government mandate and now we have that mandate being used against us," said Victor La Rosa, president of Total Transportation Systems, Inc.[1054]

The coalition's misclassification strategy sought to complement public enforcement with private litigation—and to coordinate the private litigation with driver organizing efforts. After the Clean Truck Program was enjoined, individual drivers began to file wage claims with the DLSE, challenging their misclassification as independent contractors. Acting on their own, four Long Beach drivers filed claims against Seacon Logix, which resulted in a January 2012 DLSE ruling ordering the company to pay over $100,000 in back wages and penalties.[1055] Seacon retaliated by suing the workers for breach of contract under their lease terms.[1056] David Gurley, a DLSE attorney assigned to the ports, knew of the coalition's misclassification effort and reached out to Paul to help the workers, which she did (along with private employment lawyer Stephen Glick) by assisting them in filing retaliation actions—forcing Seacon to drop the lease claims.[1057] The Seacon Logix case was prosecuted on appeal by the labor commissioner and upheld by the superior court.[1058] In commenting on the victory, Labor Commissioner Su made a statement that echoed her garment advocacy past: "In this case, drivers had signed agreements labeling them independent contractors but the Court saw the truth behind the label."[1059]

The DLSE's involvement refocused attention on the push for greater public enforcement. In February 2012, the DOL and DLSE signed a memorandum of understanding outlining their partnership to reduce misclassification.[1060] In spring, the DLSE sent out subpoenas to several trucking companies and initiated investigations; the DOL launched a similar enforcement effort, resulting in approximately fifty investigations in total.[1061] Industry decried the investigations, with a California Trucking Association representative stating: "We have a problem when companies are harassed or targeted unjustifiably simply because they use independent contractors."[1062] In response, industry lawyers conducted trainings—styled "Teamster and worker misclassification update"—instructing trucking companies on how to avoid running afoul of misclassification rules. One such update recommended that companies "DO NOT Use a Driver Handbook that looks like an employee manual," or require a driver to "Wear company logo," "Paint the truck a particular color," or "Display a company ID card."[1063] Industry representatives tried to characterize the misclassification effort as another Teamsters ploy, with the executive director of the Harbor Trucking Association pointing to a "smoking gun" letter from Hoffa to Governor Brown in April 2012, in which Hoffa stated he was "glad to know that California, in collaboration with the U.S. Department of Labor, is seeking to end this practice."[1064] In October, ten trucking companies (calling themselves the Clean Truck Coalition) escalated the fight, filing suit against Su. In the complaint, the companies sought a declaration that their "pooling agreement" to share clean trucks and lease them to independent contractors, because it was authorized by federal law, precluded Su from pursuing state enforcement actions against them; the companies also requested an injunction against further misclassification investigations.[1065] Responding to critics, Su insisted that the trucking industry was not being singled out and placed blame squarely on the trucking companies themselves:

> I think too often that entities have kept everything the same about their operation, but they once had employees and converted them to contractors to cut cost. It's bad for employees, it's bad for the competitors, and it cheats the public out of millions of dollars a year because they're not paying taxes.... I reject the notion that we should blame hardworking people for the abuse they might suffer from the people who break the law.... That's not the way our legal system is structured; that's not the way our labor laws work.[1066]

Yet the blame game continued, with industry groups insisting that they were being unfairly targeted and ratcheting up the political pressure to tamp down investigations. As government enforcement stalled, the coalition changed tack, trying to generate more bottom-up energy among workers to file wage claims, which they hoped would both put greater pressure on the DLSE to process claims coming from workers on the front lines and promote the organizing of misclassified workers. To advance this strategy, the coalition turned to Paul to help "figure out" what to do.[1067] In response, Paul planned an eight-week legal rights clinic, coordinated with state and federal enforcement agencies, beginning in September 2012. To prepare these clinics, Paul reached out to partners in the labor movement, as well as to government agency officials, for whom she provided an analysis of legal violations in the port trucking industry.[1068] In August, Change to Win organizers passed out leaflets to stopped trucks inviting them to attend an initial meeting to be held at the Teamsters Local 848 office in Long Beach.[1069] At the meeting were representatives from the DLSE, DOL, and California Division of Occupational Safety and Health (Cal/OSHA), as well as labor lawyers and Teamsters organizers—all of whom provided information and encouraged the drivers to pursue their rights.[1070] At this meeting, Paul facilitated a know-your-rights training for workers and organizers[1071]—explaining what facts to look for in support of misclassification.[1072]

From there, Paul instituted a regular legal clinic, open two nights per week, in which she helped drivers identify employment violations, provided counseling on legal options, assisted in the preparation of administrative claims, determined wages owed, and made connections to private attorneys.

Through this process, roughly fifteen cases were filed.[1073] Although Paul did not represent the drivers directly, once they filed claims, she helped calculate damages, coordinated with DLSE attorneys, and used her private bar connections to find plaintiff-side lawyers to represent the drivers in the ensuing proceedings.[1074] Paul also provided private attorneys with supporting legal analysis and developed creative theories for company liability. The number of these "first-generation" cases was deliberately limited to those with strong legal claims in order to create good precedent for high-volume filings later.[1075] In February 2013, as she was preparing to leave LAANE, Paul joined the Wage Justice Center in a class action misclassification suit against QTS, Inc., seeking more than $5 million in damages for violations including unpaid minimum wages, willful misclassification, unlawful pay deductions, and unfair competition.[1076] In May, two drivers sued Wilmington-based Harbor Express on behalf of a broader class of drivers for misclassification. Describing the suit, Brian Kabateck, one of the plaintiffs' lawyers, stated: "It looks like a traditional employment, but they slap the title of independent contractors on them."[1077] Then, in June and July, forty-seven drivers filed DLSE claims against Pacific 9 Transportation (Pac 9) alleging more than $6 million in damages.[1078] In addition, coalition organizers supported en masse truck driver wage filings with the DLSE starting in the spring of 2013.[1079] Going all in on misclassification, the message from the coalition was: "We're going to continue to be here and be a problem."[1080]

An updated version of *The Big Rig* research—released by NELP, Change to Win, and LAANE in 2014—suggested the scope of the misclassification effort. Looking at cases since January 2011, it reported that "[s]ome 400 port drivers have filed labor law complaints" with the DLSE, resulting in "19 decisions finding that drivers are employees" and assessing "more than a million dollars in wages, unlawful deductions, and penalties on behalf of 19 drivers against at least five companies: Green Fleet Systems, Seacon Logix, Western Freight Carrier, Total Transportation Services, and Mayor Logistics."[1081] In addition, based largely on coalition efforts to place driver cases with private lawyers, the report noted that there were nine pending private lawsuits against trucking companies for violations related to driver misclassification (eight of which, including Harbor Express, were class actions).[1082] In December 2015, the DLSE ordered Pac 9 to pay almost $7 million in back wages to drivers on the ground that they had been improperly classified as independent contractors.[1083]

Union Organizing

Misclassification litigation was always understood as a means to an end—a way to pressure companies to accept employees and, perhaps, even a union.[1084] As such, litigation was meant to complement the final element of the coalition's plan: organizing drivers toward the goal of winning union contracts. Unionization of port drivers, of course, was the prize that drove Teamsters involvement in the clean trucks campaign. And in the immediate wake of the Clean Truck Program's passage in Los Angeles, the Teamsters initiated union organizing campaigns at companies that had converted to employee drivers. However, when the district court in the ATA litigation preliminarily enjoined employee conversion in April 2009, these companies shifted back to an independent-contractor format and the union campaigns fizzled. As a result, the Teamsters were forced to refocus organizing on the handful of employee-based companies that—for idiosyncratic reasons—remained.

Of the hundreds of trucking companies that serviced the Port of Los Angeles, only a few had employee drivers. Pursuing unionization at them posed obvious risks. Employee drivers could lose their jobs, the Teamsters could lose the campaigns, and the companies could decide to do what all the other companies already did—contract out their driving. Yet there were also significant benefits. In the wake of the stymied clean trucks campaign, a victory was badly needed to show drivers that the Teamsters—and the broader coalition—could deliver tangible benefits. In addition, a unionized company could be held out as a successful model for others to follow—proving that employee-based drayage trucking could be economically viable. As CLUE Director Jonathan Klein put it: "We needed to have a win. And we knew that it was important for all of the port truck drivers to see us win . . . to make people aware that this effort is brought to you by the Teamsters."[1085] The union, with coalition support, thus sought to "build some density,"[1086] however modest, in the port drayage sector, with the hope of creating a foundation for further growth.

To advance the union strategy, Teamsters Local 848 took the lead, with a "big investment from Change to Win" and the Teamsters' national office.[1087] The Teamsters' Organizing Department assigned organizer Jason Gateley, who had organized Coca-Cola workers in Las Vegas, to run the campaign. The union's crucial first decision was selecting an initial target, which had to be a firm against which the union could exert maximum pressure without risking its withdrawal from the port market or conversion to contractors. The campaign thus chose Toll Group, Inc., an $8.8-billion Australia-based logistics company whose main U.S. activity was importing retail goods and shipping them to warehouses and retail outlets throughout the country. In Los Angeles, Toll employed seventy-five local port drivers. The key leverage against Toll was that the company was heavily unionized in Australia, where the Transport Workers Union represented twelve thousand Toll workers, thus forming a powerful block that could pressure management to support the U.S. workers.[1088]

To organize Toll drivers, the Teamsters ran a "traditional corporate campaign" that sought to gain union certification through an NLRB-sponsored election.[1089] After several months of Teamsters organizing, drivers at Toll filed an NLRB petition for a union election in January 2012.[1090] When a female driver was fired in February for stopping at McDonald's, the organizing campaign kicked into high gear. Local

Teamsters organizers, alongside their Australian union counterparts, protested in front of Toll's Los Angeles office in March,[1091] while Teamsters President Hoffa and Los Angeles Mayor Villaraigosa made strong statements in support of the workers at the Los Angeles Good Jobs, Green Jobs Regional Conference a few weeks later.[1092] The coalition lent organizing support, with clergy, community members, and environmental activists standing by workers during protests.[1093] CLUE's Klein joined a delegation to Toll's Los Angeles office to protest driver terminations, asking management to "rehire these people" and emphasizing the "injustice of firing them."[1094] Another rally featured speeches by Janice Hahn and Teamsters Local 848 Secretary-Treasurer Eric Tate. Teamsters counsel Mike Manley did NLRB-related legal work, filing unfair labor practice charges in response to employee firings and, when Toll refused to agree to a bargaining unit limited to drivers, successfully litigating that issue at the NLRB.[1095]

On April 11, 2012, in a historic vote, Toll drivers voted 46-15 in favor of representation by Teamsters Local 848.[1096] As Weiner recalled, it was "the first Teamster contract in L.A. in 30 years.... Big deal!"[1097] Sounding a call to action, one driver cast the vote in these terms: "Our victory means we are finally getting closer to the American Dream. If we can win, I know other port truck drivers across the U.S. can unite just like we did."[1098] The contract, unanimously ratified on December 30, 2012,[1099] gave drivers a nearly $6-per-hour pay raise with additional increases over

Figure 6.15 Mike Manley speaking at a Teamsters rally. *Source*: Jeff Gritchen/Digital First Media/*Orange County Register* via Getty Images (2014).

the life of the contract (to take effect on January 1, 2013); made all Toll drivers part of the company's retirement plan and guaranteed company pension contributions of $1 per hour in the contract's first two years; reduced driver payments for health insurance; provided paid vacation; and prohibited Toll from subcontracting out driving services.[1100] Highlighting the hope that the Toll contract would be only the industry's first, the coalition announced that to "encourage a more level playing field and wide-scale unionization, the contract provides drivers the ability to re-negotiate for higher wages when a simple majority of the Southern California market is organized."[1101] In exchange for accepting the union, Toll received some benefits. The Teamsters agreed not to make Toll follow the more stringent national Master Freight Agreement and also sought to promote Toll as a model worthy of additional business.[1102]

With the Toll victory in hand, the Teamsters pursued other companies with employees—Green Fleet (mostly employee drivers) and American Logistics (all employee drivers)—while also moving more boldly against companies with only independent-contractor drivers, starting with Pac 9. Although there were common patterns and coordinated actions (in November 2013, for instance, drivers from all three companies went on a day-and-a-half strike protesting labor practices),[1103] organizing proceeded differently across employee and nonemployee firms.

Organizing at employee-based firms followed the Toll template, in which Teamsters Local 848 initiated organizing, picketed company offices, and filed unfair labor practice charges against driver terminations.[1104] Beginning in 2013, drivers at Carson-based Green Fleet, which had a majority of employee drivers, conducted weekly picketing to protest the company's labor practices. In early 2013, the DLSE ordered the company to pay $280,822 in back wages and penalties to four misclassified drivers. In August 2013, approximately thirty of the company's ninety drivers went on strike, claiming that supervisors hired union busters and asked employees to sign an antiunion petition.[1105] The Teamsters then filed an NLRB complaint protesting the company's actions, which ultimately produced a ruling against Green Fleet in April 2015.

Building on the Green Fleet model, at Pac 9 (and later at other all-independent-contractor firms) campaign leaders began coordinating misclassification litigation with union organizing as part of a new "suing-and-striking" strategy. At Pac 9, organizers supported workers filing misclassification claims with the DLSE,[1106] attempting to use litigation as leverage to advance subsequent unionization. If the claims resulted in drivers being reclassified as employees, the Teamsters could run an NLRB campaign; if not, the threat of damages could be used to bargain for employee conversion and employer neutrality vis-à-vis subsequent union organizing. In addition, successful DLSE cases built precedent establishing the crucial legal element of drivers' employee status since the DLSE could only issue awards for employment violations on the basis of a predicate finding of employment itself. This precedent could then be used to directly organize truck drivers at independent-contractor firms: supporting their legal claim in front of the NLRB to be employees entitled to unionize under federal labor law. In this way, instead of asking (or having the government require) trucking firms to convert drivers to employees, the drivers could simply assert their status as employees. On that basis, they could engage in unfair labor practice strikes in protest of their misclassification in order to pressure firms to unionize. Because a handful of firms accounted for a large share of port drayage services, a few successful campaigns at the biggest firms could reshape the labor market. As longtime supporter Janice Hahn urged activists to "keep on trucking,"[1107] labor leaders carefully rolled out this suing-and-striking strategy, demonstrating their resilience in the face of the Clean Truck Program setback and intent to persevere in the struggle for economic justice at the ports.

Although suing and striking did not contain a systemic solution to the fundamental driver contracting problem that sparked the monumental Campaign for Clean Trucks in the first instance, it did produce concrete gains for port drivers burdened with the costs of port growth and truck conversion. The Teamsters' effort to unionize Toll and extend its reach to companies like Green Fleet showed that the fight was not over but rather had entered another phase of its long history.[1108] By 2018, the suing-and-striking strategy had resulted in $35 million in DLSE judgments, several million dollars in class action settlements, over thirty strikes, and six labor contracts (three collective bargaining agreements and three labor peace agreements) with trucking firms in an industry that had not seen any in nearly forty years. In this sense, the Green Fleet campaign could be understood as aptly named coda—and a new beginning—to the ongoing struggle to transform port trucking.

Analysis

At the Los Angeles and Long Beach ports, a coalition of labor, environmental, and community groups—held together by a collective commitment to advancing the interests of low-wage workers—took on some of the most powerful economic actors in the global economy. And they won—for a moment, they won big, and even in the end, they won something substantial. That victory was cut back by court decisions does not negate the achievement. But it does invite appraisal of how the campaign arrived at the point it did—bereft of structural labor policy reform, but still tenaciously in pursuit of innovative efforts to link misclassification litigation to driver organizing. This part examines how law informed campaign *strategy*—mobilizing a blue-green coalition to change driver status through city policy—and how that strategy affected the *outcome* achieved for the labor and environmental coalition partners, as well as the truck drivers for whom they were fighting.

Strategy

Explaining why and how a blue-green coalition emerged to mobilize local government law to redress the labor and environmental harms of port trucking draws attention to the legal opportunity structure that caused labor activists to focus on the ports as a local government target, to ally with environmentalists, and to mobilize in the local policy arena in pursuit of clean truck and employee conversion. The following analysis considers how law shaped the campaign's essential strategy: defining problems and solutions, turning legal weakness into strength, and welding labor and environmental partners together in ways that created unique roles for movement lawyers.

Turning Problems into Solutions

The history of blue-green mobilization around port trucking shows how legal rules actively contributed to the creation of profound social problems—air pollution, community congestion, and labor precarity—in ways that made the modification of legal rules a central part of the solution advanced by the labor and environmental movements. The problem targeted in the Campaign for Clean Trucks had its origins in the conservative push for trade liberalization and industry deregulation decades before. Beginning in the 1970s, legal rules promoting free trade transformed the ports from engines of regional growth to conduits of globalization, imposing negative externalities on surrounding communities in the form of pollution and incompatible development. Deregulation facilitated the explosion of trade by reducing the cost of transport, while also producing the specific problem of fragmentation in the drayage trucking industry and the shift toward independent-contractor drivers. Once that fragmentation occurred, starting in the 1980s, the independent-contractor relation became the crucial legal barrier to unionization, since independent contractors received no labor protection and were legally proscribed from organizing under antitrust law. Therefore, from the perspective of organized labor looking at port trucking at century's end, weak federal labor law interacted with federal deregulation and antitrust law to put port drivers in a legal box: economically marginalized, but unable to organize to improve their dismal working conditions. These working conditions, in turn, interacted with port expansion to produce pollution. As the size of the drayage industry grew in relation to imports, independent-contractor drivers unable to afford to maintain and upgrade their vehicles to current environmental standards became stuck with aging diesel trucks that were central sources of port air pollution. In the coalition's terms, the port was where old, dirty diesel trucks "went to die." In Los Angeles and Long Beach, pollution grew consistently worse with the arrival of ever-larger ocean carriers, which strained port capacity and continuously motivated official calls for more growth. As a result, city government officials in the early 2000s promoted port expansion as an engine of job creation but lacked the legal tools and political will to directly regulate the labor and environmental externalities.

For the gathering Coalition for Clean and Safe Ports, crafting a solution to the economic and environmental impacts of port trucking required identifying the institutional space, political power, and legal strategy to address the underlying legal problems. Coalition partners approached these problems from distinct points of view. For organized labor, finding a way to restructure the industry on the legal foundation of employment was the central aim. The Teamsters, in particular, had devoted significant internal resources to experimenting with possible legal solutions to the independent-contractor problem, which included supporting recognition strikes and advancing state legislation to permit independent-contractor organizing in the late 1990s and early 2000s. But none of these early efforts gained political traction and fizzled out.

The labor movement kept a hopeful eye on port trucking as a potential organizing target, not because of its size (it was a relatively small proportion of the overall trucking industry), but because of its strategic importance in the logistics supply chain—with the ports viewed as a key "choke point" to exert organizing pressure on warehouses and big retailers like Wal-Mart. It was in the context of this broader strategy that labor movement leaders conceived the idea of leveraging the ports' contracting power to change driver status and transform drayage labor relations. The specific idea of embedding employee conversion in port contracts with trucking firms had roots in Los Angeles campaigns to win living wage laws and attach labor-friendly requirements to city concession agreements at LAX and redevelopment agreements relying on public subsidies. The legal foundation of many of these efforts was the doctrine of market participation, which justified a local government's proprietary action to enact labor-enhancing regulation without running afoul of federal preemption. For organized labor facing the independent-contractor problem in port trucking, the legal calculus thus converged around a local policy campaign to use the ports' contracting power to reclassify port drivers as employees.

For environmentalists, the ports presented a different legal problem, but one that ultimately was seen as connected enough to the independent-contractor status of drivers (which caused driver dependence on old, cheap diesel trucks) to warrant a joint solution. By the early 2000s, environmentalists began drawing a link between port air pollution and drayage trucking, noting that idling trucks queuing up for port entry were spewing diesel fumes and that port terminal operators and trucking company owners, because they did not bear the costs of long wait times, had no incentive to take remedial action. As the Sierra Club's Tom Politeo recalled, environmentalists began arguing to port officials that port truck drivers "should be paid by the clock and not by the can"—and thus the idea of reforming drayage trucking as a solution to the twin port problems of economic and environmental injustice was born of "multiple inventors."

As the labor and environmental movements converged around a common analysis of the problem to be addressed—a dysfunctional drayage trucking market producing labor precarity and air pollution—their formulation of a solution necessarily came to be shaped by the legal possibilities for local reform. The Ports of Los Angeles and Long Beach were targeted together by the coalition as a strategic site precisely because each was a city entity with authority to enact a city policy to address truck emissions and driver status. To achieve this result, the policy had to be crafted to take advantage of local government power while avoiding federal preemption under the FAAAA, which prohibited localities from enacting a law "related to a price, route, or service of any motor carrier."

The result was a policy solution to port trucking nested in local government law that provided the crucial legal fix to the independent-contractor and pollution problems—but also built in legal vulnerabilities. The fix, enacted in the Los Angeles Clean Truck Program in 2008, was to modify the port's concession agreement—the legal contract between the port as a city entity and trucking firms seeking to enter its property—to require conversion to clean fuel trucks and employee drivers. Under the program, the environmental movement achieved one of its long-standing goals—emission reduction in the drayage trucking fleet as a step toward "greening" the port—while the Teamsters won employee status for drivers that enabled potential unionization. It was a mutually beneficial solution: by taking maintenance out of the drivers' hands and making trucking companies internalize the costs, the program promised to create a sustainable foundation for clean trucking and driver prosperity over time.

The Clean Truck Program mandated truck and employee conversion, and required trucking firm compliance with operational standards such as off-street parking and placard posting as a way to solve the port's central proprietary problem: its inability to achieve necessary growth due to legal fights over environmental pollution caused by diesel trucks. Failure to comply on the part of trucking firms subjected them to penalties—including contract termination and port disbarment. The program hinged on enforcement by terminal operators, which were prohibited from admitting noncompliant trucks on the threat of port-imposed criminal sanctions. These features of the policy solution succeeded in leveraging local government power to address the structural legal problems at the heart of port trucking, but in doing so also provided the basis for the program's legal demise in the ATA preemption lawsuit. In that suit, the program's legal assets—fusing together truck and employee conversion and enforcing concession agreements through the port's police power—became legal liabilities. The Ninth Circuit ruled that employee conversion was too tenuously connected to environmental remediation to qualify as permissible market participation, while the Supreme Court invalidated the concession plan's off-street parking and placard provisions on the ground that their enforcement via criminal sanctions constituted a regulatory, not proprietary, act.

For organized labor, the failure of employee conversion in the Clean Truck Program required reframing the legal problem in terms that could mobilize a different set of actors and resources. "Misclassification" became the organizing frame that defined the legal problem in the post-Clean Truck Program phase of the campaign—and pointed toward a new set of legal solutions. Misclassification, of course, was also the underlying problem targeted by employee conversion in the Clean Truck Program; but the local policy campaign to promote clean trucks turned on suppressing the labor law dimension of fighting misclassification (especially its relation to unionization) in favor of stressing its connection to combating pollution. When the Clean Truck Program failed to achieve employee status for drivers, labor leaders decided to reframe the industry problem explicitly in terms of misclassification and to amplify the labor law consequences of that reframing.

Drawing attention to pervasive drayage industry misclassification in Los Angeles and Long Beach was deemed necessary to advance the campaign's new "suing-and-striking" strategy: challenging independent-contractor firms at the California DLSE and in court; using the precedent from successful cases in those venues to pursue federal labor protection for misclassified drivers at the NLRB; and leveraging that federal protection to launch driver strikes against targeted trucking firms, which along with litigation liability, could pressure firms to negotiate union contracts. This strategy hinged on defining the problem in terms of misclassification in order to draw crucial legal enforcement resources from sympathetic government labor officials, while building a pipeline of cases against campaign targets at the DLSE and in court. Redefining the port trucking problem more explicitly around misclassification thus facilitated the campaign's pivot away from the local policy arena toward state and federal administrative agencies, where campaign leaders believed they could build favorable misclassification precedent that would buttress their organizing campaign.

Turning Weakness into Strength

How the campaign defined problems and solutions influenced not only where it mobilized law, but also how it did so—shaping the nature of legal advocacy it deployed and its relation to other tactics. In the port struggle, law was always an intrinsic part of overall campaign strategy—neither a centerpiece nor an afterthought—its role shaped by the specific campaign goals pursued. Campaign planning consistently integrated advocacy tactics in ways designed to maximize their collective impact. Because the Campaign for Clean Trucks and the subsequent suing-and-striking strategy each focused on different types of legal solutions to address driver misclassification, at each phase, campaign leaders had to devise new ways of converting an initial legal weakness—the rules governing independent contractors—into strength. Because it was launched from a position of relative disadvantage, this project necessarily required campaign leaders to combine legal concepts and advocacy tactics that had previously been viewed as distinct: linking environmental litigation to labor law reform, employee reclassification to emission reduction, port concession agreements to environmental and labor lawmaking, suing to striking, and misclassification to labor peace.

Throughout the port struggle, leaders integrated legal and other modes of advocacy in campaign strategies that were both proactive and responsive to unplanned events. Port advocacy thus evolved in relation to the development and revision of campaign goals and targets—an evolution that hinged on converting legal liabilities into opportunities for change. Throughout this process, campaign leaders on both the environmental and labor sides had to invest in research and planning in order to be nimble enough to seize opportunities when they were presented.

The formative period leading to the launch of the Campaign for Clean Trucks provides an important illustration. On the organized labor side, the Teamsters began to develop a strategic approach to the nation's ports in 2000, when the union announced a nationwide port trucker initiative focused on promoting policy solutions to address driver misclassification. However, this initiative did not get support from national labor leaders until the creation of Change to Win in 2005 and the launch of its Strategic Organizing Center. It was there that Nick Weiner, national campaigns organizer, and John Canham-Clyne, ports campaign director, developed a national plan focused on leveraging "potential hooks" for organizing port drivers at five ports in friendly political jurisdictions, including the port complex at Los Angeles–Long Beach. That plan enlisted the help of labor lawyers from progressive unions—like the SEIU, and well-known labor law firms, like Davis, Cowell & Bowe in San Francisco—to develop a legal framework for using the ports' concession authority to convert drivers into employees. Thus, by 2006, the national labor movement had a working theory to advance a concession-based model of employee conversion and union organizing at the Los Angeles and Long Beach ports—but lacked a specific political strategy that identified concrete levers of power or that made any connections to environmental issues.

It was against this backdrop that the opportunity to advance a serious local campaign to achieve employee status for drivers came in an unforeseen package: an environmental legal challenge to port expansion that laid the groundwork for a sweeping environmental overhaul at the ports. This challenge itself was created by sustained community pushback against port growth, amplified by the Los Angeles port's 2001 announcement that it was expanding into adjacent communities to accommodate a massive new China Shipping terminal. In response, NRDC sued on behalf of resident groups under CEQA, winning a 2002 state court ruling that enjoined terminal completion on the ground that the port had not complied with its duty to identify and mitigate environmental harm resulting from the China Shipping project.

The legal challenge to China Shipping—strengthened by the simultaneous effort by San Pedro to secede from the City of Los Angeles—extracted political concessions from local politicians: James Hahn's election as Los Angeles mayor, accompanied by his sister Janice Hahn's election to the Los Angeles City Council, were built on promises to community groups to mitigate the port's impact. At the height of the China Shipping dispute, Mayor Hahn committed his administration to a policy of "no net increase"—promising to cap port emissions at 2001 levels—which sparked a policy dialogue that led to the 2004 creation of a No Net Increase Task Force, comprised of the NRDC lawyer who had brought the China Shipping lawsuit, Gail Ruderman Feuer, along with labor and community representatives who would become central to the Campaign for Clean Trucks. The work of this Task Force laid the groundwork for the next Los Angeles mayor, Antonio Villaraigosa, to initiate discussions in 2005 between the Los Angeles and Long Beach ports around a comprehensive environmental policy: CAAP. It was CAAP that introduced standards for reducing emissions by diesel trucks, which provided the policy framework and political leverage for the labor movement to finally translate employee conversion from theoretical concept to concrete reform—embedded in a local policy designed to promote environmental remediation.

The pursuit of this end shaped the legal and political advocacy that the campaign pursued. To achieve the Clean Truck Program, campaign leaders combined an outside game of protest and public relations with an inside game focused on alliance formation and lobbying within government policymaking arenas. In Los Angeles, pressure by labor and environmental activists locked Mayor Villaraigosa into a process of genuine port reform, which he strategically advanced through his appointments to the Harbor Commission and his selection of Port of Los Angeles Executive Director Geraldine Knatz, who was a supporter of "greening and growing" and seen as well positioned to build bridges to the Port of Long Beach, where she had been managing director. With these personnel in place, CAAP was launched to advance green growth through coordinated action at both ports, but without specific attention to implementing employee conversion for port truck drivers.

Coalition advocacy followed a carefully designed script. Because CAAP required its own EIR for approval, it gave the coalition, led by LAANE's Jon Zerolnick along with campaign lawyers, the Teamsters' Mike Manley and NRDC's Adrian Martinez, a formal opportunity to weigh in on its terms. The coalition thus submitted a comment letter that made the case for a "long-term solution" in which the ports would implement the concession model developed by Change to Win—with trucking firms required to comply with "clear standards" to be admitted to the ports, including the promise of "employee status for drivers" and "labor peace." After the CAAP framework was approved by both ports in 2006, the coalition initiated an internal policy process to develop an implementation plan for truck and employee conversion, conducted in coordination with external political and legal advocacy.

It began in Los Angeles with a high-level contact by Teamsters President James Hoffa and a commitment by Mayor Villaraigosa to support the campaign in November 2006. With local official support thus secured, the campaign proceeded through a series of negotiations among industry, labor, environmental, and community stakeholders. Inside pressure on local decision-makers was brought to bear by the unions; outside pressure was exerted by community groups as well as ongoing legal challenges by NRDC, most notably around the TraPac terminal expansion at the Los Angeles port. This advocacy created the conditions for policy success, which the mayor's staff reinforced through key decisions: placing the Port of Los Angeles's Deputy Executive Director of Operations John Holmes—a credible insider supportive of the program with deep operational knowledge—in charge of concession plan development, while commissioning BCG to reanalyze the industry impact of employee conversion, which was essential to convince port officials and city policymakers of the economic viability of the program in response to an earlier economic report raising red flags.

After the ATA litigation invalidated the Clean Truck Program's employee provision, the goals of the labor movement shifted in ways that reshaped its strategy and tactics. The pivot away from local policy reform toward misclassification enforcement required a new power analysis informing a revised advocacy strategy to rebuild legal and political strength. The ascension of pro-labor leadership at key enforcement agencies at the federal and state levels provided a transformative opportunity. At the federal DOL, Obama appointees were supportive of targeting misclassification throughout the economy and agreed to allocate specific resources to port trucking, filing a 2012 lawsuit against Shippers Transport Express seeking reclassification at the Los Angeles and Long Beach ports. In California, the 2010 appointment of Julie Su as state labor commissioner at the DLSE also changed the legal calculus. Su's pathbreaking challenge to sweatshops in the garment industry connected labor abuse at the production level to retailers with industry power—and thus focused legal attention on abuse at the heart of contracting relationships like those characterizing the drayage trucking industry. Although her role required evenhanded enforcement of state employment law, she could appreciate the systemic barriers to enforcement and use her discretion to allocate resources to spotlight misclassification, which she did by prosecuting notable port trucking claims, like Seacon Logix, and permitting the adjudication of multiple cases against the same company en masse.

Having an effective DLSE enabled a strong play at the NLRB, which was also undergoing a transformation under President Obama that created new possibilities to organize misclassified drivers. The campaign's advocacy centerpiece—the suing-and-striking model—aimed to leverage litigation to win tangible misclassification victories with economic bite that would provide the legal foundation for NLRB-sanctioned unfair labor practice strikes by drivers, thus enabling collective action without fear of reprisal. With a functioning pro-labor NLRB during the Obama administration and sympathetic regional directors and staff attorneys, after the seminal organizing victory at Toll, the Teamsters could begin to contemplate a strategy that only a few years before would have seemed unthinkable: directly organizing independent-contractor drivers as misclassified workers whose status was protected under the NLRA.

Building Coalition Around Interest Convergence

In the Campaign for Clean Trucks, complementary legal and political needs coalesced around a common legal analysis of the preemption doctrine to draw the blue-green coalition together. The campaign offered a pivotal moment of labor and environmental interest convergence: the legal framing of the concession plan as a win-win for the labor and environmental movements—simultaneously addressing the twin problems of air pollution and low-wage work at the ports—was the crucial foundation for a coalition building process in which each side had something to offer the other.

Labor leaders saw the environmentalists as bringing legal power and political appeal. Framing the campaign as primarily about cleaning the environment was an important strategic move that provided political and legal benefits for labor: minimizing the salience of unionization in an industry context hostile to that aim, while also emphasizing the threat of litigation if the campaign failed and thus crystallizing the market participation argument against preemption. The employee provision of the Los Angeles Clean Truck Program was presented as a way to strengthen the green growth project through enhancing job quality for drivers, not to permit an independent mechanism for unionization, an issue on which NRDC lawyers took no official position.

For their part, environmentalists appreciated the local power of the labor movement to move policy and mobilize on the ground, and were eager for an intermovement alliance that would alleviate tensions over development, which labor unions (particularly the longshoremen) often promoted for the job benefits, but which environmentalists opposed on pollution grounds. In fact, it was during the first meeting in 2006 between Sierra Club director, Carl Pope, and Change to Win leaders to build the national Blue-Green Alliance that the seeds of the Campaign for Clean Trucks were sewn: Pope's mention of the China Shipping litigation and CAAP, though "just happenstance," was the spark that caused Change to Win's Nick Weiner to "connect the dots" and see the potential benefits to labor of a local coalition with environmentalists in Los Angeles to address port trucking.

What labor gave to environmentalists was also critical. Although NRDC lawyers could threaten additional port slowdowns, they needed proactive policy reform that would guide future port development toward sustainable green goals. CAAP promised that and, along with structures like the Port Community Advisory Committee and No Net Increase Task Force, provided critical institutional frameworks connecting activists and putting pressure on local political officials to come up with genuine reform. But the details of CAAP were vague and environmentalists' influence in city hall limited. Folding employee conversion into the Clean Truck Program thus created the opportunity for stronger environmental policy—leveraging organized labor's interest in driver status for a more aggressive attack on air pollution and comprehensive drayage fleet conversion. Although there were important local environmental and community organizations working on port trucking, none had the staff and political connections to mount a decisive policy campaign on their own. Change to Win's entry on the local scene and collaboration with LAANE altered that equation. Change to Win provided money and staff to craft a concession model linking air pollution to employee status and to mobilize the formidable local labor movement political machine in its favor. Supported by Change to Win funding and expertise, LAANE became the organizational control center of the campaign—able to draw upon a store of local contacts and internal experience built upon two decades of policy work in Los Angeles.

A shared legal interest in using local power to craft progressive policy reform within the crevices of federal preemption doctrine also cemented the blue-green partnership at the heart of the Coalition for Clean and Safe Ports. Because the political climate was inhospitable to progressive policy change at the federal level, even during the Obama presidency, the labor and environmental movements promoted state and local policy experiments to advance goals that could not be achieved nationwide. In the early 2000s, on the cusp of the Campaign for Clean Trucks, there was limited legal precedent guiding local lawmakers on the scope of what they could do legislatively to affect labor and environmental regulation in ways that departed from federal standards. Although the Supreme Court had held federal labor law did not preempt active city participation in supporting project labor agreements, the Court had given ambiguous signals about whether local governments could regulate emission standards under the market participant exception to Clean Air Act preemption, and had not weighed in on the scope of FAAAA preemption of local action around trucking. In this murky legal space, environmental and labor lawyers had incentives to interpret the doctrine of market participation broadly to support local policy, like the Clean Truck Program, that sought to enhance labor and environmental standards. This common doctrinal analysis was a key factor that solidified the Coalition for Clean and Safe Ports. By developing this common analysis, Teamsters and NRDC lawyers played an important brokerage role, helping to bridge gaps in social movement networks and thereby link together labor and environmental stakeholders to facilitate campaign development.

Ultimately, however, the legal and political interests of the blue-green coalition were not completely aligned. Legal tensions that were baked into the coalition at the outset emerged as fissures as the policy campaign resulted in mixed success. Environmentalists could claim victory with a program that banned dirty trucks and promoted the acquisition of new clean vehicles, while labor needed employee conversion to win. The linked package of Clean Truck Program reforms—the dirty truck ban, financial incentives for clean truck conversion, and a concession plan with employee conversion—constituted a political compromise that deftly advanced all stakeholder interests. However, when that compromise was pulled apart in court, the tight legal bond holding the coalition together was also weakened.

After this occurred, each side of the coalition responded by pursuing parallel agendas. Empowered with a new regulatory tool, environmentalists shifted toward enforcement of port air quality standards. On the other side, deprived of policy success, labor leaders from the Teamsters and Change to Win did not want to see their massive investment of political and financial capital produce no gain, but understood that the path forward had to proceed outside of the blue-green coalition—at least in the short term. This decision was the product of political expedience and legal calculation. Politically, the misclassification strategy focused singularly on mobilizing traditional employment and labor law to protect the rights of misclassified workers, which caused the coalition's labor partners to break away from their environmental counterparts. Legally, the Ninth Circuit's decision in the ATA case made clear that for organized labor to pass local policy requiring employee reclassification, it would have to detach its rationale from environmental remediation and instead make an independent case for avoiding preemption on the basis of the ports' proprietary interest in reducing the costs of labor unrest.

Lawyering for Local Change

The coalition format and local focus of the Campaign for Clean Trucks also influenced the nature of lawyering connected to it, shaping legal mobilization in relation to the movement's effort to create city policy, defend it from attack, and then reformulate strategy to challenge misclassification head on. Retracing this effort spotlights five essential roles for movement lawyers—disruption, validation, protection, authorization, and inspiration—that are described as follows.

Disruption
Throughout the "Hundred Years' War" between the ports and communities challenging its expansion, there was a steady-state equilibrium. The ports, supported by cities eager for revenue and corporations eager for profit, would advance capital projects that incurred progressively on adjacent communities, which were treated as adjuncts of the ports themselves. Those communities would complain, attend port meetings, even threaten to secede, largely to no avail. The China Shipping lawsuit disrupted this equilibrium by asserting the real possibility that future development would become embroiled in lengthy legal dispute. This disruption produced a scramble for a new equilibrium that environmentalists would support, which led to the creation of the policy process that resulted in the Clean Truck Program.

The disruptive effect of China Shipping was essential to give leverage to environmentalists and community residents to negotiate emission standards from a stronger position with both ports. Within the initial CAAP platform, designed to be a "living document," the emission control framework for heavy-duty vehicles like port trucks did not specify enforceable remedies but did identify drayage trucks as a significant source of air pollution—asserting an aspirational goal of replacing or upgrading port trucks to meet lower-emission standards and outlining several different plans to achieve it. By asking port staff to develop an "implementation plan" by a fixed date, CAAP established no firm rules, but created the bargaining framework within which the campaign elaborated and advocated for the Clean Truck Program. The key point is that the disruptive force of litigation not only enabled the blue-green coalition to win soft law standards in CAAP, but also to mobilize other forms of power within the negotiation framework set in motion by that policy to achieve deeper change built on hard law enforcement mechanisms: mandatory fleet and employee conversion imposed on penalty of port exclusion.

Validation

What movement lawyers do to analyze proposed legislation in light of existing legal standards and how they wield legal interpretations as resources for advancing policy in the face of resistance by lawmakers or career government attorneys is a critical dimension of mobilizing law in local campaigns. In the Campaign for Clean Trucks' policy development phase, movement lawyers from the coalition's labor and environmental wings circulated and defended legal opinions on the market participant doctrine in order to minimize concerns over the well-known risk of FAAAA preemption. This advocacy occurred far from the glare of the courtroom in the more prosaic—but no less critical—process of administrative review through meetings with elected officials, city attorneys, and port staff. In this process, city officials ultimately had to sign off on legislation that they were confident passed relevant legal standards. These officials cared both as a matter of principle and because they did not want to be on the hook for provoking, and potentially losing, expensive litigation when strong arguments did not support their positions.

Although city officials understood that a litigation challenge to the Clean Truck Program would ensue, the movement lawyers' preemption analysis was critical to providing those officials with some degree of confidence in the outcome in the face of doctrinal uncertainty. In general, legal opinions generated by lawyers invested in a movement may be discounted as biased in favor of the lawyers' own reform position. Yet, in policy campaigns, movement-side legal opinions must have enough credibility to be accepted by lawyers on the inside of the political decision-making process. In this regard, the Teamsters and NRDC's preemption analysis was also vetted by Los Angeles port counsel, as well as the mayor's general counsel—which enhanced opportunity for independent review. The presence of Teamsters and NRDC lawyers in this vetting process meant that government lawyers were accountable to a wider audience for their own internal judgments. In the end, movement and government lawyers converged around the same ultimate conclusion: The Clean Truck Program was a legally defensible exercise of local power under the market participant exception to preemption. Legal review acknowledged the risk of litigation failure, but ultimately concluded that it was a risk worth taking.

For their part, by signing off on the Clean Truck Program, port lawyers (both inside counsel at the city attorney's office and outside counsel at Kaye Scholer) were acting in accord with their traditional advising role: presenting a client with the strongest defense of its proposed course of action. When port lawyers evaluated the Clean Truck Program, there were strong political currents already in its favor and therefore port lawyers viewed their job as advancing the wishes of their client, the Harbor Commission. (The mayor's general counsel played a similar role relative to his client.) The fact that campaign and government lawyers all understood that the ATA would sue the ports *no matter what their programs required* strengthened political resolve, at least in Los Angeles, to press for the most ambitious set of policy changes.

Legal review was also intimately connected to an assessment of political risk by public officials. For the Los Angeles mayor's office, the political upside of the Clean Truck Program was transformative policy that made two important constituencies happy—and advanced goals that Mayor Villaraigosa believed in. On the other hand, losing the entire program in court would have been another political failure (following the mayor's defeated bid to take over the Los Angeles school district). The political compromise embodied in the Clean Truck Program's severability provision addressed this risk by fusing together reforms, truck and employee conversion, that were legally independent of one another. This meant that in the event employee conversion was struck down, the environmental provisions could survive—allowing the mayor to claim a major environmental win, while leaving the Teamsters (though not the truck drivers) no worse than where they started.

Protection

Once policy reform is enacted, lawyers must defend it from attack. This protective lawyering function is intrinsically connected to the lawyer's role in providing ex ante policy validation, which makes a prediction about what legal challenges will occur and whether they will succeed. Thus, the protective element of lawyering for local policy reform—defensive strategies to convince judges that validation arguments are correct—is the ex post counterpart to the groundwork that lawyers do in advance of policy enactment. Although defending policy requires the entity that enacts it—in this case, the city—to use its own counsel, movement lawyers play ancillary, though important, roles.

NRDC played such a role in the ATA litigation through its "joint defense agreement" with port counsel. During that litigation, Kaye Scholer partner Steven Rosenthal understood his role as outside port counsel in conventional client-centered terms—defending his client's policy from preemption attack—yet saw the benefits of coordinating legal strategy with NRDC as intervenor and dividing up advocacy from trial through the Supreme Court to best present the city's market participation argument and defend the program. At trial and in the Ninth Circuit, NRDC lawyers took the lead in arguing in favor of employee conversion as a way to advance the port's proprietary interest in environmental compliance since they were deemed to have no essential political stake in that position. The division of labor persisted through the Supreme Court phase, where NRDC was tasked with stressing the positive environmental and public health impacts of Los Angeles's concession plan. During the ATA litigation, the Teamsters' legal team largely faded into the background, particularly when the employee conversion issue was still alive. Nonetheless, Teamsters' counsel remained active behind the scenes in helping NRDC frame its preemption arguments given the union's ongoing stake in protecting local authority to enact progressive legislation through the market participant exception.

Authorization

One of the most significant and least appreciated elements of legal mobilization in the suing-and-striking phase of the campaign was the way in which Teamsters' lawyers built the legal authority for strikes protected under labor law. This effort was crucial to *enabling driver collective action in the first instance*—reinterpreting labor rights to create the conditions for organizing success. The campaign's suing-and-striking phase started with the unionization of the employee-based trucking firm Toll, which created the momentum pushing forward the Teamsters' decision to directly organize drivers misclassified as independent contractors. Doing so required seeking the appropriate legal authorization from the relevant government agency, the NLRB, to assure drivers that any striking activity to challenge their treatment would be legally protected—which meant that drivers could not be terminated and permanently replaced by their firms. Such authorization required Teamsters' lawyers to develop internal legal analyses marshaling precedent and making creative arguments supporting their central claim that misclassification constituted an unfair labor practice committed against drivers as employees, thereby entitling them to the protections of the NLRA—despite their formal status as independent contractors. To build a test case around this claim, lawyers incrementally advanced their misclassification arguments in the NLRB: through one-on-one conversations with board staff, in unfair labor practice charges against campaign targets, and ultimately in formal hearings in front of NLRB judges. The lawyers' ultimate goal was to reclaim the arcane striking rules as a tool to benefit drivers misclassified as independent contractors, rather than a barrier to their collective action, by convincing the NLRB to undertake two critical legal changes: (1) extending the meaning of who counted as statutory employees under the NLRA to include workers misclassified as independent contractors, and (2) extending the meaning of what counted as a violation of the NLRA to encompass the practice of misclassification by trucking firms. The lawyers' success in both regards permitted the Teamsters to run traditional organizing campaigns against key trucking firm targets with independent contractor workforces, using strikes as crucial levers of economic pressure.

Inspiration

In the misclassification phase of the campaign, the strategic counterpart to striking was suing, which involved combining individual wage claims (through the DLSE), public enforcement actions (by the DOL), and private class actions against trucking firm targets (by plaintiff-side lawyers). In each category, movement lawyers sought to *inspire, but not control* litigation in order to build financial liability against trucking firms that, in tandem with economic loss from striking, would promote negotiated labor agreements.

Movement lawyers were key architects of the suing strategy, even though they were not centrally involved in its execution. For example, the Teamsters' Mike Manley and the National Employment Law Project's Rebecca Smith were important voices persuading the DOL that misclassification was an extensive labor problem that warranted a concentrated enforcement effort. Manley played a similar role helping to lay out the legal case for enforcing port driver wage and business expense claims at the DLSE. Manley and LAANE's Sanjukta Paul also provided critical support for private misclassification lawsuits. Manley helped design the campaign's suing model in which private suits would complement organizing goals even though proceeding at arm's length from the campaign. The model was predicated on initial success by individual workers in the DLSE wage claim process proving that misclassification lawsuits could pay off. That success depended on Paul building a pipeline of DLSE cases through the campaign's legal clinic, creating a track record that, as it became publicized, underscored the potential for economic returns on private lawsuits. And Paul's involvement in the lawsuit against QTS provided a class action template that could be followed by other private counsel. Because the QTS case was launched in close concert with the campaign, Manley helped supply its lawyers with strategic research and backup support during its early stage and met with the QTS owners in efforts to facilitate a resolution. In the cases brought by plaintiff-side law firms, Manley had more limited conversations, in which he explained the campaign's organizing goals as a way of expanding the lawyers' conception of what constituted a successful settlement. Although the plaintiff-side lawyers showed varying degrees of interest in the campaign's organizing goals, their lawsuits consistently, even if unintentionally, bolstered the campaign's central objective: demonstrating to port trucking firms that so long as they continued to misclassify drivers, such suits would continue to be filed, thereby strengthening the campaign's argument that the route to eliminating litigation liability was through bargained-for labor peace.

Outcome

The Los Angeles Clean Truck Program was the culmination of two years of organizing by the Coalition for Clean and Safe Ports: a compelling campaign, brilliantly executed. Under the program, the environmental movement achieved one of its long-standing goals—"greening" the port—while the Teamsters could pursue unionization of the newly converted employee drivers.

However, despite the impressive local policy win, the program was quickly swept into court, subject to a lawsuit by the ATA on FAAAA preemption grounds. The case bounced back and forth between the district and appellate courts in the Ninth Circuit. Los Angeles's employee conversion provision was preliminarily enjoined in 2009, but after trial held to be a valid exercise of local government power under the market participant exception to the preemption doctrine. The Ninth Circuit disagreed in 2011 and reversed the trial court on that point. The case went to the Supreme Court on other grounds and, in a unanimous 2013 decision, the Court struck down two additional minor provisions of the Los Angeles port's Clean Truck Program. However, by this point, the dream of employee conversion and possible unionization on a mass scale had already died. The city did not contest the invalidation of employee conversion on appeal to the Supreme Court, so that chapter had already closed. The one silver lining of the Court's decision was that it did not erode the underlying doctrinal basis for local government efforts to intervene in labor issues through the market participant exception, so long as the local intervention was "contract-based" and did not wield the coercive power of criminal punishment to execute.

But that was likely cold comfort to the activists who had worked so hard to get the Clean Truck Program passed in the first instance. It was also a setback for the Los Angeles port, which viewed itself as caught in a bind: accountable for pollution and other negative externalities, but without complete authority to redress them. And the litigation delivered another blow to port drivers, who found themselves additionally burdened: obliged to acquire and maintain new, more expensive low-emission trucks, yet still in the degraded economic position of independent contractors. It is from the vantage point of these different constituencies that this part evaluates the outcomes of the campaign: examining the meaning of "success" as a function of the distinctive legal starting points of the blue-green partners and in relation to industry countermobilization. It then considers outcomes in terms of movement adaptation in the face of legal setback and how well the campaign ultimately represented the interests of port truck drivers.

Success as a Function of Legal Endowment

Because the labor and environmental movements, as a matter of strategy, mobilized around different legal strengths, it was inevitable that those strengths defined the boundaries of what outcomes each was able to achieve. Given the exclusion of independent contractors from the protections of federal labor law, the labor movement from the outset of the campaign was cast in the difficult position of having to use alternative legal regimes as proxies to leverage stronger labor rights. The Campaign for Clean Trucks was therefore an instance in which the Teamsters, lacking legal power because of independent-contractor rules, sought to build on the power that NRDC litigation created to change the union's structural bargaining position—using environmental law as a springboard to surmount legal barriers to organizing independent contractors. However, once labor movement leaders decided to take advantage of the opportunity that environmental law afforded, they simultaneously became bound by countervailing legal constraints: tethering labor goals to environmental policy in a way that ultimately undermined the market participation argument for employee conversion.

For the environmental coalition partners, in contrast, litigation was a strong tool in the port context to advance emission reduction objectives. The NRDC challenge to China Shipping changed the power dynamic of port growth by demanding greater accountability in port expansion plans. Environmental review, while affecting process not outcomes, could prove costly if the ports had to redo EIRs for failing to consider and mitigate significant impacts. At the ports, environmental litigation had the power to force environmental reform in a context in which two factors were present: first, the polluting industry was fixed in place based on massive upfront infrastructure investment and, second, there was intense interregional competition for the industry's service. Because the ports were geographically bound, but could potentially lose business to other regional competitors, delay and uncertainty were potent bargaining chips. Since litigation could impede port expansion plans and shippers could reroute cargo to other West Coast ports (or eventually through the Panama Canal), the Los Angeles and Long Beach ports had a strong incentive to mitigate uncertainty to maintain profitability. This incentive gave NRDC negotiating power through lawsuits to enforce environmental compliance. In addition, because environmental review of port development ultimately had to be approved by City Council, it provided a means for exerting political influence in that body.

It was political influence that organized labor brought to bear in passing the Clean Truck Program, though on terms that could not ultimately overcome its structural legal deficits. To win the concession plan, labor's argument for driver employee status was firmly connected to the idea of environmental sustainability: without employee drivers, a short-term incentive program might produce clean truck conversion, but over time drivers would be unable to maintain truck quality, reprising air quality concerns, and producing new cycles of environmental litigation over port expansion. That argument proved compelling as a way of advancing the Clean Truck Program through political channels. However, it was legally insufficient to survive preemption, with the Ninth Circuit characterizing employee conversion as an effort to "impact third party behavior unrelated to the performance of the concessionaire's obligations to the Port"[1109]—in other words, an attempt to change trucking company labor practices to enable unionization. The court thus did not buy the argument that employee conversion was about environmental sustainability first and unionization second (if at all). As a result, the environmental components of the

Los Angeles Clean Truck Program were left standing, while the labor and community provisions were gutted.

This outcome correlated to ex ante legal strength: because environmental law was the most potent weapon in thwarting port growth, mitigating environmental concerns was ultimately viewed as most central to the ports' role as market actors in stopping ongoing litigation. Conversely, requiring employee conversion (and thereby strengthening labor law) was not seen as market participation, despite arguments attempting to connect conversion to long-term environmental sustainability. In this way, labor lawmaking was doubly disadvantaged by its relationship to federalism: the weakness of the NLRA regime pushed labor law down to the local level, where that same weakness made it too insignificant to count toward legitimate city market participation—at least in relation to a Clean Truck Program designed around environmental redress.

From this perspective, the campaign outcome was a product of the deeply uneven playing field on which organized labor sought to advance. The campaign itself spotlighted the high threshold barrier to effective local labor activism in low-wage sectors defined by contracting: specifically, the legal predicate for unionization—employee status—had to be in place before local-government-based legal strategies to facilitate it could work. In industries in which statutory employees already existed, local governments could bargain with employers for labor neutrality in exchange for public benefits in order to enable union organizing without running afoul of federal labor preemption.[1110] However, the Campaign for Clean Trucks underscored the challenge of even getting to a position of bargaining for labor neutrality in low-wage industries characterized by pervasive independent contracting and thus outside the purview of labor law. In such industries, where baseline employee status was not established, federal preemption on *non-labor law* grounds (i.e., deregulatory transportation rules codified in the FAAAA) precluded local legal reforms to create employment relationships and thus get to the locally mediated bargaining process in the first instance.

As a result, the legal structure of low-wage industries defined by independent contracting created a formidable double barrier to labor organizing since unions had to *first* overcome the legal challenge of transforming the employment status of workers in the industry in order to even create the *possibility* for collective bargaining—which still had to be fought for and won. Because this weak starting position was a product of federal law—and organized labor was too politically disfavored to change that law outright—the labor movement sought to anchor reform in receptive local government law processes. But doing so subjected labor efforts to the risk of non-labor-law preemption—underscoring the movement's deeply disadvantaged position in pursuing unionization. Thus, it was *both* the weakness of labor law *and* the strength of non-labor law (antitrust and deregulation) that converged to erect substantial challenges to organizing industries—like port trucking—in which workers were assigned the label of "owner-operators" but lived a reality indistinguishable from that of low-wage employees. In such industries, even if (against the odds) campaigns managed to succeed, they did so merely by restoring workers back to the baseline of being *organizable*—aligning their legal label with their lived reality—and thus removing extant legal barriers that precluded even the possibility of demanding better conditions.

The suing-and-striking strategy endeavored to get out of this difficult box by bypassing the need to establish employee status *before* initiating collective action. Initially considered a long shot, this strategy proved legally potent: resulting in $35 million in DLSE awards against port trucking firms and extending protection for misclassified drivers in the NLRB. This legal success resulted in tangible union advances: collective bargaining agreements at Toll (2012), Eco Flow (2016), and Shippers Transport Express (2015); and labor peace agreements at Green Fleet (2015), Pac 9 (2016), and Gold Point (2016).

Progress as a Function of Legal Opposition

Where the protagonists of port struggle ended up was not simply a function of how law structured legal endowments—but how industry opponents mobilized them to contest movement progress. For the trucking industry, conditions at the outset of the campaign were the mirror image of those confronted by labor—and thus placed industry in a favorable starting position. The legal playing field that disadvantaged labor mobilization empowered industry countermobilization. Just as the structure of local government law and its relation to preemption placed limits on coalition efforts to reform port trucking, it facilitated industry resistance and, ultimately, industry success in overturning the Los Angeles concession plan. Industry began from a position of strength—seeking to protect the legal and economic status quo against change. Its strategy from the outset was to defend against structural market reform and thus keep labor in the posture of litigating individual misclassification suits, which the industry could defend in a war of attrition.

Politically and legally, industry sought to sow division where the coalition had attempted to build unity. When industry could not stop the Clean Truck Program in Los Angeles, it ramped up lobbying pressure on Long Beach and succeeded in defeating employee conversion there. The Los Angeles–Long Beach split paid political and legal dividends. Politically, it heightened inter-union division, further undercutting the support of already unionized longshoremen by increasing the risk that the Los Angeles program would divert cargo to neighboring Long Beach. The split also eroded the support of Los Angeles officials who confronted the prospect of lost economic benefit to the city and the real chance of political failure. As this suggests, the split between the two ports also produced legal benefits for the ATA: sharpening the legal focus on employee conversion (and its connection to unionization), facilitating the ultimate legal settlement with Long Beach (thus allowing the ATA to direct its full resources to defeating the Los Angeles plan), and adding weight to the ATA's preemption claim (by revealing the danger of inconsistent port regulation).

In similar fashion, industry also sought to weaken the ties binding labor and environmental allies—using litigation to promote the breach it could not achieve during the policy campaign. This divide-and-conquer strategy was enabled by the industry's favorable legal starting point. Labor and environmental partners had to overcome substantial legal uncertainty weighing against their core argument that local government had authority to enact joint clean truck and employee conversion as a coherent—and intrinsically connected—market participation strategy. Recognizing this vulnerability, industry pushed against the weakest part of the coalition's argument: that employee conversion was central to the port's proprietary interests in cleaning the environment. And industry pitted the coalition partners' ultimate interests against each other. Although the labor and environmental movements stood firm in their commitment to the entire Los Angeles Clean Truck Program, they ultimately had distinct aims. The industry plan was to drive a wedge by effectively conceding on emission reduction in order to thwart unionization. This plan was advanced through the industry's litigation decision not to challenge the dirty truck ban and its public relations strategy repeatedly linking the concession plan to the Teamsters. Although NRDC lawyers valiantly defended the environmental-labor linkage, they could not convince the courts to agree on the intrinsic connection between employee conversion and long-term environmental sustainability. In the end, while NRDC litigation brought the coalition together, ATA litigation succeeded in dividing the coalition's achievement apart.

As organized labor turned to the suing-and-striking model to reignite the quest for unionization, industry actors took affirmative legal steps to undercut its power. In perhaps the boldest effort, companies filed lawsuits seeking to preclude state labor enforcement efforts under a theory of FAAAA preemption. This strategy was used in a number of cases: by Pac Anchor to challenge the California attorney general's 2008 lawsuit against it on unfair competition grounds (rejected by the California Supreme Court); by Shippers Transport Express in a 2012 class action summary judgment motion (denied by the federal district court); and most radically in a 2016 suit filed by the California Trucking Association arguing that the entire system of DLSE wage claim adjudication was preempted (rejected by the Ninth Circuit). There were also examples of industry actors using litigation to chill strikes: In response to a 2016 strike against two trucking firms, the Law Office of Jewels Jin filed suit on behalf of a group of independent-contractor drivers against terminal operators and the Teamsters for conspiracy to interfere with business operations. Taken together, these efforts augured a mounting legal counteroffensive by the trucking industry to undermine the advantages the campaign built through DLSE claim-making and picketing at the ports. They also reflected industry's persistent strategy of treating the environmental and labor movements differently. While environmental subsidies and the promise of greater energy efficiency made it politically and economically possible for industry to support green truck initiatives, industry resistance to organized labor—perceived as presenting zero-sum trade-offs between worker wages and corporate profits—remained implacable.

Adaptation

As the suing-and-striking campaign underscores, the legal invalidation of employee conversion did not end the clean trucks campaign, but rather caused it to adapt and retool. As in any campaign for social change, the coalition had a range of goals and fallback positions, as well as linkages to related campaigns to which resources could be redeployed (and lessons applied). In the Campaign for Clean Trucks, failure to achieve the highest order goal (passage and validation of a Clean Truck Program with employee conversion at both ports) channeled resources into backup goals: ensuring enforcement of the clean truck mandate while continuing the fight to convert drivers to employees, even if in more piecemeal fashion.

At each stage of the campaign, the coalition planned for and (when necessary) pivoted to pursue alternatives to its primary goal of implementing the full Clean Truck Program. After the Ninth Circuit's unfavorable March 2009 preliminary injunction decision, the coalition swiftly adapted its strategy—deploying Plan B (and then C). Plan B focused on passing federal legislation explicitly exempting the Clean Truck Program from the FAAAA—a move that failed when the Democrats lost control of Congress in 2010. The campaign was then forced backed to its default position (Plan C): facilitating misclassification lawsuits, brought by governmental and private lawyers, to impose costs on companies that wrongfully denied drivers employee status, while simultaneously organizing to unionize trucking firms (like Toll) that already recognized their drivers as employees. The goal of the misclassification campaign was to expand the number of companies that hired employee drivers and then to increase union density company-by-company. This was, of course, where the campaign started—and where industry preferred to be—but the aggressive nature of the Plan C litigation phase, buttressed by government agency support, showed that the coalition was not willing to give up without a fight to expose the pervasive nature of truck driver misclassification—a fight ultimately coalescing around the suing-and-striking strategy.

In addition, as the misclassification fight persisted, elements of the Clean Truck Program were redesigned to advance a parallel campaign to organize city waste haulers—in which the hard lessons of port failure were used to strengthen the legal grounds for securing victory in a distinct sector of the local trucking industry. Failure to achieve one of the movement's biggest prizes—unionization of port trucking as the supply chain "choke point"—produced important learning that informed policy cycles in which labor movement actors were repeat political players. Beginning in 2011, LAANE led a campaign to require private sanitation companies servicing Los Angeles businesses and some residential properties to obtain city-issued franchises for waste hauling to and from eleven designated city zones. Titled "Don't Waste L.A.," the campaign brought together the same environmental and labor alliance that sought to green the ports around the mutual objectives of converting the waste fleet of over one thousand trucks to clean emission technology, while improving conditions for waste drivers and promoting recycling to achieve the city's "zero waste" goal.[1111]

This time around, the coalition—drawing upon its port experience—designed the policy to avoid the litigation that undercut the Clean Truck Program. Instead of granting concessions to all companies that agreed to employee conversion, the waste-hauling plan awarded an exclusive franchise for trucking companies selected through a competitive bidding process (one franchise per zone), in which bids were judged based on a range of good business practices that included using clean trucks, following efficient routing, promoting recycling and organic waste diversion, and implementing strong driver work standards. In so doing, the plan operated outside the scope of FAAAA preemption (not regulating interstate motor carriers in the transportation of property) and also fit squarely within the heart of market participation (dealing with the efficient procurement of city services). The waste-hauler plan passed the Los Angeles City Council in April 2014 and, after a rollout process in which the Bureau of Sanitation solicited bids, the city approved a final waste collection program in 2016, awarding exclusive franchises to seven garbage hauling companies that agreed to labor peace. This new achievement was another indication that the labor movement's investment in the Clean Truck Program—though itself disappointing—was not wasted.

Representation

Looking back at the Campaign for Clean Trucks shows how leaders struggled to bridge differences, promote stakeholder participation, and make critical decisions with serious consequences for drivers; and how, even with the best intentions, there was never an easy way to make uncomplicated, strictly accountable choices to any specific constituency with monolithic interests. For labor leaders seeking a vehicle for organizing supply chain workers, their approach was to establish good processes and exercise judgment in ways that represented what they viewed as the best interests of drivers in Los Angeles and Long Beach, while also advancing the larger goals of the national labor movement. Considering how well they did so, and what consequences flowed from their choices, is a critical dimension of outcome evaluation.

The coalition that would guide the Campaign for Clean Trucks was forged at the intersection of top-down planning and bottom-up resistance and reflected a genuine effort to promote inclusion and participation among a broad range of stakeholders affected by the port trucking industry. From the top-down, Teamsters and Change to Win leaders developed a campaign plan, reached out to LAANE to host local campaign staff, and hired the LAANE port team (Jon Zerolnick and Patricia Castellanos), who then undertook extensive outreach to local union leaders, NRDC lawyers and representatives from other key environmental justice groups, like East Yard Communities, as well as public health groups, like LBACA. Some of these environmental and public health organizations were already involved in bottom-up advocacy—led by the Sierra Club, East Yard Communities, and the Coalition for a Safe Environment—which had sought a larger voice in Harbor Commission governance and came together in formal networks, like the Green LA Port Working Group, created after Mayor Villaraigosa's election to develop plans for port environmental cleanup and CAAP development.

In this way, the Coalition for Clean and Safe Ports brought together national labor leaders focused on the independent-contractor problem with local organizations fighting against the environmental and community impact of port expansion. As it formally convened in 2006, the coalition operated through representatives from these diverse groups. The coalition did not formally include drivers themselves, whose interests were deemed to be represented by the Teamsters. Decision-making processes were established in democratic fashion: major decisions required a supermajority of all coalition members (though were typically by consensus); policy development on issues like truck routes and parking was assigned to subcommittees staffed by members with relevant expertise; time-sensitive strategic issues were delegated to an elected steering committee, whose members thought of themselves as representing the campaign, even as they also worked to ensure that their particular group interests were heard. Some coalition members acknowledged that organized labor, because of its political clout, and LAANE, because of its full-time staffing, had more power to set the agenda and influence strategy. As one coalition member put it, LAANE was "really in the driver's seat." This power sharing arrangement worked well as the interests of labor, environmental, and community groups aligned around the finely wrought package of changes in the Clean Truck Program. When that package unraveled in court, however, it drew attention to how the loss was distributed—and particularly whether the decision-making process adequately addressed the potential for harm to drivers who, without employee conversion, were saddled with the costs of clean trucks without the benefits of employee status.

From labor's perspective, the problem at the campaign's outset was how to evaluate the legal viability of the Clean Truck Program in relation to the ambiguous boundaries of preemption—and how to pursue the program in a way that served the interests of port drivers while also advancing the labor movement's broader ambitions for organizing supply chain workers and rebuilding its national power to promote workers' rights. The decision to advance employee conversion as part of an integrated Clean Truck Program, although resting upon legal analysis, was ultimately one made by top campaign leadership, which included key nonlawyer members of the campaign team from the Teamsters, Change to Win, and LAANE. The crucial legal prediction centered on the risk of litigation failure—specifically, the risk that the program in general and the employee conversion piece in particular would be struck down. Movement lawyers from the Teamsters and NRDC believed that the ports would win a FAAAA challenge to the Clean Truck Program at the Ninth Circuit and that the Supreme Court would not grant certiorari. This prediction turned out to be wrong: only the concession plan was challenged, the Ninth Circuit struck down the critical employee conversion provision, and the Supreme Court decided to consider, and reject, the remaining concession provisions.

At one level, this outcome, while disappointing for the campaign, is analytically mundane. Legal predictions turn out to be wrong all the time, in part because law is indeterminate and judges have significant discretion, in part because lawyers and their clients are fallible. However, the nature and process of legal analysis in relation to the Clean Truck Program was itself not mundane. As part of a social movement-led local policymaking campaign, the movement lawyers drafting the preemption analysis were not representing drivers directly, but rather were representing their own organizational interests. And the stakes were high: the legal judgment about preemption affected passage of a significant social policy reform affecting a critical national industry. Although legal judgments from government lawyers routinely precede the enactment of significant policies, a unique feature of the Campaign for Clean Trucks was the extent to which movement-generated doctrinal analysis informed internal government legal and political decision-making. Understanding the process of that movement analysis and how it misjudged the legal outcome, then, presents the accountability question most directly: Given the risk of error, was analysis and decision-making sufficiently accountable to the group upon whom error would fall most heavily?

Coalition leaders knew that there was a small, but nontrivial, risk that if clean truck conversion passed without employee conversion, drivers could be left worse off: remaining independent contractors forced to bear the cost of acquiring and maintaining more expensive clean trucks. In a context in which the prize was so big (trucking industry transformation with the possibility of organizing the entire logistics supply chain) and the legal analysis suggested that the risk of losing was so small, coalition leaders decided to pursue the policy in the face of risk. Because drivers were not independent members of the coalition, there was no mechanism for them to formally weigh in on the risk, though it is reasonable to believe that those who were active in the campaign would have agreed with the coalition's analysis and thus supported the policy. On the ground, organizers promoted the promised benefits of the Clean Truck Program to drivers without engaging in deep analysis of potential costs. This was, undoubtedly, because the campaign was so invested in playing to win—and believed winning was likely—that it did not want to dwell on the complexities of what it would mean to lose.

Yet, even with activist-driver support of the plan, the accountability problem in the Campaign for Clean Trucks was a thorny one. The activist drivers were only a fraction of the total port trucker population and could not claim representative status (and, indeed, there were challenger groups, like the National Port Drivers Association, which purported to represent thousands of owner-operators who wanted to maintain that status). Without organizing and polling all drivers, coalition leaders had to rely on the support of those drivers most committed to the clean truck project.

Moreover, the nature of the coalition itself—while strengthening its claims to broad stakeholder representation—complicated its members' representative roles. Environmentalists were committed to emission reduction and not in a position of direct accountability to the drivers. Although the Teamsters' constituency, broadly defined, included port truck drivers, the drivers were not union members—only potential ones. The Teamsters and their allies at Change to Win had to consider the impact of a successful Clean Truck Program not just on port truck drivers, but on the union movement more generally. And this was a judgment ultimately made by labor movement leaders, *not* the movement lawyers, who were in a more conventional position of general counsel to the unions—thus shifting the crucial representational decisions to the client level. In the end, labor movement leaders concluded that the campaign was strategically important enough (with significant potential benefits to a much wider universe of workers), and the downside limited enough, that it was worth the risk—that to change the equation for organized labor in the United States, it was necessary to seize the once-in-a-generation chance to go big at the ports. Once the political decision was made to pursue this chance in tandem with clean truck conversion, the potential conflict with driver interests was unavoidable: If the total package succeeded, drivers would benefit, but if employee status failed, the largest cost would fall on the constituency with the most to lose and the weakest voice in movement decision-making. That it ended precisely so underscores the unequally distributed risks of movement ambition and the challenge of ever neatly resolving the accountability dilemma in complex and high-stakes campaigns for transformative social change.

Had organized labor's gamble for employee conversion paid off, its claim to represent port truck drivers would have been put to the ultimate test in the unionization drive that ensued. Although not exactly what labor leaders had envisioned, the subsequent misclassification campaign nonetheless sought to make the case for representation through its suing-and-striking strategy. While campaign leaders did not have to directly navigate the complexity of blue-green collaboration, they did continue to confront the dual challenge of representing the interests of disaffected drivers and the broader labor movement. Lawyers sought to align these interests through the campaign's clinic-based organizing. Many aggrieved drivers, rubbed raw by mistreatment, arrived at the campaign's legal clinic already activated to pursue change. There, lawyers counseled drivers on their entitlement to legal recovery for misclassification, while also educating them on the connection between the pursuit of monetary redress for past wrongs and the campaign's efforts to change the system going forward. While clinic lawyers helped drivers through the initial process of assembling and presenting their claims to the DLSE, they also emphasized that wage claims were leverage to fight for union contracts. Thus, when lawyers sympathetic to the campaign agreed to represent drivers in the DLSE process and on appeal in court, they took on driver clients who generally had a clear understanding of how their wage claims related to the organizing goals already established.

This process of driver outreach and representation raised potential conflicts: particularly, the possibility of coercion both in terms of pressuring drivers to accept organizing goals as a quid pro quo for legal assistance and in terms of steering drivers toward settlements sacrificing short-term monetary rewards for the uncertain promise of longer-term economic benefits resulting from unionization. Yet, in lawsuits against port trucking firms, drivers were active and empowered participants in reaching settlements that struck a balance between their personal interests in recovering for past harms and the future economic benefits of labor agreements. Moreover, the campaign's striking strategy, winning legal protection for misclassified drivers under labor law, demonstrated to drivers that campaign leaders were taking care to minimize the risks of collective action—sending the message that leaders were acting as accountable stewards helping drivers accrue tangible economic benefits and political power.

As this suggests, out of the devastating loss of employee conversion in the Campaign for Clean Trucks came no small amount of redemption through labor's surprisingly successful suing-and-striking approach of contesting driver misclassification in the courts and on the streets. As this effort gained momentum at the Los Angeles and Long Beach ports, the campaign asserted its resolve to transform the conditions of thousands of drayage drivers who continued to toil long hours for low pay in a model of "ownership" forced upon them rather than chosen. From this vantage point, the decades-long story of struggle at the ports can be read as a parable of resilience and optimism, serving notice that—in the face of overwhelming odds and frequent setback—the fight for economic and environmental reform never ends, but rather takes different shapes and forms, finding ways to circumvent barriers and relentlessly forge new legal and political paths on the long road to justice.

7

An Equal Place?

Empirical Appraisal and Theoretical Implications

Overview

This book began by asking how lawyers have contributed to local movements challenging low-wage work in Los Angeles during a transformational period in the city's history: from the 1992 riots to the 2008 recession. It has explored this question through an original history of five pivotal campaigns: challenging sweatshop production in the garment industry, anti-solicitation ordinances depriving day laborers of the right to work, city-subsidized redevelopment producing low-wage jobs, big-box retailers undermining the unionized grocery sector, and port trucking firms exploiting drivers by misclassifying them as independent contractors. The central inquiry cutting across these campaigns has been how local legal mobilization to reform distinct industry sectors develops and what impact it has on the conditions of low-wage workers and the political balance of power in the city. The book has pursued this inquiry through a comparative institutional approach, in which legal mobilization is viewed in relation to wider social movement campaigns, focusing analysis on how lawyers' representational choices and strategic decisions are shaped by other actors and structured by the political system, thus providing a fuller fact base on which to judge outcomes.

By presenting an account of legal mobilization around work in a specific urban geography, the book has ultimately sought to uncover how lawyers help construct the meaning of equality in the progressive city. Its basic claim is that local movements to make Los Angeles a more equal place—one in which marginalized workers have greater protections, better wages and benefits, and a larger voice in the workplace and politics—have depended on a new generation of lawyers, embedded in local networks and committed to local action, who have negotiated an equal place of their own in advancing economic justice campaigns. The book ends, therefore, by considering the larger contributions of the five case studies: exploring what they teach about *the meaning of equality both as a process and an outcome of legal advocacy* in the contemporary American metropolis. To do so, this concluding chapter offers two perspectives on local legal mobilization: one empirical and the other theoretical. First, from an empirical perspective, the chapter synthesizes evidence from the case studies to evaluate the central role that lawyers have played in the struggle for economic justice in Los Angeles and how that role has contributed to regulatory change strengthening workers' economic rights and political representation. Second, from a theoretical perspective, the chapter reflects more broadly on lessons from the study of the L.A. campaigns for movement lawyering, labor organizing, and the possibility of meaningful economic reform in the city.

Empirical Appraisal
Equality in the Process of Struggle

To analyze the role of lawyers in the struggle for Los Angeles, this part relies on a systematic review of participants in the book's five campaigns based on information about their background, organizational affiliation, and contributions.[1] From this review, it is evident that—across the five campaigns—lawyers did what lawyers typically do: They advised clients of their legal rights, filed lawsuits, negotiated agreements, provided legal opinions, and drafted model legislation. Although the lawyers were never neutral—they were all motivated by distinctive normative visions of the political cause[2]—they were committed client agents, using legal expertise to serve ends defined by those they served. In doing so, they generally expressed a sense of humility about their roles and sensitivity to power dynamics with other activists and community members. Jerilyn López Mendoza, the Environmental Defense lawyer who was one of the architects of the community benefits campaign, summarized her own conception of role in a way that captured this broader sentiment: "I didn't want to push too hard and dominate the agenda."

Yet, in every campaign, movement lawyers at the center of the action—like López Mendoza, APALC's Julie Su, MALDEF's Tom Saenz, and LAANE's Madeline Janis—were always more than agents. While careful not to "dominate the agenda," as an empirical matter, the movement lawyers did help to set its terms and methods, ultimately playing crucial leadership roles.[3] How they negotiated their dual identities—as representatives of clients and leaders of campaigns—is a question that goes to the core of a half-century of scholarly debate over the relation of lawyers to progressive social movements.[4] At one level, it is clear—echoing Harvard Law Professor Gary Bellow—that the lawyers in the L.A. campaigns developed an "enduring alliance" with the low-income communities and communities of color on whose behalf they mounted challenges to the structure of low-wage work.[5] The lawyers were intentional about creating "bonds and dependencies" with social movement organizations and constituencies that anchored their legal work and engaged them in sustained conversations about how to best mobilize law.[6] In describing this type of movement lawyering, Austin Sarat and Stuart Scheingold have suggested that lawyers "sign over elements of their independence" to other movement actors, often finding "themselves relegated to 'second-chair' status within the movement."[7]

However, by choosing to enter social movement alliances, lawyers in the L.A. campaigns did not accept self-demotion. To the contrary, they consistently asserted standing as "political equals" with nonlawyer allies in an effort to redefine the very meaning of representation: away from traditional client service toward active participation in movement building.[8] What is most distinctive—and thus important to underscore—is that in pursuing campaigns to reform low-wage work, the L.A. movement lawyers did not simply enter movements with preexisting organizational resources and leadership structures; in each case, they worked to create partnerships where they did not exist or strengthen those that did. That is, the lawyers committed *to building movement alliances from the ground up*. In so doing, they uplifted voices of community actors and validated other forms of community knowledge—*while simultaneously asserting the equal value of their own contributions*. The lawyers' aims were twofold. By building alliances, they sought to deepen representational ties in order to promote accountability to movement clients and constituents, while also strengthening the broader movement infrastructure in order to increase the potential for having a meaningful impact on policy and practice. It is in this way that the lawyers claimed an equal place in movement decision-making, not because they sought control, but because they believed in a lawyering method in which robust dialogue and engagement of dissent among lawyers, activists, and workers could produce more effective representation based on political solidarity and shared political vision.[9] This part examines how and why movement lawyers did this, focusing on their efforts to redefine the relationship between top-down and bottom-up reform, legal and political action, and elite and grassroots knowledge.

Patterns: Beyond Top Down Versus Bottom Up

Movement lawyers in the L.A. campaigns pursued reform from the top down and bottom up—while problematizing the division between levels. To illustrate this pursuit, it is useful to start by recalling the basic goals of the campaigns and the strategies they deployed.

Table 7.1 provides an overview. Of the five campaigns documented in the book, the first two—focusing on the garment and day labor industries—had their origins in immigrant rights organizations (APALC and MALDEF) and were oriented primarily around affirmative litigation. In contrast, the last three campaigns—around the retail, grocery, and trucking sectors—were generated by community–labor coalitions, in which LAANE played a key role, and were directed primarily at producing reform in the local policy arena. This basic distinction has important implications for the nature of local legal mobilization. For one, immigrant rights advocacy against sweatshops and anti-solicitation ordinances was explicitly framed

Table 7.1 Overview of low-wage work campaigns in Los Angeles.

Campaign	Problem	Solution	Key Groups	Litigation	Legislation	Organizing	City Role	Outcomes
Garment	Retailers and manufacturers subcontracting production to sweatshops that exploited garment workers	Establish joint employer liability to make retailers and manufacturers responsible for meeting wage standards	APALC, Sweatshop Watch, Garment Worker Center	Six major lawsuits all settled for monetary damages	• State law establishing guarantor liability enforced through DLSE • City procurement ordinance	• All suits coordinated with media strategy • Large protests against Forever 21 led by GWC • Failed GUESS union campaign	+ Passed procurement ordinance	• $8 million in monetary recovery for garment workers • State guarantor law passed, although weak enforcement • Built movement infrastructure • Heightened awareness and public enforcement • Garment industry jobs decreased due to outsourcing
Day Labor	City ordinances in greater L.A. area banning public solicitation of day labor work, contributing to exploitation in underground economy	Devise impact-litigation strategy to invalidate anti-solicitation ordinances under theory of protecting day labor speech	MALDEF, ACLU, NDLON	Eight major lawsuits, seven resulting in ordinances being blocked or changed	• Home Improvement Stores Ordinance allowed city to require day labor site in exchange for conditional use permit (CUP) • Defeated federal legislation barring local ordinances	• NDLON organized corners in each lawsuit • AFL-CIO National Partnership Agreement	– Used land use power to outlaw solicitation as nuisance + Passed Home Improvement Stores Ordinance built on CUP	• Won federal appellate court decision invalidating 31 ordinances in greater L.A. area • Built movement infrastructure • Ongoing day labor harassment and exploitation • Some cities passed "smarter" anti-solicitation ordinances imposing significant barriers to day labor work

(*continued*)

Table 7.1 Continued

Campaign	Problem	Solution	Key Groups	Litigation	Legislation	Organizing	City Role	Outcomes
Retail	Publicly subsidized development producing low-wage jobs	Leverage city land use and subsidy approval process to negotiate CBAs, scaling up to citywide policy	LAANE, SAJE, Environmental Defense	Threat of environmental litigation used to gain bargaining power	Citywide policy failed CRA adopted several community benefits policies	Coalitions finalized three major CBAs before recession Provisions applying living wage to project tenants supported union organizing	+ Land use review provided key leverage + City Council and CRA supported Staples and Grand Ave. CBAs + LAWA agreed to LAX CBA	First ever private CBA with Staples providing nearly $10 million in benefits First ever public CBA with LAX providing $500 million in benefits Labor gained power in CRA Agreements substantially but not fully implemented and were affected by recession and demise of the CRA
Grocery	Threat of nonunionized Wal-Mart Supercenters in L.A. area undercutting unionized grocery sector	Block approval of Supercenter through site fight then pass ordinance limiting Wal-Mart entry	LAANE, UFCW	Lost suit to block Wal-Mart Inglewood ballot initiative, although suit spurred organizing	Superstores Ordinances passed in Los Angeles and Inglewood, conditioning entry on economic impact report	Coalition blocked Inglewood Supercenter and helped pass ordinances	+ L.A. and Inglewood passed ordinances that built economic impact review into CUP	Wal-Mart failed to win approval for Supercenter in L.A. area Superstores Ordinances created framework for community benefits negotiations UFCW negotiated favorable union contract with groceries Wal-Mart Chinatown opened but failed

Trucking	Independent-contractor status of port drivers degraded labor conditions and prohibited unionization	Pass and defend new port law, the Clean Truck Program, conditioning trucking company entry on hiring employee drivers	LAANE, NRDC, Teamsters	L.A. port lost industry preemption challenge to Clean Truck Program	• Clean Truck Program passed at Ports of Los Angeles and Long Beach	• Coalition won Clean Truck Programs • Teamsters union organized Toll and some independent-contractor firms	+ Passed ordinance built on city contracting power − Inter-jurisdictional competition (L.A. vs. Long Beach) undermined L.A. effort to upgrade driver status	• Successful policy campaign in L.A. and Long Beach • Long Beach did not pass employee conversion • L.A. employee driver provision invalidated by federal appeals court • Won cleaner trucks but drivers still exploited as independent contractors • As of 2018, campaign-sponsored misclassification lawsuits and union organizing ("suing and striking") resulted in $35 million in judgments by DLSE and six labor agreements with trucking firms

around the subordination of workers of color in a system of racial capitalism,[10] in which labor inequality was a product of racial caste. In contrast, the community–labor campaigns were framed around class-based exploitation: contesting the conditions of low-wage work, disproportionately affecting workers of color, toward the goal of strengthening workplace representation. This was, in part, a function of the nature of the campaigns' organizational sponsors and their relation to broader social movements. APALC and MALDEF were civil rights groups, while LAANE came from the labor movement. The difference in strategic framing was also a function of distinct campaign goals. At bottom, the immigrant rights campaigns focused on raising baseline working conditions to the minimum floor: using litigation to stop labor exploitation in racially segmented markets in order to achieve compliance with existing legal standards. In contrast, the community–labor campaigns were focused on promoting class solidarity and creating the conditions of possibility for union organizing.

Because the essential goals of the immigrant rights and community–labor campaigns were different, they also had distinct relationships to local government. In the immigrant rights campaigns, the city was either a passive actor enabling private sector labor abuse or a hostile force punishing vulnerable workers. In the community–labor campaigns, by contrast, the city was both an important site of legal leverage and an affirmative source of pro-worker law. These differences in objectives and approaches yield distinctive patterns of local legal mobilization across the immigrant rights and community–labor campaigns.

Because the immigrant rights campaigns were geared toward disciplining recalcitrant local actors, they followed a classical civil rights logic, depicted in Figure 7.1, in which higher-level institutions were asked to generate legal norms that lawyers and activists mobilized locally to change employer policy and practice. Mobilizing law from the top down, lawyers undertook *strategic litigation*, adapting the test case model—pioneered in the NAACP's national attack on school segregation—for locally defined ends. In the garment campaign, courts were asked to impose joint employer liability on retailers and manufacturers that used subcontracting relationships to escape responsibility for contractor labor abuse. In the day labor campaign, courts were asked to invalidate anti-solicitation ordinances on the ground that they prohibited day labor speech and thus violated the First Amendment. In both campaigns, adversaries—garment companies resisting application of joint employer status and cities seeking to preserve anti-solicitation ordinances—undertook defensive action to block higher-level legal interference in their practices.

Following the test case model, immigrant rights lawyers moved carefully and incrementally, starting with egregious cases, winning early precedent, and then gradually building cases toward more significant targets. However, unlike the NAACP's quest for a definitive Supreme Court ruling in *Brown v. Board of Education*,[11] in the immigrant rights campaigns, lawyers deployed the test case model for tailored ends. In the garment industry, the APALC lawyers' goal was to use strategic litigation to

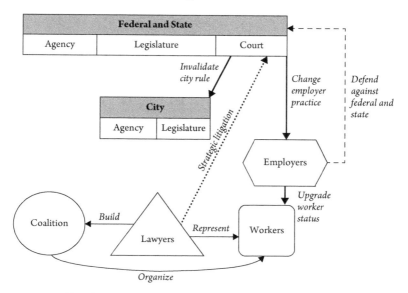

Figure 7.1 Local legal mobilization in immigrant rights campaigns.

extract settlements against high-profile industry leaders, imposing monetary costs and using public pressure in an effort to force those firms to restructure—and then building from the beachhead of that success to reform the industry. In the day labor context, MALDEF lawyers sought to limit the scope of legal challenge to the Ninth Circuit (which covered an area with the highest concentration of day laborers in the country): winning a limited geographical victory that would nonetheless provide sweeping relief.

Although the focus of immigrant rights campaigns was on courts, movement lawyers did not limit themselves to court-based struggle and, at various times, petitioned state and federal officials for policy change. For example, advocates in the early 1990s pursued a statewide anti-sweatshop law; only when that effort failed did they pivot toward strategic litigation, powered by the success of APALC's Thai worker lawsuit. After that case brought attention to the anti-sweatshop cause, advocates were able to persuade labor officials to engage in stronger industry monitoring and enforcement efforts, and eventually won passage in the California legislature of A.B. 633, which established joint liability for garment manufacturers. At every step, movement adversaries sought to block pro-worker efforts. For example, in the day labor struggle, Home Depot attempted to piggyback on the 2005 federal immigration bill sponsored by U.S. Congressman James Sensenbrenner to legally preclude local governments from tying store approval to benefits for day laborers, like on-site day labor centers.

Figure 7.2 maps the pattern of local legal mobilization in the community–labor campaigns—the mirror image of that seen in the immigrant rights

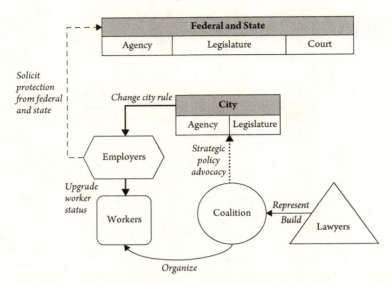

Figure 7.2 Local legal mobilization in community–labor campaigns.

context. In the community–labor campaigns, lawyers mobilized law from the bottom up: representing community–labor coalitions in their efforts to undertake *strategic policy advocacy* to change local law and thereby reform low-wage industries. Here, local government institutions played positive roles. In the CBA campaign, coalitions leveraged agency land use review to negotiate benefits and lobbied the CRA to codify community benefits policy. The anti-big-box coalition blocked Wal-Mart approval at the ballot and then mobilized to pass Superstores Ordinances in city legislatures. The coalition for clean trucks helped to pass concession programs at the Los Angeles and Long Beach ports, the former of which required truck drivers be employees of trucking firms. Across these cases, coalitions worked to *keep law local*—using their political advantage in the city to deepen worker protection and promote unionization.

Movement adversaries took the exact opposite tack: seeking to circumvent local processes that empowered community–labor action or to move legal struggles into higher institutional tiers in order to limit or shut down local action. In the CBA context, the goal of private developers was generally to limit community–labor mobilization to individual disputes resolved through private contract rather than permitting city regulation that would transform the entire development process. In the big-box campaign, Wal-Mart attempted to circumvent the local land use process through city initiative, Measure 04-A; when that backfired, the company lobbied against ordinances imposing an outright big-box ban by threatening litigation; and when the Superstores Ordinances were passed to require economic impact analysis, Wal-Mart again skirted the law by quietly gaining approval for a small-format grocery store in Chinatown. Finally, in the ports campaign, the trucking industry successfully undercut the Los Angeles Clean Truck Program through a preemption lawsuit in federal court (and also tried, unsuccessfully, to pressure the Federal Maritime Commission to enjoin the program).

These contrasting mobilization patterns yield two insights. First, in a multilevel system, local legal mobilization *necessarily involves advocacy at higher levels* (state and federal). This is true either because, as in the immigrant rights campaigns, higher-level support in the form of federal or state court orders is necessary to force local actors to change their practices or, as in the community–labor campaigns, efforts to change local policy necessarily provoke employer countermobilization at higher levels to seek protection from local rules. It is in this sense that local legal mobilization is never entirely local—rather, it always operates vertically across national, state, and local scales. Movement actors—and their adversaries—invariably seek the most advantageous arenas for their demands. If local actors are subordinating workers, advocates seek state and federal relief; if state and federal venues are foreclosed, then advocates pursue local reform. Even within institutional levels, opportunities for advocacy may vary across different governmental branches. For instance, in the ports campaign, after the Clean Truck Program was enjoined in federal court, labor advocates went to Congress to amend the federal law that preempted the program—attempting to carve out a specific exception to permit driver reclassification as employees. When Congress shifted to Republican control after the 2010 election, thwarting the amendment effort, campaign leaders enlisted federal support from the Obama Department of Labor, whose leaders agreed to increase enforcement efforts against trucking firms that misclassified drivers. In a system of fragmented power, port advocates were able to gain administrative agency support even though legislative change was foreclosed.

The second important insight from this review is that the form of legal representation lawyers undertake *necessarily depends on the pattern of legal mobilization.* When mobilization is organized around strategic litigation, as in the immigrant rights campaigns, lawyers represent workers in claiming rights through courts. When it occurs through strategic policy advocacy, as in the community–labor campaigns, lawyers represent coalitions of groups by providing legal advice on how to navigate planning or legislative approval processes, drafting model legislation, and intervening to defend legislation if necessary. The form of representation affects the degree of lawyer influence. Immigrant rights lawyers assumed more control in navigating the technically arcane litigation process on behalf of less sophisticated individual clients entering hostile legal forums, while community–labor lawyer control was checked by more powerful client groups, led by sophisticated activists, who understood the process for policy reform as well as (or better than) the lawyers. This meant that immigrant rights lawyers were more apt to encounter conflicts of interest between their own vision of structural change and the immediate interests of low-wage clients seeking financial redress, while the community–labor lawyers regularly had to negotiate conflicts among the groups forming client coalitions, which challenged the lawyers' ability to advance unified client goals.

Features: Beyond Law Versus Politics

Rejecting a sharp law–politics divide, lawyers advanced a nuanced vision of equality in advocacy: asserting professional parity with nonlawyer leaders, while affirming the essential value of law as a constituent element of effective political action. There were two key features of this vision. First, as a representational matter, movement lawyers enacted a model of *integrated leadership*, endorsing a conception of professional role that elevated the lawyers' own standing to formulate movement goals and guide movement development within the confines of accountability structures internal to the movement. Rejecting the traditional separation between lawyer-as-servant and client-as-leader, movement lawyers made self-conscious choices to ensure that their judgments were informed by the voices of those they claimed to help. Mobilizing law within a campaign framework necessarily required lawyers to account to a wider audience, defend decisions in public forums, negotiate conflict, and make advocacy choices in dialogue with other movement stakeholders asserting their own representational claims.

Where such structures of lawyer accountability did not exist within movements, lawyers helped to create them. For example, lawyers in the day labor campaign supported establishment of NDLON, coordinated with NDLON on litigation strategy throughout the challenge to anti-solicitation ordinances, and worked with NDLON to create day labor committees to act as organizational plaintiffs in order to give day laborers a strong voice in litigation and to protect undocumented workers from harassment. While engaged in litigation, anti-sweatshop lawyers created two organizations to coordinate overall strategy: Sweatshop Watch, the public relations and policy arm of the movement, and the Garment Worker Center, the organizing arm. Similarly, lawyers were critical institution builders in the community–labor campaigns. They created key organizations (such as LAANE) and helped to build the very coalitions that they represented in the local policy arena. In so doing, lawyers enacted a form of leadership in which their own judgments about how to interpret the movement's best interests and formulate appropriate strategy shaped and were informed by institutions of countervailing power. Lawyers thereby pursued a middle ground between "second-chair" status as outside counsel to movement actors and campaign architects in the legal liberal model.[12] This approach did not avoid struggles over legitimacy and control, but rather surfaced conflict through governance structures that created venues for disagreement and debate. As a result, lawyers did not feel compelled to choose between client interests and their own vision of the movement's "cause"[13]—instead negotiating the meaning of movement representation through ongoing cycles of community engagement. Integrated leadership did not mean that relations with organizers always were smooth—for example, in the anti-sweatshop fight, the Garment Worker Center ultimately opted out of APALC's litigation campaign when their mutual vision for challenging the industry broke down. Yet the very fact that inter-organizational disagreement produced a collective decision to dissolve the litigation campaign underscored the importance of the checks and balances created by the integrated leadership model.

The second feature of movement lawyering in the L.A. campaigns was that, as a tactical matter, lawyers adopted a model of *integrated advocacy* rejecting the boundary between legal and political action in favor of coordinating advocacy across institutional spaces—inside and outside of formal lawmaking arenas—to achieve short-term policy reform and longer-term social change. These boundary-crossing efforts were advanced through the lawyers' approach to comprehensive campaign planning, in which they worked proactively with activists and community members to place legal and political tactics on an equal advocacy plane—neither prioritized over nor subordinated to one another. In this way, campaign actors systematically combined modes of advocacy—litigation, lobbying, transactional work, organizing support, media relations, and community education—in order to push forward interconnected goals: enforcing legal mandates, exerting political pressure to reform rules, and building precedent to mobilize workers and change public attitudes.[14] The crucial point is that *these modes of advocacy were deliberately coordinated by movement lawyers and other actors, and executed according to an overarching strategic plan designed to maximize their combined power to advance collectively defined goals*. Central to this approach was the idea that because law was an essential tool used to subordinate workers, changing law had to be a central target of any reform. The key question in each campaign was therefore *how* the law is used, not *whether* it was used.

As a result, across campaigns, there was never any clear border at which legal mobilization stopped and political mobilization commenced. In the anti-sweatshop campaign, for instance, litigation was used to win monetary redress for aggrieved workers and force industry actors to comply with joint employer law, thereby building support for A.B. 633, which itself created new possibilities for litigation and organizing in an iterative cycle of enforcement and mobilization. In the day labor campaign, organizing on the corners in cities with draconian laws formed the foundation for litigation, which in turn emboldened laborers to engage in more organizing, which itself became a way to enforce the right to solicit work after MALDEF's victory in the Ninth Circuit against Redondo Beach. Similarly, in the CBA campaign, the threat of environmental litigation created negotiating space for private contracts, which were crafted with provisions that empowered community oversight and permitted enforcement in court. By filing suit against Wal-Mart's ballot measure seeking preemptory land use approval for a Supercenter in Inglewood, lawyers rebuked Wal-Mart's disrespect for legal process, contributing to the coalition's successful effort to defeat the measure at the polls and then to create citywide policy that could be enforced on a site-by-site basis. Finally, environmental litigation stopping port development created the political opportunity for the Clean

Truck Program, which established concession agreements legally enforceable against trucking firms, while misclassification claims against those same firms in the DLSE formed the foundation for union organizing resulting in labor contracts that provided guarantees of employment status and associated economic benefits.

Foundations: Beyond Elite Versus Grassroots

In the L.A. campaigns, equality as a process norm was double-faced: Movement lawyers rejected the idea that there was a superior form of legal knowledge, either emanating from the grassroots or handed down by elites, and instead sought to mesh expertise in crafting the most effective means to challenge systems of power. What accounts for the L.A. movement lawyers' pursuit of this position of equipoise—determined to make a difference but sensitive not to overreach? Analyzing lawyers across campaigns, two important foundations for their role definition emerge.

The first is what the lawyers themselves brought to the campaigns—their *legal endowment*—in the form of individual backgrounds, political ideology, and intellectual capital. In the immigrant rights campaigns, the key lawyers—Julie Su and the legal team at APALC, and Tom Saenz and the legal team at MALDEF—combined elite credentials with backgrounds that aligned them with the communities they served. The daughter of Chinese immigrants who grew up outside of Los Angeles,[15] Su earned a degree from Harvard Law School and then won a prestigious Skadden Fellowship to launch a project on workplace abuse at APALC—known for its antidiscrimination work on behalf of Asian American immigrant communities. At APALC, she built an anti-sweatshop team that included three other Asian American lawyers (Muneer Ahmad, Betty Hung, and Christina Chung) from elite law schools (Harvard, Yale, and Michigan, respectively).

Saenz grew up on the east side of Los Angeles, born to parents who did not go to college. His grandparents on his mother's side were from Mexico and Spain; on his father's side, his family came from a region of Mexico that was annexed by the United States after the Mexican-American War.[16] He went to Yale Law School, earned the Potter Award for best moot court oralist, and clerked for Stephen Reinhardt on the Ninth Circuit—one of the most competitive clerkships in the country. At MALDEF, over the course of the anti-solicitation campaign, there were eight other lawyers of Latin American descent, most from elite law schools: Vibiana Andrade (Harvard), Antonia Hernández (UCLA), Belinda Escobosa Helzer (Southwestern), Shaheena Simons (Yale), Hector Villagra (Columbia), Araceli Perez (Hastings), Cynthia Valenzuela (UCLA), and Gladys Limón (Stanford). The immigrant rights campaigns were thereby powered by a new generation of lawyers of color, who sought to mobilize their professional capital to challenge racialized systems of labor subordination, while maintaining more horizontal relations with the communities they served—and of which they viewed themselves a part. This identification with community, though complicated by class and ethnicity, permitted a type of solidarity often absent from first-wave public interest lawyering.

The backgrounds of lawyers in the community–labor campaigns established different bases for solidarity. CBA lawyer Jerilyn López Mendoza grew up in an industrial part of Montebello, a working-class Mexican American neighborhood in East Los Angeles, where she was sensitized to the environmental impacts of nearby chemical plants and freight traffic. She left to attend Stanford, became interested in environmental racism upon hearing a presentation from an African American activist at a protest, and—after studying environmental justice at the UCLA School of Law—was hired at Environmental Defense.[17] Madeline Janis grew up in a middle-class neighborhood in the San Fernando Valley, taking frequent trips to Mexico with her mother, who was an artist. At Amherst College, she became active protesting U.S. involvement in Central America in the late 1970s and returned to Los Angeles in 1982 to support the sanctuary movement for refugees from El Salvador.[18] Although she started at L.A. corporate law powerhouse Latham & Watkins, she soon moved to direct the Central American Resource Center and was then recruited by Miguel Contreras to start LAANE. Julian Gross, the main outside counsel to the CBA movement, also had a middle-class progressive upbringing and an entrepreneurial streak, attending Berkeley Law School, winning a Skadden Fellowship the first year it was awarded, and then starting his own solo law firm representing community–labor coalitions in local redevelopment processes at a time when that was a risky business model.

The grocery campaign similarly enlisted white progressive lawyers from small firm practice: Margo Feinberg, the Bay Area labor lawyer who was hired by LAANE and UFCW to coordinate legal strategy and draft the Superstores Ordinances; and Jan Chatten-Brown, a UCLA School of Law graduate and environmental review specialist whose law firm worked on the challenge to Measure 04-A (Chatten-Brown also sued over the LAX Master Plan, represented groups in CBA negotiations, and challenged expansion at the Los Angeles port). The port trucking campaign was the most dependent on lawyers from the labor movement, mostly white men who had come out of organized labor and either worked in house (like Mike Manley and Pat Szymanski at the Teamsters) or at labor law firm boutiques (like Richard McCracken and Andrew Kahn at Davis, Cowell & Bowe). While outside counsel had elite law school credentials, the in-house labor lawyers generally came from less elite schools: Manley graduated from Kansas Law School and Szymanski from Wayne State, which had a strong tradition of labor activism. LAANE's port lawyer was an exception: Sanjukta Paul took the position as LAANE's legal coordinator for the port trucking campaign after graduating from Yale, clerking on the Ninth Circuit, and working for a civil rights boutique. On the environmental side of the ports coalition, lawyers from NRDC came from Harvard (Gail Ruderman Feuer), UCLA (David Pettit), Georgetown (Melissa Lin Perrella), and Colorado (Adrian Martinez). These lawyers brought different motivations to the port campaign, with

Pettit, the former legal aid lawyer, dedicated to antipoverty principles and sound land use management, while Martinez was committed to environmental justice. As this suggests, part of the crucial solidarity-building work holding community–labor coalitions together centered on combining the diverse credentials and commitments of the *lawyers*, and meshing their expertise to produce a convergence of interests strong enough to survive industry efforts to divide and conquer.

Second, on top of individual endowment, the role of lawyers in the L.A. campaigns was built upon a unique foundation of *legal density*: the concentration of interrelated legal organizations engaged in low-wage worker advocacy in Los Angeles at the time. Density shaped intracity legal networks, organized around movement hubs like LAANE and the UCLA Downtown Labor Center, which permitted the circulation of innovative advocacy models. The law and organizing approach pioneered by APALC's Su and MALDEF's Saenz was followed closely by advocates in subsequent low-wage worker campaigns in other industries, like the car wash sector. Similarly, LAANE's comprehensive campaign model established the benchmark for community–labor mobilization, while the Downtown Labor Center became the central intermediary fostering coalitions between the immigrant rights and labor movements.

Legal density also helped to attract crucial funding to local hub organizations to strengthen mobilization. Legal hubs spearheading movement campaigns served as magnets: accruing funding in layers that built from initial investments in personnel. Externally funded fellowships were particularly important in the immigrant rights campaigns, in which lawyers received six Skadden Fellowships, one Equal Justice Works Fellowship, one Echoing Green Fellowship, and three Fried Frank Fellowships (designated exclusively for MALDEF). These fellowships were awarded by grantors that deliberately sought to build on preexisting organizational strength to advance campaigns. After initial fellows (like Julie Su) forged innovative paths at lead organizations, new fellows were added to help achieve scale (during the anti-sweatshop campaign, APALC was awarded four Skadden Fellows). In the community–labor campaigns, unions and foundations channeled money to LAANE to fund legal support: helping to retain Gross in the CBA campaign, Feinberg in the Wal-Mart site fight, and Paul in the ports campaign.

Over time, legal density enabled an important type of career mobility: establishing networks that created pathways to influential positions contributing to campaigns over the long haul. Julie Su, champion of exploited immigrant workers in garment contract shops, rose to be the California labor commissioner presiding over claims of misclassification in the ports campaign. Tom Saenz, defender of day labor, became Mayor Antonio Villaraigosa's general counsel, signing off on the legality of the Clean Truck Program at the Los Angeles port. After working on day labor issues at MALDEF, Victor Narro moved to oversee worker rights advocacy at CHIRLA, became co-executive director of Sweatshop Watch, and then assumed an essential coordinating role as project director at the Downtown Labor Center. Jerilyn López

Mendoza, who cut her teeth on the LAX CBA campaign, was tapped by Mayor Villaraigosa for her knowledge of public agency law to serve on the Los Angeles Board of Harbor Commissioners in order to guide passage of the Clean Truck Program. Madeline Janis pioneered the movement to require community benefits from publicly subsidized developments and was then appointed to the CRA board, where she helped design internal policies attaching labor standards to such projects. As these career trajectories underscore, investment in movement lawyering not only paid professional dividends but positioned advocates to influence the broader struggle for economic justice through positions of governmental power.[19]

Equality as an Outcome of Struggle

Throughout the L.A. movement for economic justice, egalitarian process norms were put in service of improving conditions for low-wage workers in defined industry sectors—creating a more equal place as an outcome of struggle. Drawing on evidence from the L.A. campaigns, this part offers three different perspectives on their impact. First, it examines law on the books, measuring outcomes from the campaigns in terms of the achievement of specific policy reforms designed to raise standards in the low-wage market. Second, it considers law in action, assessing outcomes in relation to the extent that campaign wins were implemented in practice. Third, it explores law as a lever for redistributing power, tracing the trajectory of the campaigns as both a cause and effect of the widening influence of organized labor in city politics.

Policy: Law on the Books

Table 7.2 lists the major policy outcomes of the five campaigns. A "policy" is defined as a rule change achieved through legal channels: a ruling in court setting forth a broad legal principle, a statute enacted through the legislative process, a rule promulgated by an administrative agency, or a private contract enforceable by worker representatives. In the table, "outcome" refers to the formal terms of policy reform—the law on the books—and is limited to rule changes bearing on the quality of work (i.e., housing and environmental aspects are not included).

As the table highlights, the L.A. campaigns won significant policy gains. The two policy victories achieved through courts were *Bureerong v. Uvawas*, the 1996 federal district court decision affirming the workers' right to bring suit against garment manufacturers that had contracted with the El Monte sweatshop; and *Comite de Jornaleros v. City of Redondo Beach* in 2011, which invalidated the Redondo Beach anti-solicitation ban. Both decisions produced policy change, albeit with different force. In *Bureerong*, the district court validated an expansive reading of joint employer status that transcended prior rulings by holding that manufacturers could be liable for contract shop labor violations based on the "economic realities"—namely,

Table 7.2 Outcomes by campaign.

Campaign	Organization	Policy	Venue	Outcome	Impact
Garment	APALC	Bureerong v. Uvawas (1996)	District Court (C.D. Cal.)	• Federal district court denied defendant manufacturers' motion to dismiss lawsuit, ruling that by alleging manufacturers contracted out to avoid liability and set unfairly low prices, workers stated a claim of manufacturer control under Fair Labor Standards Act's joint employer test	• Forced settlement in case resulting in $3.5 million in back pay award to workers • Set strong standard for joint employer liability that formed template for A.B. 633, although the legal ruling was limited by later cases • Launched the anti-sweatshop movement
	Sweatshop Watch	A.B. 633 (2000)	California state legislature	• Made garment manufacturers jointly and severally liable for minimum wage and overtime payments by contractors • Enforced through expedited process in California DLSE, appealable to state court (attorney's fees granted to lawyers for prevailing workers)	• 2005 report found contractors settled for 30% of what workers were owed • Only 15% of guarantors paid anything to workers and, when they did, paid an average of only 16% of what workers claimed
	Sweatshop Watch	Sweat-Free Procurement Ordinance (2004)	City of Los Angeles	• Required city garment contractors to pledge compliance with employment and labor laws and pay workers at the living wage rate	• Small number of garment contracts terminated by city and one contractor upgraded wages to comply with ordinance • Effectively superseded by passage of L.A. Minimum Wage Ordinance in 2015

Day Labor	NDLON	Home Improvement Stores Ordinance (2008)	City of Los Angeles	At city's discretion, big-box home improvement stores required to establish sites for day laborers, when necessary to accommodate their job-seeking, as a condition of project approval	• No evidence of day labor sites created under this ordinance • Recession plus changed market conditions caused big-box stores like Home Depot to decline
	MALDEF	Comite de Jornaleros v. City of Redondo Beach (2011)	Ninth Circuit (en banc)	Permanently enjoined Redondo Beach's anti-solicitation ordinance under First Amendment on ground that it was not a narrowly tailored speech restriction since it prohibited day laborers from communicating their availability to work and the city had other means to enforce traffic violations	• Invalidated 31 complete citywide solicitation bans around greater L.A. area
Retail	SAJE, LAANE	Staples/L.A. Live Community Benefits Agreement (2001)	Contract between coalition and developer incorporated in city development agreement	• Developer required to make reasonable efforts to meet 70% living wage goal for 5,500 permanent jobs • Developer required to fund First Source Referral System and ensure project employers make efforts to hire local residents • Developer, contractors, and tenants required to follow the city's Worker Retention and Responsible Contractor Ordinances	• 70% living wage goal met in 2013, although this included workers covered by the Living Wage Ordinance and hotel labor agreement • 50% of jobs in Phase One of development met local hiring requirements • As of 2006, developer had provided $62,000 in seed funding to support job training program

(continued)

Table 7.2 Continued

Campaign	Organization	Policy	Venue	Outcome	Impact
	Environmental Defense, LAANE	LAX Community Benefits Agreement (2004)	Contract between coalition and LAX	• LAX required to establish a First Source Hiring Program, included as a material term in all airport contracts, with first priority for the program given to low-income individuals in the project area • LAX required to provide $15 million over 5 years for job training with priority to low-income individuals in the project area • LAX required to apply the Living Wage, Worker Retention, and Contractor Responsibility Ordinances to all contracts with airport contractors, lessees, and licensees	• The FAA only certified local hiring and job training for jobs created directly by the airport, not airport contractors • In 2008, LAX reported 2,015 first source referrals resulting in 423 hires; in 2016, it reported 67,674 referrals resulting in 166 hires • In 2016, LAX reported 518 people had completed job training • All LAX contracts were certified to comply with the Living Wage, Worker Retention, and Contractor Responsibility Ordinances • Application of living wage to LAX contractors and lessees facilitated unionization
	SAJE, LA CAN	Grand Avenue Community Benefits Agreement (2007)	Term Sheet incorporated in development agreement	• Developer agreed to 30% local hiring goal (which included a 10% at-risk hiring goal) for construction and permanent jobs • Developer required to pay $500,000 for job training • All permanent jobs required to pay living wage	• Estimated to create 29,000 construction and 5,900 permanent jobs, which would equate to 8,700 local hires for construction and 1,770 local hires for permanent jobs • Because of recession, development is still incomplete

	LAANE	CRA Living Wage, Worker Retention, and Contractor Responsibility Policies (2003)	CRA	• Applied city Living Wage, Worker Retention, and Contractor Responsibility Ordinances to CRA contractors, lessees, and recipients of financial assistance	• Attached labor requirements to redevelopment projects until the CRA dissolved in 2012
Grocery	LAANE, UFCW	Superstores Ordinances (2004, 2006)	City of Los Angeles and City of Inglewood	• Big-box retail stores with groceries required to conduct economic impact report and mitigate negative economic impacts as a condition of project approval	• No Wal-Mart Supercenters opened in Los Angeles • In 2007 union contract negotiations with Los Angeles-area groceries, the UFCW won repeal of a two-tier employment benefits structure implemented in 2003 • Small-format Wal-Mart grocery opened in Chinatown in 2013, but closed in 2016
	LAANE, UFCW	Grocery Worker Retention Ordinance (2005)	City of Los Angeles	• Required new owners of supermarkets to retain existing workforce for at least 90 days	• Implementation delayed pending legal challenge by grocery industry, resulting in 2011 California Supreme Court ruling upholding law • No evidence of the ordinance being used but had potential deterrent effect on union-busting sales

(*continued*)

Table 7.2 Continued

Campaign	Organization	Policy	Venue	Outcome	Impact
Trucking	LAANE, Teamsters	Clean Truck Program (2008)	Port and City of Los Angeles	• Required trucking companies to enter concession agreements as a condition of accessing port • Key provision of concession agreement mandated companies hire employee drivers in phases culminating in 100% employee drivers by 2013 • Terminal operators required to deny entry to noncompliant trucking companies upon penalty of criminal sanction	• Forecast to convert approximately 15,000 truck drivers to employees • Employee status projected to raise truck driver wages by an estimated 40%, resulting in increased driver income of approximately $175 million annually, while permitting unionization • Program struck down by Ninth Circuit in 2011
	LAANE, Teamsters	S.B. 459 Willful Misclassification Law (2011)	California state legislature	• Imposed civil penalties of up to $15,000 for individual violations or $25,000 for a pattern or practice of willful misclassification of independent contractors	• No systematic evidence of enforcement available • 18 positive legal rulings upholding claims against trucking firms with one appellate decision extending liability to joint employers

that their contract rates could not have objectively covered the costs of garments produced. While this case sent a powerful policy message, its force was limited by the fact that it was issued by a lower court on a motion to dismiss and thus lacked ultimate precedential weight (and, indeed, later cases chipped away at *Bureerong*'s strong joint employer theory). In contrast, the *Redondo Beach* case, issued by an en banc panel of the Ninth Circuit Court of Appeals, had a sweeping policy impact: announcing a First Amendment right to communicate with potential employers that invalidated solicitation bans across the region.

The campaigns also won policy change through government bodies at all levels. The state legislature passed two significant bills: the garment joint employer bill (A.B. 633) and the willful misclassification bill (S.B 459). Locally, the campaigns successfully supported enactment of five L.A. city ordinances (Sweat-Free Procurement, Home Improvement Stores, Superstores, Grocery Worker Retention, and Clean Truck Program) and one in Inglewood (Superstores). At the agency level, the community benefits campaign succeeded in converting provisions fought for in site-specific agreements into policy: applying the L.A. Living Wage Ordinance, Worker Retention Ordinance, and Contractor Responsibility Ordinance to all development projects subsidized by the CRA. These state and local governmental policies, except for the Clean Truck Program (wiped away by the Ninth Circuit) and the CRA policies (eliminated by the dissolution of the CRA), remain on the books.

Finally, the community benefits campaign resulted in three major agreements—the Staples, LAX, and Grand Avenue CBAs (as well as several less prominent ones, most significantly at NoHo Commons in North Hollywood). The work-related outcomes in the major agreements included provisions establishing an unprecedented 70% living wage goal for permanent jobs at L.A. Live and a 100% living wage requirement at Grand Avenue; local hiring requirements at all sites; and commitments at Staples and LAX by developers to ensure their contractors and tenants, which produced permanent jobs, followed the living wage law. The Staples and LAX CBAs were both contracts between the developer and coalition, permitting direct coalition enforcement, while the Grand Avenue CBA was only incorporated in the agreement between the city and developer.

Overall, the body of law created by the campaigns contributed substantially to a pro-worker policy shift at the state and local level that transformed the regulatory architecture of low-wage work. The scope of reform varied by governmental tier and the regulatory authority of the body issuing the rule change. Courts were most useful in invalidating governmental overreach (*Redondo Beach*) and only marginally helpful in checking corporate abuse (*Bureerong*). In the legislature, state law changes transformed the class of responsible parties and the mechanics of adjudication in garment industry wage claims, while raising penalties on bad actors deliberately abusing the independent-contractor form in the port trucking industry and beyond. At the local level, city policy filled in gaps strengthening labor law and laid the foundation for collective action. Most significantly, CRA policy extended laws designed to increase wages and create the possibility for union organizing to the substantial number of retail jobs created by redevelopment. Retailers in redevelopment projects—not otherwise covered by the city's Living Wage, Worker Retention, and Contractor Responsibility Ordinances—for the first time came within these laws' reach. As a result, retailers had to agree to a living wage and labor peace, offering a route for workers to unionize. The remaining city policies did not mandate labor upgrades but rather gave the city new levers to shape the nature of work: by terminating noncompliant contractors (Sweat-Free Procurement), mandating information disclosure on wages to bolster collective bargaining (Superstores), ending trucking firm misclassification (Clean Truck Program), and requiring stores selling to contractors benefiting from day labor to provide space to protect those laborers' right to work (Home Improvement Stores).

Impact: Law in Action

To evaluate the impact of policy reform won by the L.A. campaigns, Table 7.2 summarizes evidence obtained from public reports and assessments conducted by third parties or campaign participants involved in outcome monitoring. "Impact" is meant to capture "law in action," which is the degree to which reforms were implemented and their wider social effect. As the table suggests, the criteria for assessing impact depend both on the legal mechanism through which policy is realized and on how policy goals are defined.

In terms of mechanism, it is useful to separate out policy reform achieved through litigation: the joint employer liability standard articulated in the *Bureerong* case and the endorsement of day labor solicitation rights in *Redondo Beach*. In both instances, litigation was used to achieve direct effects. In the *Bureerong* case, the narrow goal was to compensate sixty-four Thai workers for the deprivation of wages resulting from their enslavement. When filed, the suit sought hundreds of millions of dollars from the sweatshop owners for claims including involuntary servitude and false imprisonment, as well as from ten manufacturers that did business with the sweatshop for employment violations. The plaintiffs' lawyers did not believe that they would recover against the sweatshop owners, who were separately prosecuted and had their assets confiscated, but were able to settle for $3.5 million against the main manufacturer defendants—a figure augmented by public enforcement efforts that ultimately gave the workers nearly all of what they were owed in back wages. This, of course, could not compensate workers for the extreme harm imposed by their enslavement, but restored their economic loss.

While the Thai worker case sought compensation for past harm, the *Redondo Beach* day labor lawsuit, in contrast, was filed to permit prospective action. In this respect, the day labor case was quintessentially libertarian in its aims: seeking to eliminate government restrictions in order to enable private economic transactions between willing parties. Its success was therefore immediate and widespread, resulting in an injunction against the Redondo Beach ordinance and the invalidation of thirty other copycat ordinances throughout the greater L.A. area. Although elimination of the ordinances could not stop day laborer harassment by local law enforcement officials or stem employer abuse, it did eradicate the most overt threat to day laborers' economic livelihood: the criminalization of the very act of seeking work.

With respect to the legislative and agency-based policies, it is useful to consider impact in relation to policy goals, which can be grouped into four categories. First are those policies meant to *strengthen existing systems of worker protection* in order to deter workplace abuse, ensure compliance with minimum labor standards, and to compensate workers for past harms. The two policies in this category are A.B. 633, creating guarantor liability for garment manufacturers, and S.B. 459, imposing penalties for willful misclassification. Evidence of A.B. 633 enforcement against manufacturers was mixed. Five years after the law's enactment, a comprehensive analysis found that workers were recovering less than one-third of back wages claimed and that identified guarantors paid only 16% of back wages—with 60% of guarantors paying nothing despite being ordered by the labor commissioner to do so. While these figures are shockingly low, they must be considered against the liability baseline prior to the law, which required workers to sue manufacturers under the more onerous joint employment test—a barrier that meant many workers simply did not even try because of evidentiary standards of proof and because it was difficult to find willing legal counsel (a problem eliminated by A.B. 633's self-help system and its provision of attorney's fees).

S.B. 459 imposes civil penalties against willfully misclassifying employers enforceable by public agencies, like the Labor Commission, or by private plaintiffs under the state's private attorney general law, which only permits injunctive relief.[20] Although there is no systematic evidence of S.B. 459's enforcement, a review of state and federal court decisions in the *Westlaw* legal opinion database finds thirty cases addressing claims brought under the law. Of these, eighteen court decisions upheld willful misclassification claims against employers, three were dismissed on the merits, and nine were dismissed on technical grounds (mostly for improperly claiming a private right of action)—suggesting the law is providing redress for misclassified workers in most cases filed. In the most sweeping case, the California Court of Appeal held that the law applies to the acts of co-employers, like companies that contract with food vendors knowing that those vendors willfully misclassify workers—extending the scope of the law as a tool for challenging misclassification.[21]

The second category of policy change was designed to *increase wages above the minimum floor*: the Sweat-Free Procurement Ordinance, requiring city contractors to pay garment workers a living wage; and the CRA policies applying city labor ordinances to CRA-subsidized projects. Available evidence shows that the Sweat-Free Procurement Ordinance resulted in the termination of a handful of city supply contracts and, in one instance, caused a supplier to upgrade wages after violations were found.[22] The CRA policies had a broader reach—applying to tenants of development projects not otherwise covered (and also helping spur unionization). These policies enhanced labor standards in a decade's worth of redevelopment projects—with the dissolution of the CRA in 2012 limiting their temporal scope.

The third category of labor policies included those designed to *promote unionization*. In this vein, the Superstores Ordinances were crafted to protect the region's unionized grocery sector, blocking the incursion of nonunion big-box groceries that could undermine the UFCW's bargaining power. These ordinances prevented Wal-Mart from opening a Supercenter in Los Angeles—a fact that was credited with allowing grocery workers to negotiate significantly better terms in their 2007 master union contract with area grocery chains. The Grocery Worker Retention Ordinance was similarly designed to protect unionized groceries by preventing worker termination for ninety days in the event of a grocery sale, thereby giving unions the power to strike new owners to force them to retain a unionized workforce. The impact of this law has been blunted by legal challenge and industry decline. It was tied up by an industry preemption lawsuit through 2011 and, although ultimately upheld by the California Supreme Court, the lack of grocery sales has meant that the law has not played a significant role in grocery sector union campaigns (although it operates as a background deterrent on sales to undercut existing union agreements).[23] The Clean Truck Program was designed to end driver misclassification and thus permit unionization, but its invalidation meant it was never implemented.

The fourth and final category of governmental policy reform is a category of one: the Home Improvement Stores Ordinance designed to *protect the right to work and engage in collective action* by day laborers. This ordinance was, by its own terms, relatively soft, merely permitting the city to require day labor sites at stores like Home Depot as a condition for land use permit approval. By the late 2000s, there were no cases of day labor sites approved under this ordinance, perhaps in part because of the discretionary nature of its terms, but more likely because the Great Recession stalled big-box home improvement store development and, when the market rebounded, the increasing power of online sales made big-box sites less profitable for chain stores.[24]

The CBAs, because they are private contracts with developers rather than court or city-imposed rules, invite separate review. In each case—Staples, LAX, and Grand Avenue—the evidence shows modest benefits to labor (relative to overall development costs), although once again the benefits must be judged against the prior development baseline, in which communities received no benefits at all. At Staples—a $1 billion project with a $177-million city financial assistance package—a 2006 status update provided by the developer stated that a job training program had been established and that the developer had provided $62,000 in seed funding to support the program.[25] By 2009, according to the developer, all of the jobs in Phase One—the construction of the Nokia Theater—met the living wage requirements of the CBA, and half of the jobs were held by local residents in compliance with the local hiring requirement.[26] An independent analysis concluded that the developer met the project-wide 70% living wage goal in 2013, although this included jobs already covered by the citywide Living Wage Ordinance and a collective bargaining agreement with the hotel at L.A. Live.[27]

The labor provisions of the LAX CBA, approved by the city in 2004 in relation to the $3-billion LAX modernization project, were slow to proceed, not for economic reasons, but because of the relationship between the city-owned airport and FAA regulators, who had the power to approve airport expenditures. Three years after the CBA, LAX reported that the promised allocation of $15 million in job training funds had been held up by the failure to gain FAA approval and that the local hiring provisions, which had been approved for airport jobs only (not jobs created by airport contractors), were still "in progress."[28] In its 2016 annual report on CBA compliance, LAX stated that 518 people had completed job training that year and over sixty-seven thousand job seekers had been referred to employers through the First Source Hiring Program, resulting in 166 hires.

In addition, the LAX CBA included provisions requiring contractors and lessees to comply with the city's Living Wage Ordinance. This proved to be significant because it meant that most employers at LAX were contractually bound to pay employees at the higher living wage rate or enter into a union contract. According to a comprehensive study, of the nearly ninety-six hundred workers who received pay increases as a result of the Living Wage Ordinance, nearly two-thirds were in jobs at the Los Angeles or Ontario airports and most were in firms that were service contractors to the city or the airlines.[29]

When established, the Grand Avenue CBA was forecast to create twenty-nine thousand construction jobs, 30% of which (eighty-seven hundred) would go to local residents and at-risk individuals under the local hiring provisions.[30] The CBA was also forecast to create fifty-nine hundred permanent living wage jobs with the same proportion dedicated for local residents.[31] However, because development of the $3-billion project was massively delayed by the recession and only commenced in 2018, there are no jobs to report. On paper, the Grand Avenue CBA contained the strongest living wage terms, requiring all permanent jobs to comply with the city's Living Wage Ordinance. However, it has been effectively superseded by the passage of Los Angeles's higher citywide minimum wage ordinance.

Stepping back from the details of enforcement, three general themes emerge from this assessment of policy impact. First, implementation of formal policy change to enhance the conditions of low-wage work is *difficult across the board*. Industry leaders have an enormous amount of power and range of tools to resist, undermine, and circumvent policies designed to control industry behavior. This is true even in clear-cut cases of legal wrongdoing, as the striking noncompliance with A.B. 633's guarantor mandate highlights. Overall, industry is able to play a war of attrition, forcing workers into individualized processes for redress, which favor powerful repeat players.

The second theme emerging from this policy review is that the nature of the L.A. city ordinances, agency rules, and CBAs—and the scope of their implementation—is *fundamentally shaped by the local government tools through which they are created*. The city has a limited range of regulatory powers at its disposal,[32] which in the L.A. campaigns were used to craft policies that had *indirect* impacts on low-wage work: imposing conditions through contracting (Sweat-Free Procurement, CRA policies, and Clean Truck Program) or land use powers (Home Improvement Stores and Superstores Ordinances). The Grocery Worker Retention Ordinance, which rested on an assertion of the city's general regulatory power, also had an indirect impact on workplace conditions by preventing grocery chain sales designed to undercut unions. However, unlike other policies, it did not impose conditions in exchange for a city benefit (contract or land use permit), which made it vulnerable to legal attack. From a local government perspective, CBAs are unique, leveraging local government processes but ultimately not dependent on them for enforcement. However, the virtues of CBAs in this regard are also potential vices because the leverage that CBA coalitions use to execute a deal depends, in part, on the legitimate threat of disruption, which in the Staples and LAX campaigns came from threatened political and legal opposition. Once that threat disappears after a contract is signed, so does a significant part of the leverage to hold developers to account, leaving coalitions only with the power of contract enforcement. In addition, monitoring CBA compliance requires extended community engagement and oversight, which can be taxed by the lengthy nature of the development process.

Finally, the third key finding from the L.A. campaigns is that implementation is *massively influenced by factors outside of advocates' control*, such as macro-level policy changes and large-scale unpredictable events. This was true in the garment campaign, which was ultimately limited by shifting trade policy that enabled garment manufacturers to exercise their enormous power to outsource production to foreign countries. The judicial luck of the draw was also crucial. When APALC lawyers filed the Thai worker case, they drew Judge Audrey Collins, a former legal aid lawyer who took an aggressive stance on joint employer liability; when they later litigated against Forever 21, they drew Judge Gary Fees, who adopted a more formalistic and less favorable view. In the community–labor campaigns, local policies conditioned on the city's land use power (CBAs, Home Improvement Stores, and Superstores Ordinances) were heavily dependent on robust development—and thus were vulnerable to downturns in development cycles, like the Great Recession, which undercut promised benefits.

Power: Law in Political Transformation

Ultimately, social movements mobilize law and politics to achieve greater power: a more equal place in the crucial decision-making structures of governance. It is therefore important to consider the wider impact of the L.A. campaigns on the role of workers and their representatives in the transformation of city politics. In Los Angeles over the past quarter century, the campaigns documented in this book have been enabled by broader trends influencing the rise of labor and other progressive social movements in the city, while simultaneously contributing to the conditions for these movements' success. The history recounted in this book cannot disentangle the relative contributions of social movement campaigns to the pro-labor shift of L.A. city government with any precision. Yet their successes, as well as their failures, are an essential part of the story of how organized labor and the broader worker rights movement gained power in the field of local politics.

From the riots to the recession, labor influence in local politics shifted from reliance on outsider challenges to business elites to insider strategies to mold pro-worker policy. The shift was built on strategic investments in organizational structure, carried forward by leaders who helped win policy reform, which itself contributed to increased union density, growing political clout, more resources for mobilization, and new policy reform—in a virtuous cycle. In this cycle, labor movement actors and their allies identified opportunities in the existing political and legal structure for sectoral reform, leveraged those opportunities to produce new policies that extended the opportunity structure in pro-worker directions, and then jumped off from that new boundary to push for change in other industries.

The starting point was bleak. As documented in chapter 1, by the 1990s, union density was at its nadir and organized labor had been pushed out of the local power sharing arrangement it enjoyed with Mayor Tom Bradley, who was replaced in 1993 by pro-business Republican Mayor Richard Riordan. New immigrants, mostly from Latin America, were alienated from the labor movement and black political leadership. Riordan's rise was built on a promise to "Rebuild LA" after the 1992 civil unrest by investing in law enforcement and opening up public coffers to subsidize business development, giving little thought to the degraded nature of the jobs created or the growing number of working poor and new immigrants who grasped hold of them. Organized labor, on the outside of local governance and unable to rely on traditional union organizing strategies in the post-industrial urban landscape, had to reinvent itself in order to devise a pathway back to political influence. Reinvention occurred in several steps—propelled forward at critical junctures by the low-wage worker campaigns.

In the first step, demographic transformation and economic realignment asserted immediate challenges to labor's influence—while also creating conditions of possibility for resurgence. As immigration reached its peak in the early 1990s—buoyed by an influx of Mexican immigrants, many undocumented—workers encountered an economic landscape reshaped by the decline of Los Angeles's heavy manufacturing base and the expansion of service industries, like retail and hospitality, in which union representation had either never had a strong foothold or been decimated by industry union-busting and subcontracting. Organized labor, met by a new generation of worker rights advocates, confronted this crossroads. The anti-sweatshop campaign described in chapter 2 illustrated the divergent fortunes of traditional labor organizing and new-wave legal mobilization in the shrinking but still significant light-manufacturing sector. UNITE's failed campaign to organize Guess contract workers, launched in 1994, occurred alongside APALC's powerful legal challenge to sweatshops, sparked by the *Bureerong* case in 1995. The anti-sweatshop campaign marked the collapse of unionization in L.A. manufacturing while illustrating the power of immigrant worker organizing and strategic litigation to reframe workplace norms—if not industry-wide practice—in an important sector of the regional economy. Although limited in its impact by outsourcing, the anti-sweatshop campaign sent a potent message to organized labor: To succeed in the new environment, it would need to devise its own sectoral strategies that targeted opportunities presented by the non-exportable service economy, mobilized immigrant workers, and built ties to new community-based legal and organizing partnerships like those representing the anti-sweatshop movement.

The second step toward labor's political revitalization thus centered on building organizational capacity, which occurred on the labor and community sides in the latter half of the 1990s. The same year that UNITE launched the Guess campaign, the L.A. labor movement, led by the County Fed, started LAANE, designed to make connections with community partners to inform organizing strategy and build political power. Through the late 1990s, authentic community–labor partnerships were still nascent, and LAANE's efforts largely ran in parallel to community organizing, led by new groups like SAJE, and immigrant worker mobilization, exemplified by the anti-sweatshop struggle. As chapter 3 showed, the day labor campaign, which also took off at this precise time, developed its own sectoral approach, combining law and organizing, which (like its anti-sweatshop counterpart) demonstrated the will of some of the nation's most marginalized workers to fight their oppression and the equal will of movement lawyers to devise innovative legal strategies to advance their cause. Although organized labor in this phase did not provide direct support to day laborers, who did not fit into the traditional model of unionism, the day labor campaign—which took off after the creation of NDLON—nevertheless sent a message of resistance demanding organized labor recognize that, for unions to be relevant in immigrant communities, they would have to stand with "unorganizable" workers when they stood up for themselves.

In the third step of labor's rebuilding, beginning in the early 2000s, authentic community–labor partnerships were forged in the crucible of strategic campaigns designed to advance sectoral organizing. The legal foundation for these campaigns was the 1997 Living Wage Ordinance, unanimously supported by the City Council (and passed over a Riordan veto) as a modest wage increase with a facially narrow scope (estimated to cover only five thousand workers). Yet, despite its narrow formal application, the law contained the seeds of significant potential union expansion by permitting employers with city contracts and subsidies to *opt into union contracts in lieu of paying the living wage*. This provided leverage for unions to negotiate collective bargaining agreements to build density over time. It was precisely this potential that sparked the 1998 Respect at LAX organizing campaign to extend living wage requirements to screeners, security workers, janitors, and other workers employed by airlines and their subcontractors.

The Respect at LAX campaign, recounted in chapter 4, fed into and helped galvanize the first major community–labor coalition in the CBA movement. On the community side, the CBA movement brought together community development, immigrant rights, and environmental justice groups seeking resources for housing, jobs for disadvantaged local workers, and environmental remediation. On the labor side, the movement mobilized labor groups to extend the reach of the Living Wage Ordinance by applying it to retail and hospitality workers in the Staples CBA (2001) and to airport contract workers in the LAX CBA (2004). As a coalition predicated on interest convergence, each side was critical to the other. Community groups brought credibility and local knowledge, as well as legal power (in the form of the environmental lawsuit), while organized labor brought influence with city council members, who had authority over land use permits, environmental clearance, and subsidies. In the Staples campaign, the building and trades unions agreed not to enter into a project labor agreement with the developer, AEG, until the developer agreed to a CBA, which significantly increased the coalition's negotiating power. The Staples and LAX CBA campaigns catalyzed the 2004 community–labor challenge to the proposed Inglewood Wal-Mart Supercenter, detailed in chapter 5. Out of these CBA and big-box victories came tangible benefits for organized labor that helped to rebuild political capital. Success at LAX increased union density at the airport, while thwarting Wal-Mart strengthened the UFCW's hand in labor negotiations with grocery chains. Both outcomes demonstrated labor's renewed vitality, expanded resources for subsequent unionization drives, and increased capacity for mobilization in favor of pro-labor political candidates.

In step four, labor converted enhanced political capital and increased financial resources into crucial ballot-box success that laid the groundwork for pro-labor policy reform and labor's larger role in local governance. Although the County Fed supported challenger Antonio Villaraigosa over James Hahn for mayor in 2001, when Hahn won, he worked hard to support labor priorities (wishing to receive labor's endorsement in his reelection bid). During the Hahn administration, the City Council also tilted further toward the labor movement, powered by get-out-the-vote drives by the County Fed targeting occasional voters, which resulted in the election of new pro-labor council members in 2003.[33] In addition, pro-labor candidates during this period began to dominate political offices representing the L.A. area (Hilda Solis was elected to Congress in 2000, Fabian Nuñez to the State Assembly in 2002). In this evolving context, organized labor moved incrementally, investing in attainable legal reforms that built density and demonstrated that the labor movement could deliver policy wins[34]—both to union members and the broader community—which justified bolder requests over time. Acceding to one of these requests, in 2002, Mayor Hahn appointed Madeline Janis to the CRA, where she spearheaded passage of pro-labor reforms in the agency the following year. (The Los Angeles Sweat-Free Procurement and Superstores Ordinance were also passed during Hahn's tenure.)

On the strength of this growing clout, in step five of Los Angeles's political transformation, organized labor reestablished its central role *inside* city politics. Villaraigosa's election as mayor in 2005 constituted the defining moment. Swept to power by a progressive coalition built on the very community–labor alliance that had formed around the L.A. campaigns, the ascent of Villaraigosa as a genuine labor movement candidate (having started his career as a teachers' union organizer) marked the culmination of organized labor's reintegration into city politics, allowing labor to lean more heavily on insider political strategies. During the Villaraigosa administration, labor achieved significant policy victories prior to the Great Recession. In 2006, the City Council passed the Grocery Worker Retention Ordinance, which further solidified UFCW gains in the industry. In 2008, the council enacted a living wage law that applied to all hotels around LAX, which contributed to their substantial unionization (only three out of twelve airport hotels remain nonunion). That same year, the Home Improvement Stores Ordinance was passed, as was the Los Angeles Clean Truck Program. The Clean Truck Program, in particular, reflected the degree to which labor could mobilize through internal political channels. Although conceived under Hahn, the program was completed under Villaraigosa, due in significant part to his strategic appointments of labor supporters to key commission posts and mayor's office staff positions.

As these policy wins reflected, this pre-recession period also witnessed a crescendo of community–labor mobilization. The ports campaign, chronicled in chapter 6, used the full power of the blue-green alliance, first brought together in the CBA context, to win transformative local policy change—by mandating clean trucks and employee drivers in the port trucking industry. Although it was a policy victory undone in court, its local realization represented the apex of community–labor coordination in achieving mutually beneficial policy goals—and translated into a subsequent blue-green campaign winning a citywide waste hauling policy that resulted in the unionization of waste truck drivers. The 2006 day labor partnership with the AFL-CIO, though symbolic, underscored the strategic bargain between labor and immigrant rights upon which the L.A community–labor alliance ultimately depended.

In the final step of its political resurrection, as labor consolidated power after the recession, it achieved long-sought, highly ambitious goals: culminating in the 2015 passage of a citywide $15-per-hour minimum wage law. By more than doubling the federal standard, establishing an enforcement arm within the city, and incorporating a union opt-out provision, the labor movement attained an outcome inconceivable two decades before—and delivered on its promise to uplift workers of color and immigrant workers in the formal economy. However, labor's return to a position of insider power created fissures with community partners that had powered its ascendance. This was most striking in tensions with housing activists around post-Staples CBAs. In the Grand Avenue CBA campaign, although labor representatives in the CRA pushed hard for affordable housing in the downtown luxury project, the unions themselves balked at coalition membership, prompting housing advocates in subsequent CBAs to move forward without labor backing (and, in the Farmers Field CBA, over labor's objection). Although labor leaders have continued to search for common ground with housing advocates—for example, supporting a sweeping 2016 city initiative, Measure JJJ, attaching affordable housing and prevailing wage requirements to high-density development—the building trades in particular remain ardent supporters of a high-end housing construction boom that has made Los Angeles one of the most expensive housing markets in the United States. While the renaissance of organized labor in local politics has produced meaningful gains for workers and ongoing policy influence, it has also accentuated power dynamics at the heart of the complex relationship between labor and its multifaceted community partners that has defined the long struggle for Los Angeles.

Theoretical Implications

This book has presented a contemporary history of legal mobilization in Los Angeles that stands on its own terms as a powerful testament to how innovative advocacy can advance equality in a profoundly unequal city. It has also, through this history, aspired to draw out lessons for scholars working in intersecting fields touched by the L.A. campaigns: lawyering, labor, and local government law. This last part explores those lessons in more depth, drawing theoretical attention to how they inform critical normative aspirations within each field—the possibility of reviving progressive lawyering to address the challenges of neoliberalism, rehabilitating federal labor law to contest economic inequality, and reimagining local government law as a catalyst for national reform.

Lawyers: Rethinking Legal Liberalism in Neoliberal Times

Accounts of progressive lawyers mobilizing for social change, try as they might to escape the critical legacy of Civil Rights era lawyering—packaged under the label of "legal liberalism"—are inevitably overtaken by its gravitational pull.[35] Within the legal liberal frame, lawyers are made to answer for their representational and tactical choices, and held up against standards of community empowerment and democratic transformation that have defined "critical legal consciousness" over the past generation.[36] Against these standards, progressive lawyers are often viewed skeptically: too quick to make decisions for marginalized clients (the critique of lawyer *accountability*) and too eager to resolve problems by turning to court (the critique of legal *efficacy*).

Drawing on interdisciplinary insights from law and social science, this book's comparative institutional approach has sought to reappraise progressive lawyers by situating them in the wider field of social movement politics, in which their actions can be evaluated in relation to available alternatives. Doing so casts empirical doubt on strong versions of the legal liberal critiques, while also raising important theoretical questions about the meaning of legal liberalism itself. These questions are already being interrogated by scholars who suggest that, before and during the Civil Rights movement, progressive lawyers did not naively pursue the "hollow hope" of court-centered reform, but rather were guided by complex visions of social change.[37] Even this scholarship, however, by seeking to distance civil rights lawyering from legal liberalism's foundational critiques, implicitly accepts their force, rather than attempting to defend the legal liberal project itself. Yet such a defense seems crucial, especially in the current political moment, in which attacks on progressive lawyers feed into broader conservative assaults on technical expertise, government regulation, and even the rule of law itself—reinforcing the turn to neoliberal (and increasingly illiberal) policy. From this perspective, rather than viewing legal liberalism in relation to the (historically exaggerated) turn to courts by progressive lawyers, one might begin to understand it in more nuanced terms as the use of law to bend government policy back in progressive directions.

A key goal of legal liberalism in this view is to restore (and ultimately enlarge) redistributive and regulatory functions of government degraded by neoliberalism. In contrast to romantic progressive accounts of community mobilization outside structures of government power, this vision *centers the state* as a site of legal contestation and views changes in economic policy as a critical focus of progressive struggle in an era of spiraling inequality. It therefore draws attention to the crucial importance of lawyers working with social movements to generate and codify new meanings of equality under law. From this perspective, liberal lawyers are reconceived as inheritors of the positive legacy of egalitarian state-building, from the New Deal through the Civil Rights era, in which they act as architects of equality: using technical skill to translate social movement claims into legal regimes that empower marginalized communities. This new vision of legal liberalism, in short, rejects outmoded critiques of lawyers, calling instead for a renovated theory of lawyer accountability and legal efficacy in support of movements for progressive reform in contemporary American politics.

Accountability

The legal liberal critique of lawyer accountability has centered on the risk to client and community autonomy posed by activist lawyers' pursuit of social change.[38] The basic critical claim is that, by substituting their own vision of justice for that of groups they purport to represent, progressive lawyers reproduce the very disempowerment they seek to contest.[39] The most forceful articulation of this critique was

Derrick Bell's contention that NAACP lawyers in school desegregation cases engaged in conflicts of interest—"serving two masters"—by pressing integration over the objections of black families who preferred to improve the quality of existing schools.[40] Underlying this account was a vision of client control articulated in professional terms (the lawyer, as agent, should follow goals set by the client, as principal[41]), alongside an implicit critique of race and class privilege: lawyers advancing integration were middle-class, many white, pursuing their own visions of what was good for the black community.

This critique of lawyer accountability expressed a strong admonition against what lawyers should *not* do—override client control in contexts where it would undermine group interests. But it offered weak guidance on how lawyers *should* act in large-scale campaigns for "policy impact,"[42] in which client control in the conventional sense is not feasible or even desirable, either because group interests are not unified or because individual clients might prefer their own short-term gain over long-term group benefits. In such campaigns, lawyers are asked to play multiple roles in which agency-based notions of client control are inapt: (1) articulating and advancing a conception of group interests in situations where the group is not yet mobilized around an issue and there is no existing organizational infrastructure to do so; (2) working in a strategic capacity with existing social movement organizations to execute campaigns in institutional arenas (like regulatory agencies) in which lawyers do not account to specific clients in traditional control relationships; and (3) filing lawsuits conceived as part of an overarching reform plan in which the political outcome is more important than individual redress. Although these roles raise distinctive challenges, they all require the exercise of judgment under conditions of extreme uncertainty where the stakes are high—judgment that inevitably empowers certain group interests over others and must be made across chasms of privilege. Political scientists have argued that, in such contexts, the question should not be whether representation meets professional standards of control, but whether it meets political standards of legitimacy achieved through sustained engagement with group stakeholders that incorporates dissent into responsive policy demands.[43] The legal liberal critique misses this critical insight by defining the accountability problem exclusively in relation to professional standards governing *lawyers* and thereby confining assessment of accountability to the client's power of control *within* the lawyer–client relationship itself.

In contrast, the comparative institutional approach taken in this book, by illuminating the range of representative relationships within social movement campaigns, pushes away from the legal liberal preoccupation with lawyer accountability by permitting appraisal of alternative structures of representation and how well they advance group interests. Doing so underscores the crucial point that the accountability problem in complex, policy-oriented campaigns is *transprofessional*. Indeed, a central lesson from this book is that the challenge of accountable leadership *cuts across different forms of representation*—legal, political, and social movement—and *there is no reason to presume that lawyers are any worse, or any better, than nonlawyers in exercising it*. For its part, the legal liberal critique assumes that there are unique problems with professional training, asymmetrical expertise, and ethical duties that make lawyers ill-suited to effective representation in social movements.[44] And while it is true that lawyers can more easily enter and influence movements by filing lawsuits, and that professional obligations to maintain confidences and avoid conflicts impose special barriers to collaboration, what emerges from this book's analysis is that lawyers are no more prone to unresponsive representation than nonlawyers. Organizers can and do sometimes overreach and make what turn out to be suboptimal decisions based on insufficient community engagement. Acknowledging this fact, and incorporating it as part of the baseline against which lawyer representation is judged, reveals the accountability problem to be less about the specific limits of legal professionalism and more about the general dilemmas of social movement leadership.[45]

In Los Angeles, leaders seeking to represent marginalized communities across campaigns all faced the inherent challenge of "serving two masters." Just as APALC lawyers, funded by private philanthropy, made decisions about which companies to sue to promote garment industry transformation in light of their own normative commitment to integrated advocacy, so too did Garment Worker Center organizers make decisions about which companies to organize against—or whether to organize at all—in the context of their own funding constraints and ideological commitment to popular education. In the Wal-Mart and ports campaigns, labor leaders, many of whom were *not* lawyers, made crucial decisions about goals and strategies in a context in which coalition funding came primarily from organized labor, which was motivated to build union density. In the ports campaign, in particular, labor leaders' decision to pursue truck and employee conversion as legally severable components of the Clean Truck Program had negative consequences when the program failed in court, as drivers were forced to purchase expensive new low-emission vehicles without the economic benefits of employee status promised by the campaign. This campaign decision—made on behalf of, but without systematic input by, drivers on the policy details—highlights how self-motivated leaders can make good faith policy judgments that produce bad results for those they seek to help.

Just as comparative institutional analysis shifts assessment of accountability away from a singular focus on lawyers, it also broadens appreciation of the range of factors contributing to accountability beyond the lawyer–client relationship— thereby drawing attention to the *structural determinants of accountability*. Legal scholars, again by virtue of their focus on individual lawyer agency in relation to professional rules, often overlook how structural factors influence the meaning of legal representation: applying an abstract conception of control divorced from the context in which legal mobilization takes place.[46] Yet, as the L.A. campaigns show, context matters profoundly in evaluating the legitimacy of lawyers' representational choices.

In evaluating context, theorists have largely focused on representational legitimacy from an *institutional* perspective, arguing that legitimacy is promoted when leaders advance goals that are consistent with core values of the institutions within which representation occurs. As Mark Aaronson observes, in democratic institutions, like legislative or administrative bodies, built on values of inclusion and participation, "group legal representation" is legitimate when it "facilitates the influence of otherwise unrepresented or underrepresented interests."[47] In the litigation context, David Luban posits that models of legal representation fall along a spectrum running from direct delegation from strong clients to "best-world" representation—a "last resort" in which lawyers make "unilateral decisions and value choices" to pursue institutionally legitimate goals when more direct mechanisms of client control are not feasible.[48]

While it is useful to look to broad institutional values to justify representational choices, legitimacy also derives from more granular sources that are equally, if not more, important. Significantly, the *organizational* context in which representation occurs can build in mechanisms of accountability that orient lawyer behavior toward collectively defined goals and limit the potential for domination or deviation. As the earlier discussion of integrated leadership showed, even in contexts of weak or nonexistent client control, L.A. movement lawyers self-consciously sought to promote structural accountability to campaigns through deliberate choices about the design of the campaigns' organizational architecture. Operating within the bounds of professional rules on confidentiality and conflicts, these efforts allowed lawyers to coordinate individual cases with broader political mobilization in the immigrant rights campaigns, while promoting the formal organization of disadvantaged groups into community–labor coalitions that could be effective protagonists in the pursuit of local policy reform. In both instances, movement lawyers established sustained relationships with social movement partners that promoted community monitoring and responded to accountability problems associated with legal liberalism.[49]

Just as it is shaped by organizational factors, accountability is also influenced by the ideals and backgrounds that individual lawyers bring to the representation. In exercising discretion to make choices for client groups, legal scholars stress the importance of moral character and judgment, and emphasize that legal education should do more to inculcate judgment in order to promote ethical lawyering in the public good.[50] Yet this focus on judgment can obscure other individual characteristics that may be more important in ensuring accountability, including the lawyer's own ideological approach. The lawyers in this book came of age in the legal academy at a time of critical reaction against legal liberalism and many were steeped in approaches to progressive lawyering, built on critical theory and clinical pedagogy, that emphasized client deference and community empowerment.[51] The principles movement lawyers used to guide their roles thus foregrounded concerns about accountability that shaped how their representation was received by clients and judged by other campaign stakeholders. As a result, lawyers throughout the L.A. campaigns distinguished themselves as effective stewards of marginalized group interests precisely because of their critical training and community-based sensibilities. As the earlier analysis of legal endowment highlights, effective stewardship also grew out of lawyers' individual experiences and cultural backgrounds, which often fostered shared understandings and identity-based solidarity that gave lawyers more space to act in what they understood as the community interest.

On the flip side, the L.A. campaigns caution against placing too much weight on identity-based affiliation as a basis for representational legitimacy. As suggested in the context of Bell's "serving two masters"—a deliberately racialized conception of the accountability problem—the failure of white liberal leadership in struggles by communities of color has been an important theme in critical accounts of legal liberal lawyers.[52] However, while identity-based affiliation is an important foundation for solidarity, it is not decisive—and sometimes obscures other dynamics, either by presuming effective representation by virtue of racial affiliation or assigning representational failure to lack of racial sensitivity. Time and again, the movement for economic justice in Los Angeles featured lawyers representing groups across racial lines—at times mobilizing against members of their own group. This intersectional lawyering occurred most prominently in the anti-sweatshop campaign, in which APALC lawyers deliberately chose cases permitting them to represent Latina garment workers against Asian American contract shop owners in order to build cross-racial class identity. Cross-racial representation was central in the community–labor campaigns as well: three white women negotiated a groundbreaking CBA on behalf of a mostly Latino community in the Figueroa Corridor; Jerilyn López Mendoza, a Latina lawyer, represented the successful LAX CBA coalition anchored in predominantly African American communities; and the mostly white male Teamsters leadership led a campaign that challenged misclassification on behalf of Latino truck drivers at the Port of Los Angeles.

As these experiences suggest, effective representation in transformative struggles against systems of power may depend less on client control and more on lawyer-client solidarity. Particularly as movements like the one for economic justice in Los Angeles confront sophisticated and well-resourced opponents that fund their own lawyers to redefine law in neoliberal terms, movement lawyers fighting back must be empowered to make difficult judgments in designing long-term strategy and exercise discretion to respond to short-term challenges. As they do, movement lawyers' contributions should be valued on equal terms as those of nonlawyers, judged against the metric of responsible representation and human fallibility, not an aspirational standard of empowerment to which other leaders are not held. This metric should incorporate how active community members are in devising movement goals, how open the process for exchange and dissent is, and how transparent and responsive leaders are in making choices. And evaluation under these criteria should account for the more difficult burden *progressive* lawyers, in particular, must face in exercising leadership: asked to balance the need to centralize authority to make decisive judgments against a progressive value system that places a premium on decentralizing power by uplifting voices from below.

Efficacy

In addition to building a deeper understanding of lawyer accountability, the lessons from this book help rethink legal liberalism by providing a new perspective on the efficacy of legal mobilization. Within the legal liberal tradition, the critique of law as a vehicle of social change has revolved around three central claims: first, that court mandates are difficult to enforce and thus prone to erode over time;[53] second, that court decisions asserting bold policy changes are likely to provoke countermobilization and, in extreme cases, popular backlash;[54] and third, that repackaging movement claims in the language of law coopts a movement's transformative ambition and props up the legitimacy of an unjust system by buying into formal principles of individual rights that obscure structural barriers to equality.[55] By framing the efficacy problem in relation to the limits of *law*, the legal liberal critique confines its target to the deficits of litigation and courts—captured in Stuart Scheingold's famous indictment of the "myth of rights"[56]—and narrows assessment of law to its effects on building extra-legal power and leveraging policy gains in nonlegal arenas. Embedded in this critique is a notion of legal exceptionalism— that there are unique problems with law as a social change tool that do not infect other forms of mobilization—coupled with an implicit argument in favor of the superiority of nonlegal alternatives—mobilization *outside* of court, in the streets and through politics—in producing sustainable, culture-shifting change.[57] This book's comparative institutional approach, by drawing on interdisciplinary research showing parallel constraints on nonlegal challenges to power,[58] reorients the legal liberal fixation on law's limits by widening the scope of evaluation to permit relative comparison with other tools of social change.

Doing so invites reconsideration of each dimension of the legal liberal critique—enforcement, countermobilization, and cooptation—by highlighting the *transubstantive* nature of the efficacy problem. As this chapter's earlier analysis of policy implementation in the L.A. campaigns demonstrated, there are substantial barriers to the enforcement of rules resulting from social movement action *irrespective of the venue through which rule change occurs*. This does not mean that all rule change confronts identical enforcement problems. The effectiveness of different levers of reform depends on context. Litigation works well in knocking out government regulation that allows private market action, as in the day labor litigation.[59] It works less well when it hinges on bureaucratic enforcement of rules resisted by private interests in case-by-case fights, as the garment campaign underscores.[60] Yet a crucial takeaway from this book is that litigation is not unique in its inability to achieve sustained reform of complicated systems dominated by powerful actors. To the contrary, a key lesson is that *any* policy change that seeks to benefit marginalized groups—whether it occurs through legislation (A.B. 633), regulation (CRA rules), or contract (CBAs)—regularly stumbles at the level of implementation given the complexity of regulatory systems and the strength of opponents' tools of resistance. In struggles for redistributive reform, enforcement gaps are the rule, not the exception.

Just as enforcement falters irrespective of the institutional channel through which it flows, countermobilization surges to contest movement gains in whichever institutional venue they are achieved. In the L.A. campaigns, highly mobilized opponents challenged *every* movement advance by low-wage worker advocates— not simply those proceeding through court. Countermobilization was expressed in different forms and levels of intensity depending on context. Although opponents did not succeed in sparking widespread political backlash against the L.A. struggle overall, they did manage to conjure significant forces of resistance in particular cases. In the day labor campaign, business interests aligned with xenophobic groups to pressure local governments to engage in enforcement crackdowns and mobilized counterprotests against day laborers who litigated for their rights. Similarly, in the ports campaign, trucking firms sought to galvanize opposition to the Clean Truck Program among those independent contractors who claimed to prefer their non-employee status: turning out contractor drivers at public meetings to advance industry interests. In all cases of countermobilization, industry actors were deeply advantaged by their ability to use law backed by power. Opponents could move from one domain to another in order to thwart movement efforts or circumvent rules in a game of "whack-a-mole": when the ports campaign won local policy reform, industry went to federal court to prevail; when the grocery coalition stopped Wal-Mart big-box stores in Los Angeles, the company opened a smaller store in Chinatown; when MALDEF won a ban of anti-solicitation ordinances, cities drafted smarter ordinances to avoid the legal ruling or ramped up enforcement of preexisting traffic laws. As this suggests, across campaigns for economic reform, countermobilization does not emerge in episodic fashion, particularly attracted to one type of movement win over another. Rather, it is an intrinsic feature of contentious politics[61]—in symbiotic relationship with social movement success.

Similarly, endemic in social movements is the potential for political cooptation, which cuts across modes of advocacy. A central claim of critical legal scholars was that rights-based legal mobilization was especially prone to reinforce the legitimacy of liberal individualism in ways that conflicted with deeper equality claims.[62] And there is certainly evidence from this book in support of this critical view. Specifically, in the day labor campaign after the failed Agoura Hills case, lawyers deliberately opted for a more moderate, less controversial legal argument—basing anti-solicitation lawsuits on day laborers' free speech rights rather than discrimination—in order to maximize the potential for success in front of a conservative judiciary. This rankled some in the movement, who preferred to make stronger normative claims attacking racism in the public sphere. Yet this book provides evidence for a broader critical point, which is that *any* mobilization challenging powerful interests, whether it occurs through legal or political channels, can operate to legitimate the status quo by using normative frames aligned with mainstream values and accepting political compromise that can deradicalize movements.[63] Indeed, framing choices in the L.A. campaigns often sought to draw attention *away* from more radical appeals: in the garment campaign, emphasizing the elimination of egregious abuse ("modern day slavery") on which all could agree in ways that obscured more controversial structural demands for improving conditions for average workers; and in the community–labor campaigns, elevating claims of environmental and housing justice, while submerging the radical potential of union organizing. These choices were politically astute, but nonetheless deliberately cautious. In a similar vein, political compromise was a pervasive feature of reform efforts, curtailing the transformative scope of policy through the political process: Notably, policy compromise resulted in ceding a private right of action in the statewide garment manufacturer liability and willful misclassification laws, while giving up mandatory community benefits and big-box regulations for site-specific economic impact review.

While the comparative institutional approach broadens evaluation of efficacy beyond the legal liberal focus on law, it also expands the meaning of *what counts as law* in the first instance: pushing analysis outside the domain of litigation and courts, and thus reframing the relationship between law and other forms of social movement activism. Viewing law through this wider lens makes two important contributions to legal mobilization theory.[64] First, decentering litigation highlights the crucial, yet theoretically underappreciated, roles that lawyers play *behind the scenes* in creating new legal knowledge and thus reorients evaluation of legal impact toward understanding how such knowledge contributes to the design and outcome of policy campaigns. Second, this wider perspective, while providing an important corrective to legal liberalism's overemphasis on litigation, simultaneously draws theoretical attention to the multifaceted ways in which litigation *does* continue to play central—though often nontraditional—roles in reform campaigns: offensively, as one piece of larger integrated campaigns to win policy, and defensively, as an important tool to resist opponents' legal challenges to undo those victories.

As to the first point, pulling the curtain back on the L.A. campaigns reveals how lawyers integrate legal and community knowledge in policy design, and then mobilize that knowledge in advancing policy through the political process. In the private law context, scholars have noted that, as legal processes and institutions are broken down into more discrete parts, lawyers add value by assimilating information about complicated systems.[65] The L.A. campaigns spotlight similar dynamics in the public law domain. As political governance becomes increasingly fragmented and specialized, a significant part of what movement lawyers do involves *integrating knowledge across disciplines and institutions in order to create solutions to complex problems*. Specifically, by nesting labor policy in local government law frameworks not precisely created for it, lawyers engage in a form of legal triage in which new regulatory regimes are assembled from different legal materials. Lawyers do this by weaving together legal rules from distinct substantive areas into innovative regulatory fabrics that bolster labor rights (using zoning rules to require economic impact reports or to promote the development of day labor organizing sites), or by leveraging legal opportunities in one institution (agency-level environmental review) to advance goals in another (establishing living wage provisions in CBAs or creating legislative space for the Clean Truck Program). This integrative role requires movement lawyers to be interdisciplinary thinkers—seeing the possibility for legal synergies across formally disconnected legal areas—while also assessing risks that reliance on interdisciplinary strategies for labor rights will backfire (as they did in the Campaign for Clean Trucks). In deploying these triage strategies, lawyers with integrative knowledge oversee a complex division of labor, linking together legal specialists with knowledge specific to one element of the problem (such as filing environmental challenges or analyzing labor preemption), whose involvement is episodic but no less consequential. This integrative role further requires that movement lawyers work with other lawyers across the public and private sectors: for example, in the ports campaign, engaging with government lawyers asked to draft and sign off on the validity of the Clean Truck Program, and collaborating with corporate lawyers called in as outside counsel to defend the program against attack.

Tracing legal development behind the scenes of movement campaigns also provides new insight on how lawyers synthesize community knowledge in *designing policy from the ground up*. In the L.A. movement, ad hoc legal victories responding to specific community grievances served as a foundation to build out more systematic policy: CBAs and the Inglewood site fight generated the legal template for citywide policy, just as A.B. 633 codified principles underlying anti-sweatshop litigation. In these cases, by addressing community concerns *first*, movement lawyers generated the fact base and regulatory expertise that permitted them to appreciate what provisions needed to be included in broader policy to effectively address underlying problems, while strengthening lawyers' credibility by allowing them to point to previous legal success as precedent demonstrating that reform could produce positive results. In the policy development process, lawyers also played crucial information-transfer roles by designing coalition governance structures that took seriously the input of community members, who contributed important features of campaign policy—such as the Clean Truck Program provision barring port trucks from parking in residential areas, which was a source of community irritation. These efforts to incorporate community knowledge into formal policy tailors legal solutions to problems defined by community members, while also giving policy greater legitimacy in their eyes. As this shows, law did not "belong" exclusively to the L.A. movement lawyers—community members were instrumental in creating legal meaning through protests on the street and input into policy design. However, the meaning of law was democratized not just because nonlawyers wrested it away, but also because the movement lawyers themselves were committed to the democratization project.

Looking behind the scenes of the lawyering process further underscores how some of the most influential work that lawyers do in movement campaigns involves developing new legal theories and mobilizing them in strategy discussions and policy processes to facilitate their enactment. This was particularly true in the community–labor campaigns in which lawyers had to amass sophisticated knowledge of city contracting, land use approval, and project finance systems in order to draft policies redesigning those systems to enhance conditions for low-wage workers. Crucially, once a new policy was designed, legal expertise was needed to vouch for the policy's validity as an essential predicate for advancing through the gauntlet of political decision-making. This was again evident in the Campaign for Clean Trucks, where lawyers had to shepherd policy through administrative agency review: drafting legal opinions supporting the authority of cities to require employee conversion under the market participant exception to federal preemption. Those opinions provided legal legitimacy, giving city officials confidence that if they spent political capital on passing the Clean Truck Program, there was a credible chance it would be upheld in court.

That the Clean Truck Program was not ultimately upheld spotlights this book's second important contribution to legal mobilization theory: Although litigation matters profoundly in campaigns for progressive reform, it often does so in ways that break from conventional understandings and therefore calls for new thinking on evaluating its role. Across the campaigns, litigation was never conceived as a solution to the problem of low-wage work; yet it was nonetheless an essential piece of every struggle, whether as a threat to be planned around and defended against, or an affirmative tool within a broader framework of integrated advocacy.

From a defensive standpoint, as the ports campaign highlights, even as movement lawyers attempt to avoid litigation they must nonetheless anticipate the grounds on which opponents might mount a legal challenge, seek to prospectively minimize the risk of loss, and defend against legal challenge when it comes. That they sometimes lose such a challenge despite taking careful steps to avoid it underscores the uncertainty of such defensive strategies in the face of doctrinal ambiguity and ideological variation among judges. Defensive litigation is also crucial in campaigns that rely on protest. In addition to defending protesters criminally charged with breaking the law, in the legalized arena of social movement conflict, movement lawyers can also be called on to defend protesters from civil defamation lawsuits designed to shut down legitimate boycotts—such as that filed by Forever 21 against garment workers and activists in the final phase of the anti-sweatshop campaign.

When affirmative litigation *is* a key campaign feature, movement lawyers view it as *a tactic not a strategy*—integrated into a larger plan rather than an end in itself. On the front end of movement campaigns, lawyers design litigation in relation to other modes of advocacy—especially organizing and public relations—to exert coordinated pressure on litigation targets as part of an integrated approach. In the anti-sweatshop campaign, impact cases were coordinated with media and protests, like the Forever 21 boycott, to place additional pressure on garment companies. A similar strategy was used by NDLON and MALDEF, which—after a lawsuit was filed—would stage a public event, marching from the day labor site to city hall to attract press attention. At the back end of campaigns, the tactical use of litigation anticipates enforcement problems and seeks to proactively address them. The failure of garment workers to recover against employers led lawyers in 2007 to launch a new organization, Wage Justice, dedicated to using "innovative legal theories and legal tools borrowed from commercial collections law" to collect "back wages and penalties owed to low-income workers."[66] Wage Justice, in turn, anchored the new Los Angeles Coalition Against Wage Theft,[67] which produced groundbreaking reports documenting the extent of wage theft in Los Angeles,[68] and successfully lobbied for local wage enforcement divisions.[69] The critical point is that, in movement campaigns, affirmative litigation constitutes an essential part of the overall strategic plan, the impact of which should be evaluated as a whole.

In the final analysis, evaluating the efficacy of legal mobilization ultimately turns on the meaning of "success,"[70] which is a contested idea that shifts over time in reaction to events. The book's ground-level view reveals that, while substantive outcomes matter profoundly, the process by which those outcomes are achieved is also crucial. Who has a voice in shaping movement choices is a fundamental part of the legitimacy of the choices themselves—and in long-term social change cycles, legitimacy is essential to sustain commitment and adapt to setbacks. Reflecting back on the highs and lows of the L.A. movement for economic justice over a two-decade-long arc of monumental struggle calls into question the very notion of success and failure as useful concepts, pointing instead to the value of more limited, fine-grained analyses of how law and politics interact, for better or worse, at particular moments. For scholars moving forward to undertake such analyses, the lessons derived from this book's approach suggest five final points to consider.

First, by spotlighting the inseparability of legal and political action, the book questions the utility of evaluating outcomes in terms of the direct versus indirect impacts of law on politics. Scholars in the sociolegal tradition have thoroughly developed this line of impact analysis, differentiating between legal outcomes that directly modify the behavior of officials in charge of implementing policy and those that indirectly affect public attitudes, spark grassroots mobilization, or raise legal consciousness.[71] However, this division is problematic. For one, it assesses direct enforcement against an unrealistic standard of full compliance. Policy that falls short is deemed unsuccessful—even though, as this chapter has suggested, enforcement gaps are the norm not the exception. More significantly, the direct–indirect impact division obscures the complex relationship of law and politics in integrated campaigns seeking, for example, to use organizing to promote the enforcement of legal rights (as worker-led protests sought to do in the anti-sweatshop case) or to use litigation to leverage reforms with their own internal enforcement mechanisms (as with CBAs or the Clean Truck Program).

Second, impact analysis should attend more carefully to the appropriate baseline for assessment. Social movement campaigns are not similarly situated with respect to the power they wield or the tools at their disposal. Accordingly, campaign success—in both the litigation and policy arenas—must be judged against a benchmark that accounts for preexisting political and legal resources. The political vulnerability of immigrant workers made litigation a crucial strategy in the antisweatshop and day labor cases, but also set the limits of what could be achieved. Particularly for undocumented immigrants, there was ultimately little law could do for a class of workers defined as formally outside its scope. Antecedent legal and political strength also shaped outcomes in the community–labor campaigns. Because environmental partners in the ports coalition started from a position of relative legal strength—using environmental legal challenges to stop development—they wielded greater power in the policymaking process. The labor movement sought to build on that power to change the status of drivers, but ultimately labor's legal weakness undercut its cause as courts held that it was only the port's interest in stopping environmental lawsuits that had legal significance in avoiding preemption.

The third point to consider in assessing legal impact is that countermobilization is not evenly distributed. An opponent's resources, sophistication, and ferocity affect how far movements can advance in particular cases. Moreover, opponents do not treat all parties in coalition-based campaigns similarly, but rather may seek to strategically cleave coalitions apart. This happened in the big-box campaign, where Wal-Mart paid off local civil rights groups to support its store, and in the ports campaign, where the trucking industry capitulated to environmental demands in order to sharpen its attack on labor.

Fourth, because local campaigns are connected through leaders and resources, evaluation should consider adaptive processes through which lessons learned in one campaign's failure are mobilized to achieve success in another. In Los Angeles, CBA advocates could not win a citywide community benefits policy, but the anti-Wal-Mart coalition was able to build on its template to pass the Superstores Ordinances' economic impact framework. The ports campaign failed to win employee status for drivers, but the Teamsters succeeded in crafting a local policy promoting employee status for waste truck haulers and unionizing that sector. Tracing these interconnections is essential to telling the whole story of social change.

Understanding the role of adaptation in waves of social movement contention links to the fifth and final dimension of evaluative analysis: time. Ultimately, the types of legal, policy, and culture-shifting projects illustrated by the L.A. campaigns are dynamic and iterative. They play out over multiple cycles in complex ways that can never be fully predicted or mapped out. What looks like failure at one point, turns into success at another—and vice versa. This book has spotlighted how lawyers respond to these dynamics: as facts to be studied, understood, planned for, and (when things do not go as planned) revised. Instead of viewing success as advancing policy change that constitutes a decisive victory, movement lawyers appreciate that struggle is an unending process in which wins must be defended and extended over time.

Labor: Reforming Low-Wage Work in the Age of Affluence

Just as this book's account of local legal mobilization raises fundamental questions about the role of lawyers in contemporary social movements, so too does its focus on low-wage work draw attention to the current relevance and possible future of American labor law. The book's temporal focus—tracing the labor movement's response to deindustrialization and the ascent of the service economy in Los Angeles—precisely tracks the scholarly response to the same structural transformation, which has interrogated the legal and economic underpinnings of the labor movement's decline, while putting forth strategies for labor law's revitalization.[72] In this literature, scholars disillusioned with well-documented barriers to unionization posed by federal labor law have looked for inspiration in local struggle. Following the trend of mining social movements for radical reconceptions of law,[73] scholars have sought to map the future of labor law based on practices of the labor movement that have demonstrated signs, no matter how small or localized, of success. At one level, this book follows in this tradition. By providing close accounts of local legal mobilization, when it succeeds, and how it reshapes labor law in the process, the book enshrines a process of social movement-driven "labor law renewal" from the "bottom up."[74] Building on this lineage, a central contribution of the book is to document the architecture of local labor-enhancing regulation that may serve as a model for other cities—and from which may be derived a template for national-level reform should the political opportunity arise.

Yet the book goes beyond documentation to address theoretical problems at the heart of debate over the role of labor law in the future of the American labor movement. A central claim in this debate is that the federal labor law paradigm, codified in the NLRA, is "failing,"[75] which raises the question of whether it should be defended, revised, or scrapped.[76] Responding to this question, Kate Andrias has promoted a "new labor law"—illustrated in efforts like the Fight for $15—which moves beyond the NLRA system of private bargaining with individual employers to embrace strategies that reimagine unions as "political actors" enlisting state and local government in a process of "social bargaining" oriented toward broad policy reform that takes wages out of competition in a sector.[77] This book's account of Los Angeles's community–labor campaigns resonates with this approach: providing an inside view of sectoral organizing that mobilizes local government law to reset rules of the game within regionally sticky service industries where unionization may potentially occur.

However, by tracing the longer arc of "labor activism in local politics,"[78] the history presented in this book also provides a critical perspective on the claim that local labor struggle, both as a descriptive and normative matter, contains a vision of labor law that transcends the framework inherited from the New Deal. Rather, this history cautions against neat dichotomies: between old and new paradigms of labor law, private and public bargaining frameworks, labor and nonlabor law regimes, and the economic and political roles of unions. Instead of marking a rupture with the past, the L.A. campaigns reveal an essential continuity: demonstrating the labor movement's sustained effort to engage in politics in order to establish legal rules of the game—at all levels of government—that allow unions to organize in favor of better working conditions.

The Resilience of Labor Law

Looking to Los Angeles for signs of labor law's future, one is struck by how much the "new" labor law aspires to operate a lot like the "old." Indeed, a critical through line of this book is not the "failure" or "ossification" of traditional labor law,[79] but rather its *resilience*: specifically, the ability of the labor movement to adapt the traditional paradigm to respond to ongoing threats and to devise legal pathways to advance the NLRA's core principles in the face of implacable employer opposition. Key to this idea of resilience is the notion that federal labor law actually works well when unions are permitted to play the role originally envisioned by the act—which explains why the NLRA has been subjected to systematic employer efforts to undermine it. Much of what the labor movement has done in response to these employer efforts has been to design legal alternatives to return unions to the basic ground rules of collective bargaining established by federal law. These alternatives have involved private ordering, such as card-check neutrality agreements, supplemented (and often enabled) by state and local law designed to create conditions of possibility for organizing.[80] As the CBA, Wal-Mart, and ports campaigns in this book illustrate, when organized labor has succeeded in building union density in Los Angeles, it has been by clearing out the legal impediments to effective organizing that have been created by employer opposition and then using federal labor law to win collective bargaining agreements.

This does not mean that the existing federal framework should be clung to without modification. But it does illuminate legal dynamics that argue against the narrative of labor law's "failure" and the idea that the federal framework should be jettisoned in favor of radically different labor regimes—even if such regimes were politically feasible. Rather, the L.A. campaigns spotlight how the labor movement's legal approach to unionization necessarily turns on developing effective counters to corporate strategies to undermine and avoid federal labor law. The key point is that these counters do not constitute inherent defects in labor law, but rather demonstrate the power of employer interests to effectuate labor law avoidance strategies *no matter what the formal rules of labor law say*. Put differently, rather than viewing the decline of the labor movement as a product of *law's failure*, it is more accurate to think of it in terms of the *success of the anti-labor movement*—which has far more resources and power at its disposal—in distorting law's aims, exploiting its gaps, and using corporate influence over politics to rewrite the legal rules of work in ways that undercut unionization. From this perspective, the labor movement's responses—like card-check neutrality agreements or local minimum wage ordinances—are not "outside" of labor law,[81] but *part of its essential architecture*.

This book demonstrates how this legal architecture develops in response to multipronged corporate avoidance strategies. On top of underscoring the well-documented point that employers circumvent unionization by abusing the NLRA election process through intimidation, propaganda, and retaliation, the book also brings to light other legal mechanisms used by companies to unravel work relationships and intensify labor marginality. Most significantly, it shows how corporate interests have used political and legal strategies to move workers, as Noah Zatz describes, outside the "reach or grasp" of labor law altogether.[82] Central to these strategies is the pervasive expansion of *contracting relationships* that separate economic power from legal responsibility—creating legal "fissures" that make it difficult to enforce basic labor standards and even harder to engage in collective action.[83]

As the L.A. experience illustrates, these contracting relationships are a product of corporate legal maneuvering around labor law—which invites legal responses by the labor movement to reset baseline rules. In practice, contracting reflects a range of distinct corporate strategies for moving work outside of the firm, and often beyond state control, in order to impose legal barriers to rights enforcement and unionization. In one contracting model, work is transferred to different companies within the supply chain, although workers retain their formal status as employees. This is what has occurred in the garment industry, where large manufacturing companies have contracted out central aspects of work to smaller shops with fewer workers; these shops are forced to take the price offered by large players and eke out profit by slashing labor standards. They attract precarious workers, often with multiple barriers to employment (including immigration status), which make them reluctant to complain about labor abuse. Workers in these shops are not formally outside of labor law, but practically speaking, the barriers to enforcement and collective action are so significant as to undermine enforcement and prevent organizing.

The other model of contracting out, increasingly prevalent in relation to the so-called gig economy, is the transfer of work outside firms altogether by reclassifying (and, in the labor movement's view, misclassifying) workers as independent contractors. This model is deployed by trucking firms in the port drayage industry, which have used deregulation as a justification for converting unionized drivers into "owner-operators" denied all the protections and benefits of employee status—particularly, the right to organize, which independent contractors, as legal businesses, are precluded from doing under antitrust law.

Where labor could push back against contracting strategies, they have done so toward the goal of reestablishing the labor law status quo to facilitate union organizing. The garment campaign, for its part, succeeded in making retailers and manufacturers responsible for labor violations of their contractors as a matter of state *employment* law (governing individual worker rights), but were unable to reconstitute joint employment and triangular bargaining in the garment sector under *labor* law (governing worker collective action). In contrast, the ports campaign succeeded in convincing the labor board to treat misclassified drivers as statutory employees entitled to organize under federal labor law: setting the stage for the first labor contracts in the port trucking industry in nearly forty years. The unifying theme of these campaigns is their commitment to using state and local government law to reconstruct baseline employee status and firm-level responsibility disrupted by contracting in order to place back into motion federally protected union organizing.

Although this same strategy could not be used to address labor's other central challenge—the exclusion of workers from the protections of labor law by virtue of their immigration status—organized labor throughout this book made efforts to lay the groundwork for expanding labor law protections to immigrants at a future political moment. This was most evident in the AFL-CIO day labor National Partnership Agreement, which elevated worker centers to nonvoting member status on local labor boards, like the L.A. County Fed. Although this status could not confer formal labor protections, it constituted an important symbolic act demonstrating the labor movement's commitment to fighting for the legal inclusion of undocumented workers in the federal labor law system—and its faith that the federal system, properly implemented, could serve as a catalyst for immigrant worker organizing.

The Public Foundations of Private Ordering

As its response to the contracting problem highlights, the labor movement's turn to public law in support of local campaigns is *deliberately linked to private unionization strategies*. Organized labor's involvement in the CBA campaign provides one illustration. By using CBAs and CRA policy to apply the Living Wage Ordinance to tenants in city-subsidized projects, labor's ultimate goal was to use the ordinance's union opt-out to win collective bargaining agreements. Unionization, in other words, was not an incidental goal, but rather the *primary* aim (from organized labor's standpoint) of the CBA campaign—and of the broader living wage movement. As this underscores, public-facing sectoral strategies like those advanced by the L.A. community–labor campaigns do not represent an abandonment of traditional union approaches but rather an effort to revive their effectiveness. From this perspective, critics of traditional labor law present a false choice between social bargaining and firm-level bargaining. In fact, public law reform at the local level is an essential predicate to enable private ordering by creating new legal rules of the game within which traditional unionization can take place.

In this sense, there is an important distinction to be made between: (1) a collective bargaining strategy that asks the government to provide a *specific benefit* to a private employer in exchange for accepting labor peace, and (2) a broader political strategy of lobbying for passage of local laws—like community benefits policies, the Superstores Ordinances, and the Clean Truck Program—that *create conditions of possibility* for organizing. Exemplifying the first strategy, card-check neutrality is a private contract designed to address gaps in the federal labor system, which employers exploit to harass union organizers and delay organizing drives. Card-check requires employers to agree not to engage in such tactics, which levels the playing field and gives unions a stronger chance to win contracts. As scholars like Ben Sachs have shown, employers typically have to be induced to accept card-check or labor peace arrangements by government entities since unions have no independent power to cause employers to do so.[84] This is the origin of "tripartite" unionism, in which local government gives employers a benefit, such as a permit to operate, in exchange for card-check agreements that enable unions to bargain effectively.[85] This is an important strategy and one used to positive effect in the L.A. campaigns.

However, this model of tripartism must be distinguished from the broader effort to create labor-enhancing laws to take wages out of competition in a sector, as seen in this book's community–labor campaigns. This sectoral approach is continuous with a century of labor-backed local lawmaking in which unions seek state and local protections as a foundation for union organizing *but do not ask government to intervene in specific negotiations.* In the pre-New Deal era, the labor movement used state laws establishing minimum wage and other protections to create baseline rights to support unionization.[86] These laws were targeted by employers' freedom of contract claims in court, culminating in *Lochner v. New York,*[87] which placed the Supreme Court on the side of laissez faire capitalism and against the labor movement. Organized labor's success building power and passing federal labor law during the New Deal constituted the breakthrough moment—defeating Lochnerism by codifying a public law framework to promote private bargaining rights—but that moment was a high-water mark that quickly passed.

Organized labor confronts a historical moment with structural similarities to the *Lochner* era. In the contemporary political context, corporate interests are mobilizing a portfolio of federal laws—from the First Amendment to statutes governing arbitration and trucking regulation—to advance a New Lochnerism that seeks to enforce a stringent free market vision in which private contract trumps worker-protective standards. It is in this environment that organized labor has reverted back to its earlier strategy of establishing local legal frameworks to counteract this deregulatory push—and to use those frameworks to buttress core principles of federal labor law. This strategy creates new struggles over federal versus local power, which play out in relation to the legal terms of preemption.[88] From this point of view, labor's localism, rather than avoiding federal regulation and courts, merely changes the legal terms of struggle: forcing labor to thread a difficult needle by simultaneously defending local lawmaking against a hostile federal system, while ultimately depending on that system to effectuate union contracts.

That this effort has concentrated on contesting rising inequality in increasingly affluent big U.S. cities simply represents the newest frontier in the long history of struggle. In this struggle, the distinction between public and private bargaining blurs as labor advances a three-pronged local strategy. First, labor identifies legal changes in the nature of work, such as contracting out, that challenge the traditional union organizing model. Second, labor pinpoints local government law powers that give it leverage to address those challenges and pursues local reform to reestablish the legal foundations for union organizing. Third, with local legal changes in place, organized labor runs traditional organizing campaigns against employers through the NLRA system, using tools like card-check neutrality to prevent the types of abuse that are well-documented in the literature. This strategy necessarily depends on federal labor law and mobilization within the federal labor system to succeed. Therefore, rather than thinking of local strategies as promoting a public bargaining framework outside of the federal system, it is more apt to think of them as ultimately designed to bolster that system in ways that strengthen opportunities for unionization.

The Interdisciplinary Nature of Labor Law

In addition to revealing the public foundations of private bargaining, labor's turn to local lawmaking shows how labor law necessarily interacts with other legal regimes in ways that make any affirmative unionization strategy intrinsically interdisciplinary. This interdisciplinarity is both *tactical and substantive*. Tactically, labor groups turn to legal strategies—litigation and legislative initiatives—as a way to mobilize workers and enhance labor standards adjacent to the federal collective bargaining framework. Indeed, as the book has showed, legal strategies constitute an essential element of comprehensive labor campaigns, responding to the legal underpinnings of de-unionization and labor abuse. Critical scholars have cautioned that rights-based advocacy coopts labor struggle, arguing that the legalization of collective bargaining and the pursuit of rights-based employment claims have weakened the labor movement.[89] However, the L.A. campaigns mobilized rights as a pragmatic response to constraints on the traditional union organizing paradigm: for example, supporting misclassification litigation in an effort to restore port drivers to the baseline of employee status. Similarly, rather than coopting labor activism, local legislative initiatives, such as the Living Wage Ordinance, have established legal frameworks designed to incentivize bargaining in which labor groups can effectively negotiate benefits for workers.

Substantively, labor law's interdisciplinarity hinges on alternative legal frameworks to facilitate its aims. As the book documents, contemporary labor law has been inexorably pulled in two directions—both of which strengthen its foundations while also presenting significant trade-offs. In one direction, labor law, which governs collective bargaining, increasingly interacts with employment law, which governs individual worker rights.[90] While the line between these two legal regimes has long been blurry, the rise of contracting has pushed them together more forcefully because organizing under labor law depends on fortifying employment law concepts of joint employership and misclassification to succeed. Thus, mobilization to strengthen these concepts has become an essential element of local labor campaigns, which are forced to fight over the basic terms of employment status in order to reestablish the baseline right to organize.

Moving in a different direction, labor law has been pulled toward and melded with quite distinct regulatory regimes embedded in local land use law. Here, too, labor's interdisciplinarity adds legal strength while carrying trade-offs. To work, these local policies must avoid traditional labor and employment law, instead framing their objectives in terms that fit neatly within justifications for the exercise of local land use power. For example, the Superstores Ordinance was framed around eliminating economic "blight," while the Clean Truck Program emphasized the need for trucking firms to hire employee drivers as a way to internalize the costs of compliance with environmental regulation. While the benefits of this strategy have been made clear, the trade-offs have also been significant. Specifically, by nesting labor-enhancing policy in local laws framed around land use planning and environmental mitigation, such policy becomes accountable to a different set of legal standards that constrain its scope and may make it vulnerable to legal challenge (as in the case of the Clean Truck Program). As this suggests, labor's engagement with local land use law is both necessary in an era of federal constraint and second-best relative to restoring the federal labor system to full strength.

The Political Role of Unions

The labor movement's investment in the city as the key battleground for rebuilding American unionism highlights a final theme that speaks directly to ongoing debates about the role of unions in politics.[91] As the L.A. campaigns underscore, in addition to being an economic bargaining agent, unions are *inherently political actors* seeking to represent workers in the public domain in order to design legal frameworks within which to effectively advocate for workers' economic interests. Precisely because there is no dividing line between the market and politics in American capitalism, unions are constantly required to play dual roles: bargaining for workers in the private sector to enhance workers' rights and engaging in politics in the public sector to defend and extend the rules of the game within which bargaining occurs. These dual roles must interlock for the labor movement to be successful. It is only through economic representation that unions are able to generate the resources and standing to engage politically, and political engagement is essential for long-term economic success. Labor's local turn is a product of this dual role because, for the time being, it is primarily in big cities with favorable political environments where unions can exercise political power.

Historically, unions' political engagement has been important not just for protecting union bargaining rights, but for advancing broader redistributive policy—from minimum wage to welfare—serving as the foundation for America's shared postwar prosperity. This is one reason why corporate interests have targeted union representation, through right-to-work laws depriving unions of membership dues and the evisceration of nonmember "fair share" fees.[92] Corporate success in undercutting union density has contributed to weaker economic regulation and the rise of inequality throughout the American economy that labor's efforts in cities like Los Angeles have sought to address. It is against this backdrop that scholars have debated the nature of labor's political role and how it should relate to unions' core function of workplace organizing. In this vein, Ben Sachs has argued that labor's political function should be legally severed from its economic function, with workers empowered to vote in favor of unions as political representatives even if those workers do not want union representation in the workplace.[93] Putting feasibility aside (it seems unlikely that unions could make the case for broader political representation if they cannot convince workers of the immediate benefits of economic representation), there is merit in thinking more systematically about the link between firm-level bargaining and unions' wider participation in politics.

In this regard, the L.A. experience makes a strong case that union efforts to promote local policy benefiting community members *outside* of the workplace may pay direct union organizing dividends *inside*. This occurs both through changing public perception of unions and by embedding specific mechanisms in local policy that directly support unionization. From a normative standpoint, by demonstrating that they can deliver benefits to low-income communities and communities of color around issues like housing and environmental justice, unions may overcome the negative stereotype of labor as a special interest group and improve long-term prospects for increasing union density. However, in order to continue promoting wider redistributive reform, labor's local policies—even as they aim to transcend unionism—must still provide a means to directly strengthen collective bargaining in order to maintain unions' political power under the current system of campaign finance, which depends on dues collection. In Los Angeles, the paradigm of this type of reform—simultaneously promoting unionism while benefiting workers outside its scope—was the Living Wage Ordinance, which contained an opt-out for companies with unions that helped increase union density in the retail and hospitality sectors. This increased density, in turn, strengthened labor's power, creating the political possibility for the $15 minimum wage (which itself has an opt-out). Although such opt-outs have been controversial, portrayed as a retreat from the principle of minimum labor standards,[94] and therefore cutting against the goal of promoting a positive public image for unions, from a long-term perspective, they serve as critical tools in building union density that politically empowers unions to provide broader community benefits.

The development of local policies like the living wage also illuminates a representational division of labor: While community–labor alliances play a vanguard role in politics, unions remain central in the workplace. This division of labor spotlights a final point about political unionism, which is that while it fundamentally depends on *inter-movement solidarity* in the public domain, it must nonetheless continue to fight for a traditional notion of *intra-labor solidarity* in private firms in order to maintain and potentially strengthen unions' role in promoting workplace equity. Trying to mediate between these different forms of solidarity creates synergies and tensions for the labor movement. In the public domain, this book has traced how labor's political resurgence has relied on identifying and capitalizing upon interest convergence with other social movements, which have contributed the resources, power, and legitimacy necessary to build credible political organization and enact labor-friendly law. This interest convergence was the essential predicate for solidarity, while also testing its limits. The blue-green alliance converged around overlapping interests in truck drivers in the ports campaign, but industry strategy (supporting clean trucks while attacking employee drivers) drove a policy wedge that broke the coalition apart. Labor partnerships with housing advocates produced important CBAs, but also flared over the optimal distribution of limited developer funds, revealing how labor's growing political clout was a double-edged sword: reducing incentives for solidarity with movements whose aims could be perceived to conflict with job growth. Scaling up to the national level, in a conservative political environment in which opportunities for policy success by progressive movements across issue areas are highly constrained (and thus victories may appear to create zero-sum trade-offs), one would expect inter-movement solidarity to remain difficult to forge, and yet crucial to achieve, in order to rebuild labor's political power.

The challenges to building solidarity in the workplace are also substantial, though quite different, as labor shifts from strategies to promote inter-movement solidarity to reshape politics to those designed to strengthen intra-labor solidarity to effectively fight for worker power in the rapidly changing labor market. In pursuit of community relevance and policy influence, unions have supported new forms of worker collectivism that break the traditional mold.[95] Early worker centers, like that in the garment industry, came from outside the labor movement. Over time, organized labor came to appreciate the potential of worker centers to foster organizing and thus took on a stronger role incubating and financially supporting them. Despite worker center growth, however, and wider discussion of more flexible forms of workplace representation,[96] unions have continued to assert their primacy as the only vehicles capable of winning employer recognition and bargaining for stronger worker rights because worker centers and other community-based labor groups have not shown themselves capable of achieving an influential voice in the workplace. Perhaps as the workplace itself fractures in the contemporary market, such forms of solidarity will prove less important, and sectoral policy strategies will take precedence. However, unions have not been willing to bet the future of American workers' rights on ceding control to unproven alternatives, and—particularly so long as unions' political effectiveness depends on density—the argument for alternative representational forms risks undermining the labor movement's political potency.

This is, for now, especially true at the local level, where the political role of unions goes beyond expanding unionism to serving as the anchor for broader efforts to spur progressive political change. In Los Angeles, union leadership in developing alliances with other movements has been essential to reclaiming the city as a space for social inclusion and economic equality, visible in efforts to promote sanctuary for undocumented immigrants confronting the Trump crackdown and to combat climate change through environmentally friendly, Green New Deal–style reforms. These efforts, to be sure, remain outmatched against broader structural forces that continue to drive forward neoliberalism and that have bolstered the growth of affluence concentrated in America's big cities. Yet without such efforts to build the labor movement's base at the local level and to connect labor organizing to other strands of progressive action—as continues to occur in Los Angeles and cities where the majority of Americans reside—there will be even fewer institutional checks on inequality, and the pernicious environmental and social forces that it unleashes.

Localism: Reimagining the City as Catalyst of National Reform

The city has long reflected a fundamental American contradiction: a site of direct democracy and beacon of inclusion, but also the place where social divisions erupt and elites exercise power to etch those divisions into place.[97] Home to robber barons and immigrant slums during the Industrial Revolution, American cities became magnets for African Americans fleeing Southern persecution and searching for good jobs during World War II. As racial covenants, redlining, and white violence maintained the boundaries of rigid racial segregation in the postwar years, the Civil Rights movement brought the fight for integration to Northern cities. This, in turn, provoked "white flight" that transformed the urban landscape—creating inner cities populated by people of color ringed by newly created affluent white suburbs. Within this geography of racial and economic division, suburbs detached themselves from the inner-city tax base, extracting resources that sent cities into deep economic decline, decimating urban schools and services.

Coming out of this urban transformation, scholars sought to map the ways in which local government law had been used to inscribe inequality through rules permitting the creation of separate suburban enclaves zoned to keep out the poor and people of color. In this vein, Gerald Frug argued that the city should be understood as a "legal concept," highlighting the ways in which local government rules were essentially distributive in nature.[98] Scholars in this tradition, led by Richard

Thompson Ford, revealed how local government lawmaking, and the judicial doctrine built around it, permitted a spatial geography of racial exclusion, which locked residents of color into inferior housing, low-performing schools, and neighborhoods cut off from jobs.[99] Social movements by those residents to gain urban power and engage in productive redevelopment confronted the persistent legacy of political disenfranchisement and the challenge of reconstructing city economies within regional spaces in which investment could be directed to adjacent suburbs with resources to subsidize business development.

This book has explored the potential of local government law as a vehicle for low-income communities to seize back power during the most recent transformation of the city: from a place of disinvestment and decline to one defined by rampant reinvestment and unprecedented inequality. This transformation has unsettled boundaries set in the prior period, as new immigrants and older communities of color vie for space with affluent whites returning to claim property in precisely those neighborhoods redlined and abandoned during the era of white flight. The current urban transformation thus presents a new puzzle.[100] As cities like Los Angeles become "majority-minority," they have also become home to global economic elites and white professionals attracted back by the promise of proximity to jobs and cultural amenities. In this fractured environment, where the power of the majority clashes with that of the "one percent," the question of who controls the levers of local government power, and to what ends those levers can be put to address the crosscurrents of development and displacement, is at the forefront of the new struggle for the city.

Based on the recent history of Los Angeles, it is fair to say that this struggle has yielded mixed results that raise important questions going forward about the potential of localism to redress American inequality. As this book has shown, local government law processes have been at the center of the fight over who benefits from urban economic development, historically appropriated by elites to pursue goals at odds with equitable growth. In the wake of deindustrialization, Los Angeles—desperate for tax revenue—aggressively used the redevelopment process to subsidize projects that generated large property and sales tax revenue, but in so doing placed the city in the role of financially supporting projects that produced thousands of minimum wage jobs. Empowered actors used local government law in other ways to reinforce the marginality of already vulnerable workers. Perhaps most egregiously, across the greater L.A. area, city restrictions on day labor solicitation were designed to remove day laborers from plain sight, driving them further underground, undermining their ability to organize collectively on street corners, and thus increasing the potential for their exploitation.

These examples underscore an enduring lesson of this book, which is that control over space has profound implications for the nature of work and therefore the content of economic justice in the contemporary metropolis. Seeking a voice over how that control is exercised, the L.A. campaigns achieved concrete improvements measured in job quality and enhanced political power for workers. And yet, despite workers' increased standing, Los Angeles remains one of the most unequal and segregated cities in the country—a place where high-end development and gentrification reproduce cycles of displacement and economic precarity for those on the bottom. Whether the social movements that have cracked open local government to more forcefully address these problems can amass power to further democratize development and increase the economic return to labor are crucial questions in the phase to come. As scholars and activists seek to answer them, the L.A. experience teaches that local government law does, in fact, offer significant opportunities for meaningful labor reform. But these opportunities occur within a framework that limits the degree to which cities can meaningfully address structural inequality without a national movement to rein in wealth accumulation at the top, and bridge the gaping urban–nonurban divide, which has established rigid new borders that challenge the quest for economic justice.

Opportunity: The City as a Tool and Target

On the positive side of the ledger, this book's account of the L.A. campaigns maps the ways in which city rules can be tilted toward pro-labor ends—drawing theoretical attention to the potential for innovation in local government law design. From this standpoint, the city is reimagined as a tool and a target of labor reform. As a *tool*, city legal processes provide leverage for social movements to advance new norms of inclusion and equality. The city, in this view, is a means to an end: providing levers that can be used by social movements to advance substantive policy benefiting the working poor. The land use system is the central fulcrum: requiring city compliance with standards for environmental clearance and zoning, and making the city accountable for allocating public subsidies—in both instances, codifying public participation rights that permit mobilized groups to demand greater equity. In this system, social movements can use legal action (threatening lawsuits) and public pressure (threatening to withdraw support from politicians responsible for issuing approvals) to push back against development and thus create space to bargain for pro-labor policy change.

As a *target*, the city is the site where reform actually occurs. From this perspective, the city is reimagined as the level of governmental power where policy can be effectively designed to improve working conditions. Viewing the city as the locus for progressive labor policymaking flows from the city's comparative advantages, while also reflecting pragmatic political calculation. As Richard Schragger has argued, one advantage of the city is its relative openness to social movement-led campaigns for change to advance innovative solutions to local problems.[101] Another advantage is that cities like Los Angeles have unique public assets, like LAX and the port, over which they can exercise political influence to enter agreements (like the LAX CBA) or change rules (like the Clean Truck Program) to promote labor standards. From a pragmatic standpoint, demographic shifts making cities younger, more educated, and more diverse create political opportunities for progressivism that do not exist—and may not for the foreseeable future—at the national level. This has clearly been the case in places like Los Angeles, San Francisco, Seattle, and New York, where organized labor has built local power to pass labor reforms in a political context in which cities are the best and sometimes only hope.

However, beyond simply reimagining the city as an important site of policy innovation, by *reframing the specific relationship between cities and work*, the L.A. campaigns revise traditional conceptions of local government law in theoretically significant directions. The conventional view of local government law has focused primarily on how that law shapes what a city does as a matter of service provision and apportioning space. This perspective flows from the peculiar legal authority American municipalities exercise over *property*: Cities are empowered to collect taxes on property (not income), allocate those taxes to support public services deemed essentially local in character (education, police, and fire), and define what type of property gets built and how it is used in different city zones. From a redistributive perspective, programs for greater urban equity have generally concentrated on how to increase the public return on city investments in what have been deemed quintessentially public functions: designing new methods to finance better schools, promote affordable housing, and entice economic development that benefits the community and augments the tax base.

The critical intervention of the L.A. community–labor campaigns has been to demonstrate how pervasively the city's "public" functions shape the operation of the "private" labor market[102]—and then to argue in favor of revamping those functions to redefine how the market works for the working class. In particular, the campaigns reveal that municipal decisions about which companies receive city contracts (and on what terms) and how land is redeveloped for economic growth profoundly influence *the nature of jobs and therefore the quality of work* that the city produces.[103]

By empirically linking local government law to the *quality* of work, the labor movement has been able to make normative claims on city power in which the city itself can be held accountable for its contribution to the expansion of low-wage jobs. Showing how the tentacles of local government law reach into the employment relationship allows the labor movement to build the case that local government powers of contracting, land use allocation, and service delivery are not disconnected from work, but actually integral to it in ways that put cities to a fundamental choice: between supporting labor flexibility and inequality on the one hand, and promoting workplace stability and shared prosperity on the other. From organized labor's perspective, the fact that municipal lawmaking shapes work no matter what (and historically has been used to degrade labor standards) means that local authority could, and should, be legitimately deployed to redefine work in terms of higher wages and benefits, stronger workplace protections, and a meaningful opportunity to organize collectively. In this way, the labor movement's normative claim on city authority challenges traditional conceptions of local government law focused on the distribution of property and services—showing how that distribution contains implicit policy choices about what type of work city residents are entitled to have. By bringing those choices to the surface, and demanding that the city make them with job quality in mind, the L.A. campaigns have enlarged the opportunity for local government lawmaking and stimulated development of a new body of local labor law—from living wage to antidiscrimination policy to the Fight for $15—that expands city authority to regulate the private market.

Challenge: Vertical Power and Horizontal Equity

As the intense conflict surrounding the L.A. campaigns makes clear, the labor movement's push for expanded local government authority to regulate work has not gone unchallenged. Opponents of local labor law question its legitimacy, charging that the appropriation of local government tools designed to regulate development to enhance workplace standards distorts valid local goals for special interest purposes.[104] From the perspective of progressive skeptics of localism, the problem is not legitimacy but rather scale. Their concern is that labor activism in local politics cannot do enough to address regional inequality and build a foundation for broader reform. These critical perspectives point toward two challenges to local labor lawmaking: defending its role against adversaries wielding *vertical power* to abrogate city authority, and extending its reach beyond big-city boundaries to promote *horizontal equity* across metropolitan regions—potentially serving as a catalyst of national change.

From a vertical perspective, local labor law has drawn attention from critics concerned with the legitimacy of local authority in a federalist system, in which there are two layers of higher-order law—state and federal—that constrain the exercise of city power. A central ambiguity of local government law is whether there exist any quintessentially local functions over which cities have absolute autonomy or whether the city is a mere instrumentality of the state,[105] empowered to act only if and to the degree that the state gives it permission. Doctrinally, this ambiguity is resolved by reference to the terms under which a state delegates local power and the scope of home rule authority.[106] However, even when a home rule city, like Los Angeles, is granted authority over "municipal affairs,"[107] there are conflicts over the outer boundaries of what that term encompasses.

Los Angeles and other cities have sought to manage these conflicts by incrementally building out local labor law: starting from labor reforms attached to "core" local functions, like contracting and land use, which have generally avoided legal challenge on *state law* preemption grounds on the theory that a city can reasonably impose contractual conditions (like the living wage) on the use of public funds or create frameworks for evaluating land use impacts (like the Superstores Ordinance) that indirectly affect conditions of work. However, when cities move beyond these core functions to assert direct authority to regulate work—such as in citywide minimum wage ordinances—the threat of state preemption grows larger. This has pushed labor activists to seek state-level reform first when possible (as seen in the anti-sweatshop and ports campaigns); however, when the state is closed to such reform, local labor law inevitably confronts the preemption threat.

Over the past decade, the specter of state preemption has produced different types of state–local dynamics. In states with large nonurban populations and conservative state governments, local labor lawmaking has been thwarted by the corporate countermovement to assert state preemption. According to the Economic Policy Institute, there are twenty-six states that prevent local governments from setting minimum wages higher than the state wage level, and twenty-three that preempt local paid leave policies—most in the Midwest and Deep South.[108] A growing number of states have also preempted local efforts to regulate ride-sharing companies, like Uber, by requiring special licenses or imposing operational taxes. Alternatively, in progressive states like California, the development of city minimum wage and other local worker rights laws has been the vanguard pushing state law forward. It was only after cities like Los Angeles passed the $15 minimum wage that the State of California followed suit in 2016 and (because of its phased-in implementation) by the time California reaches the $15 level, in 2020, there will already be more than twenty-five local jurisdictions that mandate that pay rate. As the campaign to win employee conversion at the Los Angeles port highlights, cities have also taken the lead fighting misclassification, building local precedent and pressure on the state that culminated in the 2019 passage of A.B. 5.[109] That law has transformed the landscape of misclassification by codifying a legal standard for determining employee status—creating a presumption in favor of employment if someone does work within a company's direct line of business—that makes it significantly more difficult (and perhaps impossible) for trucking firms and gig economy businesses like Uber to label their workers as independent contractors. Yet even in California, where momentum for statewide labor change has surged from the cities, industry opponents have found ways to contest such labor laws in other venues: in the case of A.B. 5, seeking to block it through a ballot initiative that would amend the state constitution while instituting federal free speech and equal protection lawsuits supported by conservative legal organizations, like the Pacific Legal Foundation.

As the legal challenges to A.B. 5 highlight, *federal law* can also be a significant barrier to local labor lawmaking. The L.A. campaigns constantly operated in, and attempted to maneuver around, the shadow of federal law—and not, it is important to emphasize, federal *labor* law, but rather other forms of federal regulation mobilized by opponents of local labor policy. In this regard, federal preemption under the FAAAA and the Dormant Commerce Clause has loomed over the labor movement's effort to transform drayage trucking—and indeed, the FAAAA is the basis for a lawsuit brought by the California Trucking Association against A.B. 5.[110] In the L.A. campaigns, federal law imposed other limits. The LAX CBA ran into the buzz saw of federal transportation law, which was used by FAA regulators to strike down job training and referral programs deemed unrelated to airport operations. Although CBAs were never directly challenged, critics suggested that they could run afoul of federal takings law if a city were to intervene in negotiations to condition land use approval on community benefits as an unrelated or disproportionate exaction under Supreme Court doctrine.[111] These conflicts underscore a key insight from this book, which is that localism is a legal battlefield, in which invocations of city power continuously clash with, and seek to redefine, claims of higher-order law.

The critique of local labor law asserted by opponents—that it operates outside the bounds of appropriate city authority—is the mirror image of that advanced by erstwhile allies of progressive labor reform, who are less concerned with the legitimacy of local action than with its potential to achieve transformative scale. As Schragger notes, progressive suspicion of localism stems from its historical association with the conservative rhetoric of "states' rights" as a dog whistle for discrimination and exploitation, alongside the dark history of municipal complicity in income inequality and racial segregation through suburbanization and white flight.[112] This history has framed contemporary debate over progressive localism around two critical perspectives.

The first questions the effectiveness of local labor law in promoting horizontal equity among cities and suburbs in a regional economy. In a fragmented metropolitan area composed of multiple municipalities, there is a significant risk that economic regulation targeting business in one jurisdiction will be undermined if mobile capital flees to neighboring jurisdictions with lower labor costs. In this view, because adjacent cities compete for business through lucrative tax breaks and other subsidies, local labor law may do more harm than good by driving business to seek out better deals elsewhere in the region. This risk highlights a fundamental dilemma of economic decentralization, which gives cities an incentive to attract mobile capital and keep it from fleeing by slashing regulation.[113] Because this race-to-the-bottom is a product of inter-jurisdictional competition, proponents of regional equity have long argued that the best solution is to create regional governmental structures that prevent such strategic behavior by corporations.[114]

While regional governance provides an important (though thus far politically untenable) response to the risk of capital flight, the L.A. experience suggests that—at least in some circumstances—regional capital flight might not be such a significant risk in the first instance. For one, not all jobs are equally exportable, and well-targeted municipal regulation can upgrade locally tethered jobs without the risk that they will flee.[115] In this vein, the L.A. community–labor campaigns have been careful to target jobs tied to the city—jobs of municipal workers, hotel employees, truck drivers, and others whose work must be done locally. The political theory of these campaigns is that, once a significant number of a city's workers obtain higher wages and more job protections, there will be upward pressure placed on other employers to raise wages as well. And as wages rise across the board, the absence of catastrophic capital flight and job loss will bolster organized labor's political argument that upgrading work does not produce the worst-case economic scenarios business opponents often proclaim. This could produce positive ripple effects in the city itself and regionally as well.

The L.A. campaigns also spotlight the importance of informal mechanisms for promoting regional equity. As community-labor coalitions have pushed back against the conventional wisdom that a single city could not effectively pursue redistributive economic policy, they have also pursued efforts to regionalize the movement for economic justice: establishing networks of activists to coordinate campaigns (as in efforts to block Wal-Mart around Los Angeles) and share strategic information beyond the local level (as in the struggle to stop anti-solicitation ordinances in the greater L.A. area). The existence of these networks does not overcome many of the challenges of localism—including the risk of inconsistent standards and the absence of regulation in localities that lack a strong labor presence. However, by facilitating the exchange of information, regional networks allow activists to more easily learn about successful models, avoid mistakes, and draw upon allies for technical assistance and resource support.

Considering the efficacy of local policy diffusion connects to the second critical perspective on progressive localism, which questions the extent to which localism can—or should even aspire to—achieve transformative national scale. Within this debate, a threshold question is whether decentralization constitutes a first- or second-best solution to problems of poverty, inequality, and racism that are national in scope but local in effect. For those in the old labor and civil rights traditions, localism is absolutely second best: perhaps a way station on the path toward a broader national progressive movement, but not a substitute for it. Schragger and other commentators, like Bruce Katz and Jeremy Nowak, offer a different view, suggesting that progressive localism can be considered an end in itself—a way to more effectively tackle difficult distributional problems in diverse settings affecting a significant proportion of the American populace.[116]

This book has looked beyond this either/or framing to suggest how local and federal mobilization are intrinsically linked and thus must always be pursued in tandem. On one side, the history of labor law's renaissance in Los Angeles lends weight to the idea that cities can be effective sites for tailoring solutions to problems that have unique impacts in one place (such as the proliferation of low-wage jobs in the tourism industry or the specific challenges of immigrant labor). On the other, precisely because of the power of labor's opponents to elevate struggle to different regulatory scales and the omnipresent threat of preemption that presents, this history has also shown that localism is never enough: It must constantly be fortified and defended at higher levels in order to be effective on the ground.

In the end, the history of struggle in Los Angeles points beyond the difficult challenge of scaling up to the existential need to link localism to a broader politics of national reconciliation in contemporary American politics—one that transcends romantic localist visions of building bipartisan community through interpersonal "reciprocity and trust."[117] Although important in theory, this interpersonal vision misses the degree to which localities themselves have become deeply polarized, swept up into broader partisan fights in which national political actors reward localism they like and punish that which deviates from the party line, as legal disputes around city climate change and immigrant sanctuary laws illustrate. Although scholars of "cooperative federalism" may be correct that such problems are better solved through partnership not conflict,[118] the question remains how to create a stable political foundation for such partnership when national partisan conflict tears apart the fabric of cooperative regulatory schemes and conservatives at the center of federal power steadfastly deny the possibility that progressive localism could ever serve as a template for national policy.

As the struggle for scale plays out in an environment of hyper-polarization organized across the urban–nonurban divide, a central concern is whether labor and other left social movement investment in big "blue" cities like Los Angeles will produce islands of progressivism that actually widen the distance between two Americas: one embracing multiculturalism, secularism, and constraints on economic power, and the other defined by white nationalism, hostility toward non-Christian religions, and a commitment to deregulatory economics. It is one thing for local experimentation to solve discrete problems, but for it to serve as a model for wider transformation, it has to invite dialogue rather than simply assert an alternative world view. In this respect, the L.A. campaigns presented in this book may offer a tentative roadmap for sparking national change: communicating common challenges faced by low-wage workers throughout the country and offering a message of solidarity across difference to serve as a clarion call for a better American future.

Coda

In a contemporary context in which so much looks dire for labor rights in the United States, it is easy to idealize the successes of progressive cities like Los Angeles as bellwethers of a future that improves on the recent past. And although there is clearly cause for hope and inspiration in the struggle for economic justice in Los Angeles, it would be wrong to think of Los Angeles as a place for advocacy and reform in idealized terms. The city has far to go to achieve the promise that many outsiders have assigned to it. To do so will require concerted efforts not just to create better jobs, but to preserve jobs in the face of automation and to address other barriers, particularly the skyrocketing cost of housing, which makes cities like Los Angeles out of reach even for working people with good jobs. Meaningful steps to address inequality also require serious efforts to rein in spiraling compensation at the top of the income scale, which feeds into the gentrification that pushes working people further to the city's margins.

In this sense, the history of community and labor activism presented in this book, and the leadership of lawyers within it, is not written as an instruction manual for reform, but rather as a portrait in time of the extraordinary effort and courage that it takes to mount large-scale challenges to powerful systems that keep people locked in poverty and exploitation. It is a portrait of Los Angeles that belies the ready-made image of a city of superficiality and glamour, revealing the bedrock of grit and determination fortifying those who work daily to make the city live up to its better angels and make real the dreams that it presents to the world. That lawyers have been at the center of this movement underscores not only that law has come to define the fundamental landscape of contemporary political struggle, but also that the legal profession can still serve as a wellspring for social change in a moment in which change is so desperately needed.

NOTES

Chapter 1

1. For this book, I conducted interviews with sixty-six subjects pursuant to UCLA Institutional Review Board protocol #G08-06-076-02. In addition, I used another thirteen interviews conducted by students under the supervision of Richard Abel in his 2005 Law and Social Change course at the UCLA School of Law. I also reviewed campaign materials drawn from court files, public records, and archived documents from the Asian Pacific American Legal Center; Los Angeles Alliance for a New Economy; Mexican American Legal Defense and Educational Fund, Inc.; Strategic Actions for a Just Economy; and UCLA Downtown Labor Center.
2. *See, e.g.*, Lani Guinier & Gerald Torres, *Changing the Wind: Notes toward a Demosprudence of Law and Social Movements*, 123 YALE L.J. 2740, 2748 (2014) (describing the "liberal strategy" of the NAACP as seeking "to change the governing rules institution by institution with the hope that linking those changes together would transform the culture").
3. There has been important recent historical work challenging the conventional account of civil rights advocacy as overly focused on impact litigation. *See, e.g.*, SUSAN D. CARLE, DEFINING THE STRUGGLE: NATIONAL ORGANIZING FOR RACIAL JUSTICE, 1880–1915 (2015); CHRISTOPHER W. SCHMIDT, THE SIT-INS: PROTEST AND LEGAL CHANGE IN THE CIVIL RIGHTS ERA (2018); Kenneth W. Mack, *Rethinking Civil Rights Lawyering and Politics in the Era Before Brown*, 115 YALE L.J. 256 (2005).
4. For examples of contemporary movement lawyering, see JENNIFER GORDON, SUBURBAN SWEATSHOPS: THE FIGHT FOR IMMIGRANT RIGHTS (2005); Amna A. Akbar, *Toward a Radical Imagination of Law*, 93 N.Y.U. L. REV. 405 (2018); Anthony V. Alfieri, *Inner-City Anti-Poverty Campaigns*, 64 UCLA L. REV. 1374 (2017); Gabriel Arkles, Pooja Gehi & Elana Redfield, *The Role of Lawyers in Trans Liberation*, 8 SEATTLE J. SOC. JUST. 579 (2010); Michael Grinthal, *Power With: Practice Models for Social Justice Lawyering*, 15 U. PA. J. L. & SOC. CHANGE 25 (2011); Nan D. Hunter, *Varieties of Constitutional Experience: Democracy and the Marriage Equality Campaign*, 64 UCLA L. REV. 1662 (2017); Doug NeJaime, *The Legal Mobilization Dilemma*, 61 EMORY L.J. 663 (2012); and Deborah L. Rhode, *Public Interest Law: The Movement at Midlife*, 60 STAN. L. REV. 2027 (2008).
5. *See* RISA L. GOLUBOFF, THE LOST PROMISE OF CIVIL RIGHTS (2007).
6. The book uses comparative case study methodology. *See* Kathleen M. Eisenhardt, *Building Theories from Case Study Research*, 14 ACAD. MGMT. REV. 532 (1989); Theda Skocpol & Margaret Somers, *The Uses of Comparative History in Macrosocial Inquiry*, 22 COMP. STUD. SOC'Y & HIST. 174 (1980).

7. Ruth Milkman, L.A. Story: Immigrant Workers and the Future of the U.S. Labor Movement (2006).
8. *See, e.g.*, Suzanne Staggenborg, *The Consequences of Professionalization and Formalization in the Pro-Choice Movement*, 53 Am. Soc. Rev. 585 (1988); *see also* Suzanne Staggenborg, The Pro-Choice Movement: Organization and Activism in the Abortion Conflict (1991).
9. For key contributions to the law and social movements literature, see Sameer M. Ashar, *Public Interest Lawyers and Resistance Movements*, 95 Cal. L. Rev. 1879 (2007); Jack M. Balkin, *Brown, Social Movements, and Social Change*, in Choosing Equality: Essays and Narratives on the Desegregation Experience 246 (Robert L. Hayman, Jr. & Leland Ware eds., 2009); Tomiko Brown-Nagin, *Elites, Social Movements, and the Law: The Case of Affirmative Action*, 105 Colum. L. Rev. 1436 (2005); William N. Eskridge, Jr., *Channeling: Identity-Based Social Movements and Public Law*, 150 U. Pa. L. Rev. 419 (2001); Linda Greenhouse & Reva B. Siegel, *Before (and After) Roe v. Wade: New Questions About Backlash*, 120 Yale L.J. 2028 (2011); Guinier & Torres, *supra* note 2; Douglas NeJaime, *Winning Through Losing*, 96 Iowa L. Rev. 941 (2011); Reva B. Siegel, *Constitutional Culture, Social Movement Conflict and Constitutional Change: The Case of the De Facto ERA*, 94 Cal. L. Rev. 1323 (2006); and Louise Trubek & M. Elizabeth Kransberger, *Critical Lawyers: Social Justice and the Structures of Private Practice*, in Cause Lawyering: Political Commitments and Professional Responsibilities 261, 201–26 (Austin Sarat & Stuart Scheingold eds., 1998).
10. *See* Michael McCann & Helena Silverstein, *Rethinking Law's "Allurements": A Relational Analysis of Social Movement Lawyers in the United States*, in Cause Lawyering, *supra* note 9, at 266.
11. *See* Stuart Scheingold, The Politics of Rights: Lawyers, Public Policy, and Political Change (1974). For a synthesis of the progressive critique of law, see Orly Lobel, *The Paradox of Extralegal Activism: Critical Legal Consciousness and Transformative Politics*, 120 Harv. L. Rev. 937 (2007).
12. *See* Derrick Bell, Jr., *Serving Two Masters: Integration Ideals and Client Interests in School Desegregation Litigation*, 85 Yale L.J. 470 (1976).
13. *See* Gerald Rosenberg, The Hollow Hope: Can Courts Bring About Social Change? (1991); Scheingold, *supra* note 11; Alan David Freeman, *Legitimizing Racial Discrimination Through Antidiscrimination Law: A Critical Review of Supreme Court Doctrine*, 62 Minn. L. Rev. 1049 (1978); Michael J. Klarman, *How Brown Changed Race Relations: The Backlash Thesis*, 81 J. Am. Hist. 81 (1994).
14. Austin Sarat & Stuart Scheingold, *What Cause Lawyers Do For, and To, Social Movements: An Introduction*, in Cause Lawyers and Social Movements 1 (Austin Sarat & Stuart A. Schengold eds., 2006).
15. Scott L. Cummings, *Rethinking the Foundational Critiques of Lawyers in Social Movements*, 85 Fordham L. Rev. 1987 (2017).
16. *See* Richard L. Abel, Politics by Other Means: Law in the Struggle Against Apartheid, 1980–1994 (1995); Catherine R. Albiston, Institutional Inequality and the Mobilization of the Family and Medical Leave Act: Rights on Leave (2010); Joel F. Handler, Social Movements and the Legal System: A Theory of Law Reform and Social Change (1978); Gerald P. López, Rebellious Lawyering: One Chicano's Vision of Progressive Law Practice (1992); Michael W. McCann, Rights at Work: Pay Equity Reform and the Politics of Legal Mobilization (1994); Stuart A. Scheingold & Austin Sarat, Something to Believe In: Politics, Professionalism, and Cause Lawyering (2004).
17. *See* Doug McAdam, Political Process and the Development of Black Insurgency, 1930–1970 (1982); Charles S. Bullock & Charles M. Lamb, Implementation of Civil Rights Policy (1984); John D. McCarthy & Mayer N. Zald, *Resource Mobilization*

and Social Movements: A Partial Theory, 82 AM. J. SOC. 1212 (1977); Jack L. Walker, *The Origins and Maintenance of Interest Groups in America*, 77 AM. POL. SCI. REV. 390 (1983).
18. The comparative institutional approach builds on dispute transformation studies. *See* William L.F. Felstiner, Richard L. Abel & Austin Sarat, *The Emergence and Transformation of Disputes: Naming, Blaming, Claiming*, 15 L. & SOC'Y REV. 631 (1980–81).
19. Scott L. Cummings, *Empirical Studies of Law and Social Change: What Is the Field? What Are the Questions?*, 2013 WIS. L. REV. 171 (2013).
20. *See* Scott L. Cummings, *The Social Movement Turn in Law*, 42 LAW & SOC. INQUIRY 369–74 (2018).
21. Roscoe Pound, *Law in Books and Law in Action*, 44 AM. L. REV. 12 (1910).
22. SIDNEY G. TARROW, POWER IN MOVEMENT: SOCIAL MOVEMENTS AND CONTENTIOUS POLITICS (3rd ed. 2011).
23. *See* Cummings, *supra* note 15.
24. The campaign perspective flows from similar approaches adopted by other scholars, whose work has used movement decision-making as the lens of analysis. *See* MCCANN, *supra* note 16; GORDON SILVERSTEIN, LAW'S ALLURE: HOW LAW SHAPES, CONSTRAINS, SAVES, AND KILLS POLITICS (2009); MARK V. TUSHNET, THE NAACP'S LEGAL STRATEGY AGAINST SEGREGATED EDUCATION, 1925–1950 (1987); Peter Houtzager & Lucie E. White, *The Long Arc of Pragmatic Economic and Social Rights Advocacy*, *in* STONES OF HOW: HOW AFRICAN ACTIVISTS RECLAIM HUMAN RIGHTS TO CHALLENGE GLOBAL POVERTY 172 (Lucie E. White & Jeremy Perelman eds., 2011).
25. KATHERINE V.W. STONE, FROM WIDGETS TO DIGITS: EMPLOYMENT REGULATION FOR THE CHANGING WORKPLACE (2004); Cynthia L. Estlund, *The Ossification of American Labor Law*, 102 COLUM. L. REV. 1527 (2002).
26. *See* Estlund, *supra* note 25, at 1533–69.
27. Noah D. Zatz, *Working Beyond the Reach or Grasp of Employment Law*, *in* THE GLOVES-OFF ECONOMY: WORKPLACE STANDARDS AT THE BOTTOM OF AMERICA'S LABOR MARKET 31 (Annette Bernhardt, Heather Boushey, Laura Dresser & Chris Tilly eds., 2008).
28. *See* Catherine L. Fisk, *Reimagining Collective Rights in the Workplace*, 4 UC IRVINE L. REV. 523 (2014).
29. MILKMAN, *supra* note 7, at 114–44.
30. Llezlie Green Coleman, *Rendered Invisible: African American Low-Wage Workers and the Workplace Exploitation Paradigm*, 60 HOW. L.J. 61 (2016).
31. Ben Sachs, *Employment Law as Labor Law*, 29 CARDOZO L. REV. 2685 (2008).
32. JANICE FINE, WORKER CENTERS: ORGANIZING COMMUNITIES AT THE EDGE OF THE DREAM (2006); WORKING FOR JUSTICE: THE L.A. MODEL OF ORGANIZING AND ADVOCACY (Ruth Milkman, Joshua Bloom & Victor Narro eds., 2010).
33. *See* Veena Dubal, *Winning the Battle, Losing the War?: Assessing the Impact of Misclassification Litigation on Workers in the Gig Economy*, 2017 WIS. L. REV. 239 (2017).
34. *See, e.g.*, Janus v. AFSCME, 138 S. Ct. 2448 (2018) (striking down forty-year-old precedent to hold that unions could not charge "fair share dues" to nonmembers to pay for the costs of representation).
35. Katherine Stone & Scott Cummings, *Labor Activism in Local Politics: From CBAs to 'CBAs'*, *in* THE IDEA OF LABOUR LAW 273 (Guy Davidov & Brian Langille eds., 2011).
36. Richard C. Schragger, *Is a Progressive City Possible? Reviving Urban Liberalism for the Twenty-First Century*, 7 HARV. L. & POL'Y REV. 231 (2013).
37. *See* Richard Thompson Ford, *The Boundaries of Race: Political Geography in Legal Analysis*, 107 HARV. L. REV. 1841 (1994).
38. LOS ANGELES ALLIANCE FOR A NEW ECONOMY, THE ROAD TO SHARED PROSPERITY: THE REGIONAL ECONOMIC BENEFITS OF THE SAN PEDRO BAY PORTS' CLEAN TRUCKS PROGRAM (2007).

39. *See* Richard Schragger, *Mobile Capital, Local Economic Regulation, and the Democratic City*, 123 HARV. L. REV. 482 (2009).
40. U.S. CENSUS BUREAU, 2017 AMERICAN COMMUNITY SURVEY 5-YEAR ESTIMATE, https://factfinder.census.gov/faces/nav/jsf/pages/index.xhtm (last visited Sept. 29, 2019).
41. *See* MIKE DAVIS, CITY OF QUARTZ: EXCAVATING THE FUTURE IN LOS ANGELES (1990); MIKE DAVIS, ECOLOGY OF FEAR: LOS ANGELES AND THE IMAGINATION OF DISASTER (1998); WILLIAM FULTON, THE RELUCTANT METROPOLIS: THE POLITICS OF URBAN GROWTH IN LOS ANGELES (1997); MICHAEL STORPER, THOMAS KEMENY, NAJI P. MAKAREM & TANER OSMAN, THE RISE AND FALL OF URBAN ECONOMIES: LESSONS FROM SAN FRANCISCO AND LOS ANGELES (2015).
42. *See* ROBERT GOTTLIEB, REINVENTING LOS ANGELES: NATURE AND COMMUNITY IN THE GLOBAL CITY (2007); ROBERT GOTTLIEB, MARK VALLIANATOS, REGINA M. FREER & PETER DREIER, THE NEXT LOS ANGELES: THE STRUGGLE FOR A LIVABLE CITY (2005).
43. *See* ALEXANDER VON HOFFMAN, HOUSE BY HOUSE, BLOCK BY BLOCK: THE REBIRTH OF AMERICA'S NEIGHBORHOODS (2003); PRISMATIC METROPOLIS: INEQUALITY IN LOS ANGELES (Lawrence D. Bobo, Melvin L. Oliver, James H. Johnson, Jr. & Abel Valenzuela, Jr. eds., 2000).
44. GOTTLIEB ET AL., *supra* note 42, at 76.
45. UNDERSTANDING THE RIOTS: LOS ANGELES BEFORE AND AFTER THE RODNEY KING CASE (1992).
46. *Id.* at 6.
47. *Id.* at 9.
48. *Id.* at 25, 31.
49. *Id.* at 130.
50. On the nature and extent of residential segregation, *see* GOTTLIEB ET AL., *supra* note 42, at 34; Camille Zubrinsky Charles, *Residential Segregation in Los Angeles*, in PRISMATIC METROPOLIS, *supra* note 43, at 167, 170–71.
51. UNDERSTANDING THE RIOTS, *supra* note 45, at 26.
52. *See* Jack Schneider, *Escape from Los Angeles: White Flight from Los Angeles and Its Schools, 1960–1980*, 34 J. URB. HIST. 995 (2008).
53. VON HOFFMAN, *supra* note 43, at 210.
54. MILKMAN, *supra* note 7, at 85–86.
55. *See* David M. Grant, *A Demographic Profile of Los Angeles County, 1970 to 1990*, in PRISMATIC METROPOLIS, *supra* note 43, at 51, 55.
56. EDWARD W. SOJA, SEEKING SPATIAL JUSTICE 122 (2010).
57. GOTTLIEB ET AL., *supra* note 42, at 83–87; *see also* MILKMAN, *supra* note 7.
58. SOJA, *supra* note 56, at 125.
59. *Id.* at 126.
60. *Id.*
61. GOTTLIEB ET AL., *supra* note 42, at 85.
62. SASKIA SASSEN, THE GLOBAL CITY: NEW YORK, LONDON, TOKYO (1991).
63. Ruth Milkman, *Introduction*, in WORKING FOR JUSTICE, *supra* note 32, at 5–6.
64. GOTTLIEB ET AL., *supra* note 42, at 86–88; MILKMAN, *supra* note 7, at 90, 101.
65. GOTTLIEB ET AL., *supra* note 42, at 85–86; Grant, *supra* note 55, at 56.
66. ROBERT POLLIN & STEPHANIE LUCE, THE LIVING WAGE: BUILDING A FAIR ECONOMY 31 fig.2.1 (1998).
67. PAUL MORE ET AL., THE OTHER LOS ANGELES: THE WORKING POOR IN THE CITY OF THE 21ST CENTURY 8–9 (2000).
68. Lawrence D. Bobo, Melvin L. Oliver, James H. Johnson & Abel Valenzuela, Jr., *Analyzing Inequality in Los Angeles*, in PRISMATIC METROPOLIS, *supra* note 43, at 3, 18 tbl.1.6; *see also* STORPER ET AL., *supra* note 41, at 12 tbl.1.1 (showing growth of wage and salary income Gini coefficients in the L.A. region from .463 in 1980 to .482 in 1990).

69. Bobo et al., *supra* note 68, at 18 tbl.1.6.
70. GOTTLIEB ET AL., *supra* note 42, at 92. These figures are from 2000.
71. MORE ET AL., *supra* note 67, at 15–16.
72. *Id.* at 10, 12.
73. *Id.* at 15.
74. *Id.* at 19, 24.
75. MILKMAN, *supra* note 7, at 81.
76. Bobo et al., *supra* note 68, at 16 tbl.1.5.
77. *Id.* at 13.
78. Bobo et al., *supra* note 68, at 15; George Sabagh & Mehdi Bozorgmehr, *From "Give Me Your Poor" to "Save Our State": New York and Los Angeles as Immigrant Cities and Regions*, in NEW YORK AND LOS ANGELES: POLITICS, SOCIETY, AND CULTURE—A COMPARATIVE VIEW 99, 106 (David Halle ed., 2003).
79. SOJA, *supra* note 56, at 122.
80. UNDERSTANDING THE RIOTS, *supra* note 45, at 26.
81. GOTTLIEB ET AL., *supra* note 42, at 78.
82. Grant, *supra* note 55, at 58.
83. Andrew A. Beveridge & Sydney J. Beveridge, *The Big Picture: Demographic and Other Changes*, in NEW YORK AND LOS ANGELES: THE UNCERTAIN FUTURE 33, 51 fig.2 (David Halle & Andrew A. Beveridge eds., 2013). The percentage of foreign-born Latinos is countywide. Grant, *supra* note 55, at 52 fig.2.1.
84. SOJA, *supra* note 56, at 121–22.
85. VON HOFFMAN, *supra* note 43.
86. Bobo et al., *supra* note 68, at 24.
87. *Id.* at 25–26.
88. Grant, *supra* note 55, at 73–74.
89. Yu Eui-Young, *"Koreatown" Los Angeles: Emergence of a New Inner-City Ethnic Community*, 14 BULL. POPULATION & DEV. STUD. CTR. 29, 36, 40 (1985).
90. *Id.* at 38 tbl.3.
91. UNDERSTANDING THE RIOTS, *supra* note 45, at 37.
92. *Id.* at 72.
93. MIKE DAVIS, MAGICAL URBANISM: LATINOS REINVENT THE U.S. BIG CITY (2000).
94. MILKMAN, *supra* note 7.
95. *Id.* at 38.
96. *Id.* at 74.
97. *Id.* at 45–70.
98. *Id.* at 59–60.
99. *Id.* at 79 fig.2.1.
100. *Id.* at 7.
101. *Id.* at 84–87.
102. Gilda Haas & Rebecca Morales, *Plant Closures and the Grassroots Response to Economic Crisis in the United States* 13 (Paper Submitted to the International Research Center on Environment and Development, 1986).
103. *Id.* at 14–19.
104. Milkman, *supra* note 63, at 8.
105. Christopher L. Erickson, Catherine L. Fisk, Ruth Milkman, Daniel J.B. Mitchell & Kent Wong, *Justice for Janitors in Los Angeles: Lessons from Three Rounds of Negotiations*, 40 BRIT. J. INDUS. REL. 543 (2002).
106. Milkman, *supra* note 63, at 6.
107. SOJA, *supra* note 56, at 140.
108. Erickson et al., *supra* note 105, at 548.

109. MILKMAN, *supra* note 7, at 147; *see also* Richard W. Hurd & William Rouse, *Progressive Union Organizing: The SEIU Justice for Janitors Campaign*, 21 REV. RADICAL POL. ECON. 70 (1989).
110. Larry Frank & Kent Wong, *Dynamic Political Mobilization: The Los Angeles County Federation of Labor*, 8 WORKING USA 155, 157 (2004).
111. MILKMAN, *supra* note 7, at 114.
112. Frank & Wong, *supra* note 110, at 160.
113. *Id.* at 161.
114. GOTTLIEB ET AL., *supra* note 42, at 82.
115. For an analysis of the development of multiracial "Third World Left" activism, *see* LAURA PULIDO, BLACK, BROWN, YELLOW & LEFT: RADICAL ACTIVISM IN LOS ANGELES (2006).
116. GOTTLIEB ET AL., *supra* note 42; WORKING FOR JUSTICE, *supra* note 32.
117. SOJA, *supra* note 56, at 133.
118. *Id.*; *see also* VON HOFFMAN, *supra* note 43, at 214–17.
119. VON HOFFMAN, *supra* note 43, at 218.
120. *Id.* at 218–20.
121. Martha Matsuoka, From Neighborhood to Global: Community-Based Regionalism and Shifting Concepts of Place in Community and Regional Development (2005) (unpublished Ph.D. thesis, Department of Urban Planning, UCLA).
122. *Id.* at 189.
123. VON HOFFMAN, *supra* note 43, at 228.
124. *Id.* at 237.
125. *Id.* at 236–43.
126. UCLA LABOR CENTER & LOS ANGELES ALLIANCE FOR A NEW ECONOMY, WHO BENEFITS FROM REDEVELOPMENT IN LOS ANGELES? AN EVALUATION OF COMMERCIAL DEVELOPMENT ACTIVITIES IN THE 1990S (1999); *see also* SHEA CUNNINGHAM ET AL., TAKING CARE OF BUSINESS: AN EVALUATION OF THE LOS ANGELES BUSINESS TEAM (2000).
127. Phill Ansell et al., Accidental Tourism: A Critique of the Los Angeles Tourism Industry and Proposals for Change (UCLA Master of Arts in Urban Planning 1992).
128. THE LABOR/COMMUNITY STRATEGY CENTER, RECONSTRUCTING LOS ANGELES FROM THE BOTTOM UP: A LONG-TERM STRATEGY FOR WORKERS, LOW-INCOME PEOPLE, AND PEOPLE OF COLOR TO CREATE AN ALTERNATIVE VISION OF URBAN DEVELOPMENT (1993).
129. David R. Rice, *The Bus Rider's Union: The Success of the Law and Organizing Model in the Context of an Environmental Justice Struggle*, 26 ENVIRONS 187, 197 (2003).
130. Robert D. Wilton & Cynthia Cranford, *Toward an Understanding of the Spatiality of Social Movements: Labor Organizing at a Private University in Los Angeles*, 49 SOC. PROBS. 374 (2014).
131. *See generally* FINE, *supra* note 32.
132. Milkman, *supra* note 63, at 16.
133. GOTTLIEB ET AL., *supra* note 42, at 81.
134. *See* Jong Bum Kwon, *The Koreatown Immigrant Workers Alliance: Spatializing Justice in an Ethnic "Enclave," in* WORKING FOR JUSTICE, *supra* note 32, at 23; Victor Narro, *Impacting Next Wave Organizing: Creative Campaign Strategies of the Los Angeles Worker Centers*, 50 N.Y. L. REV. 465, 482 (2005–2006).
135. Susan Garea & Sasha Alexandra Stern, *From Legal Advocacy to Organizing: Progressive Lawyering and the Los Angeles Car Wash Campaign, in* WORKING FOR JUSTICE, *supra* note 32, at 125, 129.
136. Frank & Wong, *supra* note 110, at 171.
137. Overall employment grew 5.9% between 1998 and 2008; manufacturing employment decreased by 29% while total service employment was up by 13.2%. David L. Gladstone & Susan S. Fainstein, *The New York and Los Angeles Economies from Boom to Crisis, in* NEW YORK AND LOS ANGELES, *supra* note 83, at 79, 85 tbl.3.4.
138. In Tables 1.1, 1.2, and 1.4, the categories are defined by occupations within the relevant industry. Garment workers include the following occupations within the apparel industry: "Knitting,

looping, taping, weaving machine operators," "Textile cutting machine operators," "Sewing machine operators," "Shoe Machine Operators," "Pressing machine operators," "Laundering and dry clean machine operators," "Misc textile machine operators," "Dressmakers," "Tailors," "Shoe repairers," and "Misc precision apparel workers." Retail workers exclude grocery store, car dealership, auto part, and gas station workers. In Table 1.3, the categories are defined by industry only because publicly available census data do not include earnings data by occupation within a particular industry. Figures for white workers, when reported, are for non-Hispanic whites.

139. SARAH FLOOD ET AL., INTEGRATED PUBLIC USE MICRODATA SERIES, CURRENT POPULATION SURVEY (version 6.0 [dataset], 2018), https://doi.org/10.18128/D030.V6.0 (last visited Sept. 29, 2019).

Chapter 2

1. Kenneth B. Noble, *Thai Workers Are Set Free in California*, N.Y. TIMES, Aug. 4, 1995, at A1; *see also* Julie A. Su, *Making the Invisible Visible: The Garment Industry's Dirty Laundry*, 1 J. GENDER RACE & JUST. 405, 406 (1998).
2. George White, *Workers Held in Near-Slavery, Officials Say*, L.A. TIMES, Aug. 3, 1995, at A1.
3. Julie Su, *El Monte Thai Garment Workers: Slave Sweatshops*, in NO SWEAT: FASHION, FREE TRADE, AND THE RIGHTS OF GARMENT WORKERS 143, 143 (Andrew Ross ed., 1997).
4. Bureerong v. Uvawas, 922 F. Supp. 1450, 1469 (C.D. Cal. 1996).
5. Katie Quan, *Use of Global Value Chains by Labor Organizers*, 12 COMPETITION & CHANGE 89, 91 (2008).
6. EDNA BONACICH & RICHARD P. APPELBAUM, BEHIND THE LABEL: INEQUALITY IN THE LOS ANGELES APPAREL INDUSTRY 80–81 (2000).
7. *Id.* at 27–28; *see also* ASIAN PAC. AM. LEGAL CTR. ET AL., REINFORCING THE SEAMS: GUARANTEEING THE PROMISE OF CALIFORNIA'S LANDMARK ANTI-SWEATSHOP LAW 10 (2005).
8. BONACICH & APPELBAUM, *supra* note 6, at 135–37.
9. *Id.* at 137.
10. *Id.* at 135–40.
11. *The Garment Industry*, SWEATSHOP WATCH (2001).
12. BONACICH & APPELBAUM, *supra* note 6, at 3; *see also* Jerry Loo, *Fashion's Dirty Laundry: A Brief History of Sweatshops*, in SWEATSHOP SLAVES: ASIAN AMERICANS IN THE GARMENT INDUSTRY 2 (Kent Wong & Julie Monroe eds., 2006).
13. Katie Quan, *Strategies for Garment Worker Empowerment in the Global Economy*, 10 U.C. DAVIS J. INT'L L. & POL'Y 27, 29 (2003).
14. National Labor Relations Act § 8(e)v, 29 U.S.C. § 158(e) (2000 & Supp. V. 2006).
15. Quan, *supra* note 13, at 30.
16. *Id.*
17. *See* James J. Brudney, *Neutrality Agreements and Card Check Recognition: Prospects for Changing Paradigms*, 90 IOWA L. REV. 819, 832–33 (2005); Benjamin I. Sachs, *Employment Law as Labor Law*, 29 CARDOZO L. REV. 2685, 2694–97 (2008). Because of the adverse legal environment, garment unions—like other private sector unions—saw their ability to successfully organize diminish, which contributed to a decline in membership. Nationwide, total garment union membership fell from eight hundred thousand in the early 1970s to less than three hundred thousand in 1997—a more than 60% reduction. *See* Edna Bonacich, *Intense Challenges, Tentative Possibilities: Organizing Immigrant Garment Workers in Los Angeles*, in ORGANIZING IMMIGRANTS: THE CHALLENGES FOR UNIONS IN CONTEMPORARY CALIFORNIA 130, 137 (Ruth Milkman ed., 2000). During roughly the same period, total domestic employment in the garment industry fell just over 40%. *See* BONACICH & APPELBAUM, *supra* note 6, at 16.

18. Ruth Milkman, L.A. Story: Immigrant Workers and the Future of the U.S. Labor Movement 84–85 (2006).
19. *Id.* at 89 tbl.2.2 (showing that the number of workers in the L.A. apparel and textile industry grew from 55,500 in 1971 to 98,800 in 1992).
20. *Id.* at 88.
21. *See* Ruth Milkman & Kent Wong, *Organizing Immigrant Workers: Case Studies from California*, *in* Rekindling the Movement: Labor's Quest for Relevance in the 21st Century 100, 112 (Lowell Turner et al. eds., 2001).
22. Milkman, *supra* note 18, at 85 tbl.2.1.
23. Bonacich, *supra* note 17, at 137.
24. Edmond McGovern, International Trade Regulation: GATT, The United States and the European Community 507 (2nd ed. 1986).
25. Arrangement Regarding International Trade in Textiles (Multifibre Arrangement), Dec. 20, 1973, 25 U.S.T. 1001 (entered into force Jan. 1, 1974).
26. Bonacich & Appelbaum, *supra* note 6, at 56–57.
27. *Id.* at 16, 55–57.
28. *Id.* at 55.
29. *Id.* at 56–57.
30. Agreement on Textiles and Clothing, *opened for signature* Apr. 15, 1994, 1868 U.N.T.S. 14.
31. Bonacich & Appelbaum, *supra* note 6, at 16.
32. Bonacich, *supra* note 17, at 137.
33. Lab. Mkt. Info. Div., Cal. Emp. Dev. Dep't, Industry Employment & Labor Force (2007). The reported figures for cut-and-sew garment workers are based on employer payrolls for the entire apparel industry.
34. Bonacich & Appelbaum, *supra* note 6, at 17–18.
35. *Id.* at 16; Jack Kyser & George Huang, L.A. Econ. Dev. Corp., The Los Angeles Area Fashion Industry Profile 2 (2003).
36. Bonacich & Appelbaum, *supra* note 6, at 18.
37. Immigration and Citizenship: Process and Policy 158–62 (Thomas Alexander Aleinikoff, David A. Martin & Hiroshi Motomura eds., 2003).
38. Immigration and Nationality Act, Pub. L. No. 89-236, 79 Stat. 911 (1965).
39. Douglas S. Massey, Jorge Durand & Noland J. Malone, Beyond Smoke and Mirrors: Mexican Immigration in an Era of Economic Integration 43–44 (2002). In the 1970s, an estimated 900,000 of the 1.4 million Mexican immigrants who entered the United States were undocumented. *See* Jeffrey S. Passel, Pew Hispanic Center, Unauthorized Migrants: Numbers and Characteristics 37 (2005); Jeffrey S. Passel, *Undocumented Immigration*, 487 Annals Am. Acad. Pol. & Soc. Sci. 181, 190 (Sept. 1986).
40. 8 U.S.C. 1101 (2006).
41. Passel, *supra* note 39, at 6.
42. Massey et al., *supra* note 39, at 120–23, 128–33.
43. Aiko Joshi, *The Face of Human Trafficking*, 13 Hastings Women's L.J. 31, 46 n.136 (2002); *see also* Jennifer M. Chacón, *Misery and Myopia: Understanding the Failures of U.S. Efforts to Stop Human Trafficking*, 74 Fordham L. Rev. 2977 (2006).
44. George Sabagh & Mehdi Bozorgmehr, *From "Give Me Your Poor" to "Save Our State": New York and Los Angeles as Immigrant Cities and Regions*, *in* New York and Los Angeles: Politics, Society, and Culture—A Comparative View 99, 106 (David Halle ed., 2003).
45. *Id.* at 105.
46. Paul Ong & Tania Azores, *Asian Immigrants in Los Angeles: Diversity and Divisions*, *in* The New Asian Immigration in Los Angeles and Global Restructuring 100, 102 (Paul Ong, Edna Bonacich & Lucie Cheng eds., 1994).
47. Sabagh & Bozorgmehr, *supra* note 44, at 106.
48. Bonacich & Appelbaum, *supra* note 6, at 170–74.

49. Bonacich, *supra* note 17, at 138.
50. BONACICH & APPELBAUM, *supra* note 6, at 174–75. In 2000, garment workers were 70% Latino (mostly Mexican) and 20% Asian (mostly Chinese and Korean). *See* GARMENT WORKER CTR. & SWEATSHOP WATCH, CRISIS OR OPPORTUNITY? THE FUTURE OF LOS ANGELES' GARMENT WORKERS, THE APPAREL INDUSTRY AND THE LOCAL ECONOMY 6 (2004), https://digitalcommons.ilr.cornell.edu/cgi/viewcontent.cgi?article=1914&context =globaldocs (last visited Mar. 17, 2019) [*hereinafter* CRISIS OR OPPORTUNITY?].
51. BONACICH & APPELBAUM, *supra* note 6, at 139–40. Based on 1998 Department of Labor figures, Bonacich and Appelbaum estimated that there were forty-five hundred registered contract shops in Los Angeles.
52. Lora Jo Foo, *The Vulnerable and Exploitable Immigrant Workforce and the Need for Strengthening Worker Protective Legislation*, 103 YALE L.J. 2179, 2187–88 (1994).
53. *Cf.* Shirley Lung, *Exploiting the Joint Employer Doctrine: Providing a Break for Sweatshop Garment Workers*, 34 LOY U. CHI. L.J. 291, 302 (2003) (noting that in 1994, "the GAO estimated that less than 1,000 manufacturers, who outsourced work to 20,000 contractors and subcontractors, dominated the industry").
54. Nelson Lichtenstein, *Wal-Mart: A Template for Twenty-First-Century Capitalism*, *in* WAL-MART: THE FACE OF TWENTY-FIRST-CENTURY CAPITALISM 3, 9 (Nelson Lichtenstein ed., 2006).
55. Bonacich, *supra* note 17, at 132.
56. *Id.*
57. Lung, *supra* note 53, at 302.
58. BONACICH & APPELBAUM, *supra* note 6, at 223; Foo, *supra* note 52, at 2198.
59. Foo, *supra* note 52, at 2188, 2196.
60. BONACICH & APPELBAUM, *supra* note 6, at 223–40.
61. *See, e.g.,* CAL. DEP'T OF INDUST. REL., TARGETED INDUSTRIES PARTNERSHIP PROGRAM, FIFTH ANNUAL REPORT AND RETROSPECTIVE (1997) (describing program that coordinated federal and state agencies to collect more than $1 million in penalties from garment shops in 1997); *see also* Wendy Williams, *Model Enforcement of Wage and Hour Laws for Undocumented Workers: One Step Closer to Equal Protection Under the Law*, 37 COLUM. HUM. RTS. L. REV. 755, 778 (2006) (describing the California Joint Enforcement Strike Force, which was created in 1995 to coordinate state agencies in an effort to enforce labor laws in targeted sectors, including the garment industry).
62. Lung, *supra* note 53, at 303–04; Catherine K. Ruckelshaus, *Labor's Wage War*, 35 FORDHAM URB. L.J. 373, 375–78 (2008).
63. BONACICH & APPELBAUM, *supra* note 6, at 227–28.
64. Ruckelshaus, *supra* note 62, at 385–87.
65. Lung, *supra* note 53, at 305.
66. U.S. GEN. ACCT. OFF., REPORT NO. GAO/HEHS-95-29, GARMENT INDUSTRY: EFFORTS TO ADDRESS THE PREVALENCE AND CONDITIONS OF SWEATSHOPS 5 (1994).
67. Stuart Silverstein, *Survey of Garment Industry Finds Rampant Labor Abuse*, L.A. TIMES, Apr. 15, 1994, at D1.
68. BONACICH & APPELBAUM, *supra* note 6, at 3.
69. *Id.* at 225.
70. KATIE QUAN, CTR. FOR LABOR RES. & EDUC.—INST. OF INDUS. REL., LEGISLATING SWEATSHOP ACCOUNTABILITY 5 (2001).
71. *Id.* at 4–6.
72. Quan, *supra* note 13, at 32.
73. Ruth Needleman, *Building Relationships for the Long Haul: Unions and Community-Based Groups Working Together to Organize Low-Wage Workers*, *in* ORGANIZING TO WIN: NEW RESEARCH ON UNION STRATEGIES 71, 74–75 (Kate Bronfenbrenner et al. eds., 1998).
74. *Id.* at 76–77.

75. Email from Julie Su, Litig. Dir., Asian Pac. Am. Legal Ctr., to Scott Cummings, Professor, UCLA Sch. of Law (Apr. 11, 2008).
76. *Id.*
77. Telephone Interview with Julie Su, Litig. Dir., Asian Pac. Am. Legal Ctr. (Feb. 19, 2008).
78. Telephone Interview with Julie Su, Litig. Dir., Asian Pac. Am. Legal Ctr. (July 13, 2006).
79. *Id.*
80. Telephone Interview with Julie Su, *supra* note 77.
81. Telephone Interview with Julie Su, *supra* note 78.
82. Telephone Interview with Julie Su, *supra* note 77.
83. *Id.*
84. *Id.*
85. James Sterngold, *Agency Missteps Put Illegal Aliens at Mercy of Sweatshops*, N.Y. TIMES, Sept. 21, 1995, at A16.
86. Su, *supra* note 1, at 406. There was evidence that the INS was aware of the Thai workers' plight well before the 1995 raid. In 1992, an INS agent investigating the El Monte compound had written several memos to his superiors detailing suspicious activity there; although the INS asked federal authorities for a search warrant, the U.S. Attorney's office in Los Angeles did not seek court permission to execute it, citing a lack of evidence. *See* Paul Feldman, Patrick J. McDonnell & George White, *Thai Worker Sweatshop Probe Grows*, L.A. TIMES, Aug. 9, 1995, at A1; Patrick J. McDonnell & Paul Feldman, *Wilson Attacks INS over Sweatshop Probe Politics*, L.A. TIMES, Aug. 25, 1995, at B1.
87. Patrick Lee & George White, *INS Got Tip on Sweatshop 3 Years Ago*, L.A. TIMES, Aug. 4, 1995, at A1.
88. *Id.*
89. Su, *supra* note 1, at 407.
90. *Id.*
91. *Id.* at 408.
92. Karl Schoenberger, Patrick J. McDonnell & Shawn Hubler, *21 Thais Found in Sweatshop Are Released*, L.A. TIMES, Aug. 12, 1995, at A1.
93. Su, *supra* note 1, at 408.
94. K. Connie Kang, *Final $1.2 Million Added to Thai Workers' Settlement*, L.A. TIMES, July 29, 1999, at A1; Pamela Warrick, *The Freedom Fighter; Lawyer Julie Su Finds Inspiration in the Thai Garment Workers She's Assisting*, L.A. TIMES, Sept. 4, 1995, at E1.
95. Peter Hong, *Speaking Up for the Silent*, L.A. TIMES, Aug. 23, 1995, at B2.
96. Patrick J. McDonnell & Maki Becker, *7 Plead Guilty in Sweatshop Slavery Case*, L.A. TIMES, Feb. 10, 1996, at A1.
97. Paul Feldman & Patrick J. McDonnell, *Sweatshop Operators Indicted*, L.A. TIMES, Nov. 10, 1995, at B3.
98. McDonnell & Becker, *supra* note 96, at A1.
99. 8 U.S.C. § 1101(a)(15)(S).
100. Kenneth Chang, *Not Home Free; Thais Freed from Sweatshop Are Adjusting to Life in U.S., but the Future Is Uncertain*, L.A. TIMES, June 19, 1996, at B4.
101. 8 U.S.C. §§ 1255(j)(1)(B), 1255(l)(1)(A).
102. K. Connie Kang, *Once Virtual Slaves, 71 Thai Workers Win U.S. Residency*, L.A. TIMES, Nov. 18, 2002, at B1.
103. Julie A. Su, *The Progressive Critique of the Current Socio-Legal Landscape: Corporations and Economic Justice*, 4 SEATTLE J. SOC. JUST. 237, 242 (2005).
104. *Id.*; *see also* Kang, *supra* note 102, at B1.
105. The U.S. Department of Labor was also involved in investigations into allegations that some of the products from the El Monte shop ended up on the racks at retailers Neiman Marcus, Robinsons May, and Macy's, and asked that the retailers contribute toward the $5 million owed to the workers. *See Balanced Solution Is Required for Garment Industry Trouble*, L.A. TIMES,

Aug. 20, 1995, at M4; *see also* Kenneth B. Noble, *U.S. Warns Big Retailers About Sweatshop Goods*, N.Y. TIMES, Aug. 15, 1995, at A14 (stating that Labor Secretary Robert Reich called a meeting of major apparel retailers, including Federated and May, to "discuss ways to prevent goods made by slave labor from being sold").

106. Kenneth B. Noble, *Manufacturers Fined in Sweatshop Inquiry*, N.Y. TIMES, Aug. 16, 1995, at A22.
107. The state senate placed additional pressure on the manufacturers, at one point calling them to testify at a public hearing in the El Monte City Hall. *See* Paul Feldman & Carl Ingram, *8 Suspects in Sweatshop Ring Plead Not Guilty*, L.A. TIMES, Aug. 22, 1995, at B1.
108. George White, *Sweatshop Workers to Receive $1 Million*, L.A. TIMES, Mar. 8, 1996, at B1.
109. Ian James, *Freed Thai Workers File Lawsuit*, L.A. TIMES, Sept. 6, 1995, at B3.
110. Bureerong v. Uvawas, 922 F. Supp. 1450, 1458 (C.D. Cal. 1996). "The high damage amount was partly symbolic, Su said, because the alleged operators could not totally repay the victims for what she called their 'recklessness' and 'inhumanity.'" James, *supra* note 109.
111. *Bureerong*, 922 F. Supp. at 1458; K. Connie Kang, *Thai Workers Sue Top Clothing Businesses over El Monte Plant*, L.A. TIMES, Oct. 26, 1995, at B1.
112. *Bureerong*, 922 F. Supp. at 1459.
113. Telephone Interview with Julie Su, Litig. Dir., Asian Pac. Am. Legal Ctr. (Aug. 9, 2007).
114. *Id.*
115. *Id.*
116. *Id.*
117. Email from Julie Su to Scott Cummings, *supra* note 75.
118. *Id.*; *see also* Kang, *supra* note 94 (noting that Su met with the sweatshop workers nightly for eight months).
119. Telephone Interview with Julie Su, *supra* note 113.
120. *Id.*
121. Email from Julie Su to Scott Cummings, *supra* note 75.
122. Su, *supra* note 1, at 416–17.
123. Email from Julie Su to Scott Cummings, *supra* note 75.
124. *Id.*
125. *Id.*
126. *See, e.g.*, Real v. Driscoll Strawberry Assocs., Inc., 603 F.2d 748 (9th Cir. 1979) (reversing a district court dismissal of a claim by agricultural workers that they were employees of a strawberry grower and its contractor under the joint employer test of FLSA); *see also* Rick McHugh, *Recognizing Wage and Hour Issues on Behalf of Low-Income Workers*, 35 CLEARINGHOUSE REV. 289, 296 (Sept.–Oct. 2001).
127. Leo L. Lam, Comment, *Designer Duty: Extending Liability to Manufacturers for Violations of Labor Standards in Garment Industry Sweatshops*, 141 U. PA. L. REV. 623, 646–52 (1992).
128. *Bureerong*, 922 F. Supp. at 1468–69.
129. *Id.*
130. *39 Garment Workers File Suit to Recover $1.8 Million in Wages*, L.A. TIMES, Apr. 5, 1996, at B4.
131. Su, *supra* note 3, at 146; *see also* Gowri Ramachandran, Hon. Audrey B. Collins, Julie Su, Scott Cummings & Muneer Ahmad, *Panel Discussion: The El Monte Sweatshop Slavery Cases*, 23 SW. J. INT'L L. 279, 283 (2017).
132. Bureerong v. Uvawas, 959 F. Supp. 1231 (C.D. Cal. 1997).
133. *Id.* at 1237–38.
134. Su, *supra* note 1, at 413.
135. Patrick McDonnell & George White, *Sweatshop Workers to Get $2 Million*, L.A. TIMES, Oct. 24, 1997, at D1.
136. *Id.*
137. Telephone Interview with Julie Su, *supra* note 113; Email from Julie Su to Scott Cummings, *supra* note 75.

138. Telephone Interview with Julie Su, *supra* note 113.
139. Kang, *supra* note 94.
140. *Id.*
141. MILKMAN, *supra* note 18, at 89 tbl.2.2; Milkman & Wong, *supra* note 21, at 105. Union density in the garment industry, at 2%, was much lower than in the L.A. region as a whole.
142. MILKMAN, *supra* note 18, at 163.
143. *Id.* at 162–63.
144. BONACICH & APPELBAUM, *supra* note 6, at 214 tbl.8 (showing that Guess was Southern California's most profitable apparel manufacturer in 1996–1997, with nearly $67 million in annual profit, and a sales volume that ranked it as the twenty-first largest domestic apparel manufacturer).
145. MILKMAN, *supra* note 18, at 162, 164.
146. *Id.* at 162–63.
147. Milkman & Wong, *supra* note 21, at 113.
148. MILKMAN, *supra* note 18, at 164.
149. Milkman & Wong, *supra* note 21, at 113.
150. MILKMAN, *supra* note 18, at 164.
151. *Id.*
152. Milkman & Wong, *supra* note 21, at 112.
153. MILKMAN, *supra* note 18, at 164–65; Milkman & Wong, *supra* note 21, at 115.
154. *See* Cynthia L. Estlund, *The Ossification of American Labor Law*, 102 COLUM. L. REV. 1527, 1538 n.50 (2002) ("'Unfair labor practice strikers,' whose strike is provoked or prolonged by the employer's illegal conduct, are not subject to permanent replacement.").
155. MILKMAN, *supra* note 18, at 165.
156. *Id.* at 170.
157. BONACICH & APPELBAUM, *supra* note 6, at 229–30.
158. *Id.* at 230.
159. MILKMAN, *supra* note 18, at 166.
160. *Id.* at 167.
161. Charles Heckscher, *Living with Flexibility*, *in* REKINDLING THE MOVEMENT, *supra* note 21, at 59, 74.
162. Telephone Interview with David Prouty, Gen. Couns., UNITE HERE (Mar. 3, 2008).
163. *Id.*
164. Stuart Silverstein & George White, *"Good Guy" Labor List Gets a Bad Rap*, L.A. TIMES, Dec. 6, 1995, at D1.
165. Thomas J. Ryan, *Guess Finally Floats IPO but It Comes in at $18; Firm also Hit by New Labor Troubles*, DAILY NEWS REC., Aug. 8, 1996, at 3.
166. Stuart Silverstein & Vicki Torres, *String of Illegal Home-Sewing Sites Found, Regulators Say*, L.A. TIMES, July 31, 1996, at D1.
167. Stuart Silverstein, *Guess Fires Back at Charges of Illegal Sewing Operations*, L.A. TIMES, Aug. 6, 1996, at D2.
168. Milkman & Wong, *supra* note 21, at 116.
169. MILKMAN, *supra* note 18, at 167.
170. The contractors named in the suit were: A&B Contractors Inc.; Buzz Sportswear International, dba Indigo Denim; Elkay Corp., dba Infinity Jeans; Evan's Apparel; Hong Kong Garment Corp., dba Joyce Fashion; Il Hong Sangsa Inc., aka Wu Yung; Jeans Plus; Kelly Sportswear; L.A. Industrial Laundry; Mona Maris; Monterey Fashion; P&K Fashions; Parks Fashion; Pride Jeans; Select Sewing; and Total Denim Concepts. *See* Ryan, *supra* note 165.
171. *See* Kristi Ellis, *Guess, Contractors Hit with Class Action Suit*, WOMEN'S WEAR DAILY, Aug. 8, 1996, at 7; *see also* Stuart Silverstein, *Workers Sue Guess, 16 Contractors*, L.A. TIMES, Aug. 8, 1996, at D2.
172. Ryan, *supra* note 165.

173. Ellis, *supra* note 171.
174. Telephone Interview with Della Bahan, Bahan & Assocs. (Mar. 10, 2008).
175. *Id.*
176. *Id.*
177. *Id.*
178. Ryan, *supra* note 165; Janet Ozzard, *New Challenges Push Guess into Changing Corporate Culture*, WOMEN'S WEAR DAILY, Nov. 7, 1996, at 1.
179. Ryan, *supra* note 165; Ozzard, *supra* note 178.
180. The Guess class action lawsuit, combined with subsequent ULP charges, also prompted action from the Department of Labor, which announced a "thorough review" of Guess in October 1996. *See* George White, *Labor Department to Investigate Guess Apparel: It Says Firm Was Selling Garments Made at Alleged Sweatshop; Company Denies Wrongdoing*, L.A. TIMES, Oct. 5, 1996, at D2. This was followed by Guess's suspension from the department's "Trendsetter List" in November. *See* Stuart Silverstein, *Guess Is Left Off "Good Guy" List Pending Labor Inquiry; Apparel: The L.A. Company Says the Censure Is Based on Flawed Government Evaluations*, L.A. TIMES, Nov. 28, 1996, at D1.
181. Telephone Interview with Della Bahan, *supra* note 174.
182. *Id.*
183. *Id.*
184. *Id.*
185. Telephone Interview with David Prouty, *supra* note 162.
186. *Id.*
187. Ozzard, *supra* note 178.
188. Plaintiffs' Points and Auths. Re: Referee's Report and Recommendations; Declarations of Brenda Figueroa and Juan Ruiz at 1–3, Figueroa v. Guess?, Inc., No. BC 155 165 (L.A. Super. Ct. 1997).
189. Stuart Silverstein, *Guess Ordered to Halt Alleged Coercion*, L.A. TIMES, June 20, 1997, at D2.
190. Telephone Interview with Della Bahan, *supra* note 174.
191. Email from Della Bahan, Bahan & Assocs., to Scott Cummings, Professor, UCLA Sch. of Law (Apr. 10, 2008).
192. *Id.*
193. *See, e.g.*, Sachs, *supra* note 17, at 2695.
194. Stuart Silverstein, *NLRB Prepares Complaint Against Apparel Firm Guess; Labor: Accusations Include Firing Pro-Union Workers. Guess Disputes Allegations*, L.A. TIMES, Nov. 22, 1996, at D2.
195. Stuart Silverstein, *A UNITEd Effort*, L.A. TIMES, Feb. 16, 1997, at D1.
196. Mary Beth Sheridan, *Guess Inc. to Move Much of L.A. Work South of the Border*, L.A. TIMES, Jan. 15, 1997, at A1.
197. Rhonda Rundle, *Guess Shifts Apparel-Making to Mexico from Los Angeles Amid Labor Charges*, WALL ST. J., Jan. 14, 1997, at A2.
198. Letter from UNITE Gen. Couns. Max Zimny to Fred Feinstein, Gen. Couns., Nat. Lab. Rel. Bd., Re: Guess? Inc., N.L.R.B. Case No. 21-CA-31807.
199. Kristi Ellis, *NLRB Sets Complaint on Guess*, WOMEN'S WEAR DAILY (L.A.), Nov. 20, 1997, at 12.
200. John R. Emshwiller & Frederick Rose, *Guess Jeans Falters in Trying to Expand; Clothing Maker Faces Bitter Fight with Union, Problems with Stores*, CONTRA COSTA TIMES, Nov. 28, 1997, at C8; George White, *Guess Workers Stage Anti-Union Demonstration*, L.A. TIMES, May 17, 1997, at D1.
201. Appellant's Opening Br. at 2–3, AFL-CIO v. Guess?, Inc., No. B117317 (Cal. Ct. App. June 26, 1998).
202. *Id.* at 3.
203. *Calif. Court Nixes UNITE Bid in Guess Contempt Lawsuit*, WOMEN'S WEAR DAILY (L.A.), Mar. 26, 1998, at 4.

204. UNITE v. Super. Ct., 65 Cal. Rptr. 2d 838 (Cal. Ct. App. 1997).
205. *Guess Pulls Part of UNITE Suit*, DAILY NEWS REC. (L.A.), Mar. 26, 1997, at C2; Julia Stein, *Yet Another SLAPP: A Guess Inc. Lawsuit against a Literary Reading in Los Angeles*, ACTIVIST TIMES, Feb. 23, 1997.
206. *Id.*
207. Vicki Young, *Congress Seeks Data on Claiborne Payments to Union*, WOMEN'S WEAR DAILY (N.Y.) Mar. 26, 1998, at 1.
208. Milkman & Wong, *supra* note 21, at 117; *see also* Email from David Prouty, Gen. Couns., UNITE HERE, to Scott Cummings, Professor, UCLA Sch. of Law (Apr. 15, 2008) (noting that the amount of the legal fees was around $500,000).
209. *See* Patrick J. McDonnell, *Marchers Protest Garment Sweatshops*, L.A. TIMES, Oct. 5, 1997, at B1.
210. *33 Are Arrested at Guess Protest in Santa Monica*, L.A. TIMES, Dec. 14, 1997, at B5.
211. Emshwiller & Rose, *supra* note 200, at C8.
212. BONACICH & APPELBAUM, *supra* note 6, at 270.
213. Stuart Silverstein, *Guess to Rehire Laid-Off Workers, Pay Back Wages*, L.A. TIMES, Apr. 22, 1998, at D2.
214. *Id.*
215. *Id.*
216. *See* Guess?, Inc. and UNITE, 2003 WL 21514151 (N.L.R.B. June 30, 2003); Guess?, Inc. and UNITE, 2000 WL 33664316 (N.L.R.B. Div. of Judges, July 6, 2000).
217. Teena Hammond, *UNITE Carrying Fight Abroad in Attempt to Organize Guess*, WOMEN'S WEAR DAILY, July 1, 1998, at 5 (stating that "[u]nions in Argentina, Australia, Belgium, Brazil, France, Germany, Holland, Israel, Italy, Japan, Philippines, South Africa, Spain and the United Kingdom have agreed to support UNITE in its ongoing battle to organize the manufacturer" by distributing leaflets at retail stores).
218. *See* MILKMAN, *supra* note 18, at 168–69.
219. Interview with Sean Hecht, Exec. Dir., UCLA Sch. of Law Envtl. Law Ctr., Los Angeles, Cal. (Apr. 2, 2008).
220. Nancy Cleeland, *Guess to Pay up to $1 Million to End Suit*, L.A. TIMES, July 21, 1999, at C2.
221. *Id.* To the consternation of some of the workers who did recover, Strumwasser & Woocher took a cut of the award as attorney's fees to compensate the firm for the below-market fees that it had been receiving from UNITE.
222. Nancy Cleeland, *Garment Jobs: Hard, Bleak and Vanishing*, L.A. TIMES, Mar. 11, 1999, at A1 (stating that the rate of outsourcing to Mexico was accelerating, with 64% of L.A. manufacturers sourcing some work to Mexico in 1999, more than triple the percentage in 1992).
223. CRISIS OR OPPORTUNITY?, *supra* note 50, at 8; KYSER & HUANG, *supra* note 35, at 2.
224. Cleeland, *supra* note 222.
225. *See, e.g.*, Don Lee, *State Will Increase Its Inspections of Clothing Makers*, L.A. TIMES, Jan. 11, 1996, at D1.
226. BONACICH & APPELBAUM, *supra* note 6, at 228–29.
227. *Id.* at 242–43. Although the Apparel Industry Partnership was launched with much fanfare, it ultimately broke apart around the question of monitoring, as union and human rights groups pulled out after the formation of the Fair Labor Association, which they viewed as too weak to enforce the already watered-down standards contained in the Code of Conduct. *See id.* at 244.
228. George White, *El Monte Case Sparked Efforts to Monitor, Root Out Sweatshops*, L.A. TIMES, Aug. 2, 1996, at D1.
229. Email from Muneer Ahmad, Professor, Am. U. Wash. C. of Law, to Scott Cummings, Professor, UCLA Sch. of Law (May 10, 2008).
230. Telephone Interview with Julie Su, *supra* note 78.
231. Email from Julie Su, Litig. Dir., Asian Pac. Am. Legal Ctr., to Scott Cummings, Professor, UCLA Sch. of Law (Apr. 14, 2008).

232. Email from Muneer Ahmad to Scott Cummings, *supra* note 229.
233. *Id.*
234. Email from Julie Su to Scott Cummings, *supra* note 231.
235. Kristi Ellis, *BCBG, City Girl, Hobby Horse Settle Unfair Labor Practices Suit*, WOMEN'S WEAR DAILY, May 31, 2000, at 11.
236. *Garment Workers Fight for Justice*, ASIAN PAC. AM. LEGAL CTR. NEWSL. (Asian Pac. Am. Legal Ctr., Los Angeles, Cal.), Fall 2000, at 3, 7.
237. *Id.*
238. City Girl Settlement Agreement and Mutual General Releases (May 2000).
239. Kristi Ellis, *Settlement in Sweatshop Case*, WOMEN'S WEAR DAILY, Sept. 25, 2000, at 22.
240. BONACICH & APPELBAUM, *supra* note 6, at 304.
241. Seconded Amended Complaint for Injunctive and Declaratory Relief and Damages for Violation of the Fair Labor Standards Act and California Labor Code; Unfair Business Practices; Negligence; Wrongful Termination at 2, Benavides v. J.H. Design Group, No. 99-11389 WMB(BQRx) (C.D. Cal. Dec. 1999).
242. *Id.* at 8–9.
243. *Id.* at 10–13.
244. *Id.* at 12–13.
245. Settlement Agreement and Mutual Release, Benavides v. J.H. Design, No. 99-11389 WMB(BQRx) (C.D. Cal. Mar. 2000).
246. Marla Dickerson, *XOXO Sued by Contractor's Unpaid Garment Workers*, L.A. TIMES, Nov. 22, 2000, at C2; *Two Groups Plan Suit Against XOXO*, WOMEN'S WEAR DAILY, Nov. 21, 2000, at 11.
247. *Garment Workers Win Major Victory*, ASIAN PAC. AM. LEGAL CTR. NEWSL. (Asian Pac. Am. Legal Ctr., Los Angeles, Cal.), Spring 2001, at 1, 3.
248. *Id.*
249. Telephone Interview with Julie Su, *supra* note 77.
250. Natasha H. Leland, *Supporters Hold Vigil for Law Students*, THE HARVARD CRIMSON, Apr. 11, 1992, https://www.thecrimson.com/article/1992/4/11/supporters-hold-vigil-for-law-students/ (last visited Mar. 17, 2019).
251. Telephone Interview with Julie Su, *supra* note 77.
252. Email from Julie Su to Scott Cummings, *supra* note 75.
253. Email from Julie Su to Scott Cummings, *supra* note 231.
254. *History*, SWEATSHOP WATCH, http://web.archive.org/web/20071203153130/http://www.sweatshopwatch.org/index.php?s=53 (last visited Aug. 27, 2009).
255. Email from Julie Su to Scott Cummings, *supra* note 231.
256. *10th Anniversary, 1995–2005*, SWEATSHOP WATCH, https://web.archive.org/web/20070715212926/http://www.sweatshopwatch.org/media/powerpoint/SWhistory_whtback.ppt (last visited Mar. 17, 2019).
257. Patrick J. McDonnell, *Retailers Assailed in Sweatshop Protest*, L.A. TIMES, Feb. 24, 1996, at B1.
258. BONACICH & APPELBAUM, *supra* note 6, at 313.
259. Telephone Interview with Julie Su, *supra* note 77.
260. Lora Jo Foo, *Negotiating AB 633, The Garment Accountability Bill*, CAL. LAB. & EMP. L.Q., Winter 1999, at 5.
261. *Id.*
262. CAL. LAB. CODE § 2675 (West 2003).
263. Foo, *supra* note 260, at 5.
264. *Id.*
265. *See* Catherine Bridge, *Union's Fight over Fashion Factories Goes Domestic*, THE RECORDER, July 13, 1999, at 4.
266. *Garment Industry Bill Advances*, L.A. TIMES, Sept. 15, 1995, at A22.
267. Quan, *supra* note 13, at 32–34.

268. Dan Morain, *Bill Advances to Ensure Garment Workers' Pay*, L.A. TIMES, Sept. 10, 1999, at C2.
269. Foo, *supra* note 260, at 5.
270. Kang, *supra* note 94.
271. Foo, *supra* note 260, at 5.
272. Bridge, *supra* note 265, at 4.
273. Foo, *supra* note 260, at 5, 34.
274. *Id.* at 5.
275. *Id.*
276. *Id.*
277. *Id.* at 34.
278. CAL. LAB. CODE § 2673.1(a) (West 2003).
279. *Id.* § 2673.1(c).
280. *Id.* § 2673.1(d).
281. *Id.* § 2673.1(g).
282. *Id.* § 2673.1(e).
283. *Id.* § 2673.1(f).
284. *Id.*
285. *California's Sweatshop Reform Law: Two Years Later*, SWEATSHOP WATCH (Sweatshop Watch, Los Angeles, Cal.), Dec. 2001, at 5–6, http://digitalcommons.ilr.cornell.edu/cgi/viewcontent.cgi?article=1033&context=globaldocs (last visited Aug. 27, 2009).
286. CAL. LAB. CODE § 2671(b).
287. California Labor Commissioner, Notice of Proposed Rulemaking, AB 633, at 4, http://www.dir.ca.gov/dlse/GMT-NOTICE.pdf (last visited Mar. 17, 2019).
288. PROPOSED AMENDMENT AND ADOPTION OF REGULATIONS BY THE STATE LABOR COMMISSIONER TO IMPLEMENT THE PROVISIONS OF AB 633 AND OTHER STATUTES GOVERNING ENFORCEMENT OF MINIMUM WAGE AND OVERTIME REQUIREMENTS IN THE GARMENT INDUSTRY, AND THE REGISTRATION OF PERSONS ENGAGED IN GARMENT MANUFACTURING 3, http://www.dir.ca.gov/dlse/633FSOR2.doc (last visited Mar. 17, 2019).
289. *California's Sweatshop Reform Law*, *supra* note 285, at 5.
290. PROPOSED AMENDMENT AND ADOPTION OF REGULATIONS, *supra* note 288, at 6.
291. *Id.* at 5.
292. *Id.* at 8.
293. *Sweatshop Watch Scores Major Policy Victories: Assembly Bill 633 Regulations*, SWEATSHOP WATCH (Sweatshop Watch, Los Angeles, Cal.), Dec. 2002, at 6, http://digitalcommons.ilr.cornell.edu/cgi/viewcontent.cgi?article=1037&context=globaldocs (last visited Aug. 27, 2009).
294. The interpretation of "garment manufacturing" in A.B. 633 to include retailers was stated by the California Court of Appeal in Fashion 21 v. Coal. for Humane Immigrant Rights of Los Angeles, 117 Cal. App. 4th 1138, 1153 (2004); *see also* Br. of Amicus Curiae State of Cal. in Support of Plaintiffs-Appellants, Castro v. Fashion 21, 88 Fed. Appx. 987 (9th Cir. 2004) (No. 02-55629) (supporting the view that a retailer engaged in garment manufacturing may be held jointly liable under A.B. 633).
295. *Sweatshop Watch Scores Major Policy Victories*, *supra* note 293, at 6.
296. Telephone Interview with Kimi Lee, Dir., Garment Worker Ctr. (Mar. 3, 2008).
297. Victor Narro, *Finding the Synergy Between Law and Organizing: Experiences from the Streets of Los Angeles*, 35 FORDHAM URB. L.J. 339, 346–47 (2008).
298. JANICE FINE, WORKER CENTERS: ORGANIZING COMMUNITIES AT THE EDGE OF THE DREAM 8–11 (2006).
299. *Id.* at 13.
300. Telephone Interview with Julie Su, *supra* note 77.
301. *Garment Workers Fight for Justice*, *supra* note 236, at 7.

302. *Frequently Asked Questions*, GARMENT WORKER CENTER, http://www.garmentworkercenter.org/background.php?itemid=236 (last visited Mar. 5, 2009).
303. Telephone Interview with Julie Su, *supra* note 77.
304. *See, e.g.*, Patrick J. McDonnell, *Center Offers Garment Workers a Voice*, L.A. TIMES, Apr. 14, 2001, at B1.
305. Telephone Interview with Kimi Lee, *supra* note 296.
306. *See* David Greenberg, *Workers' Woes: Kimi Lee's Parents Fled the Oppressive Regime in Burma. Today, She's an Activist Fighting for the Rights of Those Exploited in Sweatshops*, L.A. BUS. J., June 28, 2004, at 48.
307. *See id.*
308. McDonnell, *supra* note 304; Telephone Interview with Kimi Lee, *supra* note 296.
309. FINE, *supra* note 298, at 50; McDonnell, *supra* note 304.
310. McDonnell, *supra* note 304.
311. FINE, *supra* note 298, at 62–63; Telephone Interview with Kimi Lee, *supra* note 296.
312. JENNIFER GORDON, SUBURBAN SWEATSHOPS: THE FIGHT FOR IMMIGRANT RIGHTS 121–22 (2005); Telephone Interview with Kimi Lee, *supra* note 296.
313. Telephone Interview with Kimi Lee, *supra* note 296; *see also Workers Prepare to Take Leadership in the Garment Worker Center*, SWEATSHOP WATCH (Sweatshop Watch, Los Angeles, Cal.), Summer 2002, at 3, http://digitalcommons.ilr.cornell.edu/cgi/viewcontent.cgi?article=1035&context=globaldocs (last visited Aug. 27, 2009).
314. FINE, *supra* note 298, at 93; McDonnell, *supra* note 304; Telephone Interview with Kimi Lee, *supra* note 296.
315. FINE, *supra* note 298, at 86; Telephone Interview with Kimi Lee, *supra* note 296.
316. Telephone Interview with Kimi Lee, *supra* note 296.
317. *Id.*
318. Narro, *supra* note 297, at 348.
319. Press Release, Asian Pac. Am. Legal Ctr. & Garment Worker Ctr., Garment Workers Celebrate End of Year with a New Beginning (Dec. 14, 2004), https://web.archive.org/web/20070811153116/www.garmentworkercenter.org/media/f21/GWC_F21_settlement.pdf (last visited Mar. 17, 2019).
320. *Id.*
321. *Id.*
322. *Boycott Forever 21!*, SWEATSHOP WATCH (Sweatshop Watch, Los Angeles, Cal.), Dec. 2001, at 1, http://digitalcommons.ilr.cornell.edu/cgi/viewcontent.cgi?article=1033&context=globaldocs (last visited Mar. 5, 2009).
323. Narro, *supra* note 297, at 349.
324. GARMENT WORKER CENTER, FOREVER 21 CAMPAIGN TIMELINE (2004), http://www.garmentworkercenter.org/media/f21/2004_05_f21_Timeline.pdf (last visited Mar. 5, 2009).
325. Nancy Cleeland, *Lawsuit Against Forever 21 Alleges Unfair Labor Practices*, L.A. TIMES, Sept. 7, 2001, at C2.
326. FINE, *supra* note 298, at 104.
327. *Id.*
328. Kristin Young, *Bebe Hit by Worker Lawsuit*, WOMEN'S WEAR DAILY, Dec. 19, 2001, at 4, http://www.wwd.com/fashion-news/article-1174836 (last visited Mar. 5, 2009). APALC filed another suit against Bebe in May 2002 on behalf of six Chinese garment workers for labor violations at the factory of Bebe contractor S&W Manufacture, Inc. Kristin Young, *Bebe Sacked with Labor Lawsuit*, WOMEN'S WEAR DAILY, May 24, 2002, at 3. Settlement negotiations in this suit proceeded in tandem with the original suit.
329. Appellants' Opening Br. at 5–6, Castro v. Fashion 21, Inc., 88 Fed. Appx. 987 (9th Cir. 2004) (No. 02-55629).
330. *Id.* at 8.

331. As in the *Forever 21* case, Bird Marella provided pro bono assistance.
332. Zhao v. Bebe Stores, Inc., 247 F. Supp. 2d 1154, 1154 (C.D. Cal. 2003); *see also Seven Chinese Garment Workers Sue Bebe Clothing Stores, Inc. for Sweatshop Abuses*, ASIAN PAC. AM. LEGAL CTR. NEWSL. (Asian Pac. Am. Legal Ctr., Los Angeles, Cal.), Spring 2002, at 7, http://www.apalc.org/newsletters/newsletter_2002_spring_pdf (last visited Mar. 5, 2009).
333. First Amended Complaint for Injunctive and Declaratory Relief and Damages for Violation of the Fair Labor Standards Act and Cal. Lab. Code; Negligence; Unfair Business Practices; Wrongful Termination; Retaliation, Zhao v. Bebe Stores, Inc., 247 F. Supp. 2d 1154 (C.D. Cal. Feb. 2002) (No. 01-10950 GAF (CTx)). The complaint also included claims under state law alleging failure to provide meal and rest breaks, and failure to provide accurate wage statements in writing. *Id.* at 16–17.
334. Plaintiffs' Mot. for Partial Summ. Judgment at 2, Zhao v. Bebe Stores, Inc., 247 F. Supp. 2d 1154 (C.D. Cal. Sep. 2002) (No. 01-10950 GAF (CTx)).
335. *Zhao*, 247 F. Supp. 2d at 1155.
336. *Id.*
337. *Id.* at 1160.
338. Bureerong v. Uvawas, 922 F. Supp. 1450, 1468 (C.D. Cal. 1996).
339. Telephone Interview with Julie Su, *supra* note 77.
340. Katherine Bowers, *Calif. Court Exonerates Stores on Sweatshops*, WOMEN'S WEAR DAILY, Nov. 18, 2002, at 2, http://www.wwd.com/fashion-news/calif-court-exonerates-stores-on-sweatshops-744574 (last visited Mar. 5, 2009).
341. *"To Be . . . or Not to Be" a Sweatshop?*, SWEATSHOP WATCH (Sweatshop Watch, Los Angeles, Cal.), Spring 2003, at 3, http://digitalcommons.ilr.cornell.edu/cgi/viewcontent.cgi?article=1038&context=globaldocs (last visited Mar. 5, 2009).
342. *Id.*
343. Press Release, Asian Pac. Am. Legal Ctr., "Bebe" Settles Two Lawsuits Alleging Sweatshop Abuses (Mar. 3, 2003), http://www.apalc.org (follow links: Newsroom/Press Releases/2004) (last visited Nov. 2, 2009); Email from Julie Su, Litig. Dir., Asian Pac. Am. Legal Ctr., to Danae McElroy, Res. Assistant to Scott Cummings, Professor, UCLA Sch. of Law (Aug. 9, 2007).
344. Email from Julie Su, Asian Pac. Am. Legal Ctr., to Danae McElroy, Res. Assistant to Scott Cummings, Professor, UCLA Sch. of Law (Aug. 7, 2007).
345. Appellants' Opening Br. at 5–6, Castro v. Fashion 21, Inc., *supra* note 329.
346. *Id.* Julia Figueira-McDonough, who arrived at APALC in October of 2000, was also listed as a lawyer on the federal court complaint.
347. Victor Narro, *Impacting Next Wave Organizing: Creative Campaign Strategies of the Los Angeles Worker Centers*, 50 N.Y. L. SCH. L. REV. 465, 473 (2005–2006).
348. Appellants' Opening Br. at 10, Castro v. Fashion 21, Inc., *supra* note 329. One Clothing agreed to pay seven of the nineteen plaintiffs $175,400. This amount included back wages as well as statutory damages and penalties. Additionally, One Clothing signed a consent decree that it would "take reasonable steps to ensure that its garments are not produced under sweatshop conditions." The decree required One Clothing to establish a multilingual toll-free number that workers could use to report sweatshop conditions to the manufacturer, organize annual trainings for workers and factories on federal and state labor laws, and guarantee that factories were sanitary. *Garment Workers Announce Major Victory Against One Clothing and Forever 21*, ASIAN PAC. AM. LEGAL CTR. NEWSL. (Asian Pac. Am. Legal Ctr., Los Angeles, Cal.), Spring 2002, at 5, https://web.archive.org/web/20041015143058/http://www.apalc.org/newsletters/newsletter_2002_spring.pdf (last visited Mar. 17, 2019).
349. Appellants' Opening Br. at 11, Castro v. Fashion 21, Inc., *supra* note 329.
350. *Id.* at 13.
351. Garment Workers Ctr. v. Super. Ct., 117 Cal. App. 4th 1156 (Cal. Ct. App. 2004).

352. Fashion 21 v. Coal. for Humane Immigrant Rights of Los Angeles, 117 Cal. App. 4th 1138 (Cal. Ct. App. 2004).
353. CAL. CIV. PROC. CODE § 425.16(b)(1).
354. *See* Narro, *supra* note 297, at 350–51.
355. *See id.* at 351.
356. *Forever 21 Boycott Gains Momentum*, SWEATSHOP WATCH (Sweatshop Watch, Los Angeles, Cal.), Fall 2002, at 6, http://digitalcommons.ilr.cornell.edu/cgi/viewcontent.cgi?article=1036&context=globaldocs (last visited Mar. 5, 2009).
357. *Id.*
358. *Forever 21 Boycott Goes National*, SWEATSHOP WATCH (Sweatshop Watch, Los Angeles, Cal.), Dec. 2002, at 3.
359. Garment Workers Ctr. v. Super. Ct., 117 Cal. App. 4th 1156, 1160–61 (Cal. Ct. App. 2004).
360. *Fashion 21*, 117 Cal. App. 4th at 1144.
361. *Garment Workers Ctr.*, 117 Cal. App. 4th at 1159.
362. *Fashion 21*, 117 Cal. App. 4th at 1150–53.
363. *See* Narro, *supra* note 297, at 353–54.
364. FINE, *supra* note 298, at 105.
365. Narro, *supra* note 297, at 354.
366. *See* Appellants' Opening Br. at 16, Castro v. Fashion 21, Inc., *supra* note 329.
367. Castro v. Fashion 21, Inc., 88 Fed. Appx. 987 (9th Cir. 2004).
368. Press Release, *supra* note 319.
369. *Id.*
370. Narro, *supra* note 297.
371. Press Release, *supra* note 319.
372. FINE, *supra* note 298, at 105; Narro, *supra* note 297, at 358.
373. Telephone Interview with Julie Su, *supra* note 77.
374. Telephone Interview with Kimi Lee, *supra* note 296.
375. JOEL F. HANDLER, SOCIAL MOVEMENTS AND THE LEGAL SYSTEM: A THEORY OF LAW REFORM AND SOCIAL CHANGE 18–22 (1978).
376. *See generally* GARY BLASI & ASSOCIATES, IMPLEMENTATION OF AB 633: A PRELIMINARY ASSESSMENT (July 26, 2001), https://web.archive.org/web/20060920040051/http://www.law.ucla.edu/docs/ab633_preliminary_assessment.pdf (last visited Mar. 17, 2019).
377. *Id.* at 3.
378. *Id.* at 4.
379. *Id.* at 6.
380. Leslie Earnest, *Wet Seal Faces Wage Claims*, L.A. TIMES, Oct. 20, 2003, at C1.
381. Order, Decision or Award of the Lab. Comm'r, Oct. 24, 2002, Lab. Comm'r State of Cal., Dep't of Indus. Rel., DLSE, *quoted in* FINE, *supra* note 298, at 90.
382. Earnest, *supra* note 380; Leslie Earnest, *Wet Seal Trial Could Assign Duty to Pay Contractor Workers*, ORANGE CTY. REG., Nov. 29, 2003.
383. Leslie Earnest, *Wet Seal Is Set to Settle Wage Claim*, L.A. TIMES, Jan. 21, 2004, at C1.
384. FINE, *supra* note 298, at 91. In a subsequent case, retailer Charlotte Russe agreed to pay $800 to a garment worker for minimum wage and overtime violations after the labor commissioner ruled in the worker's favor. *See* Amanda Bronstad, *Clothing Lines*, L.A. BUS. J., Aug. 1, 2005, at 12.
385. ASIAN PAC. AM. LEGAL CTR. ET AL., *supra* note 7.
386. *Id.* at 37.
387. *Id.* at 19.
388. *Id.* at 26.
389. *Id.* at 20.
390. *Id.* at 22.
391. *Id.* at 24.

392. *Id.* at 22.
393. *Id.* at 25.
394. *Id.* at 30.
395. *Id.* at 23.
396. Cal. Rev. & Tax. Code § 19290 (West 2003).
397. Cal. State Auditor, Franchise Tax Board, Significant Program Changes Are Needed to Improve Collections of Delinquent Labor Claims 1, 13 (2004), http://www.bsa.ca.gov/pdfs/reports/2003-131.pdf (last visited Mar. 17, 2019).
398. *Id.*
399. Am. Textile Mfrs. Inst., The China Threat to World Textile and Apparel Trade 2 (2003), https://web.archive.org/web/20070213110416/http://www.ncto.org/textilecrisis/china.pdf (last visited Mar. 17, 2019).
400. David Greenberg, *Impact of China on Apparel World Is Debated*, L.A. Bus. J., Nov. 22, 2004, at 3.
401. *The Future of California's Garment Industry: Strengthening Opportunities for Immigrant Workers*, Sweatshop Watch (Sweatshop Watch, Los Angeles, Cal.), Nov. 11–12, 2004, http://digitalcommons.ilr.cornell.edu/cgi/viewcontent.cgi?article=1010&context=globaldocs (last visited Mar. 17, 2019).
402. Crisis or Opportunity?, *supra* note 50, at 11–14.
403. *Asia's Economic Outlook Is Bright, but Risks Loom*, IMF Survey (Int'l Monetary Fund, Wash. D.C.), May 23, 2005, at 142, https://web.archive.org/web/20050527014951/http://www.imf.org/external/pubs/ft/survey/2005/052305.pdf (last visited Mar. 17, 2019).
404. Vivian C. Jones, Cong. Res. Serv., CRS Report for Congress, Safeguards on Textile and Apparel Imports from China 3 (2006).
405. Jack Kyser, L.A. Cty. Econ. Dev. Corp., Manufacturing in Southern California 4 (Mar. 2007).
406. Aurelio Rojas, *Furor over Apparel Job Losses: Industry Cites Sweatshop Laws; Worker Advocates Say They're Ineffective*, Sacramento Bee, May 25, 2003, at A3.
407. Fine, *supra* note 298, at 86.
408. *Id.*
409. *Id.*
410. *Id.* at 86–87.
411. *Id.*
412. Telephone Interview with Kimi Lee, *supra* note 296.
413. *Id.*
414. *Id.*
415. *Id.*
416. Narro, *supra* note 347, at 481.
417. *Id.*
418. Michael Barbaro, *Reborn in the U.S.A.*, N.Y. Times, Sept. 26, 2007, at H1.
419. Email from Julie Su to Scott Cummings, *supra* note 231.
420. Telephone Interview with Julie Su, *supra* note 77.
421. Email from Julie Su to Scott Cummings, *supra* note 231.
422. Telephone Interview with Rini Chakraborty, Exec. Dir., Sweatshop Watch (Feb. 19, 2008); *see also* Adam Tschorn & Booth Moore, *Bringing the Business Home; The City, Hoping to Raise Its Industry Profile, Creates a Made in L.A. Logo*, L.A. Times, Oct. 21, 2012, at 2.
423. *Transforming LA into the Sweat-Free Capital*, Sweatshop Watch (Sweatshop Watch, Los Angeles, Cal.), Spring 2006, at 2, http://digitalcommons.ilr.cornell.edu/cgi/viewcontent.cgi?article=1024&context=globaldocs (last visited Aug. 27, 2009).
424. Telephone Interview with Rini Chakraborty, *supra* note 422.
425. *Id.*
426. Doe I v. The Gap, No. CV-01-0031, 2001 WL 1842389 (D. N. Mar. I. Nov. 26, 2001).
427. Does I thru XXIII v. Advanced Textile Corp., 214 F.3d 1058 (9th Cir. 2000).

428. Jenny Strasburg, *Saipan Lawsuit Terms OKd: Garment Workers to Get $20 Million*, S.F. Chron., Apr. 25, 2003, at B1.
429. Cal. Econ. Dev. Dep't, Labor Market Information, Employment by Industry (2019), https://www.labormarketinfo.edd.ca.gov/data/employment-by-industry.html (last visited Oct. 1, 2019).
430. Email from Kimi Lee, Dir., Garment Worker Ctr., to Scott Cummings, Professor, UCLA Sch. of Law (June 22, 2009).
431. Telephone Interview with Julie Su, *supra* note 77.
432. *Id.*
433. Karen Robinson-Jacobs, *From Virtual Slavery to Being Boss; Entrepreneurs: Couple Once Indentured in a Garment Sweatshop Now Run Their Own Successful Restaurant*, L.A. Times, Oct. 25, 2001, at C1.
434. Teresa Watanabe, *Home of the Freed*, L.A. Times, Aug. 14, 2008.
435. James Sterngold, *Civil Warrior: When It Comes to Battling the Garment Industry's Threadbare Labor Practices, Julie Su Has a Particular Genius*, L.A. Mag., Nov. 1, 2002, at 58; Reebok Human Rights Award, https://www.sourcewatch.org/index.php/Reebok_Human_Rights_Award (last visited Mar. 17, 2019).
436. Andrea Adelson, *Look Who's Minding the Shop: California Garment Makers Try to Police Workplace*, N.Y. Times, May 4, 1996, at 33; White, *supra* note 228.
437. Adelson, *supra* note 436.
438. Telephone Interview with Julie Su, *supra* note 77.
439. *Id.*
440. On the basis of Wal-Mart's code of conduct, the International Labor Rights Fund in 2005 sued the company on behalf of workers in Africa, Central America, and Asia, claiming that contractor labor abuses violated the workers' rights as third-party beneficiaries to Wal-Mart supplier contracts. Press Release, Int'l Lab. Rights Forum, Sweatshop Workers on Four Continents Sue Wal-Mart in California Court (Sept. 13, 2005). The workers' suit was dismissed.
441. Telephone Interview with Julie Su, *supra* note 77.
442. Nancy Cleeland, *Clothing Firm Adopts Non-Sweatshop Concept: It Hopes to Stay Competitive and Turn a Profit*, L.A. Times, Apr. 9, 2002, at C1.
443. Adelson, *supra* note 436.
444. Alexis M. Herman, *After El Monte an Upswing; Labor: Conditions Are Better, But Unscrupulous Independents Bear Watching*, L.A. Times, Aug. 4, 1997, at 5.
445. Khahn T.L. Tran, *Schwarzenegger Takes Aim at Sweatshops*, Women's Wear Daily, Dec. 7, 2005, at 14.
446. Susan Ferriss, *Wage Probe Criticized*, Monterey Cty. Herald, Apr. 24, 2006.
447. L.A., Cal., Admin. Code div. 10, art. 17, §§ 104.43.3, 10.43.5 (2005); *see also* Narro, *supra* note 297, at 357–58.
448. Robert J.S. Ross, *Worker Rights Consortium*, in The Wiley-Blackwell Encyclopedia of Globalization (George Ritzer ed., 2017).
449. *Independent Monitor Hired to Enforce Los Angeles' SweatFree Law*, Sweatshop Watch (Sweatshop Watch, Los Angeles, Cal.), Spring 2007, at 6, http://digitalcommons.ilr.cornell.edu/cgi/viewcontent.cgi?article=1026&context=globaldocs (last visited Aug. 27, 2009).
450. Cal. Lab. Code § 2810 (2004).
451. Grace Chang & Kathleen Kim, *Reconceptualizing Approaches to Human Trafficking: New Directions and Perspectives from the Fields*, 3 Stan. J. Civ. Rts. & Civ. Liberties 317, 335 (2007).
452. *California's Garment Workers Receive Owed Wages Through Garment Special Account*, Sweatshop Watch (Sweatshop Watch, Los Angeles, Cal.), Spring 2007, at 3, http://digitalcommons.ilr.cornell.edu/cgi/viewcontent.cgi?article=1026&context=globaldocs (last visited Aug. 27, 2009).
453. *Id.*

454. MILKMAN, *supra* note 18, at 169.
455. Kent Wong & Victor Narro, *Educating Immigrant Workers for Action*, 32 LAB. STUD. J. 113, 114 (2007).
456. WAGE JUSTICE, *About Us*, http://wagejustice.org/our-team/ (last visited Mar. 17, 2019).
457. A 2008 enforcement sweep conducted by state investigators from the California Economic and Employment Enforcement Coalition cited fourteen garment businesses (out of twenty-one that were inspected) for labor violations, including failure to pay minimum wage and overtime, maintain workers' compensation insurance, and provide itemized deduction statements. Press Release, Econ. & Emp. Enf't Coal., EEEC Cites LA Garment Businesses for Labor Violations (Dec. 22, 2008), http://www.dir.ca.gov/DIRNews/2008/IR2008-73.html (last visited Mar. 17, 2019).
458. *See* Richard Abel, *Speaking Law to Power: Occasions for Cause Lawyering*, in CAUSE LAWYERING: POLITICAL COMMITMENTS AND PROFESSIONAL RESPONSIBILITIES 69, 70 (Austin Sarat & Stuart Scheingold eds., 1998) (describing the "spatial organization of power").
459. Hoffman Plastics Compound, Inc. v. NLRB, 535 U.S. 137 (2002).
460. Telephone Interview with Julie Su, *supra* note 77.
461. Su, *supra* note 103, at 239.
462. Narro, *supra* note 347, at 497–505.
463. S.B. 1818 is codified at CAL. CIV. CODE § 3339 (West 2008), CAL. GOV. CODE § 7285 (West 2008), CAL. HEALTH & SAFETY CODE § 24000 (West 2006), and CAL. LAB. CODE § 1171.5 (West 2003).
464. Telephone Interview with Julie Su, *supra* note 77.
465. Zhao v. Bebe Stores, Inc., 247 F. Supp. 2d 1154, 1156 (C.D. Cal. 2003).
466. *Id.* at 1161.
467. *See* Luis Artieda-Moncada, Exploring the Collegiate Apparel Industry: A Look at the Role and Labor Conditions of the Los Angeles Garment Industry (Comprehensive Project Submitted for the Degree of Master of Urban and Regional Planning, UCLA 2014); Luis Artieda-Moncada et al., Fast Fashion Faster! An Analysis of the Cut-and-Sew Apparel Manufacturing Sector in Los Angeles (Sectoral Analysis Final Project for the Degree of Master of Urban and Regional Planning, UCLA 2013); Alina Mehvesh Din, Threads Unraveled: An Analysis of LA County's Cut-and-Sew Sector and Ability to Thrive in the Future (Client Project Submitted for the Degree of Master of Urban and Regional Planning, UCLA 2014); Chloe Green et al., The Garment Industry: Sewing Together the Apparel Manufacturing Industry in Los Angeles 89–98 (Sectoral Analysis Conducted for Urban Planning 237, UCLA 2012); *see also* Kristi Ellis & Khanh T.L. Tran, *Sweatshops Persist in U.S. Garment Industry*, WOMEN'S WEAR DAILY (Dec. 5, 2016), https://wwd.com/business-news/government-trade/sweatshops-persist-in-u-s-garment-industry-10716742/ (last visited Mar. 18, 2019) ("Of the 77 cases investigated between November 2015 and April 2016 in Los Angeles, Orange and San Bernardino counties, the government disclosed on Nov. 16 that officials had found violations in 85 percent of them, calculating more than $1.3 million owed to workers in back wages.").
468. RUTH MILKMAN, ANA LUZ GONZÁLEZ & VICTOR NARRO, WAGE THEFT AND WORKPLACE VIOLATIONS IN LOS ANGELES: THE FAILURE OF EMPLOYMENT AND LABOR LAW FOR LOW-WAGE WORKERS 31, 35 (2010).
469. Alice Hines, *Forever 21 Under Investigation for Using "Sweatshop-like" Factories in Los Angeles*, HUFFINGTON POST (Oct. 26, 2012), https://www.huffingtonpost.com/2012/10/26/forever-21-sweatshop-investigation_n_2025390.html (last visited Mar. 20, 2019).
470. Tiffany Hsu & Chris Kirkham, *Getting Stripped of Pay; Garment Industry Dominates U.S. Probes of Wage Theft*, L.A. TIMES, Nov. 15, 2014, at A1 (stating that Los Angeles workplaces had "all the features of a sweatshop").
471. Din, *supra* note 467, at 4.

472. See Alice Hines, *Forever 21 Class Action Lawsuit Filed by Employees*, HUFFINGTON POST (Jan. 18, 2018), https://www.huffingtonpost.com/2012/01/18/forever-21-lawsuit-class-action_n_1214359.html (last visited Mar. 20, 2019); Hines, *supra* note 469. The class action was filed by the law firms Norton & Melik, APC and Kitchin Legal.
473. Din, *supra* note 467, at 28.

Chapter 3

1. Abel Valenzuela, Jr., *Working on the Margins in Metropolitan Los Angeles: Immigrants in Day-Labor Work*, 2 MIGRACIONES INTERNACIONALES 5, 15 (2002).
2. ABEL VALENZUELA, JR., UCLA CTR. FOR THE STUDY OF URBAN POVERTY—ISSR, DAY LABORERS IN SOUTHERN CALIFORNIA: PRELIMINARY FINDINGS FROM THE DAY LABOR SURVEY 8 (1999).
3. *Id.* at v, 7–8.
4. ABEL VALENZUELA, JR., NIK THEODORE, EDWIN MELÉNDEZ & ANA LUZ GONZALEZ, ON THE CORNER: DAY LABOR IN THE UNITED STATES iii (2006).
5. VALENZUELA, *supra* note 2, at 5 (noting that there were eighty-seven day labor sites in Southern California, eight of which were formal centers controlled by the city or a community group). *See generally* DAY LABOR RESEARCH INST., COMPARING SOLUTIONS: AN OVERVIEW OF DAY LABOR PROGRAMS (2004).
6. VALENZUELA, *supra* note 2, at 13.
7. Valenzuela, *supra* note 1, at 22–23.
8. VALENZUELA ET AL., *supra* note 4, at 14. Safety violations were also a major concern. *See* Juno Turner, Note, *All in a Day's Work? Statutory and Other Failures of the Workers' Compensation Scheme as Applied to Street Corner Day Laborers*, 74 FORDHAM L. REV. 1521, 1529 (2005).
9. U.S. GOV'T ACCOUNTABILITY OFF., GAO-02-925, WORKER PROTECTION: LABOR'S EFFORTS TO ENFORCE PROTECTIONS FOR DAY LABORERS COULD BENEFIT FROM BETTER DATA AND GUIDANCE 3 (2002). Day laborers faced significant barriers to asserting the rights they did possess, ranging from lack of knowledge to structural impediments such as the policy in some federal courthouses of requiring identification upon entry.
10. Jill Esbenshade, *The "Crisis" over Day Labor: The Politics of Visibility and Public Space*, 3 WORKING USA 27, 46 (Mar.-Apr. 2000).
11. *See, e.g.*, Carla Rivera, *"Intent" Clause Fuels Dispute on Day Labor Law*, L.A. TIMES, Oct. 3, 1989, § 1, at 3 (quoting Costa Mesa City Councilman Ed Glasgow, who called day labor "a nuisance for people in town").
12. Kristina Campbell, *The High Cost of Free Speech: Anti-Solicitation Ordinances, Day Laborers, and the Impact of "Backdoor" Local Immigration Regulations*, 25 GEO. IMMIGR. L.J. 1, 24 (2010).
13. *See* Scott L. Cummings & Steven A. Boutcher, *Mobilizing Local Government Law for Low-Wage Workers*, 2009 U. CHI. LEGAL F. 187, 203 (2009).
14. David Reyes, *At Sidewalk Hiring Hall, It's Laborers vs. Establishment*, L.A. TIMES (Orange Cty. ed.), Mar. 30, 1985, § 2, at 1.
15. *Id.*
16. Roxana Kopetman, *Police Put Crimp in Hiring of Workers on Street Corners*, L.A. TIMES (Orange Cty. ed.), Apr. 23, 1986, § 2, at 1.
17. *Id.*
18. Immigration Reform and Control Act of 1986, Pub. L. No. 99-603, 100 Stat. 3359 (codified as amended in scattered sections of 8 U.S.C. and 42 U.S.C.).
19. Hector Tobar, *Success of Day Labor Hiring Site Delays Council Curbs*, L.A. TIMES (Glendale ed.), Dec. 8, 1988, § 9, at 1.
20. Marita Hernandez, *Fear Prevails: Amnesty Law Takes Toll on Day Laborers*, L.A. TIMES, May 9, 1987, § 2, at 1.

21. 798 F.2d 1260 (9th Cir. 1986).
22. *Id.* The Phoenix ordinance stated: "No person shall stand on a street or highway and solicit, or attempt to solicit, employment, business or contributions from the occupants of any vehicle." *Id.* at 1262 (citing Phoenix City Ordinance § 36.101.01).
23. *See id.* at 1264–73.
24. Dave Lanson, *Day-Laborer Traffic Rules Please No One*, L.A. TIMES, Apr. 20, 1986, at 1.
25. *Id.*
26. REDONDO BEACH, CAL., MUN. CODE § 3-7.1601(a) (1987).
27. *See, e.g.,* Louise Woo & Enrique Rangel, *Group Walks Streets to Educate Laborers About Their Rights*, ORANGE CTY. REG., Mar. 2, 1988, at B1.
28. Stephanie O'Neill, *City Seeks Ban to Keep Job-Seekers Off Streets*, L.A. TIMES, Aug. 4, 1988, at 1 (quoting the Glendale City Manager).
29. *Id.*
30. *Id.*
31. Caitlin C. Patler, *Alliance-Building and Organizing for Immigrant Rights: The Case of the Coalition for Humane Immigrant Rights of Los Angeles*, in WORKING FOR JUSTICE: THE L.A. MODEL OF ORGANIZING AND ADVOCACY 71, 73 (Ruth Milkman, Joshua Bloom & Victor Narro eds., 2010).
32. Telephone Interview with Nancy Smyth (formerly Cervantes), Staff Dev. Dir., L.A. All. for a New Econ. (Dec. 20, 2010).
33. *See* Stephanie O'Neill, *Pact Reached on Day Labor Pickup Site*, L.A. TIMES, Sept. 22, 1988, at 1.
34. *Id.*
35. *Id.*
36. *Id.*
37. Tobar, *supra* note 19.
38. The owner of one company, Sierra Leasing, agreed to pay for six months of the hiring center costs in order to facilitate the deal. O'Neill, *supra* note 33.
39. *See* Marita Hernandez, *Advocates Assail Arrests of Street Corner Laborers*, L.A. TIMES, Feb. 18, 1989, § 1, at 23.
40. Maria Dziembowska, *NDLON and the History of Day Labor Organizing in Los Angeles*, in WORKING FOR JUSTICE, *supra* note 31, at 145.
41. Telephone Interview with Victor Narro, Project Dir., UCLA Downtown Lab. Ctr. (Nov. 10, 2010); *see also* Hector Tobar, *Street-Corner Immigrant Workers Get Hot Line for Legal Assistance*, L.A. TIMES, Nov. 16, 1989, § 2, at 1 (describing CHIRLA's legal help hotline). Cervantes later changed her name to Nancy Smyth.
42. Hector Tobar, *Hope of Jobs Surmounts Illegals' Fears: Immigration: 150 Workers—and No INS Agents—Turn Out as Los Angeles Opens Its First Day-Laborer Hiring Site*, L.A. TIMES, Oct. 28, 1989, § 2, at 1.
43. Telephone Interview with Victor Narro, *supra* note 41.
44. Jeffrey Miller, *Day Labor Now a City Hall Concern*, ORANGE CTY. REG., Sept. 24, 1989, at B1.
45. Charles Strouse, *Job Center a Year Later: Costa Mesa Plan to Get Dayworkers Off Street Lauded, Assailed*, L.A. TIMES (Orange Cty. ed.), Sept. 3, 1989, § 4, at 7.
46. Jeffrey Miller, *Costa Mesa Continues Day-Labor Crackdown With 12 More Arrests*, ORANGE CTY. REG., Sept. 21, 1989, at B3.
47. Miller, *supra* note 44.
48. Carla Rivera, *Need Outstrips Fear of Arrest: Employers Resisting Costa Mesa Labor Law*, L.A. TIMES (Orange Cty. ed.), Oct. 1, 1989, § 1, at 1.
49. Miller, *supra* note 46; Rivera, *supra* note 11.
50. A private lawsuit was also filed. Jeffrey Miller, *2nd Suit Challenges Intent Provision of Costa Mesa Day-Labor Ordinance*, ORANGE CTY. REG., Jan. 24, 1990, at B3.
51. *Illegals, Day Laborers Win in 2 Rulings*, L.A. TIMES, June 23, 1990, at A30.

52. Jeff D. Opdyke, *State Will Take over Costa Mesa Job Center*, ORANGE CTY. REG., Feb. 5, 1991, at B2.
53. DANA POINT, CAL., MUN. CODE § 5.06.020(a) (repealed 2007).
54. Miller, *supra* note 44. The Telephone Hiring Exchange, which cost $9,000 a year and was staffed by a part-time coordinator and volunteers, was found by the city to have assisted in placing roughly three-fourths of participating workers with employers. Jim Carlton, *More Cities Turning to Hiring Halls to Solve Day Laborer Problems*, L.A. TIMES (Orange Cty. ed.), Feb. 19, 1990, at B1.
55. Carlton, *supra* note 54; *Orange—Day Labor Laws Begin*, ORANGE CTY. REG., Apr. 26, 1990, at B2; *see also* Bob Schwartz, *INS Chief Calls Arrests in Church 'Regrettable,'* L.A. TIMES, Sept. 29, 1988, § 1, at 38. The Orange ordinance made it a misdemeanor to solicit work, punishable by a fine of up to $1,000 and six months in jail. *Orange—Day Labor Laws Begin, supra.*
56. Carlton, *supra* note 54; *Orange—Day Labor Laws Begin, supra* note 55.
57. Carlton, *supra* note 54; Danielle A. Fouquette, *Brea City Taking over Day Labor Program*, L.A. TIMES (Orange Cty. ed.), Oct. 5, 1990, at B3.
58. Miller, *supra* note 44.
59. *See* Abel Valenzuela, Jr., *Controlling Day Labor: Government, Community, and Worker Responses, in* CALIFORNIA POLICY OPTIONS 41 (Daniel J.B. Mitchell & Patricia Nomura eds., 2001).
60. Sebastian Rotella & Steve Padilla, *Finding Work, Conflict in Suburbia*, L.A. TIMES (Valley ed.), July 21, 1991, at B3.
61. Michael Coit, *Workers Taken Off Streets: Agoura Hills Plan Controls Day Labor*, L.A. DAILY NEWS, Nov. 4, 1990, at T1.
62. *Id.*
63. Amy Louise Kazmin, *Dayworker Ordinance Is Challenged*, L.A. TIMES (Valley ed.), June 11, 1991, at B3.
64. AGOURA HILLS, CAL., ORDINANCE No. 172 (1991).
65. *See* Memorandum From Joseph Donofrio, Dir. of Cmty. Servs., to David Carmany, City Manager of Agoura Hills (Jan. 16, 1991).
66. Kazmin, *supra* note 63.
67. *Id.*
68. Curtis S. Updike, *Day Laborer Enforcement Effort Yields 21 Arrests*, L.A. DAILY NEWS, Sept. 5, 1991, at 1.
69. Complaint for Damages, Declaratory, and Injunctive Relief, Xiloj-Itzep v. City of Agoura Hills, 29 Cal. Rptr. 2d 879 (Ct. App. 1994) (No. LC011284) [hereinafter Xiloj-Itzep Complaint].
70. Telephone Interview with Robin Toma, Exec. Dir., L.A. Hum. Rel. Comm. (Jan. 4, 2011).
71. *Id.*
72. Telephone Interview with Nancy Smyth, *supra* note 32.
73. *Id.*
74. *Id.*
75. Telephone Interview with Robin Toma, *supra* note 70.
76. Xiloj-Itzep Complaint, *supra* note 69.
77. Telephone Interview with Robin Toma, *supra* note 70.
78. Xiloj-Itzep Complaint, *supra* note 69, at 1.
79. *Id.* at 2–3.
80. Michael Connelly, *Laborers Fail to Win Ruling to Nullify Law*, L.A. TIMES (Valley ed.), Dec. 31, 1991, at B3.
81. Telephone Interview with Robin Toma, *supra* note 70.
82. *Id.*
83. *Id.*
84. *Id.*
85. Xiloj-Itzep v. City of Agoura Hills, 29 Cal. Rptr. 2d 879 (Ct. App. 1994).
86. Appellants' Opening Br. at 1–2, 29, *Xiloj-Itzep*, 29 Cal. Rptr. 2d 879 (No. B067188).

87. *Xiloj-Itzep*, 29 Cal. Rptr. 2d at 886 n.3.
88. *Id.* at 887.
89. Telephone Interview with Robin Toma, *supra* note 70.
90. *Xiloj-Itzep*, 29 Cal. Rptr. 2d at 889–92.
91. Telephone Interview with Robin Toma, *supra* note 70.
92. Telephone Interview with Pablo Alvarado, Exec. Dir., Nat'l Day Laborer Org. Network (Jan. 4, 2011).
93. Tracy Kaplan, *Supervisors Ban Curbside Job Solicitation*, L.A. TIMES, May 25, 1994, at B1 (attributing the following statement to ACLU Director Ramona Ripston: "The courts are clearly not very hospitable places when it comes to protecting civil liberties and civil rights.").
94. See Table 3.2: Anti-solicitation ordinances (original form) in the greater L.A. area, 1987–2011, for a list of ordinances and their dates of enactment. For a discussion of the Laguna Beach ordinance, see Leslie Earnest, *Council Endorses Day Labor Penalties*, L.A. TIMES (Orange Cty. ed.), Jan. 7, 1993, at B2.
95. Telephone Interview with Thomas Saenz, President, Mexican Am. Legal Def. & Educ. Fund (Dec. 14, 2010).
96. *Id.*
97. Telephone Interview with Pablo Alvarado, *supra* note 92.
98. Telephone Interview with Thomas Saenz, *supra* note 95.
99. Dziembowska, *supra* note 40, at 143.
100. *Id.* at 144.
101. Telephone Interview with Nancy Smyth, *supra* note 32.
102. Robert J. Lopez, *Day Laborers Face Opposition From Merchants*, L.A. TIMES (Ventura W. ed.), Mar. 6, 1994, at B22.
103. *Id.*
104. Dziembowska, *supra* note 40, at 145.
105. Erin J. Aubry, *Proposed Limits on Laborers Protested*, L.A. TIMES, Jan. 30, 1994, at 8.
106. Telephone Interview with Victor Narro, *supra* note 41.
107. Telephone Interview with Nancy Smyth, *supra* note 32.
108. Telephone Interview with Robin Toma, *supra* note 70.
109. Telephone Interview with Victor Narro, *supra* note 41.
110. Telephone Interview with Nancy Smyth, *supra* note 32.
111. *Id.*; see also Kaplan, *supra* note 93.
112. Lopez, *supra* note 102 (quoting HomeBase Manager Frank Gomez).
113. Telephone Interview with Victor Narro, *supra* note 41.
114. Aubry, *supra* note 105.
115. Nancy Cervantes, Joe Hicks & Niels Frenzen, Op-Ed, *A Case of Overkill to Curb Day Laborers*, L.A. TIMES, Jan. 25, 1994, at B7.
116. Telephone Interview with Nancy Smyth, *supra* note 32.
117. Dziembowska, *supra* note 40, at 145.
118. Telephone Interview with Nancy Smyth, *supra* note 32.
119. Telephone Interview with Victor Narro, *supra* note 41.
120. Ronni Cooper, *Regulating Day Laborers*, L.A. TIMES, Feb. 1, 1994, at B6.
121. Telephone Interview with Nancy Smyth, *supra* note 32.
122. *Id.*
123. *Id.*
124. Telephone Interview with Victor Narro, *supra* note 41.
125. Lopez, *supra* note 102.
126. Telephone Interview with Nancy Smyth, *supra* note 32.
127. Telephone Interview with Victor Narro, *supra* note 41.
128. Kaplan, *supra* note 93. Supervisor Ed Edelman was absent for the vote. *Id.*

129. L.A. CTY., CAL., CODE § 13.15.011 (1994). The ordinance also applied to drivers and passengers in moving vehicles. *Id.* § 13.15.012.
130. Telephone Interview with Victor Narro, *supra* note 41.
131. *Id.*
132. *Conversation with Day Labor Activist Pablo Alvarado*, L.A. TIMES, Sept. 7, 1996, at B7.
133. *Id.*
134. Telephone Interview with Pablo Alvarado, *supra* note 92.
135. Dziembowska, *supra* note 40 (quoting Pablo Alvarado).
136. Telephone Interview with Pablo Alvarado, *supra* note 92.
137. Telephone Interview with Victor Narro, *supra* note 41.
138. Dziembowska, *supra* note 40, at 146.
139. *Conversation with Day Labor Activist Pablo Alvarado*, *supra* note 132.
140. Telephone Interview with Victor Narro, *supra* note 41.
141. Interview with Chris Newman, Legal Programs Dir., Nat'l Day Laborer Org. Network, in Los Angeles, Cal. (Feb. 5, 2011).
142. Complaint ¶ 13, Coal. for Humane Immigrant Rights of L.A. v. Burke (*CHIRLA I*), 1999 WL 33288183 (C.D. Cal. Oct. 29, 1999) (No. CV 98-4863-GHK).
143. Telephone Interview with Victor Narro, *supra* note 41.
144. Complaint, *supra* note 142, ¶ 7.
145. *Id.* ¶¶ 8–9.
146. Coal. for Humane Immigrant Rts. of L.A. v. Burke (*CHIRLA II*), No. CV 98-4863-GHK(CTX), 2000 WL 1481467, at *2 (C.D. Cal. Sept. 12, 2000).
147. *CHIRLA I*, 1999 WL 33288183, at *8.
148. *CHIRLA II*, 2000 WL 1481467, at *13.
149. *Id.* at *5 n.1.
150. *Id.* at *5.
151. *Id.* at *6.
152. *Id.* at *10.
153. *Id.* at *12.
154. David Rosenzweig, *Federal Judge Voids Ban on Soliciting by Day Laborers*, L.A. TIMES, Sept. 15, 2000, at B1. Robin Toma, who had left the ACLU after the Agoura Hills case to head the Los Angeles County Human Relations Commission, coauthored a book highlighting collaborations to defuse day labor conflicts, ROBIN TOMA & JILL ESBENSHADE, DAY LABORER HIRING SITES: CONSTRUCTIVE APPROACHES TO COMMUNITY CONFLICT (2001), which he used to urge the county counsel not to appeal. Telephone Interview with Robin Toma, *supra* note 70.
155. Telephone Interview with Nancy Smyth, *supra* note 32.
156. *Id.*
157. Telephone Interview with Victor Narro, *supra* note 41.
158. Telephone Interview with Nancy Smyth, *supra* note 32.
159. *CHIRLA II*, 2000 WL 1481467, No. CV 98-4863-GHK (CTX) (C.D. Cal. Sept. 12, 2000).
160. *See* Table 3.2: Anti-solicitation ordinances (original form) in the greater L.A. area, 1987–2011.
161. Telephone Interview with Thomas Saenz, *supra* note 95. Rosenberg had earlier given $25,000 to CHIRLA to promote day labor outreach. Leslie Berestein, *Workshops Planned on Laborers' Rights*, L.A. TIMES, Apr. 9, 1995, at 10.
162. Telephone Interview with Thomas Saenz, *supra* note 95.
163. Karima A. Haynes, *Day-Labor Conference Begins in Northridge*, L.A. TIMES, July 27, 2001, at B3.
164. Telephone Interview with Thomas Saenz, *supra* note 95.
165. *See* Dziembowska, *supra* note 40, at 147.
166. Telephone Interview with Victor Narro, *supra* note 41.
167. Telephone Interview with Pablo Alvarado, *supra* note 92.
168. Telephone Interview with Victor Narro, *supra* note 41.

169. Id.
170. Id.
171. Id.
172. Dziembowska, *supra* note 40, at 149.
173. *Id.* at 150.
174. *Id.* at 151.
175. Telephone Interview with Pablo Alvarado, *supra* note 92.
176. Dziembowska, *supra* note 40, at 151.
177. *Building Community: An Integral Approach to Addressing Day Laborer Related Concerns*, NAT'L DAY LABORER ORG. NETWORK, http://www.mayorsinnovation.org/pdf/PabloAlvarado.pdf (last visited May 18, 2011).
178. Telephone Interview with Pablo Alvarado, *supra* note 92.
179. Interview with Chris Newman, *supra* note 141.
180. Telephone Interview with Thomas Saenz, *supra* note 95.
181. There were some cities that adopted ordinances but took a "watch and see" approach to enforcement. *See, e.g.,* Greg Sandoval, *No Citations Issued as Enforcement of Day-Laborer Law Begins*, L.A. TIMES (Valley ed.), May 15, 1997, at B6 (discussing Santa Clarita).
182. Telephone Interview with Thomas Saenz, *supra* note 95.
183. 8 C.F.R. § 274a.1(f)–(g) (2010).
184. Telephone Interview with Thomas Saenz, *supra* note 95.
185. Telephone Interview with Chris Newman, Legal Programs Dir., Nat'l Day Laborer Org. Network (Jan. 31, 2011).
186. Telephone Interview with Thomas Saenz, *supra* note 95.
187. Id.
188. Id.
189. Telephone Interview with Pablo Alvarado, *supra* note 92.
190. Id.
191. Id.
192. Complaint for Injunctive and Declaratory Relief, Comite de Jornaleros de Rancho Cucamonga y Upland v. City of Rancho Cucamonga & City of Upland (Sept. 19, 2002).
193. Telephone Interview with Pablo Alvarado, *supra* note 92.
194. Telephone Interview with Belinda Escobosa Helzer, Dir., ACLU of S. Cal., Orange Cty. Office (Dec. 16, 2010).
195. City of Upland Police Dep't, San Bernardino Cty. Sheriff—Rancho Cucamonga, *Training Update on Amended City Solicitation Ordinances* (quoting City of Upland Ordinance No. 1733 and City of Rancho Cucamonga Ordinance No. 695, which were identical).
196. Settlement Agreement and Mutual Release 2.
197. Stephen Wall, *Rialto, Calif., Church Seeks to Open Center for Day Laborers*, SAN BERNARDINO CTY. SUN, June 16, 2004.
198. Jennifer Mena, *Cities Back Off Bans on Seeking Jobs in Public*, L.A. TIMES (Orange Cty. ed.), Aug. 25, 2001, at B1.
199. Id.
200. Id.
201. Id.
202. *Id.* (quoting Alvarado).
203. Steve Ryfle, *2-Pronged Plan for Street-Side Job Seekers*, L.A. TIMES, Sept. 13, 1996, at B4.
204. Jennifer Oldham, *Proposed Laborer Ban Awaits Action*, L.A. TIMES (Valley ed.), June 17, 1994, at B3.
205. Id.
206. *Id.* (attributing the statement to Glendale City Attorney Scott Howard).
207. Ryfle, *supra* note 203.
208. Id.

209. GLENDALE, CAL., MUN. CODE § 9.17.030 (1996).
210. Ryfle, *supra* note 203.
211. Naush Boghossian, *Laborers Sue City over Solicitation of Jobs Prohibition*, L.A. DAILY NEWS, May 21, 2004, at N3.
212. Ryfle, *supra* note 203 (quoting Robin Toma of the ACLU).
213. Boghossian, *supra* note 211.
214. *Id.*
215. Telephone Interview with Belinda Escobosa Helzer, *supra* note 194.
216. Naush Boghossian, *Glendale May Cut Fees for Day Laborers*, L.A. DAILY NEWS, June 12, 2004, at N8.
217. Telephone Interview with Belinda Escobosa Helzer, *supra* note 194.
218. *Id.*
219. *Id.*
220. *Id.*
221. *Id.*
222. *Id.*
223. Telephone Interview with Veronica Federosky, Organizer, Nat'l Day Laborer Org. Network (Feb. 16, 2011).
224. *Id.*
225. *Id.*
226. *Id.*
227. *Id.*
228. *Id.*
229. Telephone Interview with Belinda Escobosa Helzer, *supra* note 194.
230. *See* Boghossian, *supra* note 211.
231. Complaint for Injunctive and Declaratory Relief, Comite de Jornaleros de Glendale v. City of Glendale, 2005 U.S. Dist. LEXIS 46603 (C.D. Cal. May 19, 2004) (No. CV 04-3521 SJO (Ex)).
232. Telephone Interview with Belinda Escobosa Helzer, *supra* note 194.
233. *See* Complaint, *supra* note 231, at 3.
234. GLENDALE, CAL., MUN. CODE § 9.17.030 (2004).
235. First Amended Complaint for Injunctive and Declaratory Relief at 4, *Comite de Jornaleros de Glendale*, 2005 U.S. Dist. LEXIS 46603 (No. CV 04-3521 SJO (Ex)).
236. Plaintiffs' Memorandum of Points and Auths. in Support of Plaintiffs' Ex Parte Application for Temporary Restraining Order and Order to Show Cause Re Preliminary Injunction at 6–15, *Comite de Jornaleros de Glendale*, 2005 U.S. Dist. LEXIS 46603 (No. CV 04-3521 SJO (Ex)).
237. Plaintiffs' Reply in Support of Plaintiffs' Mot. for Preliminary Injunction at 3–4, *Comite de Jornaleros de Glendale*, 2005 U.S. Dist. LEXIS 46603 (No. CV 04-3521 SJO (Ex)).
238. *Id.* at 4–5.
239. Order Granting Mot. for Preliminary Injunction at 15–16, *Comite de Jornaleros de Glendale*, 2005 U.S. Dist. LEXIS 46603 (No. CV 04-3521 SJO (Ex)).
240. *Id.* at 22.
241. *Id.* at 24.
242. Plaintiffs' Memorandum of Points and Auths. in Support of Their Mot. for Summ. Judgment, *Comite de Jornaleros de Glendale*, 2005 U.S. Dist. LEXIS 46603 (No. CV 04-3521 SJO (Ex)).
243. *Comite de Jornaleros de Glendale*, 2005 U.S. Dist. LEXIS 46603, at *16–20.
244. Br. of Appellant, Comite de Jornaleros de Glendale v. City of Glendale, No. 05-55880 (9th Cir. Oct. 14, 2005).
245. Telephone Interview with Belinda Escobosa Helzer, *supra* note 194; Telephone Interview with Shaheena Simons, Senior Trial Att'y, U.S. Dep't of Just. (Dec. 21, 2010).
246. Petition to Withdraw as Couns. and Addition of New Att'y of Record, *Comite de Jornaleros de Glendale*, No. 05-55880.

247. Telephone Interview with Veronica Federosky, *supra* note 223.
248. *See* Stipulation of Dismissal and [Proposed] Order of Dismissal (FED. R. CIV. P. 41(a)) at 2, Ex. A, *Comite de Jornaleros de Glendale*, 2005 U.S. Dist. LEXIS 46603 (No. CV 04-3521 SJO (Ex)).
249. GLENDALE, CAL., MUN. CODE § 9.17.030(a) (2008).
250. *Id.*
251. REDONDO BEACH, CAL., MUN. CODE, § 3-7.1601 (1987).
252. Victor Narro, *Impacting Next Wave Organizing: Creative Campaign Strategies of the Los Angeles Worker Centers*, 50 N.Y.L. SCH. L. REV. 465, 490–91 (2005–2006).
253. Telephone Interview with Chris Newman, *supra* note 185.
254. Narro, *supra* note 252, at 491.
255. Telephone Interview with Pablo Alvarado, *supra* note 92.
256. Telephone Interview with Veronica Federosky, *supra* note 223.
257. *Id.*
258. *Id.*
259. Telephone Interview with Chris Newman, *supra* note 185.
260. *Id.*
261. *Id.*
262. *Id.*
263. *Id.*
264. *Id.*
265. *Id.*
266. *Id.*
267. Telephone Interview with Veronica Federosky, *supra* note 223.
268. Narro, *supra* note 252, at 492–93.
269. Complaint for Injunctive and Declaratory Relief, Comite de Jornaleros de Redondo Beach v. City of Redondo Beach, 475 F. Supp. 2d 952 (C.D. Cal. Nov. 16, 2004) (No. CV 04-9396 CBM).
270. Telephone Interview with Chris Newman, *supra* note 185.
271. Telephone Interview with Thomas Saenz, *supra* note 95.
272. Telephone Interview with Shaheena Simons, *supra* note 245.
273. Temporary Restraining Order and Order to Show Cause Re Preliminary Injunction, *Comite de Jornaleros de Redondo Beach*, 475 F. Supp. 2d 952 (No. CV 04-9396 CBM).
274. Findings of Fact and Conclusions of Law at 7–13, *Comite de Jornaleros de Redondo Beach*, 475 F. Supp. 2d 952 (No. CV 04-9396 CBM).
275. *Comite de Jornaleros de Redondo Beach*, 475 F. Supp. 2d at 956.
276. Order Granting in Part and Denying in Part Plaintiffs' Mot. for a Protective Order at 2, *Comite de Jornaleros de Redondo Beach*, 475 F. Supp. 2d 952 (No. CV 04-9396 CBM).
277. Order Granting Plaintiffs' Mot. for Reconsideration of Magistrate Judge's Order Granting in Part and Denying in Part Plaintiffs' Mot. for a Protective Order at 10, *Comite de Jornaleros de Redondo Beach*, 475 F. Supp. 2d 952 (No. CV 04-9396 CBM).
278. Telephone Interview with Shaheena Simons, *supra* note 245.
279. Telephone Interview with Philip Hwang, Staff Att'y, Laws.' Comm. for Civil Rts. (Jan. 5, 2011).
280. *Comite de Jornaleros de Redondo Beach*, 475 F. Supp. 2d 952. The court also upheld plaintiffs' standing. *Id.* at 956–58. In a later decision, Judge Marshall awarded the plaintiffs' lawyers more than $208,000 in attorney's fees. Comite de Jornaleros de Redondo Beach v. City of Redondo Beach, No. CV 04-9396 CBM, 2006 U.S. Dist. LEXIS 95610, at *2 (C.D. Cal. Dec. 12, 2006).
281. Telephone Interview with Veronica Federosky, *supra* note 223.
282. The injunction remained in effect pending appeal. Order Granting Defendant's Ex Parte Application for Order Granting Partial Stay of 4-27-06 Order Pending Appeal, *Comite de Jornaleros de Redondo Beach*, 475 F. Supp. 2d 952 (No. CV 04-9396 CBM).

283. Telephone Interview with Veronica Federosky, *supra* note 223.
284. Telephone Interview with Nora Preciado, Staff Att'y, Nat'l Immigr. L. Ctr. (Dec. 17, 2010).
285. *See* Table 3.2: Anti-solicitation ordinances (original form) in the greater L.A. area, 1987–2011.
286. William Wheeler, *Immigration Debate Gets Contentious in Laguna*, ORANGE CTY. REG., Jan. 8, 2006, http://www.ocregister.com/articles/-19225--.html (last visited Mar. 23, 2019).
287. Chris Caesar, *State Supreme Court Won't Hear Suit on Day-Labor Site*, ORANGE CTY. REG., Feb. 23, 2009, http://www.ocregister.com/articles/daylabor-137370-lagunabeach-daylaborsite.html (last visited Mar. 23, 2019).
288. LAKE FOREST, CAL., MUN. CODE § 5.06.020 (1993).
289. Jack Leonard & Alex Katz, *Sherriff Acts on Laborers' Complaints*, L.A. TIMES, Oct. 6, 1999, at B1.
290. Jennifer Delson, *New Front on Day-Labor Battle Opens*, L.A. TIMES (Orange Cty. ed.), Dec. 9, 2006, at B1.
291. Telephone Interview with Nora Preciado, *supra* note 284.
292. Telephone Interview with Hector Villagra, Legal Dir., ACLU of S. Cal. (Nov. 29, 2010).
293. Telephone Interview with Nora Preciado, *supra* note 284.
294. Telephone Interview with Hector Villagra, *supra* note 292.
295. Telephone Interview with Nora Preciado, *supra* note 284.
296. Telephone Interview with Hector Villagra, *supra* note 292.
297. Telephone Interview with Veronica Federosky, *supra* note 223.
298. *Id.* The cold reception by locals persisted even after the day laborers organized a community service day to rebuild the houses of Orange County fire victims in an effort to "change hearts and minds." *Id.*
299. Telephone Interview with Hector Villagra, *supra* note 292.
300. Telephone Interview with Nora Preciado, *supra* note 284.
301. Telephone Interview with Hector Villagra, *supra* note 292.
302. *Id.*
303. Telephone Interview with Nora Preciado, *supra* note 284.
304. *Id.*
305. Complaint for Declaratory and Injunctive Relief, Asociación de Trabajadores de Lake Forest v. City of Lake Forest (*ATLF*), No. SA CV 07-250 DOC (ANx) (C.D. Cal. Mar. 1, 2007).
306. *See* Order to Withdraw Plaintiffs' Mot. for Preliminary Injunction and Take Hearing Re: Preliminary Injunction Off Calendar, *ATLF*, No. SA CV 07-250 DOC (ANx) (C.D. Cal. Mar. 19, 2007).
307. Alejandra Molina, *Lake Forest Eliminates Day Labor Law*, ORANGE CTY. REG., Apr. 4, 2007, http://www.ocregister.com/articles/city-184848-ordinance-day.html (last visited Mar. 23, 2019).
308. Telephone Interview with Hector Villagra, *supra* note 292.
309. First Amended Complaint, *ATLF*, No. SA CV 07-250 DOC (ANx) (C.D. Cal. Apr. 19, 2007).
310. *Id.* Plaintiffs filed a second amended complaint in June 2007 that incorporated more factual allegations to establish the individual defendants' personal liability for acting "within the course, scope, and authority of [their] agency or employment" "to violate Plaintiffs' constitutional rights," in conformity with "official policy, custom, or practice." Second Amended Complaint at ¶¶ 15, 24, *ATLF*, No. SA CV 07-250 DOC (ANx) (C.D. Cal. June 19, 2007).
311. Defendants' Notice and Mot. to Dismiss for Failure to State a Claim Upon Which Relief Can Be Granted, *ATLF*, No. SA CV 07-250 DOC (ANx) (C.D. Cal. June 29, 2007).
312. Proceeding (in Chambers): Denying Defendants' Mot. for Failure to State a Claim Upon Which Relief Can Be Granted at 3, 5, *ATLF*, No. SA CV 07-250 DOC (ANx) (C.D. Cal. July 18, 2007).
313. Telephone Interview with Nora Preciado, *supra* note 284.
314. *Id.*
315. *Id.*
316. Third Amended Complaint, *ATLF*, No. SA CV 07-250 DOC (ANx) (C.D. Cal. Dec. 5, 2007).

317. Proceedings on Plaintiffs' Mot. for a Protective Order at 2, *ATLF*, No. SA CV 07-250 DOC (ANx) (C.D. Cal. Feb. 28, 2008).
318. *Id.* at 9.
319. *Id.* at 11.
320. Alejandra Molina, *Lake Forest Attorney Says ACLU Suit Is Frivolous*, ORANGE CTY. REG., May 14, 2008, http://www.ocregister.com/articles/aclu-184961-city-suit.html (last visited Mar. 23, 2019).
321. Proceedings: Settlement Conference (Session One), *ATLF*, No. SA CV 07-250 DOC (ANx) (C.D. Cal. June 19, 2008); Proceedings: Settlement Conference (Session Two), *ATLF*, No. SA CV 07-250 DOC (ANx) (C.D. Cal. June 20, 2008).
322. Plaintiffs' Mot. in Limine to Exclude Any Evidence or Argument Relating to the Immigration Status of Any Witness or Federal Law Regulating the Hiring of Aliens, *ATLF*, No. SA CV 07-250 DOC (ANx) (C.D. Cal. Aug. 14, 2008).
323. Memorandum of Points and Auths. Regarding Standing, *ATLF*, No. SA CV 07-250 DOC (ANx) (C.D. Cal. Aug. 13, 2008).
324. *Id.* at 4–12.
325. Order Granting in Part and Denying in Part Mot. Regarding Standing, *ATLF*, No. SA CV 07-250 DOC (ANx) (C.D. Cal. Aug. 18, 2008).
326. Telephone Interview with Hector Villagra, *supra* note 292.
327. Order Regarding Settlement Agreement and Release of Claims at 3–4, *ATLF*, No. SA CV 07-250 DOC (ANx) (C.D. Cal. Aug. 18, 2008). The defendants admitted no wrongdoing. *Id.* at 2.
328. Asociación de Trabajadores de Lake Forest v. City of Lake Forest, 624 F.3d 1083, 1090 (9th Cir. 2010).
329. Telephone Interview with Hector Villagra, *supra* note 292.
330. Ellyn Pak, *Orange Tightens Day Laborer Rules*, ORANGE CTY. REG., Dec. 11, 2007, http://www.ocregister.com/articles/city-142049-problems-laborers.html (last visited Mar. 23, 2019).
331. Eugene W. Fields & Rosalba Ruiz, *Day-Labor Numbers Dropping in Orange*, ORANGE CTY. REG., Apr. 3, 2008, http://www.ocregister.com/articles/day-144791-laborers-city.html (last visited Mar. 23, 2019).
332. *Id.*
333. Eugene W. Fields, *Advocacy Group Finds Way Around Day-Labor Law*, ORANGE CTY. REG., Nov. 17, 2008, http://www.ocregister.com/articles/day-144322-laborers-streets.html (last visited Mar. 23, 2019).
334. *See* Stephen Wall, *Case Closed: Job Center Stays, City Council Says*, ORANGE CTY. REG., Dec. 17, 1998, at 18.
335. Brian Martinez, *Center of Contention*, ORANGE CTY. REG., Apr. 3, 2005, www.ocregister.com/ocr/2005/04/03/sections/local/local/article_466862.php (last visited Mar. 23, 2019) (quoting an email distributed by the California Coalition for Immigration Reform urging support for Costa Mesa's decision to close the center).
336. Rachana Rathi, *Job Center's End Won't Still Debate*, L.A. TIMES, Mar. 17, 2005, at B1.
337. COSTA MESA, CAL., MUN. CODE § 10-354(a) (2005).
338. *Id.* § 10-354.2(1).
339. Costa Mesa, Cal., Ordinance of the City Council of the City of Costa Mesa, California, Amending Title 10, Chapter XIX of the Costa Mesa Municipal Code Regarding Solicitation of Employment, Business or Contributions From Streets and Certain Commercial Parking Lots (codified as amended in COSTA MESA, CAL., CODE § 10-354).
340. Cindy Carcamo & Ellyn Pak, *ACLU Sues Costa Mesa over Day Laborer Issue*, ORANGE CTY. REG., Feb. 3, 2010, http://www.ocregister.com/news/city-232185-day-ordinance.html (last visited Mar. 29, 2019).
341. *See* John Earl, *"Chilling Effect": Costa Mesa Day Laborers Claim Police Harassment Under Enforcement of Sign Ordinance*, ORANGE COAST VOICE, Oct. 5, 2007, at 1.
342. Telephone Interview with Hector Villagra, *supra* note 292.

343. Telephone Interview with Veronica Federosky, *supra* note 223.
344. *Id.*
345. Complaint for Injunctive and Declaratory Relief, Asociación de Jornaleros de Costa Mesa v. City of Costa Mesa, No. SA CV 10-00128 CJC (RNBx) (C.D. Cal. Feb. 2, 2010). NDLON was not named as a plaintiff, but Newman was co-counsel. MALDEF also co-counseled this lawsuit.
346. Ellyn Pak & Cindy Carcamo, *Costa Mesa Won't Enforce Anti-Solicitation Law*, ORANGE CTY. REG., Mar. 2, 2010, https://www.ocregister.com/2010/03/02/costa-mesa-wont-enforce-anti-solicitation-law/ (last visited Mar. 23, 2019).
347. Nisha Gutierrez, *City Bans Solicitation in Some Areas*, SAN GABRIEL VALLEY TRIB., June 8, 2007.
348. Staff Report From Stephanie Scher, City Att'y, to Mayor and City Council members (May 2, 2007) (regarding Baldwin Park's "commercial solicitation ordinance").
349. BALDWIN PARK, CAL., ORDINANCE No. 1302 (May 2, 2007) (amendment to BALDWIN PARK, CAL., MUN. CODE § 97.136(A)).
350. *Id.* (amendment to BALDWIN PARK, CAL., MUN. CODE § 97.137(A)).
351. Telephone Interview with Kristina Campbell, Assistant Professor of Law, U. of the D.C. Sch. of Law (Dec. 2, 2010).
352. *Id.*
353. *Id.*
354. *Id.*
355. *Id.*
356. Complaint for Injunctive and Declaratory Relief, Jornaleros Unidos de Baldwin Park v. City of Baldwin Park, No. CV 07-4135 ER (MANx) (C.D. Cal. June 25, 2007).
357. Fred Ortega, *Day Laborers Protest New Law*, SAN GABRIEL VALLEY TRIB., June 21, 2007.
358. 466 F.3d 784 (9th Cir. 2006).
359. *Id.* at 796–97.
360. Order Granting Preliminary Injunction at 3–4, *Jornaleros Unidos de Baldwin Park*, No. CV 07-4135 ER (MANx) (C.D. Cal. July 17, 2007).
361. Telephone Interview with Kristina Campbell, *supra* note 351.
362. Tania Chatila, *Solicitation Ban Overturned*, SAN GABRIEL VALLEY TRIB., Aug. 16, 2007.
363. Telephone Interview with Kristina Campbell, *supra* note 351.
364. Stipulation to Dismiss, *Jornaleros Unidos de Baldwin Park*, No. CV 07-4135 ER (MANx) (C.D. Cal. Oct. 5, 2007).
365. Telephone Interview with Kristina Campbell, *supra* note 351.
366. *Id.* (stating that she and Chris Newman spoke to staff members of Representative Solis in Washington, D.C. while they were in town attending an immigrant rights conference). In addition, Solis met directly with the Baldwin Park day laborers, who urged her to help in their struggle; it was on the heels of that meeting that Solis asked Mayor Lozano to withdraw the proposed ordinance. Telephone Interview with Chris Newman, Legal Programs Dir., Nat'l Day Laborer Org. Network (June 28, 2011).
367. Telephone Interview with Kristina Campbell, *supra* note 351.
368. Tania Chatila, *BP Day Laborers Organize*, SAN GABRIEL VALLEY TRIB., Nov. 8, 2007.
369. Telephone Interview with Chris Newman, *supra* note 185.
370. Julie Tamaki, *Hardware Chain Adds a Depot for Hiring Laborers*, L.A. TIMES, Dec. 11, 1997, at B1.
371. License Agreement (Dec. 11, 2000).
372. Victor Narro, Project Dir., UCLA Downtown Lab. Ctr., Presentation to Problem Solving in the Public Interest Seminar, UCLA Sch. of Law (Sept. 4, 2008).
373. In 2004, the Burbank City Council voted to approve a Home Depot store conditioned on the creation of a day labor center. Alex Dobuzinskis, *Day-Laborer Center Sees Mixed Usage*, L.A. DAILY NEWS, May 2, 2004, at N3.

374. CITY PLANNING COMM'N, L.A. CITY PLANNING DEP'T, CITY PLAN CASE NO. 2005-3903-CA (2005).
375. Border Protection, Anti-Terrorism, and Illegal Immigration Control Act of 2005, H.R. 4437, 109th Cong., 2d Sess.
376. *Id.* §§ 705, 708.
377. Richard Simon, *Day Labor Site Mandate Riles D.C.*, L.A. TIMES, Apr. 23, 2006, http://articles.latimes.com/2006/apr/23/nation/na-daylabor23 (last visited Mar. 23, 2019).
378. Telephone Interview with Pablo Alvarado, *supra* note 92.
379. *Id.*
380. *See* Victor Narro, *Si Se Puede! Immigrant Workers and the Transformation of the Los Angeles Labor and Worker Center Movements*, 1 L.A. PUB. INT. L.J. 65, 100 (2009).
381. Telephone Interview with Pablo Alvarado, *supra* note 92.
382. *Id.* The relationship between NDLON and the AFL-CIO had begun before the delegation's visit, dating back to NDLON's first general assembly, which was attended by representatives of the Laborers' International Union of North Am., an AFL-CIO affiliate. Telephone Interview with Chris Newman, *supra* note 366.
383. Telephone Interview with Pablo Alvarado, *supra* note 92.
384. The original Change to Win coalition included the International Brotherhood of Teamsters; Laborers' International Union of North America; Service Employees International Union; UNITE-HERE; and United Food and Commercial Workers International Union. They were quickly joined by the United Brotherhood of Carpenters and the United Farm Workers.
385. Telephone Interview with Pablo Alvarado, *supra* note 92.
386. National Partnership Agreement Between the AFL-CIO and the National Day Laborer Organizing Network (NDLON); *see also* Jill Tucker, *AFL-CIO, Nonunion Day Laborers Team Up to Fight for Worker Rights*, S.F. CHRON., Aug. 10, 2006, http://articles.sfgate.com/2006-08-10/bay-area/17305996_1_afl-cio-worker-centers-day-laborers (last visited Mar. 23, 2019).
387. Narro, *supra* note 380, at 100.
388. Dziembowska, *supra* note 40, at 152.
389. Comprehensive Immigration Reform Act of 2007, S. 1348.
390. Anna Gorman, *Day Labor Sites at Issue in Immigration Bill*, L.A. TIMES, June 23, 2007, at B3; *see also* Editorial, *Home Depot Amendment*, N.Y. TIMES, June 22, 2007, https://www.nytimes.com/2007/06/22/opinion/22fri2.html (last visited Mar. 23, 2019).
391. *See* S. Amend. 1982, Offered by Sen. John Isakson (June 5, 2007).
392. Telephone Interview with Chris Newman, *supra* note 366.
393. Dziembowska, *supra* note 40, at 152.
394. Telephone Interview with Chris Newman, *supra* note 366.
395. David Zahniser, *Council Targets Large Stores*, L.A. TIMES, Oct. 13, 2007, at B3.
396. L.A., CAL., ORDINANCE 180,174 (Aug. 22, 2008) (codified as amended in L.A., CAL., MUN. CODE § 12.24 (2008)).
397. Anna Gorman, *Day Laborer Rules OKd*, L.A. TIMES, Aug. 14, 2008, at B3.
398. L.A., CAL., MUN. CODE § 12.24U.14(a), (e)(2)(i).
399. Cummings & Boutcher, *supra* note 13, at 239.
400. Fernanda Santos, *In the Shadows, Day Laborers Left Homeless as Work Vanishes*, N.Y. TIMES, Jan. 2, 2010, at A16.
401. S.B. 1070, 49th Leg., 2d Reg. Sess. (Ariz. 2010).
402. *Id.* § 13-2928(B) ("It is unlawful for a person to enter a motor vehicle that is stopped on a street, roadway or highway in order to be hired by an occupant of the motor vehicle and to be transported to work at a different location if the motor vehicle impedes the normal movement of traffic.").
403. Narro, *supra* note 252.
404. Telephone Interview with Chris Newman, *supra* note 185.

405. Answering Br. of Appellees, Comite de Jornaleros de Redondo Beach v. City of Redondo Beach, 607 F.3d 1178 (July 10, 2007) (No. 06-55750).
406. Telephone Interview with Philip Hwang, *supra* note 279.
407. *Id.*
408. 569 F.3d 1029 (9th Cir. 2009) (en banc).
409. *Id.* at 1034, 1059.
410. Telephone Interview with Philip Hwang, *supra* note 279; *see also* Supplemental Letter from Philip Hwang to Molly Dwyer, Comite de Jornaleros de Redondo Beach (July 20, 2009).
411. Comite de Jornaleros de Redondo Beach v. City of Redondo Beach, 607 F.3d 1178, 1186-87 (9th Cir. 2010). The court distinguished *ACLU v. Las Vegas* on the ground that the Las Vegas ordinance had "prohibited the distribution of handbills 'requesting financial or other assistance' while permitting the distribution of handbills that did not make such a request.'" *Id.* at 1186.
412. *Id.* at 1190.
413. *Id.* at 1191.
414. *Id.* at 1192.
415. Petition for Rehearing En Banc at 1, *Comite de Jornaleros de Redondo Beach*, 607 F.3d 1178 (No. 06-55750). In support of the plaintiffs' petition, an amicus curiae brief was filed on behalf of prominent workers' rights organizations, which reinforced the day laborers' First Amendment arguments. *See* Br. of Amici Curiae Nat'l Domestic Worker All., National Employment Law Project, Restaurant Opportunities Center—United, and Right to the City in Support of Appellees' Petition for Rehearing En Banc, *Comite de Jornaleros de Redondo Beach*, 607 F.3d 1178 (No. 06-55750). This was in addition to the amicus brief filed in connection with the original appeal by UCLA Professor Abel Valenzuela, Jr., a pioneering day labor researcher. Saenz was formally added to the case on July 28, 2010. As the case proceeded, Cynthia Valenzuela withdrew from the legal team, replaced by MALDEF lawyer Nicholas Espiritu, who sat with Saenz at counsel's table during the en banc oral argument.
416. Petition for Rehearing En Banc, *supra* note 415, at 2–20.
417. Erwin Chemerinsky, *The Myth of the Liberal Ninth Circuit*, 37 LOY. L.A. L. REV. 1 (2003). In 2011, of the twenty-eight active judges in the Ninth Circuit, eleven were appointed by Republican presidents (seven by George W. Bush); and of Clinton's thirteen appointments, five (Silverman, Graber, Gould, Tallman, and Rawlinson) were considered conservative.
418. Comite de Jornaleros de Redondo Beach v. City of Redondo Beach, 657 F.3d 936 (9th Cir. 2011) (en banc).
419. Emily Bazelon, *The Big Kozinski*, LEGAL AFF., Jan./Feb. 2004, at 23.
420. Oral Argument, Comite de Jornaleros v. City of Redondo Beach, 657 F.3d 936 (9th Cir. 2011) (argued on Mar. 21, 2011), https://www.c-span.org/video/?298623-1/comite-de-jornaleros-v-city-redondo (last visited Mar. 29, 2019). The quoted exchanges are all excerpted from this source.
421. *Comite de Jornaleros de Redondo Beach*, 657 F.3d at 940.
422. *Id.* at 946.
423. *Id.* at 947.
424. *Id.* at 948.
425. *Id.* at 949.
426. *Id.* at 949–50.
427. *Id.* at 945.
428. *Id.* at 943.
429. *Id.* at 953. Judge Gould, in his own concurrence, would have found in favor of the city if it "had designated a permissible area for day laborer solicitation, in a convenient area for day laborers and potential employers alike." *Id.* at 951.
430. *Id.* at 957.
431. *Id.* at 958.

432. *Id.* at 959.
433. *Id.* at 960.
434. *Id.* at 961.
435. *Id.* at 956–57.
436. Editorial, *They Want Work*, N.Y. TIMES, Apr. 4, 2012, at A20.
437. *Id.*
438. Hannah Fry, *Costa Mesa Repeals Ban on Day Laborer Solicitation*, L.A. TIMES, Oct. 7, 2013, https://www.latimes.com/local/lanow/la-me-ln-costa-mesa-day-laborer-solicitation-20131007-story.html (last visited Mar. 29, 2019).
439. Valle Del Sol Inc. v. Whiting, 709 F.3d 808, 819 (9th Cir. 2013).
440. *Id.*
441. *Id.* at 826.
442. Saenz also hired Augustín Corral, the paralegal who created the ordinance database.
443. Telephone Interview with Victor Narro, *supra* note 41.
444. Telephone Interview with Veronica Federosky, *supra* note 223.
445. Telephone Interview with Belinda Escobosa Helzer, *supra* note 194.
446. Interview with Chris Newman, *supra* note 141.
447. Sonja Steptoe, *25 Most Influential Hispanics in America: Pablo Alvarado*, TIME, Aug. 22, 2005, at 53.
448. Telephone Interview with Shaheena Simons, *supra* note 245.
449. Telephone Interview with Chris Newman, *supra* note 185.
450. Telephone Interview with Hector Villagra, *supra* note 292.
451. *See generally* Hiroshi Motomura, *The Curious Evolution of Immigration Law: Procedural Surrogates for Substantive Constitutional Rights*, 92 COLUM. L. REV. 1625 (1992).
452. *See* Campbell, *supra* note 12.
453. *Cf.* Scott L. Cummings & Douglas NeJaime, *Lawyering for Marriage Equality*, 57 UCLA L. REV. 1235, 1312 (2010) (explaining the multidimensional advocacy approach used by LGBT movement lawyers).
454. Editorial, *Day Laborers and the Law*, L.A. TIMES, Mar. 29, 2011, http://articles.latimes.com/2011/mar/29/opinion/la-ed-daylabor-20110329 (last visited Mar. 23, 2019).
455. Telephone Interview with Belinda Escobosa Helzer, *supra* note 194.
456. *Id.*
457. Telephone Interview with Nora Preciado, *supra* note 284.
458. Telephone Interview with Chris Newman, *supra* note 185.
459. Telephone Interview with Hector Villagra, *supra* note 292.
460. Telephone Interview with Thomas Saenz, *supra* note 95.
461. Telephone Interview with Victor Narro, *supra* note 41.
462. Telephone Interview with Nancy Smyth, *supra* note 32.
463. Interview with Chris Newman, *supra* note 141.
464. Telephone Interview with Chris Newman, *supra* note 185.
465. Telephone Interview with Philip Hwang, *supra* note 279.
466. *Id.*
467. Telephone Interview with Belinda Escobosa Helzer, *supra* note 194.
468. Telephone Interview with Shaheena Simons, *supra* note 245.
469. Telephone Interview with Kristina Campbell, *supra* note 351.
470. *Id.*
471. Email from Chris Newman, Legal Programs Dir., Nat'l Day Laborer Org. Network, to Scott L. Cummings, Professor, UCLA Sch. of Law (July 1, 2011).
472. Telephone Interview with Pablo Alvarado, *supra* note 92.
473. Telephone Interview with Veronica Federosky, *supra* note 223.
474. Telephone Interview with Thomas Saenz, *supra* note 95.
475. Telephone Interview with Kristina Campbell, *supra* note 351.

476. Telephone Interview with Thomas Saenz, *supra* note 95.
477. Telephone Interview with Kristina Campbell, *supra* note 351.
478. *Id.*
479. Telephone Interview with Hector Villagra, *supra* note 292.
480. In the Lake Forest case, in addition to NDLON and ATLF, Colectivo Tonantzin was named as a plaintiff. In Costa Mesa, NDLON was not listed as a plaintiff—reflecting the negative standing decision in the Lake Forest case.
481. Comite de Jornaleros de Redondo Beach v. City of Redondo Beach, 657 F.3d 936, 943 (9th Cir. 2011).
482. Telephone Interview with Hector Villagra, *supra* note 292.
483. Telephone Interview with Chris Newman, *supra* note 185.
484. *Id.*
485. Julia Preston, *Lack of Consensus in Legislatures Slows Tough Measures on Immigration*, N.Y. TIMES, Mar. 14, 2011, at A13.
486. Telephone Interview with Belinda Escobosa Helzer, *supra* note 194.
487. Interview with Chris Newman, *supra* note 141.
488. Telephone Interview with Chris Newman, *supra* note 185.
489. *Id.*
490. Adam Liptak, *How Conservatives Weaponized the First Amendment*, N.Y. TIMES, June 30, 2018, https://www.nytimes.com/2018/06/30/us/politics/first-amendment-conservatives-supreme-court.html (last visited Mar. 30, 2019).
491. Telephone Interview with Michael Kaufman, Staff Att'y, ACLU of S. Cal. (Dec. 21, 2010).
492. Of the jurisdictions originally enacting complete citywide bans, five provided statutory exceptions for solicitation from day labor centers (El Monte, Glendale, Laguna Beach, Pomona, and Rialto). The City of Orange added such an exception when it amended its ordinance in 2007.
493. Of the original citywide bans, thirty-seven applied to both workers and employers, four to workers only, and one (Pasadena's) to employers only.
494. *See* Table 3.2: Anti-solicitation ordinances (original form) in the greater L.A. area, 1987–2011. Twenty-six cities also had commercial parking lot bans in addition to bans on solicitation in public space. These came in a variety of forms, with seventeen prohibiting such solicitation if the lot owner both established a lawful area for solicitation and posted appropriate signs. Eight of the bans prohibited commercial parking lot solicitation only upon posting of signs, one prohibited it with either a lawful area or a sign, and one prohibited it without conditions.
495. Nik Theodore, Abel Valenzuela, Jr. & Edwin Meléndez, *Worker Centers: Defending Day Labor Standards for Migrant Workers in the Informal Economy*, 30 INT'L J. MANPOWER 422, 425 (2009).

Chapter 4

1. Scott L. Cummings & Ingrid V. Eagly, *A Critical Reflection on Law and Organizing*, 48 UCLA L. REV. 443 (2001); *see also* ANDREA GIBBONS & GILDA HAAS, REDEFINING REDEVELOPMENT: PARTICIPATORY RESEARCH FOR EQUITY IN THE LOS ANGELES FIGUEROA CORRIDOR (Dep't of Urb. Plan., Sch. of Pub. Pol'y & Soc. Res., UCLA, Sept. 2002).
2. George Ramos, *The Upgrading of Figueroa Becomes a Two-Way Street; Development: A Group of Merchants and Another of Residents Want to Spruce Up the 2 ½-mile Corridor*, L.A. TIMES, Aug. 21, 2000, at B1.
3. *See Who We Are*, CRA/LA, http://www.crala.org/internet-site/About/who_we_are.cfm (last visited Oct. 19, 2019).
4. MARTIN ANDERSON, THE FEDERAL BULLDOZER: A CRITICAL ANALYSIS OF URBAN RENEWAL 1949–1962 (1964).

5. *See* PETER DREIER, JOHN MOLLENKOPF & TODD SWANSTROM, PLACE MATTERS: METROPOLITICS FOR THE TWENTY-FIRST CENTURY 120 (2000).
6. *See* Benjamin Quinones, *Redevelopment Redefined: Revitalizing the Central City with Resident Control*, 27 U. MICH. J.L. REFORM 689 (1994).
7. The Hoover Redevelopment Project area, created in 1966, covered USC and Exposition Park. *See* Amy Young, *Plans for Figueora Corridor Remain Troubling Question*, THE LANTERN (Columbus), Sept. 25, 2000. The Central Business District redevelopment project area, established in 1975, included approximately 1,549 acres bounded by the Hollywood 101 Freeway to the north, the Harbor 110 Freeway to the west, the Santa Monica 10 Freeway to the south, and Alameda Street to the east. Howard Fine & Elizabeth Hayes, *Officials Eye Redevelopment Boost for Downtown*, L.A. BUS. J., May 22, 2000, at 1. In addition, parts of the Figueroa Corridor also sat within the City Center project area, established in 2002; the Adams-Normandie project area, established in 1979; and the Council District 9-South of Santa Monica Freeway project area, established in 1995.
8. *See* CRA/LA, MAP OF HOOVER PROJECT AREA, http://www.crala.org/internet-site/Projects/Hoover/upload/Hoover-Map-in-PDF.pdf (last visited Oct. 19, 2019).
9. Travis James Tritten, *USC Growth Causes Land Clash With Locals*, THE LANTERN (Columbus), Sept. 25, 2000.
10. Jocelyn Y. Stewart, *Activists Seek Agreement with USC; Coalition Wants the University to Provide Housing and Job Aid to the Campus' Neighbors*, L.A. TIMES, Oct. 8, 2003, at B1.
11. *See* George Ramos, *Special Report: Recent Actions by the University Have Given Some Neighbors . . . New Worries About Being Displaced by USC*, L.A. TIMES, May 21, 2000, at B1; *see also* Steve Kawashima, *Coalition Wants to Lift Community Voice*, OUR TIMES (Crenshaw), Nov. 19–25, 1999; John M. Cleary, *Editorial, Selling Out Our Neighbors*, DAILY TROJAN (L.A.), Sept. 7, at 4.
12. FIGUEROA CORRIDOR COALITION FOR ECONOMIC JUSTICE, REPORT TO THE COMMUNITY REDEVELOPMENT AGENCY ON THE GALEN CENTER PROPOSAL (Oct. 2003).
13. Tritten, *supra* note 9; Erica Werner, *$26 Million Downtown Hotel Latest Real Estate Grab for USC*, ASSOCIATED PRESS STATE & LOC. WIRE, Aug. 12, 2000. In August 2000, USC bought the 240-room Radisson Hotel across the street from campus for $26 million. David Kesmodel, *USC to Buy Radisson Hotel Across the Street from Campus*, L.A. TIMES, July 28, 2000, at C2. Despite concerns regarding USC's expansion, residents recognized some of the university's positive contributions, including investing resources in five local public schools and providing campus police to patrol the surrounding neighborhood.
14. *See* Ramos, *supra* note 2.
15. *Id.*
16. *See* Sam Farmer, *Delay of NFL Game in LA*, L.A. TIMES, Dec. 24, 2004, at D1.
17. *See* Fine & Hayes, *supra* note 7.
18. *See* Patrick McGreevy, *City OKs Hotel Subsidy Deal*, L.A. TIMES, Feb. 12, 2005, at B1.
19. *See* CRA/LA, BUILDING A WORLD CLASS CITY: CENTRAL BUSINESS DISTRICT REDEVELOPMENT PROJECT, 1975–2010 (2010), http://www.crala.org/internet-site/upload/CBDBooklet_July2010.pdf (last visited Oct. 19, 2019).
20. Anschutz owned AEG, which owned or controlled the Staples Center and several other arenas, as well as sports franchises including the Los Angeles Kings and several pro soccer teams; AEG also managed shares of the Los Angeles Lakers and Sparks. *See About Us*, STAPLES CENTER, http://www.staplescenter.com/about/about-staples-center (last visited Feb. 1, 2006).
21. Robert A. Baade, *Los Angeles City Controllers Report on Economic Impact: Staples Center* (July 21, 2003), https://controllerdata.lacity.org/views/uu9w-6f5z/files/IgxMBgs3lGqmsO1sJyHultg2fcA_WwrIjOcazFn4e9k (last visited Oct. 19, 2019).
22. *See id.* The city obtained $20 million of the $58.5-million loan from the Convention Center Debt Service Reserve Fund and borrowed the remaining $38.5 million by issuing bonds. *Id.* The $58.5-million city loan was personally guaranteed by the developer, who planned to repay

it from admission fees, parking revenues, property tax revenues, and other taxes from business-related activities. Matthew J. Parlow, *Publicly Financed Sports Facilities: Are They Economically Justifiable? A Case Study of the Los Angeles Staples Center*, 10 U. MIAMI BUS. L. REV. 483, 536, 538 (2002). The grant from the CRA to fund the Staples Center, however, did not need to be repaid. Tatiana Siegel, *You Can Forget All Your Cares and Go Downtown: Five Years After Opening Its Doors, Staples Center Has Silenced Critics by Revitalizing Downtown L.A. and Becoming One of the World's Finest Sports and Entertainment Venues* (Special Report), AMUSEMENT BUS., Nov. 1, 2004.
23. *See* CRA/LA, *supra* note 19.
24. Carla Rivera, *Staples Center's Displaced Have New Homes and New Worries; Housing: Many Families Are Living in Cleaner Places, but Some Wonder How They Will Pay the Rent After Subsidies Run Out*, L.A. TIMES, Oct. 9, 1999, at B1.
25. *Id.*
26. *Id.*
27. *Id.*
28. James B. Goodno, *Feet to the Fire: Accountable Development Keeps Developers and Community Groups Talking—and Walking*, 70 PLAN. 14 (2004).
29. JENNIFER GORDON, SUBURBAN SWEATSHOPS: THE FIGHT FOR IMMIGRANT RIGHTS 62–63 (2005); KATHERINE V.W. STONE, FROM WIDGETS TO DIGITS: EMPLOYMENT REGULATION FOR THE CHANGING WORKPLACE 224–25 (2004).
30. COMMUNITY SCHOLARS PROGRAM, UCLA SCHOOL OF PUBLIC POLICY AND SOCIAL RESEARCH, DEPARTMENT OF URBAN PLANNING, A "JUST" REDEVELOPMENT: LESSONS FROM THE FIGUEROA CORRIDOR COALITION FOR ECONOMIC JUSTICE (Final Project Report 2004).
31. CAROL ZABIN & ISAAC MARTIN, LIVING WAGE CAMPAIGNS IN THE ECONOMIC POLICY ARENA: FOUR CASE STUDIES FROM CALIFORNIA (Center for Labor Research and Education, Institute of Industrial Relations, UC Berkeley for The Phoenix Fund for Workers and Communities, The New World Foundation, June 1999). For analysis of LAANE's efforts to extend living wage, see Kathleen Erskine & Judy Marblestone, *The Role of Lawyers in Santa Monica's Struggle for a Living Wage*, in CAUSE LAWYERS AND SOCIAL MOVEMENTS (Austin Sarat & Stuart Scheingold eds., 2006).
32. L.A., CAL., ADMIN. CODE div. 10, ch. 1, §§ 10.37.1, 10.37.2 (1997).
33. L.A., CAL., ADMIN. CODE div. 10, ch. 1, § 10.36.1 (1995).
34. Bob Rector, *Valley Perspective Interview: Madeline Janis-Aparicio; Union Leader Aims to Tie Labor Issue to Development in Universal's Expansion Plan: Valley Edition*, L.A. TIMES, July 26, 1998, at B15.
35. Subsidy Accountability Project, Subsidy Accountability and Economic Development in LA: An Outline (1998).
36. Subsidy Accountability Project Advisory Committee, *Minutes of Meeting* (Aug. 27, 1998).
37. Subsidy Accountability Project, Flowchart: Developing a Cradle to Grave Process for Subsidy Accountability (The CRA Example) (May 21, 1999).
38. *See* UCLA LABOR CENTER & LOS ANGELES ALLIANCE FOR A NEW ECONOMY, WHO BENEFITS FROM REDEVELOPMENT IN LOS ANGELES? AN EVALUATION OF COMMERCIAL DEVELOPMENT ACTIVITIES IN THE 1990S (Los Angeles Alliance for a New Economy 1999).
39. Response to LAANE Report from Community Redevelopment Agency of the City of Los Angeles (Apr. 22, 1999).
40. *About Us*, STRATEGIC ACTIONS FOR A JUST ECONOMY, http://www.saje.net/site/c.hkLQJcMUKrH/b.2315795/k.C925/About_Us.htm (last visited Mar. 23, 2015).
41. Margaret Ramirez, *25 Arrested at USC Labor Protest Dispute: Activists Target University for Refusing to Give Job Security to Workers. School Officials Say They Need Flexibility*, L.A. TIMES, Sept. 1, 1999, at B4. USC responded that it did not plan to subcontract out employee jobs but did not want to lose flexibility; it also stated that it had offered a wage increase totaling $1 million plus full benefits. *Id.*

42. Howard Padwa, *Development for the People*, Lab. Res. Ass'n, June 15, 2001; Bobbi Murray, *Unite and Conquer*, The Nation, July 12, 2001, https://www.thenation.com/article/unite-and-conquer/ (last visited Oct. 19, 2019); Gilda Haas, *Economic Justice in the Los Angeles Figueroa Corridor*, in Teaching for Change: Popular Education and the Labor Movement (Linda Delp & Miranda Outman-Kramer et. al., 2002).
43. Edith Chan, *Behind the Line*, Daily Trojan (L.A.), Nov. 19, 1998, at 11; Edith Chan, *More Than 200 March for Union*, Daily Trojan (L.A.), Nov. 19, 1998; Hugo Martin, *Students, Clergy March to Support USC Workers' Contract Demands*, L.A. Times, Sept. 3, 1998, at B3; Ramirez, *supra* note 41; Rhonda Roumani, *USC Workers Declare Victory as City Council Passes Worker-Retention Law*, Metro. News Enterprise, Sept. 16, 1999, at 10. Employees were concerned about job security in part because of USC's tuition remission benefit, which allowed workers to send their children to USC for free while employed by the university or after five years of service. Chan, *Behind the Line, supra*.
44. L.A., Cal., Admin. Code div. 10, ch. 1, § 10.36.1(c) (1999).
45. *See USC Settles 4-Year Dispute with Cafeteria, Janitorial Workers*, L.A. Times, Oct. 5, 1999, at B3.
46. Murray, *supra* note 42.
47. Haas, *supra* note 42; *see also* Gilda Haas, *Mapping (In)justice*, 15 City: Analysis of Urb. Trends, Culture, Theory, Pol'y, Action 87 (2011).
48. *About Us*, Strategic Actions for a Just Economy, *supra* note 40.
49. Lee Romney, *Community, Developers Agree on Staples Plan; Deal; The Proposed Entertainment and Sports District Could Become a Model for Urban Partnerships*, L.A. Times, May 31, 2001, at A1; *see also* Letter from William J. Fujioka, City Admin. Officer & Ronald F. Deaton, Chief Legis. Analyst, to Ad Hoc Comm. on the LA Sports and Ent. Dist. Master Plan, Re: Initial Actions for Review and Negotiation of the Master Plan (June 12, 2000).
50. *See* Romney, *supra* note 49; Rick Orlov, *No Public Funds for L.A. Hotel; Instead, Developers Seek 20 Years of Bed Tax Diversion*, Daily News of L.A., July 15, 2004, at N16; Ray Waddell, *AEG Has Big Plans for L.A. Venues, On the Road*, Billboard, July 31, 2004, at 21.
51. Lee Romney, *Staples Plan Spotlights "Invisible" Communities*, L.A. Times, June 2, 2001, at C1.
52. Lynn Lunsford, *Staples Center Plan Required to Provide Community Services*, Wall St. J., June 1, 2001, at B8.
53. Nancy Cleeland & Jeffrey Rabin, *Gore's Presence at Rally Boosts Janitors' Spirits*, L.A. Times, Apr. 17, 2000, at B1.
54. Antonio Olivo, *Hotel Workers, Riot Police Clash During Protest*, L.A. Times, July 4, 2000, at B1.
55. Figueroa Corridor Coalition for Economic Justice, Strategy Meeting re: Staples Development, Coalition LA (July 7, 2000).
56. Lunsford, *supra* note 52.
57. Figueroa Corridor Coalition for Economic Justice, Notes of Meeting on Staples Center Development (Sept. 7, 2000).
58. Memorandum from Misty Sanford, Envtl. Def., to FCCEJ Res. Comm. (Sept. 20, 2000).
59. Agenda for Meeting of Staples Accountable Development Working Groups (Oct. 11, 2000).
60. *See* Romney, *supra* note 49. Coalition recruitment built on work started while SAJE was conducting a neighborhood survey shortly before the Democratic National Convention. *Id.* Originally, there were twenty-nine community groups in the coalition; however, one dropped out because the coalition did not address its concerns regarding liquor licenses. *Id.*
61. Haas, *supra* note 42.
62. Bill Delvac, Partner, Latham & Watkins, Presentation to Cmty. Econ. Dev. Clinic, UCLA Sch. of Law (Mar. 28, 2005).
63. Julian Gross, Greg LeRoy & Madeline Janis-Aparicio, Community Benefits Agreements: Making Development Projects Accountable 29–30 (Good Jobs First and the California Partnership for Working Families 2005). For analysis of CBAs, see Murtaza H. Baxamusa, *Empowering Communities through Deliberation: The Model of Community Benefits Agreements*, 27 J. Planning Education & Research 261 (2008); David A. Marcello,

Community Benefit Agreements: New Vehicle for Investment in America's Neighborhoods, 39 URB. LAW. 657 (2007).
64. Telephone Interview with Gilda Haas, Exec. Dir., Strategic Actions for a Just Econ. (Jan. 20, 2005).
65. *See, e.g.*, Christopher L. Erickson, Catherine L. Fisk, Ruth Milkman, Daniel J.B. Mitchell & Kent Wong, *Justice for Janitors in Los Angeles: Lessons from Three Rounds of Negotiations*, 40 BRIT. J. INDUS. REL. 543 (2002).
66. Disposition and Development Agreement of the Los Angeles Community Redevelopment Agency and TrizecHahn Hollywood LLC (Feb. 10, 1999).
67. REPORT FROM CITY ADMINISTRATIVE OFFICER TO THE MAYOR AND THE COUNCIL, RE: COUNCIL ACTION OF MAY 15, 1998, APPROVING HOLLYWOOD AND HIGHLAND PROJECT 2 (Mar. 3, 1999).
68. Disposition and Development Agreement, *supra* note 66, at 49, 52.
69. *Id.* at 52.
70. Ronald F. Deaton, Chief Legis. Analyst, to Members, Housing and Cmty. Redev. Comm., Re: CRA-Cinerama Dome Entertainment Center-Parking Revenue Bonds (May 31, 2000).
71. Owner Participation Agreement, Cinerama Dome 44 (July 17, 2000).
72. Living Wage Incentive Plan Appendix to Owner Participation Agreement, Cinerama Dome 2–3 (July 17, 2000).
73. Nona Liegeois, Francisca Baxa & Barbara Corkrey, *Helping Low-Income People Get Decent Jobs: One Legal Services Program's Approach*, 33 CLEARINGHOUSE REV. 279, 290 (1999).
74. *See id.* at 286–89.
75. LAANE, Draft of Proposed Steps to Reform the Process of Subsidy Accountability (Jan. 1, 2000).
76. Agenda for Policy Development Subcommittee Meeting of Living Wage Coalition (Feb. 22, 2000).
77. Memorandum from Jessica Goodheardt, Co-Dir. of Res., LAANE, to Subsidy Accountability Team (Mar. 15, 2000).
78. Email from Jessica Goodheart to Erika Zucker et al., Re: Notes from CD 13 Meeting (May 10, 2000).
79. Preliminary Outline of Report on Subsidy Accountability from Los Angeles Alliance for a New Economy to City Council (2000).
80. LAANE, Draft of How It Adds Up: An Accounting of the City of Los Angeles Economic Development Expenditures in the 1990s (June 16, 2000).
81. LAANE, Presentation of Research to Participants in the Public Subsidies Project (July 27, 2000).
82. Meeting of State Network Exploration on Forming a California Alliance (Sept. 15, 2000).
83. Meeting of California Public Subsidies Project Partners (Nov. 13, 2000) (discussing whether an economic impact analysis should track the environmental review format and which equity standards could be adopted as a platform for seeking city and statewide laws); *see also* Meeting of California Public Subsidies Project Partners (Nov. 13, 2000) (seeking to create a statewide equity impact analysis); Email from Sarah Zimmerman to Jessica Goodheart et al., Re: Definition of EIA (Feb. 8, 2001).
84. *See* Telephone Interview with Gilda Haas, *supra* note 64.
85. *Id.*
86. *Id.*
87. Notes from FCCEJ De-Briefing Conference Call (Nov. 16, 2000).
88. Notes from Meeting of FCCEJ, Staples World Sports and Entertainment District "Big Brains" (Dec. 14, 2000).
89. Notes from Meeting of the Staples World Ad Hoc Housing Committee (Jan. 3, 2001).
90. Meeting of Figueroa Corridor Coalition for Economic Justice, Specific Plan (Jan. 10, 2001).
91. Email from Jessica Goodheart to Madeline Janis-Aparicio (Feb. 12, 2001).

92. *Id.*
93. *Id.*
94. *See* Padwa, *supra* note 42.
95. With HERE Local 11 and the SEIU Local 1877 as coalition members, FCCEJ had the benefit of labor's established track record and excellent relations with the media and key city politicians in strengthening its bargaining position. *See* Padwa, *supra* note 42.
96. Presentation by Bill Delvac, *supra* note 62.
97. Telephone Interview with Julian Gross, Law Off. of Julian Gross (Jan. 20, 2005).
98. *Id.*
99. *Id.*
100. *Id.* Gross was hired after the coalition decided its pro bono lawyer "was not working out."
101. *Id.*
102. During negotiations, Haas also invited attorneys from LAFLA and Public Counsel to review CBA drafts.
103. Jacqueline Leavitt, *Linking Housing to Community Economic Development with Community Benefits Agreements: The Case of the Figueroa Corridor Coalition for Economic Justice*, in JOBS AND ECONOMIC DEVELOPMENT IN MINORITY COMMUNITIES (Paul Ong & Anastasia Loukaitou-Sideris eds., 2006).
104. Gilda Haas, Exec. Dir., Strategic Actions for a Just Econ., Presentation to Cmty. Econ. Dev. Clinic, UCLA Sch. of Law (Mar. 28, 2005).
105. *Id.*
106. Telephone Interview with Julian Gross, *supra* note 97.
107. *Id.*
108. *Id.*
109. Presentation by Gilda Haas, *supra* note 104.
110. Presentation by Bill Delvac, *supra* note 62.
111. Telephone Interview with Julian Gross, *supra* note 97.
112. *Id.*
113. Telephone Interview with Jerilyn López Mendoza, Pol'y Dir., Envtl. Def. (Jan. 21, 2005).
114. *Id.*
115. *Id.*
116. *Id.*
117. 14 CAL. CODE REGS. § 15002 (2000).
118. CAL. PUB. RES. CODE § 21080(d) (2000).
119. 14 CAL. CODE REGS. § 15230 (2000).
120. Jerilyn López Mendoza, Pol'y Dir., Envtl. Def., Presentation to Problem Solving in the Public Interest Seminar, UCLA Sch. of Law (Sept. 23, 2004).
121. Jerilyn López Mendoza, Letter on behalf of FCCEJ to Lateef Sholebo, Project Coordinator, Envtl. Rev. Sec., L.A. City Plan. Dep't (Feb. 26, 2001).
122. Presentation by Gilda Haas, *supra* note 104.
123. Third Implementation Agreement to Disposition and Development Agreement among the City of Los Angeles, CRA, and L.A. Arena Land Co. (2001), Modifying Original Disposition and Development Agreement for Los Angeles Arena Project (Oct. 31, 1997). The Final EIR incorporated much of what the coalition had asked for in its comments. FINAL ENVIRONMENTAL IMPACT REPORT, LOS ANGELES SPORTS AND ENTERTAINMENT DISTRICT (Apr. 2001). However, by the time the Final EIR was issued in April 2001, the CBA had been nearly finalized. As López Mendoza recalled, "we didn't have to pay much attention to the Final EIR because we got what we really wanted out of the CBA process." Email from Jerilyn López Mendoza, Pol'y Dir., Envtl. Def., to Scott Cummings, Professor, UCLA Sch. of Law (May 9, 2005).
124. FCCEJ member Environmental Defense—Environmental Justice Project agreed not to oppose the project and was specifically exempted from the support obligations. *See* Los Angeles Sports and Entertainment District Cooperation Agreement § 12 (May 29, 2001).

125. In the final agreement, only nine organizations were named as signatories: CARECEN, CHIRLA, Concerned Citizens of South Central Los Angeles, Coalition LA, Environmental Defense–Environmental Justice Project, Esperanza Community Housing Corporation, HERE Local 11, LAANE, and SAJE. This was owing to the timing of the agreement, with the parties pushing to announce it by the end of May in order to leave time to finalize city approvals before the July 1 mayoral and city council transition. Because each FCCEJ member had to ratify the agreement through its own internal organizational process, not every group could meet the May deadline. However, the developer made it clear that it wanted at least eighteen FCCEJ members as signatories, with particular members identified as key parties. Accordingly, in the month after the agreement was announced, another twelve FCCEJ members signed onto the agreement. Only AGENDA and the Community Coalition refused to sign out of principle. A few other groups did not get around to signing in a timely fashion, and as the project moved forward their formal status as parties to the contract became irrelevant.
126. Presentation by Bill Delvac, *supra* note 62.
127. *See* Cooperation Agreement, *supra* note 124, at § 11.
128. *See* Los Angeles Sports and Entertainment District Community Benefits Program (May 29, 2001).
129. The project was set to be reviewed by the City Council in July 2004. Orlov, *supra* note 50.
130. Tina Daunt, *Plan for L.A. Times Square to Get Key Airing*, L.A. TIMES, Sept. 3, 2001, (Metro), at 1.
131. Beth Barrett, *No Subsidy, No Hotel*, L.A. DAILY NEWS, June 17, 2001, at N1.
132. *See* Daunt, *supra* note 130.
133. Chris Modrzejewski, *Anschutz's Public Affairs VP Is on Top of His Development Game*, L.A. DOWNTOWN DEV. NEWS, Feb. 17, 2003, at 13.
134. In 1977, then-Councilman Ernani Bernardi brought a lawsuit that resulted in a court judgment limiting the CRA from receiving more than $750 million in tax increment funds from the Central Business District, on the theory that above that level, the city should have to share in the economic return of downtown development. Patrick McGreevy & Daren Briscoe, *Judge Deals Blow to Downtown Plan; Court Says That Los Angeles' Approval of the 879-Acre City Center Redevelopment Project Violates an Earlier Settlement*, L.A. TIMES, June 26, 2003, at 3 (Metro).
135. *Id.*
136. Troy Anderson, *Downtown Redevelopment Blocked*, L.A. DAILY NEWS, June 26, 2003, at N5
137. *Id.*
138. Orlov, *supra* note 50. The developer announced a deal with Nokia to name the Nokia Theater, Nokia Plaza, and Club Nokia. Waddell, *supra* note 50.
139. Rick Orlov, *Miffed About Hotel Plans—Downtown Los Angeles Hotel Project Critics Voice Reservations about Subsidies*, L.A. DAILY NEWS, July 25, 2004, at N1.
140. *See* McGreevy, *supra* note 18. The hotel subsidy could not be paid for by TIF revenues because the Central Business District had already hit the TIF ceiling imposed by the 1977 Bernardi lawsuit settlement.
141. Nicholas J. Marantz, *What Do Community Benefits Agreements Deliver? Evidence from Los Angeles*, 81 J. AM. PLAN. ASSOC. 251, 262 (2015); *see also* Leland Saito & Jonathan Troung, *The L.A. Live Community Benefits Agreement: Evaluating the Agreement Results and Shifting Political Power in the City*, 51 URBAN AFF. REV. 263 (2014).
142. Leavitt, *supra* note 103.
143. *Id.*
144. As López Mendoza suggested, "the most difficult part is implementation. It lasts for years. It is boring, not public, and therefore takes a long time and patience keeping the coalition together." *See* Telephone Interview with Jerilyn López Mendoza, *supra* note 113.
145. Marantz, *supra* note 141.
146. *Id.*
147. *Id.*

148. *Id.*
149. *Id.*; Memorandum on Private Enforcement by Figueroa Corridor Coalition for Economic Justice or L.A. Arena Land Co. of Affordable Housing Requirements of Community Benefits Program against Figueroa South Land LLC (Sept. 2005).
150. Marantz, *supra* note 141; *see also* Letter from L.A. Arena Land Company to FCCEJ, YWCA & Figueroa South Land LLC, Re: LASED-Affordable Housing Credit Agreement (Oct. 3, 2005).
151. L.A. Live, *Community Benefits Program, Status Update* (Mar. 2006).
152. Telephone Interview with Martha Saucedo, Vice President of Cmty. Affs., AEG Worldwide (Aug. 26, 2009).
153. Marantz, *supra* note 141.
154. *Id.*
155. *Id.*
156. Beginning in 2006, community–labor organizations following the LAANE model succeeded in passing community benefits policies in San Diego, San Jose, and Emeryville.
157. Valley Jobs Coalition, Working Harder, Earning Less: Why We Need Smart Public Investment (Dec. 4, 2000).
158. Patrick McGreevy, *NoHo Project Backed for More Public Funding*, L.A. Times, Nov. 22, 2001, at B3.
159. Patricia E. Salkin & Amy Lavine, *Negotiating for Social Justice and the Promise of Community Benefits Agreements: Case Studies of Current and Developing Agreements*, 17 J. Affordable Housing & Cmty. Dev. L. 113, 119 (2008).
160. McGreevy, *supra* note 158.
161. North Hollywood Mixed-Use Redevelopment Project, Community Benefits Program 4 (Nov. 2001), https://www.laane.org/wp-content/uploads/2012/03/NoHo20CBA.pdf (last visited Oct. 19, 2019).
162. *Id.*
163. *Id.* at 2-3.
164. Amy Lavine, *NoHo Commons CBA*, Cmty. Benefits Agreements (Jan. 28, 2008), http://communitybenefits.blogspot.com/2008/01/2001-deal-in-relation-to-large-mixed.html (last visited Oct. 22, 2019). In 2007, the NoHo developer, J.H. Snyder Co., agreed to pay $1.5 million to build the child care center. As of January 2008, 80% of project tenants had used the first-source hiring program set up by the developer, which found tenants willing to pay a living wage. *See* Salkin & Lavine, *supra* note 159, at 119. In 2010, Keys Consulting Group conducted an analysis of the NoHo CBA finding that the retail space was 100% leased but the office space was only 50% leased (although the office space was not completed until August 2009 due to the recession). The report found that, overall, "a total of 476 jobs have been created"; of the office jobs, there were 267 created by the California Arts Institute, all of which at or above the living wage threshold. In addition, there were roughly 200 other retail jobs (with no wage data) in businesses like Panera Bakery, Cold Stone Creamery, the Coffee Bean & Tea Leaf, and HOWS Market, which had the most jobs (55) but was closing. *See* Memorandum to Cmty. Dev. Dep't. & J.H. Snyder Co. from Keys Consulting Group 1–7 (2010).
165. *CBAs Currently in Effect*, Partnership for Working Families, http://www.forworkingfamilies.org/page/policy-tools-community-benefits-agreements-and-policies-effect (last visited Oct. 19, 2019).
166. SunQuest Industrial Park Project, Community Benefits Plan (Oct. 25, 2001), http://juliangross.net/docs/CBA/Sunquest_Agreement.pdf (last visited Oct. 19, 2019).
167. *Id.* at 5.
168. *Id.* at 2.
169. *Id.* at 3.
170. *Id.* at 4–5, 8.

171. *See* REPORT FROM OFFICE OF THE CITY ADMINISTRATIVE OFFICER, TO THE INFORMATION TECHNOLOGY AND GENERAL SERVICES COMMITTEE (Dec. 17, 2001); File History, Final Ordinance No. 174403 (Feb. 2, 2002). In 2002, after the SunQuest CBA was inked, the developer sought to purchase an adjacent landfill owned by the city in order to expand its project footprint. Because the site had significant environmental problems, the city agreed to sell it to SunQuest for $2.55 million, requiring SunQuest to conduct environmental remediation. As part of the sale, the city promised to work with SunQuest and the coalition to "develop a mutually agreeable Community Benefits Plan" in connection with the expanded project (the city was not party to the original CBA, which was not incorporated in the city's development agreement). Under the terms of the sale, the city was to lease back a portion of the land for city office space. Although the City Council agreed to the sale, which was finalized in January 2003, the CBA was not recorded in the purchase or development agreements. *See* REPORT FROM OFFICE OF THE CITY ADMINISTRATIVE OFFICER TO THE INFORMATION TECHNOLOGY AND GENERAL SERVICES COMMITTEE (Dec. 17, 2001); File History, Final Ordinance No. 174403 (Feb. 2, 2002). In 2006, the developer filed for bankruptcy. The bankruptcy court permitted the developer to sell the SunQuest property to a new owner, which was a company legally related to SunQuest Development LLC—the original developer. However, the court concluded that the new owner was not an "insider" of SunQuest and thus did not have to take on SunQuest's contractual obligations. As a result, the bankruptcy sale negated the CBA and, although LAANE and Gross attempted to find a way to impose the CBA on the new purchaser, because the city's benefit plan was never recorded, the purchaser was released from community benefit obligations by the bankruptcy court.

172. In April 2002, during an implementation meeting to discuss next steps after NoHo and SunQuest, the Valley Jobs Coalition planned a citywide community benefits policy campaign. *See* Meeting of Valley Jobs Coalition on CBP Implementation (Apr. 25, 2002); *see also* Lee Romney, *Making Builders Do More*, L.A. TIMES, Mar. 18, 2002, at A1 ("Now, those receiving public dollars increasingly are being called on to deliver improved wages, health benefits, subsidized housing, child-care centers, and parks.").

173. The Marlton Square Redevelopment Project in Crenshaw was a $125 million, 22-acre CRA-sponsored retail and residential project originally advanced by Magic Johnson, who lost the deal in 2002 to Capital Vision Equities. A CBA was finalized in 2002 and incorporated into the CRA's development agreement. In 2004, Capital Vision Equities dissolved, and the property was transferred to a new owner with the CRA taking a 20% share. As of 2015, no community benefits had been provided by the project, which was plagued by delay and cost overruns. *See* Ralph Rosado, *What Will the Neighbors Say? How Differences in Planning Culture Yield Distinctive Outcomes in Urban Redevelopment: The Example of the Community Benefits Trend* 1, 176 (2015) (Ph.D. thesis, University of Pennsylvania Department of City & Regional Planning).

174. Hollywood & Vine Community Benefits Agreement (2004), http://www.laane.org/whats-new/2009/09/25/hollywood-and-vine-community-benefits-agreement/#more-771 (last visited Sept. 25, 2009). The Hollywood and Vine development was a $326 million revitalization project that included a W Hotel, condominiums, 350 apartments, and more than 32,000 square feet of retail space, including a Trader Joe's grocery. It was a joint development between Legacy Partners and Gatehouse Capital, in cooperation with the City of Los Angeles (which contributed $5 million), the CRA (which contributed $2 million), and the Metropolitan Transportation Authority (which donated land in connection with the Red Line station). The coalition was composed of LAANE, Yucca Residents' Group, and L.A. Voice. The CBA was facilitated by Councilman Eric Garcetti, whose district included Hollywood. The coalition's lawyer was Julian Gross, and the CBA was completed in 2004. In 2010, the developer claimed 83% of 597 project tenant employees were paid a living wage. Letter from Jeffrey A. Cohen, Gatehouse Hollywood Development, to Zach Hoover, LA Voice/PICO, Re: Hollywood & Vine Mixed-Use Development Project (Apr. 8, 2010).

175. *See* Goodno, *supra* note 28.
176. Torrie Osborn, *Do Good and Do Good Business: What Better Place Than L.A. for Ethical Capitalism?*, L.A. TIMES, July 24, 2002, at B13.
177. Jessica Goodheart, A Model Community Impact Report (Aug. 15, 2002).
178. *Id.*
179. Email from Donald Spivack, CRA, to Scott Cummings, Professor, UCLA Sch. of Law (May 18, 2005).
180. Harold Meyerson, *L.A. Story*, THE AMERICAN PROSPECT (Aug. 6, 2013), https://prospect.org/article/la-story-0 (last visited July 3, 2019).
181. For a review of CRA policies, *see* Patrick Burns, Daniel Flaming & Brent Haydamack, *Benefits of CRA/LA Social Equity Policies* (Mar. 2004). In 2009, after a strong push from LAANE, the Los Angeles County Fed, and other labor and community allies, the CRA adopted a Construction Careers and Project Stabilization Policy that required project developers to hire more low-income residents from the neighborhoods in which projects were being built.
182. Larry Kanter, *Furor over Airport Expansion Plan Grows*, L.A. BUS. J., Mar. 23, 1998.
183. *See* L.A., CAL., ADMIN. CODE art. VI, § 630 (2000).
184. 49 U.S.C. § 47133 (2000).
185. LAURIE KAYE & JERILYN LÓPEZ MENDOZA, EVERYBODY WINS 3.21 (Environmental Defense 2008).
186. *Id.* at 3.14 (citing LAX Master Plan Supplement to the Draft EIS/EIR).
187. Data comes from the 2000 U.S. Census and the *Los Angeles Times*, Mapping L.A. database. U.S. CENSUS BUREAU, U.S. CENSUS DATA 2000, AMERICAN FACTFINDER, https://factfinder.census.gov/faces/nav/jsf/pages/index.xhtml (last visited Oct. 19, 2019); *Mapping L.A. Neighborhoods*, L.A. TIMES, http://maps.latimes.com/neighborhoods/ (last visited Oct. 19, 2019).
188. KAYE & MENDOZA, *supra* note 185, at 3.14–3.15.
189. *LAX Modernization Plans Released to Public*, BUSINESS WIRE, Dec. 13, 1996.
190. Notice of Public Scoping Meetings, FAA/LAWA for Preparation of an EIS/EIR for the LAX Master Plan Project (July 12, 1997); Text of Notice of Intent to Appear in the Federal Register on June 11, 1997, FAA, Intent to Prepare an EIR and Hold Scoping Meetings for LAX (June 11, 1997).
191. Jim Newton, *Opponents of Airport Plan Assail Riordan*, L.A. TIMES, Mar. 14, 1998, at B1.
192. Jim Newton, Jodi Wilgoren & Lorenza Munoz, *Battle over LAX Expansion Leaves Behind Turbulence*, L.A. TIMES, May 29, 1998, at A1.
193. Newton, *supra* note 191.
194. Jim Newton, *L.A.'s Chief of Airports Ousted*, L.A. TIMES, May 9, 1998, at B1.
195. Jim Newton, *Ballot Item on Expansion of LAX Urged*, L.A. TIMES, Aug. 1, 1998, at B1.
196. U.S. DEP'T OF TRANSP. & CITY OF LOS ANGELES, DRAFT ENVIRONMENTAL IMPACT STATEMENT/ENVIRONMENTAL IMPACT REPORT (California State Clearinghouse No. 1997061047, Jan. 2001).
197. Douglas Shuit, *Mayoral Hopefuls Keep Their Distance from LAX Expansion*, L.A. TIMES, Mar. 1, 2001, at B1.
198. KAYE & MENDOZA, *supra* note 185, at 3.14.
199. LAX Master Plan Supplement to the Draft Environmental Impact Statement/Environmental Impact Report, Executive Summary, Table ES-1, Summary of Activity, Comparison of Alternatives ES-2 (2001).
200. Jean Merl, *The Mayor Who Rallied LAX Foes*, L.A. TIMES, Feb. 6, 2001, at A1.
201. *Id.*
202. *Id.*
203. Douglas Shuit, *Pilots, Controllers Warn of Dangers at "Outdated" LAX*, L.A. TIMES, Apr. 6, 2001, at B9.
204. Interview by Students from UCLA Sch. of Law Course on Law & Soc. Change (taught by Professor Richard Abel) with Valeria Velasco, President, All. for a Reg'l Sol. to Airport Congestion (Apr. 27, 2005).

205. Matea Gold & Jennifer Oldham, *Hahn Faces Litmus Test on LAX Expansion*, L.A. TIMES, July 16, 2001, at B3.
206. Inglewood Unified School District, Response and Comments on the Draft LAX Master Plan and Draft EIS/EIR 3, 5-6, 13, 19, 34 (Sept. 21, 2001).
207. Lennox School District, Comments on the Draft LAX Master Plan and Draft EIS/EIR Submitted to FAA and LAWA (Sept. 21, 2001).
208. Jennifer Oldham, *$9.6-Billion Make-Over for LAX?*, L.A. TIMES, July 2, 2002, A1.
209. *Id.*
210. Jennifer Oldham, *Air Carriers Attack Hahn's Plan for Renovating LAX*, L.A. TIMES, Aug. 3, 2002, at B3. Hahn enlisted support for Alternative D from law enforcement officials from the Department of Homeland Security, Customs and Border Protection, Transportation Security Administration, Federal Bureau of Investigation, California Highway Patrol, Los Angeles Police Department, L.A. sheriff, and LAX police.
211. Patrick McGreevy & Jennifer Oldham, *Report Finds Pluses in LAX Plan*, L.A. TIMES, July 13, 2003, at B1; Jennifer Oldham & Patrick McGreevy, *No Benefit Found in Plan to Modernize LAX*, L.A. TIMES, July 9, 2003, at B3.
212. David Zahniser, *Hahn Wants Expanded Comment Period for LAX Plan*, COPLEY NEWS SERV., July 28, 2003.
213. David Zahniser, *Supervisors Deny Request from LAX to Delay Vote*, COPLEY NEWS SERV. (Aug. 19, 2003).
214. David Zahniser, *Miscikowski Airs Own Plan for Better Security at LAX*, COPLEY NEWS SERV. (Sept. 2, 2003).
215. Rick Orlov, *Miscikowski Presses Case*, L.A. DAILY NEWS, Sept. 11, 2003, at N5; Rick Orlov, *Slowing Down LAX Fast Track*, L.A. DAILY NEWS, Sept. 17, 2003, at N3.
216. Jennifer Oldham, *LAX Check-In Site Is Mired in Delays*, L.A. TIMES, Sept. 21, 2003, at B1.
217. David Zahniser, *Ethics Commission Seeks Greater Disclosure of Fund Raising by City Commissioners*, COPLEY NEWS SERV., Nov. 4, 2003; *see also* Rick Orlov, *Airport Board Oks Consultant Contract Extension*, PASADENA STAR-NEWS, Dec. 1, 2003. On March 25, 2004, Deputy Mayor Troy Edwards, who was Hahn's liaison to the airport, resigned amid continuing investigations into pay-for-play fundraising (Edwards had raised $5.7 million during the 2001 mayoral campaign). This was followed in early April by the resignation of Airport Commission President Ted Stein. Jennifer Oldham, Noam N. Levey & Jessica Garrison, *Mayor's Man at the Airport Quits amid Contract Probes*, L.A. TIMES, Apr. 7, 2004, at A1.
218. Rick Orlov, *Fund-Raising Probe Reaction Is Mixed*, L.A. DAILY NEWS, Nov. 25, 2003, at N4.
219. Los Angeles World Airports, Final Environmental Impact Report, Los Angeles International Airport Proposed Master Plan Improvements (California State Clearinghouse No. 1997061047, Apr. 2004).
220. *LAX*, CITY NEWS SERV., Apr. 15, 2004.
221. Jia-Rui Chong, *Petition Drive Begun Against Hahn's Modernization Plan*, L.A. TIMES, May 9, 2004, at B3.
222. Erin Park, *Los Angeles*, CITY NEWS SERV., May 24, 2004.
223. Erin Park, *Hahn, Miscikowski Reach Agreement over LAX Revamp*, CITY NEWS SERV., June 11, 2004.
224. Jennifer Oldham, *Panels Vote to Revamp LAX*, L.A. TIMES, June 15, 2004, at B1.
225. Letter from Madeline Janis-Aparicio, LAANE, to City Council member Jackie Goldberg (Sept. 18, 1997).
226. DAVID FAIRRIS, DAVID RUNSTEN, CAROLINA BRIONES & JESSICA GOODHEART, EXAMINING THE EVIDENCE: THE IMPACT OF THE LOS ANGELES LIVING WAGE ORDINANCE ON WORKERS AND BUSINESSES 9 (UCLA Institute for Research on Labor and Employment, 2005).
227. Letter from Margo Feinberg, Schwartz Steinsapir Dohrmann & Sommers, to Frederick C. Merkin, Los Angeles City Att'y, Re: Los Angeles Living Wage (Dec. 3, 1997).
228. LAX Organizing Project Proposal between SEIU, HERE and the AFL-CIO (1998).

229. L.A., CAL., ADMIN. CODE, Ordinance No. 171547, § 10.37.1 (1997).
230. *Id.* § 10.37.1(h).
231. Overall, the SEIU and HERE agreed to commit $738,340 while the AFL-CIO committed $185,062.
232. Agenda for Meeting of LAX Organizing Project (Mar. 9, 1998).
233. Memorandum from Mike Garcia, Eddie Iny (SEIU); Tom Walsh, Jennifer Skurnik (HERE); and Madeline Janis-Aparicio (TIDC) to Miguel Contreras, Re: Service Worker Organizing Campaign at LAX (Mar. 16, 1998).
234. *Id.*
235. Agenda for LAX Meeting (Mar. 18, 1998).
236. Draft Op-Ed by Miguel Contreras to *La Opinión* (1998).
237. Letter from Madeline Janis-Aparicio to Harold Meyerson, Editor, *L.A. Wkly.* (Apr. 3, 1998).
238. *See* Memorandum from Jon Barton, SEIU 1877, to List, Re: LAX Campaign Infrastructure Needs (Apr. 7, 1998) (listing campaign infrastructure needs including office space, equipment, furniture, personnel forms, a bank account, and a budget tracking system); Proposed Agenda for LAX Strategy Retreat (Apr. 22, 1998) (discussing strategy and campaign structure).
239. Proposed Agenda for LAX Strategy Retreat (Apr. 24–25, 1998).
240. Memorandum from Lety S. to Marianne H et al., Re: May 1, Meeting Agenda (Apr. 30, 1998).
241. Letter from Margo Feinberg to Jon Barton, Maria Elena Durazo, Tom Walsh, Madeline Janis-Aparicio, Re: Los Angeles Airport Organizing Project (Apr. 27, 1998).
242. *Id.*
243. Memorandum from Lety Salcedo & Madeline Janis-Aparicio to Andy Levin & Larry Englestein, Re: Legal Retainer for the Political/Legislative Components of the LAX Project (May 8, 1998).
244. Letter from C. Bernard Gilpin, Dir., Bureau of Cont. Admin., to John J. Driscoll, Exec. Dir., LAWA (May 6, 1998). Similar letters were sent regarding American Airlines, Continental, SkyWest, Federal Express, Korean Airlines, Lufthansa, Singapore Air, Southwest, TWA, United, Virgin Atlantic, and others.
245. Letter from Madeline Janis-Aparicio to John Van De Kamp, Dir., United Airlines Corporation (May 20, 1998).
246. Agenda for Meeting with Jackie Goldberg, Re: LAX (1998).
247. Memorandum from Eddie Iny to Lety Salcedo, Re: Pending Lease Expirations That Trigger the LWO (June 5, 1998).
248. Respect at LAX, LAX Political/Legislative Strategy (1998).
249. *Id.*
250. Letter from Schwartz Steinsapir Dohrmann & Sommers to Frederick C. Merkin, Senior Assistant City Att'y, Re: Application of Living Wage Ordinances to Airline Leases (July 24, 1998).
251. First Draft Letter from Madeline Janis-Aparicio to Current Allies (July 30, 1998).
252. Letter from Madeline Janis-Aparicio to the Honorable Jackie Goldberg (July 31, 1998).
253. Respect at LAX, Strategy Discussion (1998).
254. Memorandum from Eddie Iny to Miguel Contreras, Re: Working Conditions and Safety and Security at LAX (Aug. 24, 1998).
255. Memorandum from Commissioner Miguel Contreras to Jack Driscoll, Exec. Dir., Los Angeles World Airports (Sept. 9, 1998).
256. Memorandum from Jon Barton to List (Oct. 22, 1998).
257. Letter from R. Thomas Buffenbarger, Int'l President, Int' Ass'n of Machinists & Aerospace Workers, to Herbert Kelleher, Chairman, President and CEO, Southwest Airlines (Oct. 20, 1998).
258. Press Release, Off. of the Mayor Richard Riordan, Mayor Hails United Airlines' Support of Living Wage Ordinance (Jan. 11, 1999).

259. Letter from Dale J. Goldsmith, Greenberg Glusker Fields Claman & Machtinger LLP, to the Honorable Com., Energy and Nat. Res. Comm. (May 24, 1999).
260. Memorandum from Mary Anne Hohenstein, Local 1877, to Jackie Goldberg, Re: LAX Update (Feb. 3, 1999).
261. Letter from Henry F. Anthony, Vice President-Hum. Res., Argenbright, to Mike Garcia, President, SEIU Local 1877 (Apr. 15, 1999).
262. Letter from Charlie Costello, LEC President, Ass'n of Flight Attendants, AFL-CIO, to Jim Goodwin, CEO United Airlines (May 18, 1999).
263. Letter from Mike Garcia, President, SEIU Local 1877, to Peter McDonald, Managing Dir., United Airlines (June 17, 1999).
264. Memorandum from United Fin. Team, Re: Financing for United's Proposed Cargo Facility at LAX (May 19,1999).
265. Letter from Raymond S. Ilgunas, Assistant City Att'y, to Bd. of Airport Comm'rs (July 29, 1999).
266. Letter from Michael E. Wall to the Honorable City Councilors, Re: Inadequate Environmental Review (Oct. 21, 1999).
267. Potential Components of a Settlement with LAWA, the City and UAL (1999).
268. LAX Project Memorandum (Mar. 12, 2000).
269. Id.
270. Collective Bargaining Agreement between Argenbright and SEIU Local 1877 (effective Mar. 1, 2001 through July 1, 2003).
271. Draft Outline of the Los Angeles Economic Impact Task Force (Oct. 6, 2001).
272. Letter from Tom Walsh, HERE, to Paul L. Green, Chief Operating Officer, Los Angeles World Airports (Dec. 13, 2001).
273. Fax from Maria Elena Durazo to Eddie Iny (Mar. 14, 2002).
274. Interview by Students from UCLA Sch. of Law Course on Law & Soc. Change (taught by Professor Richard Abel) with Nancy Cohen, Senior Pol'y Analyst, Los Angeles All. for a New Econ. (Apr. 4, 2005).
275. KAYE & MENDOZA, *supra* note 185, at 3.15.
276. *Id.*
277. *Id.* at 3.16 (citing South Camden Citizens in Action v. N.J. Dep't of Environ. Protection, 254 F. Supp. 2d 486 (D.N.J. 2003)).
278. Alexander v. Sandoval, 532 U.S. 275 (2001).
279. KAYE & MENDOZA, *supra* note 185, at 3.16.
280. *Id.*
281. Telephone Interview by Students from UCLA Sch. of Law Course on Law & Soc. Change (taught by Professor Richard Abel) with Jerilyn López Mendoza, Pol'y Dir., Envtl. Def. (Apr. 4, 5 & 28, 2005).
282. KAYE & MENDOZA, *supra* note 185, at 3.16.
283. *Id.* at 3.17.
284. *Id.*
285. Interview by Students from UCLA Sch. of Law Course on Law & Soc. Change (taught by Professor Richard Abel) with Jennifer Oldham, Reporter, *L.A. Times* (Apr. 2005).
286. *Id.*
287. Interview by Students from UCLA Sch. of Law Course on Law & Soc. Change (taught by Professor Richard Abel) with William Smart, Dir. of Training & Outreach, Los Angeles All. for a New Econ. (Mar. 7 & 25, 2005).
288. Presentation by Los Angeles Alliance for a New Economy on LAX Modernization, Prepared for SEIU 347 (2003).
289. *Id.*
290. *Id.*
291. KAYE & MENDOZA, *supra* note 185, at 3.17.

292. *Id.*
293. *Id.*
294. *Id.* at 3.19.
295. *Id.* at 3.17-3.18.
296. *Id.* at 3.17.
297. *Id.*
298. *Id.* at 3.18.
299. *Id.*
300. Interview with William Smart, *supra* note 287.
301. Interview by Students from UCLA Sch. of Law Course on Law & Soc. Change (taught by Professor Richard Abel) with Edgar Saenz, Bd. Member, All. for a Reg'l Sol. to Airport Congestion (Apr. 27, 2005).
302. Telephone Interview with Jerilyn López Mendoza, *supra* note 281.
303. KAYE & MENDOZA, *supra* note 185, at 3.19.
304. *Id.*
305. Meeting Agenda for LAX Coalition (Jan. 8, 2004).
306. In early 2004, Smart also focused on outreach at Black History Month events, mobilizing community partners to meet at the Los Angeles County Fed Security Coalition Meeting and Black Press Conference, and planned a "major action" in downtown on February 23. To Do for Rev. William Smart, Black History Month Events (2004).
307. KAYE & MENDOZA, *supra* note 185, at 3.19.
308. Interview with William Smart, *supra* note 287.
309. KAYE & MENDOZA, *supra* note 185, at 3.19.
310. Telephone Interview with Jerilyn López Mendoza, *supra* note 281.
311. *Id.*
312. Interview by Students from UCLA Sch. of Law Course on Law & Soc. Change (taught by Professor Richard Abel) with Jim Ritchie, Deputy Exec. Dir., Los Angeles World Airports (Apr. 25, 2005).
313. KAYE & MENDOZA, *supra* note 185, at 3.22.
314. *Id.*
315. Culling stated: "What kept [LAWA] in the room was the thought of the Coalition not supporting the plan." Interview by Students from UCLA Sch. of Law Course on Law & Soc. Change (taught by Professor Richard Abel) with Claudia Culling, Los Angeles City Att'y (Apr. 7, 2005).
316. *Id.*
317. *Id.*
318. Interview with Jim Ritchie, *supra* note 312.
319. KAYE & MENDOZA, *supra* note 185, at 3.20.
320. Interview with William Smart, *supra* note 287.
321. KAYE & MENDOZA, *supra* note 185, at 3.20.
322. *Id.*
323. *Id.*
324. *Id.* at 3.19.
325. *Id.* at 3.20 (quoting López Mendoza).
326. Interview by Students from UCLA Sch. of Law Course on Law & Soc. Change (taught by Professor Richard Abel) with Shirlene Sue, Senior Mgmt. Analyst, Los Angeles World Airports (Apr. 18, 25 & May 5, 2005).
327. Interview with William Smart, *supra* note 287.
328. KAYE & MENDOZA, *supra* note 185, at 3.21.
329. Interview with William Smart, *supra* note 287.
330. Interview by Students from UCLA Sch. of Law Course on Law & Soc. Change (taught by Professor Richard Abel) with Bob Gilbert, Chief Operating Officer, Los Angeles World Airports (Apr. 25, 2005).

331. Interview with Nancy Cohen, *supra* note 274.
332. Interview with William Smart, *supra* note 287.
333. *Id.*
334. KAYE & MENDOZA, *supra* note 185, at 3.21–3.22.
335. *Id.* at 3.21 (quoting López Mendoza).
336. Interview with William Smart, *supra* note 287.
337. Interview with Jim Ritchie, *supra* note 312.
338. Draft LAX Plan 4, 10–12 (Mar. 25, 2004).
339. Interview with Bob Gilbert, *supra* note 330.
340. *Id.*
341. Interview with Jim Ritchie, *supra* note 312.
342. Interview with Nancy Cohen, *supra* note 274.
343. *Id.*
344. Telephone Interview by Students from UCLA Sch. of Law Course on Law & Soc. Change (taught by Professor Richard Abel) with Maria Verduzco-Smith, Dir., Lennox Coordinating Council (Mar. 25, 2005).
345. Interview with Claudia Culling, *supra* note 315.
346. KAYE & MENDOZA, *supra* note 185, at 3.21.
347. Interview with Claudia Culling, *supra* note 315.
348. Interview with Jim Ritchie, *supra* note 312.
349. Interview by Students from UCLA Sch. of Law Course on Law & Soc. Change (taught by Professor Richard Abel) with Bruce McDaniel, Superintendent, Lennox Sch. Dist. (Apr. 25, 2005).
350. Interview with Nancy Cohen, *supra* note 274.
351. Interview with Claudia Culling, *supra* note 315.
352. *Id.*
353. Telephone Interview by Students from UCLA Sch. of Law Course on Law & Soc. Change (taught by Professor Richard Abel) with Julian Gross, Law Off. of Julian Gross (Mar. 18, 2005).
354. Jia-Rui Chong, *Petition Drive Begun Against Hahn's LAX Modernization Plan*, L.A. TIMES, May 9, 2004, at B3.
355. *Id.*
356. *Id.*
357. Erin Park, *Council Vote Puts LAX Modernization Plan on Takeoff Rollout*, CITY NEWS SERV., Oct. 20, 2004.
358. LAX Coalition Summary Proposal (May 10, 2004).
359. *Id.*
360. Media Plan for LAX Community Benefits Agreement Campaign (2004).
361. LAX Coalition Queries for 5-20-04 Negotiation (May 7, 2004).
362. LAX Coalition Response to LAWA Counter-Proposal, Construction-Related Diesel Emissions Reduction Requirements (93-102) (May 2004).
363. Meeting of the Steering Committee of the LAX Coalition (May 19, 2004).
364. Agenda for LAX CBA Negotiation Session No. 11 (May 20, 2004, 9:00 AM – 12:00 PM).
365. Confidential Memorandum from LAX Coal. Negot. Team to LAWA Staff, Re: Air Toxics Study (May 20, 2004).
366. Ian Gregor, *LAX Plan Clears Hurdle*, DAILY BREEZE, June 15, 2004, at A1.
367. Ian Gregor, *LAX Agency Negotiating Pact to Help Neighbors*, DAILY BREEZE, June 17, 2004, at A1.
368. Jennifer Oldham, *Coalition Seeks Deal on LAX Fallout*, L.A. TIMES, June 17, 2004, at B1.
369. *Id.*
370. Confidential/Privileged Draft of Community Benefits Agreement, LAX Master Plan (Aug. 3, 2004).
371. Interview with Nancy Cohen, *supra* note 274.

372. Kerry Ezard, *LAX Modernization Plan Garners ATA Endorsement*, AIR TRANSP. INTELLIGENCE (Sept. 27, 2004).
373. *Business, Labor Forms Alliance over Plan to Modernize Los Angeles Airport*, L.A. DAILY NEWS, Oct. 20, 2004.
374. Jennifer Oldham & Jessica Garrison, *Council Backs LAX Project*, L.A. TIMES, Oct. 21, 2004, at A1; *see also* Park, *supra* note 357.
375. Erin Park, *Los Angeles*, CITY NEWS SERV., Nov. 30, 2004; David Zahniser, *County Supervisors Poised to File Suit against LAX Plan*, COPLEY NEWS SERV., Nov. 30, 2004.
376. Draft of Cooperation Agreement, Los Angeles International Airport Master Plan Program (Nov. 24, 2004).
377. Press Release, LAX Coal., Highlights of the LAX Community Benefits Agreement (Nov. 24, 2004). The press release highlighted the following elements of the LAX deal: $1.7 million annually for residential soundproofing, $15 million in job training for airport and aviation-related jobs, and $200 million for soundproofing and air filtration in Lennox and Inglewood schools. In addition, the press release stressed that the CBA provided for gate electrification; conversion to low-emission construction equipment, tarmac equipment, and airport vehicles; studies of airport emissions and community health impacts; and LAWA's commitment to ask the FAA to restrict nighttime eastward departures.
378. LAWA Resolution No. 22554 (Dec. 6, 2004); *see also* Ian Gregor, *Board Oks Deal with LAX Neighbors*, DAILY BREEZE, Dec. 7, 2004, at A1.
379. Jennifer Oldham, *L.A. to Fund Upgrades Near LAX*, L.A. TIMES, Dec. 4, 2004, at B1; *see also* Rick Orlov, *Council OKs LAX Master Plan*, L.A. DAILY NEWS, Dec. 8, 2004, at N3.
380. Ian Gregor, *Millions for LAX Impacts?*, DAILY BREEZE, Dec. 4, 2004, at A1; *see also* Oldham, *supra* note 379. Because the Lennox and Inglewood school districts were negotiating to amend a prior 1980 settlement, they had to gain separate approval from LAWA and the FAA before the school components of the CBA could take effect. Accordingly, the school districts entered their own settlement agreement with LAWA in December. The Inglewood settlement provided for a ceiling of $118.5 million in mitigation funding, which included $45 million for the relocation of Oak Street Elementary, as well as money for noise and pollution abatement, double-paned windows, roofing upgrades, and temporary locations during school construction. Settlement Agreement, Los Angeles International Airport Master Plan, between LAWA and Inglewood around Inglewood Challenge to Draft EIS/EIR and Supplement to Draft EIS/EIR (2004).
381. Oldham, *supra* note 379.
382. *Id.*
383. Rick Orlov & Troy Anderson, *Council OKs LAX Master Plan*, L.A. DAILY NEWS, Dec. 8, 2004, at N3.
384. Sheila Muto, *Residents Have Their Say on LAX Expansion Plans*, WALL ST. J., Dec. 15, 2004; *see also* David Zahniser, *Council Approves LAX Agreement*, COPLEY NEWS SERV., Dec. 14, 2004. In addition to the CBA, the City Council had to approve three plans: the LAX Master Plan; general guidelines for development; and the LAX Specific Plan, which included changes to zoning and procedures for future environmental approval.
385. The signatories were: AGENDA, AME Minister's Alliance, CLUE, Coalition for Clean Air, Communities for a Better Environment, Community Coalition, Community Coalition for Change, Environmental Defense, Inglewood Coalition for Drug and Violence Prevention, Inglewood Democratic Club, Lennox Coordinating Council, LAANE, Los Angeles Council of Churches, Nation of Islam, NRDC, Physicians for Social Responsibility in Los Angeles, SEIU Local 347, and Teamsters Local 911. Cooperation Agreement, Los Angeles International Airport Master Plan Program 17-35 (2005).
386. Cooperation Agreement, Los Angeles International Airport Master Plan Program, Section III.C. (2005); *see also* KAYE & MENDOZA, *supra* note 185, at 3.22; Ian Gregor, *LAX-Area Residents to Benefit from Plan*, DAILY BREEZE, Dec. 14, 2004, at A1.
387. KAYE & MENDOZA, *supra* note 185, at 3.22.

388. Oldham, *supra* note 379.
389. Telephone Interview with Jerilyn López Mendoza, *supra* note 281.
390. *See* KAYE & MENDOZA, *supra* note 185, at 3.23–3.24.
391. Telephone Interview with Maria Verduzco-Smith, *supra* note 344.
392. David Zahniser, *Officials Set to File LAX Suit*, DAILY BREEZE, Dec. 1, 2004, at A1.
393. *LAX Agreement*, CITY NEWS SERV., Dec. 22, 2004.
394. Orlov, *supra* note 379; *see also* Erin Park, *LAX Plans Set for Final Vote, County Agrees to Sue*, CITY NEWS SERV., Dec. 7, 2004; KAYE & MENDOZA, *supra* note 185, at 3.26.
395. Telephone Interview with López Mendoza, *supra* note 281.
396. *Id.*
397. Petition for Writ of Mandate, City of El Segundo v. City of Los Angeles, No. BS094279 (Super. Ct. L.A. Cty. filed Jan. 3, 2005) (consol. into City of El Segundo v. City of Los Angeles, No. RIC 426822 (Super. Ct. Riverside Cty. Feb. 24, 2005)).
398. Petition for Writ of Mandate, Cty. of Los Angeles v. City of Los Angeles, No. BS094320 (Super. Ct. L.A. Cty. filed Jan. 6, 2005) (consol. with City of El Segundo v. City of Los Angeles, No. RIC 426822 (Super. Ct. Riverside Cty. Feb. 24, 2005)).
399. Petition for Writ of Mandate, All. for Reg'l Sol. to Airport Congestion v. City of Los Angeles, No. BS094359 (Super. Ct. L.A. Cty. filed Jan. 6, 2005) (consol. with City of El Segundo v. City of Los Angeles, No. RIC 426822 (Super. Ct. Riverside Cty. Feb. 24, 2005)).
400. Fed'n of Hillside and Canyon Ass'ns v. City of Los Angeles, No. BS094503 (Super. Ct. L.A. Cty. filed Jan. 7, 2005) (consol. with City of El Segundo v. City of Los Angeles, No. RIC 426822 (Super. Ct. Riverside Cty. Feb. 24, 2005)).
401. U.S. Dep't of Transp., Fed. Aviation Admin., Final Environmental Impact Statement, Los Angeles International Airport Proposed Master Plan Improvements (Jan. 2005).
402. *Noise Mitigation*, CITY NEWS SERV., Feb. 22, 2005.
403. U.S. Dep't of Transp., Fed. Aviation Admin., Record of Decision, Proposed LAX Master Plan Improvements (May 20, 2005).
404. Jennifer Oldham & Jessica Garrison, *FAA Approves LAX Modernization Plan*, L.A. TIMES, May 21, 2005, at B1.
405. Jennifer Oldham & Richard Fausset, *Mayor Picks Airport Commissioners*, L.A. TIMES, July 26, 2005, at B4. Villaraigosa's Airport Commission picks also included the dean of the UCLA School of Public Affairs, vice-president of the California Labor Federation, and a regional planner from the Southern California Association of Governments.
406. Jennifer Oldham, *LAX Expansion Will Raise Cancer Risk, Study Finds*, L.A. TIMES, Aug. 1, 2005, at B1. Community groups representing Los Angeles County, Inglewood, Culver City, El Segundo, and others filed comments criticizing the EIR. Jennifer Oldham, *LAX Runway Plan Lands with a Thud*, L.A. TIMES, Sept. 17, 2005, at B3.
407. David Zahniser, *Airport Commissioner's Conflicts Still Under Question*, COPLEY NEWS SERV., Sept. 13, 2005.
408. Beth Barrett, *Kennard Returns to Head LAWA*, L.A. DAILY NEWS, Oct. 5, 2005, at N4.
409. Jennifer Oldham, *Airport Agency Chief Has Steered LAX out of Turbulence*, L.A. TIMES, Nov. 13, 2006, at B1.
410. Judgment Pursuant to Stipulated Settlement, City of El Segundo v. City of Los Angeles, No. RIC426822 (Super. Ct. Riverside Cty. filed Feb. 17, 2006).
411. KAYE & MENDOZA, *supra* note 185, at 3.26.
412. *Id.* at 3.25.
413. Community Benefits Agreement, LAX Master Plan Program, Section XVI.A-B (2005).
414. Cooperation Agreement, LAX Master Plan Program, Section V.A.5 (2005).
415. LAX CBA Implementation Work Plan (2005). In addition to coalition oversight, LAWA—pursuant to the community-based research provisions of the CBA—initiated a stakeholder liaison program to ensure that community members had time to review and provide input on Master Plan projects and Specific Plan amendments.

416. LAX Coalition's Position on Reallocation of LAX Community Benefits Agreement Job-Training Dollars (Aug. 12, 2005).
417. KAYE & MENDOZA, *supra* note 185, at 3.25.
418. Letter from Jim Ritchie, Deputy Exec. Dir., LAWA, to William Smart, LAX Coal., Re: Cooperation Agreement—LAX Master Plan Program Annual Status Report (Mar. 1, 2006).
419. Letter from Jim Ritchie, Deputy Exec. Dir., LAWA, to Mark A. McClardy, Manager, Airports Div., FAA, Re: Request for FAA Advisory Opinion (Mar. 6, 2006).
420. Letter from Jim Ritchie, Deputy Exec. Dir., LAWA, to Mark A. McClardy, Manager, Airports Div., FAA, Re: Request for FAA Advisory Opinion (Mar. 23, 2006).
421. Letter from Mark A. McClardy, Manager, Airports Div., FAA, to Jim Ritchie, Deputy Exec. Dir., LAWA (May 16, 2006).
422. Letter from Patricia V. Tubert, Deputy Exec. Dir., LAWA, to Catherine Lang, Deputy Assoc. Admin. for Airports, FAA (Aug. 25, 2006).
423. Letter from Jim Ritchie, Deputy Exec. Dir., LAWA, to Mark A. McClardy, Manager, Airports Div., FAA (Sept. 6, 2006).
424. Letter from Mark A. McClardy, Manager, Airports Div., FAA, to Jim Ritchie, Deputy Exec. Dir., LAWA (Oct. 6, 2006).
425. Dan Laidman, *FAA Changes Course on Airport-Related Jobs*, COPLEY NEWS SERV. (Dec. 13, 2006).
426. Jennifer Oldham, *If You Think LAX Is Busy Now, Just Wait a Month*, L.A. TIMES, July 2, 2006, at A1 (noting that moving the runways farther apart was necessary to make room for the impending arrival of the Airbus A380).
427. David Zahniser, *Shooting Down Trains*, L.A. WKLY., July 5, 2006.
428. Jean Merl, *Residents Weigh In on LAX Modernization Plan*, L.A. TIMES, Aug. 27, 2006, at B6.
429. *LAX Requires Hotels to Consolidate Courtesy Shuttle Trips to Improve Air Quality, Reduce Congestion*, MKT. WIRE, Dec. 4, 2006.
430. Tami Abdollah, *Study to Gauge LAX's Role in Pollution*, L.A. TIMES, Feb. 26, 2008, at B3.
431. LOS ANGELES WORLD AIRPORTS, LAX MASTER PLAN, COMMUNITY BENEFITS AGREEMENT (CBA), 2008 ANNUAL PROGRESS REPORT (Jan. 2009).
432. LOS ANGELES WORLD AIRPORTS, LAX MASTER PLAN, COMMUNITY BENEFITS AGREEMENT (CBA), 2016 ANNUAL REPORT, 9-10 (2017).
433. *Id.*
434. *Id.* at 13.
435. Cara Mia DiMassa, *Grand Avenue Project; Gehry Sees His Glass Towers Transforming Downtown L.A*, L.A. TIMES, Apr. 24, 2006, at A1; *see also* Amy Lavine, *Grand Avenue Community Benefits Package*, COMMUNITY BENEFITS AGREEMENTS (May 19, 2008), http://communitybenefits.blogspot.com/2008/05/grand-avenue-community-benefits-package.html (last visited Oct. 19, 2019).
436. For a history of redevelopment, see WILLIAM H. SIMON, THE COMMUNITY ECONOMIC DEVELOPMENT MOVEMENT: LAW, BUSINESS AND THE NEW SOCIAL POLICY 8 (2001); *see also* BERNARD J. FRIEDEN & LYNNE B. SAGALYN, DOWNTOWN DEVELOPMENT, INC.: HOW AMERICA REBUILDS CITIES (1989).
437. *See* MIKE DAVIS, CITY OF QUARTZ: EXCAVATING THE FUTURE IN LOS ANGELES 226 (1990).
438. Nicolai Ouroussoff, *A Core Dilemma*, L.A. TIMES, Aug. 2002, at F4.
439. *Id.*
440. Joel Kotkin, Opinion, *L.A.'s Core Already Has a 'There' There*, L.A. TIMES, Oct. 26, 2003, at M1.
441. Louise Roug, *$1.2-Billion Downtown L.A. Project Draws Top Architects*, L.A. TIMES, Dec. 24, 2003, at B1.
442. *Id.*
443. Louise Roug, *Finalists Face Off in Grand Ave. Project Bid*, L.A. TIMES, June 29, 2004, at B1.

444. Noam N. Levey & Louise Roug, *New York Developer Chosen to Make Grand Ave. Grander*, L.A. TIMES, Aug. 10, 2004, at A1.
445. Cara Mia DiMassa & Nicholas Shields, *Will This Time Be Different?*, L.A. TIMES, May 26, 2005, at B1.
446. Cara Mia DiMassa, *Grand Plan Approved to Give LA a Heart*, L.A. TIMES, May 24, 2005, at A1.
447. *Id.*
448. *Id.*
449. *Id.*
450. Cara Mia DiMassa, *Aid but No Subsidy for Grand Ave.*, L.A. TIMES, Aug. 9, 2005, at B1.
451. *Id.*
452. *Id.*
453. Rents were to be divided between the government agencies based on proportionate ownership and renegotiated after twenty years based on market conditions. *Id.*
454. Cara Mia DiMassa, *Grand Ave. Questions Raised*, L.A. TIMES, Aug. 19, 2005, at B1.
455. *Id.*
456. Cara Mia DiMassa, *2 Projects, 2 Visions of Downtown's Future*, L.A. TIMES, Sept. 15, 2005, at B1.
457. DiMassa, *supra* note 450.
458. CMTY. REDEVELOPMENT AGENCY OF LOS ANGELES, CRA HOUSING POLICY (Aug. 4, 2005).
459. Madeline Janis changed her name from Janis-Aparicio in 2002.
460. Cty. of L.A. v. Bd. of Dirs. of Cmty. Redevelopment Agency, No. BC276472 (Super. Ct. L.A. Cty. filed June 25, 2002).
461. Wiggins v. Cmty. Redevelopment Agency, No. BC277539 (Super. Ct. L.A. Cty. filed July 12, 2002).
462. *Id.* at 2.
463. Cty. of Los Angeles v. Cmty. Redevelopment Agency, Nos. B169633, B172113, B171510, B173554, 2005 WL 8957009 (Cal. Ct. App. 2d Dist. Apr. 19, 2005).
464. The county case continued, ultimately resulting in another appellate court victory for the county plaintiffs reaffirming the invalidity of the City Center plan carve out. Cty. of Los Angeles v. Cmty. Redevelopment Agency, Nos. B191095, B194315, 2007 WL 2729839 (Cal. Ct. App. 2d Dist. Sept. 20, 2007).
465. CRA/LA, A DESIGNATED LOCAL AUTHORITY, REPORT TO GOVERNING BOARD ON ANNUAL REPORT ON IMPLEMENTATION OF THE WIGGINS SETTLEMENT AGREEMENT (Mar. 2, 2017).
466. *Id.* As of December 2016, permanent employers at the Alexandria Apartments, Van Nuys project, and Hope St. Family Recreation Center had hired 40 local residents out of 148 total employees for a 33% local employment rate.
467. *See* FIGUEROA CORRIDOR COALITION FOR ECONOMIC JUSTICE & LA COALITION TO END HUNGER & HOMELESSNESS, SHARE THE WEALTH: A POLICY STRATEGY FOR FAIR REDEVELOPMENT IN L.A.'S CITY CENTER (2002).
468. Ben Beach, *Strategies and Lessons from the Los Angeles Community Benefits Experience*, 17 J. AFFORDABLE HOUSING & CMTY. DEV. L. 78, 92 (2008).
469. DiMassa, *supra* note 435.
470. *Id.*
471. Christopher Hawthorne, *Grand, Yes, but Public Expects More*, L.A. TIMES, Apr. 24, 2006, at A1.
472. DiMassa, *supra* note 435; *see also* Hawthorne, *supra* note 471.
473. Cara Mia DiMassa & Roger Vincent, *Retailers Not Sold on Grand Avenue*, L.A. TIMES, Apr. 25, 2006, at A1.
474. Editorial, *Grand Avenue Is the Wrong Path*, L.A. TIMES, Feb. 7, 2007, at A20.
475. Lavine, *supra* note 435.
476. *Id.*
477. Telephone Interview with Becky Dennison, Exec. Dir., Venice Cmty. Hous. (Sept. 25, 2018).
478. *Id.*
479. *Id.*

480. *Id.*
481. *Id.*
482. *Id.*
483. *Id.*
484. *Id.*
485. Telephone Interview with Madeline Janis, Exec. Dir., Jobs to Move Am. (June 17, 2019).
486. Telephone Interview with Becky Dennison, *supra* note 477.
487. *Id.*
488. Telephone Interview with Ben Beach, Legal Dir., Cmty. Benefits L. Ctr. (Sept. 5, 2018).
489. Telephone Interview with Becky Dennison, *supra* note 477.
490. Telephone Interview with Ben Beach, *supra* note 488.
491. Beach, *supra* note 468, at 92–93.
492. *Id.*
493. *Id.* at 93; *see also* Cara Mia DiMassa, *Mega-Projects Could Reshape L.A. Growth*, L.A. TIMES, Dec. 13, 2006, at A1. Critics worried that the sheer size of the Grand Avenue Project would overwhelm any small improvements made by increasing the number of people who used mass transit. The EIR found that development could significantly worsen downtown traffic—even though it would be built along the Metro Red Line.
494. Telephone Interview with Becky Dennison, *supra* note 477.
495. *Id.*
496. *Id.*
497. *Id.*
498. *Id.*
499. Telephone Interview with Madeline Janis, *supra* note 485.
500. Roger Vincent, *Developer Works by Building Consensus*, L.A. TIMES, May 14, 2006, at C1.
501. Cara Mia DiMassa, *"Hello, Columbus": L.A. Street Looks to a New York Circle*, L.A. TIMES, June 19, 2006, at A1.
502. Scott Timberg, *Rising Construction Costs Boost Price Tag for Grand Avenue Project*, L.A. TIMES, Sept. 21, 2006, at B4.
503. Cara Mia DiMassa, *$2-Billion Downtown Overhaul in the Red*, L.A. TIMES, Nov. 17, 2006, at A1.
504. FINAL ENVIRONMENTAL IMPACT REPORT, THE GRAND AVENUE PROJECT (California State Clearinghouse No. 2005091041, Nov. 2006).
505. Cara Mia DiMassa, *Grand Avenue Development Clears First Hurdle*, L.A. TIMES, Nov. 21, 2006, at B1.
506. *Id.*
507. Telephone Interview with Becky Dennison, *supra* note 477.
508. Grand Avenue Project, Summary of Community Benefits, Attachment H to the CRA/LA Development Agreement (2006).
509. Telephone Interview with Becky Dennison, *supra* note 477.
510. *Id.*
511. Grand Avenue Project, Summary of Community Benefits, *supra* note 508.
512. Term Sheet of Negotiations by and among the Grand Avenue Community Benefits Coalition, the Related Companies, and CRA/LA (2006).
513. Grand Avenue Project, Summary of Community Benefits, *supra* note 508.
514. Telephone Interview with Ben Beach, *supra* note 488.
515. Telephone Interview with Becky Dennison, *supra* note 477.
516. *Id.*
517. Grand Avenue Project, Summary of Community Benefits, *supra* note 508.
518. *Id.*
519. *Id.*
520. Term Sheet, *supra* note 512.

521. Troy Anderson, *CRA Backs Grand Avenue Project*, L.A. DAILY NEWS, Feb. 2, 2007, at N4; Jeffrey L. Rabin & Cara Mia DiMassa, *Redevelopment Agency to Vote on the Grand Avenue Project*, L.A. TIMES, Feb. 1, 2007, at B1.
522. Cara Mia DiMassa, *Grand Avenue Project Needs Help, Report Says*, L.A. TIMES, Feb. 3, 2007, at B1.
523. Steve Lopez, *66 Million Reasons to Re-Examine Grand Ave*, L.A. TIMES, Feb. 7, 2007, at B1.
524. Rick Wartzman, *A Grand Vision for Affordable Housing*, L.A. TIMES, Feb. 9, 2007, at C1.
525. Editorial, *Grand, and Good*, L.A TIMES, Feb. 12, 2007, at A18.
526. Cara Mia DiMassa & Jack Leonard, *Grand Avenue Project Passes Go*, L.A. TIMES, Feb. 13, 2007, at A1.
527. Michael Antonovich, *Not a Grand Deal for Taxpayers*, L.A. TIMES, Feb. 13, 2007, at A21.
528. Term Sheet, *supra* note 512; *see also* THE PUBLIC LAW CENTER, SUMMARY AND INDEX OF COMMUNITY BENEFIT AGREEMENTS (2011), https://law-ektron.tulane.edu/uploadedFiles/Institutes_and_Centers/Public_Law_Center/Summary%20and%20Index%20of%20%20Community%20Benefit%20Agreements.pdf (last visited Oct. 21, 2019).
529. Term Sheet, *supra* note 512.
530. Telephone Interview with Becky Dennison, *supra* note 477.
531. *Id.*
532. Anderson, *supra* note 521.
533. David Zahniser, *Grand Ave. Project Backed*, L.A. TIMES, Sept. 12, 2007, at B4.
534. *Council Rejects Bid to Block Grand Ave. Project*, L.A. TIMES, Sept. 20, 2007, at B4.
535. Cara Mia DiMassa, *Funding Gets Grand Plan Going*, L.A. TIMES, Mar. 18, 2008, at B1.
536. Cara Mia DiMassa, *Grand Avenue Snags on Loans*, L.A. TIMES, Apr. 29, 2008, at A1.
537. Cara Mia DiMassa, *Grand Ave. Faces a New Snag*, L.A. TIMES, June 8, 2008, at B3.
538. Cara Mia DiMassa, *Board Denies Grand Avenue Delay*, L.A. TIMES, June 10, 2008, at B1.
539. Rich Alossi, *Turn Signals on Grand*, L.A. TIMES, June 29, 2008, at M7.
540. Cara Mia DiMassa, *Grand Avenue Delay Is OKd*, L.A. TIMES, July 29, 2008, at B1.
541. Cara Mia DiMassa & Molly Hennessy-Fiske, *Grand Ave. Developer Seeks Waiver*, L.A. TIMES, Feb. 13, 2009, at B1.
542. Kate Linthicum, *Downtown Project Facing More Delays*, L.A. TIMES, Aug. 27, 2010, at AA1.
543. David Zahniser, *L.A. Hotel Tax Breaks Questioned*, L.A. TIMES, May 4, 2011, at AA.1; *see also* Sam Allen, *A Simpler Grand Plan*, L.A. TIMES, June 3, 2012, at A1.
544. Cara Mia DiMassa, *Board OKs Civic Park Pacts*, L.A. TIMES, Feb. 17, 2010, at AA5; Kate Linthicum, *Ground Is Broken on Civic Park in Downtown*, L.A. TIMES, July 16, 2010, at AA3.
545. Allen, *supra* note 543. As of 2015, the park was the only completed part of the Grand Avenue Project. Rosado, *supra* note 173.
546. David Zahniser & Jessica Garrison, *L.A. Assesses Costs of Shuttering Redevelopment Agency*, L.A. TIMES, Jan. 11, 2012.
547. Madeline Janis, *Rethinking Redevelopment*, L.A. TIMES, Feb. 8, 2012, at A13.
548. Zahniser & Garrison, *supra* note 546.
549. The final phase of the Grand Avenue Project was set to be completed by 2021. Bianca Barragan, *Here's the Latest Look for the Frank Gehry-Designed Grand Avenue Project*, CURBED LOS ANGELES, Jan. 22, 2018, https://la.curbed.com/2018/1/22/16919512/frank-gehry-los-angeles-grand-avenue-project (last visited Oct. 21, 2019).
550. Lorenzo Project Cooperation Agreement (Feb. 9, 2011). For a description of the agreement, *see* Patrick J. McDonnell, *City Planners Approve South L.A. Project*, L.A. TIMES, Feb. 11, 2011, at AA3; *see also* Alejandro E. Camacho, *Community Benefits Agreements: A Symptom, Not the Antidote, of Bilateral Land Use Regulation*, 78 BROOK. L. REV. 355, 356 (2013).
551. Complaint for Declaratory and Injunctive Relief, Play Fair at Farmers Field v. State of California, No. BC 491200 (Super. Ct. L.A. Cty. filed Aug. 30, 2012).
552. Play Fair at Farmers Field Settles Lawsuit Challenging Proposed Downtown Stadium (Nov. 1, 2012), https://playfairfarmersfield.wordpress.com/ (last visited June 18, 2019).

553. Robert Halpren, Rebuilding the Inner City: A History of Neighborhood Initiatives to Address Poverty in the United States (1995).
554. Paul Grogan & Tony Proscio, Comeback Cities: A Blueprint for Urban Neighborhood Revival (2001).
555. Telephone Interview with Julian Gross, *supra* note 97.
556. *Id.*
557. *Id.*
558. Telephone Interview with Jerilyn López Mendoza, *supra* note 113.
559. Telephone Interview with Julian Gross, *supra* note 97.
560. *See* Stephen Ellman, *Client-Centeredness Multiplied: Individual Autonomy and Collective Mobilization in Public Interest Lawyers' Representation of Groups*, 78 Virginia L. Rev. 1103 (1992).
561. *See* Gross, LeRoy & Janis-Aparicio, *supra* note 63.
562. Telephone Interview with Ben Beach, *supra* note 488.
563. *Id.*
564. Michael W. McCann, Rights at Work: Pay Equity Reform and the Politics of Legal Mobilization 513–14 (2004).
565. Telephone Interview with Jerilyn López Mendoza, *supra* note 281.
566. The public relations functions of CBAs are in line with new governance theory. *See* Orly Lobel, *The Renew Deal*, 89 Minn. L. Rev. 342 (2004); William H. Simon, *Solving Problems v. Claiming Rights: The Pragmatist Challenge to Legal Liberalism*, 46 Wm. & Mary L. Rev. 127 (2004).
567. Vicki Been, *Community Benefits Agreements: A New Local Government Tool or Another Variation of the Exactions Theme?*, 77 U. Chi. L. Rev. 5 (2010); Edward W. De Barbieri, *Do Community Benefits Benefit Communities?*, 37 Cardozo L. Rev. 1773 (2016).
568. Dolan v. City of Tigard, 512 U.S. 374 (1994); Nollan v. Cal. Coastal Comm'n, 483 U.S. 825 (1987).
569. DeBarbieri, *supra* note 567.
570. *See* Been, *supra* note 567, at 27-29.
571. Lavine, *supra* note 164.
572. Telephone Interview with Becky Dennison, *supra* note 477.

Chapter 5

1. *See* Gerald E. Frug, *Is Secession from the City of Los Angeles a Good Idea?*, 49 UCLA L. Rev. 1783, 1784 (2002).
2. *See* William Fulton, The Reluctant Metropolis: The Politics of Urban Growth in Los Angeles 3 (1997). On Los Angeles's history of decentralized urban planning, *see* Mike Davis, City of Quartz: Excavating the Future in Los Angeles 165–69 (1990).
3. *See* Tracy Gray-Barkan, *Southern California's Wal-Mart Wars*, 35 Soc. Pol'y 31 (Fall 2004).
4. *See Inglewood Household Income in 1999*, http://www.city-data.com/city/Inglewood-California.html (last visited Apr. 13, 2019)
5. In addition to Vons, Inglewood also had a Costco, which opened in 1984.
6. *See* Industry at a Crossroads: What L.A.'s Supermarket Chains and City Leaders Should Do to Restore Good Jobs, Increase Food Access, and Build Healthy Communities in Los Angeles 9 (Mar. 2007); Ross D. Petty et al., *Regulating Target Marketing and Other Race-Based Advertising Practices*, 8 Mich. J. Race & L. 335, 357 (2003); *see also* William H. Simon, The Community Economic Development Movement: Law, Business and the New Social Policy 95 (2001).
7. The Supercenter designation was given to Wal-Mart stores defined by their massive linear space (upwards of two hundred thousand square feet), which allowed them to house grocery departments and Wal-Mart's traditional discounted consumer merchandise under one

roof. Tracy Gray-Barkan, Wal-Mart and Beyond: The Battle for Good Jobs and Strong Communities in Urban America 17 (2007).
8. Nelson Lichtenstein, *Wal-Mart: A Template for Twenty-First-Century Capitalism*, in Wal-Mart: The Face of Twenty-First-Century Capitalism 3, 4 (Nelson Lichtenstein ed., 2006).
9. *See* Gray-Barkan, *supra* note 7, at 23.
10. *See* Nancy Cleeland & Debora Vrana, *Wal-Mart CEO Takes His Case to California; He Says the Retailer Erred in Its Aggressive Pursuit of the Crucial Market but Won't Back Down*, L.A. Times, Feb. 24, 2005, at A1.
11. *See* Gray-Barkan, *supra* note 7, at vii.
12. One public poll reported that nearly 80% of Inglewood residents "supported the sale of groceries in Wal-Mart." Gray-Barkan, *supra* note 3, at 32.
13. *See* Ruth Milkman, L.A. Story: Immigrant Workers and the Future of the Labor Movement 3 (2006) (calling Los Angeles "a crucible of labor movement revitalization in the 1990s"); *see also* Mike Davis, Magical Urbanism: Latinos Reinvent the Big U.S. City 145 (2000).
14. *See* Annette Bernhardt et al., What Do We Know About Wal-Mart? An Overview of Facts and Studies for New Yorkers 1 (Brennan Center for Justice Economic Policy Brief No. 2, Aug. 2005) (reporting 2005 profit figures).
15. *See* Lichtenstein, *supra* note 8, at 3–5.
16. *See* Abigail Goldman & Nancy Cleeland, *The Wal-Mart Effect: An Empire Built on Bargains Remakes the Working World*, L.A. Times, Nov. 23, 2003, at A1.
17. *See* Lichtenstein, *supra* note 8, at 9–11.
18. Transaction costs include the costs of acquiring information, bargaining, and enforcing decisions. *See* Ronald Coase, *The Nature of the Firm*, 3 Economica 386 (1937).
19. *See* Lichtenstein, *supra* note 8, at 11.
20. *See id.*
21. *See* Benedict Sheehy, *Corporations and Social Costs: The Wal-Mart Case Study*, 24 J.L. & Com. 1, 36 (2004); Nancy Cleeland et al., *Scouring the Globe to Give Shoppers an $8.63 Polo Shirt*, L.A. Times, Nov. 24, 2003, at A1.
22. *Compare* Global Insight, The Economic Impact of Wal-Mart (2005) (stating that disposable income had risen nearly 1% as a result of Wal-Mart's reduction in consumer prices), *with* David Neumark et al., The Effects of Wal-Mart on Local Labor Markets (2005) (finding that payrolls per person declined by about 5% after the opening of Wal-Mart stores).
23. *See* Lichtenstein, *supra* note 8, at 26–27.
24. *See* Bernhardt et al., *supra* note 14, at 3–4 (noting that those Wal-Mart employees covered by insurance were forced to pay high premiums and medical deductibles); *see also* Steven Greenhouse & Michael Barbaro, *Wal-Mart Memo Suggests Ways to Cut Employee Benefit Costs*, N.Y. Times, Oct. 26, 2005, at C1; Bernard Wysocki Jr. & Ann Zimmerman, *Bargain Hunter: Wal-Mart Cost-Cutting Finds a Big Target in Health Care*, Wall St. J., Sept. 30, 2003, at A1.
25. *See* Steven Greenhouse, *Parrying Its Critics, Wal-Mart Says Its Wages Must Stay Competitive*, N.Y. Times, May 4, 2005, at C1.
26. *See* Nelson Lichtenstein, State of the Union: A Century of American Labor 30–38 (2002).
27. *See* Lichtenstein, *supra* note 8, at 4.
28. *See* Lichtenstein, *supra* note 26, at 54.
29. The Taylorist production model was characterized by the scientific management of production processes, whereby workers were assigned to specialized tasks that presaged the subsequent rise of the assembly line mode of production. *See* Daniel Nelson, Frederick W. Taylor and the Rise of Scientific Management (1980).

30. *See* Wal-Mart, *Economic Opportunity* 1–1, WAL-MART FACTS, http://www/walmartfacts.com/FactSheets/8292006_Economic_Benefits.pdf (last visited May 18, 2007).
31. *See* BERNHARDT ET AL., *supra* note 14, at 1.
32. *See* Jim Pope, *Next Wave Organizing and the Shift to a New Paradigm of Labor Law*, 50 N.Y. L. SCH. L. REV. 515, 516 (2005–2006).
33. *See* James J. Brudney, *Neutrality Agreements and Card Check Recognition: Prospects for Changing Paradigms*, 90 IOWA L. REV. 819, 821 (2005); Paul Weiler, *Striking a New Balance: Freedom of Contract and the Prospects for Union Representation*, 99 HARV. L. REV. 351, 412–19 (1984); *see also* Eric Tucker, *"Great Expectations" Defeated?: The Trajectory of Collective Bargaining Regimes in Canada and the United States Post-NAFTA*, 26 COMP. LAB. L. & POL'Y J. 97, 139–140 (2004). According to one report, unions lost about half of the board-certified elections that they were involved in. *See* Wendy Zellner, *How Wal-Mart Keeps Unions at Bay: Organizing the Nation's No. 1 Employer Would Give Labor a Lift*, BUS. WEEK, Oct. 28, 2002, at 94.
34. *See* Brudney, *supra* note 33, at 821.
35. See discussion of Wal-Mart's anti-union policy, *infra*.
36. *See* KATHERINE V.W. STONE, FROM WIDGETS TO DIGITS: EMPLOYMENT REGULATION FOR THE CHANGING WORKPLACE 210 (2004).
37. Wal-Mart attempted to place the legal ownership of Wal-Mart stores under separate companies to limit union organizing across stores. *See* Thomas Jessen Adams, *Making the New Shop Floor: Wal-Mart, Labor Control, and the History of the Postwar Discount Retail Industry in America*, in WAL-MART: THE FACE OF TWENTY-FIRST-CENTURY CAPITALISM, *supra* note 8, at 213, 219.
38. *See* Dukes v. Wal-Mart Stores, Inc., 222 F.R.D. 137, 161 (N.D. Cal. 2004).
39. *See* Steven Greenhouse & Michael Barbaro, *Wal-Mart to Add More Part-Timers and Wage Caps*, N.Y. TIMES, Oct. 2, 2006, at A1.
40. *See* Brad Seligman, *Patriarchy at the Checkout Counter: The Dukes v. Wal-Mart Stores, Inc. Class-Action Suit*, in WAL-MART: THE FACE OF TWENTY-FIRST-CENTURY CAPITALISM, *supra* note 8, at 231, 237.
41. *See id.* at 236.
42. *See id.* at 237–38.
43. Right-to-work laws prevent a union from requiring employees to join the union as a condition of employment. *See* Paul C. Weiler, *A Principled Reshaping of Labor Law for the Twenty-First Century*, 3 U. PA. J. LAB. & EMP. L. 177, 180 (2001).
44. *See* Lichtenstein, *supra* note 8, at 17.
45. *Id.*
46. *See* Anna M. Archer, *Shopping for a Collective Voice when Unionization is Unattainable*, 42 HOUS. L. REV. 837, 845 (2005).
47. *See* Jeffrey A. Botelho, *Who Should Pay the Human Price of "Every Day Low Prices"?*, 18 ST. THOMAS L. REV. 825, 841–42 (2006).
48. *See* Lichtenstein, *supra* note 8, at 14.
49. *See* George Lefcoe, *The Regulation of Superstores: The Legality of Zoning Ordinances Emerging from the Skirmishes Between Wal-Mart and the United Food and Commercial Workers Union*, 58 ARK. L. REV. 833, 834 (2006); Zellner, *supra* note 33. Wal-Mart opened its first Supercenter in 1998; by 2003, there were over 1,400. *See* Liza Featherstone, *Rollback Wages: Will Labor Take the Wal-Mart Challenge?*, THE NATION, June 28, 2004, at 11.
50. Botelho, *supra* note 47, at 841 (quoting Wal-Mart management directive).
51. *See* Archer, *supra* note 46, at 862.
52. *See* Zellner, *supra* note 33.
53. *See* Botelho, *supra* note 47, at 843.
54. *See* NIK THEODORE & CHIRAG MEHTA, UNDERMINING THE RIGHT TO ORGANIZE: EMPLOYER BEHAVIOR DURING UNION REPRESENTATION CAMPAIGNS (2005) (finding that 30% of employers in Chicago study fired workers in union organizing campaigns); *see also* Wal-Mart

Stores, Inc. v. United Food & Com. Workers Int'l Union, No. 12-CA-20882, 2003 WL 22532371 (N.L.R.B. Div. of Judges).
55. *See* No Sweat, Briefing: Wal-Mart's Anti-Union Practices, https://web.archive.org/web/20061003113451/http://www.nosweat.org.uk/node/32 (last visited Apr. 10, 2019); *see also* HUM. RTS. WATCH, DISCOUNTING RIGHTS: WAL-MART'S VIOLATION OF US WORKERS' RIGHT TO FREEDOM OF ASSOCIATION 112 (2007), http://hrw.org/reports/2007/us0507/us0507web.pdf (last visited Apr. 13, 2019) ("Between January 2000 and July 2005, NLRB regional directors issued thirty-nine 'complaints' against Wal-Mart. The complaints consolidated 101 cases, combining those charges involving the same stores and, in some cases, combining charges against stores located near each other.").
56. *See The Real Facts About Wal-Mart: Wal-Mart Anti-Union Policy*, WAKE-UP WAL-MART, http://www.wakeupwalmart.com/facts/#anti-union (last visited May 18, 2007).
57. *See* Doug Struck, *Wal-Mart Leaves Bitter Pill: Quebec Store Closes After Vote to Unionize*, WASH. POST, Apr. 14, 2005, at E1.
58. Wal-Mart had recognized unions in several other countries. *See* Wade Rathke, *A Wal-Mart Workers Association? An Organizing Plan*, in WAL-MART: THE FACE OF TWENTY-FIRST-CENTURY CAPITALISM, *supra* note 8, at 261, 262–63.
59. *See* Featherstone, *supra* note 49.
60. *See* Rathke, *supra* note 58, at 269.
61. *See* Featherstone, *supra* note 49.
62. *See* Rathke, *supra* note 58, at 270.
63. *See* Katherine V.W. Stone, *Flexibilization, Globalization, and Privatization: The Three Challenges to Labor Rights in Our Time*, 44 OSGOODE HALL L.J. 77, 90–92 (2006).
64. *See* JENNIFER GORDON, SUBURBAN SWEATSHOPS: THE FIGHT FOR IMMIGRANT RIGHTS 178 (2005).
65. *See* Goldman & Cleeland, *supra* note 16.
66. *See* Lisa Alcalay Klug, *Jury Rules Wal-Mart Must Pay $172 Million over Meal Breaks*, N.Y. TIMES, Dec. 23, 2005, at A22.
67. *See* Steven Greenhouse, *Wal-Mart Told to Pay $78 Million*, N.Y. TIMES, Oct. 14, 2006, at C4.
68. *See* Steven Greenhouse, *In-House Audit Says Wal-Mart Violated Labor Laws*, N.Y. TIMES, Jan. 13, 2004, at A16.
69. *See* Russell Gold & Ann Zimmerman, *Papers Suggest Wal-Mart Knew of Illegal Workers*, WALL ST. J., Nov. 5, 2005, at A3; *see also* Ann Zimmerman, *After Huge Raid on Illegals, Wal-Mart Fires Back at U.S.*, WALL ST. J., Dec. 19, 2003, at 1.
70. *See, e.g., The Real Facts About Wal-Mart: Wal-Mart Wages and Workers Rights*, WAKE-UP WAL-MART, http://www.wakeupwalmart.com/facts/ (last visited May 18, 2007).
71. *See* David Streitfeld, *It's Berkeley vs. Bentonville as Lawyers Take On Wal-Mart*, L.A. TIMES, June 28, 2004, at A1.
72. Dukes v. Wal-Mart Stores, Inc., No. C 01-02252 MJJ, Order Granting in Part and Denying in Part Mot. for Class Certification (N.D. Cal. June 21, 2004), *aff'd* Dukes v. Wal-Mart, Inc., 474 F.3d 1214 (9th Cir. 2007); *see also* Lisa Girion & Abigail Goldman, *Wal-Mart Must Face Huge Sex-Bias Suit*, L.A. TIMES, June 23, 2004, at A1.
73. *See, e.g.*, Archer, *supra* note 46, at 880 (arguing that the class action vehicle is a viable means of obtaining collective voice for Wal-Mart workers unable to form unions).
74. *See* John Grant, General Counsel, United Food and Commercial Workers, Local 770, Presentation to Problem Solving in the Public Interest Seminar, UCLA School of Law (Nov. 2, 2006).
75. *See* Ritu Bhatnagar, *Dukes v. Wal-Mart as a Catalyst for Social Activism*, 19 BERKELEY WOMEN'S L.J. 246, 248 (2004).
76. *Cf.* Clayton P. Gillette, *Local Redistribution, Living Wage Ordinances, and Judicial Intervention*, 101 NW. U.L. REV. 1057 (2007).
77. *See* Lefcoe, *supra* note 49, at 4.

78. Nancy Cleeland & Abigail Goldman, *The Wal-Mart Effect: Grocery Unions Battle to Stop Invasion of the Giant Stores*, L.A. TIMES, Nov. 25, 2003, at A1 (quoting Rick Icaza, president of UFCW Local 770, stating that "The No. 1 enemy has still got to be Wal-Mart."); *see also* Barbara Ehrenreich, Editorial, *Wal-Mars Invades Earth*, N.Y. TIMES, July 25, 2004, at D11.
79. *See* Merritt Quisumbing, *Choosing Where to Buy Groceries: The High Prices of Wal-Mart's "Always Low Prices. Always."*, 7 J. L. & SOC. CHALLENGES 111 (2005).
80. Cleeland & Goldman, *supra* note 78; *see also* Lefcoe, *supra* note 49, at 835 (stating that wages and benefits at Wal-Mart "average about 20–40% less than those of union grocery workers").
81. Cleeland & Goldman, *supra* note 78; *see also The Wal-Mart Threat*, UFCW, http://www.ufcw.org/take_action/walmart_workers_campaign_info/index.cfm (last visited May 18, 2007).
82. *See* Cleeland & Goldman, *supra* note 78; *see also* VICKY LOVELL ET AL., INSTITUTE FOR WOMEN'S POLICY RESEARCH, THE BENEFITS OF UNIONIZATION FOR WORKERS IN THE RETAIL FOOD INDUSTRY 2 (2002), http://www.iwpr.org/pdf/c352.pdf (last visited May 18, 2007).
83. *See* Max Vanzi, *Bill Passed to Ban Warehouse Sales of Foods, Drugs*, L.A. TIMES, Sept. 11, 1999, at C1.
84. *See* Carl Ingram, *Davis Vetoes Ban on Grocery Sales at 'Big Box' Stores*, L.A. TIMES, Sept. 23, 1999, at 3; Cleeland & Goldman, *supra* note 78.
85. *See* Lefcoe, *supra* note 49, at 836.
86. Telephone Interview with John Grant, In-House Couns., UFCW Local 770 (Mar. 16, 2007).
87. *See* CAROL ZABIN & ISAAC MARTIN, LIVING WAGE CAMPAIGNS IN THE ECONOMIC POLICY ARENA: FOUR CASE STUDIES FROM CALIFORNIA 9 (Center for Labor Research and Education, Institute of Industrial Relations, UC Berkeley for The Phoenix Fund for Workers and Communities, New World Foundation, June 1999).
88. Telephone Interview with John Grant, *supra* note 86.
89. *Id.*
90. Telephone Interview with Margo Feinberg, Partner, Schwartz Steinsapir Dohrman & Sommers (Mar. 13, 2007).
91. *Id.*
92. *Id.*
93. *Id.*; *see also* Lefcoe, *supra* note 49, at 860 (stating that courts disfavor land use controls designed to protect local merchants from competition, citing KENNETH H. YOUNG, 1 ANDERSON'S AMERICAN LAW OF ZONING § 7.28, at 805 (4th ed. 1996)). In 2006, Estolano would become CEO of the CRA, championing the Grand Avenue CBA.
94. *See* Gray-Barkan, *supra* note 3, at 36.
95. *See* Patrick McGreevy & Sue Fox, *Election 2001*, L.A. TIMES, June 6, 2001, at A19.
96. The proposed ban applied to big-box stores larger than one hundred fifty thousand square feet that devoted more than 10% of their floor area to non-taxable items. *See* Jessica Garrison & Sara Lin, *Wal-Mart vs. Inglewood a Warm-Up for L.A. Fight*, L.A. TIMES, Apr. 2, 2004, at 7; Abigail Goldman, *Wal-Mart Still Raises Concern in Inglewood*, L.A. TIMES, Jan. 10, 2006, at C1.
97. Telephone Interview with Margo Feinberg, *supra* note 90.
98. *See* Robert Greene, *Thinking Outside the Big Box: L.A.'s New Law to Rein in Wal-Mart Isn't Sweeping, but It May Be Smart*, L.A. WKLY., Aug. 13-19, 2004, at 17.
99. Telephone Interview with Margo Feinberg, *supra* note 90.
100. Steven Greenhouse, *How Costco Became the Anti-Wal-Mart*, N.Y. TIMES, July 21, 2005, at BU2.
101. Telephone Interview with Margo Feinberg, *supra* note 90.
102. Robert L. Gard, *L.A. Looks to Wall out "Superstores": Buffer Zones Would Prevent Walmart, Others*, PARK LA BREA NEWS/BEVERLY PRESS, Dec. 25, 2003, at 1.
103. RODINO ASSOCIATES, FINAL REPORT ON RESEARCH FOR BIG BOX RETAIL/SUPERSTORE ORDINANCE (Oct. 28, 2003); *see also* Nancy Cleeland, *City Report Is Critical of Wal-Mart Supercenters*, L.A. TIMES, Dec. 6, 2003, at C1 ("A report commissioned by two Los Angeles city councilmen warns that Wal-Mart Stores Inc.'s Supercenters could harm the local economy

and recommends that the company be required to raise its pay and benefits if it wants to operate in the city."); Jessica Garrison, *Battles over Mega-Stores May Shift to New Studies; Law Requiring Economic Impact Reports Could Set the Stage for Skirmishes Across Los Angeles*, L.A. TIMES, Aug. 12, 2004, at B1 ("In December, city officials released a $30,000 study, prepared by the consulting firm Rodino Associates, that said Supercenters—which can run to 200,000 square feet—could harm the local economy, push down wages, strain public services and hurt smaller businesses.").

104. See LOS ANGELES CITY ATTORNEY, OPTIONS FOR REGULATING THE DEVELOPMENT OF SUPERSTORES (Report No. R03-0585) (2003).
105. See Lawrence Kootnikoff, *Wal-Mart Takes on Inglewood Store*, DAILY J., Dec. 24, 2003, at 1.
106. Telephone Interview with Margo Feinberg, *supra* note 90; *see also Alameda County Sued by Wal-Mart*, L.A. TIMES, Jan. 27, 2004, at C3.
107. Telephone Interview with Margo Feinberg, *supra* note 90.
108. See Shirley V. Svorny, *Banning Wal-Mart May Prove Costly*, L.A. TIMES, Jan. 30, 2004, at B15.
109. Telephone Interview with Margo Feinberg, *supra* note 90.
110. See Gray-Barkan, *supra* note 3, at 35.
111. See James F. Peltz, *3 Months, and Still No Deal: Latest Grocery Talks Collapse*, L.A. TIMES, Jan. 12, 2004, at A1.
112. See Cleeland & Goldman, *supra* note 78.
113. See Peltz, *supra* note 111.
114. See Garrison & Lin, *supra* note 96; *see also* Kelly Candaele & Peter Dreier, *A Watershed Strike*, THE NATION, Oct. 23, 2003, http://www.thenation.com/doc.mhtml?i=20031110&s=dreier (last visited May 18, 2007); Daniel B. Wood, *A Strike That's Struck a Chord Nationwide: Los Angeles Grocery Walkout Taps into Labor Solidarity and Woes of a Shrinking Middle Class*, CHRISTIAN SC. MONITOR, Dec. 11, 2003, at 2.
115. See John O'Dell, *Workers OK Grocery Pact to End Strike*, L.A. TIMES, Mar. 1, 2004, at B1. Safeway reported losses of over $100 million attributed to the strike. *See* James F. Peltz, *Safeway Reports $696 Million Loss; Company Says Red Ink Includes $103 Million from Strike, Less Than Analysts Had Forecast*, L.A. TIMES, Feb. 13, 2004, at C1.
116. See Garrison & Lin, *supra* note 96. Critics charged that the UFCW ran a botched campaign that failed to respond clearly to Wal-Mart's media message (which suggested that the dispute was simply about workers contributing $5 per week to their own healthcare) and to nationalize the boycott to respond to the grocery chains' ability to offset losses in California with profits from other states. *See* Andrew Pollack, *Southern California Grocery Strike Defeated— How Can Labor Pick Up the Pieces?*, FRONTLINE 13, http://www.redflag.org.uk/frontline/13/13grocers.html (last visited May 18, 2007).
117. See Nancy Cleeland & Abigail Goldman, *Wal-Mart Trying to Put Plan on Ballot; the Retailer Is Seeking Approval for a New Store in Inglewood from the City's Voters, Not Its Council Members*, L.A. TIMES, Aug. 30, 2003, at A1.
118. Gray-Barkan, *supra* note 3, at 32.
119. See GRAY-BARKAN, *supra* note 7, at 10–11. At the national level, Wal-Mart's strategy involved hiring former civil rights leader and U.S. Ambassador to the United Nations Andrew Young to lead the Working Families for Wal-Mart initiative—a position he left in controversy after he suggested that Jewish, Arab, and Korean shop owners had "ripped off" black communities for years. *See* Michael Barbaro & Steven Greenhouse, *Wal-Mart Image-Builder Resigns*, N.Y. TIMES, Aug. 28, 2006, at C3.
120. See Garrison & Lin, *supra* note 96. In its Baldwin Hills campaign, Wal-Mart made contributions to local school and youth programs, donated $10,000 for baseball field lights to a local park, and gave $3,000 to the Urban League, after which its director, John Mack, issued a statement in support of Wal-Mart's "economic benefits." Cleeland & Goldman, *supra* note 78; *see also* Gayle Pollard-Terry, *Rallying Around Wal-Mart*, L.A. TIMES, Apr. 2, 2004, Calendar Section, at 22 (citing Mack's support of Wal-Mart).

121. Martha L. Willman & Carol Chambers, *Back at Home, the Issues Were Store, School and Airport*, L.A. Times, Nov. 8, 2000, at B1. Not all of Wal-Mart's zoning initiatives passed. In particular, Wal-Mart lost rezoning measures in Eureka in 1999 and Yucaipa in 2000. *See* Mike Anton & Seema Mehta, *Voters Take the Initiative to Control Growth Themselves*, L.A. Times, Nov. 12, 2001, at A1; Eric Malnic, *Eureka Voters Reject Plan for Wal-Mart*, L.A. Times, Aug. 25, 1999, at A3.
122. Natasha Lee & David Pierson, *L.A. County Gets Its First Wal-Mart Supercenter*, L.A. Times, Aug. 31, 2005, at B1.
123. Karen Alexander, *Voters Approve 2 "Big Box" Store Plans, Reject 2 Others*, L.A. Times, Mar. 7, 2002, at B16. Wal-Mart subsequently developed a Supercenter in Calexico, which opened in 2005. *See Calexico Wal-Mart Supercenter Celebrates Grand Opening*, Wal-Mart Facts (May 18, 2005), http://www.walmartfacts.com/articles/2139.aspx (last visited May 18, 2007).
124. *See* Seema Mehta, *Wal-Mart Superstores Find Their Niche*, L.A. Times, Sept. 10, 2004, at B1 (noting that a Wal-Mart Supercenter had opened in La Quinta and another was slated to open in Hemet).
125. *See id.*; *see also* Patricia E. Salkin, *Supersizing Small Town America: Using Regionalism to Right-Size Big Box Retail*, 6 Vt. J. Envtl. L. 9 (2005).
126. *See* Nancy Cleeland & Abigail Goldman, *Wal-Mart Blocked by Union Lobbying*, L.A. Times, Oct. 25, 2002, at C1.
127. *See* Cleeland & Goldman, *supra* note 78 ("[The site fight] strategy can temporarily save union jobs and give leaders victories to celebrate, but it does little to stop the long-term march of Wal-Mart, critics say. After all, there are 478 cities in California, 88 in Los Angeles County alone.").
128. *See* Gray-Barkan, *supra* note 3, at 32.
129. Tracy Gray-Barkan, Dir. Retail Pol'y & Senior Res. Analyst, Los Angeles All. for a New Econ., Presentation to Cmty. Econ. Dev. Clinic, UCLA Sch. of Law (Mar. 21, 2007).
130. *See* Gray-Barkan, *supra* note 3, at 32.
131. *See* Jean Merl, *Inglewood Voters Go to Polls, Again; For the Fifth Time in Less Than a Year, They'll Choose a District 4 Council Member*, L.A. Times, Sept. 14, 2003, at B3.
132. Telephone Interview with John Grant, *supra* note 86.
133. *See* Gray-Barkan, *supra* note 3, at 32.
134. Telephone Interview with John Grant, *supra* note 86.
135. *See* Cleeland & Goldman, *supra* note 126.
136. *See id.*; Inglewood, Cal., Ordinance 02-30 (Oct. 22, 2002), http://www.cityofinglewood.org/civica/filebank/blobdload.asp?BlobID=1651 (last visited May 18, 2007).
137. *See* Gray-Barkan, *supra* note 3, at 32.
138. *See id.*
139. *See* Hannah Cho et al., *Inglewood Reverses Itself on Wal-Mart; Following Legal Advice, City Council Abandons Decision to Back Union Bid to Keep Store from Being Constructed*, L.A. Times, Dec. 5, 2002, at C4.
140. *See* Inglewood, Cal., Ordinance 02-35 (Dec. 3, 2002) (repealing Ordinance 02-30).
141. *See* Cleeland & Goldman, *supra* note 78.
142. Telephone Interview with John Grant, *supra* note 86.
143. *See* Jean Merl, *Franklin Wins Inglewood Council Seat*, L.A. Times, Sept. 17, 2003, at B4; Merl, *supra* note 131.
144. *See* Gray-Barkan, *supra* note 3, at 34.
145. *See* Proposed Inglewood, Cal., Initiative Measure 04-A [hereinafter Measure 04-A], http://www.cityofinglewood.org/pdfs/Home%20Page/doc.pdf (last visited May 18, 2007).
146. Measure 04-A § 12-200.1.B.
147. *See* Cleeland & Goldman, *supra* note 117; *see also* Measure 04-A § 12-200.1 G.8 ("The Home Stretch Specific Plan is a comprehensive, stand alone planning document that preempts and replaces all of the standards, criteria, [and] procedures for review . . . .").

148. Measure 04-A § III.
149. *Id.* § VI.
150. WAL-MART WATCH, SHAMELESS: HOW WAL-MART BULLIES ITS WAY INTO COMMUNITIES ACROSS AMERICA 23 (2005).
151. *See* Gray-Barkan, *supra* note 3, at 34.
152. Telephone Interview with John Grant, *supra* note 86.
153. Presentation by Tracy Gray-Barkan, *supra* note 129.
154. *See* Gray-Barkan, *supra* note 3, at 35.
155. *See* CLERGY AND LAITY UNITED FOR ECONOMIC JUSTICE, http://www.cluela.org (last visited June 26, 2007).
156. ACORN, a national membership-based organizing group, focused on building power for low- to moderate-income families. *See* GARY DELGADO, ORGANIZING THE MOVEMENT: THE ROOTS AND GROWTH OF ACORN (1986).
157. The CBI members were Reverend Altagracia Perez, Reverend Jarvis Johnson, Reverend Harold Kidd, Bishop Gregory Dixon, Juanita Ducros, Diane Johnson, Mary Bueno, Cleveland Brown, Cresia Davis, Irene Cowley, Gary Cowley, Gill Mattheiu, Elliott Petty, Danny K. Tabor, Walter Johnson, Eliani Padilla, Sylvia Hopper, Aisha Young, Paulette Francis, Doug Appel, and Lizette Hernandez. *See* SOUTHERN CALIFORNIA LIBRARY, *The Southern California Library's 2005 Annual Dinner, Mover and Shaker Award: Coalition for a Better Inglewood,* http://www.socallib.org/SCLWebSite/events/dinner05/cbi.html (last visited May 18, 2007).
158. *See* Garrison & Lin, *supra* note 96; Sara Lin, *Wal-Mart and Its Foes Vie for Support,* L.A. TIMES, Apr. 4, 2004, at B1.
159. *See* Earl Ofari Hutchinson, *Commentary: Inglewood Opens the Wal-Mart Wars,* L.A. TIMES, Apr. 8, 2004, at B15.
160. *Id.*
161. *See* WAL-MART WATCH, *supra* note 150, at 23.
162. Telephone Interview with John Grant, *supra* note 86.
163. *See* Tentative Decision, Coal. for a Better Inglewood v. City of Inglewood, No. BS087433 (Feb. 27, 2004).
164. *See* Gray-Barkan, *supra* note 3, at 35 (noting that CBI's materials were used to help "shape specific messages for different segments of the community, including homeowners, women, African-Americans, Latinos and union members").
165. RODINO ASSOCIATES, FINAL REPORT ON RESEARCH FOR BIG BOX RETAIL/SUPERSTORE ORDINANCE (Oct. 28, 2003).
166. Nancy Cleeland & Abigail Goldman, *Report: Wal-Mart Will Create Jobs,* L.A. TIMES, Jan. 28, 2004, at C2.
167. Rodino Comments on Wal-Mart Report.
168. Email from BobRodino@aol.com to JKamensk@council.lacity.org, re: LAEDC-a response- another factor (Jan. 17, 2004).
169. *See* Gray-Barkan, *supra* note 3, at 35.
170. *See* Garrison & Lin, *supra* note 96.
171. *See id.*
172. *See* Gray-Barkan, *supra* note 3, at 35–36.
173. *See id.* at 35.
174. *See id.*
175. *See id.* at 36; *see also* Sara Lin, *Activists Blast Wal-Mart Bid in Inglewood,* L.A. TIMES, Mar. 30, 2004, at B3. Clerics opposed to the initiative included the Southern Christian Leadership Conference and Nation of Islam, as well as St. Michael's Catholic Church and the Holy Faith Episcopal Church in Inglewood. *See* John M. Broder, *Voters in Los Angeles Suburb Say No to a Big Wal-Mart,* N.Y. TIMES, Apr. 8, 2004, at A20; Sara Lin & Monte Morin, *Voters in Inglewood Turn Away Wal-Mart,* L.A. TIMES, Apr. 7, 2004, at A1.

176. *See* Editorial, *A Big-Box Ballot Bully*, L.A. TIMES, Mar. 28, 2004, at 4; Patt Morrison, *Can You Hear That, Inglewood?*, L.A. TIMES, Mar. 30, 2004, at B3; *see also* Gray-Barkan, *supra* note 3, at 36.
177. *See* Gray-Barkan, *supra* note 3, at 36.
178. *See id.*; Telephone Interview with John Grant, *supra* note 86.
179. *See* Gray-Barkan, *supra* note 3, at 36.
180. *See id.*; Telephone Interview with John Grant, *supra* note 86.
181. *See* Madeline Janis-Aparicio & Roxana Tynan, *Power in Numbers: Community Benefits Agreements and the Power of Coalition Building*, SHELTERFORCE ONLINE, no. 144, Nov.–Dec. 2005, http://www.nhi.org/online/issues/144/powerinnumbers.html (last visited Apr. 13, 2019); *see also* GRAY-BARKAN, *supra* note 7, at 37.
182. *See* Candid Enters., Inc. v. Grossmont Union High Sch. Dist., 705 P.2d 876, 882 (Cal. 1985); Assoc. Home Builders, Inc. v. City of Livermore, 135 Cal. Rptr. 41, 51 (Ct. App. 1976).
183. *See* Daniel J. Curtin, Jr., *Regulating Big Box Stores: The Proper Use of the City or County's Police Power and Its Comprehensive Plan—California's Experience*, 6 VT. J. ENVTL. L. 8 (2004–2005).
184. DANIEL J. CURTIN, JR. & CECILY T. TALBERT, CURTIN'S CALIFORNIA LAND USE AND PLANNING LAW 5–6 (5th ed. 2005).
185. *See* Lefcoe, *supra* note 49, at 860.
186. *See id.* at 840–42.
187. *See* DeVita v. Cty. of Napa, 9 Cal.4th 763, 775 (Cal. 1995) (affirming that "the local electorate's right to initiative and referendum is guaranteed by the California Constitution, article II, section 11, and is generally co-extensive with the legislative power of the local governing body").
188. *See id.* at 774.
189. *See generally* Karen Alexander, *Increasingly, Voters Decide Fate of Big Stores*, L.A. TIMES, Mar. 5, 2005, at B6.
190. The use of the referendum to gain voter approval of pro-Wal-Mart land use changes occurred in Palmdale. *See* Willman & Chambers, *supra* note 121; *see also* WAL-MART WATCH, *supra* note 150, at 23 (noting also that Wal-Mart won voter approval for a Supercenter in Glendora).
191. The use of the referendum to repeal big-box bans happened in Calexico and Contra Costa County. *See* Alexander, *supra* note 123; Garrison & Lin, *supra* note 96 (noting also that Wal-Mart successfully campaigned for a referendum to repeal a big-box ban in Contra Costa County).
192. *See, e.g.*, *San Marcos Vote Puts End to Second Wal-Mart*, SAN DIEGO TRIB., Mar. 4, 2004, at NC-1.
193. Telephone Interview with Margo Feinberg, *supra* note 90.
194. *Id.*
195. CHATTEN-BROWN & CARSTENS, http://cbcearthlaw.com (last visited Apr. 13, 2019).
196. *See, e.g.*, CAL. CIV. PROC. CODE § 1021.5 (West 2006) (authorizing court-awarded attorney's fees where "a significant benefit . . . has been conferred on the general public or a large class of persons" and "the necessity and financial burden of private enforcement are such as to make the award appropriate").
197. Telephone Interview with Jan Chatten-Brown, Partner, Chatten-Brown & Carstens (July 26, 2004).
198. Telephone Interview with Jan Chatten-Brown, Partner, Chatten-Brown & Carstens (Mar. 14, 2007).
199. *Id.*
200. Telephone Interview with Margo Feinberg, *supra* note 90.
201. David Pettit, Partner, Caldwell Leslie Proctor & Pettit, Presentation to Problem Solving in the Public Interest Seminar, UCLA School of Law (Nov. 16, 2006).
202. Telephone Interview with David Pettit, Partner, Caldwell Leslie Proctor & Pettit (Mar. 7, 2007).
203. *Id.*

204. *Id.*
205. Interview with Sean Hecht, Exec. Dir., UCLA Sch. of Law Envtl. Law Ctr., in Los Angeles, Cal. (Mar. 15, 2007).
206. Telephone Interview with Jan Chatten-Brown, *supra* note 198.
207. *Id.*; Interview with Sean Hecht, *supra* note 205.
208. *See* Brosnahan v. Eu, 31 Cal.3d 1, 4 (Cal. 1982); Save Stanislaus Area Farm Econ. v. Bd. of Supervisors of the Cty. of Stanislaus, 13 Cal. App. 4th 141 (1993).
209. Telephone Interview with Jan Chatten-Brown, *supra* note 198; Interview with Sean Hecht, *supra* note 205.
210. *See* Gray-Barkan, *supra* note 3, at 33.
211. *See id.*
212. *See id.*; *see also* Dennis Romero, *Walling Off Wal-Mart: Inglewood Activists File Suit to Prevent Their Own Town from Being Wal-Martyred in the War over Big-Box Retail*, L.A. CITY BEAT, Dec. 24, 2003, at http://www.lacitybeat.com/article.php?id=505&IssueNum=29 (last visited May 18, 2007).
213. Press Release, Coal. for a Better Inglewood, Lawsuit to Challenge Wal-Mart Ballot Initiative (Dec. 17, 2003), http://www.laane.org/pressroom/releases/walmart031217.html (last visited May 18, 2007).
214. *See* Abigail Goldman, *Wal-Mart Maneuver Draws Suit*, L.A. TIMES, Dec. 19, 2003, at C2.
215. Petition for an Alternative and Peremptory Writ of Mandate; Complaint for Declaratory and Injunctive Relief, Coal. for a Better Inglewood v. City of Inglewood, Case No. BS087433 (Cal. Super. Ct. Dec. 17, 2003).
216. *Id.* at 5–6.
217. *Id.* at 7. At oral argument, Chatten-Brown contended that the initiative would displace the redevelopment plan in Inglewood by giving land use powers covered by the plan to Wal-Mart. Ruling on Hearing on Petition for Writ of Mandate, Coal. for a Better Inglewood et al. v. City of Inglewood et al., Case No. BS087433, at 4 (Cal. Super. Ct. Feb. 27, 2004).
218. Petition for an Alternative and Peremptory Writ of Mandate; Complaint for Declaratory and Injunctive Relief, Coal. for a Better Inglewood v. City of Inglewood, Case No. BS087433, at 8–10 (Cal. Super. Ct. Dec. 17, 2003).
219. *Id.* at 7, 10–11.
220. Tentative Decision, Coal. for a Better Inglewood v. City of Inglewood, No. BS087433 (Feb. 27, 2004).
221. *See* Gray-Barkan, *supra* note 3, at 34; *see also* V. Dion Haynes, *Wal-Mart Tries End Run Around Balky City*, CHI. TRIB., Jan. 12, 2004, at Zone CN8; Daniel B. Wood, *Wal-Mart Rollout—or Rollback?*, CHRISTIAN SCI. MONITOR, Dec. 24, 2003, at USA1.
222. Telephone Interview with David Pettit, *supra* note 202.
223. Telephone Interview with Margo Feinberg, *supra* note 90; Interview with Sean Hecht, *supra* note 205; Telephone Interview with David Pettit, *supra* note 202.
224. Interview with Sean Hecht, *supra* note 205; Telephone Interview with David Pettit, *supra* note 202.
225. Telephone Interview with Margo Feinberg, *supra* note 90.
226. *Id.* Feinberg also spent time before the election coordinating public statements and appearances by other elected officials, like State Assemblyman Jerome Horton. *Id.* Horton campaigned vigorously against Measure 04-A, vowing to sponsor a law "requiring developers to comply with local building and safety codes" in the event the initiative passed. Lin, *supra* note 158.
227. Interview with Sean Hecht, *supra* note 205.
228. Presentation by Tracy Gray-Barkan, *supra* note 129.
229. Telephone Interview with David Pettit, *supra* note 202.
230. *See* Lin & Morin, *supra* note 175, at A1; *see also Inglewood Community Decisively Defeats Wal-Mart Initiative*, LAANE, http://www.laane.org/ad/walmart.html (last visited May 18, 2007).

231. *See* Broder, *supra* note 175; Editorial, *Global Retailing: WalMart's Waterloo*, GUARDIAN (LONDON), Apr. 9, 2004, at 25; Jennifer Ordonez, *Wal-Mart Hits a Wall in California*, NEWSWEEK, Apr. 19, 2004, at 54; Christopher Parkes, *California Residents Spurn Wal-Mart Store*, FIN. TIMES OF LONDON, Apr. 8, 2004, at 9; Daniel B. Wood, *California's Chilly Welcome for Wal-Mart*, CHRISTIAN SCI. MONITOR, Apr. 8, 2004, at USA3; *Voters in Inglewood, CA Reject Wal-Mart Superstore* (transcript of Democracy Now! Radio broadcast, Apr. 22, 2004), http://www.democracynow.org/print.pl?sid=04/04/22/150248 (last visited May 18, 2007).
232. *See* Jessica Garrison et al., *Wal-Mart to Push Southland Agenda*, L.A. TIMES, Apr. 8, 2004, at B1 (noting that prior to Inglewood, "Wal-Mart had not lost a Superstore fight at the ballot box").
233. *See* Broder, *supra* note 175.
234. *See Wal-Mart: Aim for Fairness*, L.A. TIMES, Apr. 8, 2004, at B14.
235. *See* Lefcoe, *supra* note 49, at 846–47.
236. *See* AFL-CIO, WAL-MART: AN EXAMPLE OF WHY WORKERS REMAIN UNINSURED AND UNDERINSURED (2003); GEORGE MILLER, EVERYDAY LOW WAGES: THE HIDDEN PRICE WE ALL PAY FOR WAL-MART: A REPORT BY THE DEMOCRATIC STAFF OF THE COMMITTEE ON EDUCATION AND THE WORKFORCE (Feb. 16, 2004); UC BERKELEY LAB. CTR., HIDDEN COSTS OF WAL-MART JOBS: USE OF SAFETY NET PROGRAMS BY WAL-MART WORKERS IN CALIFORNIA (2004); *see also* AFL-CIO, THE WAL-MART TAX: SHIFTING HEALTH CARE COSTS TO TAXPAYERS (Mar. 2006); BERNHARDT ET AL., *supra* note 14; *Wal-Mart and Cost to Taxpayers*, WAKE-UP WAL-MART, http://www.wakeupwalmart.com/downloads/wal-mart-cost-to-taxpayers-facts.pdf (last visited May 18, 2007). Wal-Mart responded by commissioning its own studies. *See* GLOBAL INSIGHT, THE ECONOMIC IMPACT OF WAL-MART (2005) (finding that Wal-Mart increased real disposable income by nearly 1%). There were also attempts by independent researchers to weigh Wal-Mart's economic impact. *See* David Neumark et al., *The Effects of Wal-Mart on Local Labor Markets* (Nat'l Bureau of Econ. Res., Working Paper No. 11782, 2005), http://www.nber.org/papers/w11782 (last visited May 18, 2007) (concluding that Wal-Mart reduced local retail employment by 2 to 4%).
237. The Rodino study elicited a response from Wal-Mart, which paid the Los Angeles County Economic Development Corporation $65,000 to produce a report finding that Supercenters would increase the overall number of jobs in Los Angeles. Amanda Bronstad, *Wal-Mart Study Has LAEDC Defending Consulting Practice*, L.A. BUSINESS J., Feb. 2, 2004, at 3.
238. *See* GOOD JOBS FIRST, SHOPPING FOR SUBSIDIES: HOW WAL-MART USES TAXPAYER MONEY TO FINANCE ITS NEVER-ENDING GROWTH (2004); *see also* DAVID KARJANEN & MURTAZA BUXAMUSA, SUBSIDIZING WAL-MART: A CASE STUDY OF THE COLLEGE GROVE REDEVELOPMENT PROJECT (Nov. 2003).
239. *See* Lefcoe, *supra* note 49, at 859–66. There were questions about whether a big-box ban was subject to environmental review under CEQA.
240. *See Alameda County Sued by Wal-Mart*, L.A. TIMES, Jan. 27, 2004, at C3; Wal-Mart Stores, Inc. v. City of Turlock, 138 Cal. App. 4th 273, 284 (Cal. Ct. App. 5th Dist. 2006). Alameda County repealed its ban soon after the suit was filed. *See* Guy Ashley, *Supervisors Repeal "Big-Box" Ordinance: Alameda County Board Sends Matter Back to the Planning Commission*, CONTRA COSTA TIMES, Mar. 31, 2004, at A03.
241. *See* Jessica Garrison, *L.A. Council Votes to Restrict Superstores*, L.A. TIMES, Aug. 11, 2004, at A1.
242. *See* Gray-Barkan, *supra* note 3, at 37.
243. *See id.* at 38.
244. *See id.* at 38 ("[I]n March, . . . state Senator Richard Alarcon introduced a law (later vetoed by Governor Schwarzenegger) that required local officials to prepare a 'business impact report' (BIR) prior to the approval of big box stores over '100,000 square feet of gross buildable area' and with 'more than 10,000 square feet of floor space to be used for selling non-taxable merchandise.'").
245. Letter from Margo Feingold to Ricardo Icaza, President, UFCW Local 770 (May 14, 2004).

246. *See* David Greenberg, *Officials Propose New Tactics in Restrictions on Superstores*, L.A. DAILY BUS. J., May 24, 2004, at 7.
247. Telephone Interview with Margo Feinberg, *supra* note 90 (noting that the ordinance formally came from the city attorney's office, though the UFCW and LAANE had input into its content).
248. There was a question, raised by representatives from the Westfield mall, about the extent to which the ordinance would cover retail malls. This issue was disposed of by carving out malls from the Supercenter definition. Telephone Interview with Margo Feinberg, *supra* note 90.
249. Email from Margo Feinberg to Roxana Tynan, Re: idea! (June 23, 2004).
250. Telephone Interview with Margo Feinberg, *supra* note 90.
251. LAANE put out a flyer answering the question: "Why a Community Impact Report?" *See* LAANE, The Community Impact Report: A Proposed New Policy (2004).
252. Talking Points for Superstores Ordinance—General (2004).
253. Letter from Beth Steckler, Pol'y Dir., Livable Places, to Joseph Klein, President, L.A. City Plan. Comm'n (June 21, 2004).
254. Letter from Roxana Tynan to Los Angeles Plan. Comm'n re: Proposed Amendment (June 21, 2004).
255. *Id.*
256. *Id.*
257. *Id.*
258. Letter from Philip R. Recht, Mayer Brown Rowe & Maw, to Los Angeles City Plan. Comm'n (June 22, 2004).
259. See Letter from Gregory S. Pettis, Mayor Pro Tem, Cathedral City, Cal., to the Honorable Eric Garcetti and Ed Reyes, L.A. City Council (Aug. 4, 2002).
260. *See* Greene, *supra* note 98.
261. *See* Jessica Garrison, *City, Wal-Mart Step Up Hostilities*, L.A. TIMES, June 24, 2004, at B10.
262. *See* Jessica Garrison, *Los Angeles City Panels Back Plan to Hinder Wal-Mart Stores*, L.A. TIMES, Aug. 5, 2004, at B3; Garrison, *supra* note 241; *see also* Rene Sanchez, *L.A. City Council Considers Putting Lid on Big-Box Retailers*, WASH. POST, Aug. 15, 2004, at A02; Daniel B. Wood, *A New Twist in the Wal-Mart Wars*, CHRISTIAN SCI. MONITOR, Aug. 12, 2004, at USA2.
263. L.A., CAL., MUN. CODE § 12.24(U)(14)(a) (2004). The "Superstore" designation was meant to indicate that the ordinance applied to all big-box stores that met the statutory definition, not just Wal-Mart Supercenters.
264. *Id.* § 12.24(U)(14)(a).
265. *Id.* § 12.24(U)(14)(a).
266. *See* Lefcoe, *supra* note 49, at 845.
267. L.A., CAL., MUN. CODE § 12.24(U)(14)(d)(2)(i)-(ix).
268. *Id.* § 12.24(U)(14)(d)(2)(x).
269. *Id.* § 12.24(U)(14)(d)(3).
270. *Id.* § 12.24(U)(14)(d)(1).
271. Presentation by David Pettit, *supra* note 201.
272. *See* Goldman, *supra* note 96.
273. *See Inglewood Campaign: Ensuring Community Control over Development Decisions in Key Southland City*, LAANE, http://laane.org/projects/inglewood/index.html (last visited May 18, 2007).
274. *See* Ronald D. White, *Inglewood Delegation Tries to Air Concerns at Wal-Mart Conference*, L.A. TIMES, Apr. 6, 2005, at C2; Press Release, Coal. for a Better Inglewood, Inglewood, CA Leaders Urge Wal-Mart Chief to Invest in Employees and Communities—Not PR (Apr. 5, 2005).
275. Telephone Interview with Margo Feinberg, *supra* note 90.
276. *See* Goldman, *supra* note 96.

277. *See* Josh Grossberg, *Inglewood Law Scrutinizes Superstores: A New Ordinance Makes It Even More Difficult for Potential Big Boxes to Build by Requiring Them to Pay for an Economic Impact Analysis*, DAILY BREEZE, July 13, 2006, at A3. There were two differences of note in the Inglewood ordinance. First, it dealt with the possibility that Wal-Mart might attempt to circumvent the ordinance's minimum square footage requirement by building two smaller adjacent stores by prohibiting stores from being within three hundred feet of one another. *See When One Is Too Much, Build Two*, L.A. TIMES, Mar. 14, 2005, at C3; *cf.* OAKLAND, CAL., MUN. CODE § 17.09.040 (avoiding this problem by aggregating square footage of adjacent stores that share common management, check stands, warehouses, and distribution). Second, the Inglewood ordinance was written to apply retroactively if Wal-Mart succeeded in gaining approval before the ordinance formally passed.
278. *See* Dan Levine, *Wal-Mart's Big City Blues*, THE NATION, Nov. 24, 2003, http://www.thenation.com/doc/20031208/levine (last visited May 18, 2007).
279. *See Council Fails to Override Veto of Living Wage*, L.A. TIMES, Sept. 14, 2006, at A18; Chi. Living Wage Ordinance, http://www.wakeupwalmart.com/community/ChicagoLivingWage.pdf (last visited May 18, 2007).
280. *See* Michael Barbaro & Steven Greenhouse, *Wal-Mart Chief Writes Off New York*, N.Y. TIMES, Mar. 28, 2007, at C1.
281. *See* Alan Clendenning, *Wal-Mart Moves in on Brazil: Retail Giant Buys 140 Stores in Effort to Expand Globally*, HOUS. CHRON., Dec. 15, 2005, at 2; Evelyn Iritani, *Unions Go Abroad in Fight with Wal-Mart*, L.A. TIMES, Aug. 24, 2005, at A1.
282. *See* WAL-MART WATCH, *supra* note 150.
283. Presentation by Tracy Gray-Barkan, *supra* note 129.
284. *See* Cleeland & Vrana, *supra* note 10.
285. Through 2005, Wal-Mart had generally been able to capitalize on consumer support for its discount prices to win most of the local fights against Supercenters, prompting CEO Lee Scott to boast at Wal-Mart's 2005 Annual Shareholders Meeting that the company had won twenty-two out of twenty-seven California ballot contests. *See* WAL-MART WATCH, *supra* note 150, at 25. For a compilation of local big-box battles, *see* ADAM CLANTON & KERRY DUFFY, CALIFORNIA RESPONSES TO SUPERCENTER DEVELOPMENT: A SURVEY OF ORDINANCES, CASES AND ELECTIONS, HASTINGS COLLEGE OF LAW PUBLIC LAW RESEARCH INSTITUTE REPORT (Spring 2004).
286. Save Our Cmty. v. Rosemead, No. BS903012 (Cal. Sup. Ct. Apr. 22, 2005).
287. *See* Hector Becerra, *Wal-Mart Foes Face Setback in Rosemead; Opponents of a Planned Superstore Find Their Efforts Have Worked in the Discounter's Favor*, L.A. TIMES, Dec. 16, 2004, at A1. The Rosemead community–labor coalition subsequently tried to vote out pro-Wal-Mart city council members. *See* Jason Felch, *3 Candidates Hope to Rout Wal-Mart; Challengers in Rosemead's Election on Tuesday Seek to Unseat Incumbents Who Backed the Store's Move into the Community of 53,000*, L.A. TIMES, Mar. 6, 2005, at B1. This campaign, however, also failed. *See* Jason Felch, *Wal-Mart Foes Claim Win in Rosemead: Voters Oust Two Council Members Who Backed Chain, Which Still Plans to Build a Store There*, L.A. TIMES, Mar. 10, 2005, at B1.
288. *See* Hector Becerra, *Wal-Mart Wages Fight for Suburbs; As Efforts to Open Its Supercenters in Urban Areas Have Failed, the Retail Giant Finds Success in Rosemead. But Some Local Officials Face Recall*, L.A. TIMES, Sept. 19, 2006, at B1.
289. *See* Greene, *supra* note 98.
290. *See* GRAY-BARKAN, *supra* note 7, at 18.
291. Wal-Mart Stores, Inc. v. City of Turlock, 138 Cal. App. 4th 273 (2006). The reasoning, though not the holding, of the *Turlock* case was disapproved by the California Supreme Court in Hernandez v. City of Hanford, 41 Cal. 4th 279, 297 (2007).
292. *See Council Votes to Ban Wal-Mart*, L.A. TIMES, Nov. 30, 2006, at B4. The San Diego ban was pushed by the Joint Labor Management Committee. *See* Penni Crabtree, *Proposed Ordinance in San Diego Takes Aim at Wal-Mart Supercenters*, S.D. UNION-TRIBUNE, Nov. 20, 2003, at C1.

293. See Dave McKibben, *Santa Ana Prepares to Ban Supercenters*, L.A. TIMES, Jan. 18, 2007, at B5.
294. See Nancy Wride, *Big-Box Grocery Ban Is Headed for the Ballot Box in Long Beach*, L.A. TIMES, Jan. 8, 2007, at B3.
295. See Chris Thompson, *Hercules vs. Wal-Mart*, EAST BAY EXPRESS, Dec. 20, 2006, http://eastbayexpress.com/2006-12-20/news/hercules-vs-wal-mart (last visited May 18, 2007).
296. *See, e.g.*, Save Our Gateway v. Town of Paradise, 2007 WL 106189 (Cal. App. 3d Dist. Jan. 17, 2007).
297. Bakersfield Citizens for Local Control v. City of Bakersfield, 124 Cal. App. 4th 1184, 1207 (2004).
298. See Fred Alvarez, *No Big Boxes in Store for Ventura Group*, L.A. TIMES, Sept. 15, 2005, at B1.
299. See CITIZENS AGAINST WAL-MART IN MARINA, *Local Information*, http://www.nowalmartinmarina.org/local-information.htm (last visited July 2, 2007).
300. See Emili Vesilind, *Wal-Mart Foes Try to Slow California Growth*, WOMEN'S WEAR DAILY, Sept. 20, 2006, at 14; *see also* Marcus Kabel, *Wal-Mart to Slow Pace of Store Openings*, WASH. POST, Oct. 23, 2006, http://www.washingtonpost.com/wp-dyn/content/article/2006/10/23/AR2006102300332.html (last visited May 18, 2007).
301. See WAL-MART FACTS, *California Community Impact*, http://www.walmartfacts.com/StateByState/?id=5 (last visited July 2, 2007).
302. L.A., CAL., MUN. CODE § 181.00 (2005).
303. See Grocery and Retail Campaign, Alliance for Healthy and Responsible Grocery Stores (2007).
304. Press Release, All. for Healthy & Responsible Grocery Stores, Southern California Groups Ask TESCO to Put Promises in Writing as It Prepares to Open First U.S. Stores (Sept. 6, 2007); *see also* Jacob Adelman, *Tesco Makes First Foray into State Grocery Market*, SAN MATEO CTY. TIMES, Nov. 9, 2007; Cynthia E. Griffin, *Community Group Seeking Written Promises from Tesco*, OUR WKLY., Sept. 13, 2007.
305. Alliance for Healthy and Responsible Grocery Stores, Fact Sheet: The Supermarket Chains' Broken Promises to Poor and Minority Communities (2007).
306. *Id.*
307. Letter from Barack Obama to Tim Mason, CEO, Fresh & Easy Neighborhood Mkt., Inc. (Nov. 5, 2007).
308. Press Release, All. for Healthy & Responsible Grocery Stores, Hundreds of Activists Rally to Show TESCO Investors that Fresh & Easy Faces Powerful Resistance (Nov. 26, 2007); Press Release, All. for Healthy & Responsible Grocery Stores, Community Alliance Delivers Message to Andrew, Duke of York, Urging Fresh & Easy to Negotiate and Fulfill Its Promises (Feb. 7, 2008); *see also* Hannah Chu, *Britain's Prince Andrew Visits Fresh & Easy Opening*, LONG BEACH PRESS-TEL., Feb. 8, 2008, at 3A.
309. Blue Ribbon Commission on L.A.'s Grocery Industry and Community Health, Feeding Our Communities: A Call for Standards for Food Access and Job Quality in Los Angeles' Grocery Industry (July 2008).
310. Mot. No. 09-1251 by Councilman Ed Reyes, Planning & Land Use Management Committee (May 27, 2009).
311. Jacquelyn Ryan, *Downtown L.A. Greets Wal-Mart*, L.A. BUS. J., Feb. 27–Mar. 4, 2012, at 1.
312. Mot. No. 12-0382 by Councilman Ed Reyes, Planning & Land Use Management Committee (Mar. 16, 2002).
313. David Zahniser, *Council Votes Too Late to Block Chinatown Wal-Mart Project*, L.A. TIMES, Mar. 24, 2012, at AA1.
314. Ari Bloomekatz, *Thousands Rally against Wal-Mart in Chinatown*, L.A. TIMES, July 1, 2012, at A27.

315. *Judge Refuses to Block Wal-Mart Project in Chinatown*, L.A. NOW BLOG (Sept. 7, 2012), https://latimesblogs.latimes.com/lanow/2012/09/wal-mart-chinatown.html (last visited Apr. 12, 2019).
316. CITY OF LOS ANGELES, *Council File: 12-0382, New Formula Retail Uses in Chinatown*, https://cityclerk.lacity.org/lacityclerkconnect/index.cfm?fa=ccfi.viewrecord&cfnumber=12-0382 (last visited Apr. 12, 2019); *see also Judge Again Refuses to Block Wal-Mart Construction in L.A. Chinatown*, L.A. NOW BLOG (Nov. 12, 2012), https://latimesblogs.latimes.com/lanow/2012/11/judge-again-refuses-block-los-angeles-wal-mart-chinatown-construction.html (last visited Apr. 12, 2019).
317. Tiffany Hsu, *Protesters Greet Chinatown's New Wal-Mart Store*, L.A. TIMES, Sept. 14, 2013, at B2.
318. Samantha Masunaga, *Wal-Mart to Close 269 Stores, Including 154 in the U.S. and 9 in California*, L.A. TIMES, Jan. 15, 2016.
319. *See* Michael McCann & Jeffrey Dudas, *Retrenchment ... and Resurgence? Mapping the Changing Context of Movement Lawyering in the United States*, *in* CAUSE LAWYERS AND SOCIAL MOVEMENTS 37 (Austin Sarat & Stuart Scheingold eds., 2006).
320. To the extent that the Superstores Ordinance operated to keep Wal-Mart out altogether, the distinction between hard and soft law may be of little practical use in this context.
321. *See* JULIAN GROSS, GREG LEROY & MADELINE JANIS-APARICIO, COMMUNITY BENEFITS AGREEMENTS: MAKING DEVELOPMENT PROJECTS ACCOUNTABLE (Good Jobs First and the California Partnership for Working Families 2005).
322. Telephone Interview with Margo Feinberg, *supra* note 90.
323. *See* Steven Greenhouse, *Opponents of Wal-Mart to Coordinate Efforts*, N.Y. TIMES, Apr. 3, 2005, at A20.
324. Telephone Interview with Margo Feinberg, *supra* note 90.
325. *See* GRAY-BARKAN, *supra* note 7. The Advancement Project, a national social justice organization, also sought to promote anti-Wal-Mart activism through developing and disseminating a case study on Inglewood. *See* Elliot Petty, *The People vs. Wal-Mart: Strategies That Work*, ADVANCEMENT PROJECT, NL VOL. 12 CASE STUDIES (July 15, 2005).
326. The Partnership for Working Families' selection of target cities for anti-Wal-Mart campaigns was based on established criteria, including the presence of a strong labor board, receptive local governmental officials, and significant communities of color, whose members were viewed as sympathetic to new labor organizing campaigns.
327. Retail Indus. Leaders Assoc. v. Fielder, 435 F. Supp. 2d 481 (D. Md. 2006) (holding Maryland Fair Share Act preempted by ERISA); *see also* Edward A. Zelinsky, *Maryland's "Wal-Mart" Act: Policy and Preemption*, 28 CARDOZO L. REV. 847 (2006).
328. *See* William H. Simon, *Solving Problems vs. Claiming Rights: The Pragmatist Challenge to Legal Liberalism*, 46 WM. & MARY L. REV. 127, 147–57 (2004).
329. Legal mobilization in Inglewood conforms to that described by Michael McCann and Helena Silverstein in their analysis of the pay equity and animal rights movements, in which they found that lawyers "*did not view litigation as an exclusive end in itself*" but instead were "*very committed to encouraging, enhancing, and supplementing*" movement activity. *See* Michael McCann & Helena Silverstein, *Rethinking Law's "Allurements": A Relational Analysis of Social Movement Lawyers in the United States*, *in* CAUSE LAWYERING: POLITICAL COMMITMENTS AND PROFESSIONAL RESPONSIBILITIES 261, 269 (Austin Sarat & Stuart Scheingold eds., 1998).
330. *See* Abigail Goldman, *Grocers Lose Their Wal-Mart Leverage*, L.A. TIMES, Apr. 12, 2007, at C1.
331. *See* Jerry Hirsch, *Stater May End Two-Tier Pay*, L.A. TIMES, Jan. 13, 2007, at C1.
332. *See* Jerry Hirsch, *A Change in Strategy; Scarred by a Long Grocery Work Stoppage in 2003–04, Union Leaders Plan this Time Around to Negotiate with One Supermarket Chain at a Time*, L.A. TIMES, Sept. 24, 2006, at C1; Jeremy Hirsch, *Union to Seek Strike Vote from Albertsons Workers*, L.A. TIMES, Mar. 21, 2007, at C3.
333. Jerry Hirsh, *Grocery Union Fought for Unity*, L.A. TIMES, July 24, 2007, at C1.

334. *See* INDUSTRY AT A CROSSROADS, *supra* note 6, at 7.
335. *See* Scott L. Cummings, *The Politics of Pro Bono*, 52 UCLA L. REV. 1 (2004).
336. *See* STUART A. SCHEINGOLD & AUSTIN SARAT, SOMETHING TO BELIEVE IN: POLITICS, PROFESSIONALISM, AND CAUSE LAWYERING 3 (2004) ("At its core, cause lawyering is about using legal skills to pursue ends and ideals that transcend client service—be those ideals social, cultural, political, economic or, indeed, legal.").
337. Telephone Interview with Jan Chatten-Brown, *supra* note 198.
338. Telephone Interview with David Pettit, *supra* note 202.
339. Interview with Sean Hecht, *supra* note 205.
340. *Id.*
341. *Id.*
342. *See* Michael Barbaro, *Wal-Mart to Expand Health Plan for Workers*, N.Y. TIMES, Oct. 24, 2005, at C1; Michael Barbaro & Steven Greenhouse, *Wal-Mart Says Thank You to Workers*, N.Y. TIMES, Dec. 4, 2006, at C1.
343. *See* Michael Barbaro, *A New Weapon for Wal-Mart: A War Room*, N.Y. TIMES, Nov. 1, 2005, at A1; Michael Barbaro, *Wal-Mart Enlists Bloggers in Its P.R. Campaign*, N.Y. TIMES, Mar. 7, 2006, at C1.
344. *See* Abigail Goldman, *Wal-Mart Goes "Green,"* L.A. TIMES, Nov. 13, 2006, at C1.
345. *See* Michael Barbaro, *Wal-Mart to Offer Help Near Urban Stores*, N.Y. TIMES, Apr. 4, 2006, at C1.
346. *See* Austin Sarat & Stuart Scheingold, *Cause Lawyering and the Reproduction of Professional Authority: An Introduction*, *in* CAUSE LAWYERING, *supra* note 329, at 3; *cf.* William H. Simon, *The Ideology of Advocacy*, 1978 WIS. L. REV. 30 (1978).
347. Telephone Interview with David Pettit, *supra* note 202.
348. *See* DAVID A. BINDER ET AL., LAWYERS AS COUNSELORS: A CLIENT-CENTERED APPROACH (2nd ed. 2004).
349. Telephone Interview with David Pettit, *supra* note 202.
350. Telephone Interview with Margo Feinberg, *supra* note 90.
351. *See* Model Rule of Prof'l Conduct r. 1.7 (2004).
352. *See* Stephen Ellman, *Client-Centeredness Multiplied: Individual Autonomy and Collective Mobilization in Public Interest Lawyers' Representation of Groups*, 78 VA. L. REV. 1103 (1992).
353. LAANE paid $100,000 for Chatten-Brown's services by raising $85,000 from small donors and some unions through an Internet campaign and taking $15,000 from its general operating funds.
354. Telephone Interview with Jan Chatten-Brown, *supra* note 198.
355. Email from David Pettit, Partner, Caldwell Leslie Proctor & Pettit, to Scott Cummings, Professor of Law, UCLA Sch. of Law (Mar. 7, 2007).
356. Telephone Interview with Margo Feinberg, *supra* note 90.
357. Interview with Sean Hecht, *supra* note 205.
358. *See* GRAY-BARKAN, *supra* note 7, at 10, 13.

Chapter 6

1. See EDNA BONACICH & JAKE B. WILSON, GETTING THE GOODS: PORTS, LABOR, AND THE LOGISTICS REVOLUTION 45 (2008).
2. *Id.* (noting that, as of 2004, the two ports combined were the third largest in the world). As of 2011, the Port of Los Angeles was the sixteenth largest in the world by container volume, while the Port of Long Beach was ranked twenty-first; combined, they formed the eighth largest port in the world. Marsha Salisbury, *The JOC Top 50 World Container Ports*, J. COM., Aug. 20–27, 2012, at 24, 26.
3. *See* STEVEN P. ERIE, GLOBALIZING L.A.: TRADE, INFRASTRUCTURE, AND REGIONAL DEVELOPMENT 47 (2004). *See generally* BD. OF HARBOR COMM'RS, THE PORT OF LOS ANGELES 23–38 (1913) (providing a history of the Port of Los Angeles); CHARLES

F. QUEENAN, THE PORT OF LOS ANGELES: FROM WILDERNESS TO WORLD PORT 27–56 (1983) (discussing the growth and evolving role of the Port of Los Angeles between the late nineteenth and early twentieth centuries).
4. See CHARLES F. QUEENAN, LONG BEACH AND LOS ANGELES: A TALE OF TWO PORTS 13–16 (1986).
5. See REMI A. NADEAU, CITY-MAKERS: THE MEN WHO TRANSFORMED LOS ANGELES FROM VILLAGE TO METROPOLIS DURING THE FIRST GREAT BOOM, 1868–76, at 24 (1948).
6. QUEENAN, *supra* note 4, at 26.
7. NADEAU, *supra* note 5, at 78.
8. ERIE, *supra* note 3, at 49.
9. *Id.* at 54.
10. ROBERT M. FOGELSON, THE FRAGMENTED METROPOLOIS: LOS ANGELES, 1850–1930, at 114–15 (1967).
11. See ERIE, *supra* note 3, at 65.
12. FOGELSON, *supra* note 10, at 115.
13. See QUEENAN, *supra* note 4, at 63; *see also Fleming Tells of Campaign to Secure Harbor*, L.A. HERALD, Aug. 25, 1909, at 1.
14. L.A., CAL., CITY CHARTER art. XVI, § 176 (1911) (amended 1913). The proprietary nature of the Port of Los Angeles is atypical: Only 17% of U.S. ports are governed by municipal authorities and of the eight ports in the largest American cities, Los Angeles's is the only one under city control. See ERIE, *supra* note 3, at 31.
15. FOGELSON, *supra* note 10, at 119.
16. ERIE, *supra* note 3, at 71; QUEENAN, *supra* note 4, at 82.
17. ERIE, *supra* note 3, at 72.
18. QUEENAN, *supra* note 4, at 89. There was some cooperation between the ports, most crucially the joint establishment of the Harbor Belt Line Railroad in 1929, which linked multiple harbor rail lines to permit seamless rail travel around the two port complexes. *Id.* at 92.
19. Shipping Act, ch. 451, §§ 3, 14–22, 39 Stat. 728, 729, 733–36 (1916) (repealed in part and amended in part 1984).
20. Interstate Commerce Act, ch. 104, 24 Stat. 379 (1887).
21. Motor Carrier Act, ch. 498, 49 Stat. 543 (1935).
22. See Fred Thompson III, Note, *Challenges to the Legality of Minibridge Transportation Systems*, 1978 DUKE L.J. 1233, 1236–37 (1978).
23. See Wayne K. Talley, *Wage Differentials of Intermodal Transportation Carriers and Ports: Deregulation Versus Regulation*, 3 REV. NETWORK ECON. 207, 211–12 (2004).
24. See QUEENAN, *supra* note 4, at 96.
25. *See id.*
26. BONACICH & WILSON, *supra* note 1, at 173–74.
27. RUTH MILKMAN, L.A. STORY: IMMIGRANT WORKERS AND THE FUTURE OF THE U.S. LABOR MOVEMENT 49 (2006).
28. *Id.* at 51. Michael Belzer reported that in the 1970s, the trucking industry was almost completely under union contract. MICHAEL H. BELZER, SWEATSHOPS ON WHEELS: WINNERS AND LOSERS IN TRUCKING DEREGULATION 107 (2000).
29. BONACICH & WILSON, *supra* note 1, at 47.
30. *Id.* at 51.
31. Dan Weikel, *Freighters Enter the Age of the Mega-Ship*, L.A. TIMES, June 15, 1999, at A1.
32. WAYNE K. TALLEY, PORT ECONOMICS 150 (2009).
33. BONACICH & WILSON, *supra* note 1, at 50–54.
34. QUEENAN, *supra* note 4, at 147, 149; *see also* BONACICH & WILSON, *supra* note 1, at 47.
35. QUEENAN, *supra* note 4, at 147.
36. *See id.* at 149.
37. See ERIE, *supra* note 3, at 22.

38. BONACICH & WILSON, *supra* note 1, at 47.
39. *See* Daryl Kelley, *Edgerton on Junket with Port Officials to Asia*, L.A. TIMES, June 27, 1985, at LB8. Politicians did outreach to other regions, such as Latin America, to promote harbor trade. *See The Region*, L.A. TIMES, Oct. 2, 1985, http://articles.latimes.com/1985-10-02/news/mn-16051_1_los-angeles-mayor-tom-bradley (last visited June 14, 2017).
40. BELZER, *supra* note 28, at 64–65.
41. EDWARD JAMES TAAFFE ET AL., GEOGRAPHY OF TRANSPORTATION 161 (1996).
42. Talley, *supra* note 23, at 211–12.
43. *Id.* at 212, 214.
44. QUEENAN, *supra* note 4, at 156–57; *see also* Tim Waters, *Railhead Is Competitive Edge for Port*, L.A. TIMES, Nov. 23, 1986, at SB1 ("The new rail facility was financed primarily through the sale of $53.9 million in bonds that will be paid back with money collected by a $30-per-container gate charge that shippers must pay."). The ICTF is now operated by UP; the other major rail line, BNSF, does not use the ICTF, but rather has its Los Angeles Intermodal Facility downtown at Hobart. BONACICH & WILSON, *supra* note 1, at 108. In May 2013, the Los Angeles City Council approved the Southern California International Gateway, a new BNSF rail yard in Wilmington, adjacent to one of the city's major high schools. Dan Weikel, *Rail Yard for Port Complex OKd*, L.A. TIMES, May 9, 2013, at AA3. "The 153-acre project would be capable of handling up to 2.8 million 20-foot shipping containers a year by 2035 and 8,200 trucks a day." *Id.* Public officials and advocates disputed its environmental impact, with proponents claiming that it would reduce the number of truck trips each year by one million, while opponents argued that overall emissions would increase and local community residents would be disproportionately affected. *Id.*
45. BONACICH & WILSON, *supra* note 1, at 108; ERIE, *supra* note 3, at 93.
46. MYRA L. FRANK & ASSOCS., INC., ALAMEDA CORRIDOR: ENVIRONMENTAL IMPACT REPORT S-1 (1993); *see also* Nona Liegeois et al., *Helping Low-Income People Get Decent Jobs: One Legal Services Program's Approach*, 33 CLEARINGHOUSE REV. 279, 289 (1999).
47. Liegeois et al., *supra* note 46, at 289.
48. ERIE, *supra* note 3, at 147; *see also* Daryl Kelley, *L.B. Port Looks to New Growth Spurt in 1985: Harbor's 35-Year Plan Will Expand Size to Match Its Increasing Cargo*, L.A. TIMES, Jan. 6, 1985, at SE1 ("The Port of Long Beach, straining at its seams after two decades of robust growth, is looking to 1985 to complete $150 million in wharf, road and rail construction and to firm up another $400 million in building for 1986.").
49. ERIE, *supra* note 3, at 92; *see also* Dean Murphy, *Ports Cheer Promising Major Growth of Harbor*, L.A. TIMES, Oct. 26, 1986, at SB1.
50. ERIE, *supra* note 3, at 119–23.
51. *Id.* at 141 tbl.5.4.
52. BONACICH & WILSON, *supra* note 1, at 45.
53. Tim Waters, *Activity Rises Sharply at Port of Los Angeles*, L.A. TIMES, Sept. 19, 1985, at SD C1 ("The Port of Los Angeles lured six steamship companies from berths at rival Long Beach last year and, as a result, handled a third more general cargo. According to figures released this week, 22.2 million metric tons of general cargo—that is, containerized cargo and all loose cargo except liquid or dry bulk—passed through the Los Angeles port during the 12 months ended June 30, a 34.5% increase from the 16.5 million tons the year before.").
54. Edmund Newton, *The Ship Has Come In: Long Beach Steams Past L.A. to Become Nation's No. 1 Port*, L.A. TIMES, Apr. 23, 1995, at D1.
55. ERIE, *supra* note 3, at 142–43.
56. BONACICH & WILSON, *supra* note 1, at 57 ("Ports used to invest mainly for the benefit of their region. Now they are being asked to invest for the benefit of the entire country, without the security of knowing that the investment will pay off. Even if a port is successful, the regions that are nearby may have to bear additional costs on top of the financial ones, such as congestion and pollution.").

57. Erie, *supra* note 3, at 109; *see also* Mark Gladstone & Ralph Frammolino, *Funds of San Diego, Other Port Districts Under Siege*, L.A. Times, July 8, 1992, at A1.
58. Erie, *supra* note 3, at 126–29.
59. Jean-Paul Rodrigue et al., The Geography of Transport Systems 90, 259 (2009).
60. The port, in an effort to mitigate the negative impact of its facilities in San Pedro, created the Cabrillo Beach Recreational Complex on the peninsula's southern tip, containing a park, picnic area, bird sanctuary, and marina. Queenan, *supra* note 4, at 157. Developers built up the surrounding area, which included an $18 million, 216-room hotel two blocks from the port. *$18-Million Hotel Planned in San Pedro*, L.A. Times, Nov. 3, 1985, at H26.
61. *See Mapping L.A., San Pedro*, L.A. Times, http://projects.latimes.com/mapping-la/neighborhoods/neighborhood/sanpedro/?q=San+Pedro%2C+Los+Angeles%2C+CA%2C+USA&lat=33.7360619&lng=-118.2922461&g=Geocodify (last visited Oct. 2, 2013).
62. *Mapping L.A., Wilmington*, L.A. Times, http://projects.latimes.com/mapping-la/neighborhoods/neighborhood/wilmington/?q=Wilmington%2C+CA%2C+USA&lat=33.7857948&lng=118.2643567&g=Geocodify (last visited Oct. 2, 2013).
63. *See generally* Bonacich & Wilson, *supra* note 1, at 159–240; Arin Dube et al., On the Waterfront and Beyond: Technology and the Changing Nature of Cargo-Related Employment in the West Coast (2004) (unpublished manuscript).
64. David Jaffee, Kinks in the Intermodal Supply Chain: Longshore Workers and Drayage Drivers 14 (June 2010) (unpublished manuscript), https://www.unf.edu/uploadedFiles/aa/coas/cci/ports/REPORT_Port%20Paper%2010-%20SASE-Kinks%20in%20the%20Intermodal%20Supply%20Chain.pdf (last visited Nov. 11, 2019).
65. Talley, *supra* note 23, at 216.
66. David Bensman, *Port Trucking Down the Low Road: A Sad Story of Deregulation*, Dēmos 3 (2009), http://www.demos.org/sites/default/files/publications/Port%20Trucking%20Down%20the%20Low%20Road.pdf (last visited June 14, 2017).
67. Bonacich & Wilson, *supra* note 1, at 209–10.
68. *Id.* at 211–12.
69. Contracting out was part of an overall employer strategy to promote labor flexibility. Jaffee, *supra* note 64, at 11.
70. Despite the "independent" designation, researchers suggested that contract relationships between trucking companies and drivers were not that distinct from the preregulatory employment system. *See* Rebecca Smith et al., The Big Rig: Poverty, Pollution, and the Misclassification of Truck Drivers at America's Ports 26 (2010) (concluding that "[t]rucking companies exert a high degree of control over the work activities of the truck drivers"); *see also* Belzer, *supra* note 28, at 37; Bensman, *supra* note 66, at 11–12. David Jaffee noted that independent-contractor drivers were typically prevented from working for more than one company. Jaffee, *supra* note 64, at 17. Ruth Milkman and Kent Wong found that drivers relied on companies to finance the acquisition of trucks and insurance. Ruth Milkman & Kent Wong, *Organizing Immigrant Workers: Case Studies from Southern California*, *in* Rekindling the Movement: Labor's Quest for Relevance in the 21st Century 99 (Lowell Turner, Harry C. Katz & Richard W. Hurd eds., 2001).
71. Jaffee, *supra* note 64, at 17.
72. Bonacich & Wilson, *supra* note 1, at 104.
73. *See, e.g.*, Columbia River Packers Ass'n v. Hinton, 315 U.S. 143 (1942); *see generally*, *Employee Bargaining Power Under the Norris-LaGuardia Act: The Independent Contractor Problem*, 67 Yale L.J. 98 (1957) (arguing that there should be exceptions to the ban on organizing for independent contractors). On the challenges to unionization after deregulation, *see* Michael H. Belzer, *Collective Bargaining After Deregulation: Do the Teamsters Still Count?*, 48 Indus. & Lab. Rel. Rev. 636 (1995).
74. *See, e.g.*, Ronald D. White, *The Ports' Short-Haul Truckers Endure Long Hours, High Costs*, L.A. Times, Nov. 21, 2005, at C1.

75. Dale L. Belman & Kristen A. Monaco, *The Effects of Deregulation, De-Unionization, Technology, and Human Capital on the Work and Work Lives of Truck Drivers*, 54 INDUS. & LAB. REL. REV. 502, 502 (2001).
76. Jaffee, *supra* note 64, at 18.
77. Bensman, *supra* note 66, at 1.
78. Some studies of the overall industry, not just the Los Angeles and Long Beach ports, put the wage rate much lower. *See* Ted Prince, *Endangered Species*, J. COM. 12, 13 (2005); *see also* Edna Bonacich, *Pulling the Plug: Labor and the Global Supply Chain*, 12 NEW LAB. F. 41, 46 (2003). Studies of drivers at other ports have found similarly low pay. *See, e.g.*, EAST BAY ALLIANCE FOR A SUSTAINABLE ECONOMY, TAKING THE LOW ROAD: HOW INDEPENDENT CONTRACTING AT THE PORT OF OAKLAND ENDANGERS PUBLIC HEALTH, TRUCK DRIVERS & ECONOMIC GROWTH (2007), http://www.workingeastbay.orgdownloads/Coalition%20Port%20Trucking%20Report.pdf (last visited June 14, 2017) (finding that Oakland drivers made $10.69 per hour on average and that one-quarter made less than $7.64 per hour).
79. KRISTEN MONACO, INCENTIVIZING TRUCK RETROFITTING IN PORT DRAYAGE: A STUDY OF DRIVERS AT THE PORTS OF LOS ANGELES AND LONG BEACH 18–19 (2008) (finding that 91.24% of port truck drivers were Hispanic and 44% were noncitizens). Edna Bonacich and Jake Wilson cited sources estimating that 90% of port truckers were from Central America, while the remainder were Mexican. BONACICH & WILSON, *supra* note 1, at 218.
80. BONACICH & WILSON, *supra* note 1, at 212 (quoting Ernesto Nevarez, a port trucking activist).
81. *Id.*
82. *Id.* at 212–13.
83. *Id.*
84. *Id.* at 223–24 (noting also that some longshoremen viewed immigrants as responsible for the labor movement's decline).
85. *See* Bensman, *supra* note 66, at 8–10.
86. *See id.* at 10; *see also* ANTOINE FRÉMONT, EMPIRICAL EVIDENCE FOR INTEGRATION AND DISINTEGRATION OF MARITIME SHIPPING, PORT AND LOGISTICS ACTIVITIES (2009) (OECD/ITF Joint Transport Research Centre Discussion Paper); David Bensman, Barriers to Innovation in Global Logistics: The Deregulated Port Trucking Sector (2009) (unpublished presentation to the Industry Studies Association).
87. One study found that, for each trip, port truck drivers spent more time waiting than driving. Kristen Monaco & Lisa Grobar, A Study of Drayage at the Ports of Los Angeles and Long Beach 11 (2005) (unpublished manuscript).
88. Jaffee, *supra* note 64, at 24.
89. *Id.* at 9.
90. *See* Deborah Schoch, *Study Details Port Pollution Threat*, L.A. TIMES, Mar. 22, 2004, at C1.
91. SMITH ET AL., *supra* note 70, at 10 (quoting Art Marroquin, *Judge Rules Port of L.A. Can Fully Implement Clean Trucks Program*, DAILY BREEZE, Aug. 27, 2010, https://www.dailybreeze.com/2010/08/26/judge-rules-port-of-la-can-fully-implement-clean-trucks-program/amp/ (last visited Nov. 11, 2019). In 2008, Monaco reported that the median model year of trucks driven by independent contractors in Los Angeles was 1995–1996. MONACO, *supra* note 79, at 12. The Port of Los Angeles's Deputy Executive Director of Operations John Holmes described the market this way: "Generally, big companies like Swift would own trucks for 5 years, then sell to regional carriers which would own them for a few years, then the trucks would be sold into the drayage market." Interview with John Holmes, Deputy Exec. Dir., Port of L.A. (July 19, 2013). A survey commissioned by the ports in 2007 found that the "vast majority of drivers engaged in Port drayage" were independent owner operators and that the average truck was from 1994. CGR MGMT. CONSULTANTS, A SURVEY OF DRAYAGE DRIVERS SERVING THE SAN PEDRO BAY PORTS 1 (2007).

92. *See, e.g.,* Diane Bailey et al., *Driving on Fumes: Truck Drivers Face Elevated Health Risks from Diesel Pollution,* 8 tbl.1, NAT. RES. DEF. COUNCIL, http://www.nrdc.org/health/effects/driving/driving.pdf (last visited June 14, 2017).
93. *Id.* at 4.
94. PINGKUAN DI, DIESEL PARTICULATE MATTER EXPOSURE ASSESSMENT STUDY FOR THE PORTS OF LOS ANGELES AND LONG BEACH: FINAL REPORT 2 (2006) (Report for the California Environmental Protection Agency, Air Resources Board), http://www.arb.ca.gov/ports/marinevess/documents/portstudy0406.pdf (last visited June 14, 2017).
95. *Id.*
96. 49 U.S.C. § 14501 (2012).
97. Californians for Safe & Competitive Dump Truck Transp. v. Mendonca, 152 F.3d 1184, 1187 (9th Cir. 1998).
98. 49 U.S.C. § 14501(c)(1).
99. Whether federal law is determined to preempt a specific local act depends not just on the scope of the federal law, but also on the nature of the local act itself. *See* Michael Burger, *"It's Not Easy Being Green": Local Initiatives, Preemption Problems, and the Market Participant Exception,* 78 U. CIN. L. REV. 835, 843–44 (2010).
100. Wis. Dep't of Indus., Lab. & Hum. Rel. v. Gould Inc., 475 U.S. 282, 289 (1986).
101. Bldg. & Constr. Trades Council v. Assoc. Builders & Contractors of Mass./R.I., Inc., 507 U.S. 218, 227 (1993). The market participant doctrine had its origins in dormant commerce clauses cases, where it was used to permit some local action impacting interstate commerce if done for proprietary reasons. *See generally* Hughes v. Alexandria Scrap Corp., 426 U.S. 794 (1976). Although the market participant doctrine developed to permit state lawmaking, some jurisdictions, like the Ninth Circuit, have applied the exception to municipal government entities as well. *See* Big Cty. Foods, Inc. v. Bd. of Educ. 952 F.2d 1173, 1178–79 (9th Cir. 1992).
102. *See* Engine Mfrs. Ass'n v. S. Coast Air Quality Mgmt. Dist., 498 F.3d 1031, 1041 (9th Cir. 2007).
103. Engine Mfrs. Ass'n v. S. Coast Air Quality Mgmt. Dist., 541 U.S. 246 (2004). The SCAQMD's jurisdiction is over the South Coast Air Basin, which includes most of Los Angeles County, all of Orange County, and parts of San Bernardino and Riverside counties.
104. Engine Mfrs. Ass'n v. S. Coast Air Quality Mgmt. Dist., No. Cv00-09065FMC(BQRX), 2005 WL 1163437, at *12 (C.D. Cal. May 5, 2005), *aff'd* Engine Mfrs. Ass'n v. South Coast Air Quality Mgmt. Dist., 498 F.3d 1031, 1041 (9th Cir. 2007).
105. Tocher v. City of Santa Ana, 219 F.3d 1040 (9th Cir. 2000), *abrogated on other grounds by* City of Columbus v. Ours Garage & Wrecker Serv., Inc., 536 U.S. 424 (2002) (reversing that part of *Tocher* which held that a state may not delegate its regulatory authority to a municipality under the FAAAA's safety exception).
106. *See* Donna St. George, *Wilmington: Community of Contradictions,* L.A. TIMES, Oct. 6, 1985, at SB1.
107. *Id.*
108. *See* Dean Murphy, *Port in a Storm: Harbor Profits Are Rising, but So Are Neighbors' Complaints,* L.A. TIMES, Nov. 27, 1987, at SB12.
109. Donna St. George, *Wilmington—Battered but Not Broken: Pride and Community Spirit Persevere Despite Area's Problems,* L.A. TIMES, Oct. 10, 1985, at SB1. The *Los Angeles Times* reported that "[a]bout 45% of Wilmington's 11,518 dwelling units are owner-occupied homes"; "the area remains largely blue-collar and union-oriented, with 63% of its population employed as laborers and 12 union halls located in the community"; and "Latinos now make up at least 67% of Wilmington's population, compared to 27.5% citywide." The remaining population was 22% Anglo, 8% Asian and American Indian, and 4% black. Unemployment stood at 8%. Undocumented immigrants were estimated at 10%–20% of the population. *Id.*
110. Murphy, *supra* note 108.

111. *See* Dean Murphy, *As Wilmington Suspected, Study Finds Port Gets More Containers Than It Ships*, L.A. TIMES, Nov. 16, 1989, at 3.
112. Sheryl Stolberg, *End to Traffic Sought: Wilmington Residents Hungry for Truck Stop*, L.A. TIMES, Oct. 18, 1987, at SB1.
113. *Id.*
114. Sheryl Stolberg, *Cement Plant OKd Despite Traffic Fear*, L.A. TIMES, Nov. 19, 1987, at SE14; Murphy, *supra* note 108.
115. Greg Krikorian, *Plan to Expand Ports Meets with Public Criticism*, L.A. TIMES, Oct. 11, 1990, at B3 (South Bay ed.).
116. *Id.*
117. Murphy, *supra* note 108.
118. *Id.*
119. *Id.* ("When completed in the next few years, the new development will provide slips for more than 3,000 private boats and will include a hotel, a youth aquatics camp, restaurants, shops, offices, parks, a salt marsh and bicycle paths.").
120. St. George, *supra* note 106; *see also* Sheryl Stolberg, *L.A. Port's New Terminal Ready for Cruise Ships, Era of Growth*, L.A. TIMES, Apr. 29, 1988, at E1.
121. *See* Eric Malnic, *Harbor Area Secession Drive Nears Key Number of Backers*, L.A. TIMES, July 3, 1999, at B5. Wilmington had joined an earlier effort by westside communities to secede in 1990. Greg Krikorian, *Grass-Roots Unrest; Wilmington, Westside Areas to Join in Bid to Secede from L.A.*, L.A. TIMES, Oct. 3, 1990, at B3 (South Bay ed.).
122. *See* Sharon Bernstein, *Report Bolsters Bid to Secede*, L.A. TIMES, Mar. 7, 2002, at B1.
123. Dan Weikel, *Port Officials Extend Olive Branch to Communities*, L.A. TIMES, Jan. 11, 2001, at B1.
124. Matea Gold & Patrick McGreevy, *Hahn, Council Woo Harbor Area with Visit*, L.A. TIMES, Dec. 13, 2001, at B3. In August 2001, it was revealed that the Harbor Commission had scaled back its contract with the community relations firm hired to promote a better community partnership because the firm was too supportive of community concerns. Louis Sahagun, *Local Storm Clouds Brew over Port*, L.A. TIMES, Aug. 10, 2001, at B4.
125. Patrick McGreevy, *New Slant on Harbor Area Bottom Line*, L.A. TIMES, June 10, 2001, at B1.
126. Kristina Sauerwein, *Fever for Secession in Harbor Area Cools*, L.A. TIMES, Sept. 15, 2002, at B3; *see also* Patrick McGreevy, *Harbor Cityhood Found Unfeasible*, L.A. TIMES, Apr. 26, 2001, at B1; McGreevy, *supra* note 125.
127. Sharon Bernstein, *Panel Urges Port Remain with L.A.*, L.A. TIMES, Apr. 10, 2002, at B5.
128. Dan Weikel, *Barrier Rift*, L.A. TIMES, Jan. 30, 2001, at B1.
129. *See* Telephone Interview with Jesse Marquez, Exec. Dir., Coal. for a Safe Env't (May 20, 2013).
130. Weikel, *supra* note 128, at B4.
131. *See* Telephone Interview with Jesse Marquez, *supra* note 129.
132. *Id.*
133. *Id.*
134. *Id.*
135. *Id.*
136. *See* Louis Sahagun, *Evictions Loom for Many in Wilmington's "Third World,"* L.A. TIMES, May 13, 2001, at B1.
137. Telephone Interview with Angelo Logan, Co-Dir., East Yard Communities for Envtl. Just. (May 1, 2013).
138. *Id.*
139. *Id.*
140. *Id.*
141. *Id.*
142. *Id.*
143. *Id.*
144. *Id.*

145. BONACICH & WILSON, *supra* note 1, at 210–11.
146. James Peoples, *Deregulation and the Labor Market*, 12 J. ECON. PERSP. 111, 112 (1998).
147. BONACICH & WILSON, *supra* note 1, at 211.
148. *See* Chris Woodyard, *Truckers Told to Avoid Violence in Port Strike*, L.A. TIMES, July 22, 1988, at D1 (stating that the union's goal was to get companies to agree to talks with container terminals to decrease wait times of up to eight hours; the union asked the Federal Maritime Commission to make terminals pay $68 per hour of wait time).
149. BONACICH & WILSON, *supra* note 1, at 219.
150. *See* Anthony Millican, *IRS Probing Trucking Companies: Possible Reclassification of Drivers as Employees Could Cost Area Firms Millions*, L.A. TIMES, Aug. 29, 1991, at B3.
151. *Id.*
152. *See* Jesus Sanchez, *Wildcat Strike Idles Cargo at L.A.-Area Ports*, L.A. TIMES, Nov. 13, 1993, at D1.
153. MILKMAN, *supra* note 27, at 179.
154. *Id.*
155. *Id.*
156. *Id.* Some insiders speculated that the alliance between the CWA and the truckers may have been orchestrated by the ILWU to keep the Teamsters out of the harbor, which is the ILWU's base. BONACICH & WILSON, *supra* note 1, at 220.
157. MILKMAN, *supra* note 27, at 179–80.
158. *Court Order Limits Picketing of Truckers at Port Gates*, L.A. TIMES, May 9, 1996, at B5.
159. MILKMAN, *supra* note 27, at 180–81.
160. *Id.* at 181.
161. Jeff Leeds, *Long Beach, L.A. Ports Face Crisis in Labor Dispute*, L.A. TIMES, May 8, 1996, at A1.
162. MILKMAN, *supra* note 27, at 182.
163. *Id.* at 183–84.
164. Milkman & Wong, *supra* note 70, at 101–02. Ruth Milkman and Kent Wong noted that as a result of the campaign, the ILWU was able to win the right to represent intra-harbor truckers. *Id.* at 129.
165. BONACICH & WILSON, *supra* note 1, at 222.
166. MILKMAN, *supra* note 27, at 181.
167. Jeff Leeds, *Transport Firms Sued on Behalf of Port Truck Drivers*, L.A. TIMES, July 12, 1996, at B3.
168. *Id.* In addition to claims under the Labor Code, the drivers also brought claims for unfair business practices under section 17200 of the California Business and Professions Code. Albillo v. Intermodal Container Servs., Inc., 8 Cal. Rptr. 3d 350, 354 (Cal. Ct. App. 2003).
169. Leeds, *supra* note 167.
170. *Id.*
171. *Id.* ("Cardoza, 34, said he grossed $42,000 last year, but that deductions and the costs of maintaining the truck left him with only $12,000. With his daughters Samantha, 3, and Jennifer, 11, at his feet, he told reporters that he has been borrowing money from family members to make ends meet.").
172. *Albillo*, 8 Cal. Rptr. 3d at 353.
173. *Id.*
174. *Id.* at 354.
175. *Id.* at 362.
176. MILKMAN, *supra* note 27, at 184.
177. Nancy Cleeland, *Harbor Drivers Independent, Panel Says*, L.A. TIMES, Jan. 19, 2000, at C2.
178. Telephone Interview with Michael Manley, Staff Att'y, Int'l Bhd. of Teamsters (Feb. 20, 2013).
179. *Id.*
180. BONACICH & WILSON, *supra* note 1, at 211, 222.
181. Telephone Interview with Michael Manley, *supra* note 178.
182. *Id.*
183. *Id.*

184. Id.
185. Id.
186. Id.
187. Id.
188. Id.
189. Id.
190. Id.
191. Telephone Interview with John Canham-Clyne, Campaign Dir., Change to Win (May 20, 2013).
192. Telephone Interview with Nick Weiner, Nat'l Campaigns Organizer, Change to Win (Apr. 17, 2013).
193. Id.
194. Id.
195. Canham-Clyne and Weiner also worked with Rich Yeselson. Id.; see also Telephone Interview with Michael Manley, supra note 178.
196. Telephone Interview with John Canham-Clyne, supra note 191.
197. Id.
198. Id.
199. Weiner had started in the AFL-CIO's Food and Allied Service Trade department. Telephone Interview with Nick Weiner, supra note 192. In 2004, HERE joined with the Union of Needletrades, Industrial, and Textile Employees (UNITE) to form UNITE-HERE, which withdrew from the AFL-CIO to join Change to Win a year later.
200. Id.
201. Telephone Interview with John Canham-Clyne, supra note 191.
202. Id.
203. Telephone Interview with Nick Weiner, supra note 192.
204. Telephone Interview with Michael Manley, supra note 178.
205. Telephone Interview with John Canham-Clyne, supra note 191.
206. Telephone Interview with Michael Manley, supra note 178.
207. Telephone Interview with Nick Weiner, supra note 192.
208. Telephone Interview with Michael Manley, supra note 178.
209. Id.
210. Id.
211. Id.
212. Telephone Interview with Nick Weiner, supra note 192.
213. For example, attorney Richard McCracken had advised UNITE-HERE on the market participant exception in connection with city contracting projects. Telephone Interview with John Canham-Clyne, supra note 191.
214. Engine Mfrs. Ass'n v. S. Coast Air Quality Mgmt. Dist., No. CV00-09065FMC(BQRX), 2005 WL 1163437, at *12 (C.D. Cal. May 5, 2005).
215. Deborah Schoch, *Port Air Cleanup Plan May Become a Model*, L.A. TIMES, Apr. 1, 2003, at B1 ("On an average day, 16 ships arrive at Los Angeles and Long Beach, releasing more pollution than a million cars.").
216. See, e.g., Bigelow v. Virginia, 421 U.S. 809 (1975); see also *Pioneering Cleanup at Ports*, L.A. TIMES, Mar. 17, 2003, at B10. The United States failed to ratify a 1978 treaty setting global environmental standards on ships.
217. Engine Mfrs. Ass'n v. E.P.A., 88 F.3d 1075 (D.C. Cir. 1996).
218. Daryl Kelley, *Port Employers Attack Plan to Curb Ship Smog*, L.A. TIMES, Mar. 8, 1987, at SE1.
219. Id.
220. 42 U.S.C. § 7543(d) (2012).
221. In 2000, the EPA issued regulations requiring diesel trucks to dramatically reduce emissions beginning in the 2007 model year. EPA, EPA420-F-00-026, REGULATORY

ANNOUNCEMENT: FINAL EMISSION STANDARDS FOR 2004 AND LATER MODEL YEAR HIGHWAY HEAVY-DUTY VEHICLES AND ENGINES (2000).
222. Marla Cone, *Diesel—the Dark Side of Industry*, L.A. TIMES, May 30, 1999, at A30.
223. *Id.*
224. S. COAST AIR QUALITY MGMT. DIST., MULTIPLE AIR TOXICS EXPOSURE STUDY FINAL REPORT (MATES II) ES-3 (2000) [hereinafter MATES II], http://www.aqmd.gov/docs/default-source/air-quality/air-toxic-studies/mates-ii/mates-ii-contents-and-executive-summary.pdf?sfvrsn=4 (last visited July 5, 2017).
225. *Id.* at ES-5.
226. *Id.* at ES-5 to ES-12. Some efforts to reduce pollution were spurred by the MATES II findings. For example, Marine Terminals Corp. purchased five low-emission trucks under a state incentive program. *Cargo Terminal Operator Using Low-Emission Trucks*, L.A. TIMES, Sept. 16, 2000, at B4. In 2001, the EPA settled a suit by Bluewater Network under which it agreed to "begin developing rules to cut smog-forming exhaust from the largest, diesel powered ships, including cargo vessels, tankers and cruise liners." Gary Polakovic, *EPA Settlement Seeks to Curb Air Pollution from Big Ships*, L.A. TIMES, Jan. 17, 2001, at A15.
227. *See* Schoch, *supra* note 215.
228. *See* Martha M. Matsuoka & Robert Gottlieb, *Environmental and Social Justice Movements and Policy Change in Los Angeles: Is an Inside-Outside Game Possible?*, *in* NEW YORK AND LOS ANGELES: THE UNCERTAIN FUTURE 445, 452 (David Halle & Andrew A. Beveridge eds., 2013).
229. Jeff Leeds, *Long Beach Port Faces Rising Tide of Criticism*, L.A. TIMES, Mar. 24, 1997, at B1.
230. To secure COSCO's business, each port sent delegations to lobby Chinese officials. *Id.*
231. Jeff Leeds, *Ruling May Block Long Beach Port Project*, L.A. TIMES, May 21, 1997, at B1 (The naval station had been closed in 1991 and turned over to the port in 1995).
232. *Id.*; Jeff Leeds, *Coastal Commission Oks Permit for Long Beach Port Terminal*, L.A. TIMES, Jan. 9, 1997, at B3.
233. City of Vernon v. Bd. of Harbor Comm'rs of Long Beach, 74 Cal. Rptr. 2d 497 (Cal. Ct. App. 1998).
234. Dan Weikel, *Port Shifts Focus After Cosco Deal for Base Unravels*, L.A. TIMES, Sept. 19, 1998, at B1.
235. NRDC v. City of Los Angeles, 126 Cal. Rptr. 2d 615, 622 (Cal. Ct. App. 2002).
236. Louis Sahagun, *Lawsuit Seeks to Block Shipping Terminal Plan*, L.A. TIMES, June 15, 2001, at 5.
237. Louis Sahagun, *Judge Halts Work on New Port of L.A. Terminal*, L.A. TIMES, July 24, 2002, at B3; Sahagun, *supra* note 236.
238. NRDC, 126 Cal. Rptr. 2d at 622.
239. *Id.*; Sahagun, *supra* note 237.
240. Schoch, *supra* note 215.
241. *Id.*
242. Petition for Writ of Mandate, NRDC v. City of Los Angeles, No. BS070017, 2002 WL 34340562 (Cal. Super. Ct. May 30, 2002) (filed June 14, 2001).
243. *Id.* at 13–19. Petitioners also argued that the port's approval of the project violated the city's general plan. *See id.* at 20. Petitioners filed an amended complaint with two additional causes of action, one for abuse of discretion for approving a project inconsistent with the port's master plan and the second for violating the coastal act. Amended Petition for Writ of Mandate at 26–29, NRDC, No. BS070017, 2002 WL 34340562 (filed Oct. 19, 2001).
244. For CEQA rules, see CAL. PUB. RES. CODE §§ 21000 et seq. (West 2007).
245. Petition for Writ of Mandate, *supra* note 242.
246. Sahagun, *supra* note 236.
247. Amended Petition for Writ of Mandate, *supra* note 243, at 9.
248. NRDC v. City of Los Angeles, 126 Cal. Rptr. 2d 615, 617–20 (Cal. Ct. App. 2002).

249. *Id.* at 620. In April 2001, the Army Corps issued China Shipping a permit to build the first wharf, which the coalition also challenged under NEPA. Louis Sahagun, *Work to Resume on Port of L.A.*, L.A. TIMES, July 27, 2002, at B4.
250. NRDC, 126 Cal. Rptr. 2d at 622 (citation omitted).
251. *Id.*
252. *Id.*
253. *Id.* at 623.
254. *Id.*
255. *Id.* at 622.
256. Answer to Amended Petition for Writ of Mandate, *NRDC*, No. BS070017, 2002 WL 34340562 (filed Dec. 31, 2001).
257. Louis Sahagun, *Anger at Hahn Brings Unusual Allies Together*, L.A. TIMES, Feb. 21, 2002, at B3.
258. *Id.* Hahn's father, Kenneth Hahn, was a longtime member of the Los Angeles County Board of Supervisors, serving the predominately African American Baldwin Hills community. *Id.*
259. *Id.*
260. *Id.*
261. *Id.*
262. Judgment Denying Petition for Writ of Mandate, *NRDC*, No. BS070017, 2002 WL 34340562 (Cal. Super. Ct. May 30, 2002).
263. *Id.* at 9–11.
264. Appellants' Opening Br. at 3, NRDC v. City of Los Angeles, 126 Cal. Rptr. 2d 615 (Cal. Ct. App. 2002) (No. B159157) (filed Aug. 23, 2002).
265. *Id.* at 1.
266. Amicus Br. of the State of Cal., Ex Rel. Att'y Gen. Bill Lockyer in Support of Appellants at 4, *NRDC*, 126 Cal. Rptr. 2d 615 (No. B159157) (filed Oct. 2, 2002).
267. Petition for Writ of Supersedeas or Other Appropriate Stay Order, and for an Immediate Stay; Memorandum of Points and Auths.; Supporting Declaration, *NRDC*, 126 Cal. Rptr. 2d 615 (No. B159157) (filed June 7, 2002).
268. Order Denying Petition for Writ of Supersedeas and Setting Expedited Briefing Schedule and Oral Argument for Appeal, *NRDC*, 126 Cal. Rptr. 2d 615 (No. B159157) (filed Aug. 5, 2002).
269. *Court Expected to Rule on Port Injunction*, L.A. TIMES, July 23, 2002, at B4.
270. Sahagun, *supra* note 237.
271. *Id.*
272. Sahagun, *supra* note 249.
273. Eric Malnic, *Environmentalists Win a Battle over L.A. Port Terminal*, L.A. TIMES, Oct. 24, 2002, at B4.
274. NRDC, 126 Cal. Rptr. 2d at 625.
275. *Id.* at 627.
276. *Id.* at 617.
277. Louis Sahagan, *Court Halts Work at L.A. Port*, L.A. TIMES, Oct. 31, 2002, at B1.
278. NRDC, 126 Cal. Rptr. 2d at 628.
279. Stipulated Judgment, Modification of Stay, and Order Thereon, NRDC v. City of Los Angeles, No. BS070017, 2002 WL 34340562 (Cal. Super. Ct. May 30, 2002) (filed Mar. 6, 2003).
280. *Id.* at 6.
281. *Id.* at 16.
282. *Id.* at 17.
283. *Id.* at 18.
284. *Id.* at 18–19.
285. *Id.* at 19–23.
286. *Id.* at 20–22.
287. Deborah Schoch, *Port Project Suit Settled*, L.A. TIMES, Mar. 6, 2003, at B1. The environmental groups also settled the federal action (contingent on approval of the state court settlement),

which required the Army Corps of Engineers to conduct "a full environmental impact review of the project and reconsider its issuance of the permits in light of the review." Press Release, NRDC, City of Los Angeles and Community and Environmental Groups Reach Record Settlement of Challenge to China Shipping Terminal Project at Port (Mar. 3, 2005), http://www.nrdc.org/media/pressreleases/030305.asp (last visited July 5, 2017).

288. Deborah Schoch & Peter Nicholas, *Plans for 1st "Green" Ship Terminal in U.S. Stall*, L.A. TIMES, June 14, 2003, at B3.
289. *Id.*
290. *Id.*
291. *Id.*
292. *Id.*
293. Deborah Schoch, *Residents Feel Ignored in L.A. Harbor Deal*, L.A. TIMES, Mar. 11, 2004, at B11.
294. *Id.*
295. Deborah Schoch, *Accord Clears Way for '03 Plan to Clean Up Air at Port*, L.A. TIMES, Mar. 12, 2004, at B3. The final amended agreement was filed with the court on June 21, 2004. Amended Stipulated Judgment, Modification of Stay, and Order Thereon, NRDC v. City of Los Angeles, No. BS070017, 2002 WL 34340562 (Cal. Super. Ct. May 30, 2002) (filed June 21, 2004).
296. *See* Deborah Schoch, *Port and Shipper End Fight*, L.A. TIMES, May 26, 2005, at B6. Although the terminal opened in May 2004, the legal wrangling continued, with the port settling a lawsuit by China Shipping for more than $20 million to compensate the company for delays. *Id.*
297. *See Port of Los Angeles Hosts First Plugged In Container Ship*, ENV'T NEWS SERV. (June 21, 2004), www.ens-newswire.com/ens/jun2004/2004-06-21-04.asp (last visited June 21, 2004). The port circulated draft EIRs in July 2006 and then again in April 2008. ENVTL. MGMT. DIV., PORT OF L.A. REGULATORY BRANCH, BERTH 97-109 [CHINA SHIPPING] CONTAINER TERMINAL RE-CIRCULATED DRAFT EIS/EIR (2008), http://www.portoflosangeles.org/EIR/ChinaShipping/DEIR/_Public_Meeting_Presentation.pdf (last visited July 5, 2017). The port approved the EIRs at the end of 2008. Press Release, Port of L.A., China Shipping Container Terminal Expansion Is Approved by Port of Los Angeles (Dec. 19, 2008), http://www.portoflosangeles.org/newsroom/2008_releases/news_121908cs.asp (last visited July 5, 2017). China Shipping completed phase II in 2011. *See China Shipping Celebrates Major Terminal Expansion at Port of Los Angeles*, LONGSHORE & SHIPPING NEWS (Apr. 28, 2011), http://www.longshoreshippingnews.com/2011/04/china-shipping-celebrates-major-terminal-expansion-at-port-of-los-angeles/ (last visited July 5, 2017).
298. *Port of Los Angeles Hosts First Plugged In Container Ship*, *supra* note 297.
299. Deborah Schoch, *City Downplays Port Pollution, Critics Say*, L.A. TIMES, July 9, 2004, at B4.
300. *Id.*
301. Deborah Schoch, *Plan to Cut Port Smog to Be Unveiled*, L.A. TIMES, Dec. 27, 2004, at B1.
302. Deborah Schoch, *Hahn Shift on Port Cleanup Is Criticized*, L.A. TIMES, Nov. 16, 2004, at B3.
303. Louis Sahagun, *Hahn Outlines His Vision for Port*, L.A. TIMES, Dec. 7, 2002, at B4.
304. *See* DIANE BAILEY ET AL., NRDC, HARBORING POLLUTION: THE DIRTY TRUTH ABOUT U.S. PORTS 11 (2004), http://www.nrdc.org/air/pollution/ports1/ports.pdf (last visited July 5, 2017).
305. Press Release, Nat. Res. Def. Council, New Study Says U.S. Seaports Are Largest Urban Polluters (Mar. 22, 2004), http://www.nrdc.org/media/pressreleases/040322.asp (last visited July 5, 2017).
306. DIANE BAILEY ET AL., NRDC, HARBORING POLLUTION: STRATEGIES TO CLEAN UP U.S. PORTS at ix–xii (2004), http://www.nrdc.org/air/pollution/ports/ports2.pdf (last visited July 5, 2017).
307. *Id.* at 43.
308. *Id.* at 21.
309. *Id.* at 49.

310. *Id.* at 73. The idling bill was supported by the Teamsters. Bill Mongelluzzo, *Big Win for Truckers*, TEAMSTERS NATION BLOG (Sept. 9, 2002), http://www.teamster.org/content/joc-big-win-truckers (last visited July 5, 2017).
311. CAL. AIR RES. BOARD, FINAL STATEMENTS OF REASONS FOR RULEMAKING (2004), http://www.arb.ca.gov/regact/idling/fsor.pdf (last visited July 2017) (discussing rationales for and evolution of proposed regulation titled "Airborne Toxic Control Measure to Limit Diesel-Fueled Commercial Motor Vehicle Idling"). The rule was codified at CAL. CODE REGS. tit. 13, § 2485 (2012). CARB later approved a rule requiring 2008 and newer trucks to be equipped with a sleeper switch to automatically shut down idling trucks after five minutes. CAL. CODE REGS. tit. 13, § 1956.8 (2012).
312. Schoch, *supra* note 299.
313. Port of Los Angeles Community Advisory Committee, Joint Subcommittee Meeting with Wilmington Waterfront Development Subcommittee Traffic Committee: Minutes (Jan. 13, 2105).
314. *Id.* Truck pollution remained a significant concern despite the Alameda Corridor rail project, which proved disappointing. By August 2004, only 40 trains per day ran on the corridor, which was built for 150; in contrast, there were 47,285 trucks per weekday traveling on the 710 Freeway, a number expected to increase to 99,300 in 2020. This was the result of changes in the shipping industry in which shippers, instead of loading cargo directly to trains, hauled "most of their imports by truck to hubs in Riverside and San Bernardino counties," where the cargo was repackaged before being sent to recipients, such as large retail chains. Sharon Bernstein & Deborah Schoch, *New Routes Just for Trucks Urged*, L.A. TIMES, Aug. 22, 2004, at B1.
315. Deborah Schoch, *Mayor Tells Port to Create New Air Plan*, L.A. TIMES, Aug. 13, 2004, at B3.
316. Patrick McGreevy & Deborah Schoch, *L.A. Port Director Resigns*, L.A. TIMES, Sept. 18, 2004, at B1.
317. Schoch, *supra* note 302.
318. Schoch, *supra* note 301.
319. Jack Leonard & Deborah Schoch, *Plans for L.A. Port Focus on Pollution*, L.A. TIMES, Dec. 30, 2004, at B3.
320. Deborah Schoch, *Meeting Delay for Hahn Task Force Stirs Concern*, L.A. TIMES, Feb. 10, 2005, at B6.
321. Deborah Schoch, *Panel Backs Plan to Curb Pollution at Port*, L.A. TIMES, Mar. 4, 2005, at B3.
322. Deborah Schoch, *Port Clean-Air Plan Nearly Set*, L.A. TIMES, Mar. 3, 2005, at B3.
323. Deborah Schoch, *2 Ports Split on How to Clear the Air*, L.A. TIMES, Mar. 13, 2005, at B1.
324. Deborah Schoch, *Hahn's Harbor Pollution Plan Faces an Uncertain Future*, L.A. TIMES, June 22, 2005, at B10.
325. *Id.*
326. NO NET INCREASE TASK FORCE, REPORT TO MAYOR HAHN AND COUNCILWOMAN HAHN (2005), http://www.portoflosangeles.org/DOC/REPORT_NNI_Final.pdf (last visited July 5, 2017).
327. *Id.*
328. *Id.* at ES-2. The control measures included proposals to move ocean vessel engines to low sulfur fuel, mandate low-emission rail engines, electrify the Alameda Corridor, expand the low-emission truck conversion program, retrofit diesel trucks with filters, and impose truck idling reduction measures. *Id.* at 3-4 to 3-9.
329. *Id.* at 5-1 to 5-100.
330. *Id.* at 5-44.
331. *Id.* at 5-50.
332. Deborah Schoch, *Hahn Supports Port Task Force's Plan*, L.A. TIMES, June 30, 2005, at B10.
333. *Id.*
334. Telephone Interview with Jerilyn López Mendoza, Comm'r, L.A. Bd. of Pub. Works & Former Comm'r, L.A. Bd. of Harbor Comm'rs. (Apr. 26, 2013).

335. Id.
336. Id.
337. Id.
338. Id.
339. Id.
340. Id.
341. Id.
342. Id.
343. Id.
344. Deborah Schoch & Richard Fausset, *Villaraigosa's Port Panel Choices Suggest New Direction*, L.A. TIMES, July 27, 2005, at B3.
345. Id.
346. Deborah Schoch, *A Radical Shift in Tone for L.A. Harbor Panel*, L.A. TIMES, Sept. 16, 2005, at B4.
347. Deborah Schoch, *Wilmington Looks to Step Out from Under Port's Shadow*, L.A. TIMES, Sept. 14, 2005, at B4.
348. Schoch, *supra* note 346.
349. Deborah Schoch, *New Harbor Panel Aims to Cut Pollution While Expanding Port*, L.A. TIMES, Sept. 29, 2005, at B6.
350. AIR RES. BD., CAL. ENVTL. PROT. AGENCY, DIESEL PARTICULATE MATTER EXPOSURE ASSESSMENT STUDY FOR THE PORTS OF LOS ANGELES AND LONG BEACH 2 (2005), http://www.arb.ca.gov/ports/marinevess/documents/100305draftexposrep.pdf (draft version) (last visited July 5, 2017).
351. Deborah Schoch, *Study Links Diesel Fumes to Illnesses*, L.A. TIMES, Dec. 3, 2005, at B3.
352. AIR RES. BD., *supra* note 350, at 4.
353. Janet Wilson, *Pollution Plan on Haulers Nears OK*, L.A. TIMES, Apr. 20, 2006, at B3.
354. Id.
355. Telephone Interview with S. David Freeman, Interim Gen. Manager, L.A. Dep't of Water & Power Water Sys. & Former Comm'r, L.A. Bd. of Harbor Comm'rs (Apr. 29, 2013).
356. Telephone Interview with Jerilyn López Mendoza, *supra* note 334.
357. Id.
358. Telephone Interview with David Libatique, Senior Dir., Gov't Aff., Port of L.A. (June 2, 2013).
359. Id.
360. Id. Libatique also vetted the candidates for the Harbor Commission.
361. Id.
362. Jim Newton, *Once Rivals, Local Ports Clear Air in Partnership*, L.A. TIMES, July 4, 2006, at A1.
363. Id.
364. Telephone Interview with Adrian Martinez, Staff Att'y, Nat. Res. Def. Council (Apr. 1, 2010).
365. Telephone Interview with David Libatique, *supra* note 358.
366. Id.
367. Newton, *supra* note 362.
368. Telephone Interview with S. David Freeman, *supra* note 355.
369. In 2013, at the Port of Los Angeles, approximately 50% of containers were routed locally to Los Angeles, Riverside, San Bernardino, and Ventura Counties. Interview with John Holmes, *supra* note 91.
370. Newton, *supra* note 362.
371. Id.
372. Id.
373. Other CAAP proposals were also important, including the recommendation to require ships to burn sulfur fuel within twenty miles of the port and dock with electrical power. PORT OF LONG BEACH & PORT OF L.A., SAN PEDRO BAY PORTS CLEAN AIR ACTION

PLAN: TECHNICAL REPORT 6, 87 (2006), http://www.portoflosangeles.org/CAAP/CAAP_Tech_Report_Final.pdf (last visited July 5, 2017).
374. Janet Wilson, *Diesel Trucks Target of Port Plan*, L.A. TIMES, Nov. 7, 2006, at B3.
375. PORT OF LONG BEACH & PORT OF L.A., *supra* note 373, at 4.
376. *Id.* at 57.
377. *Id.* at 59. The report assumed that five hundred trucks would be replaced through the China Shipping-created Gateway Cities program. *Id.*
378. *Id.* at 58.
379. *Id.* at 62–63.
380. *Id.* at 71.
381. *Id.* at 59. The report estimated that LNG trucks would cost $188,500, while clean diesel trucks would cost $129,500 to replace. Retrofitting was estimated at $19,500 per truck. *Id.* at 60.
382. *Id.* at 67–70.
383. *Id.* at 68.
384. The deadlines were "so that the community would know that we were taking their concerns seriously but also so that our business contacts, our tenants and our customers would know and have certainty about what was going to be expected of them in terms of delivering cleaner air to the public." Telephone Interview with Jerilyn López Mendoza, *supra* note 334.
385. PORT OF LONG BEACH & PORT OF L.A., *supra* note 373, at 73.
386. *See San Pedro Bay Ports Clean Air Action Plan Joint Board Meeting* (Nov. 20, 2006), http://lacity.granicus.com/MediaPlayer.php?view_id=14&clip_id=1211 (last visited Dec. 1, 2017).
387. The Los Angeles mayor urged the port to "grow green, but grow indeed," noting that port growth would support 1.9 million regional jobs. Janet Wilson, *Port Panels OK Plan to Cut Pollution*, L.A. TIMES, Nov. 21, 2006, at B3.
388. *Statements of the Presidents of the Los Angeles Board of Harbor Commissioners and the Long Beach Board of Harbor Commissioners, in* PORT OF L.A. & PORT OF LONG BEACH, *supra* note 373.
389. *Id.*
390. *Id.*
391. *Id.*
392. Louis Sahagun, *Port OKs "Green" Cargo Fee*, L.A. TIMES, Dec. 18, 2007, at B1. As part of the emission-reduction effort, the Los Angeles port and SCAQMD funded the production of electric drayage trucks in conjunction with Balqon Corporation. *See* Press Release, Port of Los Angeles, Mayor Villaraigosa Drives First Heavy-Duty, Electric Port Drayage Truck off the Assembly Line at New Harbor City Factory (Feb. 24, 2009), http://www.portoflosangeles.org/newsroom/2009_releases/news_022409_etruck.asp (last visited July 5, 2017).
393. Janet Wilson, *Trucks Targeted in Clean-Air Drive*, L.A. TIMES, Nov. 12, 2006, at B1.
394. *Id.*
395. Carl Pope, *A New Blue-Green Alliance Is Born*, HUFFINGTON POST (June 8, 2006, 4:53 PM), http://www.huffingtonpost.com/carl-pope/a-new-bluegreen-alliance-_b_22558.html (last visited July 10, 2017).
396. The video was narrated by Diane Keaton. See NAT. RES. DEF. COUNCIL, *Terminal Impact*, YouTube (Sept. 1 2006), http://www.youtube.com/watch?v=qOUbj1ssjKs (last visited July 10, 2017).
397. Telephone Interview with Nick Weiner, *supra* note 192.
398. *Id.*
399. *Id.*
400. Telephone Interview with John Canham-Clyne, *supra* note 191.
401. Jon Zerolnick, The Clean and Safe Ports Campaign: False Dichotomies and the Underground Economy Versus Coalition-Building and the Power of Local Government 9 (unpublished manuscript).
402. Telephone Interview with Nick Weiner, *supra* note 192.
403. *Id.*

404. Telephone Interview with John Canham-Clyne, *supra* note 191.
405. Interview with Patricia Castellanos, Dir. of Clean & Safe Ports Project, in Los Angeles, Cal. (Feb. 23, 2012).
406. Interview with Jon Zerolnick, Senior Res. & Pol'y Analyst, L.A. All. for a New Econ., in Los Angeles, Cal. (Feb. 23, 2012).
407. *Id.*
408. *Id.*
409. *Id.*
410. *Id.*
411. Interview with Patricia Castellanos, *supra* note 405.
412. Telephone Interview with John Canham-Clyne, *supra* note 191.
413. Interview with Patricia Castellanos, *supra* note 405.
414. *Id.*
415. *Id.*
416. *Id.*
417. *Id.*
418. *Id.*
419. Telephone Interview with Nick Weiner, Nat'l Campaigns Organizer, Change to Win (Apr. 25, 2013).
420. Telephone Interview with Nick Weiner, *supra* note 192.
421. Interview with Jon Zerolnick, *supra* note 406.
422. Telephone Interview with Michael Manley, *supra* note 178.
423. *Id.*
424. *Id.*
425. Telephone Interview with Nick Weiner, *supra* note 192.
426. *See, e.g.*, Colleen Callahan, Clean Trucks Program Case Study (unpublished manuscript).
427. *See* Press Release, Int'l Bhd. of Teamsters, Teamsters and ILWU Announce Port Legislation Strategy (Feb. 4, 2002), http://teamster.org/content/teamsters-and-ilwu-announce-port-legislation-strategy (last visited July 10, 2017) (noting that the unions were joining to support state bills to force terminal operators to pay fines for making truckers idle while waiting for cargo and to require trucks to be safety certified).
428. Telephone Interview with Adrian Martinez, *supra* note 364.
429. Telephone Interview with Melissa Lin Perrella, Staff Att'y, Nat. Res. Def. Council (Apr. 2, 2010).
430. Interview with Patricia Castellanos, *supra* note 405.
431. *See* Dep't of Transp. v. Public Citizen, 541 U.S. 752 (2004) (holding that neither the NEPA nor Clean Air Act required the Federal Motor Carrier Safety Administration to evaluate the environmental impact of cross-border trucking).
432. Telephone Interview with Adrian Martinez, *supra* note 364.
433. Engine Mfrs. Ass'n v. S. Coast Air Quality Mgmt. Dist., 498 F.3d 1031 (9th Cir. 2007).
434. Telephone Interview with Adrian Martinez, Staff Att'y, Nat. Res. Def. Council (Apr. 2, 2010).
435. *Id.*
436. *Id.*
437. Telephone Interview with Adrian Martinez, *supra* note 364.
438. Telephone Interview with David Pettit, Senior Att'y, Urb. Program, Nat. Res. Def. Council (Apr. 5, 2010).
439. *Id.*
440. Telephone Interview with Melissa Lin Perrella, *supra* note 429.
441. *Id.*
442. Telephone Interview with Adrian Martinez, *supra* note 434.
443. Telephone Interview with Melissa Lin Perrella, *supra* note 429.
444. *Id.*

445. Telephone Interview with Adrian Martinez, *supra* note 434.
446. *Id.*
447. Telephone Interview with Melissa Lin Perrella, *supra* note 429.
448. *See* Telephone Interview with Elina Green-Nasser, Adm'r, UCLA Sch. of Pub. Health & Former Project Manager, Long Beach All. for Children with Asthma (Apr. 23, 2013) (Green changed her name to Green-Nasser after the campaign); Telephone Interview with Angelo Logan, *supra* note 137.
449. Interview with Jon Zerolnick, *supra* note 406.
450. Telephone Interview with Nick Weiner, *supra* note 192.
451. Telephone Interview with John Canham-Clyne, *supra* note 191.
452. *Id.*
453. Telephone Interview with Tom Politeo, Volunteer, Sierra Club Harbor Vision Task Force (Mar. 26, 2013).
454. *Id.*
455. *Id.*
456. *Id.*
457. *Id.*
458. *Id.*
459. *Id.*
460. *Id.*
461. *Id.*
462. *Id.*
463. *Id.*
464. Telephone Interview with Candice Kim, Senior Campaign Assoc., Coal. for Clean Air (Apr. 26, 2013).
465. Telephone Interview with Tom Politeo, *supra* note 453. The group was coordinated by Martha Matsuoka, a Ph.D. candidate in Urban Planning at UCLA and now professor at Occidental College. Telephone Interview with Candice Kim, *supra* note 464.
466. Telephone Interview with Tom Politeo, *supra* note 453.
467. *Id.*; Telephone Interview with Jesse Marquez, *supra* note 129.
468. Telephone Interview with Colleen Callahan, Deputy Dir., UCLA Luskin Ctr. for Innovation & Former Manager of Air Quality Pol'y, Am. Lung Ass'n (Apr. 15, 2013).
469. *Id.*
470. *Id.*
471. *Id.*
472. Telephone Interview with Elina Green-Nasser, *supra* note 448.
473. *Id.*
474. *Id.*
475. Telephone Interview with Tom Politeo, *supra* note 453.
476. *Id.*
477. *Id.*
478. *Id.*
479. Telephone Interview with Jonathan Klein, Exec. Dir., Clergy & Laity United for Econ. Just. (May 8, 2013).
480. Port truckers had heavily participated in the 2006 May Day immigration demonstrations, angered by immigration raids.
481. Interview with Patricia Castellanos, *supra* note 405.
482. *Id.*
483. *Id.*
484. *Id.*
485. Interview with Jon Zerolnick, *supra* note 406.
486. *Id.*

487. Interview with Patricia Castellanos, *supra* note 405.
488. *Id.*
489. *Id.*
490. *Id.*
491. *Id.*
492. *Id.*
493. Telephone Interview with Colleen Callahan, *supra* note 468. Callahan stated that the American Lung Association senior managers wanted to make sure "the campaign was truly about... clean air and not just about... labor issues." *Id.*
494. Telephone Interview with Elina Green-Nasser, *supra* note 448.
495. Telephone Interview with Angelo Logan, *supra* note 137.
496. *Id.*
497. Coal. for Clean & Safe Ports, Draft Mission Statement (unpublished document).
498. Telephone Interview with Adrian Martinez, *supra* note 364.
499. Interview with Jon Zerolnick, *supra* note 406.
500. *Id.*
501. *Id.*
502. Telephone Interview with Adrian Martinez, *supra* note 364.
503. Interview with Jon Zerolnick, *supra* note 406.
504. Letter from LAANE et al. to Geraldine Knatz, Exec. Dir., Port of L.A. & Richard D. Steinke, Exec. Dir., Port of Long Beach (Aug. 28, 2006). The coalition partners included at that point were Change to Win, CLUE, Coalition for Clean Air, CHIRLA, Communities for a Better Environment, Harbor Watts Economic Development Corporation, the Teamsters, the Los Angeles County Federation of Labor, and NRDC.
505. *Id.* at 2.
506. *Id.* at 3–4.
507. *Id.* at 5–6.
508. *Id.* at 6.
509. *Id.* at 7.
510. Interview with Jon Zerolnick, *supra* note 406.
511. Interview with Patricia Castellanos, *supra* note 405; Interview with Jon Zerolnick, *supra* note 406.
512. Interview with Jon Zerolnick, *supra* note 406.
513. Interview with Patricia Castellanos, *supra* note 405 (noting that End Oil joined the coalition after the initial launch).
514. There were approximately thirty initial members in the coalition, which grew to around forty members. *See id.*
515. Telephone Interview with Adrian Martinez, *supra* note 434.
516. Coal. for Clean & Safe Ports, Structure & Decision-Making (2006).
517. *Id.* The first steering committee, not yet at full strength, included Adrian Martinez of NRDC, Elina Green of LBACA, Louis Diaz from Teamsters Local 848, Nativo Lopez from Hermandad Mexicana, Rafael Pizarro of Coalition for Clean Air, a representative from Teamsters Local 63, and Tom Politeo from the Sierra Club.
518. Interview with Patricia Castellanos, *supra* note 405.
519. Steering committee decisions were by consensus; if no consensus could be achieved, decisions went to the full coalition. *See* Coal. for Clean & Safe Ports, Structure & Decision-Making, *supra* note 516.
520. Interview with Patricia Castellanos, *supra* note 405.
521. Port of Long Beach & Port of L.A., San Pedro Bay Ports Clean Air Action Plan Implementation Stakeholder Meeting (PowerPoint presentation).
522. *See* Port of L.A. & Port of Long Beach, San Pedro Bay Ports Clean Air Action Plan, CAAP Stakeholder Group Members.

523. *See* San Pedro Bay Ports Clean Air Action Plan Implementation Stakeholder Meeting, *supra* note 521.
524. Telephone Interview with Melissa Lin Perrella, *supra* note 429.
525. Interview with Jon Zerolnick, *supra* note 406.
526. *Id.*
527. *Id.*
528. *Id.*
529. Telephone Interview with Angelo Logan, *supra* note 137.
530. Interview with Jon Zerolnick, *supra* note 406.
531. Interview with Patricia Castellanos, *supra* note 405.
532. Coal. for Clean & Safe Ports, Request for Proposals: Port Drayage Service Contract, Executive Summary 5 (Apr. 2007).
533. *Id.* at 5–6.
534. Interview with Jon Zerolnick, *supra* note 406.
535. *Id.*
536. Coal. for Clean & Safe Ports, Request for Proposals, *supra* note 532, at 2.
537. *Id.* at 3.
538. *Id.*
539. Interview with Jon Zerolnick, *supra* note 406.
540. Coal. for Clean & Safe Ports, Request for Proposals, *supra* note 532, at 10–11.
541. *Id.* at 4.
542. *Id.* at 3. The RFP also stated that 25% of the converted fleet had to be natural gas trucks.
543. *Id.* at 12–13.
544. *Id.* at 4.
545. Telephone Interview with Jon Zerolnick, Dir. of Clean & Safe Ports Project, L.A. All. for a New Economy (Feb. 20, 2013).
546. Janet Wilson & Ronald D. White, *2 Ports Aim to Slash Diesel Exhaust*, L.A. Times, Apr. 14, 2007, at B1.
547. *Id.*
548. Port of Long Beach & Port of L.A., Ports of Long Beach and Los Angeles Proposed Clean Trucks Program 1 (2007).
549. *Id.* at 1–2.
550. *Id.* at 2.
551. Port of Long Beach & Port of L.A., Proposed Clean Trucks Program Fact Sheet (2007).
552. Port of Long Beach & Port of L.A., *supra* note 548, at 8.
553. Ports of Los Angeles and Long Beach, Clean Trucks Program: Program Elements for Stakeholder Discussion, CAAP HDV1 (Apr. 11, 2007) (PowerPoint presentation).
554. Interview with Jon Zerolnick, *supra* note 406.
555. Wilson & White, *supra* note 546.
556. Interview with Jon Zerolnick, *supra* note 406.
557. *Id.*
558. Letter from Coal. for Clean & Safe Ports to Dr. Geraldine Knatz, Exec. Dir., Port of L.A. & Richard D. Steinke, Exec. Dir., Port of Long Beach, at 1 (May 10, 2007).
559. *Id.* at 2.
560. *Id.* The letter reiterated its argument for imposing minimum business standards on LMCs, requiring labor peace agreements, mandating some alternative fuel trucks, and developing an off-street parking and community impact plan. *Id.* at 5–9.
561. Interview with Patricia Castellanos, *supra* note 405.
562. Interview with Jon Zerolnick, *supra* note 406.
563. Telephone Interview with David Pettit, *supra* note 438 (recalling statement by Tom Russell, the port's general counsel).

564. Interview with Jon Zerolnick, *supra* note 406.
565. Louis Sahagun & Ronald D. White, *Port Drivers Steer Toward Clean-Truck Program*, L.A. TIMES, June 6, 2007, at B2.
566. Interview with Jon Zerolnick, *supra* note 406.
567. *See Agenda of the Regular Meeting of the Los Angeles Board of Harbor Commissioners* (Oct. 12, 2007), http://lacity.granicus.com/MediaPlayer.php?view_id=14&clip_id=2191&meta_id=27885 (last visited July 10, 2017).
568. *See* Telephone Interview with Elina Green-Nasser, *supra* note 448.
569. Tiffany Hsu & Rong-Gong Lin II, *Taking a Message to the Streets*, L.A. TIMES, June 28, 2007, at B1.
570. Telephone Interview with Candice Kim, *supra* note 464.
571. Telephone Interview with Nick Weiner, *supra* note 419.
572. Telephone Interview with Candice Kim, *supra* note 464.
573. Interview with Patricia Castellanos, *supra* note 405.
574. Telephone Interview with Jerilyn López Mendoza, *supra* note 334.
575. Telephone Interview with Elina Green-Nasser, *supra* note 448.
576. *Id.*
577. Interview with Patricia Castellanos, *supra* note 405.
578. *Id.*
579. Telephone Interview with Angelo Logan, *supra* note 137; Telephone Interview with Jesse Marquez, *supra* note 129.
580. Telephone Interview with Colleen Callahan, *supra* note 468.
581. *Id.*; Telephone Interview with Elina Green-Nasser, *supra* note 448.
582. David Zahniser & Louis Sahagun, *Truckers' Status Is a Hitch in Port Plan*, L.A. TIMES, Mar. 6, 2008, at B1.
583. Telephone Interview with Sean Arian, President, Eos Consulting (Apr. 26, 2013).
584. Telephone Interview with Nick Weiner, *supra* note 192.
585. Telephone Interview with David Libatique, *supra* note 358.
586. *Id.*
587. *Id.*
588. Telephone Interview with Sean Arian, *supra* note 583.
589. *Id.*
590. Telephone Interview with Michael Manley, *supra* note 178.
591. *Id.*
592. *Id.*
593. *Id.*
594. Telephone Interview with Nick Weiner, *supra* note 419.
595. Telephone Interview with Adrian Martinez, *supra* note 364.
596. Telephone Interview with David Pettit, *supra* note 438.
597. Email from Joy Crose, Assistant Gen. Couns., Off. of the City Att'y, to Scott Cummings, Professor, UCLA Sch. of Law (May 7, 2013).
598. Telephone Interview with Steven S. Rosenthal, Partner, Complex Commercial Litig. Dep't, Kaye Scholer (Dec. 16, 2013).
599. *Id.*
600. Telephone Interview with Nick Weiner, *supra* note 192.
601. Telephone Interview with Adrian Martinez, *supra* note 364.
602. *Id.*
603. *Id.*
604. Telephone Interview with David Libatique, *supra* note 358; see also Telephone Interview with Sean Arian, *supra* note 583 ("[W]e were very confident that we had strong legal justification for [the program] to pass.").

605. Howard Blume & Joel Rubin, *Judge Tosses Out Mayor's Takeover of L.A. Schools*, L.A. TIMES, Dec. 22, 2006, at A1.
606. Louis Sahagun, *Ports Complex Plans to Grow Bigger, Cleaner*, L.A. TIMES, May 28, 2007, at B1.
607. *Id.*
608. *Id.*
609. *Id.*
610. Interview with Patricia Castellanos, *supra* note 405.
611. Ronald D. White, *Record Southland Imports Predicted*, L.A. TIMES, May 1, 2007, at C6.
612. Ronald D. White, *Exporters Making Waves over Ports' Clean-Air Plan*, L.A. TIMES, June 1, 2007, at C3.
613. JOHN E. HUSING ET AL., SAN PEDRO BAY PORTS CLEAN AIR ACTION PLAN, ECONOMIC ANALYSIS: PROPOSED CLEAN TRUCK PROGRAM (2007), http://www.cleanairactionplan.org/civica/filebank/blobdload.asp?BlobID=2260 (last visited July 10, 2017).
614. *Id.* at iv–v.
615. *Id.* at 6.
616. *Id.* at iii.
617. *Id.* at 39–41.
618. *Id.* at 66–69.
619. *Id.* at v.
620. Interview with Jon Zerolnick, *supra* note 406.
621. JON ZEROLNICK, THE ROAD TO SHARED PROSPERITY: THE REGIONAL ECONOMIC BENEFITS OF THE SAN PEDRO BAY PORTS' CLEAN TRUCKS PROGRAM 6–7 (2007), http://www.cleanandsafeports.org/fileadmin/files_editor/Road_to_Shared_Prosperity.pdf (last visited July 10, 2017).
622. HUSING ET AL., *supra* note 613, at i.
623. *Id.* at 74.
624. *Id.* at vi, 17 (predicting loss of 376 "mostly smaller LMCs" out of a total of 800 to 1,200 LMCs overall).
625. Ronald D. White, *Plan to Cut Port Air Pollution Assailed*, L.A. TIMES, Sept. 28, 2007, at C3.
626. Ronald D. White & Janet Wilson, *Opposition Grows to Ports' Clean-Air Plan*, L.A. TIMES, Sept. 29, 2007, at C1.
627. Ronald D. White, *Changes Urged in Proposal for Ports*, L.A. TIMES, Oct. 10, 2007, at C2.
628. White & Wilson, *supra* note 626.
629. Telephone Interview with David Libatique, *supra* note 358.
630. Telephone Interview with Sean Arian, *supra* note 583.
631. *Id.*
632. *Id.*
633. *Id.*
634. *Id.*
635. *Id.*
636. Telephone Interview with Nick Weiner, *supra* note 419.
637. Telephone Interview with Sean Arian, *supra* note 583.
638. Telephone Interview with John Holmes, Deputy Exec. Dir., Port of L.A. (Apr. 29, 2013).
639. *Id.*
640. *Id.* The placard and parking programs were in the version that Holmes received.
641. *Id.*
642. *Id.*
643. Telephone Interview with Nick Weiner, *supra* note 419.
644. *Id.*
645. *Id.*
646. *Id.*
647. *Id.*

648. *Id.*
649. *Id.*
650. Telephone Interview with John Holmes, *supra* note 638.
651. Telephone Interview with Sean Arian, *supra* note 583.
652. *Id.*
653. Telephone Interview with Nick Weiner, *supra* note 192.
654. Telephone Interview with Sean Arian, *supra* note 583.
655. *Id.*
656. Interview with John Holmes, *supra* note 91.
657. *Id.*
658. *Id.*
659. *Id.*
660. *Id.*
661. *Id.*
662. Telephone Interview with John Holmes, *supra* note 638.
663. *Id.*
664. Interview with John Holmes, *supra* note 91.
665. Telephone Interview with John Holmes, *supra* note 638.
666. *Id.*
667. Telephone Interview with Jerilyn López Mendoza, *supra* note 334.
668. Telephone Interview with Sean Arian, *supra* note 583.
669. Telephone Interview with Jerilyn López Mendoza, *supra* note 334.
670. Telephone Interview with S. David Freeman, *supra* note 355.
671. *Id.*
672. Telephone Interview with Jerilyn López Mendoza, *supra* note 334.
673. *Id.*
674. Telephone Interview with S. David Freeman, *supra* note 355.
675. Louis Sahagun, L.A. *Panel OKs Plan to Cut Port Truck Soot*, L.A. TIMES, Nov. 2, 2007, at B1.
676. Memorandum from Ralph G. Appy & Michael R. Christensen, Envtl. Mgmt. Div., Permanent Order Amending Port of L.A. Tariff No. 4 (Oct. 29, 2007).
677. L.A. Bd. of Harbor Comm'rs., Order 6935, Items 2010, 2015, 2020 (Nov. 1, 2007). The progressive ban operated by barring drayage trucks built before 1989 by October 1, 2008; barring unretrofitted trucks built before 2004 (and retrofitted trucks built before 1994) by January 1, 2010; and completely barring any trucks that did not meet EPA 2007 model year standards by January 1, 2012. *Id.*
678. L.A., Cal., Ordinance 165789 (Apr. 10, 1990) (adopting L.A. Bd. of Harbor Comm'rs, Order No. 5837 (July 12, 1989) (adopting Port of L.A. Tariff No. 4)).
679. L.A. Bd. of Harbor Comm'rs, Order 6935, Items 2010, 2015, 2020 (Nov. 1, 2007).
680. *Id.* ¶ 12.
681. *Id.* ¶¶ 13, 14.
682. *Id.* at Items 2000, 2005, 2025.
683. Long Beach Bd. of Harbor Comm'rs, *Minutes of a Special Meeting*, PORT LONG BEACH 20 (Nov. 5, 2007). At this meeting, during which the board approved the ordinance's first reading, the coalition turned out several drivers who spoke, as did NRDC's Martinez, the Coalition for Clean Air's Kim, and the American Lung Association's Callahan. *Id.* at 3–10. The Long Beach harbor commissioners approved the ordinance's "second and final reading" on November 12. Long Beach Bd. of Harbor Comm'rs, *Minutes*, PORT LONG BEACH 9 (Nov. 12, 2007). The ordinance, as adopted, was No. HD-1997, which amended Long Beach Tariff No. 4 to include findings and policy language that were identical to Los Angeles Order 6935. Long Beach, Cal., Ordinance HD-1997 (Nov. 12, 2007) (amending Ordinance HD-1357, Tariff No. 4 (Dec. 27, 1983)). The Long Beach Clean Truck Program was drafted by City Attorney Robert Shannon.
684. Louis Sahagun, *Long Beach Joins Port Ban on Old Trucks*, L.A. TIMES, Nov. 6, 2007, at B4.

685. Sahagun, *supra* note 675.
686. *Id.*
687. *Id.*
688. Sahagun, *supra* note 684.
689. Sahagun, *supra* note 392. The Ordinance, No. HD-2005, was unanimously approved in its second and final reading (with one commissioner absent) on January 7, 2008. *See* Long Beach, Cal., Ordinance No. HD-2005 (Jan. 9, 2008); *Long Beach Bd. of Harbor Comm'rs, Minutes*, PORT LONG BEACH 9 (Jan. 7, 2008).
690. Long Beach Bd. of Harbor Comm'rs, *Clean Truck Tariff Amendment and Fee*, Item 1030 (Dec. 11, 2007), http://www.polb.com/civica/filebank/blobdload.asp?BlobID=4708 (last visited July 10, 2017).
691. Sahagun, *supra* note 392.
692. Long Beach Bd. of Harbor Comm'rs, *Clean Truck Tariff Amendment and Fee*, *supra* note 690, at Item 1035.
693. L.A. Bd. of Harbor Comm'rs Order No. 6943 (Dec. 20, 2007). This order also followed a strong staff endorsement. *See* Memorandum from Ralph G. Appy & Michael R. Christensen to L.A., Cal. Bd. of Harbor Comm'rs (Dec. 20, 2007).
694. Telephone Interview with Nick Weiner, *supra* note 419.
695. Telephone Interview with S. David Freeman, *supra* note 355.
696. *Id.*
697. Sahagun, *supra* note 392.
698. Louis Sahagun, *Ports Turn over a New, Green Leaf*, L.A. TIMES, Dec. 25, 2007, at A1.
699. Louis Sahagun, *Unsafe Trucks Stream Out of L.A.'s Ports*, L.A. TIMES, Jan. 21, 2008, at A1.
700. Sahagun, *supra* note 698.
701. *Id.*
702. *Id.*
703. *Id.*
704. *See* ENVTL. MGMT. DIV., PORT OF L.A., DRAFT FINDINGS OF FACT AND STATEMENT OF OVERRIDING CONSIDERATIONS, BERTHS 136–147 [TRAPAC] CONTAINER TERMINAL PROJECT (2007).
705. L.A. Bd. of Harbor Comm'rs, *Minutes of the Special Meeting of the Los Angeles Board of Harbor Commissioners*, PORT L.A. (Dec. 6, 2007).
706. Letter from David Pettit et al. to Members of the Los Angeles City Council, Re: Appeal from Board of Harbor Commissioners Decision to Approve the Final EIR for TraPac Container Terminal (Dec. 14, 2007).
707. Telephone Interview with Kathleen Woodfield, Member, Sierra Club (May 14, 2013). Woodfield was also a member of the Port Community Advisory Committee. *Id.*
708. *Id.*
709. *See* Am. Trucking Ass'ns, Inc. v. City of Los Angeles, No. CV 08-4920 CAS (RZx), 2010 WL 3386436, at *8 (C.D. Cal. Aug. 26, 2010).
710. David Zahniser & Louis Sahagun, *Harbor Reaches Pollution Accord*, L.A. TIMES, Apr. 3, 2008, at B1.
711. Louis Sahagun, *Long Beach Port Faces Suit Threat*, L.A. TIMES, Feb. 7, 2008, at B3.
712. *Id.*
713. *Id.*
714. Louis Sahagun, *Officials of Area Ports Split over Truck Issue*, L.A. TIMES, Feb. 19, 2008, at B1.
715. *Id.*
716. Long Beach, Cal., Ordinance No. HD-2011, ¶ 14 (Mar. 17, 2008).
717. *Id.* at Item 1030.
718. Long Beach Bd. of Harbor Comm'rs, *Minutes*, PORT LONG BEACH 5–6 (Feb. 19, 2008).
719. A second and final reading of the ordinance was approved on March 17, 2008, with two commissioners (Doris Topsy-Elvord and Mike Walter) absent. Long Beach Bd. of Harbor

Comm'rs, *Minutes*, PORT LONG BEACH 6–7 (Mar. 17, 2008). The board authorized the port director to execute the concession agreements on June 2. Long Beach Bd. of Harbor Comm'rs, *Minutes*, PORT LONG BEACH 10 (June 2, 2008).
720. Louis Sahagun, *Public Health, Labor Groups Decry Harbor Panel's Air Plan*, L.A. TIMES, Feb. 20, 2008, at B4.
721. The Long Beach port's concession agreement stated that a concessionaire "shall give a hiring preference to drivers with a history of providing drayage services to the port," but did not require employee conversion. Long Beach Bd. of Harbor Comm'rs, Port of Long Beach Concession Agreement § III(e). Like the Los Angeles program that would follow, the Long Beach agreement required compliance with truck routes and parking restrictions, a maintenance plan, and placards, though it reduced the concession fee to $250 per concessionaire. *Id.* §§ III(f), (g), (m) & 2.1.1.
722. Sahagun, *supra* note 714.
723. Sahagun, *supra* note 720. The coalition appealed the board's decision to the City Council to no avail. NRDC then filed a Freedom of Information Act suit to get all documents relevant to the Clean Truck Program. "We just wanted to find out what was going on because they just kept on making these bizarre decisions behind closed doors, with no public process." Telephone Interview with Adrian Martinez, *supra* note 434.
724. Telephone Interview with Adrian Martinez, *supra* note 434.
725. Sahagun, *supra* note 714.
726. Editorial, *A Storm in Every Port*, L.A. TIMES, Feb. 24, 2008, at M2.
727. *Id.*
728. *Id.*
729. Martin Schlageter, *Letter to the Editor, Delays in Cleaning Up the Ports*, L.A. TIMES, Mar. 1, 2008, at A20.
730. Telephone Interview with Nick Weiner, *supra* note 419.
731. Telephone Interview with David Pettit, *supra* note 438.
732. L.A., Cal., Ordinance 179707 (Feb. 27, 2008) (adopting L.A. Bd. of Harbor Comm'rs, Order No. 6935 (Nov. 1, 2007) (progressive truck ban)); L.A., Cal., Ordinance 179708 (Feb. 27, 2008) (adopting L.A. Bd. of Harbor Comm'rs Order No. 6943 (Dec. 20, 2007) (clean truck fee)).
733. Zahniser & Sahagun, *supra* note 582.
734. *Id.*
735. *Id.*
736. *Id.*
737. *Id.*
738. THE BOS. CONSULTING GRP., SAN PEDRO BAY PORTS CLEAN TRUCK PROGRAM: CTP OPTIONS ANALYSIS 6 (2008).
739. *Id.*
740. *Id.* at 10.
741. *Id.* at 9.
742. *Id.*
743. *Id.* at 68.
744. *Id.* at 70, 79.
745. *Id.* at 74.
746. *Id.* at 9.
747. *Id.* at 74.
748. Ronald D. White & Louis Sahagun, *Risk Seen in Port Plan*, L.A. TIMES, Mar. 8, 2008, at C1.
749. Memorandum from John Holmes, Deputy Exec. Dir. of Operations & Molly Campbell, Deputy Exec. Dir. of Fin. & Admin., to the Bd. of Harbor Comm'rs (Mar. 12, 2008).
750. Telephone Interview with Sean Arian, *supra* note 583.
751. Editorial, *Harbor No Illusions*, L.A. TIMES, Mar. 20, 2008, at A20.

752. Telephone Interview with David Libatique, *supra* note 358.
753. The presentation of the concession plan provided at the meeting drew heavily on the BCG findings. *See The Port of Los Angeles Clean Truck Program: Program Overview & Benefits*, PORT OF L.A., http://www.portoflosangeles.org/ctp/CTP_O&B.pdf (last visited Apr. 2, 2014).
754. L.A. Bd. of Harbor Comm'rs, Order No. 6956 ¶ 3 (Mar. 20, 2008).
755. L.A. Bd. of Harbor Comm'rs, Port of L.A., Tariff No. 4, Item No. 2040 (Mar. 20, 2008).
756. *Id.* at Item No. 220(b).
757. L.A. Bd. of Harbor Comm'rs, Order No. 6956 ¶¶ 16, 19.
758. *Id.* ¶ 24.
759. Transmittal 1, Port of Los Angeles Drayage Truck Concession Requirements ¶ (b).
760. *Id.* ¶¶ (f), (m), (o).
761. L.A. Bd. of Harbor Comm'rs, Port of L.A., Tariff No. 4, Item No. 2095 (Mar. 20, 2008).
762. Telephone Interview with S. David Freeman, *supra* note 355.
763. L.A. Bd. of Harbor Comm'rs, Resol. 6522, at 1 (Mar. 20, 2008).
764. *Id.* ¶¶ a–o.
765. *Id.* at 7.
766. *Id.*
767. Louis Sahagun, *Port Shifts Plan's Cost to Shippers*, L.A. TIMES, Mar. 21, 2008, at B5.
768. Telephone Interview with Tom Politeo, *supra* note 453.
769. Telephone Interview with Kathleen Woodfield, *supra* note 707.
770. *Id.*
771. Telephone Interview with Tom Politeo, *supra* note 453.
772. *See* Press Release, Port of Los Angeles, Mayor Villaraigosa, Councilwoman Hahn Announce Historic Agreement That Will Allow TraPac Terminal Renovations to Go Forward at Port of L.A. (Apr. 3, 2008); *see also* Zahniser & Sahagun, *supra* note 710.
773. Telephone Interview with Kathleen Woodfield, *supra* note 707. Woodfield also noted the contributions of Serena Lin, a lawyer at Public Counsel Law Center. *Id.*
774. L.A. Harbor Dep't Agreement 09-2764, Memorandum of Understanding 4 (Apr. 2, 2008); *see also* Zahniser & Sahagun, *supra* note 710.
775. *See* L.A. Harbor Dep't Agreement 09-2764, *supra* note 774, at 4.
776. *Id.*
777. *Id.* at 3; *see also* L.A. Bd. of Harbor Comm'rs, *Minutes of a Special Meeting*, PORT L.A. 15–16 (Oct. 26, 2010) (approving creation of nonprofit organization to administer the Mitigation Trust Fund).
778. *See* L.A. Harbor Dep't Agreement 09-2764, *supra* note 774, at 2–3.
779. Zahniser & Sahagun, *supra* note 710.
780. *Id.*
781. L.A. Bd. of Harbor Comm'rs, Drayage Services Concession Agreement for Access to the Port of Los Angeles ¶ III(d).
782. *Id.*
783. *Id.* ¶¶ III(f), (g), (l), (n) & § 2.1.1.
784. *Id.* §§ 4.3 & 4.4.
785. *See* L.A. Bd. of Harbor Comm'rs, *Minutes of the Regular Meeting*, PORT OF L.A. 19–20 (May 15, 2008).
786. *See* L.A., Cal., Ordinance No. 179981 (June 17, 2008).
787. Phil Willon, *Mayor Signs Law to Clean Port Air*, L.A. TIMES, June 27, 2008, at B4. There were several subsequent technical amendments that clarified exemptions to the Clean Truck Fee, clarified the basis for charging the Clean Truck Fee, delayed the implementation of the fee, and made other adjustments. *See* L.A., Cal., Ordinance No. 180681 (Aug. 21, 2008); L.A., Cal., Ordinance No. 180679 (May 5, 2009); L.A., Cal., Ordinance No. 180923 (Oct. 14, 2009); L.A., Cal., Ordinance No. 1809253 (Oct. 14, 2009); L.A., Cal., Ordinance No. 180942 (Oct.

27, 2009); L.A., Cal., Ordinance No. 181125 (Mar. 12, 2010); L.A., Cal., Ordinance No. 181126 (Mar. 12, 2010); L.A., Cal., Ordinance No. 181255 (June 27, 2010).
788. Telephone Interview with Nick Weiner, *supra* note 419.
789. Telephone Interview with Jon Zerolnick, *supra* note 545.
790. Ronald D. White & Louis Sahagun, *National Trucking Group to Sue Ports over Cleanup Plan*, L.A. TIMES, July 26, 2008, at B9.
791. Complaint for Declaratory Judgment and Injunctive Relief, Am. Trucking Ass'ns, Inc. v. City of L.A., 577 F. Supp. 2d 1110 (C.D. Cal. 2008) (No. CV 08-04920 CAS (CTx)) (filed July 28, 2008). The ATA was represented by its in-house counsel, Robert Digges; outside law firm Constantine Cannon LLP, appearing pro hac vice; and local counsel Christopher C. McNatt, Jr. of Scopelitis, Garvin, Light, Hanson & Feary, LLP, in Pasadena. *Id.*
792. 49 U.S.C. § 14501(c)(1) (2012).
793. Complaint for Declaratory Judgment and Injunctive Relief, *supra* note 791, ¶ 2.
794. *Id.* ¶ 3.
795. *Id.* ¶ 4.
796. *Id.*
797. Louis Sahagun, *Truck Group Sues Ports*, L.A. TIMES, July 29, 2008, at B4.
798. Complaint for Declaratory Judgment and Injunctive Relief, *supra* note 791, ¶¶ 37–47 (Count I), ¶¶ 48–54 (Count II). Count III argued that both plans were preempted by the Commerce Clause. *Id.* ¶¶ 55–66.
799. Notice of Mot. and Mot. for Preliminary Injunction on Counts I and II of Plaintiff's Complaint, *Am. Trucking Ass'ns, Inc.*, 577 F. Supp. 2d 1110 (No. CV 08–04920 CAS (CTx)) (filed July 30, 2008).
800. Louis Sahagun & Ronald D. White, *Truckers and Ports Head to Court*, L.A. TIMES, Sept. 8, 2008, at B3.
801. Telephone Interview with Adrian Martinez, *supra* note 434.
802. Notice of Mot. and Mot. to Intervene of Natural Resources Defense Council, Sierra Club and Coalition for Clean Air at 1–2, *Am. Trucking Ass'ns, Inc.*, 577 F. Supp. 2d 1110 (No. CV 08-04920 CAS (CTx)) (filed July 31, 2008).
803. Opposition of Proposed Defendant-Intervenors Natural Resources Defense Council, Sierra Club and Coalition for Clean Air to Plaintiff's Mot. for Preliminary Injunction at 3, *Am. Trucking Ass'ns, Inc.*, 577 F. Supp. 2d 1110 (No. CV 08-04920 CAS (CTx)) (filed Aug. 20, 2008).
804. *Id.* at 5.
805. Telephone Interview with Melissa Lin Perrella, *supra* note 429.
806. Telephone Interview with Adrian Martinez, *supra* note 434.
807. *Id.*
808. Telephone Interview with David Pettit, *supra* note 438.
809. Telephone Interview with Melissa Lin Perrella, *supra* note 429.
810. Telephone Interview with David Pettit, *supra* note 438.
811. Telephone Interview with Melissa Lin Perrella, Staff Att'y, Nat. Res. Def. Council (Apr. 23, 2013).
812. Telephone Interview with Melissa Lin Perrella, *supra* note 429.
813. *Id.* Rosenthal suggested that although the city was "aligned" with NRDC in the litigation, they had "differing interests," noting that "NRDC certainly supported what we were doing, but NRDC sues the port as well." Telephone Interview with Steven S. Rosenthal, *supra* note 598.
814. Telephone Interview with Melissa Lin Perrella, *supra* note 811.
815. Telephone Interview with Michael Manley, *supra* note 178.
816. Telephone Interview with Michael Manley, Staff Att'y, Int'l Bhd. of Teamsters (Mar. 29, 2013).
817. The outside counsel was Paul L. Gale from Ross, Dixon & Bell, LLP, and C. Jonathan Benner and Mark E. Nagle, appearing pro hac vice, from Troutman Sanders, LLP. *See* Defendants'

Opposition to Plaintiff's Mot. for Preliminary Injunction, *Am. Trucking Ass'ns, Inc.*, 577 F. Supp. 2d 1110 (No. CV 08–04920 CAS (CTx)) (filed Aug. 20, 2008).
818. *Id.* at 17.
819. *Id.* at 22.
820. Engine Mfrs. Ass'n v. S. Coast Air Quality Mgmt. Dist., 498 F.3d 1031 (9th Cir. 2007).
821. Defendants' Opposition to Plaintiff's Mot. for Preliminary Injunction, *supra* note 817, at 26–29.
822. 49 U.S.C. § 14501(c)(2)(A) (2012).
823. Defendants' Opposition to Plaintiff's Mot. for Preliminary Injunction, *supra* note 817, at 38.
824. Declaration of John M. Holmes in Support of Defendants' Opposition to Plaintiff's Mot. for Preliminary Injunction at 4, Am. Trucking Ass'ns, Inc. v. City of L.A., 577 F. Supp. 2d 1110 (C.D. Cal. 2008) (No. CV 08–04920 CAS (CTx)) (filed Aug. 20, 2008). Affidavits of other port officials, including Los Angeles Executive Director Geraldine Knatz and Long Beach Executive Director Richard Steinke, were also submitted to support the defendants' broader market participant arguments. Declaration of Dr. Geraldine Knatz in Support of Defendants' Opposition to Plaintiff's Mot. for Preliminary Injunction, *Am. Trucking Ass'ns, Inc.*, 577 F. Supp. 2d 1110 (No. CV 08–04920 CAS (CTx)) (filed Aug. 20, 2008); Declaration of Richard Steinke in Support of Defendants' Opposition, *Am. Trucking Ass'ns, Inc.*, 577 F. Supp. 2d 1110 (No. CV 08–04920 CAS (CTx)) (filed Aug. 20, 2008).
825. Susan Gordon, *Beverly Hills Bar Association Honors the Honorable Christina A. Snyder and Top Trial Attorney Marshall B. Goldman*, WESTSIDETODAY (Feb. 6, 2013), http://www.westsidetoday.com/s7-8972/beverly-hills-bar-association.html (last visited July 11, 2017).
826. *Id.*
827. Order Denying Plaintiff's Mot. for Preliminary Injunction at 26, *Am. Trucking Ass'ns, Inc.*, 577 F. Supp. 2d 1110 (No. CV 08–04920 CAS (CTx)) (filed Sept. 9, 2008).
828. *Am. Trucking Ass'ns, Inc.*, 577 F. Supp. 2d at 1117.
829. *Id.* at 1125.
830. *Id.* at 1124–25.
831. *Id.* at 1121–23.
832. Preliminary Injunction Appeal, *Am. Trucking Ass'ns, Inc.*, 577 F. Supp. 2d 1110 (No. CV 08–04920 CAS (CTx)) (filed Sept. 10, 2008).
833. CONSUMER FED'N OF CAL. ET AL., FORECLOSURE ON WHEELS: LONG BEACH'S TRUCK PROGRAM PUTS DRIVERS AT HIGH RISK FOR DEFAULT (2008), http://laane.org/downloads/B568P314C.pdf (last visited July 11, 2017). The coalition included the NAACP, Consumer Federation of California, the League of United Latin American Citizens, and LAANE.
834. *Id.* at 2.
835. *Id.*
836. Louis Sahagun, *Long Beach Port's Truck Loans Criticized*, L.A. TIMES, Aug. 20, 2008, at B3.
837. Louis Sahagun, *Truckers Blast Long Beach Loan Program*, L.A. TIMES, Aug. 23, 2008, at B4.
838. Ronald D. White & Louis Sahagun, *2 Big Haulers Accept L.A. Port's Clean-Truck Criteria*, L.A. TIMES, Aug. 22, 2008, at C2.
839. Ronald D. White, *Truckers on Board with Clean-Air Plans*, L.A. TIMES, Sept. 6, 2008, at C1.
840. Louis Sahagun & Ronald D. White, *Local Ports Initiate Antipollution Program*, L.A. TIMES, Oct. 2, 2008, at B2 (noting a 9.9% decrease in container traffic at the Long Beach port and a 4.6% decrease at the Los Angeles port).
841. Francisco Vara-Orta, *Clean Air Program Revs Up Truck Sales*, L.A. BUSINESS J., May 25, 2009, https://labusinessjournal.com/news/2009/may/25/clean-air-program-revs-up-truck-sales/ (last visited Nov. 11, 2019).
842. Ronald D. White, *Truckers Unload Fuel Costs*, L.A. TIMES, Apr. 10, 2012, at A1.
843. Sahagun & White, *supra* note 840.
844. *Id.*

845. Br. of Appellant Am. Trucking Ass'ns, Inc. at 15, Am. Trucking Ass'ns, Inc. v. City of Los Angeles, 559 F.3d 1046 (9th Cir. 2009) (No. 08-56503) (filed Oct. 8, 2008).
846. Opening Br. for Appellees, *Am. Trucking Ass'ns, Inc.*, 559 F.3d 1046 (No. 08-56503) (filed Nov. 26, 2008).
847. Intervenor-Appellees' Br. at 3–4, *Am. Trucking Ass'ns, Inc.*, 559 F.3d 1046 (No. 08-56503) (filed Nov. 5, 2008).
848. Br. for the U.S. as Amicus Curiae in Support of Reversal, *Am. Trucking Ass'ns, Inc.*, 559 F.3d 1046 (No. 08-56503) (filed Oct. 21, 2008).
849. Br. of Amicus Curiae the Nat'l Indus. Transp. League in Support of Appellant Am. Trucking Ass'ns, Inc., *Am. Trucking Ass'ns, Inc.*, 559 F.3d 1046 (No. 08-56503) (filed Oct. 20, 2008).
850. Br. of Amicus Curiae Nat'l Ass'n of Waterfront Employers in Support of Appellant Am. Trucking Ass'ns, *Am. Trucking Ass'ns, Inc.*, 559 F.3d 1046 (No. 08-56503) (filed June 30, 2009).
851. Br. of the Att'y Gen. of the State of Cal. as Amicus Curiae in Support of Appellees the City of L.A., *Am. Trucking Ass'ns, Inc.*, 559 F.3d 1046 (No. 08-56503) (filed Dec. 18, 2008). In 2008, CARB was finalizing its own emission rules to phase out old, dirty diesel trucks by requiring all diesel trucks to meet 2010 standards by the year 2023. Margot Roosevelt, *Community Groups, State Battle Pollution*, L.A. TIMES, Dec. 11, 2008, at B1. The *Los Angeles Times* editorial board praised the CARB plan but also used it to take another jab at the Los Angeles port's employee conversion program: "The port needs a separate truck plan because it has a separate mechanism for funding cleaner vehicles, but it would be better off imitating state regulators and focusing on cleaning the air, not trying to reinvent the steering wheel." Editorial, *A New Day for Diesel*, L.A. TIMES, Dec. 12, 2008, at A32. Industry groups challenged the CARB standard and NRDC intervened to support it. Telephone Interview with Melissa Lin Perrella, *supra* note 811. The standard was approved in 2008, although by 2014, it still had not been fully implemented. Tony Barboza, *Date for Cleaner Trucks Delayed*, L.A. TIMES, Apr. 26, 2014, at AA1 (stating that CARB agreed to postpone the compliance deadline for "small fleets, lightly used trucks and those operating in rural areas"). The Port of Los Angeles subsequently amended Tariff No. 4 to be consistent with the CARB standards. L.A. Bd. of Harbor Comm'rs, Order No. 09-7031 (Dec. 8, 2009).
852. *Am. Trucking Ass'ns, Inc.*, 559 F.3d at 1060.
853. *Id.* at 1057.
854. *Id.* at 1053.
855. *Id.* at 1055.
856. *Id.*
857. *Id.* at 1056.
858. *Id.*
859. *Id.* at 1056–57.
860. *Id.* at 1057–58.
861. *Id.* at 1059–60.
862. *Id.* at 1060.
863. Notice of Plaintiff's Mot. on Remand for Entry of a Preliminary Injunction on Counts I and II of Complaint, Am. Trucking Ass'ns, Inc. v. City of L.A., No. CV 08-4920 CAS (CTx), 2009 WL 1160212 (C.D. Cal. Apr. 28, 2009) (filed Apr. 3, 2009).
864. Los Angeles Defendants' Opposition to ATA's Mot. on Remand for a Preliminary Injunction at 6–11, *Am. Trucking Ass'ns, Inc.*, No. CV 08-4920 CAS (CTx), 2009 WL 1160212 (filed Apr. 13, 2009). The provisions of Los Angeles's concession plan not addressed by the Ninth Circuit order included those requiring concessionaires to prepare maintenance plans; ensure driver enrollment in TWIC; guarantee compliance with federal, state, and local laws (including other provisions of the Clean Truck Program); and post placards.
865. Long Beach Defendants' Memorandum in Opposition to Plaintiff's Mot. on Remand for Preliminary Injunction at 2–3, *Am. Trucking Ass'ns, Inc.*, No. CV 08-4920 CAS (CTx), 2009 WL 1160212 (filed Apr. 13, 2009). Long Beach also argued that its plan should be examined

in the first instance by the Secretary of Transportation, which had statutory authority to determine whether its plan could be enforced. *Id.* at 7.
866. Reply of ATA in Support of Mot. on Remand for Preliminary Injunction at 22–23, Am. Trucking Ass'ns, Inc., No. CV 08-4920 CAS (CTx), 2009 WL 1160212 (filed Apr. 17, 2009).
867. Editorial, *Let's Get Truckin,'* L.A. TIMES, Apr. 24, 2009, at A32. As he had in the past, the Coalition for Clean Air's Martin Schlageter responded to the *Times*: "Without a systemic fix, today's new trucks will be tomorrow's broken-down trucks." Martin Schlageter, *The Road We're On*, L.A. TIMES, Apr. 28, 2009, at A22 (letter to editor).
868. Am. Trucking Ass'ns, Inc., No. CV 08-4920 CAS (CTx), 2009 WL 1160212.
869. *Id.* at *20–21. The court also enjoined Long Beach's driver health insurance provision, and both ports' truck tariffs and concession fees. *Id.* However, in a subsequent ruling, responding to a motion by the ATA to modify the April 28 order so that it would not have to post bond, the court reinstituted the Port of Los Angeles's concession fee. Am. Trucking Ass'ns, Inc. v. City of L.A., No. CV 08-4920 CAS (CTx), 2009 WL 2412578, at *2–3 (C.D. Cal. Aug. 4, 2009).
870. Am. Trucking Ass'ns, Inc., No. CV 08-4920 CAS (CTx), 2009 WL 1160212, at *11–18. In total, the court let stand nine provisions requiring concessionaires to: (1) be LMCs; (2) use permitted trucks; (3) ensure driver compliance with concession agreement; (4) prepare a maintenance plan; (5) ensure driver enrollment in TWIC; (6) ensure that trucks had compliance tags; (7) ensure compliance with security laws; (8) post placards; and (9) keep records. *Id.* at *21.
871. *Id.* at *19–20.
872. Ronald D. White, *Judge Restricts Ports' Truck Plan*, L.A. TIMES, Apr. 30, 2009, at B2.
873. Br. of Appellant Am. Trucking Ass'ns at 13–16, Am. Trucking Ass'ns, Inc. v. City of L.A., 596 F.3d 602 (9th Cir. 2010) (No. 09-55749) (filed June 11, 2009).
874. Stipulation of Settlement and Joint Mot. for Voluntary Dismissal with Prejudice between Plaintiff ATA and Long Beach Defendants, Exhibit A, Motor Carrier Registration and Agreement at 1–2, Am. Trucking Ass'ns, Inc. v. City of L.A., No. CV 08-4920 CAS (CTx) (filed Oct. 19, 2009). The settlement was approved by the Long Beach Board of Harbor Commissioners after a closed session meeting, with Commissioner Cordero voting against. Long Beach Bd. of Harbor Comm'rs, *Minutes of a Special Meeting*, PORT LONG BEACH 1 (Oct. 19, 2009).
875. Ronald D. White, *Port Settles Truckers' Lawsuit*, L.A. TIMES, Oct. 21, 2009, at B4.
876. Exhibit A, Motor Carrier Registration and Agreement, *supra* note 874, at 2–4. The settlement also required the Long Beach port to amend provisions of its Clean Truck Program to be consistent with the settlement terms, which it did after a full hearing at which Pettit, Zerolnick, Schlageter, and other coalition members spoke out against the changes. Long Beach Bd. of Harbor Comm'rs, *Minutes*, PORT LONG BEACH 9–11 (Nov. 16, 2009).
877. Order of Voluntary Dismissal with Prejudice of Long Beach Defendants, *Am. Trucking Ass'ns, Inc.*, No. CV 08-4920 CAS (CTx) (filed Oct. 20, 2009). NRDC and other environmental groups challenged the Long Beach settlement on CEQA grounds, arguing that it "substantially weakened the environmental benefits of the Port's Clean Truck Program" and that the Long Beach port violated CEQA by failing to conduct an appropriate environmental review. NRDC, Inc. v. City of Long Beach, No. CV 10-826 CAS (PJWx), 2011 WL 2790261, at *1–2 (C.D. Cal. July 14, 2011). The district court agreed, ordering an initial environmental study in July 2011. *Id.* at *5. The city conducted a study and issued a negative declaration, stating that the proposed project would not have a significant effect on the environment. THOMAS JOHNSON ENVTL. CONSULTANT LLC, PORT OF LONG BEACH ATA LITIGATION SETTLEMENT AGREEMENT: INITIAL STUDY (2011), http://www.polb.com/civica/filebank/blobdload.asp?BlobID=9236 (last visited July 11, 2017).
878. Ronald D. White, *Ports Split on Union Stance*, L.A. TIMES, Nov. 28, 2009, at B1.

879. Joint Stipulation Regarding Plaintiff's Mot. to Compel Production of Documents Withheld Due to the Deliberate Process Privilege at 1–3, *Am. Trucking Ass'ns, Inc.*, No. 08-4920 CAS (RZx), 2010 WL 3386436 (filed Oct. 19, 2009).
880. Order Re: Plaintiff's Mot. for Rev. of the Order of the Magistrate Judge Declining to Require Production of Documents Withheld Due to the Deliberative Process Privilege at 13, *Am. Trucking Ass'ns, Inc.*, No. 08-4920 CAS (RZx), 2010 WL 3386436 (filed Dec. 21, 2009).
881. Seema Mehta, *Truckers Protest New Rules*, L.A. TIMES, Nov. 14, 2009, at A3.
882. Bill Mongelluzzo, *ILWU Backs Long Beach Clean Trucks Program*, J. COM. (Jan. 7, 2010), http://www.joc.com/maritime-news/ilwu-backs-long-beach-clean-trucks-program_20100107.html (last visited July 11, 2017).
883. Am. Trucking Ass'ns, Inc. v. City of Los Angeles, 596 F.3d 602, 606 (9th Cir. 2010). The panel consisted of a staunch liberal, Harry Pregerson, appointed by President Jimmy Carter; Ronald M. Gould, a conservative appointed by President Bill Clinton in a deal to break a nominations impasse; and Myron H. Bright, a senior Eighth Circuit judge (appointed by President Lyndon Johnson) sitting by designation.
884. *Id.*
885. On February 25, 2010, the district court denied both the ATA and Port of Los Angeles's cross-motions for summary judgment, clearing the way for trial. Civil Minutes—General, *Am. Trucking Ass'ns, Inc.*, No. 08-4920 CAS (RZx), 2010 WL 3386436 (proceedings in chambers on Feb. 25, 2010).
886. Telephone Interview with Jon Zerolnick, *supra* note 545.
887. *Id.*
888. *Id.*
889. *Id.*
890. Patrick J. McDonnell, *Truckers Caught in a Tight Spot*, L.A. TIMES, Nov. 27, 2009, at A18. Critics charged that most port incentives went to fund big trucking companies (Swift Transportation received $12 million for 591 clean trucks, while Knight Transportation got $4.4 million for 172 trucks), although the port stated that $200 million went to small firms. *Id.*
891. *Id.*
892. *Id.*
893. Patrick J. McDonnell, *Truckers Assail "Green" Cost*, L.A. TIMES, Dec. 7, 2010, at A1.
894. *Id.*
895. *Id.*
896. *Id.* Similar reports of driver hardship came out of Long Beach. *See* Kristopher Hanson, *Straining Under the Load*, LONG BEACH PRESS-TEL., Aug. 23, 2009, at 3A (quoting one driver as saying: "Between payments for the new truck, insurance, fuel, taxes and the lack of work, I'm barely making it").
897. Complaint for an Injunction Pursuant to Section 6(h) of the Shipping Act of 1984 46 U.S.C. § 41307, Fed. Mar. Comm'n v. City of L.A., 607 F. Supp. 2d 192 (D.D.C. 2009) (No. 08-1895 (RJL)) (filed Oct. 31, 2008).
898. 46 U.S.C. § 41307(b)(1) (2012).
899. SEJAL PATEL, FROM CLEAN TO CLUNKER: THE ECONOMICS OF EMISSIONS CONTROL 5 (2010), https://perma.cc/M8QN-WBQR (last visited July 11, 2017).
900. Plaintiff's L.R. 16-10 Trial Br. at i, Am. Trucking Ass'ns, Inc. v. City of L.A., No. 08-4920 CAS (RZx), 2010 WL 3386436 (C.D. Cal. Aug. 26, 2010) (filed Apr. 13, 2010). That the commerce argument was relegated to a subsidiary position did not surprise NRDC's Martinez, who reflected that the freight industry "lawyers will scream commerce clause violations to the top of their lungs during the advocacy or administrative stage, . . . [b]ut ultimately I haven't found them to want to litigate it because . . . there's fear of bad precedent . . . [since] I don't think their case is that strong." Telephone Interview with Adrian Martinez, *supra* note 434.
901. *Am. Trucking Ass'ns, Inc.*, No. 08-4920 CAS (RZx), 2010 WL 3386436, at *2–3.
902. Castle v. Hayes Freight Lines, Inc., 348 U.S. 61, 63–64 (1954).

903. Am. Trucking Ass'ns, Inc. v. City of Los Angeles, 596 F.3d 602, 607 (9th Cir. 2010).
904. Plaintiff's L.R. 16-10 Trial Br., *supra* note 900, at 25.
905. Defendants' Trial Br. (L.R. 16-10) at 1, *Am. Trucking Ass'ns, Inc.*, No. 08-4920 CAS (RZx), 2010 WL 3386436 (filed Apr. 13, 2010).
906. Telephone Interview with David Pettit, *supra* note 438.
907. Defendants' Trial Br. (L.R. 16-10), *supra* note 905, at 22–23 n.10, 24–25.
908. Telephone Interview with David Pettit, *supra* note 438.
909. Tr. of Defendant the City of Los Angeles' Opening Statement at 35, *Am. Trucking Ass'ns, Inc.*, No. 08-4920 CAS (RZx), 2010 WL 3386436.
910. *Id.* at 28, 33.
911. *Id.* at 30, 41.
912. Tr. of Intervenor Nat. Res. Def. Council's Opening Statement at 49, *Am. Trucking Ass'ns, Inc.*, No. 08-4920 CAS (RZx), 2010 WL 3386436.
913. *Id.* at 52–53.
914. Tr. of Testimony of Defendant's Witness, Dr. Geraldine Knatz, *Am. Trucking Ass'ns, Inc.*, No. 08-4920 CAS (RZx), 2010 WL 3386436.
915. Tr. of Testimony of Defendant's Witness, Simon David Freeman, *Am. Trucking Ass'ns, Inc.*, No. 08-4920 CAS (RZx), 2010 WL 3386436.
916. Tr. of Testimony of Defendant's Witness, John Merrill Holmes at 84, *Am. Trucking Ass'ns, Inc.*, No. 08-4920 CAS (RZx), 2010 WL 3386436.
917. Tr. of Testimony of Defendant's Expert Witness, Jeffrey Walter Brown, *Am. Trucking Ass'ns, Inc.*, No. 08-4920 CAS (RZx), 2010 WL 3386436; Tr. of Testimony of Defendant's Expert Witness, James Evan Hall, *Am. Trucking Ass'ns, Inc.*, No. 08-4920 CAS (RZx), 2010 WL 3386436; Tr. of Testimony of Defendant's Witness, Bruce Charles Wargo, *Am. Trucking Ass'ns, Inc.*, No. 08-4920 CAS (RZx), 2010 WL 3386436.
918. Tr. of Testimony of Defendant's Expert Witness, Dr. Elaine Chang, *Am. Trucking Ass'ns, Inc.*, No. 08-4920 CAS (RZx), 2010 WL 3386436.
919. Tr. of Testimony of Intervenor's Witness, Bernice Banares, *Am. Trucking Ass'ns, Inc.*, No. 08-4920 CAS (RZx), 2010 WL 3386436.
920. Telephone Interview with Melissa Lin Perrella, *supra* note 811.
921. *Am. Trucking Ass'ns, Inc.*, No. 08-4920 CAS (RZx), 2010 WL 3386436, at *20.
922. *Id.* at *22–23.
923. *Id.* at *19–22.
924. *Id.* at *26.
925. *Id.*
926. *Id.* at *27.
927. *Id.* at *28.
928. *Id.* at *29–32. In reaching its conclusion, the court dismissed the port's tideland trust power claim. *Id.* at *23.
929. Memorandum of Points & Auths. on Mot. to Stay Final Judgment Pending Appeal, *Am. Trucking Ass'ns, Inc.*, No. 08-4920 CAS (RZx), 2010 WL 3386436 (filed Sept. 24, 2010).
930. Civil Minutes—General on Plaintiff's Mot. for Injunction Pending Appeal at 8, *Am. Trucking Ass'ns, Inc.*, No. 08-4920 CAS (RZx), 2010 WL 3386436 (proceedings in chambers Oct. 25, 2010).
931. *Compare* Br. of Appellant Am. Trucking Ass'ns, Inc., Am. Trucking Ass'ns, Inc. v. City of L.A., 660 F.3d 384 (9th Cir. 2011) (No. 10-56465) (filed Dec. 28, 2010), *with* Br. for Appellees, *Am. Trucking Ass'ns, Inc.*, 660 F.3d 384 (No. 10-56465) (filed Jan. 31, 2011) *and* Br. for Intervenor-Appellees, *Am. Trucking Ass'ns, Inc.*, 660 F.3d 384 (No. 10-56465) (filed Jan. 31, 2011).
932. Intermodal Ass'n of N. Am., Inc. to Participate as Amicus Curiae, *Am. Trucking Ass'ns, Inc.*, 660 F.3d 384 (No. 10-56465) (filed Jan. 4, 2011).
933. Mot. for Leave to File Amicus Br. in Support of Appellant by Raymond Porras, et al., *Am. Trucking Ass'ns, Inc.*, 660 F.3d 384 (No. 10-56465) (filed Jan. 4, 2011).

934. Br. of the Owner-Operator Indep. Drivers Ass'n, Inc., as Amicus Curiae in Support of Appellant Am. Trucking Ass'ns, Inc., for Reversal of District Court's Findings of Fact and Conclusions of Law, *Am. Trucking Ass'ns, Inc.*, 660 F.3d 384 (No. 10-56465) (filed Jan. 4, 2011).
935. Br. Amicus Curiae of Ctr. for Const'l Juris. & Harbor Trucking Ass'n in Support of Plaintiff-Appellant at 9, *Am. Trucking Ass'ns, Inc.*, 660 F.3d 384 (No. 10-56465) (filed Jan. 4, 2011). The California attorney general again supported the port. *See* Amicus Curiae Br. of the State of Cal., ex rel. Att'y Gen. Kamala Harris in Support of Appellees and Affirmance, *Am. Trucking Ass'ns, Inc.*, 660 F.3d 384 (No. 10-56465) (filed Feb. 17, 2011).
936. *Am. Trucking Ass'ns, Inc.*, 660 F.3d 384 (filed Sept. 26, 2011). Dissenting, Judge Smith would have held the entire plan to be preempted, that market participant status did not apply because the relevant market was trucking services (in which the port did not participate), and that the safety exception was precluded by *Castle*. *Id*. at 410–15 (Smith, J., dissenting).
937. *Id*. at 401.
938. *Id*. at 401–02.
939. *Id*. at 402.
940. *Id*. at 403–09.
941. *Id*. at 408.
942. *Id*.
943. *Id*.
944. *Id*.
945. *Id*.
946. Louis Sahagun, *Panel Throws Out Part of Port's Clean Truck Program*, L.A. TIMES, Sept. 27, 2011, at AA3.
947. Editorial, *Truckin' Toward a Cleaner Port*, L.A. TIMES, Sept. 28, 2011, at A12.
948. Telephone Interview with David Pettit, *supra* note 438.
949. Telephone Interview with Adrian Martinez, *supra* note 434.
950. Telephone Interview with Adrian Martinez, Staff Att'y, Nat. Res. Def. Council (Mar. 29, 2013).
951. Petition for a Writ of Certiorari, Am. Trucking Ass'ns, Inc. v. City of L.A., 133 S. Ct. 2096 (2013) (No. 11-798) (filed Dec. 22, 2011).
952. Telephone Interview with Melissa Lin Perrella, *supra* note 811.
953. *Id*.
954. Petition for a Writ of Certiorari, *supra* note 951, at 2. In their amicus briefs, the Chamber of Commerce and National Industrial Transportation League, Center for Constitutional Jurisprudence and Harbor Trucking Association, and Airlines for America (the airline trade group) all sided with the ATA in arguing for limiting the market participant exception. *See* Br. for the Chamber of Commerce of the United States of America & Nat'l Indus. Transp. League as Amici Curiae in Support of Petitioner, *Am. Trucking Ass'ns, Inc.*, 133 S. Ct. 2096 (No. 11-798) (filed Jan. 23, 2012); Mot. for Leave to File and Br. Amicus Curiae of Ctr. of Const'l Juris. & Harbor Trucking Ass'n in Support of Petitioner, *Am. Trucking Ass'ns, Inc.*, 133 S. Ct. 2096 (No. 11-798) (filed Jan. 23, 2012); Br. of Amicus Curiae Airlines for Am. in Support of Petitioner, *Am. Trucking Ass'ns, Inc.*, 133 S. Ct. 2096 (No. 11-798) (filed Jan. 23, 2012).
955. City of L.A. Br. in Opposition at 9–38, *Am. Trucking Ass'ns, Inc.*, 133 S. Ct. 2096 (No. 11-798) (filed Feb. 21, 2012).
956. NRDC Br. in Opposition at 5–14, *Am. Trucking Ass'ns, Inc.*, 133 S. Ct. 2096 (No. 11-798) (filed Feb. 21, 2012).
957. Telephone Interview with Adrian Martinez, *supra* note 950.
958. Br. for the United States as Amicus Curiae Supporting Reversal, *Am. Trucking Ass'ns, Inc.*, 133 S. Ct. 2096 (No. 11-798) (filed Feb. 22, 2013).
959. David G. Savage, *High Court to Hear Case on Port's Clean Truck Program*, L.A. TIMES, Jan. 12, 2013, at B2.
960. Br. for the United States as Amicus Curiae Supporting Reversal, *supra* note 958, at 6.

961. The ATA technically did not seek review of the Ninth Circuit holding that the truck maintenance provision fell under the safety exception; it did ask for review of the financial capability provision, but the Supreme Court refused to grant it. *Am. Trucking Ass'ns, Inc.*, 133 S. Ct. at 2102 n.3.
962. Telephone Interview with Melissa Lin Perrella, *supra* note 811.
963. Br. for the City of L.A. Respondents at 15, *Am. Trucking Ass'ns, Inc.*, 133 S. Ct. 2096 (No. 11-798) (filed Mar. 18, 2013).
964. *Id.* at 29–30.
965. Br. for Respondents Nat. Res. Def. Council, et al. at 10, *Am. Trucking Ass'ns, Inc.*, 133 S. Ct. 2096 (No. 11-798) (filed Mar. 18, 2013).
966. Telephone Interview with Michael Manley, *supra* note 816.
967. Telephone Interview with Melissa Lin Perrella, *supra* note 811. Perrella also recalled circulating information on the Supreme Court case on a port listserv, responding to listserv questions, and explaining the case to coalition members. *Id.*
968. Tr. of Oral Argument at 30, *Am. Trucking Ass'ns, Inc.*, 133 S. Ct. 2096.
969. *Id.* at 31.
970. Telephone Interview with Melissa Lin Perrella, *supra* note 811.
971. Tr. of Oral Argument, *supra* note 968, at 39.
972. *Id.* at 44–51.
973. *Am. Trucking Ass'ns, Inc.*, 133 S. Ct. at 2102.
974. *Id.*
975. *Id.* at 2103.
976. *Id.*
977. *Id.*
978. *Id.* at 2104.
979. *Id.* at 2105.
980. *Id.* In a concurrence, Justice Thomas, while agreeing entirely with the opinion, noted an issue that the port failed to raise but, in his view, should have: The FAAAA's application to port trucking, which was entirely intrastate, was quite likely unconstitutional under the Commerce Clause and thus the FAAAA itself would lack preemptive force. *Id.* at 2106 (Thomas, J., concurring): "Although respondents waived any argument that Congress lacks authority to regulate the placards and parking arrangements of drayage trucks using the port, I doubt that Congress has such authority." *Id.*
981. *Id.* at 2102 n.4 (majority opinion).
982. *Id.* at 2102.
983. Interview with John Holmes, *supra* note 91.
984. Ronald D. White, *Cleaner Port Air, but How?*, L.A. TIMES, Jan. 9, 2010, at B1 (noting that the Los Angeles port had given out $44 million in incentives); David Zanhiser, *Trucking Group to Appeal Port Ruling*, L.A. TIMES, Aug. 28, 2010, at AA3 (stating that the harbor department had given out $57 million to subsidize vehicles).
985. The Clean Truck Program did not mandate that truck drivers purchase and maintain their own trucks. Rather, it directed terminal operators to bar noncompliant dirty trucks, while stating that trucking companies "shall be responsible for vehicle condition and safety and shall ensure that the maintenance of all Permitted Trucks . . . is conducted in accordance with manufacturer's instructions." L.A. Bd. of Harbor Comm'rs, Drayage Services Concession Agreement for Access to the Port of Los Angeles, *supra* note 781, ¶ III(g). The program did not preclude trucking companies from passing on the purchase and maintenance costs to drivers and, as a matter of practice, that is what the companies did. *See* McDonnell, *supra* note 893.
986. Telephone Interview with Melissa Lin Perrella, *supra* note 429.
987. Am. Trucking Ass'ns, Inc. v. City of L.A., 559 F.3d 1046, 1056 (9th Cir. 2009).

988. Louis Sahagun & Ronald D. White, *Groups to Ask Congress for Help on Port*, L.A. TIMES, Apr. 15, 2009, at A12.
989. Telephone Interview with Jon Zerolnick, *supra* note 545.
990. Telephone Interview with Melissa Lin Perrella, *supra* note 429.
991. Coal. for Clean & Safe Ports, Background on the Port of Los Angeles Clean Trucks Program (July 15, 2009).
992. Art Marroquin, *Port Panel Extends Lobbying Contract*, PASADENA STAR-NEWS (Jan. 20, 2010), http://www.pasadenastarnews.com/20100121/port-panel-extends-lobbying-contract (last visited July 11, 2017).
993. Telephone Interview with Jon Zerolnick, *supra* note 545.
994. LAANE, BRIEFING BOOK, CLEARING THE ROADBLOCKS: A MAP TO GREEN AND GROW A KEY AMERICAN INDUSTRY TO CREATE 85,000 MIDDLE-CLASS JOBS AT OUR NATION'S PORTS (2009).
995. Coal. for Clean & Safe Ports, Background on the Port of Los Angeles Clean Trucks Program, *supra* note 991.
996. Letter from Zoe Lofgren et al., Representatives from the State of Cal., U.S. House of Representatives, to James L. Oberstar, Chairman of the Transp. & Infrastructure Comm., U.S. House of Representatives (Nov. 4, 2009).
997. Antonio Villaraigosa, *Clean Trucks: One Year Later*, HUFFINGTON POST GREEN (Dec. 1, 2009), http://www.huffingtonpost.com/antonio-villaraigosa/clean-trucks-one-year-lat_b_307158.html (last visited July 11, 2017).
998. White, *supra* note 875.
999. Ronald D. White, *L.A. Port Urged to Stop Lobbying over Clean Truck Program*, L.A. TIMES, Aug. 26, 2009, at B2.
1000. Telephone Interview with Nick Weiner, *supra* note 419.
1001. Telephone Interview with Jonathan Klein, *supra* note 479.
1002. Telephone Interview with Nick Weiner, *supra* note 419.
1003. *Id.*
1004. Letter from LAANE et al. to James B. Oberstar, Chairman of the Transp. & Infrastructure Comm., U.S. House of Representatives, & John Mica, Ranking Member of the Transp. & Infrastructure Comm., U.S. House of Representatives (Apr. 22, 2010).
1005. *Id.*
1006. *Assessing the Implementation and Impacts of the Clean Truck Programs at the Port of Los Angeles and the Port of Long Beach: Hearing Before the Comm. on Transp. & Infrastructure*, 111th Cong. 2 (2010).
1007. Telephone Interview with Jon Zerolnick, *supra* note 545.
1008. Telephone Interview with Nick Weiner, *supra* note 419.
1009. Clean Ports Act of 2010, H.R. 5967, 111th Cong. (2010); *see also* Darren Goode, *E2 Morning Round-up: Green Groups Highlight Oil Accidents, Spill Response Debate Heats Up, Nadler Floats "Clean Ports" Bill and Oil Spill Threatens Lake Michigan*, THE HILL (July 29, 2010), http://thehill.com/blogs/e2-wire/111569-e2-morning-round-up-green-groups-highlight-oil-accidents-spill-response-debate-heats-up-nadler-floats-clean-ports-bill-and-oil-spill-threatens-lake-michigan (last visited July 11, 2017).
1010. H.R. 5967.
1011. COAL. FOR CLEAN & SAFE PORTS, LONGER HOURS, LOWER WAGES & LITTLE HOPE 1 (2010).
1012. *Id.*
1013. Telephone Interview with Nick Weiner, *supra* note 419.
1014. Clean Ports Act of 2011, H.R. 572, 112th Cong. (2011). The new legislation added three words to the last clause of proposed section 14501(c)(2)(A) so that it exempted local or state laws related to environmental, traffic, or operational concerns so long as "adoption or enforcement of such requirements" did not conflict with other federal laws. *Id.*

1015. *The Clean Ports Act of 2011 (H.R. 572), in* COAL. FOR CLEAN & SAFE PORTS (May 2011).
1016. Clean Ports Act of 2011, S. 2011, 112th Cong. (2011). Gillibrand had five co-sponsors: Senators Barbara Boxer (CA), Sherrod Brown (OH), Al Franken (MN), Robert Menendez (NJ), and Charles Schumer (NY).
1017. A.B. 950, 2011–2012 Leg., Reg. Sess. (Cal. 2011).
1018. Assembly Third Reading, A.B. 950 (Feb. 18, 2011); Assemb. Comm. on Lab. and Emp., Hearing on A.B. 950 (May 4, 2011).
1019. *California Bill Seeking to Ban Independent Truck Operators Shelved*, PAC. MAR. ONLINE (June 7, 2011), http://www.pmmonlinenews.com/2011/06/california-bill-seeking-to-ban.html (last visited July 11, 2017).
1020. *Id.*
1021. A 2007 report found that only 9% of Los Angeles and Long Beach port truck drivers worked as employees. *See* GREENBERG QUINLAN ROSNER RESEARCH, DEMOGRAPHIC OVERVIEW OF TRUCK DRIVERS AT THE PORTS OF LOS ANGELES AND LONG BEACH 3 (2007), https://perma.cc/B6CD-2FAT (last visited July 20, 2017).
1022. *See* Albillo v. Intermodal Container Servs., Inc., 8 Cal. Rptr. 3d 350, 354 (Cal. Ct. App. 2003); BONACICH & WILSON, *supra* note 1, at 219.
1023. Telephone Interview with Jon Zerolnick, *supra* note 545.
1024. *See* Lambert v. Ackerley, 180 F.3d 997, 1012 (9th Cir. 1999); S.G. Borello & Sons, Inc. v. Dep't of Indus. Rel., 769 P.2d 399, 403–05 (Cal. 1989).
1025. Press Release, Cal. Att'y Gen., Attorney General Brown Sues Three Trucking Companies in Ongoing Worker Abuse Crackdown at Los Angeles and Long Beach Ports (Oct. 27, 2008), https://oag.ca.gov/news/press-releases/attorney-general-brown-sues-three-trucking-companies-ongoing-worker-abuse (last visited July 17, 2017).
1026. The companies sued by Attorney General Brown included Pacifica Trucks, Guasimal Trucking, Jose Maria Lira Trucking, Esdmundo Lira Trucking, and Noel and Emma Moreno Trucking. Press Release, Cal. Att'y Gen., Brown Wins Fifth Suit Against Port Trucking Companies that Violated Workers' Rights, (Feb. 4, 2010), http://oag.ca.gov/news/press-releases/brown-wins-fifth-suit-against-port-trucking-companies-violated-workers-rights (last visited July 17, 2017).
1027. CAL. BUS. & PROF. CODE §§ 17200–17210 authorizes injunctive relief and civil restitution against anyone engaged in "unfair competition," defined broadly as "any unlawful, unfair or fraudulent business act or practice."
1028. Press Release, Cal. Att'y Gen., *supra* note 1026.
1029. Telephone Interview with Michael Manley, *supra* note 816.
1030. *See* Complaint for Restitution, Penalties and Injunctive Relief, State v. Pac Anchor Transp., Inc., No. BC397600 (Sept. 4, 2008), http://oag.ca.gov/system/files/attachments/press_releases/n1606_complaint_pac_anchor.pdf (last visited July 17, 2017).
1031. *Truckers Claim Brown's Frivolous Lawsuit Designed to Curry Political Favor*, LEGAL NEWSLINE (Nov. 25, 2008), http://legalnewsline.com/news/217658-truckers-claim-browns-frivolous-lawsuit-designed-to-curry-political-favor (last visited July 17, 2017).
1032. Marc Lifsher, *Her Job: Putting a Stop to Wage Theft*, L.A. TIMES, May 22, 2013, at B1.
1033. *See* Bureerong v. Uvawas, 922 F. Supp. 1450, 1459–61 (C.D. Cal. 1996).
1034. SMITH ET AL., *supra* note 70, at 6.
1035. Isaías Alvarado, "We Are at the Mercy of God," LA OPINIÓN, Dec. 8, 2010, http://cleanandsafeports.org/fileadmin/pdf/La_Opinion_december_article_Eng.pdf (last visited July 17, 2017).
1036. RUTH MILKMAN ET AL., WAGE THEFT AND WORKPLACE VIOLATIONS IN LOS ANGELES 2 (2010) (finding that 30% of L.A. workers were paid less than minimum wage in the week preceding the survey, while 21.3% were not paid overtime).
1037. James Rufus Koren, *Truckers Want Break on Audits*, L.A. BUS. J., Oct. 1, 2012, at 1, 35.
1038. Telephone Interview with Sanjukta Paul, Legal Coordinator, L.A. All. for a New Econ. (May 9, 2013).

1039. *Id.* Initial funding came from the Public Welfare Foundation. *Id.*
1040. *Id.*
1041. *Id.*
1042. *Id.*
1043. Telephone Interview with Michael Manley, *supra* note 816.
1044. *Id.*
1045. Telephone Interview with Nick Weiner, *supra* note 419.
1046. James Rufus Koren, *Port Access Still Drives Teamsters*, L.A. BUS. J., Dec. 12, 2011, at 1.
1047. *Id.*
1048. Howard Fine, *Leasing Could Be Roadblock for Trucking Companies*, L.A. BUS. J., Oct. 24, 2011, at 51.
1049. Howard Fine, *Contracting May Squeeze Employers*, L.A. BUS. J., Oct. 24, 2011, at 1, 51.
1050. Telephone Interview with Sanjukta Paul, *supra* note 1038.
1051. CAL. LAB. CODE §§ 226.8 & 2753 (Deering 2013).
1052. The act imposed penalties of up to $15,000 for individual violations and $25,000 for violations that showed a "pattern or practice" of misclassification. *Id.* § 226.8 (b) & (c).
1053. Sanjukta Paul, Synopsis of the California Willful Misclassification Law 3 (2011).
1054. Koren, *supra* note 1046.
1055. Order of the Lab. Comm'r, Garcia v. Seacon Logix, Inc., Order, No. 05-52821-LT (Cal. Lab. Comm'r Jan. 10, 2012); Order of the Lab. Comm'r, Urbina v. Seacon Logix, Inc., Order, No. 05-53002-LT (Cal. Lab. Comm'r Jan. 10, 2012).
1056. Telephone Interview with Sanjukta Paul, Clinical Fellow, UCLA Sch. of Law (Jan. 23, 2014).
1057. *Id.*
1058. Tom Gilroy, *Shipping Company Drivers Are Employees, Not Contractors, California Court Decides*, BLOOMBERG BNA, Mar. 4, 2013, at A-5.
1059. Press Release, Dep't of Indus. Rel., California Labor Commissioner Prevails in Misclassification Case Against Port Trucking Company (Mar. 1, 2013), http://www.dir.ca.gov/DIRNews/2013/IR2013-11.html (last visited July 17, 2017).
1060. Press Release, U.S. Dep't of Lab., US Labor Department, California Sign Agreement to Reduce Misclassification of Employees as Independent Contractors (Feb. 9, 2012), http://www.dol.gov/opa/media/press/whd/WHD20120257.htm (last visited July 17, 2017).
1061. Koren, *supra* note 1037. The DOL investigations resulted in some misclassification findings and orders of back pay. *See, e.g.,* Wage & Hour Div. Investigation Findings Letter, Container Connection of S. Cal., Inc., Case No. 1634525 (Jan. 22, 2013) (finding that two workers were owed one day of back pay for $211.52 and $26.17 respectively). In August 2012, the DOL sued Shippers Transport Express on behalf of Oakland port truckers. *See* Complaint for Violations of the Fair Labor Standards Act, Solis v. Shippers Transp. Express, Inc., No. 12-4249 (N.D. Cal. Aug. 13, 2012).
1062. Koren, *supra* note 1037.
1063. CAMERON W. ROBERTS & SEAN BREW, ROBERTS & KEHAGIARAS LLP, UNDERSTANDING THE CLEAN TRUCK LITIGATION PART VI, at 1, 30–31 (Nov. 13, 2013), https://perma.cc/E7YZ-Z2NR (last visited July 18, 2017).
1064. Bill Mongelluzzo, *Feds Take on Drayage Misclassification*, J. COM. (July 16, 2012), http://www.teamsters492.org/docs/Feds%20Take%20on%20Drayage%20Misclassification.pdf (last visited July 18, 2017).
1065. Complaint for Declaratory and Injunctive Judgment at 12–13, Clean Truck Coal., LLC v. Su, No. 12-08949 (Oct. 17, 2012). The coalition included Green Fleet Systems, LLC, Pacific 9 Transportation, Inc., Southern Counties Express, Inc., and Total Transportation Services, Inc., among others. *Id.* at 3.
1066. Joseph Lapin, *Notes from the Underground Economy: Are Companies at the Port of Long Beach Cheating Truckers Out of Their Rightful Wages?*, OC WKLY., Jan. 10, 2013, https://ocweekly.com/notes-from-the-underground-economy-6425266/ (last visited July 18, 2017).

1067. Telephone Interview with Sanjukta Paul, *supra* note 1038.
1068. Telephone Interview with Sanjukta Paul, *supra* note 1056.
1069. Telephone Interview with Sanjukta Paul, *supra* note 1038; *see also* Joseph Lapin, *Local Coalition Tries to Organize Misclassified Workers*, LONG BEACH POST, Aug. 24, 2012, https://lbpost.com/news/local-coalition-tries-to-organize-misclassified-port-truckers-2/ (last visited Nov. 11, 2019).
1070. Telephone Interview with Sanjukta Paul, *supra* note 1038. Paul was joined by Carlos Bowker, deputy labor commissioner at the DLSE; Abel Gervacio, an investigator with the DOL; Victor Narro, project director at the UCLA Labor Center; Peter Riley, regional manager of Cal/OSHA Region 3; Rebecca Smith, attorney at the National Employment Law Project; and Michael Manley from the Teamsters.
1071. *See, e.g.*, Teamsters Local 848, Know Your Rights Workshop, Sept. 14, 2012 (asking: "What is employee misclassification and what can you do to end it at the ports?").
1072. Telephone Interview with Sanjukta Paul, *supra* note 1038.
1073. Telephone Interview with Sanjukta Paul, *supra* note 1056.
1074. *Id.*
1075. *Id.*
1076. Class Action Complaint at 17, Talavera, Jr. v. QTS, Inc., No. BC501571 (Cal. Super. Ct. Feb. 22, 2013). The class action against QTS was settled in 2016 for $5 million.
1077. Ricardo Lopez, *Truck Drivers Sue for Overtime*, L.A. TIMES, May 15, 2013 at B2.
1078. Paula Winciki, *Port Truck Drivers Owed Millions in Wages*, CITY WATCH (Sept. 13, 2013), http://www.citywatchla.com/in-case-you-missed-it-hidden/5708-port-truck-drivers-owed-millions-in-wages (last visited Feb. 15, 2014).
1079. Telephone Interview with Sanjukta Paul, *supra* note 1056.
1080. Telephone Interview with Michael Manley, *supra* note 816.
1081. REBECCA SMITH ET AL., THE BIG RIG OVERHAUL: RESTORING MIDDLE-CLASS JOBS AT AMERICA'S PORTS THROUGH LABOR LAW ENFORCEMENT 14 (2014); *see also* Dan Weikel, *Campaign Questions Status of Port Truck Drivers*, L.A. TIMES, Feb. 19, 2014, at AA3).
1082. SMITH ET AL., *supra* note 1081, at 20–22; *see also* Ricardo Lopez, *Port Truckers Load Up on Labor Suits*, L.A. TIMES, July 5, 2014, at B1).
1083. James Rufus Koren, *Port Drivers Win Back Wages*, L.A. TIMES, Dec. 22, 2015, at C1).
1084. There were some examples of companies converting to a company driver model. *See* Sheheryar Kaoosji, *Port Trucking Companies Big and Small Changing Their Business Strategy, Convert to Company Driver Model*, PORT INNOVATIONS (Nov. 23, 2015), https://perma.cc/7F8S-3JP6 (last visited July 18, 2017).
1085. Telephone Interview with Jonathan Klein, *supra* note 479.
1086. *Id.*
1087. Telephone Interview with Nick Weiner, *supra* note 419.
1088. *See* Press Release, Grim Truth at Toll Grp., America's Port Truckers Deliver a Resounding Yes Winning Union Recognition as Teamsters in Historic Vote (Apr. 11, 2012), https://perma.cc/4A33-TV9Q (last visited July 18, 2017); *Jobs Can't Be Good or Green If They're Not Union!*, COAL. FOR CLEAN & SAFE PORTS (Mar. 20, 2012), https://perma.cc/5ETU-7JC7 (last visited July 18, 2017).
1089. Telephone Interview with Nick Weiner, *supra* note 419; Telephone Interview with Michael Manley, *supra* note 816.
1090. James Rufus Koren, *Toll Group Drivers File with NLRB*, L.A. BUS. J. (Jan. 27, 2012), http://labusinessjournal.com/news/2012/jan/27/toll-group-drivers-file-nlrb (last visited July 18, 2017).
1091. *Toll Group in Dispute with Los Angeles Truck Drivers*, AUSTL. BUS. REV. (Mar. 10, 2012), http://www.theaustralian.com.au/business/toll-group-in-dispute-with-los-angeles-truck-drivers/story-e6frg8zx-1226295773360 (last visited July 18, 2017).
1092. *Jobs Can't Be Good or Green If They're Not Union!*, *supra* note 1088. Teamsters officials also initiated a federal investigation into Toll driver misclassification at the New York and New

Jersey ports. *See* U.S. Dep't of Labor, Wage & Hour Div., Compliance Action Report, Toll Global Forwarding, Case ID 1647833 (Mar. 1, 2012).

1093. Telephone Interview with Jon Zerolnick, *supra* note 545.
1094. Telephone Interview with Jonathan Klein, *supra* note 479.
1095. Telephone Interview with Michael Manley, *supra* note 816.
1096. Press Release, Grim Truth at Toll Grp., *supra* note 1088; Laura Clawson, *Truck Drivers Win Union Representation at Toll Group*, DAILY KOS (Apr. 12, 2012), www.dailykos.com/story/ 2012/04/12/1082732/-Truck-drivers-win-union-representation-at-Toll-Group.
1097. Telephone Interview with Nick Weiner, *supra* note 419.
1098. Press Release, Grim Truth at Toll Grp., *supra* note 1088.
1099. *Toll Drivers Unanimously Ratify First Time Contract*, TEAMSTERS LOCAL 848, http://www.teamsters848.org/toll-drivers-unanimously-ratify-first-time-contract/ (last visited Feb. 16, 2014).
1100. *The Road to the Middle Class: Teamster Contract with Toll Group Fuels Port Driver Hope*, COAL. FOR CLEAN & SAFE PORTS, http://toll.cleanandsafeports.org/files/2013/01/TollContract_Highlights.pdf (last visited Feb. 16, 2014).
1101. *Id.*
1102. Telephone Interview with Michael Manley, *supra* note 816.
1103. *Port of L.A. Truck Drivers Stage 36-Hour Strike*, L.A. TIMES, Nov. 18, 2013, http://articles.latimes.com/2013/nov/18/local/la-me-ln-port-truck-drivers-strike-20131118 (last visited July 18, 2017). In July 2014, drivers conducted a job action against Total Transportation Services, Inc., Green Fleet Systems, and Pac 9, walking off the job in protest of what they claimed to be their wrongful classification as independent contractors. Andrew Khouri, *Truckers Put Breaks on Protest at Twin Ports*, L.A. TIMES, July 12, 2014, at 30. Some drivers from Total Transportation Services were fired. In November 2014, workers fired from Green Fleet Systems were reinstated as employees after a district court ruling that they had been misclassified as independent contractors. *Two Fired Port Truck Drivers Return to Work in Landmark Case*, CAPITAL & MAIN, http://www.laane.org/capitalandmain/two-fired-port-truck-drivers-return-to-work-in-landmark-case/ (last visited Nov. 7, 2014).
1104. *Two Fired Port Truck Drivers Return to Work in Landmark Case*, *supra* note 1103.
1105. Ricardo Lopez, *Truckers Strike, Push to Unionize*, L.A. TIMES, Aug. 27, 2013, at B1.
1106. Email from Jon Zerolnick, Res. Dir., L.A. All. for a New Econ., to Scott Cummings, Professor, UCLA Sch. of Law (Jan. 10, 2014).
1107. *See* Janice Hahn, Op-Ed., *To Keep on Trucking*, L.A. TIMES, Nov. 25, 2013, at A11.
1108. Steve Lopez, *Truck Drivers at Port of L.A. Want a Fair Shake*, L.A. TIMES, May 18, 2014, at A1.
1109. Am. Trucking Ass'ns, Inc. v. City of L.A., 660 F.3d 384, 408 (9th Cir. 2011).
1110. *See* Benjamin I. Sachs, *Despite Preemption: Making Labor Law in Cities and States*, 124 HARV. L. REV. 1153 (2011).
1111. *Don't Waste LA Facts and Impacts*, DON'T WASTE LA, http://www.dontwastela.com/wp-content/uploads/2014/08/DWLAFactsandImpacts.pdf (last visited Dec. 18, 2017); *see also* SABRINA BORNSTEIN, DON'T WASTE L.A.: A PATH TO GREEN JOBS, CLEAN AIR AND RECYCLING FOR ALL (Jan. 2011), http://www.dontwastela.com/wp-content/uploads/2013/06/DWLA_Report_Finalweb1.pdf (last visited Dec. 18, 2017).

Chapter 7

1. The analysis of participants in this chapter uses a qualitative empirical methodology following New Legal Realist scholars. *See* Elizabeth Mertz, *New Legal Realism: Law and Social Science in the New Millennium*, *in* THE NEW LEGAL REALISM: TRANSLATING LAW-AND-SOCIETY FOR TODAY'S LEGAL PRACTICE 1 (Elizabeth Mertz, Stuart Macaulay & Thomas W. Mitchell eds., 2016).

2. *See* STUART A. SCHEINGOLD & AUSTIN SARAT, SOMETHING TO BELIEVE IN: POLITICS, PROFESSIONALISM, AND CAUSE LAWYERING (2004).
3. DEBORAH L. RHODE, LAWYERS AS LEADERS (2013).
4. *See generally* JOEL F. HANDLER, SOCIAL MOVEMENTS AND THE LEGAL SYSTEM: A THEORY OF LAW REFORM AND SOCIAL CHANGE (1978); MICHAEL W. MCCANN, RIGHTS AT WORK: PAY EQUITY REFORM AND THE POLITICS OF LEGAL MOBILIZATION (1994); STUART A. SCHEINGOLD, THE POLITICS OF RIGHTS: LAWYERS, PUBLIC POLICY, AND POLITICAL CHANGE (1974); GERALD N. ROSENBERG, THE HOLLOW HOPE: CAN COURTS BRING ABOUT SOCIAL CHANGE? (1991).
5. Gary Bellow, *Steady Work: A Practitioner's Reflections on Political Lawyering*, 31 HARV. C.R.-C.L. L. REV. 297, 302 (1996).
6. *Id.* at 303.
7. Austin Sarat & Stuart Scheingold, *What Cause Lawyers Do For, and To, Social Movements: An Introduction*, *in* CAUSE LAWYERS AND SOCIAL MOVEMENTS 1, 2 (Austin Sarat & Stuart Scheingold eds., 2006).
8. DAVID LUBAN, LAWYERS AND JUSTICE: AN ETHICAL STUDY 337 (1988); *see also* Mark Aaronson, *Representing the Poor: Legal Advocacy and Welfare Reform during Reagan's Gubernatorial Years*, 64 HASTINGS L.J. 933 (2013).
9. *See, e.g.*, Clyde Spillenger, *Elusive Advocate: Reconsidering Brandeis as People's Lawyer*, 105 YALE L.J. 1445 (1996).
10. Nancy Leong, *Racial Capitalism*, 126 HARV. L. REV. 2151 (2013).
11. 347 U.S. 483 (1954).
12. For a characterization of legal liberal lawyering, see Lani Guinier & Gerald Torres, *Changing the Wind: Notes Toward a Demosprudence of Law and Social Movements*, 123 YALE L.J. 2740 (2014).
13. *See* SCHEINGOLD & SARAT, *supra* note 2, at 2.
14. *See generally* ALAN K. CHEN & SCOTT L. CUMMINGS, PUBLIC INTEREST LAWYERING: A CONTEMPORARY PERSPECTIVE 201–72 (2013).
15. Pamela Warrick, *The Freedom Fighter: Julie Su Finds Inspiration in the Thai Garment Workers She's Assisting*, L.A. TIMES, Sept. 4, 1995, at 1.
16. Suzanne Gamboa, *Latino Lawyer Putting Human Face on Immigration Case in SCOTUS Debut*, NBC NEWS (Apr. 17, 2016).
17. David Zahniser, *Jerilyn Lopez Mendoza*, L.A. WKLY., May 9, 2007, https://www.laweekly.com/jerilyn-lopez-mendoza/ (last visited Jan. 23, 2020).
18. Jose Cardenas, *She's Working Overtime for L.A.'s Living Wage Battle*, L.A. TIMES, Aug. 21, 2000, at 1.
19. Douglas NeJaime, *Cause Lawyers Inside the State*, 81 FORDHAM L. REV. 649 (2013).
20. There is no private right of action to enforce S.B. 249 under Noe v. Super. Ct., 237 Cal. App. 4th 316, 340 (Ct. App. 2d Dist. 2015).
21. *Id.* at 328.
22. Bjorn Claeson & Eric Dirnbach, *Making City Hall Sweat: Using Procurement Power for Worker Rights*, 18 NEW LAB. FORUM 89 (2009).
23. The Grocery Worker Retention Ordinance was upheld by the California Supreme Court in Cal. Grocers Ass'n v. City of Los Angeles, 52 Cal. 4th 177 (Cal. 2011). LAANE intervened in the lawsuit in support of the city.
24. Email from Victor Narro, Project Dir., UCLA Downtown Lab. Ctr., to Scott Cummings, Professor of Law, UCLA Sch. of Law (June 25, 2009).
25. L.A. Live, Community Benefits Program, Status Update (Mar. 2006).
26. Telephone Interview with Martha Saucedo, Vice President of Cmty. Aff., AEG Worldwide (Aug. 26, 2009).
27. Nicholas J. Marantz, *What Do Community Benefits Agreements Deliver? Evidence from Los Angeles*, 81 J. AM. PLAN. ASSOC. 251, 262 (2015).

28. Los Angeles World Airports, LAX Master Plan, Community Benefits Agreement (CBA) 2007 Annual Progress Report 12–13 (2008).
29. David Fairris, David Runsten, Carolina Briones & Jessica Goodheart, Examining the Evidence: The Impact of the Los Angeles Living Wage Ordinance on Workers and Businesses 2 (2005).
30. Grand Avenue Project, *Summary of Community Benefits*, Attachment H at 1, http://www.crala.org/internet-site/Meetings/upload/01042007_1.pdf (last visited Aug 27, 2009).
31. *Id.*
32. Scott L. Cummings & Steven A. Boutcher, *Mobilizing Local Government Law for Low-Wage Workers*, 2009 U. of Chi. Legal F. 187 (2009).
33. Amy B. Dean & David Reynolds, A New New Deal: How Regional Activism Will Reshape the American Labor Movement 64 (2010).
34. Marco Hauptmeier & Lowell Turner, *Political Insiders and Social Activists: Coalition Building in New York and Los Angeles*, in Labor in the New Urban Battlegrounds: Local Solidarity in a Global Economy 129, 132 (Lowell Turner & Daniel B. Cornfield eds., 2018).
35. On legal liberalism, see Laura Kalman, The Strange Career of Legal Liberalism (1998). For accounts of progressive lawyers in social movements, see generally Tomiko Brown-Nagin, Courage to Dissent: Atlanta and the Long History of the Civil Rights Movement (2011); Susan D. Carle, Defining the Struggle: National Organizing for Racial Justice, 1880–1915 (2013); Anthony V. Alfieri, *Faith in Community: Representing "Colored Town,"* 95 Cal. L. Rev. 1829 (2007); Lynette J. Chua, *Pragmatic Resistance, Law, and Social Movements in Authoritarian States: The Case of Gay Collective Action in Singapore*, 46 Law & Soc. Rev. 713 (2012); Guinier & Torres, *supra* note 12.
36. Orly Lobel, *The Paradox of Extralegal Activism: Critical Legal Consciousness and Transformative Politics*, 120 Harv. L. Rev. 937 (2007).
37. *See* Carle, *supra* note 35; Christopher W. Schmidt, The Sit-Ins: Protest and Legal Change in the Civil Rights Era (2018); Kenneth W. Mack, *Rethinking Civil Rights Lawyering and Politics in the Era Before Brown*, 115 Yale L.J. 256 (2005). The "hollow hope" reference is to Gerald Rosenberg's classic critique of litigation. Rosenberg, *supra* note 4.
38. As David Luban put it, expansive notions of activist reform-oriented lawyering have foundered because of concerns about lawyers using client cases as vessels to advance lawyers' own visions of social change (the "double agent" problem). Luban, *supra* note 8, at 319.
39. For a synthesis of this critique, see Scott L. Cummings, *The Social Movement Turn in Law*, 43 Law & Soc. Inquiry 360, 368 (2018).
40. Derrick Bell, Jr., *Serving Two Masters: Integration Ideals and Client Interests in School Desegregation Litigation*, 85 Yale L.J. 470 (1976).
41. Model Rules of Prof'l Conduct r. 1.2(a) (A.B.A. 2018).
42. *See* Aaronson, *supra* note 8; Nan D. Hunter, *Varieties of Constitutional Experience: Democracy and the Marriage Equality Campaign*, 64 UCLA L. Rev. 1662, 1670 (2017).
43. Aaronson, *supra* note 8, at 960 (discussing Hannah Pitkin, The Concept of Representation (1967)).
44. William H. Simon, *Solving Problems vs. Claiming Rights: The Pragmatist Challenge to Legal Liberalism*, 46 Wm. & Mary L. Rev. 127, 162 (2004).
45. Rhode, *supra* note 3, at 180–84.
46. For an analysis of legal mobilization that explores structural accountability factors, see Mark V. Tushnet, The NAACP's Legal Strategy Against Segregated Education, 1925–1950 (1987).
47. Aaronson, *supra* note 8, at 965.
48. Luban, *supra* note 8, at 351–55.

49. *But cf.* Simon, *supra* note 44, at 162 (arguing that professional norms inhibit lawyers from "establishing relations with both individuals and organizations" that could play productive roles monitoring legal liberal lawyers).
50. The focus on judgment as a source of public-oriented lawyering comes from the left, *see* Aaronson, *supra* note 8; and the right, *see* ANTHONY T. KRONMAN, THE LOST LAWYER: FAILING IDEALS OF THE LEGAL PROFESSION (1993).
51. *See* Scott L. Cummings, *Movement Lawyering*, 2017 U. ILL. L. REV. 1645, 1686-87 (2017).
52. The theme of race and representation runs from Bell's critique of white NAACP lawyers like Jack Greenberg, Bell, *supra* note 40, at 490; to later poverty law critiques, including Gerald López's manifesto against "regnant lawyers," who "consider themselves the preeminent problem-solvers," GERALD P. LÓPEZ, REBELLIOUS LAWYERING: ONE CHICANO'S VISION OF PROGRESSIVE LAW PRACTICE 24 (1992); and Lucie White's narrative account of her own representation of African American welfare recipient Mrs. G, Lucie E. White, *Subordination, Rhetorical Survival Skills, and Sunday Shoes: Notes on the Hearing of Mrs. G.*, 38 BUFF. L. REV. 1 (1990).
53. *See* ROSENBERG, *supra* note 4, at 21.
54. *See* MICHAEL J. KLARMAN, FROM JIM CROW TO CIVIL RIGHTS: THE SUPREME COURT AND THE STRUGGLE FOR RACIAL EQUALITY (1987).
55. *See* MARK KELMAN, A GUIDE TO CRITICAL LEGAL STUDIES 6 (1987).
56. *See* SCHEINGOLD, *supra* note 4.
57. *See* Guinier & Torres, *supra* note 12, at 2748.
58. *See, e.g.*, EUGENE BARDACH, THE IMPLEMENTATION GAME: WHAT HAPPENS AFTER A BILL BECOMES A LAW (1977); ROBERT T. NAKAMURA & FRANK SMALLWOOD, THE POLITICS OF POLICY IMPLEMENTATION (1980).
59. ROSENBERG, *supra* note 4, at 33.
60. *Cf.* HANDLER, *supra* note 4, at 192.
61. SIDNEY G. TARROW, POWER IN MOVEMENT: SOCIAL MOVEMENTS AND CONTENTIOUS POLITICS (3rd ed. 2011).
62. *See* Duncan Kennedy, *Form and Substance in Private Law Adjudication*, 89 HARV. L. REV. 1685 (1976).
63. *See* David A. Snow & Robert D. Benford, *Master Frames and Cycles of Protest*, *in* FRONTIERS IN SOCIAL MOVEMENT THEORY 133 (Aldon D. Morris & Carol McClurg Mueller eds., 1992).
64. MCCANN, *supra* note 4, at 5–12.
65. *See* RICHARD SUSSKIND, TOMORROW'S LAWYERS: AN INTRODUCTION TO YOUR FUTURE 32-36, 135 (2nd ed. 2017).
66. *Legal Strategies*, WAGE JUST., http://wagejustice.org/?page_id=4 (last visited Aug. 4, 2017).
67. *See Los Angeles Coalition Against Wage Theft*, FACEBOOK, https://www.facebook.com/stopLAwagetheft?ref=br_tf (last visited Aug. 4, 2017).
68. ANNETTE BERNHARDT ET AL., BROKEN LAWS, UNPROTECTED WORKERS: VIOLATIONS OF EMPLOYMENT AND LABOR LAWS IN AMERICA'S CITIES (2009), http://nelp.3cdn.net/e470538bfa5a7e7a46_2um6br7o3.pdf (last visited Apr. 22, 2017); RUTH MILKMAN ET AL., WAGE THEFT AND WORKPLACE VIOLATIONS IN LOS ANGELES (2010).
69. *See, e.g.*, Abby Sewell, *L.A. County Sets Up Wage Enforcement Program to Police New Minimum Wage Rules*, L.A. TIMES (Nov. 17, 2015), http://www.latimes.com/local/lanow/la-me-ln-county-wage-enforcement-20151117-story.html (last visited Jan. 25, 2019).
70. *See* SCHMIDT, *supra* note 37.
71. *See* HANDLER, *supra* note 4, at 191–92; *see also* ROSENBERG, *supra* note 4, at 25; Marc Galanter, *The Radiating Effects of Courts*, *in* EMPIRICAL THEORIES ABOUT COURTS 117, 117–42 (Keith O. Boyum & Lynn Mather eds., 1983). For an assessment of the enforcement value of litigation, *see* Joanna Schwartz, *Myths and Mechanics of Deterrence: The Role of Lawsuits in Law Enforcement Decisionmaking*, 57 UCLA L. REV. 1023 (2010).

72. On the restructuring of the economy and workplace and its impact on the labor movement, see KATHERINE V.W. STONE, FROM WIDGETS TO DIGITS: EMPLOYMENT REGULATION FOR THE CHANGING WORKPLACE (2004); Cynthia L. Estlund, *The Ossification of American Labor Law*, 102 COLUM. L. REV. 1527 (2002); Paul Weiler, *Promises to Keep: Securing Workers' Rights to Self-Organization Under the NLRA*, 96 HARV. L. REV. 1769 (1983). On strategies for labor revitalization, see Matthew Dimick, *Productive Unionism*, 4 U.C. IRVINE L. REV. 679 (2013); Ben Sachs, *Labor Law Renewal*, 1 HARV. L. & POL'Y REV. 375 (2007).
73. *See* Cummings, *supra* note 39; *see also* Amna Akbar, *Toward a Radical Imagination of Law*, 93 N.Y.U. L. REV. 405 (2018).
74. Michael M. Oswalt & César F. Rosado Marzán, *Organizing the State: The "New Labor Law" Seen from the Bottom-Up*, 39 BERKELEY J. EMP. & LAB. L. 415 (2018); Sachs, *supra* note 72. For key contributions to the labor literature focusing on the relation between social movements and labor law, see WILLIAM E. FORBATH, LAW AND THE SHAPING OF THE AMERICAN LABOR MOVEMENT (1992); Kate Andrias, *The New Labor Law*, 126 YALE L.J. 2 (2016); James Gray Pope, *Labor's Constitution of Freedom*, 106 YALE L.J. 941 (1997).
75. Andrias, *supra* note 74, at 2.
76. *See* Cynthia L. Estlund, *The Death of Labor Law?*, 2 ANN. REV. L. & SOC. SCI. 105 (2006).
77. Andrias, *supra* note 74, at 8–10.
78. Katherine Stone & Scott Cummings, *Labor Activism in Local Politics: From CBAs to 'CBAs,'* in THE IDEA OF LABOUR LAW 273 (Guy Davidov & Brian Langille eds., 2011).
79. Andrias, *supra* note 74; Estlund, *supra* note 76.
80. Benjamin I. Sachs, *Despite Preemption: Making Labor Law in Cities and States*, 124 HARV. L. REV. 1153, 1155 (2011).
81. Craig Becker, *Labor Law Outside the Employment Relation*, 74 TEX. L. REV. 1527 (1996).
82. Noah D. Zatz, *Working Beyond the Reach or Grasp of Employment Law*, in THE GLOVES-OFF ECONOMY: WORKPLACE STANDARDS AT THE BOTTOM OF AMERICA'S LABOR MARKET 31 (Annette Bernhardt, Heather Boushey, Laura Dresser & Chris Tilly eds., 2008).
83. DAVID WEIL, THE FISSURED WORKPLACE: WHY WORK BECAME SO BAD FOR SO MANY AND WHAT CAN BE DONE TO IMPROVE IT (2014).
84. Sachs, *supra* note 80; at 1155–57.
85. *Id.*
86. FORBATH, *supra* note 74.
87. 198 U.S. 45 (1905).
88. Sachs, *supra* note 80.
89. *See* NELSON LICHTENSTEIN, STATE OF THE UNION: A CENTURY OF AMERICAN LABOR 178–211 (2002).
90. Ben I. Sachs, *Employment Law as Labor Law*, 29 CARDOZO L. REV. 2685 (2008).
91. Ben I. Sachs, *The Unbundled Union: Politics Without Collective Bargaining*, 123 YALE L.J. 148 (2013).
92. Janus v. Am. Fed'n of State, Cty., & Mun. Emps., Council 31, 138 S. Ct. 2448 (2018).
93. Sachs, *supra* note 91.
94. *See* Andrias, *supra* note 74, at 71.
95. *Cf.* STONE, *supra* note 72, at 227 (describing forms of "citizen unionism").
96. *See, e.g.*, David Rolf, *Toward a 21st Century Labor Movement*, AM. PROSPECT (Apr. 18, 2016).
97. For the classic debate on the virtue and vice of localism, compare ALEXIS DE TOCQUEVILLE, 1 DEMOCRACY IN AMERICA 63 (Phillips Bradley ed., Alfred A. Knopf 1945) (1835) ("A nation may establish a free government, but without municipal institutions it cannot have the spirit of liberty."), with THE FEDERALIST NO. 10, at 133–34 (James Madison) (Benjamin F. Wright ed., 1961) (arguing in favor of federal government to control the negative effects of factions in local democracy). For seminal accounts of the benefits of urban life, see JANE JACOBS, THE DEATH AND LIFE OF GREAT AMERICAN CITIES (1961); IRIS MARION YOUNG, JUSTICE AND THE POLITICS OF DIFFERENCE (1990).

98. Gerald E. Frug, *The City as a Legal Concept*, 93 HARV. L. REV. 1057 (1980).
99. *See* Richard Thompson Ford, *The Boundaries of Race: Political Geography in Legal Analysis*, 107 HARV. L. REV. 1843, 1844 (1994); *see also* GERALD E. FRUG, CITY MAKING: BUILDING COMMUNITIES WITHOUT BUILDING WALLS 132–38 (1999).
100. For scholarship dealing with the "puzzle" of the contemporary city, see RASHMI DYAL-CHAND, COLLABORATIVE CAPITALISM: REFORMING URBAN MARKET REGULATIONS (2018); LEGAL SCHOLARSHIP FOR THE URBAN CORE: FROM THE GROUND UP (Rashmi Dyal-Chand & Peter Enrich eds., 2019); Brandon Weiss, *Progressive Property Theory and Housing Justice Campaigns*, 10 UC IRVINE L. REV. 251 (2019).
101. Richard Schragger, *The Progressive City* (University of Virginia School of Law Public Law and Legal Theory, Research Paper Series No. 2009-16, 2009); *see also* Nestor Davidson, *The Dilemma of Localism in an Era of Polarization*, 128 YALE L.J. 954 (2019).
102. On the instability of the public-private distinction in municipal law, see Frug, *supra* note 98, at 1099, 1028.
103. Early minority business contracting rules made a link between city authority and work, but those rules did not define the quality of jobs, just who received them.
104. *See, e.g.*, Vicki Been, *Community Benefits Agreements: A New Local Government Tool or Another Variation of the Exactions Theme?*, 77 U. CHI. L. REV. 5, 21–29 (2010) (questioning whether CBAs disrupt appropriate land use planning).
105. *See* Kathleen S. Morris, *The Case for Local Constitutional Enforcement*, 47 HARV. C.R.-C.L. L. REV. (2012) (critiquing the rule of *Hunter v. City of Pittsburgh*, 207 U.S. 161 (1907), holding that cities are powerless instrumentalities of the state).
106. *See* Frug, *supra* note 98, at 1109–20 (discussing development of Dillon's Rule vs. Home Rule conceptions of city authority).
107. The California Constitution permits charter cities, like Los Angeles, to "make and enforce all ordinances and regulations in respect to municipal affairs . . . ." CAL. CONST. art. XI, § 5(a).
108. *Worker Rights Preemption in the U.S.*, ECONOMIC POLICY INSTITUTE, https://www.epi.org/preemption-map/ (last visited Dec. 28, 2019).
109. Assemb. B. 5, 2019–2020 Leg., Reg. Sess. (Cal. 2019).
110. *See Cal. Trucking Ass'n v. Att'y Gen. Xavier Becerra*, No. 3:18-cv-02458-BEN-BLM (S.D. Cal. 2019).
111. Been, *supra* note 104, at 27.
112. Schragger, *supra* note 101, at 2.
113. Richard C. Schragger, *Mobile Capital, Local Economic Regulation, and the Democratic City*, 123 HARV. L. REV. 482 (2009).
114. *See, e.g.*, REFLECTIONS ON REGIONALISM (Bruce Katz ed., 2000).
115. Economists debate whether local regulation increasing wages causes employers to reduce jobs. *See, e.g.*, DALE BELMAN & PAUL J. WOLFSON, WHAT DOES THE MINIMUM WAGE DO? (2014).
116. BRUCE KATZ & JEREMY NOWAK, THE NEW LOCALISM: HOW CITIES CAN THRIVE IN THE AGE OF POPULISM (2017); Schragger, *supra* note 101.
117. David Brooks, *The Localist Revolution*, N.Y. TIMES, July 19, 2018.
118. *See, e.g.*, Susan Rose-Ackerman, *Cooperative Federalism and Co-optation*, 92 YALE L.J. 1344 (1983); Philip J. Weiser, *Towards a Constitutional Architecture for Cooperative Federalism*, 79 N.C. L. REV. 663 (2001); *but see* Jessica Bulman-Pozen & Heather Gerken, *Uncooperative Federalism*, 118 YALE L.J. 1256 (2009).

INDEX

Note: Tables and figures are indicated by *t* and *f* following the page number.

Aaronson, Mark, 481
Abasto, Cristian, 234–35
Abercrombie and Fitch, 79
Academy Awards, 175–76
Accidental Tourism report (Ansell et al.), 18–19
accountability
    in big-box campaign, 306–10
    in Campaign for Clean Trucks, 443–45
    in CBA campaigns, 178, 208–9, 241, 255, 258
    democratic, 88
    in garment industry, 32, 38–39, 40, 61, 77, 79–80
    lawyer, 306–8, 477, 478–83
    leadership and, 250, 456–57, 479–80
    in local campaigns generally, 7–8, 448
    in redevelopment, 165, 208–9, 218, 255, 258
    in relation to legal liberalism, 5, 477, 478–83
    solidarity and, 482–83
    specific challenges for progressive lawyers, 482–83
    structural determinants of, 480, 481
    transprofessional nature of, 479–80
    in trucking industry, 359, 361, 362, 398–99, 405
accountable development, 192–93, 262, 289–90
    coalitions, 217–18
ACJC. *See* Alameda Corridor Jobs Coalition
ACLU. *See* American Civil Liberties Union
ACLU v. City of Las Vegas, 124–26
ACORN. *See* Association of Community Organizations for Reform Now
Action for Grassroots Empowerment and Neighborhood Alternatives (AGENDA), 19–20, 174, 177, 178, 179, 181–82, 185, 192–93, 203–4, 212, 257, 278–79, 295, 351
    Valley Jobs Coalition and, 192

ACTWU. *See* Amalgamated Clothing and Textile Workers Union
Adams La Brea neighborhood, 193
administrative agencies, 424, 455, 461, 487
Adopt-a-Corner program, 97, 105. *See also* CHIRLA
advocacy
    decentralized, 262
    integrated, 457
    mobilization and, 302–3
    multidimensional, 1–2, 144–45
    multi-level, 298–302
    nontraditional, 304
    political cooptation and, 484–85
AEG. *See* Anschutz Entertainment Group
aerospace, 12, 327–28
affirmative litigation, 448–52, 487–88
affordable housing, 179, 189, 233–34, 251, 256
AFL. *See* American Federation of Labor
AFL-CIO. *See* American Federation of Labor and Congress of Industrial Organizations
African Americans
    conflict around Inglewood Wal-Mart, 279, 306, 308–9
    demographics in Los Angeles, 13–14
    in industries targeted by L.A. campaigns, 20–22, 21*t*, 23*t*, 26*t*
    in Inglewood, 29–30, 264, 265, 275–76
    judges, 47, 117
    Korean community tensions with, 14–15
    labor organizing and, 19–20, 275–76, 281
    in Ladera Heights, 103
    Latino community tensions with, 104, 473
    in L.A. workforce, 13–14, 16

625

African Americans (*cont.*)
  in LAX workforce, 202
  around LAX, 195, 217, 482
  in Los Angeles government, 15
  migration to Los Angeles, 12, 499
  1992 civil unrest and, 11–12
  redevelopment and, 166, 237
  in South Los Angeles, 12, 13, 14–15, 236
AGENDA. *See* Action for Grassroots Empowerment and Neighborhood Alternatives
Agoura Hills, 99–101, 102, 103, 110–11, 142, 144, 484–85
Agreement on Textiles and Clothing, 36
Ahmad, Muneer, 58, 59–60, 458
Airbus, 197–98
Air France, 205
Airline Deregulation Act, 200–1, 204–5
air pollution
  at LAX, 198, 216, 218, 223, 228
  at ports, 30–31, 322–24, 335–36, 339, 343, 346, 347, 348, 350, 356–57, 364–65, 373–74, 378, 381, 389–90, 398–99, 421–22, 423, 428–29, 430–31
  regulation of, 324, 335
Airport Commission, 195–96, 197–98, 206, 219–20, 226. *See also* Board of Airport Commissioners
  settlement of lawsuits over LAX modernization, 226–27
Air Transport Association, 206–7, 219–20
Alameda Corridor Jobs Coalition (ACJC), 18, 181
Alameda Corridor project, 317–19, 320, 327–28, 337–38, 593
  impact on community, 318
Alameda County, 274, 289–90, 294
Alatorre, Richard, 15
Albertsons, 275, 303
Albillo v. Intermodal Container Services, 331, 410–11
Alexander v. Sandoval, 209–10
Alhambra, 102, 157*t*
Alien Tort Statute, 79
Allen, Donald, 330
Alliance for a Regional Solution to Airport Congestion (ARSAC), 196–97, 211–12, 213, 218, 225–27
Alliance for Healthy & Responsible Grocery Stores, 303, 309–10
  members, 295
All People's Christian Center, 174
Alossi, Rich, 244
Altshuler Berzon, 54, 79, 207–8, 333–34
Alvarado, Pablo, 105, 108, 109–10, 115–16, 127–28, 129*f*, 139–40, 141, 146
Amador, Marco, 124

Amalgamated Clothing and Textile Workers Union (ACTWU), 51
Amazon, 297
American Apparel, 82
American Civil Liberties Union (ACLU), 28–29, 41, 46–47, 97, 98, 99–101, 105, 449*t*
  Immigrants' Rights Project, 45–46
  Orange County office, 119, 120, 121–22, 122*f*, 123–24
  S.B. 1070 fight and, 130–31
American Federation of Labor (AFL), 15–16
American Federation of Labor and Congress of Industrial Organizations (AFL-CIO), 16, 80–81
  Campaign for Clean Trucks and, 332, 351
  LAX Organizing Project and, 201, 203–5
  NDLON partnership with, 126–29, 129*f*, 139–40, 449*t*, 476, 493
  position on immigration, 16–17
  Thai workers and, 80–81
American Logistics, 419
American Lung Association, 358, 359–60, 381
American Trucking Associations (ATA), 30–31, 353, 365, 369, 370, 382, 383, 388–89, 427, 432–33, 435, 438–39
American Trucking Associations v. City of Los Angeles
  appeals, 399–400, 432–33
  Commerce Clause arguments, 388, 397–98, 399
  complaint for injunctive relief filed, 388
  coordination between Ports of Los Angeles and Long Beach, 390
  employee conversion preempted, 400–1
  FAAAA preemption arguments, 391, 394, 402, 403–4
  impact on Campaign for Clean Trucks (*see* Campaign for Clean Trucks)
  injunctive phase, 388–96
  intervenors, 389–90
  market participant argument, 389–90, 393, 399, 400–1, 403–4, 405
  merits phase, 396–401
  petition for certiorari, 402
  Port of Long Beach settlement, 394–95
  preliminary injunction, 388–96
  role of Teamsters in, 390
  safety exception, 392–93, 395, 399, 400–1
  Supreme Court phase, 401–5
  trial court ruling, 399
American University Washington College of Law, 81–82
Andrade, Vibiana, 100, 102, 458–59
Andrias, Kate, 490
Anschutz Entertainment Group (AEG), 167–68, 188–90, 233–34, 246–47, 256–57, 258, 259, 475

Anschutz, Phillip, 167–68
anti-big-box coalition, 306, 453–54
anti-big-box ordinances, 294
anti-idling bill, 357–58
anti-immigrant sentiment, 118
anti-solicitation campaign, 28–29, 91
    ACLU role in, 97, 98, 100, 101, 103–4, 119, 120, 121, 122, 123, 449t
    adaptation over time, 149
    CHIRLA role in, 97, 98, 99–100, 103–4, 105, 107, 108, 118–19, 127, 139–40
    city-by-city approach, 107–26
    coalition, 97
    dual-plaintiff structure of lawsuits, 146
    evaluation of, 138–41, 142, 143t, 151–55, 449t, 461–77, 462t
    federal court-civil liberties approach, 102–26, 142, 143t
    goals, 94–95, 109
    immigration politics and, 91–95
    integrated advocacy in, 141–48
    lawyers' attitudes about lawyering, 144–46
    LCCR role in, 114, 118, 132, 144
    leadership in, 138–40
    limitations of, 155
    litigation campaign, 95–101, 102–26, 129–38, 141–44, 449t
    MALDEF role in, 93–94, 95–138, 449t
    mobilization template, 107–9
    NDLON role in, 108, 109, 112, 115, 117, 119, 120, 122, 124–26, 127–29, 135–36, 139–40, 141, 146
    networks role in, 140–41
    outcomes, 142, 143t
    political environment and, 148–49
    conflicts of interest and, 146–48
    state court-civil rights approach, 95–101
    targets (*see* anti-solicitation ordinances)
    test-case strategy, 93–94
anti-solicitation ordinances, 3, 28–29, 446, 449t
    Agoura Hills, 99–100, 102
    applied to sidewalks, 110, 111, 112–13, 114, 122
    Baldwin Park, 124
    changes to, as result of litigation campaign, 94, 151–55, 154f, 157t
    CHIRLA v. Burke impact on, 107, 150
    citywide ban, 98, 99, 142, 149, 150f, 150–55, 157t
    commercial parking lots, bans in, 150f, 150–55, 157t, 545
    complete ban in designated areas, 150f, 150–51, 157t
    Costa Mesa, 123, 137
    enforcement of, 96, 98, 99–100, 105–6, 109, 111–12, 115, 117, 118, 119, 120, 121, 122, 123–24, 142, 155
    First Amendment and legality of, 96–97, 101, 104, 106, 109, 113–14, 117, 127, 135–36, 137, 138, 141–42
    Glendale, 111
    growth of, 150f, 150
    jurisdictions with, 96–97, 149–50, 157t
    Ladera Heights, 103
    Laguna Beach, 102
    Lake Forest, 118–19, 120, 122
    list of, by type in greater L.A. area, 157t
    Los Angeles County, 104, 105–6
    in Orange County, 118, 119
    origins of, 95–99
    Phoenix tagging ordinance as model, 96
    Redondo Beach, 4, 28–29, 96–97, 115–18, 129–36
    "smart" ordinances, 155
    spread of, 118
    traffic interference ban, 150f, 150–55, 157t
    types of, 150–51
    urban geography of, 149–56, 152f, 153f, 154f
anti-sweatshop campaign, 28, 32, 39–80. *See also* Assembly Bill 633; garment lawsuits
    APALC role in (*see* APALC)
    beginnings of, 40–41
    challenges to, 84–88
    collaboration with industry, 78
    end of impact litigation campaign, 72, 73
    evaluation of, 80–88, 449t, 457–58, 461–77, 462t
    goals, 33, 39–40, 58
    globalization and, 85–86
    Guess campaign, relation to, 49–57
    GWC role in, 64–66, 68, 77
    high-road production, 77
    impact of, 80–82, 84
    industry countermobilization, 72
    lawyers, 58, 81–82
    limits of law in, 58–60
    litigation campaign, 58–73
    Made in L.A., 78
    outcomes, 80–84
    strategies, 46–47
    Sweatshop Watch role in, 61–64, 66–67, 68, 77
    Thai worker case and (*see Bureerong v. Uvawas*)
antitrust law, 317, 321–22, 330, 421–22, 437–38, 492–93
anti-Wal-Mart campaign. *See* big-box campaign
Antonovich, Mike, 195–96, 243, 244
APALA. *See* Asian Pacific American Labor Alliance
APALC. *See* Asian Pacific American Legal Center
Apex Clothing Corporation, 67–68
APL, 371
Apparel Industry Partnership, 58, 82–83
Apparel Resources, 87
ArcLight, 176–77

628   INDEX

Argenbright Security, 203, 205, 207–9, 255
Arian, Dave, 353–54
Arian, Sean, 373–74, 375, 384
Arizona Senate Bill (S.B.) 1070, 130–31, 138
Army Corps of Engineers, 338–40
ARSAC. *See* Alliance for a Regional Solution to Airport Congestion
Asian Americans, 41–44, 48–49, 58–59, 65
　in Los Angeles, 13–14, 20–22, 21*t*, 23*t*
Asian Immigrant Women Advocates, 41, 61
Asian Law Caucus, 41, 46–47, 61, 62
Asian Pacific American Labor Alliance (APALA), 296–97
Asian Pacific American Legal Center (APALC), 28, 32, 33, 41–42, 45–47, 48–49, 58–59, 60, 61, 64, 68, 80, 81–82, 85, 86–87, 88, 447–52, 449*t*, 458, 473–74, 480. *See also* anti-sweatshop campaign
　collaboration with industry, 78
　cross-racial representation and, 482
　development of law and organizing model, 58–59
　GWC and, 65, 66, 456–57
　role in building anti-sweatshop coalition, 41
　shift to worker rights, 41–42
　litigation and, 58–60, 66–73, 452–53, 462*t*
　tensions with Asian American community, 72–73
　Thai worker case and, 41–49
Asociación de Trabajadores de Lake Forest (ATLF), 120, 121–22, 147–48
Assembly Bill (A.B.) 5, 504–5
Assembly Bill (A.B.) 292, 246–47
Assembly Bill (A.B.) 633, 60–64, 80, 83–84, 457–58, 462*t*, 467, 469, 471, 485–86
　application to retailers, 74
　definition of garment manufacturing, 64, 524
　enactment, 63, 73
　enforcement of, 62–63, 73–74, 75
　fight over inclusion of retailers as guarantors, 63
　GWC self-help model and, 76
　history of, 62
　implementing regulations, 63–64, 73–74
　lack of recovery from guarantors, 36, 73
　private right of action, 62–63
　process, 63
　remedies, 63, 74–75
　safe harbor, 64
　UCLA report on, 73
　worker participation in development of, 62
Assembly Bill (A.B.) 950, 410, 413–14
Assessment of Fifty Years of Redevelopment in Los Angeles (UCLA), 170
Association of Community Organizations for Reform Now (ACORN), 96, 179–80
Association of Community Organizations for Reform Now (ACORN) v. City of Phoenix, 96, 100–1, 106–7, 131–32, 133, 134, 135–36

Association of Day Laborers of Pasadena, 102–3
ATA. *See* American Trucking Associations
Atlantic Yards, 259–60
ATLF. *See* Asociación de Trabajadores de Lake Forest
Auer, Roxane, 203–4
avigation easement, 217, 221, 228–29

Baca, Lee, 107–8
backlash, 2, 5, 7, 15, 28–29, 82–83, 91, 483, 484
Bahan, Della, 45–47, 48–49, 53, 54
Baldwin Park, 124, 126, 144, 145–46, 541
Banares, Bernice, 398–99
Banning, Phineas, 313
Barton, Jon, 203–4, 206–7
Bas, Nikki Fortunato, 61
BCBG Max Azria, 59
BCG. *See* Boston Consulting Group
Bea, Carlos, 132–33, 136
Beach, Ben, 189, 238, 239, 241, 251, 252
Bebe lawsuit, 85, 86–87
　contractor liability, 67–68
　coordination with grassroots campaign, 68
　federal law claims, 67
　filing of, 67
　joint employer status under FLSA, 67–68
　ruling, 67–68
　settlement of, 68, 80
Beers, Roger, 337
Beezer, Robert, 393
Beistline, Ralph, 131
Bell, Derrick, 478–79, 482
Bellow, Gary, 447–48
Belman, Dale, 322
Bensman, David, 412
Bentonville, 266–70, 377
Berger v. City of Seattle, 131, 149
Berk, Ed, 331
Berkeley, 204, 271–72, 273–74
Bernardi, Ernani, 551
Berzon, Marsha, 132–33
Berzon, Stephen, 333–34
Bet Tzedek, 61, 74
Beverly Hills, 41, 55–56, 184–85, 189–90, 231–32, 264
BID. *See* business improvement district
big-box campaign. *See also* Inglewood site fight
　accountability in, 270–72
　effort to pass big-box ban, 274
　evaluation of, 298–310
　goals, 273, 276
　lawyers' role in, 304–7, 308
　outcomes, 294, 310, 449*t*, 461–77, 462*t*
　policy diffusion, 301
　political opportunity structure, 298
　relation to grocery sector, 273, 303, 449*t*

big-box stores, 3, 272, 274, 289–90, 292, 293, 294, 299
Bigin, 45
The Big Rig (Smith, Bensman, and Marvy), 412, 413, 416
Bird Marella, 48–49, 67
Blake & Uhlig, 331–32
Blasi, Gary, 73
Blazers Youth Services, 174
Bloomberg, Michael, 407–8
Blue-Green Alliance, 350, 408, 428
blue-green coalition, 29, 30–31, 311–12, 353–54, 421, 498
BNSF. *See* Burlington Northern and Santa Fe
Board of Airport Commissioners, 198–99, 207–8, 226. *See also* Airport Commission
Bonacich, Edna, 322
Bond, Julian, 392
Boston Consulting Group (BCG), 375, 377–78, 426–27
  Report on Clean Truck Program, 383–85
Boyle Heights, 97
Bradley, Tom, 15, 16–17, 18, 473
Brennan, Cecilia, 178–79
Brewster, Rudi, 400
Broad, Eli, 230–33, 240, 242–43
Brown, Jerry, 81–82, 410, 411–12
Brown, Scott, 408
Brown v. Board of Education, 2, 452–53
BRU. *See* Bus Rider's Union
Budlong and Jefferson Block Club, 174
Building and Trades Council, 353–54
B.U.M. International, 45, 48
Bunker Hill, 165, 230–34
  history of, 230
Bunker Hill Urban Renewal Project, 230
Bureau of Contract Administration, 205
Bureau of Sanitation, 441
Bureerong v. Uvawas
  attorney's fees, 48–49
  claims, 45, 47–48
  complaint, 45, 48
  litigation team, 45–46, 468
  manufacturer defendants, 48
  motion to dismiss, 47, 48
  outcome, 449t, 462t, 473–74
  RICO claims, 45
  rulings, 47, 48
  settlements, 48–49, 49f
Burke, Yvonne Brathwaite, 103, 104, 144, 220
Burlington Northern and Santa Fe (BNSF), 327–28, 358
Bush, George W., 113–14
Business and Professions Code § 17200, 60, 67
business improvement district (BID), 167
busing, 11–12
Bus Rider's Union (BRU), 18–19

Bybee, Jay, 132–33

CAAP. *See* Clean Air Action Plan
Cabrillo Beach, 326
Caldwell Leslie Proctor & Pettit, 284–85
Calexico, 276
California Air Resources Board (CARB), 322–24, 335, 346
California attorney general, 285–86, 304, 392–93, 411–12, 439–40
California Coalition for Immigration Reform, 118
California Coastal Commission, 345
California Community Foundation, 242–43
California Court of Appeal, 55–56, 71, 234–35, 246–47, 294, 331, 469
California Division of Occupational Safety and Health (Cal/OSHA), 415–16
California Economic and Employment Enforcement Coalition, 530
California Environmental Quality Act (CEQA)
  environmental review process, 184, 194–95
  exemptions from, 246–47
  role in Campaign for Clean Trucks, 337–38, 339, 378
  role in CBA movement, 184, 207–8, 209–10, 213, 225–27, 255
California Environmental Rights Alliance, 214–15
California Franchise Tax Board, 75
California Labor Code, 410
California Labor Federation, 40
California Public Employees' Retirement System, 244
California State Lands Commission, 326
California state legislature, 40, 462t
  Labor and Employment Committee, 410
California Trucking Association, 410, 414–15, 439–40
Callahan, Colleen, 358, 359–60, 368
Callahan, Consuelo, 132–33
Cal/OSHA. *See* California Division of Occupational Safety and Health
campaign
  comprehensive (*see* comprehensive campaign)
  policy-oriented, 479–80
  as unit of analysis, 7
campaign finance, 497–98
Campaign for Clean Trucks, 30–31, 324, 349–420, 487. *See also American Trucking Associations v. City of Los Angeles*; Clean Truck Program; Coalition for Clean and Safe Ports
  accountability in, 443–45
  adaptation in, 440–41
  aftermath, 405–20
  ATA v. City of Los Angeles impact on, 405, 406, 462t
  birth of, 349

630　INDEX

Campaign for Clean Trucks (*cont.*)
　campaign to organize city waste haulers and, 440–41
　coalition, 349–62, 428–30, 443, 444
　comments on CAAP, 361
　concession agreements and, 334, 352–53, 357, 385
　decision-making processes in, 442
　defensive phase, 388–405
　division between Los Angeles and Long Beach, 367–68
　drafting policy, 366–67
　employee conversion and, 379, 423, 445
　environmental justice framing, 428
　evaluation of, 420–45, 449t, 461–77, 462t
　FAAAA amendment (*see* Federal Aviation Administration Authorization Act)
　formative period leading to, 425
　goals, 311–12
　independent contractor status of port drivers as target, 311, 449t
　inside game, 368–77
　integrated advocacy and, 424–25
　interest convergence and, 422–23, 428–30
　labor interests in, 437
　legal endowments and, 435–38
　legal opportunity structure, 421, 437
　legal opposition to, 438–40
　legal planning for, 333–34
　legislative strategy, 406–10
　local legal mobilization, 363–87
　meaning of success in, 435
　meetings with government officials, 368–77
　misclassification litigation, 410–16, 440–41 (*see also* misclassification litigation)
　opportunity for, 349–50
　outcomes, 406, 434–45
　outside game, 363–68
　partnerships, 353–60
　personnel, 349–53
　policy development phase, 360–62, 431
　port truck drivers, impact on, 444
　preemption analysis, 431
　representation of workers in, 441–45
　response to failure of employee conversion, 424
　role of environmental litigation in, 436
　role of law in shaping problems and solutions, 421–22
　role of lawyers in, 430–34
　strategy, 421–34
　suing-and-striking strategy, 438
　Supreme Court and, 401–5
　top-down planning, 350, 368
　union organizing, 416–20, 462t
Campbell, Kristina, 124, 126, 131, 132, 145–46, 147

Campbell, Molly, 384
Canham-Clyne, John, 332–33, 350–51, 352–53, 356, 368, 425
Cannon, Chris, 127
Capital Vision Equities, 192, 553
CARB. *See* California Air Resources Board
card-check neutrality, 175–76, 179, 193, 201–2, 203–4, 205, 207, 208, 491–92, 494, 495
Cardenas, Tony, 15, 210, 226
CARECEN. *See* Central American Resource Center
Carson, 327–28
Carstens, Doug, 284
Carter, David, 120, 121–22
Carver, Ron, 331, 333, 380–81
Car Wash Campaign, 19–20
Castellanos, Patricia, 351–53, 352f, 359–60, 366–67, 368, 374, 401, 413
Castle v. Hayes Freight Lines, 397, 399, 402, 403, 405
Catholic Youth Organization, 97–98
CBA. *See* community benefits agreement
CBA campaign
　dependence on redevelopment, 166–68, 263
　evaluation of, 247–53, 449t, 462t
　goals, 164, 256
　impact on lawyers' careers, 251–52
　interest convergence and, 164–65, 248
　key actors, 164–65, 168–74, 209–25, 234–38
　labor's role in, 168–74, 199–209, 262–63
　lawyers' professional self-conceptions, 249–50
　lawyers' role in, 248–53
　leverage in, 180, 209–10, 213, 239, 253–58
　litigation in, 449t
　outcomes, 185–87, 191, 221–24, 228–29, 242, 258–63, 462t
　strategies, 174–75, 253–58
CBI. *See* Coalition for a Better Inglewood
CD Tech. *See* Community Development Technologies Center
Ceja, Garciela, 59
Center for Community Change, 175
Center for Constitutional Jurisprudence, 399–400
Center for Food and Justice, 358
Center for Law in the Public Interest, 53
Center on Policy Initiatives, 178
Central American Resource Center (CARECEN), 97–98, 100, 459, 551
Central Business District, 167, 187, 234
Central District of California, 117
Century Cargo Facilities Lease, 207–8
Century City, 16
CEQA. *See* California Environmental Quality Act
Cervantes, Nancy, 98, 100, 102–4, 107, 139, 145
Cesar Chavez Avenue, 232, 296

Chamber of Commerce, 99, 199, 208, 220
Chang, Do Won, 66
Chang, Elaine, 398–99
Change to Win, 128, 332, 333–34, 350–51, 352–53, 358–59
　Campaign for Clean Trucks and, 363–64, 368, 369, 415–16, 441–42
　national ports campaign, 350
　Strategic Organizing Center, 425
CHARO Community Development Corporation, 17–18
Chatten-Brown, Jan, 284–86, 303, 304, 305, 307, 308, 336–37, 459–60
　role in Farmers Field lawsuit, 252–53
　role in Inglewood site fight, 284
　role in LAX modernization, 225–26
Chemerinsky, Erwin, 284–85
Cheunchujit, Rojana, 62*f*
China, 13–14, 428
　garment production and, 75–76
　as Los Angeles trading partner, 336–37
　Sweatshop Watch and, 79
　trade with, 317
　WTO and, 75–76
China Ocean Shipping Company (COSCO), 336–37
China Shipping Holding Company (China Shipping), 335–49, 350, 357–58, 371, 425–26, 430–31, 436
　lease with Port of Los Angeles, 337, 338, 342
　NRDC CEQA lawsuit against (*see* China Shipping lawsuit)
　protests against, 338–39
　refusal to retrofit, 341
　terminal, 337, 342
China Shipping lawsuit, 336–42
　CAAP and, 425–26, 428
　CEQA challenge filed, 337
　as example of disruptive litigation, 430
　impact on efforts to reduce port emissions, 342, 345, 425–26
　impact on port development, 380–81, 386–87
　NRDC and, 337–40, 354–55
　relation to Clean Truck Program, 436
　settlement of, 340–42, 365
Chinatown
　in Los Angeles, development of, 14–15
　Wal-Mart in, 295–97, 297*f*, 303, 310
CHIRLA. *See* Coalition for Humane Immigrant Rights of Los Angeles
CHIRLA v. Burke, 105–6, 107, 110, 111, 144, 149
Chung, Christina, 58, 67, 71, 74, 81–82, 458
Cinerama Dome theater, 176–77
CIO. *See* Congress of Industrial Organizations
CIR. *See* Community Impact Report

cities
　as catalyst of national reform, 499–507
　contemporary transformation of, 500
　control over property, 502
　as legal concept, 499–500
　preemption and, 503–7
　regional inequality and, 503–7
　social movements and, 499–500
　as tool and target of labor reform, 501–3
　as unit of analysis, 10
　work, relationship to, 502
Citizens Committee to Welcome Wal-Mart to Inglewood, 277–78
City Center Redevelopment project, 187, 234, 235, 242
City Girl, Inc., 59, 67, 80
citywide ban on day labor solicitation, 98, 99, 142, 149, 150*f*, 150–55, 157*t*
civil defamation lawsuits, 487
civil liberties, 93
civil rights, 2–3, 4, 7–8, 19, 41–42, 45–46, 65, 95–101, 145, 164, 247, 252–53, 279, 306, 392, 412, 448–52, 478, 489, 506
Civil Rights Act of 1964
　Title VI, 209–10
　Title VII, 271–72
Civil Rights era, 15, 477
Civil Rights movement, 11–12, 478
CLEAN. *See* Community Labor Environmental Action Network
Clean Air Act, 324, 335, 344, 391, 429
Clean Air Action Plan (CAAP), 335–49, 353–54, 355–56, 425–26, 430–31
　approval of, 349, 363
　Clean Truck Program and, 368, 428
　coalition comments on, 360–61
　Control Measure HDV1, 348
　diesel trucks as target, 348
　directive on port truck drivers, 348
　EIR, 360–61
　implementation, 363
　leverage for, 347–48
　relation to Clean Truck Program, 363–65
　RFP and, 364–65
　technical report, 348
Clean Ports Act, 409–10
Clean Truck Coalition, 414–15
Clean Truck Fee, 379, 380, 381–82
Clean Truck Program, 30–31, 311–12, 348, 356, 382, 430, 439, 440, 449*t*, 454–55, 457–58, 460–61, 467, 470, 476, 480, 485–86, 487, 494, 496, 613. *See also American Trucking Associations v. City of Los Angeles*; Campaign for Clean Trucks
　BCG report on, 383–84
　Clean Truck Fee, 379

INDEX

Clean Truck Program (*cont.*)
  Clean Truck Fund, 379
  components of, 366
  concession agreement, 385, 387, 390, 397, 423, 424
  costs and benefits of, 372
  dirty truck ban, 378
  drafting of, 370
  economic analysis of, 372, 373–74, 375
  employee conversion and, 384–87, 428–29, 442–43
  Federal Maritime Commission lawsuit, 396–97
  fees, 364–65, 379, 380, 381–82
  financing of, 387
  Great Recession impact on, 392
  identifying clean trucks, 378–79
  industry opposition to, 371, 373, 376, 382
  Joint Public Workshop, 366–67
  lawsuit challenging, 427, 435 (*see also* American Trucking Associations v. City of Los Angeles)
  legal analysis, 369–71, 432, 443
  market participant rationale for, 378, 386
  negotiations over, 366, 373, 379, 380
  as "operational issue," 374, 375
  Order 6935, 378, 384
  passing of, 377–87, 436–37
  placards, 366–67, 385, 387, 397
  political calculation around, 371
  port lawyers and, 432
  proposals for, 362, 365–66
  provisions challenged in *ATA v. City of Los Angeles*, 397
  outcome, 462t
  RFP model, 364–65
  rollout of, 392, 395–96
  severability clause, 385
  Tariff No. 4 and, 385
  union support for, 395
clean trucks campaign. *See* Campaign for Clean Trucks
Clean Trucks Center, 392
Clearing the Roadblocks (LAANE), 407
Clergy and Laity United for Economic Justice (CLUE), 171–73, 191, 278–79
client-community accountability, in big-box campaign, 308–10
client control, 479, 481
climate change, 506–7
Clinica Oscar Romero, 174
Clinton, Bill, 47, 58, 82–83, 85
CLUE. *See* Clergy and Laity United for Economic Justice
Coalition for a Better Inglewood (CBI), 278–81, 285–86, 289, 308–9
  legal strategy, 282–87
Coalition for a Responsible USC, 170–71

Coalition for a Safe Environment, 327, 335–36, 356–57, 359, 363, 381, 441–42
Coalition for a Truly Regional Airport Plan, 196–97
Coalition for Clean Air, 295, 337, 342–43, 358, 363, 367, 381, 382–83, 389
Coalition for Clean and Safe Ports, 30–31, 365–66, 381, 422, 429, 442
  accountability to constituents, 441–45
  Change to Win role in, 332–34, 350–51
  governance of, 362
  impact of *ATA v. City of Los Angeles* on, 430
  LAANE role in, 350–53
  members, 353–54, 368
  messaging by, 382–83
  mission statement for, 360
  NRDC role in, 356
  official convening of, 362
  organizing by, 366–67, 380f, 382, 383
  origins of, 349–62
  outreach to members, 353–60
  power dynamics in, 368
  reaction to *ATA v. City of Los Angeles*, 392, 405–20
  representation in, 444–45
  Teamsters role in, 333, 353–54, 358, 363, 368, 383, 395–96, 408
  role of networks, 358–59
  shared interests of labor and environmentalists, 354–55, 369–70, 428–30
Coalition for Community Health, 174
Coalition for Humane Immigrant Rights of Los Angeles (CHIRLA), 61, 64, 69, 71, 84, 99–100, 103–4, 105–6, 108, 127, 173, 551
  Adopt-a-Corner program, 97, 105
  Coalition for Clean and Safe Ports and, 358–59
  day labor hiring centers and, 108, 127
  Day Labor Outreach Project, 97–98, 139
  Valley Jobs Coalition and, 191
  Workers' Rights Project, 102–3, 139
Coalition for Justice in the Maquiladoras, 79
Coalition LA, 173, 174, 179–80, 181–82, 551
Coalition of Immigrant Workers Advocates, 19–20, 84, 85
coalitions
  conflicts in, 88, 262–63, 308–10, 443–45
  interest convergence and, 441–42
  leadership, 250, 443
  organizing by, in Los Angeles, 18
  representation of, 248–53, 302–3, 306–8, 453–56, 453f, 454f
  role of organized labor in, 16, 168–74, 254, 270–72, 422, 453–54
  tensions in, 234–38, 262–63, 308–10, 444, 498
Coalition to Eliminate Sweatshop Conditions, 40, 41–42

INDEX

Cohen, Ben, 82
Cohen, Nancy, 208–9, 210, 214–16, 219
Colectivo Tonantzin, 120, 121–22, 123–24, 147–48
collective bargaining. *See* labor law
Collins, Audrey, 47, 48, 86–87
Columbia Law School, 373
comeback cities, 248
Comite de Jornaleros v. Redondo Beach, 91, 137, 138, 142, 147, 148–49, 461–67, 468–69
   appeal to Ninth Circuit, 118, 131–32
   denial of certiorari, 136–37
   en banc rehearing, 132–33, 134–36
   federal court filing, 117
   impact on other anti-solicitation ordinances, 137, 151–55
   litigation team, 117–18, 131
   outcome, 462t
   plaintiffs, 117
   preliminary injunction, 117
   ruling on legal status of workers, 117
   summary judgment, 117–18
Commerce (city), 327–28
commercial parking lot only ban on day labor solicitation, 150–51
commercial speech, 28–29, 134, 137, 148–49
Common Threads, 56
Communication Workers of America (CWA), 329, 330, 331
Communities for a Better Environment, 245–46
Community Action to Fight Asthma, 212
Community and Economic Development Committee, Los Angeles, 170
community benefits agreement (CBA), 3, 29, 248, 299–300, 453–54, 459, 470–71, 485–86, 491, 552, 553
   conflicts over terms, 256
   contracting problems and, 257–58
   cooperation provisions, 185
   critiques of, 259
   defining, 165
   developer response to, 259
   development of model for, 175
   as development regulations, 259
   direct enforcement by community as feature of, 177
   enforceability of, 253, 256–57
   equity criticisms of, 259–60
   evaluation of, 253–58, 260–61, 462t
   exactions and, 259
   as induced agreement, 180–81
   institutionalization of, 258–63
   legal issues with, 259
   legal representation and, 251
   leverage for, 253–54, 254f, 255, 258, 449t
   Living Wage Ordinance and, 256

living wage requirements, 165, 186, 191–92, 223, 242, 256
local hiring and, 242, 243, 471
organized labor involvement in, 493–94
origins of, 175
as political resource, 258
private CBA, 253, 449t
public CBA, 221, 255, 449t
public-private enforcement of, 258
redevelopment and, 165, 166, 170, 177, 187, 189–91, 193, 230, 242, 245, 247
relation between leverage and enforceability, 255–56
rights-stripping, 257
as second-best solution, 262
successor liability and, 258
Superstores Ordinance, relation to, 300–1
unionization and, 493–94
community benefits campaign. *See* CBA campaign; Grand Avenue CBA; LAX CBA; Staples CBA
Community Benefits Law Center, 251–53
community benefits policy, 193, 210, 261–62, 453–54, 489
Community Coalition, 178, 185, 214–15, 257
Community Coalition for Change, 211
community development corporations, 17–18
Community Development Technologies Center (CD Tech), 236, 237, 238, 240–41
Community Economic Development Clinic, UCLA, 78
Community Economic Development Unit, LAFLA, 238
community empowerment, 477
Community Impact Report (CIR), 193
community knowledge, 485, 486–87
community-labor alliances, 16, 164, 168–74, 248–49, 476, 498
community-labor campaigns, 452, 489
   lawyers in, 456–57, 459, 460, 482, 487
   legal mobilization in, 453–56, 454f
   strategic policy advocacy and, 453–54
   mobilization and, 16, 460
   reshaping work, 502, 505–6
   unionism and, 493–94
community-labor coalitions, 258–59, 272, 276, 294, 302–3, 448–52, 453–54, 459, 475, 481, 505–6
   foundations for, in Los Angeles, 17–18
Community Labor Environmental Action Network (CLEAN), 19–20
Community Legal Services of Phoenix, 124
community mobilization, 234
   against Grand Avenue Project, 234
   against port expansion, 325–29
   against Wal-Mart, 302–3

Community Redevelopment Agency (CRA), 166, 167–68, 237, 291, 449t, 475–76, 553
    Bunker Hill and, 230
    CBAs and, 176–77, 178, 180, 187, 191, 192, 233–34, 238
    CIR policy, 193
    contractor responsibility policy, 193, 462t
    Development and Disposition Agreement with TrizecHahn, 175–76
    dissolution of, 245
    Figueroa Corridor shaped by, 166–67
    Grand Avenue Project and, 230–32, 233–36, 237, 238, 241, 242–43
    labor peace policy, 193
    living wage policy, 237, 462t
    Local Hiring Requirements, 242
    Owner Participation Agreement with Dome Entertainment Center, 176–77
    Prevailing Wage Policy, 242
    San Fernando Valley and, 191
    subsidy accountability and, 170
    successor agency, 245
    worker retention policy, 193, 462t
Community Reinvestment Act, 175
Community Scholars program, 18–19
comparative institutional analysis, 6f, 446, 478
    accountability and, 478–83
    actors in, 5
    campaign as unit of analysis, 7
    definition of, 5
    efficacy and, 485
    lawyers and, 7–8
    means and ends, 7
    prospective orientation of, 7
complete ban on day labor solicitation in designated areas, 150f, 150–51, 157t
comprehensive campaign, 282, 304, 457, 460
Compton, 202, 295, 317–18
Comunidad Presente, 246–47
Concerned Citizens of South Central Los Angeles, 237, 238, 239–41, 243, 551
concession agreement
    as goal of Campaign for Clean Trucks, 333–34, 350, 352–53, 357, 369–70
    implementation of, 387
    legal justification for, 334, 385
    as model for Clean Truck Program, 334
    as policy solution to independent contractor problem in port trucking, 423
conditional use permit (CUP), 291–92, 295, 303, 449t
Congress of Industrial Organizations (CIO), 15–16
Congress Watch, 332
ConocoPhillips, 320, 321
containerization, 316–17

contentious politics, 7, 484
contracting relationships
    CBAs and, 257–58
    challenges to labor protection and, 427, 492–93
    Living Wage Ordinance and, 201–2
Contractor Responsibility Ordinance, 223, 228–29, 467–68
Contreras, Miguel, 16–17, 193, 198–99, 202, 203, 206, 210, 288f, 459
Control Measure HDV1, 348
cooperative federalism, 506–7
Corona, Mike, 118–19, 120
COSCO. *See* China Ocean Shipping Company
Costa Mesa, 137, 142
    ACLU lawsuit against, 98, 100–1, 123
    anti-solicitation ordinance, 123
    day labor hiring center, 98
    day labor protests in, 125f
    Saenz role in anti-solicitation challenge, 124, 125f
Costco, 266–67, 274
Cotrell, Sharon, 357–58
countermobilization, 28, 80, 435, 438, 455, 483, 484, 489
County Fed. *See* Los Angeles County Federation of Labor
CRA. *See* Community Redevelopment Agency
critical legal consciousness, 477
Crose, Joy, 369, 370, 378, 386, 390
cross-racial organizing, 48, 58–59
Culling, Claudia, 214–15, 217–18
Culver City, 213
CUP. *See* conditional use permit
cut-and-sew apparel workers, 36, 52
CWA. *See* Communication Workers of America

Dana Point, 98–99
Daniels, Paula, 345
Davis, Cowell & Bowe, 333–34, 353, 425, 459–60
Davis, Gray, 62, 63, 346, 458–59
Davis, Mike, 15, 230
day labor, 3, 28–29, 113f, 446, 449t, 452, 456–57
    advocacy, 93–95
    business support for, 93
    campaign to defend, 95–138
    city responses to, 99
    on the corners, 97, 98
    as "crisis," 92–93
    definition, 91
    demographic overview and earnings, 26t
    discrimination against, 100–1, 141–42
    economics of, 91–92, 129–30
    growth of, 92
    hiring centers, 97–99, 103–4, 108, 118, 119, 127
    home improvement stores and, 102–3

immigration status and, 92, 98
impact of IRCA on, 96
impact of recession on, 129–30
integrated advocacy and, 141–48
labor abuse, 92
local regulation of, 91–95
as part of underground economy, 91
political environment and, 92–93, 94, 129–31, 148–49
regulation as public nuisance, 92–93, 99
resident opposition to, 103, 104
in Southern California, 91–92
visibility of, 91
wage theft and, 129–30, 130f
Day Labor Outreach Project, 97–98, 139
Day Labor Union, 105
day labor worker committees, 112, 114, 117, 120, 123–24, 126, 146
Deep South, 12
defamation, 56, 59, 69, 487
defensive litigation, 487
deindustrialization, 15–16, 318, 490, 500
Delgadillo, Rocky, 226
Delvac, Bill, 182–83, 185
demobilization, as consequence of legal action, 5, 33
Democratic National Convention of 2000, 171–73
Democratic Party, 9
demographic overview of industries targeted by L.A. campaigns, 1990, 21t
demographic overview of industries targeted by L.A. campaigns, 2010, 23t
Dennison, Becky, 237, 238, 239, 241, 243, 260–61
Denver International Airport, 351
Department of Labor, 39, 58, 61, 82–83, 85, 411, 434, 455
garment industry compliance program, 51
misclassification initiative, 411–12, 413, 414–15
No Sweat Initiative, 87
Wage and Hour Division, 39
Department of Transportation, 408–9
deradicalization, 484–85
deregulation
drayage trucking and, 321–22, 421–22, 492–93
intermodalism and, 317
ports and, 315–19
Teamsters and, 329
trade growth and, 421–22
truck drivers, impact on, 329
desegregation, 478–79
Deukmejian, George, 40
deunionization, 15–16, 37

Development Guidelines and Controls for Residential Hotels in the City Center and Central Industrial Project Areas, 235
diesel fuel, 219, 223, 322–24, 335
diesel truck pollution. See truck pollution
Digges, Robert, 398
dirty truck ban, 378–79. See also Clean Truck Program
disinvestment, 248, 500
displacement, 17–19, 29, 166–93, 237, 248, 263, 272, 291–92, 500–1
Division of Labor Standards Enforcement (DLSE), 39, 42, 44–45, 48–49, 80, 82–83, 416, 424, 427, 434, 438. See also Labor Commission
A.B. 633 and, 62–63, 74, 75
misclassification and, 411, 412, 414–15, 419–20
DLC. See Downtown Labor Center
DLSE. See Division of Labor Standards Enforcement
Dockside electrical power (also cold ironing), 335, 342, 343–44, 346, 347–48
Dolores Mission, 97
Dome Entertainment Center, 176–77
Donoghue, Diane (Sister), 17–18, 181–82, 183f
Don't Waste L.A. campaign, 440–41
Dormant Commerce Clause, 504–5
Dorn, Roosevelt, 225, 276–77, 279
Dorothy Chandler Pavilion, 230–31
Downtown Labor Center (DLC), 19–20, 141, 460–61
downtown Los Angeles
gentrification in, 232
plan to revitalize, 230–31
Downtown Women's Center, 235–36
drayage trucking, 311, 320, 327–28, 410, 504–5
Clean Truck Program and, 352–53, 356, 361, 364–65, 369, 379, 383–85, 386, 393–94, 400, 402–3
conditions, 322
deregulation and, 321–22, 421–22
environmental impacts of, 322–24
growth in Los Angeles, 322–24, 421–22
handoff from steamships, 322
idling, 322, 323f, 335, 342–43, 357
immigration and, 322
impact on port communities, 320
independent contracting and, 321–22
labor force of, 322
labor hierarchy and, 321–22
misclassification and, 410–16
size of trucking firms, 322–24
unionization and, 322, 417, 419–20
DreamWorks, 177
Dreier, Peter, 358

INDEX

Driscoll, John, 202–3, 205, 206
D.T. Sewing, 74
Dukes v. Wal-Mart, 271–72
Dunlap, Judy, 276–77
Durazo, Maria Elena, 179–80, 350–51

earnings distribution in industries targeted by L.A. campaigns, 1990-2010, 22, 24*t*
East Asian Tigers, 317
East Bay Alliance for a Sustainable Economy (EBASE), 178
East Lawrence Improvement Association, 331–32
East Los Angeles, 13
East Palo Alto, 181
East Wilmington, 325, 327–28
East Yard Communities for Environmental Justice, 327–28, 358, 359–60, 363, 441–42
EBASE. *See* East Bay Alliance for a Sustainable Economy
Echoing Green Fellowship, 84, 460
Economic and Employment Enforcement Coalition, 82–83
Economic Development Committee of City Council, 274
economic impact analysis, 289–90, 291–92, 293, 294, 300–1, 454–55, 549
economic impact report, 290–91, 449*t*
economic justice, 164, 170–71, 174, 210–11, 419–20, 446–47, 461, 482, 488, 500–1, 505–6, 507
Economic Policy Institute, 504
Economics & Politics, Inc., 372
education, citizenship, and nativity in industries targeted by L.A. campaigns, 25*t*
efficacy
  challenges to legal enforcement, 483–84
  cooptation and, 484–85
  countermobilization and, 484
  as foundational legal liberal critique, 5, 477
  lawyers and, 5, 483
  in legal mobilization, 483–90
  litigation and, 487–88
  measurement of, 8
  in relation to policy change, 468–72, 483–84
  transsubstantive nature of challenges to, 483–84
EIR. *See* environmental impact report
EIS. *See* environmental impact statement
Elmendorf, James, 173, 179, 181–82
El Monte, 42, 43*f*, 461–67
El Rescate, 97–98
El Salvador, 13–14
El Segundo, 211–12, 213, 225–26
  noise mitigation and, 228–29
eminent domain, 166, 294
empirical appraisal of L.A. campaigns, 447–77

employee conversion, 379, 380, 383, 400–1, 423, 424, 428–29, 442–43, 445
employer verification of day labor legal status, in Sensenbrenner bill, 127
employment law, 57, 88, 411, 493, 495–96
Employment Law Center, 18, 81–82, 181
Empowerment Zones, 18
endowments, of lawyers in L.A. campaigns, 458
Engine Manufacturers Association v. SCAQMD, 354–55, 391
Engineers Local 501, 174–75
Englert, Roy, 401
Environmental Defense, 447, 449*t*, 459
  Campaign for Clean Trucks and, 345, 354
  LAX CBA campaign and, 199–210, 214–15, 462*t*, 551
  Staples CBA campaign and, 173, 183–84, 249
Environmental Defense Fund. *See* Environmental Defense
Environmental Health Coalition, 178
environmental impact report (EIR)
  CAAP and, 360–61
  in CBA campaigns, 184, 194–95, 196–99, 209–19, 225–27, 233, 236, 239–40, 246–47, 255, 256
  China Shipping and, 337–38, 340–41, 342
  Port of Los Angeles and, 337
  TraPac terminal expansion and, 381, 386–87
environmental impact statement (EIS), 194–95, 196, 197, 198, 199, 209–10, 212, 213, 225–26, 338
environmental justice, 9, 164–65, 194–230, 252, 262–63, 335–36, 351, 353, 355, 356, 358, 459–60, 475, 497–98
Environmental Justice Project at Environmental Defense, 183–84, 345
environmental movement, 1, 30–31, 262–63, 305, 335, 349–50, 405–6, 421–22
Environmental Protection Agency (EPA), 335, 359–60
  emission standards of 2007, 348
environmental remediation, 165, 211, 354, 373–74, 423, 425–26, 430, 475, 553
EPA. *See* Environmental Protection Agency
Episcopal Church of St. Phillip the Evangelist, 174
equality
  constructing meaning of, 446–47
  as outcome of struggle, 461–77
  policies advancing in Los Angeles, 461–68
  in process of struggle, 447–61
Equal Justice Works, 238
equal place, 7–8
  meaning of, 1
  promoting economic equality in city as goal of L.A. campaigns, 1, 446–47, 461
  role of lawyers in L.A. campaigns (*see* lawyers in L.A. campaigns)

Equal Rights Advocates (ERA), 41, 61
equitable development, 164
equity
　CBAs and, 254, 258–60
　regional, 10, 503–7
　workplace, 498
ERA. *See* Equal Rights Advocates
Esperanza Community Housing Corporation, 17–18, 97, 164–65, 181–82, 551
Estolano, Cecilia
　as CEO of CRA, 238, 239–40, 241
　as city attorney, 273–74, 289–90
　as member of Villaraigosa transition team, 345
Ethics Commission, 198–99
expertise, 4, 458, 459–60, 486–87
Expo Line, 246–47
Exxon, 373

F-40, 45
FAA. *See* Federal Aviation Administration
FAAAA. *See* Federal Aviation Administration Authorization Act
"Fabulous" Forum, 264
Fair Labor Association, 59–60
Fair Labor Fashions Trendsetter List, 51–52, 82–83
Fair Labor Standards Act (FLSA), 39, 58, 67, 68–69
　economic realities test, 86–87, 411, 412, 461–67
　hot goods provision, 48, 59–60
　joint employer test, 47, 67
fair share fees, 497
fair share laws, 301–2
Faithful Central Bible Church, 264, 276–77
Farmers Field, 246–47, 252–53
fast fashion, 88–89
FCCEJ. *See* Figueroa Corridor Coalition for Economic Justice
Federal Aviation Administration (FAA), 197–98, 206–7, 226–27, 229, 471, 554
　aviation-related requirement, 194–95, 216, 220
　LAX CBA and, 227
Federal Aviation Administration Authorization Act (FAAAA)
　Clean Truck Program and, 391, 392–93, 394, 395, 397–98, 402, 406–10, 440, 442–43
　effort to amend, 406–10
　market participant exception and, 324
　preemption of state and local trucking laws, 324, 406–7, 431, 435, 439–40, 504–5
　safety exception, 392–93
federalism, 2–3, 437
federal labor law. *See* labor law
Federal Maritime Commission, 353, 373, 396–97, 454–55

Federal Motor Carrier Safety Administration, 392–93
Federation of Hillside and Canyon Associations, 225–26
Federosky, Veronica, 112, 115, 117, 118, 119, 123–24, 139, 147–48
Feess, Gary, 67–68, 86–87
Feinberg, Margo, 459–60
　role in Inglewood site fight, 273–74, 277, 284–85, 286, 290–91, 301, 304, 305
　role in Los Angeles Living Wage Campaign, 273–74
　role in Respect at LAX, 204–5, 206
Feinstein, Diane, 128
Feinstein, Fred, 127–28
fellowships, role in supporting lawyers in L.A. campaigns, 460
Fernandez, Ferdinand, 393
Feuer, Gail Ruderman, 337, 339–41, 341*f*, 343, 425–26, 459–60
Feuer, Mike, 179
Fight for $15, 9, 490, 502–3
Figueira-McDonough, Julia, 59–60, 81–82
Figueroa Corridor, 166–93, 237, 257–58
　CRA and, 166–67
　geography of, 166, 172*f*
　SAJE and, 170–71
Figueroa Corridor Coalition for Economic Justice (FCCEJ)
　Ad Hoc Housing Committee, 179
　community organizing efforts, 173
　developer meeting with, in Staples CBA, 175
　first assembly meeting, 173–74
　list of members, 174, 551
　map, 172*f*
　origins of, 171
　response to L.A. Live EIR, 184
　SAJE role in, 171, 173
　Staples Accountable Development Working Groups, 173
　in Staples CBA campaign, 174–75, 179–80, 190–91, 255, 257
　Staples CBA negotiating team and, 181–83
　UNIDAD as successor, 245–46
Figueroa Corridor Community Land Trust, 188–89
Figueroa Corridor Partnership, 167
Figueroa South Land LLC, 189
First Amendment, 100–1, 106, 109, 127, 137, 141–42, 452
first-source hiring, 186, 191–92, 218, 220, 223, 228–29, 235, 462*t*, 471
Fletcher, Betty, 400
FLSA. *See* Fair Labor Standards Act
Foo, Lora Jo, 41–42, 45–46, 61, 62

Ford Foundation, 115–16, 170
Ford Motor Company, 448–52
Ford, Richard Thompson, 499–500
foreclosures on wheels, 392
Forest City Enterprises, 232
Forever 21, 28, 66–73, 449t
Forever 21 lawsuit, 28, 66–73, 76, 80–81, 86–87, 88–89, 487–88
   appeal, 71
   coordination with anti-sweatshop campaign, 66–67
   dismissal, 69
   filing of, 66–67
   Forever 21 response, 69–71
   goal of extending joint liability to retailers, 67
   plaintiffs, 66
   reason for targeting by anti-sweatshop campaign, 66–67
   removal to federal court, 68–69
   settlement, 72, 80
   SLAPP suits, 69, 71
   state law claims, 67
   as turning point in anti-sweatshop campaign, 72
Foster, Bob, 367–68, 378–79, 382, 383
   effort to defeat Clean Truck Program, 379
   public records act request against, 383–84
Fox Group, 167–68
Francine Browner Inc., 59
Frank, Larry, 351–52
Franklin, Ralph, 277, 292–93
Freeman, S. David, 346, 371, 376, 377, 379, 385, 386, 398–99
free trade, 36, 315–19, 421–22
Freire, Paulo, 102–3
Frenzen, Niels, 100
Fresh & Easy, 295
Fried Frank fellowship, 114, 124, 460
Frug, Gerald, 499–500
Fua, Rose, 41–42
Fulbright fellowship, 373
The Future of California's Garment Industry: Strengthening Opportunities for Immigrant Workers (Sweatshop Watch), 75

Galanter, Ruth, 195–96
Galen Center, 166–67
Garcetti, Eric, 274, 289, 290–91
Garcetti, Gil, 103–4
Garcia, Mike, 207
garment contractors
   labor abuse by, 33–34
   in Los Angeles, 39
   pressure to reduce costs, 33–34
garment industry, 3, 32–33
   changing structure of, 38
   codes of conduct in, 59–60, 82
   corporate organization of, 38
   economic division of labor in, 38–39
   high fashion, 36, 88–89
   growth, 35
   immigration and, 35, 37
   impact of Great Recession on, 79–80
   international trade in, 36, 57, 75–76
   labor enforcement in, 38–39
   labor monitoring programs in, 58
   labor standards in, 39
   legal division of accountability in, 38–39
   in Los Angeles, 20–26, 36
   manufacturers' role in, 33–34
   ongoing abuse in post-recession era, 88–89
   outsourcing, 36
   regulatory environment after El Monte, 87
   retailers' role in, 33–34
   shift from New York to Los Angeles, 36, 38
   shrinking of, 88–89
   structure of, 33–34, 34f
   subcontracting in, 38, 449t
   as target of labor movement, 58
   triangular bargaining and, 35
   undocumented labor and, 37
   unionization of, 26, 35, 515
garment lawsuits
   Bebe (*see* Bebe lawsuit)
   City Girl, Inc., BCBG Max Azria, and Hobby Horse, Inc., 59
   Forever 21 (*see* Forever 21 lawsuit)
   J.H. Design Group, 59–60
   John Paul Richards Inc. and Francine Browner Inc., 59
   XOXO Clothing Company, 60
Garment Registration Act, 61
Garment Special Account, 83–84
Garment Worker Center (GWC), 64–66, 68, 71, 80–81, 84, 449t, 456–57, 480
   A.B. 633 enforcement and, 65–66, 73–74
   divestment from legal activities, 76
   founding of, 64, 65
   legal clinic, 76
   mission, 65
   popular education, 77
   relations with APALC, 66, 72–73
   separation from Sweatshop Watch, 76–77
   steering committee, 64
   worker organizing and, 76–77
   workshops, 65–66
Garment Workers Collaborative, 74, 84
Garment Workers Justice Center, 65
Gateley, Jason, 417
Gates, Daryl, 11
Gateway Cities program, 365
GE. *See* General Electric
Gehry, Frank, 230–32, 236, 240

General Agreement on Tariffs and Trade, 36, 317
General Electric (GE), 16
General Motors, 267, 373
gentrification, 3, 29, 164
　　legal origins of, 166–68
Georgetown Law School, 356
Gephardt Group, 407
Gephardt, Richard, 407, 408
Gerald Desmond Bridge, 371, 383
Gibson, Dunn & Crutcher, 345
gig economy, 9
Gilbert, Bob, 214–17
Gill, Paul, 64
Gillibrand, Kirsten, 341
Gini coefficient, 13
Gladstein, Reif & Meginniss, 81–82
Glendale, 97–98, 110–14, 113f
Glick, Stephen, 414
global financial crisis of 2007, 244
globalization
　　garment industry and, 85–86
　　ports and, 315–19
global trade. See trade
Goldberg, Jackie, 105, 175–77, 178, 200–1, 205, 206, 273–74, 290–91
Gonzalez, Favian, 207–8
Gonzalez, Paulina, 173
Goodheart, Jessica, 178, 179–80, 193
Good Jobs First, 168–69
Good Jobs, Green Jobs Regional Conference, 417–18
Goodwin, Jim, 207
Gordon, Mike, 196, 199, 218
Gore, Al, 171–73
Gottlieb, Robert, 358
Gould, Ronald, 132–33
Graber, Susan, 132–33
Grand Avenue Authority, 240–41
Grand Avenue CBA, 29, 165, 230–47, 248–49, 252, 467, 470–71
　　coalition (see Grand Avenue Coalition for Community Benefits)
　　leverage, 239
　　living wage requirements, 242
　　local hiring and job training requirements, 242
　　organizing for, 238, 239
　　outcomes, 241, 242, 462t
　　political pressure for, 239–40
　　unions interest in project labor and labor peace agreements, 239–40
Grand Avenue Coalition for Community Benefits, 238, 242–43, 254
　　formation of, 236
　　goals, 238
　　LA CAN role, 237
　　members, 236, 237
　　negotiations with developer, 239–43

　　organizing, 239–41
　　SAJE role, 237
　　unions' decision not to join, 237
Grand Avenue Committee, 231, 242–43
Grand Avenue Project, 29, 237, 246f
　　affordable housing and, 233–34, 238, 241, 256
　　alternatives to, 240
　　announcement of, 231
　　approval of, 242–43
　　as Champs-Élysées of Los Angeles, 231–32
　　community mobilization against, 234
　　concerns about gentrification, 232
　　cost projections, 244
　　County Office Building Option, 240
　　economic impact projections, 232
　　EIR, 236, 240
　　financing of, 232–33, 240, 244
　　Grand Park, 208, 211
　　impact of CRA dissolution on, 245
　　impact of Great Recession on, 244
　　incentive rents and, 233
　　income diversity and, 233–34
　　job projections, 242
　　job training and, 257–58
　　local hiring provisions, 243
　　Master Plan, 232
　　public funding for, 244–45
　　Related Companies and, 232
　　scaling back of, 245
Grant, John, 273, 277, 290–91, 304, 305, 308
grassroots organizing
　　in anti-sweatshop campaign, 39–40, 57–75
　　in big-box campaign, 281, 309–10
　　day labor and, 93–94, 97
Gray-Barkan, Tracy, 276–77, 278–79, 284, 285, 287f, 308
Great Depression, 314
Great Recession, 1, 77, 165, 392, 470, 476
greater L.A. area, 10, 28–29, 91, 94, 95, 96–97, 101, 102, 104, 118, 130–31, 138, 149–50, 151, 155, 298, 468–69, 500, 505–6
Green, Elina, 358, 363, 367–68, 371, 379
Green Fleet Systems, 416, 419, 420
Green LA, 358
　　Port Working Group, 358, 441–42
grocery industry, 3, 446
　　in California, 273
　　master labor agreement with Southern California chains, 303, 449t
　　Wal-Mart and, 273
Grocery Reinvestment Act, 295–96, 299–300, 303
Grocery Worker Retention Ordinance, 295, 462t, 470, 476
grocery workers, in Los Angeles, 20–26
Gross, Julian, 181, 182–83, 214–15, 217–18, 249–50, 251–52, 459, 460

guarantors, in garment industry, 63, 65–66, 73, 74–75, 87, 449t
Guerra, Samuel, 59
Guess, 32–33, 41–42, 473–74
    Clinton administration investigation of, 51
    Fair Labor Fashions Trendsetter List, 51–52
    legal strategies against UNITE, 54–56
    Made in USA, 50
    opposition to unionization, 53–54
    state labor raids of, 51–52
Guess campaign, 49–57, 449t, 474.
    See also anti-sweatshop campaign
    air war, 50–51, 52–53, 56
    challenges to, 50
    class action (see Guess class action)
    goal, 49–50
    ground war, 50–51
    Guess response, 54–55
    initial public offering as leverage, 51–52
    origins, 50
    outcome, 56–57
    sectoral organizing in, 50
    UNITE role in (see Union of Needletrades, Industrial and Textile Employees)
Guess class action
    claims, 52
    defendants, 52
    ethical conflicts, 53, 54
    goal, 52–53
    legal response by Guess, 54
    litigation team, 53
    relation to union organizing, 52–53
    settlement of, 57
Gunning, Isabelle, 103–4
Gurley, David, 414
Guttentag, Lucas, 45–46
GWC. See Garment Worker Center

Haas, Gilda, 18–19, 173, 175, 179–80, 181–82, 182f, 183, 184–85, 237, 241, 250
Hadsell & Stormer, 45–46, 252–53, 412–13
Hahn, James, 180, 193, 475–76
    election as mayor, 425–26, 459–60
    LAX CBA and, 196–200, 208–9, 210, 211–12, 218, 222f, 226
    Port of Los Angeles and, 338–39, 342, 343–44, 357–58
    response to secessionists, 326
Hahn, Janice, 338–39, 342, 343, 368, 381, 386–87, 417–18, 419–20, 425–26
Hancock Park, 14–15
Harbor Commission, Long Beach, 382.
    See also Long Beach Board of Harbor Commissioners
Harbor Commission, Los Angeles, 325–26, 337–39, 345, 356–57, 368, 371, 381, 426, 432,

442. See also Los Angeles Board of Harbor Commissioners
Harbor Community Benefit Foundation, 386–87
Harbor Express, 416
Harbor Freeway (110), 320, 321
harbor railroads, 314–15
Harbor Trucking Association, 414–15
Harbor Vision Task Force, 357–58
Harbor-Watts Economic Development Corporation, 358–59
Harlins, Latasha, 14–15
Harris-Dawson, Marqueece, 214–15
Harry Bridges Boulevard, 321, 326–27
Harvard Law School, 58, 447–48, 458
Hastings School of Law, 458–59
Hayden, Tom, 62, 195–96
Hayes, Genethia, 103–4
heat islands, 192
heavy-duty vehicle (HDV), 348, 364–65
Hecht, Sean, 54, 284–85, 286, 304, 306
Helzer, Belinda Escobosa, 111–13, 114, 117–18, 119, 122f, 123–24, 139, 144–46, 148, 458–59
HERE. See Hotel Employees and Restaurant Employees
Hermandad Mexicana, 358–59
Hernández, Antonia, 104, 114, 242–43, 458–59
Hernandez, Lizette, 284, 308
Hernandez, Mike, 127, 173, 179
Heru, Shabaka, 211
Hicks, Joe, 103–4
Hispanic workers in industries targeted by L.A. campaigns, 20–26, 21t, 23t, 26t
H&M Terminals Transport, 329
Hobby Horse, Inc., 59
Hoffa, James, 368, 408, 413, 414–15, 417–18, 426–27
Hoffman Plastic Compounds, Inc. v. NLRB, 85
Ho, Laura, 41, 45–46
Holden, Nate, 48–49
hollow hope, 478
Hollywood, 10, 108, 175–76, 192–93
Hollywood and Highland project, 176–77, 290–91
    Development and Disposition Agreement, 176
Hollywood and Vine project, 553
Hollywood Park, 264–65, 275–76
Holmes, John, 374, 375, 377, 378, 384, 391, 398–99, 405, 426–27
HomeBase, 103–4
Home Depot, 110–11, 124, 126, 127, 128, 145–46
Home Improvement Stores Ordinance, 126–29, 144, 449t, 462t, 470
home-sewing operations, 51–52
Home Stretch Specific Plan Zone, 277–78
Hong, Roy, 41
Hoover Redevelopment Project, 166–67

INDEX

Hope and Peace Park, 187–88, 257–58
Horizon, 331
horizontal equity, in relation to local government regulation of work, 503–7
Horton, Jerome, 207–8, 292–93
hospitality industry, 12, 20–26, 29, 164–65, 169–70, 193, 470–71, 475, 497–98
Host Marriott, 208
Hotel Employees and Restaurant Employees (HERE), 169–70, 332–33
    Grand Avenue CBA and, 236, 242
    LAX CBA and, 208, 212, 214–15
    Local 11, 16–17, 171, 173, 174, 175, 180, 191, 212, 214, 236, 242, 351, 551
    Local 814, 203–4
    Staples CBA and, 170–73, 174–75, 179–80, 181–82
    Valley Jobs Coalition and, 191
House Committee on Transportation and Infrastructure, 407, 408–9
Howard, Scott, 112
Hricko, Andrea, 358
Hub Distributing, Inc., 45, 48
human trafficking, 37, 44
Hundred Years' War, 325–29
Hung, Betty, 58, 81–82, 458
Husing, John, 372, 373–74, 375
Husing Report, 372, 383–84
Hwang, Philip, 114, 117–18, 131, 145

Ibarra, Cecilia, 379
Icaza, Rick, 308
ICTF. *See* Intermodal Container Transfer Facility
identity-based affiliation, 482
IDEPSCA. *See* Institute of Popular Education of Southern California
Ikuta, Sandra, 131, 132–33
ILGWU. *See* International Ladies' Garment Workers' Union
immigrant rights campaigns, 452–53
    efforts outside of court, 453
    legal mobilization in, 452, 453*f*
immigrant rights movement, 142, 164
immigrant rights organizations, 40, 94, 97, 100, 138, 174, 358–59, 448–52
immigrant sanctuary laws, 506–7
Immigrants' Rights Project, ACLU, 45–46, 100
immigrant workers, 9, 19, 28
immigration
    AFL-CIO position on, 16–17
    day labor and, 91–95
    drayage trucking labor force and, 322
    garment industry and, 37
    land use law as a tool for controlling, 91–95
    Los Angeles and, 3, 13–14, 37
    opposition to, 118, 130–31
    political environment and, 148
    Sensenbrenner bill and, 127, 128
Immigration and Nationality Act of 1965, 37
Immigration and Naturalization Service (INS), 41–42, 44, 96
Immigration Reform and Control Act (IRCA), 16–17, 37, 96
impact analysis, 488–89
Impact Fund, 271–72
impact litigation, 2, 39–40, 58–60, 66–73, 78, 86–87, 93–94, 138, 144
implementation of legal reform, 7, 471, 472, 483–84
import quotas, 36, 57, 75–76
incentive zones, 291
independent contractors, 30–31, 109, 311, 424, 435–36, 446
    misclassification of (*see* misclassification)
    municipal strategy to address status of port truck drivers, 329–34
    port truck drivers as, 321–22, 380, 388–89
    preclusion from union organizing, 321–22
    Teamsters and, 330–31, 422
    unionization and, 421–22
Industrial Areas Foundation, 281
industrialization, ports and, 314–15
Industrial Revolution, 499
industries targeted by L.A. campaigns, 20–26
    demographics of, 20–26
    reasons for, 20
inequality
    challenge to, 1, 8, 27
    cities and, 500
    income, 13
    in Los Angeles, 11–20, 500–1
    labor law and, 477, 490–99, 503–7
    local government law and, 10
informal economy, 12, 91–92, 97
Inglewood
    African Americans in, 12, 264
    City Council, 206–7, 277, 287
    demographics of, 195
    as food desert, 264–65
    LAX and, 195, 197, 202, 210, 211–12, 213, 214, 221, 225–26, 228, 255
    location, 264
    Measure 04-A, 277–82
    noise mitigation and, 228–29
    soundproofing grants for, 227–28
    Wal-Mart and, 29–30, 264–65, 272–97, 306, 308–9, 457–58, 467, 475, 486–87
Inglewood Coalition for Drug and Violence Prevention, 214–15
Inglewood Democratic Club, 212
Inglewood Ministerial Alliance, 212

Inglewood site fight. *See also* big-box campaign
   community-labor coalition (*see* Coalition for a Better Inglewood)
   connection to LAX CBA campaign, 272
   consequences of, 287, 293–94
   goal, 276
   as legal reform from the bottom up, 298–99
   legal strategy, 282–87
   leverage, 283
   Measure 04-A, 277–78, 283–84, 287*f*
   nontraditional advocacy in, 304
   organizing, 277, 278–82, 280*f*
   origins of, 275–78
   public relations, 281–82
Inglewood Unified School District, 197, 212
Inland Empire, 276
Inner City Law Center, 81–82
INS. *See* Immigration and Naturalization Service
insider political strategies, of organized labor, 29, 476
Institute of Popular Education of Southern California (IDEPSCA) (also Instituto de Educación del Sur de California), 84, 102–3, 108, 112, 295
integrated advocacy, 7–8, 141–48, 457, 480, 487
   role of interdisciplinary knowledge, 485–86
integrated leadership, 456, 481
Intercorner Day Labor Conference, 108
interest convergence, 164–65, 248, 262–63, 311–12, 349–50, 354–55, 428–30, 475, 498
Interim Control Ordinance to ban Chinatown Wal-Mart, 296–97
Intermodal Association of North America, 399–400
Intermodal Container Transfer Facility (ICTF), 317–19, 321, 583
intermodalism, 316, 317–18, 327–28
International Alliance of Local Stage Employees Local 33, 174–75
International Brotherhood of Boilermakers, 331–32
International Brotherhood of Electrical Workers, 358
International Labor Rights Fund, 529
International Ladies' Garment Workers' Union (ILGWU), 40, 41, 53
   in Los Angeles garment industry, 50
   merger with ACTWU to form UNITE, 51
   triangular bargaining and, 35
   unionization of garment workers, 35
International Longshore and Warehouse Union (ILWU)
   Campaign for Clean Trucks and, 354, 358
   Local 13, 353–54, 395
   at Ports of Los Angeles and Long Beach, 314–15

international trade. *See* trade
intersectional lawyering, 482
Iny, Eddie, 203–4, 206
IRCA. *See* Immigration Reform and Control Act
Isakson, Johnny, 128
Italian Club, 45

Jack-in-the-Box, 100–1
Jackson, Jesse (Reverend), 281–82, 282*f*
Janavs, Dzintra, 340–41
Janis-Aparicio (also Janis), Madeline, 169*f*, 169–70, 177, 179–80, 181–82, 183, 193, 200–1, 203–5, 206, 208–9, 210–11, 233–34, 238, 245, 249, 250, 251–52, 284–85, 288*f*, 290–91, 304, 306–7, 308, 350–51, 447–48, 460–61, 475–76
janitors, 13, 15–16, 18–19, 171–73, 200, 203, 271, 474–75
Jewels Jin, Law Office of, 439–40
JfJ. *See* Justice for Janitors
J.H. Design Group, 59–60, 80
J.H. Snyder Co., 552
Joaquin, Linton, 100
John Paul Richards Inc., 59, 80
Johnson, Lorraine, 276–77
Johnson, Lyndon, 86–87
joint employer liability
   in anti-sweatshop campaign, 32–33, 35, 38–39, 40, 61, 449*t*, 467
   employment law test, 47
jornalero, 91
Jornaleros Unidos de Baldwin Park, 124–26
Justice for Janitors (JfJ), 16–18, 168–69

Kabateck, Brian, 416
Kagan, Elena, 403–4
Kahn, Andrew, 353, 459–60
Kahn, Simon, 390, 398
Kanjobal Indians, 100
Kanter, Robert, 343–44
Karp, Jessica, 140
Katz, Bruce, 506
Kaye Scholer, 370, 390, 398, 432–33
Keller, Larry, 343, 347
Kennard, Lydia, 226–27, 228
Kieffer, George, 208, 220
Kim, Candice, 358, 363, 367
Kim, Kaylynn, 346
King, George, 106
King, Rodney, 11
KIWA. *See* Koreatown Immigrant Workers Alliance
Klein, Jonathan, 408, 417–18
Knabe, Don, 220
Knatz, Geraldine, 347, 368, 374, 379, 386–87, 394–95, 398–99, 426

Knight, 376, 392
Knoll Hill, 338–39
Kodak Theatre, 175–76
Koff, David, 174–75, 181–82
Korean immigrants, 14–15, 19, 37
Koreatown, 14–15
Koreatown Immigrant Workers Alliance (KIWA) (also Korean Immigrant Workers Advocates), 19, 41, 60, 61, 64, 84
Kotkin, Joel, 231
Kozinski, Alex, 132–33, 134, 136, 137, 138, 148–49
Krause, Doug, 346
Kroger, 275
Kumetz, Fred, 330–31
Kwoh, Stewart, 45–46

LAANE. *See* Los Angeles Alliance for a New Economy
L.A. Arena Land Company, 167–68, 173, 174–75, 178–79, 187
labor, 8–9, 490–99
labor activism, 9, 10, 32–33, 270–71, 437, 459–60, 491, 495, 503, 508
Labor Commission, 74, 469. *See also* Division of Labor Standards Enforcement
Labor/Community Strategy Center, 18–19
labor contingency, 1
labor-environmental coalition, 210, 349–62, 382. *See also* blue-green coalition
labor flexibility, 3, 37, 265–66, 502–3
labor law. *See also* National Labor Relations Act
 collective bargaining and, 8–9
 contracting and, 492–93
 critique of, 490
 garment industry and, 35
 interdisciplinary nature of, 495–96
 labor movement future and, 490
 living wage and, 191–92
 local lawmaking and, 504–5
 ossification of, 8–9
 outside of federal system, 9, 10, 33
 port trucking and, 314–15, 321–22, 324
 preemption and, 494–95, 503–5
 private ordering and, 493–95
 resilience of, 491–93
 strikes and, 433
 Wal-Mart and, 267–68
 workers beyond "reach and grasp" of, 8–9
labor law theory
 connection between local policy and unionization, 493–94
 immigration and, 493
 implications of L.A. campaigns for, 490–99
 interdisciplinary nature of labor law, 495–96
 political role of unions, 496–99
 preemption and, 494–95, 503–5
 resilience of labor law, 491–93
 sectoral strategies, 493–94
 solidarity, 498
 tripartite unionism, 494
 role of cities, 496, 502–3
 weakness of nonunions as bargaining agents, 498–99
labor movement
 decline of, 8–9, 13, 27f, 491–92
 demographic changes and, 9
 garment industry as target of, 58
 labor law role in future of, 490
 LAX and, 200
 local government law and, 270–72, 498, 502–7
 in Los Angeles, 16
 as part of community-labor coalitions, 9, 16, 448–52
 political strategy of, 9
 role in L.A. political transformation, 472–77
labor organizing, 26, 30–31, 57, 102–3, 209–10, 262–63, 267–69, 307, 310, 437–38, 446–47, 473–74, 499
labor peace agreement, 202–3, 204–5, 237, 239–40, 420
labor studies, 4
L.A. Business Team, 170, 347, 373
LA CAN. *See* Los Angeles Community Action Network
Ladera Heights, 103
Ladera Heights Civic Association, 103, 104
Ladera Heights Task Force, 105
LAFCO. *See* Los Angeles County Local Area Formation Commission
La Feria, 219, 286
LAFLA. *See* Legal Aid Foundation of Los Angeles
L.A. Grand Avenue Authority, 231–32, 239, 240, 244
Laguna Beach, 102, 118, 119
Lake Forest, 118–19, 120, 122, 142, 147
L.A. Live, 171, 189–90, 190f, 233–34, 467
LA Metro, 281, 282–83
L.A. Metropolitan Churches, 212
land use
 in big-box campaign, 303
 CBAs and, 180, 253–54, 453–54
 Home Improvement Stores Ordinance and, 129
 Superstores Ordinance and, 292
 as tool to influence labor standards, 496
 as tool for controlling day labor, 91–95, 449t
L.A. Olympics of 1984, 18
La Opinion, 203, 412
La Raza Centro Legal, 84
La Rosa, Victor, 413–14
Latham & Watkins, 181–83, 459

Latin America
  as source of garment exports, 36
  as source of immigration to Los Angeles, 13–14, 37, 473
Latin American Truckers' Association, 329
Latinos
  in L.A. politics, 15
  in labor movement, 19–20
  in Los Angeles, 13–15
  in garment industry, 48
  in industries targeted by L.A. campaigns, 20–26
law, role in L.A. political transformation, 472–77
LAWA. *See* Los Angeles World Airports
law and organizing, 3, 57–75
law and social movements, 4
L.A. Weekly, 304–5
law in action, 468–72
law on the books, 461–68
law-politics divide, 456
lawyer accountability, 477, 478–83
lawyer-client accountability, in big-box campaign, 306–8
lawyering for local change, 430–34
  authorization, 433
  disruption, 430–31
  inspiration, 434
  protection, 432–33
  validation, 431–32
lawyering theory
  accountability, 478–83
  coalitions and, 248–53
  efficacy, 483–90
  implications of L.A. campaigns for, 477–90
  integration of legal and community knowledge, 448, 485–86
  interdisciplinary nature of lawyering, 485–86
  intersectional, 482
  lawyering behind the scenes, 485, 487
  meaning of law, 485
  meaning of success, 488
  policy design from the ground up, 486–87
  representation, 481–83
  role of lawyers in campaigns for policy impact, 479
  role of litigation in social change, 487–88
lawyers
  accountability and, 5, 478–83
  comparative institutional analysis as framework for studying, 5–8
  debate over social change role, 5–8
  efficacy and, 5, 483–90
  in Los Angeles, 2–4
  role in L.A. campaigns (*see* lawyers in L.A. campaigns)
  social movements and, 1–4, 5
Lawyers' Committee for Civil Rights (LCCR), 114, 132, 145

lawyers in L.A. campaigns
  backgrounds of, 458, 459–60
  career mobility of, 460–61
  cross-racial representation, 482–83
  diverse commitments of, 459–60
  elite credentials, 458–67
  evaluation of, 447–77
  fellowships, 460
  integration of legal and community knowledge, 448, 485–86
  integration of law and politics, 456–58
  leadership, 447–48, 456, 479–80
  race and, 458–60
  representation, 480
  role in movement-building, 448
LAX. *See* Los Angeles International Airport
LAX Air Quality and Source Apportionment Study, 219
LAX CBA, 29, 165, 194–230, 251–52, 262–63, 460–61, 467, 470–71, 475, 504–5
  Airport Commission and, 219–20, 221, 224
  amount of benefits, 221
  announcement of, 222f
  approval, 221
  coalition, 200, 201, 209–10, 212 (*see also* LAX Coalition for Economic, Environmental, and Educational Justice)
  community participation and, 213
  draft proposal, 220
  FAA and, 216, 227
  financing of, 221
  as first public CBA, 221
  gate electrification, 215–17, 219, 223
  implementation of, 227, 228–29
  labor roots of, 199–209
  LAWA's interest in, 213–14
  leverage for, 213, 255
  litigation around and enforcement of, 225–30
  Mayor Hahn role in, 210
  negotiations with LAWA over, 209–25
  noise mitigation, 221, 227–29
  organizing for, 209–25
  origins of, 209–10
  outcomes, 229–30, 462t
  proposal for, 210–11
  provisions of, 221–24, 471
  Respect at LAX and, 199–209
  role of EIR/EIS in, 209–10, 212, 213, 215–16, 218, 219
  unresolved issues, 224–25
LAX Coalition for Economic, Environmental, and Educational Justice
  celebrating LAX CBA, 224f
  committees, 214–15
  environmental groups in, 200, 211
  formation, 210–12
  governance, 212

labor unions in, 210
media program, 218–19
members, 212
negotiation plan, 214, 219
negotiation teams, 214–15
negotiations with LAWA, 213, 215–18
organizing, 209–25
strategy, 212–13
LAX Master Plan
Alternative C, 196
Alternative D (Enhanced Safety and Security Alternative), 197–98, 199, 218, 226
approval of, 220–21
CEQA lawsuits against, 209–10, 213, 225–27, 459–60
Consensus Plan, 199, 219–20, 226
county opposition to, 195–96, 198–99, 213, 220
debate over, 196–97
EIS/EIR, 196, 197, 198, 199, 209–10, 218, 225–26
external challenges to, 218
green light projects, 199, 226, 228
implementation of, 229
LAX CBA and, 213, 220
phases of, 195
Respect at LAX and, 204–6
September 11 attacks and, 208
yellow light projects, 219–20, 226–27
LAX modernization, 194–96, 210, 220–21, 471. *See also* LAX Master Plan
LAX Organizing Project
allies, 203
goals, 201
as foundation for Respect at LAX, 203–4
proposal for, 201, 202
strategies, 201–2
LBACA. *See* Long Beach Alliance for Children with Asthma
LCCR. *See* Lawyers' Committee for Civil Rights
leadership
accountability and, 456–57, 479–80, 481, 482
in anti-solicitation campaign, 102–3, 105, 138–40
in anti-sweatshop campaign, 76–77, 80–81
in big-box campaign, 285, 307
in Campaign for Clean Trucks, 442–43
in CBA campaigns, 203–4, 250, 251–52
integrated, 456–57, 481
lawyers and, 7–8, 447–48, 508
unions and, 499
Leadership in Energy and Environmental Design (LEED), 217
lease-to-own truck program, 392
LEED. *See* Leadership in Energy and Environmental Design
Lee, Kimi, 65

Legal Aid Foundation of Los Angeles (LAFLA), 18, 59–60, 61, 84, 189, 251, 252–53
anti-solicitation ordinances and, 96–97
Community Economic Development Unit, 238
Employment Project, 81–82
Immigrants' Rights Office, 100
legal analysis
centrality in organizing strategy, 9
of FAAAA preemption, 344, 370, 428, 443
port as a unit of, 324
legal density, 460–61
legal endowments, movement success as function of, 435–38
legal liberalism
accountability and, 477, 478–83
critique of, 477, 478–79
defense of, 478
efficacy and, 483–90
lessons of L.A. campaigns for, 478
relation to Civil Rights era lawyering, 477
rethinking, 477–90
legal mobilization, 32–33, 446–47, 452. *See also* local legal mobilization
in anti-sweatshop campaign, 32–33
in Campaign for Clean Trucks, 363–87, 421–22, 430–34
in community-labor campaigns, 453–54, 454*f*
critiques of, 47–48
in day labor campaign, 155–56
in immigrant rights campaigns, 452, 453*f*
in L.A. campaigns, 1–2
at local level, 4–10, 446
legal opinions, 203–4, 370–71, 388, 431, 447, 487
legal profession, 480, 508
legal reform, in big-box campaign, 298–304
legitimation of status quo as a result of legal action, 5
Leiweke, Tim, 173, 178–79
Lennox, 195, 197, 202, 207–8, 210, 211–12, 213–14, 218, 219–20, 221, 228
Lennox Coordinating Council, 211, 214–15, 217
LeRoy, Greg, 251–52
Levis, 79
Levy, Stanley, 62
LF Sportswear, 45, 48
Libatique, David, 347, 369, 370–71, 373
libel, 56, 69
Liberty Hill Foundation, 65
licensed motor carriers (LMCs), 365, 400–1
Clean Truck Program and, 372, 385
Limón, Gladys, 124, 132, 458–59
Lin Perrella, Melissa, 356, 363, 366–67, 368, 389–90, 398, 401, 402–3, 404*f*, 408–9, 459–60
liquid natural gas (LNG), 376, 383–84

litigation
  affirmative, 487–88
  critique of, 483
  defensive, 487
  in L.A. campaigns, 487–88
  representational legitimacy and, 481
  strategic, 452
Little Tokyo, 14–15, 171–73
Little Tokyo Service Center, 17–18
Littler Mendleson, 413
Livable Places, 291
living wage
  CRA policy and, 237
  Grand Avenue CBA and, 242
  LAX CBA and, 223
  Staples Center CBA and, 186
Living Wage Campaign, 284–85
Living Wage Coalition, 178, 200–1, 202–3, 204
living wage movement, 29, 176–77
Living Wage Ordinance
  application to airlines, 201–2
  Contractor Responsibility Ordinance and, 178
  CBAs and, 29, 169–70, 175–76, 178, 179, 189–90, 200, 201–3, 256, 471, 475
  concessionaires and, 169–70
  CRA policy and, 467–68
  extension to tenants in publicly subsidized projects, 175–76, 449t
  gaps in coverage, 169–70
  LAANE and, 169–70
  LAX and, 200, 201, 202, 203–4, 205, 206–7
  legal ambiguity in, 201–2
  relation to union organizing, 201, 474–75
  supersession clause in, 201, 206–7
  union opt out and, 474–75
  unionization and, 169–70, 178, 200, 474–75, 493–94, 497–98
  Worker Retention Ordinance and, 169–70
llanteros, 380
LMCs. *See* licensed motor carriers
local dissent, politics of, 258–63
local government law (also municipal law)
  authority, 180, 248, 254, 472, 501
  as site for labor law reform, 2–3, 10, 272, 301, 423, 437–38, 502
local government law theory
  city as catalyst of national reform, 499–507
  city as tool and target of reform, 501–3
  conventional view of local government law, 502
  implications of L.A. campaigns for, 499–507
  horizontal equity, 505
  localism as first- or second-best solution, 506
  partisanship and localism, 506–7
  potential of localism to redress inequality, 500
  preemption, 504–5
  progressive critique of localism, 505
  regionalism, 505
  relation between local government law and work, 500–1, 502–3
  relation of social movements to cities, 500–1, 502–3
  vertical power, 503
local hiring, 186, 242, 243, 256–57, 471
localism, 10, 499–507. *See also* local government law theory
  as alternative labor strategy, 270–72
  challenges to, 437–38
  relation to federal power, 7–8, 270–71
local lawmaking, 502–3, 504–5
  social movements and, 4, 7
local legal mobilization, 4–10, 31
  accountability, 478–83
  community-labor campaigns and, 453–54, 454f
  efficacy, 483–90
  expanded conception of law, 485
  forms of representation, 455–56
  immigrant rights campaigns and, 452, 453f
  higher level advocacy and, 455
local policy diffusion, 301–2, 506
local politics
  labor activism in, 9
  unions and, 497–98
Lochner v. New York, 494
Lockyer, Bill, 285–86
Loeb & Loeb, 69
Logan, Angelo, 327–28, 328f, 358, 359–60, 363
logistics industry, 315–19, 422
Lo, Joann, 65, 71
Long Beach,
  big-box ban in, 294
  oil and, 313–14
  development of port, 313–14 (*see also* Port of Long Beach)
Long Beach Alliance for Children with Asthma (LBACA), 358, 359–60, 363, 366–68, 371, 379
Long Beach Board of Harbor Commissioners. *See also* Harbor Commission, Long Beach
  approval of concession plan, 381–82
  passage of Clean Truck Fee, 379
  passage of dirty truck ban, 378–79
Long Beach Freeway (710), 321
Long Beach Press-Telegram, 383
Long Beach Yacht Club, 357–58
longshoremen, 321, 357–58, 373
López Mendoza, Jerilyn, 173, 179, 181–82, 183–84, 209–10, 211, 213, 214–16, 219–20, 221f, 249, 250, 251, 255, 345, 346–47, 354, 367–68, 376, 377, 447–48, 459, 460–61
Lopez, Miguel, 353–54, 358, 363
Lopez, Steve, 242–43

Lorenzo CBA, 245–46
Los Angeles
    activism in, 17–20
    deindustrialization in, 500
    demographics of, 13–15
    diversity in, 11, 13–14
    economic realignment in, 3
    greater area of, 10, 94
    history of, 11–20
    immigration and, 13–14, 37
    industries targeted by campaigns in, 20–26, 21t, 23t, 24t, 25t, 26t
    inequality in, 13, 500–1
    lawyers and social movements in, 2–4
    low-wage worker campaigns and, 1, 10
    middle-class in, 12
    organized labor in, 474–76
    population growth, 313–14
    residential patterns by race, 14–15
    smog in, 335
Los Angeles Alliance for a New Economy (LAANE), 4, 29–31, 97, 164, 208, 249, 284, 302–3, 308, 358–59, 441–42, 447–52, 449t, 459–60, 462t, 474, 551
    Campaign for Clean Trucks and, 311–12, 351–52, 354, 360–61, 362, 363–64, 368, 369, 442
    CBA development and, 177
    Change to Win and, 350–51, 428–29
    Cinerama Dome and, 176–77
    formation of, 18–19
    Grand Avenue Project and, 234, 236, 237
    Grocery Worker Retention Ordinance and, 295
    Inglewood site fight and, 272–97
    lawsuit against TraPac terminal expansion, 381
    Living Wage Ordinance and, 168–69, 272
    Respect at LAX and, 199–209
    role in CBA campaigns, 169–70, 171–73, 174–76, 177, 178, 181, 192–93, 199–200, 208–9, 210, 211, 212, 214–15, 227, 234
    subsidy accountability and, 170, 175–76, 178
    Valley Jobs Coalition and, 191, 192
Los Angeles Board of Harbor Commissioners, 30–31, 460–61. *See also* Harbor Commission, Los Angeles
    approval of concession plan, 387
    passage of Clean Truck Fee, 379
    passage of dirty truck ban, 378
Los Angeles Catholic Archdiocese, 231
Los Angeles Chamber of Commerce, 220
Los Angeles city attorney, 273, 289–90, 390, 407
Los Angeles City Council, 15, 17, 459–60, 475–76
    anti-solicitation ordinance proposal, 98
    anti-sweatshop ordinance, 83
    big-box ban, 274
    CBAs and, 187, 191–92, 254

Clean Truck Program, 387
composition of, 15, 17
Economic Development Committee, 274
Grand Avenue Project, 243
Hollywood and Highland project, 175–76
Home Improvement Stores Ordinance, 129, 144
LAX modernization and, 194, 199, 219, 220, 221
Living Wage Ordinance, 18–19, 474–75
Planning and Land Use Management Committee, 274, 295–96
pro-labor, 475–76
redevelopment and, 180
Respect at LAX and, 205
Superstores Ordinance, 291
term limits, 180
waste-hauler plan, 441
Worker Retention Ordinance, 170–71
Los Angeles City Hall, 178, 195–96, 230–31, 232, 395–96
Los Angeles Coalition Against Plant Shutdowns, 16
Los Angeles Coalition Against Wage Theft, 487–88
Los Angeles Coalition to End Hunger and Homelessness, 234–36
Los Angeles Community Action Network (LA CAN), 235–36, 237, 238, 462t
Los Angeles Community College, 228–29
Los Angeles Convention Center, 166, 167–68, 245–46
Los Angeles County
    airport noise mitigation and, 221, 228–29
    anti-solicitation ordinance, 103–7, 118, 142, 151
    Board of Supervisors (*see* Los Angeles County Board of Supervisors)
    cities in, 10, 94, 275–76
    garment production in, 36
    immigration and, 13–14
    inequality in, 13
    lawsuit against downtown redevelopment, 187
    opposition to LAX Master Plan, 221, 225
    unincorporated areas of, 195
    union density in, 26, 27f
    Wal-Mart in, 276
Los Angeles County Board of Supervisors, 177, 179, 198–99, 232, 243
Los Angeles County Day Labor Association, 108
Los Angeles County Economic Development Corporation
    Clean Truck Program report, 371
    Grand Avenue Project report, 232
    Wal-Mart report, 279–80

INDEX

Los Angeles County Federation of Labor (County Fed), 16–17, 19–20, 174–75, 193, 220, 474, 475–76
   campaign support from, 280–81
   LAX Organizing Project and, 202
   role in election of Villaraigosa as mayor, 17
   role in reversing AFL-CIO anti-immigration policy, 17
Los Angeles County Local Area Formation Commission (LAFCO), 326
Los Angeles Department of Water and Power, 346
Los Angeles Economic Impact Task Force, 208
Los Angeles Harbor Department, 337–38
Los Angeles International Airport (LAX)
   air pollution, 195
   airline lease renewals, 205, 207
   cargo, 194
   CBA (see LAX CBA)
   communities around, 195, 202
   community impacts, 195
   concessions at, 208–9, 210
   as environmental justice problem, 195, 200, 216–17, 219
   labor movement and, 200
   Living Wage Coalition and, 200–1
   Living Wage Ordinance and, 200
   modernization of (see LAX modernization)
   nighttime departures from, 227–28, 229
   noise, 195, 197, 198, 207–8, 213–14, 216, 217, 218, 225–26
   passengers, 194
   as public asset, 194–99
   as target of union organizing, 200
   workforce at, 202
Los Angeles Kings, 167–68
Los Angeles Labor Defense Network, 97, 140
Los Angeles Lakers, 167–68
Los Angeles Living Wage Campaign, 273–74
Los Angeles-Long Beach port complex, 312f
   cargo, 319f
   city control over, 318–19
   community mobilization against, 325–29
   as conduit of global trade, 317
   environmental impacts, 335
   expansion, 318
   as growth ratchet, 37
   historical evolution of, 312–24
   impact of globalization on, 315
   increase of imports at, 316–17
   as integrated unit, 312–13
   inter-port cooperation, 317–18, 347
   investment in infrastructure, 317–18
   labor impacts of, 321–22
   local impact of, 319–24
   map of, 320f
   passage of Clean Truck Programs, 377–78
   pursuit of tax-revenue-generating projects, 318–19
   role in city-building, 313
   role in global supply chain, 319–20
   role of law in development of, 312–24
   role of organized labor at, 314–15
   role in promoting service industry, 318–19
Los Angeles Memorial Coliseum, 166, 167
Los Angeles Music Center, 230–31
Los Angeles Sports and Entertainment District, 171, 173, 174–75, 180, 187, 188–89, 251, 258
Los Angeles Superior Court, 54, 285–86
Los Angeles Times, 104, 144, 170, 206, 210, 219–20, 231, 232–33, 236, 242–43, 244, 281–82, 325, 335–36, 340, 380, 396
   opposition to Clean Truck Program, 382, 384–85, 394, 401
Los Angeles Unified School District, 371
Los Angeles Urban League, 208
Los Angeles Workers Advocates Coalition, 76–77
Los Angeles World Airports (LAWA), 194–95, 197, 198, 205, 226
   Century Cargo Facilities Lease for United Airlines, 207–8
   CEQA lawsuits settlement, 226–27
   First Source Hiring Program, 228
   implementation of LAX CBA, 227
   LAX CBA approval and, 224, 228
   negotiation over LAX CBA, 213–14, 215–17, 219
   negotiation with school districts over LAX Master Plan, 217
   noise mitigation and, 227–28
Lowenthal, Alan, 342–43, 357–58
low-wage economy, 1
   growth of, 13–14
low-wage work, 88–89, 428, 446
   black workers and, 9, 20–23
   campaigns to reform, 1–2, 448
   changing demographics of, 9
   immigrants and, 13–14, 22
   law and structure of, 3, 437–38
   lawyers in challenge to, 4, 7–8, 447–48
   policy reform targeting, 467–68, 471, 472
   role of city in contributing to, 18
   role of labor movement in addressing, 490–99
   role of local government law in addressing, 499–507
   in service sector, 12
Loya, Maria, 210, 219
Loyola Marymount University, 228–29
Lozano, Manny, 124, 126, 541
Luban, David, 481
Ludlow, Martin, 15, 17, 347
Lujan, George, 395
Lyou, Joe, 214–15

MacArthur Fellowship, 81–82
machinists union, 206–7
Mack, Chuck, 333, 413
Made in L.A., 78
Made in L.A. (documentary), 80–81
Mahony, Roger (Cardinal), 231
Maintenance Cooperation Trust Fund, 84
MALDEF. *See* Mexican American Legal Defense and Educational Fund
Manatt, Phelps & Phillips, 62, 208
Mandarin Hotel, 244
Manley, Mike, 331–32, 333–34, 353, 361, 363–64, 369, 388, 390, 402–3, 413, 417–18, 418*f*, 426, 434, 459–60
Mann, Eric, 18–19
Mansoor, Allan, 123
manufacturing
  boom after World War II, 12
  garment, 33, 36, 75–76, 79–80
  in Los Angeles, 12, 13, 18, 20, 473–74
  ports' relation to, 313–14
  union density in, 15–16
maquiladoras, 36, 79
Marblestone, Judy, 81–82
Marciano, Maurice, 55
marginalized communities, 478, 480
Marin, Nadia, 140
market participant doctrine, 324, 334, 335, 344–45, 354–55, 369–70, 390, 391–92, 393, 398, 399, 400, 402, 403, 405, 431, 487, 586
Marlton Square, 192, 553
Marquez, Jesse, 327*f*, 327, 335–36, 339–40, 356–57, 358, 363
Marshall, Consuelo, 117–18
Martinez, Adrian, 355*f*, 355–56, 361, 362, 363–64, 368, 369–70, 380–81, 382, 386–87, 388–90, 426, 459–60
Marvy, Paul, 412
Maryland Fair Share Health Care Fund Act, 301–2
Mashouf, Manny, 68
Master Freight Agreement, 418–19
Masters, Julie, 337
MATES II. *See* Multiple Air Toxics Exposure Study
Matsuoka, Martha, 18
Mayer Brown Rowe & Maw, 291
Mayor Logistics, 416
McClardy, Mark, 227–28, 241
McClendon, Noreen, 239–41, 243
McClintock, Jessica, 41, 60, 65
McCracken, Richard, 202, 333–34, 353, 459–60
McCutchen, Doyle, Brown & Enersen, 338
McDaniel, Bruce, 214–15, 217
McKinsey & Company, 373
McNatt, Christopher, Jr., 398
McNeill, Sandra, 171, 173, 181, 183

Measure 04-A, 277–78, 280*f*, 302, 303, 454–55, 459–60
  on ballot, 286
  election results, 287
  organizing against, 278–82, 283
Measure JJJ, 476–77
Medrano, Ernesto, 203–4
megaships, 316
Mengitsu, Samson, 214–15
Mercedes-Benz/Daimler Truck Finance Company, 392
Merkin, Frederick, 200–1
Merrill Lynch, 52
Mervyn's, 45, 48
Metropolitan Transportation Authority (MTA), 18–19
Metro Green Line, 196, 197–98, 199, 228
Metro Red Line, 175–76
Mexican American Legal Defense and Educational Fund (MALDEF), 28–29, 91, 93–94, 100, 102–4, 107–8, 112, 114, 117–18, 124–26, 130–31, 136–37, 141, 370–71, 447–53, 449*t*, 457–59, 460, 462*t*, 484, 487–88
  alliance with NDLON, 109
  challenge to Costa Mesa anti-solicitation ordinance, 124
  challenge to Glendale anti-solicitation ordinance, 112
  challenge to Los Angeles County anti-solicitation ordinance, 105–6
  challenge to Rancho Cucamonga-Upland anti-solicitation ordinances, 109–10
  challenge to Redondo Beach anti-solicitation ordinance, 115–18, 132
  high-water mark of day labor legal capacity, 111–12
  leadership in day labor campaign, 139
  leadership transition at, 119
  legal challenges to cities after *Redondo Beach* decision, 137
  origins of anti-solicitation campaign and, 102
  mobilization template and, 107
  strategy for challenging anti-solicitation ordinances, 106
Mexican-American War, 458–59
Mexico
  garment production in, 36
  immigration from, 13–14
Meyerson, Harold, 203
MFA. *See* Multi-Fiber Agreement
Miami port, 368
Michigan Law School, 58, 59–60
Midnight Special, 56
midterm elections of 2010, 409–10
Milberg Weiss Hynes & Lerach, 79
Milkman, Ruth, 15–16

Miller, John, 357–58
Millman, Robert, 413
Minato, Susan, 214–15
minimum wage, 9, 13, 497, 500
    at city level, 504
Minutemen, 118–19, 148
Miracle Mile, 14–15
Miscikowski, Cindy, 179, 198–99, 219–20, 226, 357
misclassification, 311–12, 410, 411, 419–20, 424, 427, 433, 440–41, 492–93
misclassification litigation, 410–16, 449t
    business deductions and, 413–14, 416
    class actions, 416
    individual port driver wage claims, 416
    industry response to, 414–15
    legal analysis of, 413–14
    origins of in port trucking industry, 410–11
    public enforcement, 410–11, 414–15
    as response to failure of employee conversion at ports, 424
    trucking leases and, 413–14
Mitchell Silberberg & Knupp, 51–52
MOCA. *See* Museum of Contemporary Art
Molina, Gloria, 232
Monaco, Kristen, 322
Montebello, 459
Montgomery Ward, 45, 48
Morales, Eloy, Jr., 277
Morello, Tom, 56
Morrison & Foerster, 338
Morrow, Margaret, 339–40
Motor Carrier Act of 1980, 321–22, 324, 397
movement lawyers
    accountability and, 478–83
    beyond elite versus grassroots, 458–61
    building movement alliances, 448
    integrated advocacy and, 457
    integrated leadership and, 456
    interdisciplinary thinking and, 485–86
    in Los Angeles, 1–2
    role in movement decision-making, 448
    work outside of courtrooms, 453
Ms. Tops, 45
MTA. *See* Metropolitan Transportation Authority
Multicultural Collaborative, 103–4
Multi-Ethnic Immigrant Workers Organizing Network, 84
Multi-Fiber Agreement (MFA), 36, 75
multi-level legal advocacy, in big-box campaign, 298–302
Multiple Air Toxics Exposure Study (MATES II), 335–36, 336f, 356–57
multi-tier accountability, in big-box campaign, 306–10

municipal lawmaking. *See* local lawmaking
Murdoch, Rupert, 167–68
Museum of Contemporary Art (MOCA), 230–31
myth of rights, 483

NAACP. *See* National Association for the Advancement of Colored People
Nadler, Jarrold, 408–10
NAFTA. *See* North American Free Trade Agreement
Narro, Victor, 69, 71, 102–3, 104, 105, 108, 127, 139, 141, 144, 460–61
National Association for the Advancement of Colored People (NAACP), 2, 18–19, 308–9, 392, 452–53, 478–79
National Association of Public Interest Law fellowship, 41
National Association of Waterfront Employers, 392–93
National Day Laborer Organizing Network (NDLON), 19–20, 28–29, 84, 91, 93–94, 109–10, 115–16, 117, 119, 120, 121–22, 123–26, 139–40, 449t, 456–57, 462t, 474, 487–88
    AFL-CIO partnership, 128, 129f, 493
    alliance with MALDEF, 109
    founding of, 108
    goal of protecting solicitation on corners, 108
    as plaintiff in anti-solicitation litigation, 109
National Employment Law Project (NELP), 412, 434
National Environmental Protection Act (NEPA), 194, 378
National Football League (NFL), 167
National Immigration Law Center (NILC), 95–96, 100
National Industrial Transportation League, 373, 392–93
National Labor Relations Act (NLRA), 427, 490, 491, 492, 495
    deficiencies of, 35
    election process, 35
    employer practices in unionization campaigns and, 54–55
    future of, 491
    garment industry organizing and, 38
    LAX Organizing Project and, 203–4
    misclassification claims and, 419–20, 424
    port workers and, 314–15
    section 8(e), 35
    Toll Group and, 417–18
    triangular bargaining and, 35
    truck drivers and, 433
    unionism and, 267
    Wal-Mart and, 267–68
National Labor Relations Board (NLRB)

Guess and, 53, 54, 55, 56–57
  misclassification and, 424, 427, 438
  port trucking and, 417–18, 419, 433
  Respect at LAX and, 207
  Wal-Mart and, 267–68, 269–70
National Lawyers Guild (NLG), 69, 97
National Partnership Agreement Between the AFL-CIO and NDLON, 128, 449t, 493
National Port Drivers Association, 395
national reform, cities as catalyst of, 499–507
National Right to Work Legal Defense Foundation, 399–400
Nation of Islam, 212
Native Americans, in industries targeted by L.A. campaigns, 21t, 23t
Natural Resources Defense Council (NRDC)
  ATA v. City of Los Angeles and, 389–90
  Campaign for Clean Trucks and, 354–56, 359, 360–61, 363–64, 366, 368, 369–70, 380–81, 382, 425–26, 432–33, 439, 449t
  CBA campaigns and, 211, 252–53
  challenge to China Shipping, 337, 339, 340–41, 342, 436
  challenge to TraPac terminal expansion, 381
  environmental report card on ports, 342–43
  joint defense agreement with Port of Los Angeles lawyers, 390
  preemption analysis, 344, 431, 442–43
  representing organizational interests, 389–90
  representing Sierra Club and Coalition for Clean Air, 389–90
NDLON. *See* National Day Laborer Organizing Network
negligence per se theory, 48
Neighborhood Services office of L.A. Mayor, 351–52
Neighbors for an Improved Community, 174
neoliberalism, 15–16, 477–90
NEPA. *See* National Environmental Protection Act
networked expertise, in big-box campaign, 304–6
New America Foundation, 242–43
New Boys, 45
New Deal, 314, 494
New Lochnerism, 494–95
Newman, Bob, 54
Newman, Chris, 115–16, 117–18, 124, 126, 127–28, 139–40, 144, 145–46, 148
New Otani Hotel, 171–73
Newton, Jim, 206
New York–New Jersey port, 333
New York Times, 41, 137
New York University School of Law, 238
NFL. *See* National Football League
NILC. *See* National Immigration Law Center
Ninth Circuit Court of Appeals, 93, 107
  ACLU v. City of Las Vegas, 126

ACORN v. City of Phoenix, 96, 131
ATA v. City of Los Angeles, 393–95, 396–97, 400, 401, 402, 406, 423, 436–37
Berger v. City of Seattle, 131
Comite de Jornaleros v. Redondo Beach, 28–29, 118, 131–33, 134, 135, 136, 148–49, 457–58
Forever 21, 71, 86–87
Lake Forest, 122
S.B. 1070, 138
nitrogen oxide, 335, 342
NLG. *See* National Lawyers Guild
NLRB. *See* National Labor Relations Board
NoHo Commons CBA, 177, 181, 191, 260–61
Nokia Theater, 189–90, 470–71
no net increase policy, 342, 343, 344–45, 346, 357–58, 425–26
No Net Increase Task Force, 343–44, 346, 355, 425–26, 428–29
North American Free Trade Agreement (NAFTA), 36, 57, 85–86
Northern Mariana Islands, 79
Northwest Airlines, 208
No Sweat Garment Enforcement Report, 58
No Sweat Initiative, 87
Nowak, Jeremy, 506
Nuncio, Marissa, 124
Nuñez, Fabian, 475–76
Nutter, Steve, 41, 45–46

Obama, Barack, 406–7, 408, 427
Oberstar, James, 407, 408–9
Occidental College, 358
Occupational Safety and Health Administration, 88–89
Office of Contract Compliance, 200–1
oil refineries, 320, 321
Oldham, Jennifer, 210
Olivares, Luis, 97
One Clothing, 69, 526
Operating Engineers Local 501, 174–75
Operation Hammer, 11
Orange, City of, 95–97, 98–99, 119, 123, 144, 151–55
Orange County, 55–56, 209–10, 357–58
  day labor restrictions in, 95–96, 98–99, 118, 119–26
Orbach & Hoff, 197
organizational standing, 109, 122, 135–36, 146, 147
organized labor
  city politics and, 473, 474–76
  coalitions and, 16, 168–74, 254, 270–72, 422, 453–54
  corporate attack on, 13
  demographic changes and, 9
  localism as alternative strategy for, 9, 468–72
  political revitalization of, 473–75, 476–77

Ortiz, Michael, 100
Otero, S. James, 113–14
outcome evaluation, 8. *See also* impact analysis
outcomes of L.A. campaigns, 449t, 461–77, 462t
  CBAs, 470–71
  court cases, 468–69
  policy change, 461–68
  policy implementation, 468–72
  political power of organized labor, 472–77
  tensions between labor and community goals, 476–77
outsourcing, 20
  domestic, 13, 18–19, 169–70
  in garment industry, 33, 36, 38, 66–67, 472
  global, 1, 316
overtime laws, 39
overview of low-wage work campaigns in Los Angeles, 449t
Ovram, Bud, 347
Owner Operator Independent Drivers Association, 399–400
Owner Participation Agreement, 176–77

Pac Anchor Transportation, 411–12, 439–40
Pacific Legal Foundation, 504–5
Pacific Maritime Association (PMA), 329
Pacific Merchant Shipping Association (PMSA), 344, 373
Pacific 9 Transportation, 416, 419–20
Pacific Rim, 316–17
Pacific Theaters, 176–77
Pacoima Beautiful, 191
Padilla, Alex, 15, 179
Paez, Richard, 393
Palmdale, 195–96, 276
Palmer, Geoffrey, 245–46
Palos Verdes Peninsula, 312–13
Panama Canal, 316, 436
Parker, Sarah Jessica, 60
Park, Noel, 337, 341f, 343, 356–58
Parks, Bernard, 129, 211–12, 338–39
Park, Yungsuhn, 81–82
Partnership for Working Families, 217–18, 251–52, 301
part-time employment, Wal-Mart use of, 268
patterns of legal mobilization in L.A. campaigns
  in community-labor campaigns, 453–55, 454f
  contrasts between immigrant rights and community-labor campaigns, 448–52
  in immigrant rights campaigns, 452–53, 453f
  lessons from, 455–56
  local legal mobilization linked to higher level advocacy, 455
  relation to form of legal representation, 455–56
Paul, Sanjukta, 412–13, 416, 434, 459–60
Pelosi, Nancy, 127–28, 408

Perez, Altagracia, 281f
Perez, Araceli, 114, 139, 458–59
Perez, John, 410
Perry, Jan, 237, 239–40, 243, 244, 254
Petrocelli, Daniel, 51–52, 54
Pettit, David, 284–85, 286, 303, 305, 307–8, 355–56, 366, 368, 369–70, 373, 381, 386–87, 389–90, 398, 401, 404f, 459–60
Philippines, 13–14
Phillips Temple CME Church, 211
Physicians for Social Responsibility, 212, 246–47
Pilipino Workers Center of Southern California, 84
Pineda, Miguel, 380
Planning and Land Use Management Committee, 273–74
Planning Commission, 180, 254, 273–74, 290–92
Plan to Achieve No Net Increase of Air Emissions at the Port of Los Angeles, 343
Playa del Rey, 196–97
Playa Vista, 213
Play Fair at Farmers Field Coalition, 246–47, 252–53
PMA. *See* Pacific Maritime Association
PMSA. *See* Pacific Merchant Shipping Association
police brutality, 11
policy design, from the ground up, 487
PolicyLink, 178
policy outcomes of L.A. campaigns, 461–72, 462t
Politeo, Tom, 356–59, 371, 422
political cooptation
  as critique of legal liberalism, 483–84
  in relation to social movements, 484–85
political mobilization, 5, 7–8
political opportunity structure, 7, 298
Poor People's Preferential Parking District, 188
Pope, Carl, 350, 428
port communities. *See* San Pedro and Wilmington
Port Community Advisory Committee, 338–39, 428–29
Port of Long Beach, 30–31, 311, 312f, 320f, 480
  air quality at, 335–36
  breaking ranks with Los Angeles on Clean Truck Program, 381–82
  CAAP approval, 349
  Campaign for Clean Trucks and, 363
  competition with Los Angeles, 315–16, 318–19, 462t
  concession plan, 381–82
  COSCO and, 336–37
  emission control plan, 347
  employee conversion and, 381–82, 451t
  expansion projects, 318
  intermodalism and, 317–18
  law in development of, 312–24
  local impact of, 319–24

public actions against, 367
Registration and Agreement, 394–95
settlement of *ATA v. City of Los Angeles,* 394–95
size, 312–13
Port of Los Angeles, 3, 30–31, 311, 312*f,* 320*f*
air quality at, 335–36
annexation by Los Angeles, 313–14
CAAP approval, 349
Campaign for Clean Trucks and, 363, 370, 378
China Shipping lawsuit against, 311–12, 337–38, 339, 340–41, 342
Clean Truck Program and, 378, 384–85
competition with Long Beach, 315–16, 318–19, 462*t*
efforts to control diesel emissions at, 342, 343, 344, 608
employee conversion and, 383, 385, 451*t*
establishment of, 313–14
expansion projects, 318, 337–38
growth, 313–14, 318
intermodalism and, 317–18
law in development of, 312–24
lawsuit over Clean Truck Program (*see American Trucking Associations v. City of Los Angeles*)
local impact of, 319–24
location, 312–13, 320
NRDC coordination with lawyers for, 390
San Pedro and, 320
size, 312–13
terminal expansion, 371
TraPac terminal, 381, 386–87
truck emissions, 322–24
Wilmington and, 325
Port of Oakland, 333
Ports O' Call Village, 326
port transportation, federal regulation of, 314
port truck drivers
clean truck leases and, 396
demographics of, 322
diesel fuel trucks and, 322–24
health issues, 322–24
impact of Clean Truck Program on, 396, 435
impact of deregulation on, 321–22
impact of Great Recession on, 392, 396
independent associations of, 329
as independent contractors, 311, 321–22
labor conditions of, 322
lease-to-own programs for, 392
at Los Angeles-Long Beach port complex, 322
misclassification of, 410–16, 427, 433
NLRA and, 433
unionization and, 331–32
port trucking
firms, as non-asset-based companies, 322
impact of Great Recession on, 392

independent contracting in industry, 321–22
safety of, 380
Port Working Group, 358–59, 441–42
post-Panamax ships, 316*f,* 316
poverty, in Los Angeles, 13
power
community, 250
federal, 7–8, 314–15
global, in relation to ports, 315–19
local, in relation to ports, 313–14
mapping, 7
as outcome of social movement mobilization, 472–77
state, 503–7
practice sites of lawyers in Inglewood site fight, 304–5
Preciado, Nora, 119, 120–21
preemption
federal, 9, 206–7, 334, 344, 353, 370, 388, 390, 392–93, 406, 409, 429, 437, 487, 504–5
state, 503–4
Prevailing Wage Policy at CRA, 242
Prince Andrew, Duke of York, 295
private sector union membership in Los Angeles County, 1990-2010, 27*f*
pro bono, 48–49, 67, 69, 131, 284, 304–5
professional interdisciplinarity, as feature of big-box advocacy, 305–6
project labor agreement, 175–76, 181–82, 206, 237, 238, 242, 429, 475
Proposition 1B, 349
Proposition 187, 104, 105–6
Prouty, David, 53
Public Citizen, 332–33
Public Counsel, 105, 246–47, 252–53, 391
Immigrant Rights Project, 100
public law, as leverage in CBA campaigns, 248, 253–58
publicly subsidized development, 18, 29, 164, 165, 166, 167, 170, 184, 187, 191, 199–200, 240–41, 242–43, 245–46, 449*t*
public participation rights, as leverage in CBA campaigns, 180

QTS, Inc., 416, 434
Quan, Katie, 41
Qwest Communications, 167–68

racial capitalism, 452
racial covenants, 499
racial segregation, 11–12, 313, 499, 505
Racketeer Influenced and Corrupt Organizations Act (RICO), 45, 79
Radisich, Joe, 346
Rafeedie, Edward, 126
Rage Against the Machine, 56

railroads
    Alameda Corridor project (*see* Alameda Corridor project)
    harbor, 314–15
    intermodal transport and, 317–18
    on-dock, 320, 337–38
    transcontinental, 313, 317–18
Ralphs, 303
Rancho Cucamonga-Upland day labor case, 109–10, 112
Raymond, Brad, 333–34
Reagan, Ronald, 126, 132–33, 393, 400, 401
Real, Manuel, 69, 86–87
Rebuild LA (RLA), 18, 473
recession of 2008 (*see* Great Recession)
reclassification, 424–25, 427, 430, 455, 492–93
red-blue state division, 9
redevelopment
    changing context of, 247, 248
    gentrification and, 237
    impact of CBA campaigns on, 247
    law of, 166
    living wage requirements and, 165
    relocation and, 167–68, 186–87
    role in low-wage job creation, 164–65, 446
    role in reshaping Los Angeles, 166–67, 230
    subsidies and, 166, 254
    tax increment and, 166
    unionization and, 165
redlining, 303, 499
Redondo Beach
    anti-solicitation ordinance, 96–97
    campaign against anti-solicitation, 28–29, 115–18, 129–36, 142, 149, 457–58
    day labor in, 115*f*
    MALDEF lawsuit against (*see* Comite de Jornaleros v. Redondo Beach)
    protests against, 116*f*
Reebok International Human Rights Award, 81–82
Reed, Kevin, 54
refugees, 97
region
    inequality in, 10
    movement to promote equity in, 10, 505
    organizing in, 18, 505–6
Reich, Adell & Crost, 53, 82–83
Reich, Robert, 58
Reinhardt, Stephen, 102, 114, 458
reinvestment, 500
Related Companies, 232–34, 244, 259
    Grand Avenue CBA negotiations with, 239–40, 241
Reno, Janet, 44
representation
    alternative structures of, 479–80
    coalition, 251, 307–8

    legitimacy of, 481, 482
    organizational context of, 481
Republican National Convention, 184–85
Republican Party, 9
request for proposal (RFP), 364–65
resilience of labor law, 491–93
Resource Conservation and Recovery Act, 381
resources, in comparative institutional analysis, 7
Respect at LAX campaign, 208–9, 210, 262–63, 334, 459–60, 474–75
    Argenbright Security, 205, 207, 208
    goals, 208
    launch of, 203–4
    leadership, 203–4
    legal team, 204
    Living Wage Ordinance and, 200–2, 206
    organizing, 205
    relation to LAX modernization, 202
    September 11 attacks and, 208
    strategies, 205–7
    United Airlines, 203, 207
Retailer Accountability Campaign, 61
retail industry, 164
    as focus of garment litigation, 67
    as target of CBA campaigns, 164
retail workers, 3, 208–9
    in Los Angeles, 12, 20–26, 21*t*–25*t*
Reyes, Ed, 15, 274, 296–97
RFP. *See* request for proposal
Rhow, Ekwan, 48–49
RICO. *See* Racketeer Influenced and Corrupt Organizations Act
Ridley-Thomas, Mark, 15
right to the city, 164–65
right-to-work laws, 497
    Wal-Mart and, 268–69
Riordan, Richard, 15, 18–19, 169–70, 180, 184–85, 194, 195–97, 206, 209–10, 230–31, 232, 273–74, 326, 473
riots of 1992, 1, 11
    as political pivot point, 15
    progressive activism and, 19–20
    roots of, 11–12
Ritchie, Jim, 210, 213–15, 216, 227–28
Riverside County, 94, 149–50, 225–26
RLA. *See* Rebuild LA
The Road to Shared Prosperity (LAANE), 372
Roberts, John, 403
Robinsons-May, 56
Rockefeller Foundation Next Generation Leadership Program, 108–9
Rodeo Drive, 55–56
Rodino Associates, 274, 295–96
Rodino, Bob, 279–80, 289, 291
Rosemead, 293–94
Rosenbaum, Mark, 46

Rosenberg Foundation, 107, 139
Rosendahl, Bill, 226
Rosenthal, Steven, 370, 390, 398–99, 403, 432–33
Roski, Ed, Jr., 167–68
Ross, Stephen, 232
Rothbart Development Corporation, 275–76
Rothner, Segall, Bahan & Greenstone, 45–46, 53
Rubin, Michael, 54, 79
Rubin, Robert, 114, 117–18, 131
Russell, Thomas, 369, 375, 386–87, 390, 398
Russia, 13–14

Sachs, Ben, 494, 497
Sacramento, 62
Saenz, Edgar, 211–12
Saenz, Thomas, 105–6, 109, 111–12, 113*f*, 115–16, 117–18, 119, 124, 125*f*, 131, 132–33, 134, 136–37, 141, 145, 147, 447–48, 458–59, 460
    as general counsel to mayor, 370–71, 460–61
    at MALDEF, 102–3, 132, 139, 458
Safeway, 275
St. Agnes Catholic Church, 174
St. John's Episcopal Church, 174
St. John's Well Child Center, 174
St. Mark's Lutheran Church, 174
Saipan, 79
SAJE. *See* Strategic Actions for a Just Economy
Salas, Angelica, 173
Salcedo, Leticia, 203–5
Salek, Sima, 214–15
Salvation Army, 97–98
Sam's Club, 273–74, 277–78
San Bernardino County, 94, 109–10, 149–50
Sanchez, Edgar, 366
Sanchez, Juan, 203
sanctuary movement, 97, 459, 499, 506–7
San Diego, 276, 294, 400
San Fernando Neighborhood Legal Services, 191
San Fernando Valley, 99, 326, 459
    CRA and, 191
Sanford, Misty, 173
San Pedro
    demographics of, 320
    environmental activism in, 338–39, 356–57
    port relations to, 326
    as recreational and commercial site, 326
    secession efforts, 326
San Pedro and Peninsula Homeowners Coalition, 337, 381
San Pedro harbor, 313
San Pedro Harbor Administration Building, 346
San Pedro Peninsula Homeowners United, 337
Santa Ana, 294
Santa Monica, 54, 56, 68, 171–73, 203–4, 264, 284–85, 312–13

Santa Monica Freeway (10), 167
Sany Fashion, 69
Sarat, Austin, 447–48
Scalia, Antonin, 403
SCAQMD. *See* South Coast Air Quality Management District
Scheingold, Stuart, 447–48, 483
Schlageter, Martin, 382–83, 392
Schneider, 376
school desegregation, 478–79
Schragger, Richard, 501–2
Schultz, Barbara, 234–35
Schwab, Gertrude, 325–26
Schwartz, David, 45–46
Schwartz, Steinsapir, Dohrmann & Sommers, 204, 273–74
Schwarzenegger, Arnold, 82–83, 330, 346
SCLC. *See* Southern Christian Leadership Conference
Scopelitis, Garvin, Light, Hanson & Feary, 398
Scott, Judy, 333–34
Scott, Lee, 578
Scrap Truck Buyback Program, 386
Scully, Jack, 103–4, 105
Seacon Logix, 414, 416
Seattle-Tacoma port, 333
secondary effects doctrine, 113–14
Secretary of Labor, 58, 408
sectoral organizing, 18, 474–75, 490, 493–94
Securtec, 120–22
SEIU. *See* Service Employees International Union
self-help model, 76, 469
Senate Bill (S.B.) 179, 83–84
Senate Bill (S.B.) 459, 413–14, 467, 469
Senate Bill (S.B.) 1070, 130–31, 138
Senate Bill (S.B.) 1818, 85
Senate Committee on Commerce, Science, and Transportation, 407, 409–10
Sensenbrenner, Jim, 127, 148
Sensenbrenner immigration bill, 127, 148
September 11, 2001 terrorist attacks
    anti-immigrant sentiment after, impact on day labor campaign, 118, 148
    LAX Master Plan process and, 208
service economy, as focus of L.A. campaigns, 200, 473–74, 490
Service Employees International Union (SEIU), 15, 168–69, 175, 206–7, 242, 333–34, 425
    Argenbright campaign and, 207
    Grand Avenue Project and, 236
    Justice for Janitors campaign (*see* Justice for Janitors)
    LAX and, 203–4, 207–8, 210–11
    Local 34, 210–11
    Local 399, 16
    Local 1877, 174–75, 203–4, 207, 208
    Respect at LAX and, 201, 203–4, 206, 207

service sector
  growth of, 12
  immobility of, 20, 270–71, 490
  labor abuse in, 12
  in Los Angeles, 12, 20
  low wages in, 12, 248
  as site of labor organizing, 3, 16, 20, 490
Service Worker Retention Ordinance. *See* Worker Retention Ordinance
serving two masters, 478–79, 480, 482
7-Eleven, 97
SG&A, 279–80, 281–82
shared prosperity, 502–3
Share the Wealth Coalition, 235–36, 238, 252
shippers, at ports, 314, 315–16, 317, 318, 322, 344, 347, 372, 379, 384, 387, 436
Shippers Transport Express, 427, 439–40
Shipping Act, 353, 396–97
shoestring district, 313–14
short-haul trucking. *See* drayage trucking
Shropshire, Adrianne, 181–82
Shute, Mihaly & Weinberger, 207–8
Sierra Club, 350, 357–58, 371, 381, 389, 441–42
Silva, Beatriz, 214–15
Simi Valley, 11
Simons, Shaheena, 114, 117–18, 139, 458–59
Single Room Occupancy (SRO), 234–36
site fight, as a labor strategy, 265, 272.
  See also Inglewood site fight
Skadden Fellowship, 41, 58, 59–60, 74, 81–82, 181, 458, 459, 460
SK Fashions, 44–45, 47
Skid Row, 230, 235–36, 237
Skurnik, Jennifer, 203–4
SLAPP. *See* Strategic Litigation Against Public Participation
slip seat, 376
SL NO HO LLC, 191
Smart, William, 211–13, 214–16, 217, 278–79, 280f, 367–68
Smith, Gary, 357–58
Smith, Milan, Jr., 132–33, 134, 135, 148–49
Smith, Randy, 132–33, 400
Smith, Rebecca, 412, 413, 434
smog, 335
SMOs. *See* social movement organizations
Snyder, Christina, 391–93, 396–97, 399
Soboroff, Steve, 196–97
social bargaining, 490, 493–94
social movement campaigns, evaluation of, 489
social movement lawyers. *See* movement lawyers
social movement organizations (SMOs), 4, 5, 7
social movements
  building power and, 472–77
  cities and, 499–500
  comparative institutional analysis of, 5
  cooptation of, 484–85
  and lawmaking, 4
  lawyers and, 1–4, 5, 447–48, 490
  in Los Angeles, 2–4
  in promoting equality, 447–61
soft law, 299–301
Soja, Edward, 12
solicitation, day labor, 92, 93, 95–96, 98–99, 103, 104, 106, 109–10, 111, 112–13, 114, 117, 123, 124–26, 131–32, 134, 136, 138
solidarity
  inter-movement, 498
  intra-labor, 498
  lawyer-client, 482–83
Solis, Hilda, 126, 145–46, 408, 413, 475–76, 541
soundproofing around LAX, 229
South America, 55
South Bay, 95–97, 98, 225, 351, 359
South Coast Air Quality Management District (SCAQMD), 324, 335, 344, 348, 349, 354–55, 372, 391
South Coast Plaza, 55–56
Southern California Association of Governments, 196
Southern California Association of Nonprofit Housing, 290–91
Southern California Edison, 367–68
Southern California grocery strike, 275, 278–79, 280–81
Southern California International Gateway, 358
Southern Christian Leadership Conference (SCLC), 103–4
Southern Counties Express, 395–96
Southern Pacific Railroad, 317–18
South Los Angeles, 13, 14–15, 103
Southwestern Law School, 103–4, 111–12
spatial geography of racial exclusion, 499–500
SRO. *See* Single Room Occupancy
Stanford Law School, 458–59
Staples Accountable Development Working Groups, 173
Staples CBA, 166–93, 251–52, 467, 470–71, 475
  affordable housing, 179, 186–87, 189, 256
  community benefits program, 185
  cooperation agreement, 185
  developer compliance with, 189–90
  developer incentives for, 180–81
  evaluation of, 260–61, 261t
  final agreement, 185
  impact of, 190–91
  implementation of, 187–93
  as "induced agreement," 180–81
  interested organizations, 185
  key provisions, 185–87
  living wage program, 186, 189–90, 256
  local hiring and job training, 186, 256–57

outcomes, 190–91, 462t
parking permit area, 185
parks and recreation, 185
service worker retention and responsible contracting, 186
Staples CBA campaign
    affordable housing as goal, 179
    coalition, 178–79, 180
    EIR challenge, 184
    evaluation of, 191, 260, 261t
    goals, 173–74
    key actors, 168–74, 249
    leverage, 180–81
    living wage as goal, 178
    negotiating team, 181–82, 183–84
    negotiation, 180, 182–83
    organizing, 171–73, 178, 180
    outcomes, 185–87, 189–91, 248–49, 260, 261t
    relation to L.A. Live labor negotiations, 174–75
    subsidy accountability campaign and, 178–79
    tensions between labor and housing advocates, 179–80
    union support for, 175
Staples Center, 171, 173, 174–75, 182–83, 231, 234, 246–47, 470–71
    community impacts of, 167–68, 171–73
    CRA financial assistance to, 168
    development of, 167–68
    displacement caused by, 167–68
    Sports and Entertainment District (see L.A. Live)
Staples Center Specific Plan, 179
Staples Foundation, 179
Starcrest Consulting Group, 343
Stater Bros., 303
states' rights, 505
Steckler, Beth, 291
Steinberg, Darrell, 62
Steinke, Richard, 394–95
Stein, Ted, 198–99
Stormer, Dan, 45–47, 48–49, 54, 247
Strategic Actions for a Just Economy (SAJE), 18–19, 29, 164–65, 182f, 238, 449t, 462t, 474, 551
    FCCEJ and, 171, 174
    Figueroa Corridor and, 170–71
    Grand Avenue CBA and, 234, 236, 237
    origins, 170–71
    Staples CBA and, 171–73
strategic litigation, 32, 452–56
Strategic Litigation Against Public Participation (SLAPP), 69, 71, 87
Strategic Organizing Center, Change to Win, 332, 425
strategic policy advocacy, 453–54, 455–56

strikes, 267–68, 314–15, 321, 329, 419–20, 422, 424, 433, 439–40
Strumwasser & Woocher, 54
Stubbs, Cassandra, 74
Student Coalition Against Labor Exploitation, 174
subcontracting, 13, 16, 32, 473–74
    in garment industry, 28, 32–33, 34f, 449t, 452
    Living Wage Ordinance and, 201–2
    port trucking and, 388
subprime market collapse, 244
subsidy accountability, 170, 175–76, 178–79, 193, 262–63
Subsidy Accountability Project, 170
successor liability, in CBAs, 258
suing-and-striking strategy, in ports campaign, 384, 419–20, 424–25, 433, 438, 439–40, 444–45, 449t
Su, Julie, 41–44, 45–47, 46f, 48–49, 58, 59–60, 61, 62, 67–68, 78, 80–82, 447–48, 458, 460
    as Labor Commissioner, 412, 413, 414–15, 427, 460–61
SunQuest CBA, 192, 553
SunQuest Development LLC, 192
Sun Valley Neighborhood Improvement Association, 192
Supercenter, 264–65, 269, 272, 273–75, 276, 277, 278, 279–80, 282–83, 287, 291, 292–94, 298, 300–1, 302–3, 306, 309, 310, 457–58, 470, 475, 566–67
Superstores Ordinance, 293, 298, 300, 303, 449t, 453–55, 459–60, 467, 470, 472, 475–76, 489, 494, 496
    definitions, 291–92
    distinguished from CBAs, 300–1
    Economic Assistance Areas, 274, 291–92
    economic impact analysis, 289
    example of policy reform built from community struggle, 299
    example of "soft law," 299
    impact of, 300–1
    in Inglewood, 292–93
    legal analysis of, 289–90
    in Los Angeles, 291
    origins of, 274
    outcome, 462t
    provisions, 291–92
    Rodino report, 274
    Wal-Mart's opposition to, 291
Supreme Court, 9, 85, 130–31, 136–37, 209–10, 259, 271–72, 324
S visa program, 44
Swanson, Sandre, 410
Sweat-Free Procurement Ordinance, 83, 462t, 469–70
sweatshops, 3, 28, 32, 446, 461–67, 468, 473–74
    definition, 33–34

658 INDEX

sweatshops (*cont.*)
    garment industry structure and, 33–34
    law in construction of, 32–33
    law in resistance to, 39–80
    in Los Angeles, 39
Sweatshop Watch, 64, 65, 66–67, 68, 69, 77, 79, 83, 84, 456–57, 460–61, 462*t*
    A.B 633, 61, 62, 63, 64
    closure, 79–80
    collaborative strategies, 78
    formation, 61
    founding organizations, 61
    mission, 61
    Retailer Accountability Campaign, 61
    transnational advocacy, 79
SweatX, 82
Sweeney, John, 129*f*
Swift, 395–96
Szymanski, Pat, 331–32, 333–34, 459–60

Tabor, Danny, 214–15, 215*f*
tactical pragmatism, in big-box campaign, 302–4
tagging, 96, 110, 131, 134, 141
takings law, 504–5
Tallman, Ann Marie, 114, 124
Tanner, Ted, 178–79, 187
Target, 33
Tariff No. 4, 378, 384, 385
Tate, Eric, 417–18
tax increment financing (TIF), 166
Taylorist production model, 267, 567
Teamsters, 30–31, 321–22, 329, 331, 333–34, 427, 442, 459–60, 462*t*
    Campaign for Clean Trucks and, 353, 357–59, 361, 363–64, 368, 369, 380–81, 382, 416–20, 441–43, 444, 449*t*
    decline in port trucking, 322
    impact of deregulation on, 329
    independent contractors and, 422
    lobbying for amendment to FAAAA, 408
    Local 63, 353–54
    Local 848, 353–54, 415–16, 417, 418–19
    Local 911, 174–75, 212
    misclassification litigation, 330–31, 413–15
    port driver unionization as goal, 331–32
    preemption analysis of Clean Truck Program, 431
    strategy to address independent contracting, 330–34
    success in California after World War II, 314–15
    suing and striking, 419–20, 433
    tensions with ILWU, 353–54
    Toll and, 417–19
    trucking deregulation and, 329
Tea Party movement, 130–31, 148, 408
TELACU. *See* The East Los Angeles Community Union

1010 Hope Development Corporation, 186–87
Terminal Island, 320
Terminal Impact (video), 350
terminal operators, 321, 343–44, 378, 379, 384–85, 387, 403–4, 422, 423, 439–40
term limits, as leverage in CBA campaigns, 180
TESCO, 295, 299–300
Tesoro, 321
Thai Community Development Corporation, 42–44
Thai workers, 28, 32, 41–49, 80, 468
    back wages owed to, 44–45
    discovery of, 42
    El Monte sweatshop, 42–44, 43*f*
    immigration status of, 44
    lawsuit on behalf of (*see Bureerong v. Uvawas*)
    total recovery by, 48–49
The East Los Angeles Community Union (TELACU), 17–18
theoretical implications, 446–47
    for labor law (*see* labor law theory)
    for lawyering (*see* lawyering theory)
    for local government law (*see* local government law theory)
Thigpenn, Anthony, 178–79, 203–4
Thomas, Jim, 231
Thomas, Sidney, 132, 136
TIDC. *See* Tourism Industry Development Council
TIF. *See* tax increment financing
Time Warner Center, 232, 240
TMA. *See* Transport Maritime Association
Todd Shipyard, 337
Tokaji, Daniel, 46
Toll Group Inc., 413, 417–18, 420, 427
    collective bargaining agreement with Teamsters, 418–19, 462*t*
Toma, Robin, 100–1
Tomato, Inc., 45, 48–49
Tom Bradley International Terminal, 199, 229
Topson Downs of California, 45
Torres, Benjamin, 240–41
Total Distribution Service, 379
Total Transportation Systems, Inc., 413–14, 416
Tourism Industry Development Council (TIDC), 169–70, 200–1, 202
trade
    deficit, 317
    garment industry and, 36
    global, 313
    import quotas on garments, 36, 57, 75–76
    international, 85–86
    liberalization, 36, 317, 421–22
    ports and, 315–17, 318
traffic interference ban on day labor solicitation, 114, 137, 148–49, 150–55
Trafficking Victims Protection Act of 2000, 83–84
transportation law, 504–5

deregulation of, 317
drayage trucking and, 321–22
ports and, 324
Transportation Workers Identification Credential (TWIC card), 372, 400–1
Transport Maritime Association (TMA), 330
Transport Workers Union, 417
TraPac container terminal, 321, 326–27, 371, 373, 380–81, 386–87
Trasviña, John, 124
triangular bargaining, in garment industry, 35
tripartite unionism, 494
TrizecHahn, 175–76
Truck Driver Employment and Public Safety Act, 410
truck drivers, 329. *See also* port truck drivers
in Los Angeles, 20–26
Truck Impact Fee, 365
trucking industry
impact of deregulation on, 329
as target of L.A. campaigns, 3, 20–26
unionization of, 329, 416–20
truck pollution, 322–24, 335, 349, 356, 398, 593, 608
Truck Procurement Assistance Program, 386
Trump, Donald, 231–32
Turlock, 294
twenty-foot equivalent units (TEUs), 316, 318, 319*f*, 337
2020 Plan, 317–18, 325–26
TWIC card. *See* Transportation Workers Identification Credential
Tynan, Roxana, 175–76, 289–91, 351–52

Uber, 504
UCLA. *See* University of California, Los Angeles
Ueberroth, Peter, 18
UFCW. *See* United Food and Commercial Workers
ULP. *See* unfair labor practice
underground economy, 28–29, 91, 449*t*
undocumented immigrants
AFL-CIO and, 16–17
day laborers and, 92, 98, 121–22
employer sanctions for hiring, 16–17, 96
garment industry and, 37
labor law protections and, 85
in Los Angeles, 13–14, 37
S.B. 1070 and, 130–31, 138
unfair labor practice (ULP), 53, 54–55, 56–57, 417–18, 419
strikes, 50–51, 419–20, 427, 433
UNIDAD. *See* United Neighbors in Defense Against Displacement
Union Cities, 168–69
union density, 497

corporate strategies to undermine, 13
in Los Angeles over time, 26, 27*f*
unionism, 16, 19–20, 27
decline in Los Angeles, 15–16, 26, 27*f*
decline nationally, 26, 27*f*
garment sector and, 35, 38
grocery sector and, 280–81
tripartite, 494
Wal-Mart and limits of, 266–70
unionization
barriers to, 490
big-box campaign and, 289–90
CBA campaigns and, 29, 164–65, 169–70, 175, 191–92, 193, 201, 207, 208–9, 262–63
in garment industry, 35, 38, 53–54, 73
as goal of L.A. campaigns, 20, 454
independent contractors and, 419–20, 421–22, 427, 433
living wage law and, 476
local government law and, 2–3, 9, 493–94
local labor policies promoting, 470
and organized labor's political resurgence, 476
port truck drivers and, 30–31, 311–12, 321–22, 330, 331–32, 416–20, 421–22, 428, 433, 436–37, 439, 444–45
trend in Los Angeles, 26, 27*f*
Wal-Mart and, 266, 306
Union of Needletrades, Industrial and Textile Employees (UNITE), 32–33, 41, 45–46, 82
formation of, 51
as founder of Sweatshop Watch, 61
Garment Workers Justice Center, 65
Guess class action and, 52, 53–56
role in Guess campaign, 51–57, 58, 473–74
Union Pacific (UP), 317–18, 327–28
unions, political role of, 496–99
UNITE. *See* Union of Needletrades, Industrial and Textile Employees
United Airlines, 202, 203, 205, 207–8, 255
United Electrical Workers, 16
United Farm Workers, 16, 351
United Food and Commercial Workers (UFCW), 303, 449*t*, 459–60, 462*t*, 470, 475, 476, 571
CBAs and, 191–92, 251
Inglewood site fight and, 267, 270, 272, 273–75, 276–77, 280–82, 289–90, 293, 302–3, 308
Local 770, 191–92, 273, 284, 290–91
Wal-Mart and, 270, 295, 301–2
United Neighbors in Defense Against Displacement (UNIDAD), 245–47, 252–53
United States Attorney, 67–68, 106
United States Steel, 267
United Steel Workers, 350
United Students Against Sweatshops, 59–60, 68

United Teachers Los Angeles, 15
United University Church, 174
Universal City Walk, 233–34
Universal Studios, 170
University of California, Berkeley, 41, 53, 119, 459
University of California, Irvine School of Law, 402–3
University of California, Los Angeles (UCLA), 170
  Community Economic Development Clinic, 78
  Community Scholars, 18–19
  Department of Urban Planning, 18–19, 181–82
  Downtown Labor Center, 141, 460
  Environmental Law Center, 284–85
  Labor Center, 19–20
  School of Law, 78, 100, 459
University of Colorado Law School, 355
University of Denver College of Law, 115–16
University of Richmond Law School, 102–3
University of Southern California (USC), 18–19, 59–60, 84, 98, 166–67, 170–71, 245–46, 284–85, 335–36
University Village, 166–67
UP. *See* Union Pacific
Urban League, 308–9
urban planning, 4, 248
urban renewal, 166, 230
USC. *See* University of Southern California

Valenzuela, Cynthia, 124, 131, 132, 458–59
Valley Jobs Coalition, 177, 191, 192, 251
Van Nuys Worksource Center, 191
Velasco, Val, 196–97, 199, 218, 226
Velasquez, Enrique, 173
Ventura County, 94, 149–50
Verduzco-Smith, Maria, 211, 214–15, 217, 225
Verrilli, Donald, 402
vertical power, in relation to local government regulation of work, 503–7
Villagra, Hector, 114, 119, 120, 122*f*, 122, 123–24, 141–42, 144–45, 147, 458–59
Villaraigosa, Antonio, 114, 180, 343–44, 351–52, 417–18, 460–61, 475–76
  addressing pollution at the port, 344–45, 347, 425–26, 441–42
  Clean Truck Program and, 368, 370–71, 378–79, 386–87, 394, 407–8, 426–27, 432
  election to City Council, 15, 17
  election as mayor, 17, 226, 358
  Grand Avenue Project and, 232, 238
  as labor organizer, 476
  LAX Master Plan and, 196–97, 226
  school board takeover and, 371
  as Speaker of California Assembly, 345
Vincent Thomas Bridge, 337
Volpp, Leti, 41, 45–46
Vons, 303

wage-and-hour cases, 32–33, 41–42, 52, 57
wage enforcement, at the city level, 487–88
Wage Justice Center, 84, 416, 487–88
wage theft, 19, 487–88
  in day labor industry, 129–30
  in port trucking industry, 412
Wakeupwalmart.com, 301–2
Waldorf-Astoria hotel, 52
Wall Street Journal, 55
Wal-Mart, 3, 38, 82, 299–300, 422, 453–55, 460, 480, 484, 489, 491, 505–6
  aftermath of Inglewood site fight and, 293–94
  anti-union policy, 269–70
  bargaining strength with suppliers, 266
  Chinatown store, 295–97, 296*f*, 297*f*, 303, 310, 449*t*
  Clean Truck Program and, 373, 377
  code of conduct, 529
  command-and-control structure of, 266
  consumer support for, 578
  contesting at the local level, 265
  culture of, 268–69
  economic impact of stores, 279–80, 289
  economic power of, 266
  efforts to divide anti-big-box coalition, 306
  election defeat in Inglewood, 287
  employment practices, 268
  expansion of, 264–65, 273
  garment industry and, 33, 38
  gender discrimination and, 271–72
  grocery industry and, 273
  Home Stretch at Hollywood Park site, 278*f*, 292–93
  Inglewood and, 29–30, 264–65, 272–97, 308–9
  labor law and, 267–68
  labor policies of, 269–70
  labor standards of, 266–67, 271
  legal strategy of anti-big-box coalition against, 282–87
  litigation against, 271–72
  local policy reform in challenge to, 272, 289
  organizational structure, 268
  organized labor and, 266–67, 270
  origins of, 266
  neighborhood market, 296
  public relations, 279
  public subsidies for, 289
  response to union organizing, 269–70
  size, 266
  strategy to pass Measure 04-A, 279
  Supercenter, 264–65, 269, 272, 273–75, 276, 277, 278, 279–80, 282–83, 287, 291, 292–94, 298, 300–1, 302–3, 306, 309, 310, 457–58, 470, 475, 566–67
  Supercenter expansion plan in California, 264–65

targeting African American communities, 275–76
traditional unionism and, 266–70
unfair labor practices, 269–70
use of ballot initiatives and referenda, 283
worker intimidation by, 269–70
workforce, 267, 268
Walmartwatch.com, 301–2
Walsh, Tom, 203–4, 208
Walt Disney Concert Hall, 230–32, 236, 244
Walters, Rita, 178–79, 180
Walton, Sam, 266
Wardlaw, Kim, 131–32
Waterfront Rail Truckers Union (WRTU), 329, 330–31, 410–11
Waters, Maxine, 211–12, 226, 281–82, 282f
Watts Labor Community Action Committee, 17–18
Watts protests of 1965, 11
Waxman, Seth, 402–3
Webb, Michael, 133
Weiner, Nick, 332–33, 334f, 350–51, 352–53, 356, 358–59, 367, 368, 374, 375, 379, 406, 408, 409, 413, 418–19, 425, 428
Weiss, Jack, 220
welfare, 13, 205, 497
West Basin Transportation Project, 337–38
Westchester, 195, 196–97, 211–12, 213–14, 228
Western Center on Law and Poverty, 54
Western Freight Carrier, 416
West Hollywood, 264
Westin Bonaventure, 243, 244
Westwater, Brady, 232
Westwood, 284
Wet Seal, 74
Whalen, Curtis, 365, 383, 386
white flight, 14–15, 247, 499, 500, 505
whites, in Los Angeles, 13–14, 20–26, 21t, 23t, 26t
Who Benefits from Redevelopment in Los Angeles? (LAANE), 170
Wiggins v. CRA, 237, 239–40
as foundation of no net loss policy, 235–36
role in Share the Wealth Coalition, 235–36
rulings, 234–35
settlement, 235
Willful Misclassification Law, 413–14, 416, 462t, 467, 469. *See also* S.B. 459
Williams and Dame, 189
Wills, Doug, 219–20
Wilmington, 320, 346
as adjunct to port transportation system, 321
demographics of, 321
environmental hazards in, 325
impact of trucking on, 325–26
impact of ports on, 325

secession efforts, 326
zoning in, 326
Wilmington Coalition, 327
Wilmington Home Owners, 325–26
Wilmington Liquid Bulk Terminals, 325–26
Wilmington oil field, 325
Wilshire Boulevard, 14–15
Wilson, Jake, 322
Wilson, Pete, 18, 40
Witte, Bill, 240, 241, 244
Wong, Kent, 203
Woocher, Fred, 54
Woodfield, Kathleen, 381, 386–87
worker centers
definition of, 19
development in Los Angeles, 19–20, 64
relation to union movement, 9, 493, 498–99
worker organizing, 1–2, 27, 73, 79–80
"hydraulic pressure" for, 9
immigrants and, 474, 493
integration with strategic litigation, 28, 32
outside of traditional labor law, 9
Worker Retention Ordinance, 169–71, 179, 200, 201–2, 206, 207, 220, 223, 228–29, 467–68
Worker Rights Consortium, 83
workers' compensation, 82–83, 330–31, 411–12
Workers' Rights Project at CHIRLA, 69, 102–3, 139
Working Families for Wal-Mart initiative, 571
Working Partnerships, 178
workplace
abuse in, 66–67, 458, 469
changing nature of, 8–9, 12
corporate strategies to restructure, 13
solidarity in, 498–99
Workplace Project, 144–45
World Trade Organization (WTO), 36, 75–76
World War II, 12, 315, 499
WRTU. *See* Waterfront Rail Truckers Union
WTO. *See* World Trade Organization
Wyenn, Morgan, 404f

XOXO Clothing Company, 60, 67, 80

Yale Law School, 41, 58, 81–82, 102, 114, 458
Young, Andrew, 571
Young, David, 53
YWCA, 189–90

Zatz, Noah, 492
Zerolnick, Jon, 351, 352–53, 359–61, 363–64, 365–67, 372, 382, 388, 395–96, 406–7, 426, 441–42
Zucker, Erika, 173, 178, 204